OM on Site

PayPal: The Worst Idea of the Year? 7	Should Employees Talk to Customers? 389
Eliminating Customer Risk-Taking at Borders 15	Cutting Employee Perks: With or Without Cutting Employee Morale 392
Profitability Requires Adaptation 40	Reducing Turnover in the Fast-Food Industry 394
Adobe: Turning a Popular Product into a Profitable Product 55	Making Overbooking a Win–Win Situation 441
At Starbucks, Suppliers Bring More than Beans 77	What Should Happen to Employees When Demand Drops Suddenly? 445
Home Depot Improves the Shopping Experience 82	New Markets Mean More Than Just Moving ... 466
The Battle over Who Has the Greenest Wood 84	Oops—Maybe that Move Was a Bad Idea 468
A Focused Strategy in the Women's Clothing Industry 103	Office Layouts Change to Reduce Noise Levels 482
Changing Strategy to Match a Changing Environment 104	"Flow" Drives Layout for Kohl's 497
Business Method Patents: Good or Bad? 135	Ski Resorts: Improving Customer Relationships when 85 Percent Never Return 518
Minimills Make Money, Not Steel 136	A Case Study in Losing Customer Loyalty 521
Cost versus Price: Surcharges, "Taxes," and User Fees 164	Increased Loyalty through Increased Convenience 523
Online Contacts Reduce Costs 167	97X—A Broadcasting Phenomenon 528
Quality, Productivity, and Inventory Reduction: Inseparable Goals 188	Maintaining Inventory Access during a Tragedy 550
Quality and Consistency Are Key for Wilson Tennis Balls 210	A Precious Metal Disaster 554
What Does Six Sigma Really Mean? 216	Supplier Relationships: Key to Successful Inventory Reduction 555
Better Tools Enhance Timeliness 234	TQM Results 574
Fast versus Slow in the Fashion Industry 240	Standardizing Election Processes 580
Airport Lines: Why Airlines Want Them 244	Constraint Management at Amazon.com 602
Planning Is Complicated by Changes in Customer Behavior 293	A Constraint Management Case 608
Are Second Phone Lines on the Declining Side of Their Life Cycle? 295	SCM and Profit for Amazon 629
Eliminating Inventory through Mass Customization: Build-to-Order 342	Communication Enhances Supply Chain Connections 631
It's Not Just "When" and "How Many," but also "How" and "Where" 350	Reduced Time Can Mean Reduced Opportunity for Disruptions in Tightly Linked Supply Chains 641

OperationsNow.com

LIST OF TITLES

OperationsNow.com
MCGRAW-HILL/IRWIN SERIES
Operations and Decision Sciences

OPERATIONS MANAGEMENT

Bowersox and Closs, *Logistical Management: The Integrated Supply Chain Process,* First Edition

Chase, Aquilano, and Jacobs, *Operations Management for Competitive Advantage,* Ninth Edition

Chu, Hottenstein, and Greenlaw, *PROSIM for Windows,* Third Edition

Cohen and Apte, *Manufacturing Automation,* First Edition

Davis, Aquilano, and Chase, *Fundamentals of Operations Management,* Third Edition

Dobler and Burt, *Purchasing and Supply Management,* Sixth Edition

Fitzsimmons and Fitzsimmons, *Service Management: Operations, Strategy, Information Technology,* Third Edition

Flaherty, *Global Operations Management,* First Edition

Gray and Larson, *Project Management: The Managerial Process,* First Edition

Hill, *Manufacturing Strategy: Text and Cases,* Third Edition

Hopp and Spearman, *Factory Physics,* Second Edition

Lambert and Stock, *Strategic Logistics Management,* Third Edition

Leenders and Fearon, *Purchasing and Supply Chain Management,* Eleventh Edition

Moses, Seshadri, and Yakir, *HOM Operations Management Software for Windows,* First Edition

Nahmias, *Production and Operations Analysis,* Fourth Edition

Nicholas, *Competitive Manufacturing Management,* First Edition

Olson, *Introduction to Information Systems Project Management,* First Edition

Pinedo and Chao, *Operations Scheduling,* First Edition

Sanderson and Uzumeri, *Managing Product Families,* First Edition

Schonberger and Knod, *Operations Management,* Seventh Edition

Schroeder, *Operations Management: Contemporary Concepts and Cases,* First Edition

Simchi-Levi, Kaminsky, and Simchi-Levi, *Designing and Managing the Supply Chain: Concepts, Strategies, and Case Studies,* First Edition

Sterman, *Business Dynamics: Systems Thinking and Modeling for a Complex World,* First Edition

Stevenson, *Production/Operations Management,* Seventh Edition

Vollmann, Berry, and Whybark, *Manufacturing Planning and Control Systems,* Fourth Edition

Zipkin, *Foundations of Inventory Management,* First Edition

QUANTITATIVE METHODS AND MANAGEMENT SCIENCE

Alwan, *Statistical Process Analysis,* First Edition

Bodily, Carraway, Frey, and Pfeifer, *Quantitative Business Analysis: Casebook,* First Edition

Bodily, Carraway, Frey, and Pfeifer, *Quantitative Business Analysis: Text and Cases,* First Edition

Bonini, Hausman, and Bierman, *Quantitative Analysis for Business Decisions,* Ninth Edition

Hesse, *Managerial Spreadsheet Modeling and Analysis,* First Edition

Hillier, Hillier, and Lieberman, *Introduction to Management Science: A Modeling and Case Studies Approach with Spreadsheets,* First Edition

OperationsNow.com
PROCESSES, VALUE, AND PROFITABILITY

BYRON J. FINCH
Miami University

McGraw-Hill
Irwin

Boston   Burr Ridge, IL   Dubuque, IA   Madison, WI   New York   San Francisco   St. Louis
Bangkok   Bogotá   Caracas   Kuala Lumpur   Lisbon   London   Madrid   Mexico City
Milan   Montreal   New Delhi   Santiago   Seoul   Singapore   Sydney   Taipei   Toronto

McGraw-Hill Higher Education

*A Division of The **McGraw-Hill** Companies*

OPERATIONSNOW.COM: PROCESSES, VALUE AND PROFITABILITY
Published by McGraw-Hill/Irwin, a business unit of The McGraw-Hill Companies, Inc., 1221 Avenue of the Americas, New York, NY, 10020. Copyright © 2003 by The McGraw-Hill Companies, Inc. All rights reserved. No part of this publication may be reproduced or distributed in any form or by any means, or stored in a database or retrieval system, without the prior written consent of The McGraw-Hill Companies, Inc., including, but not limited to, in any network or other electronic storage or transmission, or broadcast for distance learning. Some ancillaries, including electronic and print components, may not be available to customers outside the United States.

This book is printed on acid-free paper.

domestic   1 2 3 4 5 6 7 8 9 0 VNH/VNH 0 9 8 7 6 5 4 3 2
international 1 2 3 4 5 6 7 8 9 0 VNH/VNH 0 9 8 7 6 5 4 3 2
ISBN   0-07-241640-8

Publisher: *Brent Gordon*
Executive editor: *Scott Isenberg*
Developmental editor: *Cynthia Douglas*
Senior marketing manager: *Zina Craft*
Producer, media technology: *Anthony Sherman*
Project manager: *Scott Scheidt*
Manager, new book production: *Melonie Salvati*
Coordinator freelance design: *Mary L. Christianson*
Photo research coordinator: *Jeremy Cheshareck*
Photo researcher: *Jennifer Blankenship*
Supplement producer: *Vicki Laird*
Senior digital content specialist: *Brian Nacik*
Freelance interior, cover, and content manager: *Amanda Kavanaugh Design*
Cover photographs left to right: *airplane/©Digital Vision, circuit board/©PhotoDisc; flight schedule/©PhotoDisc; shopping cart/©PhotoDisc; assembly line/©Tony Stone; dollar signs/©PhotoDisc.*
Typeface: *10.5/12 Goudy*
Compositor: *Lachina Publishing Services*
Printer: *Von Hoffman Press, Inc.*

Library of Congress Cataloging-in-Publication Data
Finch, Byron J.
    OperationsNow.com : process, value, and profitability / Byron J. Finch
      p. cm.—(McGraw-Hill/Irwin series Operations and decision sciences)
    Includes index.
    ISBN 0-07-241640-8 (alk paper).—ISBN 0-07-112334-2 (international : alk. paper)
    1. Production management. I. Title: OperationsNow.com. II. Title. III. Series.
TS155 .F556 2003
658—dc21

2002027882

INTERNATIONAL EDITION ISBN 0-07-112334-2
Copyright © 2003. Exclusive rights by The McGraw-Hill Companies, Inc. for manufacture and export. This book cannot be re-exported from the country to which it is sold by McGraw-Hill. The International Edition is not available in North America.

www.mhhe.com

With love to my wife, Kim,
my son, Matt,
and my daughter, Meredith.
— *Byron J. Finch*

ABOUT THE AUTHOR

BYRON J. FINCH

Byron J. Finch is a Professor of Operations Management in the Richard T. Farmer School of Business Administration at Miami University, Oxford, Ohio. He earned his BS and MS degrees from Iowa State University and received his doctorate from the William Terry College of Business Administration at the University of Georgia in 1986. He began teaching and research responsibilities in 1987 at Miami University, where he has taught operations management courses at the undergraduate and graduate levels.

Dr. Finch's research interests have evolved from the topic of manufacturing planning and control systems early in his career, to spreadsheet models, to his most recent research endeavors involving the use of Internet-based conversations as information to improve product and service quality. As the U.S. economy has shifted to a service orientation, Dr. Finch's research interests have become more inclusive of services as well, particularly online services. Research projects that Dr. Finch has been involved with have resulted in numerous publications in such outlets as the *Journal of Operations Management, International Journal of Production Research, Quality Management Journal, Academy of Management Journal, Production and Inventory Management Journal,* and *International Journal of Quality and Reliability Management.* Dr. Finch is also the author or co-author of *The Management Guide to Internet Resources* (1997), *Operations Management: Competing in a Changing Environment* (1995), *Spreadsheet Applications for Production and Operations Management* (1990), and *Planning and Control System Design: Principles and Cases for Process Manufacturers* (1987). In addition to the traditional print publications, Dr. Finch has been the managing editor for the Operations Management Center website (http://www.mhhe.com/pom/) since 1998. Dr. Finch serves on the editorial boards of the *Journal of Operations Management* and the *Quality Management Journal.*

Dr. Finch has been actively involved in teaching innovation since beginning his academic career in 1986. He received the Southern Business Administration Innovative Teaching Award in 1987, the NCR Computer Innovation Award in 1990, and the Richard T. Farmer School of Business Teaching Award in 1996. Dr. Finch was nominated for the Miami University Associated Student Government Teaching Award in 2002.

Dr. Finch has held various offices in the Midwest Decision Sciences Institute, including president. He has also been involved in Decision Sciences Institute at the national level and is currently a vice president. Dr. Finch is also a member of the Production and Operations Management Society (POMS).

LIST OF CONTRIBUTORS

TEXT REVIEWERS

John Nicholas
Loyola University, Chicago
Joe Felan
Baylor University
Victor Sower
Sam Houston State University
Ken Klassen
California State University, Northridge
Brad Meyer
Drake University
Chwen Sheu
Kansas State University
Scott Dellana
East Carolina University
Tom Wilder
California State University, Chico
Gene Fliedner
Oakland University
Barb Flynn
Wake Forest University
Keith Willoughby
Bucknell University
Stella Hua
Oregon State University

FOCUS GROUP ATTENDEES

Bill Tallon
Northern Illinois University
Rhonda Lummus
Iowa State University
Vijay Agrawal
University of Missouri at Kansas City
Bharatendu Srivastava
Marquette University
Donald A. Carpenter
University of Nebraska at Kearney
Paul Hong
University of Toledo
T. J. Wharton
Oakland University
Francis O. Pianki
Anderson University
Mehmet Barut
Wichita State University
Lawrence Fredendall
Clemson University

Britt Shirley
University of Tampa
Nancy Hyer
Vanderbilt University
Marilyn Smith
Winthrop University
Gene Fliedner
Oakland University
Ann Marucheck
University of North Carolina at Chapel Hill
Richard Reid
University of New Mexico
Charles Petersen
Northern Illinois University
Zhimin Huang
Adelphi University
William Pinney
Alcorn State University
Daniel Krause
Arizona State University
Alan Khade
California State University—Turlock
Nael Aly
California State University—Turlock
Gilvan Souza
University of Maryland at College Park
Joel Wisner
University of Nevada at Las Vegas
Rajesh Srivastava
Florida Gulf Coast University
Henry Aigbedo
Oakland University
Bob Ash
Indiana University at New Albany
Christopher Craighead
University of North Carolina at Charlotte
Edie Schmidt
Purdue University
Mary J. Meixell
George Mason University
Vicente Vargas
Emory University
Madeline (Mellie) Pullman
Colorado State University
Michael Mancuso
Purdue University

BRIEF CONTENTS

Preface xvi

Acknowledgments xix

UNIT ONE FOUNDATIONS FOR SUCCESS 1
CHAPTER ONE Introduction to OperationsNow.com 2
CHAPTER TWO Profitability 34
CHAPTER THREE Value 72
CHAPTER FOUR Strategy 96

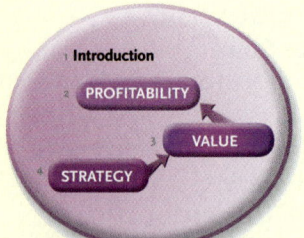

UNIT TWO COMPONENTS OF VALUE 128
CHAPTER FIVE Processes and Capabilities 130
CHAPTER SIX Cost 158
CHAPTER SEVEN Quality 182
CHAPTER EIGHT Timeliness 230

UNIT THREE MANAGING RESOURCES TO CREATE VALUE 284
CHAPTER NINE Resource Planning 286
CHAPTER TEN Inventory 338
CHAPTER ELEVEN Workforce 384
CHAPTER TWELVE Capacity 416
CHAPTER THIRTEEN Facilities 458
CHAPTER FOURTEEN Customer Relationships 514

UNIT FOUR INTEGRATIVE MANAGEMENT FRAMEWORKS 538
CHAPTER FIFTEEN Just-in-Time Management 540
CHAPTER SIXTEEN Total Quality Management 566
CHAPTER SEVENTEEN Constraint Management 594
CHAPTER EIGHTEEN Supply Chain Management 622

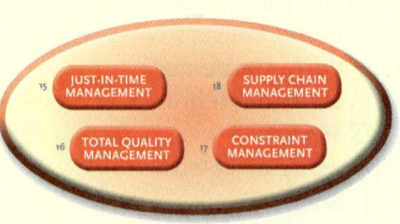

Appendix A Areas of the Standard Normal Distribution 651

Appendix B Areas of the Cumulative Standard Normal Distribution 652

Glossary 654

Index 662

CONTENTS

Preface xvi

Acknowledgments xix

UNIT ONE: Foundations for Success

CHAPTER ONE: INTRODUCTION TO OperationsNow.com 2

Introduction: Why "Operations Management" Is Critical to a Career in Business 4
  Why "Now"? 5
  Why ".com"? 7
A New Business Environment 8
Overview of the Resource/Profit Model 9
  Foundations for Success 9
  Profitability 9
  Value 11
  Strategy 13
Components of Value 14
  Processes and Capabilities 14
  Cost 16
  Quality 17
  Timeliness 17
Managing Resources Used to Create Value 17
  Inventory 18
  Workforce 19
  Capacity 19
  Facilities 19
  Customer Relationships 20
  Resource Planning 20
Integrative Management Frameworks 20
  Just-in-Time Management 21
  Total Quality Management 22
  Constraint Management 22
  Supply Chain Management 22
Environmental Forces 22
  Globalization 22
  The Internet 23
  The Natural Environment 23
  Regional Pressures 24
The Resource/Profit Model in Review 24
Business Outputs: Products and Services 24
  Products 25
  Services 25
Customers 28
Operations, Other Business Functions, and You 28
  Chapter Summary 30

CHAPTER TWO: PROFITABILITY 34

Introduction: The Link Between Value and Investment Results 36
Profitability Measures 40
  Profit Margin 41
  Return on Assets 42
  Return on Equity 43
Economic Value Added: A New Profitability Measure 43
Profitability from Operation Resources 44
  Inventory 45
  Workforce 47
  Capacity 50
  Facilities 52
  Customer Relationships 53
Local Versus Global Optimization 53
Measurement Improvement 54
Decision-Making Tools: Breakeven Analysis 56
A Broader Approach to Productivity Measurement: The Balanced Scorecard 59
  Chapter Summary 59

CHAPTER THREE: VALUE 72

Introduction: The Customer Determines Product and Service Value 74
Supply Chains 74
Value Determination by Customers 78
Value Attributes of Consumer Customers 80
   Cost 81
   Quality 81
   Convenience 81
   Response Time 83
   Personalization 83
   Ethical Issues 83
   Style and Fashion 84
   Use of Technology 85
Value Attributes of Business Customers 85
   Cost 86
   Quality 87
   Dependability of Delivery 88
   Response Time 88
   Flexibility 89
A Common Set of Value Attributes 90
The Link Between Customer Value Attributes and Value Creation 90
Chapter Summary 92

CHAPTER FOUR: STRATEGY 96

Introduction: A Plan for Creating Value 98
The Strategic Hierarchy 99
   Corporate Strategy 100
   Business Strategy 101
   Operations Strategy 102
Strategic Decision Categories 105
Strategic Decisions and Competitive Priorities 105
   Capacity Decisions 109
   Facility Decisions 111
   Process Technology Decisions 112
   Vertical Integration and Supplier Relationship Decisions 113
   Human Resources Decisions 115
   Quality Decisions 117
   Production Planning/Inventory Control Decisions 118
   New-Product or Service Development Decisions 119
   Performance/Reward System Decisions 120
   Organization System Decisions 121
Complexity of Relationships Among Strategic Decisions and Competitive Priorities 122
Process and Volume Choices: Strategic Tradeoffs for Manufacturers 122
Customer Contact and Process Efficiency: Strategic Tradeoffs for Services 124
Chapter Summary 125

UNIT TWO: Components of Value

CHAPTER FIVE: PROCESSES AND CAPABILITIES 130

Introduction: Converting Resources to Value 132
Capabilities Versus Processes 132
Order Qualifiers and Order Winners 135
General Layout Decisions: Strategic Decisions for Process Requirements 137
   Layout Alternatives 137
   The Impact of Volume Requirements 140
   Demand Linkages 142
   Service Process Considerations 143
   Determining New-Process Requirements 144
   Product, Service, and Process Design 145
   Quality Function Deployment 146
Process Improvement Tools 150
   Business Process Analysis 151
   Reengineering 151
   Concurrent Engineering 152
   Poka-Yoke 152
Service Blueprinting 154
Capability Chains 154
   Chapter Summary 155

CHAPTER SIX: COST 158

Introduction: Paying for Value 160
Cost and Perceived Value 161
    What Is a "Cost"? 162
    Cost and Profitability 162
    Types of Costs 163
    Average Costs 163
The Value Chain 164
An Overview of Operations Cost Measurement 166
    Assigning Operations Costs 166
    Traceability of Direct Operations Costs 167
    Allocating Indirect Operations Costs 168
    Components of Product Cost 169
Productivity Improvement and Cost Reduction 170
    Putting Cost Information to Work for Operations: Standards and Variances 170
Total Cost Versus Cost per Unit 173
Cost Tradeoffs 173
Nonfinancial Costs 173
    Chapter Summary 174

CHAPTER SEVEN: QUALITY 182

Introduction: Product and Service Quality Defined 184
Quality and Value 184
Quality and Profitability 186
Proaction Versus Reaction in Quality Management 189
Cost of Quality 190
    External Failure Costs 190
    Internal Failure Costs 191
    Appraisal Costs 191
    Prevention Costs 192
General-Purpose Quality Analysis Tools 193
    Flowcharts 193
    Run Charts 194
    Cause and Effect Diagrams 195
    Pareto Charts 195
    Histograms 198
    Check Sheets 198
    Scatter Diagrams 199
    Control Charts 199
Statistical Process Control 200
Acceptance Sampling 210
The Next Level: Moving Beyond Merely Satisfying the Customer 211
    The Kano Model 212
    Six Sigma Quality 213
Service-Oriented Quality Improvement 216
    Service Blueprinting 216
    Moment-of-Truth Analysis 217
Technological Advances in Quality Information Management: Customer Relationship Management 218
When Something Still Goes Wrong: Recovery 219
Total Quality Management 220
    Chapter Summary 220

CHAPTER EIGHT: TIMELINESS 230

Introduction: Time *Really Is* Money 232
Time and Profitability 232
    The Effect of Time on Profit Margin 232
    The Effect of Time on Return on Assets 237
    Time-Related Productivity Measures 237
Feedback Delay: A Frequently Overlooked Time Penalty 239
General Time Reduction Strategies 240
Scheduling 243
Scheduling Techniques 244
The Gantt Chart 245
Controlling Manufacturing Task Sequences with Traditional Job Sequencing 246
    Sequencing Rules 246
Trends in Resource Scheduling 250
Managing Queues of Customers 251
    Physical Features of Queues 251
Psychological Features of Queues 256
    Keep Customers Busy 256
    Keep Customers Informed 256
    Treat Customers Fairly 256
    Start the Service As Soon As Possible 257
    Exceed the Customer's Expectations 257
Project Management 257
    A Network Approach to Project Scheduling 258
    Developing the Network 258
    Project Scheduling with Uncertain Time Estimates 263
    Crashing Projects 265
    Project Management Caveats 268
Chapter Summary 269

CONTENTS

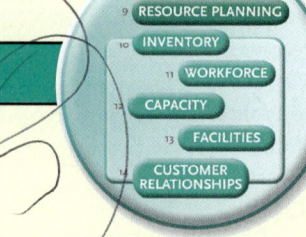

UNIT THREE: Managing Resources to Create Value

CHAPTER NINE: RESOURCE PLANNING 286

Introduction: Why Do We Plan? 288
Planning Fundamentals 290
    The Financial Benefits
      of Effective Planning 290
    Looking into the Future:
      The Planning Horizon 291
The Impact of Product and Service Life Cycles 294
A Strategy for More Successful Plans: Compressing
    Lead Times 297
Demand Forecasting 297

Causal Forecasting 298
Time Series Forecasting 298
    Components of a Time Series 300
    Time Series Techniques 302
Forecast Accuracy 312
    Measuring Absolute Error 312
    Measuring Forecast Bias 314
Integrated Resource Planning Systems 315
Supply Chain Management 320
    Chapter Summary 321

CHAPTER TEN: INVENTORY 338

Introduction: A Balancing Act
    for Management 340
Why Should Businesses Carry Inventory? 341
Why Should Businesses Avoid Carrying
    Too Much Inventory? 341
Different Types of Inventory: Costs
    and Benefits 342
Retailing and Finished-Product Inventories 344
Component and Raw Materials Inventory 348

Inventory Decisions 349
Managing Independent Demand Inventory 350
    Fixed Quantity, Variable Interval Systems 351
    Fixed Interval, Variable Quantity Systems 357
Managing Dependent Demand Inventory 360
Prioritizing Inventory: ABC Analysis 370
Measuring Inventory Productivity 371
    Chapter Summary 373

CHAPTER ELEVEN: WORKFORCE 384

Introduction: Using the Workforce as a Key to
    Competitive Success 386
Employee/Customer Interaction, Value,
    and Profitability 386
The Employee Contribution to
    Value Attributes 390
Employee Interaction with Customers:
    A Prerequisite to Good Service 391
The Most Important Employee Contribution to
    Value: Sound Decisions 394
Increasing the Contribution of Employees
    Through Teams 395
    Why Use Teams? 396

Appropriate Uses for Teams 397
Structure for Team Processes 398
Team Decision-Making Tools 399
Increased Need for Workforce Flexibility 400
    The Use of Cross-Training 400
    The Use of Contingent Workers 400
Who's in Charge? 401
The New Working Environment 402
Workforce Productivity Improvement 402
    Productivity Measurement and
      Improvement Tools 403
    Learning Curves 406
    Chapter Summary 409

CHAPTER TWELVE: CAPACITY 416

Introduction: Matching Resource Availability to Market Demand 418
Capacity Defined 418
Capacity and Value 421
The Financial Impact of Capacity Decisions 423
Individual Resource Influence on System Capacity 425
A Broader View: Supply Chain Capacity 427
Managing the Demand–Capacity Match in Manufacturing 428
Demand Chase Aggregate Planning 429
Level Production Aggregate Planning 431
Detailed Capacity Planning in Manufacturing 433
Managing the Demand–Capacity Match in Services 439
   Yield Management 440
   Overbooking 441
Current Trends in Capacity Management 444
Chapter Summary 444

CHAPTER THIRTEEN: FACILITIES 458

Introduction: Making Decisions for What May Be the Largest Investment 460
Strategic Importance of Facilities 460
Facility Location Decisions 463
   Locating a New Business 463
   Relocating an Existing Business 465
   Choosing a Location for Business Expansion 465
Location Decision-Making Criteria 465
   International Issues 466
   Domestic Location Decisions 467
   Geographic Information Systems 471
Location Decision-Making Techniques 472
   Multifactor Rating 472
   Center-of-Gravity Method 474
   Decision Tree Analysis 477
   Breakeven Analysis 479
Business Location Trends 481
Facility Layouts 481
   Process-Oriented Layouts 483
   Product-Oriented Layouts 490
   Cellular Layouts 496
   Service Layouts 496
Chapter Summary 498

CHAPTER FOURTEEN: CUSTOMER RELATIONSHIPS 514

Introduction: The Value of Strong Customer Relationships 516
Perceived Value: A Prerequisite to a Relationship 517
Extending Customer Relationships 519
   Win Back or Save 519
   Prospecting 520
   Loyalty Building 520
   Cross-Sell/Upsell 523
Customer Loyalty and Profitability 525
Customer Loyalty: A Cycle of Value Enhancement 526
Customer Relationship Management: Investing in the Valuable Customers 529
   Information Technology: The Enabling Force Behind CRM 531
   Outsourcing CRM 534
   CRM in an Enterprise Resource Planning Environment 534
Chapter Summary 534

UNIT FOUR: Integrative Management Frameworks

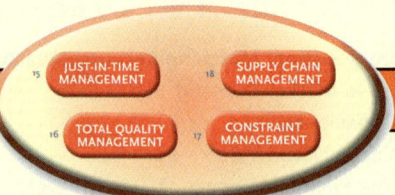

CHAPTER FIFTEEN: JUST-IN-TIME MANAGEMENT 540

Introduction: A Management Framework for Waste Elimination 542
Eliminate Waste: The Focus of the JIT System 542
   Operations Resources and Waste 545
JIT Waste Reduction Techniques 546
Enterprisewide JIT Techniques 546
   Quality Management 546
   Kaizen 547
Inventory-Focused Techniques 548
   Matching Production to Demand 548
   Kanban 548
   Component Standardization 551
   Small-Batch Production 552
   Reduced Changeover Times 553
   Frequent Deliveries 553
   Paperless Transactions 553
   Improved Supplier Relationships 554

Workforce-Focused Techniques 555
   Employee Involvement 555
   Employee Cross-Training 556
   Improvement Teams 556
Capacity-Focused Techniques 556
   Process Focus 556
   Eliminate Non-Value-Adding Steps 556
   Automation 557
   Small-Scale Equipment 557
   Protective Capacity 557
   Level Loading of Capacity 558
   Increased Preventive Maintenance 558
Facility-Focused Techniques 559
   Cellular Layouts 559
   U-Shaped Production Lines 559
   Chapter Summary 560

CHAPTER SIXTEEN: TOTAL QUALITY MANAGEMENT 566

Introduction: Building a Culture of Continuous Improvement 568
A Brief History of TQM 568
   Walter A. Shewhart 568
   W. Edwards Deming 569
   Joseph M. Juran 570
   Philip B. Crosby 571
Components of TQM 571
An Enterprise View of Quality 573
The TQM Process 576

Obtaining Continuous Improvement 577
   The Plan, Do, Check, Act Cycle 577
   The Quality Improvement Story 578
Benchmarking 581
Quality Certification Programs 584
Quality Awards 586
   The Malcolm Baldrige National Quality Award 586
   The Quality Cup 588
   Chapter Summary 589

CHAPTER SEVENTEEN: CONSTRAINT MANAGEMENT 594

Introduction: Maximizing System Output 596
Defining a Constraint 596
Global Performance Measures 599
The Constraint Management
    Focusing Process 600
    Step 1. Identification 601
    Step 2. Exploitation 601
    Step 3. Elevation 601
    Step 4. Subordination 601
    Step 5. Repeat 601
The Role of Disruptions in
    Productive Systems 603
Protecting the System from Disruptions 604
Buffering to Protect Constraints 604
Constraint Management and Batch Sizes 607
The Role of the Constraint: A Product
    Mix Example 609
JIT and Constraint Management 612
    Chapter Summary 612

CHAPTER EIGHTEEN: SUPPLY CHAIN MANAGEMENT 622

Introduction: A Systemwide Perspective 624
Supply Chain Management: The
    Motivating Forces 624
    Increased Competition 626
    The Impact of Customers on Suppliers 628
    The Impact of Suppliers on Customers 630
    Technological Advances 630
Supply Chain Management Components 630
    Distribution Network Configuration 631
    Inventory Management 632
    Distribution Strategy 632
    Strategic Partnering 633
    Cooperative Product Design 635
    Information Management 636
    Policy, Procedure, and Product
        Standardization 636
    Electronic Commerce 637
Supply Chain Management: A Typical
    Example 637
Extending the Supply Chain Globally 639
A Closer Look at the Bullwhip Effect 640
A Closer Look at Risk Pooling 645
    Chapter Summary 645

Appendix A: Areas of the Standard Normal Distribution 651

Appendix B: Areas of the Cumulative Standard Normal Distribution 652

Glossary 654

Name Index 662

Subject Index 663

PREFACE

In the years since I began studying and teaching operations management, dramatic changes have occurred both in the business environment that informs the operations management course and in the classroom where it is conducted. Certainly what we teach our students has changed over the years in ways that might have seemed inconceivable only a decade or two ago.

The discipline itself has changed in at least three fundamental ways. First, its focus is no longer limited to manufacturing concerns but, reflecting the direction in which our economy is moving, has broadened to include a focus on services as well. Second, the body of knowledge constituting "operations management" has expanded considerably in recent years. Lately such areas of study as supply chain management, project management, ebusiness and ecommerce, and ERP systems have found their way into the operations management curriculum. Finally—and this is perhaps the most critical change—it has become increasingly difficult to carry on a meaningful discussion of the operations function without discussing other functional areas of business. Regardless of the vantage point from which one begins the study of operations management, sooner or later one observes the operations function interacting with other business functions—intersecting with marketing here, nudging up against finance there. In short, it is no longer possible to view operations as less critical than, or in isolation from, other key functional areas of business. Well-designed, well-implemented operations, like a soundly devised and executed marketing plan, are vital to achieving and maintaining a company's competitive edge. This last observation is critical for students to understand.

Beyond the changes in our discipline, however, an even more fundamental change in our students has occurred. As primary beneficiaries of rapid advances in information technology, students today have easier and quicker access to more information than any previous generation of students. Such access has made them arguably more sophisticated than their counterparts of a decade earlier; but having access to such an abundance of information has just as often led to information overload. Students are exposed to more information, but, because of its sheer volume, are often discouraged from absorbing it. If their desire for or access to information is greater, their willingness to analyze and assess that information is not always evident. Students are indisputably more knowledgeable today than ever before, but is their ability to acquire knowledge matched by their ability to use it?

These are some of the fundamental issues that I found facing me as I began to write this book. How can I create a table of contents that accurately reflects the state of operations management today? How can I package this information in a way that will be both appealing and digestible to today's students—not just to operations management majors, but to all business students? Finally, how can I exploit the new information technology to produce better, more relevant instruction and learning materials?

OperationsNow.com is my attempt to answer these questions. I have tried to address both the changing field of operations management—hence the "Now" of the title—and the variety of media—suggested by the ".com" of the title—currently at our disposal that we can use to help improve the quality of the instruction we deliver. The ".com" of the title is also an acknowledgment of our changing economy and, hence, our changing view of operations. Finally, ".com" is meant to signal to students that this book not only recognizes the new frontier of cyberspace, but it makes use of it as well. Every attempt has been made to ensure that the website accompanying *OperationsNow.com* is a seamless extension of the text rather than simply an appendix to it—that it is more than a repository for ancillaries that might just as effectively have been produced in print. From its conception, the website was intended to host those activities that are best carried out on the Internet and that could not be done, or could be done less effectively, in print. It is certainly possible to use the textbook independently of the website and the website independently of the text. But using the two together provides an infinitely richer and more rewarding learning experience for students.

Just as the website differs from others in its degree of integration with the printed text, the textbook itself is organized differently from other books written for the introductory operations management course. At the core of every business is the need to create products and services of value and sell them at a price that is greater than the cost of creating them. Operations management is the management of the processes used to create that value and the resources needed to make those processes possible. Business profitability—measured by profit margin, return on assets, and return on equity—depends on a firm's ability to generate sales of the products and services created, and to manage the associated costs, so that a margin of profit is attained. Because it falls within the scope of the operations function both to control the cost of resources required to create and manage the processes needed to produce the value that customers purchase, operations management has a significant impact on the profitability of a business, its ability to compete, and its ultimate success.

Advances made in product and service quality evolve from pressures that force businesses to differentiate themselves from their competition. New products and services often start with the idea of "building a better mousetrap." A different perspective on solving an old problem, combined with the availability of new technologies, is often all that is needed to form the impetus for a product or service that is truly different. It is precisely this series of events that resulted in *OperationsNow.com*, which takes a giant step forward that differentiates it from other operations management texts.

Because it dictates the financial productivity of a firm's assets, operations management is at the core of business success; yet operations is often viewed by business students as an inessential part of their business education. This misperception makes the course difficult to teach. More important, it can result in students entering the workforce who are insufficiently acquainted with operations management and the pivotal role it plays in the success of virtually any business. *OperationsNow.com* addresses this challenge by dramatically changing the context in which operations management is presented. *OperationsNow.com* places operations decisions and concepts into their real-world context—the financial performance of the firm—through the use of a unique organizational model: the resource/profit model. Introduced in detail in Chapter 1, this model places the content of the text within the context of financial performance and provides students with an intuitive organizational framework within which the operations function can be regarded. The model's financial foundation enables *OperationsNow.com* to present operations management concepts and tools in a way that will interest all students whose futures will include increasing business profitability.

Used in conjunction with the integrated website, *OperationsNow.com* makes a significant step forward in the delivery of operations management content. *OperationsNow.com* is an unconventional yet appropriate title for a textbook that is not a traditional text. It moves beyond the traditional framework by exploiting Internet technologies to provide a wealth of content and support that is accessible online at http://www.operationsnow.com. To maximize the effectiveness of both delivery channels, each is used for what it presents best. The text is used to deliver a basic narrative covering the fundamental concepts of operations management. The website, by contrast, is used to deliver what it is best at delivering: dynamic content, video, interactive models, and resources maintained online by businesses. By using the resource/profit model as an organizational framework for the text and as a navigational framework for the website, *OperationsNow.com* provides an integrated "multichannel" learning/teaching environment that is greater than the sum of its components.

Using this text in their courses, students will learn that a fundamental prerequisite to the success of any business is its ability to combine resources to create value. It will become clear that in order to compete effectively, the value created must exceed that of competitors. The ownership of the resources is necessary but is not alone sufficient to ensure that enhanced levels of value are created. The firm must creatively combine resources into value-creating processes. Students using this text will further learn that for many businesses, enhancing product value by adding services has proven to be a very successful way to differentiate.

The same principle applies to this textbook in relation to its competitors. Like other innovative products and services, *OperationsNow.com* differentiates itself by combining traditional resources with exciting new pedagogical assets never before utilized in operations management education. It is ultimately not what *OperationsNow.com* offers but how its assets are used that will enhance the value of the class. The combination of the text "product" and cutting-edge online "services" creates a learning/teaching environment that is exciting, challenging, different, and—I believe—better equipped than traditional textbooks to serve the needs of today's students.

The resources—both text and web-based—designed to enhance *OperationsNow.com* are discussed in detail in the Guided Tour, which begins on page xx.

ACKNOWLEDGMENTS

The first edition of any book succeeds because of the combined efforts of a number of people who contribute in a variety of ways, and I owe all of those people my thanks. First of all, thanks to my family, Kim, Matt, and Meredith, for supporting and tolerating my work on this project and occasional need to be away from home. I would also like to thank my colleagues at the Richard T. Farmer School of Business Administration at Miami University for their support.

As in any large project, one person cannot contribute all of the content. I would like to thank Jaideep Motwani for his work on the test bank, Sean Lancaster for the end-of-chapter problems, and Joe Felan for accuracy checking. I would like to thank the following for reviewing and/or focus group participation: John Nicholas, Loyola University, Chicago; Joe Felan, Baylor University; Victor Sower, Sam Houston State University; Ken Klassen, California State University, Northridge; Brad Meyer, Drake University; Chwen Sheu, Kansas State University; Scott Dellana, East Carolina University; Tom Wilder, California State University, Chico; Gene Fliedner, Oakland University; Barb Flynn, Wake Forest University; Keith Willoughby, Bucknell University; Stella Hua, Oregon State University; Bill Tallon, Northern Illinois University; Rhonda Lummus, Iowa State University; Vijay Agrawal, University of Missouri at Kansas City; Bharatendu Srivastava, Marquette University; Donald A. Carpenter, University of Nebraska at Kearney; Paul Hong, University of Toledo; T. J. Wharton, Oakland University; Francis O. Pianki, Anderson University; Mehmet Barut, Witchita State University; Lawrence Fredendall, Clemson University; Britt Shirley, University of Tampa; Nancy Hyer, Vanderbilt University; Marilyn Smith, Winthrop University; Ann Marucheck, University of North Carolina, Chapel Hill; Richard Reid, University of New Mexico; Charles Petersen, Northern Illinois University; Zhimin Huang, Adelphi University; William Pinney, Alcorn State University; Daniel Krause, Arizona State University; Alan Khade, California State University, Turlock; Nael Aly, California State University, Turlock; Gilvan Souza, University of Maryland at College Park; Joel Wisner, University of Nevada at Las Vegas; Rajesh Srivastava, Florida Gulf Coast University; Henry Aigbedo, Oakland University; Bob Ash, Indiana University at New Albany; Christopher Craighead, University of North Carolina, Charlotte; Edie Schmidt, Purdue University; Mary J. Meixell, George Mason University; Vicente Vargas, Emory University; Madeline Pullman, Colorado State University; and Michael Mancuso, Purdue University.

I would like to express thanks to the editorial staff and project team at McGraw-Hill/Irwin for their commitment to this project. At the top of that list are Scott Isenberg and Cynthia Douglas, who lived with this project day in and day out for over two years. As sponsoring editor and good friend, Scott was willing to take a chance on a project that was very different from the norm. Cynthia, the developmental editor, worked tirelessly on the details of this project and, toward the project's completion, dealt with issues on a daily basis. I would also like to thank Tony Sherman, media technology producer, for his help, flexibility, and ideas on creating the text-support website. Thanks to Brent Gordon, publisher, for his support of this project, and to marketing manager Zina Craft and marketing coordinator Dave Kapoor. A special thanks to Scott Scheidt, project manager, who kept the project on schedule and saw it through to its ultimate publication. Thank you to Vicky Laird for coordinating the supplements, Mary Christianson for her contribution to the text and website design, Jeremy Cheshareck and Jennifer Blankenship for their photo research, and Carole Schwager for copyediting.

Guided Tour

Text Resources

The resource/profit model is used as an organizational framework throughout the text. It appears on all unit and chapter openers, with the current unit or chapter highlighted, emphasizing the conceptual structure of the text. This content model also serves as the navigation tool to the website, further integrating the online and text resources.

Learning Objectives

This is a list of key points that should be understood when the student has finished reading the chapter.

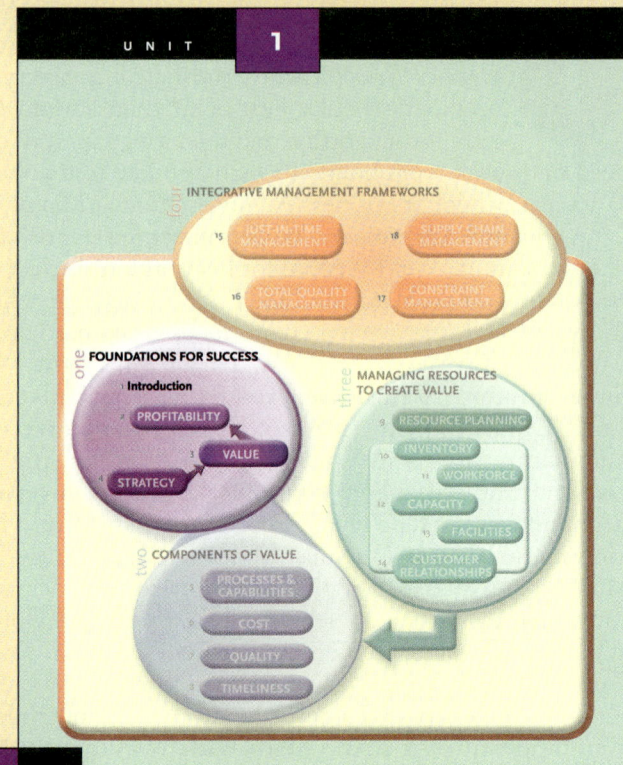

Chapter Outline

The chapter outline pulls out the main topic headings with page numbers for easy reference.

Text Resources

Examples

Throughout the chapters, problems are worked through and solved in examples, which give the student hard numbers to apply to realistic situations. The examples provide students with the quantitative tools they'll need to use in their careers and demonstrate their use. Each example in the text has an associated Excel Tutor available on the OperationsNow.com website, which solves the problem using the most common spreadsheet program in use. Excel Tutors are described in more detail in the Web Resources section of this Guided Tour.

Example 2.3 — Utilization Calculation

A newly purchased welding robot has been monitored for the past week to provide information to be used for scheduling. The observations are noted in Exhibit 2.6. What was the total utilization of the robot? What impact on utilization did each category of downtime have?

EXHIBIT 2.6 Utilization Calculations for Example 2.3

Reason for Downtime	Minutes	Utilization Impact (%)
Operator/monitor not present	107	4.46
Preventive maintenance	149	6.21
Breakdown	40	1.67
Adjustments and programming	160	6.67
Material quality problems	46	1.92
Total downtime	502	20.92
Total uptime	1,898	
Total time available:	2,400	
Total utilization:	79.08%	

Solution

Total utilization can be calculated by dividing the minutes of total uptime by the total time available. The utilization impact of each category of downtime is determined by dividing the minutes of downtime for each category by the total available minutes. The results of these calculations are presented in Exhibit 2.6. Spreadsheet calculations to obtain utilization values are presented in Excel Tutor 2.3.

www.OperationsNow.com

OM on Site

These boxes call attention to and discuss real businesses that exemplify (for better or worse) the topic at hand in the text. They put a business that students will recognize into the context of the chapter, and also into the context of the resource/profit model, showing how operations management has affected that company's profits or creation of value.

Every company profiled in the chapter's OM on Site sidebars is linked to the OperationsNow.com website.

OM on Site — Adobe: Turning a Popular Product into a Profitable Product

In 1992, Adobe Systems demonstrated software that enables a document created on one computer to be opened, edited, and saved on another computer, even with different applications and operating systems. Despite the fact that this was three years before the introduction of the World Wide Web, it was lauded as the most significant technology at Comdex, an annual technology show. The concept of document sharing was new, it was viewed positively, but its importance was not really known.

In the years since its introduction, 320 million copies of the Adobe Acrobat Reader have been distributed. The Reader, however, is free. Since 1993, fewer than 6 million copies of the full program have been sold. Adobe products have a tradition of dominating their market segments. They are driven by the pledge to allow users to publish content wherever the user wants, whether it's a printer, web page, cell phone, handheld device, PC, or Internet appliance.

But in the early and mid-1990s, the concept of electronically sharing documents wasn't on anyone's radar screen. Over time, the number of Acrobat Reader users grew. By the end of 1997, some 11.7 million had been distributed. By the end of 1998 that figure had jumped to 57.4 million. During that time, however, the sale of the full program still represented less than 7 percent of Adobe's $894 million in revenues.

Increasing the sales of the complete program was critical to Acrobat's success, but Adobe was not successful at doing it. Finally, by building alliances with system integrators that are specific to certain industries (government, pharmaceutical companies, banks, and so on), Adobe began to educate potential users about the software's capabilities. The effect of this education has been dramatic. Sales for Adobe's ePaper Solutions, which is predominantly Acrobat, reached $129.3 million in 1999 and $207 million in 2000.

R&D efforts in fast-paced technology-driven organizations may create products and services that are ahead of their time. Patience and educating customers may be required to bring about profitability.

Source: "Adobe Had a Popular Product—Making It Profitable Took Some Work," *The Wall Street Journal*, October 15, 2001, pp. R18–R19; http://www.adobe.com/aboutadobe/pressroom/pressmaterials/networkpublishing/main.html.

xxi

Guided Tour

Review Questions
Review questions test the student's knowledge of concepts—they reinforce the reading and are a great way for students to study for quizzes and tests. They can also be assigned as homework if the instructor so chooses.

Key Terms
A list of key terms at the end of each chapter presents the vocabulary a student will need to know to thoroughly understand the material. Each term is followed by the page on which it is introduced, and all terms are defined formally in the Glossary.

REVIEW QUESTIONS

1. Who determines value?
2. How are value and costs related to the potential for profit?
3. Why is net present value (NPV) often so difficult to determine accurately?
4. Describe the three global measures of profitability.
5. What are two general ways profit margin can be improved?

DISCUSSION QUESTIONS

1. Describe a business you are familiar with whose product or service value was reduced, not by what it did, but by what a competitor did. How could the business you chose have reacted to maintain the value of its product or service?
2. Identify a business you are familiar with. What could be done to increase the value of its product or service? Trace the effects of those changes to determine how they would change profit margin and ROA. Include specific effects on the components of net income.

Discussion Questions
Discussion questions are useful for student review or homework as well as for spurring class or group discussions. They are designed to require critical thinking and reasoning in situations that often lack a "right" answer.

End of Chapter Materials

Problems

The end-of-chapter problems test the students' understanding of the quantitative material presented in the chapter. They require that the student perform calculations or analyses using the equations and other tools presented in the chapter. Again, these will be helpful for individual or group practice, in-class demonstration, or assignments.

PROBLEMS

1. Morris Machining's plant diagram is below. A distance of 20 feet separates departments that are next to each other. Departments across the center hall from each other are separated by 10 feet, and those that are diagonal from each other are separated by 30 feet. Use the trips matrix and the cut-and-try layout method to create a diagram that would reduce the total distance.

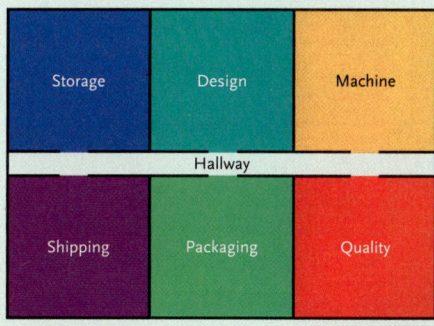

INTERACTIVE ANALYSIS 3.2

THE PROCESS-ORIENTED LAYOUT INTERACTIVE MODEL

The Process-oriented Layout Interactive Model demonstrates how different arrangements in a process-oriented layout result in different costs for transporting material. The model is sited in Chapter 13, on page 490, and is used in Interactive Analysis 13.2 on page 508. A small production facility that produces three different products in a layout with 6 departments forms the basis for the model. The three products have different routings and demands. The demands can be changed, but not the routings. You can change the layout by dragging a department to a different "room."

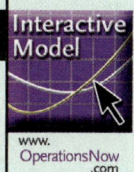
www.OperationsNow.com

Interactive Analysis

Each interactive analysis provides an experimental environment for using the interactive models available at www.operationsnow.com. For each interactive model available online, Interactive Analysis experiments guide the student through a step-by-step process that demonstrates the model and adds to the student's understanding of the concepts demonstrated in it. The interactive models are described in greater detail in the following section on Web Resources.

Guided Tour

Chapter Enhancement Resources

The resources found on this part of each chapter's website reinforce and expand upon the subject presented in the chapter. Together with the print elements within and at the end of each chapter, these resources complete the coverage of the chapter's topic and give students a broad understanding of that subject while allowing them to see how the issues raised come up in the real world.

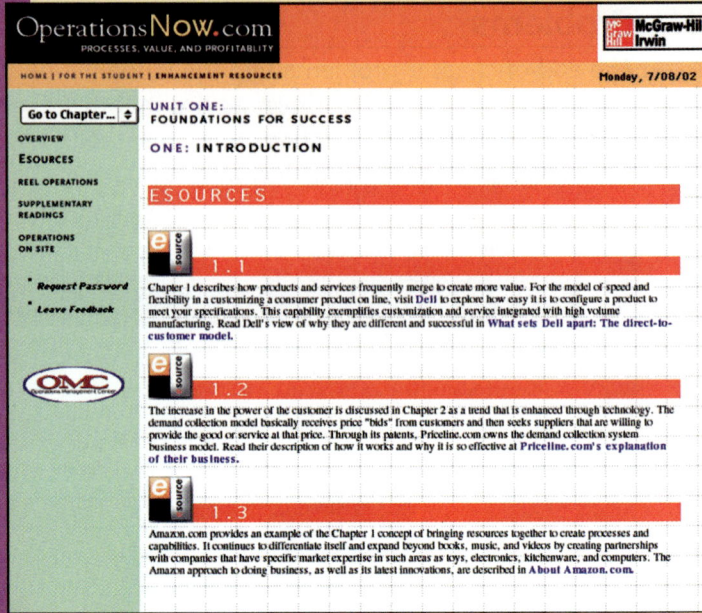

Esources

In the text, Esource icons alert the students to related content on the website. Each chapter contains two to three Esources pertaining to the topic at hand—like a traditional boxed insert found in a textbook—giving a real-world example of the topic under discussion. However, because online information can change quickly, the Esources are not discussed specifically in the text; their references are general so that the content of the website can be updated if necessary.

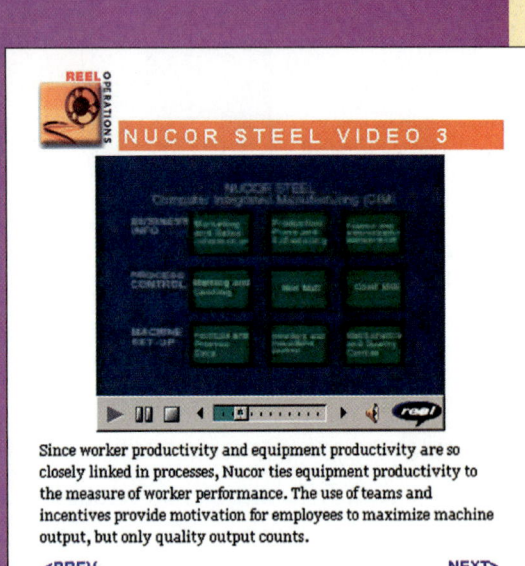

Reel Operations Video Clips

Called to the reader's attention in the text by a marginal icon, Reel Operations video clips—each an annotated series of 30- to 60-second videos presented in streaming format—comprise a video essay that illustrates the topic being discussed by providing real company footage.

Web Resources at www.operationsnow.com

Interactive Models

The interactive models are an excellent tool for increasing student comprehension of often complicated concepts through quantitative models and simulations. Marginal icons in the text let the students know that the concept at hand has an accompanying interactive model on the website that will allow students to experiment with the materials they are studying. Interactive models are used to assist students in understanding two distinctly different types of material. In some cases, the way a complex system works can be better understood if it can be seen to actually function. For example, the way queues build up in front of servers, the way inventory moves through a series of work centers, or the way a kanban

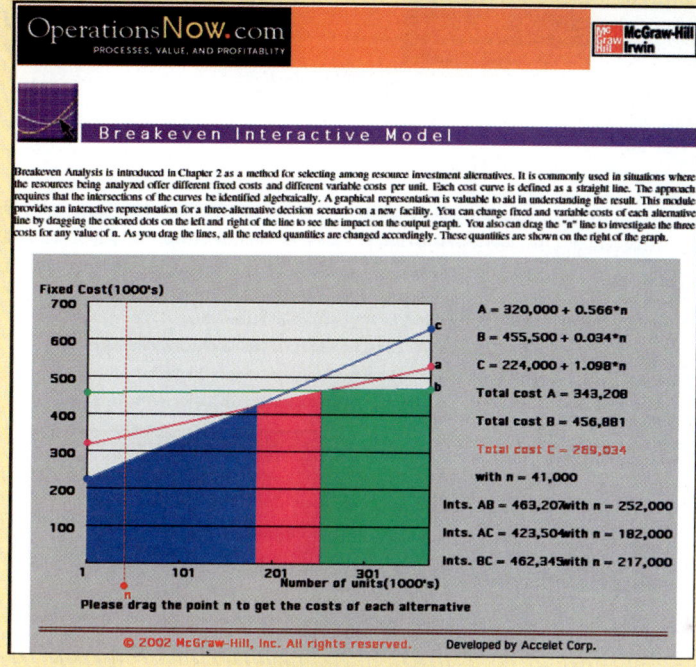

system functions can be difficult to show and describe. The interactive models show these systems in action, and the student's understanding is enhanced by being able to see the system actually work and make changes that affect it. In other cases, quantitative models can be made more easy to understand if students can see how changing one variable affects others. Changing the fixed cost of an alternative in a breakeven analysis, changing the service level in a reorder point model, changing the inventory carrying cost in an aggregate planning problem, and changing the learning rate in a learning curve problem are examples. In these situations students can see in graphs and tables exactly what the effect of the change was.

Sophisticated Java programming enables these models to be kept online for access from anywhere, eliminating the need for a student CD-ROM. The programs download quickly and run with any Java-enabled browser.

Interactive models provide the models for end-of-chapter Interactive Analysis exercises and can also be used in class for demonstration purposes.

OM on Site

Each OM on Site sidebar in the text has an accompanying link on the website, which allows the student easy access to visit the company's website to explore it more completely.

xxv

Guided Tour

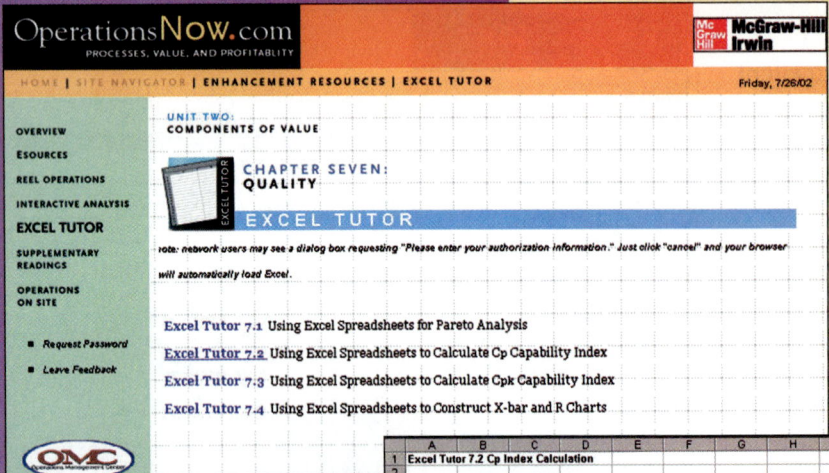

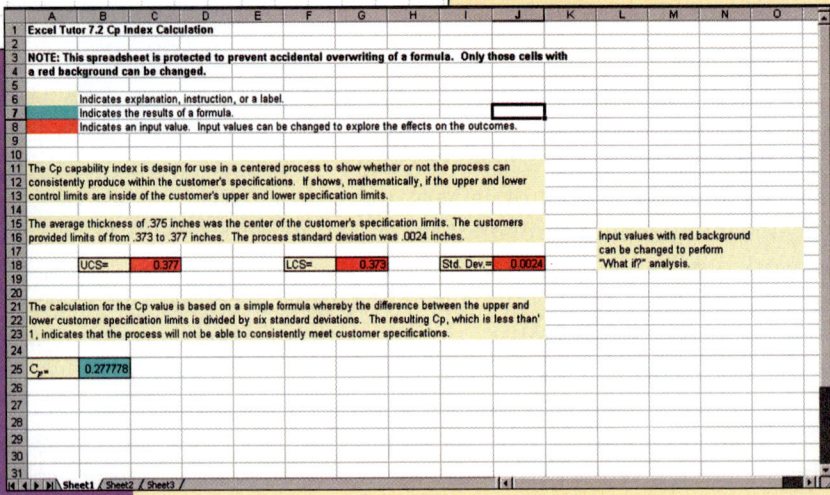

Supplementary Readings

Supplementary readings identify and present current online articles that further explore or demonstrate a specific discussion in the text. Though there is no reference to the website in the book (allowing the website to be enhanced when new articles appear online), each article on the website refers the reader to the specific page in the text that the article relates to, adding to the integration of the text and website resources. Supplementary readings include topical online articles from such general business publications as *BusinessWeek* and *Fast Company* as well as articles from publications devoted to specific topics such as quality, inventory management, and resource planning.

Excel Tutors

For every Example presented in the text, Excel spreadsheets are provided online to demonstrate how that problem is solved in a spreadsheet environment. The spreadsheets are color-coded for easy understanding and annotated, and they walk the student through the problem-solving process—equations and all—rather than simply churning out the answer. By simply clicking on the spreadsheet name on the website, Excel is automatically loaded and the spreadsheet brought up.

Web Resources at www.operationsnow.com

OM Exploration

Resources in this section of the chapters' website point the student to sites and activities that will extend the coverage of the chapter beyond the basic concepts and into the real world, where students can see how operations affect business every day. These resources can be assigned for homework or can be completed in class, as most include questions and assigned activities.

Check It Out Internet Reference Sites

Check It Out sites are dedicated to a certain topic that is discussed in the text. The primary intent of Check It Out sites is to give students a starting point for further investigation. Students can use these sites as research aide or to get more detailed information about a certain topic that is covered in the chapter.

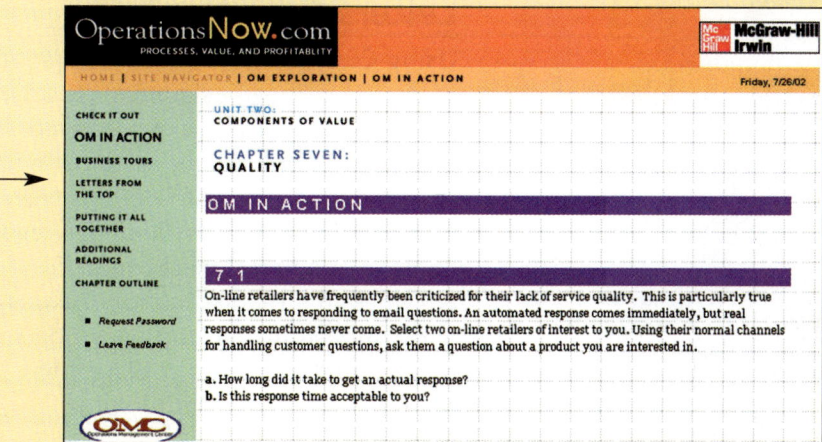

OM in Action

This resource points the student to a specific company website that relates to the text discussion of a specific topic or concept. Questions are posed requiring the student to think critically about what he or she has seen in the company website and how it applies to the subject under discussion.

Guided Tour

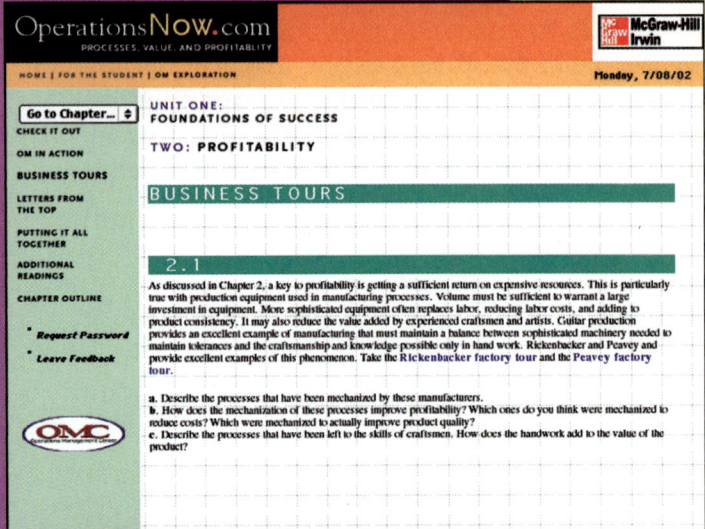

Online Business Tours

These activities take students on a virtual tour of a business or businesses and then extend beyond the basic look-and-see approach by asking questions that require the student to consider specific aspects of the tours; apply critical thinking skills by analyzing or comparing competing companies; or giving some other thoughtful reaction to the tour.

Letters from the Top

Using CEO letters to shareholders that appear in companies' annual reports, this feature increases the perceived relevance of operations management by illustrating how operations is relevant to the financial success and high-level strategy of a firm. Questions and activities that require further analysis and critical thinking lead the student to explore the letter and relate it to the topic covered in the chapter.

Web Resources at www.operationsnow.com

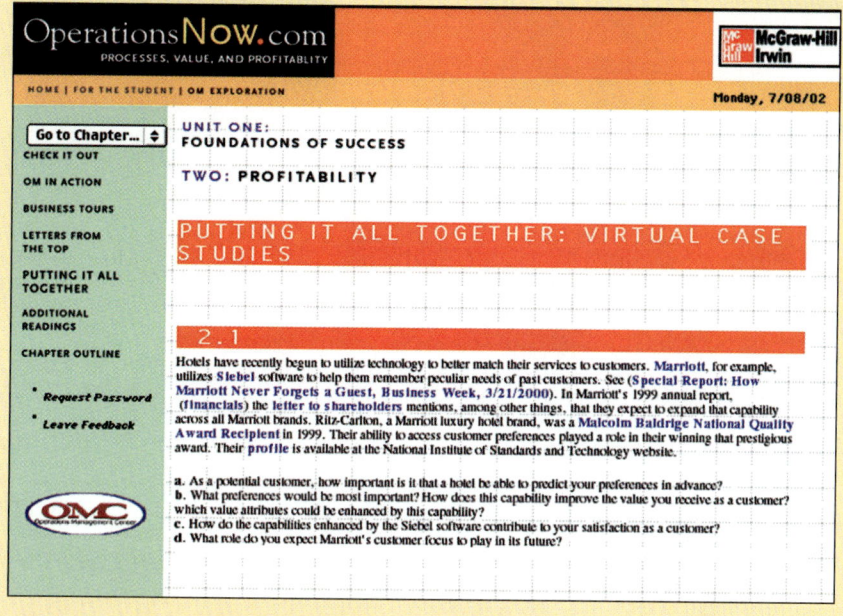

Putting It All Together: Virtual Case Studies

Analogous to an end-of-chapter minicase, Putting It All Together activities are in-depth exercises that require students to gather information from different online sources, including articles, company websites, annual reports, and government sites, to explore a topic or company, then answer questions based on their findings. Putting It All Together cases often involve more than one company and more than one area of a company's organization, illustrating again the inter-relatedness of business functions.

Additional Readings

This feature provides additional online articles that may enhance the chapter coverage or simply provide additional choice for the instructor who wishes to supplement text material with outside articles.

Review and Assessment

For further review, each chapter has self-grading quizzes available online, as well as PowerPoint slides of lecture notes prepared by the author.

UNIT 1

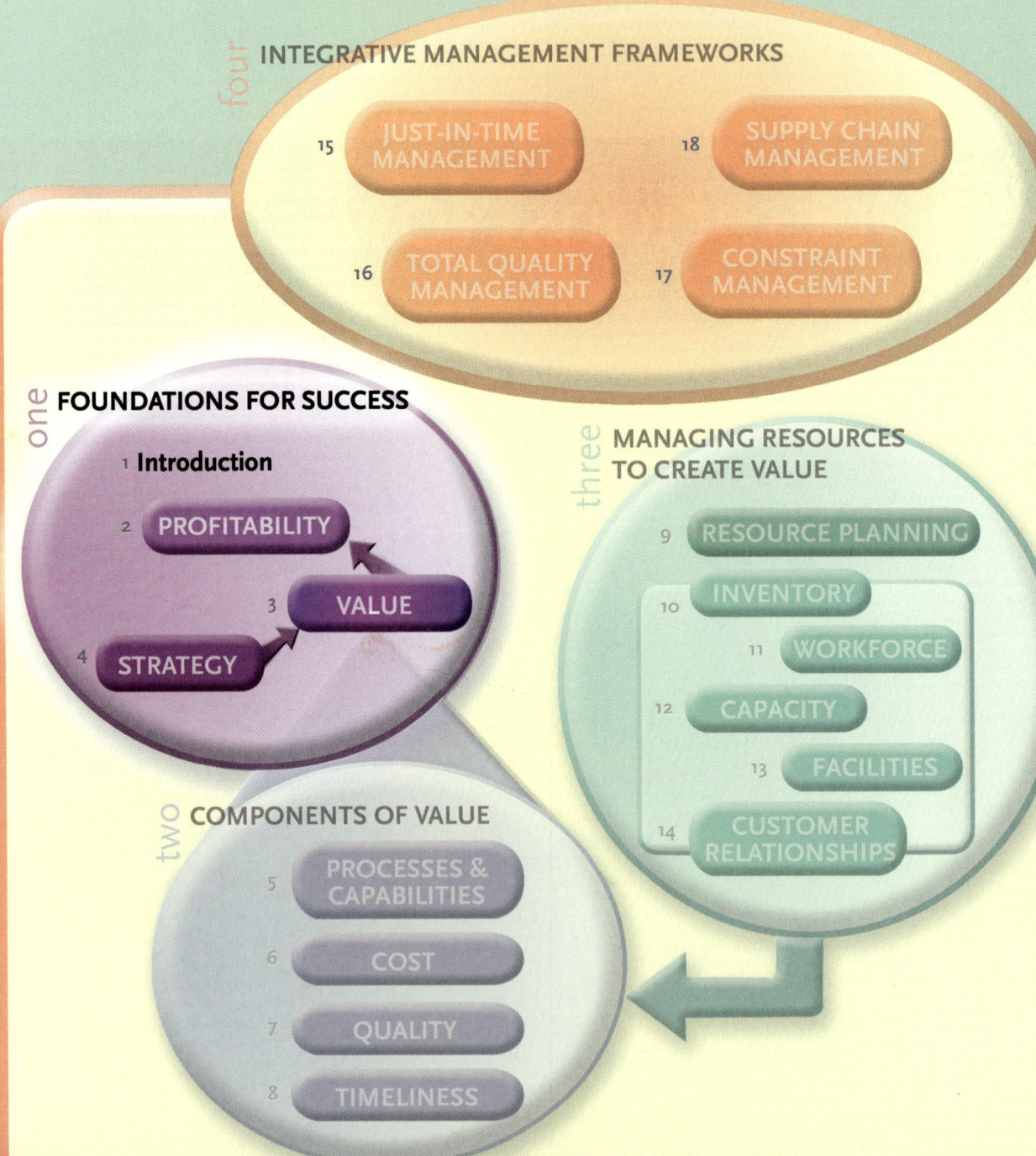

Foundations for Success

- **Chapter 1:** Introduction
- **Chapter 2:** Profitability
- **Chapter 3:** Value
- **Chapter 4:** Strategy

INTRODUCTION

Operations management is best described when it is placed in the context in which it exists—the business. As we'll soon understand, operations management is necessary for the financial success of the business. To see how operations decisions affect financial performance, several foundation components that form the context of operations must be understood. These components, which are at the heart of the business itself, are not exclusive to operations management, but without them as context, any explanation of operations would lose its relevance. The "foundations for success" that form fundamental prerequisites for business success are profitability, value, and strategy. Each is presented in detail following the introductory chapter, which covers the basics of operations management.

Operations management is the management of the resources a business uses to create value. Value creation from resources lies at the heart of all businesses—those that make consumer products, products for other businesses, or consumer or commercial services. Without resources management, value is never formed, products and services are never sold, there is no profit, and the business fails. Chapter 1 introduces operations management and the unique approach OperationsNow.com uses to integrate operations management and the success of the business.

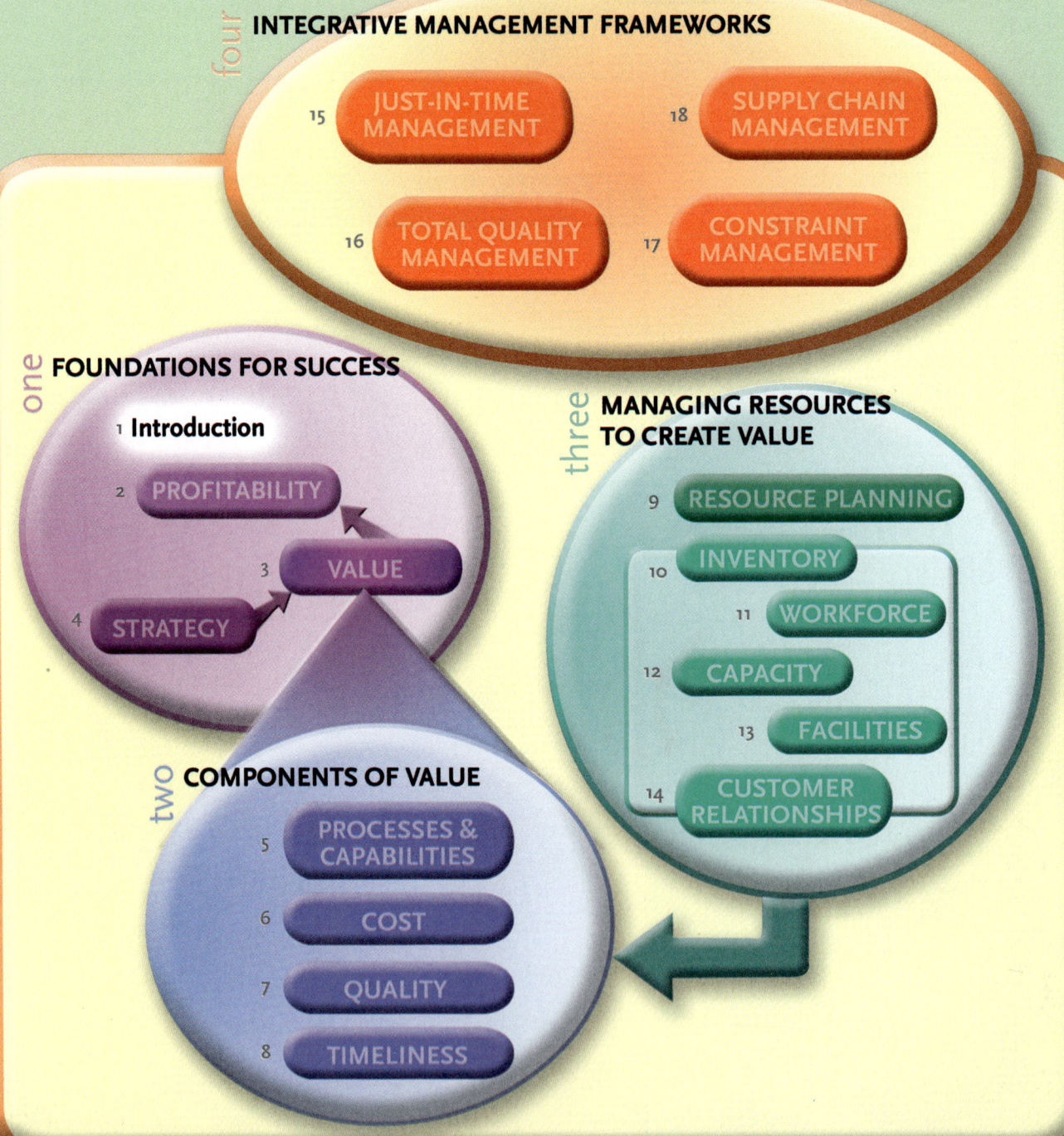

CHAPTER 1

Introduction

LEARNING OBJECTIVES

Upon completion of Chapter 1, you should be able to

- Describe the meaning of "operations," "now," and ".com" as they apply to the current coverage of operations management.

- Understand and describe the impact changes in the business environment have had and will continue to have.

- Describe the components and the relationships among the components of the resource/profit model.

- Describe external forces that affect the resource/profit model.

Introduction: Why "Operations Management" Is Critical to a Career in Business
A New Business Environment
Overview of the Resource/Profit Model
Components of Value
Managing Resources Used to Create Value
Integrative Management Frameworks
Environmental Forces
The Resource/Profit Model in Review
Business Outputs: Products and Services
Customers
Operations, Other Business Functions, and You
Chapter Summary

INTERNET RESOURCES

 Excel Tutors provide annotated spreadsheets for every solved problem that automatically load Excel.

 Esources provide an online version of the more traditional boxed insert.

 Reel Videos provide streaming video footage for company applications of chapter concepts.

 Interactive Models provide an experimental environment for quantitative concepts and simulations.

INTRODUCTION

Why "Operations Management" Is Critical to a Career in Business

What is operations management? Why is operations management a critical topic of business study? Operations management is the management of resources used to create salable products and services. It consists of those tasks necessary to turn business inputs into more valuable outputs. The inputs consist of the traditional business resources—employees, equipment, inventory, and facilities—combined with some not-so-traditional assets—knowledge, skills, customer relationships, and reputation. For an increasing number of firms, the resources include such things as Internet server speed and capacity, the technical acumen of staff, and bandwidth. The salable outputs are products, services, information, experiences, and, increasingly, combinations of all of these components. The challenge of operations management is to manage these resources effectively so that the investment made in them generates a positive financial return.

For decades, operations management has been described as a business function, analogous to accounting, marketing, and finance. To be fair, there's nothing inherently wrong with that statement. It used to be accurate, but it isn't always true now. Many businesses have taken on a very different look in recent years. Business functions look different, too. Responsibilities have changed, decisions have changed, and the role of traditional business functions within the business has changed. In many firms it has become difficult to identify and distinguish between some of these functions. For example, despite the fact that marketing, engineering, and operations tasks are still accomplished, their role as distinct and independent functions is changing. Managers in each function find that they must interact and coordinate their decision-making processes. In some businesses, traditionally named departments like marketing, finance, and operations no longer exist. The lack of a distinct department in the organization doesn't mean that the department's tasks don't get done, however. It means that businesses have begun to integrate the tasks. Many companies bring experts together into cross-functional teams rather than have them continue to function behind the barriers that have traditionally separated business functions.

Many businesses rely heavily on an organization that integrates teams of people around a common project or goal. The teams change as each goal or project is accomplished and as new ones arise. The teams encompass a variety of expertise, but all members must be cognizant, from a broad business perspective, of what has to be done and why. The isolated departments that once existed, sometimes referred to as "functional silos," have seen their walls disappear. The business where people interact only with their own kind—accountants, human resource managers, or information systems staff—is no longer effective.

Put more simply, and from the perspective students must have for their future: Businesses want to hire bright people, trainable people, who can ultimately make decisions that are best for the business. They don't want employees who cannot grasp the big picture or who cling to a belief that what looks best for marketing or finance is obviously the best decision for the entire business. The present and future manager must have functional expertise with an enterprise perspective, not functional expertise with a functional perspective.

If a student imagines herself as a marketing brand manager for a consumer products firm, a president of a bank, or a consultant working for a Big Five (or is it Four?) accounting firm, and assumes she will be working with people whose expertise and background are the same as hers, she should think again. She is placing constraints on her career potential. She'll work with systems experts. She'll work with engineers. She'll work with people whose expertise lies in areas that haven't even been thought of yet. She needs to understand what they do and why they do it. She needs to understand how her business converts resources and capabilities into a healthy profit. She needs to understand operations management.

Today's managers require continuous education to keep them apprised of advancements made in their areas of expertise *and* in other aspects of the business that have broad implications. As business decision-making becomes more cross-functional and global measures of business performance continue to increase in importance, a foundation that provides an enterprise perspective, enhanced by ongoing educational efforts to maintain currency, is critical.

Why "Now"?

"Now" appears in the title of this book because "now" implies that times have changed (they have) and that operations management "now" is quite different from operations management "then" (it is). Service-oriented businesses, whether they are banks, retail stores, insurance companies, or hairdressers, have long recognized the customer as an integral part of the firm's formula for success. The firm's location, design, and layout, as well as the training of employees, have always had a customer focus. Manufacturers, on the other hand, have been able to isolate themselves from the consumer with barriers of distributors, wholesalers, and retailers. Now, however, even such hardcore manufacturers as auto producers have recognized that service-related issues are as important as—if not more important than—the product they sell.

All businesses received a not-so-gentle shove down a slippery slope when personal computer (PC) manufacturers began to sell customized PCs directly to the public. That business model was immediately copied. Toyota, Ford, and General Motors are rapidly approaching the day when the customer will have the ability to configure a car over the Internet and climb behind the wheel in days, not weeks.[1] Internet speed forces a company to place the customer at the center of everything and design itself for customer satisfaction rather than mass production. Today's definition of customer satisfaction extends beyond product quality to incorporate speed, flexibility, and other service-related issues. Esource 1.1 provides an example of one implementation of the direct-to-customer model.

It's true that the Internet has not removed all the stumbling blocks to good customer service. We all still occasionally encounter products of poor quality. We encounter poor quality service like slow responses and long delays much too frequently. Is this Internet speed? No, it's simply a great opportunity for a competitor.

United Parcel Service (UPS) has experienced the dramatic change in consumer expectations for customer service. In December 1995 it experienced its first month with 100,000 online tracking requests. In December 1996 it experienced its first month with 1 million online tracking requests. In December 1997 it experienced its first *week* with 1 million online tracking requests. In December 1998 it experienced its first *day* with 1 million online tracking requests. In December 1999 it experienced its first day with 2.5 million online tracking requests. In December

2000, it experienced its first day with 5 million online tracking requests. In five years the demand for that service grew by a factor of 1,500.[2]

It used to be easy to distinguish between manufacturers and services. Manufacturers made products, things you could get your hands around. Services fulfilled needs, but their outputs were intangible. Today all successful firms must deliver services. Companies *know* this. They even provide the mechanisms—customer service hotlines and websites with "Contact Us!" buttons. These mechanisms can be effective, but for the business that doesn't take them seriously, they can also be dangerous. Expectations actually increase because customers think the businesses mean what they say. Unfortunately, many companies don't know how to follow through on their implied promises. They raise the customers' hopes that their comments are important and then dash them.

Whether customers want to believe it or not, in the not-too-distant future many traditional manufacturing firms, including automobile manufacturers, computer manufacturers, and other consumer product manufacturers, will no longer manufacture at all; they'll merely assemble components provided by a deep network of suppliers. Some won't even assemble but will invest their expertise in product development and look outside the company for manufacturing capability. In fact, the notion of vertical integration is beginning to take on a new look. In the past, manufacturers were likely to buy up suppliers in order to have better control over quality and costs. They were quite disconnected from the consumer, however, because of a series of distributors and independent retailers.

The pendulum has now swung the other way. Manufacturers are outsourcing more and more of their needs and at the same time becoming more directly linked to the customer through services. Even Japanese manufacturers, despite decades of close-knit supplier networks known as **keiretsu**, are beginning to outsource manufacturing processes to contract manufacturers.[3] These changes are made possible by advancements in technology that enable firms to maintain accurate and almost instantaneous communication up and down the supply chain. Some manufacturers maintain that level of communication. Some recognize they need to do it. Is this the way of the future? No one knows for sure. When the pendulum swings, it often swings too far. There are many examples of companies that outsourced their production capability and then lost their competitive position in the market.

Clearly speed is important, but how does it all happen? Computers quickly process information over the Internet, but how can the actual physical systems move goods and services so fast? In the current business environment, speed is critical. How can an order for a customized automobile be completed in five days when many of us can't get a response from an email in 48 hours? How are many businesses able to react that quickly and why can't they all? How can machines produce products so swiftly? How can products be moved that rapidly? The answers are that the processes must not only accomplish their objectives quickly, but they must also be designed for almost split-second response to change. Suppliers must provide instantaneous replenishment and production processes must be totally flexible. Services must meet customer needs immediately. They must, and in many cases they do know in advance what individual customers want. That's operations *now*.

The world economy itself is changing drastically, and businesses must exist within that changing environment. We often hear reference to a "knowledge-based" economy, but what exactly does that mean? And, more to the point, "So what?" In a knowledge-based economy, innovations substitute knowledge for other capital. Some creative person comes up with a great idea, and suddenly some other product or service is obsolete. Someone gets rich, and someone else is looking for a new job. But more important, we, as a society, gain knowledge. Knowledge breeds more knowl-

CHAPTER 1 Introduction 7

> **om on site**
>
> **PayPal: The Worst Idea of the Year?**
>
> PayPal, the largest Internet payment network, allows money to be sent by email. It has dominated the auction company Ebay as a safe and convenient way to transfer money from buyer to seller. It has a customer base of 10 million and has grown rapidly. It expects $3 billion in transactions per year. Surprisingly, PayPal didn't start out with that concept in mind at all. Originally, PayPal started in 1999 as a specialized service for owners of Palm computers who needed to transmit funds to each other using the device's infrared port. In its early days, however, to actually use the feature the two Palm users had to be so close they could have easily handed checks to each other. One trade publication voted the idea the worst of the year. PayPal also provided a means for non-PayPal users to transfer money, and it was this capability that began to become popular. The Palm-only service was dumped and PayPal began to grow. PayPal is expanding its position to be the online means of transferring money for all types of online business transactions, including traditional bills like phone and utility bills.
>
> PayPal's success lies in the fact that it doesn't try to reinvent everything. It recognizes what needs to be reinvented and does that very quickly. The rest PayPal leaves alone. PayPal has been particularly attractive to small merchants that can be charged as much as 5 percent by credit card companies. PayPal charges only 2.9 percent plus 30 cents per transaction.
>
> Source: "Fix It and They Will Come," *The Wall Street Journal*, February 12, 2001, p. R4; www.paypal.com, August 9, 2001; "These Guys Will Make You Pay," *Fast Company*, November 2001, Online Edition.

edge. Just imagine the ideas and wealth that have been dependent on the development of the first web browser created by graduate students at the University of Illinois. The World Wide Web wasn't their idea. Their creative input was in developing a different way *to use it*. So often we find that the creativity that sparks innovation is the ability to recognize another use or potential for someone else's idea.

Knowledge expands at an even faster rate when more people talk to each other and share ideas. This principle has expanded to create a global business network—enhanced even more by close relationships between companies that trade with each other to the point that they invest in each other, help develop each other's new products and services, and help each other solve problems.

Rapid change, driven by technology and expanding global markets, is changing the way we make business decisions, the way we value assets, and the way we calculate costs. The traditional understanding of value and how customers perceive it has been turned inside out. For a while, even the way people thought about profit changed. Market share was the only important measure. Profit didn't matter. Just ask shareholders of "pavingstones.com" or "petfoodinbulk.com" For some bizarre reason, customers just wouldn't pay $13 for a $15 bag of dog food when shipping costs were $7. That was then. This is now. Profit matters.

Why ".com"?

What does ".com" mean? Back in the late 1990s it meant instant money. Get rich quick. All efforts were devoted to that initial public offering (IPO). After that, who cares? The business plan started out with an exit strategy. Something was wrong with that picture. Managers compared their projected rate of cash outflow ("burn rate") to the rate of getting venture capital. If inflow was greater than outflow, business was fine. Then it hit the proverbial fan. Dot-coms hemorrhaged investors. Investors again became interested in companies that actually make a profit, companies that actually own *something* and make *something*. There aren't nearly as many dot-coms as there used to be. More will disappear, not from lack of bandwidth or from being short of spinning gizmos on the splash page. It's simpler than that. They have disappeared and will continue to disappear because they aren't profitable. Of course, that attrition has been good for those that are effective producers of goods and services.

That dot followed by three letters has now come to define a business that not only utilizes the Internet but also leverages it to accomplish more than it could without it. This configuration means that the company wants to deal directly with a customer. It might mean that the company is merely selling consumer products and consumer services via the Internet. It might mean that the company is selling products and services to other companies selling products or services via the Internet. It might even mean that the company sells traditional products, but its suppliers can access important information through the Internet. It could also mean that a service or product being offered didn't even exist four years ago. It definitely implies speed. It implies that information is changing hands rapidly. It means quick response. It means the company wants its customers to have access to more information. That's what ".com" has come to mean in a business context. It used to mean a lot less, but those companies are gone.

In the context of this book, ".com" has two meanings. First, ".com" is recognition that operations cannot be separated from the technological changes that are occurring all around us. The age of the dot-com company has arrived and has already been through one major transition. There will be more. Any coverage of the operations management topic must integrate this phenomenon and address its implications. Successful businesses use what is necessary to accomplish their goals. The integration of a technology can become so universal that separating it has no meaning. The "e" in ecommerce really means that the business is using modern business techniques. It's as simple as that. Why would any business that hopes for success not use current business methods and resources? It wouldn't.

Second, ".com" means that this book utilizes these same current technologies. Why would a book not use current technologies and resources? It should take advantage of modern technologies to provide a better way to communicate knowledge, a better way to keep up-to-date, and a better way to keep the reader informed. Just like in a business, those technologies provide a more efficient and higher-quality link to the customer—you. That's *OperationsNow.com*.

A NEW BUSINESS ENVIRONMENT

Businesses today range from a traditional manufacturer of corrugated paper containers (cardboard boxes to you and me) to one running an online auction of banner space on web pages. Imagine selling, through a virtual auction, a virtual commodity (web page advertising space) that may even be purchased by companies wishing to advertise their virtual services. Boxes are traditional products that have been around for years and will be needed for years to come. Both have value. Both companies have potential to be profitable. Virtual products and services that are now commonplace could barely be imagined seven or eight years ago. An online auction of *anything* would have seemed unlikely. An auction of advertising banner space on websites would have been ridiculous. Will online auctions exist in 10 years? That's hard to say. You can bet, however, that we'll still be using cardboard boxes.

In addition to the added pressures and capabilities resulting from technological progress, many other pressures exert forces on business. Pressures vary in different industries. Obviously the external pressures on a box manufacturer are different from those on an Internet auction business. Like any organic system, a business must adapt.

The vast range of products and services, many in a medium that didn't even exist just five years ago and others basically unchanged for a hundred years, makes it difficult to come up with a general model that perfectly represents operations in all businesses. In fact, it makes it impossible. A model is important, however, to understand operations and its role in businesses. An effective model makes it possible to organize operations concepts and place them in the context of the entire business. It shows how operations management contributes to the business's goals. Such a model is critical if operations concepts are to be integrated into the firm's success, not as independent entities. The resource/profit model, shown in Exhibit 1.1, provides an organizational framework for examining operations in the larger business context. It has the level of simplification necessary to be generalizable but has sufficient detail to provide a framework for examining operations management.

OVERVIEW OF THE RESOURCE/PROFIT MODEL

Foundations for Success

The resource/profit model begins, quite logically, with the overriding objective of the business—profitability—and proceeds with two of its most critical prerequisites—value and strategy. These three concepts are presented in Exhibit 1.2 as "foundations for success" because they form the foundation for decision making throughout the business. It is no coincidence that there are parallels between finance classes and the coverage of profitability, as it relates to operations management, in this book. This connection is critical because finance exists in the environment of operations management decisions. Operations management, on the other hand, exists within an environment of financial decision making. It is also no coincidence that the coverage of value will link closely to classes in marketing. The creation of value is often thought of as the root of operations management responsibility. Determining what customers actually value is at the root of marketing responsibility.

Profitability

Every business organizes resources into processes and uses these processes to create goods and/or services and then it sells these goods or services. Ideally, the sale results in a positive financial return on the investments that were utilized to create the goods and services. **Profitability** is the primary objective of any business. It is the answer to the question "Why?" when asked about the existence of any business. The bookstore where you purchased this text has invested tens of thousands of dollars in resources and processes to get books to you not because it wants you to read more. The copy shop across the street made its investments for the same reason. So has the restaurant. It seems simple, but it can also be extremely complex.

It is important to notice that the goal of the business is profitability, not profit. When most people say profit, they really are talking about "net income." Net income doesn't provide enough information to allow for the evaluation of a business's success. It's simply the measure of an output. If a business's net income was $100,000, it's impossible to know whether it was successful. Profitability measures, including those that measure profit, compare outputs to inputs to determine how productive the money invested was.

Businesses have other objectives, including employment and development of individuals and contributing to society as a whole, but none can be accomplished without

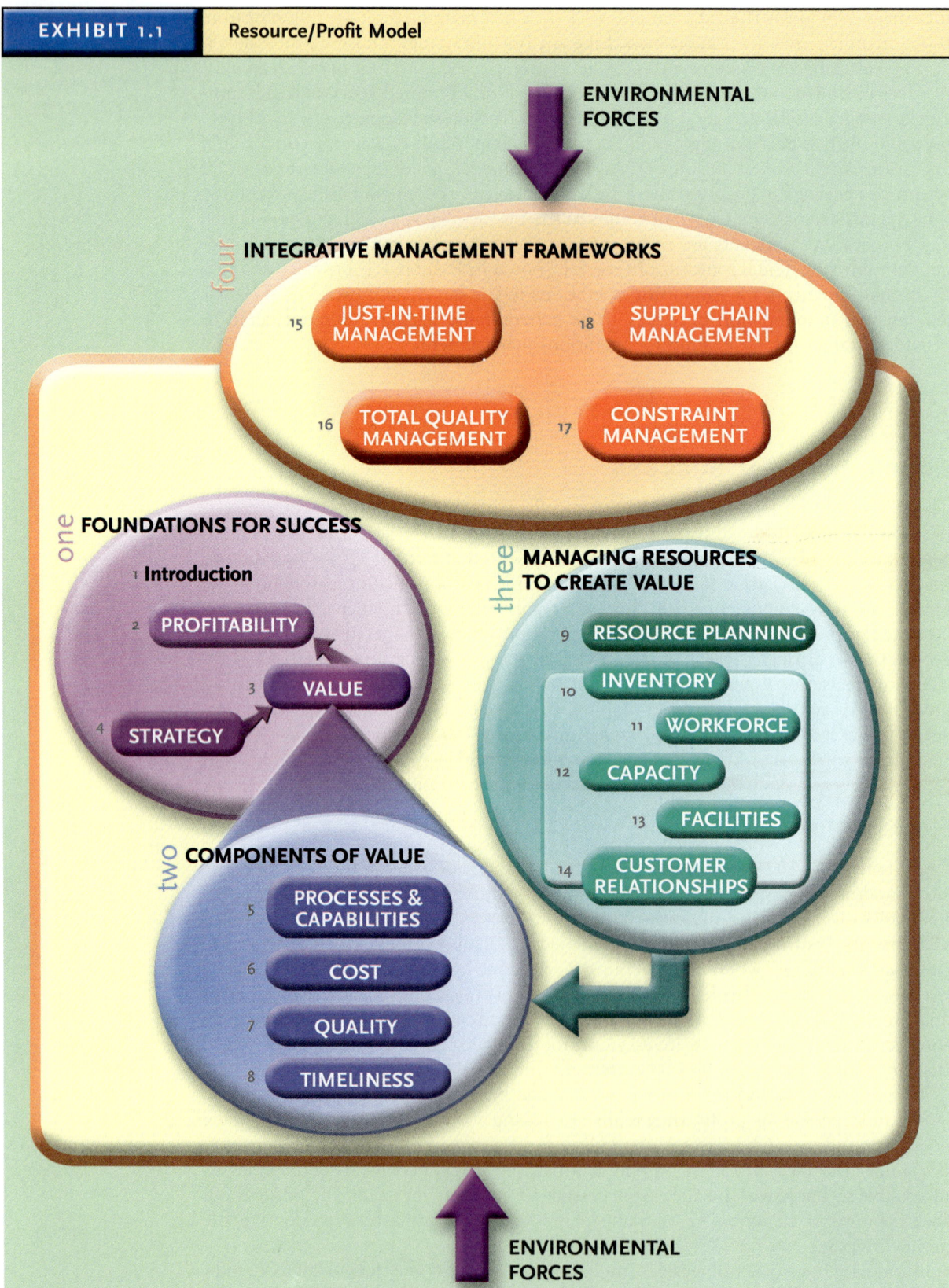

EXHIBIT 1.1 Resource/Profit Model

> **Foundations of Success Excerpt from the Resource/Profit Model** — EXHIBIT 1.2

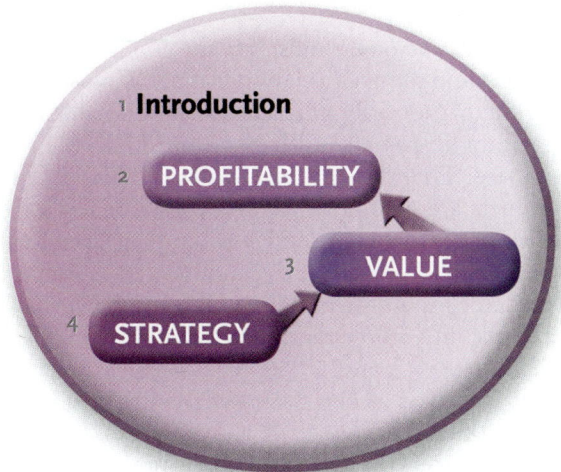

profitability. Financial return, short and long term, at a rate that is greater than other alternatives must be at the forefront or all other objectives will fail when the company folds. Operations management is at the heart of that cycle, managing the productive resources to provide profitability. Operations manages the inputs used to get that profitability.

Value

The goal of any investor is to find an investment that will create value for the owner. Resources and processes are company assets that, like any other investment, are expected to provide a financial benefit to the owner. If the answer to the "Why?" question of a business's existence is profitability, then the answer to the "How?" question is value. Customers seek value. **Value** is added through processes. You bought the shoes you're wearing because you thought they were a better value than other alternatives. You prefer one restaurant to another because of how you define value. You get copies made at that copy shop because it's a better value than paying 10 cents each on a machine at the library.

Customers are willing to pay for value, and therein lies the potential for the business's owners to benefit from their investment. The difference between the amount customers are willing to pay for the value of something and the cost of creating that something establishes the primary motivation for the enterprise. It provides the opportunity for profitability. From a financial perspective, the difference between something's market value and the cost of creating it is referred to as the **net present value (NPV)** of an investment.

For someone trying to make money in the stock market, investment decisions ultimately determine the return on the dollars invested. Make a good decision—get a good return. Make a poor decision—get a poor return. For product- and service-oriented businesses, processes act in a manner similar to that of a stock fund manager. Processes define how operating resources are used. If resources are used well, the return will be good. Processes play two critical roles in defining the NPV of a resource investment. First, the lower the cost (as long as value remains the same), the greater the difference between cost and market value. Second, the process is a major factor in the customer's perceived value. The more value added by the process, the greater the difference between market value and cost (as long as cost remains the same). Processes define the way resources are exploited (or not) through design, implementation, and use.

For profitability to result, customers must buy the goods or services produced. They must view those products and services as having value. Without that perceived value, consumers won't buy them. Not only must customers see value and be willing to pay for it, they must be willing to pay a sum that's greater than the total cost of producing the product or service. That difference provides the potential for profit.

The amount customers are willing to pay for a good or service is defined by their perception of the value of that good or service when compared to alternatives. Value is what processes are supposed to add to the inputs. For example, a pizza restaurant utilizes a variety of resource inputs—a building, tables and chairs, ovens, recipes, skills of employees, cars, boxes, and a process that combines them—to create a pizza and get it to the customer's door.

Without value that is viewed as being greater than that of competitors' offerings, no one will buy a product once they've made a comparison. Despite the fact that producers often set price, producers do not determine value. The customer does that.

Suppose a student is in the market for a PC. He sees one of those "for sale" signs with the little tear-off phone number tabs at the bottom. The sign extols the virtues of a 550-megahertz Pentium PC, complete with a 1-gigabyte hard drive, a good-sized monitor, and 64 megabytes of RAM. Old, but functional. Price: $500. The ad also used sentiment in comments like "reliable," "hate to part with it," and "need the money for spring break." The student is thinking, "I only need a PC for word processing, spreadsheets, and email. This machine would work for me." But $500 seems high and he knows he can buy a brand-new system with far greater capabilities for about $800. So he calls the number and offers $100. The owner seems extremely insulted, claiming that the PC is worth far more than that because *he* paid more than $2,000 for it.

Should the price someone else paid for the computer two years earlier have any impact on its current value? Absolutely not. Its value to this student is determined by the capabilities it offers to him now, compared to current alternatives. That logic holds for all products and services. The customer determines the value. Always. The customer's ability to determine value has traditionally resulted in the customer either accepting the merchant's quoted price or walking away. Either it is a good deal, or it isn't.

In most transactions, the customer has had to accept or reject the seller's price, despite the fact that the customer actually determines the value. This paradigm may be changing as consumers become more exposed to a variety of pricing approaches. Online auctions like Ebay are now available for virtually any product or service imaginable. PNC Bank, for example, auctions certificates of deposit as small as $5,000. The best 25 bids win.[4] Another new pricing approach, known as a "demand collection system," has also become popular. In this system, customers submit a price they are willing to pay for a product or service,[5] and the seller then locates a producer willing to sell at that price. This is a major shift in power that has huge implications for firms seeking the customer's dollar. Esource 1.2 provides an example of how the demand collection system approach works.

Value is the basis on which potential customers make decisions. It is often measured by how much the consumer would be willing to pay. Creating value is the only way a business can expect the customer to buy from it in the long term. Everyone has made mistakes on purchases. They've paid for something and ultimately decided it was a big mistake. "That wasn't worth it!" might have been their complaint. The *it* they refer to is whatever amount they paid for the product or service. Their recourse was to return it for a refund or just write it off as one of life's unpleasant experiences. Any discussion of value leads us to the adage "you get what you pay for," which, in many ways, is true. Better product or service quality generally will cost more, although paying more doesn't always guarantee a higher-quality product or service.

This discussion of value has been one-sided. The value of a transaction goes beyond the characteristics of the product or service. It must also include the price. Reconsider the used computer example. Changing the price changes the value. That computer, for $100, would have been a good value. For $500 it wasn't. The computer didn't change value, but its price did. To include the price of a product or service and the benefits received from it, value is sometimes thought of as

$$\text{Value} = \frac{\text{Benefits}}{\text{Price}}$$

Changes in pricing approaches have dramatically changed the way customers must determine value. As businesses gather more data about customers' purchasing habits, they are slowly moving toward setting different prices for different individuals. This has been a standard practice for airlines, hotels, and car rental companies. In mortgage lending, different interest rates are applied for different risk distinctions. This is actually advantageous for some, because they would pay an even higher rate elsewhere. Grocery stores are expected to follow, offering reduced prices automatically for customers who normally buy certain products only during promotions or with coupons. Customers who guard their privacy, however, will not have access to the lower prices.[6]

For producers of goods and services, improving processes provides the opportunity to increase value. The processes add the benefits that make the product or service attractive to consumers. But once again, the price side must be considered, since adding steps to a process almost always increases its cost to the producer. If, to improve a service, process steps must be added whose cost is greater than the consumer's perception of the value added, then the increased cost may require an increase in the price, which may actually decrease the value because the price is now greater relative to the benefits perceived.

The relationship between value and profit leads firms to try to continuously increase value. One way is to reduce costs, which allows them to reduce price. A common way to reduce costs is to analyze processes and eliminate steps that do not add value. Eliminating non-value-adding steps reduces the cost of producing the product or service but doesn't decrease the benefits perceived by the customer. In fact, this is the crux of process improvement.

Strategy

The business must also identify how, in the future, it will continue to add value to its inputs in ways that customers will desire. What type of customer will the business seek to attract? What will customers want? What will competitors do to meet customer wants? What must a business do to compete against them? The business must continue to determine how it can create value as its environment changes and as customer desires change. The business must plan its **strategy**, which sets the direction for the future. Planning for a particular way of offering value to a specific set of customers is a tremendous challenge, but it provides the means by which the company positions itself for future profitability. By establishing goals for the future, and creating the mechanisms to reach them, the business is able to adapt to changing customer expectations and changing environmental pressures. Detailed examinations of profitability, value, and strategy are presented in Chapters 2, 3, and 4 respectively.

COMPONENTS OF VALUE

In the resource/profit model the components of value are presented to provide a close-up view of value. Many things, until examined up close, are difficult to understand. Salt looks like little cubes until magnified. Then crystalline structures become apparent. Pond water looks nasty and green until magnified. Then hundreds of small organisms are exposed. Value is taken for granted until its components are identified and examined. The resource/profit model provides an organization for examining value by breaking it into the components of processes and capabilities, cost, quality, and timeliness, as shown in the model excerpt in Exhibit 1.3.

Processes and Capabilities

One might argue that—unlike cost, quality, and timeliness—processes and capabilities are not viewed by customers as a component of value. This argument is often valid when one looks only at product-oriented processes, because customers aren't as concerned about how a product is produced. However, customers care very much about the **processes** they must interact with to purchase that product. They care very much about service-oriented processes, such as those they must interact with to get assistance when they need it. It turns out that customers care deeply about many business processes—particularly those that affect them directly. While they don't pay much attention to the processes used to assemble a product, they care very much about the capabilities those processes give the company. They view these as important because they judge that company by those capabilities. Those capabilities generate value.

The **capabilities** the company has formulated are the answer to the customer's questions, "What exactly can you do for me?" and "What is it that I'm paying for?"

The answer to those questions can be, simply, "This company can sell you a collar for your dog cheaper than anyone else." Or it can be "This company can offer you a selection of 50 different dog collars on our website. Our website is easy to navigate and quick to download. Purchasing products on the site is simple, secure, and quick. We can deliver the collar you prefer in 48 hours at a price lower than anyone else. If,

| EXHIBIT 1.3 | Components of Value Excerpt from the Resource/Profit Model |

> **om on site**
>
> **Eliminating Customer Risk-Taking at Borders**
>
> We've all considered purchasing a CD when we're not entirely sure we'll like it. Maybe we've heard a song or two but hate to shell out $16 for one that will never be played. Some stores have dealt with that problem by offering to open any CD that a customer wishes to listen to. This satisfies the customer but creates logistical issues for the store trying to deal with all of those opened CDs. Technological advancements have enabled Borders to eliminate that dilemma for its customers in a much more elegant way. In the past, Borders had listening carrels and a selection of several CDs to choose from. Using new technology, a customer can scan the bar code of any CD, which remains unopened, and the entire contents of the CD can be played. With this capability, risk is eliminated for the customer through unlimited preview options that are available. For Borders, CDs need not be opened for a customer to listen to them, but customers are able to sample everything offered.

when you get the dog collar, you don't like it, you can return it simply by putting it back in the box and dropping it off at any UPS pickup point. Nothing more. You'll receive an immediate credit." Are the processes and capabilities that enable a company to make such claims of value? Certainly.

Customers perceive value in different ways. Clearly, the processes and capabilities of a business allow it to create value consistent with the product or service design, which should also be consistent with customer expectations. Processes are made up of tasks. Tasks are specifically designed to contribute to a product or service in a way that will be perceived as valuable by a customer. The grouping of simple tasks into processes, and the grouping of processes in a way that creates capabilities, is at the core of creating something of value. A company whose capabilities are different from those of a competitor can produce products and services that differ, as well. Different doesn't necessarily mean more valuable, but to create greater perceived value a company must have processes and capabilities that differ from competitors.

Processes and capabilities are a dominant responsibility of operations management. They range from being extremely simple to extremely complex. For some businesses, the need for consistency mandates that processes be standardized and accurately documented. For others, the need for customization requires processes to be flexible in order to satisfy each customer's special needs. Processes range tremendously, from the method used to ensure that a small paper bag is full of french fries, to the steps taken when auditing a Fortune 500 firm's books, to how a credit card account number is transferred securely online. Most firms utilize a variety of processes that create capabilities of interest to customers. Often these capabilities set one firm apart from another. Capabilities, when compared to those of competitors, provide customers with what they need to determine a service or product's value. The capability might be to make a tangible good or it might be to perform a service. If the customer wants what the business capability provides, the processes have created value.

Capabilities are not all of equal value, however. Some are so fundamental that possessing them doesn't translate into a competitive advantage for the firm. For example, the ability to deliver a pizza isn't very valuable, because virtually all pizza restaurants can do it. It's necessary, but not sufficient. The capabilities that competitors don't have are often the most valuable. These **differentiating capabilities** distinguish one company from another and often mean success or failure for the firm in the marketplace. Understanding the concepts of processes and capabilities is critical to understanding

Unique products or services depend on the business's ability to create capabilities that are distinctive. Entrepreneurs have responded to Bangkok, Thailand's air pollution problem with oxygen bars. In this bar, named "O2O," curious Thais and foreign tourists pay 90 baht (US$1.80) for 20 minutes of oxygen. The ability to add oxygen to other services a business offers requires an investment in sophisticated equipment, facilities in a high-traffic location, current and interesting reading material for a broad range of interests, and personalized music selection.

operations because designing and managing the processes used to create value is one of the most important responsibilities of operations.

Cost

When a customer orders a pizza, he is certainly thinking about the taste of that pizza. When the manager of the pizza restaurant orders flour, she is certainly concerned about the flour, but other aspects of the business transaction have an impact on value of that dough as well. The first of these aspects is the cost associated with obtaining the product or service. **Cost** can be defined as the amount of scarce resources consumed to achieve a specified objective. The cost of owning a new car, for example, is not just the price one has to pay to drive it off the dealer's lot. The total cost of owning the new car includes all costs associated with it over a specified period of time. If the customer wishes to own the car for six years, for example, the cost must include expenditures over that time period. Certainly, the price paid is part of the total cost, but so is the interest on the loan, as are the price of insurance, the cost of maintenance and repair, and the value depreciation on the car over the six years.

Costs can have very different meanings to different customers. In the previous example, the customer was assumed to be a consumer. A business customer might have a very different view of cost. A car dealer, for example, would view the cost of purchasing a car as more of a financial investment. The total costs would include the cost of the space it would take on the lot, work that would need to be done on the car to get it ready to sell, administrative costs associated with ownership transfer, advertisement costs, and opportunity cost of the dollars invested in it that could be used for something else.

Costs are important not only to the customer, but they are very important for the business as well. For example, the costs associated with getting a car ready to sell and advertising it, as well as the cost of administrative work involved in these tasks, are determined by the actual processes used to accomplish them. Processes and capabilities cost money. The costs of employee time, materials consumed, and electricity are passed on to the customer and contribute to her costs as well. Cost is both a critical component of value and a critical operations concept.

Quality

The quality of the product or service is another component of its value. For virtually any product or service, different levels of quality exist. Why? Because customers view quality very differently. What's high quality for one customer is not important for another. Higher levels of quality don't always translate into higher levels of value. Remember, value is in the eye of the beholder. **Quality** has very different meanings when products are compared to services. As mentioned earlier, outcomes dominate the customer's perception of value *and* quality when products are considered. However, as soon as services are examined, the concept of quality becomes broader and more difficult to define. For consumers, quality is often judged by how well the product or service met the customer's expectations. Did the product last as long as it should have? In other words, was it durable? Was it reliable? Did it do what it was designed to do? In a service, however, expectations change. Were the employees friendly? Was the service quick? Did I have to wait in line long? The answers to each of these questions, under identical situations, can be different for different customers. No matter what the customer's definition, however, the perception of quality will be a major determinant of value.

Timeliness

The fourth component of value consists of the **timeliness** associated with the product's or service's creation, delivery, and availability. However, something *now* is generally perceived as more valuable than the same thing *later*. Timeliness is probably less critical for consumers than it is for a business customer, but it is a component of value nevertheless. Timeliness is often lumped together with quality when services are evaluated. When products are evaluated, particularly those purchased by a business in the form of inventory, the product quality is certainly important, but issues of timeliness can be equally or even more important. For a business, time has a critical role in determining financial return on any investment. If the time to obtain a given financial return is reduced, the return is increased. If the time is halved, the return is doubled. Processes take time and the same principle applies.

MANAGING RESOURCES USED TO CREATE VALUE

Resources provide the direct inputs that either are converted into salable goods and services or enable that conversion to happen. As presented in Exhibit 1.4, among the most important tangible resources managed by any business and specifically under the auspices of operations are inventory, workforce, capacity, facilities, and customer relationships. These resources provide the critical inputs to creating the product and service attributes customers seek. Operations, although critical in the creation of value, can't claim responsibility for all value added. There are other important resources as well, such as intangibles like patents that result from the creativity of engineers and research and development specialists. Employee knowledge and skills—instilled in

> **EXHIBIT 1.4** | **Managing Resources to Create Value Excerpt from the Resource/Profit Model**

the workforce through training and development—and the creativity that emerges with the help of the business culture are also important. Looking even deeper, other necessary resources include the transportation system that brings inventory to the store, including trucks, drivers, and warehouses. This infrastructure is critical to making the goods and services available and valuable to the customer. The communication networks that provide management with the data needed to make timely and appropriate decisions are also essential to the success of the business. This large pool of resources is tapped for various tasks that can differentiate a business from its competition. Nonetheless, a very significant portion of the success of the business is under the auspices of operations.

Inventory

A retailer performs what appears to be a simple function—selling products to consumers. It's easy to assume that the products, or **inventory**, would be one of its most important resources. The retailer must have it when the customer needs it, or sales are lost. However, this seemingly simple relationship is actually much more complicated. To produce the product being sold, a manufacturer needs raw materials, which are used to create component parts, which in turn are assembled into finished products and sold to the retailer. All forms of materials make up a category of resources known as inventory. Inventory serves many critical functions. It buffers one work center from direct dependency on another. It allows customers to be satisfied immediately. It enables retailers to offer their customers many choices. It is an asset on the balance sheet, but it is widely recognized by managers as a liability as well. Despite all of its benefits, surplus inventory has been blamed for many business failures. A resource that, when in either short supply or excess, can destroy a business must be managed with extreme care.

Workforce

Most managers will claim that the **workforce** is their business's most critical resource. Inventory can be purchased, capacity can be purchased, facilities can be purchased, but good, talented, skilled employees are not easy to come by. They are developed, over a long period of time and at great expense. They are also the only resource that can leave the business for a better offer elsewhere.

Employees' skills and talents differ greatly. Their experiences, attitudes, and backgrounds also range tremendously. The diversity adds to the potential capabilities of the firm and also adds to the skills necessary at the managerial level. Great potential isn't free. The diversity of ideas, the creativity, and the ability to recognize potential value can come only from the widest possible set of experiences. The result of this diversity is truly any business's most valuable resource, but it is also the most difficult to manage.

Capacity

Capacity can be summed up as the level of productive output of an organization in a specified period of time. Productive output results from a variety of resources, but in most cases it is dominated by the availability of labor and/or equipment. An income tax service's ability to meet its demand is dictated by the number of skilled employees who can complete the IRS forms. A bank's ability to keep up with demand at its drive-up service is determined by the number of drive-up bays and tellers. A department store's ability to keep pace with customers making their purchases is determined by the number of cash registers and operators. The tax service can complete an average of three "basic" income tax filings per hour. The bank can handle, on average, 22 customers an hour per staffed drive-up bay. The store can check out approximately 14 customers per hour for each staffed cash register. A pediatrician, on average, can consult with 16 patients per hour. An automated teller machine (ATM) can complete an average of 35 transactions per hour.

One similarity should stand out in each of the above examples. Capacity is almost always an average. Why? Because the time required per unit can vary. In some cases that variability is a function of what's required. One person's income taxes are more complex than another's. Drive-up banking customers have different needs. Retail customers purchase varying amounts of products. In other cases, the employee or equipment varies in its ability to complete the required tasks. One cashier is faster than another. One physician is slower than another. In addition, the rate at which a single person accomplishes his task varies. One particular accountant is faster in the morning and slower in the late afternoon. Ultimately, the management of capacity is to match the firm's productive capabilities to the demand for them. Excess productive resources result in a financial return on those resources that is lower than that desired. A shortage of productive resources results in an inability to meet demand.

Facilities

The land and the building that houses a business can be the least important decision for management, as in the case of where to place a web server, or it can be the most important decision, as when a retailer is determining store location. In addition to facility location, **facility** decisions also include how the facility should be arranged, known as a facility layout. The facility layout can have tremendous implications for the business's ability to meet customer expectations. It determines such important outcomes as the ability to customize products and services and the ability to produce in high volumes, and it dictates the type of skills needed from employees. In many businesses, the layout determines the ease with which employees can interact with each other and with customers.

Every business has to be somewhere. The location decision makes that determination. Within that facility, every thing and every person also has to be somewhere. Where they are matters. The layout dictates possible processes and capabilities, as well as the costs, the quality, and the timeliness.

Customer Relationships

In addition to tangible resources just discussed, among the most important resources a company can have are the relationships it has with its customers. **Customer relationships** are different from the other resources managed by operations in that they are intangible. They have always been valued highly by successful companies, but new technological advancements have increased their importance, as well as business's ability to manage them.

Businesses invest a tremendous amount of money in the creation of customer relationships, and they do it for a reason. The better the relationships with customers, the more profitable the company. Like the investment in inventory, workforce, capacity, and facilities, the investment in customer relationships can have a very positive financial return. And just as with those other resources, no intelligent manager would waste them. No intelligent manager would ignore them.

Resource Planning

Simply owning inventory, capacity, and facilities, paying a workforce, and managing customer relationships does not result in the production of goods and services or the creation of value. These resources must be brought together into processes that provide the firm with capabilities. The firm's level of success or failure will be determined not by what resources the company owns, but by how it uses them. Resources aren't free, so the business must possess them in the appropriate quantity and at the appropriate time. If a company has invested in too many resources, it has invested money poorly because the resources won't contribute to making value. If the firm has too few resources, it can't meet demand. If the resources arrive too early, they aren't used. If they arrive too late, customer needs aren't met. Resource planning provides the mechanism that obtains the correct resources, in the correct quantities, at the correct time, and at the lowest cost.

INTEGRATIVE MANAGEMENT FRAMEWORKS

Managers universally acknowledge the link between the effective management of resources and the creation of value. On a day-to-day basis, however, it is often difficult to know exactly how a particular resource decision will affect current and future profitability. For example, when a retailer is considering the quantity of a particular CD to order from a supplier, does he compute the impact on the end-of-quarter profitability figures? Not likely. When a manufacturer determines what quality level is required of a particular product, does she compute the impact on profitability and make the decision accordingly? Probably not. When a restaurant chef is deciding which supplier to use for vegetables, is he calculating the impact on net income? No. It is impossible to make many day-to-day decisions using global measures like net income, profitability, or return on assets as criteria, although that is what management really wants to know. In order to create guidance for managerial decision making, various integrative management frameworks have been developed, as illustrated in Exhibit 1.5.

Integrative management frameworks provide a set of principles that eliminate the need to evaluate day-to-day decisions on the basis of profitability. They are, in a

Integrative Management Frameworks Excerpt from the Resource/Profit Model — EXHIBIT 1.5

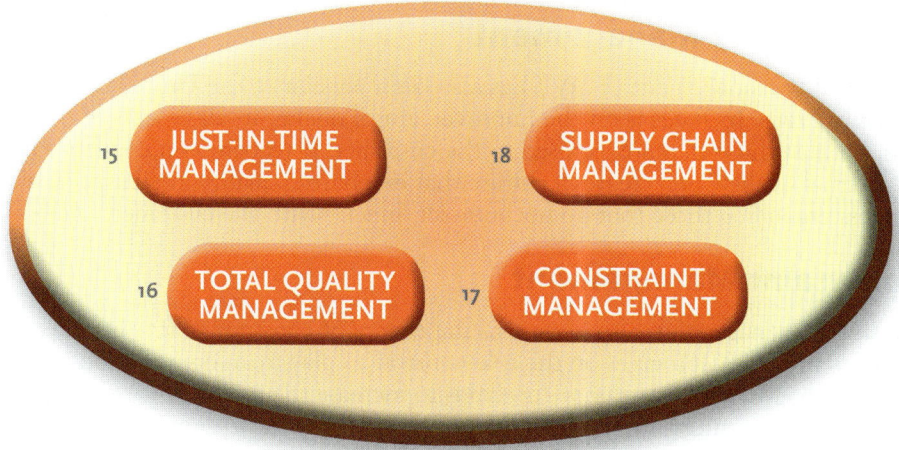

sense, an intermediate standard on which to evaluate decisions. A good analogy would be the way different basketball, football, and hockey teams identify a particular offensive or defensive *system* to run. The system provides guidance for players' actions, no matter what the opposing team does. Each system comes with a general objective and a specific set of rules of behavior that, if implemented effectively, should result in the team being able to compete. Different systems emphasize a different approach to utilizing resources (player talent or capabilities). One system might be used if a team is extremely fast but not very tall. Another system might be more effective if the team has two very tall players but no outside shooters. Integrative management frameworks are similar in that each has a general objective, each comes with a set of techniques or tools, and each focuses on specific resources.

The rise of integrative management frameworks has been interesting to observe. In virtually every case, they have been born out of the need to adapt to changing external forces. Each has become very popular, creating a frenzy to learn and adopt the system, as well as charge countless billable hours for consulting firms. Each has been labeled a "new philosophy of management." Some have gained an almost cultlike following. And then each has declined in popularity—not because managers no longer believe in their value, but because they have been absorbed into mainstream management practice. They become such a part of good management practices that they are no longer viewed as a distinctive way of doing things. Once managers accept the techniques and apply them on a routine basis, the framework that espoused them is no longer as important. Managers just do it. They don't need a philosophy or guru to preach the word to them.

The resource/profit model includes four integrative management frameworks. Each has made dramatic contributions to good management practice. Many of the techniques used today have their roots in these frameworks. Each has its own focus, but they are not exclusionary. In other words, businesses can incorporate all four into their decision-making processes if they so choose.

Just-in-Time Management

Just-in-time (JIT) management has been implemented in the United States since about 1980 after being practiced in Japan since the 1960s. Its primary focus is on the elimination of waste in producing goods and services. It is frequently used to eliminate waste related to inventory, processes, and the workforce, and it is also used when inventory reduction is desired.

Total Quality Management

Total quality management (TQM) has also been popular in the United States since the early 1980s. Its focus is on the improvement of quality in all aspects of the business, not just those that are exposed to the customer. It recognizes a concept known as "internal quality" and creates a culture that emphasizes quality in all aspects of the business, including those that do not interact directly with the customer.

Constraint Management

Constraint management, also known as the theory of constraints, first attained visibility around 1987. It focuses on the role constraints play in an organization and how best to manage those constraints. Its goal is to increase the productivity of the system as a whole by focusing on its constraints and recognizing that optimizing specific parts of the system will not optimize the entire system.

Supply Chain Management

Supply chain management focuses on the relationships among customers and suppliers, recognizing that the effects of decisions aren't limited to the business that made them but extend to suppliers and customers as well. Ultimately, the entire supply chain creates the value a customer perceives and receives. Optimizing that value and minimizing its costs require a decision-making perspective that includes the entire supply chain.

The integrative management frameworks tie together the foundations for success, the components of value, and the resources used to create value in a consistent set of decision-making priorities. Managers familiar with the objectives and the techniques inherent in each framework are provided with a systematic approach to decision making that will be consistent with global performance measures. Each provides a means of making day-to-day decisions consistent with the firm's profitability goals.

ENVIRONMENTAL FORCES

A business is an open system. No business that has an impact on external entities (customers, demand, and so on) can function without itself being influenced by external forces. The forces that exist within a particular business's environment often depend on competitive and regulatory forces within the industry, but there are also many environmental forces that cross industry boundaries. The resource/profit model you saw in Exhibit 1.1 depicts environmental forces as arrows providing pressure against the business because that is exactly what these forces do.

Globalization

The first and probably the strongest environmental force that product- and service-oriented firms must cope with is the increased competition and emerging markets resulting from the globalization of most businesses. This phenomenon has resulted in increased competitive pressures in a firm's home country from foreign firms and also in increased opportunities in foreign markets. This trend will have a negative impact on firms unable to mobilize and seek new markets, but firms looking for opportunities and wishing to expand their markets will perceive this as a wide-open field in which they can excel. However, it's important to remember that along with expansion into emerging markets comes risk associated with political unrest, unknown competitive forces in those markets, unexpected expectation for products and services, and uncertainties associated with transportation, supplies, labor, and financial exchange rates.

The globalization of business affects operations. Moving into global markets with products and services creates entirely new definitions of value, because there is a different customer base involved. As value changes, so does the creation of value. This has implications for processes and capabilities, costs, quality, and timeliness. It creates new objectives, but it also creates new challenges. Different cultures have different expectations and needs. Geographic distances translate into time differences. Time increases create an entirely new set of challenges for managing all resources.

In addition to moving into global markets with products and services, businesses also move readily into global markets for purchasing products and services they need. Extending the supply base into global markets creates an entirely new set of advantages and management challenges as well. Time necessary to obtain inputs increases. Infrastructures must be built. Employees must be trained. Along with these challenges, however, come advantages. New ideas are generated. New skills and talents are identified. Extending the supplier base sometimes involves extending the location of facilities into foreign countries to take advantage of resources, talents, and markets. All of these decisions affect the way resources are obtained, utilized, and brought together in the value-creation process. They provide great potential, but they require managers to recognize the diversity of cultures and the talent, creativity, and views those cultures bring as well.

The Internet

The second environmental force being felt by most businesses is coming from the increased levels of communication and competition brought about by the Internet. The Internet has created a business environment that makes geography a nonissue for many firms. Businesses that were successful simply because of their location must develop other capabilities to maintain a competitive advantage.

The Internet has also placed a tremendous amount of pressure on businesses that act primarily as intermediaries between the producer and consumer. Manufacturers can deal directly with consumers, and do so at low cost. Intermediaries are finding it difficult to add enough value to warrant their markup. This phenomenon is not limited to product-oriented firms. Banks, investment houses, insurance companies, and numerous types of retailer must compete against firms that exist solely online, with no expenses tied to brick and mortar facilities.

The Natural Environment

Changes in the natural environment constitute a third force exerting pressures on businesses. Air and water pollution are still a vital concern, even though the "point-source" origin of these pollutants is no longer the most significant source. Automobiles and homes have become the most significant threat to the health of our air and water. Greenhouse gas levels have raised global warming concerns. Household consumption levels threaten to overflow landfills, endanger drinking water supplies, and fuel a demand for agricultural products that may cause deforestation half a world away. Businesses now assess environmental impact as part of their decision-making processes. They have begun to accept the fact that sustainable use patterns must be developed for many of our resources, including process inputs as far-ranging as timber, fossil fuels, and fish.

Minimizing environmental impact has numerous implications for a business. Sometimes it increases processing costs in the short term. Sometimes it means that what appears to be a prime location from one perspective really isn't acceptable. Sometimes it opens new markets for "greener" products and actually gives the firm a competitive advantage over firms that haven't addressed these issues.

Regional Pressures

In addition to global forces, regional pressures also influence business decisions. Included among these pressures are population growth and land development in rural areas. In some parts of the country there are concerns about maintaining the levels of undisturbed forests or wildlife habitat. In other parts of the country, such as the Midwest, there are concerns about the loss of farmland and the family farm. In the West, there are concerns about water use and water rights. In large cities there are health worries related to the number of smog days. Clearly, businesses have begun to recognize their role in a larger natural system and are learning how to minimize the negative impact on that system. The importance of these issues for future decisions can only be expected to increase.

THE RESOURCE/PROFIT MODEL IN REVIEW

The resource/profit model, initially presented in Exhibit 1.1, provides an organizing framework for the study of operations management. It views operations issues in a way that acknowledges the relationships among these concepts and the role they play in the enterprise, but like all models, it doesn't represent every detail of operations, or every detail of how operations fits into the business context. To include more detail would detract from its value as an organization framework. Ultimately, the student of operations management will learn the most about the importance of operations management and its role in the enterprise *in an actual business*. That is where the concepts presented here come to life.

An examination of two fundamental business entities—what is sold and who buys it—is necessary to understand how profitability, value, and strategy emerge from the apparent chaos of business management. In the following sections, the business outputs of products and services are examined first, followed by a brief examination of different types of customers.

BUSINESS OUTPUTS: PRODUCTS AND SERVICES

In today's economy, it is impossible to completely separate service-producing industries (traditionally known as "services") from product-producing businesses (traditionally known as "manufacturers"). Successful firms have recognized that potential customers do not compartmentalize value that way. Customers look at the total package, which includes aspects of both services and products. Failure to recognize this greatly reduces a firm's ability to compete. Studies by the American Society for Quality Control (ASQC) confirm this perspective. Since 1994, despite significant improvement in product quality, overall customer satisfaction has continued to drop, leaving no doubt that the service aspects of doing business are not meeting expectations. From a competitive standpoint, it means that providing a high-quality product is necessary, but not sufficient, to effectively compete.[7]

Despite the integrated nature of business outputs and the difficulty in defining a business as a service or a manufacturer, it is important to understand that business outputs can be defined distinctly as either a service or a product. Even though these components come together for the customer (and are perceived by the customer as one entity), they are often produced separately. Furthermore, examination and comparison of the characteristics of products and services contribute to an understanding of value.

Products

Products are *things*. They're tangible. They can be seen, they can be touched, they can be counted, they can be measured, and they can be stored for later use. They are produced by manufacturers. The fact that products are tangible has many management implications, most of them advantageous to the tasks facing managers.

Because a product is tangible, its quality can be measured in a relatively straightforward manner before a customer has a chance to examine the product. The function of the product can be measured and actually tested to make sure it works properly. This allows management to avoid exposing customers to poor quality, even if it is produced. Electronic products are tested upon completion. Automobiles are examined for defects. Clothing is inspected for flaws in the fabric. In all cases, finding a problem results in the defective product being separated from the good products and being either fixed or destroyed. Reel Operations Video 1.1 provides an excellent discussion of many of the characteristics of products by using a product of Federal Signal as an example.

www
OperationsNow
.com

A completed product can be stored in finished-goods inventory until needed, or it can be shipped anywhere in the world for use. Whereas some products are stored for only a short time before being consumed (some food, pharmaceuticals, stylish clothing, and newspapers, for example), other products have an extremely long shelf life (furniture, books, and toys, for example). When products can be stored for later use, their actual rate of production does not have to match the rate of demand in the short term. Demands fluctuate. Matching output rate to a fluctuating demand is extremely difficult, particularly when materials have to be ordered from suppliers in advance and employees have to be hired and trained in advance, so the ability to inventory products is extremely important to the effective management of their production and all resources associated with that production.

When a product is purchased, the customer typically has no idea of the conditions associated with its production. She doesn't care if processes are noisy, if they smell bad, or if the machines are dirty. In most cases she doesn't care anything about the process, because it's the outcome of those processes that matters. The finished product is evaluated in terms of quality, but the process used to create it isn't. As consumers become more aware of production, however, they have also become more concerned. Consumers were shocked, for example, when they found out that certain clothing items they wore were being manufactured by children and in unacceptable conditions. In some cases, the companies that purchased the goods weren't even aware of the conditions in which they were manufactured. Issues such as employee exploitation and impact on environment have begun to be of interest to manufacturing customers. Attributes such as the friendliness of the employees or the ambiance of the factory, however, make no difference to the customer.

Services

Services are intangible. They can't be touched or counted or examined the way a product can. Services are tasks that are done for the customer or done to the customer. Because they are intangible, they can't be stored for later use. They can't be examined or tested for quality before the customer gets them. In fact, they are often produced in a process that the customer is actually a part of. Sometimes it is the customer that is actually processed. The intangibility and direct customer involvement create a situation that can be quite difficult to manage. In a service, the customer *does* care about the production process because he spends time in it, and the process can be as important as outcome to that customer. The process utilized to entertain a customer at a theme park matters a great deal. The process a retailer uses to sell products defines the quality of service a customer perceives. The process a financial consultant uses to plan investments for a client matters to the client because she is a player in that process.

A close match between the output rate and the demand rate is critical for services because people aren't willing to wait for a process to catch up with them. Access to an online retailer, for example, must be immediate or the customer will click on another alternative. A seat on an airplane must be available when a customer wants it or he'll simply buy a ticket on a competing airline. If either business has idle server capacity or empty seats at a particular time, it can't store that capacity for later use.

Unfortunately for managers of services, service quality cannot be determined until after the fact. For customers, this means that they're exposed to poor quality service more often than they're exposed to poor quality products. Unlike manufacturing managers, who can "scrap" or "rework" defective products, service managers must attempt a "recovery" when customers are exposed to quality failures. When a restaurant finds out that a customer is dissatisfied, management attempts the recovery by providing complimentary drinks or a gift certificate for free meals at a later date.

Customers place higher expectations on the employees in services because they are often face to face with them. When the customer watches a service production process and is involved in it, expectations for "special treatment" are common. A rule of thumb is that the greater the customer contact, the greater the expectation for customization, and the more difficult it is to maintain efficient processes. Banking by ATM, phone, and online removes customers from direct contact with bank personnel. For students, online registration has improved the efficiency of that process by removing direct student contact. The need to meet varied expectations and customize the service can make the management of a service more difficult and customer expectations harder to meet. Many services have removed service processes from customer access to increase productivity. In a close look at a banking operation, Reel Operations Video 1.2 provides a summary of how management can combine the practices used for managing services and products. Exhibit 1.6 summarizes the characteristics of products and services by comparing them.

As can be seen in Exhibit 1.7, business outputs often blend product and service components. For example, you might order a product directly from a manufacturer, but along with that product comes a lot of services. Dell Computer Corporation provides an excellent example of a manufacturer that has blended products and services. A customer buys a computer directly from Dell and along with the computer receives specific services. One is fast delivery. The second is free on-site support for one year. The customer can also buy additional services, such as extended support. Dell's success, particularly in quantity purchases for businesses and schools, is not dependent solely on the quality of its products but can also be traced directly to its reputation for after-the-sale support. Dell's success is incontrovertible: A $1,000 investment in Dell in 1989 was worth $890,052 at the end of 1999.[8] Since the turn of the century, Dell has taken its service efforts a step further. In early 2000, Dell announced Dellhost.com in an effort to provide website hosting and ecommerce Internet service. This service is part of an even larger service, Dell E Works, that will sell procurement, job recruiting, and direct mail services.[9]

For many traditional product-oriented companies, managers are finding that good service not only helps sell products but can also be profitable. Auto companies dra-

EXHIBIT 1.6 Summary of Product and Service Output Differences

Products	Services
Products are tangible.	Services are intangible.
Products are easy to measure.	Services are difficult to measure.
Products can be stored for later use.	Services can't be stored for later use.
Products can be checked for conformance to quality prior to customer receiving them.	Services can't be checked for conformance to quality prior to customer receiving them.
Production processes for products are relatively unimportant to customers.	Production processes for services are very important to customers.
Producers of defective products can repair or scrap the defects.	Producers of defective services must attempt to recover to retain the customer.

EXHIBIT 1.7 Continuum of Service and Product Producers

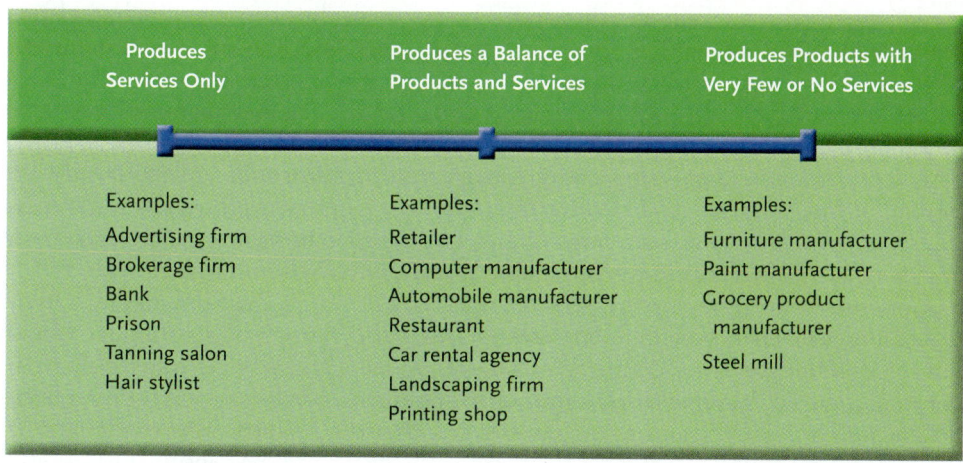

matically increased incentives to buyers in 2001 in response to declining sales during the economic downturn. This resulted in record sales. They expected a sharp decline in 2002 and hoped to balance that decline by improved used car sales, which actually have higher margins than new cars. The economic slowdown resulted in customers keeping cars longer. Those older cars needed more service. At large dealer chains, repairs and service part sales made up 10–12 percent of revenues but created up to 35 percent of the net profits.[10]

Generally, service management tends to follow manufacturing management in adoption of new management approaches. Productivity and quality improvement efforts initiated in manufacturing often move to the service sector. In the past decade it has become increasingly common for manufacturers to outsource labor-intensive aspects of production to countries with cheaper labor. That has been made possible by the ease of transporting products, compared to the difficulty in transporting services. Services have recently begun to follow suit, however. The tight labor markets in the United States have increased the incentive for U.S. services to seek labor from outside the country.

An excellent example of this trend is the **maquiladoras**. Maquiladoras have traditionally been known as foreign-owned manufacturing (usually assembly) plants in Mexico. A company establishes a plant in Mexico, usually just across the border from the United States. Since the plant is company-owned, the company could import the components into Mexico duty-free and then export finished products back to the United States. Maquiladoras have been very popular as a means of lowering labor expenses in a variety of manufacturing industries, including automotive, electronics, and garment manufacturing. They have also been controversial in that some companies' primary motivation to manufacture in Mexico has been to avoid Environmental Protection Agency (EPA) requirements. The use of maquiladoras has recently been extended into the service sector. In early 2000, approximately 50,000 Mexican workers were employed by service maquiladoras. That's small compared to the 350,000 employed in electronics maquiladoras or the 450,000 employed in textiles and automotive, but it has grown 30-fold compared to what it was in 1990.[11]

CUSTOMERS

The impact customers have on a business is enormous. They determine the value of what the business produces. Unfortunately, what's valuable to one is worthless to another. For a successful business, knowing which is which is critical. One important way to categorize customers is by their use of the product or service being sold.

Businesses buy material goods for their own consumption, and also as components used in the products or services they sell. The materials they consume, such as cleaning compounds, lubricants, or machine repair parts, are known as maintenance, repair, and operating (MRO) inventory. Component parts that end up in the product or service they sell, such as memory chips for a computer manufacturer, also become part of the company's inventory. A business also purchases services. It might contract with a firm to provide security, hire a consulting firm to design an information system, or hire a transportation company to deliver its products. Business-to-business transactions have become such a major part of the economy that they have taken on an acronym—B2B. Business-to-consumer transactions have been tagged B2C.

Consumers buy products and services that they utilize in their day-to-day activities. Businesses have very different uses for what they buy than a consumer would have. Consequently, they define the value of products and services differently than consumers would. In some cases, a firm might produce a product or service for a business as well as for a consumer. Despite the fact that the product or service might be the same for each type of customer, the business customer and the consumer would still define value differently. Exhibit 1.8 shows a comparison of companies that produce different types of outputs and serve different types of customer. This matrix will be revisited in Chapter 3 in a detailed examination of value.

OPERATIONS, OTHER BUSINESS FUNCTIONS, AND YOU

A business environment characterized by speed and flexibility cannot afford to be constrained by the boundaries imposed by traditional departmental barriers. Business decisions must be made quickly and made from an enterprise perspective, considering implications for all aspects of the business. For this very reason, many companies have increased their utilization of cross-functional teams on tasks such as new product and service development, systems implementation, and process improvement. These companies have become more organized around their products and services, and less organized around the functional areas within their organizations. For many firms, particularly small ones, responsibilities can be dispersed among a variety of staff. It is not

EXHIBIT 1.8 Business Output/Customer Matrix

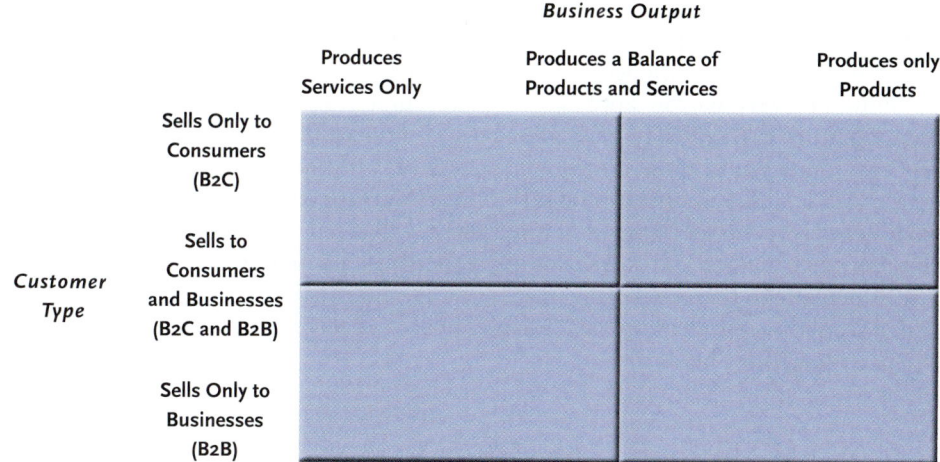

at all uncommon for someone with financial expertise to be involved in what have traditionally been marketing issues or for someone with marketing expertise to be involved in quality management.

As businesses continue to break down functional barriers, functional experts will continue to take on broadened responsibilities that relate to product and service design and processes, rather than traditional department functions. For business functions like operations, marketing, finance, accounting, and information systems, departmental affiliations will continue to become less meaningful than the needs of the organization. The functional responsibilities and tasks must still be accomplished, but not necessarily by a functional department per se. As these trends continue we will likely see all business functions take on new shapes and new roles in the business.

Value derives from processes. A process is an accretion of resources. The resources necessary to create a value-adding process often come from different parts of the business. Amazon.com provides an excellent example of how differentiating capabilities emerge from bringing together very different resources. Amazon.com's ability to provide a book (or other product) at a very low price and do it very quickly sets it apart from competitors. There is no need to go elsewhere, because if the book exists, Amazon can probably get it. An examination of all the processes required to take the order, process the credit card information, and deliver the book to the customer clearly shows that resources from many different parts of the company have to come into play: marketing and information technology experts develop the customer interface; financial, accounting, and computer experts develop the mechanisms necessary to handle the credit card transactions online; purchasing and contract experts develop relationships with suppliers; logistics and operations experts design and maintain the outgoing flow of products. Amazon.com could be broken into a series of small processes, but they must all interact with each other. Without any single piece, the system never emerges, and the differentiating capability doesn't exist. Amazon.com has continued to expand its businesses into new areas by linking up with traditional retailers. It continues to have difficulty showing profitability, however. Esource 1.3 provides a company's expansion history to demonstrate the role different resources play in business success.

www.OperationsNow.com

The interaction among processes makes it particularly important for all managers to have, in addition to a functional expertise, a basic knowledge of all business functions.

As transaction speeds increase, and as companies interact more directly with customers, the need to see across boundaries and recognize potentially valuable resources will increase. An employee who can recognize resources in other areas of the business that can be combined with resources of his own to form new processes has mastered one of the most difficult and valuable aspects of new product and service development. Without the knowledge of how all functions interact in the business, ideas will be limited to very narrow applications of resources. There is little remaining "low-hanging fruit" in the area of new products and services. The lack of an enterprise perspective limits the firm's potential for success, and it limits the career potential of its employees as well. A business student's differentiating capability, which separates her from her classmates in the eyes of a recruiter, will not be her major. Even when she compares her preparation to that of any other business major, the difference is only 10–15 percent of the courses taken. The differentiating capability is something special: Any ability a student has that enables her to perceive the business from a broader perspective will set her apart.

CHAPTER SUMMARY

This chapter introduced operations management as a critical component of the successful management of a business. Operations management is the management of productive resources that are used to create salable products or services. It is that sale of products and services that provides an opportunity for profitability.

The resource/profit model was introduced as an organizing framework of operations concepts. The model provides four primary elements. The first, foundations for success, consists of profitability, value, and strategy. The second, components of value, consists of processes and capabilities, cost, quality, and timeliness. The third, managing resources used to create value, consists of resource planning, followed by inventory, workforce, capacity, facilities, and customer relationships. The final element of the model is integrative management frameworks consisting of just-in-time management, total quality management, constraint management, and supply chain management. Environmental forces are recognized as pressures that initiate responses from the entire business and from operations.

An overview of the resource/profit model shows that profitability results from the creation of value and a strategy for maintaining a link to the customers that define it. The components of value come together to give customers their value perceptions. The creation of value at a level that exceeds the cost of creating it provides the potential for profitability. The resources owned and managed as a part of operations management are brought together to create the value customers seek.

Operations management has responded to and will continue to respond to three dominant environmental forces: competition resulting from the globalization of business, increasing levels of communication and competition brought about by the Internet, the impact on and changes in the way businesses interact with the natural environment, and regional pressures that have varying impacts on business decisions.

Two business outputs—products and services—are critical to the management of operations resources. Effective operations management must acknowledge the differences and similarities of those environments. Two different types of customer—B2B and B2C—are examined. They must also be recognized and the differences in expectations and needs must be incorporated into business processes to succeed in these relationships.

Last, but certainly not last in importance, the importance of operations familiarity—and familiarity with all aspects of the enterprise—is discussed as an important way for the business student to differentiate himself or herself from other students. It is an employee's ability to make the best decisions for the business, after all, that is most highly prized.

KEY TERMS

capabilities, 14
capacity, 19
cost, 16
customer relationships, 20
differentiating capabilities, 15
facility, 19
integrative management frameworks, 20
inventory, 18
keiretsu, 6
maquiladoras, 28
net present value (NPV), 11
processes, 14
profitability, 9
quality, 17
strategy, 13
timeliness, 17
value, 11
workforce, 19

REVIEW QUESTIONS

1. Why is it important for students with any business major to have a basic understanding of all aspects of a business?
2. What does operations management mean?
3. Describe the resource/profit model. What are the foundations for success? What are the components of value? What resources are managed to create value?
4. What is the relationship between value created and profitability?
5. How does cost affect the amount of profitability that results from value?
6. Why do resources alone not create value for a business?
7. Who ultimately defines value?
8. What are "differentiating capabilities"?
9. Provide an example of how inventory, workforce, capacity, facilities, and customer relationships can each contribute to value.
10. What are integrative management frameworks? What do they provide for managers?
11. How do products and services differ?
12. What is the management impact of the intangibility of services?
13. Why are most manufacturers also typically service providers?
14. What do B2B and B2C mean? Why is the difference important?

DISCUSSION QUESTIONS

1. How has the speed of transactions made possible by the Internet had a positive impact on your life? What are some of the ways the impact has been negative?
2. What are the positive and negative connotations of ".com"? Are these stereotypes deserved?

3. Identify a product or service that you frequently purchase. Identify all of its value components. Which are the most important? Which are you are most frequently dissatisfied with?

4. Examine a process on your campus that you are familiar with. What steps in it do not add value? What are the costs, for the customer, associated with these steps? What are the costs for the university? In terms of the other components of value, how would the value resulting from the process be improved if the non-value-adding steps were removed?

5. Identify and describe a business you are familiar with that has had to adapt to increasing levels of competition. Where has the competition come from? How has the business changed in response? Have its changes been successful?

6. Identify and describe a business you are familiar with that has had to adapt to increasing competition from an Internet-based business. How has it changed? Has it been successful?

7. How do most students prioritize the components of value for services? For products?

8. Consider a recent significant purchase you made. What were the costs associated with that purchase?

9. What changes have you observed in the products and services you buy that indicate pressures on business to have less impact on the natural environment? Have these changes had an impact on the way you purchase products or services?

10. Describe a business whose major focus is difficult to classify as either a product or a service. What makes it difficult to categorize? Which parts of the business would be the most difficult to manage—producing the services or producing the products? Why?

11. Identify a product or service that would likely be purchased by both consumers and businesses. How might the B2B and the B2C customers differ in terms of how each defines value? What components of value would be the most important for each?

ENDNOTES

1. "Customers Move into the Driver's Seat," *Business Week,* October 4, 1999, pp. 103–106.
2. "People Who Need People," *The Wall Street Journal,* February 12, 2001, p. R20.
3. "Why Some Sony Gear Is Made in Japan—By Another Company," *The Wall Street Journal,* June 14, 2001, pp. A1, A10.
4. "How Technology Tailors Price Tags," *The Wall Street Journal,* June 21, 2001, p. A1.
5. "How to Use Priceline.com," *Web's Best* 5, no. 11, pp. 30–32.
6. "How Technology Tailors Price Tags."
7. Deloitte Research, *Making Customer Loyalty Real,* New York: Deloitte & Touche, 1999.
8. "The Best and Worst Performing Companies," *The Wall Street Journal,* February 24, 2000, p. B4.

9. "Dell to Offer Hosting of Small-Business Web Sites," *The Wall Street Journal*, February 22, 2000, p. B23.
10. "Can Car Dealers Keep the Profits Rolling?" *BusinessWeek*, January 14, 2002, p. 37.
11. "First Came Assembly, Now Services Soar," *The Wall Street Journal*, February 28, 2000, p. A1.

OperationsNow.com LEARNING ACTIVITIES

CHAPTER ENHANCEMENT RESOURCES
- Esources
- Reel Operations Video Clips
- Interactive Models
- Excel Tutors
- Supplementary Readings
- Links to Operations On-Site Companies

OM EXPLORATION
- Check It Out
- OM in Action
- Online Business Tours
- Letters from the Top
- Putting It All Together: Virtual Case Studies
- Additional Reading

After dot-coms suffered more than a year of stagnant performance in the Dow Jones Industrial Average, S&P 500, and the Nasdaq, the Wall Street Journal ran a front-page article headlined "Latest Dot-Com Fad Is a Bit Old-Fashioned: It's Called 'Profitability.'"[1] Profitability is presented in the resource/profit model as the first of three foundations for success. It is the overriding objective of any business. It is the end that justifies the money invested in all of the firm's resources. While the "whats" and "hows" of business drive many business decisions, profitability is the "why."

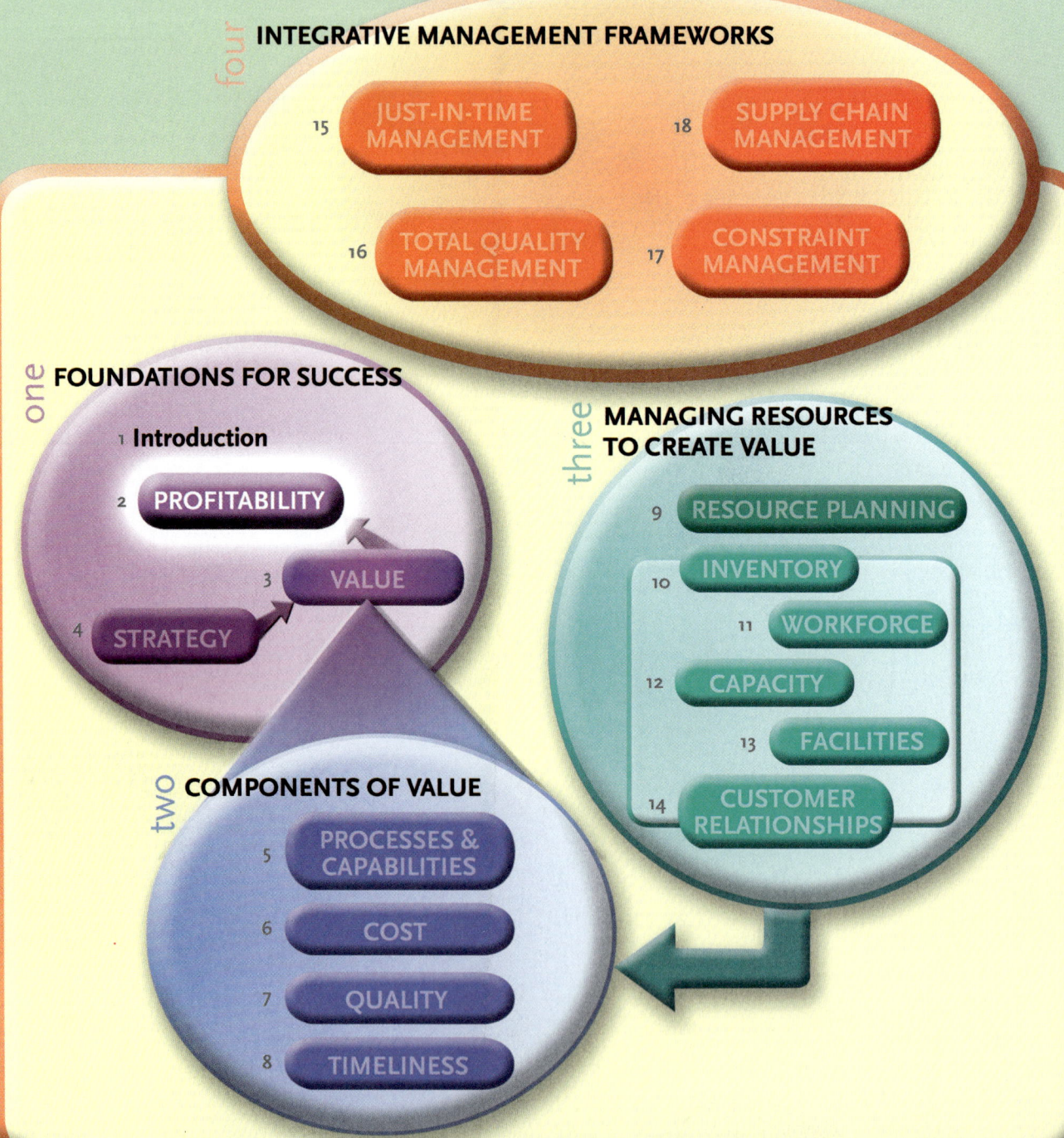

CHAPTER 2

Profitability

LEARNING OBJECTIVES

Upon completion of Chapter 2, you should be able to

- Understand and describe the concepts of value and profitability.
- Understand and describe the effects operations management has on profitability measures.
- Describe economic value added (EVA).
- Calculate the average level of inventory from a delivery pattern.
- Understand productivity measures for resources.
- Calculate utilization and efficiency.
- Explain the importance of customer relationships.
- Distinguish between local and global productivity measures.
- Identify conflicts between productivity measures.
- Describe how to increase productivity measures.
- Conduct a breakeven analysis.
- Describe the balanced scorecard approach.

Introduction: The Link Between Value and Investment Results
Profitability Measures
Economic Value Added: A New Profitability Measure
Profitability from Operation Resources
Local versus Global Optimization
Measurement Improvement
Decision-Making Tools: Breakeven Analysis
A Broader Approach to Productivity Measurement: The Balanced Scorecard
Chapter Summary

INTERNET RESOURCES

 Excel Tutors provide annotated spreadsheets for every solved problem that automatically load Excel.

 Esources provide an online version of the more traditional boxed insert.

 Reel Videos provide streaming video footage for company applications of chapter concepts.

 Interactive Models provide an experimental environment for quantitative concepts and simulations.

INTRODUCTION
The Link Between Value and Investment Results

There may be many reasons for the existence of a business, but none are as fundamental as profitability. Without it, no other objectives can be achieved because the business will die. Profitability is at the beginning of the resource/profit model in Exhibit 2.1 because it provides the motivation for the rest of the model. The primary objective of this chapter is to put operations into the context in which it exists: that of using resources to generate value, which can be sold at a profit. The chapter defines profitability measures as they relate to operations management and discusses the impact that operations resources have on those measures by sampling resource productivity measures that link directly to profitability.

It is no coincidence that the content of this chapter will be familiar to students of finance. Although not often emphasized in finance texts, operations management is the context of many financial decisions. Operations management provides the means to accomplish the financial goals detailed in the measures held dear by financial specialists.

The owner of any investment expects a financial return on that investment. It doesn't matter if the investment is a share of stock, a rental property, a restaurant, or a shoelace factory. The money is tied up. If it wasn't, it could be invested somewhere else. For an investor, merely getting a financial return from owning a business isn't enough—the financial return must be good enough, *given other alternatives for investing the money*, to warrant keeping the money invested there. The same holds for any part of that business. For example, when a restaurant owner invests in a new computer system, a financial return is expected, because the money could have been invested in a new stove, new dishes, or any number of other functional assets. When a bank invests in more ATMs, it expects a financial return. Money available for those capital investments is almost always limited. A business invests in resources—inventory, equipment, facilities, and staff—and expects a financial return that is acceptable.

But what is acceptable? Simply earning a financial return on the investment isn't enough. The investor must gauge the potential return of the investment compared to what could be earned on alternative investments. Just as mutual fund managers utilize various measures to assess investment productivity for stocks or bonds, managers of product- and service-oriented businesses use various measures to monitor and assess investment productivity for their resources.

Like any other financial investments, operations resources are associated with varying degrees of uncertainty. Higher potential gains are often accompanied by higher potential losses. For operations resources, a key source of uncertainty is net present value (NPV), which cannot be known before the fact. The *expected* return of one investment must be compared to the *expected* return on another. To understand this, NPV must be clearly understood.

The NPV is the sum of the discounted cash flows received or disbursed over the life of the investment. The cash flows are discounted to take into account the time value of the money received and spent. As mentioned briefly in Chapter 1, it is the difference between the ultimate worth to the customer (as determined by the customer's perception of value) and the cost of adding that value. If there were no uncertainty concerning cash to be disbursed and no uncertainty concerning cash to be received, the business would be a classic example of "a sure thing." But there is no sure thing. Businesses do not typically go bankrupt because they erred in their calculation of the NPV. They go bankrupt because their estimate of future cash disbursals

EXHIBIT 2.1 The Role of Profitability in the Resource/Profit Model

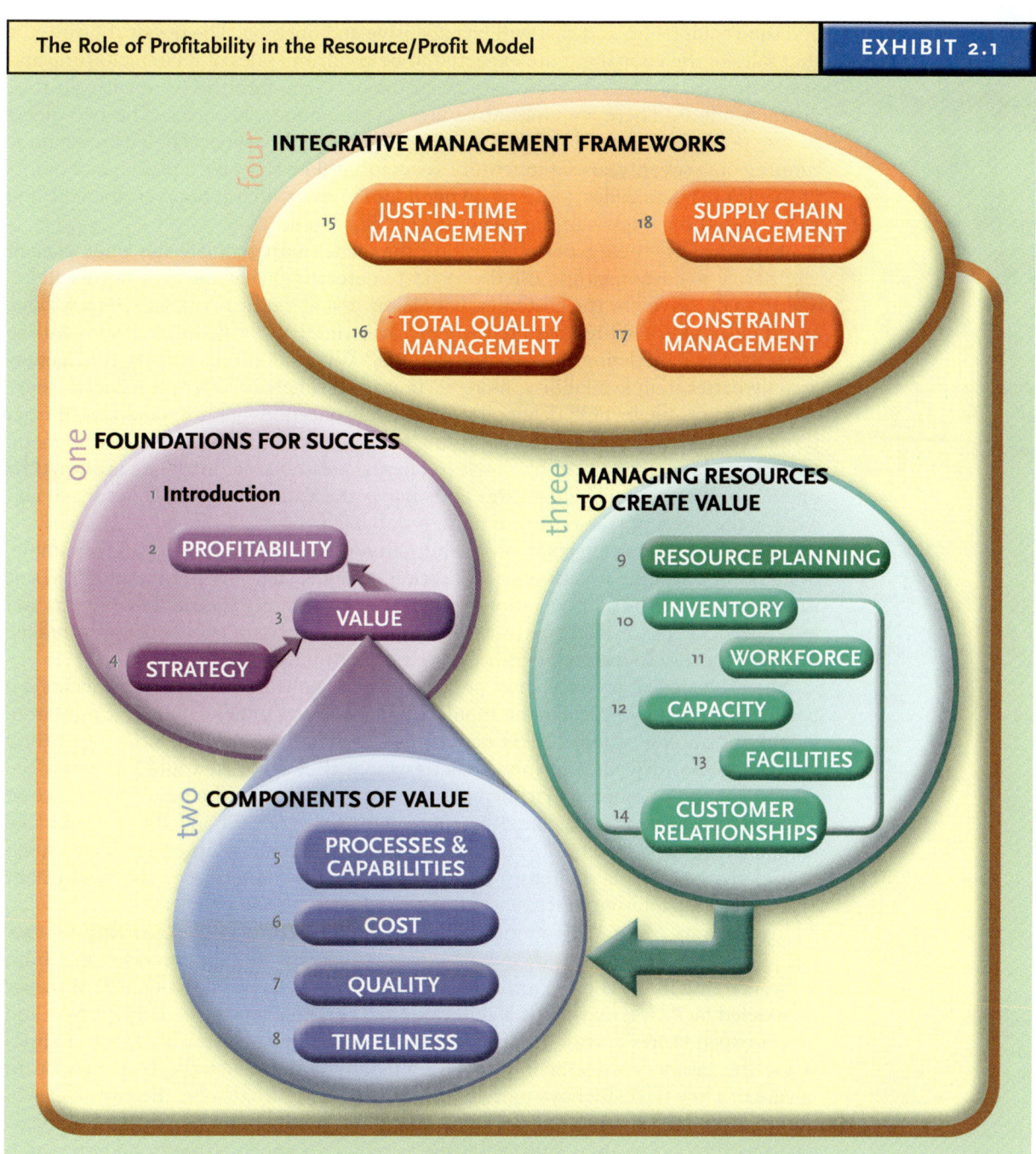

and/or receipts was wrong. Operations generates many of the costs through the creation of products and services. Through the creation of the products and services, operations also generates the receipts. An example provides some possible reasons why this happens.

A small retail sporting goods chain has six stores. The owner is considering expanding into the snow ski and snowboarding market. In addition to the floor space and fixtures required for the stock, expanding into that market requires significant investment in equipment for mounting bindings and for tuning skis (waxing, sharpening edges, repairing, and so on). Personnel must be trained to correctly fit, mount, adjust, and tune equipment, and that will be expensive and ongoing. The upside, however, is that sales of the equipment are expected to be good, and sales of related clothing and accessories should also increase as new customers come into the store with ski trips on their minds. There are alternative uses for the money, however. The two oldest stores could use a general upgrading in appearance and fixtures. The entire chain is running on a seven-year-old inventory system that does not take advantage of point-of-sale (POS) data collection. The owner doesn't have the cash reserves or credit line to do everything. How can the owner decide what to do?

When making these types of decisions, the owner must estimate the value of each alternative to customers and use the result to determine what the cash flows will be. Value, as perceived by the customer, will determine what the financial return will be. What will sales of ski-related products be, over time? What additional sales will be generated by remodeling the two oldest stores? What additional sales will be generated by better item availability, more accurate and timely orders, and reduced stockouts made possible by POS data collection? These questions are not too different from those a broker might consider when trying to decide between recommending General Electric and Procter & Gamble stock to clients, but these questions are answered by operations managers. The question is, What is the expected return, over time, and what is the value of that return in present dollars?

Certainly the sporting goods store alternatives have been simplified. For example, in addition to adding to customer perception of value, some alternatives might result in a reduction of costs for operations. A remodeled store might need fewer repairs and less maintenance. A better inventory management system might actually reduce inventory levels, reducing inventory carrying costs.

Manufacturers of products must perform similar analyses when trying to decide if a particular product improvement should be made. For example, should a miniature global positioning system (GPS) be added as standard equipment in a sport utility vehicle so that drivers will know exactly where they are? Or would customers see equal value in a compass that merely told them which way their car was pointing? The expected return, as dictated by customers' perception of added value, must be compared to the cost. The cost will be the result of the materials and processes used to include the GPS. Is the return positive and, if so, is the return on the investment better than the alternatives?

Investments require that money be spent. Investments in operations require that money be spent to purchase, maintain, and power a particular resource and train workers to use it. Maybe the resource is a machine, maybe it's additional facilities or remodeled facilities, maybe it's a skill obtained through training. Many current and future expenditures contribute to the total cost for that investment. In most situations, the business is reasonably capable of determining what the costs will be in advance. They typically have more difficulty predicting what *value* the customer will put on a product or service prior to its design and production. It is that value, compared to alternatives, that determines the potential financial return. Market research provides some information, but forecasting for a new product or service is always a very subjective process. For that matter, forecasting for *anything* is fraught with error. For a product that has been around a while and has an established market, that uncertainty is somewhat reduced, but even then, the value can decline as competing products become more popular. The business must try to predict when this might happen and what its effect will be.

Managers cannot escape the customer's perception of value as being the most critical component of success for any operations investment *and* one of the most difficult to predict. That's the business's uncertainty. Notice that care has been taken here to use the word "uncertainty" rather than "risk." It is important to note that risk is measurable uncertainty. Businesses have the ability to measure some uncertainties, but the uncertainty associated with customer perception of value is very difficult to accurately determine.

Usually an investment decision in an operations resource is more complicated than the sporting goods store example. A business cannot assume, for example, that whether it makes a particular choice or not, its competitors will maintain the status quo. Looking back at the retail sporting goods example, it should be acknowledged that the store's competitors have options as well. If the owner of the sporting goods chain decides not to enter the snow ski market, and neither does the competitor, the owner can reasonably assume that the customer base will remain constant. But what happens if he doesn't enter the ski market and his biggest competitor does? Will he lose customers? What if he decides not to remodel the oldest store and his competitor opens a brand new store nearby? What if he doesn't invest in a new inventory system, but his competitor does and is therefore able to promise 48-hour availability on any item currently not in stock in the store?

The estimation of the customer's perception of value must recognize that customers also make comparative judgments. The value of a product or service is always related to the alternatives available to customers. If the alternatives change, the value of all competing products changes as well. The decision isn't simply a matter of deciding between making the investment and not making it. It is much more complex, as shown in Exhibit 2.2.

Management must try to predict not only how customers will value what the business does, but also how that value will be affected by what competitors decide to do. And they must recognize that competitors are making those same analyses. In even the simplest of scenarios, many predictions are required. Realistically, the decision requires an analysis of even more outcomes because predicting a competitor's actions would include more than one possible act. The difficulty is compounded when more than one competitor is involved. Analyses of potential outcomes of investment decisions frequently assume that competitors will do nothing. This is obviously a dangerous assumption to make.

After a positive investment decision is made, the resource is purchased and put to use. Operations resources become inputs to processes. The purchase of the resource doesn't guarantee the expected return on the investment; the return is dependent on how the resource will be used. Just like giving money to a stockbroker, there are no guarantees and the return depends on how the broker uses the money. Thus one

Realistic Cost/Benefit Decision — EXHIBIT 2.2

	Cost and Benefits of Making the Investment	Cost and Benefits of Not Making the Investment
Competitor Acts		
Competitor Does Nothing		

UNIT ONE   Foundations for Success

> **om on site**
>
> ### Profitability Requires Adaptation
>
> Many industries must cope with short product life cycles, fast rates of technological change, or thin profit margins. Disk-drive manufacturers face all three of these challenges and more. As competition has pushed them, they have increased the capacity of storage devices to the point that they've exceeded the needs of the typical PC user. Disk drives have reached "commodity" status, so costs have been cut, prices have been cut, and profit margins are slim. R&D costs, however, remain high. Now, in order to stay profitable, the manufacturers are faced with finding demand for the high-capacity drives they have created.
>
> The need to find new markets for high-capacity storage devices has caused manufacturers to look to the future. They must wait for a new technology to generate the need for more storage space. Napster and the surge in consumer desire to store MP3s created the last peak in demand. New consumer devices, from digital TVs to personal digital assistants (PDAs), offer potential future applications for high-capacity storage devices. Currently, consumer products account for only 2 percent of disk-drive sales. That figure is expected to rise to 12 percent by 2004.
>
> With high R&D costs, profitability rests on increasing sales volumes. One of the biggest potential applications is TV. Building digital video storage capacity directly into a TV set is not as easy as it might appear. The added complexity causes a TV to more closely resemble a PC.
>
> Looking to the future for profitability enhancement forces a disk-drive manufacturer to anticipate what new features might be needed. Reducing the noise made by the disk drive has been one priority. The result has been millions of dollars spent on acoustic improvement. The other issue for disk-drive manufacturers that hope to utilize their designs in consumer products is to make them robust enough to handle the shocks they must be able to withstand as PDAs are dropped in briefcases or carried around in pockets. Disk-drive manufacturers are also struggling to create devices that run cooler, eliminating the heat generation of disk drives.
>
> For disk-drive manufacturers, profitability requires investing in the appropriate R&D while patiently hoping and waiting for someone else to develop a technology that will depend on data storage. Predicting the needed future capabilities of the device, to provide guidance to R&D, is a forecast with all the inherent risks of any forecast.
>
> Source: "Disk-Drive Makers Have Reached a Profitability Wall—And They're Looking for Ways Around It," *The Wall Street Journal*, October 15, 2001, p. R21.

---

important role of managers is to ensure that the value created by processes is at least equal to the initial NPV estimate, thereby providing the necessary return on the investment. The opportunity for profit is the difference between actual process cost and the perceived value that it creates. Like the mutual fund manager with a specific strategy for identifying "buy" and "sell" opportunities to maximize fund owners' investment return, the effectiveness of processes determines the investment outcomes for operations resources.

PROFITABILITY MEASURES

To earn a profit is the goal of a business enterprise. Although that goal certainly simplifies the objectives of a business nicely, as a measure of performance to provide direction for day-to-day decisions, it falls short for several reasons.

First, it is difficult to predict the impact daily operations decisions have on profit. There is too much separation between daily decisions and a measure like profit. In Chapter 1, integrated management frameworks were briefly discussed as one solution to this problem. Managerial accounting has also evolved into a system designed to provide that link. Managerial accounting for operations decisions will be addressed in detail in Chapter 6.

Second, profit alone isn't a measure of investment success. Any measure of investment success must measure the **productivity** of the resources involved. For example, suppose I tell you I have made $500 on an investment. Is that good? You don't know because you don't know how much money was invested. Suppose I tell you I made the $500 on a $1,000 investment. Is that good? You still don't know because without knowing how long it took to gain that $500, you can't evaluate the performance of the investment. Likewise, suppose I painted my house. Was I productive? Again, you don't know. If it took me eight months you'd conclude that I probably wasn't, but you couldn't be certain. If I did it in a weekend you'd think I was either very productive or lived in a very small place. To understand productivity, you need a measure of inputs, a measure of outputs, *and* you need to know the amount of time it took to get from inputs to outputs.

Financial productivity frequently is referred to in terms of profit. The term *profit* is often misused, however. When people say "profit," many times they actually mean "net income." Net income provides an absolute measure but lacks the input comparison necessary for a measure of productivity. It doesn't really tell us anything about the productivity of resources. Profitability measures, on the other hand, are measures of the productivity of money. They relate outputs (net income) to inputs. The three most common measures of profitability are **profit margin**, **return on assets**, and **return on equity**. Each compares net income to a particular input and each is a critical measure of the success of operations. Equations 2.1, 2.2, and 2.3 are the formulas for these profitability measures:

$$\text{Profit Margin} = \text{Income}/\text{Sales} \tag{2.1}$$

$$\text{Return on Assets} = \text{Net Income}/\text{Total Assets} \tag{2.2}$$

$$\text{Return on Equity} = \text{Net Income}/\text{Total Equity} \tag{2.3}$$

Before examining each in detail, let's take a closer look at net income, which is used in all three. To determine net income, we start out with net sales, subtract the cost of goods sold and depreciation, and then subtract interest paid to provide taxable income. Subtracting the taxes gives us net income, as seen in Equation 2.4.

$$\text{Net Income} = \text{Net Sales} - \text{Cost of Goods Sold} - \text{Depreciation} - \text{Interest Paid} - \text{Taxes} \tag{2.4}$$

Net income is often expressed on a per-share basis for shares outstanding to give us earnings per share (EPS). As an output measure, it shouldn't be surprising that net income provides a critical measure of success. It is, in fact, *the bottom line*. Without being compared to inputs, however, it doesn't provide us with a sense of how productive our assets were. Now that we have a conceptual understanding of net income, let's examine each of the profitability measures.

Profit Margin

Profit margin tells us how much profit is generated per dollar of sales. It measures the productivity of our entire business. A high profit margin, which is desirable, can result

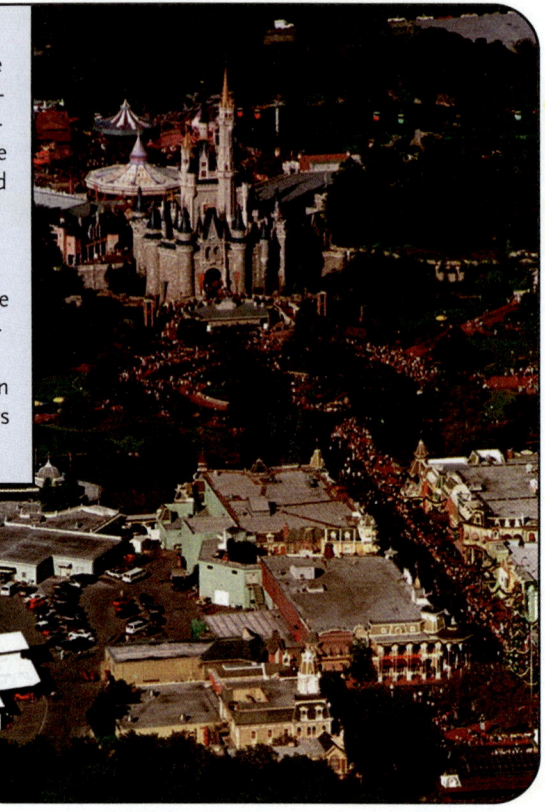

Financial investment in productive assets, such as those at Disney World, can be staggering. Assets that must provide a financial return include not only those directly related to the visitors' experiences and visible to everyone, but also the supporting facilities and equipment that make the customers' experience enjoyable. Here we get a glimpse of what lies behind the "Main Street" facade that customers see.

from low expenses relative to sales or high sales relative to expenses. Operations decisions have a significant impact on profit margin by influencing both the numerator and denominator. High levels of sales result from products and services valued highly by customers. Customers determine the value, but the value is created by the processes. Low costs result from processes that make good use of inventory, workforce, equipment capacity, and facilities. Processes that do not waste resources have low costs. Processes are at the root of many costs, and they are also key to adding the value that leads to sales. Effectively designed and managed processes can provide a double impact on net income by increasing net sales through value enhancement *while at the same time* decreasing costs of goods sold by using resources productively. This is why the effective design and management of processes are so critical to a business's success. They hit profit margin from both directions.

The most immediate way to reduce processing costs relative to sales is to identify steps in processes that do not add value and then eliminate them. This action is a significant part of process improvement efforts such as just-in-time (JIT) management (discussed in Chapter 15), as well as business process analysis and reengineering (both discussed in Chapter 5). By using this approach, costs are reduced but value isn't. Net income jumps. Reduction of non-value-adding steps can provide a nice boost to profit margin by increasing net income, but focusing only on cost reduction as a way to increase profit margin can be a mistake. Costs have an absolute minimum—zero. For most firms, the minimum is really a lot more than zero, and trying to squeeze out that extra dollar can take a tremendous amount of effort and may not provide much benefit. And it might result in an actual reduction in value. In addition, the same amount of effort devoted to increasing value and net sales may have a greater impact on the bottom line. The key to increasing sales relative to processing costs is to effectively design and manage processes to create products or services for which the customer is willing to pay more: Make a better product or a better service. To do that you must know what the customer wants, produce what the customer wants, and then deliver it and service it in a way that delights the customer.

Return on Assets

The second profitability measure, return on assets (ROA), is an indication of profit per dollar of assets. It is the broadest measure of asset productivity. ROA is to operations as an overall GPA is to a student. It measures how well assets are used to generate income. Return on assets is extremely relevant to operations because operations controls an extremely valuable set of assets. While ROA is a critical measure, it does not provide specific direction for improvement, just as a student's overall GPA doesn't provide information useful for directing improvement efforts. If the ROA is lower than desired, a red flag is raised, but management still has to identify those assets not being used to their fullest. More narrowly defined measures of asset productivity are needed to provide more direction and are more useful as an evaluative tool of asset productivity. To carry the GPA analogy further, a student needs to examine grades in individual courses to begin to direct improvement efforts. Then she must look at her grades on exams or homework within those courses to determine where the improvement efforts should be directed.

Return on Equity

Return on equity (ROE) quantifies how well stockholders did during a year by providing a measure of the productivity of *their* investment. ROE is important because providing a good investment for stockholders is important. It is the stockholders' gauge of the effectiveness of *their* investment, which, in turn, becomes *their* evaluation of how well the firm's management utilized its assets. For operations, ROE is not typically used as a performance measure because ROA and profit margin provide more transparent indicators of asset productivity. Ultimately, however, the performance of the operations resources dictates net income, given a fixed amount of equity. Increasing value and reducing costs, once again, increases net income, and increases ROE.

All three profitability measures are important for the business and important for operations. Once again, notice that all have net income in the numerator. Net income is the overriding indicator of the firm's output. It is the most relevant measure of output at that level. When focusing on the productivity of assets at a lower and more specific level, other measures of inputs and outputs are used.

ECONOMIC VALUE ADDED: A NEW PROFITABILITY MEASURE

A fourth profitability measure that is gaining popularity is economic value added (EVA). EVA is the after-tax operating profit minus the annual cost of capital:

$$\text{EVA} = \frac{\text{Net Operating}}{\text{Profit after Taxes}} - \left(\frac{\text{Average Cost}}{\text{of Capital}} \times \frac{\text{Total Capital}}{\text{Employed}} \right) \quad (2.5)$$

A positive EVA indicates that the company is creating wealth from its capital. A negative EVA means that it is actually destroying wealth—it ends up worse than it started. For most companies, the difficulties associated with using EVA are that the average cost of capital is a *weighted* average. To calculate the weighted average cost of capital, companies consider capital obtained from different sources, including capital obtained from borrowing and capital obtained from issuing stock. Borrowed money includes an interest rate that is adjusted for appropriate tax deductions, so its cost is easy to determine. The cost of equity financing, on the other hand, is the opportunity cost to investors. Historically, stockholders have received an average return that is six percentage points higher than the return on long-term government bonds. Riskier stocks command higher returns, and more stable stocks command a somewhat lower return. If, for example, bond rates are 6 percent, the average cost of equity would be

12 percent. The proportionate share of each financing method is multiplied by its percentage cost and totaled to provide the weighted average cost of capital.[2]

Once the cost of capital is determined, the actual EVA value is easy to determine. Let's look at a simple example. Suppose you decided to start a small business to help you earn money in your spare time. You are able to borrow $3,000 at 8 percent interest. Your EVA will be your net operating profit after taxes, minus the $240 cost of capital (8 percent of $3,000). If your after-tax profit is less than $240, you have not successfully added economic value. The amount of after-tax profit above $240 is your EVA.

EVA is very relevant to operations for the same reasons other profitability measures are relevant to operations. Operations generates many of the costs associated with the after-tax profit. In addition, through value creation, operations generates net income. In addition to the impact on value and costs, financing operations resources creates a demand for capital that has an impact on capital costs.

EVA differs from the other three profitability measures in that it is not a ratio of net income to a business input, but it is an absolute measure of dollars. Examples of industries that use EVA to help guide decisions are mining, pulp and paper, and high-volume manufacturers. All are extremely capital-intensive. For many of them, capital costs include about everything that goes into their businesses: buildings, equipment, inventory, property, and so on. When a company earns greater than a certain after-tax threshold on capital, a positive EVA results. The importance of operations in generating that return should be obvious, given the fact that operations decisions dictate how those buildings, equipment, inventory, and property are used. As EVA is improved, shareholder value is created. Esource 2.1 provides one company's perspective on the use of EVA.

www
OperationsNow
.com

Employees can improve EVA directly in three different ways. First, they can improve profitability without increasing the investment required. The most frequent use of this method is reducing the costs associated with production processes. Second, they can recommend investments to grow the business; investing in certain technologies, for example, could improve efficiency and therefore improve EVA. And third, they can reduce investments that don't enhance earnings. Reducing inventory is an example of this method. Notice that these efforts would result in positive impact on the other profitability measures as well. All three of these EVA improvement approaches require operations decisions.

PROFITABILITY FROM OPERATION RESOURCES

Processes are derived from grouping resources together. These processes create value. Profitability is generated by selling that value. Without the effective use of resources, value isn't created, and the potential for profitability is lost. Clearly, operations resources are critical to a firm's profitability. Operating resources are often broken into the four broad categories of inventory, workforce, capacity, and facilities. Additionally, customer relationships are used as a resource to add value. Customer relationships are not traditionally considered an "operating resource," but when the creation of value is examined it becomes clear that customer relationships are similar to other assets. In other words, they're scarce, they're expensive, and their effective use enhances profitability. Customer relationships are an asset to be managed very carefully by all parts of the business, particularly operations.

Measures of how well resources are used are generally thought of as productivity measures, but viewing them as local profitability measures can be enlightening. They provide important insights into how various operations resources contribute to the firm's profitability. Literally hundreds of performance measures are used to evaluate the productivity of these resources. The following sections demonstrate how such measures can be used and how they link to profitability through a common example for each resource group.

Inventory

Inventory consists of products and the components of products sold. Some items, like an inventory of retail items, are sold in the same form they were in when purchased. Others, like the raw material inventory of a manufacturer, are changed substantially before being sold. For services and manufacturers, no other resource group has come under as much scrutiny as inventory in the last 15 years. As just-in-time (JIT) manufacturing approaches were introduced in the early 1980s, U.S. manufacturers quickly came to realize that excess inventory was a huge drain on the productivity of assets. As we'll see in Chapter 15, excess inventory, though just one of many wastes attacked by JIT, became symbolic of the quest to become more productive. Many services, including retailers and financial services, followed the manufacturers' lead. They streamlined processes and slashed inventory. They didn't call it JIT, however; they called it "reengineering" and "continuous replenishment." A quick examination of inventory levels during those times reveals levels that look extremely high by today's standards. Before examining the inventory reduction phenomenon, let's look, for a moment, at an example of the use of inventory as an investment.

Inventory investment varies among different types of businesses, and even among different types of retailers. A retailer of fine wines, for example, would probably have greater investment in inventory than a typical liquor store. Individual bottles could cost hundreds of dollars. A lack of customers would result in slow turnover, and a low return on that inventory investment. A key to success would be obtaining sales volumes necessary to move the inventory. That would require high levels of customer traffic and customers interested in purchasing expensive wines.

An electronics retailer's inventory exists to satisfy demand. If demand for a specific CD player, for example, is 100 units per month, evenly dispersed through the month, the retailer must receive 100 units per month from the supplier. The retailer might receive 100 units on the first day of the month, or 25 units every Monday (assuming four weeks per month), or 5 units every weekday (assuming five days per week). As long as delivery costs are the same, from the standpoint of meeting a steady demand, it wouldn't matter *when* these units are delivered. From the standpoint of getting a financial return on that investment in inventory, however, it makes a huge difference. Let's suppose the retailer buys each CD player for $200 and sells it for $249. What are the financial implications of different delivery patterns?

If the retailer takes delivery and pays for all 100 units on the first day of the month, she has invested $20,000 in inventory at the beginning of the month. If demand is even through the month, her investment drops to zero by the end of the month. Her average investment level in that inventory would be $10,000:

$$\text{Average Inventory} = \frac{100 + 0}{2} = 50 \quad (2.6)$$

$$\text{Average Inventory Investment} = 50 \times \$200 = \$10,000 \quad (2.7)$$

For that $10,000 investment, which was held, in effect, for the entire month, she earns $4,900 (100 units sold and $49 contribution margin on each). That's a 49 percent return (4,900/10,000) in one month. Obviously, when all of the expenses of running the store are included, things won't look as good, but it's still a good return.

Now, what would happen if, instead of one monthly delivery, she took a daily delivery of 5 units every weekday and paid for them as she received them, instead of one monthly delivery? Exhibit 2.3 provides a graphical comparison of these two scenarios. With daily delivery, her inventory would start out at 5 units and drop to zero at the end of the day. Her average level of inventory would be 2.5 units, or $500:

$$\text{Average Inventory} = \frac{5 + 0}{2} = 2.5 \tag{2.8}$$

$$\text{Average Inventory Investment} = 2.5 \times \$200 = \$500 \tag{2.9}$$

At the end of the month she would have sold her 100 units and made $4,900 on an average daily investment of $500. That's a 980 percent return in a month, or 20 times what her return was with monthly deliveries, simply by changing the timing of delivery. Add to these numbers the fact that her average investment in inventory is $500 instead of $10,000, which gives her $9,500 to invest somewhere else. Besides that, she doesn't need as much space to store inventory, *and* the risk of inventory becoming damaged during storage is decreased.

This simplified example demonstrates how powerful inventory productivity's effect on the return on investment can be. For services and manufacturers that turn over millions of dollars in inventory annually, it's no wonder that effective inventory management is a critical responsibility of operations management. The following example demonstrates how to calculate average inventory levels for different delivery patterns.

EXHIBIT 2.3   Daily Orders versus Monthly Orders to Meet 100 Unit/Month Demand

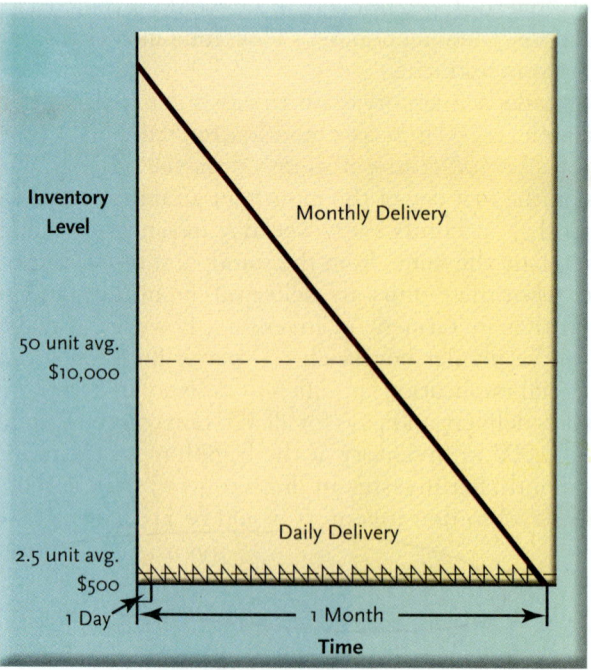

> **Example 2.1**
>
> ### Average Inventory Calculations from Delivery Pattern
>
> A distributor of novelty items has asked a manufacturer of incense sticks to begin daily deliveries instead of weekly. The manufacturer currently delivers 800 cases each Monday. Cases are valued at $265. What is the average level of incense inventory in units before the change? In dollars? What will the average level of inventory be after the change?
>
> **Solution**
>
> The average level of inventory for a period is the average of the beginning and ending period levels. In this example, the average level of inventory with weekly shipments is
>
> $$\frac{800 + 0}{2} = 400 \text{ cases} \tag{2.10}$$
>
> $$400 \text{ cases} \times \$265 \text{ per case} = \$106,000 \tag{2.11}$$
>
> For the daily delivery pattern, assuming 20 days/month, the average level of inventory would be
>
> $$\frac{160 + 0}{2} = 80 \text{ cases} \tag{2.12}$$
>
> $$80 \text{ cases} \times \$265 \text{ per case} = \$21,200 \tag{2.13}$$
>
> Excel Tutor 2.1 demonstrates how this problem can be solved in a spreadsheet.

www.OperationsNow.com

The most frequently used measure of inventory productivity is known as **inventory turnover**, or "inventory turns." Inventory turnover compares annual sales generated by the inventory (cost of goods sold) to the average level of inventory. The intent is to show how many times the inventory "turns over" as a result of sales. The more frequently it turns over, the greater its productivity. In Example 2.1, assuming a 52-week year, we can compare the inventory turns for monthly delivery to the turns for daily delivery. For the monthly delivery pattern, the annual cost of goods sold was $240,000. For the electronics retailer the average level of inventory for the CD player was $10,000 initially. Inventory turnover was 24. For the daily delivery pattern, cost of goods sold was still $240,000, but the average level of inventory was $500, yielding an inventory turn value of 480. To provide a point of reference, in the early 1980s, prior to lean manufacturing approaches, many manufacturers experienced inventory turns of less than 5.

Workforce

The workforce consists of all of the employees of the company. Employees are often described as being a company's most important asset. Employees are also commonly accepted as the source of a manager's greatest problems. Certainly they are expensive, and they are getting more and more difficult to attract as labor markets become tighter in some industries. Hiring, training, and managing employees has always been expensive. One can argue that many businesses, particularly manufacturers, have moved toward increasing levels of automation to eliminate the need for as many employees. Many would gladly trade all of the costs associated with employees for a sizable up-front cost of a numerically controlled machine or robot. Automated machines and robots do not, however, provide the flexibility and critical thinking of a human worker. The increasing importance of response and flexibility has resulted in some businesses eliminating automated equipment in favor of hiring more workers.

In some manufacturing industries, the percentage of total product costs resulting from direct labor is less than 10 percent. The service activities of those manufacturers, however, including sales, delivery, and after-sale service, as well as internal business services such as information systems, human resources, facility management, and equipment maintenance, are still very labor-intensive.

In the service sector of the economy, where the labor market can often be tight, good service can be difficult to find. A tight labor market often means tight competition for the most qualified workers and high levels of employee turnover. When poor service quality is received, it is often perceived as the result of employees' actions or inactions. Whether the employee is rude, slow, or just generally inept, poor service quality is often blamed on the employee. Sometimes low-quality service is the employee's fault, but it may well be caused by systems and processes that don't take advantage of the employee's strengths and weaknesses. Those processes are the management's responsibility. Employees, like other productive resources, are utilized in those processes, and like other resources, an employee can be part of an ineffective process that does not add value.

Employees, whether they are white or blue collar, are increasingly finding themselves the subject of productivity measures that compare outputs, like sales dollars and units produced, to inputs, like hours, weeks, customers, and calls. A quick examination shows a very close relationship between a ratio such as the dollars generated by an individual per week and the number of phone calls made, and a broader profitability measure like ROA. Ratios of outputs to inputs for individuals can create productivity measures that are like local profitability measures for individual salespersons. Productivity measures for employees, particularly white-collar employees, vary tremendously across industries. It is important to ensure that assets, including human assets, are as productive as possible. Productivity measures aid in decision making for those assets. Despite the fact that broader measures indicate business success, it is at the level of the individual asset that many decisions are made. At that level management can intervene and change processes so that those assets can be more productive.

A particularly relevant example of a measure of an employee's productivity is one typically used at universities, student credit hours generated per full-time equivalent faculty (FTE). One student taking a 3-credit-hour course generates 3 student credit hours. Thus, a 3-hour course with 40 students would generate 120 credit hours. Credit hours is an important output measure because it determines tuition revenues, state subsidy revenues, and so on. FTE is important as an input measure because it defines the equivalent of one full-time faculty member. Faculty frequently have fractional appointments, so it allows two half-time faculty, for example, to be counted as one FTE. University administrators make comparative analyses of departments across campus by looking at the average student credit hours generated per FTE for each department. This measure helps explain why class sizes for freshman and sophomore courses are often larger than those taught for juniors and seniors. The large classes provide a way to keep the average class size up when departments want to have small class sizes for their advanced courses. Granted, in the university setting, profitability of the firm isn't the objective, but a financial return of operational resources is still critical. Salaries and utility bills must be paid, and buildings must be maintained. Operational dollars come from tuitions and, in the case of state schools, state subsidy. Both are driven by student credit hours generated.

Value added by a good employee or value lost by a lousy one contributes directly to net income in a number of ways. Obviously, a customer's decision to return to a business can be greatly influenced by interactions with employees, so as a crucial part of the process for most services, employees add or detract value. Like any resource in any process, employees must add value to contribute to profitability. Chapter 11 examines more closely how employees contribute to value. Besides adding value through direct interaction with customers in service environments and with products for manufacturers, employees add value in other ways, such as through creative decision making and problem solving that reduces costs or improves processes.

Productivity measures for employees are often a challenge to create and interpret, and they can be quite deceiving. This phenomenon can best be understood through the use of an example. Example 2.2 provides the calculations for several relevant

> **Example 2.2**
>
> ### Calculating Productivity Measures
>
> Exhibit 2.4 presents productivity measures for a three-person sales force. A cursory examination of the data in Exhibit 2.4 shows that performance measures are variable and that different salespeople perform differently, depending on the measure. Use the performance measures provided in Exhibit 2.4 to create productivity measures for the three salespeople. Compare their productivity.
>
> **EXHIBIT 2.4** Monthly Performance Data for Sales Force
>
> | | Jeannie | Al | Carla |
> |--------------------|----------|----------|----------|
> | Sales dollars | $26,000 | $31,000 | $37,000 |
> | Clients visited | 95 | 109 | 67 |
> | Clients in region | 130 | 127 | 198 |
> | Miles traveled | 3,900 | 3,150 | 2,070 |
> | Salary (monthly) | $5,800 | $4,200 | $7,300 |
>
> **Solution**
>
> Exhibit 2.5 provides several productivity measures for the sales force.
>
> **EXHIBIT 2.5** Possible Productivity Measures for Sales Force
>
> | | Jeannie | Al | Carla |
> |--|----------|----------|----------|
> | Sales dollars per mile | $6.67 | $9.84 | $17.87 |
> | Sales dollars per visit | $273.68 | $284.40 | $552.24 |
> | Sales dollars per client | $200.00 | $244.09 | $186.87 |
> | Percent of clients visited | 73% | 86% | 34% |
> | Sales dollars generated per dollar of salary | $4.48 | $7.38 | $5.07 |
> | Clients visited per day | 4.75 | 5.45 | 3.35 |
>
> One measure of the productivity of the salesperson's activity with clients could be represented by the sales dollars per visit, showing Carla to be the most productive. Sales dollars per client in their region, however, provides a very different result, with Al being highest and Carla being the lowest. Carla appears to make the most of her visits, as measured by sales dollars per mile traveled and sales dollars per visit. One could conclude that Carla doesn't waste visits and visits only clients with a high likelihood of
>
> *(continues)*

> **Example 2.2** *(continued)*
>
>
>
> ordering. One might also conclude that she isn't very effective at reaching all of her region's potential clients. Al, on the other hand, seems to be the best at visiting clients, which may be important for maintaining relationships and getting future sales. Al also had the highest number of clients visited per day. The productivity of the salary paid to the sales staff seems to be highest with Al and lowest with Jeannie.
>
> Excel Tutor 2.2 demonstrates how these productivity measures can be derived using a spreadsheet.

productivity measures and also demonstrates how it can be difficult to determine which are the most important.

Capacity

Capacity is the capability of workers, machines, plants, servers, or organizations to produce output in a specific period of time. Capacity, particularly that associated with equipment utilized in the production of a service or product, is expensive. Maximizing the return on equipment investments is a high priority for any manager. Ineffective measurement of the productivity of equipment has long resulted in disagreement and poor decision making for many businesses. The logical approach to justifying the large cost of equipment has been to look at it from a "cost per unit" point of view. Basically, the question was: Could the purchase of a bigger (faster) machine reduce the per-unit cost of what it makes? To justify a large piece of equipment, its cost must be spread among a large number of units. That seems quite logical on the surface. This led to a measure of machine productivity known as **machine utilization**. Utilization is computed as another ratio of output over input:

$$\text{Utilization} = \frac{\text{Actual Running Time}}{\text{Time Available}} \quad (2.14)$$

In this case the output is the amount of time the machine was actually running divided by the total time the machine could have been running, which is the input. For example, a machine running for seven hours of an eight-hour shift would have a utilization of 87.5 percent. Increasing that utilization to 100 percent will result in more units being produced and a corresponding reduction in the cost per unit. Example 2.3 provides an example of calculating utilization.

Producing more units will spread the fixed costs associated with a resource over more units, but it won't necessarily result in an increase in net income, particularly if the production rate exceeds the demand rate in the marketplace. Producing at a rate greater than the demand rate actually results in a reduction in net income because costs are increasing, but sales revenues aren't. This is a narrow or resource-specific productivity measure that is out of sync, or even in direct conflict with a broader measure of productivity. Logic and intuition dictate that producing more products than demand will consume is probably a pretty dumb idea. All productivity measures, if used incorrectly, can cause problems that lead to bad decisions. Utilization can be an important measure of resource productivity when used appropriately, for example, on a resource that needs to run 100 percent of the time in order to meet demand.

Another often used, but misunderstood, capacity-related measure is **efficiency**. People typically use the term to describe how well something works or how effective

> **Example 2.3** **Utilization Calculation**
>
> A newly purchased welding robot has been monitored for the past week to provide information to be used for scheduling. The observations are noted in Exhibit 2.6. What was the total utilization of the robot? What impact on utilization did each category of downtime have?
>
> **EXHIBIT 2.6** Utilization Calculations for Example 2.3
>
> | Reason for Downtime | Minutes | Utilization Impact (%) |
> |---|---|---|
> | Operator/monitor not present | 107 | 4.46 |
> | Preventive maintenance | 149 | 6.21 |
> | Breakdown | 40 | 1.67 |
> | Adjustments and programming | 160 | 6.67 |
> | Material quality problems | 46 | 1.92 |
> | Total downtime | 502 | 20.92 |
> | Total uptime | 1,898 | |
> | Total time available: | 2,400 | |
> | Total utilization: | 79.08% | |
>
> **Solution**
>
> Total utilization can be calculated by dividing the minutes of total uptime by the total time available. The utilization impact of each category of downtime is determined by dividing the minutes of downtime for each category by the total available minutes. The results of these calculations are presented in Exhibit 2.6. Spreadsheet calculations to obtain utilization values are presented in Excel Tutor 2.3.

www
OperationsNow
.com

EXCEL TUTOR

it is. Efficiency is actually a productivity measure that is calculated using the following formula:

$$\text{Efficiency} = \frac{\text{Actual Output}}{\text{Standard Output}} \qquad (2.15)$$

In other words, it compares what should have happened to what actually did happen.

This productivity measure also creates a ratio of outputs to inputs. It's not as direct a comparison as some, however. The outputs are obviously the actual machine output. The input, however, is a standard that represents the resource's proven or documented potential. The machine should be able to operate at the standard rate. If the standard was 1,000 units per hour, for example, that is the expectation of the machine under normal circumstances. Efficiency, then, is a measure of what the machine actually did divided by a measure of what the machine could have or should have done. Employees are also measured by their efficiency when there is a standard of performance in place. Unlike utilization, efficiency can actually be greater than 100 percent in cases where a resource is performing better than the standard. Reel Operations

Video 2.1 examines how Nucor Steel integrates productivity measures of human and equipment resources.

Efficiency calculations are quite straightforward, as demonstrated in Example 2.4.

Facilities

Facilities consist of the buildings used to house all aspects of a business. In the discussion of employee productivity, it was mentioned that the measurement of productivity was very specific to what the employees are used for, and it often varied a great deal from company to company. The same situation exists for facilities. Facilities are expensive, they are frequently a long-term investment, and they are used for a variety of important purposes. The size of an investment in a particular facility is often closely related to the cost of the land on which it is located. Land costs and building costs mean that facility cost is almost always associated with the facility's size. To

---

Example 2.4

Efficiency Calculation

A bank's check-clearing operation uses automated machines to read and sort checks. A newly purchased machine has been monitored for two months in order to develop a standard. The standard developed was 5,400 checks per hour. Hourly counts of checks in a recent eight-hour study are reported in Exhibit 2.7.

Calculate the efficiency of the bank's check-reading machine.

EXHIBIT 2.7 Check Reading Data for Example 2.4

Hour	Quantity Read
1	5,756
2	5,235
3	5,540
4	4,886
5	5,267
6	4,656
7	5,346
8	5,104

Total read: 41,790
Standard: 43,200
Efficiency: 96.74%

Solution

Efficiency is calculated by dividing the total number of checks read by the number that should have been read during that period of time. Over an eight-hour period, 43,200 checks should have been read according to the standard. Only 41,790 were actually read, resulting in an efficiency of 96.74 percent.

Excel Tutor 2.4 provides an example of how efficiency calculations are made in a spreadsheet.

determine how well such an investment generates a financial return, output measures (sales revenues, customers served, and so on) must be compared to the input measure most closely tied to the initial investment. An input measure frequently used is the size of the facility in square feet.

For retailers, a commonly used measure of facility productivity is sales revenues per square foot. Not only can this measure be used to compare stores to each other, but standards can be generated based on the return desired from that facility investment. These standards can be used for evaluation purposes or to make expansion decisions. Performance of other stores can be used as a basis for determining whether the costs of a particular new facility can be justified, given likely sales volumes.

Customer Relationships

Treating customer relationships as a resource results from two distinct pressures. First, research has shown that the longer the customer relationship with a business is, the more profitable that customer is. The length of this relationship is synonymous with customer loyalty. This results from several factors that are discussed in more detail in Chapter 14, including reductions in costs as customers become more loyal and benefits they provide the business by being advocates for it. Second, advances in technology have made it feasible for companies to manage their customer relationships as scientifically as they manage other resources. If managing them provides benefits, and if technology enables businesses to manage them relatively easily, they should be managed. Besides the obvious need and ability to manage customer relationships, another recent trend in business supports the practice. The use of the balanced scorecard method of performance measurement, discussed later in this chapter, places customer outcomes as one of four primary perspectives (the others are financial objectives, internal business processes, and learning and growth) necessary for evaluating organizational performance. But how does one measure productivity of this resource?

One common approach to measuring customer loyalty is to collect data on sales to see what percentage of customers have made a previous purchase within a specified length of time. Another is to track the sales associated with specific customers to identify which customers are most valuable to the organization. Increased investment in the relationships identified, such as increased levels of personal attention, is then warranted.

LOCAL VERSUS GLOBAL OPTIMIZATION

The gradual trend for businesses to pay more attention to broad profitability measures by widening management's perspective and eliminating functional boundaries has implications for resource-specific performance measures. Global measures—profit margin, ROA, ROE—are very important, but since they are acceptable only when resources are used effectively, measures of resource effectiveness are needed as well. The challenge arises when these resource-specific "local" measures are in conflict with broader "global" measures. This can lead to situations where management makes decisions to improve resource-specific measures only to find that the decisions actually harm global measures—profit margin, ROA, or ROE. How does this happen?

Earlier in this chapter, in the discussion of measuring generated profitability, the issue of productivity measures being out of sync or even in direct conflict with each other was mentioned. This phenomenon also appears when local and global productivity measures are compared. It may seem logical to assume that optimizing or maximizing all of the local or "resource-specific" measures of performance will also optimize global measures. If all of the resources are at the highest level of productivity, the system must also be at its highest level of productivity, right? Wrong. For example, if utilization of all work centers in a factory were maximized, would ROA be maximized as a result? Probably not. Products do not require exactly equal time on all equipment. If equipment utilizations were maximized, there might be too much inventory of some items.

It doesn't take long to discover that there are many examples of conflict between local and global productivity measures. Optimization of global measures, like the company's profitability, generally requires coordination and balance that precludes optimization of all local measures.

Inventory turns have long been the dominant measure for identifying inventory productivity. The lower the level of inventory, the higher the turns. A manufacturer that fulfills orders from a finished goods warehouse might initiate an inventory reduction effort by simply making substantial across-the-board cuts in inventory. A retailer could accomplish the reduction by decreasing the quantity ordered and increasing the frequency of orders to suppliers. A manufacturer would have to decrease the production quantity ordered while increasing the frequency of production orders to the factory. Initially, given a substantial amount of excess inventory, there would probably be no detrimental effect. As inventory is reduced, however, another measure—service level—will be affected. This measure isn't typically thought of as a measure of productivity, but it is. The **service level** of a particular inventory is the number of orders satisfied from the inventory divided by the total number of orders. In other words, it is the percentage of demand satisfied from stock.

Whenever demand occurs that cannot be met directly from inventory, a **stockout results**. The relationship between product demand, order delivery frequency, order quantity, and customer service is an interesting one. Obviously, if demand were 10 units per day and 10 units per day were received from the supplier, demand would be met. However, demand is not always even. A demand pattern that averaged 10 units per day would likely have days of higher and lower demand. That uncertain aspect of demand creates the possibility of stockouts, even though, on average, supply and demand are equal. Additional inventory, known as **safety stock**, is used to help cope with demand uncertainty. Once a certain point in an inventory reduction effort is reached, the low inventory can start to have a negative impact on service level because of the variability of demand. The problem can be magnified when an unforeseen problem arises. A supplier strike, for example, could quickly result in stockouts if there were initially low levels of finished products.

The conflict between measures of performance arises quite often. Businesses are complex systems. It's not possible to change the way any one resource is being used without having an impact somewhere else. Quite often that impact is far-reaching and unexpected.

MEASUREMENT IMPROVEMENT

Most productivity measures can be thought of as local profitability measures. Most are ratios of an output measure to an input measure. Obviously, increasing the numerator or decreasing the denominator can improve such a measure. A balanced approach to productivity improvement, and one that is more likely to be successful, focuses on the numerator and denominator in a measure *and* targets more than one measure. The focus on more than one measure reduces the likelihood that one measure is improved at the expense of another.

An attempt to increase the numerator of a productivity measure is an attempt to increase a measure of output. As long as that output level is in sync with product or

Adobe: Turning a Popular Product into a Profitable Product

In 1992, Adobe Systems demonstrated software that enables a document created on one computer to be opened, edited, and saved on another computer, even with different applications and operating systems. Despite the fact that this was three years before the introduction of the World Wide Web, it was lauded as the most significant technology at Comdex, an annual technology show. The concept of document sharing was new, it was viewed positively, but its importance was not really known.

In the years since its introduction, 320 million copies of the Adobe Acrobat Reader have been distributed. The Reader, however, is free. Since 1993, fewer than 6 million copies of the full program have been sold. Adobe products have a tradition of dominating their market segments. They are driven by the pledge to allow users to publish content wherever the user wants, whether it's a printer, web page, cell phone, handheld device, PC, or Internet appliance.

But in the early and mid-1990s, the concept of electronically sharing documents wasn't on anyone's radar screen. Over time, the number of Acrobat Reader users grew. By the end of 1997, some 11.7 million had been distributed. By the end of 1998 that figure had jumped to 57.4 million. During that time, however, the sale of the full program still represented less than 7 percent of Adobe's $894 million in revenues.

Increasing the sales of the complete program was critical to Acrobat's success, but Adobe was not successful at doing it. Finally, by building alliances with system integrators that are specific to certain industries (government, pharmaceutical companies, banks, and so on), Adobe began to educate potential users about the software's capabilities. The effect of this education has been dramatic. Sales for Adobe's ePaper Solutions, which is predominantly Acrobat, reached $129.3 million in 1999 and $207 million in 2000.

R&D efforts in fast-paced technology-driven organizations may create products and services that are ahead of their time. Patience and educating customers may be required to bring about profitability.

Source: "Adobe Had a Popular Product—Making It Profitable Took Some Work," *The Wall Street Journal*, October 15, 2001, pp. R18–R19; http://www.adobe.com/aboutadobe/pressroom/pressmaterials/networkpublishing/main.html.

---

service demand, and is not increased at the detriment of other measures, this approach can be effective. An examination of what is required to increase the ROA provides a good example of why one must give attention to *both* the numerator and denominator. Recall that ROA is net income divided by total assets. On paper, increasing net income can be accomplished in a number of ways, including increasing net sales, reducing the cost of goods sold, reducing interest paid, or reducing taxes. The most direct approach would be to increase net sales, which could be accomplished by increasing the volume of goods sold, or by increasing the selling price, or both. Increasing the selling price is a somewhat risky approach, however, because its impact on the volume of goods sold is difficult to predict, and the increase could actually result in a reduction in net sales.

The other approach to increasing ROA is to decrease the value of assets required. In other words, the output stays the same, but ROA improves because the denominator (input) is reduced. This approach to productivity improvement is often thought of as "cost cutting" and is quite common. When applying this approach to more local measures of productivity, such as the productivity of a particular department or the productivity of equipment, a change in productivity may be demonstrated more quickly than would be the case if one were trying to increase the output measure. Unfortunately, a productivity-improvement effort based solely on cost cutting often leads to undesirable side effects. Keep in mind that there is an absolute limit to how much the inputs can be reduced. After all, they can't go below zero. As they are reduced, other measures—particularly those related to customer service or service quality—can be harmed.

Quite often, a cost-focused effort to improve productivity of operations resources and overall profitability is aimed at getting short-term results. For example, one can lay off workers quickly, and the results will appear on financial reports almost as quickly. Such efforts frequently end up as a tradeoff between short-term performance and long-term performance, however. The short-term benefits of reduced labor expense can later be outweighed by the costs associated with retraining new, inexperienced workers or by a reduction in sales that can be a response to poor-quality service.

DECISION-MAKING TOOLS: BREAKEVEN ANALYSIS

Because of the nature of operations, managers are bombarded with questions that start with the two words: "Should we?" Should we bring that new service online? Should we bring that new product into production? Should we expand? Should we upgrade our information system? Should we purchase that new piece of equipment? Should we build a new facility in another city? Often implicit in the question "Should we?" is a more detailed question: "Of these alternatives, which is the best investment?" Which is the best new product to produce? Which expansion design is the best? Which piece of equipment is the most desirable? Alternatives are often examined from a perspective of different costs associated with different alternatives. These questions are asked when managers consider the purchase of a variety of resources. Resources aren't free, after all, and there are always choices. Two types of cost are usually involved. **Fixed costs** are unrelated to the volume of output and include such costs as facility construction or other start-up costs. **Variable costs** are directly related to volume of output and include such costs as material costs and transportation costs. Labor costs are often considered to be variable costs, but in reality they usually aren't. Direct labor is generally paid by the week or month, no matter what the employee output, even though salaries are described as "hourly." In some cases, expected revenues are also different for the different alternatives. The analysis of decision alternatives in such situations is known as **breakeven analysis**. When fixed costs are high relative to variable costs, large volumes are needed to spread out that large fixed cost over a large number of units. However, when variable costs are high relative to the fixed costs, the alternative is more advantageous for small volumes. Conceptually, breakeven analysis seeks to identify the volumes that support different combinations of fixed versus variable costs.

Breakeven analysis is a relatively straightforward approach to comparing the total cost curves for each alternative. The total cost curves are assumed to be linear and can be created by using the basic formula for a line:

$$y = a + bn \qquad (2.16)$$

where y is the total cost for producing n units or serving n customers, a is the Y intercept (and equals the fixed cost), and b is the slope of the line forming the total cost curve (and equals the variable cost per unit). The problem can be solved graphically by identifying the intersections of the cost curves and interpreting their meaning, or by identifying the intersections algebraically by setting the equations for the cost curves equal to each other and solving for n. A conceptual understanding of breakeven analysis can be enhanced by examining Interactive Model 2.1.

An example of breakeven analysis used in a software selection scenario is described in Example 2.5.

Example 2.5 Breakeven Analysis

The ability to identify, understand, analyze, and track customer wants and needs has become extremely important to businesses. This has extended to the ability to access this information immediately as a customer calls to place an order. It is actually possible, for example, to know what a customer is likely to want prior to his asking for it. Technological advancements in data analysis and data mining techniques have made this possible, and customer relationship management (CRM) software combined with call-center technologies has made this practice commonplace for large mail-order retailers.

Like many software-related markets, a large share of the market for such technology is held by a very small set of companies, but there are also some "small players" with good products. There are also companies willing to collect and analyze the data on a contract basis, creating the potential to outsource this function entirely. It should not be a surprise that performing this function in-house using the largest and best-known software, as compared to outsourcing, is a tradeoff. Management must weigh a large fixed cost with small variable costs against a small fixed cost but significant costs per unit down the road.

The management of a mail-order retailer has identified three alternatives for CRM software purchase. The market leader is Market Probe. It is very expensive, but well known and popular. WEEZL is a small upstart in the business. Prophecy is a subcontractor and a well-known provider of these types of services. Exhibit 2.8 compares the cost information of these alternatives.

EXHIBIT 2.8 CRM Software Choice Alternatives

Company	Description	Total Installation Costs ($)	Variable Costs ($ per customer)
Market Probe	Market upstart	360,000	0.38
Prophecy	Market leader	480,000	0.07
WEEZL	Contractor of services	224,000	0.97

Installation costs include software licensing, server and other hardware upgrades, and initial staffing expense associated with the CRM software installation (consultant fees included). Variable costs per customer include such costs as ongoing staffing time for data entry, data maintenance, and analysis, as well as the per-customer fees assessed by the subcontractor. Complete a breakeven analysis for the CRM software alternatives.

Solution

Exhibit 2.9 graphically analyzes the total costs given different numbers of customers and shows that at lower numbers of customers (below roughly 225,000 customers) WEEZL is

(continues)

Example 2.5 (continued)

the low-cost alternative. At very high numbers of customers (above about 380,000), Prophecy is the low-cost alternative. Between 220,000 and 375,000, Market Probe is the low-cost alternative.

EXHIBIT 2.9 Call Management Software Cost Comparison

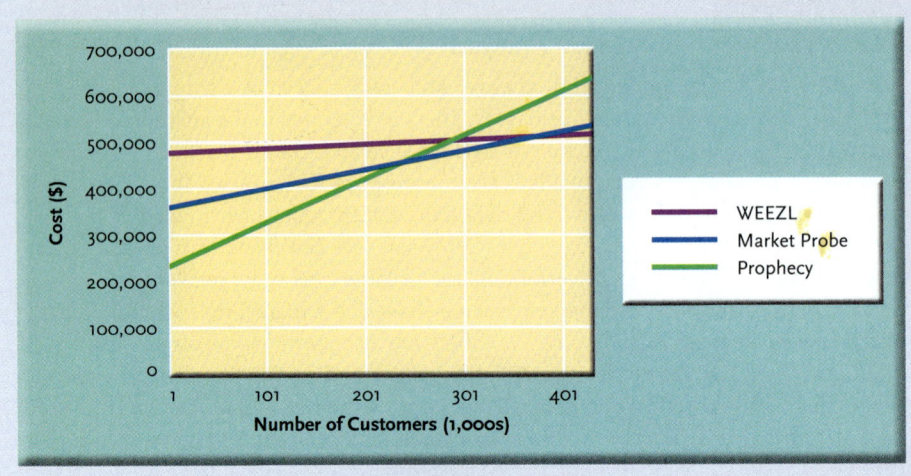

A more precise result can be obtained by identifying the intersections of the three lines as follows:

$$360{,}000 + 0.38n = 224{,}000 + 0.97n$$
$$136{,}000 + 0.38n = 0.97n$$
$$136{,}000 = 0.59n$$
$$230{,}508 = n$$
$$480{,}000 + 0.07n = 360{,}000 + .38n$$
$$120{,}000 + 0.07n = 0.38n$$
$$120{,}000 = 0.31n$$
$$387{,}097 = n$$

For a company with fewer than 230,508 customers, WEEZL is the low-cost alternative. For more than 387,097 customers, Prophecy is the low-cost alternative. For a company that falls in the middle, Market Probe is the low-cost alternative. The intersection of WEEZL and Prophecy is not needed because it does not form an endpoint of a line segment that is part of the solution.

An example of how breakeven analysis can be accomplished in a spreadsheet can be found at Excel Tutor 2.5.

www
OperationsNow
.com

At the functional level, for almost any department in a business, these types of decision are commonplace. Keep in mind, however, that the decisions are still dependent on uncertain data. In Example 2.5, for instance, we are not certain of the number of eventual customers, so we must make an educated estimate. Like any financial manager, the decision maker must consider not only the size and timing of cash to be received from an investment in an operating resource, but also the likelihood of receiving it. Uncertainty is a constant.

A BROADER APPROACH TO PRODUCTIVITY MEASUREMENT: THE BALANCED SCORECARD

This chapter has discussed global performance measures and local, resource-specific measures. It has looked at a sampling of resource-specific performance measures, along with a frequently used technique for choosing among resource alternatives. It has also identified the dangers of local measures that conflict with each other and with global measures. We've seen that the use of several different measures simultaneously provides the best and most objective way to examine resource productivity. The potential for measures to conflict and result in poor business decisions has been recognized in recent years and has given rise to an increasingly popular method of measuring and evaluating the global performance of the business. This method is known as the **balanced scorecard**. The balanced scorecard was introduced in 1992.[3] The method argued that the performance of a business cannot be captured with financial measures alone, and other measures that are more difficult to quantify are also important. In addition, financial measures look only at the past, and businesses need to look into the future.

Consistent with recommendations to use several performance measures simultaneously, the balanced scorecard approach is based on four perspectives:

- Financial objectives
- Customer outcomes
- Internal business processes
- Learning and growth

Rather than merely looking at past performance, the balanced scorecard approach examines past performance and future plans so that efforts can be aligned with needed improvement. The balanced scorecard approach, combined with productivity and performance measures that provide useful information, help a firm keep up with changing markets and changing environments. Esource 2.2 provides additional information about the use of balanced scorecards.

CHAPTER SUMMARY

In this chapter, three profitability measures were reviewed: profit margin, return on assets, and return on equity. Profit margin provides a measure of productivity of the entire business. Return on assets provides a measure of the productivity of all of its assets. Return on equity provides a measure of productivity of the investment the company's owners have made. Although each measure may appear to be separate from day-to-day activities, management's challenge is to understand the linkage between their actions and these measures. Each profitability measure is tightly linked to a firm's ability to create value and sell it for an amount greater than its cost.

A common theme of all operations-oriented decisions is the direct impact on net income. By managing resources effectively, businesses can reduce costs associated with the production of goods and services by making processes more effective. A reduction in costs translates directly into an increase in net income. Net income can also be increased by enhancing product or service value, which enables the business to increase the sales price. Both approaches require effective operations decision-making regarding productive processes. Net income increases provide profitability increases because net income is the denominator for all three profitability measures.

This chapter introduces each of the five resources presented in the profit model: inventory, workforce, capacity, facilities, and customer relationships. Links to profitability are created for each resource through a cursory examination of typical resource-specific productivity measures. Calculations for several common resource-specific productivity measures, including inventory turns, utilization, and efficiency, are presented. A common approach to choosing among alternative resources by analyzing their cost curves, known as breakeven analysis, was also described.

The balanced scorecard, a relatively new global performance measurement approach that addresses quantitative and qualitative measures of performance, was introduced.

KEY TERMS

balanced scorecard, 59
breakeven analysis, 56
economic value added (EVA), 43
efficiency, 50
fixed costs, 56
inventory turnover, 47
machine utilization, 50
productivity, 41

profit margin, 41
return on assets, 41
return on equity, 41
safety stock, 54
service level, 54
stockout, 54
variable costs, 56

REVIEW QUESTIONS

1. Who determines value?
2. How are value and costs related to the potential for profit?
3. Why is net present value (NPV) often so difficult to determine accurately?
4. Describe the three global measures of profitability.
5. What are two general ways profit margin can be improved?
6. What are the two general ways return on assets (ROA) can be improved?
7. Why would ROA be important to the owner of a business?
8. Why is economic value added (EVA) becoming so popular?
9. How can employees of a company improve EVA?
10. Describe common productivity measures for inventory, workforce, capacity, facilities, and customer relationships. How do these measures link to profitability measures?
11. What is meant by "local" versus "global" optimization? Which is more important? Why can't both occur?
12. What is the objective of breakeven analysis? What are its potential weaknesses?
13. Describe the balanced scorecard approach to performance measurement. What are its advantages?

DISCUSSION QUESTIONS

1. Describe a business you are familiar with whose product or service value was reduced, not by what it did, but by what a competitor did. How could the business you chose have reacted to maintain the value of its product or service?
2. Identify a business you are familiar with. What could be done to increase the value of its product or service? Trace the effects of those changes to determine how they would change profit margin and ROA. Include specific effects on the components of net income.
3. Some people have said that inventory should actually be considered to be similar to a loan that the company takes out, rather than an asset. Why might someone promote such a view?
4. Identify local performance measures you are familiar with that are not in sync with global performance objectives. What do you think was the motivation for the development of these local measures? Why do they remain in existence? What behaviors do they motivate?
5. Many people have criticized the use of academic grades as the sole criterion for evaluating a student's performance in college, just as others have insisted that financial performance measures can't be the sole measure of a business's performance. Design a balanced scorecard approach for evaluating college students.

PROBLEMS

1. PetToys, a national pet supply warehouse store, takes delivery of all products at its central warehouse in St. Louis. It then ships products to its store on a weekly basis, based on individual store purchases. One particular product, the Doggie Jolt Training Collar, is shipped every other month from a manufacturer in China. The PetToys warehouse, on average, ships 800 collars per month to its retailers. At a value of $80 per unit, how much can PetToys reduce its inventory investment by changing to a monthly delivery pattern from China?

2. Ron's Music Supply currently sells 18 units of a particular CD player per week, on average. The inventory manager takes monthly delivery of 72 units. The CD players cost Ron's Music Supply $100 each.
   a. What is the average investment in the inventory of the CD player?
   b. Ron needs to free up $2,700 to help pay for a new promotional campaign. Can he accomplish this by increasing the delivery frequency of the CD player? How?

3. TiteRite manufactures a variety of plastic containers that are sold nationally at discount stores. The molding process used to produce the popular container is accomplished by a machine that also produces three other products. Currently, the machine produces three-day production runs of each product, changing molds after each run. Management has inquired about the possibility of investing in quick-change molds that would make the changeover easier and make it possible to reduce the production runs to one day in length. Current batch size and product values are presented on the following page:

3 day production

Product	Batch Size		Product Value ($)
Product 1	1,800	600	1.32
Product 2	2,400	800	1.69
Product 3	2,000	667	1.74
Product 4	2,600	867	1.86

How much money could be spent on changeover improvement if it was limited to the money made available by an inventory reduction resulting from one-day production runs?

4. Ward's Sporting Collectibles has an eclectic supply of antique sports memorabilia, from antique fishing gear to baseball, football, and basketball memorabilia. Mark Ward, the business owner, buys items from 12 "pickers" he has contracted with around the country. Pickers search for items, buy them, and send $100,000 worth of products to him four times per year, on the first of January, April, July, and October. Considering these four peaks in his inventory level, Mark estimates his average inventory level to be $600,000, peaking at about $1.2 million at delivery time. Customers have complained that his inventory doesn't change much. Mark would like to reduce his inventory and increase the turnover in his shop by having pickers deliver more products, but deliver monthly. He wants deliveries of $50,000 per month from each of the 12 pickers. What would his average inventory level drop to?

5. A small law firm with two partners and four associates has begun to evaluate the productivity of the four associates. The following data were assembled:

Associate	Clients Served in Current Year	Total Hours Billed This Year	New Clients Served This Year	Experience at This Firm (years)
Sam	37	1,910	28	6
Sarah	42	2,430	24	5
Nick	56	1,870	33	3
Julie	32	2,200	12	2

a. What productivity measures would be useful for these associates?
b. From a strict "profitability" standpoint, which measure would be most appropriate?
c. What measure might indicate the associate that can provide the greatest growth for the firm?
d. What measure might indicate the best productivity, given the person's experience level?

6. The following table provides production, price, and sales data for two models of CD player:[4]

Year	Product	Units Produced	Price ($)	Sales ($)
2001	Z40	12,000	60.00	720,000.00
2001	Z60	12,000	120.00	1,440,000.00
2002	Z40	6,000	150.00	900,000.00
2002	Z60	18,000	120.00	2,160,000.00

a. Identify different ways of comparing the productivity of 2002 to that of 2001.
b. What happens to production? What happens to sales revenue?
c. What is your assessment of the changes in productivity if 2001 prices are used for the evaluation of 2002?
d. Overall, do you think productivity has increased from 2001 to 2002?

7. A brokerage firm provides newly hired associates a list of contacts that they are required to call on in hopes of building their client base. The first contact is by mail with a personal letter. The second call is by telephone, with the objective of setting up a face-to-face meeting to discuss investments. The following table shows data collected over the past year for five new associates:

Broker	Number of Contacts Given	Mailings	Phone Calls Made	Meetings Scheduled	Meetings Completed	Meetings Resulting in Investments	Total Investments ($)
Armstrong	450	450	450	43	42	28	724,000.00
Frederickson	450	450	450	64	52	16	380,000.00
Davis	450	450	450	85	55	12	520,000.00
Foster	450	450	450	70	61	32	643,000.00
Kinney	450	450	450	30	26	19	256,000.00

a. Who was best able to convert a phone call into an agreement to meet face-to-face?
b. Who was best able to convert a commitment to meet into an actual meeting?
c. When meeting, which broker seems best able to turn the client into an investor?
d. Who is the most productive of the brokers? Why did you select the measure you used?

8. A manufacturer of paper has three paper machines of various ages. The oldest was installed in 1961, the second oldest was installed in 1983, and the newest was installed in 1998. The following production statistics have been collected over the past six months of operation:

Machine	Total Production (hours)	Total Paper Produced (tons)	High-Grade Paper Produced (tons)	Low-Grade Paper Produced (tons)	Labor Required (hours)	Maintenance Required (hours)
1961	3,000	39,000	4,000	35,000	6,000	760
1983	2,500	28,000	28,000	0	6,000	510
1998	4,000	33,000	14,000	19,000	4,000	420

a. Which machine is most productive, per hour of operation?
b. Which machine is most productive, per hour of labor?
c. If high-grade paper generates twice the profit of low-grade paper, which machine is most productive per hour of labor?

d. What other productivity measures might be useful in looking for improvements in paper machine productivity?

9. Spotted Cow Dairy collected the following downtime data on its bottle-filling machine:

Categories of Downtime	Minutes
Breakdowns	70
Changeover time	189
Restocking	221
Worker break and lunch	300
Total time available	2,400

What was the utilization of the filling machine?

10. The faculty in the Management Department office have complained about having to wait in line for the copying machine. The department chair, always tight with his money, has resisted buying an additional one. His data show that for the week studied, the machine was used the following amount:

Day	Time in Use (minutes)
Monday	420
Tuesday	180
Wednesday	244
Thursday	171
Friday	143
Total	1,158

The department chair claims that since there are 10,080 minutes in a week, the utilization is just over 10 percent, making it unnecessary to purchase an additional machine.

   a. What is wrong with that argument?
   b. What do you think the appropriate utilization is?

11. The standards for each of three scanning robots used in the shipping department of a major online retailer are presented below:

   Scanner 1   3,600 pieces per hour
   Scanner 2   3,000 pieces per hour
   Scanner 3   2,150 pieces per hour

   Actual output of the three scanners averages:

   Scanner 1   3,200 pieces per hour
   Scanner 2   2,650 pieces per hour
   Scanner 3   2,400 pieces per hour

   a. What is the standard output for the entire scanning department?
   b. What is the efficiency of each machine?
   c. What is the department efficiency?

12. The standard for manual entry of check information for those checks rejected by an automatic check reader is 265 checks per hour. The actual output of three check readers is presented on the next page:

Reader	Output
1	218
2	269
3	253

a. Compute the efficiency of each reader.
b. What is the efficiency of the group?

13. A local one-hour film developing lab recently purchased a new automated developer. The machine was described by the supplier as being able to develop and print 720 prints per hour, with a trained operator. After 30 days of operation, management collected the following data for one 40-hour week:

Total hours available	40.0
Hours down for maintenance	3.5
Hours down for chemical refill	0.5
Hours down for cleaning	0.8
Hours down for paper jam	0.2
Total hours downtime	5.0

The following data were collected on 35 full hours of operation:

Hour	Output	Hour	Output
1	723	19	735
2	694	20	740
3	790	21	701
4	719	22	729
5	702	23	717
6	753	24	687
7	698	25	729
8	707	26	691
9	709	27	724
10	697	28	710
11	680	29	701
12	739	30	679
13	702	31	725
14	715	32	686
15	736	33	726
16	684	34	716
17	687	35	733
18	684		

a. Calculate the utilization and efficiency of the new machine.
b. To increase output, management plans on scheduling the machine for 50 hours next week. What would the expected output be, based on past efficiency and utilization?

14. The student government at a small university is in charge of all logistics for an upcoming concert. The band coming in has included, as a part of their contract, a clause that mandates every entrant to the coliseum must pass through a metal detector. Because 11,000 tickets were sold, an opening act was scheduled as a means of spreading out the arrival period. Concert planners expect that the arrival of the 11,000 attendees will be spread out over one and one-half hours. Metal detectors are rented from a security firm. They are delivered, set up, and calibrated on site, at a cost of $1,300 each. That includes the cost of two operators for each. The security firm claims that each metal detector can process 11 people per minute. However, recalibration and adjustment result in an average utilization of 91 percent.

    a. How many metal detectors will be needed to process all concert attendees in time?
    b. The opening act costs $8,500. Without the opening act, the arrival period is projected to be 45 minutes. Would it be cheaper to cancel the opening act and rent enough metal detectors for a 45-minute arrival period? Justify your answer.

15. Stevens Fabrication, a small manufacturing firm, has just won a long-term contract for the manufacture of motor mounting plates for refrigerators. The contract is with a high-volume appliance manufacturer. For its test run of parts, Stevens produced the parts with a process that was predominantly manual, using existing equipment. An automated stamping press would significantly lower the cost per unit by eliminating most of the labor, but such a press is expensive. After a cost analysis of the current process and an investigation of the purchase and setup of a new press, Stevens projects the following fixed and variable costs:

Alternative	Fixed Cost ($)	Variable Costs per Unit ($)
Automated	27,000	0.16
Manual	2,000	1.85

How much production volume is necessary to make the automated stamping press economically attractive?

16. A&F Tax service wishes to store data electronically, rather than in hard copy format. The owner has collected cost information on three different approaches to scanning and storing documents. All involve leased equipment with all hardware and software maintenance provided. Annual cost information for the alternatives is presented below:

Alternative	Fixed Cost ($)	Variable Costs ($)
1	1,000	0.02
2	800	0.08
3	500	0.25

Identify the breakeven points for the three alternatives. If A&F expects to scan 1,500 documents in the upcoming year, which alternative should be selected?

17. Junktractorparts.com provides a clearinghouse for antique tractor collectors to locate parts for their tractors. The site offers information on tractor restoration, links to new part suppliers, and discussion groups. Its owner wishes to begin collecting statistics on website traffic. Several online services exist with essentially

the same services. They track hits per page, unique visitors, new visitors, return visitors, referring search engines, duration of visit, path taken, entry page, domain, and other useful information. As would be expected, the services offer different cost structures. Three alternatives that are in the ballpark of the Junktractorparts.com budget are presented below:

Alternative	Monthly Fee Up to 10,000 Hits ($)	Cost per Hit for Those Above 10,000 ($)
HitCount.com	35	0.001
QuickStat	25	0.0035
TrafficCounter	50	unlimited hits

With a prediction of 20,000 hits for the next month, which service will be the low-cost provider? The owner has tracked the growth of Internet traffic and expects it to increase at a rate of an additional 1,000 hits per month. Each of the providers offers a $10 discount on the installation fee to customers signing a one-year contract. With next month's forecasted traffic at 20,000 hits, should a contract be signed? Explain your answer.

18. Elizabeth Wise is a very talented but unknown author. For years she has tried to get a book published, but no major publishing house has been willing to publish her product. She took advantage of Amazon.com's willingness to stock and sell any book and has begun to sell her books without the aid of a publisher. She is about to run out of the small quantity she had produced, however. Because publishers have never been willing to give her the chance she thought she deserved, she has decided not to use one, even though the sales volumes are creeping up. She is determined to produce her books herself through the use of an independent printer. Elizabeth's desktop publishing capabilities have resulted in a very nice looking product, but one with no cover or binding. She wants to make as much money as possible, so she will have an income while working on her next book, but she also recognizes the need for a quality printing and binding job. Elizabeth wishes to publish her book in paperback and has found four printers that can do the work she needs to have done. The fixed and variable costs associated with the four printers are presented below:

Printer Alternative	Fixed Costs ($)	Cost per Unit ($)
1	3,000	4.00
2	7,000	3.75
3	8,000	2.70
4	11,000	0.80

At the current demand rate, Elizabeth predicts sales of 4,000 units in the next six months. Her book sells for $7.95. Which printer should she select? What will be her profit for the next six months if she sells 4,000 units?

19. Tom Owens, the owner of Mr. T's Custom-Printed Shirts, is investigating the purchase of new silk screening equipment. Silk screening machines are expensive, but the better machines create a reduction in the amount of labor required for production. They also produce shirts at a faster rate. Tom wishes to reduce labor costs and improve his response time to customers. In general, the more automated the machine, the more expensive it is, but the costs per unit drop

because both labor costs and the time to complete an order drop as well. Material use is the same for each machine. The fixed and variable costs associated with each machine are presented below:

Alternative	Fixed Cost ($)	Variable Costs ($)
R&I Screener	10,500	6.24
Thomson Controls	24,000	4.20
Swede	39,000	3.10

Tom projects a demand of 26,000 shirts for next year alone. Which machine would be his best alternative?

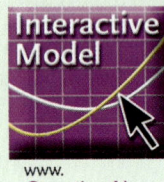
www.OperationsNow.com

INTERACTIVE ANALYSIS 2.1

THE BREAKEVEN INTERACTIVE MODEL

The Breakeven Interactive Model is accessed through Chapter 2 of the *OperationsNow.com* website. It offers an interface to manipulate the fixed and variable costs of a three-alternative breakeven analysis. Although the breakeven points can easily be determined through calculations, the interactive model provides a more visual representation that makes it easier to understand the interactions involved in this type of situation.

The Breakeven Interactive Model provides the user with the ability to drag the Y intercept and the right endpoint for any of the three cost curves. This results in a change in fixed costs and/or a change in the slope (variable cost per unit). The formulas for each alternative adjust to reflect those changes. The user can also drag the red "n" below the x axis to determine the cost of producing a particular volume with each of the alternatives. The system identifies the low-cost alternative by highlighting the total cost in red.

Experiment 1: System Fundamentals

1. The default values of the system are set to the following:

Alternative	Fixed Cost ($)	Variable Cost ($ per unit)
A	320,000	0.57
B	455,500	0.034
C	224,000	1.10

  a. What is the total cost, for each alternative, of producing 220,000 units?
  b. If the fixed cost of Alternative C is reduced to $100,000, what happens to the cost of producing 220,000 units on that alternative?
  c. What must the fixed cost of Alternative A be reduced to in order for it to be the low-cost alternative when producing 220,000 units?
  d. Click on your browser's "refresh" button to bring the parameters back to the default values. If the company wishes to negotiate to bring down the per-unit cost of Alternative C, what must it come down to in order to be the low-cost alternative for values of n up to 371,000?

Experiment 2: Fixed Costs

1. Set the values to the default settings by downloading a fresh page. Record the equations for all three alternatives and the intersection points.

   a. Change Alternative C to fixed costs of $225,000 and keep the variable costs at $1.10. At what volume does Alternative A now become the low-cost alternative?

   b. If fixed costs for Alternative C remain at $225,000, to what level must the variable costs drop to eliminate Alternative A and B as ever being the low-cost alternative?

2. Set the cost curves for the three alternatives to be:

Alternative	Fixed Cost ($)	Variable Costs ($ per unit)
A	252,500	0.53
B	275,000	0.46
C	225,000	1.16

   a. The fixed costs and cost per unit can often be known with some certainty, but sometimes the variable cost is difficult to determine. In this case, a small error in projecting the variable cost can make what seemed to be a correct alternative choice end up being the wrong one. Forecasts are frequently wrong. What are the potential ramifications of demand forecast error in this situation? As a vendor selling Alternative C, what could you do to make it more attractive to the customer?

   b. Alternative C also appears to be the low-cost alternative in only a small volume range. If the demand forecast is off significantly, a choice of Alternative B may end up being a costly one. What could the vendor of Alternative B do to make it more attractive?

Experiment 3: Variable Costs

There are times when a reduction in variable costs per unit can result in a business being able to delay a costly investment in new equipment.

1. Set the cost curves for the three alternatives to be:

Alternative	Fixed Cost ($)	Variable Costs ($ per unit)
A	295,500	0.67
B	327,500	0.52
C	225,000	1.08

   a. Currently, a business projects sales of 215,000 units per year and uses Alternative A for its production needs. If the forecast is low, and demand increases as is hoped, Alternative B very soon becomes attractive. That will require a $225,000 investment. The business wishes to delay that occurrence and has charged its engineering staff with reducing the cost per unit so that Alternative A remains the low-cost alternative through a volume of 300,000 units. What cost per unit will accomplish this objective?

   b. What happens if the engineers are able to cut $0.10 per unit off the variable cost of Alternative A?

2. Set the values as below:

Alternative	Fixed Cost ($)	Variable Costs ($ per unit)
A	295,500	0.52
B	327,500	0.32
C	407,599	0.06

When fixed costs are similar, as in this case, a small change in variable cost can drastically change the results of the analysis. If there is uncertainty concerning the variable cost, identifying a definite low-cost alternative is difficult. A business currently projects sales of 233,000 units.

a. If the variable cost of Alternative B is underestimated, Alternative C could be the low-cost alternative. What amount of error in the computation of the variable cost per unit of Alternative B would eliminate it as an alternative at any volume? Do you think this amount of error is possible?

b. Reduction of cost per unit is often possible, but there are limits. It would be impossible, for example, for total costs to drop as volume increases. Because of this limit, there are situations that require the reduction of a fixed cost if an alternative is to be adjusted to be economically preferable. With the total cost curves defined as they were for 2a above, what must be done to the fixed cost of Alternative C to make it preferable at a volume of 233,000 unit?

SELECTED RESOURCES

Hansen, D. R., and Mowen, M. M. *Cost Management,* Cincinnati: South-Western College Publishing, 1997.

Ross, S. A., Westerfield R.W., and Jordan, B. D. *Essentials of Corporate Finance,* New York: Irwin McGraw-Hill, 1999.

ENDNOTES

1. "Latest Dot-Com Fad Is a Bit Old-Fashioned: It's Called 'Profitability,'" *The Wall Street Journal,* August 14, 2001, p. A1.
2. D. R. Hansen and M. M. Mowen, *Cost Management* (Mason, OH: South-Western College Publishing, 1997), p. 785.
3. R. S. Kaplan and D. P. Norton, "The Balanced Scorecard—Measures That Drive Performance," *Harvard Business Review,* January–February 1992, pp. 71–79.
4. Adapted from W. B. Chew, "No-Nonsense Guide to Measuring Productivity," *Harvard Business Review,* January–February 1988, pp. 110–118.

CHAPTER 2 Profitability 71

OperationsNow.com LEARNING ACTIVITIES

CHAPTER ENHANCEMENT RESOURCES
- Esources
- Reel Operations Video Clips
- Interactive Models
- Excel Tutors
- Supplementary Readings
- Links to Operations On Site Companies

OM EXPLORATION
- Check It Out
- OM in Action
- Online Business Tours
- Letters from the Top
- Putting It All Together: Virtual Case Studies
- Additional Reading

The resource/profit model depicts value as a foundation for success because without it, there is no potential for profitability. When examined more closely, the model shows the components of value to be the company's processes and capabilities, costs, quality, and timeliness. Profitability answers the "why" question, value answers the "how" question, and the components of value provide the means.

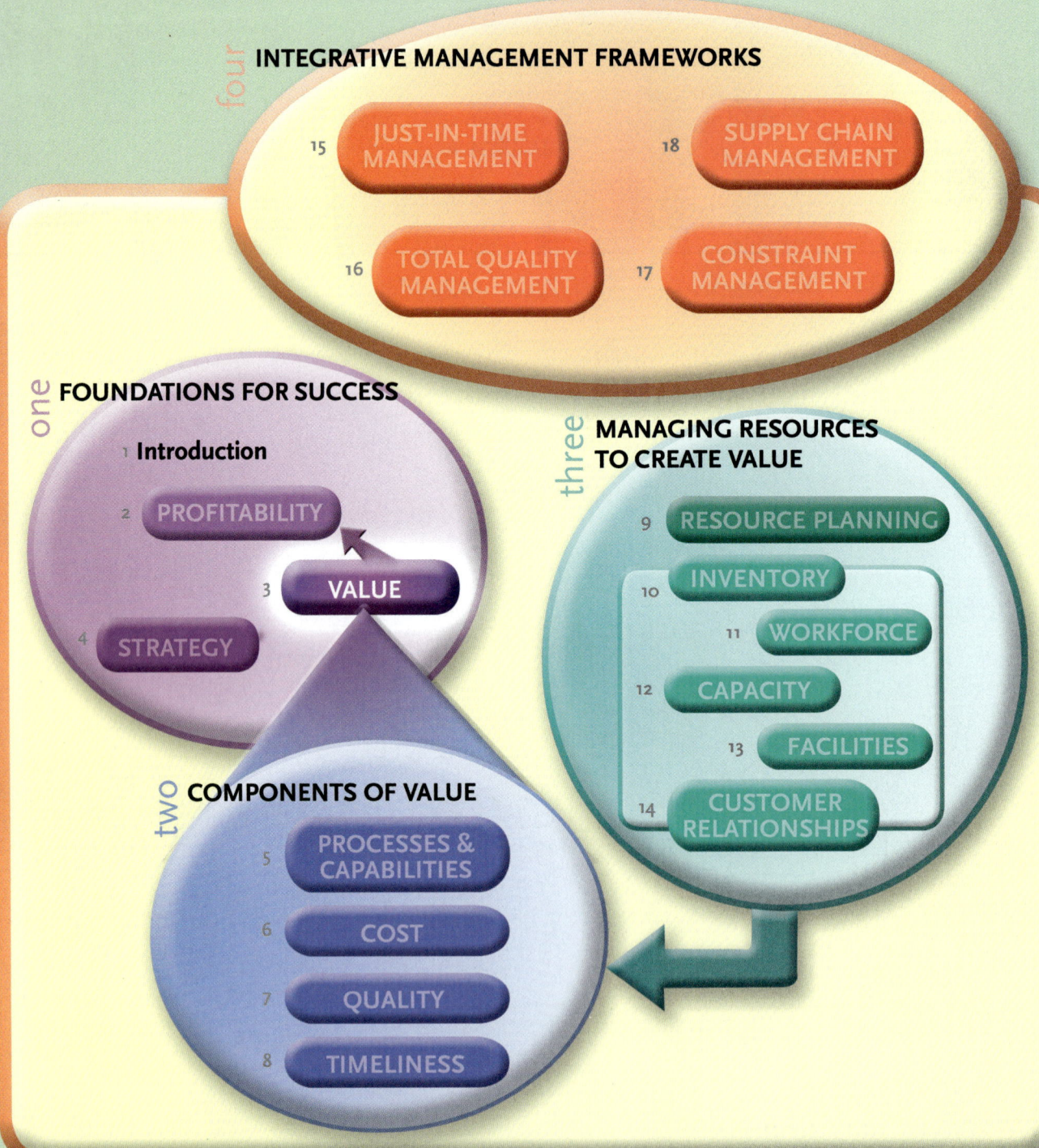

CHAPTER 3

Value

LEARNING OBJECTIVES

Upon completion of Chapter 3, you should be able to

- Describe the concepts of business-to-business (B2B) and business-to-consumer (B2C) interactions.

- Define the concept of a supply chain.

- List and describe value attributes commonly associated with B2B customers.

- List and describe value attributes commonly associated with B2C customers.

- Describe the value attributes common to B2B and B2C customers.

- Describe the four basic components of value.

Introduction: The Customer Determines Product and Service Value
Supply Chains
Value Determination by Customers
Value Attributes of Consumer Customers
Value Attributes of Business Customers
A Common Set of Value Attributes
The Link Between Customer Value Attributes and Value Creation
Chapter Summary

INTERNET RESOURCES

 Excel Tutors provide annotated spreadsheets for every solved problem that automatically load Excel.

 Esources provide an online version of the more traditional boxed insert.

 Reel Videos provide streaming video footage for company applications of chapter concepts.

 Interactive Models provide an experimental environment for quantitative concepts and simulations.

INTRODUCTION

The Customer Determines Product and Service Value

The previous chapter established the fact that value creation is the key to successful investment in operating resources. The resource/profit model in Exhibit 3.1 shows value to be a prerequisite to profitability. It is the difference between the customer's perception of value and the cost of creating it that provides the opportunity for profitability. This chapter investigates value, identifies value attributes that customers seek, examines the importance of those attributes for different types of customers, and identifies the role operations plays in these processes. Customers see value differently than those producing it. Customers deem many products and service attributes valuable, but the product or service provider "assembles" them all from a relatively small set of value components.

It is no coincidence that you will find close links between material in this chapter and basic marketing concepts. After all, an important responsibility of marketing is to educate customers about the value of products and services. This, in itself, adds to their value. The contribution of processes to the value of products and services, however, is the most basic function of operations. Reel Operations Video 3.1 examines how Trek (the bicycle producer) builds value into its products.

The introductory chapter examined the components of the resource/profit model as well as two dominant outputs for businesses—products and services—and two primary customers—consumers (B2C) and businesses (B2B). To understand how perception of value differs from one customer to another, the implications of different relationships between customers and suppliers must be clear. Products and services move from business to business and ultimately to a consumer. These relationships are examined in the following section, which introduces the concept of supply chains.

SUPPLY CHAINS

To acquire a "big-picture" understanding of the role customers must play in business decisions, it is necessary to look at the entire network of producers and customers for both products and services. The creation of product value begins with **basic producers**, which mine minerals or harvest trees and other agricultural products. It then shifts to **converters**, which refine those natural resources. Next, **fabricators** take over to transform these inputs into usable product components. Finally, **assemblers** put them all together. The path ends with the sale of a consumer product or service. This entire network is known as a **supply chain**. Supply chains consist of both products and services, and they can be dominated by either. For example, automotive supply chains are dominated by the products used in manufacturing automobiles, but they contain many services as well, including transportation, distribution, and warehousing services. Financial services can play an important role as well, as do services provided by dealerships. Examination of a banking supply chain shows that it is dominated by service providers but also uses some products. Most supply chains, like most companies, are involved with products and services, making it difficult to distinguish between value added by products and value added by services. All product-oriented supply chains require support services. All service-oriented supply chains consume materials.

Whether the supply chain is oriented toward a product or a service is often simply a matter of perspective. A service-oriented business, for example, will have that perspective when examining its supply chain. Likewise, if a company supplies products to the supply chain, it will view it from a product perspective. A retailer will view the supply chain differently from a basic producer, even though they may be at opposite

EXHIBIT 3.1 The Role of Value in the Resource/Profit Model

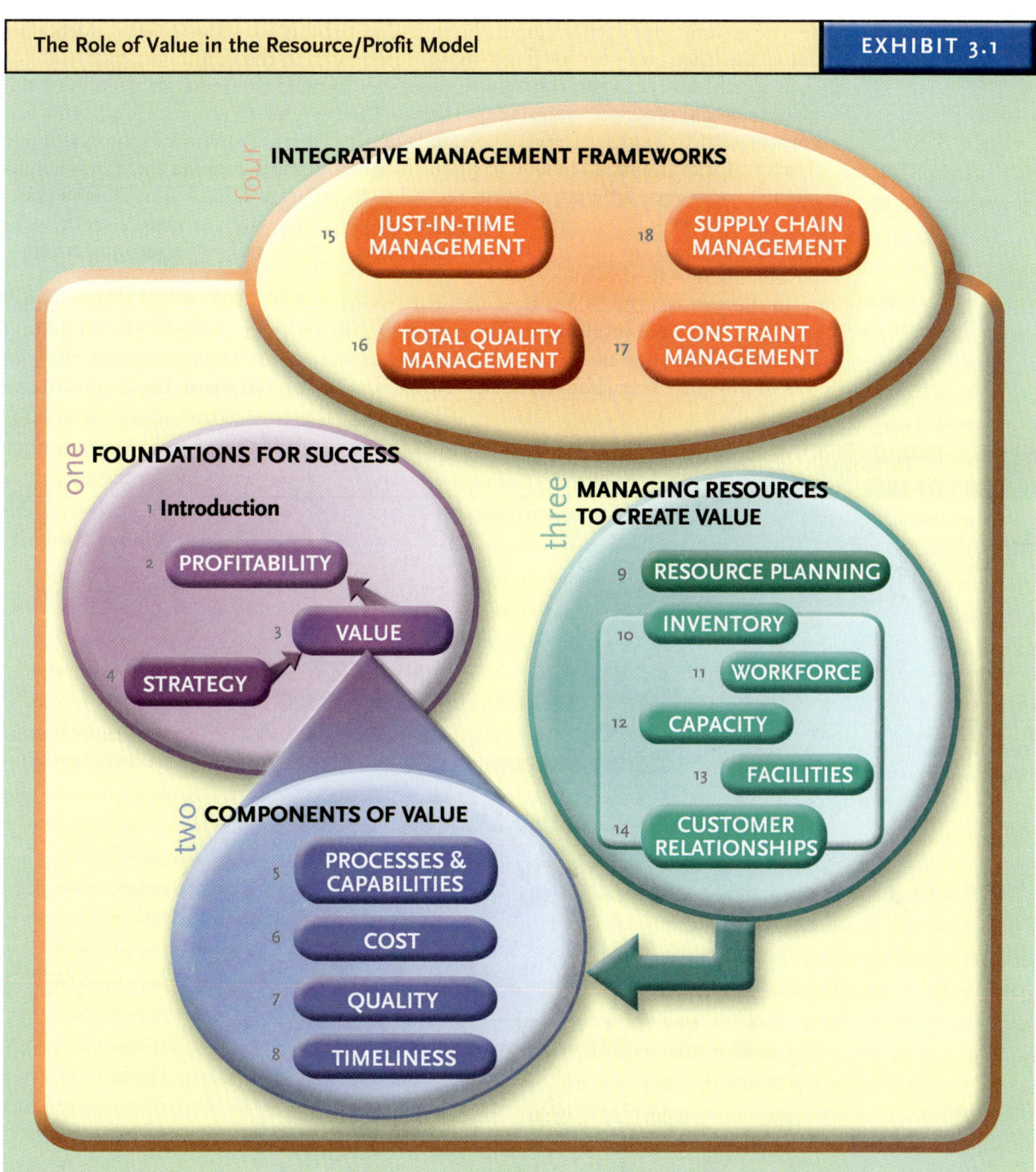

ends of the same supply chain. A comprehensive definition of a supply chain follows. A supply chain

> *encompasses all activities associated with the flow and transformation of goods from the raw material stage (extraction), through to the end user, as well as the associated information flows. Material and information flow both up and down the supply chain.*[1]

The generic supply chain model presented in Exhibit 3.2 shows how products start out at the basic producer level and move, ultimately, to the consumer.

It should not be a surprise that services can provide a significant portion of the value added in product-oriented supply chains and products can provide a significant contribution to value in service-oriented supply chains. Transportation and timely delivery, for example, add value to products in many ways. In addition, many manufacturers outsource different services related to their business, including such necessities as employee selection and training, uniform services, database management, website development and maintenance, marketing, advertising, and even new-product development. All add value.

In the past, supply chains were vertical arrangements of buyers and suppliers that started at the basic producer level, progressed through the converter, fabricator, and assembler stages, and ultimately ended at the consumer. For many businesses, the goal was to integrate vertically until they owned and controlled the entire chain. In the

EXHIBIT 3.2 Generic Supply Chain Model

Supply Chain Functions
- Retailers
- Distributors and Warehousers
- Transportation and Storage
- **Assemblers** and Associated Services
- Transportation and Storage
- **Fabricators** and Associated Services
- Transportation and Storage
- **Converters** and Associated Services
- Transportation and Storage
- **Basic Producers** and Associated Services

Supply Chain Level
- Product and Service Consumers
- Transportation, Storage, and Delivery Services
- Assembly/Manufacturers
- First-Tier Suppliers
- Second-Tier Suppliers

↑ = Business-to-Business   ⬆ = Business-to-Consumer   ⬭ = Manufacturing-Oriented Business   ▭ = Service-Oriented Business

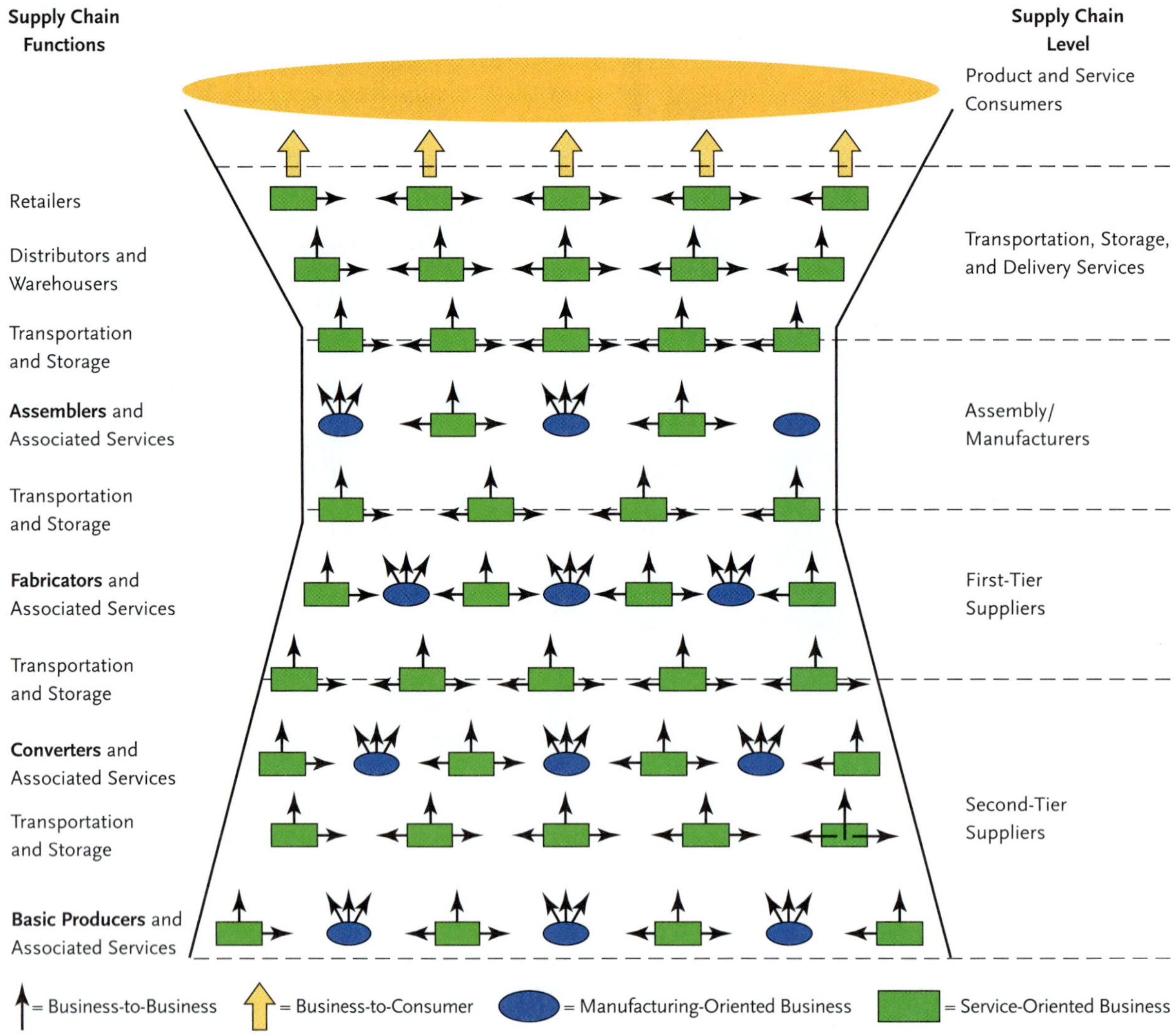

At Starbucks, Suppliers Bring More Than Beans

When we think about suppliers, it is often assumed that we're talking about businesses that ship inventory for use by manufacturers and services. We know, though, that increasingly, businesses are outsourcing services as well. Suppliers can provide human resource expertise, product design services, and a host of other business needs. Starbucks's suppliers bring to mind companies that provide coffee and other edibles, packaging, paper products, and so on. Starbucks also has a supplier that may seem a bit unusual. Hear Music supplies music to enhance the atmosphere at all Starbucks stores.

Hear Music is dedicated to finding great music beyond the Top 40. The company looks for new and old albums and brings them together for Starbucks. Initially Hear Music was a catalog retailer, then it opened stores in Berkeley, Palo Alto, Santa Monica, Chicago, and Seattle. Hear Music joined Starbucks in 1999 to add an identifiable type of music to its coffeehouses worldwide.

Source: http://www.starbucks.com/hearmusic/default.asp, October 30, 2001.

last 15 to 20 years, however, changes have taken place. First, a more global economy has resulted in a tremendous increase in competition. This has led to outsourcing of components and products to reduce costs and add focus to what a firm does. Second, firms have increased the amount of business services they outsource as well. Businesses formerly provided various nonmaterial needs for themselves. If they needed additional staff, for example, they'd advertise, interview, hire, and train them. If they needed engineering work done, they'd hire engineers. If they needed products distributed to customers, they'd buy trucks and build warehouses. Businesses wanted to depend on others as little as possible. They wanted total control of their destiny, or "mastery of their domain."

Today firms are much more likely to outsource material and service needs, resulting in a supply chain that involves many different businesses and many more relationships. In many industries, the supply chain viewed from a particular company's perspective might show a vertical structure; when all of the players in the market are included, however, a web of relationships would be a more appropriate description. It is possible for two companies to be head-to-head competitors while at the same time being suppliers for each other and even strategic business partners in another market. They might share suppliers and share customers as well. Firms no longer have an overall goal of owning the entire supply chain. In fact many firms have divested themselves of major components of that chain in order to remain more responsive to market changes and focus on the processes they do best. The Internet has made outsourcing service and product needs easier because of the networks of business-to-business (B2B) contacts that can be found there. Businesses now frequently compete as providers of manufacturing capabilities, expertise in human resources, engineering, product design, information technology, purchasing, and other capabilities. Esource 3.1 provides an example of the breadth of B2B services offered by some firms.

www
OperationsNow
.com

Despite the trend toward outsourcing as a way to enhance value while at the same time remaining focused on core capabilities, some firms resist outsourcing and maintain control of all of their processes. In some cases this is viewed as enhancing quality because the company can maintain tighter control over processes. In other situations, the business's expertise is so narrow and it produces such a specialized product that finding capable suppliers is impossible.

To understand value, it is important to understand the various types of customers that exist in today's supply chains. Customers have different priorities and different needs. They create different perspectives on value. The supply chain, similarly, is often defined by a firm's role in the chain. A company defines it by its own interactions. If it supplies products directly to a retailer, it sees that part of the supply chain. It is most concerned with its immediate suppliers and immediate customers.

VALUE DETERMINATION BY CUSTOMERS

Value means different things to different people. The old saying "One person's trash is another person's treasure" simply means that individual perceptions of value differ. In the simplest possible context, the value of a product or service is the amount of money a particular customer is willing to pay for it. The seller is interested in increasing the difference between the customer's perception of value and production cost to maximize profitability. It is important to know how and why a customer ended up with a certain dollar figure in mind. Exactly what is it that a particular customer sees as valuable? To understand this, it is necessary to understand what value means to different types of customers.

Exhibit 3.3 shows how the customer's perception of value depends on the types of business outputs being produced and on the type of customer buying them. Consumer customers have a different frame of reference from business customers because they use the product or service to fulfill different needs. But do they evaluate the services separately from the products that the services accompany? Not necessarily. From the standpoint of the producer that must manage their creation, it may make sense to separate issues related to the production of services from issues related to the production of products. After all, there are differences in the management of processes used to create them. For customers, however, whether they are consumers or businesses, there is little separation. Customers buy the "total package." They also tend to judge the value of the entire package, rather than separate it into its product and service components. For the purpose of identifying components of value, this chapter will distinguish between different types of customers and their differing views on value but will

EXHIBIT 3.3   **Business Output/Customer Matrix**

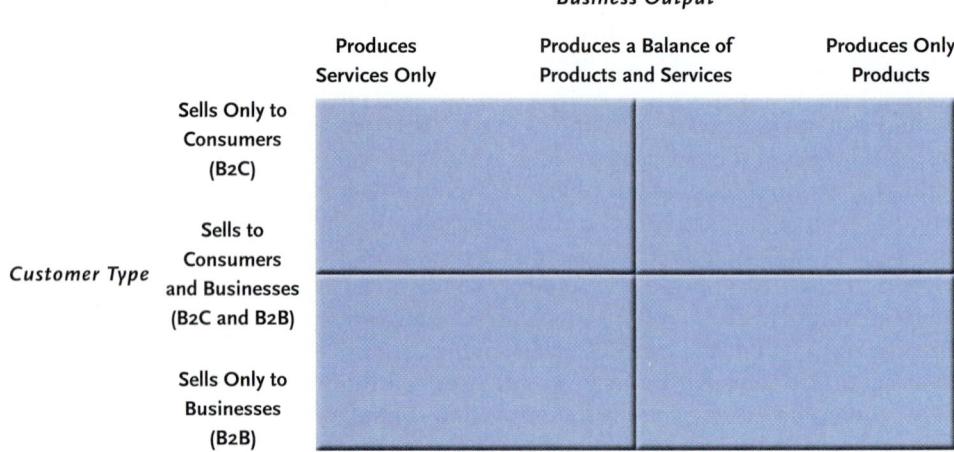

Value truly is in the eyes of the beholder. The books, movies, and products surrounding the Harry Potter phenomenon demonstrate how even producers can be mistaken about who will find value in a product. While there was really no question that young children would be attracted to the Harry Potter movie, adults also added to the long lines and formed a surprisingly large segment of the demand.

not distinguish between value for products and value for services. Customers typically don't make that distinction.

Consumers evaluate the alternatives when faced with a potential purchasing decision. Most people do this many times a day. Every time someone sees something that is for sale, a decision concerning its value is made. Usually it happens so quickly that it doesn't even register as being a conscious thought.

Recall the value formula:

$$\text{Value} = \frac{\text{Benefits}}{\text{Cost}} \qquad (3.1)$$

Whereas a consumer judges value based on the specific product or service performance and benefits desired, a business seeking to purchase a service or product considers a very different set of potential benefits. A business's goal is to create value for its customers in such a way as to also end up with value added that is greater than its cost. It is seeking a service or a product that is expected to add value to what it sells and to enhance profitability. It might be seeking consulting services to improve business processes, an information system to improve the ability to make quick decisions, components of one of the products it produces, or it might just seek mops to clean the cafeteria floor. Its decision-making process is a little more complex than the consumer's, but the ultimate objective is the same. It wants to ensure that it makes the best choice, given present and future alternatives. It must include not only the various purchase alternatives, however, but also the alternative of producing the product or service itself, instead of buying it.

A business's decision to buy, rather than produce, results from thinking that it can get a better return on its investment. There are various reasons why buying a product or service may provide a better return than producing it in-house. In many cases, the costs of gearing up to produce a product or service are prohibitive and more expensive than outsourcing, particularly if a supplier can take greater advantage of economies of scale, thereby offering it cheaper. The argument is frequently made that a company should be able to do something cheaper than an outside firm because it doesn't need to make a profit on it. That's actually not true. In a sense, the company *does* need to make a profit on it. A company needs to get a financial return on any investment it makes—investments in services it performs for itself *and* investments in components it produces itself to go into its own products. Frequently, the financial return obtained from in-house production of a product or service is less than that obtained had the company outsourced it and invested the difference in a part of its business that could use the funds in a more productive manner. Consumers do the same thing when they purchase services rather than perform them for themselves. They could select their own investments. They could change the oil in their cars. They could sew their own clothes. They could even cut their own hair. But they've decided, in most cases *very wisely*, to outsource.

VALUE ATTRIBUTES OF CONSUMER CUSTOMERS

Several researchers have attempted to categorize consumer customers by the way they shop. One theory that has been particularly popular, originated by Stone,[2] dates back to 1954. Stone's list of classifications has been modified[3] in the past, and it is modified again in Exhibit 3.4, because decisions and alternatives are different than they were in 1954.

It is not accurate to identify certain consumers as always being driven by certain attributes related to product or service value. "Always" and "never" can be dangerous words to use. It does make sense, however, to recognize that a relatively short list of product and service attributes represents the basis on which most people calculate the value of the products or services they buy. Some of the attributes are more often associated with products, some more often associated with services, and some are equally applicable to both. Before looking at different value attributes, however, it must be emphasized again that every consumer purchase, in the consumer's own mind, is based on value. It doesn't make sense to say that some consumers are more value-conscious than others. All are value-conscious; they just value different things. The differences in actions are simply the result of different people placing higher value on different things.

EXHIBIT 3.4	Value Attributes for Consumer Customers	
	Attribute	**Consumer Concern**
	Cost	What does it cost for the total time of ownership?
	Quality	Does it meet my needs?
	Convenience	How easy is it to get?
	Timeliness	How quickly can I get it?
	Personalization	Will the business treat me as special?
	Ethical issues	Is the business acting responsibly, according to my values?
	Style/fashion	Is the product the most current style?
	Technology	Does purchasing the product or service require that I have technological skills?

Cost

Cost is a key attribute of value for most consumers. It is composed not only of price, but every expense associated with ownership of the product or obtaining the service. Despite the fact that cost would seem to be a critical component of value for everyone, it is far more important to some than others. Some consumer customers are very *cost-conscious,* and this is reflected in a preoccupation with the price of the product or service. A low price, however, might not be indicative of low cost. Being seduced by a low price and then finding that the total cost is very high is a common experience for "bargain-hunting" consumers. In some cases price is the most important value attribute for customers because they do not have enough money to purchase any alternative but the cheapest. In other situations it may be that none of the other attributes of the product or service are important to them.

For some products, particularly those that can be purchased at a variety of outlets and have little need for after-the-sale service, price can be critical. For these products, price is the entire cost of ownership. The importance of price in some retail markets can easily be seen when examining the recent problems of some so-called category killer retailers. Category killers are those retailers that specialize with a narrow product line but also attempt to offer discount prices. Stores like Toys "R" Us, Just For Feet, Sports Authority, and Builder's Square are examples of category killers. Most have had difficulty keeping their prices below those of the larger discounters like Wal-Mart. In 1998, for example, Wal-Mart surpassed Toys "R" Us as the largest toy retailer in the United States.[4] The result has been that customers have moved away from specialty stores, with a larger selection, to stores with lower prices.

It is important to remember that there is a difference between cost and price. Cost includes price but also has other components. For many consumer products, however, price is the largest single component of cost and often dominates the customer's perception of cost.

Quality

The second value attribute is product or service quality. For the purposes of this discussion, quality is defined as meeting the consumer's expectations. Characteristics associated with product quality include reliability, durability, appearance, workmanship, and other product-specific attributes. For an audiotape, it might include such measures as the amount of signal drop, dynamic range, output, and accuracy. For a service, quality-related characteristics might include helpfulness of the contact personnel, atmosphere, cleanliness, wait time, and the quality of products that come with the service (food, for example). Quality and price are often related. Higher quality often, but not always, means higher price. (It doesn't necessarily cost more to produce higher quality, but businesses can charge a higher price because many customers feel it is *worth* more.)

For example, if the author takes a trip out west with his family, they will have specific requirements for lodging. They will stay at hotels with large rooms, they want a pool, they want a kitchenette, and they want to be close to other activity-oriented sites. When he goes to the same town on a fishing trip with an old college buddy, they stay at the cheapest place they can find. They're not going to spend much time at the hotel. Basically, they need two beds and that's all they're willing to pay for. Amenities add costs, but not value.

Convenience

Convenience has become increasingly important as a criterion for making value determinations. As jobs place increasing demands on people's time, and home life

Home Depot Improves the Shopping Experience

Retail businesses need to focus on sales. That's a given. But retailers are increasingly trying to find ways, beyond price, to improve the customer's perception of value. This has come to include many aspects of the customer experience unrelated to what happens at checkout. Home Depot, Inc., headquartered in Atlanta, has launched a new, more customer-friendly approach to store management that has taken two years to formulate. The founders of the home improvement chain wanted customers to experience a busy, active sales floor. That included pallets of merchandise being unloaded, forklifts beeping through the aisles, and employees stocking shelves, to give the store an actual "warehouse" feel. Recently, customers have reacted to what they perceive as levels of customer service lower than those of competitor Lowe's. They've complained about cluttered aisles, and falling merchandise has caused injuries. Store sales are down since 1999 and fourth quarter 2000 figures report the chain's first failure to show rising sales since 1985.

New CEO Bob Nardelli wishes to increase sales growth from existing facilities, rather than obtain new growth from expansion. This means using current facilities more efficiently and providing the customer with an experience that is more highly valued than that of the competition. The new approach, known as Service Performance Improvement (SPI), resulted in significant change in policy and a resulting change in facility appearance. Some of the more obvious changes are summarized below:

Policy	Old Way	New Way
Wooden pallets on sales floor	No limits (Some managers had as many as 90 wooden pallets on the sales floor.)	Absolutely no wooden pallets on the sales floor
Stocking shelves with merchandise	Shelves stocked throughout the day by sales personnel	No stocking of shelves between 8 A.M. and 8 P.M.
Forklifts	Forklifts allowed throughout store any time	No forklifts allowed on sales floor between 8 A.M. and 8 P.M.
Sales displays	Small sales displays, called wingstacks, cluttered aisles throughout the store	No more than three wingstacks per aisle
Role of sales personnel	Shelf stocker and occasional salesperson	Salesperson
Truck deliveries	Throughout the day	None during daytime hours

SPI was expected to be in every store by the end of 2001. In addition to changing the role of sales staff, from shelf stocker to salesperson, management is monitoring interaction with customers. Managers spend several hours each day counting customers actually interacting with an employee. This interaction is increasing under the new policies.

Source: "Home Depot's Home Improvement," *The Wall Street Journal*, March 8, 2001, pp. B1, B6; Home Depot, 2000 Annual Report, http://www.homedepot.com/HDUS/EN_US/compinfo/financial/annual/2000/pdf.html.

and work life become harder to separate, the value of convenience keeps rising. Convenience, along with price, is also a very important value attribute for busy college students. Placing a high degree of importance on convenience means that customers place a high value on their own time. They view consumption of their time as a very significant component of the overall cost of a purchase. Like money, time becomes more valuable when it is in short supply. Convenience-oriented customers tend to be busy with other things. They like to "multitask." They don't like to spend unproductive time driving or waiting and are more likely to be attracted to products and services that offer delivery. Location plays a very important part in their patronage of a particular business. They like to accomplish tasks on their way to doing other tasks. Business hours that fit their schedule best will be very important to customers that place a high priority on convenience.

Response Time

Many customers, given all other things equal, would rather get a product or service now than get it later. When they go into a store to purchase something, they're there to buy it now because they want it now. They expect it to be available immediately. If they had wanted to wait several days, they'd have mail-ordered it. Many customers may even pay a premium for faster delivery of a product. Virtually all mail-order retailers offer express shipping, and some provide it as standard service at no extra charge.

The speed associated with the Internet has raised the expectations of many customers. For online retailers, the most difficult challenge is to get the actual physical product to the customer quickly. Some customers grow to almost expect the product to actually be delivered "online" or beamed to them.

Personalization

The perception of value is enhanced when contact personnel recognize customers or even know their name. Some people find it important to be treated as a "regular." Depending on the experience desired by the customer, an environment characterized in the old TV show *Cheers* can be a desirable one. Retail store personnel often try to know all of their customers. Clothing store personnel might try to know a customer's size, for example. Pizza deliverers might know exactly what a customer wants before the order, based on previous orders. In some cases the information actually adds to the efficiency of the processes. In other situations it may give the customer a bit of an ego boost to be recognized. It makes the customer feel important. Data collection and storage technologies have made personalization easier, giving many businesses an easy way to track customer purchases and maintain a file of personal preferences.

Ethical Issues

Increasingly, ethical, political, and religious beliefs are having an impact on purchase decisions. Awareness of company practices has resulted in customers expressing their support, or lack of support, through their wallets. Customers prone to this behavior are known as ethical customers. As examples, customers have expressed support or lack of support of company practices on issues related to environmental concerns, religious beliefs, tobacco use, animal testing, working conditions in manufacturing plants, and TV programs in which their commercials were aired. In many areas these pressures have forced businesses to do a better job of policing themselves and their suppliers.

In some areas of concern, particularly those related to the environment and human rights, entirely new business strategies have sprung up, promoting "green," or "environmentally safe," processes. Green labeling requirements and human rights have

become so strategically important that conflicts have taken place over whose product is greenest. Esource 3.2 is an example of a company's reaction to pressure from ethical customers.

Watchdog groups have proliferated as these areas of concern have grown. This phenomenon has occurred in other areas as well. In late 1999, for example, Kathy Levinson, the president and chief operating officer of E-Trade, made a $300,000 pledge to combat California's proposed ban on same-sex marriages (Proposition 22). Even though the donation was a personal donation by Levinson, the fact that it was made in the form of shares of E-Trade stock linked it to E-Trade. Many who opposed her actions withdrew their support by withdrawing business from E-Trade. Six months after the initial negative response, however, email was overwhelmingly in favor of her action and many investors were opening accounts specifically because of the donation.[5]

Style and Fashion

Some product or service attributes can be viewed as an enhancement for some people and detractor for others. The style or fashion statement made by a product or service can have very unpredictable results. Manufacturers, distributors, and retailers of men's and women's clothing have been grappling with this problem for decades. This

The Battle over Who Has the Greenest Wood

The concept of harvesting trees using sustainable approaches has finally become an important marketing tool. This is what environmentalists have been working for and they devised a seal from the Forest Stewardship Council that would identify such wood for consumers. The Forest Stewardship Council is active in North America, South America, and Europe. The American Forest and Paper Association, made up of forest land owners, plans to market its products with a logo that designates compliance with its own sustainable forestry initiative. It hired a marketing firm to wage a large advertising campaign.

Pressure has been directed toward Home Depot to favor the Forest Stewardship Council logo. The Forest Stewardship Council claims that the American Forest and Paper Association is soft on major players like Pacific Lumber Company. The Forest Stewardship Council also maintains that the program rules are not strict enough and put no restrictions on chemical herbicides, which are restricted under the Forest Stewardship Council rules.

Others look at the battle as a distraction that takes away from what is really happening. The reality is that certification, no matter by whom, is becoming important because consumers are including it in their buying decisions. They now consider the practices of the company as part of the value they are paying for. The demand for certified wood products now exceeds supply. The Forest Stewardship Council plans to increase its certification capacity.

Despite this seemingly important victory, the battle wages on. The website http://www.fscfacts.com/ blasts the Forest Stewardship Council and lists numerous reasons why companies should avoid its certification program. Nowhere on the website, however, is the sponsoring organization listed.

Source: "Battle Breaks Out over Rival Seals for 'Green' Wood," *The Wall Street Journal*, May 23, 2001, pp. B1, B4; http://www.fsc-bc.org/default.asp, June 7, 2001; http://www.fsccanada.org/, June 7, 2001; http://www.fscfacts.com/, June 7, 2001.

is prevalent not only in the apparel industry, but in sporting goods, shoes, outerwear, stereo and sound equipment, and so on.

For some customers, what's in style is exactly *not* what they want to purchase. Companies often discover that too much success or visibility of their clothing can actually reduce its attractiveness to those who place a high priority on wearing the absolute latest fashion. If everyone else is wearing that T-shirt, for example, it can't be the latest. The scarcity of an item can often add to its perceived value. Once it is commonplace, it may lose its appeal. Some recent examples are worthy of a closer look.

In 1998, The Limited, Inc., spun off Abercrombie & Fitch. A&F's clothing, although expensive, was extremely popular on campus, but by early 2000 it had become so popular that the image began to wear off. From 1998 to 1999 sales for stores open at least one year rose 26 percent, but from 1999 to 2000 the same stores' sales rose only 3 percent. It became "too hot to be cool."[6] Another example of the impact scarcity can have on desirability can be found with Krispy Kreme doughnut shops.[7] Openings of Krispy Kreme doughnut shops have been celebratory events in towns beyond its traditional home in the Southeast. Despite its slow growth and popularity, franchise owners expressed concern about an upcoming initial public offering (IPO), hypothesizing that such visibility would damage the unique appeal.

Chrysler's PT Cruiser may succumb to a similar fate. During the summer of 2000, dealers had nine-month waiting lists for the retro car. The following summer, however, sales were flat, and in some areas a customer could walk into a dealership and buy one off the lot.[8] Producers that must conform to the current style or fashion must be prepared to face this backlash when a stylish product becomes so successful and so popular that the real hip customers don't want it any more for that very reason. Depending on the customer, value may be increased by the presence of style or may actually be decreased by it.

Use of Technology

The degree to which a product or service incorporates technology may also enhance its perceived value for some customers and be a detractor for others. Many customers are becoming more familiar with technology and more open to utilizing it, but others still resist. In the frontier days of the Internet, say around 1996, the demographics of the typical Internet user were very different from those of the general population. That is obviously not true today. Many customers see technology as a way to improve convenience and will adopt it for that reason only. Others enjoy it for its own sake. They enjoy gadgets and gizmos and are the very "early adopters" that businesses seek out when developing new high-tech products and services. For some, even if it is actually more time-consuming and more difficult to utilize technology in a task, they'd rather incorporate technology than do it in the traditional manner. Others will avoid it at all costs. They don't want it and they don't like it. Maybe they even fear it.

In the grand scheme of things, most customers tend to resist utilizing a new technology until they are convinced that it has a real benefit. Potential benefits might be a price reduction, less time required, more convenience, and so on. If one of these is important to the customer, the technology might be accepted and used.

VALUE ATTRIBUTES OF BUSINESS CUSTOMERS

In typical B2B relationships, business customers are seeking one thing from the supplier: the potential to increase the value they can pass on to their customers.

Archer Daniels Midland (ADM), a large producer of food products, animal feed products, and industrial products made from agricultural products, sums up the definition of value in a B2B relationship in a very succinct "value promise":

> *Value is defined by the customer, the ultimate judge. At ADM, our focus on value creation is directed and measured continuously by the customer's need to improve its own products, quality and costs.*[9]

The B2B customer determines the value of what it purchases based on its potential to improve the value of what the company sells. A consumer service company should not expect that all of the value being transferred to the consumer would come from its suppliers. Some will, but the company must add value as well. The same holds for a consumer products producer. If suppliers contribute all of the value, and the consumer products producer contributes none, it will not be in business long because it adds costs but not value. When a business's role in the supply chain is examined, customers quickly discover that without adding value, there really isn't one. Customers quickly figure out that buying directly from that company's suppliers is a better value. The "middleman" that performs no value-adding function, merely linking customers to suppliers, is becoming extinct. The Internet is the great big impending comet that future historians will identify as the cause of this extinction. This phenomenon of eliminating intermediaries in supply chains has been coined by some as "disintermediation," a very big word for a simple principle: If a company offers nothing of value, it can't survive.

Specifically, what do businesses want, in terms of value attributes, from a supplier of goods or services? Some value attributes desired by businesses are identical to those of consumers but are important for very different reasons. Businesses view five criteria as being extremely important when deciding whether to order from a particular supplier: cost, quality, dependability of delivery, response time, and flexibility, as depicted in Exhibit 3.5. Depending on the product or service, and on the customer, the value attributes will be priority-ranked differently from one situation to another. They are so important, however, that they provide a framework for firms trying to identify a strategic focus. They are often referred to as the five competitive priorities for operations strategy. The following sections take a detailed look at each.

Cost

It should be no surprise that cost is a high-priority value attribute for a business customer. For a business customer, cost involves far more than price. Price is critical in

EXHIBIT 3.5	Value Attributes for Business Customers	
	Attribute	**Business Concern**
	Cost	What does it cost for the total time of ownership?
	Quality	Does it meet our specifications?
	Dependability of delivery	Does the firm meet its delivery promises?
	Response time	How quickly can they get it to us?
	Flexibility	Can they adapt to special needs?

most consumers' determination of value, however, so its impact on value is reflected all the way through the supply chain. Business customers must endure many additional costs of ownership for products and services because they can affect production processes, resulting in other costs associated with their use. For equipment purchases, price is but one of many costs that may follow, including maintenance and repair costs and training costs for equipment operators. Prices charged by material and service suppliers have become so important that many businesses have reduced their costs by finding ways to deal directly with producers of goods and services rather than going through intermediaries or brokers. As a result, B2B auctions have dramatically increased their presence on the Internet. Some predictors estimate that auction sales, which amounted to $8.7 billion in 1998, will be more than $50 billion by 2002. Esource 3.3 provides an opportunity to explore the offerings of a company specializing in B2B auctions.

Quality

Quality, clearly a critical component of value for the consumer, is critical for the business customer as well. For a business customer, quality can be defined with more precision than "meeting expectations" because businesses define their expectations more precisely than consumers, in the form of carefully written **specifications**. For the business, quality is often defined as "meeting specifications." For a manufacturer of products, quality of components and materials has a broad impact. Obviously, if a component is of bad quality, the finished product will have a quality problem as well. For this reason, many manufacturers assist in the quality-related efforts of their suppliers. Quality of raw materials and components also has an impact on manufacturing costs. Components may take longer to process, may result in machine problems and breakdowns, and may require additional steps, such as inspection and sorting, which add costs but no value.

To a business, the impact of service quality is not significantly different from the impact of component or raw material quality. The costs for purchased services either come directly out of profit or are passed on to the customer, and the resulting reduction in customer perceived value (resulting from the higher price) comes out of profit. Service quality, particularly the quality of those services that support company efforts but aren't a direct part of the goods or services sold, can be a critical part of how well employees are able to do their jobs. Such frequently outsourced services as temporary staffing, information technology and database management, new-product design and development, advertising and promotion, security, and custodial services all contribute to the environment from which employees get support for their work. Poor-quality services translate directly into difficulty and frustration for employees. Creating an environment that simplifies employees' jobs is important. Employees have quality expectations, just as customers do.

Heskett and colleagues[10] introduced the **service–profit chain** as a means of showing how internal quality ultimately affects profitability. Internal quality is the quality of the environment in which people work. High levels of internal quality result in employee satisfaction and employee retention. Employees who stay with the firm longer are more experienced, more productive, and can offer customers greater value. Greater value increases customer satisfaction and customer loyalty. Higher levels of customer satisfaction and loyalty increase profitability and growth of the business. Satisfied employees mean higher profitability. In a tight labor market, employee satisfaction is even more critical.

The following three value attributes for business customers tend to be more service-related, even if what is being sold is predominantly a product.

In order for a business to maintain reliable deliveries of products, the correct item must get to the customer at the promised time. Completing the production of the product on time doesn't guarantee success. Packaging, labeling, and sorting thousands of products per day, and shipping them to their destination in a timely manner, depends on equipment, technology, and processes designed to handle high volume with accuracy.

Dependability of Delivery

The importance of time is expressed in many ways in buyer–supplier relationships. One critical aspect of time is the completion of what a supplier promises. If a supplier promises two-day delivery, does it actually keep its promise? If a supplier promises that a project will be completed by a certain date, is the project actually completed by that date? The sequential nature of events in business means that for effective completion of a task, many prerequisite events must be completed. Even one failure can have a domino effect. Dependability of all aspects of the physical productive system is critical. If made aware in advance, a business can cope with undependable suppliers, but the coping mechanisms required are expensive. One of the most popular coping mechanisms is discussed next.

Businesses have long been using large stockpiles of raw materials inventory to protect against the effects of undependable suppliers. If inventory for three weeks of demand is kept on site, a manufacturing plant can tolerate a raw material delivery that is up to three weeks late. The cost of keeping that inventory on hand is substantial, however. Many companies, manufacturers and services alike, have substituted reliable suppliers for those stockpiles of inventory. They recognize the value of reliable delivery and want to establish long-term relationships with suppliers that can provide it. A quality supplier has come to mean one that not only provides a high-quality product or service, but one that delivers it as promised. Quality service is just as important as the quality of the product.

Response Time

In addition to value added by delivering a product or service when promised, value is added by delivering it quickly. A short response time adds value in several ways. First, as product life cycles have become shorter, each day cut from the "time-to-market" means a greater sales opportunity. In a product with a five-month life, two weeks on the front end of the life cycle can easily mean the difference between a profit and a loss. This is particularly true when competitors are responding with products as quickly as possible. The beginning weeks of the life cycle represent the time when competition will be at its lowest point and opportunity to gain an advantage at its highest.

An example of the critical importance of reducing time-to-market can be seen in a recent shift in the supplier base for the electronics industry. Not so long ago, many of the electronics products sold in the United States were actually manufactured in Asia, to take advantage of low labor costs. Recently, however, product life cycles have gotten shorter, making time-to-market even more critical. While labor costs may be lower in Asia, the two weeks required to ship completed products back to the United States has become unacceptable and air freight costs are just too expensive. The result has been phenomenal growth for contract manufacturers of electronics in Guadalajara, Mexico. One particular plant, Flextronics International Ltd., opened in 1997 with $12 million in sales for its first eight months of operation; by early 2000, it had quarterly sales of $140 million.[11] Included among the products assembled at that single plant were Sony WebTV set-top boxes, Hewlett-Packard printers, 3Com PalmPilots, Johnson & Johnson blood-glucose monitors, and networking products for Cisco Systems. The rapid transition from one product to the next in these markets makes a two-week transportation lag completely unacceptable, despite cheaper labor in Asia.

Another pressure to reduce response time is the desire to minimize the cash-to-cash cycle. The **cash-to-cash cycle** is the time required between purchasing inputs, such as raw materials, and being paid by customers for products or services sold. Reduction of time in that series of events results in a quicker payback on the investments made. Halving the time required to get a payback on an investment effectively doubles the return. Since parts of that cash-to-cash cycle are dictated by supplier response time, a quicker response improves the customer's profitability.

A third reason to reduce response time is to improve forecast accuracy. Lead times associated with obtaining process inputs often require that demand be forecasted. Suppose the replenishment lead time (the time between ordering and receiving the item) for a product is three weeks. To know how many of the product to order, demand must be predicted for three weeks into the future. The further into the future the prediction, the less accurate it will be. Thus the further a business has to forecast into the future, the more extra inventory must be ordered in case its forecast is too low. The further into the future it predicts, the more "extra" it must order. To achieve a productive investment in inventory—that is, to turn inventory over as often as possible—a supplier that can provide a very quick response time for orders is advantageous. This can decrease the time horizon for forecasts, make them more accurate, and reduce the amount of inventory required.

Flexibility

Businesses need to respond quickly to special requests. Their ability to respond quickly may hinge on the abilities of their suppliers to respond quickly. Not only do customers value quick response; they also value the ability to do something different—something special. In the rapidly changing business environment, businesses must evolve quickly. Their needs can change overnight. Sometimes a customer needs treatment above and beyond the norm. Maybe it just received a unique order, and satisfying that customer might initiate a long-term relationship. Maybe another supplier failed to deliver as promised. In any event, it may need a special favor and to give it what it needs may create a new relationship or a higher level of loyalty in an existing one. A supplier that has the flexibility to meet special needs is particularly valuable.

Like the value attributes of consumers, the value attributes of business customers originate in the processes used to create the products and services they use. Those processes are designed, managed, and improved by the operations function.

EXHIBIT 3.6 — Primary and Secondary Value Attributes for Consumer and Business Customers

Value Attribute	Importance for Consumer Customers	Importance for Business Customers
Cost	Primary	Primary
Quality	Primary	Primary
Response time	Primary	Primary
Dependability of delivery	Secondary	Primary
Convenience	Primary	Secondary
Style/fashion	Primary	Secondary
Ethical issues	Secondary	Secondary
Technology	Secondary	Secondary
Flexibility	Secondary	Primary
Personalization	Primary	Secondary

A COMMON SET OF VALUE ATTRIBUTES

Exhibit 3.6 combines the product and service value attributes presented in Exhibits 3.4 and 3.5. It distinguishes those value attributes that tend to be much more important for a particular type of customer from those that tend to be less important. Keep in mind, however, that these are generalizations and there are certainly exceptions to these classifications.

Merging the value attributes for consumer customers and business customers creates a relatively short list of value attributes. They play an important role in the customer's calculation of value and, as a result, in the customer's purchase decisions, whether that customer is a consumer or a business.

If every alternative product or service possesses the same value attribute, that attribute is no longer an important part of the purchase decision process. The value attributes that make the difference in a purchasing decision are those that differentiate the product or service from the competition. Thus businesses in the same competitive market try to differentiate themselves on the basis of the value attributes they provide. Businesses routinely seek to attract customers that place a high priority on certain attributes. Some value attributes are very dominant and almost universal, whereas others tend to be less significant. It is important to recognize, however, that for a specific individual consumer or business customer, any one of the attributes could be perceived as critical. Recognize also that these attributes are changing as lifestyles change, new products and services replace old ones, and businesses create new ways to deliver products and services.

The process of alignment between what the customer wants and what a business provides, in the long term, is known as the business strategy, the topic of Chapter 4.

THE LINK BETWEEN CUSTOMER VALUE ATTRIBUTES AND VALUE CREATION

Value is passed to the consumer from many places. If the supply chain is examined from the consumer all the way upstream to its starting point, value is added by the network of service and product suppliers and is ultimately brought together by the consumer product or consumer service producer. The value that has been added along the way will be sold to the consumer. The value transfer model in Exhibit 3.7 illustrates how value is transferred from supplier to producer to consumer in a small segment of a supply chain.

The importance of the transfer of value through the supply chain is evidenced by the effort companies are willing to expend to develop and maintain good relationships with quality suppliers. The network of suppliers that a company has developed is a critical resource and should be viewed as an investment. Supplier capabilities, after all, determine a significant portion of the value the consumer sees. The management of these relationships, known as supply chain management, is the topic of Chapter 18. It is the effective combination of value from suppliers and value added to enhance it that offers great potential for profitability. No company can be best at everything. Recognizing when a particular part of the value-adding process should be outsourced to a quality product or service supplier is an important capability.

Just as a product or service is made of a set of components, value attributes are also created from a set of components assembled by the producer. The value attributes are what the customer desires; the *components of value* are what the producer uses to create them. Exhibit 3.8 provides the four basic components of value and links each to the value attributes that it helps to create.

Processes and capabilities are the most influential of the components of value. They are the end result of the business's use of its resources. They combine resources from inventory, workforce, capacity, facilities, and customer relationships to create value. The availability of these resources makes it possible for the business to create value, but it can also limit what the firm can create.

Value Transfer Model   EXHIBIT 3.7

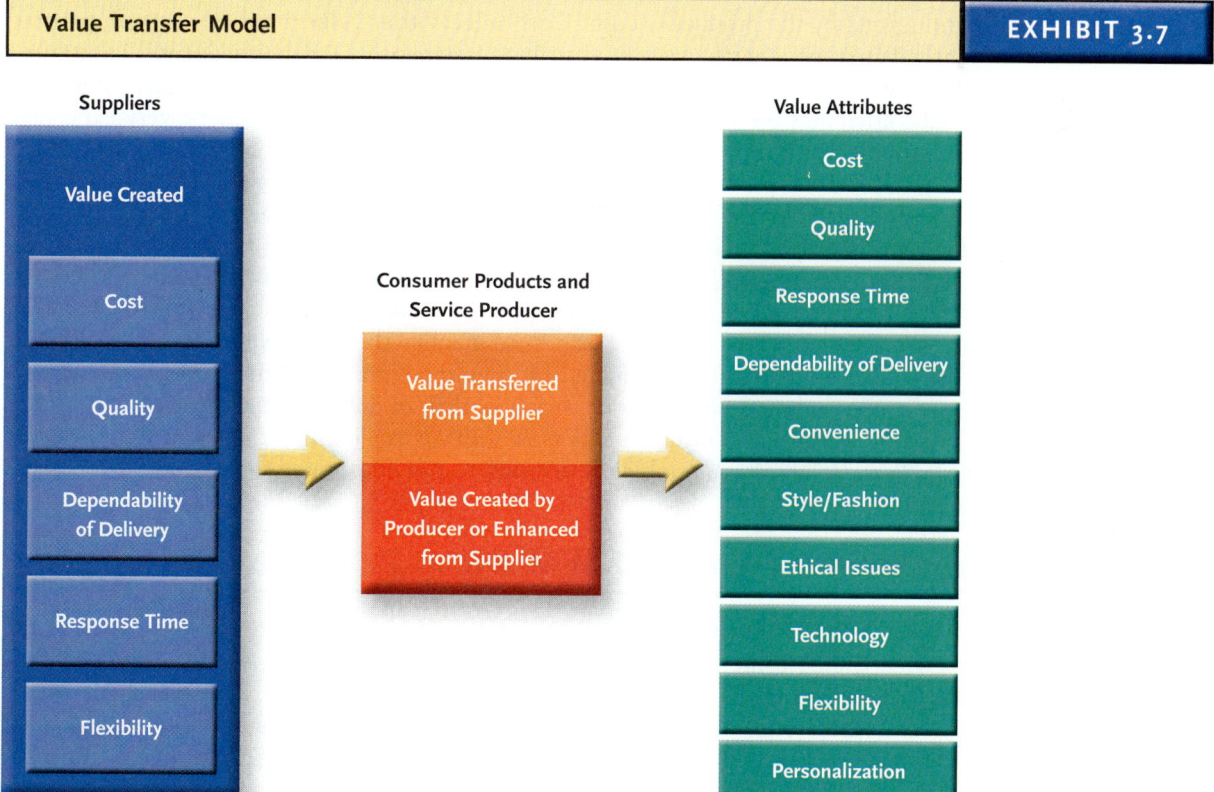

EXHIBIT 3.8 Value Components and Value Attributes

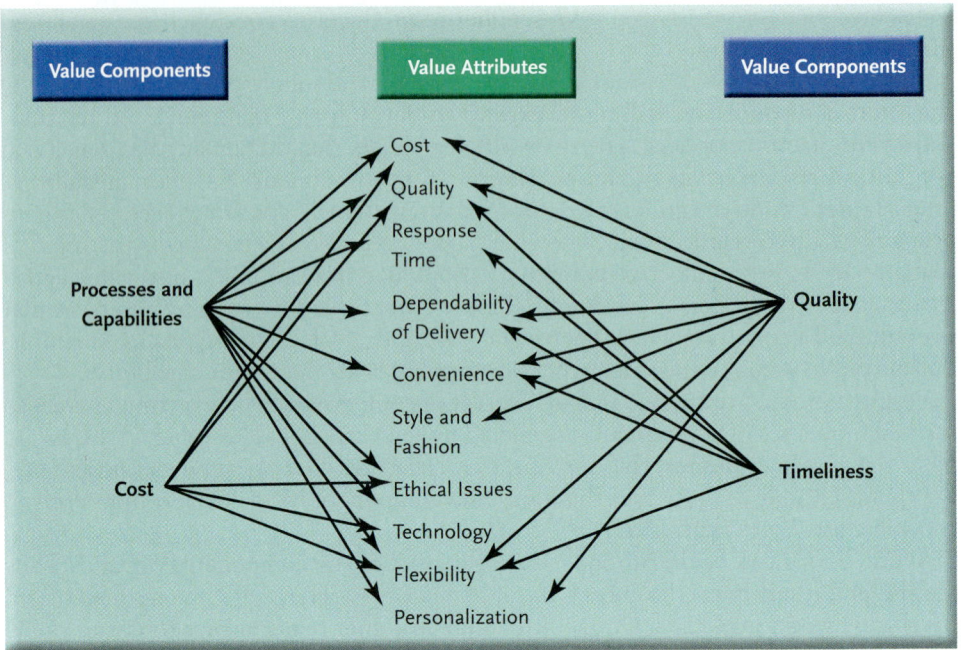

Costs are also influential to several value attributes. Obviously, costs that are incurred by the business are passed on to the customer, so the customer's costs are influenced by the producer's costs. Costs affect other value attributes as well, particularly if creating a particular value attribute is expensive for the producer. Maintaining the level of costs acceptable to stay at a particular price point may mean that some value attributes are not provided. Convenience, for example, may be very expensive to provide, resulting in a business eliminating it as a value attribute it seeks to offer.

Quality is the producer's ability to meet the expectations of the customer. For products and services, the ability to offer consistent quality translates into the customer's perception of quality, but it also affects customer impressions of accompanying services, style and fashion, and ability to be flexible in meeting special needs. Many of these value attributes are viewed as aspects of service quality.

Timeliness is the ability of a business to manage the time required for everything it does. The value attributes affected by timeliness are all of those related to service quality, including response time, dependability of delivery, convenience, and flexibility. In addition, most customers view waiting as a quality issue. Customer waiting is a direct result of the producer's inability to provide timely service.

CHAPTER SUMMARY

The prerequisite to profitability that stands out more than any other is value. Value is what the customer pays for. Value creation is the most important contribution of operations because it provides the objective for the resources being managed.

This chapter examined how two different types of customer, consumers and businesses, view value. Businesses seek products and services that can enhance value for *their* customers, whereas consumers seek those that meet their own needs. Value is transferred through products and services, from supplier to customer to consumer, within large networks of businesses called supply chains.

Those product and service characteristics consumer and business customers seek in the products and services they buy are their value attributes. Value attributes for consumer customers are cost, quality, convenience, timeliness, personalization, ethics, style/fashion, and technology. Value attributes for business customers are cost, quality, dependability of delivery, timeliness, and flexibility. A set of common value attributes can be derived from these. Value attributes are created by operations through the use of the four components of value: processes and capabilities, cost, quality, and timeliness. These four components of value are the focus of the four chapters of Unit 3.

Chapter 4 examines how businesses position themselves to win contests with their competitors to provide the most value in the present, as well as the future. It builds on profitability from Chapter 2 and value attributes from this chapter, to formulate the necessary objectives and decision patterns known as strategy. In Chapter 4 strategy is examined at the business level, as well as at the functional level, with a thorough examination of operations strategy and its impact on business success.

KEY TERMS

assembler, 74
basic producer, 74
cash-to-cash cycle, 89
converter, 74
fabricator, 74
service-profit chain, 87
specification, 87
supply chain, 74

REVIEW QUESTIONS

1. Why do firms outsource?
2. What is a supply chain?
3. How must the value added and the cost to add it relate for a profitable business?
4. Traditionally, why did businesses resist outsourcing?
5. Describe the analysis a consumer uses when faced with a potential purchase.
6. Who determines the value of a product or service? How is the value measured?
7. How does a business's purchasing decision differ from that of a consumer?
8. Describe each of the value attributes for consumer products and services.
9. Why have response time and dependability of delivery gained so much importance in dictating value for B2B transactions?
10. What are the five priorities for operations strategy? Why is it difficult to optimize all five?
11. What is meant by "value added"?
12. Why would response time be more critical for a business customer than for a consumer?

DISCUSSION QUESTIONS

1. What are some reasons a manufacturer might outsource a product when it could manufacture it?
2. What are the most common value attributes for college students?
3. Describe purchasing decisions students make that require a tradeoff between quality and convenience. How valuable is convenience for students?
4. What are some current ethical issues that dictate purchasing decisions?
5. What businesses do you frequent that seek to add value through flexibility?
6. How will the value attributes that are most important to you change when you graduate?
7. For each of the value attributes in Exhibit 3.5, identify a local business that seeks to add value with that attribute.
8. Give an example of a product or service you purchased because of the price, but later concluded that it was not a good value.
9. What is the fallacy associated with the belief that companies should always be able to do something themselves cheaper than they could outsource it because they don't need to make a profit on that activity?

SELECTED RESOURCES

Handfield, R. B., and Nichols, E. L. *Introduction to Supply Chain Management* (Upper Saddle River, NJ: Prentice-Hall Inc., 1999).

Fitzsimmons, J. A., and Fitzsimmons, M. J. *Service Management* (Boston, Mass: Irwin/McGraw-Hill, 1997).

ENDNOTES

1. R. B. Handfield and E. L. Nichols, *Introduction to Supply Chain Management* (Upper Saddle River, NJ: Prentice-Hall, 1999), p. 2.
2. G. P. Stone, "City Shoppers and Urban Identification: Observations on the Social Psychology of City Life," *American Journal of Sociology*, July 1954, pp. 36–43.
3. J. A. Fitzsimmons and M. J. Fitzsimmons, *Service Management* (New York: Irwin/McGraw-Hill, 1997), p. 247.
4. W. M. Bulkeley, "'Category Killers' Go from Lethal to Lame in the Space of a Decade,'" *The Wall Street Journal*, March 9, 2000, pp. A1, A8.
5. D. Bank, "A Big Donation for Gay Rights Puts Executive in the Spotlight," *The Wall Street Journal*, March 3, 2000, pp. B1, B6.
6. R. Quick, "Is Ever-So-Hip Abercrombie & Fitch Losing Its Edge with Teens?" *The Wall Street Journal*, February 22, 2000, pp. B1, B4.
7. J. R. Hagerty, "Krispy Kreme at a Krossroads?" *The Wall Street Journal*, February 24, 2000, pp. B1, B4.

8. "A Year Later, Some of the Thrill Is Gone," *The New York Times on the Web,* August 31, 2001.
9. Archer Daniels Midland Company, *2000 Annual Report,* p. 7.
10. J. L. Heskett, T. O. Jones, G. W. Loveman, W. E. Sasser Jr., and L. A. Schlesinger, "Putting the Service–Profit Chain to Work," *Harvard Business Review,* March–April 1994, pp.164–174.
11. J. Friedland and G. McWilliams, "How a Need for Speed Turned Guadalajara into a High-Tech Hub," *The Wall Street Journal,* March 2, 2000, pp. A1, A8.

OperationsNow.com LEARNING ACTIVITIES

CHAPTER ENHANCEMENT RESOURCES
- Esources
- Reel Operations Video Clips
- Interactive Models
- Excel Tutors
- Supplementary Readings
- Links to Operations On Site Companies

OM EXPLORATION
- Check It Out
- OM in Action
- Online Business Tours
- Letters from the Top
- Putting It All Together: Virtual Case Studies
- Additional Reading

The resource/profit model depicts strategy as an input to value, which is necessary to achieve profitability. With no direction for decisions, attempts to create value would not likely match customer desires. Just as short-term decisions, without some direction, are unlikely to be consistent with customer expectations, long-term resource decisions, made with no consideration of value creation, are not likely to produce desired outcomes either. A strategy is a long-term plan for creating the value customers seek, ensuring that the value attributes that receive highest priority—and the resources needed to create them—converge.

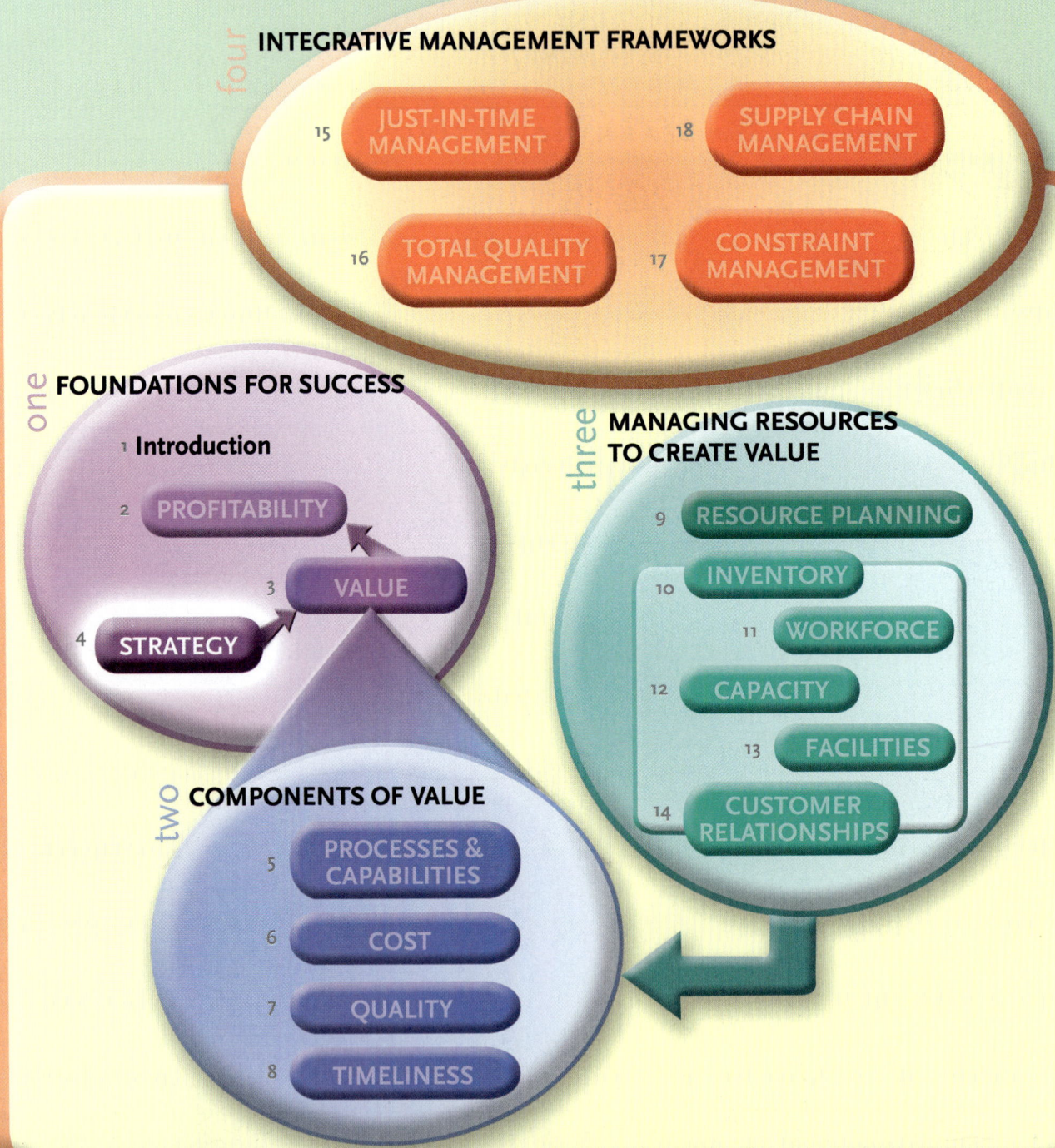

CHAPTER 4

Strategy

LEARNING OBJECTIVES

Upon completion of Chapter 4, you should be able to

- State the purpose of a strategy.
- Describe the role of the strategies that form the strategy hierarchy.
- Describe Porter's three strategies.
- Define order winners, order losers, and order qualifiers and relate them to value.
- Explain how operations affects the competitiveness of a firm.
- List and describe examples of structural and infrastructural decisions.
- Explain how the law of unexpected consequences relates to strategic decision making.
- List and describe the competitive priorities of operations.
- Summarize the effects each strategic decision category has on operations' competitive priorities.
- Describe the strategic implications of the process-oriented and product-oriented layout decisions for manufacturers.
- Describe the strategic implications of customer contact decisions for services.

Introduction: A Plan for Creating Value
The Strategic Hierarchy
Strategic Decision Categories
Strategic Decisions and Competitive Priorities
Complexity of Relationships Among Strategic Decisions and Competitive Priorities
Process and Volume Choices: Strategic Tradeoffs for Manufacturers
Customer Contact and Process Efficiency: Strategic Tradeoffs for Services
Chapter Summary

INTERNET RESOURCES

 Excel Tutors provide annotated spreadsheets for every solved problem that automatically load Excel.

 Esources provide an online version of the more traditional boxed insert.

 Reel Videos provide streaming video footage for company applications of chapter concepts.

 Interactive Models provide an experimental environment for quantitative concepts and simulations.

INTRODUCTION

A Plan for Creating Value

Simply stated, a strategy is a plan for being competitive. Despite the fact that every concept in this book is related to the firm's competitive position, the concept of operations strategy must be examined on its own. The result of an effective strategy is that customers perceive a value that is greater than that offered by competitors, and the firm has made long-term decisions to enable that to continue at an acceptable cost. The arrow that leads from strategy to value in the resource/profit model in Exhibit 4.1 depicts this.

Operations decisions are such an integral part of any company's competitive success that many long-term resource decisions are strategic in nature. Recall from Chapter 1 that a business must continue to create value for its customers. This must occur even as the customer desires change and even as the business environment changes. Since most operations decisions have implications for value, a plan for maintaining long-term consistency between the value attributes created and those desired by customers is necessary. Some operations decisions are day-to-day in nature, but many others are long term. A long-term decision made today may involve such a long-term commitment of capital or resources that it can't be "remade" in six months. The business commitments that result from these decisions are ongoing. They dictate, to a great extent, the firm's ability to succeed in the future.

Chapter 4 has two dominant themes. First, to provide a thorough understanding of operations strategy, the chapter examines in detail the strategic operations decisions and several frameworks used to organize them. Second, to provide meaning for these frameworks, it examines the impact each has on the set of value attributes identified in Chapter 3.

This chapter's treatment of strategy focuses on the role of operations in the development and implementation of a firm's strategy. Effective strategic decisions are used to position the firm so that it can compete in the future. A strategy is implemented throughout the organization to help guide the decisions of the organization's functional units. Included among these functional units are marketing, finance, human resource management, information technology, and, of course, operations.

Within operations, a strategy is used to guide decisions in a variety of areas that will affect the value attributes sought by customers. The value attributes desired establish strategic priorities to guide day-to-day decisions and have the potential to increase profitability through value enhancement. Beyond that, however, and of key importance, is that in the development of the strategy, decisions affecting long-term use of resources are made. These decisions establish the competitive future of the firm.

The term "strategy" is widely used, but it is also widely misunderstood. A company's strategy is not necessarily what the company publicly says it is. A strategy is the pattern of decisions an organization adopts in order to link resource decisions to goals.[1] The actual pattern of decisions might not be consistent with the business's stated goals. For a business to decide on a particular strategy, it must identify a pattern it wishes to follow in decision making. This often involves the development of business goals. Some of the most important goals relate to how the business wants customers to perceive the value it offers for sale. For example, a business may strive to be the most reliable supplier of printing supplies. Another might desire to be the premier low-cost provider of short-haul delivery services. Yet another might seek to be the most advanced developer of logistical computer support systems. If the business has a strategy for meeting its goals, more alternatives are available for making resource-oriented decisions, and those resource investments are more likely to provide the desired outcome.

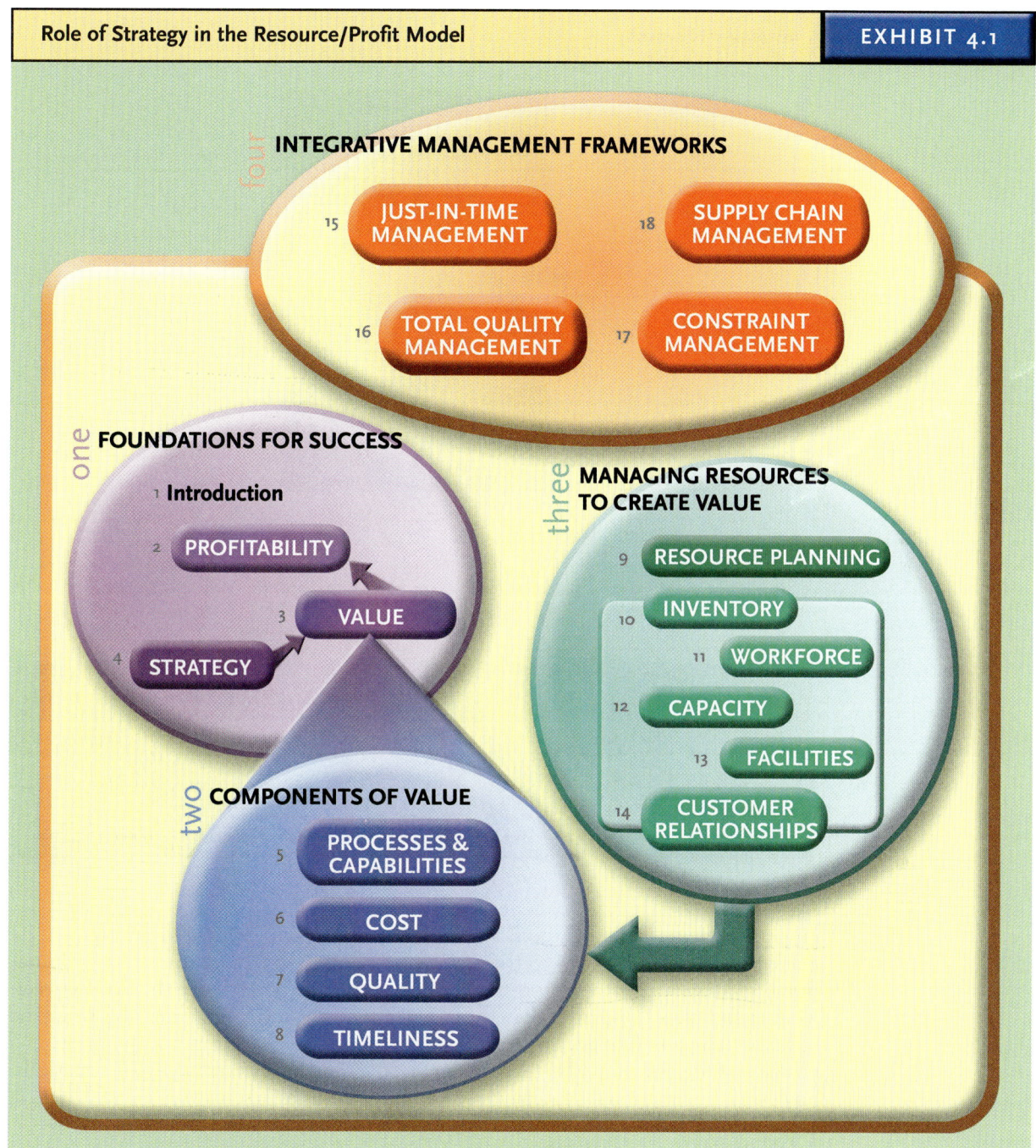

Exhibit 4.1 Role of Strategy in the Resource/Profit Model

THE STRATEGIC HIERARCHY

The concept of a functional strategy, such as an operations strategy, makes more sense when put into the context of the other levels of strategy. Exhibit 4.2 shows the hierarchical nature of the levels of corporate, business, and functional strategies.

At the broadest level is a **corporate strategy**. A corporate strategy provides a vision. It defines the businesses that the corporation will engage in and how corporate resources will be expended in those businesses. A **business strategy** defines the

> **EXHIBIT 4.2** Strategic Hierarchy

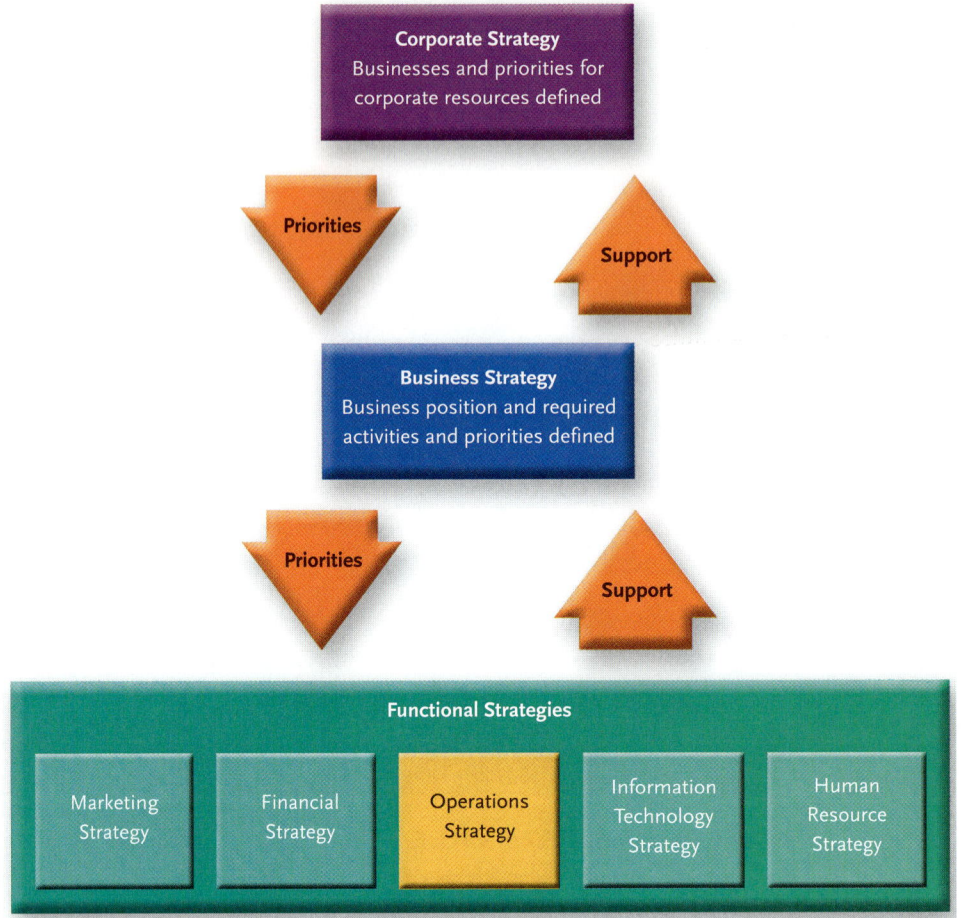

range of activities for a business, setting priorities, so that its desired position in the marketplace can contribute to the accomplishment of the corporate strategy. **Functional strategies** exist to support the business strategy. They provide the link between what each business function does, from a decision-making standpoint, and what the business is supposed to do. For businesses that do not exist within a corporation, the business strategies would be the highest strategy in the hierarchy. In all situations, however, the functional strategy must support the business strategy.

Corporate Strategy

Corporate strategies tend to be stated in broad terms because of the diversified nature of many corporations. It would be difficult, for example, to develop specific and directive language in a corporate strategy for a company like General Electric. GE's involvement in such businesses as consumer appliances, locomotives, jet engines, automotive controls, medical equipment, financial services, and broadcasting and entertainment makes it virtually impossible to provide more than general direction at the corporate level. Business strategies for GE, however, are another matter. They are focused, specific, and leave no doubt as to what the business wants to accomplish. The success of GE's businesses leads to corporate success.

Business Strategy

There are numerous effective ways of examining business strategies. One of the most popular ways to define strategies is using Michael Porter's three strategy categories: cost leader, differentiation, and focus.[2] A **cost leader strategy** seeks to price goods and services lower than competitors. Cost leadership is often viewed as a strategy for mature markets where competition is greater. A **differentiation strategy** seeks to create products and services that are different from those of competitors, resulting in the ability to charge more for them. A **focus strategy** is designed to focus products and services at a small segment of the market. Rather than seek a small portion of the broad market, the focus strategy seeks a large proportion of a smaller market segment. Porter's three strategies can be described as plans for creating value. Each seeks to identify a set of customers who will be attracted to it through their own value definition. The success or failure of a business strategy is judged by the ability of the business to attract the customers it targeted. Esource 4.1 provides an example of a successful focus strategy.

www.
OperationsNow
.com

When Porter's three strategies are examined closely, each can be seen as a way to distinguish one's products or services from the competition. Remember, different people have different perceptions of value. Specific strategies seek to attract customers who prioritize value in a particular way. A business's strategy determines how it will be profitable by identifying a certain target set of customers. For example, does it want to attract the customers whose highest priority is response time? Or does it seek the customers who value the latest fashions above all other attributes? Or can it place several issues of interest to customers at the top of its priority list? Does it seek to be a technological leader? Or does it shun technology in hopes of attracting technology-averse customers?

The business strategy seeks to identify the general basis on which the business will compete. This requires a thorough understanding of the available customers and what they want. It requires an understanding of the resources needed to create what those customers want, as well as an understanding of the types of process needed to join them together. In addition, it must project this into an uncertain business future.

In the previous chapter, customer preferences were described in terms of the value attributes reproduced in Exhibit 4.3. A framework developed by Terry Hill provides an effective means of matching value attributes and product or service characteristics to customer desires.[3] The framework uses the concepts of order winners, order losers, and order qualifiers. A product or service characteristic that is most important to a particular customer is referred to as an **order winner**. It is the characteristic that results in the order. **Order losers** are those characteristics or attributes that repel particular customers. **Order qualifiers** are those product or service characteristics that are necessary but not sufficient to result in winning the order.

In today's rapidly changing business environment, the ability to adapt quickly is a critical success factor. Without a doubt, the firm that can react quickly to a changing environment has a distinctive advantage, but being able to react quickly makes long-term decision making even more critical. For many businesses, decisions are costly to implement. Decisions such as the business location, large purchases of specific types of equipment, and workforce recruitment and training require large investments and, when changed, require additional investments. Imagine completing construction of a new store only to find that you should have built it three blocks closer to a new highway. Sometimes you simply can't reverse a decision and do it over.

A close look at customer value attributes shows that some of the business capabilities necessary to provide them can be developed quite cheaply and could be adapted and changed as needed. For example, the personalization and style/fashion value

EXHIBIT 4.3 Primary and Secondary Value Attributes for Consumer and Business Customers

Attribute	Importance for Consumer Customers	Importance for Business Customers
Price	Primary	Primary
Quality	Primary	Primary
Response time	Primary	Primary
Dependability of delivery	Secondary	Primary
Convenience	Primary	Secondary
Style/fashion	Primary	Secondary
Ethical issues	Secondary	Secondary
Technology	Secondary	Secondary
Flexibility	Secondary	Primary
Personalization	Primary	Secondary

attributes are typically the result of short-term decisions related to day-to-day practices rather than long-term resource commitments. Other value attributes, however, are expensive to provide, and their high cost makes them long-term commitments. The value attributes of quality and response time, for example, often require the development of complex management information systems that are costly to implement.

Long-term commitments involving expensive resources typify many strategic decisions. Facilities needed to house businesses are often one of the largest investments a business will make. These decisions must not only consider the initial investment and expected return, but must also include such difficult-to-predict issues such as possible trends and business conditions in the future and the potential impact competitors' decisions and actions may have.

The business strategic planning process is an attempt to identify which customers to target, through specific value attributes, and how to best appeal to them through long-term resource decisions that provide the necessary support.

Operations Strategy

For an operations strategy to be effective, the strategy must prioritize value attributes, identify which value attributes have long-term implications for operations resource (inventory, workforce, capacity, facilities) decisions, and determine what the implications are. The implementation of an operations strategy requires that decisions regarding those resources must be made. That is the execution of the plan. These decisions will require investing in resources, managing those resources, and following policies to guide day-to-day decisions.

> ### A Focused Strategy in the Women's Clothing Industry
>
> A focused strategy often evolves from learning about the market and about capabilities and finding a small match that no one else has. There are so many players in the retail clothing market, and so many that compete very effectively as cost leaders, that a focused strategy is one road to success. Many companies have attempted and failed, but one in particular, Coldwater Creek, found a narrow place in the market that has led to success selling women's clothing.
>
> Coldwater Creek started in 1984 as a home business run out of a garage. In less than 20 years, it has grown to a company with 1,600 employees and a 20-acre home office campus in Idaho. It also has an East Coast Operations Center in West Virginia. Coldwater Creek sells primarily through its catalog and website but also has retail store locations in larger cities. For five consecutive years, Coldwater Creek has been among the 500 fastest-growing companies in the United States. Its emphasis on customer service has resulted in it being ranked at the top in mail-order customer satisfaction. In 1999 Coldwater Creek filled 3.5 million customer orders. By the end of 1999, more than 8 million customers had purchased products; 2.2 million of those had made purchases within the previous 12 months. Customer loyalty remains high, and the customer retention rate was at an all-time high in 1999.
>
> High levels of service alone can provide Coldwater Creek with a different reputation than some mail order firms, but its focused strategy goes beyond that. This focused strategy is important enough that the company made sure investors are aware of it. The 1999 Annual Report provides an example of a true focus:
>
>> Thus our 35–55 year old woman with substantial discretionary income, discerning taste and little time to shop has a world of versatile clothing at her fingertips. Casual and everyday apparel. Soft career wear. Timeless, all-occasion ensembles. And wardrobe essentials she can mix, match, and combine for casual dressing on her own terms.
>
> Coldwater Creek does not sell clothing for kids. Not for teens. Not clothing for those under 30. It doesn't sell cheap clothing. It sells clothing for busy women who have money. And the strategy works. In 2000 the company was awarded the Number 1 spot for customer service via email and live chat interactions on the Internet by Customer Relationship Management Grand Prix Awards. In 2001 it was named the nation's best provider of customer service on the telephone, Internet, and email.
>
> ---
>
> Source: http://www.coldwatercreek.com, June 7, 2001; *Coldwater Creek 1999 Annual Report*; Company News on Call, "Coldwater Creek Named #1 for Customer Service Centers in U.S," http://www.prnewswire.com/cgi-bin/stories.pl?ACCT=105&STORY=/www/story/, June 19, 2001.

Effective operations strategy can have a huge financial impact. Some strategic decisions involve large investments—purchases of big-ticket items—that would require a number of years to pay off, such as a new branch for a bank or a robotic machine for a manufacturer. Generally, longer-term decisions involve the largest financial investments. If the wrong doormat is purchased, no one cares, but if the wrong building is purchased, the business is in deep trouble. A business can tolerate a poor financial return on a doormat. If the priorities of the business must change in a very short time—thus eliminating the need for the new branch or robot—the investment won't be paid off by the revenues it generates. Net income and profit margin suffer because the costs associated with the asset continue. Return on assets suffers because the asset generates no return. Return on equity suffers because the business owners receive a proportionately lower return on their investment. The business may try to sell the asset, but the likelihood that it will get back its initial investment is very low. Effective operations strategy can substantially boost all measures of profitability because it guides the purchase of resources. The remainder of this chapter is an in-depth examination of operations strategy.

The competitive power of effective operations strategy has been recognized since the 1980s, when Japanese auto manufacturers began to dominate the U.S. auto market through more effective management of operations resources. These management approaches spread throughout manufacturing and into the service sector as well.

In many cases, the resource decisions that contribute to the firm's competitive position are long term in nature. The ability to effectively make such decisions requires that the business possess a sense of what it wants to accomplish, long term, with those resources. The easiest way to determine this is by establishing goals regarding the value attributes important to the customers the firm wishes to attract. For example, an electronics retailer might be the cheapest source of the top consumer brands. Another might cater to the audiophile and carry a small inventory of top-end equipment. The selected strategy has implications that include the operations resources of inventory, workforce, capacity, and facilities.

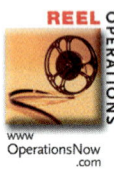
www.OperationsNow.com

The resource/profit model includes environmental forces as a dynamic that all businesses must contend with. One of these environmental forces is constant change in competitors' actions that affect the value of products and services and changes in technology that affect potential capabilities. Changes in business ownership also often result in changes in business strategy, because new owners often have different goals. Reel Operations Video 4.1 chronicles a change in the strategy of ABTCO (a producer of business products) following a change in ownership.

Changing Strategy to Match a Changing Environment

Many services depend on traffic for their customers. Customers, however, come from different sources. Some hotels, for example, may implement a strategy that seeks to attract business customers. Others may locate to attract tourists. Other service businesses in the hospitality and food service industries must make similar decisions. As U.S. business and leisure travel declined following the September 11, 2001, terrorist attacks on New York and Washington, D.C., businesses whose strategy was to seek out those customers had to change their focus.

By October 2001, business travel had dropped 80 percent from one year earlier and leisure travel had fallen off by 25 percent. Many restaurants, particularly high-end, expensive ones, depended on visiting business travelers and tourists for their demand. Restaurants in big cities were hit especially hard, while suburban and neighborhood restaurants were affected less. Expensive restaurants in cities like New York, Los Angeles, Washington, D.C., Boston, and San Francisco were directly hurt by the travel crunch. In some cities, however, New Orleans in particular, locals supported even the most expensive restaurants.

Reductions in demand can be a motivating factor for changes in business approaches. Many restaurants tried extra hard to provide better service during this period. Many needed to replace traveler customers with locals if they were to survive, meaning that they needed to attract more return customers. For many restaurants, a completely different approach to attracting customers was necessary. Changes in the market required changes in strategy for many affected by this disaster.

Source: "Across America, Restaurants Adjust to a Stay-Put Nation," *The New York Times on the Web*, October 24, 2001.

Changes in political climate, both domestic and foreign, change cost structures and market access. International businesses, however, face much greater changes and larger risks. Any change can create havoc for the unexpecting company. Companies seeking international markets must adapt their strategies to fit the expectations of new customers. In 2000, U.S. companies earned $134 billion in profits from overseas affiliates, more than double the earnings of a decade earlier.

As of 2001, exports accounted for 48 percent of the output of developed nations.[4] Many companies seek to diversify risks by expanding to international markets. However, as the global economy becomes more integrated, that diversification doesn't help because the economies of individual countries are not independent. Instead, all tend to follow the rise and fall of global economic conditions.

Even within the United States, changing demographics have resulted in companies changing their strategies to meet the needs of different customers. For the company whose strategy includes flexibility and agility, however, changing demographics may create opportunities. Can a firm make strategically sound long-term decisions in an environment that appears to be in a constant state of flux? Many decisions depend on forecasts of what is likely to happen but will be made with maintaining flexibility as an objective. For example, without a clear picture of future demand, a business might design a new facility at the minimum acceptable size while retaining the capability for expansion in the future if necessary. Esource 4.2 provides several examples of how strategic decisions affect a firm's success.

www.OperationsNow.com

STRATEGIC DECISION CATEGORIES

Grouping strategic decisions into categories of structural and infrastructural decisions is a useful way to examine them. Exhibit 4.4 lists strategic decisions and examples grouped in this way.

A quick overview of the examples listed in Exhibit 4.4 provides evidence that many of the decisions are not independent of each other. For example, the degree to which *process technology* is used in production of a service or product has implications for the skill level of *human resources*. The *capacity* of the service or manufacturing facility dictates the degree of *integration* and the emphasis placed on developing *business partners*. The degree to which the business outsources has implications for *quality management systems*. Just as operations have an impact on other business functions, strategic decisions made within operations have an impact on other decision areas of operations.

STRATEGIC DECISIONS AND COMPETITIVE PRIORITIES

The relationships between strategic decisions and value attributes are presented in Exhibit 4.5. In reality, a connecting line drawn from almost every decision box to every value attribute in Exhibit 4.5 could be justified. It is easier, however, to draw just one large arrow.

The relationships between the decision categories presented in Exhibit 4.5 and the value attributes of interest to the customer enable a business to position itself to successfully compete in the future. Structural decisions relate to such tangibles as buildings, equipment, the way equipment and personnel are organized in processes, and how the business links to other businesses. For the most part, they relate to "bricks and mortar"–type issues. Infrastructural decisions, on the other hand, relate to systems used to enhance the utilization of the structural resources and to control those resources so the business achieves high levels of productivity.

EXHIBIT 4.4 — Strategic Decisions in Operations

	Decision Categories	Examples
Structural Decisions	Capacity	High-volume vs. low-volume equipment Timing of additional capacity Flexibility of capacity Overbooking/yield management
	Facilities	Location Size Design Number Line of visibility
	Process technology	Type of equipment technology Customer involvement Layout Automation Internet presence
	Vertical integration/supplier relationships	Linkages and business partnerships Integration versus outsource
Infrastructural Decisions	Human resources	Skill level Part time vs. full time Salary position in labor market Security
	Quality	Prevention vs. detection Control systems Specifications Involvement with suppliers
	Production planning/inventory controls	Supplier decisions Inventory management systems Vendor and outsourcing policies
	New product or service development	Sequential versus parallel activities Makeup of new product or service development teams Supplier involvement
	Performance measurement and reward systems	Focus: individual vs. group incentives Types of performance measure Types of reward (bonus, stock options, etc.)
	Organization/systems	Organization structure Line and staff relationships

Source: Adapted from R. H. Hayes and S. C. Wheelwright, *Restoring Our Competitive Edge: Competing through Manufacturing* (New York: Wiley, 1984), p. 31, and R. H. Hayes, S. C. Wheelwright, and K. B. Clark, *Dynamic Manufacturing* (New York: Free Press, 1988), p. 351.

EXHIBIT 4.5 Relationships among Strategic Decisions and Value Determinants

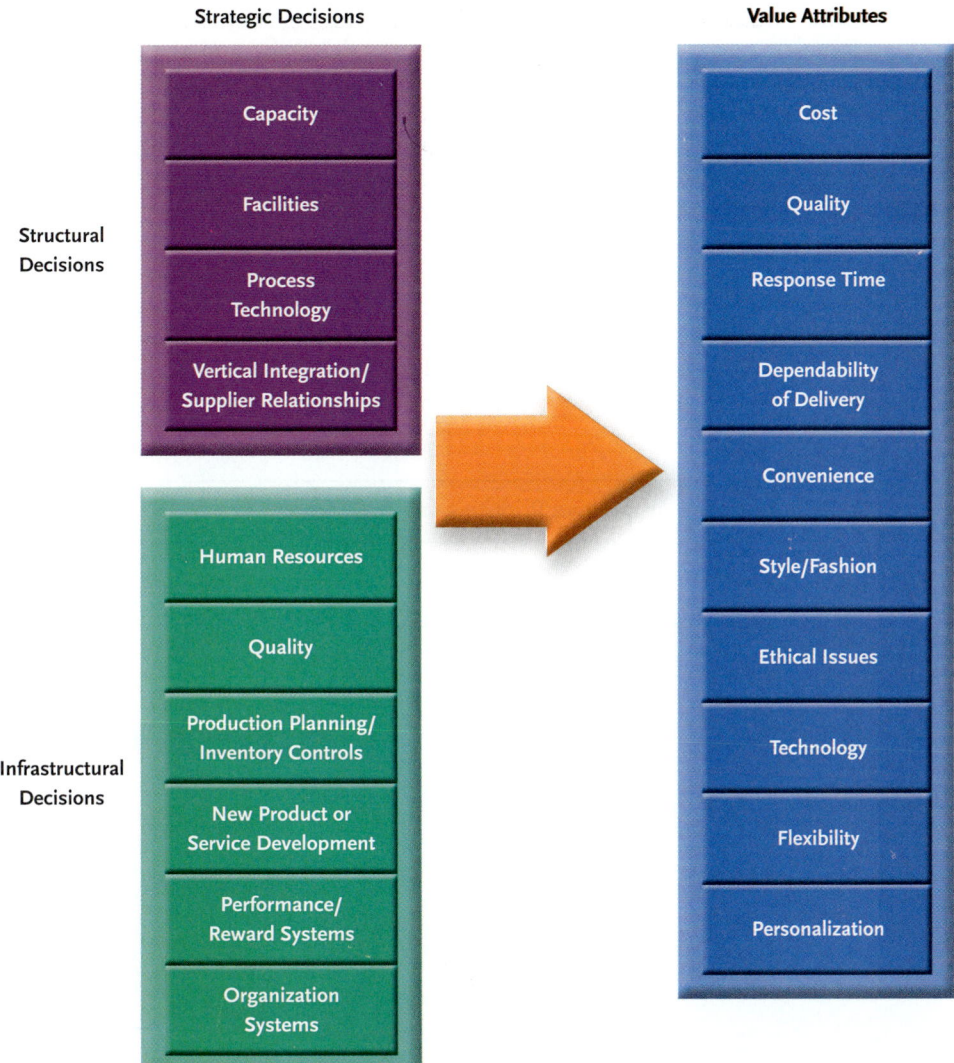

Recall that value attributes provide the means through which a firm offers the customer value. Examination of the implications strategic decisions have on value attributes illustrates how important these decisions can be. Keep in mind that the strategic decisions are not made or modified on a day-to-day basis. They are long term in nature, with impacts that can extend years into the future. For many firms, a five-year plan might have been considered long term a decade ago. Now two years may be considered long term. The result is that the time required to implement and receive a financial return from a specific strategy has been compressed as product life cycles have become shorter.

Ten strategic decisions categories and ten value attributes create a lot of relationships, but they aren't all equally important for a specific company. For example, for a bank having mostly business accounts, process technology may be closely linked to response time. Businesses may need to have electronic access to accounts and be able to make a large variety of transfers and payments using that technology. For a bank with mostly consumer accounts, however, process technology may be more closely linked to the value attribute of convenience, through its network of ATMs.

The complex network of relationships between decisions and their impacts on value increases the likelihood that a decision will have an outcome that is not anticipated. This is sometimes referred to as the *law of unintended consequences*, which simply means that in complex environments, decisions can have impacts that are unanticipated and negative. In this environment, the potential for unforeseen relationships makes it quite likely that a decision will have unintended consequences. The need to prioritize those value attributes that are more strategic in nature and that have the most significant impact on the firm's long-term competitiveness has led to an operations focus on the **competitive priorities** of cost, quality, dependability of delivery, flexibility, and response time. Exhibit 4.6 illustrates these competitive priorities compared to the complete list of value attributes. In the following discussion, the effects each strategic decision category has on the competitive priorities are summarized.

EXHIBIT 4.6 — Value Attributes and Competitive Priorities for Operations

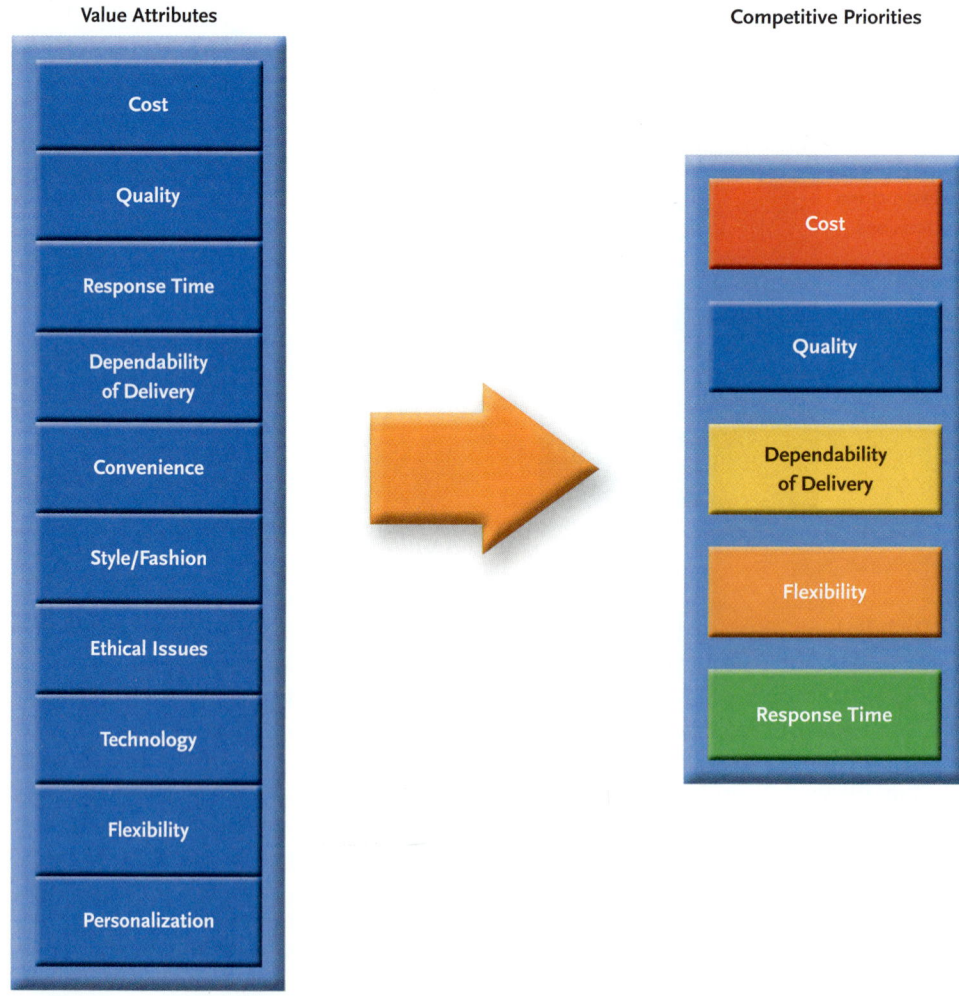

Capacity Decisions

Capacity decisions determine output capabilities. Capacity is generally defined in terms of an output measure per unit of time, or, in other words, an output rate. Customers per hour, claims per hour, units per day—all are examples of measures of capacity. Since capacity determines rate of output, competitive priorities most closely tied to capacity decisions are generally those that are related to output rate and volume. All five competitive priorities can be linked to capacity decisions, as shown in Exhibit 4.7. Exhibit 4.7 also summarizes the means by which capacity decisions affect competitive priorities.

The term "capacity" has many contexts, but an important one is **design capacity**, the capacity a facility is designed to accommodate on an ongoing basis. Design capacity may refer to a factory, a restaurant, a hotel, an airport, or any other productive system.

Cost is affected by design capacity through its impact on cost per unit. For any facility, whether it be a factory or a service business, cost per unit is at its lowest when the production or service rate matches the design capacity. For example, cost per visitor would be minimized at a theme park when the number of visitors was at the park's design capacity. Cost per unit would be minimized for a manufacturer of motorcycles when the production rate was at the factory's design capacity. Producing or serving at a rate below the design capacity means that the resources aren't being utilized as much as they could be, and the investment in the facility isn't providing its maximum return. In addition, some costs that are predominantly fixed, like utilities, maintenance, and housekeeping, as well as some labor costs, are spread over fewer customers. For a business producing at a rate greater than design capacity, cost per unit can also increase. Extra staff may need to be brought in and paid at overtime salary rates. Routine equipment maintenance might be postponed, resulting in increased levels of wear and tear, and possibly expensive breakdowns on equipment. If the appropriate

Strategic Capacity Decisions' Impact on Competitive Priorities EXHIBIT 4.7

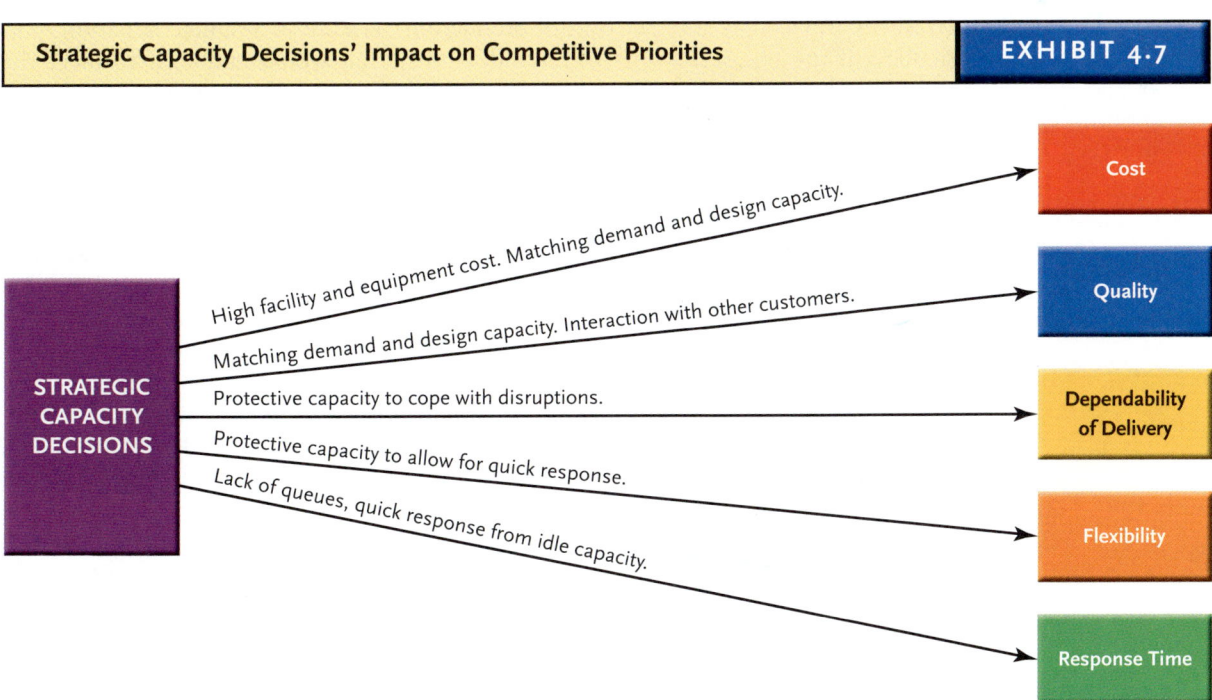

design capacity can be identified up front, demand can be matched closely, resulting in lower costs and greater financial return overall.

Quality is also affected by the match between design capacity and demand. For manufacturers, output rates lower than design capacity do not typically result in lower levels of quality directly, but they can result in increases in inventory produced, which can negatively affect quality. For some manufacturers, the rate of production has to be either completely on or completely off because it can't be "throttled back." This is especially true for manufacturers that utilize chemical reactions in their processes or use equipment that cannot be shut down for fear of serious damage. For restaurants, bars, and other activity-oriented services, lack of sufficient customers can actually harm quality because customers expect interaction with others.

Dependability of delivery has been increasing in importance for both consumers and business customers. In services and product-oriented businesses, when capacity is tight, any unexpected disruption can result in a missed due date. Protection from these disruptions can be achieved by incorporating **protective capacity**. Protective capacity is a layer of capacity above that which is absolutely required to meet known demand. It provides firms the ability to handle occasional problems that come up and also gives them the ability to handle a special request. Protective capacity is capacity whose utilization is not planned but exists "just in case." Protective capacity has traditionally been difficult to justify in the United States because of a bias toward maximizing the short-term return on investment in capacity-oriented resources. Short-term ROI will probably not be maximized if resources are idle part of the time, even though that's exactly what must be the case for long-term performance. Protective capacity provides a buffer against Murphy's law, and even if a machine breaks down, transportation problems arise, or other systems fail temporarily, protective capacity can allow production to catch up quickly. The end result is that delivery promises are met.

Flexibility, to a great extent, is determined by the relationship between design capacity and the capacity required to meet demand at any given time. When demand stabilizes, there may be excess capacity, resulting in high costs per unit and wasted resources. Or there might be a constant shortage of capacity, resulting in overstressed resources and a high cost per unit of production. The most desirable situation, particularly if the business wants to have flexibility that would enable it to meet the unexpected or unique needs of customers, would be a level of protective capacity. Flexibility can translate into new customers, stronger relationships with existing customers, and greater long-term profitability.

Response time is of interest to consumers as well as business customers. Capacity has a direct impact on response time because idle capacity can respond immediately to demand. Busy capacity cannot. A manufacturer that wishes to respond quickly can do it in two ways. One way would be to ensure that enough capacity existed to provide some idle or protective capacity that could be used if an immediate need arose. Another way would be through a buildup of finished-goods inventory. During low demand periods, inventory could be produced ahead of time (from the idle capacity), making it possible to satisfy demand directly from inventory. For many businesses, however, inventory has a shelf life. Quality of the products can suffer if too much inventory is built up, remaining on the shelf for extended lengths of time. For a firm that wishes to customize products, satisfying demand from inventory is not feasible and capacity would be the only way to respond quickly to unexpected demand.

For services, the relationship between capacity and rate of demand often results in the presence or absence of a waiting line. For many customers, the length of a wait in a line is one criterion in evaluating service quality. The longer the wait, the lower the perceived quality. Some potential customers will simply not wait in a line—they'll take their business elsewhere.

Facility Decisions

Strategic facility decisions can affect all five competitive priorities, as illustrated in Exhibit 4.8.

The impact facility decisions have on *cost* can be traced to the facility's share of the overhead costs. It has an impact on other costs as well, including the cost of labor. Costs can be influenced by various facility decisions, including facility location. Location decisions affect the initial cost of building or acquiring the facility, and taxes, utility rates, transportation costs, and labor rates. Facility location can also influence the raw material availability and cost for other inputs that might be expensive to transport.

Facility decisions also affect *quality*. Facility design and location will have a direct impact on the quality of a service that requires the customer to actually come to the service. Customers want an environment compatible with their expectations. For some services, that environment is an integral part of the total package they're paying for. Hotels, casinos, night clubs, banks, and even retail establishments sell an atmosphere that customers have come to expect.

While most customers who purchase products don't care about the "ambiance" of the factory in which they were made, facility location has an impact on the type of skilled labor force available. Many businesses require specific skills that may not be common. Skills that are available in the Silicon Valley area of California make it an attractive location for computer-oriented manufacturers. Skills available in the mountains of North Carolina make that area attractive to furniture producers. Skills of the labor force can translate directly into product and service quality.

Facility design can influence quality as well. Many service businesses must decide which parts of the service processes will be exposed to the customers and which will not. In banking, for example, some processes take place behind the scenes. The separation between these backroom activities and the customer is known as the **line of visibility**. The placement of that line of visibility must be considered during the facility design stage.

Strategic Facility Decisions' Impact on Competitive Priorities — EXHIBIT 4.8

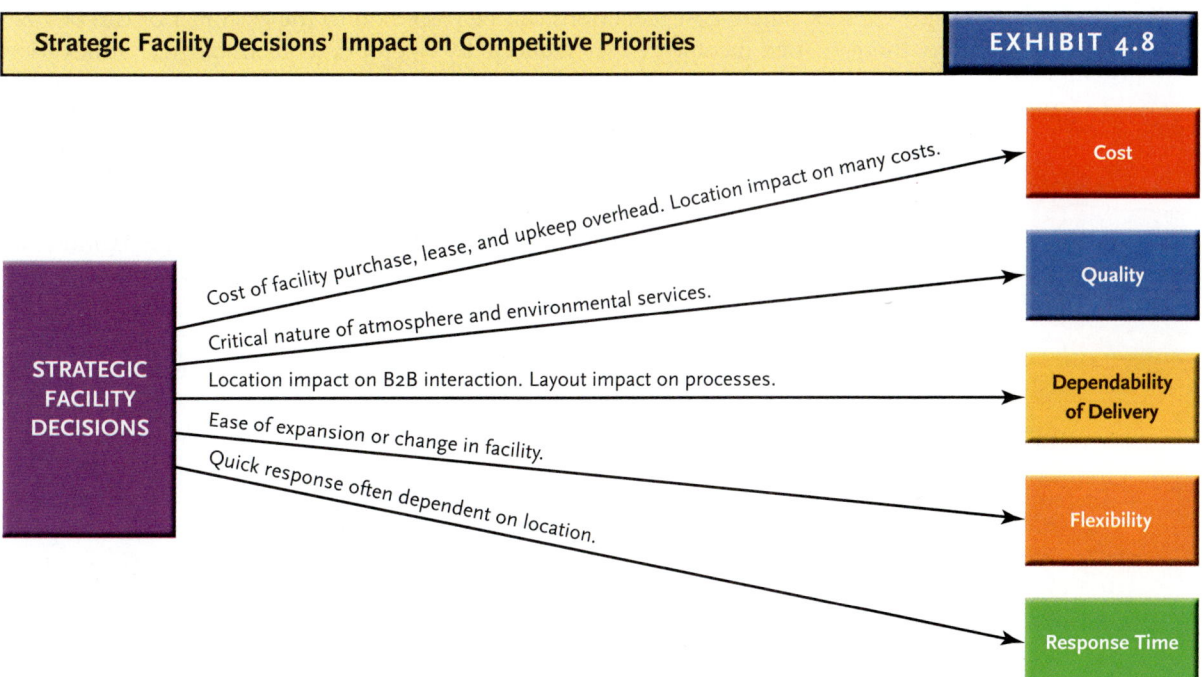

For B2B and B2C interactions, reliability depends on *dependability of delivery* at the promised time. Inventories are often held at low levels, so missing a delivery by only a day can create problems for a production schedule. Location decisions have an impact on the reliability of delivery, if only because short transportation distances offer less opportunity for disruptions. The facility layout also has an impact. Ease of shipping raw materials or components can depend on the ability to move goods out of a manufacturing plant quickly and easily. For this reason, layouts that make it easy to move materials through the production process to shipping have become commonplace in manufacturing.

Long-term facility decisions have an important impact on *flexibility*. It is often difficult to predict the ultimate success of a business. In some cases, the business flourishes, and expansion soon becomes necessary. Initial facility decisions can play a big part in the ease of an expansion to an existing facility. Or, if the possibility of expansion was never considered, a facility might be constructed in a way that makes expansion of the existing building impossible. The only business expansion alternative might be to build a new facility. Demand changes over time, delivery methods change over time, so the successful business needs to stay abreast of changing needs. Designing in flexibility not only can reduce future costs of adaptation but can also enhance adaptability.

Quick *response time*, particularly in a B2B relationship, is characterized by rapid response to requests and can depend on reliable transportation and a nearby location. Close proximity to customers has become more important as supplier relationships have become longer term and expectations have risen to daily—or even more frequent—deliveries of goods.

Process Technology Decisions

Strategic process technology decisions determine how technology will actually be used in the business. All competitive priorities have the potential to be affected by technology decisions. Exhibit 4.9 summarizes the impact that strategic process technology decisions have on the competitive priorities.

www.OperationsNow.com

Cost reduction is a frequent objective of technology in the production of products and services. These cost reductions can be passed on to the customer or can be held to increase net income. Costs reduced by appropriate technological innovation include labor costs, cost of waste, costs of carrying too much inventory, and utility costs. Technology frequently makes it possible to produce manufactured products at high volumes, reducing cost per unit. Technology can also provide the controls necessary to reduce product defects and service failures, eliminating waste at the same time. More efficient utilization of resources is made possible by technological applications such as yield management, which is used in airline and hotel reservation systems. While the use of technology solely to reduce costs is sometimes viewed as somewhat remedial, it is an important practice. Esource 4.3 is an example of how process technology can provide a competitive advantage for a firm.

Technology can also be used to improve the *quality* of goods and services. Processes that are controlled so that variability is reduced are inherently better quality. In many manufacturing processes, quality tolerances would be impossible to maintain without automated processes and controls. In many services, processes behind the line of visibility can be automated to increase processing speed and provide quicker service. Processes that involve the customer can also be enhanced technologically, but it is at that point that technology comes into play as a value attribute of the customer. Some customers will be attracted by the technology. Others will be put off by it. Decisions about using technology in processes that involve customers must be carefully considered.

Dependability of delivery can be affected by process technology decisions because technology can make processes less variable, which makes them easier to predict and

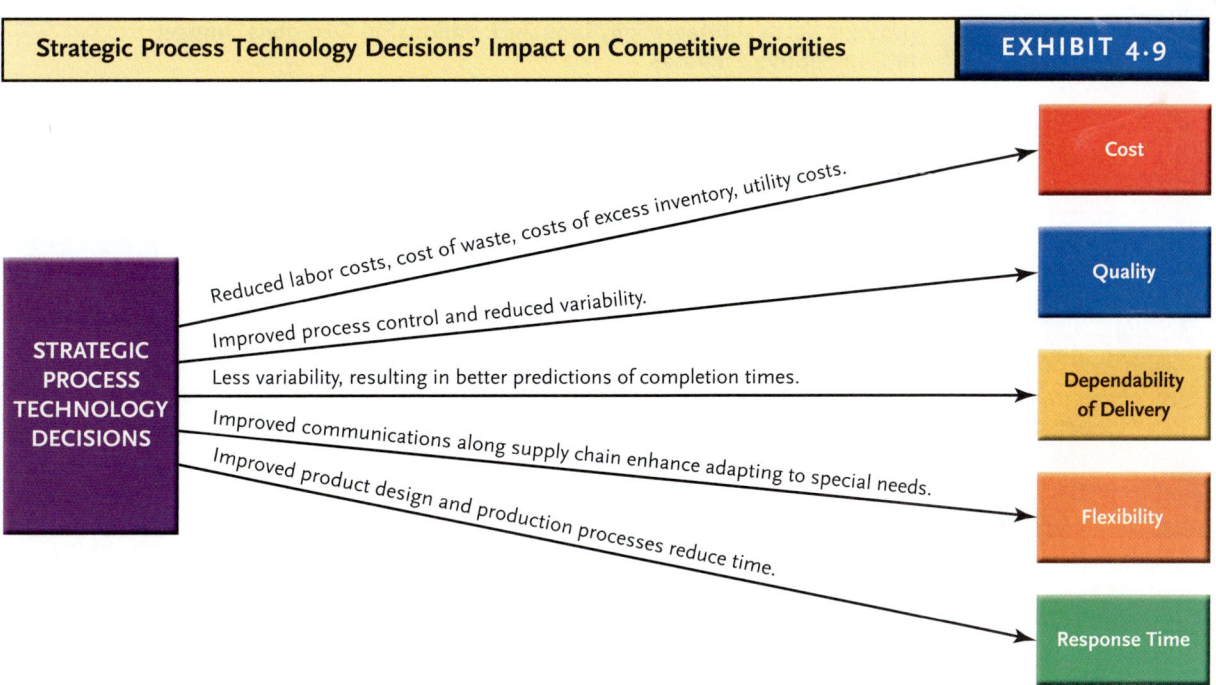

Strategic Process Technology Decisions' Impact on Competitive Priorities — EXHIBIT 4.9

more consistent. Processes with less variability do not surprise managers with long delays and the delaying impact that quality problems can bring. For services, process technology also tends to make processing each customer more consistent and timely by reducing the time for interaction and reducing the likelihood that the customer would want special treatment.

Technology, particularly when Internet based, can result in virtually seamless communication links between business partners. The result is an awareness of what each is dealing with an ability to respond more quickly and with greater *flexibility* in a business environment that continues to increase its amount of outsourcing. The end result is that customer needs requiring more than what can be done in-house can be translated immediately into requirements for suppliers. Producers of products and services alike, no matter how much they depend on suppliers and outside sources, can adapt quickly to unique customer needs.

For many situations, technology results in shorter *response time*. This is particularly true with product or service introductions. The process of designing the new product or service and then bringing it through production can take a long time, reducing the advantage gained by being first to the market. Technological enhancements to the design and engineering process enable product design and engineering tasks to be performed concurrently with process design and engineering tasks. Production processing times are often reduced when automated. Better communication with suppliers, also made possible through technological linkages, enables more and earlier involvement on their part as well.

Vertical Integration and Supplier Relationship Decisions

Strategies related to vertical integration, supplier relationships, and outsourcing also have implications for all five competitive priorities. Exhibit 4.10 summarizes these relationships.

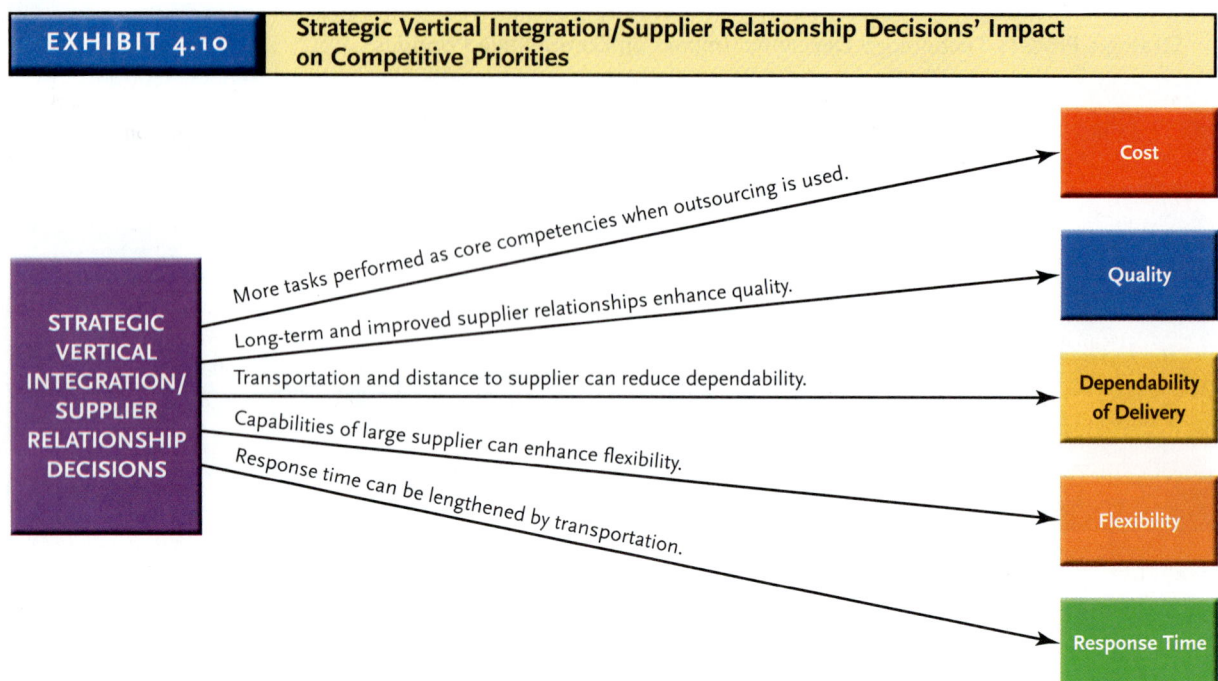

EXHIBIT 4.10 Strategic Vertical Integration/Supplier Relationship Decisions' Impact on Competitive Priorities

A little more than a decade ago, there was a strong incentive to vertically integrate, rather than depend on suppliers or subcontractors for inputs to productive systems. At that time, if you wanted it done right, you did it yourself. Doing something in-house was generally viewed as cheaper, and most businesses wanted to be able to control their own supplies of inputs. An increase in focus on core competencies has changed all that. **Core competencies** are those things a firm does really well. Sticking to what it does well keeps a business focused on those capabilities that distinguish it from others. In many cases, those capabilities are most closely related to process expertise, not product expertise. Involvement in activities that are far removed from the firm's core competencies has become recognized as a significant mistake.

Outsourcing can be a wise choice because it may take advantage of another business's core competencies. Outsourcing can reduce *costs*, increasing value contributed to the supply chain. Businesses now exist in a complex environment of contingent workforces, contract manufacturers, business partners, and long-term suppliers. A great deal of the value added to products and services results from outsourcing. The end result is better products, better services, and greater efficiencies within supply chains because companies are spending more of their time doing what they do well.

The relationships a business has with its suppliers, combined with the value-added processes it controls, have a significant impact on costs. Outsourcing can increase or decrease costs, depending on the situation. The firm outsourcing products and services must look for the best value possible because that value will be passed on to customers and be reflected in customers' purchase decisions.

Outsourcing decisions and the resulting supplier relationships can also improve *quality*. Processes controlled by suppliers and subcontractors have as much impact on quality as the processes owned by the company itself. Quality that is enhanced or reduced will become a part of the finished product or service, no matter where in the supply chain it was produced. Many companies have come to believe that long-term relationships with suppliers can result in improved levels of quality. In fact, many large firms assist their suppliers in developing quality systems. Many suppliers also assist their customers by being involved in the early stages of new product and service development to help address quality-related issues.

The processes completed by suppliers take time. All time-consuming portions of value-adding process have an impact on *dependability of delivery*. Dependability within the supply chain may be reduced as outsourcing increases because of transportation between the supplier and the producer, but if the supplier provides dependable delivery, and the communication between the supplier and producer is good, there may be no negative impact whatsoever. Good buyer–supplier relationships are the difference between an effective supply chain and a disjointed network of uncommitted suppliers. The former can work like a well-oiled machine to provide products and services on demand. The latter is slow to react, undependable, and ultimately unsuccessful, and it can lead to the failure of other members of the supply chain.

Suppliers of product and service components play a critical role in the success of their customers. Customers, after all, do not differentiate between components made by a supplier and components made by the manufacturer. No case exemplifies the importance of suppliers more than the erosion of the relationship between Ford Motor Company and Firestone. As consumer confidence in the safety of all Firestone tires on Ford SUVs slumped, on May 22, 2001, Ford announced that it would voluntarily recall 13 million Firestone Wilderness AT tires because of a lack of confidence in the tires' future performance.

The successful business must react to change. *Flexibility* is necessary to meet the needs of business customers who themselves must reduce response time and increase adaptability. For some firms, a decision to outsource increases flexibility. For example, rather than buy a required piece of equipment that will be obsolete as process requirements change, a business will outsource. The best long-term strategy for producing components that require frequent process change may be to not produce them at all. Outsourcing may increase component costs, but it will eliminate the uncertainty associated with investing in equipment that may become obsolete. As any investor knows, minimizing uncertainty is a part of any successful investment approach.

Response time can be affected negatively as the amount of outsourcing increases, but strategic placement of inventory can reduce the effect. Transportation of materials always takes time, adding to the cash-to-cash cycle. If inventory is placed well, it might not add to the waiting time of customers, however. Location of suppliers can make a big difference in the transportation time required. In many industries, suppliers locate as close to their major customers as possible to minimize that impact.

Human Resources Decisions

Strategic human resource decisions involve the skill and experience level required of employees, training commitments, staff development, contingent or temporary staffing issues, and, in general, how the organization views its investment in personnel. These critical decisions have the most implications for cost, quality, and flexibility. Exhibit 4.11 summarizes these relationships.

Cost is influenced by strategic human resource decisions because of the labor component of the firm's cost structure. Labor costs, which are present in most business environments, are often more important for services. For many manufacturers, labor costs have been reduced through advances in automation. Overhead costs, however, have often increased as a result of an increased need for nondirect labor such as administrative personnel, technicians, and managers. Labor costs can become more critical during times of labor shortages. Jobs can become so plentiful that high-quality employees can demand premium salaries. Decisions related to the use of contingent workers during peak demand periods can also have an impact on costs. Contingent or temporary employees can reduce some costs but can also create quality and morale problems, as discussed in the following section.

Quality continues to be significantly influenced by labor decisions in manufacturing and services. Manufacturing jobs are increasingly technical, requiring more expertise. Service-oriented firms struggle to find employees who can succeed when customer contact is high, and customer expectations are even higher. Employee turnover leads to an overall lowering of the experience of the workforce, reducing employee effectiveness. Firms with variable demand may attempt to maintain flexibility by hiring temporary employees through an agency. This approach has many benefits, including reduced cost of salary and benefits, as well as an opportunity to "try out" an employee prior to hiring on a permanent basis. Using temporary employees also has some negative impacts, however. Quality can be one of them. Temporary employees typically haven't had as much experience, which can result in lower levels of quality for a manufacturer or a service.

The need to continually train and retrain employees provides an excellent basis for increasing *flexibility*. As the firm needs to shift to keep up with changing and emerging markets, employees must maintain skills compatible with those requirements. These requirements result in costs that shortsighted managers often try to defer. From

EXHIBIT 4.11   **Strategic Human Resource Decisions' Impact on Competitive Priorities**

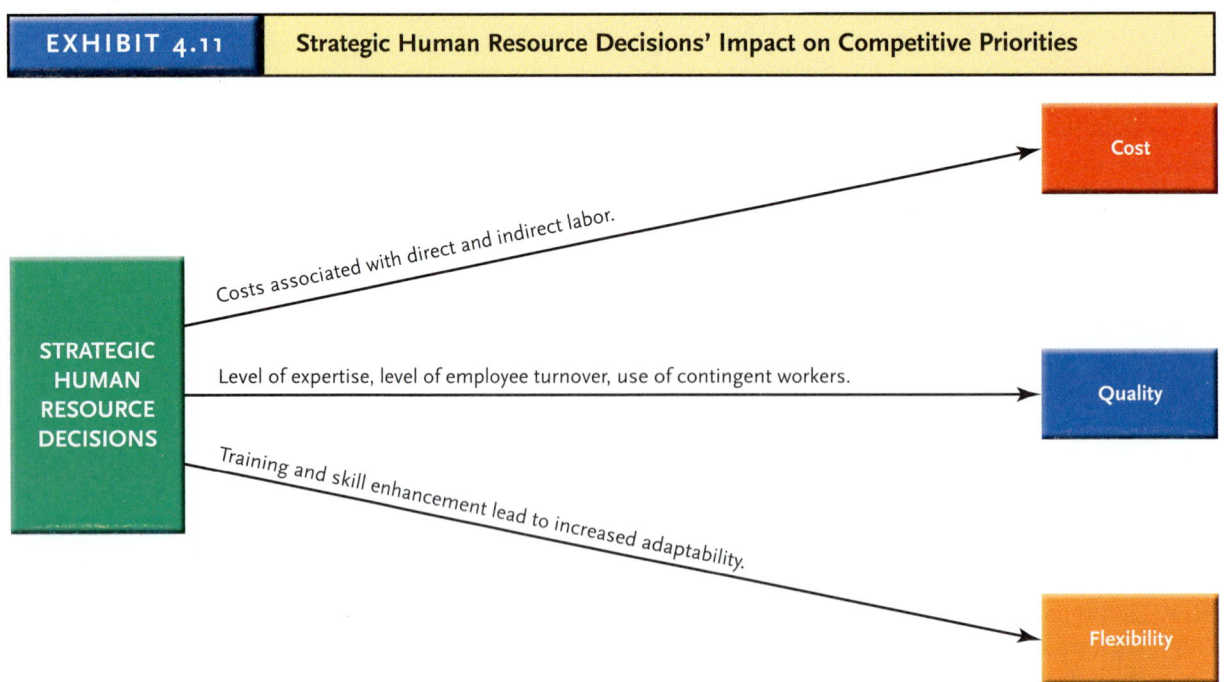

a strategic standpoint, a commitment to these efforts up front, with an acknowledgment of the expense of this type of training, serves to keep it as a high priority.

Quality Decisions

Strategic quality decisions include decisions related to the design of systems used to maintain quality. These decisions will obviously have their biggest impact on the competitive priority of quality. Decisions regarding quality systems affect other competitive priorities as well, however. Because quality means doing what the customer wants, all customers are going to consider quality as important, and many will lump other competitive priorities into what they perceive as issues of quality. Ultimately, strategic quality decisions can have significance for all five competitive priorities, as summarized in Exhibit 4.12.

Much of what the customer perceives as quality is determined by day-to-day decisions. The systems that specify how those day-to-day decisions are made, however, are the result of more strategic decisions regarding the role quality will play competitively. An example of a quality system would be a business's efforts to become quality certified through a global certification body or to seek a national or state quality award.

Strategic quality decisions affect *cost* in several ways, all generally positive. First, efforts devoted to maintaining high-quality inputs to products and services require closer relationships with suppliers and better inputs to their systems. Better relationships typically result in lower costs associated with quality. Processes with higher-quality goals may require more investment in process technology, more sophisticated equipment, or more highly trained employees, however. These may actually cause short-term cost increases, but over time costs should decrease, and value should be enhanced as well. Higher levels of quality result in less waste, less scrap for manufacturers, and less labor required to fix what should have been done correctly the first time, thereby reducing costs.

Quality systems also include the use of tools to reduce the variability in processes, which can improve *delivery dependability*. In addition, when processes are not func-

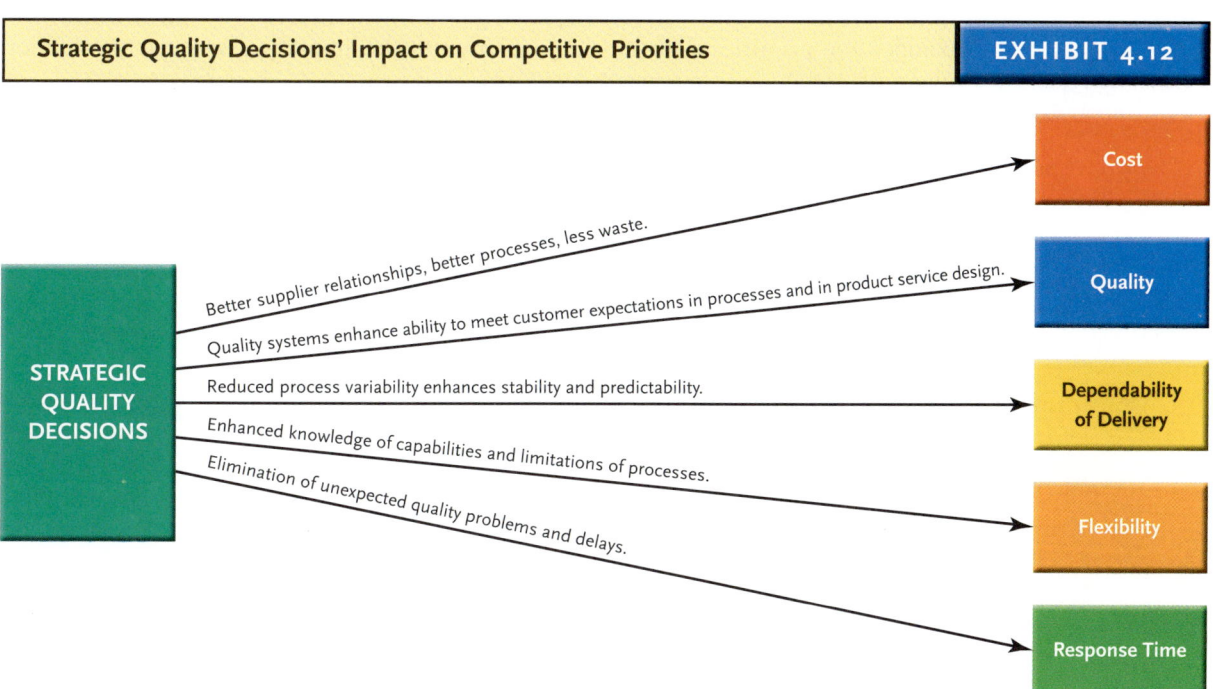

Strategic Quality Decisions' Impact on Competitive Priorities — EXHIBIT 4.12

tioning well, the length of time associated with them can be even more difficult to predict. Problems with defects can occur at the worst possible time, delaying order completion. Wide variability of processing times makes order due dates more difficult to determine reliably.

Flexibility is also enhanced by the effective use of quality management systems. Better control over processes facilitates the understanding of the capabilities of those processes. Better knowledge of process capabilities makes it easier to respond to special requests, since managers and operators are well informed of limitations and capabilities of each piece of equipment and each step in every process.

Quality enhancement, resulting from strategic quality decisions, can influence *response time* by eliminating potential delays resulting from quality problems. Defects in manufactured goods can result in delays to finish production. Defects that result in products being scrapped may result in an order for a large quantity being incomplete and unacceptable to the customer. Delays can also result from quality problems in services. Airlines, for example, frequently experience delays resulting from equipment maintenance problems. Poor-quality inputs, coming from a supplier that didn't meet specifications, can result in delays as well. Excess time is also required when employees must identify and sort poor-quality inputs. Quality problems anywhere in an organization can be expected to eventually make their way to the customer.

Production Planning/Inventory Control Decisions

Strategic production planning and inventory control decisions include the design, development, and role of systems used to manage production planning and scheduling, equipment use, capacity, and inventories. Traditionally, production planning and control systems have been used predominantly in manufacturing. However, new technologies have resulted in an influx of capacity-related planning systems being used in services as well. Inventory management systems have been used in both manufacturing and services. Integrated systems, such as enterprise resource planning (ERP) systems, have become increasingly common. Competitive priority implications for these systems vary from one application to another but can affect all five competitive priorities. Exhibit 4.13 summarizes the impact of strategic production planning and inventory control decisions.

Strategic production planning and inventory control decisions affect *costs* in different ways. Production planning and control systems contribute to the productivity of resources by making it possible to accurately match the supply of capacity and inventory to the demand. Such systems can be expensive, but like many business decisions, the benefits may justify the costs. The results obtained from such systems frequently create a better use of the resources, providing a financial return for such an investment. Inventory, for example, can be reduced if order quantities and timing of orders are more accurate, and expensive equipment can be utilized more effectively if schedules are better. An appropriate match of demand and supply creates an environment where processes can run at their optimal rates. A mismatch between the rate of demand and the capacity can reduce *quality*.

Production planning and control systems enhance *dependability of delivery* by providing a means to improve the accuracy of predicting how long processes will take. With ineffective systems, schedules used to determine completion time are not accurate reflections of reality. Accurate order promise dates depend on sophisticated resource scheduling systems.

For some firms, particularly manufacturers of products that must be customized, technologies have enhanced *flexibility*. Some sophisticated manufacturing systems allow design changes to a machined product to be made on a computer using a computer-

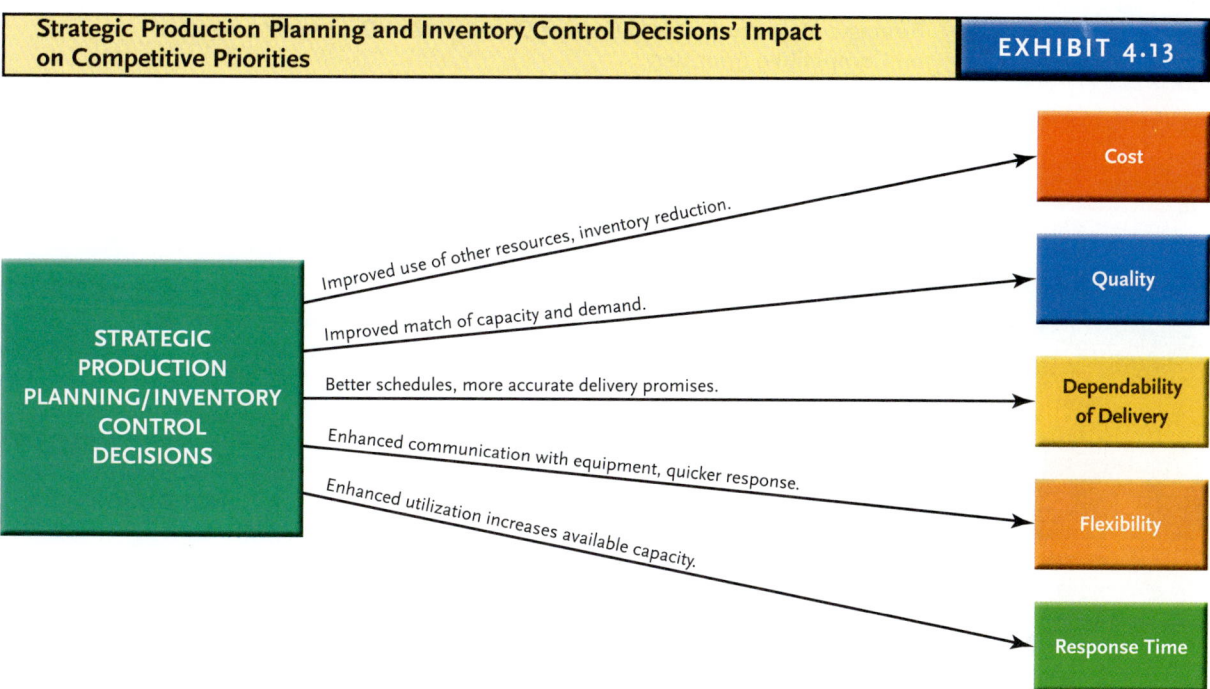

EXHIBIT 4.13 Strategic Production Planning and Inventory Control Decisions' Impact on Competitive Priorities

aided design (CAD) system. The digital information is then transferred directly to the machining centers, and the product is automatically machined to match the design changes. This flexibility has created a huge competitive advantage in some industries.

The ability to effectively plan and schedule demands on capacity and inventory can have such a positive impact on the utilization of these resources that *response time* can be greatly improved. For many businesses, scheduling products and services through a complex series of steps that require resource time can be a daunting process. Numerous systems have been developed—many that are industry-specific—to aid in this task.

New-Product or Service Development Decisions

Strategic decisions related to new-product or service development address such topics as market research, the product or service development process itself, and how the firm views itself in terms of new products or services, that is, is it an innovator or market leader or does it take on a more conservative follower role? These decisions have implications for cost, quality, flexibility, and response time, as summarized in Exhibit 4.14.

New product and service design processes dictate the product or service attributes that will provide the value customers seek. Matching the product and service design to the business's capabilities keeps *costs* in check.

New product or service development processes contribute to *quality* because they link product and service design with customer expectations. Without that link to customer needs, creating a product or service that actually met the needs of the customer would be a random event. For products and services, certainly the production process must ensure that quality levels are maintained, but with a poorly designed product or service, the best production process in the world wouldn't be able to produce quality.

Product and service design decisions have a long-term impact on *flexibility*. Robust designs enable the business to adapt in the future. Products that incorporate modular design schemes make it easier to integrate innovations when needed. Effective designs also make it easier to deal with different or changing suppliers of component parts.

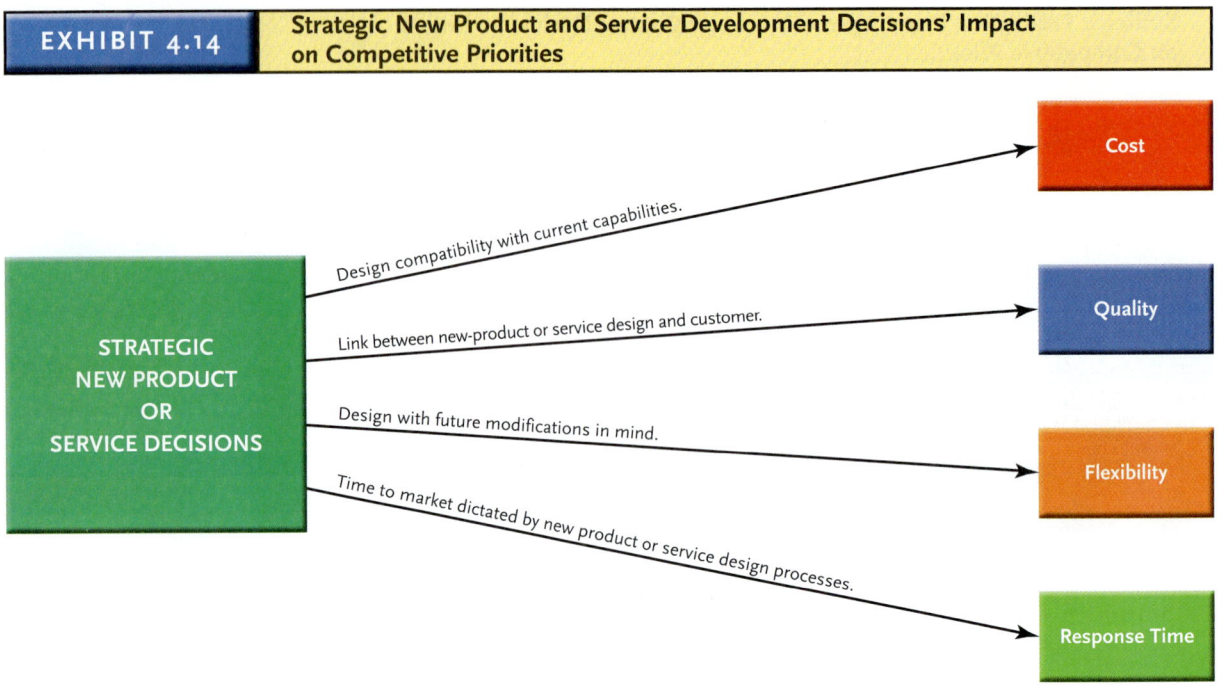

EXHIBIT 4.14 Strategic New Product and Service Development Decisions' Impact on Competitive Priorities

Flexibility can also be designed right into the processes that create services. Designing a process with steps that minimize sequence dependencies (the number of steps that must precede other steps), for example, makes the process much more flexible.

As technology has quickened the pace of innovation, product life cycles have been compressed. In this context, *response time* means responding to the market, not to an individual customer. A product life cycle is the amount of time from a product's introduction through declining demand to its disappearance because it is obsolete. These cycles are often short, so being first to market with a new product or service—or an innovation spun from an old one—is important to that product or service's financial success. The time it takes for a product or service to get from the idea stage to market is indirectly related to sales volume. In other words, the longer it takes to get the product or service to the market, the fewer units will be sold. This occurs not only because the product or service will become obsolete more quickly, but also because competitors will respond with innovations of their own.

Performance/Reward System Decisions

Strategic decisions related to performance and reward systems determine how good performance might be rewarded and how bad performance might be punished. The effects tend to be indirect but quite broad and far-reaching. Cost and quality are affected substantially by reward systems. Exhibit 4.15 shows the relationships between strategic performance and reward system decisions and these competitive priorities.

Costs are affected by reward system decisions because, in many cases, rewards are monetary. The issue isn't necessarily that the monetary rewards are given out, but it does raise the question of whether there is a return on that investment. Do the rewards result in higher retention of employees and greater levels of productivity? If so, the costs are justified by their effects. If not, the costs merely increase the cost of those employees.

The impact of the reward system on *quality* depends on the link between rewards and employee performance. Employees react to their work environment. The service–profit

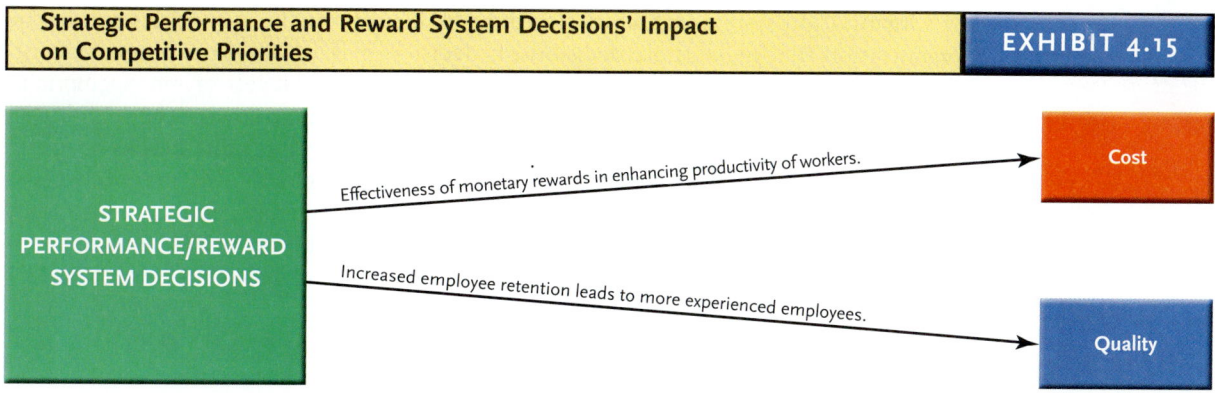

EXHIBIT 4.15 Strategic Performance and Reward System Decisions' Impact on Competitive Priorities

chain provides a model of how employee satisfaction leads to high quality in the service sector.[5] Satisfied employees are not as likely to leave to work for someone else, thus the rates of employee retention are higher. The higher retention rates result in the business having more experienced employees, and employees with greater levels of experience are able to provide higher levels of quality. These higher levels of quality result in improved customer satisfaction, higher levels of customer loyalty, and greater profit. Keep in mind, quality can be interpreted very generally. Employees' experience levels can have an impact on virtually anything they do. In a given situation, employee attitude and experience could have an impact on almost any value attribute.

Organization System Decisions

The design and structure of the organization itself dictates the chain of command, the flow of decisions, the span of responsibility of managers, and, in general, how major decisions are made and how quickly the firm can react. This issue is most significant for two time-related competitive priorities: flexibility and response time. Exhibit 4.16 summarizes the value attributes of significance for strategic organization system decisions.

Flexibility is valueless without speed. Customers who want something special or unique want to get a commitment for it within a reasonable length of time. Requests that must be passed through levels of management and then get signed off for approval take time that could be used producing what the customer wants. The customer wants a "yes" or a "no." Any delay in that response is time the customer could have been using to locate someone else to do the work. The result is that customers will go elsewhere for quick and more flexible response.

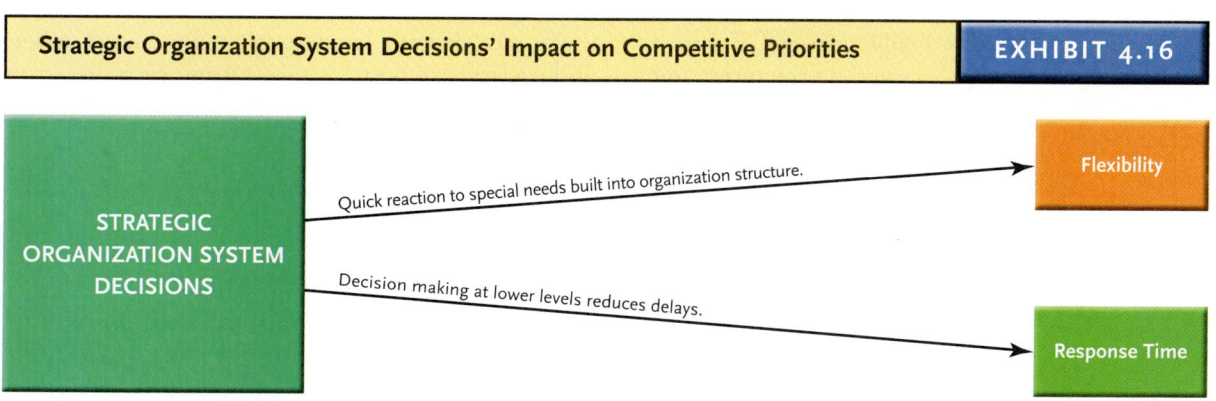

EXHIBIT 4.16 Strategic Organization System Decisions' Impact on Competitive Priorities

Organization systems influence decisions by identifying the authorities within the organization that make those decisions. Is decision-making authority given to front-line employees? Or must they seek approval from higher levels of management to make everyday decisions? The degree of autonomy given to lower-level employees plays a major role in the firm's *response time*. Decisions that must be passed up to higher levels of management invariably are in memo or email form, unread because the recipient is out, and add waiting time to the customer's experience. Autonomy can result in quick decisions and a customer that has greater confidence in the contact personnel.

COMPLEXITY OF RELATIONSHIPS AMONG STRATEGIC DECISIONS AND COMPETITIVE PRIORITIES

The previous sections provided a superficial, but broad, overview of links between strategic decision categories and competitive priorities of operations. Competitive priorities themselves, however, are not independent. Each has implications for others. Response time is related to flexibility. Flexibility can be related to cost. Quality can be related to dependability of delivery. And the list goes on and on. Some priorities can conflict with others. For example, increasing flexibility may increase costs. Reducing response time may increase costs. Improving dependability of delivery may reduce flexibility. It is not uncommon to have to make tradeoffs between these priorities. Decision categories aren't independent either. Structural decisions affect infrastructural decisions. Capacity decisions affect facility decisions. Facility decisions affect process technology decisions. Facility decisions affect organization system decisions. And they *all*, ultimately, will influence profitability measures.

A model of the relationships among and between all strategic decisions and competitive priorities very quickly resembles a plate of spaghetti. Identifying and discussing every one is overwhelming. The fact that the relationships are highly intertwined, combined with the fact that they all affect profitability, means three things:

- Managers must establish priorities and make decisions that are consistent with those priorities.
- Managers must have a view and understanding of the enterprise as a whole. The interactions between and among strategic decisions and competitive priorities are numerous, complex, and ignore departmental boundaries. Without an enterprise perspective, the law of unintended consequences will run rampant because the ability to anticipate the affect one change has on other aspects of the business will be missing.
- The relationships among some competitive priorities are well known and virtually universal. For many of these, models have been developed to aid in understanding the future impacts and tradeoffs among several strategic decisions.

The following sections examine two of the most popular models.

PROCESS AND VOLUME CHOICES: STRATEGIC TRADEOFFS FOR MANUFACTURERS

A common decision faced by many businesses provides an excellent example of how fundamental but long-term decisions can have broad impact across competitive priorities.

Companies are faced with a decision early in their life concerning the volume they intend to produce. Low-volume production of goods and services allows the firm to customize its products and services. Product variety is made possible by the flexibility of equipment. However, as higher production volumes and higher efficiencies are desired, products and services must become more standardized. Equipment needed must be able to produce at high speed. Typically this equipment doesn't have flexibility but rather is designed to complete a narrow selection of tasks very rapidly. The challenge for the business is to determine what customers will want—customization or standardization (and lower costs). For manufacturers, the choices on production volume and product variety have direct implications for the processes used. Processes designed for low volumes and high levels of customization employ specific types of equipment and require highly skilled employees. Process selection dictates equipment purchases and can even influence the facility selection process.

Flexibility usually means that a business must sacrifice any attempt at low cost per unit. Manufacturers that elect to produce high volumes employ production processes that use dedicated equipment and employees, and they compete well on a cost basis because the large volumes produced drive down costs per unit. These relationships between the type of manufacturing process used and the production volumes and level of customization desired are summarized in the product/process matrix shown in Exhibit 4.17.

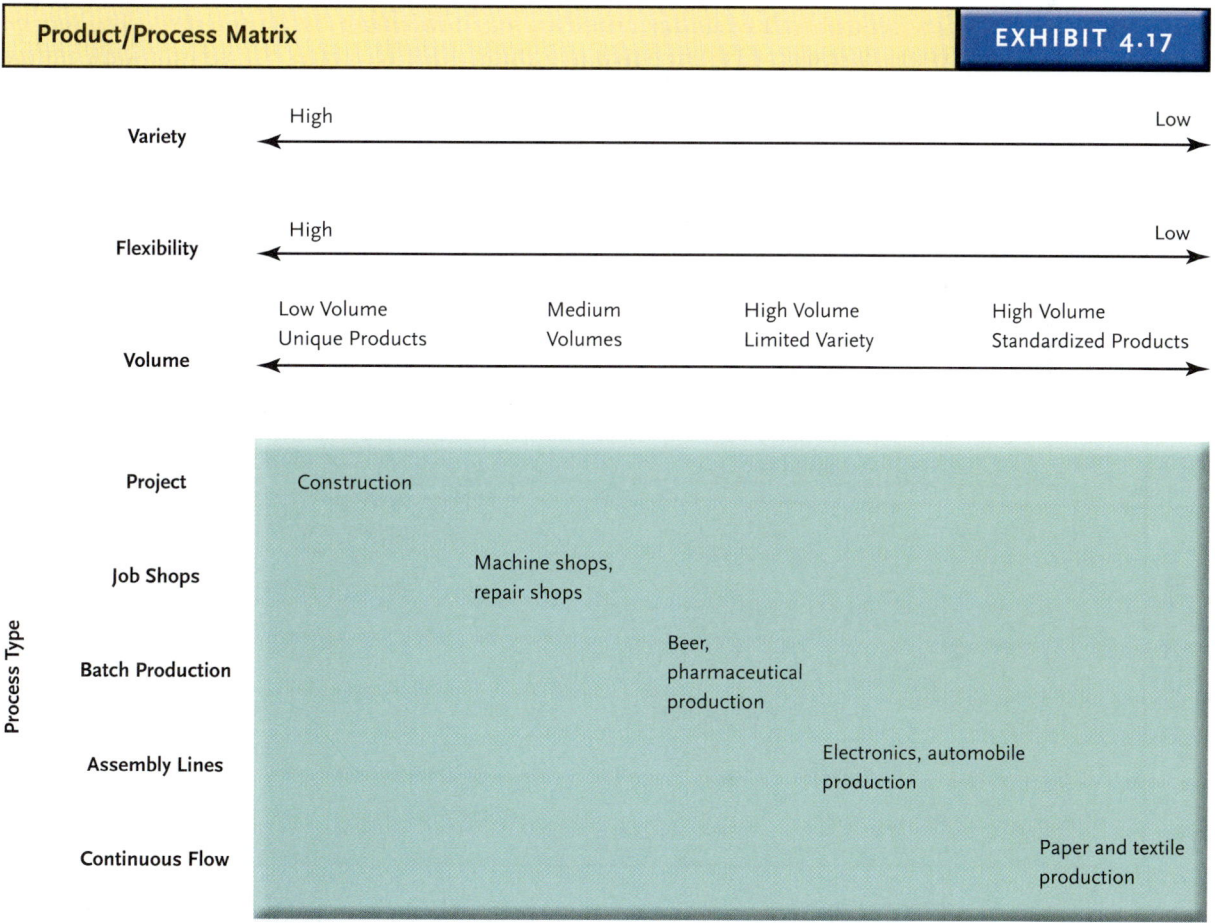

Product/Process Matrix — EXHIBIT 4.17

Source: Adapted from R. H. Hayes and S. C. Wheelwright, *Restoring Our Competitive Edge: Competing through Manufacturing* (New York: Wiley, 1984), p. 209.

The product/process matrix clearly shows how choices made on one issue dictate choices to be made elsewhere. These situations are extremely critical when choices involve long-term investments. Using the product/process matrix as an example, suppose the owner of a new business determines that customization of products will be necessary in order to compete. A job shop organization is designed that allows for significant amounts of customization. Equipment is purchased, and workers are trained. After several months of production, it becomes obvious that the great majority of customers select one of the three leading product configurations. Even though the capability to customize is present, the customers don't want it. They want lower prices. Unfortunately, the equipment, processes, facilities, and employee training investments have been geared toward customization. Given those resources, production at high volumes is impossible. A conversion to a continuous-flow process to produce high volumes of the three products on dedicated equipment would be a tremendous investment in new equipment and new employees. Reel Operations Video 4.2 provides an examination of the product/process matrix, with examples for each manufacturing type.

CUSTOMER CONTACT AND PROCESS EFFICIENCY: STRATEGIC TRADEOFFS FOR SERVICES

Services also utilize customer needs to aid in making strategic decisions. The service system design matrix, presented in Exhibit 4.18, illustrates the relationships among several key factors of customer interactions.

EXHIBIT 4.18 — Service System Design Matrix

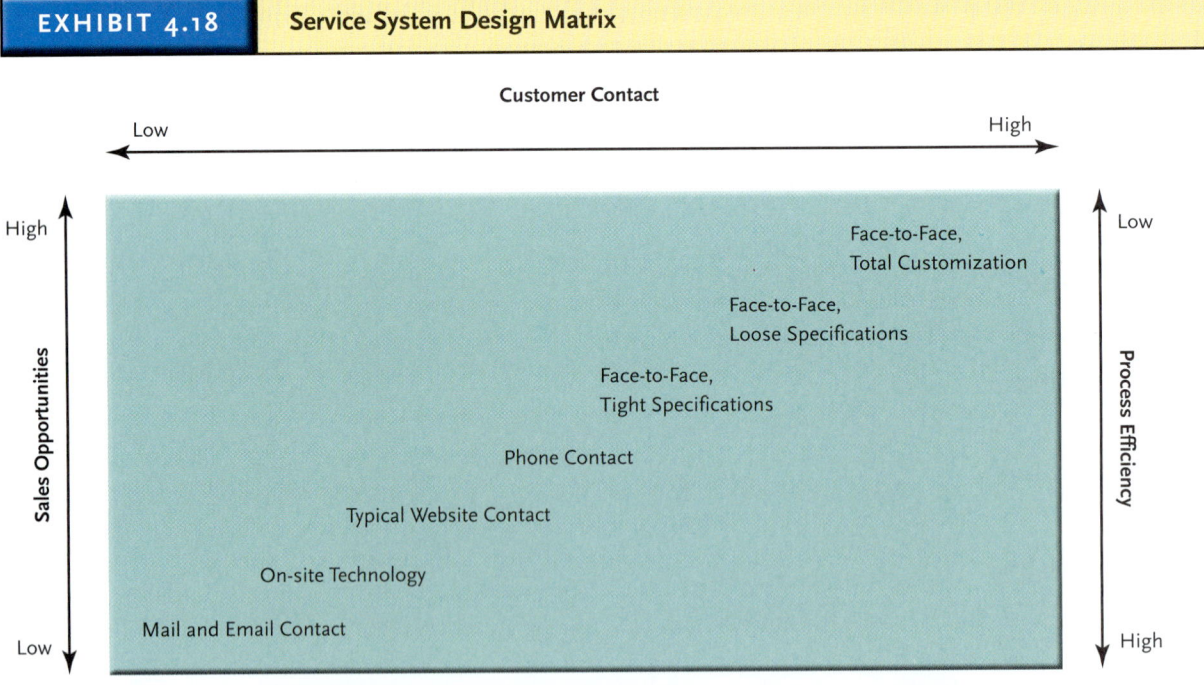

Source: Adapted from R. B. Chase and N. J. Aquilano, *Production and Operations Management* 6th ed. (Homewood, IL: Irwin, 1992), p. 123.

For a service provider, customer contact has two significant effects—one positive and one negative. First, the more customer contact, the greater the opportunity for service providers to make additional sales to the customer. Second, as customer contact increases, efficiency and productivity of the service process declines. Services must trade off their desires for efficient production processes with opportunities for sales similar to the way manufacturers must trade off flexibility and product variety for costs. The service system design matrix provides guidance for making service delivery decisions in ways that balance the desire for sales opportunities and the need for process efficiency. Starting at the lowest contact delivery system (mail or email contact) and progressing all the way to three forms of face-to-face contact, efficiency is decreased as sales opportunities increase. Face-to-face delivery offers alternatives from very tightly controlled "tight specification" interaction to wide open "total customization." Reel Operations Video 4.3 shows how First Chicago Bank capitalizes on all aspects of the service system design matrix.

Models have been created to assist managers in making the types of tradeoff decisions necessary in strategic planning. In many cases, the relationships among competitive priorities and resources are well known and predictable. In those cases the past experiences of businesses can be very beneficial.

CHAPTER SUMMARY

A firm's competitiveness rests on its ability to match functional strategies—and the day-to-day decisions they guide—to business strategies so that they can successfully compete. For operations decisions, this means recognizing the value attributes important to customers as well as the competitive priorities of cost, quality, dependability of delivery, flexibility, and response time and making strategic decisions that enhance competitive priorities.

In this chapter, the relationships among value attributes, competitive priorities for operations, and strategic decision categories were examined. Understanding these relationships is a responsibility of managers. The resources controlled by operations, including employees, equipment, inventory, and facilities, require a tremendous investment for both services and manufacturers. The return on these investments comes only through customer purchases, which result from a close match between the value resources create and the value the customers want. This is determined substantially by the way the firm capitalizes on its resources to position itself competitively in the marketplace.

The relationships among competitive priorities and operations resources are so numerous and complex that understanding all of them is a daunting task. Failure to consider them, however, can result in unexpected consequences of decisions. The large number of relationships makes prioritization critical as a means of focusing management attention on the most important issues. Experience has shown that the relationships among some competitive priorities and some resources are very important and very predictable. In many cases models have been developed to aid managers in understanding these relationships. The chapter included two such models. The first, the product/process matrix, was used to illustrate the importance of strategic decisions in creating opportunities and establishing limitations for what manufacturers can do to meet customer expectations. The second, the service system design matrix, was introduced to provide an example of similar tradeoffs that are required in the strategic decision-making processes of services.

KEY TERMS

business strategy, 99
competitive priorities, 108
core competencies, 114
corporate strategy, 99
cost leader strategy, 101
design capacity, 109
differentiation strategy, 101
focus strategy, 101
functional strategy, 100
line of visibility, 111
order loser, 101
order qualifier, 101
order winner, 101
protective capacity, 110

REVIEW QUESTIONS

1. Define and compare corporate, business, and functional strategies.
2. How are business strategies related to customers' value attributes?
3. Why is it important for a company to identify strategic priorities?
4. Describe the five competitive priorities for operations. How are they important to the profitability measures of profit margin, return on assets, and return on equity?
5. What are Porter's three strategies? How do they affect operations decisions?
6. For each of the strategic structural and infrastructural decision categories, describe the relationships to competitive priorities.
7. What is the law of unintended consequences? Why is it relevant to operations strategy?
8. Summarize how each strategic decision category affects competitive priorities.
9. Describe the product/process matrix. What does it exemplify? What are the primary tradeoffs it identifies?
10. What are the primary tradeoffs identified by the service system design matrix?

DISCUSSION QUESTIONS

1. Select a business that is familiar to you. Identify decisions it must make within each of the structural and infrastructural decision categories. How important are those decisions? What impact does each have on the firm's potential for success?
2. From your own work experience, provide examples of how performance/reward system decisions have had an impact on the strategic success of a business. Have they encouraged you to perform in a manner consistent with the business's goals? Why or why not?
3. Identify, in several businesses you frequent, the competitive priorities that appear to be most important. Rank them based on their importance.
4. How do you think organization system decisions have changed as a result of Internet technologies? Which businesses that you utilize depend heavily on this technology? Could they exist without it?
5. For businesses you frequent, what are the most important value attributes offered? Do all of the businesses you frequent emphasize the same value attributes? Are the attributes you prioritize the highest offered by all businesses you frequent?
6. From work experience you have had, identify situations where increased customer contact reduced efficiency. What tradeoff was being made that resulted in management not eliminating the customer interaction?

SELECTED RESOURCES

Porter, M. *Competitive Advantage*. New York: The Free Press, 1985.

Hill, Terry. *Manufacturing Strategy*. Burr Ridge, IL: McGraw-Hill/Irwin, 2000.

Fitzsimmons, J. A., and Fitzsimmons, M. J. *Service Management*. Boston: Irwin/McGraw-Hill, 2000.

ENDNOTES

1. S. C. Wheelwright, "Manufacturing Strategy: Defining the Missing Link," *Strategic Management Journal* 5 (January–March 1984), pp. 77–91.
2. M. E. Porter, *Competitive Advantage* (New York: Free Press, 1985).
3. T. Hill, *Manufacturing Strategy* 3rd Edition (Burr Ridge, IL: McGraw-Hill/Irwin, 2000), pp. 35–39.
4. "As G-8 Leaders Meet, U.S. Has Pivotal in Leading Recovery," *The Wall Street Journal*, July 20, 2001, pp. A1, A4.
5. J. L. Heskett, T. O. Jones, G. W. Loveman, W. E. Sasser Jr., and L. A. Schlessinger, "Putting the Service–Profit Chain to Work," *Harvard Business Review*, March–April 1994, pp. 164–174; J. A. Fitzsimmons and M. J. Fitzsimmons, *Service Management*, 3rd Edition (New York: Irwin/McGraw-Hill, 2000), pp. 216–218.

OperationsNow.com LEARNING ACTIVITIES

CHAPTER ENHANCEMENT RESOURCES
- Esources
- Reel Operations Video Clips
- Interactive Models
- Excel Tutors
- Supplementary Readings
- Links to Operations On Site Companies

OM EXPLORATION
- Check It Out
- OM in Action
- Online Business Tours
- Letters from the Top
- Putting It All Together: Virtual Case Studies
- Additional Reading

UNIT 2

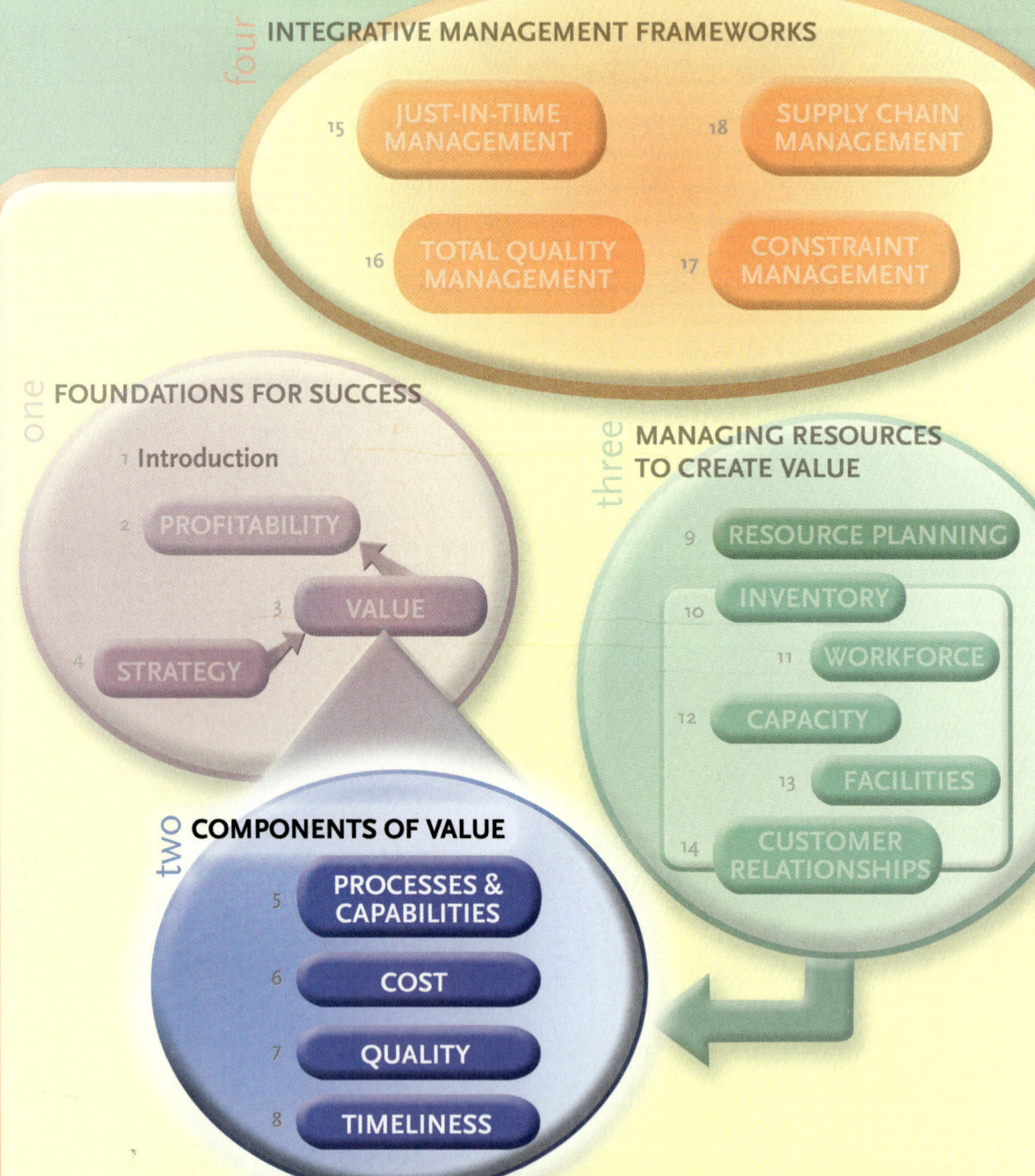

Components of Value

Chapter 5:
Processes and Capabilities

Chapter 6:
Cost

Chapter 7:
Quality

Chapter 8:
Timeliness

INTRODUCTION

Value, as described in Unit 1, is the fundamental motivation for customers purchasing products and services. Customers define value by the way they prioritize a variety of possible product and service attributes—that is, by how their priorities are satisfied. From the business's perspective, value is created from some basic components. These components of value, which form the chapter topics within this unit, are processes and capabilities, cost, quality, and timeliness. Processes and capabilities create the characteristics that define the products or services produced and many of the benefits customers receive. Costs, on the other hand, are incurred as materials are purchased, employees are paid, and facilities are maintained. Quality is embodied in the way the product or service satisfies the customers' expectations. Timeliness contributes to meeting customer expectations regarding when products and services are provided. These components of value often form the basis for compromises known as "tradeoffs."

In the resource/profit model, processes and capabilities are the first component of value. Processes, from the producer's perspective, provide an organizing structure for the resources used to create value. The business's capabilities, on the other hand, define the type of value that can be created. This chapter delves into the heart of operations: the processes and capabilities that give rise to value. It focuses on what the business controls: the way resources are used to create value.

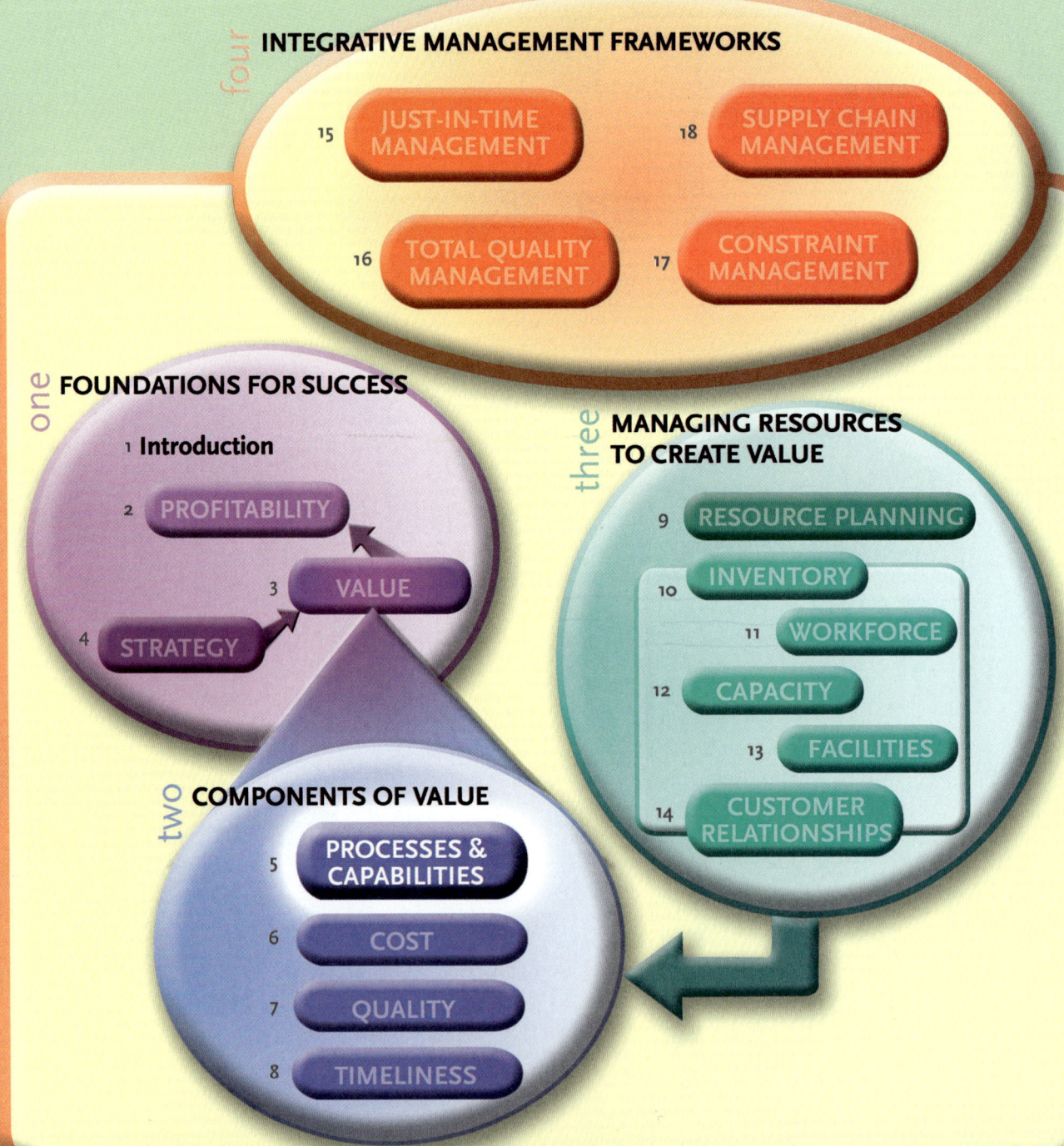

CHAPTER 5

Processes and Capabilities

LEARNING OBJECTIVES

Upon completion of Chapter 5, you should be able to

- Distinguish between capabilities and processes.

- Compare the strengths and weaknesses of process-oriented, product-oriented, and cellular layouts.

- Describe the continuum of choices related to production volume and the alternatives available for linking to customer demand.

- Explain how the four phases of quality function deployment (QFD) are used to link service and products to customer expectations.

- Describe process improvement approaches such as business process analysis, reengineering, concurrent engineering, and poka-yoke.

- Construct a service blueprint.

- Describe what is meant by a capability chain.

Introduction: Converting Resources to Value
Capabilities Versus Processes
Order Qualifiers and Order Winners
General Layout Decisions: Strategic Decisions for Process Requirements
Process Improvement Tools
Service Blueprinting
Capability Chains
Chapter Summary

INTERNET RESOURCES

 Excel Tutors provide annotated spreadsheets for every solved problem that automatically load Excel.

 Esources provide an online version of the more traditional boxed insert.

 Reel Videos provide streaming video footage for company applications of chapter concepts.

 Interactive Models provide an experimental environment for quantitative concepts and simulations.

INTRODUCTION

Converting Resources to Value

Value is not just lying around to be picked up by a savvy 17-year-old entrepreneur who already has an initial public offering (IPO) and exit strategy in mind. If value were that easy to come by, no one would be willing to pay for it. When it comes to value, there is very little in the way of low-hanging fruit. Value must be created. Once in a while it goes unrecognized until some dealmeister sees it, markets it, and makes a billion, but in 99.99 percent of the cases, it results from hard work and late nights. Someone has an idea for a product or service, but that's the easy part. The tough part is coming up with ways to produce that product or service so that it will not only satisfy the high-priority value attributes of the targeted customers, but also accomplish that goal at a cost that leaves room for profit. This is the challenge of designing and managing the processes and capabilities of the firm. As the resource/profit model in Exhibit 5.1 illustrates, the first component of value consists of the business's processes and capabilities. Without them, the business simply owns resources; it doesn't use them to create value.

If you can't increase the value added to make the product or service profitable, you must decrease the cost to add it. Even Amazon.com still has difficulty with that part of the equation. If you can't do either, the story's over—just as it has started and ended for thousands of companies in the past five years. In this chapter, we look specifically at the processes and capabilities that generate value.

CAPABILITIES VERSUS PROCESSES

The differences between capabilities and processes are sometimes subtle, but it is important to understand them because any attempt to improve value must be focused on the correct target. In general, capabilities define what a business can do. For example, a company might be able to deliver products quickly. A company might be able to design and construct skateboard parks. A company might be able to provide excellent financial or tax advice. These are all capabilities. The capabilities are the firm's ability to create an outcome that customers value. Processes provide an organizing structure for the use of resources that can create these capabilities.

It is important to recognize the difference between capabilities and processes because matching customer needs and identifying problems depend on it. Perhaps the capability matches the customer needs but the process doesn't create it effectively or the capability is wrong even though the process is effective. In a sense, customers buy the capability from the producer because they don't have it themselves. Customers generally don't care about the process required, because they don't see it. They're concerned only about the results. That's what they want to buy. In many cases, a single process isn't enough to create value for a customer. Several processes must be combined to create the value. Processes can be viewed as the components of capabilities, just as small parts are the components of finished products.

As an example, let's take a simple idea for a business, then backtrack through all of the necessary requirements. This simple analysis works quite well as a means of distinguishing between capabilities and processes.

Suppose a local entrepreneur wants to fill a void in the town's food service market with a very quick pizza delivery service. She wants to guarantee pizza delivery within 20 minutes of a phone order. That is her differentiating strategy, and it has serious implications for the way her business must operate. From a value attribute perspective, she's electing to compete on the basis of *response time* and *convenience*. She hopes

CHAPTER 5 Processes and Capabilities 133

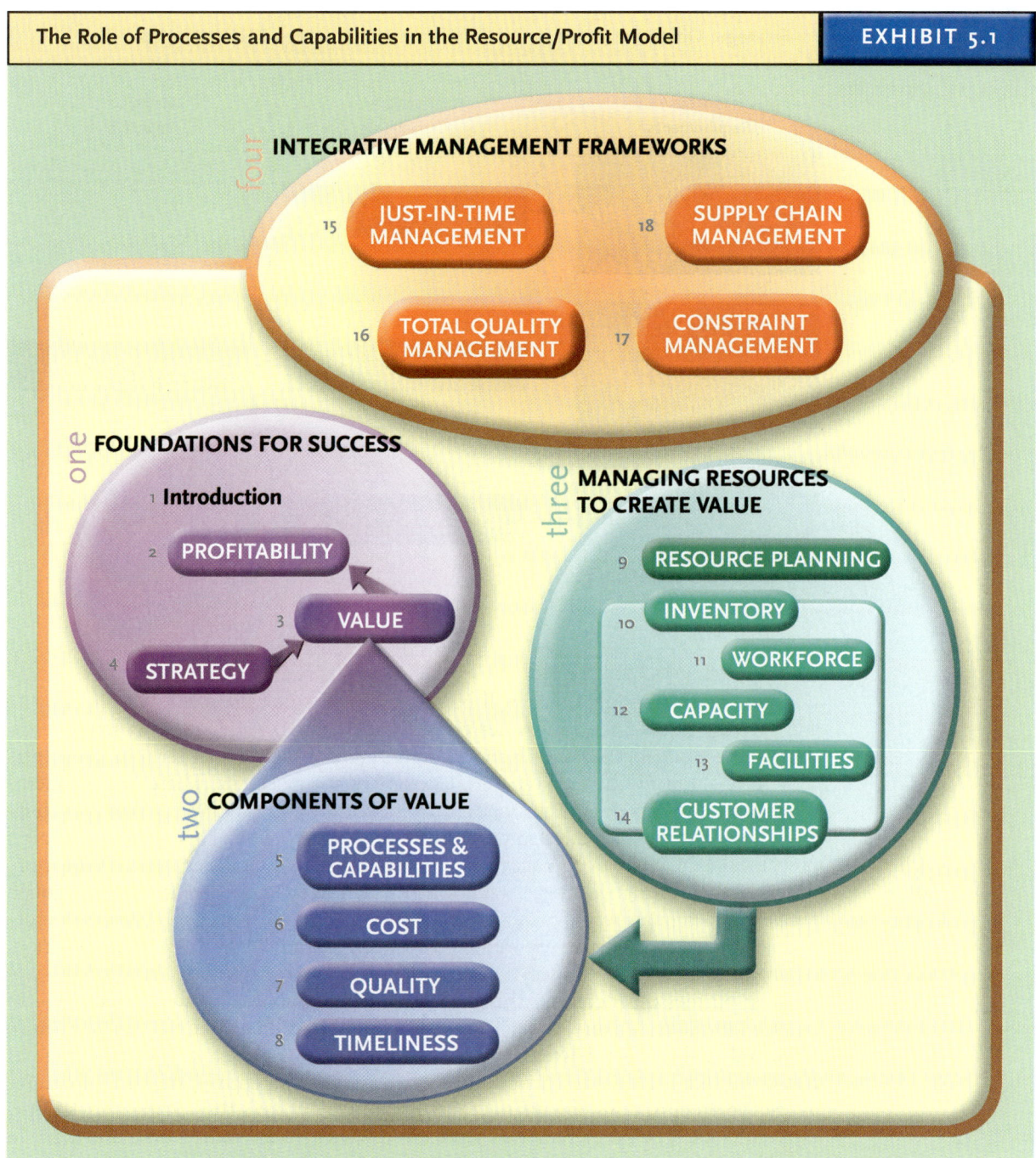

EXHIBIT 5.1 The Role of Processes and Capabilities in the Resource/Profit Model

that a delivery that is faster than everyone else will differentiate her business enough from competitors to gain substantial market share.

If the issue of "quick response time" is examined further and broken down into its components for the pizza business, we can identify three capabilities that are prerequisites to accomplishing our strategic objectives. These prerequisites are presented in Exhibit 5.2. The capabilities of fast preparation, fast baking, and fast delivery have significant impact on the process components of each. The sum must be less than 20

> **EXHIBIT 5.2** Strategic Objectives versus Capabilities versus Process Requirements

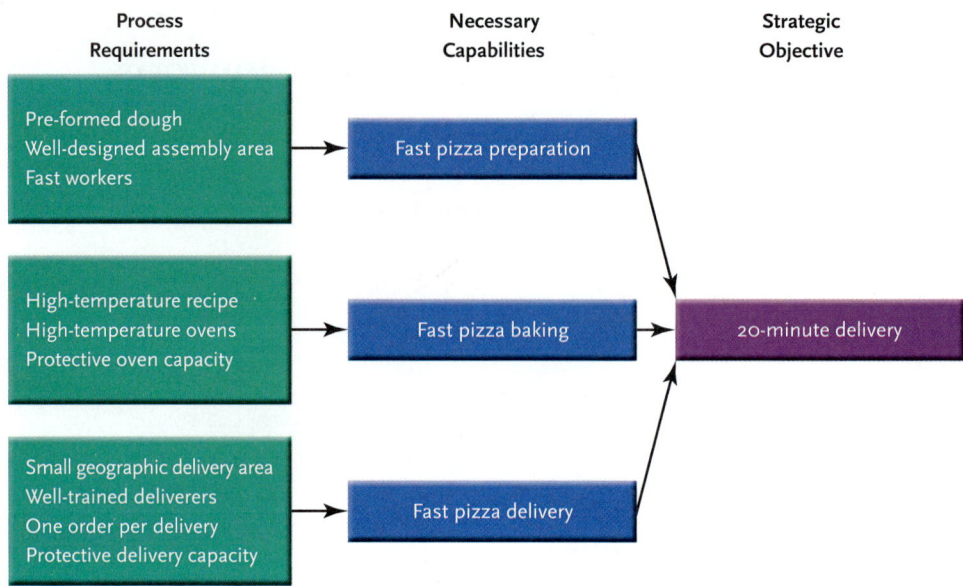

minutes. The component that will be the most difficult to control will probably be the delivery time, since the owner can't control traffic. As evident in Exhibit 5.2, each of these capabilities entails some commitments that are long term in nature and that have implications for the initial design of the business. These commitments relate directly to several of the strategic decision areas presented in the previous chapter. Those that are particularly important in this case would be capacity (such as pizza preparation capacity, oven capacity, deliverer capacity), facilities (such as location, pizza prep area design), process technology (such as oven temperature, pizza dough recipe), and human resources (such as worker speed and training). These resources will be utilized to perform very well-defined tasks that make up the pizza preparation, baking, and delivery processes.

Most businesses, including this one, have more than one strategic objective. In addition to quick delivery, the pizza business might also have an objective relative to price and quality. Fast deliveries aren't worth much if the pizza is priced too high or if it tastes like cardboard. Capabilities related to these objectives are also important, as are the process requirements necessary to actually possess those capabilities. They might include specific ingredients, suppliers, reward systems, and so on. As evident in Exhibit 5.2, each capability can be broken down into its process requirements. At the strategic level, the capability and process requirements involve significant up-front costs and would prohibit frequent change.

For some firms, the process is so critical to their success that they actually patent the process to prevent others from using it. This is particularly true when there is no way to effectively keep the process secret. But even with those breakthrough processes, other product and service attributes are necessary. The following section takes a closer look at the phenomenon of differentiation and how it impacts purchase decisions. Esource 5.1 provides an example of a business that is dependent on an unusual process.

> ### Business Method Patents: Good or Bad?
>
> Business method patents have been hotly debated since an appeals court validated them in 1998. During their first year of availability, 2,821 were issued. The next year 7,800 were issued. In the fiscal year 2000, the U.S. Patent and Trademark Office issued only 899. The Patent Office now requires a "second pair of eyes" to see business method patent applications and has also begun to send out examiners to corporations to find out about the processes. This is an attempt to identify which ones are obvious and routine and therefore not eligible for patents. These steps have resulted in patent applications being returned with questions.
>
> The debate has two distinct sides. The efforts to tighten up the issuance of business method patents are criticized by those who favor looser business patent approval processes. They claim that a patent is a patent, and these new examination procedures applied only to business method applications are, in effect, changing the law. On the other side of the argument are those who claim that many business method patents are issued for methods that are simply computerizing obvious tasks that were previously done with pencil and paper. Amazon's One Click Ordering has been a target. Barnes & Noble, for example, appealed a court decision so it could continue to use its Express Lane feature. The result of the scrutiny is that in the final quarter of 2000, only 36 percent of the business method patent applications were approved, compared to an approval rate on all patent applications of 72 percent for 2000.
>
> Clearly a business method is different from a new-product design. Many suggestions have been put forth for changing the business method patent to make it distinct. For example, a patent is good for 17 years. There have been suggestions for business method patents to be for much shorter periods of time. The average patent approval process takes 26 months. For a business method, particularly one that is technology-related, a 26-month delay could make the method obsolete before the company got the protection it sought.
>
> ---
>
> Source: "Fewer Patents on Methods Get Clearance," *The Wall Street Journal,* March 21, 2001, pp. A3, A6; "Raising the Bar on Business Patents," *BusinessWeek.com,* April 2, 2001; "In Business This Week: Patent Pounding at Amazon," *BusinessWeek.com,* February 26, 2001.

ORDER QUALIFIERS AND ORDER WINNERS

Customers have many expectations of the services and products they purchase. One way to look at a customer's purchasing decision is by identifying order qualifiers and order winners. Recall from Chapter 2 that a purchase decision is made by comparing the value of the alternatives. In addition to comparing overall value, customers will also have some minimum expectations to be met before they will even consider a particular alternative. In other words, some characteristics must be present just to get a product placed on the list of alternatives to consider. These product or service attributes were described in Chapter 4 as order qualifiers.[1] Order qualifiers may vary from one customer to another, just as the prioritization of value attributes varies from one customer to another. Order qualifiers are necessary but not sufficient to win a customer.

Once an alternative meets the order qualifiers necessary for further consideration, attributes known as order winners come into play. As described in Chapter 4, order winners are those attributes that make the difference for a particular customer. In our pizza delivery example, the owner is obviously seeking customers who will view the short delivery time as a quality attribute that is important enough to be an order winner. If,

> ### Minimills Make Money, Not Steel
>
> The U.S. steel industry has seen rough times for the past decade, with 19 mills (25 percent of the entire U.S. capacity) filing for bankruptcy since 1998.
>
> Integrated mills, which produce virgin metal from iron ore, have suffered the most. Minimills, however, utilize a high percentage of scrap in their production and typically operate at lower cost levels. Even many minimills are having difficulty maintaining levels of profitability, but those that can control raw material costs, labor costs, and electricity costs succeed.
>
> One company in particular, Steel Dynamics, has been notably successful. Its operating profit is $55 per ton produced, $12 more than its largest competitor. Its profits increased 36 percent from 1999 to 2000, with only a 12 percent increase in sales. Steel Dynamics's initial decision to focus on high-margin products meant that it would produce higher-quality steel and thinner steel. It endeavored to be the low-cost producer of automotive-quality steel, with 33 percent of its output going to automotive uses (door panels, frames, and chassis). Steel Dynamics has negotiated competitive contracts for scrap steel as well as power.
>
> Much of Steel Dynamics's success can be traced to the efficiency of its manufacturing processes. Scrap is turned into new steel in about two hours. After 55 minutes in a furnace, bringing the temperature of the scrap to 3,000 degrees, ladles of molten steel are tested by technicians and alloys are added. Ladles are then emptied and the molten steel flows into molds of a continuous caster. It exits the mold with an outside surface that is solid. Breaking the cooled surface, at this point, can result in molten steel all over equipment. The resulting cleanup costs about $10,000. A continuous ribbon of steel gradually moves through the mold and slabs are cut to length. After being processed through a second furnace, steel slabs move to rolling processes to flatten the steel to sheets as thin as 0.011 inch. Cold-rolled steel like that of Steel Dynamics is priced at $100–$150 per ton more than hot-rolled steel.
>
> Steel Dynamics's processes are complex and critical. Behind the company's success lies a hard-working and motivated workforce. Various incentives are in place to ensure that employees do everything possible to maintain the processes. When production objectives are met, employees receive a weekly bonus of $10 per hour above the $10 per hour base. In addition, meeting other objectives can add another $2. Annual profit-sharing awards also contribute to employee compensation. They averaged $6700 in 2000. For Steel Dynamics, the capability of being the low-cost producer of high-quality steel is clearly the result of combining two resource groups: very efficient processes supported by an extremely motivated workforce.
>
> Source: "America's Elite Factories," *Fortune*, September 3, 2001, pp. 206A–206L.

however, she fails to meet the order qualifiers for that customer, her business will no longer be considered by customers, and fast delivery won't matter.

The role of order qualifiers and order winners can change as markets mature. Price is often an important order winner in mature markets. Unfortunately for the producer, competing on the basis of price can often have detrimental effects on the bottom line. However, when all competitors are essentially equal on such quality measures as dependability of delivery and response time, price may be the only remaining value attribute that differentiates the rivals.

For many products, service-oriented attributes have become order winners. Desktop computers are a good example. For the most part, a computer is a computer, virtually indistinguishable once issues like memory, hard disk size, processor speed, and accessories included are resolved. However, if something else of value is added, like after-the-sale on-site service, the computer is different. In today's economy, services have become a very viable order winner for many products. It is not uncommon for order winners to gradually turn into order qualifiers as competitors and the markets embrace them, however. In our pizza example, for instance, if competitors adapted, so that most were able to deliver in 20 minutes, quick delivery could become an order qualifier for many customers. Our entrepreneur would need a new differentiating capability for an order winner.

Domino's Pizza would undoubtedly be a strong competitor of our example business. It has been a major competitor in the pizza delivery business for decades because it continues to differentiate itself, even as the market changes. Over the years, Domino's has adapted to various order winners. Initially, it focused on short delivery times. As that became an order qualifier, it found other ways to differentiate the products and service. Esource 5.2 provides an example of a capability that creates an order winner.

In most businesses, the capabilities required to create order qualifiers and order winners will mean that some initial decisions must be made relative to several strategic decision areas. Some long-term decisions are so fundamental that they must be considered for all producers of products and services, whether they sell to business or consumers. Reel Operations Video 5.1 examines how McDonald's redesigned its entire operation to add a critical capability.

GENERAL LAYOUT DECISIONS: STRATEGIC DECISIONS FOR PROCESS REQUIREMENTS

The decision as to how facilities will be arranged, known as the layout decision, is critical to enhancing or limiting the business's range of capabilities. For most businesses, the general layout decision is a strategic decision that has implications for the type of equipment the business will purchase, the design of the facility, and the skill level of the employees. This decision has long-term cost implications, so it should not be taken lightly or with the attitude that if it doesn't succeed, it can be changed. Such a change would be very costly to make.

Layout Alternatives

General facility layout decisions are often made in response to the firm's specific strategic objectives. Like many decisions, there are numerous alternatives involving general layout, but examining the two opposing ends of the continuum provides a good starting point. These concepts were introduced in the Chapter 4 discussion of the product/process matrix. The two layout extremes are product-oriented layout and process-oriented layout. In brief, a **product-oriented layout** provides the necessary resources in a fixed sequence that matches the sequence of the steps required to produce the product or service. The **process-oriented layout** provides a layout that is organized by the function of each resource, allowing steps to be done in any sequence. Let's take a closer look at each alternative.

Product-Oriented Layouts

Product-oriented layouts are designed to be efficient producers of goods and services when there is little or no variation from one item to the next. This kind of layout lets the business take advantage of repetitive tasks to gain efficiency, processing speed, and low cost per unit. Production speed is enhanced by breaking bigger tasks into smaller ones and assigning them to more workstations. If high volumes are likely, and low cost per unit is important, a product-oriented layout is probably a good alternative. Product-oriented layouts are very common in high-volume manufacturing of standardized products such as automobiles, boats, electronics, food, or other products produced in a uniform manner with little or no customization. They are common in high-volume standardized services where high volumes of customers must be processed and all customers will have the same processing needs: driver's license offices, health clinics, university registration offices, and so on.

Conceptually, a product-oriented layout can be viewed as a linear series of processing steps, as illustrated in Exhibit 5.3, which shows a hypothetical manufacturer laid out in a product-oriented fashion. Each product goes through the steps in the same sequence.

Despite its benefits, the product-oriented layout has several disadvantages. First is its lack of flexibility. Customization is virtually impossible in such a layout. Each unit being processed undergoes essentially the same processing steps. Although the layout does provide low cost per unit and high volume capability, the repetitive nature of the jobs associated with the layout can result in problems. Employees often complete the same task over and over, which can lead to boredom, job dissatisfaction, and potential quality problems. Greater volume is obtained by increasing the number of workstations or by reducing the amount of time at each workstation. That translates into chopping the work tasks into smaller and smaller pieces, making the contribution of each workstation a smaller proportion of the total production, which makes the work even more repetitive and less likely to seem meaningful. As in most decisions, tradeoffs must be made when considering the product-oriented layout alternative. The tradeoffs can be viewed from the perspective of the value attributes supported by this layout and those that would actually be reduced by it.

Process-Oriented Layouts

The process-oriented layout, sometimes called the **functional layout,** often provides advantages that the product-oriented layout lacks. The key advantages it affects are flexibility and customization. In a process-oriented layout, resources are arranged by function. This is often implemented in the form of a departmentalized organization. Each department performs a specific function. In a process-oriented layout, each functional department has a range of capabilities limited only by the extent of the

EXHIBIT 5.3 Conceptual View of a Product-Oriented Layout

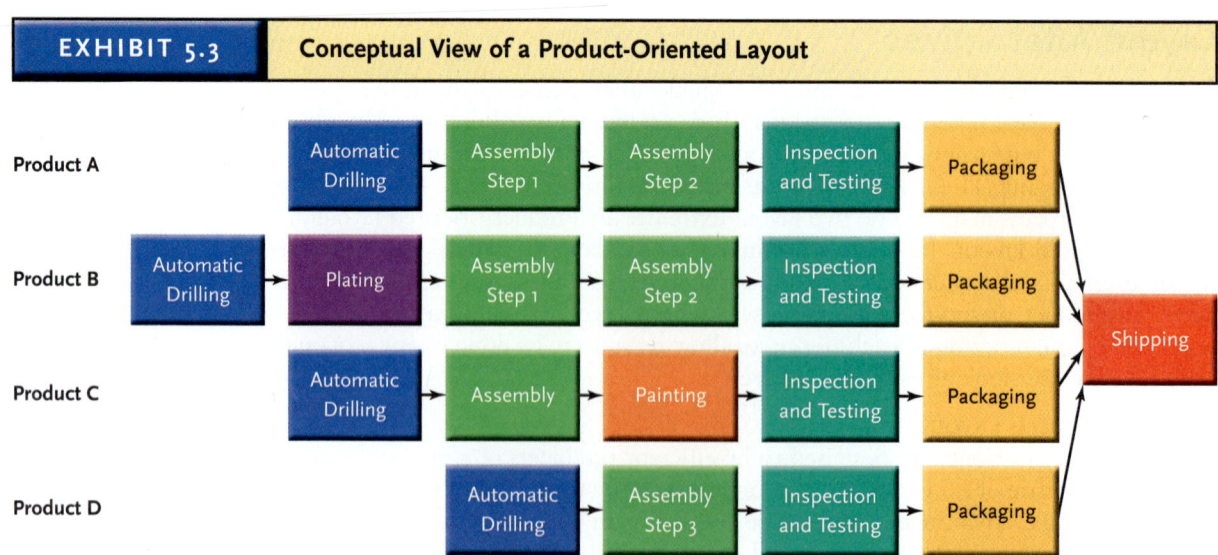

department's resources. Flexibility and the ability to customize products or services are accomplished by being able to route products or customers through the functional departments in any sequence desired. Manufacturers and businesses requiring a great degree of flexibility commonly use this layout. Service examples include hospitals, government administrative offices, large legal firms, and banks. Manufacturers that use this approach customize products and include such industries as custom machining businesses, custom furniture manufacturing, and custom electronics and chip manufacturers.

Exhibit 5.4 provides a conceptual view of a process-oriented layout for the same manufacturer presented in Exhibit 5.3. Obviously, even though similar products might be made, capabilities would be quite different. Equipment that can perform tasks with the flexibility needed to customize is available in a variety of types. The most advanced capabilities are offered by computerized numerically controlled (CNC) machines. Systems containing CNC machines are often referred to as flexible manufacturing systems (FMSs). Despite the range of flexibility within each functional department, job shops often produce batches of each product to gain some economies of scale. Washburn Guitar production is used in Reel Operations Video 5.2 to provide an example of a process-oriented layout.

www
OperationsNow
.com

As compared to product-oriented layouts, weaknesses associated with process-oriented layouts include a higher cost per unit and less consistency from unit to unit or customer to customer. The high cost per unit results from lower efficiencies, inability to take advantage of economies of scale, and costs of moving materials between departments. The nature of this layout requires judgments to be made by employees, as customizing is done in each functional department. As would be expected, better judgment comes only with employees who are more highly skilled, and such employees are generally more expensive to employ than their unskilled counterparts.

Conceptual View of a Process-Oriented Layout EXHIBIT 5.4

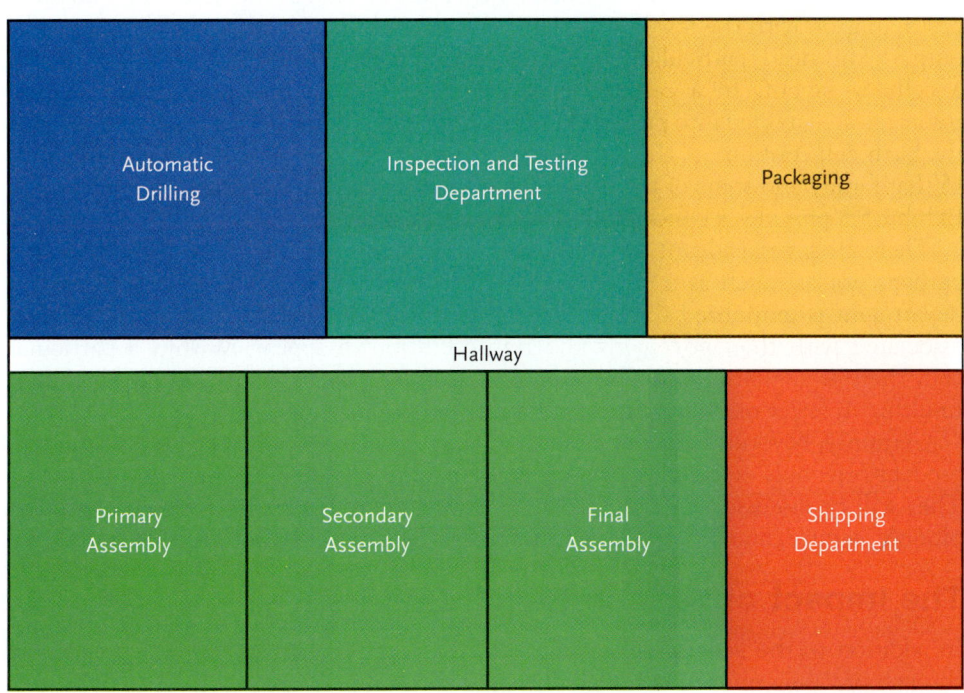

> High-volume manufacturing and assembly often depend on a product-oriented layout to maintain required production volume and low costs. In the manufacture and assembly of medical products, product-oriented layouts also contribute to the necessary consistency from one product to the next. Here we see how a product-oriented layout is used to assemble standard procedure trays with the necessary medications, sterile pads, and syringes.

www
OperationsNow
.com

Another weakness of this layout is transportation time and cost of moving customers from one department to another. A related drawback is that customers or products arriving at or moving into a department may have to wait. Time spent waiting can become problematic, particularly for services. Customers place a high level of importance on the brevity of waiting time when evaluating a business's quality. The company in Esource 5.3 uses a process-oriented layout to gain flexibility.

Mixing Product-Oriented and Process-Oriented Layouts

Many businesses find that either a pure product- or process-oriented layout doesn't exactly fit their processing needs. They need a compromise. Some of their customers may need standard services or products that must be produced in high volume and at low cost to meet demand; others may require versatility and customization. In some situations, a new product or service may be produced in a process that requires great flexibility. However, as the business's managers learn more about the market, they find that much of their demand can be satisfied with a few alternatives, and that only a small portion of the market requires customization. In many cases a portion of the processes can be designed utilizing a process-oriented layout while the remainder uses a product-oriented one.

The more difficult scenario is when a firm must be able to integrate flexibility and customization with the low cost per unit and efficient production of high volumes of output. This need, particularly in manufacturing settings, has led to the evolution of a **cellular layout**. In a cellular layout, products whose processes require similar resources are grouped into product families. One cell is designed for each product family. Each cell contains all the resources or workcenters necessary to produce products in that family and some of the cells have resources that are duplicated in other cells. Exhibit 5.5 provides a conceptual view of a cellular layout.

There are several advantages to the cellular layout. First, it has flexibility, although perhaps not as much as a process-oriented layout. Movement from department to department is minimized since all needed resources are present in the cell, so costs associated with that movement and transportation disappear. Within a particular cell, there is similarity among the processes of the product family group members, resulting in fewer machine setups and increased productivity.

Certainly, beyond the general decision that evaluates needs for process-oriented, product-oriented, or cellular layout, more specific layout decisions must be made. They will be discussed in Chapter 13. As an initial and strategic decision related to product, service, and process design, however, the general layout decision is critical.

The Impact of Volume Requirements

In addition to the general layout decision, the way products or customers will flow through processes must be considered when determining initial process design. Process

Conceptual View of a Cellular Layout EXHIBIT 5.5

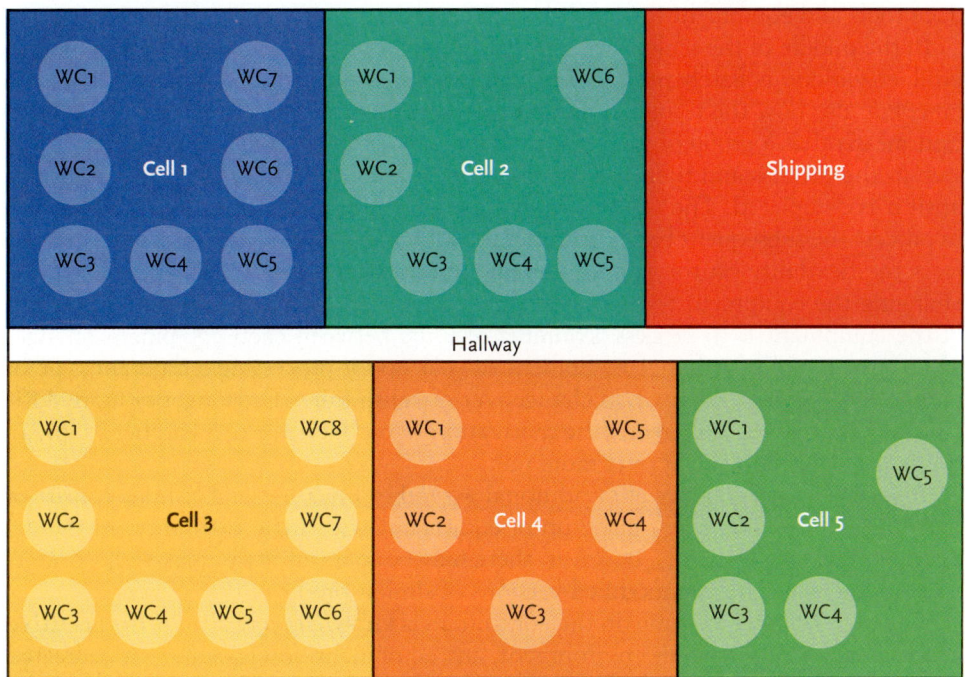

flows are dictated by several factors, including volume of demand, changes required on equipment to meet varying needs, and the nature of what is being produced.

When making early decisions and commitments regarding productive processes, the expected volume is one aspect that must be considered. Different volumes will place different requirements on the system and will result in different management approaches. Exhibit 5.6 is a continuum identifying different production volumes for products and services, based on the product/process matrix in Exhibit 4.17.

Examining the low-volume extreme first, we see processes that produce only one unique unit. Unique, one-of-a-kind, products or customers are known as **projects**. Projects are generally large in size (building a bridge, installing a software system, implementing a major improvement effort, and so on) and reasonably long in duration. In a project, resources are generally brought to the task at hand, as opposed to completing that task at the resources' location. Resources utilized in projects tend to be extremely flexible and may also be used only temporarily.

Continuum of Production Volumes for Product and Service Producers EXHIBIT 5.6

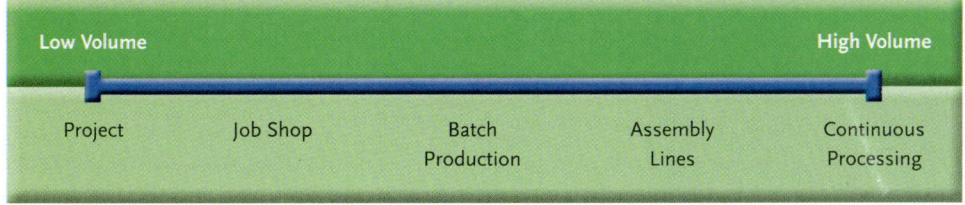

Moving to a little higher volume but maintaining a high degree of customization, we have an environment that exists predominantly in manufacturing, known as a **job shop**. Job shops provide flexibility to customers and dominate companies that produce tools and equipment for other manufacturers.

In the middle of the scale, at a slightly higher volume but still maintaining limited product variety, is **batch production**. Batch production addresses not only the volume, but also how the resources and processes deal with the volumes. Batch production means that a group of identical products or customers is processed through one step in the process and then the entire group moves to the next step, and the next, until it is completed. The equipment can then be adjusted or modified, if necessary, to process the subsequent batch. In general, batch processing is used because of a need for some flexibility on the part of the equipment. Rather than processing one unit, changing the equipment to process the next unit, and so on, a more productive use of the equipment is to process a number of units between each equipment change. The time required to change equipment or gear up for processing a different type of product or customer is known as **changeover** or **setup time**. The longer or more difficult the changeover, the greater the motivation to produce in larger batches to spread the cost of the changeover over more units.

At even higher volumes are traditional **assembly lines**. Assembly lines consist of narrowly defined processes, made up of equipment with little flexibility. In typical assembly line arrangements, however, there may be some ability to make adjustments on equipment to produce modified versions of similar products.

The high-volume extreme on the continuum is known as **continuous** or **repetitive processing**. In a continuous environment, any equipment or workstation is dedicated to one thing. High levels of efficiency can be obtained through economies of scale. An opportunity exists for automation in this environment for two reasons. First, the tasks are repetitive, and it is relatively easy to automate repetitive tasks. Second, volume is sufficient to provide a financial return on the investment in automated equipment. Automated equipment is expensive, and the investment in that equipment needs to be spread across a large volume to keep the per-unit impact on cost down. A continuous environment generally utilizes a product-oriented layout because of its compatibility with higher-volume production. There is a strong link between the volume desired from a process and the general layout decisions.

The product/process matrix presented in Chapter 4 and reproduced in Exhibit 5.7 shows the relationship between volume and general layout type. Notice that the higher the volume, the greater the tendency toward a product-oriented layout. This eliminates the ability to customize but reduces cost per unit.

Demand Linkages

In addition to general layout and volume decisions, another broad decision that has implications for processes is the link to demand. This issue has little impact on services, since they can't store capacity in the form of inventory, but it has a major impact on manufacturers. Exhibit 5.7 adds the demand linkage continuum to the bottom of the product/process matrix.

Manufacturers can produce goods to meet demand in two fundamentally different ways. First, they can produce when they receive an order. This is known as **make-to-order (MTO)** processing. The term implies that the product is customized in some way, but this isn't necessarily the case. Standardized products can be made to order also. The advantage of MTO is that finished-goods inventories are kept to a minimum. The disadvantage of this choice is that the customer must wait for the products to be made. This lengthens the response time. The opposite alternative is **make-to-stock (MTS)**. In an MTS environment, products are produced to be warehoused.

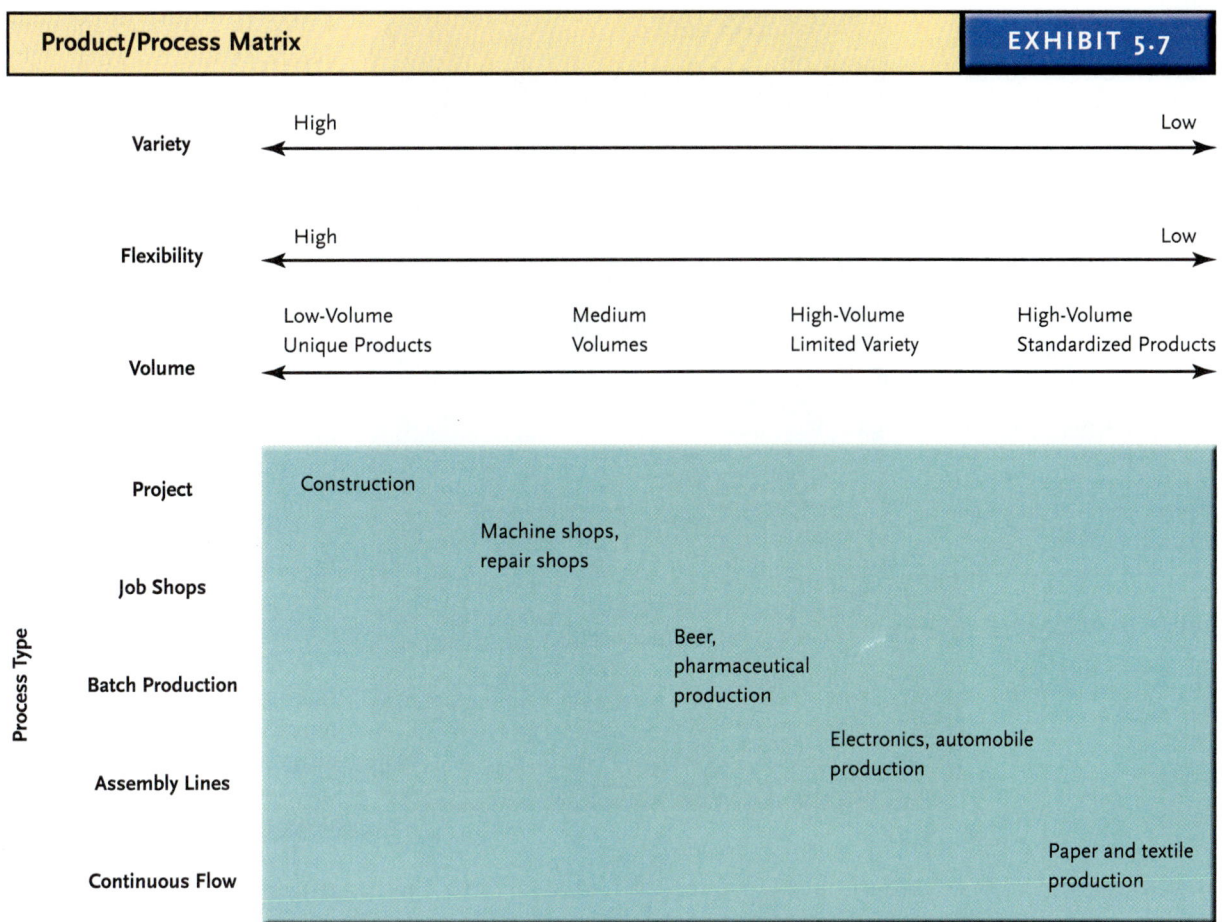

EXHIBIT 5.7 Product/Process Matrix

Source: Adapted from R. H. Hayes and S. C. Wheelwright, *Restoring Our Competitive Edge: Competing through Manufacturing* (New York: Wiley, 1984), p. 209.

The customer purchases products out of that warehouse. The advantage is that customers get an immediate response to their order. The disadvantage of this alternative is that the product offerings are limited to those listed in the catalog.

A compromise system is known as **assemble-to-order.** In this environment, products are manufactured up to a point, and then stored. Customer orders dictate the final configuration. It provides a quicker response than MTS and provides a greater ability to customize than MTO. Exhibit 5.7 shows a link between high volumes and the make-to-order end of the demand linkage continuum. Make-to-order environments are typically lower volumes.

Service Process Considerations

Prior to the initial design of any process, the potential implications of what is actually being processed must be considered. In services, for example, are people being processed? If so, is something being done *to* them or is it being done *for* them? Is something that represents a person, like an application or an insurance claim, being processed or is something being done to property like a home, a car, or money? A business that processes people has to consider whether people will like the process. Processing "things" for people tends to be more like manufacturing. The customer contact and opportunity for sales, as pointed out in the service system design matrix pre-

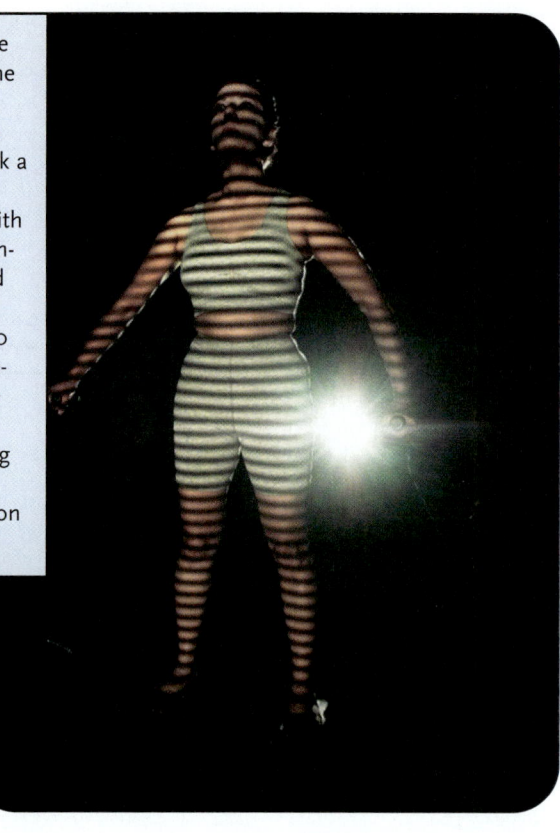

The capability to customize *and* produce at high volume had long been a goal of manufacturing and service producers. Lands' End took a significant step toward accomplishing that goal with its "My Virtual Model" technology. Here, a Lands' End employee is scanned and mapped with over 200,000 data points so that her precise measurements can be stored in the Lands' End data base. Online shopping for clothes is enhanced by more precise information on customer size.

sented in Exhibit 4.18, must also be considered when making process decisions.

Does the process go to the customers or do the customers come to the process? Response time, flexibility, and convenience are closely tied to location. For many services, the "on-site" alternative provides a way to differentiate competitively. Performing services in people's homes has serious implications for issues related to increased scrutiny of employee performance, honesty, cleanliness, and so on. More time is spent in transit, thus reducing productive capacity and increasing costs per customer. Equipment portability, transportation, communication costs, central facility location, and other costs associated with mobility also are affected.

If products or components of products are being processed, what are their characteristics? Some products can be processed in discrete units: clothing, electronics, furniture, and so on. Other products became discrete units only after packaging and are nondiscrete during actual production: many food items such as soft drinks, flour, and cereals, as well as textiles, paint, fuels, and most other liquids and powders. All of these characteristics create specific requirements for process design, packaging, staffing, storage facilities, and delivery systems.

Determining New-Process Requirements

New-product and service design, and the corresponding process design, has become increasingly important as product and service life cycles have become shorter, as customers have become more demanding, and as global levels of competition have increased. To a great extent the success of new products and services hinges on the success of the processes designed to make them happen.

If products and services do not meet customer expectations, the customer will not purchase them. Net income then drops, resulting in reduced profit margin, reduced return on assets, and reduced return on equity for the business owners. If processes are not used effectively, the investment in the processing equipment and facilities will not provide an acceptable return. ROA drops because the denominator (total assets) is large relative to the income generated. If ineffective use of processes results in increased costs (overtime labor, wasted material and supplies, and so on), net income drops, once again reducing all profitability measures. The financial implications for poor process design can be instantaneous and potentially devastating for the firm.

All of the issues just raised impact profitability, but the most serious of them is the inability of a process to create value. No value means no customers, no sales, no income, and ultimately no business. Products and services will meet customer expectations only if customer expectations are known, understood, *and* designed into them. These facts point to an obvious need to link new-product and service design to customer expectations and the design of processes. The following section examines the challenging tasks associated with new-product and service design.

Product, Service, and Process Design

The design of new products or services begins with an idea. It might be something completely new, a revision of an old concept, or a new application for a preexisting capability. New-product and new-service designs, when viewed from a broader enterprise perspective, cannot be developed in isolation from each other. The design of the process that will create a new product or service is just as important as the design of the product or service itself. The process design must be capable of producing the product or service the customer wants. Processes create the value *and* the costs. Reel Operations Video 5.3 examines Tristate, a manufacturer of carts and trailers, as it tries to adapt to changing customer needs by using a cellular design for its processes.

The importance of processes leads us to a "chicken and egg" discussion of which must come first. Ultimately, the design of the products and services and the design of the processes that create them must be an integrated single process. Processes must be designed to meet the needs of products and services. Products and services must be designed to meet the needs and limitations of the processes. Designing products and

EXHIBIT 5.8 — QFD Conceptual Model

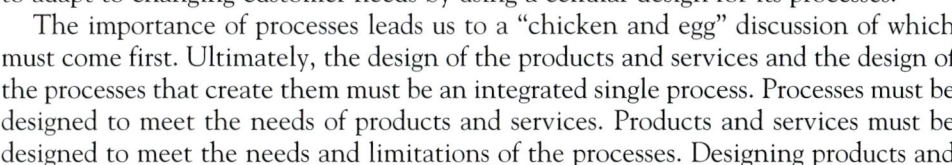

Phase 1 Product Planning: Customer wants and needs → Translate → Technical design parameters for product and/or service

Phase 2 Part Deployment: Technical design parameters for product and/or service → Translate → Target characteristics and specifications for product and service components

Phase 3 Process Planning: Target characteristics and specifications for product and service components → Translate → Requirements for processes used to create product and service components

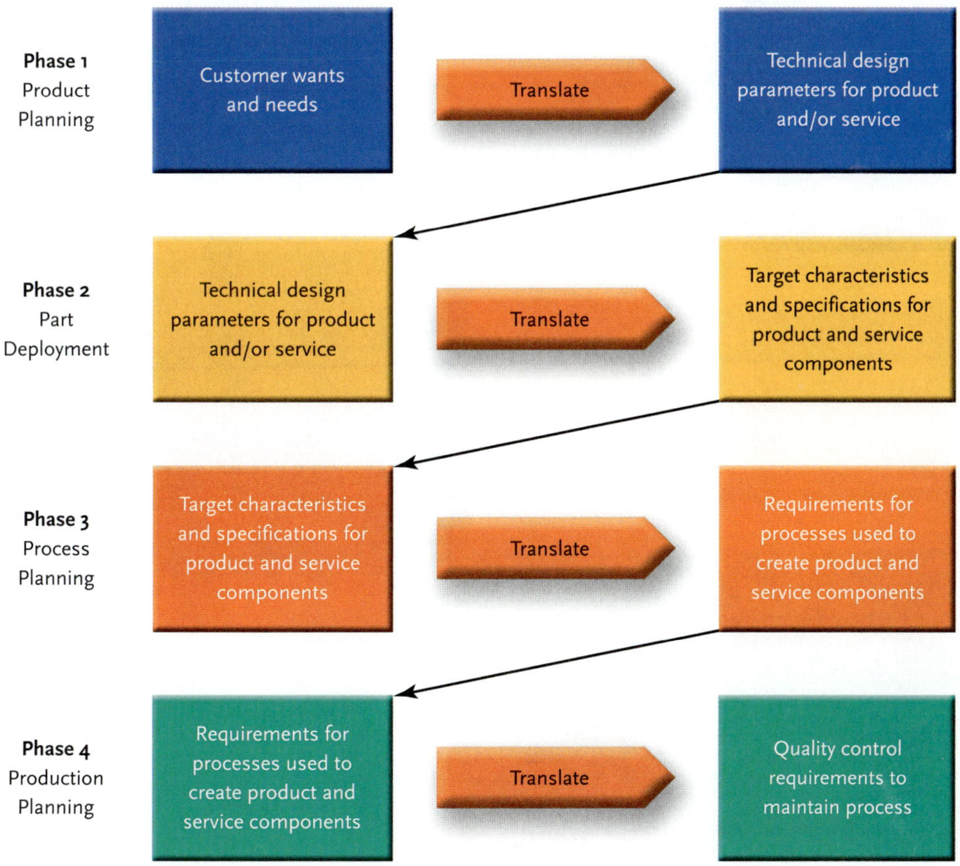

Phase 4 Production Planning: Requirements for processes used to create product and service components → Translate → Quality control requirements to maintain process

services to meet process capabilities is crucial to profitability. In manufacturing, this approach is known as **designing for manufacturability (DFM)**.

Quality Function Deployment

Quality function deployment (QFD) is a widely used approach for accomplishing product and process design tasks. Quality function deployment translates customer needs into product and service designs that guide the corresponding process requirements. This is accomplished through a four-phase procedure presented conceptually in Exhibit 5.8. The QFD process moves through the four phases with the aid of a set of intertwined matrices known as the house of quality. Exhibit 5.9 shows a generic house of quality. In the following discussion of the four phases of QFD, a more defined house of quality is developed as an example to better define this process.

Phase 1: Product Planning

The product planning phase of QFD consists of two major tasks. The first is to determine customer wants and needs. This process is often referred to as obtaining the "voice of the customer" (VOC) and is accomplished through customer interviews, customer complaints, and so on. VOC data are usually sorted into categories so that needs can be structured. Actual phrases used by customers often are listed in a table. Each need is linked to customer demographics and specific details like how the product would be used and where and when it would be needed. For example, suppose we were

EXHIBIT 5.9   **Generic House of Quality**

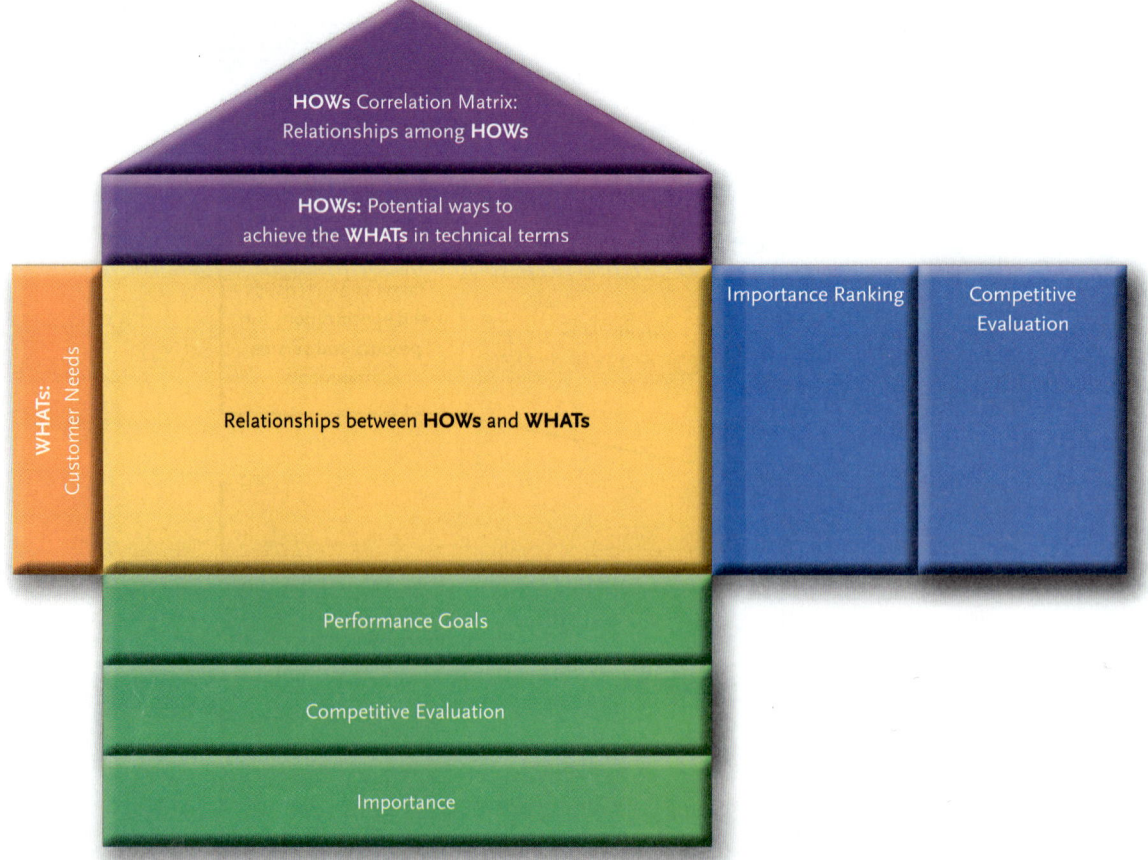

designing a product such as an emergency help kit to be kept in a car. We would want to place the customers' needs in a context of how the kit would be used (indicating the items needed in it), when it would be used (daylight, darkness, summer, winter), where it would be used (at home or on the road), and so on.

The second task associated with Phase 1 of the QFD process is to translate the customer needs into a description of the product or service that is in technical language by using **substitute quality characteristics**. Substitute quality characteristics are aspects of the product or service controlled by the development team. Customer needs are stated in terms of functions. The translation of customer needs encompasses the translation of functions the customer expects into characteristics or capabilities of the product or service design. Included in defining customer wants in technical terms is creating target values for some of the technical characteristics. A customer need such as "I want a car with quick acceleration" or "I want my pizza delivered hot" or "I shouldn't have to wait in line too long" must be translated so that it is defined precisely. Should the acceleration be zero to 60 miles per hour in four seconds or six seconds? Should the pizza be 100 degrees Fahrenheit or 120 degrees? Is "too long" 2 minutes or is it 10 minutes? If you can't measure it, you can't control it.

Phase 2: Part Deployment

The second phase of the QFD procedure is called part deployment. Customer needs that have been translated into technical design parameters create the HOWs and WHATs in the house of quality. Sticking with the pizza delivery example, suppose the customer needs presented in Exhibit 5.10 have been elicited through interviews. In Exhibit 5.11, the customer needs have been translated into technical parameters.

Technical design parameters quickly move beyond the product and "function" level to the component and "sub-function" level. The more specific a technical description of a product or service, the more precise the design of the product or service. Exhibit 5.12 shows how the

EXHIBIT 5.10 — Customer Wants and Needs for Pizza Delivery

- Pizza arrives quickly
- Pizza arrives hot
- Pizza toppings are of sufficient quantity
- Pizza tastes good
- Pizza is consistent with pizza ordered

EXHIBIT 5.11 — Technical Parameters for Pizza Delivery

Customer Wants and Needs	Technical Parameters
Pizza arrives quickly	Pizza arrives in 20 minutes or less from time of order
Pizza arrives hot	Pizza arrives with a temperature of 130°F
Pizza toppings are of sufficient quantity	Amount of each topping is consistent with pizza assembly guidelines specified for each topping and each size of pizza
Pizza tastes good	Exact recipe is followed for dough, sauce, and toppings
Pizza is consistent with pizza ordered	No orders are lost, misread, or misunderstood

| EXHIBIT 5.12 | WHATs and HOWs in House of Quality |

		Time, Minutes	Temperature at Departure, °F	Number of Pieces of Each Topping	Ranking in Annual Pizza Review in Local Magazine	Percentage of Correct Orders
WHATs: Customer Needs	Pizza arrives quickly	●				
	Pizza arrives hot	○	●			
	Toppings are of sufficient quantity			●		
	Pizza tastes good			○	●	
	Pizza is consistent with pizza ordered					●

● Direct Relationship   ○ Indirect Relationship

customer needs (WHATs) and technical design parameters (HOWs) are placed in the house of quality.

Notice also in Exhibit 5.12 that the relationships between WHATs and HOWs are provided in the central matrix. Direct relationships are designated with a solid circle and indirect relationships are designated with a hollow circle. Exhibit 5.13 shows the "roof" added, containing the relationships among the actual HOWs. The performance goals for the HOWS are provided in the row immediately below the central matrix.

Note in Exhibit 5.13 the designated relationships between measures: time and temperature, number of toppings and ranking, and so on. Also note that the performance goals are all quantitative and measurable.

Phase 3: Process Planning

In Phase 3, process planning, performance goals or targets are translated into process requirements. In our example, a desired temperature for the pizza would have implications for several processes, including the processes of baking the pizza, boxing the finished pizza, storing the boxed pizzas until delivery, and keeping the boxed pizzas warm on the way to the customer. Specific decisions related to the exact configuration of the general layout would also need to be made during this phase. Within the constraints of the general layout decision, many details need to be determined. A discussion of detailed layout decisions is presented in Chapter 13.

In these first three phases of QFD, customer needs are translated into technical definitions of product and service requirements, performance measures and targets for those technical requirements, and processes to make the requirements a reality. These three QFD phases provide a tight link between process design and what the customer needs. Customer needs define value, so the necessary link between value and process design is created. Linking value and process design in this manner ties operating

EXHIBIT 5.13 House of Quality with HOW Relationships and Performance Goals

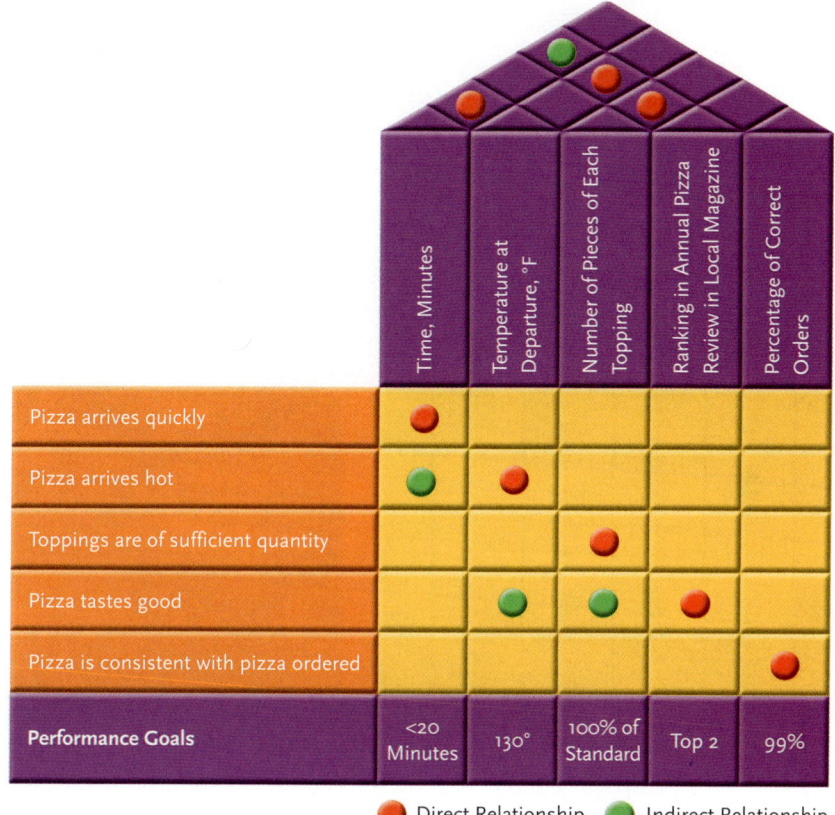

resources (investments) to net income through value. This is a critical link in the firm's ability to attract and keep customers *and* to make money.

In the previous chapter, we saw how the large number of relationships among strategic decision categories and value attributes makes it important for managers to prioritize. The same situation exists in this case, when managers are faced with many different customer needs. Some, obviously, are more important than others. The house of quality, as shown in Exhibit 5.14, aids in the prioritization process by ranking the HOWs on their importance. In addition, business performance is compared to that of competitors to help identify particular issues that need management attention.

The two additional columns added to the house of quality in Exhibit 5.14 bring a competitive assessment process into QFD by comparing performance to that of three competitors. Note the importance ranking of the five WHATs, as well as how the business performs relative to the competitors. It ranks first on "Pizza arrives quickly" and "pizza arrives hot." It ranks relatively low, however, on taste.

It is important to recognize that aspects of Phases 1, 2, and 3 are undertaken simultaneously in order to accommodate product, service, and process needs. No one aspect can have absolute priority over another. Even though product planning and part deployment are begun prior to process planning, the involvement of product engineering, process engineering, and suppliers in the development process ensures that what is designed can be produced.

EXHIBIT 5.14 Completed House of Quality

	Time, Minutes	Temperature at Departure, °F	Number of Pieces of Each Topping	Ranking in Annual Pizza Review in Local Magazine	Percentage of Correct Orders	Importance Ranking	Competitive Evaluation First			Last
Pizza arrives quickly	●					1	X			
Pizza arrives hot	● (green)	●				2	X			
Toppings are of sufficient quantity			●			4			X	
Pizza tastes good		● (green)	● (green)	●		3				X
Pizza is consistent with pizza ordered					●	5		X		
Performance Goals	<20 Minutes	130°	100% of Standard	Top 2	99%					

● Direct Relationship   ● Indirect Relationship

Phase 4: Production Planning

The production planning phase of QFD consists of translating the process requirements into a system that will be able to control processes and maintain target goals. (Quality control systems are covered in depth in Chapter 7.) This phase provides the link between the control system and customer needs. In the pizza example, Phase 4 would include the development of systems to monitor and control the WHATs and ensure that performance goals are met.

QFD has been implemented quite successfully in the United States. Most efforts, however, have been devoted to Phases 1 and 2. The effects of QFD not only have resulted in products and services that better meet customer needs, but also have reduced cycle times for product and service development. As product and service life cycles have become shorter, the need to respond with new designs has escalated, and design enhancements are begun virtually as soon as the development of a product or service is completed. The QFD process shortens that cycle time.

PROCESS IMPROVEMENT TOOLS

In addition to QFD, which can be used to improve products and services as well as to develop new ones, there are other tools used to assist in the improvement of processes. Some tend to focus on cost reduction. Some focus on efficiency and effectiveness while others focus on reduction of lead times. The remaining sections of this chapter provide brief overviews of several popular approaches to process improvement.

Business Process Analysis

Business process analysis (BPA) is used to optimize large processes in ways that increase their ability to meet customer needs. BPA is particularly useful when a business is trying to improve large processes that cross functional boundaries. Exhibit 5.15 provides a model of this type of situation by diagramming the process used to initiate new contracts with a consulting firm.

In the example, a new contract initiates with sales and is then reviewed by the purchasing and procurement department for material and staffing needs. The contract is then reviewed by the legal department and finally by finance from a profitability standpoint. It then goes back to the customer. BPA focuses on all aspects of the process, paying particular attention to the transitions between departments, which are often neglected, allowing customer needs to fall through the cracks. In focusing on the process and how it performs, instead of individuals and how they perform, BPA attempts to identify and eliminate non-value-adding activities. Non-value-adding activities add cost but not value and reduce ROA, ROE, and profit margin.

In complex business processes crossing departmental or functional boundaries, the interface between departments is particularly critical and difficult to manage. If you think back to problems you've had with bureaucracies, departmental interfaces are frequently the source. Problems you've had with your university administration, for example, probably occurred at the interface between two departments. If you've ever been dropped from a class for nonpayment of fees when you'd actually paid them, you could probably track the problem down to a mixup between the bursar's office and the registrar.

Reengineering

Reengineering designs processes starting from a clean slate rather than incrementally improving the processes, as is done in BPA. In reengineering, everything is redesigned, including forms processing and information processing. Reengineering is not limited to those processes that directly involve a product or customer, however. It includes all business processes. In fact, more often than not, reengineering focuses on behind-the-scenes activities. Reengineering is equally applicable to service- or product-oriented

Business Process Analysis Example — EXHIBIT 5.15

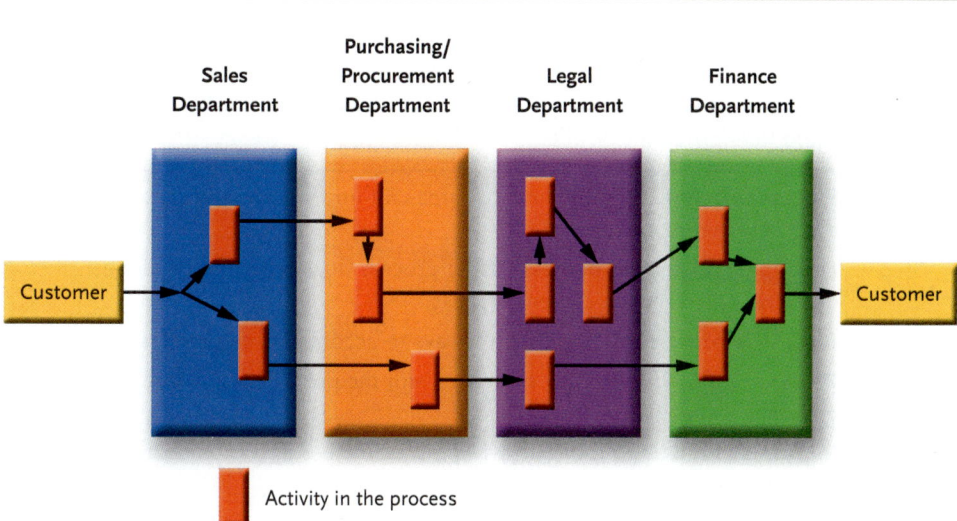

businesses. The general objective is to create leaner processes and lower costs, but quite often the result is that processes are more robust and meet customer needs better. Common outcomes of reengineering programs include reduced lead times, costs, staff (downsizing), and an overall reduction to process inputs. Reengineering has been particularly effective in service-oriented markets such as insurance and financial services.

A change in customer needs may require a completely new type of process, triggering a reengineering effort. Reengineering frequently is needed when an order winner becomes an order qualifier, and a new order winner must be developed. The changes in the McDonald's Corporation's meal preparation processes provides an interesting overview of the complexity of reengineering and is detailed in Reel Operations Video 5.4.

Since reengineering efforts focus on processes, the generic procedure follows a typical problem-solving approach, with a focus on process effectiveness. Reengineering efforts are frequently accomplished by project teams whose first responsibility is to identify potential areas for process improvement. The team then follows a rigorous, step-by-step procedure like the one in Exhibit 5.16.

Concurrent Engineering

Concurrent engineering is the ultimate in integrating process design and new product or service design. In this approach, development team members are responsible for each of the necessary tasks, but they work together throughout the development process. The traditional approach to product development is a set of sequential steps wherein each is started only after the previous one is completed. The result is a very long development time and frequent lapses in communication between functions that should communicate, like product and process engineering. In concurrent engineering, many of the steps are performed in tandem. This not only reduces the cycle time, but also enables communication and coordination between various aspects of the product and service development process. The ability to design the product/service and processes simultaneously results in a design that is more consistent with process expertise and technology. The result is higher levels of quality and reduced costs. Exhibit 5.17 compares both approaches to the new product development process for a hypothetical product.

Poka-Yoke

How many times have you realized, after leaving the drive-up window, that your fast-food order was wrong? A popular approach to minimizing mistakes made in produc-

EXHIBIT 5.16	Project Team Reengineering Procedure
	Step 1. Process selection: Identify potential areas for improvement based on need and likelihood of success.
	Step 2. Description of current process: Using process flow diagram techniques, describe, precisely, the current process.
	Step 3. Process improvement: Identify new ways to accomplish the process goals.
	Step 4. Process verification: Identify problems with the proposed changes and ensure that they can be eliminated.
	Step 5. Implementation and monitoring: Make the changes and monitor the results for effectiveness.

Comparison of Traditional New-Product Development and Concurrent Engineering — EXHIBIT 5.17

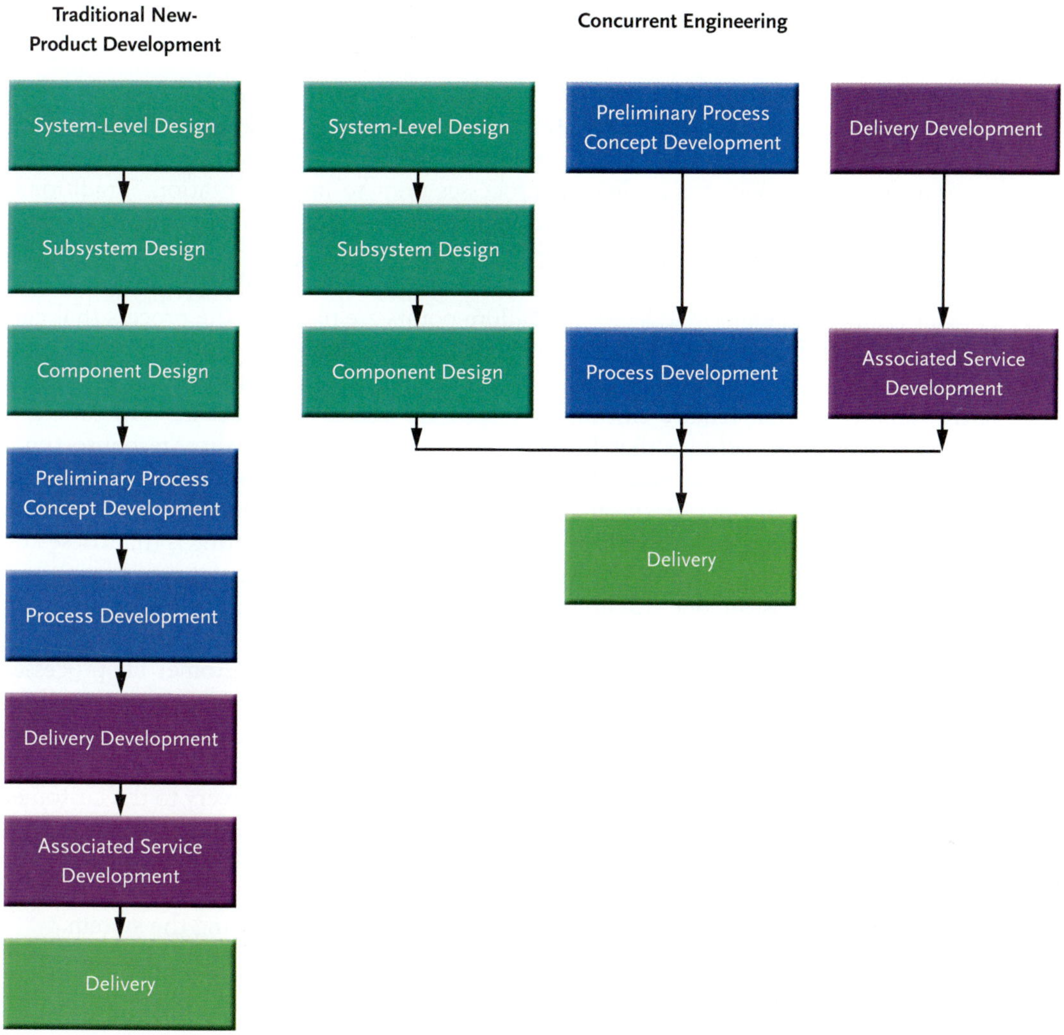

Traditional New-Product Development

System-Level Design → Subsystem Design → Component Design → Preliminary Process Concept Development → Process Development → Delivery Development → Associated Service Development → Delivery

Concurrent Engineering

System-Level Design → Subsystem Design → Component Design

Preliminary Process Concept Development → Process Development

Delivery Development → Associated Service Development

All converge → Delivery

Source: Adapted from L. Cohen, *Quality Function Deployment* (Reading, MA: Addison-Wesley, 1995), pp. 33–36.

---

tion processes is to create barriers to doing tasks any way but the correct way. These mechanisms, known in Japan as **poka-yokes**, can take a variety of forms. In some cases a product component's design can prevent it from being assembled any way but correctly. In other situations, various mechanisms are used to help reduce the likelihood of errors. Such "fail-safe" systems are common in everyday life. Cars won't start unless the transmission is in Park. Lawnmowers have a "dead-man" switch that requires that the operator hold the handle, or the mower shuts off. McDonald's uses a specially designed tool to ensure that each order of fries has the right quantity. Urinals in some European airports have the small image of a fly etched into the center of the porcelain. There are many more examples, but that's probably far enough.

In the production of goods and services, poka-yokes include tools that can be used the correct way only, checklists to follow, or alarms that sound when something is done incorrectly. A mechanism is incorporated into the system to force correct procedures.

Poka-yoke designs have gained popularity as a way to eliminate mistakes, increase quality, and reduce costs.

SERVICE BLUEPRINTING

Service blueprinting is an approach to creating a diagrammed model of a service to enhance management's ability to analyze its strengths and weaknesses.[2] Blueprinting is a modification of process flowcharting that has been used to model processes and provide a mechanism for evaluating processes prior to implementation. Traditional process flowcharting involves the development of a written model of a process, showing all activities and decisions along with their relationships and sequence. Additional key components specific to service blueprints include failure points, customer wait points, and employee decisions. Failure points are places in the process that can result in the failure of the service. Such points are critical to identify because each provides an opportunity to create a control mechanism such as a poka-yoke. Points in the process that require customers to wait are also critical because wait time is a non-value-adding activity that has an impact on perceived quality, response time, and convenience. A service blueprint shows the line of visibility (the division between "up-front" and "back-office" activities) so that its position relative to various events can be evaluated. A primary advantage of service blueprinting is that these key points can be identified and addressed prior to the development of a new service or a change in an existing one. Exhibit 5.18 is a simple service blueprint of our proposed high-speed pizza delivery business.

In Exhibit 5.18, the line of visibility separates from the customer all processes except order taking and actual delivery. Failure points are at key process steps such as the entry of the actual order (it could be entered incorrectly), the assembly of the pizza (incorrect ingredients could be added or ingredients could be omitted), the driver pickup (wrong pizza could be picked up by driver), and delivery to the customer (driver could get lost or go to the wrong address). Poka-yokes could be developed to minimize the probability that any of these errors would take place. Quite often an "as-is" service blueprint is developed to model the existing system. After an analysis, a "should-be" blueprint is developed to provide a guide for improving the system.

CAPABILITY CHAINS

Chapter 3 introduced the concept of supply chains. The network of producers and suppliers, from the consumer all the way back to the original raw materials, makes up that chain and everyone in that chain needs to add value. Integrating service and product design with capabilities and process design is also necessary given that all members of the chain are adding their capabilities to the finished product or service. Charles Fine describes this as the **capability chain**.[3] The design of the capability chain, which is, in effect, the design of the system of suppliers, subcontractors, and customers, dictates the capabilities that exist within the chain. Fine argues in his book *Clockspeed* that three critical principles related to capabilities must be observed. First, no capability lasts forever. Capabilities will and must change. Second, no capability exists alone, without interacting with and depending on other capabilities. And third, competitive advantage can be obtained by the concurrent design of capabilities along with products and processes. Without the concurrent design of capabilities, products, and processes, new products are likely to be difficult or impossible to produce. Investments in processes and capabilities that cannot produce a product—or investment in developing a product that cannot be produced by

Service Blueprint for Pizza Delivery Example   EXHIBIT 5.18

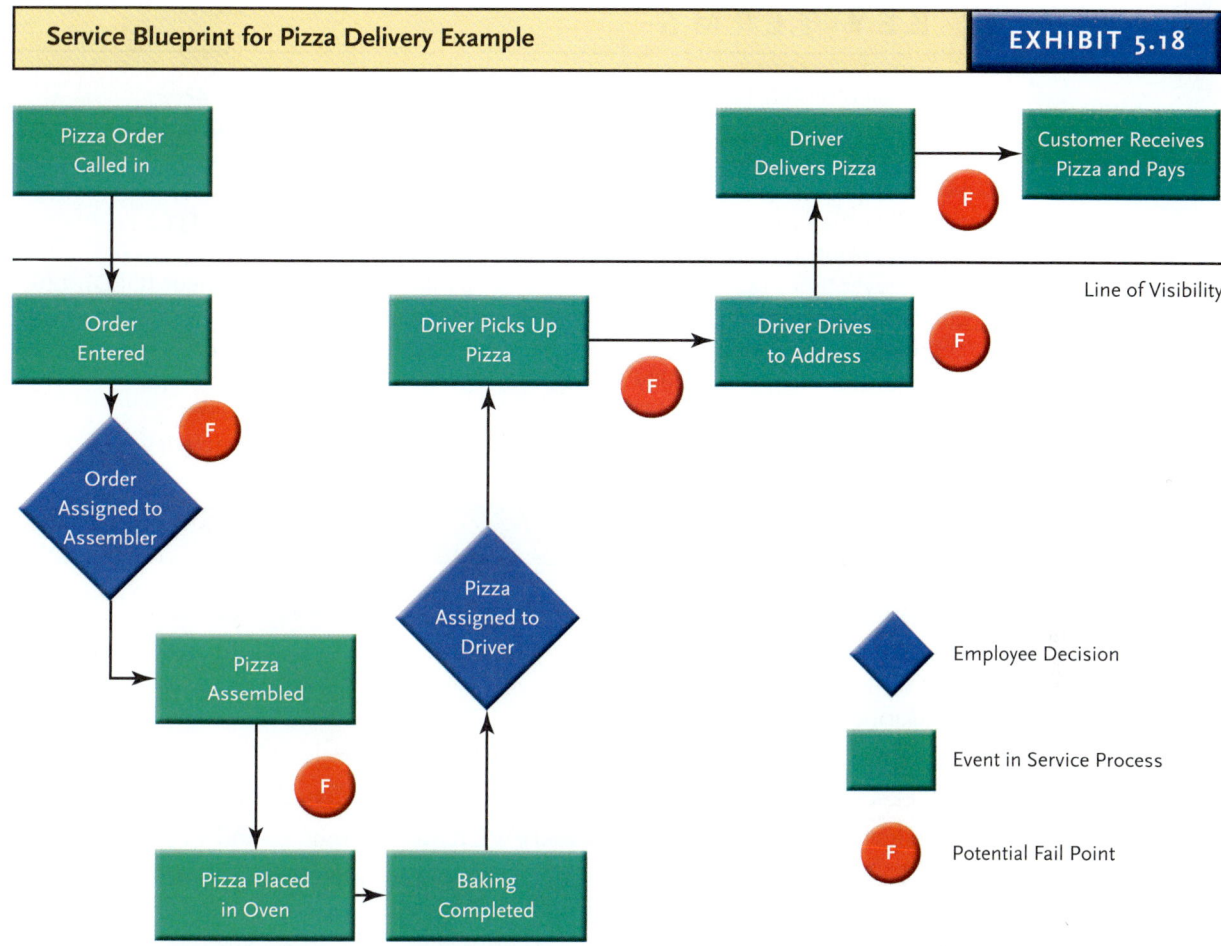

existing processes and capabilities—turn out, ultimately, to be investments that provide no financial return.

CHAPTER SUMMARY

This chapter examined the concepts of capabilities and processes. Capabilities provide value to customers by enabling a business to do things a customer can't. Processes are used by businesses of create those capabilities. One can look at the relationship from an input–output perspective, with resources being the inputs and capabilities the outputs of processes. Linking processes and capabilities to customer needs enhances value. Improving the productivity of processes reduces costs. The productivity of processes depends substantially on the costs associated with them.

In addition to a discussion of processes and capabilities, this chapter introduced quality function deployment, a very popular framework to link processes to customer needs. Methods to improve existing processes beyond the QFD product and service design process include the process improvement techniques of business process analysis, reengineering, concurrent engineering, poka-yoke, and service blueprinting. The next chapter will examine one of the unfortunate by-products of processes: costs.

KEY TERMS

- assemble-to-order, 143
- assembly line, 142
- batch production, 142
- business process analysis (BPA), 151
- capability chain, 154
- cellular layout, 140
- changeover time, 142
- concurrent engineering, 152
- continuous processing, 142
- designing for manufacturability (DFM), 146
- functional layout, 138
- job shop, 142
- make-to-order (MTO), 142
- make-to-stock (MTS), 142
- poka-yoke, 153
- process-oriented layout, 137
- product-oriented layout, 137
- project, 141
- quality function deployment (QFD), 146
- reengineering, 151
- repetitive processing, 142
- service blueprint, 154
- setup time, 142
- substitute quality characteristics, 147

REVIEW QUESTIONS

1. What is the difference between a capability and a process? Why is the difference important?
2. Why are customers usually more concerned about service than about manufacturing processes?
3. What is meant by an order winner? What are order qualifiers?
4. Describe a product-oriented layout. What are its strengths and weaknesses?
5. Describe a process-oriented layout. What are its strengths and weaknesses?
6. What capabilities can be achieved from combining process- and product-oriented layouts into a cellular layout?
7. How are facility-oriented decisions related to volume capabilities?
8. What is meant by batch production?
9. What is the impact of changeover time on batch production?
10. What is the overall objective of quality function deployment? Describe the steps of the quality function deployment process.
11. Compare and contrast business process analysis, reengineering, concurrent engineering, poka-yoke, and blueprinting.
12. What is a capability chain?

DISCUSSION QUESTIONS

1. Select a successful business you often frequent. What are its capabilities? Describe its processes. Which processes are most critical to its capabilities?
2. Capabilities that lead to market dominance often result from combining processes that originate in different parts of a business. Describe a business you are familiar with that has created a unique set of capabilities in this way.
3. What are the order qualifiers for your choice of where to eat lunch? What are the order winners for this place?

4. What capabilities are made possible when a service is designed with high volume in mind? What capabilities might a competitor try to develop as a way of differentiating itself from that service?

PROBLEMS

1. Identify a service you frequent (a sandwich shop, a doctor's office, a college administrative office, etc.). Create a service blueprint for the service. Be sure to include potential fail points and the line of visibility.
2. Create a service blueprint for your college's class registration process. Examine the completed blueprint. Examine the fail points. Do they often result in service failure? Have any resulted in service failure for you? What could be done to reduce the likelihood of service failure at these points?
3. Create a service blueprint for the checkout process of a retail store you frequent. Identify the line of visibility and fail points. How critical is the business's placement of the line of visibility to its strategic objectives? Have they placed it correctly? Which of the fail points, in your opinion, result in the most frequent service failure? How critical are these failures to the business's strategy? What is the typical reaction of the customer to these failures?

SELECTED RESOURCES

Cohen, L. *Quality Function Deployment*, Reading, MA: Addison-Wesley Publishing Company, 1995.

Fine, Charles H. *Clockspeed: Winning Industry Control in the Age of Temporary Advantage*, Reading, MA: Perseus Books, 1998.

ENDNOTES

1. T. Hill, *Manufacturing Strategy* (Homewood, IL: Irwin, 1989), pp. 36–46.
2. G. L. Shostack, "Designing Services that Deliver," *Harvard Business Review*, January–February 1984, pp. 133–139.
3. C. H. Fine, *Clockspeed: Winning Industry Control in the Age of Temporary Advantage* (Reading, MA: Perseus Books, 1998), pp. 71–76.

OperationsNow.com LEARNING ACTIVITIES

CHAPTER ENHANCEMENT RESOURCES
- Esources
- Reel Operations Video Clips
- Interactive Models
- Excel Tutors
- Supplementary Readings
- Links to Operations On Site Companies

OM EXPLORATION
- Check It Out
- OM in Action
- Online Business Tours
- Letters from the Top
- Putting It All Together: Virtual Case Studies
- Additional Reading

In the resource/profit model, cost is identified as the second of four components of value. It is important because it forms the basis for what customers must give up to purchase a product or service. Cost, for the producer, is the antithesis of profitability. The higher the costs, the lower the profitability. In most cases cost is the input for productivity measures. Reduce the cost and you improve productivity. Many operations decisions rest on the impact of cost. Costs drive much of what operations does, and the effect is an increase or decrease in value.

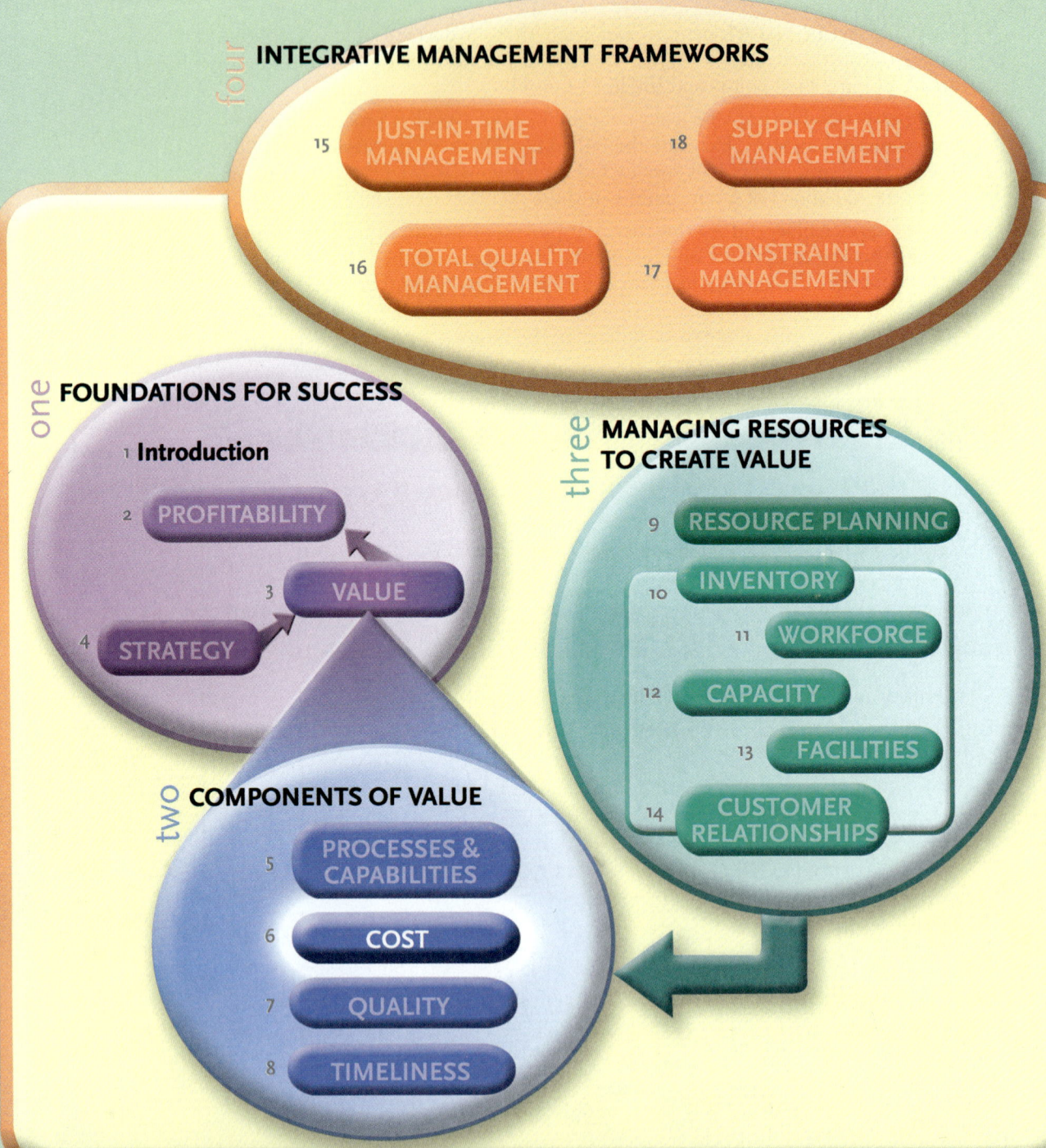

CHAPTER 6

Cost

LEARNING OBJECTIVES

Upon completion of Chapter 6, you should be able to

_____ Describe the relationship between cost and value.

_____ Understand how costs affect the three profitability measures.

_____ Describe why costs are important in operations.

_____ State the dangers of using average costs.

_____ Explain why it is important to be able to assign operations costs.

_____ Explain the concepts of tracing and allocating costs.

_____ Define the components of product cost.

_____ Describe how cost reduction relates to productivity improvement.

_____ Explain the concepts of standards and variances.

_____ Compute usage, price, and total variances.

_____ Understand the difference between total cost and cost per unit.

_____ List some cost tradeoffs.

Introduction: Paying for Value
Cost and Perceived Value
The Value Chain
An Overview of Operations Cost Measurement
Productivity Improvement and Cost Reduction
Total Cost Versus Cost per Unit
Cost Tradeoffs
Nonfinancial Costs
Chapter Summary

INTERNET RESOURCES

 Excel Tutors provide annotated spreadsheets for every solved problem that automatically load Excel.

 Esources provide an online version of the more traditional boxed insert.

 Reel Videos provide streaming video footage for company applications of chapter concepts.

 Interactive Models provide an experimental environment for quantitative concepts and simulations.

INTRODUCTION
Paying for Value

ost is shown in the resource/profit model in Exhibit 6.1 as the second of four components of value. Whereas increasing the other three components *adds* to value, increasing cost obviously *detracts* from it. Cost is often thought of as the realm of accountants, but cost drives so many decisions

EXHIBIT 6.1 — The Role of Cost in the Resource/Profit Model

four — INTEGRATIVE MANAGEMENT FRAMEWORKS
- 15 JUST-IN-TIME MANAGEMENT
- 18 SUPPLY CHAIN MANAGEMENT
- 16 TOTAL QUALITY MANAGEMENT
- 17 CONSTRAINT MANAGEMENT

one — FOUNDATIONS FOR SUCCESS
- 1 Introduction
- 2 PROFITABILITY
- 3 VALUE
- 4 STRATEGY

three — MANAGING RESOURCES TO CREATE VALUE
- 9 RESOURCE PLANNING
- 10 INVENTORY
- 11 WORKFORCE
- 12 CAPACITY
- 13 FACILITIES
- 14 CUSTOMER RELATIONSHIPS

two — COMPONENTS OF VALUE
- 5 PROCESSES & CAPABILITIES
- 6 COST
- 7 QUALITY
- 8 TIMELINESS

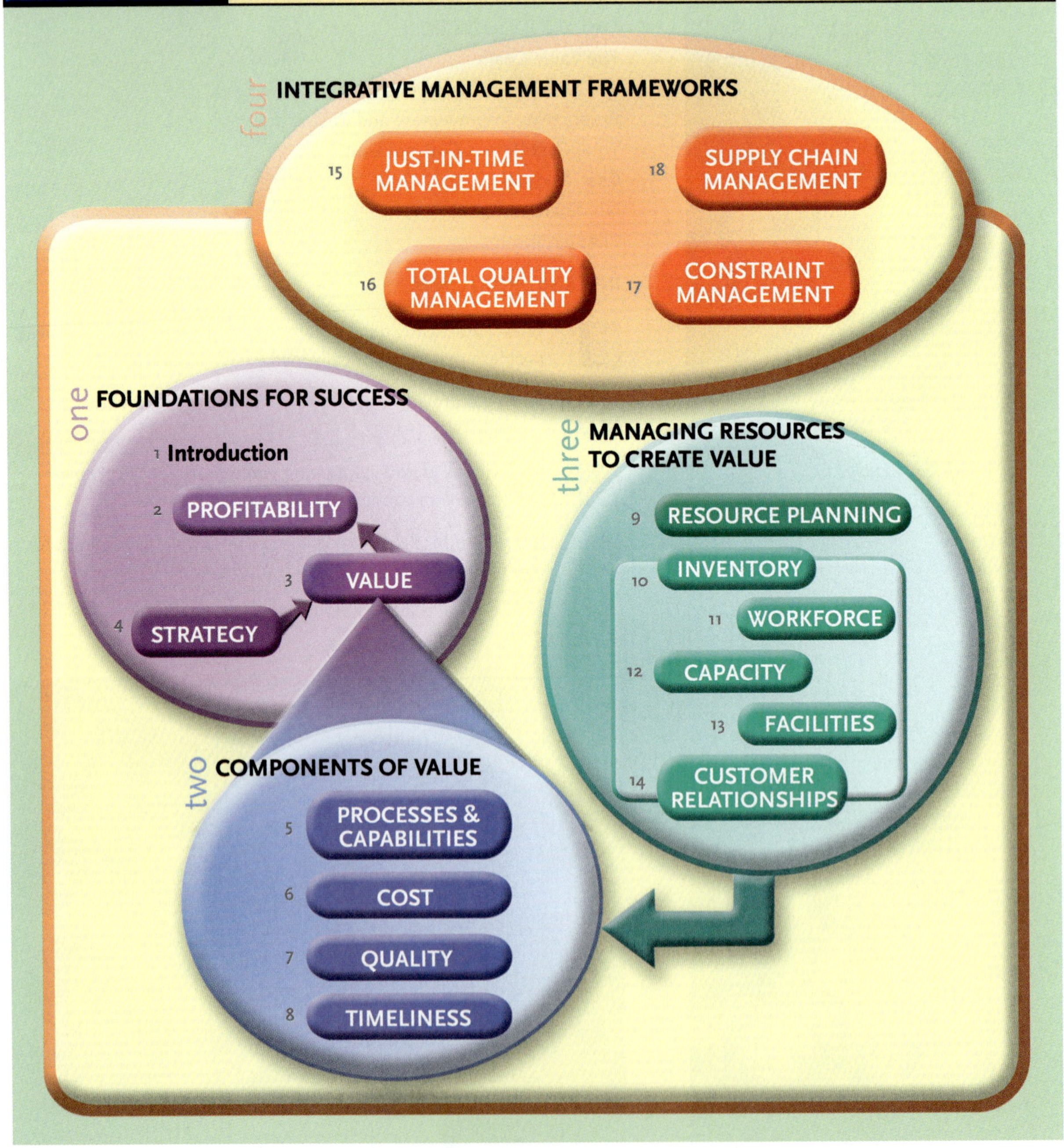

in operations that it must be examined from that perspective. Not only are operations decisions based on costs, but operations resources create many of the costs associated with products and services.

This chapter structures the examination of cost and operations around four objectives. First, it presents an overview of different types of costs as they relate to operations. Second, because of the effect of cost on value, it examines the role costs play in value chains. Third, it provides an overview of cost measurement and the operations implications of assigning, tracing, and allocating costs. Included in that examination are discussions of resource and activity drivers. Finally, because not all costs are financial, the concept of nonfinancial costs is introduced and examined as a critical component of effective decision making.

Chapter 3 presented the value attributes for business and consumer customers listed in Exhibit 6.2. The value attributes of quality, response time, dependability of delivery, convenience, ethical issues, flexibility, and personalization are often thought to enhance value. Style and fashion are occasionally viewed negatively, as is technology. Cost is almost always viewed as the overriding negative factor.

For the customer, cost is more than merely price. It includes all of the resource outlays over the life of the product or service. Cost is the currency by which the benefits of all of the other value attributes are measured. The link between costs and operations comes directly through costs added in processes. Cost's wide-ranging impact has many implications for a firm's profitability. It influences profitability indirectly through its impact on net sales via its effect on product or service demand. As costs go up, value drops and then demand drops, reducing net sales. As net sales drops, net income drops, reducing all profitability measures:

$$\frac{\text{Net}}{\text{Income}} = \frac{\text{Net}}{\text{Sales}} - \frac{\text{Cost of}}{\text{Goods Sold}} - \text{Depreciation} - \frac{\text{Interest}}{\text{Paid}} - \text{Taxes} \qquad (6.1)$$

Cost also influences profitability indirectly through the net sales calculation via the cost of goods sold. As is evident in Equation 6.1, increasing cost of goods sold decreases net income, reducing all profitability measures.

This chapter examines the concept of cost, its role in determining value and profitability, how it is measured, and how it is managed. By this point in your coursework, you have probably had one or two accounting courses. The intent of this chapter is to link operations and accounting by establishing the context for many accounting practices. This context is important for all managers because the origin of many costs is in the way resources are managed. Reducing or controlling these costs can only come from understanding the link between resource use and the costs it creates.

COST AND PERCEIVED VALUE

For any customers, whether business or consumer, cost is a key factor in the purchasing

EXHIBIT 6.2

Critical Value Attributes
Cost
Quality
Response time
Dependability of delivery
Convenience
Style/fashion
Ethical issues
Technology
Flexibility
Personalization

decision. Cost is almost always an order winner or an order qualifier and, when too high, can be an order loser. Even though a customer's cost of ownership consists of more than just the purchase price, purchase price is usually a very important component of the total cost of ownership. Purchase price is so dominant in purchasing decisions that, all other attributes being nearly equal, it frequently sways the final decision. Just think about retailers trying to increase sales or reduce inventory at the end of the season. Do they offer quicker delivery? No. Do they offer a special or more congenial salespersons? No. Instead, they reduce price. Businesses selling to other business customers pay close attention to cost because all of *their* costs are translated into what they must in turn charge customers. For example, a clothing manufacturer closely monitors the costs of fabric because those costs are passed on to the retailers that purchase the finished products. High fabric costs either cut into the profit margin or are passed on, potentially hurting sales. The business is transparent in that all of the costs incurred are eventually either passed on to the customer or deducted from net income. Esource 6.1 provides an example of a business that is able to compete on the basis of cost. Its competitive success hinges on its ability to maintain low costs.

www.OperationsNow.com

For consumers, the perceived value must be greater than the cost or they wouldn't spend the money to make the purchase. For business customers, potential for adding value to their product or service must be greater than the cost, or they will not be able to recoup the costs when they sell the product or service. From any perspective, cost has a critical impact on value.

What Is a "Cost"?

Cost is a scarce resource given up in order to obtain a current or future benefit. Cost is often measured in monetary terms but does not have to be. Instead of money, cost could be in the form of some other scarce resource, such as time or customer loyalty. With the exception of a brief overview of nonmonetary costs at the end of this chapter, most of the discussion in this chapter is limited to monetary costs. This does not imply that nonmonetary costs are not important. On the contrary, they can be extremely important. In fact, they can be the most important costs. In many cases, wrong decisions are made because nonmonetary costs are overlooked. To maintain a financial focus for this chapter, however, nonmonetary types of cost are covered in other chapters, where they more closely link to the topic.

Cost and Profitability

Costs incurred by a business have an impact on the prices the business must charge, which have an immediate impact on the customer's perception of value. But why should a company care about costs if its prices are in line with those of competitors? The answer is that cost savings that are not passed on to the customer go directly to profitability. Let's review how this happens. Recall from Chapter 2 that net income is the numerator for all profitability measures:

$$\text{Profit Margin} = \text{Net Income/Sales} \qquad (6.2)$$

$$\text{Return on Assets} = \text{Net Income/Total Assets} \qquad (6.3)$$

$$\text{Return on Equity} = \text{Net Income/Total Equity} \qquad (6.4)$$

Also recall that the net income calculation starts with net sales. Net sales is the direct result of customers' perceived value. The cost of goods sold, depreciation, and interest paid are subtracted to provide the taxable income. Subtracting the taxes gives us net income:

$$\text{Net Income} = \text{Net Sales} - \text{Cost of Goods Sold} - \text{Depreciation} - \text{Interest Paid} - \text{Taxes} \quad (6.5)$$

Costs have two direct impacts on net income. They influence the selling price, which, to a great extent, dictates value. Value creates demand, which translates into net sales. Costs also dictate the cost of goods sold, which is used in the calculation of net income. Thus, the greater the cost, the greater the price, the less the perceived value by customers, the less the net sales, and, ultimately, the less the net income. *Also*, the greater the costs, the greater the costs of goods sold, and the less the net income. No wonder many firms seem to be on a never-ending cost-cutting binge.

The concepts of price and cost frequently are misunderstood. From the buyer's perspective, they are occasionally the same thing, but usually they are different. *Price*, or, more precisely, sales price, is the amount of money a seller agrees to accept in return for something, like a product or service. That price might be the total cost of the product or service, but usually there are other costs as well. Shipping costs, for example, would add to the buyer's cost. Future repairs and maintenance would also need to be considered. There's a reason, for example, why reliability history is important when customers shop for a new car: Lack of reliability translates directly into higher cost of ownership. Consumers who have become accustomed to ordering online have rapidly come to recognize that price isn't as important as cost, since shipping and handling costs can be significant. Many Internet retailers have been criticized for providing customers with the sales price early in the purchasing decision but withholding other important cost information, like shipping and handling charges, until very late in the checkout process. This has been a major factor in customers abandoning their "shopping carts" at the online checkout. Esource 6.2 provides examples of companies that have learned to provide all cost information early.

www
OperationsNow
.com

For the seller, sales price must be greater than the cost or there is no margin for profit. A business that purchased a piece of equipment would need to install it. There would be costs associated with that installation. There would also be maintenance costs associated with keeping the equipment running. Those costs would include labor costs, costs of downtime on the equipment, and costs for repair parts.

Types of Costs

There are many different types of cost. Two very important ones are the expected cost and the actual cost. **Expected costs** are the forecasted payments for future resources. **Actual costs** are the past payments for currently owned resources. **Out-of-pocket costs** are cash payments made for resources. **Product costs** are costs of the resources used to make products. **Period costs** are costs of resources used in nonproduction elements of the business. **Total costs** include the costs of all resources obtained in a particular period. It is important to be specific when discussing a particular cost to avoid being misunderstood. This is particularly true of costs related to operations, because they motivate many operations-oriented decisions.

Average Costs

In many cases, the cost used to make an operations decision is an average cost—thus average costs can be useful, but they can also be dangerous. Average costs provide an excellent way to compare current costs with historical costs, a frequently used measure of improvement. They can be helpful when a business is making comparisons with

> **om on site**
>
> ### Cost Versus Price: Surcharges, "Taxes," and User Fees
>
> The Internet has made it relatively easy for consumers to seek out the lowest prices available. This doesn't necessarily mean they've found the lowest cost, however. A number of different industries are countering the consumers' money-saving efforts by adding extra charges to the products or services they offer. Hotels commonly add surcharges for utilities, which they call an "environmental" surcharge because that name gets a better reaction from customers than just calling it a price increase. Businesses commonly tack on surcharges to cover renovations and recycling fees. Most dry cleaners now add a 5 percent "tax." Auto dealerships add as much as $500 in charges called "documentation fees." It is becoming more common for businesses to directly charge customers for costs that formerly were considered just a cost of doing business. Preparation of documents to transfer auto ownership, for example, was one of the costs a dealership bore. Seventy-five percent of travel agencies now charge service fees for airline tickets. That number has tripled since 1997. Dialing an 800 number for Internet access used to be a $0.75 local call charge in a hotel. Today, many hotels are charging much more for that call. Some hotels add on as much as $6 per night in "resort" charges to cover the access to the pool and spa, newspapers, and housekeeping. Some automatically charge for a newspaper unless customers say they don't want one.
>
> Source: "The Little Extras That Count (Up)," *The Wall Street Journal*, July 12, 2001, pp. B1, B4.

competitors, or when a comparison of costs versus sales prices is necessary. Caution should be used, however, because average costs can be misleading, particularly when a firm is trying to assign average costs to periods of time. Average costs typically do not represent all of the costs associated with a product during a specific period of time. For example, during a particular period of time, a business might not have enough demand to fully utilize equipment and labor. Restaurant capacity typifies this danger. Suppose that on Monday through Thursday a restaurant had very little business, and waiters were idle most of the time. On Fridays and Saturdays, however, it didn't have enough wait staff, provided very slow service, and even turned significant numbers of customers away. When management compared average daily and weekly labor costs to those of other restaurants in the chain, they found that the average was not lower than that of other restaurants, and therefore concluded that there was no need to add staff. In reality, the restaurant was short of capacity on weekends and had extra on weekdays. It's like standing with one foot in a bucket of ice and one foot in a fire: On the average, your feet are comfortable, but in reality each is very uncomfortable.

Another negative aspect of using average costs is that they can lull a business into ignoring details of a situation. A comparison of average sales price to average cost, for example, might indicate that prices are sufficiently above costs. On an individual-product basis, however, some products might be priced extremely high and others priced too low relative to their costs. Even though there is an average product or service cost, for most businesses, an average product or average service doesn't exist.

THE VALUE CHAIN

One way to look at the activities of a business is in the context of a value chain. A *value chain* is a model of an organization that links all of its processes together, from the initial task of obtaining resources to the final task of delivering a product or service to the customer. The value chain approach is extremely relevant to linking costs and operations because many of the cost-adding components of the value chain fall under the realm of operations decisions.

Exhibit 6.3 provides a generic value chain. Here each link is expected to add value to the product or service being produced. Research and development provides the knowledge behind new products and services. Design utilizes that knowledge to create new product and service designs for production. Inbound logistics provides production with the necessary material inputs to processes. Operations actually produces the products or services. Marketing educates potential customers so that they will buy the product or service. Distribution handles the outbound side—making sure products and services get to the customers who've purchased them. Customer service provides after-the-sale service to customers.

Many steps, adding value and adding costs, occur between harvesting cotton and placing a denim shirt in a Gap shopping bag. Included in that value chain are all of the activities associated with textile and apparel manufacturing, but also included are activities that depend on the skills and abilities of store managers and store employees, all the way to the friendly "May I help you?" that greets a customer entering the store.

All of the value of the product or service is added in the value chain. All of the costs, however, are not necessarily incurred along the value chain. Costs are also added by administrative support services: accounting, legal services, computer services, personnel functions, and so on. The value chain is a critical concept when cost implications for operations management are examined. First, the value chain illustrates which aspects of a business add value and which do not, a critical comparison in keeping attention focused on value-adding activities and keeping costs below the customers' perception of the value. Second, with a thorough understanding of the value chain, a more detailed analysis of processes—to ensure that activities within the chain actually do add value—can be conducted. Finally, the value chain concept provides a stepping-stone to the concept of an activity. An **activity** is a basic unit of work. Each component of the value chain is made up of processes, which are in turn made up of activities. Activities play a very important role in linking costs to the products

Value Chain   **EXHIBIT 6.3**

Research & Development — Design — Inbound Logistics — Production — Marketing — Distribution — Customer Service

VALUE

and services responsible for them. The processes controlled by operations can all be broken into activities. In fact, they must be broken into activities in order to link them to product and service costs.

Recall the discussion of the supply chain in Chapter 3. The supply chain links value chains together and provides an integrative way to view how value and costs are added by the various elements of that chain. Just as value added anywhere in the chain can ultimately enhance the product or service, costs are also carried through the chain. Any focus on cost reduction must pay attention to the entire chain.

AN OVERVIEW OF OPERATIONS COST MEASUREMENT

Assigning Operations Costs

The difference between the customer's perceived value of a product or service and the cost of producing that product or service is the potential for profitability. One of the uncertainties associated with investing in operating resources is that knowing a priori what that value will be is difficult. Given the uncertainty surrounding the prediction of the value of the product or service, knowing what the cost of the product or service is and minimizing the uncertainty of the cost component are essential. Accurately assigning costs to products and services is important to potential profitability. Management accounting systems utilize cost objects as a basis for assigning costs.

A **cost object** is an item for which costs are measured and assigned. A cost object can be a customer, product, service, department, or activity. Cost objects are typically those entities management would want to know the cost of. For example, if the cost of operating a branch bank in the mall were important, that facility would be the cost object. If the cost of processing loans were important, the loan-processing department would be the cost object. If the cost of maintaining ATMs were important, the ATMs would be the cost object. Labor, equipment, inventory, and other resources are common cost objects. Activities can also be important cost objects for operations because many of the costs associated with the production of goods and services are the result of process activities. For example, a manufacturer might be interested in the cost of packaging products, so packaging would be a cost object. An architect firm might be interested in the cost of on-site consultation, so that would be a cost object.

The accurate assignment of costs to cost objects is important to good operations decision making. Without an accurate cost assessment, decisions that have financial implications can have no validity. As the saying goes, "Garbage in, garbage out." Operations decisions are often made by analyzing alternatives and selecting the one that has the highest net present value (NPV). Cost is such an integral part of NPV that if the costs associated with the alternatives are not predicted accurately, or if costs associated with existing cost objects are not assigned accurately, the expected value will be wrong, and the wrong decision could be made.

For example, the costs of a product frequently are reduced by increasing the productivity of processes. This, in fact, is a primary task of operations managers. Suppose a particular manufacturing process were used on four different products. If the estimate of the cost of that process associated with one of those products was very high, management could be motivated to reduce the cost of that particular product by improving that process. If, in reality, the costs associated with that product were small, the improvement of that process would not reduce the cost associated with the product. The result could be dollars spent on improving a process that didn't need it, which would in effect be an investment with no hope of a financial return.

Obtaining accurate costs is not just an issue of making sure the costs are accurate in terms of dollars, but it is also important to assign costs to the correct cost object.

CHAPTER 6   Cost   167

> **Online Contacts Reduce Costs**
>
> The UAL Corporation's United Airlines had a rough start using the Internet to reduce costs with a website that required special software to access, was difficult to read, and downplayed the UAL brand. After recognizing how important the website would be, however, UAL turned it into a site that is widely recognized as one of the best in the industry. A successful website is critical because online ticket purchases reduce the number of calls handled by employees, reducing labor costs. UAL expects that 20 percent of its revenues will be generated through its website by 2003.
>
> The Internal Revenue Service provides another example of the power of a website to reduce costs. IRS forms are requested by the millions. Responding to mailed-in requests requires form pullers, envelope stuffers, and label addressors. Mailed-in requests cost an average of $3 each. Online forms, which utilize Adobe's Acrobat software, look as good as the mailed forms. During tax season, more than 100 million forms are downloaded at a cost of a fraction of a cent each. The need for employees to handle hard copy forms has dropped dramatically, reducing the staffing as well. In addition to cost savings from reduced mailings, the website also offers information and assistance, which reduces the need for IRS personnel to answer phones.
>
> Source: "Fix It and They Will Come," *The Wall Street Journal*, February 12, 2001, p. R4.

Most businesses have a fairly accurate idea of what their total costs are, because they've spent the money. Their biggest difficulty comes when a business attempts to assign the costs of products or services accurately so it can obtain a reasonable idea of what a particular product or service actually costs and focus improvement efforts accordingly. The firm can never expect to know precisely, with 100 percent accuracy, what it costs to produce a product or service, however. Some costs associated with the product or service can be determined with precision, but other costs are difficult to assign accurately.

Traceability of Direct Operations Costs

From accounting we know that the ease or difficulty associated with assigning costs to cost objects is known as **cost traceability**. Direct costs are relatively easy to trace, whereas indirect costs cannot be traced at all. A particular cost, however, might be a direct cost in one situation but an indirect cost in another, depending on the cost object. For example, maintenance required on a specific piece of equipment would be a direct cost when the cost object is that piece of equipment. When the cost object is one of several products produced on that piece of equipment, however, maintenance cost is an indirect cost because it cannot be traced to a particular product.

The actual assignment of costs to a cost object is accomplished by using some measure of resources consumed by that cost object. Assigning costs to cost objects can be done with direct tracing or with driver tracing. In direct tracing, the costs are physically associated with the cost object, like the maintenance costs for the machine mentioned in the example. Assigning them is simply a matter of observation. Driver tracing, on the other hand, is used when a direct observation cannot be used. A cost driver must be used to provide the link between a cost and the cost object.

Two types of driver can be used to assign costs to cost objects. Both are important to operations. **Resource drivers** measure demands placed on resources by activities

The production of any product, even one as small and inexpensive as a golf ball, creates direct material, direct labor, and overhead costs. For a high-volume, low-cost item production processes are likely to be automated, resulting in higher overhead costs when compared to labor costs. Expensive automated equipment must produce (and the businesses must sell) high volumes to spread the high overhead costs over a large number of products.

and are used to assign the costs of those resources to activities. For example, if the activity of interest was "maintaining the lawn" for a bank, resources consumed would include labor, water, fuel, equipment, and fertilizer. Some of the resources could be measured precisely. Labor and fuel, for example, would be directly measured by observation. Water, on the other hand, would be difficult to measure specifically for grounds use, because it isn't metered separately. One way to assign water costs to grounds would be to use a driver such as "labor expended watering grounds." A relationship between watering labor and water consumption could be created. It could be as simple as determining how much water flows through the sprinkler in a minute as measured by a bucket. If it was determined that it took three minutes to fill a five-gallon bucket with water, the relationship between time and cost of water could be created. Water is consumed at the rate of 100 gallons per hour. Since the groundsperson is watering the lawn, one hour of groundsperson labor on the lawn relates directly to 100 gallons of water consumed. The cost of 100 gallons of water is directly related to a labor hour. A direct relationship is created between the particular cost of interest (water) and another resource (labor) that is easy to measure. Resource drivers are particularly useful to operations decisions because the resources are often controlled by operations.

Activity drivers measure the demands that cost objects place on activities. They are used to assign the cost of associated activities to cost objects. An activity driver might be the number of computer technician hours worked, for example. This driver could be used to assign the cost of computer programming to a cost object such as the loan-processing department. If the loan-processing department required 300 hours of computer programming that cost $28 per hour during one month, then $8,400 ($28 × 300 hours) of the total costs of computer programming would be assigned to the loan-processing department. This model for tracing costs provides the basis for activity-based costing (ABC). ABC links costs to cost objects by first assigning costs to activities and then assigning them to cost objects. Linking activities and costs can result in cost reductions because costs can be better controlled. Activity drivers are critical to operations because they are often part of processes used to create products and services.

Exhibit 6.4 provides a conceptual view of three alternatives to linking costs of resources to cost objects. Costs can be assigned directly through direct tracing, through resource drivers, and through activity drivers.

Allocating Indirect Operations Costs

Indirect costs cannot be traced precisely to cost objects, because no direct relationship exists; thus they must be *allocated* to cost objects. An example of a cost that must be allocated is the cost of electricity for a large computer system firm. Certainly each system design project would consume its share of the total amount of electricity used in a month, but if a particular project is the cost object, there would be no way to

Cost Assignment Alternatives

EXHIBIT 6.4

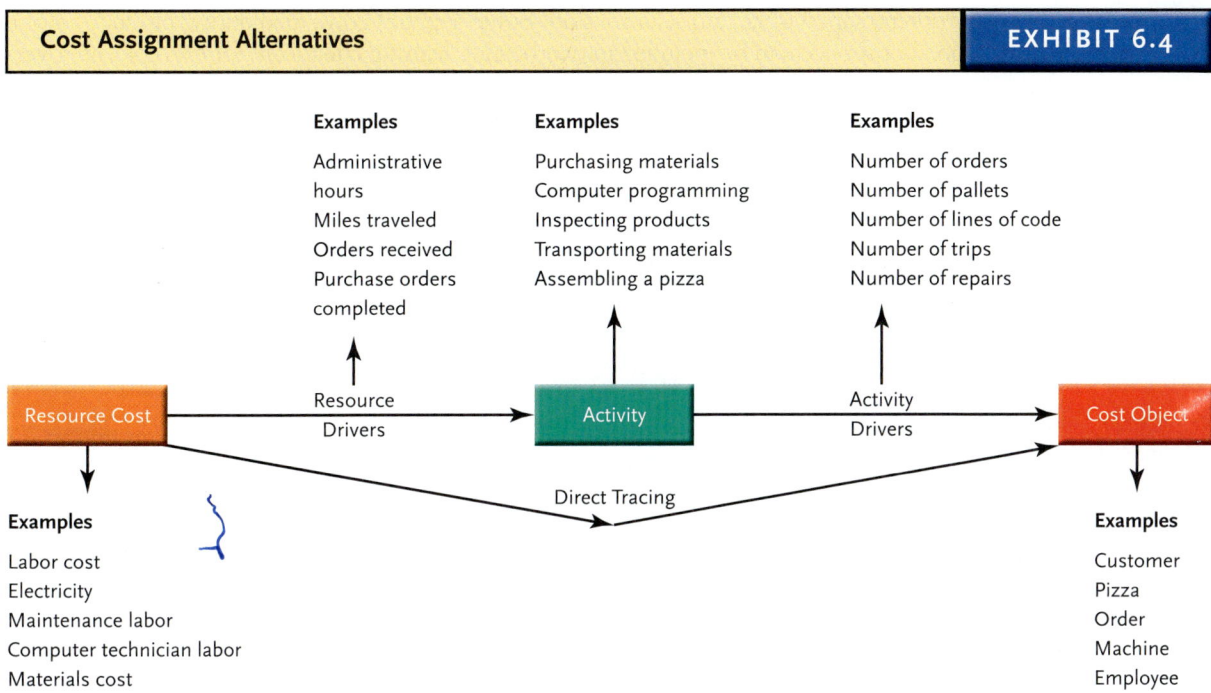

directly link electricity consumption to that project. Without that link, there'd be no way to determine what the total cost of that project was. It must be allocated in some way. One way might be to allocate electricity to projects proportionate to the number of days of project duration. Allocation of costs to cost objects, such as projects, products, or customers, is not accurate and is subject to substantial bias inherent in the assumptions used. Links between indirect costs and various cost objects may be required for external reporting, but they contribute very little to the precise needs of decision making.

Components of Product Cost

Cost management systems identify product costs for external financial reporting. Product costs are divided into two categories: production costs and nonproduction costs. **Production costs** are those costs associated with the actual production of goods or services. They are often the focus of operations-driven productivity improvement efforts. **Nonproduction costs** are the costs associated with selling and administration.

Production costs, in turn, are broken down into direct materials, direct labor, and overhead. **Direct materials** are materials that can be traced directly to the good or service being produced. The component parts of a product, for example, are direct materials. Buns at your favorite fast-food restaurant are direct materials. Those little bottles of shampoo and conditioner, bars of soap, and toilet paper are direct materials for a hotel. Peanuts provided on an airline and those little envelopes banks use to put currency in when you cash a check are other examples of direct materials in services. Materials that actually become a part of the product or are consumed during the service are considered direct materials. **Direct labor** can also be traced directly to the products or services being produced. The amount used can easily be calculated by observing the production processes. All other nondirect costs are thrown into the category of **overhead**. Examples of overhead are the costs of employing maintenance workers, supervisors, and security staff. Some supplies consumed during production of a good or service can be included in overhead. Cleaning chemicals, for example, are overhead for a hotel. Machine lubricants are an example of overhead for a manufacturer.

The operations decisions categories of inventory, workforce, capacity, and facilities are clearly significant when viewed from a product cost perspective. Direct materials, for example, are the costs of purchasing inventory. Direct labor is the cost of paying the workforce that works on the product or service. Overhead consists of the costs associated with the facility, equipment, and workforce that are not directly involved in production. Operations controls most of the costs of the product or service.

PRODUCTIVITY IMPROVEMENT AND COST REDUCTION

Measuring and managing costs, as they relate to operations resources, is an important component of decision making. As resource management is examined in detail in subsequent chapters, it will become apparent that the purpose of many of the decision models is to minimize costs.

For the operations resource categories of inventory, workforce, capacity, and facilities, managing costs is often synonymous with managing productivity. As has been mentioned previously, productivity measures are generally some measure of output divided by some measure of input, and the key input is cost. For employees, productivity can be expressed as a measure of work accomplished per labor hour. For inventory it is expressed as a measure of sales per dollar of inventory value. For equipment, it is some measure of equipment output divided by machine time. For the facility, it is a measure of facility output (sales, customers served, and so on) divided by a measure of facility investment, such as square feet. In many of these cases the denominators will look very similar to the cost objects discussed earlier in this chapter because they are resources management is interested in.

Reduction of inputs can take the form of eliminating waste, eliminating steps that don't add value, eliminating workers, and a host of other simplification and time-saving improvements. The practice of producing at minimum costs has become known as **lean production**. Reel Operations Video 6.1 examines lean production practices at Caterpillar's Aurora, Illinois, production plant.

Effort to improve any aspect of business processes invariably results in cost reduction. For many of these efforts, action is initiated by a desire to reduce the difference between the desired and actual cost or consumption rate (a standard). This difference is known as **variance**. Operations decisions are frequently motivated by the desire to decrease a variance. The following discussion introduces the use of variances to guide cost management efforts.

Putting Cost Information to Work for Operations: Standards and Variances

A **standard** is a measure that should be achieved. It provides a goal and gives operations consistency in processes, costs, and output levels. It is simply a desired measure that provides managers with a basis for comparison to determine if performance is what it should be. In the previous chapter, efficiency was defined as being the actual output divided by the standard output. Calculating efficiency is a popular use for standards. Standards that are commonly used in operations include quantity usage standards (output or usage per unit of time) and price standards (price per unit). Not surprisingly, just as output rates do not always meet quantity standards, resulting in less than 100 percent efficiency, actual prices do not always meet price standards.

Cost systems aid operations decision making. They are used to develop standard product and service costs to aid in operations planning and control functions and also help in determining product and service costs. To assist in the planning and control of operations resource usage, a process known as **variance analysis** compares what should happen to what actually is happening regarding inventory and capacity consumption. The resulting information provides a valuable input to operations so that costs are maintained and the appropriate levels of inventory and capacity can be planned for. Exhibit 6.5 illustrates how variance analysis works for products that have standards for usage of a material and the price for that material.

Variance analysis drives many operations actions because it facilitates the control of various contributors to cost. Exhibit 6.5 demonstrates how the difference between the actual quantity at the actual price minus the actual quantity at the standard price provides the price variance. Similarly, the actual quantity at the standard price minus the standard quantity at the standard price yields the usage variance. The actual quantity at the actual price minus the standard quantity at the standard price provides the total variance. Direct materials costs can be monitored and controlled from two perspectives: the quantity consumed and the price of each item. If the quantity consumed or the price strays from the standard, the costs go up or down. An unfavorable price variance occurs when box 1 minus box 2 is greater than 0: The price is greater than it should be. An unfavorable usage variance occurs when box 2 minus box 3 is greater than 0: Too much material is being consumed. Variance analysis is used to help isolate costs that are not what they should be. Many operations control functions are guided by variance analysis.

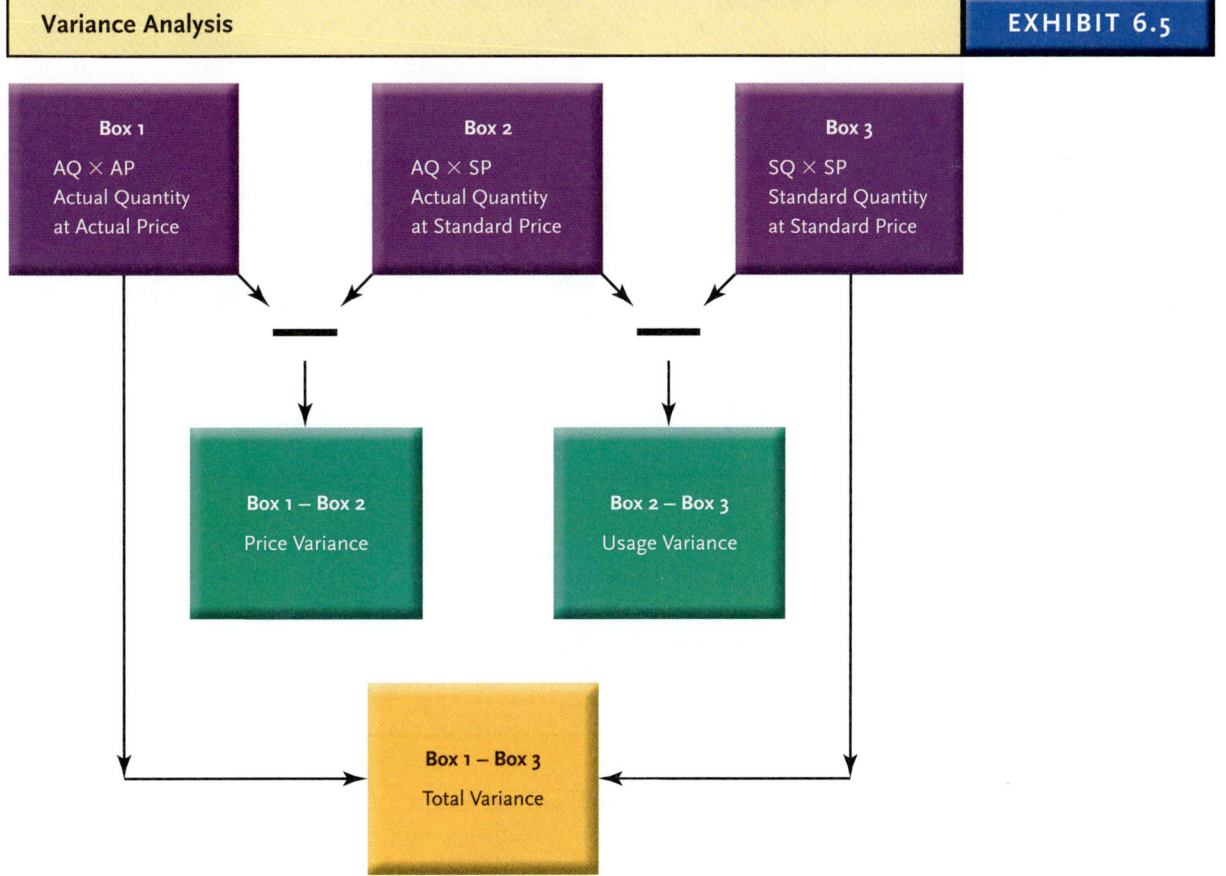

EXHIBIT 6.5 Variance Analysis

Example 6.1

Variance Analysis

A small manufacturer of organic snack foods monitors all components that go into its products. One product in particular, a very popular salsa, utilizes a number of ingredients, but two of primary importance—pepper sauce and a very high grade of fresh cilantro—are tightly controlled for both taste and costs purposes. Usage variance can result in inconsistency in taste from batch to batch. Price variance results in cost variances that can eat up the profit margins available on the product. The standard usage rate for cilantro is 15 ounces per 50-gallon batch. The standard price is $1.20 per ounce.

Current usage rates, determined by monitoring the amount of cilantro in the bin and the number of 50-gallon batches produced, average 16.3 ounces per 50-gallon batch. Cilantro prices have risen for the supplier and are now at $1.42 per ounce. Compute the usage variance, price variance, and total variance.

Solution

Exhibit 6.6 provides a framework for the solution to this problem.

EXHIBIT 6.6 Variance Analysis for Example 6.1

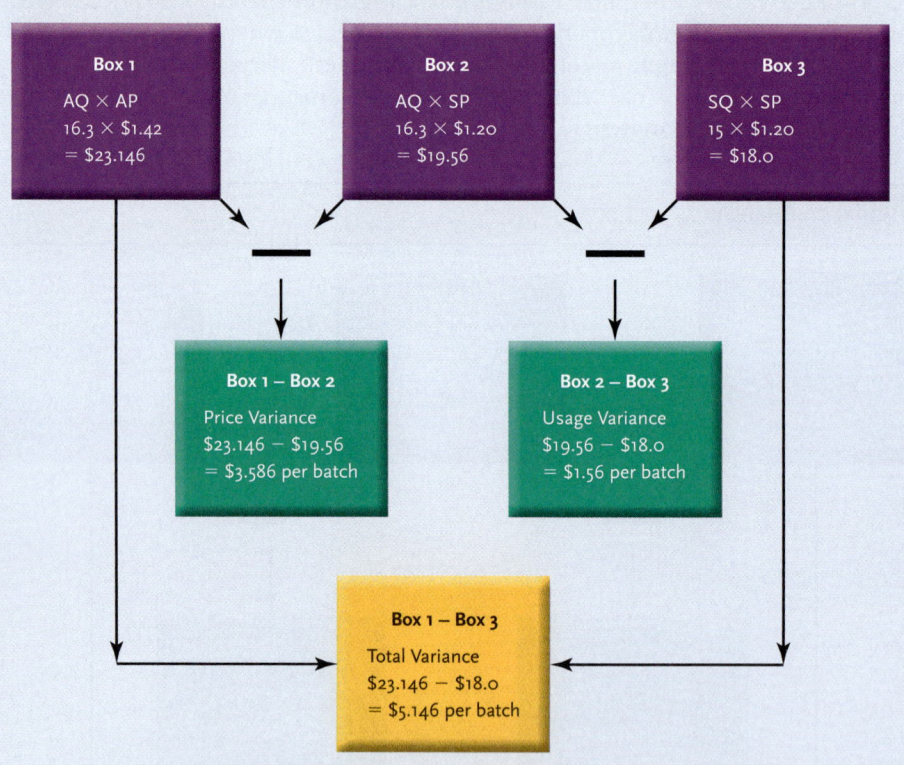

The price variance is $3.586 per batch, given the $0.22 per ounce price variance over standard. The usage variance is $1.56 per batch. Total variance is $5.146 per batch produced. Excel Tutor 6.1 demonstrates how variance analysis can be done in a spreadsheet environment.

www.OperationsNow.com

Variance analysis can be used with a variety of resources. Almost any type of resource, including inventory, labor, facilities, and equipment capacity, can be analyzed using variance analysis. For example, labor variances are used to monitor the number of hours required (usage) and the hourly pay rate. Efficiency variances can be used to compare hours actually used and those that should have been used. Interactive Model 6.1 provides an interactive environment for experimenting with usage, cost, and total variances.

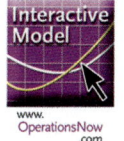

Using variance analysis, specific variances can be isolated, giving management the ability to monitor resource usage and costs—critical tasks for effectively managing operations. Unfavorable variances often provide the catalyst for productivity improvement efforts.

TOTAL COST VERSUS COST PER UNIT

Total costs were defined earlier in this chapter as the costs of all resources obtained in a particular period. Total costs are critical and have a direct impact on profitability via the net income calculation, as shown in Equation 6.1. A generic and frequently used measure of the productivity of resources purchased is known as **cost per unit**. To determine cost per unit, a particular product or service becomes the cost object. Cost per unit is determined by dividing the total cost for producing the units of interest by the number of units produced.

Cost per unit is at the root of many productivity measures, including equipment utilization. It is really the "average" cost per unit. Like many uses of average costs, cost per unit can be misleading. Any average can be reduced by increasing the number of units (the denominator). Here, it is done by increasing the number of units produced.

The misuse of the cost per unit measure often results from an inherent assumption that reducing cost per unit is the same as reducing the cost of goods sold, and it will automatically increase profitability. It isn't and it won't. There is no reason to expect that total costs will be reduced simply because cost per unit for a particular product is lower.

If total costs are reduced, a reduction in cost per unit will follow if the number of units produced remains the same. If demand increases and an increase in units produced increases the denominator, the cost per unit may decrease. Managers can play deceitful games with cost per unit. It isn't that managers are dishonest or criminal in nature, it's just that they wish to maximize the performance measures that form the basis for their evaluation. These games are not only misleading about improvements to costs, but they can result in total costs increasing while showing a decrease in cost per unit.

COST TRADEOFFS

Many business decisions require a tradeoff of one cost for another. Quite often, the tradeoff amounts to short-term costs being traded for long-term costs. This is not necessarily bad, but it frequently happens because the long-term costs aren't recognized or are given low priority. The long-term costs appear to be lower than they really are. The decision to place short-term costs above long-term costs may actually be consciously made. These decisions sometimes result from the short tenure of managers. A fast-track manager will be evaluated on this year's performance, not the financial performance five years down the road. They can also be motivated by the short-term perspective of investors. Many cost tradeoffs also trade nonfinancial costs for financial ones.

NONFINANCIAL COSTS

As mentioned early in this chapter, not all costs are monetary and many involve resources that are difficult to measure quantitatively. The fact that businesses invest in hopes of obtaining these resources, however, means that they must be considered costs when given up. Unfortunately, since the resources are difficult to quantify, the costs are open to interpretation, and they are not required in external financial reports, they often receive little priority in tradeoffs. Many nonfinancial costs will be familiar to you. Some correspond to value attributes or competitive priorities such as quality, flexibility, or response time. In other situations they are the very capabilities the company depends on to compete. Someone unfamiliar with the importance of a particular capability may be willing to sacrifice it for an apparent decrease in monetary costs. Lack of an enterprise view strikes again.

Time and flexibility are two costs that often lose to monetary cost reduction in a tradeoff because placing a value on them is extremely difficult. They are of incredible strategic importance, however. Decisions to reduce costs often result in an increase in response time or a decrease in flexibility. Let's briefly examine an example for each case.

Outsourcing has become a popular way to reduce costs. However, outsourcing can increase transportation time to get components, thereby slowing the response time for customers. As a result, a competitor with a shorter response time may become the new supplier of choice for a customer with quick response time needs.

Reducing costs by eliminating excess capacity is also a quick way to improve the appearance of periodic performance numbers. Eliminating labor through layoffs, or even by eliminating equipment, reduces total costs and costs per unit but can have devastating effects on a firm's ability to quickly react to the unique need of a customer. Protective capacity provides flexibility, and a customer who can't get the response needed is motivated to try out the competition.

Quality is also frequently sacrificed in tradeoff decisions. Pressures to improve end-of-period performance figures motivate managers to ship goods known to be defective. Substitution of cheaper and lower-quality raw materials and components for products and services is a way to reduce direct material costs. We've all experienced poor-quality service that results from too few staff at peak demand times.

Virtually any value attribute can be at risk during a cost-reduction push. Value attributes are important to customers because they cost the customer money. They're targets for cost cutting for the same reason. Activities that add the most value are often the most expensive. Businesses have begun to recognize that many nonmonetary costs are actually closely linked to future performance, although the impact on quantitative measures is merely delayed. An approach to ensure that performance measures are not improved at the expense of others, known as the balanced scorecard (BSC), was introduced in Chapter 2.

The BSC translates a business's vision and strategy into a set of performance measures distributed among perspectives beyond the purely financial. It links objectives, initiatives, *and* performance measures to the firm's strategy by integrating financial measures with nonfinancial performance indicators. Clearly, when looking at a firm's strategy, there are objectives that aren't stated in financial terms. BSC translates these objectives into a framework that provides an enterprise view of an organization's overall performance. In addition to a financial perspective, other key performance indicators relate directly to a customer perspective, internal business processes, and organizational growth, learning, and innovation. Balanced scorecards have become an increasingly popular way to ensure that a balance exists among performance indicators.

Exhibit 6.7 summarizes 10 benefits of the balanced scorecard approach.

CHAPTER SUMMARY

The first component of value, discussed in Chapter 5, is the actual processes and capabilities that a business uses to create products and services that are sold. With-

> **EXHIBIT 6.7**
>
> **Balanced Scorecard Benefits**
>
> 1. For government agencies, the BSC fulfills a legal requirement. The Government Performance and Results Act of 1993 requires a strategic plan and a method of measuring the performance of strategic initiatives for government agencies.
> 2. The BSC allows an organization to align strategic activities to the strategic plan. It supports deployment and implementation of the strategy on a continuous basis by providing feedback needed to guide efforts.
> 3. Visibility provided by a measurement system supports better and faster financial decisions and control of processes.
> 4. That visibility also provides accountability and incentives based on real data.
> 5. Measurements of process efficiency provide an objective, rational basis for selecting areas to improve first.
> 6. It allows managers to identify best practices and standardize their use elsewhere.
> 7. The measurements used make it possible to benchmark process performance against outside organizations.
> 8. The process cost data collected for past projects helps managers learn how to estimate costs more accurately for future projects.
> 9. It improves profitability by reducing process costs and improving productivity while at the same time improving mission effectiveness.
> 10. It raises the quality score of the organization as measured for the Malcolm Baldrige National Quality Award, increasing the probability of long-term success.
>
> Source: Adapted from *The Balanced Scorecard Institute*, "Top Ten Reasons for a Performance Measurement System," http://www.balancedscorecard.org/, April 27, 2000.

out them, no value would be created. In this chapter, the concept of cost was examined as the second component of value. Cost, although often thought of as the domain of accountants, drives so many critical decisions that all managers must understand its impact on the business, particularly the operational aspects of the business. Understanding costs and utilizing cost data in decision making is critical to making decisions that are financially sound *and* serve the best interests of the business owners.

This chapter examined the types of cost that are relevant to operations, including a very widely used cost: average cost. Cost data, particularly average cost data, can be misused and can be misleading. The role costs play in the value chain was also examined in this chapter.

Cost measurement is critical to operations because the results drive many decisions. Cost objects form an important basis for assigning costs to resources and activities, both important to operations managers. Tracing direct costs and allocating indirect costs are cost measurement tasks that affect many operations decisions. Productivity measures often include a cost as the denominator, motivating most productivity improvement efforts to focus on cost reduction. For productivity improvement and cost reduction efforts, variance analysis is often used to help isolate the causes of costs being higher than they should be.

When using cost measures for making decisions, caution should always be exercised. Average costs, particularly average cost per unit, can be misleading and result in behaviors not beneficial to the company. Likewise, an enterprise view should be fostered by using performance measures beyond those that have a purely financial perspective. A popular nonfinancial performance measurement tool is the balanced scorecard.

The next chapter examines one of those perspectives that must also play a role in decision making because it is such a critical component of value—quality.

KEY TERMS

activity, 165
activity drivers, 168
actual costs, 163
cost object, 166
cost per unit, 173
cost traceability, 167
direct labor, 169
direct materials, 169
expected costs, 163
lean production, 170
nonproduction costs, 169

out-of-pocket costs, 163
overhead, 169
period costs, 163
product costs, 163
production costs, 169
resource drivers, 167
standard, 170
total costs, 163
variance, 170
variance analysis, 171

REVIEW QUESTIONS

1. Define "cost."
2. Describe the difference between price and cost.
3. Why is price often considered to be the sole component of cost?
4. What role does cost play in profitability?
5. Describe two ways that increasing costs can reduce profitability.
6. Describe the following costs:
    a. Expected costs
    b. Actual costs
    c. Out-of-pocket costs
    d. Period costs
    e. Product costs
    f. Total costs
7. Why can the use of average costs be dangerous?
8. What is the value chain?
9. What is a cost object?
10. What does cost traceability mean? How does it relate to direct and indirect costs?
11. What is driver tracing?
12. What are resource drivers and activity drivers?
13. Describe the process of allocating indirect costs.
14. What are the components of production costs?
15. What is variance analysis? How can it be used to help manage the costs of resources?
16. Why is cost per unit sometimes misleading?

17. What are some common nonfinancial costs that should be considered when business decisions are made?

DISCUSSION QUESTIONS

1. What are the total costs of ownership for an automobile? Are those costs the same for students and nonstudents? How do those costs differ from one automobile to another? How important are those costs when considering an automobile purchase?
2. Identify the major categories of cost for a university. Create alternative plans for calculating the cost per student. How does the plan change if the cost object becomes a "student graduated"? If the cost object is a "chemistry major graduated," would the cost per unit be different from that of a business student graduated? Why? If the costs per student are different, should tuition be different?
3. Labor costs are often a concern for services and manufacturers. Employee salaries are the most frequently discussed labor costs, but there are others. Quite often, salaries are not increased because of the impact increases would have on labor costs. Some might argue that higher salaries would reduce total labor costs in the long term. How could this be true?
4. Much of the effort to improve cost measurement, including activity-based costing, focuses on providing more accurate ways to allocate costs to individual products. Why is it important to be able to know what a specific product costs? Which types of cost will be the most difficult to deal with?
5. Nonfinancial costs are often the most difficult to include in decision-making processes. What nonfinancial costs are most often part of financial decisions you must make? In jobs you have had, have you observed decisions made that ignored nonfinancial costs? Describe them.

PROBLEMS

1. Mayflower Department Store offers a gift-wrapping service for its customers. Ribbon is the most expensive component of gift wrapping and must be controlled for both the cost of the service and the amount used. The current cost for ribbon is $0.48 per inch. The current usage of ribbon is 10 inches per package. The standard usage is 11 inches per package, with a standard price of $0.55. What are the price, usage, and total variances for the ribbon?
2. Dee's Cookies sells chocolate chip cookies on campus. Of course, chocolate chips are the most important ingredient for taste and cost. The standard usage of chips is 11 chips per cookie. The standard price for a bag of chocolate chips is $2.05. Dee has found that students like more than the standard amount of chocolate chips in the cookies. She therefore started to make her cookies with 15 chips. The store she buys the chocolate chips from has a sale on the chips, selling them for $1.89 per bag. There are 400 chips in a bag. Calculate the price variance, usage variance, and total variance.

3. Bill Howe is a project supervisor for Regal Homes, a builder of new houses. As the project supervisor, Bill must keep a careful eye on the number of worker-hours put into the construction of a new house. The standard number of worker-hours to complete a house is 1,075 and the standard hourly wage is $20.00. The current house has taken only 1,010 worker-hours and the workers are under contract for $20.00 per hour. What are the price, usage, and total variances for this house?

4. Stan operates a copy shop. The copy machines cost $0.05 per copy to operate excluding the paper. Stan normally pays $2.90 per 500-sheet ream of paper, although he currently is buying paper from a wholesaler for only $2.50 per ream. When his copiers are running well, paper jams are infrequent, resulting in an average usage of 1.07 sheets of paper to make one copy. The weather has been quite humid lately, causing his copiers to jam more frequently. It currently takes 1.27 sheets of paper to make one copy. Calculate the current price variance, usage variance, and total variance. What would the variance be if Stan began to use a more expensive brand of paper, costing $3.20 per ream, which resulted in there never being paper jams?

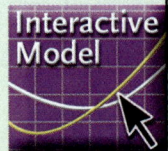
www.OperationsNow.com

INTERACTIVE ANALYSIS 6.1

THE VARIANCE ANALYSIS INTERACTIVE MODEL

The Variance Analysis Interactive Model is accessed in Chapter 6 of the *OperationsNow.com* website. It provides a conceptual view of a typical variance analysis problem in manufacturing. Recall that variance analysis is frequently used to monitor and evaluate operations actions and can be an influential force behind many operations decisions. A *variance* is the difference between a standard (what a measure should be) and the actual performance measure. Common operations-related variances enable managers to monitor the consumption of resources that relate closely to costs. A common approach to monitoring costs related to material consumption is to monitor the quantity consumed and the cost of each. The actual price (AP) for each item and the actual quantity consumed (AQ) provide the basis for knowing what reality was for the given situation. The standard price (SP) and the standard quantity (SQ) provide the standard that gives a basis for comparison.

In the Variance Analysis Interactive Model, cost and usage information is provided for a chemical manufacturer. One particular ingredient is supposed to be used at the rate of 50 gallons per batch. The final amount needed per batch depends on the quality level of the input, however. Lower quality requires more to get the desired reaction. The impact of an increase or decrease in price or quantity consumed, or an increase or decrease in the standard price or quantity, can be examined.

Default values are
SQ = 50   AQ = 60
SP = $21.00   AP = $31.00

Actual and standard amounts can be changed by dragging the top of the appropriate bar on the bar graph. The current total variance of $810 per batch is viewed as acceptable, given current price and quality availability of the ingredient.

Experiment 1: System Fundamentals
1. Using the default values, what is the current price variance? What is the current total variance? By dragging the top of the pink bar in the upper graph, reduce the actual price for the materials from $31.00 to $28.00.
   a. What is the new price variance? What is the new total variance?
   b. Does the usage variance change? Why or why not?
2. Set the model back to the default values by clicking on your browser's "refresh" or "reload" button. What is the current starting usage variance?
   a. Increase the standard quantity from 50 to 55 gallons per batch. What is the impact on the usage variance?
   b. What is the impact on the total variance? Is it what you expected? Explain the result.

Experiment 2: Exploring the Impact of Actual and Standard Quantity
1. Set the model to the default starting values.
   a. In many manufacturing situations, a higher-quality ingredient, with a higher concentration, can result in the company being able to tighten its standard quantity. This will require, however, that the actual usage be reduced as well, to maintain acceptable variances. Record the current total variance. Tighten the standard quantity by 15 gallons per batch. What happens to the total variance? What must happen to the actual quantity to maintain its total variance at approximately $800 per batch?
   b. One way to make variances *appear* more favorable is to change the standard quantity. The closer the standard gets to the actual quantity used, the less the variance. Drag the standard quantity (blue bar) to be equal to the actual quantity (pink bar). What happens to the total variance? When the actual and standard quantities are equal, a total variance of $500 remains. What is its cause?
2. Set the values back to the default settings by clicking on your browser's "refresh" or "reload" button.
   a. Under the default settings, the actual price is significantly above the standard price. As a percentage, how much higher than standard price is the actual price?
   b. Drag the actual quantity (pink bar) down until the total variance reaches zero. Describe how the relationship between actual and standard price and actual and standard quantity together dictate total variance.

Experiment 3: Exploring the Impact of Actual and Standard Price
1. Set the model to the default starting values by refreshing the page.
   a. A reduced price, achieved through the efforts of purchasing managers, can result in the company being able to tighten its standard price on raw materials purchased. For purchasing, however, that will mean actual price will need to be maintained at this level to maintain acceptable variances. Record the current total variance. Reduce the standard price by $5, to $16. What happens to the total variance? What must happen to the actual price to maintain its total variance at approximately $800 per batch?

b. One way to make variances *appear* more favorable is to increase the standard price. The closer the standard price gets to the actual price, the less the variance. Drag the standard price (blue bar) to be equal to the actual price (pink bar). What happens to the total variance? When the actual and standard quantities are equal, a total variance of $310 remains. What is its cause?

2. It is clear that the total variance results from price and usage. Look back at the results of the previous experiments.

   a. Based on the experiments you've done, what portion of the total variance results from price? What portion results from usage?

SELECTED RESOURCES

Hansen, Don R., and Mowen, Maryanne M. *Cost Management,* Cincinnati: South-Western Publishing, 1997.

Ross, S. A., Westerfield, R. W., and Jordan, B. D. *Essentials of Corporate Finance,* New York: Irwin McGraw-Hill, 1999.

OperationsNow.com LEARNING ACTIVITIES

CHAPTER ENHANCEMENT RESOURCES
- Esources
- Reel Operations Video Clips
- Interactive Models
- Excel Tutors
- Supplementary Readings
- Links to Operations On Site Companies

OM EXPLORATION
- Check It Out
- OM in Action
- Online Business Tours
- Letters from the Top
- Putting It All Together: Virtual Case Studies
- Additional Reading

The resource/profit model places quality as the third of four components of value. Quality is unique as a component of value because customer definitions vary and measurement can be difficult, both making it more challenging to manage. Quality truly is in the eye of the beholder. Although consumers need not arrive at any consensus in defining quality, businesses must define quality precisely in order to produce it and control it.

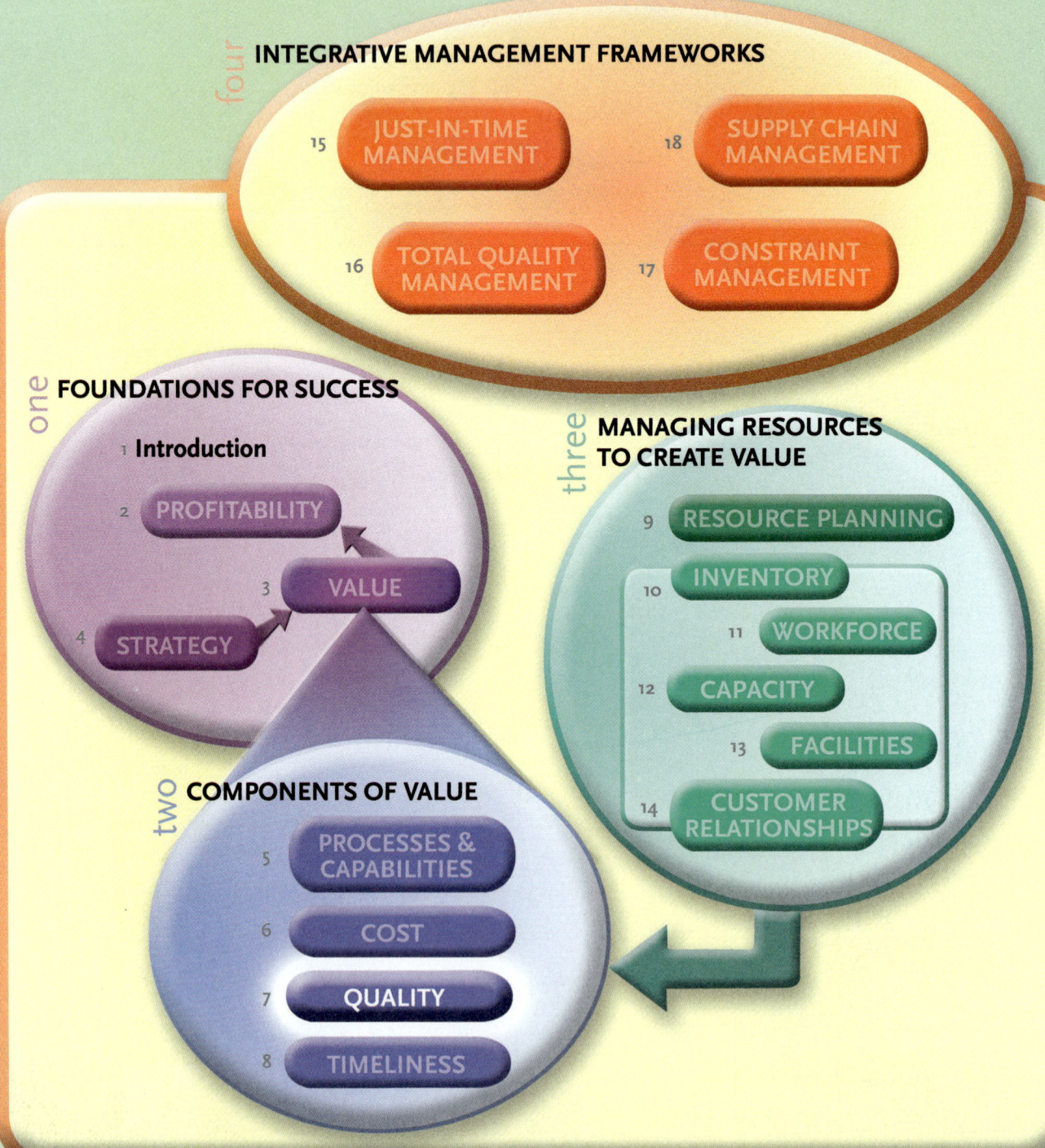

CHAPTER 7

Quality

LEARNING OBJECTIVES

Upon completion of Chapter 7, you should be able to

_____ Define quality from a customer's perspective.

_____ Describe the relationships between quality and value as well as quality and profitability.

_____ Compare proactive approaches and reactive approaches to quality management.

_____ Describe the costs of quality.

_____ Explain the function of the general-purpose quality analysis tools.

_____ Describe and make computations for process capability.

_____ Describe how acceptance sampling works and the role of the operating characteristics curve.

_____ Understand the Kano model.

_____ Explain how six sigma quality relates to process capability.

_____ Describe service quality applications, including service blueprinting and moment-of-truth analysis.

_____ Describe how "recovery" applies to quality failures.

Introduction: Product and Service Quality Defined
Quality and Value
Quality and Profitability
Proaction Versus Reaction in Quality Management
Cost of Quality
General-Purpose Quality Analysis Tools
Statistical Process Control
Acceptance Sampling
The Next Level: Moving beyond Merely Satisfying the Customer
Service-Oriented Quality Improvement
Technological Advances in Quality Information Management: Customer Relationship Management
When Something Still Goes Wrong: Recovery
Total Quality Management
Chapter Summary

INTERNET RESOURCES

 Excel Tutors provide annotated spreadsheets for every solved problem that automatically load Excel.

 Esources provide an online version of the more traditional boxed insert.

 Reel Videos provide streaming video footage for company applications of chapter concepts.

 Interactive Models provide an experimental environment for quantitative concepts and simulations.

INTRODUCTION

Product and Service Quality Defined

The concept of quality means different things to different people. Most people would agree that quality is an important characteristic of a product or service, but if you ask 10 people how a particular product or service stacks up in terms of quality, you may get 10 different responses. On the other hand, if you ask a manager to define quality, the response will probably be specific, describing the products or services the manager deals with every day and stressing how important quality is to profitability.

Links between quality and profitability are strong because quality plays such an important role in the customer's perception of value, as shown in the resource/profit model in Exhibit 7.1. Despite its importance, quality can be understood only after agreement on its definition. A concept with as many potentially different interpretations as quality needs a precise definition if it is to be measured, controlled, managed, specified to suppliers, *and* evaluated by customers. Quality is conformance to customer specifications and expectations. Recall from Chapter 3 that quality was described as a critical value component in B2B and B2C interactions. Quality is defined by the customer, but the two different types of customer may define it very differently.

The nature of today's products and services makes it difficult for companies to understand the expectations of all customers, let alone live up to them. Service quality expectations have increased the complexity of expectations that once were limited to products. Purchasing a product without at least some expectations of service is a rare experience today. Services that are purchased without associated goods are also unusual. The management of quality for a service creates challenges that are quite different from those associated with purchases of products. This can best be understood through an examination of the dimensions of product and service quality. Garvin and later Pisek summarized product quality through eight dimensions: performance, features, reliability, durability, serviceability, aesthetics, response, and reputation.[1] They are briefly described in Exhibit 7.2. A contrasting set of dimensions for service quality consists of reliability, responsiveness, assurance, empathy, and tangibles.[2] Exhibit 7.3 provides brief descriptions of these dimensions.

Note that the product quality dimensions that are associated with services seem to be lumped into the categories of reliability and response. Likewise, the product-oriented dimensions of service quality are lumped into the category of "tangibles." Exhibit 7.4 provides an integrated approach to understanding product and service dimensions of quality that fits an environment where customers expect products and services. Businesses must meet those customer expectations in order to be competitive.

QUALITY AND VALUE

The components of value (processes and capabilities, cost, quality, and timeliness) are all necessary parts of the value equation. Without them, value cannot be created and sold. The components of value do not necessarily play equivalent roles, however. Recall that value is a function of costs and benefits. The "benefit" side of the value equation consists of processes and capabilities and the resulting quality and timeliness. A product or service with "bad" quality means that the product or service doesn't meet the customer's expectations. It is difficult to imagine how purchasing something that falls short of your expectations could ever be considered to be a good value, but most of us have done it. We are sometimes seduced by the "good deal" only to be disap-

The Role of Quality in the Resource/Profit Model — EXHIBIT 7.1

four — INTEGRATIVE MANAGEMENT FRAMEWORKS
- 15 JUST-IN-TIME MANAGEMENT
- 18 SUPPLY CHAIN MANAGEMENT
- 16 TOTAL QUALITY MANAGEMENT
- 17 CONSTRAINT MANAGEMENT

one — FOUNDATIONS FOR SUCCESS
- 1 Introduction
- 2 PROFITABILITY
- 3 VALUE
- 4 STRATEGY

three — MANAGING RESOURCES TO CREATE VALUE
- 9 RESOURCE PLANNING
- 10 INVENTORY
- 11 WORKFORCE
- 12 CAPACITY
- 13 FACILITIES
- 14 CUSTOMER RELATIONSHIPS

two — COMPONENTS OF VALUE
- 5 PROCESSES & CAPABILITIES
- 6 COST
- 7 QUALITY
- 8 TIMELINESS

---

pointed later on. What actually happens is that we confuse price with cost. We see a low price and think "Hey, low cost!" Unfortunately, often it turns out that the cost isn't low at all. As the saying goes, if you buy the best, you only cry once, but if you don't buy the best, you cry over and over again. This axiom makes it seem like those purchase decisions should be simple—always buy the best. In reality most customers can't always buy "the best," and that's where the judgment of value comes into play.

Lack of quality means that the product or service doesn't meet customer expectations, which almost always means poor value. But the presence of quality doesn't necessarily

EXHIBIT 7.2 — Dimensions of Product Quality

Performance:	What are the desirable characteristics of the product?
Features:	What additional characteristics of the product are possible?
Reliability:	Is the business dependable? Does it accomplish what it promises?
Durability:	How long will the product last?
Serviceability:	Can the product be easily and inexpensively repaired?
Aesthetics:	Does the product satisfy subjective requirements, like appearance and style?
Response:	Is the interaction between the customer and the product provider pleasant and appropriate?
Reputation:	What does information on past performance say about the company?

Source: Adapted from D. A. Garvin, "What Does Product Quality Really Mean?" *Sloan Management Review* 26 (Fall 1984), pp. 29–30, and P. E. Pisek, "Defining Quality at the Marketing Development Interface," *Quality Progress* 20 (June 1987), pp. 28–36.

EXHIBIT 7.3 — Dimensions of Service Quality

Reliability:	Does the business keep its promises?
Responsiveness:	Does it promptly respond to the needs of its customers?
Assurance:	Can the employees generate customer trust and confidence?
Empathy:	Are employees approachable and sensitive to individual customers?
Tangibles:	Do the physical facilities, equipment, and written materials show care and attention?

Source: Adapted from J. A. Fitzsimmons and M. J. Fitzsimmons, *Service Management* (New York, McGraw-Hill, 2001), p. 45.

mean a good value for a customer. Outrageous costs or delays in availability may also overshadow the quality component. Quality is a necessary component of value, but it is not sufficient. Quality is so important to value that many customers try to learn about product quality before making a purchase. They seek out quality-related information from services that specialize in evaluating product quality. Esource 7.1 provides an example of this type of evaluation.

QUALITY AND PROFITABILITY

Previous chapters examined the role value plays in a firm's profitability. Recall from the discussion of cost in Chapter 6 that cost has a double influence on profitability because it affects net income in two ways. First, a cost reduction results in a reduced cost of goods sold, which, by itself, results in an increase in net income. A reduction in cost also provides an opportunity to reduce the selling price, resulting in an increase in value for the customer and increasing demand and net sales.

EXHIBIT 7.4 Dimensions of Service and Product Quality Combined

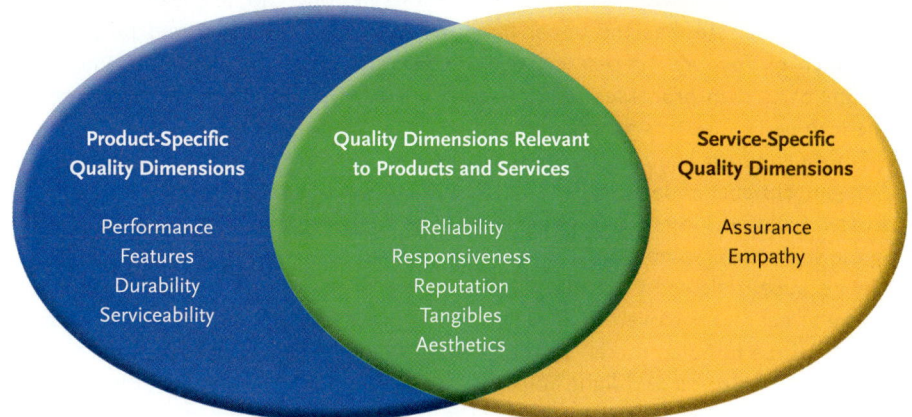

Source: Adapted from D. A. Garvin, "What Does Product Quality Really Mean?" *Sloan Management Review* 26 (Fall 1984), pp. 29–30. P. E. Pisek, "Defining Quality at the Marketing Development Interface," *Quality Progress* 20 (June 1987), pp. 28–36, and J. A. Fitzsimmons and M. J. Fitzsimmons, *Service Management* (New York, McGraw-Hill, 2001), p. 45.

Quality can also have a double effect on profitability. The most direct impact is through its relationship with value. As quality goes up, all else being equal, value goes up. If quality rises beyond the wants and needs of the customer, the customer may not recognize it as valuable and may not be willing to pay for it, however. A price increase necessary to cover the cost of added quality features may reduce value. The key is to focus on the customer by letting the customer define quality. In this way, a financial return on the quality added is ensured. Reel Operations Video 7.1 provides an overview of how Detroit Diesel focuses on the customer when designing quality products.

The increase in net income that results from enhanced value can come in several forms, including increased demand, increased customer loyalty, increased market share, and the resulting increased sales. Increased value also provides an opportunity to increase the selling price, also increasing net sales.

Quality has another, less obvious impact on net income through its link to product and service production costs. Many quality improvements in the product and service sectors create reductions in costs through a variety of means. Among these are reductions in scrap, warranty claims, labor, recalls, repairs, rework, and inventory. These costs are worthy of a more in-depth examination.

Recall from the previous chapter that production costs are those associated with the actual production of goods and services. They consist of direct materials, direct labor, and overhead. Products and services are typically of poor quality because the processes used to create them were ineffective or tasks were improperly performed. Production costs increase as a result of several influences. Labor and materials consumed in those processes are wasted because the product can't be sold or service doesn't meet the needs of the customers so they don't pay for it. Overhead costs associated with poor-quality products and services also often increase.

A defective product may lead to a number of possible cost scenarios. The defect might be discovered before the product is sold. In that case, the product might be fixed, or it might be thrown away or "scrapped." In the first case, additional labor and materials will be required to fix it. The product is eventually sold, but at higher cost. In the second case, the labor and materials consumed are discarded and provide no opportunity for a financial return. The worst case, from a total-cost perspective, is

Quality, Productivity, and Inventory Reduction: Inseparable Goals

Despite two decades of catch-up efforts by Ford, GM, and Daimler-Chrysler, Toyota still has the upper hand on auto industry quality and productivity.

Much of Toyota's success can be credited to common sense and tremendous scrutiny of its own processes. That scrutiny has been transported from Japan to the American parts suppliers as well.

Toyota engineer Hajime Oba provides a classic example in a visit to a Kalamazoo, Michigan, supplier of dashboard vents. Summit, the supplier of the vents, had recently invested $280,000 in robots and paint ovens to bake the vents. The process of painting the vents took 90 minutes. The slow process actually reduced quality and productivity because it slowed the conveyor feeding the oven, and the parts gathered dust waiting to get into the oven. Hajime Oba demonstrated that the paint could be dried in under three minutes merely by using a hair dryer. The paint system was replaced with $150 spray guns and light bulbs for drying the paint. The faster process could then be integrated into final assembly. The result was improvements in quality and productivity along with a drastic reduction in inventory. Component parts inventory fell from 14 days' worth to four hours. Finished-goods inventory fell from 30 days' worth to eight hours.

Toyota's attention to quality has not gone unnoticed. J.D. Power and Associates' rankings of four- to five-year-old vehicles has placed Toyota highest for six consecutive years. Toyota consistently lands on *Consumer Reports'* lists of top vehicles. Toyota expects that as the auto market cools in the United States, consumers will be more interested in quality and durability. This presents a challenge to Toyota, because as the company strives to increase its U.S. capacity by 60 percent, it must increasingly depend on U.S. suppliers of parts. U.S. suppliers are not as committed to the lean manufacturing principles as Toyota is. This approach to manufacturing strives to produce vehicles with one-third the defects, using half the factory space, half the capital, and half the engineering time. This results in a doubling of the productivity of most resources, at a much higher level of quality. In contrast, U.S. manufacturers use lean manufacturing techniques to reduce inventory alone.

The broad impact of lean manufacturing is demonstrated by another example of Oba's analysis of an American factory—Gentex, a high-quality supplier of self-dimming mirrors. Gentex productivity was variable, as a result of workers' hurrying on Fridays to avoid overtime on Saturdays and high levels of absenteeism on Mondays. Oba promoted *heijunka,* a practice that calls for the factory to standardize output levels. Stable production levels result in easier response to demand changes (higher levels of flexibility). In addition, if a defect or problem occurs, it is more obvious in an environment that is more stable. In the end, Gentex quality improved even more, and inventory levels dropped. Value was increased in two ways: better quality through fewer defects, and lower costs through lower levels of inventory. Both result in profitability enhancement.

Time after time, lean production efforts result in dramatic improvements in productivity, higher levels of quality, and reduced inventory. The three are quite interdependent. In the Toyota example just presented, the success can also be attributed to a much higher level of involvement with suppliers. Results of a recent supplier survey show that even though the suppliers trained by Toyota also supply Big Three auto makers with parts, they perform much better for Toyota. The table below shows how, despite improvements made in the last two decades, U.S. auto makers are signifi-

(continues)

> **(continued)**
>
> cantly behind Japanese manufacturers. Reliability of new 2000 U.S. autos was approximately at the level the Japanese manufacturers had reached in 1985.
>
> | Year | Japanese Automobile Manufacturers Problems per 100 Vehicles | American Automobile Manufacturers Problems per 100 Vehicles |
> |---|---|---|
> | 2000 | 11 | 23 |
> | 1980 | 34 | 105 |
>
> Source: "Why Toyota Wins Such High Marks on Quality Surveys," *The Wall Street Journal*, March 15, 2001, pp. A1, A11, : "Japanese Autos Lead in Quality; Gap Is Closing," *The Wall Street Journal*, March 15, 2001, p. A4; "Cruising for Quality," *Business Week*, September 3, 2001, pp. 74–75.

that the defective product is sold and the customer discovers the defect and expects a refund or exchange. In addition to all of the financial costs associated with that situation, customer loyalty decreases or is lost and that customer tells potential customers of the negative experience. No matter what the specifics, defective products always increase costs. The product always comes back, and the business incurs the costs associated with discarding it. What makes this scenario even worse, however, is when the business involves the customer in its poor performance. It has done the worst possible thing: given the customer a reason to try a competitor. The costs associated with quality will be addressed later in this chapter during the discussion of a quality management approach known as cost of quality (COQ).

The repercussions of a defective service are different from those of a defective product. Unlike product quality, service quality is difficult to measure before the customer receives it. Thus in every case of defective service, the customer is directly involved. Customer exposure to defective service can have a variety of outcomes. In the best case, employees discover the impending error and fix it before the customer encounters it. If the customer is involved, however, the outcome can range from a mild problem to a total disaster. We've all had experiences at a retailer when we couldn't find any employees to help us or at a restaurant that served us the wrong meal (and by the time the correct one was brought, everyone we were with had already finished eating). These experiences are best dealt with through a process of prevention rather than correction after the fact.

Most of our experiences as consumers of product quality are positive, because defective products are typically not allowed to get to the customer. We have a variety of products to select from, but most manufacturers are managing product quality well. Service quality, on the other hand, is often poor. A tight labor market, resulting in high levels of turnover, inexperienced employees, employees who lack the skills to interact effectively with customers, and managers who are unskilled at managing service quality all contribute to the problem.

PROACTION VERSUS REACTION IN QUALITY MANAGEMENT

When the objective of quality management is simplified to the extreme, it can change from "producing high-quality goods and services" to "making sure the customer gets

www
OperationsNow
.com

only high-quality goods and services." There is a huge difference between these two objectives. The extra step involved in the second, which might appear to be reasonable, actually does a lot of damage. Prevention of poor quality effects a substantial reduction in costs. Merely stopping poor quality from getting to the customer, however, doesn't reduce costs at all. Reel Operations Video 7.2 examines how Honda tackles cost reduction goals through effective quality management.

Costs associated with quality management are much more extensive than one might imagine. One approach to managing quality, known as "cost of quality," is discussed in the following section.

COST OF QUALITY

Studies in the late 1970s and early 1980s provided proof that the costs of quality were significant. Costs associated with producing poor-quality goods and services—things like scrap, waste, rework, inspection, warranty costs, and recalls—can make up between 15 and 20 percent of the total costs of goods sold. Some studies showed that efforts to fix things that had originally been done wrong accounted for 20 to 30 percent of operating budgets. The **cost of quality (COQ)** concept was originally developed for manufacturing, but it has also been applied to services. COQ is defined as all of the costs associated with maintaining the quality of goods and services. It includes the general categories of external failure costs, internal failure costs, appraisal costs, and prevention costs. Let's examine external and internal failure costs first.

External Failure Costs

External failure costs occur when a customer is exposed to poor quality. A quality problem that becomes an external failure is almost always more expensive than it would have been had it been dealt with internally, for several reasons. First, the fact that a product has made it all the way to the customer means that more costs have been expended on the product. Transportation and stocking costs, for example, that would not have been spent had the failure been identified internally, have now been added to the failure. In addition, sales staff time has been invested with no financial return. These quantifiable costs, though important and potentially sufficient to eliminate a profit, may not be the most critical. The most serious costs associated with an external failure may be the cost of losing a customer.

In contrast to product failures, external failures in services that involve personal experience or that require a significant investment in time can be difficult to recover from. These failures can result in dissatisfied customers, the potential loss of customers, and negative "word of mouth." In the past, managers of services routinely predicted that a customer who had a bad experience would tell 10 others about it. Today, however, with the prevalence of Internet newsgroups, chat rooms, and the potential for anyone to publicize frustrations on a website, word of mouth can be even more devastating. Just as "buzz" can cause demand for a hot product to skyrocket, negative buzz can cause demand to nosedive. Large businesses spend millions of dollars each year in what is known as "issues management," dealing with untrue rumors being spread about their products or services, or countering negative publicity posted on the Internet. Many businesses, as a means of acquiring more information about customer wants and needs, monitor Internet newsgroups, chat rooms, and mailing lists, to gain from this information.

When an external failure does occur, however, a business still has an opportunity to salvage the situation and resolve it in a way that causes the customer to want to return. The way a business deals with an external failure is known as **recovery**. Recovery practices are addressed more specifically later in this chapter.

Internal Failure Costs

Internal failure costs are costs associated with correcting a defect before the customer comes into contact with a product or service. For a manufacturing environment, where internal failures are most common, internal failure costs include the cost of scrapping the item (either discarding it or selling it for its scrap value), reworking the item so that it is no longer defective, selling the item at a reduced price as a second, or "blem," and all associated administrative costs. The costs may also include reductions in employee productivity and higher employee turnover. In some service industries, internal failure costs are comparable to those in manufacturing. Services that process documents, for example, are exposed to the possibility of defects that can be discovered internally. Restaurants can detect problems with food before it is served. Retailers can identify a defective item and remove it from the shelves. Internal failures affect consumers, however, through increased costs.

In many services quality problems are impossible to identify prior to the customer being exposed to them simply because the customer is involved in the production process itself. For example, if a customer walks out of a shop with a bad haircut, there really is no way the hairstylist could have known that it was going to be a bad haircut before it happened. The shop owner, however, should know that stylist experience and training reduce the likelihood of a bad haircut. The same holds for bank transactions, such as loan applications. Services that are experience-based, like expensive restaurants, bars and clubs, theme parks, and theaters, have great difficulty managing quality and customer satisfaction because of this very fact. Bad quality, from the consumer's perspective, cannot be identified until after the consumer experiences it.

Customer expectations for products tend to vary less noticeably. Customer reactions to service quality tend to be variable because expectations depend on individual tastes, mood, and the personalities (both customer and employee) that interact during the service encounter, whereas employee personalities or communication skills are rarely a factor in the customer's evaluation of a product's quality.

Appraisal Costs

Appraisal costs are linked to inspection and testing processes and to the auditing of quality-related systems. Inspection and testing activities ensure that products and services meet predetermined specifications. System auditing activities ensure that the systems designed to maintain quality do what is necessary to achieve specifications and not deviate from their intended objectives.

Inspection activities, used primarily in manufacturing, examine products and compare their characteristics to characteristics specified by customers. Inspections can occur at any point, from the incoming raw materials, through all production stages, to the finished product. In services, when inspections are possible, they typically precede the customer's involvement. Inspections are used to ensure that the facilities a customer will encounter will be acceptable. The hotel and lodging industry, for example, inspects to ensure that the customer's accommodations are of expected quality. When products accompany the service, as in restaurants, retailing, or health care, inspections provide one last opportunity to ensure that the customer is not exposed to bad-quality products. In other services, however, there can be no inspection prior to the customer's service encounter. Legal counseling or other services with high levels of customer interaction are good examples of businesses that cannot take advantage of inspection.

Testing is a specific type of inspection that is used when a visual inspection cannot reveal whether or not products meet specifications. Testing is frequently used with electronic and mechanical products that can be connected quickly to testing

Crash tests on automobiles, performed by the Insurance Institute for Highway Safety, as well as tests by the manufacturers themselves, provide evaluations of passenger injury potential for different models of autos as well as damage costs. Results identify areas for improvement in design. Effectiveness of process control charts depends not only on the interpretation of the data used, but also on the accuracy of the data being collected. Precision measurements require consistent techniques and employee skills in using and reading measuring instruments.

equipment in order to check out all system components. Products that are expensive or have high failure costs are often exposed to a barrage of tests prior to shipment. Testing of a service is often impossible, but testing of equipment utilized in some services is a means of ensuring that the equipment is up to the tasks required.

System auditing costs occur when in-depth analysis and improvement efforts are performed on quality management systems. A frequent cause of poor quality is the failure of systems that are intended to maintain quality. Recall the discussion of the quality function deployment (QFD) process from Chapter 5 in which the last step is the development of systems to maintain the process so that it continues to produce quality components. This is a critical part of the quality management effort. These systems must be periodically audited to make sure they continue to operate effectively and to identify ways they can be improved.

Prevention Costs

Prevention costs are those associated with efforts to prevent errors or defects from happening. They include costs of employee training, process improvement and control activity, and quality planning activity. In services, prevention costs are often a much greater portion of the total cost of quality because of the customer interaction, the higher penalty for a customer being exposed to poor quality, and the inability of management to detect most quality problems before they get to the customer.

Prevention costs are obviously the most proactive of the firm's investment in quality management. If prevention were totally successful, appraisal costs, internal failure costs, and external failure costs would disappear. It is hard to imagine total prevention of all quality problems, but that is the goal for many companies. One frequently overlooked benefit of prevention is that even though the costs of total prevention might appear to be too great compared to the costs of appraisal and external and internal failure, prevention would eliminate many nonfinancial costs as well, including reduced market share, dissatisfied customers that switch to a competitor (known as defectors), and long-term impact on profitability. Exhibit 7.5 illustrates how the four cost-of-quality categories relate to each other as quality costs are reduced.

| Cost of Quality As a Company Moves from External Failures Toward Prevention | EXHIBIT 7.5 |

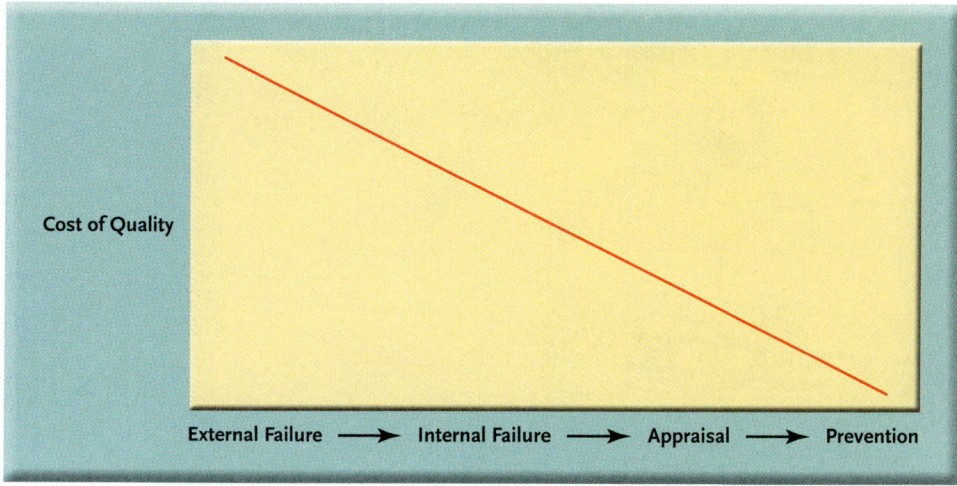

It should not be a surprise that as a company expands its efforts from eliminating external failures, to eliminating internal failures, to appraisal, and then to prevention, the total costs decline, resulting in an increase in profitability. In general, costs associated with poor quality increase the further along a product is in its process and as the poor quality gets closer to the customer. The earlier a defect is discovered, the lower its cost.

GENERAL-PURPOSE QUALITY ANALYSIS TOOLS

As quality rose to a high priority in the mid- to late 1980s, a number of tools that contributed to problem solving also became popular. The following sections provide an overview of eight of these tools. Several may seem familiar to you, because they are used in many settings, but this discussion places them in the context of quality management.

Flowcharts

Flowcharts, or "process flow diagrams," form the basis for documenting a process. The ability to represent a process visually, in a way that emphasizes relationships between various activities in the process, can contribute substantially to better understanding of the process and its weaknesses. Looking at an entire production process and understanding all the relationships among resources can be difficult. A diagram, however, can be studied and analyzed to identify logical relationships and sequences. Exhibit 7.6 is a basic flowchart of a purchasing process for an Internet retailer.

Chapter 5 introduced a modification of the flowchart known as a service blueprint. A service blueprint models the entire service process from the customer's perspective, including activities "behind the scenes" (behind the line of visibility) as well as those that result in interaction with the customer. After potential service failures, as well as customer waits and transportation activities, are identified, management can focus improvement efforts, employee education, and special attention on these problems. For many different uses of flow diagrams, different symbols are used. In service blueprinting, for example, the symbols used include fail points, customer wait points, and employee decisions. Service blueprinting is discussed again later in this chapter.

| EXHIBIT 7.6 | Flowchart |

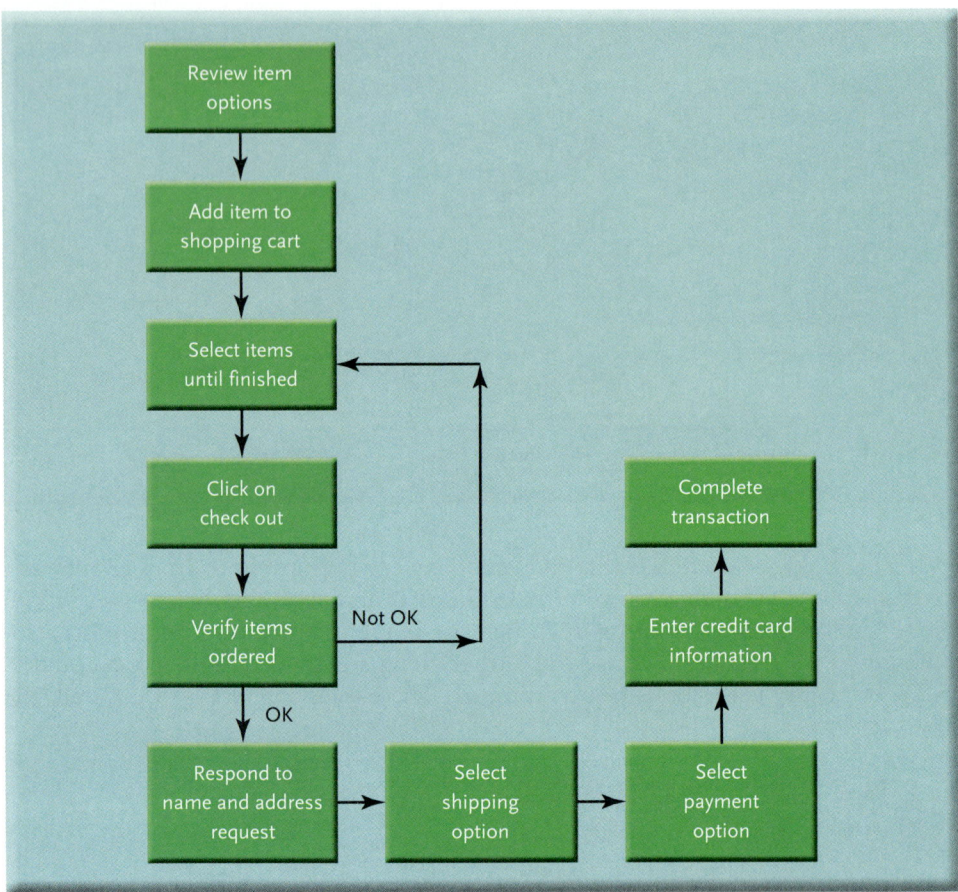

Run Charts

A **run chart** is a plot of a variable on the y axis versus time on the x axis. Run charts are helpful in understanding the relationship between changes in a variable measure over time. A measure of the problem plotted against time often reveals the cause of a problem. Identifying that the effect is related to time—that is to say, a pattern of change in the effect is linked to changes in time of day, day of the week, and so on—is often a major step toward identifying the cause. Once the time element of the problem is identified, other things that are time-related can be examined as potential causes. For example, a hotel that noticed an increase in the number of customer complaints each week might want to see if the complaints were related to time. Complaints could be examined by day or by time of day. If the increase resulted from a large number of customers arriving every Monday, that information would lead the hotel to one set of possible causes, but if the increase came every morning, it would lead them to a different set of possible causes.

Other time-related variables that could cause quality problems include temperature, traffic level, specific employees on duty, and demand patterns. Exhibit 7.7 is a sample run chart for a paper company that had problems with $8\frac{1}{2}$-by-11-inch peel-off adhesive paper curling after being cut from large rolls. After seeing the relationship between curl and certain days of June and July, the managers were then able to link the curl problem to days with high temperature and humidity. The rolled paper had

| Run Chart | EXHIBIT 7.7 |

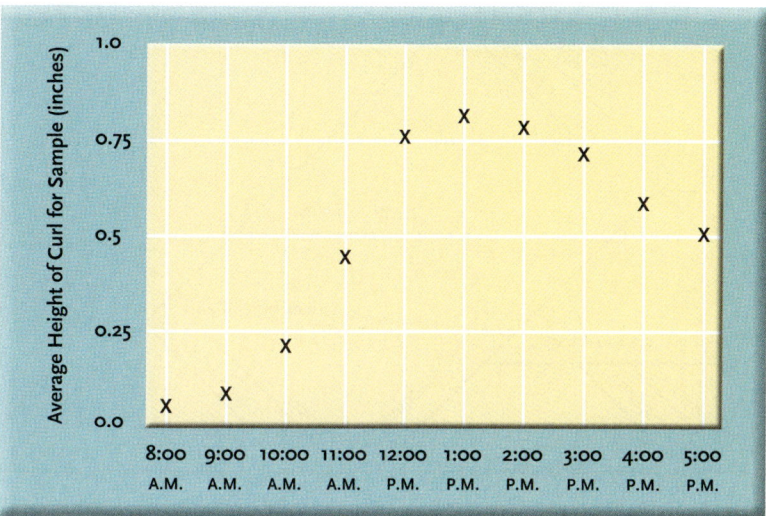

been wrapped in plastic when manufactured, and unwrapping it and exposing it to high humidity resulted in the label taking on moisture faster than the peel-off backing, causing it to curl. Ultimately, this link between humidity and curl led to the installation of an air-conditioning system in the plant.

Cause and Effect Diagrams

The **cause and effect diagram** shown in Exhibit 7.8 is used to help identify the cause of a problem. Creating the diagram typically starts with the identification of potential causes and gradually, through a process of elimination, moves to the root cause.

Sometimes referred to as a "fishbone diagram" because of its appearance, cause and effect diagrams are great tools to use with a group of individuals who first examine all possible causes of a problem and then work their way to a root cause that all agree on. The example in Exhibit 7.8 provides a sample cause and effect diagram for a pizza delivery company that was getting complaints about pizza being delivered cold. The pizza company determined that the root cause of the cold pizza was slow delivery time during high-traffic periods. Its solution was to reduce the number of orders that each driver would take during high-traffic times from four to two.

Pareto Charts

Pareto charts are simple bar graphs used to categorize data and help establish priorities for action. Often, data that are collected are difficult to interpret until they are organized. Pareto analysis is the process of identifying the most important category to give a focus to improvement efforts. Pareto charts provide a tool to display organized data in a variety of ways. A typical example of a large volume of data of little use without organization would be the calls a consumer products company receives through the 800 number printed on its products. Generally, the most valuable information companies can get through such a practice is complaints from customers. Before taking action to reduce complaints, however, a company must try to determine what initiated the complaints. A Pareto chart can be used to break the complaints down by category.

UNIT TWO Components of Value

EXHIBIT 7.8   Cause and Effect Diagram

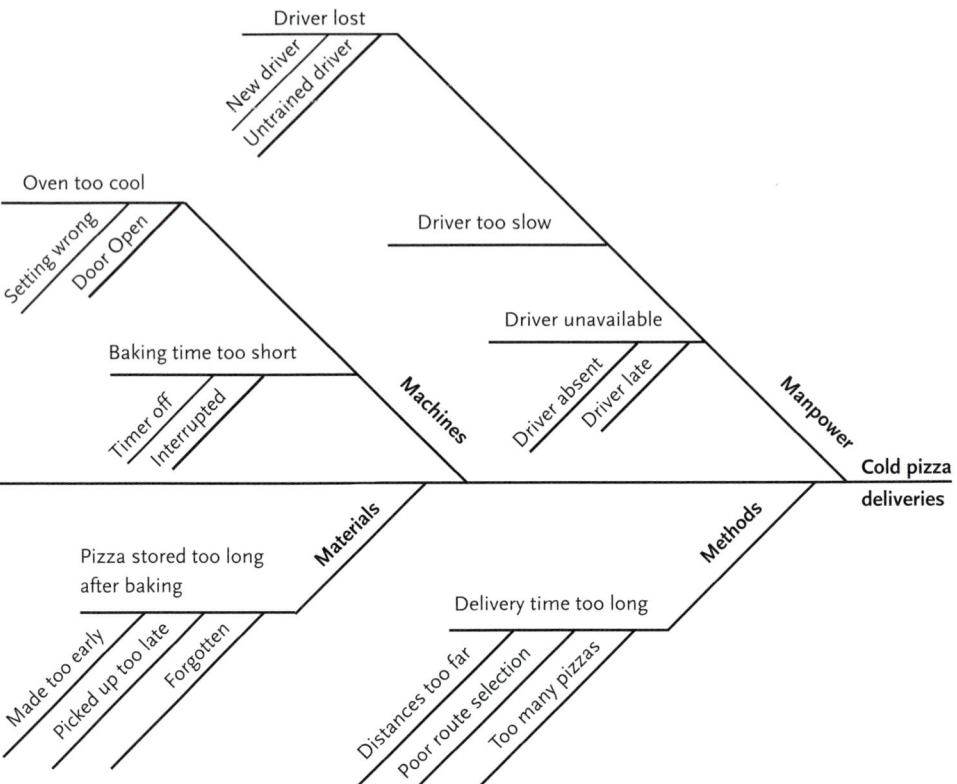

EXHIBIT 7.9   Pareto Chart

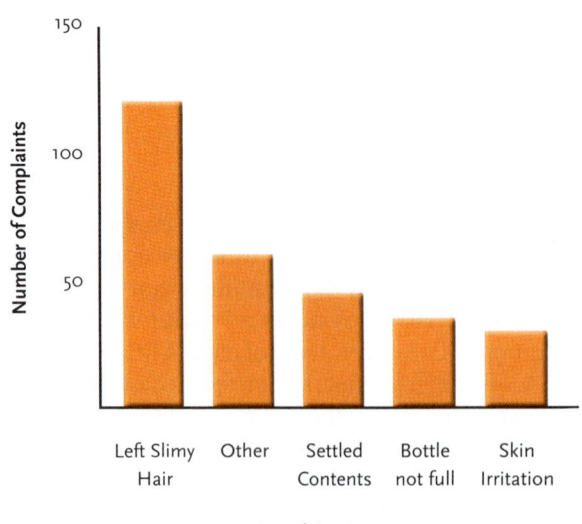

Exhibit 7.9 is a Pareto chart representation of customer complaints for a shampoo manufacturer. The most frequent complaint was related to the difficulty in rinsing the shampoo out of the customer's hair. The company took action by experimenting with formulations that were less reactive to varying degrees of water hardness. Example 7.1 provides a demonstration of **Pareto analysis**. Pareto analysis is intended to separate the relatively few important problems from the many unimportant ones.

> **Example 7.1**
>
> ### Pareto Analysis
>
> The SleepCheap Hotel chain maintains 12 hotels that provide suites to business travelers. During the past three months housekeeping staff have placed a complaint survey in each room. Each complaint was categorized in two ways. The first set of categories dealt with satisfaction with specific physical areas of the room. The second dealt with types of problems the customers had with different aspects of the room. The data collected are presented in Exhibit 7.10. Complete a Pareto analysis on the data.
>
> **EXHIBIT 7.10 SleepCheap Hotel Survey Data**
>
> | Area | Complaint Frequency | Problem Type | Complaint Frequency |
> |---|---|---|---|
> | Shower | 46 | Dirty | 105 |
> | Toilet | 23 | Not working | 45 |
> | Vanity | 63 | Missing amenities | 32 |
> | Desk | 12 | Not prepared | 26 |
> | Bed | 9 | Total | 208 |
> | Dresser | 3 | | |
> | Floor | 38 | | |
> | TV | 14 | | |
> | Total | 208 | | |
>
> In order to begin work on improving the quality levels, management performed a Pareto analysis.
>
> **Solution**
>
> After being sorted by category, the percentage of the total number of complaints is calculated. The results for both sets of categories are shown in Exhibit 7.11.
>
> **EXHIBIT 7.11 Percentages for Each Category of Complaint in Example 7.1**
>
> | Area | Complaint Frequency | Percentage | Problem Type | Complaint Frequency | Percentage |
> |---|---|---|---|---|---|
> | Shower | 46 | 22.1% | Dirty | 105 | 50.5% |
> | Toilet | 23 | 11.1 | Not working | 45 | 21.6 |
> | Vanity | 63 | 30.3 | Missing amenities | 32 | 15.4 |
> | Desk | 12 | 5.8 | Not prepared | 26 | 12.5 |
> | Bed | 9 | 4.3 | Total | 208 | |
> | Dresser | 3 | 1.4 | | | |
> | Floor | 38 | 18.3 | | | |
> | TV | 14 | 6.7 | | | |
> | Total | 208 | | | | |
>
> *(continues)*

> **Example 7.1** *(continued)*
>
> The next step is to sequence the categories by their frequency and construct a bar graph. This is presented in Exhibits 7.12 and 7.13.
>
> **EXHIBIT 7.12 Pareto Chart for Complaints by Room Area** 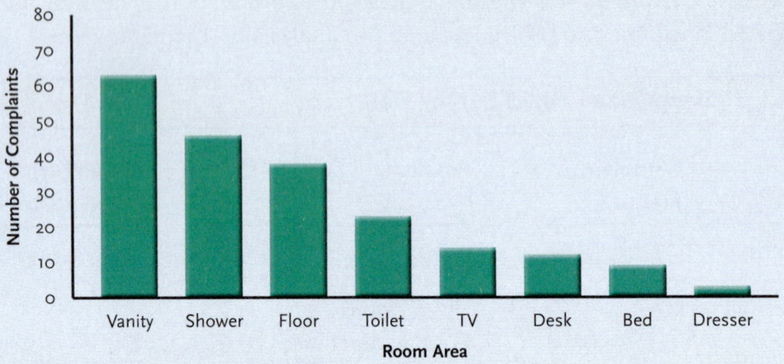
>
> *[Bar chart showing Number of Complaints by Room Area: Vanity ~62, Shower ~46, Floor ~38, Toilet ~23, TV ~14, Desk ~12, Bed ~8, Dresser ~2]*
>
> **EXHIBIT 7.13 Pareto Chart for Complaints by Type** 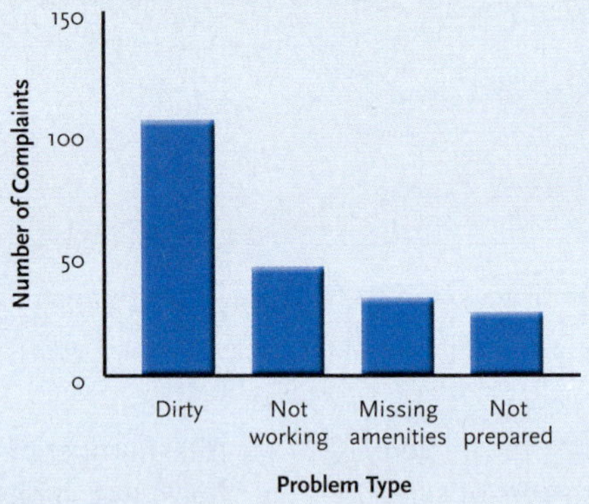
>
> *[Bar chart showing Number of Complaints by Problem Type: Dirty ~108, Not working ~45, Missing amenities ~33, Not prepared ~27]*
>
>
> www.OperationsNow.com
>
> Excel Tutor 7.1 demonstrates how easily Pareto analysis can be done in a spreadsheet.

Histograms

A **histogram** is another bar graph, but it is configured differently than a Pareto chart. Exhibit 7.14 provides a histogram for the telephone wait time being experienced during one hour at a videogame technical support center.

In a histogram, the *x* axis is used for a particular measurement and the *y* axis is used for the frequency of the occurrence of that particular measurement. Histograms are frequently used to get a rough idea of the distribution of variables. This is particularly important in many quality management situations that arise because of too much process variability. The histogram provides a visual means of presenting and understanding that variability.

Check Sheets

The **check sheet**, as shown in Exhibit 7.15, is a simple, useful way to organize and tally data. Check sheets are frequently used for collecting and recording data that might later be used in another one of the quality tools. For example, customer complaints that might ultimately go through a Pareto analysis might be tallied on a check sheet. Check sheets can take a variety of forms, but they typically have blank cells for check marks or hash marks for categories of items being counted.

Scatter Diagrams

The **scatter diagram** utilizes one variable on the *x* axis and another variable on the *y* axis to provide a visual means of identifying a correlation or a relationship between the two variables. Exhibit 7.16 is a scatter diagram plotting the number of admission tickets sold at the entry to a theme park against the number of complaints about waiting in line too long at the most popular ride.

Although the existence of a positive correlation is not sufficient to conclude that a cause and effect relationship exists, correlation is a prerequisite to cause and effect. The identification of relationships between variables is an important first step toward identifying the cause of a particular problem.

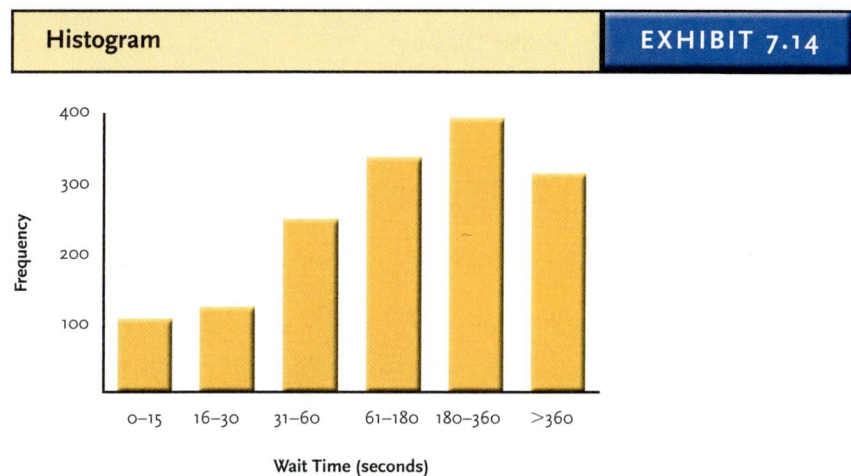

EXHIBIT 7.14 Histogram

EXHIBIT 7.15 Check Sheet

	Issue 1	Issue 2	Issue 3	Issue 4	Issue 5
Item A	✓				
Item B		✓		✓	
Item C			✓		✓
Item D		✓			
Item E	✓	✓	✓		
Item F	✓				

Control Charts

A **control chart** is a specific type of run chart used to plot measurements or test outcomes against time and distinguish between variability caused by random fluctuation and variability that has an assignable cause. The variability of a process determines whether it will be able to consistently meet customer expectations. If the range of the process variability stays inside the customer expectations, the process is viewed as being capable. Process variability creates some randomness in process outcomes. The variability can be described by its mean and standard deviation. As long as a process mean stays at the same point and the variability doesn't change, the process has not changed

| EXHIBIT 7.16 | Scatter Diagram |

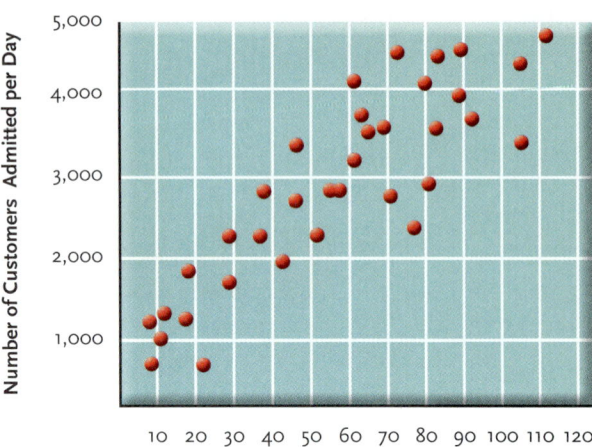

Number of Waiting Time Complaints per Day

and is said to be "in control." If, however, the process begins to create outcomes that provide evidence that the amount of variability or the mean has changed, the process is said to be "out of control."

Control charts are used to monitor processes to enable conclusions to be drawn about whether the process is in control. Data are gathered from random samples of process outputs (critical dimensions of products, times of processes, and so on). By plotting the collected data and comparing the plotted data to the known standard deviations of the process, judgment can be made as to whether the process has changed or not.

Process control charts are used to monitor a variety of process types, always with the goal of distinguishing between variability that is inherent in the process from variability that results from something being wrong with the process. In other words, the process control chart tells you that the process has changed, even though it has yet to produce a defect. This early warning gives management the ability to prevent defects from happening. Reel Operations Video 7.3 provides an example of the variables Honda monitors using control charts.

REEL OPERATIONS
OperationsNow.com

Process control charts are best understood as a part of statistical process control, which is the context in which they are most often used. Control charts are such an integral part of the broader set of quality prevention procedures that the following section is devoted to that topic.

The eight tools just described constitute a foundation for identifying and solving problems related to quality. While they can be used in many different ways and are often used independently of each other, they can also be used in conjunction with each other in a structured problem-solving process. In Chapter 15, "Total Quality Management," a framework for using these tools is presented.

STATISTICAL PROCESS CONTROL

Statistical process control (SPC) provides a preventive approach to managing quality by monitoring processes in a way that identifies potential problems before defects are even created. Fundamental to SPC are several different control charts. Some are used when the aspect of interest is a variable, that is, a measure indicating a weight, dimension, strength, or other factor. Other control charts are used when a product attribute is of interest. Unlike variables, which potentially have an infinite number of possible outcomes, attributes have only two possible outcomes, such as pass or fail, fit or nonfit, on or off, and good or bad.

A commonly used process control chart is known as the X-bar chart. The X-bar chart is used to monitor a variable that results from a particular process. A detailed examination of X-bar charts provides an overview of how all process control charts are used. The values plotted on an X-bar chart are means of subgroups, as shown below:

Effectiveness of process control charts depends not only on the interpretation of the data used, but also on the accuracy of the data being collected. Precision measurements require consistent techniques and employee skills in using and reading measuring instruments.

$$\overline{X}_1 = \frac{x_1 + x_2 + x_3 + x_4 + \cdots + x_n}{n} \tag{7.1}$$

where n is the number of units in the subgroup, X is the mean of that subgroup, and x represents each measure in the subgroup. The center line on the control chart, representing X-double bar, is the mean of the subgroup means, as shown below:

$$\overline{\overline{X}}_1 = \frac{\overline{X}_1 + \overline{X}_2 + \overline{X}_3 + \overline{X}_4 + \cdots + \overline{X}_k}{k} \tag{7.2}$$

where $\overline{X}$ is the subgroup mean and k is the number of subgroup samples of size n.

The process used for gathering data to be plotted on an X-bar chart is illustrated in Exhibit 7.17.

As an example of the use of an X-bar chart, let's examine its use to monitor the process of filling 12-ounce (355-milliliter) soft drink cans. Exhibit 7.18 shows the process was on target, as evidenced by the grand mean equaling the objective of the process (355 ml). The standard deviation of the process was 2 ml. Each data point plotted in the X-bar chart was the average from a sample of filled cans. The upper and lower **control limits** are commonly 3σ, or 3 standard deviations above and below the mean. Control limits equal to 3 standard deviations above and below the mean contain almost all of the random fluctuation. Data points outside the 3σ control limits are assumed to be the result of something other than random fluctuation, that is, a change in the process. The greater the variability of the process, the wider these 3σ limits will be apart.

The customer for whom the bottler fills cans has provided a quality specification. The customer specified that cans must be filled to plus or minus 8 ml from the target

EXHIBIT 7.17 Process Control Chart Data Gathering Process

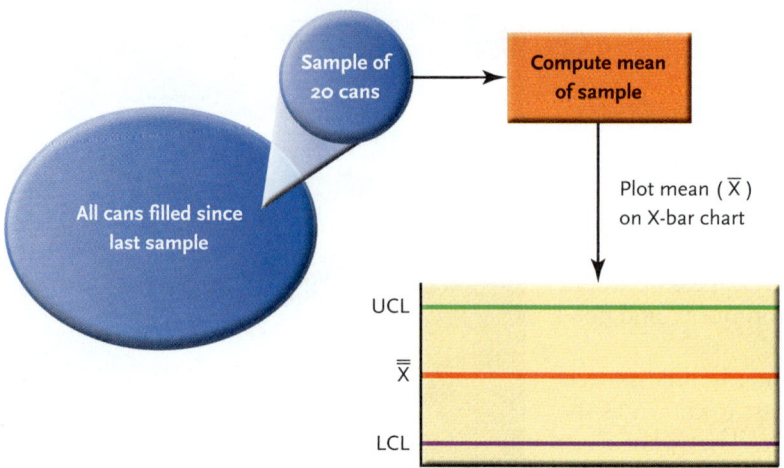

EXHIBIT 7.18 Process Control Chart for Soft Drink Can

of 355. Anything between the customer's specification limits of 347 and 363 is considered good. Anything outside these limits would be considered a defect.

The 3σ control limits must be inside the customer specification limits, because that ensures that virtually all of the random fluctuation remains inside the customer's specification limits. If the customer's specification limits were outside the upper and lower control limits, the process would produce defects as a part of its normal variability. If that were the case, the process would not be good enough to meet customer expectations. Exhibit 7.18 shows the upper and lower control limits, as well as a bell-shaped curve that has been superimposed to help illustrate how the upper and lower control limits are developed.

The ability of a process to consistently meet customer expectations, demonstrated by the control limits being inside the customer specifications, is known as **process capability**. Process capability is often measured using a **capability index**. One such capability index is the C_p index. If C_p is less than or equal to 1, the process is not able to meet the specifications of the customer. A C_p that is greater than 1 is considered acceptable. A larger C_p would be even better. The formula for computing C_p is

$$C_p = \frac{\text{Upper Specification Limit} - \text{Lower Specification Limit}}{6\sigma} \tag{7.3}$$

Example 7.2 demonstrates the calculation of the C_p capability index.

Process control requires precise measurement of the variables of interest. Without that measurement precision, the outputs are not accurate enough to provide meaningful direction. For many industries, measurement equipment is produced by companies with the expertise necessary to obtain these high necessary levels of precision. Esource 7.2 provides an example of a company that specializes in the type of equipment necessary to collect data for process control efforts.

The C_p capability index calculated in Equation 7.3 and in Example 7.2 assumes that the process is centered—in other words, that the average of the process output is centered between the customer's specification limits. There are times when it is actually desirable not to center a process within the customer's specification limits. For example, in some manufacturing processes tools will wear and cause a process to "drift." A cutting edge might wear and cause a dimension to gradually increase over time. A drill bit might wear and cause the depth of a hole to change over time. In these situations, as long as the manufacturer understands the direction of the process drift, it may make sense to start the process closer to one of the customer's specification limits and let the process drift toward the other. The manufacturer is able to reduce costs associated with tool repair or replacement by obtaining longer useful life from them. Machine utilization is also increased because tools don't need to be changed as frequently.

Example 7.2

Capability Index Calculation

Precision Machining is a subcontractor for manufacturers in the aerospace and defense industries. It was recently approached by Nuclear Triggers 'R' Us (NTRU) to machine some small parts. To determine if it had the capability to meet NTRU quality requirements, Precision Machining was asked to machine a sample batch of 100 parts. The most critical operation was that of surface grinding, which required very high tolerances. NTRU specified the thickness as 0.375 inch. Precision Machining finished the 100 parts and returned them to NTRU. NTRU technicians measured the parts and found that, indeed, the average thickness was 0.375 inch. What NTRU *did not tell* Precision Machining, however, was that the parts needed to be 0.375 inch but could not vary more than ±0.002 inch. NTRU's measurements showed that the standard deviation of the Precision Machining parts was 0.0024 inch. Can Precision Machining be counted on to provide parts that meet NTRU needs?

Solution

NTRU's upper customer specification is 0.375 + 0.002 = 0.377. Its lower customer specification is 0.375 − .002 = 0.373. Using Equation 7.3, the capability index is calculated as

$$C_p = \frac{0.377 - 0.373}{6(0.0024)}$$

$$= 0.27778$$

Since the capability index is less than 1, NTRU must conclude that Precision Machining is not capable of meeting its quality specifications.

Excel Tutor 7.2 shows how a spreadsheet can be used to aid in the calculation of the C_p capability index.

For processes that aren't centered, the C_p capability index cannot be used. Instead, the C_{pk} capability index is used. Like the C_p index, the C_{pk} index measures how the process fits into the limits established by the customer. As the mean of a process shifts, the tails of the distribution of the process get closer to the upper or lower customer specification, depending on the direction of the shift. As this shift occurs, the direction of the shift and the nearness to the customer specification limit establish limits on the process capability. C_{pk} expresses the relationship between the process and the customer's specifications by identifying the distance between the tails of the process and the specification limit in the direction of the shift.

Exhibit 7.19 shows a process that was initially centered but shifted downward. Notice how the tail of the process has moved closer to the lower customer specification limit, although it is still a long way from creating defects. As the process shifts, however, the likelihood of defects caused by violating the lower customer specification limit increases. The C_{pk} is calculated by computing the difference between the process mean and each of the customer specification limits. The result is divided by 3σ, to compute a ratio. The smallest of the two values is the one of interest, since it compares the distance between the process mean and the customer specification in the direction the process is shifting. The formula for computing the C_{pk} is

$$C_{pk} = \min\left[\frac{\bar{\bar{X}} - \text{LCS}}{3\sigma}, \frac{\text{UCS} - \bar{\bar{X}}}{3\sigma}\right] \qquad (7.4)$$

where LCS = lower customer specification and UCS = upper customer specification. As the process shifts, the distance between the distribution tail and the customer specification limit gets smaller, until the tail of the process goes beyond the customer specification, at which time the process is out of control because it will produce defects as a part of its normal variability. A C_{pk} of 1 or greater is typically considered to be representative of a "capable" process. The larger the C_{pk}, the lower the likelihood of a defect being produced. Example 7.3 demonstrates the calculation of C_{pk}.

X-bar charts are always used in conjunction with a range chart (R-chart) because the means that are plotted on the X-bar chart show the central tendency of the sample group of measurements but do not indicate anything about that group's distribu-

EXHIBIT 7.19 **Process Shifted Downward from Center**

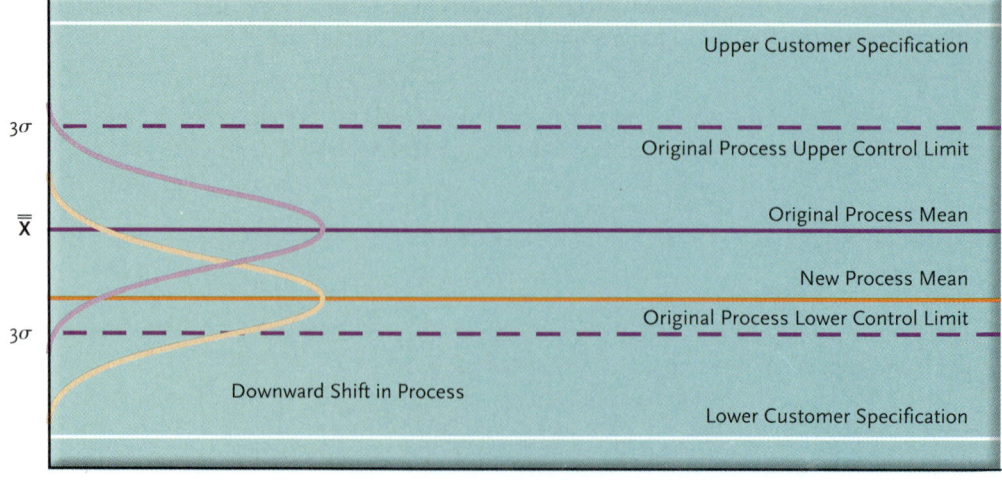

Example 7.3 C_{pk} Calculation

Since getting the NTRU contract, Precision Machining was able to dramatically tighten its surface grinding operation and reached a standard deviation of 0.0003 inch. The customer specified 0.375 ± 0.002 inch for the part, giving customer specification limits of 0.373 to 0.377 inch. The operator of the surface grinder decided that it was to his advantage not to center the process within the upper and lower customer specification limits. He figured out that in order to maximize the use of the grinding tools, he should start with the process below center, giving it more room to shift, and less frequent tool changes. As the grinding wheel wore, the process mean would shift upward. By starting out low, the operator got longer life out of each wheel and spent less time changing wheels. He had to closely monitor the shift, however, to make sure that he maintained an acceptable C_{pk}. On one Friday afternoon, he collected data that showed the process mean had shifted to 0.376. Is the C_{pk} acceptable? Or does he need to change grinding wheels?

Solution

$$C_{pk} = \min\left[\frac{\overline{\overline{X}} - \text{LCS}}{3\sigma}, \frac{\text{UCS} - \overline{\overline{X}}}{3\sigma}\right]$$

$$C_{pk} = \min\left[\frac{0.376 - 0.373}{0.0009}, \frac{0.377 - 0.376}{0.0009}\right]$$

$$= \min[3.333, 1.111]$$

$$= 1.111$$

The process has shifted upward, but since the C_{pk} is greater than 1, it is still acceptable. Excel Tutor 7.3 shows how a spreadsheet can aid in the calculation of the C_{pk} index.

www
OperationsNow
.com

tion. One could theoretically have a mean that matched the target but have no measurements in the group actually fall within the customer specifications. The R-chart plots the range for the same subgroup used to obtain the X-bar value. The range R for a subgroup is obtained by subtracting the smallest value in the group from the largest. The centerline, R-bar, is the mean of the subgroup ranges:

$$\overline{R} = \frac{R_1 + R_2 + R_3 + R_4 + \cdots + R_k}{k} \tag{7.5}$$

The upper control limits and lower control limits for the X-bar chart are

$$\text{UCL} = \overline{\overline{X}} + A_2\overline{R} \tag{7.6}$$

$$\text{LCL} = \overline{\overline{X}} - A_2\overline{R} \tag{7.7}$$

where A_2 is a constant based on the subgroup size and yields 3σ limits for X-bar when multiplied by R-bar. The upper control limits and lower control limits for the R-chart are

$$\text{UCL} = D_4\overline{R} \tag{7.8}$$

$$\text{LCL} = D_3\overline{R} \tag{7.9}$$

Exhibit 7.20 lists the values for A_2, D_3, and D_4 to provide the values for calculating 3σ control limits for X-bar and R-charts.

Quality and Consistency Are Key for Wilson Tennis Balls

Wilson U.S. Open Tournament Select tennis balls have been the official ball of the U.S. Open since 1979. Despite the evolution in rackets, from wood and metal to carbon, there has been virtually no change in the ball. As service speed exceeds 140 miles per hour, the impact on the ball has changed tremendously, making durability, as well as consistent bounce, more important. The ball is available for four playing conditions: the US Open Extra Duty, the US Open Regular Duty, the US Open High Altitude, and the US Open Grass Court.

The U.S. Open uses more than 70,000 of these tennis balls (6 tons!). Wilson has to be extremely concerned about ball quality, because with the players' names or their sponsors' names on their shoes and rackets, only the balls and umpires will be blamed when things go wrong. Every ball must meet specifications of the International Tennis Federation and United States Tennis Association for size, weight, hardness, and rebound. A sample of eight dozen balls are submitted for tournament approval a year before the start of the tournament.

The hardness test for the ball is based on how it compresses when subjected to the squeezing of a machine known as the Stevens Machine. The Stevens Machine subjects the ball to an 18-pound load. Standard balls are allowed to deform between 0.220 and 0.290 inch. Balls used in the U.S. Open are allowed only 0.005 inch variability, from 0.240 to 0.245. A professional player can feel the difference between balls on opposite ends of the range of hardness.

Natural products are always variable. With two natural products (natural rubber and wool felt), it is particularly difficult to get consistency across the 100 million tennis balls produced by Wilson each year. The most difficult part of the production process is actually getting two flat pieces of felt to smoothly fit over a round surface. The two pieces, known as "dogbones," are assembled manually by a ball-coverer. For the ball-coverers, the squarer the dogbone shapes, the more likely the cover is going to wrinkle.

The composition of the cover requires a constant tradeoff between durability and "fluffing." Durability is good. Fluffing is bad. Making the ball last longer can often make the covering fluffier. There needs to be enough hair on the ball so that the racket face will grab it, but not enough to create drag as it flies through the air. Balls that fluff up too much are known as "Don King balls" or "troll balls." Players actually sort through balls looking for those with the amount of fluff they like. For first serves, many players like a "skinny" ball, where the fluff is still down. They tend to go through the air faster and come off the court more quickly. Players like scuffed-up balls for the second serve so they can put more English on it to make sure it drops in.

Obviously, the air pressure in the ball is critical. Ten percent of the balls are actually tested by plunging a 12-gauge veterinarian's needle into the ball to make sure the ball has 12 pounds of air in it. The canning machines used by Wilson are actually from the food industry, but rather than create a vacuum as they would for food, they create a positive pressure of 13 pounds to make sure the ball maintains its pressure on the store shelf.

Source: "Under Pressure to Withstand an Unforgivable Beating," *The New York Times on the Web*, http://www.nytimes.com/2001/08/30/garden/30NOTE.html, August 30, 2001; Wilson, US Open Official Ball, http://www.wilsonsports.com/corporate/index.asp?content_id=1100, August 30, 2001.

EXHIBIT 7.20

Values for A_2, D_3, and D_4

Number of Observations in Subgroup (n)	Factor for X-bar Chart (A_2)	Lower Control Limit (D_3)	Upper Control Limit (D_4)
2	1.880	0	3.268
3	1.023	0	2.574
4	0.729	0	2.282
5	0.577	0	2.114
6	0.483	0	2.004
7	0.419	0.076	1.924
8	0.373	0.136	1.864
9	0.337	0.184	1.816
10	0.308	0.223	1.777
15	0.223	0.348	1.652

Interactive Model 7.1 provides an interactive environment that demonstrates the interaction between X-bar and R-charts as process variability changes.

Example 7.4 demonstrates the construction of an X-bar and R-chart for variable data.

As mentioned earlier, control charts can also be used for attributes. P-charts, for example, are used to monitor the percentage of products that are acceptable versus the percentage unacceptable. C-charts are used to monitor defects per part in applications where there can be several defects on a single product, such as dust specks on a car's paint finish.

Control charts are maintained on an ongoing basis so that workstation operators can ensure that a process is not changing (i.e., moving out of control). Data points that are outside the control limits, as well as other nonrandom patterns of data points, indicate that the process has changed. Any pattern that shows a lack of randomness means that the variability is not due to random fluctuation. If not caused by random fluctuation, the variability must have an assignable cause. Exhibit 7.24 on page 210 lists some nonrandom patterns that would indicate a process out of control.

Variability with an assignable cause, even though the cause might not be found, is evidence that the process is out of control. Variability that has an assignable cause can be analyzed, and the problem's cause can be corrected. This can all occur prior to the creation of any defective products when control charts are correctly used, providing that the control limits are within customer specifications. If the control limits are outside the customer specifications, the process does not have the capability to meet the customer specifications and will produce defective items as a part of the process's random fluctuation. In this situation, nothing can be done to prevent defective items from being produced and the process must be improved so that it lies entirely within customer specifications.

Like many business tasks that are labor-intensive or require extreme precision, process control tasks are sometimes performed automatically. In many industries they can be performed by equipment specifically designed to measure process outputs with high accuracy and create statistical process control charts.

Example 7.4

X-Bar and R-Chart Construction

Northeast Bottling Company is a regional contractor for a number of beverage companies. It recently acquired a new contract for a 1-liter bottle of Frantic, a new energy drink designed for 8- to 12-year-olds. Northeast is required to maintain control over a consistent volume of product in each 1-liter container. The company wishes to use an X-bar chart and an R-chart to accomplish this. For the first day of operation, machine operators took 20 samples, with 5 bottles in each sample. From that data, they calculated X-bar, X-double bar, and R-chart, as shown in Exhibit 7.21.

EXHIBIT 7.21 Bottling data for Example 7.4

Sample Number	\multicolumn{5}{c}{Sample X Values}	X-bar	UCL	LCL	Range
	1	2	3	4	5				
1	996	989	998	998	1,001	996.4	1,005.078	994.9224	12
2	1,004	1,007	1,001	1,004	1,002	1,003.6	1,005.078	994.9224	6
3	1,002	1,003	1,005	1,003	1,005	1,003.6	1,005.078	994.9224	3
4	995	996	995	999	1,001	997.2	1,005.078	994.9224	6
5	1,003	998	1,006	1,002	999	1,001.6	1,005.078	994.9224	8
6	999	997	1,006	1,003	998	1,000.6	1,005.078	994.9224	9
7	1,003	1,007	1,000	993	998	1,000.2	1,005.078	994.9224	14
8	1,002	1,003	999	1,003	998	1,001	1,005.078	994.9224	5
9	1,002	1,003	1,001	996	1,003	1,001	1,005.078	994.9224	7
10	997	997	988	1,001	999	996.4	1,005.078	994.9224	13
11	999	999	1,011	998	1,002	1,001.8	1,005.078	994.9224	13
12	1,005	1,003	995	1,000	998	1,000.2	1,005.078	994.9224	10
13	1,001	994	993	1,001	1,001	998	1,005.078	994.9224	8
14	999	1,002	999	1,002	1,002	1,000.8	1,005.078	994.9224	3
15	998	998	991	999	1,001	997.4	1,005.078	994.9224	10
16	1,002	997	1,011	998	996	1,000.8	1,005.078	994.9224	15
17	998	995	1,001	1,006	999	999.8	1,005.078	994.9224	11
18	996	1,006	997	1,003	998	1,000	1,005.078	994.9224	10
19	1,003	998	1,001	997	997	999.2	1,005.078	994.9224	6
20	1,002	1,001	1,003	996	1,000	1,000.4	1,005.078	994.9224	7
			$\overline{\overline{X}} = 1{,}000$					$\overline{R} = 8.8$	

They have been told to construct an X-bar chart and an R-chart for the data.

Solution

The construction of an X-bar chart is accomplished by using Equations 7.6 and 7.7, as well as the value for A_2 from Exhibit 7.20. The upper and lower control limits for the X-bar chart are calculated as follows:

$$UCL = \overline{\overline{X}} + A_2 \overline{R}$$

(continues)

Example 7.4 (continued)

$$= 1{,}000 + (0.577)(8.8)$$

$$= 1{,}005.078$$

$$\text{LCL} = \bar{\bar{X}} - A_2 \bar{R}$$

$$= 1{,}000 - (0.577)(8.8)$$

$$= 994.9224$$

Exhibit 7.22 provides the completed X-bar chart.

EXHIBIT 7.22 X-bar Chart for Example 7.4

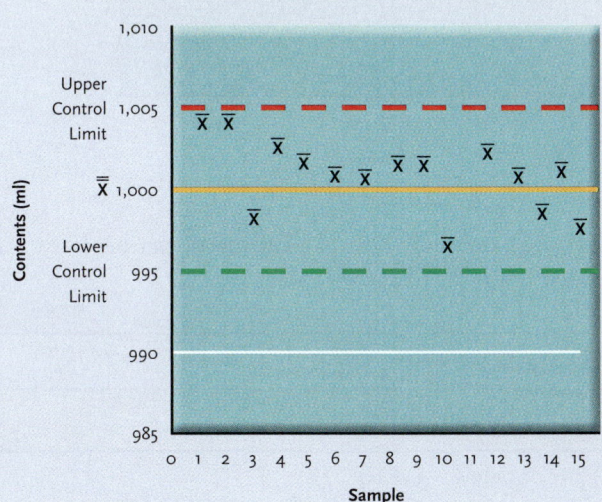

The R-chart control limits are calculated by using Equations 7.8 and 7.9, as well as Exhibit 7.16. The calculations are

$$\text{UCL} = D_4 \bar{R}$$

$$= 2.114(8.8)$$

$$= 18.6032$$

$$\text{LCL} = D_3 \bar{R}$$

$$= 0(8.8)$$

$$= 0$$

(continues)

Example 7.4 (continued)

The R-chart is presented in Exhibit 17.23.

EXHIBIT 7.23 R-Chart for Example 7.4

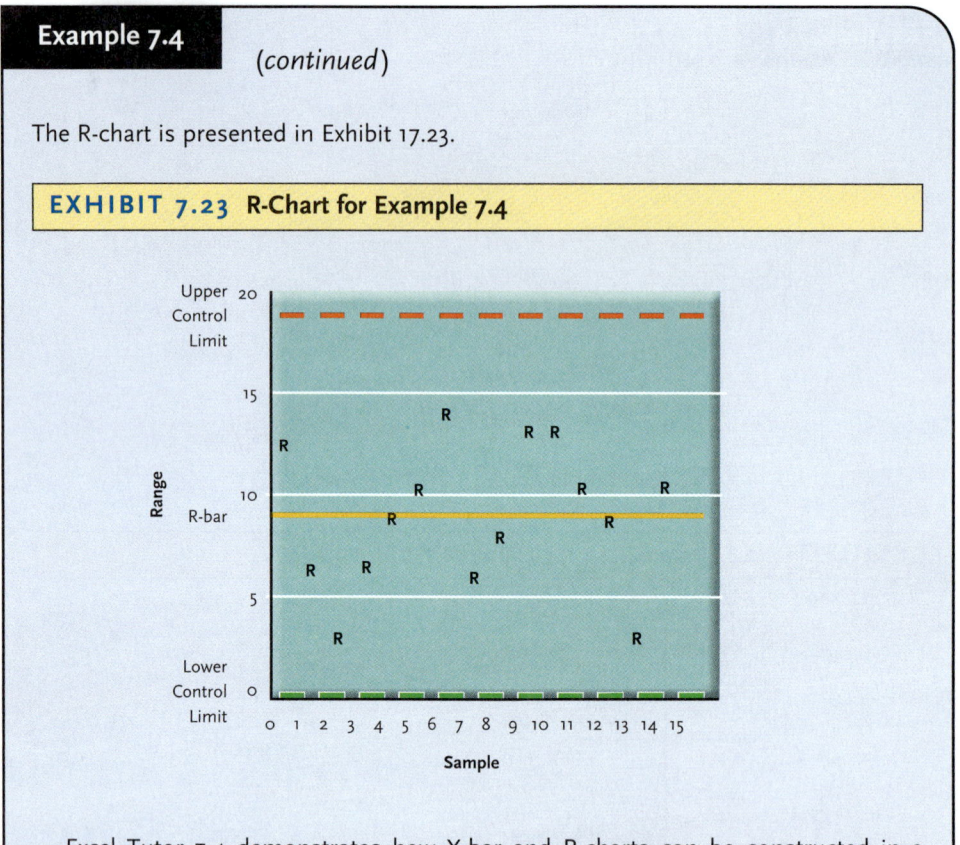

www.OperationsNow.com

Excel Tutor 7.4 demonstrates how X-bar and R-charts can be constructed in a spreadsheet.

EXHIBIT 7.24 Nonrandom Patterns on Control Charts

1 data point above $+3\sigma$ or below -3σ

2 out of 3 data points between $+2$ and $+3\sigma$ or between -2 and -3σ

4 out of 5 data points between $+1$ and $+3\sigma$ or between -1 and -3σ

8 successive points above the grand mean (X-double bar) or 8 successive points below the grand mean (X-double bar)

Source: B. Brocka and M. S. Brocka, *Quality Management: Implementing the Best Ideas of the Masters* (Homewood, IL: Business One Irwin, 1992), p. 281.

ACCEPTANCE SAMPLING

Acceptance sampling is used to identify suspect products or components of products without examining all of them. A sample group is extracted from a large quantity of products or components of interest, known as a "lot," and the entire lot is judged either good or bad based on the quality level of the sample group. Obviously, an inspection process of this type does not prevent poor quality from being produced; it merely identifies the quality after the fact. Moreover, since the decision is based on a sample, the wrong conclusions can be drawn. Sampling is always subject to the risks of sampling error, because there is always a possibility that the sample is not totally representative of the lot it comes from. It is possible to conclude from a sample that the lot is of poor quality when in fact it is good, or that the lot is good quality when in fact it is bad.

Acceptance sampling isn't as popular as it used to be, because it presumes that a given level of defects is acceptable. In addition, to reduce the potential of drawing wrong conclusions, samples must be large. Despite these problems, it is still used when the products or components of interest are produced in very high quantities, when the quality of the components or products is somewhat inconsequential, and when a supplier of incoming products or components is being monitored closely. The following discussion provides an overview of the acceptance sampling process.

Acceptance sampling for any purpose requires a sampling plan. The basis of the sampling plan is the sample size n and the largest number of defects that can be present in an acceptable sample, referred to as c. The risks inherent in acceptance sampling that arise because the sample doesn't represent the lot must be addressed in the sampling plan because they determine the level of confidence one can have in the results. To address these risks, the plan must define acceptable and unacceptable levels of quality for the lot.

The **acceptable quality level (AQL)** identifies the quality level required for lots that will be sampled. A lot is considered to be good if the actual level of quality is at the AQL or better. The AQL is typically specified by the producer and must be agreeable to the customer. The **lot tolerance percent defective (LTPD)** is the level of quality in the lot that would be unacceptable to the customer. A lot known to be at or below the LTPD would be rejected by the customer. The LTPD is typically specified by the customer and must be agreed to by the producer.

The risks inherent in a plan can be specified in terms of the AQL and LTPD. The producer is most concerned with the risk of rejecting a good lot, which would happen if a sample indicated that a lot was defective when in reality it was at or above the AQL. The probability of this happening is known as **producer's risk**, which is the probability of rejecting a good lot, indicated by α. The customer is most concerned about the sample indicating that the lot was good, when in reality it contained the LTPD level of defective products. This is known as **consumer's risk** and is designated as β.

The values for n and c are derived from the values of α, β, the AQL, and the LTPD. A trial-and-error process can be used, as can the binomial or Poisson distribution, but most businesses use standard reference tables such as the MIL STD 105D (Military Standard 105D). The result of a completed sampling plan is a graph that demonstrates how well the plan discriminates between good and bad quality by showing the probability of accepting a lot of LTPD quality (a bad lot) and the probability of rejecting a lot of AQL quality (a good lot). Such a graph is known as an **operating characteristics (OC) curve**. Exhibit 7.25 shows an OC curve for a plan that has an AQL of 0.04 and an LTPD at 0.20. Notice that the probability of accepting the lot with 4 percent defective is 0.90. The probability of accepting lots with greater numbers of defects is lower than 0.90, but it is still going to happen. The probability of accepting the lot when the quality level is at the LTPD of 0.20 is 0.05. The steeper the graph between the AQL and the LTPD, the more discriminating the plan. This steepness is obtained by manipulating n and c.

THE NEXT LEVEL: MOVING BEYOND MERELY SATISFYING THE CUSTOMER

The idea of defining quality as meeting the customer's expectations is entirely sound because it establishes a point by which the value of competitors' products or services

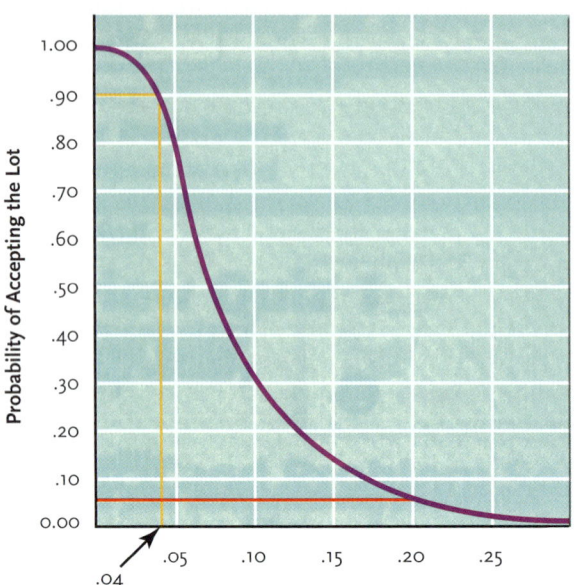

EXHIBIT 7.25 Operating Characteristics Curve

can be compared, and it allows customers to pay only for what they want. There are times, however, when merely satisfying the customer may not be enough. Some companies want to go beyond that to the point of truly delighting their customers. The rationale behind this desire isn't altruistic. If a product or service's quality reaches a new level, some customers will begin to count on that level of quality from their supplier. This gives the producer the competitive advantage of being the first in the market and an opportunity to set the standard. Two approaches to taking quality to the next level are the **Kano model**, an attempt to add product or service features that surprise or delight the customer, and **six sigma quality**, which advances process control to the point of being almost perfect, where the odds of a defect are only 3.4 per million. While the latter is sometimes taken out of necessity, it also provides a means of differentiation in an industry where high quality is the norm and increased levels of quality would be perceived as valuable.

The Kano Model

The Kano model is based on the work of a Japanese consultant, Noriaki Kano.[3] It proposes that there are actually three important levels of quality characteristics for customers. The first level is considered to be a "must-be." In other words, the characteristic has to be present for the product to be considered on the list as a possible alternative to purchase. The customer expects to find these characteristics and so is not particularly impressed when they are present. They are generally taken for granted. When these characteristics are not present, however, the customer will be very dissatisfied. An example is the availability of ATM access for a bank. It's expected, but not enough to win new customers.

The second level of characteristics covers "one-dimensional" characteristics. They are the characteristics that the customer looks for. The more products and services possess these characteristics and the better the performance on these characteristics, the more impressed the customer is. These are most frequently the characteristics that will separate a product or service from a competitor's. Examples are the friendliness of a bank's staff and the attractiveness of its lobby.

The third level of characteristics is known as exciting characteristics, or "delighters." They are a pleasant surprise to the customer. The customer doesn't expect them or look for them because he or she is unaware that they exist. These characteristics almost always set a product or service apart from its competition. Delighting characteristics do not remain delighters for long, however. They soon become expected, and competitors copy them if possible. An example of this type of characteristic is the rear seat system on the Honda Odyssey van, which allows the seat to disappear completely into the floor. Most customers were very surprised at this feature when it first came out. Over time, however, it has become expected, and competitors have been forced to provide something comparable. The Kano model offers a framework for moving customers beyond the point of being satisfied to being delighted with the quality.

Six Sigma Quality

Six sigma (6σ) is an approach used predominantly in manufacturing to improve the control of production processes so that the likelihood of producing a defect is greatly reduced. As was discussed in the section on statistical process control and process capability, the ability of a manufacturer to avoid production of defects depends on how the specifications for an item produced compare to the capabilities of the processes used to produce it. If the processes used to produce a particular component, for example, are so well controlled and so precise that meeting the specifications required for that component is very easy, there is a very small likelihood of a defect being produced. If the processes are not as precise and not as easy to control, there is an increased chance of a defect being produced. This phenomenon, known as process capability, is best understood by reexamining the role of random fluctuation in production processes.

As you know, there is some variability in all production processes, no matter how good the process. As a process becomes more tightly controlled, however, the variability is held to a narrower and narrower range. The variability of the process is measured by the standard deviation (σ). Traditional views of process capability held that when the specifications for a product or component are compared to the process capabilities, 3σ upper and lower limits must be inside customer specifications. To understand how this extends to 6σ, it helps to look at this in the form of an example.

Suppose a manufactured automotive component was specified to be 0.60 inch long. It was also specified that the upper and lower limits on that part were ±0.08 inch. In other words, parts from 0.52 to 0.68 inch were okay. The component was stamped out of sheet steel in a process that, like all processes, has a small amount of variability. When parts were measured, it was found that the average size, indeed, was 0.60 inch and the standard deviation was 0.02. Exhibit 7.26 provides a comparison of the customer specifications and process capabilities. In Exhibit 7.26 it is evident that the 3σ limits are well within the customer specifications.

Process Capability for Three Sigma Quality EXHIBIT 7.26

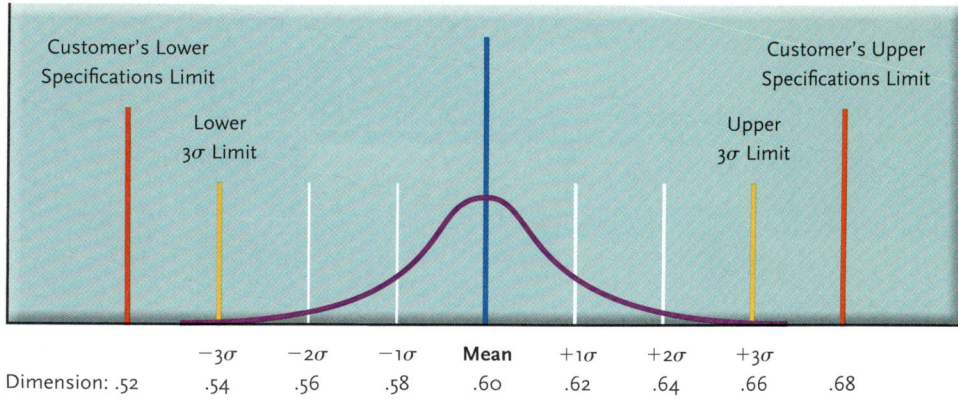

The requirement that the customer specifications be inside the 3σ limits is set because random fluctuation, for which we have no control, stays primarily within these 3σ limits. The proportion of the total amount of variability that will be within 3 standard deviations above and below the mean is 99.74 percent. For every 1,000 units, however, 16 will be outside the 3σ limits, just because of random fluctuation. As long as the 3σ limits are just inside the customer specifications, there is a small chance (0.26 percent) of producing a "defect" or an outcome outside the customer specifications as a result of random fluctuation. The important point in understanding the use of 3σ limits is that potentially, only 99.74 percent of the quantity produced are "good," and as many as 0.26 percent could be "bad." That brings us to six sigma.

Six sigma quality simply means that 6σ limits are used instead of 3σ limits. If 6 standard deviations above and below the process mean must be inside the customer specifications, the process has to be much "tighter," and the likelihood of random fluctuation extending beyond customer specifications becomes minuscule. The standard deviation must be much less (half as large) in order to fit six of them inside the customer specifications. The odds of random fluctuation creating a result that is 6 standard deviations from the mean is 2 in 1 billion. In other words, rather than being 0.9974 (99.74 percent) confident in products being within specifications as we would be using 3σ limits, 6σ limits give us 0.999999998 (99.9999998 percent) confidence. In most manufacturing applications, the process is not centered, however, and is allowed to shift from 1 standard deviation above to 1 standard deviation below the mean. One advantage to reducing the process variability is the increase in the amount the process is allowed to shift. A noncentered process results in a reduction in confidence, to 3.4 defects per million. This is still much better than 99.74 percent, which results in 26 defects per 10,000 units.

Suppose we eliminated variability in our process until the standard deviation was 0.01 rather than 0.02. That leaves 6 standard deviations above and below the mean inside the customer's specifications. Exhibit 7.27 shows how the tighter process looks with 6σ limits in place.

EXHIBIT 7.27 Process Capability for Six Sigma Quality

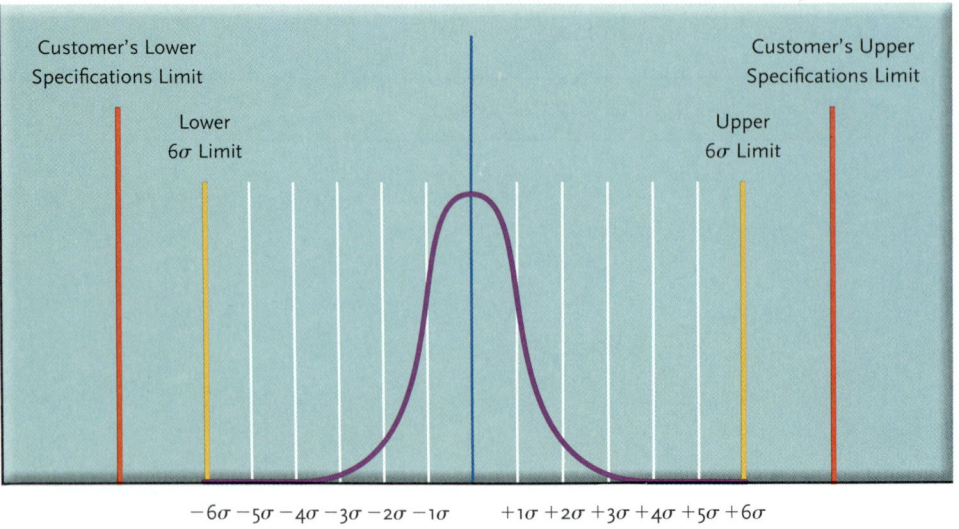

One might justifiably ask, "Why would anyone need this kind of accuracy?" There are two possible reasons. The first reason is that a company's ability to demonstrate that level of quality is an extremely important confidence-builder for customers. They know that any supplier able to meet 6σ quality levels has tremendous control of its processes and the discipline necessary to achieve a very difficult standard. Esource 7.3 provides an example explanation of how one company uses six sigma quality.

www
OperationsNow
.com

The second reason a company might use six sigma is that in some environments, the six sigma quality level is actually necessary to provide completed products of acceptable quality. Two notable companies that have committed to the six sigma level of quality are Motorola and General Electric. Both companies produce complex products that must also meet high quality standards, such as electronic components for communication equipment, medical equipment, and aviation equipment. Complex products often contain a large number of components that are interdependent. If a single component of the product fails, the entire product fails.

Suppose the small stamped part we discussed in our previous example is a component of such a product, and the product contains 125 components, each of which could cause a product failure. With 3σ limits in place, we know that there is a 99.74 percent likelihood of each component being good. With 99.74 percent confidence for

What Does Six Sigma Really Mean?

Six sigma has become synonymous with extremely high levels of reliability. With 6 standard deviations inside the customer specifications, the likelihood of a defect occurring due to random variation is less than two in one billion. With three sigma quality, there are nearly three defects in a thousand. It's hard to conceptualize the proportion of two in one billion, so here are some examples of six sigma in more visible contexts, compared to the accuracy associated with three sigma.

- A book typed with a 3σ level of accuracy would average approximately 1.5 misspelled words per page. With 6σ accuracy there would be only one misspelled word in all of the books contained in a small library.
- If the errors associated with 3σ were the months in a century, there would be $3\frac{1}{2}$ months. Six sigma would be equal to 6 seconds out of a century.
- If the error associated with 3σ was equal to a coast-to-coast trip across the United States, 6σ would be four steps.

Why would such a high level of quality be needed? Several examples drive the point home. With only three sigma quality the following disasters would happen:

- There would be 20,000 wrong prescriptions written per year.
- More than 15,000 newborn babies would be accidentally dropped by doctors and nurses each year.
- There would be nearly 500 wrong surgeries performed on patients *per week* in the United States.
- The U.S. Postal Service would lose 2,000 articles of mail each hour.
- Your drinking water would be unsafe for an hour each month, but you wouldn't know which hour.

Source: "Six Sigma: Motorola's Quest for Zero Defects," *APICS—The Performance Advantage*, July 1991, pp. 36–40; "Quality Control: U.S. Felt Earns a Business Practice Black Belt," *Midrange Enterprise*, April 2001, pp. 27–28.

each component, and 125 components, there is only a 72.22 percent (0.9974 raised to the 125th power) probability that all 125 components would be sound, and that the product would work. A 72.22 confidence in a product being usable would not be sufficient. A much higher confidence in component quality is required to bring about an acceptable level of quality for the finished product.

This scenario actually opens up an opportunity to introduce another approach to obtaining high levels of quality in complex products. The greater the number of components, the higher the level of confidence necessary for each component in order to maintain an acceptable level of finished product quality. An alternative to increasing the confidence in components by reducing process variability would be to design the product with fewer components, which would also raise system reliability. Japanese auto manufacturers have utilized this approach extensively.

SERVICE-ORIENTED QUALITY IMPROVEMENT

Service quality management must sometimes be looked at from a different perspective than product quality management. Process quality for the creation of products usually doesn't have any direct impact on the customer. It affects the customer only if the process produces a defective outcome. But because of their involvement in services, customers are interested in both the outcome *and* the process. The customer's interest in service processes *and* outcomes places much more importance on workforce skills, particularly for those processes that involve interaction with the customer. Employee characteristics related to customer interactions are covered in more detail in Chapter 11.

Management of service quality can include the use of all of the tools discussed earlier in this chapter, including statistical process control charts. This discussion of "services" includes service-oriented businesses and services that accompany products. In service environments acceptance sampling is occasionally used for incoming materials or products. In service environments that have a high degree of interaction with the customer, that interaction and the processes that the customer is involved in, known as the **service encounter**, are very important. Two approaches to enhancing the service encounter are **service blueprinting** and **moment of truth analysis**.

Service Blueprinting

As mentioned in the discussion of the general-purpose quality tools, a service blueprint is actually a special process flowchart. A service blueprint provides a model of the actual process so that the process can be examined for weaknesses and potential failure points. The identification of customer waits, employee decisions, details of the process, and the line of visibility, which separates tasks that the customer is involved in from those that take place behind the scenes, provides valuable information that can be used for service improvement. Exhibit 7.28 reproduces a service blueprint of a 15-minute oil change service. Notice the customer orientation of the blueprint. Potential failure points are identified in the blueprint as focal points for process improvement.

Notice that Exhibit 7.28 visually separates activities that occur behind the line of visibility from those that the customer sees. Moving activities behind the line of visibility is an effective means of improving productivity and efficiency by moving the customer out of the process. Removing the customer from the process removes any interaction or customer expectations for special treatment. It also allows the business to hire technicians who are good at changing oil but may not be very skilled in inter-

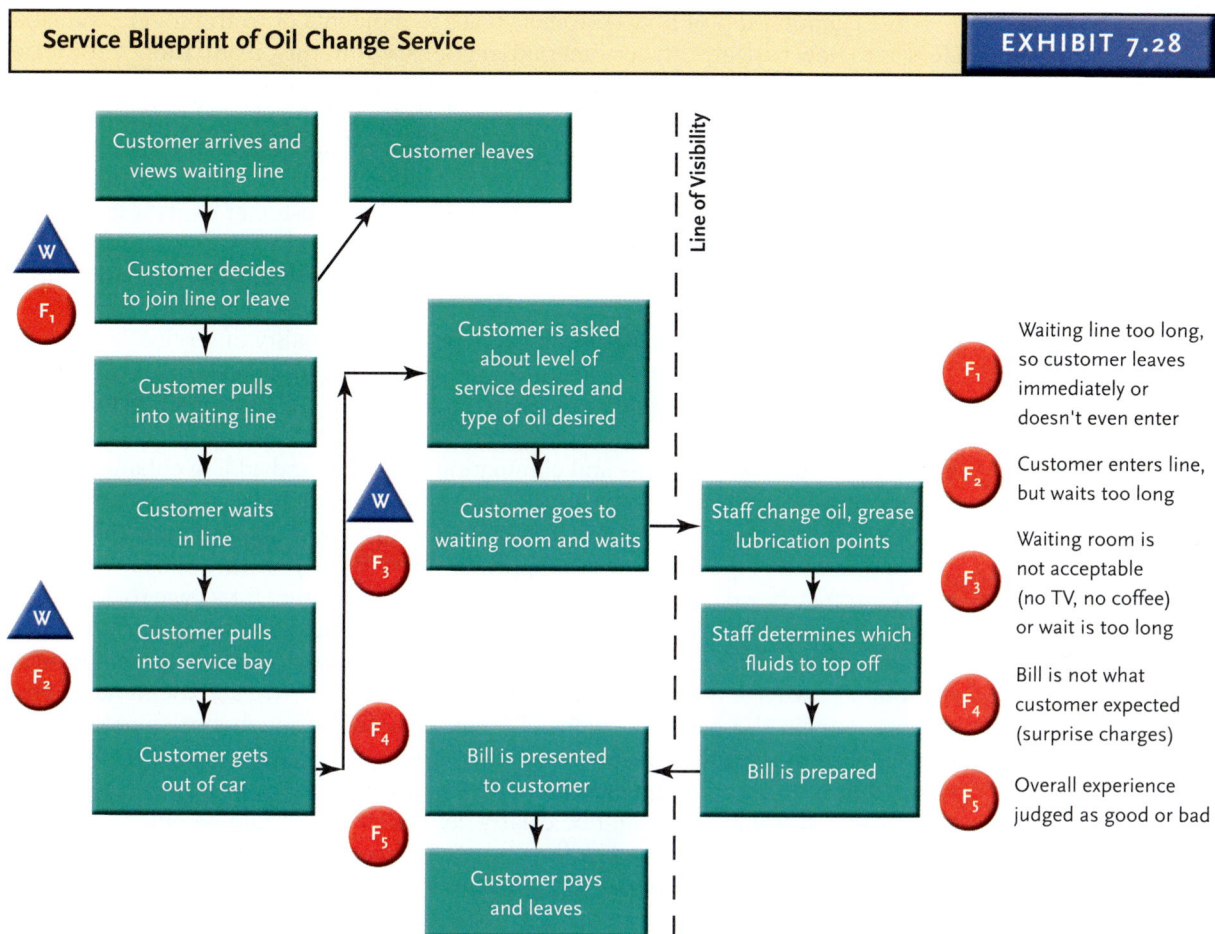

Exhibit 7.28 Service Blueprint of Oil Change Service

acting with the customer. Interaction with the customer can be accomplished by one individual who greets the customer, takes instructions from the customer, answers questions, prepares the bill, and so on. In this environment, like many services, failure points are often linked to waiting time.

Service blueprints benefit service organizations by enabling the company to closely examine its processes. Management can look at a service blueprint and see how the service processes work and how the customer is involved. Many service providers have gone a step further, examining not only how a customer is involved with the service but how that involvement compares to the customer's expectations. This process is examined in detail in the following section.

Moment-of-Truth Analysis

Certain instances in a customer's interaction with a business define the customer's perception of quality. These instances have a substantial impact and become ingrained in the customer's mind. If a service business can identify these critical instances and separate them from all other activities of the service, it can bring about a focus on issues that matter most to the customer. These instances, first identified by Jan Carlzon, CEO of Scandinavian Airlines System, are known as **moments of truth**.[4,5] Moments of truth occur whenever a customer comes in contact with an organization and judges the quality of service being provided.

Close examination of how customers react to moments of truth provides valuable clues as to how to deal with customer interactions within the organization. Customers react in three different ways to moments of truth. Certain aspects of that interaction will be considered to be experience enhancers, some will be viewed as meeting standard expectations, and some will be perceived as experience detractors. **Experience enhancers** make the customer feel good about the interaction. They make the interaction better. A **standard expectation** is just that—the customer expects it and usually gets it. While enhancers are typically unexpected and viewed as very positive, standard expectations are taken for granted. **Experience detractors** are those aspects of the interaction that take away from the quality of the service. A customer views a detractor as something that signifies a reduction in the quality of service.

A moment-of-truth analysis requires gathering data from customers about the enhancers, detractors, and standard expectations for all service encounters. Then attention can be given to the moments of truth—through process change, process improvement, and employee training—and eliminating detractors and adding enhancers.

Service processes become more critical when they are expanded to include Internet-based services. Processes that are accomplished in a brick and mortar business by interacting with employees are accomplished electronically on the World Wide Web for an Internet-based company. Entering information, waiting for a page to download, or trying to understand a checkout process on the Internet has a tangible counterpart in a traditional service. The reaction of a customer to unnecessary requests for information, a slow page download, or a confusing checkout process is the same in both settings, only in the Internet company it can be acted on much more quickly. After all, it is much easier for a customer to click to a competitor than to drive to one. Businesses that have an online presence must recognize that an "e" process is just another process to a customer. It should be clearly defined and it should be quick. Estimates range up to 75 percent for the portion of customers who abandon their shopping carts at a website checkout. Reasons vary from confusion to surprisingly large shipping costs. Billions of dollars of sales are lost because customers abandon pages that download too slowly. No one wants to wait for the three-minute download of a "splash page" that contains nothing useful to the customer anyway. Moments of truth become "seconds of truth" at Internet speed.

TECHNOLOGICAL ADVANCES IN QUALITY INFORMATION MANAGEMENT: CUSTOMER RELATIONSHIP MANAGEMENT

The discussion of quality in this chapter, from the eight tools to six sigma quality to moment-of-truth analysis, is focused on one overriding issue: pleasing the customer. Do what the customer wants. If this is accomplished, the customer comes back. Success means that the business has acquired the valuable resource of customer loyalty. Customer loyalty increases profitability. Loyal customers do not take their business to competitors. They tell their friends about their experiences and they are actually easier to please than nonloyal customers, resulting in lower costs.

Customer loyalty requires ongoing relationships with customers. Advances in technologies, applications, and techniques have enhanced companies' ability to manage relationships with customers. This relatively new focus for businesses, known as **customer relationship management (CRM)**, has set new standards for the way people are treated. Since businesses now invest more in customer relationship development, those relationships must be treated as resources. Customer relationship management is covered in depth in Chapter 14.

Recall from the discussion of the Kano model how a "delighter" can gradually become something that is taken for granted. This is definitely the case with CRM. CRM systems can consist of virtually anything that relates to customer contact. In many instances, they include call center management software; they also track all sales, marketing, and customer service interactions with customers. CRM enables anyone who interacts with a particular customer to know about all previous interactions. Different departments can have access to information related to a particular customer. Customers perceive a more consistent experience because they get a more unified interaction with the business, no matter who the contact person is. CRM is often extended to the organization's website to enable customers to interact.

When interactions with consumers in B2C relationships are necessary, CRM may include access to data on, for example, previous purchases, clothing sizes, interests, and payment modes. If you've purchased over the Internet or over the phone, you may have wondered how the call center staff person knew something about you. The answer: CRM software accessed a database that included information on previous interactions with you.

WHEN SOMETHING STILL GOES WRONG: RECOVERY

Despite every effort to ensure good quality, despite every effort to minimize variability, and despite every effort to provide customers with exactly what they want, there will still be times when customers do not get what they want. It may be because of an actual failure, or it may be because a customer has expectations that are different from the norm. In any case, because the customer defines quality, poor quality as perceived by the customer is just that—poor quality.

A failure, be it a product that didn't meet expectations or service that fell short, does not have to mean a lost customer or even lost customer loyalty. Quality-oriented businesses have in place a **recovery plan**, a plan to save the customer when a failure occurs. In some cases, a failure followed by an excellent recovery can result in the customer feeling even better about the business than if no failure had occurred.

Successful recovery plans are well thought out, well known to all employees, and designed to make the customer end up feeling good about the experience. Unsuccessful recovery plans make a token effort to please the customer, don't eliminate the bad experience, and do not result in retaining the customer. We've all experienced both situations. You've probably received bad food or bad service at an expensive restaurant, and after complaining you've been told that the meal would be free. Of course, it should be free! If you'd purchased a pair of shoes that fell apart the day after you bought them, you wouldn't hesitate to demand your money back. We tend to be very willing to demand our money back when a product is bad, but we hesitate to demand our money back when service is bad. We grumble about it, but we rarely take a stand. Even when someone asks "Was everything OK?" we are likely to say "Yeah, everything was fine," even when it wasn't. A good manager does not want to hear that things were great when they weren't. Negative comments are critical to the business that wants to improve. Negative experiences provide an opportunity to improve, and the savvy manager should be very willing to pay for those opportunities. A business should consider the cost of a recovery to be the cost of extremely valuable information. If it can help the business improve, it is worth the investment.

Returning to the restaurant example, the common practice of eliminating the charge for a bad meal isn't an acceptable recovery plan. The customer will leave feeling the service was bad and probably will not return. A successful recovery plan requires doing what it takes to make the customer feel good about the experience and want to come back—for example, eliminating the charges for the meal, having the manager apologize profusely, and offering a pair of gift certificates for a later date for any meal on the menu. This will probably get a person to return. And if the follow-up experience is a good one, the customer will come back again. You might think that such a recovery would be too expensive, but the only real cost is the cost of raw food, and that is minimal when compared to the revenue stream generated by a loyal customer.

TOTAL QUALITY MANAGEMENT

No discussion of quality would be complete without a discussion of total quality management (TQM). TQM will be discussed briefly here to put it in perspective as a way to link the management of quality to everything a firm accomplishes. It is discussed in detail as an integrative management framework in Chapter 15, which is devoted entirely to the topic.

The thrust of TQM is that quality should drive everything a company does whether or not it has direct impact on the products or services the customer will eventually receive. This focus on the internal and external aspects of quality management is based on a culture of doing "it" right the first time. The motivating logic behind this commitment is that anything not done correctly ultimately has an impact on what the customer receives. A companywide commitment to quality, treating anyone who is affected by the actions of anyone else as a "customer"—even if the recipient of those actions is another employee—creates a culture that strives for excellence. The impact of that culture enhances numerous broad-based performance measures, including profitability measures, costs, customer satisfaction, and customer loyalty.

CHAPTER SUMMARY

The quality of services and products is such an important component of value, and value is such an important prerequisite to profitability, that issues of quality arise in every facet of business management and can be found in virtually every chapter of this book. This chapter examined the link between quality and value and introduced a number of techniques to assist in the management of quality.

Whereas producers of products have begun to master quality management, providers of services are far behind. To compound the problem of service quality, consumers are being exposed to more and more services, further increasing their exposure to poor quality. Tight labor conditions make the problem even worse. Part of the overall problem, however, lies in the unwillingness of consumers to demand quality in services in the same way they demand quality in products. Good businesses recognize that when it comes to poor quality, no news is *not* good news. The quiet customers, who speak little but leave dissatisfied and never return, can kill a business. Only through actively seeking out customer wants and needs can a business actually fulfill them. In the following chapter, a concept that is, in many ways, a part of quality is addressed in detail to finish up the unit on the components of value. This final topic is timeliness.

KEY TERMS

acceptable quality level (AQL), 211
acceptance sampling, 210
appraisal costs, 191
capability index, 202
cause and effect diagram, 195
check sheet, 198
consumer's risk, 211
control chart, 199
control limits, 201
cost of quality (COQ), 190
customer relationship management (CRM), 218
experience detractors, 218
experience enhancers, 218
external failure costs, 190
flowchart, 193
histogram, 198
Kano model, 212
lot tolerance percent defective (LTPD), 211
moments of truth, 217
moment of truth analysis, 216
operating characteristics (OC) curve, 211
Pareto analysis, 196
Pareto chart, 195
prevention costs, 192
process capability, 202
producer's risk, 211
recovery, 190
recovery plan, 219
run chart, 194
scatter diagram, 199
service blueprinting, 216
service encounter, 216
six sigma quality, 212
standard expectation, 218
statistical process control (SPC), 200
testing, 191

REVIEW QUESTIONS

1. Define "quality."
2. Why is the management of service quality often more difficult than that of products?
3. How are product and service quality linked to profitability?
4. Describe the concept of "cost of quality." Why is a proactive approach to quality less costly than a reactive approach?
5. Describe the four categories of the cost of quality.
6. For each of the following eight general-purpose quality tools, describe how the tool works and provide an example application:
   a. Flowchart
   b. Run chart
   c. Cause and effect diagram
   d. Pareto chart
   e. Histogram
   f. Check sheet
   g. Scatter diagram
   h. Control chart
7. Why is the elimination of process variability important for improving quality?
8. What is meant by "process capability"?
9. Why must an X-bar chart be used in conjunction with an R-chart?

10. What is acceptance sampling? What is meant by AQL, LTPD, producer's risk, and consumer's risk?
11. Describe the Kano model. What implications does it have for competitiveness?
12. Describe the concept of six sigma quality. How does six sigma quality relate to process capability? What environments are particularly in need of six sigma?
13. How does moment-of-truth analysis improve service quality? What is meant by enhancers, expectations, and detractors?
14. How does customer relationship management improve customer loyalty?
15. What is a recovery plan? What should the objective of a good recovery plan be?
16. What is the fundamental objective underlying total quality management?

DISCUSSION QUESTIONS

1. What are the most recent examples of bad quality (product or service) you have been exposed to? What was your reaction? In hindsight, should your reaction have been different? What recovery attempts were made by the business? Were they successful?
2. What is your favorite local business? What characteristics make it your favorite?
3. Design a recovery system for a frequently experienced quality problem. How does your recovery system differ from those you typically encounter?
4. Describe the potential conflicts between customer relationship management and the desire for privacy. Where do you draw the line regarding the type of information you want businesses to have?
5. What are the dangers associated with acceptance sampling? When is it appropriate?
6. Identify the moments of truth for a business that you frequent. What are the enhancers, standard expectations, and detractors?

PROBLEMS

1. State University sent a survey to all its first-year students. The responses are given in the following table. Perform a Pareto analysis on the data and construct a Pareto chart.

Type	Number of Complaints	Cumulative Total	Percentage of Total	Cumulative Percentage
Problems with roommate	16	16	22%	22%
Lack of privacy	18	34	24	46
Community bathrooms	32	66	43	89
Noise	8	74	11	100
Total	74			

2. J&R Investments surveyed its clients on the reasons they chose to invest with the company. Some 49 percent responded that it was due to the high returns that J&R's funds offered; 15 percent attributed their selection to the variety of funds that the company offered; 23 percent felt J&R's reputation was worthy of their business; 13 percent were won over by the company's security. The company received a total of 150 responses. Perform a Pareto analysis and construct a Pareto chart for the survey results.

3. Patch is a popular manufacturer of blue jeans. The company maintains a strong quality policy with regard to its products. Last month the company held 94 pairs of blue jeans due to quality issues: 11 of the problems were due to poor fabric, 17 were related to improper stitching, 28 resulted from poor coloring, and 34 were because of irregular sizing. Management plans to present the quality information at a monthly meeting. Perform a Pareto analysis and construct a Pareto chart for this meeting.

4. Simcoe Corporation, a manufacturer of ice skates, wishes to know if the company is able to make a new type of skate blade. The blades need to be 0.48 inch from top to bottom without varying more than ±0.02 inch. The company's machine responsible for producing the blades currently offers a standard deviation of 0.005 inch. Compute the C_p for the process. Will Simcoe be able to consistently manufacture the new skate blades to specification?

5. Giftnet is a proposed ecommerce website for a large clothing retailer. The company has a large number of customers who have shown an interest in purchasing clothes online, provided delivery of the merchandise would take no longer than seven days plus or minus half a day. A prototype of the etailor showed that by using a premium shipping service, the average delivery time is 7 days, with a standard deviation of 0.17 day. Giftnet believes it can make all of the desired delivery times. Is the company correct? Explain your answer in terms of the C_p for the process.

6. Willie is the head greenskeeper at Par Four Golf Course. He recently found out that the golfers prefer the fringe of the greens to be kept between a half inch and inch in length. Willie has a riding mower that can cut a mean of 0.75 inch with a standard deviation of 0.11 inch. He also has a hand mower that can cut at 0.75 inch with a standard deviation of 0.06 inch, although it would take quite a bit more time. Compute the C_p for each mower. Should Willie use the rider or the hand mower? Explain your answer.

7. Bottoms-Up bottles soft drinks. It plans on introducing a new style of bottle to attract more drinkers. The new bottle can hold no more than 12.1 ounces of cola. The company also knows that anything less than 11.9 ounces in the new bottle will be apparent to potential customers as a less-than-full bottle because of the bottle's narrow neck. The current bottling machine is set for 12 ounces and is able to maintain a standard deviation of 0.019 ounce. Compute the C_p. Should the company adopt the new bottle? Explain your answer.

8. Anteater Skateboards outsources wheels and trucks (the axle and suspension). TuffTruck, the manufacturer of its trucks, machines axles to tolerances supplied by Anteater. Anteater requires that axles be between 0.2492 and 0.2508 inch. TuffTruck has learned to begin its axle turning process below center and allow the process to drift as the cutting tool wears. The standard deviation of the turning process is 0.0002 inch. The current process mean is at 0.2503 inch. Should the cutting tool be changed?

9. TekLane produces various diameters of extruded plastic string for use in "weed whackers." The plastic extrusion process forces molten plastic through a nozzle to form the plastic string. Weed whacker strings of various diameters are used for different brands of weed whackers. Over time, extrusion nozzles wear and the diameter of the string increases. Process variability depends on consistent temperature and pressure. The most popular string diameter is the 0.095. In order to function properly in the automatic string advance weed whackers, the string must be between 0.093 and 0.097 inch. The standard deviation of the process is 0.0004 inch. If the process is averaging a diameter of 0.096 inch, is the process in control?

10. Brittain's Fine Furniture produces customer cabinets and tables. Its production facilities utilize rough-sawn lumber from local mills. The first step in Brittain's wood processing is a planing operation, which surfaces all wood to a standard of from 0.748 to 0.752 inch thick. The planer used for surfacing has three rotating knives that must be kept extremely sharp to maintain the proper smooth finish. It maintains a process standard deviation of 0.0003 inch. As the knives wear and get resharpened, the thickness of the boards gradually increases. Eventually, the knives must be replaced. Knives are expensive, so Brittain purchases knives slightly wider than required so that as they wear, the thickness of the wood drifts through the allowable limits. Brittain wishes to know the process mean it should start at in order to maximize knife life.

11. The First Regional Bank requires its tellers to sample the amount of withdrawals customers make in order to track the amount of cash kept on hand. The withdrawal information is charted below. The R-bar value is 50. Construct an X-bar chart from the data.

Sample Number	Observation		
	1	2	3
1	$20.00	$40.00	$60.00
2	35.00	50.00	10.00
3	40.00	20.00	75.00
4	30.00	125.00	50.00
5	20.00	40.00	20.00

12. InkWell produces inkjet printers. The company must control the weight of packaging material for each packaged printer in order to maintain and control shipping costs. Sample data are given below in pounds. The R-bar value is 1.2. Construct an X-bar chart with the data.

Sample Number	Observation		
	1	2	3
1	12.2	14.1	11.9
2	12.1	12.9	12.5
3	11.8	12.4	12.1
4	12.4	13.6	12.1
5	12	12.9	12.6

13. Mr. Salty bakes and sells pretzels. The company carefully controls the amount of pretzels it puts in each bag. Below are data from the last five quality checks. Use the data to construct an R-chart.

Sample Number	Observation 1	Observation 2
1	78	76
2	78	75
3	77	77
4	79	77
5	76	78

14. You have been asked to present the accompanying R-chart (Exhibit 7.29) to top-level management at Dunham Inc. Explain the use of the R-chart and any significant conclusions that can be drawn from this chart.

EXHIBIT 7.29

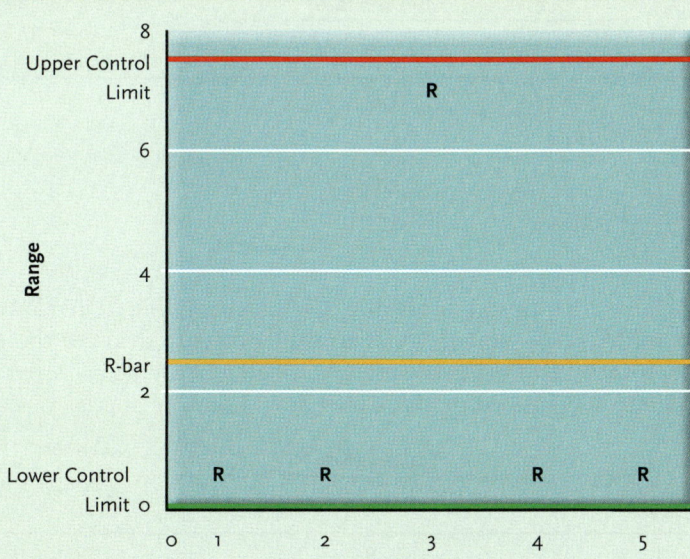

15. CarPro specializes in renting cars for students going on spring break. Due to the long travel distances, the company carefully controls the miles-per-gallon that the cars get. Sample data are given below. Construct an X-bar and R-chart with the data.

Sample Number	Observation 1	Observation 2	Observation 3
1	20.4	20.2	21.4
2	19.3	20.5	20.8
3	21.1	20.8	20.1
4	21.2	19.7	20.5
5	20.4	21.1	19.5

16. Andy's Candies sells jellybeans. Each bag of candy must be carefully monitored for the proper weight. The company samples and charts the weight of bags of jellybeans as part of its quality control program. The results are given below. Construct X-bar and R-charts using the data.

Sample Number	Observation		
	1	2	3
1	1.1	1.2	1.6
2	2	1.3	1.6
3	3.8	1.2	1.7
4	1.9	1.2	1.4
5	1.4	1.1	1.8

17. Metropolitan Airport carefully tracks the length of flight delays. The most current data are given below. Construct an X-bar and an R-chart from the data. What conclusions can be drawn?

Sample Number	Observation (minutes late)	
	1	2
1	10.1	20.2
2	19.3	94.1
3	8.1	35.8
4	21.2	43.1
5	32.1	26.7

18. Mortis Dining Hall is the primary dining hall for students living in the dormitory. It conducted a study on the amount of time students needed to use the dining hall's services. The results of the study are given below. Provide an X-bar chart, an R-chart, and any conclusions that you may draw from the charts.

Sample Number	Observation		
	1	2	3
1	30	18	47
2	8	21	32
3	16	22	26
4	32	48	53
5	16	24	19
6	12	21	27
7	22	19	32
8	26	31	15

19. Tie's Drive-In is a popular hamburger restaurant. To accommodate the large quantity of hamburgers ordered each day, the eatery has purchased a machine that will rapidly roll hamburger patties. However, the hamburgers appear to be different sizes from each other. Tie, the owner, kept track of the weights of recent hamburger patties. You have been brought in to provide your recommendations.

Should Tie continue to use the machine? Create an R-chart and an X-bar chart to support your recommendations.

Sample Number	Observation			
	1	2	3	4
1	0.35	0.36	0.35	0.34
2	0.34	0.36	0.36	0.35
3	0.21	0.26	0.36	0.35
4	0.31	0.34	0.34	0.36
5	0.47	0.49	0.36	0.35

20. You are employed by Control Consulting and have an important presentation tomorrow. The topic of the presentation is statistical process control charts. You have been given the accompanying charts (Exhibit 7.30) to use in your presentation. Describe why statistical process control charts are used. Also interpret the charts. Are the data in control?

EXHIBIT 7.30

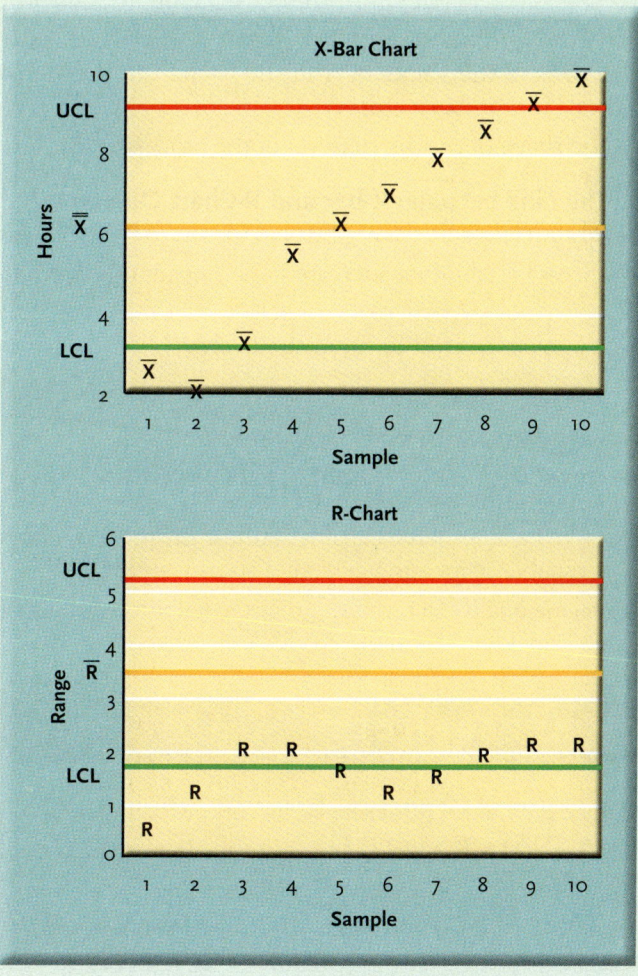

www.
OperationsNow
.com

INTERACTIVE ANALYSIS 7.1

THE PROCESS CONTROL CHART INTERACTIVE MODEL

The X-bar and R-chart Interactive Model is accessed through Chapter 7 of the *OperationsNow.com* website. It provides a visual environment for examining the interactions between an X-bar chart and an R-chart as process variability is manipulated.

The X-bar and R-chart Interactive Model allows the user to change one parameter—process variability. The outputs of the system include the graphical X-bar chart, with customer specifications, three sigma control limits, and six sigma control limits. An R-chart is also provided as an output of the system.

Experiment 1: System Fundamentals
1. Start with the process variability at its greatest level, with the slider all the way to the right.
    a. What would you say about the company's ability to consistently meet the customer specifications at this level of variability?
    b. Reduce the process variability until the three sigma control limits are inside the customer specifications. What happens to the values of *R* in the R-chart as the variability is reduced?
2. Reduce the process variability until the six sigma limits are within the customer specifications.
    a. What happens to the values of *R* in the R-chart as the variability is reduced to this level? Is that expected?
    b. What is the shape of the distribution of the process at this level of variability?

Experiment 2: The Link between X-bar and R-Chart Outcomes
1. Set the model to its default setting by clicking on the "reset" button.
    a. As the process variability is increased one step at a time, what happens to the R-chart?
2. Why is there a lower control limit on the R-chart?

Experiment 3: Process Capability
1. Set the model at the highest level of process variability.
    a. What is meant by process capability? What must the relationship between the three sigma control limits and the customer specifications be in order for the process to be considered capable? Adjust the process variability so that the process is capable of meeting customer specifications.
2. Describe six sigma quality in terms of process capability. Adjust the model so that it provides six sigma quality.

SELECTED REFERENCES

Bergeron, B. P. *The Eternal E-Customer.* New York: McGraw-Hill, 2001.

Brocka, B., and Brocka, M. S. *Quality Management: Implementing the Best Ideas of the Masters.* Homewood, IL: Business One Irwin, 1992.

Carlson, J. *Moments of Truth.* Cambridge, MA: Ballinger Press, 1987.

Cohen, L. *Quality Function Deployment.* Reading, MA: Addison-Wesley, 1995.

Juran, J. M. *Juran on Planning for Quality*. New York: Free Press, 1988.
Zemke, R., and Schaaf, D. *The Service Edge*. New York: Penguin Books, 1989.
Zemke, R. and Connellan, T. *E-service*. New York: AMACOM, 2000.

ENDNOTES

1. D. A. Garvin, "What Does Product Quality Really Mean?" *Sloan Management Review* 26 (Fall 1984), pp. 25–34; P. E. Pisek, "Defining Quality at the Marketing/Development Interface, *Quality Progress* 20 (June 1987), pp. 28–36.
2. V. Parasuraman, V. A. Zeithaml, and L. L. Berry, "A Conceptual Model of Service Quality and Its Implications for Future Research," *Journal of Marketing* 49 (Fall 1985), p. 48.
3. L. Cohen, *Quality Function Deployment* (Reading, MA: Addison-Wesley, 1995), pp. 36–40.
4. R. Zemke and D. Schaaf, *The Service Edge* (New York: Penguin Books, 1989), pp. 18–35.
5. Jan Carlson, *Moments of Truth* (Cambridge, MA: Ballinger Press, 1987).

OperationsNow.com LEARNING ACTIVITIES

CHAPTER ENHANCEMENT RESOURCES
- Esources
- Reel Operations Video Clips
- Interactive Models
- Excel Tutors
- Supplementary Readings
- Links to Operations On Site Companies

OM EXPLORATION
- Check It Out
- OM in Action
- Online Business Tours
- Letters from the Top
- Putting It All Together: Virtual Case Studies
- Additional Reading

The resource/profit model presents timeliness as the fourth of four components of value. Its relationship with processes and capabilities, cost, and quality is intricate: It is often an outcome of processes, it is a determiner of costs, and it is viewed as an aspect of quality. For consumer and business customers alike, time is as critical as any other value component. In many transactions it is the most important of all.

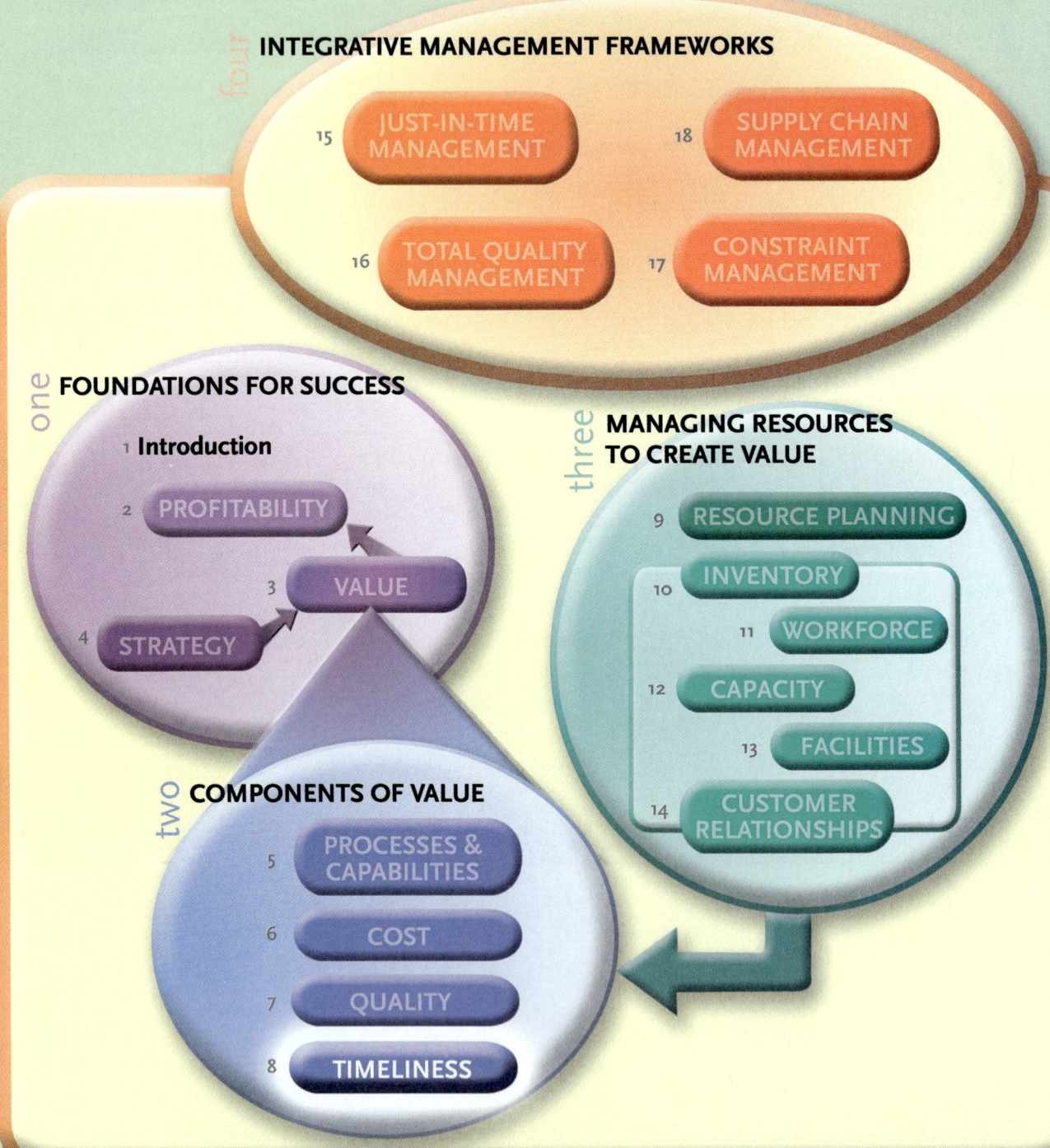

CHAPTER 8

Timeliness

LEARNING OBJECTIVES

Upon completion of Chapter 8, you should be able to

_____ Explain the effect time has on each profitability measure.

_____ Describe the impact of feedback delay on quality.

_____ Explain the common time reduction strategies.

_____ Construct a Gantt chart.

_____ Sequence orders using the traditional sequencing rules and compare rule performance.

_____ Describe the physical features of queues and describe how they affect queue performance.

_____ Compute the probability of *x* arrivals per unit time for a queue.

_____ Describe the psychological approaches to managing perception of queue length.

_____ Construct a network diagram for a project.

_____ Identify the critical path for a project using CPM calculations.

_____ Calculate the likelihood of completing a project in a specified time using CPM with activity time uncertainty.

_____ Complete the calculations necessary to effectively crash a project.

Introduction: Time *Really Is* Money
Time and Profitability
Feedback Delay: A Frequently Overlooked Time Penalty
General Time Reduction Strategies
Scheduling
Scheduling Techniques
The Gantt Chart
Controlling Manufacturing Task Sequences with Traditional Job Sequencing
Trends in Resource Scheduling
Managing Queues of Customers
Psychological Features of Queues
Project Management
Chapter Summary

INTERNET RESOURCES

 Excel Tutors provide annotated spreadsheets for every solved problem that automatically load Excel.

 Esources provide an online version of the more traditional boxed insert.

 Reel Videos provide streaming video footage for company applications of chapter concepts.

 Interactive Models provide an experimental environment for quantitative concepts and simulations.

INTRODUCTION

Time *Really Is* Money

Time has become one of the most critical aspects of business competition, if not the most critical, simply because it has so many implications for business success. As shown in Exhibit 8.1, time is a component of value. "When" can be nearly as important as "what" for a customer, and if the "when" doesn't meet customer needs, the "what" will be obtained somewhere else. Even when a customer is purchasing a product, the service aspects of the product delivery and support can be more important than attributes of the product itself. Many service quality issues are linked to timeliness.

Time-related issues and decisions also affect costs and value. Many of the effects that time-related issues have on value are direct and, as a result, seemingly small improvements in timeliness can yield huge financial payoffs. Online business entrepreneurs, for example, knew from day one that speed was critical for success. The more time downloading a screen takes, the more likely the customer will click on something else. Speed is synonymous with good service. Studies by PayPal, the money emailing system, of its signup and registration process showed that increasing the number of screens results in a dramatic loss of customers. In its original signup process, seven screens were required. Analysis showed that 25 percent of the customers would leave at each screen. Now the signup process takes only one screen.[1] Internet download speeds are very important for businesses, and most work hard to design sites that download quickly. Unfortunately, as is demonstrated in Esource 8.1, slow downloads aren't always the fault of the business.

www.OperationsNow.com

Flexibility is closely related to timeliness. Whereas time provides the measure of the speed at which a firm can react, flexibility is the breadth of possible reactions the firm can have. The business that can respond quickly to change with a wide range of possible responses is flexible. The business that can't respond quickly to change is, well, history. The operative word is "quickly." The ability to change is of little use if it takes a long time to do it. "Slow" flexibility doesn't work. The market favors a firm that responds quickly, not one that evolves. The business that can respond quickly to change, to customer needs, and to internal and external forces is a **responsive** company. Responsive companies have many advantages over those that are sluggish or resistant. Think about all the critical resources a business must possess. It can borrow more cash when cash is in short supply. It can buy more machines or outsource when machine capabilities must be increased. It can hire more people when it needs different skills. When it is short of time, however, there isn't much it can do to get more.

Timeliness has a significant impact on the financial health of the firm. Management of time-related issues through operations actions, decisions, and systems can improve profitability.

TIME AND PROFITABILITY

In Chapter 2, two profitability measures, profit margin and return on assets (ROA), were introduced. Profit margin tells how much profit is generated per dollar of sales, and return on assets tells how much profit is generated per dollar of the company's assets.

The Effect of Time on Profit Margin

A quick breakdown of profit margin into its components of net income and sales doesn't immediately indicate the key role that timeliness plays. However, when net

EXHIBIT 8.1 The Role of Timeliness in the Resource/Profit Model

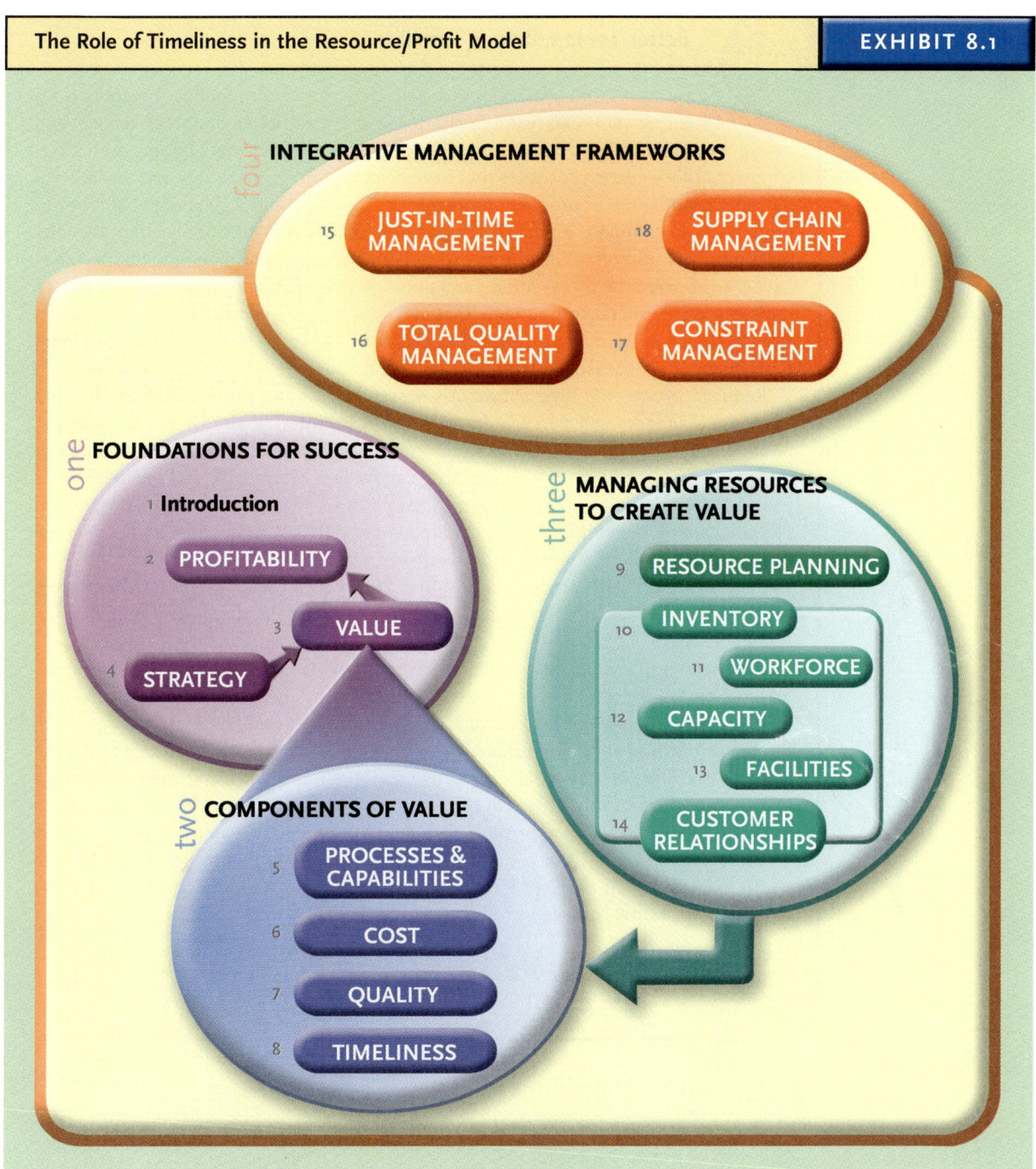

income is broken into its components of net sales and those items subtracted from net sales (costs of goods sold, depreciation, and interest paid), the importance becomes evident.

Time, like cost and quality discussed in previous chapters, has broad implications. From a customer's point of view, reductions in time associated with product- and service-related issues like order-taking, waiting in line, waiting for a product delivery, or waiting for an appointment directly enhance value. Improved response time, dependability of delivery, and convenience can all be linked to timeliness. These enhancements to value

> **om on site**
>
> ### Better Tools Enhance Timeliness
>
> Improved processing speed provides many competitive advantages to businesses. It can result in shorter lead times, better customer service, and reduced costs. In manufacturing, the simple tasks of cutting, grinding, and shaping pieces of metal are processes that have been around for a century and are still significant components of production processes. They also add a substantial amount to production lead times. Huffman Corporation makes machine tools. It makes the machines that other manufacturers use to fabricate metal components. Its machines have transformed the metal cutting and grinding tasks for many customers. Huffman tools can create metal components that vary less than a micrometer. They can accelerate a stream of water to a speed that can cut titanium. Most important, Huffman tools speed up processes, often improving productivity to five times what it was.
>
> Reduced processing time allows businesses to respond more quickly to demand changes. Managers can perceive imbalances in inventories almost as they happen. Shorter lead times mean lower levels of inventory. Increased utilization of computer technology has resulted in machines that can communicate with each other and has enabled businesses to use computer diagnostics to keep machines running better. New machining technologies have resulted in parts that fit better, last longer, and are quieter in their ultimate application. Huffman's customers are able to reduce costs through more efficient processes, and don't have to forecast as far into the future because of their reduced processing lead times. These improvements benefit customers as well.
>
> Advancements in tools have increased the flexibility of manufacturing equipment, eliminating the need to produce large batches of components. Smaller tools can produce individual products instead of large quantities. The elimination of large-batch production results in components moving through processes more quickly and lower levels of inventory. These types of improvement are not often recognized as having a strong impact on productivity, but their influence is actually quite impressive. Manufacturing productivity has improved more than the productivity in other business sectors. Machine tools like those made by Huffman have resulted in the productivity in some manufacturing markets increasing at rates greater than 25 percent, while the rest of the economy has seen productivity increases of only around 10 percent.
>
> Source: "Better Machine Tools Give Manufacturers Newfound Resilience," *The Wall Street Journal*, February 15, 2001, pp. A1, A8.

increase net income by increasing demand, market share, and net sales and may also provide an opportunity to increase the price, which will increase net sales even further.

There are several time-related components of value in B2C and B2B relationships. Increasingly, consumers are willing to pay for immediate gratification. Convenience and quick response have become a dominant priority in the marketing, production, and delivery of consumer goods and services. Customers don't want to wait. The reason they're shopping for something right now is because they want it right now. If they wanted it later, they'd shop for it later. Customers want to spend time on something enjoyable, not waiting in line, or waiting for a package to arrive, or being "on hold," or waiting for a page to download. Can there really be an emergency that would require next-day delivery for the great majority of consumer products? Not likely, but customers still value the quickest response.

Time plays equally important roles for customers and for the business selling to them. Customers want prompt delivery while businesses want prompt payment. Esource 8.2 provides an example of how important time-related issues are for both sides of a business relationship.

www
OperationsNow
.com

Time can play an even more critical role in the determination of value for a B2B customer. Unlike the consumer, who rarely absolutely *needs* a product or service immediately, a business very well could. A manufacturer might shut down an assembly line for lack of one component, resulting in employees being paid $16 an hour for doing nothing. The end product requiring that component may be part of an order that will be delivered late. The business expecting that order may reconsider its relationship with the company if it can't meet its delivery promises. How could this one component be so critical? The customer expecting it has made promises to *its* customers. And they also have expectations that are time-based because *their* customers also do. Time's impact on value and net sales is not the only issue here; it has other implications as well.

Costs associated with time reduce the bottom line for a business and for its customers in several ways. For example, direct materials costs, direct labor costs, and overhead costs are directly related to time. Materials require an investment. The longer the material is stored, the longer it takes to get a financial return on the investment. Labor is paid by the hour or by the week. Overhead costs, such as rent and utilities, are time-based as well.

Despite time's importance, wasting time is not viewed nearly as critically as wasting materials or inventory. Wasting time, however, can be worse than wasting other resources. Suppose we look back at that late component. Having idle workers does more than potentially make the delivery of that order late. Suppose, through heroic effort, the order was still delivered on time. Is all well? Probably not. The fact that labor was paid to do nothing increased the costs associated with the order. Remember that even though we paid workers once while they did nothing, we have to pay them again to do the required labor. The cost increases associated with this order could erase any profit margin that existed. In addition, some other order is likely to pay the price for the heroic action taken to save this one. Any time heroic action is needed in any endeavor, it is probably because someone botched the job and someone else had to work extra hard to save the day. Equipment was idle also, resulting in no return on that asset and the potential for a shortage of equipment capacity later on. One might think that such a small amount of idle time would have an insignificant impact on ROA, and a one-time occurrence probably would. Repeated problems, however, would not only reduce ROA but would also create a chain reaction ending with lost customers and corresponding lost sales.

Direct material costs provide another excellent example of time-related costs. First, the time it takes to receive an order when more products, components, or raw materials are needed can be critical. The longer this "replenishment" lead time, the further into the future demand must be known so the correct amount can be ordered. The further into the future a business forecasts, the less accurate the forecast. The less accurate the forecast, the greater the amount of "safety stock" inventory that must be purchased and carried. This concept is examined further in Chapter 9, which is devoted to inventory.

Direct labor costs are affected by time as well. Obviously, the greater the amount of time required in the actual processes that produce a product or service, the greater the amount of direct labor required per unit. Although labor costs aren't perfectly proportional to the units produced (businesses tend to pay people for 40-hour weeks rather than by the unit), additional labor requirements ultimately result in an increase in workforce, just as reductions in labor will eventually result in a reduction in workforce.

Many products have seasonal demand. For some, demand forecasts must be made far in advance because suppliers take weeks or months to fulfill orders. Unfortunately, some seasonal products have very low value "off-season." Prices of holiday goods, for example, are slashed after Christmas in an attempt to generate at least some revenue and make room for other products.

As we have all experienced, the amount of time a product or a customer is in a productive system isn't all devoted to processing and adding value. A lot of time can be spent waiting. Waiting time is expensive as well. We know customers get frustrated and often associate long waiting times with poor service quality. We also know that space is needed to house long lines. Look, for example, at the amount of space required in fast-food restaurants, theaters, and airports just to accommodate lines of customers. Some businesses go so far as to entertain customers waiting in line, creating an additional cost. Products that wait in queue to be processed increase the level of inventory in the system, increasing inventory carrying costs and causing congestion.

The impact time-related issues have on indirect costs is also substantial. Let's go back to the previous example of long replenishment lead times. Because the longer lead times created the need for forecasting further into the future, the likelihood of inaccurate forecasts made it necessary to buy more inventory, in the form of a safety stock. The impact is greater than that, however, since the greater amount of safety stock increases the overall inventory. As inventory levels go up, so do the indirect costs associated with storage, obsolescence, damaged goods, and so on. For a retailer, the greater the level of inventory, the more likely there will be excess at the end of the season that must be sold at a discount.

Waiting lines result in increases in indirect costs as well. In services, they can increase the need for crowd control and security. In manufacturing, waiting products require more space around work centers, more forklifts to move stuff around, more drivers needed for those forklifts, and more products being damaged by careless drivers. What's more, that waiting time adds to total lead time, and lead time contributes to the amount of time a customer must wait for delivery.

In Chapter 6, during the discussion of allocating indirect costs, several approaches were mentioned. Because time has such an impact on costs, it is often used as a cost driver. Cycle time for producing products, for example, can be used as the driver to allocate overhead costs to products. Time-conscious companies frequently use lead time as the basis for assigning overhead costs rather than the more traditional approach of using direct labor as the cost driver. Time measures are also used in the balanced scorecard approach as a nonfinancial measure.

Another significant cost related to time is the interest on borrowed money. The payback period on a capital investment is dictated by the amount of money it generates. A new building or new automated machine is paid off as it generates income.

The faster it generates income, the more quickly it can be paid off, and the less interest paid. In many cases, the revenue generated by such an improvement is dictated by the amount of products or customers that can be processed through it. Once a resource is "on line" in the productive system, time that is unavailable for use directly reduces the financial return on the resource. This is particularly true for companies that have large capital investments in resources. Esource 8.3 provides an example of one company's efforts to reduce this impact.

The Effect of Time on Return on Assets

A brief examination shows that time is a key determinant of return on assets. ROA is a motivating factor behind a retail managers' interest in such productivity measures as sales per square foot as a measure of retail store productivity or inventory turns as a measure of inventory productivity. Both of those measures are meaningless without a time context.

The faster the financial return on any investment, the greater the return, on an annualized basis. Remember from Chapter 6 that ROA is equal to net income divided by total assets. A key point in understanding the importance of time is that the increases in net income that result from time reduction occur with no increase in total assets. So, rather than invest in new equipment or new technologies as a way to boost net income (which will also result in an increase in total assets), reductions in time increase value, decrease costs, *and* do so with no increase in the denominator of the ROA formula. The result is that enhanced timeliness has a very robust impact on ROA.

Time-Related Productivity Measures

Many measures associated with productivity and quality have their roots in simple time measures. Such commonly used measures as lead time and queue time indicate how long it took for something to occur or how long a customer (or product) had to wait. Another time-based measure, due date performance, compares the actual completion of an order to its due date and calculates the percentage of orders that actually met their due date promise.

The **cash-to-cash cycle** has become a popular means of measuring the impact of time on business productivity. The cash-to-cash cycle is the amount of time between the cash outlay required for purchasing direct materials or inventory consumed during the production of the product or service and the actual receipt of the payment when it is sold. Exhibit 8.2 provides an example of a cash-to-cash cycle and some possible components of that cycle. Notice that each part of the cycle requires time.

In this example, it took approximately 17 weeks after the original expenditure on materials to obtain the financial return. With a cash-to-cash cycle of approximately 17 weeks, the inventory investment "turnover" is just over three times per year. Reductions in the amount of time required to reach any of the milestones shown in Exhibit 8.2 result in an increase in financial return through a reduction in costs. Suppose the transaction netted a $200 return on total expenditures of $1,000, a 20 percent return. The 17-week cycle enables that to occur just over three times per year, for an annual return of 60 percent ($600) on the $1,000. Reducing the cash-to-cash cycle time from 17 weeks to 13 weeks (a 23.5 percent reduction in time), however, results in the $1,000 being turned over four times instead of three. Rather than generate $600 per year on the $1,000 expenditure, $800 is generated, a shift from 60 percent to 80 percent. That is a 33 percent increase in the financial return, generated from a 23.5 percent cash-to-cash cycle improvement.

| EXHIBIT 8.2 | Cash-to-Cash Cycle |

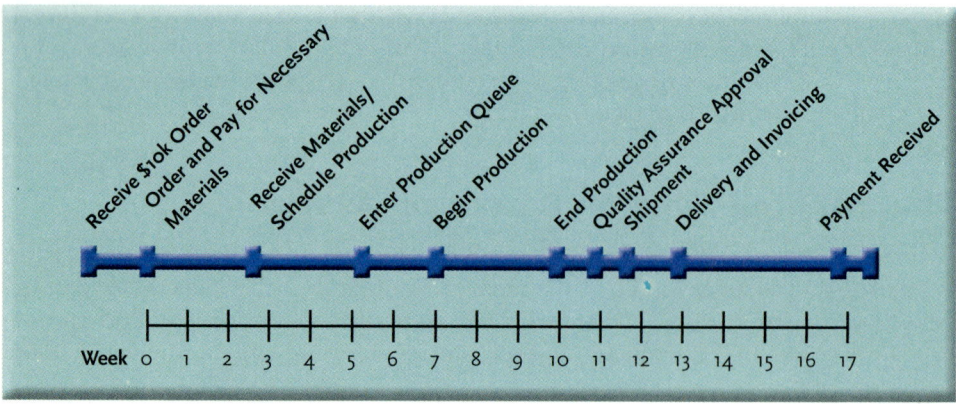

The common tendency is to focus only on production time when trying to reduce the cash-to-cash cycle, but in reality, any task in the cycle, including the time between billing the customer and receiving payment, has the same impact. All business processes, not just those involved in the direct production of the product or service, should be targets. The time that payments are kept before processing them, for example, adds to the cycle. The timing of payments to suppliers also has a dramatic effect.

Typically, a product is shipped and the customer must pay within 30 days. Compare this scenario to some that exist in Internet retailing. It is feasible for an Internet retailer to sell a product online and immediately charge the purchaser's credit card. The retailer, however, might not have to pay its supplier for 30 days. Revenue is collected immediately, but the bill payment is delayed, creating an opportunity to earn interest on the customer's payment prior to paying the supplier. This creates a negative cash-to-cash cycle, allowing the business to price the product very low, because its revenue can be supplemented by the interest income generated by the sale. The low price increases the product's value and its subsequent demand and market share. The negative cash-to-cash cycle actually makes it possible to sell below cost and make it up on volume. Some brick and mortar retailers are able to accomplish the same feat with products sold as loss leaders. Fast turnover, combined with the capacity to delay bill payments to suppliers, results in making money on the "float" while the products are sold below cost.

An important part of the cash-to-cash cycle is known as the make/market or order/deliver loop. For a new product, the loop is the time required to produce the new product and get it to market. For an existing product, the loop is the time required to take the order, make the item, and deliver it. From the customer's perspective, this loop is important because it defines the lead time required to receive an order. For the B2B customer, it defines the replenishment lead time, which determines the customer's planning horizon, forecast accuracy, and so on. Once again, reductions in time anywhere in this loop reduce the wait time for the customer, increasing the value of the product. Reduction in the loop also reduces the length of the cash-to-cash cycle, providing a better financial return for the seller. Greater value equals greater net sales and net income, improved profit margin, and improved ROA.

FEEDBACK DELAY: A FREQUENTLY OVERLOOKED TIME PENALTY

Today's successful businesses must react quickly to any problems associated with product or service quality. A company can't be responsive unless it knows what to respond to. One of the most valuable pieces of information for a responsive company is information about product or service quality problems. The elimination of the causes of such quality problems *at the source* provides the only long-term solution for a firm that emphasizes quality. In the case of a defective product, the mere identification of a defect prior to shipping is a short-term fix that does nothing to improve long-term value. After all, the costs associated with producing that defective product must still be either passed on to customers or absorbed. Prevention is the key. If poor-quality service is delivered, the horse is already out of the barn, so to speak. Quality problems, or "defects," occur because of weaknesses or faults in the productive systems. The ability to fix the system's problems, take corrective action, or design in procedures that eliminate the fault depends on feedback that can be analyzed for cause.

Quality information that is communicated through feedback is critical to quality improvement. Two characteristics of feedback must be present for it to be useful. First, the feedback must be appropriate and accurate. Information that relates to a defective product or service must very precisely describe what was wrong so relevant aspects of the productive system can be addressed. The appropriateness and accuracy of the feedback are dictated by the metrics in place and the ability to actually measure the right things. The second, and most often overlooked, requirement for feedback is that it be timely. Feedback must occur during or as soon as possible after the actual production of the product or service. The ability to create a link between cause and effect diminishes rapidly as the time between creation of a problem and the identification of that problem increases, as modeled in Exhibit 8.3.

This phenomenon becomes obvious if we examine a completely ridiculous, yet analogous, situation. Imagine yourself blindfolded and throwing darts at a target. You are required to throw a dart every 10 seconds, and after each toss, your coach gives you feedback in the form of directions and distances. You throw. Your coach says, "A little higher." You throw again. Your coach says, "A little to your right." Imagine the same situation, you throwing darts every 10 seconds, but there is 3-minute delay before you get the feedback from your coach. Thus after 3 minutes and 18 darts tossed, you are told, "Throw two feet further to the left than you did on that first dart." You throw, thinking "I can't even remember my first dart." You get the idea. Immediate feedback is a prerequisite to improvement. Without quick feedback, no connection can be made between action and outcome. In many production processes, the actual assessment of the quality cannot take place until after the product or service is completed. Therefore, the faster the completion, the quicker the feedback, and the more likely the contribution to improvement. The time between cause and effect is

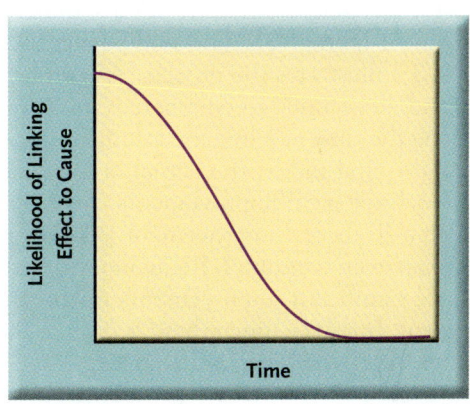

Feedback Delay and Finding Causes of Defects — EXHIBIT 8.3

> **om on site**
>
> ### Fast Versus Slow in the Fashion Industry
>
> The advantages gained by compressed "time to market" are demonstrated quite well in many consumer product retail markets. The benefits obtained in clothing retailing are obvious when large, but very different, retailers are compared. Hennes & Mauritz AB, the Swedish company that operates the H&M chain of clothing stores, exemplifies the more traditional approach to manufacturing and retailing. H&M has 900 suppliers and no factories of its own. The suppliers specialize in different things, which enables H&M to offer a wide variety. For traditional retailers, an average of six months is needed to design a new collection, and another three months is needed to manufacture it.
>
> Zara, a unit of Inditex SA, a Spanish clothing manufacturer and distributor, has 449 stores in Europe, Asia, and North America. Zara manufactures more than half of its own clothing and 40 percent of its own fabric. Zara also owns its own worldwide distribution network. Stores get deliveries twice weekly, and inventory turnover is very high. A new collection can be designed by Zara in four to five weeks and manufactured in a week. Zara is so flexible, it can send out a new style and by the end of the first day know if it is a hit or not. If it is, Zara can order more. Close contact with store managers allows Zara manufacturers to react to trends quickly.
>
> Source: "Just-in-Time Fashion," *The Wall Street Journal*, May 18, 2001, pp. B1, B4.

reduced by eliminating wait time and other time-consuming, but non-value-adding, aspects of the process.

GENERAL TIME REDUCTION STRATEGIES

Assuming that all non-value-adding time has already been removed, the actual time required to accomplish a set of tasks can be reduced in two ways. The first method is to find ways to actually reduce the amount of time required for individual tasks. Suppose a firm was interested in reducing the amount of time it takes to process a customer order. The process is fairly straightforward. The customer calls with an order and the order-taking staff person answers the call, records the customer name, address, and so on, and takes the order. The order is then repeated back for an accuracy check. Once confirmed for accuracy, an availability check is performed to make sure the desired items are in stock. Credit card information is then requested and approval is received. Total cost is calculated, shipping details and costs are determined, and an estimated delivery time is then given. The staff person then thanks the customer and hangs up.

Exhibit 8.4 illustrates the process. As can be seen, the typical order takes about 6 minutes and 40 seconds to complete. One way to reduce the total time required is compressing the time required for specific tasks. By providing the order takers with an online catalog and index, the actual order-taking task is reduced by 20 seconds. In addition, technological improvements can reduce the time for credit card approval, resulting in a 20-second improvement. As shown in Exhibit 8.5, the process has been reduced to an even 6 minutes. Reducing the time required to perform individual tasks can provide significant improvements to the entire process. There is a limit to that improvement, however, since there is only so much time to squeeze out.

Another approach, and one that can have a greater impact on the total time required to process an order, is to identify tasks that could be done concurrently,

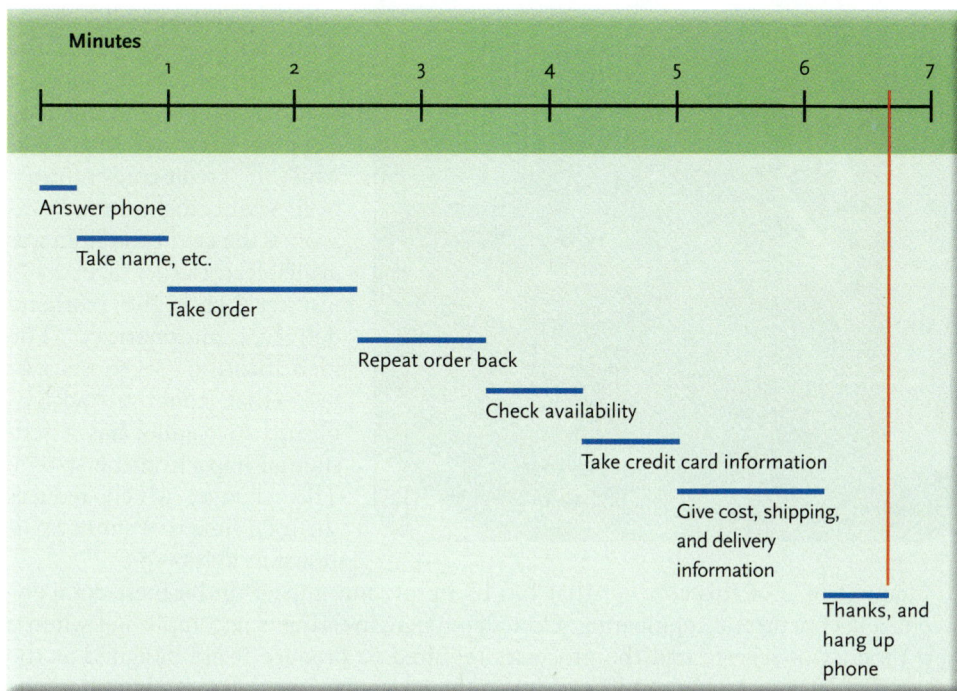

EXHIBIT 8.4 Order-Taking Process

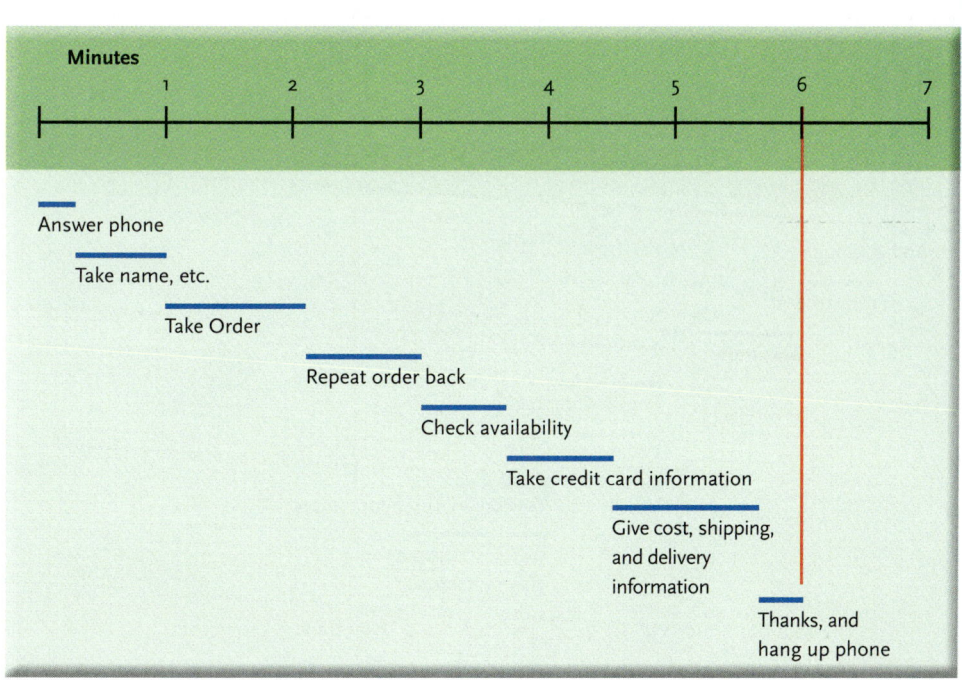

EXHIBIT 8.5 Order-Taking Process with Reduced Time on Specific Tasks

As customers, we're very cognizant of waiting in lines for products and services. We may not realize, however, that while waiting "on hold" to place a telephone order or for customer service we are also in a queue. While not visible to the customer, these queues typically function as a multiple-server, single line queuing system with a first come first served queue discipline. We may get frustrated with the waiting time and hang up, but that means we have to go back to the end of the line.

rather than in sequence. Suppose the system could check the availability of the items ordered automatically, while the order taker read back the order. In addition, suppose that the system could calculate shipping costs and total costs while the credit card information was being entered. As soon as the credit card info was available, the order taker could just read back the cost and delivery information. The identification of those two tasks that could be accomplished in parallel has a substantial impact on the system. This change, which reduces the total time to $4\frac{1}{2}$ minutes, is shown in Exhibit 8.6.

One example of this concept that has had profound impact on business competitiveness is concurrent engineering. **Concurrent engineering** is accomplished when a new product or service and the processes required to produce it are designed at the same time by one integrated team, rather than by separate teams. Rather than the product design team and process design team waiting for each other to accomplish specific tasks, the integrated team works together to accomplish tasks simultaneously. In

EXHIBIT 8.6 Order-Taking Process with Parallel Processing

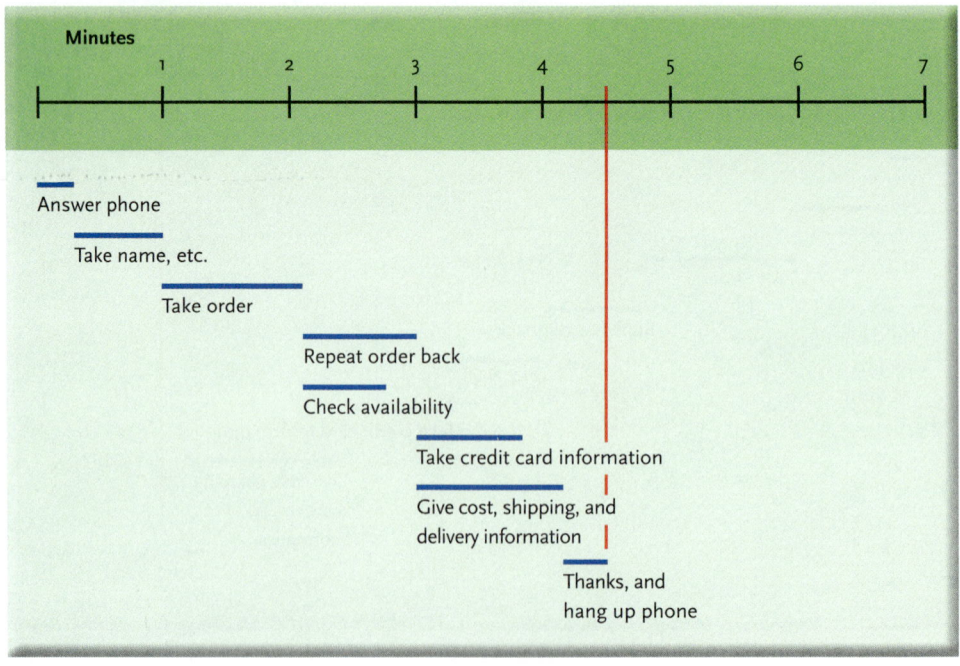

addition to reducing time to market, concurrent engineering also results in a product or service being designed with produceability in mind. Its requirements are consistent with the capabilities of the firm *and* the processes are designed as the product or service is designed. The result is a better match between product or service specifications and the processes required to make them happen. This improves product and service quality and reduces costs associated with processes. In addition, since the design functions are done concurrently instead of sequentially, the amount of time to go from new product or service idea to market is reduced.

SCHEDULING

Scheduling determines when something is to be done and the tasks and activities required to do it. Effective scheduling has two dominant effects on a company. First, the ability to schedule effectively determines whether products and services will be completed *on time*. The operative phrase here is "on time" because whether or not it is on time has a direct impact on the customer. The more complex the processes, the more difficult they will be to schedule. Scheduling effectively enables a firm to compete on the basis of time-related value attributes. And we know how important they are.

Second, in addition to the competitive attributes associated with time, scheduling has an impact on the utilization of capital resources. If an expensive piece of equipment is not scheduled appropriately, it could remain idle instead of being productive, thus generating no return on its investment. So, in addition to allowing the firm to compete on the basis of time-related attributes, the ability to schedule effectively also enables the firm to control costs and maintain an acceptable ROA.

Matching the availability of a resource with demand is a prerequisite to getting an acceptable ROA from the resource and can be accomplished in two ways. The first is to process products or customers when capacity is available. In this scenario, the availability of materials (or in the case of services, the availability of customers) dictates whether resources will be utilized, so management attempts to ensure material and customer availability. In the case of products, production can occur early and the finished products stored until needed. In the case of services, appointments and reservations are used to shift demand to best utilize capacity. The way to match demand and capacity is to schedule capacity so that it will be there when demand occurs. This may require increasing or decreasing capacity as demand shifts.

In many businesses, particularly services and businesses that sell products with very short shelf lives, resources must be available when they are needed to fill demand. If the resource is unavailable, the opportunity to process a product or customer will be lost. If you go to a restaurant on Friday night and find that it is full, you inquire about the wait time, and if it's too long, you go elsewhere. This occurs even though the restaurant may have had empty tables on Thursday night. This inability to store excess capacity, in the form of inventory, for later use is one of the most critical characteristics of services and makes them very difficult to manage. It also contributes to poor-quality service in the eyes of the customers. It is difficult to predict demand in many services, making it also very difficult to schedule capacity.

In the typical service setting, two approaches are used to match capacity with demand. One is to schedule capacity to meet the demand. The other is to attempt to control demand so that it will match the available capacity. In many services this is dealt with by requiring appointments or reservations. Appointments are used as a way to match demand and capacity when resource time is very expensive (doctors, lawyers, dentists, and so on). When the resources aren't very expensive (waiters, bartenders, and so on), management often has a staff "on call" so that if demand requires it, extra resources can be brought in, but if demand is low, the resources won't be called and

> **Airport Lines: Why Airlines Want Them**
>
> No one can argue the need for high levels of security at airports, particularly at the check-in counter. However, one might think that airlines would see lines at the check-in counters as a major problem and seek to minimize them. Not so fast. Airlines associate no cost with customers waiting in line, but they see a substantial cost to increase the staff at the counter. Airlines are actually trying to improve their performance "on the ground," but improvement will be slow for several reasons. Frequent fliers pay hundreds of dollars per year to belong to clubs that give them access to private waiting areas offering no-wait check-in. If the lines disappear, the motivation to join these clubs disappears with them. Self-service kiosks will be used more in the near future, but they are motivated primarily by the fact that they will reduce labor costs for the airline.
>
> Why aren't boarding passes issued more frequently by travel agents, allowing the customer to go directly to the gate and check in? Airlines have resisted allowing travel agents to issue boarding passes because that would encourage customers to buy their tickets from the travel agent. Since airlines have to pay travel agents a commission, they'd rather customers bought the tickets directly from the airline.
>
> Lines go beyond the check-in counter. They're often at their longest at the car rental agencies. Despite the fact that frequent-renters can get cars very quickly, the car rental agencies are in no hurry to speed up the process for the rest of us. Lines at rental counters give staff a face-to-face opportunity to "upsell" or convince the customer to upgrade to a more expensive car. For some rental companies, upselling provides as much as 20 percent of revenues. It also gives managers a chance to better manage their fleet. If they have an overabundance of full-size cars that they do not expect to rent that day, they can reduce the price and convince the customer that he is getting a good deal, even though he's paying more than he would have on a smaller car. In the trade, upselling is referred to as "one-on-one service."
>
> Source: "The Airport Waiting Game," *The Wall Street Journal*, May 24, 2001, pp. B1, B4.

won't be paid. To maximize value, capacity is usually scheduled to meet demand, as specified by the customer. The schedule of the resources needed by the customer is determined first, and it drives other schedules that provide supporting resources.

SCHEDULING TECHNIQUES

Scheduling techniques used in services and manufacturing vary tremendously, depending on the types of resource in place, the type of layout used, whether particular resources have excess capacity or are short on capacity, the variety of products or services produced, and many other factors. In some situations, scheduling might mean determining, for a specific product or customer, when each processing step will occur at each resource used. In another situation, scheduling might be focused on a particular machine and could mean determining when each of the products that utilize the machine will be processed on it. The greater the number of tasks, the more difficult it is to schedule that resource. At the opposite extreme, a resource that does only one task (known as a dedicated resource) is easy to schedule. It does the same thing all of the time.

All scheduling tools are related to two basic approaches to scheduling: forward scheduling and backward scheduling. **Forward scheduling** is utilized when a start date is known, and a completion date needs to be determined. Backward scheduling is utilized when a completion date or due date is known, and a start date must be determined. Reel Operations Video 8.1 explores how scheduling complexity challenges United Airlines. Keeping resources in use pays financial dividends but requires expertise in a variety of scheduling tools. In the following sections, several common scheduling tools are examined.

THE GANTT CHART

The **Gantt chart**, which provides a visual model of how resources are used to accomplish specific tasks, is one of the oldest scheduling tools. The diagrams used in the previous figures are Gantt charts. The Gantt chart is even more valuable as a tool to model the way resource time is utilized when several products or customers compete for resources' time. Gantt charts typically utilize a horizontal bar graph format with time on the *x* axis and the different resources on the *y* axis. In addition to displaying the time–resource interactions for an order or task in question, the Gantt chart makes it possible to see how other orders interact with resources and how resources relate to each other. Let's examine how a Gantt chart can be used.

Suppose a firm's new-media development department is charged with the design, development, and execution of a new website. The department's resources are divided among several areas of expertise, including graphics design, technical writers, interactivity experts, and Java script coders. To determine how this job (let's call it Job 100) fits into other jobs the department is involved with, and also to provide some estimate of when Job 100 might be completed, a Gantt chart could be used. Time estimates for various components of Job 100, along with the necessary resources utilized to create the Gantt chart, are presented in Exhibit 8.7.

The Gantt chart aids in answering several important questions regarding resource use. For example, it shows when each job is expected to start and finish at each resource. It shows when each job will be completed. It also shows the sequences so that each resource can prepare ahead of time for its next task.

Gantt Chart Example — **EXHIBIT 8.7**

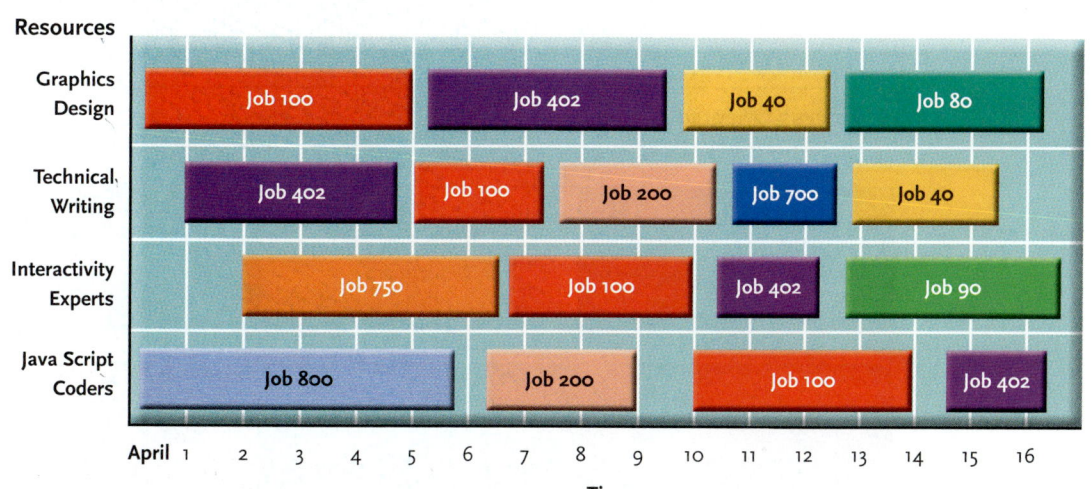

CONTROLLING MANUFACTURING TASK SEQUENCES WITH TRADITIONAL JOB SEQUENCING

In many production systems, particularly process-oriented manufacturing, orders and parts tend to queue up in front of work centers. This phenomenon occurs as a result of the process-oriented layout. Recall that a process-oriented layout is functional in nature. Its strength is its ability to customize. All similar operations are completed in the same department. That means the routings of products will vary from one product to another, depending on the order of processing steps. When a variety of products or orders enter the production system, several orders can "collide" at one department or work center, resulting in a waiting line or queue, as seen in Exhibit 8.8.

Orders entering the production system illustrated in Exhibit 8.8, for example, can have different routings, resulting in different sequences through the six departments. The different routings, combined with orders at the different departments taking different amounts of time, result in orders arriving at departments when the departments are already busy working on another order. In fact, several orders can arrive simultaneously. These "collisions" result in queues at each department. The same phenomenon occurs in organized services, including architecture, law, accounting, auditing, and consulting firms. If different skills or expertise are required for different clients, there can be similar queues of work waiting for access to specific skills. In all of these situations, a decision rule is used to determine which order or client to process next. These rules, known as sequencing or dispatching rules, have an impact on various time-related measures.

In the case of actual customers waiting in line to be served, the decision rule to determine who is served next is almost always **first come, first served (FCFS)**. This is particularly true in the United States and Great Britain. In some other cultures, forming a single-file line is not as "automatic." The actual design and management of queues will be addressed in detail in a later section. When customers are not physically present, and several different departments are used, it is common to use something other than FCFS as the decision rule.

Sequencing Rules

Sequencing rules are based on either of two critical aspects of scheduling performance. These two aspects of a job or customer order determine whether it is on time or late. The first aspect is the due date, the second is how long it will take to complete the task, that is, the processing time. When the processing time to complete the

EXHIBIT 8.8 Process-Oriented Layout

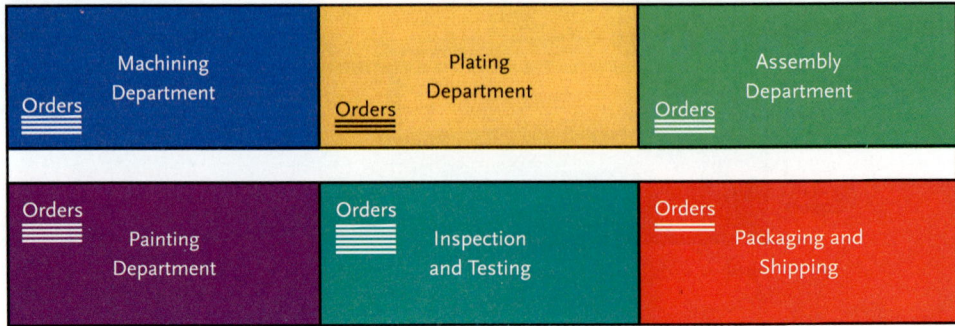

task is greater than the time remaining until the due date, the job will obviously be late. In addition to FCFS, the sequencing rules applied to queues can be based on the due date, the processing time, or a combination of both.

Getting back to the website design example, suppose the firm decided to outsource the website project to a firm specializing in website design. The website design firm is a small operation with one team working together on each project. They are most interested in maximizing customer satisfaction with regard to due date performance and try various sequencing rules to prioritize jobs in queue. Exhibit 8.9 displays basic information on the jobs in queue. There are several alternatives for sequencing these jobs.

A common sequencing rule is **earliest due date (EDD)**. Using EDD, the job or order that is due earliest gets the highest priority. The remaining orders are sequenced according to their due dates. This technique is demonstrated in Example 8.1.

Another popular sequencing rule is **shortest processing time (SPT)**. The SPT rule sequences jobs according to the expected amount of time to complete the job. SPT is demonstrated in Example 8.2.

Another popular rule, and one that provides a means of including the due date and the processing time in the priority decision, is the **critical ratio (CR)** rule. In the critical ratio rule, the time remaining until the job is due is divided by the time needed to complete the job. This creates a relationship between the necessary time and the available

EXHIBIT 8.9 Arrival Sequence, Due Date, and Estimated Completion Time for Website Design Jobs

Client	Order Arrival Sequence	Due Date	Estimated Completion Time for Design (days)
Smith Clothing	1	17	11
Thomas Retail	2	9	5
Stevens Sports	3	6	3
L&P Financial Services	4	11	4
Simmons Retailing	5	29	7

Example 8.1

Job Sequencing Using EDD

Sequence the jobs provided in Exhibit 8.9 using the EDD sequencing rule.

Solution

Exhibit 8.10 provides the sequence of the five website projects using EDD sequencing. As a means of measuring the performance of each rule, calculations for average lateness and the number of jobs late have been made. To calculate lateness for each order, the due date is compared to the expected completion date that results from the sequence. If the expected completion date is after the required completion date, the number of days late is the lateness for that order. Early orders have zero lateness. The average lateness is computed by summing the number of days late for all orders and dividing by the total number of orders. As Exhibit 8.10 indicates with shading, the EDD sequence results in three of the five jobs being late. The average number of days late is 1.6 days (8 total days late divided by 5 jobs).

(continues)

Example 8.1 (continued)

EXHIBIT 8.10 Earliest Due Date (EDD) Sequence for Website Design Jobs

Client	Estimated Completion Time (days)	Due Date	Expected Completion Date	Lateness
Stevens Sports	3	6	3	0
Thomas Retail	5	9	8	0
L&P Financial Services	4	11	12	1
Smith Clothing	11	17	23	6
Simmons Retailing	7	29	30	1
Total days late:				8
Number of jobs late:				3
Average lateness:				1.6

Using the sorting capabilities of a spreadsheet to aid in EDD sequencing is demonstrated in Excel Tutor 8.1.

www.OperationsNow.com

Example 8.2 Job Sequencing Using SPT

Given the data from Exhibit 8.9, sequence the jobs using SPT.

Solution

Exhibit 8.11 provides an analysis of the SPT sequence for the website design jobs. Note that the two shaded jobs are late and the average lateness measure for SPT is significantly longer than that of EDD. SPT has an inherent problem in that long jobs can be delayed indefinitely. When SPT is used, some type of intervention policy is usually used along with it to make sure long jobs get completed.

EXHIBIT 8.11 Shortest Processing Time (SPT) Sequence for Website Design Jobs

Client	Estimated Completion Time (days)	Due Date	Expected Completion Date	Lateness
Stevens Sports	3	6	3	0
L&P Financial Services	4	11	7	0
Thomas Retail	5	9	12	3
Simmons Retailing	7	29	19	0
Smith Clothing	11	17	30	13
Total days late:				16
Number of jobs late:				2
Average lateness:				3.2

The use of sorting capabilities in Excel to aid in SPT sequencing is demonstrated in Excel Tutor 8.2.

www.OperationsNow.com

time. If there is extra time, the critical ratio is greater than 1. The job with the smallest ratio is the highest priority. The critical ratio rule is demonstrated in Example 8.3.

One of the problems with sequencing rules such as EDD, SPT, and CR is that they do not recognize the impact that sequencing at one resource has on other resources. In this example, since only one resource was used (one team did everything), this was not an issue. In many traditional process-oriented manufacturing operations, however, these rules are used at each resource. Orders are sequenced at each resource independently, ignoring the fact that optimizing the sequence at that resource may actually be a detriment to the overall process. Interactive Model 8.1 provides an exploratory environment for comparing the performances of several common sequencing rules.

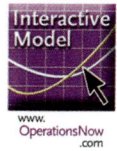

Another rule, **slack per remaining operation**, takes a step toward acknowledging that in process-oriented environments, each resource or operation does not exist in isolation. In the slack per remaining operation rule, **slack** is calculated by subtracting expected processing time from the days remaining until the due date. A positive slack implies that there are more days remaining than necessary to complete the job. As slack moves toward zero, the job becomes more problematic because the amount of time needed to complete it is equal to the time remaining until the due date. A negative slack means that even if the job is started immediately, it will be late. To compute slack per remaining operation, simply divide the slack value by the number of remaining operations to be done.

Example 8.3 Job Sequencing Using Critical Ratio

Given the data from Exhibit 8.9, sequence the jobs using the critical ratio rule.

Solution

Exhibit 8.12 provides an analysis of the website design jobs using the critical ratio technique. As shown in the exhibit, under the critical ratio rule, Smith Clothing would be done first, followed by Thomas Retail, Stevens Sports, L&P Financial Services, and Simmons Retailing.

EXHIBIT 8.12 Critical Ratio Analysis of Website Jobs

Client	Estimated Completion Time (days)	Due Date	Critical Ratio	Expected Completion Date	Lateness
Smith Clothing	11	17	1.55	11	0
Thomas Retail	5	9	1.8	16	7
Stevens Sports	3	6	2.0	19	13
L&P Financial Services	4	11	2.75	23	12
Simmons Retailing	7	29	4.14	30	1
Total days late:					33
Number of jobs late:					4
Average lateness:					6.6

Using the sorting capabilities of Excel to assist in critical ratio sequencing is demonstrated in Excel Tutor 8.3.

> **Example 8.4**
>
> ### Job Sequencing Using Slack per Remaining Operation
>
> A queue of jobs waiting for the design team is presented in Exhibit 8.13. Calculate slack per operation for each job waiting for the design team.
>
> **EXHIBIT 8.13** Slack per Remaining Operations
>
> | Client | Order Arrival Sequence | Due Date | Estimated Completion Time for Design (days) | Number of Remaining Operations | Slack | Slack per Remaining Operations |
> |---|---|---|---|---|---|---|
> | Dogs.com | 1 | 25 | 3 | 2 | 22 | 11 |
> | E-beers | 2 | 18 | 4 | 4 | 14 | 3.5 |
> | Allen Shoes | 3 | 16 | 7 | 3 | 9 | 3 |
> | Turf Grass R Us | 4 | 34 | 5 | 2 | 29 | 14.5 |
>
> **Solution**
>
> As shown in Exhibit 8.13, the first priority job would be Allen Shoes, with only three days of slack per remaining operation. The second would be E-beers, with 3.5 days of slack per remaining operation. That job would be followed by Dogs.com and finally by Turf Grass R Us.
>
> Applying the slack per remaining operation rule in a spreadsheet is demonstrated in Excel Tutor 8.4.

www.OperationsNow.com

Slack per remaining operation obviously makes no sense when there is only one resource being used, because there would never be any remaining operations. However, if the website design operation is expanded, its use might be appropriate. Suppose that as the website business grew, it decided to organize functionally, breaking its expertise into the five teams of design, coding, graphics, database integration, and quality checking. Depending on the client and order, three, four, or all five teams could be used in a particular job. Example 8.4 demonstrates how the slack per remaining operation rule would function in that setting.

TRENDS IN RESOURCE SCHEDULING

Meeting due dates and shortening response time have become more important as a result of two dominant business trends: inventory reduction and pressures added by Internet transactions.

Due date performance in B2B transactions has become more important as businesses have reduced levels of inventory. Inventory reduction in manufacturing, often a component of a management framework known as just-in-time (JIT) manufacturing, has increased in importance since the late 1980s. Inventory reduction in the service sector has also increased in importance. In retailing this practice is sometimes referred to as continuous replenishment. In manufacturing and applicable services, it is common to carry only a few days' supply of an item that is needed on an ongoing basis. The reduced supply and more frequent replenishment result in higher inventory turns and reduced costs. Both have a positive impact on profitability. The penalty, however, for a missed delivery date is likely to be a stockout. Depending on the costs associated with that stockout, the effects can be devastating. Issues related to inventory availability and associated costs of stockouts will be discussed in detail in a subsequent chapter, but suffice it to say that the importance of timeliness increases drastically as inventory levels are dropped.

The Internet has also had a dramatic impact on timeliness. Transactions that occur almost instantaneously in B2C and B2B relationships have greatly reduced the time required to make a purchase, check for product or component availability, compare prices, and so on. Unfortunately, the time required to physically move goods has hardly changed at all. Traditional transportation must still be used to get a product from point A to point B. So far, a product itself can't move at the speed of an electron, though the Internet has raised expectations of customers who are accustomed to the speed of Internet interaction. This makes timely delivery, once the product is actually ordered, even more expected. And when it doesn't happen, the dissatisfaction of the customer is that much higher.

MANAGING QUEUES OF CUSTOMERS

The treatment of orders or jobs in queue is substantially different from the treatment of actual customers in queue. Orders and jobs can be resequenced, but customers expect FCFS treatment. Customers also expect not to wait in line for what they are paying for. In many cases, the amount of time they must wait is how they define the quality of the service. Customers must wait, however, since many businesses cannot have enough capacity to eliminate all waiting by customers. (There are also some situations where a business actually wants lines to form, because lines can create an opportunity to sell products.) Despite the inevitable nature of waiting lines, there are ways to reduce the amount of time customers must wait, and there are ways to make the customer's wait seem shorter. Let's examine both issues.

Physical Features of Queues

The amount of time a customer must wait is a function of five features of every queuing system: the queue configuration, the queue discipline, the calling population, the arrival process, and the service process. Each is described in the following sections.

The Queue Configuration
The **queue configuration** is the physical design of the lines and servers. The simplest scenario is one line in front of a single process, for example, the queue at a pay phone or the queue at a stop sign.

The descriptions of various queue configurations are best understood when the concepts of servers and phases are used. A **server** is a resource that is able to complete the process or service the customers or jobs in queue wait for. A **phase** is a distinct step in the process that requires a new waiting line. Let's look at some examples. The pay phone queue is a single-phase, single-server queuing system. A fast-food restaurant that used one single line, with the person at the front of the line going to the first available server, is a single-phase, multiserver queuing system. The configuration of the ticketing staff at an airport is often a single-phase queue with multiple servers. Banks and post offices also utilize this configuration. There are often different alternatives for accomplishing the same thing, as shown in a bank example in Exhibit 8.14.

Multiphase systems are used when the services are relatively complex and some steps need to be completed before others. For example, the queuing system at a driver's license office may be a multiphase queuing system. There might be a first phase, which collects information. After the first phase, the customer must wait in line for an available computer to take the test. Upon passing the test, the customer waits in line to have a picture taken.

Drive-up windows at fast-food restaurants are also multiphase systems. Usually customers wait in line to order, then wait in line to pay, and then wait in line to receive the order. Many situations, however, involve multiple servers.

Exhibit 8.14 shows that there are different ways to accomplish the same thing. A new customer might be forced to enter one long serpentine queue, gradually moving up in line until she is asked to proceed to the next available teller. An alternative would be to allow queues to develop in front of each teller. Customers typically try to predict which queue will be faster and move into that queue. Grocery stores generally configure their queues this way. Some customers like this alternative better, because they think they are good judges of which queue will move fastest. Overall, however, this approach is not fair, because some customers do get in slower lines. Ultimately,

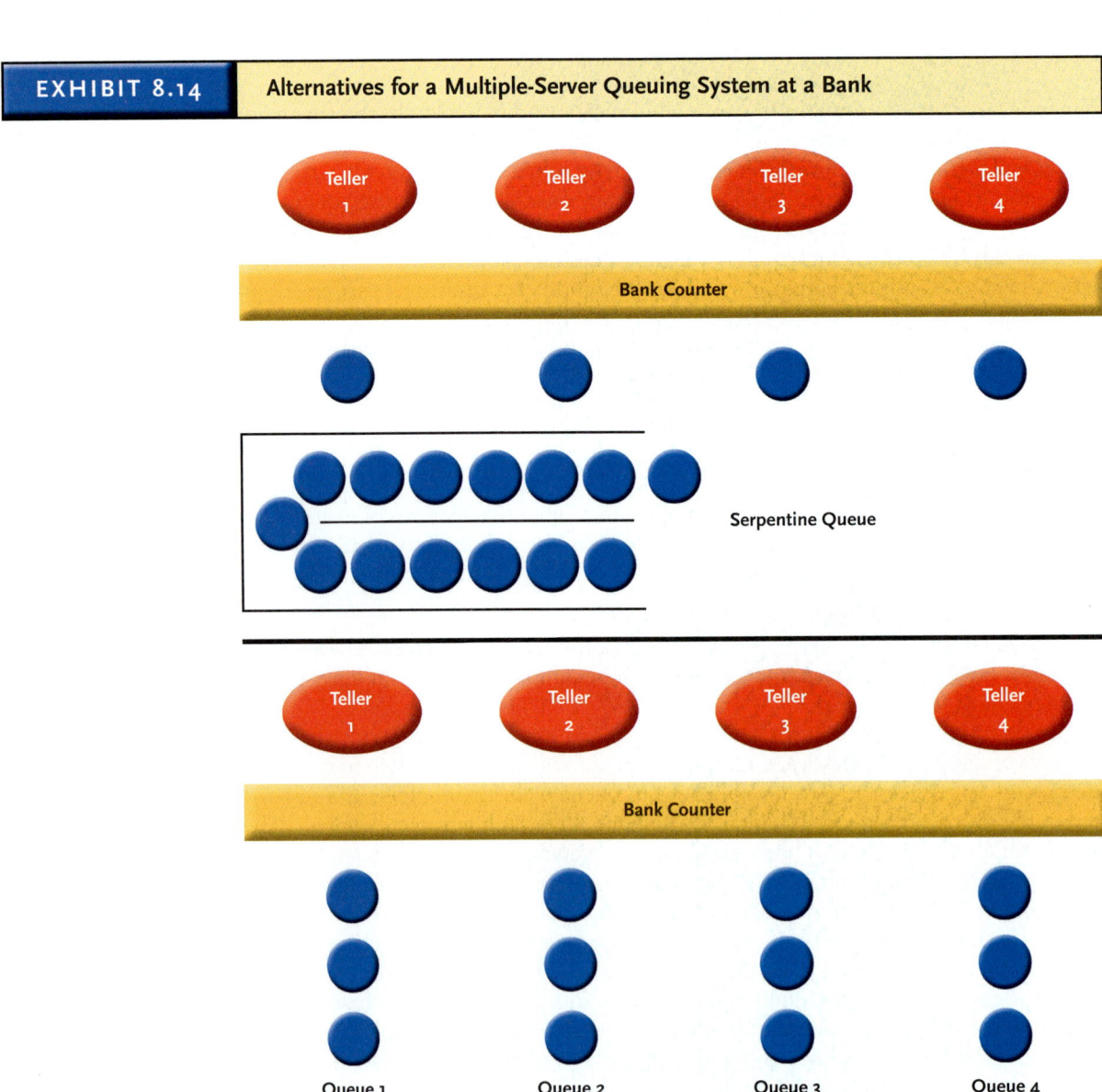

EXHIBIT 8.14 Alternatives for a Multiple-Server Queuing System at a Bank

someone who arrived later could be served sooner. A behavior common to this configuration, known as **jockeying**, occurs when customers switch lines hoping to move faster. Jockeying has actually proven to be enough of a problem in fast-food environments that most have gone to a serpentine configuration. Research has shown that instead of deciding on their order, customers spend their time trying to figure out which line to switch to—so that they arrive at the cash register unprepared to order.

The single queue, multiserver queue is commonly used in the management of call centers. Even though you don't feel like you're waiting in a line when you get placed on hold in a call center, you are, and typically it's managed on a FCFS basis. There are numerous configurations that create a variety of alternatives in virtually any queuing system. Multiphase queue configurations add complexity to queuing analysis because queues can actually interact with each other. In the fast-food drive-up window example this happens frequently. Exhibit 8.15 illustrates how the queues can interact. Notice how the queue at the pickup window can back up and prevent access to the pay window and even back up beyond the order station. The choice of the queue configuration depends on a variety of factors, including the space available for waiting lines, the nature of the actual process, and the expectations of the customers.

The Queue Discipline

The **queue discipline** consists of the rules that management enforces to determine who the next customer served is. In most cases, first come, first served (FCFS) is used when customers actually stand in line. The dispatching rules discussed earlier in this

Multiple-Phase Queuing System at a Drive-Up Window **EXHIBIT 8.15**

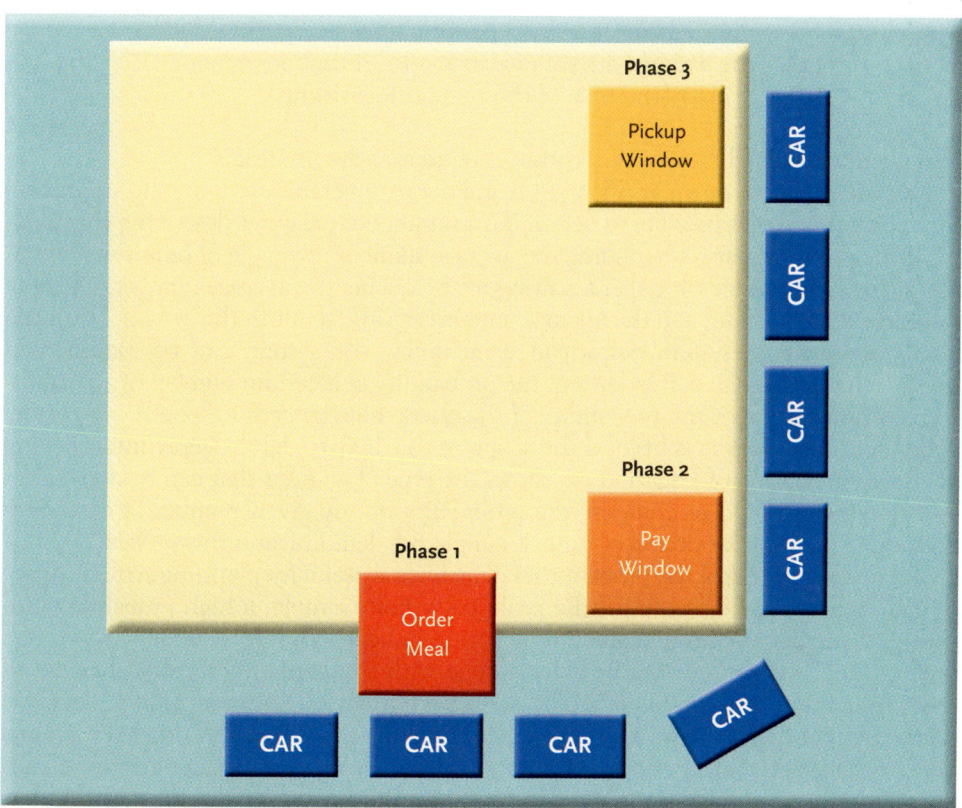

chapter are alternatives to the FCFS rule, but they aren't typically used for actual customers. They may be used, however, when a customer's order, rather than the actual customer, waits in line.

There are some variations of the traditional FCFS rule. For example, in some environments customers are directed to "take a number." This ensures that the FCFS rule is maintained. The FCFS rule is sometimes combined with a shortest processing time (SPT) rule. In essence, the express lane used in grocery stores is such a hybrid.

The Calling Population

The **calling population** consists of the population of arriving customers or orders. The size of the calling population is important because its size dictates the maximum length of the queue. While many calling populations are infinite in size, others are limited. For example, the calling population for a copying machine in an office would be limited to the number of employees in that office. The queue could never be any longer than that number.

The Arrival Process

The **arrival process** defines the pattern or frequency with which customers arrive at the queue. It defines the demand placed on the service. Queuing analysis generally requires data on the actual rates at which customers arrive, computed as the number of arrivals per unit time (four cars per hour, six customers per minute, and so on). Arrivals per unit time follow a Poisson distribution as determined by the following formula:

$$P(x) = \frac{e^{-\lambda} \lambda^x}{x!} \quad \text{for } x = 1, 2, 3, \ldots \quad (8.1)$$

where $P(x)$ = the probability of x arrivals in a time period
x = the number of arrivals per unit time
λ = the average arrival rate in a certain time increment
e = 2.7183 (the base of the natural logarithms)

Service rates typically follow a negative exponential distribution.

Knowledge of the queue configuration and the parameters describing the arrival and service rates makes it possible to determine a number of measures describing the queuing system's performance, including the average number of people or orders waiting in the queue, the average time spent waiting in the queue, the average number of people or orders in the system, and the average amount of time spent in the system. With the ability to compute system performance measures, the system can be modified to improve its performance. In addition, the probability of a certain number of arrivals in a given time period or the probability of the queue being a certain length can also be computed. Although it is beyond the scope of this text to delve deeply into queuing analysis, application of Equation 8.1 shows the type of analysis that can be done. This equation can be used to compute the probability of any given number of customers arriving in a particular period of time. Example 8.5 demonstrates this process.

An understanding of the probabilities of arrivals is useful for planning system capacity and how the system is to handle peak loads. For example, a high probability of a specified number of calls in a given time period indicates that level of demand will be predictable. The system must be able to cope with the predicted level of demand in order to maintain acceptable levels of queue performance. This may require development of some means of increasing capacity during peak loads. Fast-food restaurants demonstrate such a means of dealing with peak loads. Wendy's restaurants, for example, send an employee out in front of the counter with an order pad when the line gets

> **Example 8.5** **Determining Probabilities of Queue Arrivals**
>
> A call center for a small online retailer gets an average of 36 calls per hour. The distribution follows the Poisson distribution. What is the probability that during any given hour, the center will receive 41 calls?
>
> **Solution**
>
> Using Equation 8.1,
>
> $$P(x) = \frac{e^{-\lambda}\lambda^x}{x!} \quad \text{for } x = 1, 2, 3, \ldots \quad (8.1)$$
>
> where $P(x)$ = the probability of x arrivals in a time period
> x = the number of arrivals per unit time
> λ = the average arrival rate in a certain time increment
> e = 2.7183 (the base of the natural logarithms)
>
> In this situation,
>
> $$\lambda = 36$$
> $$x = 41$$
> $$P(x) = \frac{e^{-36}36^{41}}{41!}$$
> $$= 4.46\%$$
>
> Excel Tutor 8.5 demonstrates this computation in a spreadsheet.

www.OperationsNow.com

extremely long. Thus, the cashier has to only ring up orders and take money, increasing the speed of the service and reducing the amount of time customers must wait. This approach is used only when the waiting line is extremely long.

For certain queue configurations, analytical methods provide a convenient means of examining queuing system performance. However, for complex queuing systems, computer simulation provides a more effective means of understanding how the system performs. Computer simulation models require that data regarding the arrival and service rates be collected. The configuration of the queue can be modeled, and using the service and arrival data, the system can then be run "virtually" to simulate how the queuing system behaves over a long period of time. Interactive Model 8.2 provides a flexible simulation model for queuing systems. It is capable of modeling single-phase and two-phase queuing systems with up to four servers per phase. This model provides an interactive environment for experimentation with queuing systems and their behavior.

www.OperationsNow.com

The arrival process can be affected by several different customer behaviors. The first, known as **balking**, occurs when a customer views the queue and does not enter it because it is too long. The second, known as **reneging**, occurs when a customer joins the queue, but then leaves it because the wait was too long. Both behaviors are important considerations when designing a queue because they result in a loss of customers. Knowing, for example, that a lot of customers will balk when the line reaches a specific length can aid in determining how much capacity is needed to maintain a shorter line.

The Service Process

The **service process** consists of the capacity of the server(s), the distribution of service times, and other behaviors of the servers that affect the number of customers the servers can handle.

Clearly, modification of the capacity of the servers has a significant impact on such measures as the average time each customer waits, the average length of the queue, the average amount of time each customer spends in the system, and the average number of people in the system. Increasing capacity reduces queues and the times associated with them. In addition to the average capacity of the service, the variability of services is also important. The distribution of service times can range from being zero (all services take exactly the same amount of time) to being quite wide, with service times being quite variable. As mentioned earlier, the distribution of service times is typically a negative exponential distribution.

The variability of the arrivals and the variability of the service combine to create a significant impact on queues. Even though processing capacity appears to match the arrival rate, variability in each results in the formation of queues.

PSYCHOLOGICAL FEATURES OF QUEUES

The psychology of waiting is an interesting study of human perception. In many ways, perception is more important than reality. There are some short waits that seem like they take forever. And there are some long waits that seem to pass by very quickly. Human behavior reacts predictably to a number of features that can be included in queues. Those that are particularly noteworthy are discussed next.[2]

Keep Customers Busy

Customers waiting in line feel that their time is not being wasted if they are kept busy. This might mean that they should be able to entertain themselves or be entertained, or actually accomplish something important to the service. Being able to watch TV, for example, makes the wait seem shorter. Providing information that is needed for the service, such as filling out application forms, while waiting in line also has the same effect. During the December heavy-travel period of 2001, Chicago's O'Hare Airport hired local bands to entertain travelers while they waited at check-in or security. The placement of mirrors in elevator lobbies is a classic example of keeping people busy while they wait.

Keep Customers Informed

Customers' perception of waiting time is enhanced if they understand that they are making progress. This is particularly true when they are unable to perceive this for themselves, as is the case when waiting on the phone. A periodic update on approximately how long the remaining wait will be helps. Waiting lines at theme parks often have signs positioned at known distances from the service informing customers as to how long they can expect to wait when they've reached the sign. Phone queues can be extremely frustrating for callers because they can't see how long the queue is.

Treat Customers Fairly

Customers are less critical of their experience in a queue if the queue discipline is enforced and they think they are treated fairly. Have you ever been to a restaurant and noticed that someone who sat down after you did was served before you? The point is, you noticed. It didn't seem fair and had an impact on your perception of the wait. All of a sudden, you determined that you were waiting too long.

Start the Service As Soon As Possible

If the service can be started while the customers are still in line, customers' perception of how long they wait will be reduced. Test Track, a ride at Epcot, is a great example. For at least 30 minutes of the line, the customer goes through a mock automobile testing facility that is perceived to be an actual part of the Test Track experience. Its real purpose is to provide a way to start the experience early.

Exceed the Customer's Expectations

The final way to enhance customer perceptions is to provide service sooner than customers expect. A customer who overestimates how long he will have to wait is pleasantly surprised when the wait is actually shorter. If the customer is told that there is a 20-minute wait and he is served in 15 minutes, he is much happier than if he'd been told that the wait would be 10 minutes and the actual wait was 15 minutes.

PROJECT MANAGEMENT

A **project** is a set of activities aimed at meeting a goal, with a defined beginning and end. **Project management** consists of a variety of techniques that recognize the dependencies present among the project activities and manage those activities to complete the project on time. The length of projects can range from several months to several years. The difficulty in managing projects is that each project is somewhat distinct, adding uncertainty to process of scheduling resources. In addition, there may be competition for the resources used to complete the project because resources may be used on several projects simultaneously. This makes coordinating and scheduling their availability a challenge. Examples of projects include new-product and service development, process improvement efforts, business expansion, and site selection.

Suppose a business was developing a new computerized accounting system. The development of that system would require expertise in several areas—system design, database management, programming, software quality checking, and so on—but each category of expertise would not be needed for the entire duration of the project. The use of each kind of expertise is tied to specific activities required to complete the project. So, a particular expertise that is not needed on one project probably is needed on another project. Resources are moved from one project to another as a way to increase their utilization and productivity.

Project teams are often used to provide a way of coordinating projects because the team can be composed of people from all the functions that affect and are affected by the project. This is especially true for process improvement and quality improvement projects. The team membership gives the project cross-functional expertise and a broad "enterprise" perspective that is necessary to ensure that the project will be successful. Techniques used by project teams for decision making are covered in detail in Chapter 11, devoted to the workforce.

The key objectives of project management are to accomplish the project's goals, complete it on time, and complete it on budget. The effectiveness of the resources used and their ability to do what is required will determine if project goals are accomplished. The effectiveness of the coordination and scheduling of these resources will determine

whether the project is completed on time and on budget. Reel Operations Video 8.2 chronicles a complex project and illustrates the importance of resource scheduling.

A Network Approach to Project Scheduling

The scheduling of the resources and activities required to complete a project would be easy if a specific sequence was not required. In virtually all projects, however, events must be accomplished in a specific sequence. The sequence is critical to the effective completion of the project. For simple projects that utilize no more than five or six resources and contain only 10 or 12 activities, a Gantt chart, like the one shown in Exhibit 8.7, may provide an effective way to model these dependent relationships. For more complex projects, however, the Gantt chart would become too large and too complex to be effectively used as a management tool. The Gantt chart can provide an effective way for the manager to view the interaction of various resources and activities, but it does not provide a means of distinguishing between those resources and activities that are most critical and those that aren't.

The ability to create a **network diagram** of the project is crucial to understanding the relationships among the activities and resources, and determining the project's duration. The network diagram of a project is somewhat analogous to a flow diagram in that it illustrates the steps in the project.

Historically, two approaches were used to manage projects: the critical path method (CPM) and the program evaluation and review technique (PERT). Both approaches were developed in the 1950s. CPM was created for network analysis of deterministic projects (activity times were certain), and PERT was used in probabilistic environments (when activity times were not known with certainty). Over the years, the distinctions between the two techniques have blurred.

Developing the Network

The first task in project scheduling is to construct the network model. To do this, the project must be broken into small, specific activities. An accurate time estimate must be available for the completion of each activity. Accuracy of the final project schedule is dependent on the accuracy of these estimates. Finally, the order that the activities must follow must be developed and specified. The sequence is defined by identifying the immediate predecessors of each activity. Immediate predecessors function in much the same way as prerequisites do when you are scheduling classes. If class C is a prerequisite to class B, and class B is a prerequisite to class C, you know that both class C and class B must be taken prior to class A.

The actual network consists of circles (called nodes) and arrows. It is possible to use either the nodes or the arrows to represent activities, but we'll stick with using the nodes to represent activities. Exhibit 8.16 provides a diagram of a very simple network, with no inclusion of activity names or times.

The interpretation of the network model is important, so let's take a close look at it. The project modeled in Exhibit 8.16 consists of eight activities. The immediate predecessors are presented in Exhibit 8.17. Activity 1 must precede activity 2. Activity 2 must precede activities 3 and 4. Activity 3 must precede activity 5. Notice, however, that activity 4 is not a predecessor of activity 5. These precedence relationships create the "branching" that appears in Exhibit 8.16, immediately after activity 2. Activity 3 must precede activity 5, which must precede activity 6. In addition, activity 4 must precede activity 6, but activity 4 can be completed at any time after activity 2 and before activity 6. After activity 4 and activity 5 are completed, activity 6 can be

Network Diagram	EXHIBIT 8.16

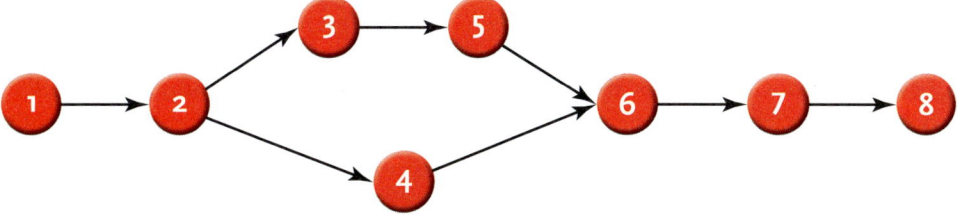

completed. Then, since activity 6 is the immediate predecessor of activity 7, activity 7 can be completed. Finally, activity 8 can be completed.

The network diagram in Exhibit 8.16 is important in providing a model of how the project activities relate to each other, but it must provide more information if it is to be used to actually schedule when things happen. One of the most important contributions of project scheduling is to help us compute the project's duration. It is the duration, after all, that will determine whether it is completed on time and, because many of the costs are time-related, whether it will be completed on budget. Let's take a closer look at the project that forms the basis for the network in Exhibits 8.16 and 8.17.

The network in Exhibit 8.16 shows the work flow, from left to right, and it shows precedence relationships, but it provides no other information. Adding additional information requires understanding the concept of a path. A **path** is a sequence of activities that begins at the start of the project and goes to the end. In our example, there are two possible paths: 1, 2, 3, 5, 6, 7, 8, and 1, 2, 4, 6, 7, 8. The number of paths depends on the complexity of the project network. The path that takes longest is called the **critical path**. The critical path defines the length of the project. If an activity on the critical path takes longer than estimated, the duration of the project is increased. If an activity is completed more quickly than expected, the project duration is decreased. The critical path can shift from one path to another if an activity on a noncritical path is lengthened enough or an activity on the critical path is reduced enough. Managing the activities on the critical path is important in project management because those activities dictate the completion time, which determines whether or not the project is completed on time. Focusing on the critical path places management's attention on those activities that are the most important. Activities that aren't on the critical path generally can be delayed without having any impact on the completion of the project. The amount of time an activity on a noncritical path can be delayed without affecting the duration of the project is known as that activity's slack. Those activities with zero slack define the critical path. Example 8.6 demonstrates the process of identifying the critical path.

Precedence Relationships		EXHIBIT 8.17
Activity	Predecessors	
1	—	
2	1	
3	2	
4	2	
5	3	
6	4,5	
7	6	
8	7	

Example 8.6 — CPM Calculations

A small printing shop has determined that it has the demand and market potential to build a new, larger facility. It has identified eight activities necessary to bring the new facility into production, as listed in Exhibit 8.18. Precedence relationships and an estimated time are included for each activity. Identify the critical path for the project.

EXHIBIT 8.18 Project Detail

Activity ID No.	Activity Description	Predecessors	Estimated Time (weeks)
1	Needs analysis	—	4
2	Architect plans	1	10
3	Equipment selection	2	2
4	Building permits and zoning	2	4
5	Vendor ID and equipment order	3	3
6	Construction	4,5	16
7	Interior finish	6	4
8	Installation and setup	7	1

Solution

The slack of an activity is determined by computing four different values for each activity in the project. They are early start (ES), early finish (EF), late start (LS), and late finish (LF). The ES for any activity (other than the first activity) is computed by processing from left to right through the network. ES for an activity is equal to the EF of the activity of the immediate predecessor. The EF time for an activity is the early start time plus the estimated time to complete it:

$$EF = ES + t \qquad (8.2)$$

where t is the time estimated to complete the activity.

The ES for the first activity is usually zero. If an activity anywhere in the project has more than one predecessor, the ES is the largest or latest of the EF times of the predecessors. This is because an activity cannot begin until all of its predecessors are completed. The one that takes the longest would be the last one completed. The completion of the ES and EF times is known as the forward pass or **early start schedule** of the network.

To present all of the information on the network itself, a standard notation is used to designate the ES, EF, LS, and LF values. This notation is presented in Exhibit 8.19.

EXHIBIT 8.19 ES, EF, LS, and LF Notation

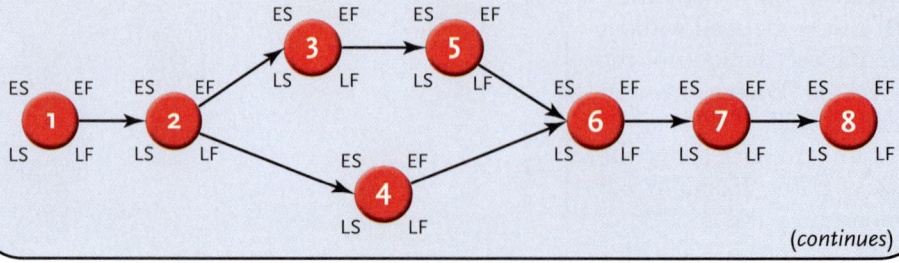

(continues)

Example 8.6 (continued)

The ES and EF values can be computed following Equation 8.2. For example, the ES for activity 1 is 0. EF for activity 1 is 4, and the ES for activity 2 is 4. This follows the process of the EF being the ES plus the estimated time, and the ES for the next activity being the EF for the preceding activity. Exhibit 8.20 provides these values for the entire network. Note that the ES for activity 6 is the "latest" EF from its predecessors, which in this case is 19 from activity 5.

EXHIBIT 8.20 Early Start and Early Finish Calculations

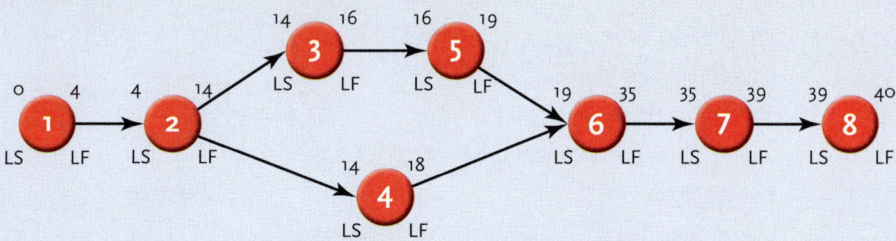

The LS and LF values are computed next, proceeding from right to left, beginning at the last activity. The LF for the last activity is equal to the EF of the last activity or the target date, if different from LF. The LS for the last activity is equal to the LF minus the estimated time:

$$LS = LF - t \qquad (8.3)$$

The LF for any other activity is equal to the LS for the activity that follows it. In other words, for activity 8, the LS and LF values are 39 and 40. This means that the LF value for activity 8 is equal to 39. The process of computing the LS and LF values is known as the backward pass or **late start schedule**. The LS and LF values are presented in Exhibit 8.21. In a manner similar to that of the forward pass, if an activity is the predecessor of more than one activity, the LF is equal to the smallest (earliest) LS value for all activities that immediately follow it. For example, activity 2 is the predecessor of activities 3 and 4. The LF value for activity 2 is the smallest LS value from activities 3 or 4. Since the LS for activity 3 is smaller (14) when compared to the LS of activity 4 (15), the LF value for activity 2 is equal to 14.

EXHIBIT 8.21 Computation of LS and LF Values

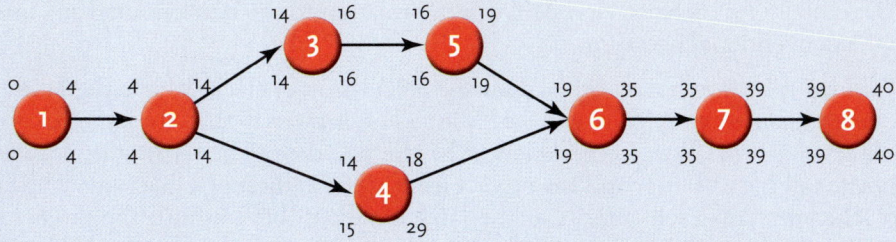

(continues)

> **Example 8.6** *(continued)*
>
> The ES, EF, LS, and LF values are presented in tabular form in Exhibit 8.22. Values for slack are computed by either LS − ES or LF − EF. The activities with zero slack are activities 1, 2, 3, 5, 6, 7, 8, so that is the critical path.
>
> ### EXHIBIT 8.22 ES, EF, LS, LF, and Slack Values
>
> | Activity ID No. | Activity Description | ES | EF | LS | LF | Slack |
> |---|---|---|---|---|---|---|
> | 1 | Needs analysis | 0 | 4 | 0 | 4 | 0 |
> | 2 | Architect plans | 4 | 14 | 4 | 14 | 0 |
> | 3 | Equipment selection | 14 | 16 | 14 | 16 | 0 |
> | 4 | Building permits and zoning | 14 | 18 | 15 | 19 | 1 |
> | 5 | Vendor ID and equipment order | 16 | 19 | 16 | 19 | 0 |
> | 6 | Construction | 19 | 35 | 19 | 35 | 0 |
> | 7 | Interior finish | 35 | 39 | 35 | 39 | 0 |
> | 8 | Installation and setup | 39 | 40 | 39 | 40 | 0 |
>
>
> www.OperationsNow.com
>
> Notice in Exhibit 8.22 that the only activity with slack is activity 4 (permits and zoning). This makes the project very difficult to complete on time. With very little slack, any disruption can delay the start of an activity enough that it will affect the completion of the project.
>
> Excel Tutor 8.6 shows how Excel can be used to assist in the process of identifying the critical path.

The process followed in project scheduling can be organized into the following sequence:

1. Determine the activities that need to be accomplished to complete the project.
2. Determine the precedence relationships and estimated completion times for each activity.
3. Construct a network diagram for the project.
4. Determine the critical path by identifying the path that takes the longest.
5. Determine the early start schedule and late start schedules by calculating ES, EF, LS, and LF for each activity. Add this information to the network diagram, using the conventional notation.

You might be wondering, other than the calculation of slack, what's the point of the two schedules: early start and late start? The answer is that they provide two schedules that will allow for completion by the due date. The early start schedule completes all the activities and the project itself at the earliest possible time. The late start schedule starts each activity at the latest time possible to finish the project on time. You would use the early start schedule to complete the project as early as possible. You would use the late start schedule to take advantage of the occasional cost-saving opportunities made possible by delaying some aspects of activities. There might be an advantage to purchasing needed materials, for example, as late as possible. It is also possible that resources might not be available for the early start because they are being used on another project. The late start shows the latest possible time the resources must become available without causing a project delay.

In some projects, the times for activities are pretty rough estimates. In these projects, rather than determining the critical path and identifying the ES and LS schedules for completing by a specified time, we're more interested in if we could complete a project by a specified time and what the likelihood of completing it is. In that situation, we use a slightly different approach that allows us to include uncertainty in the process. That procedure is described in the next section.

Project Scheduling with Uncertain Time Estimates

When a project in question is completely new and not similar to projects attempted before, the activity time estimates are likely to be inaccurate. In these situations, it is typically assumed that the activity times follow the beta distribution. Uncertainty is factored into the problem by identifying three time estimates for each activity: an optimistic (o) situation, a pessimistic (p) situation, and a most likely (m) situation. These values are used to compute an expected time (T_e) using the formula for computing the mean of the beta distribution as follows:

$$T_e = \frac{o + 4m + p}{6} \qquad (8.4)$$

where
o = the optimistic expected completion time
m = the most likely completion time
p = the pessimistic expected completion time

The variance (σ^2) for a single activity is calculated as follows:

$$\sigma^2 = \left(\frac{p - o}{6}\right)^2 \qquad (8.5)$$

Although the standard deviation of the critical path cannot be computed by summing the standard deviations (σ) of the activities because standard deviations are not additive, since variances are additive, the variance for the critical path is calculated by summing the activity variances. Then, since the standard deviation (σ) is the square root of the variance,

$$\sigma_p = \sqrt{\Sigma(\text{variances on the critical path})} \qquad (8.6)$$

The uncertainty related to the time estimates can be measured using this standard deviation. Assuming the completion times of the activities on the critical path are distributed normally (according to the Central Limit Theorem), the probability of completing the path by any specified due date D can be computed. The difference between the expected completion time and the desired due date is $D - T_e$. Dividing that difference by the standard deviation σ_p gives us the number of standard deviations D is from T_e. This value, commonly referred to as Z, is

$$Z = \frac{D - T_e}{\sigma_p} \qquad (8.7)$$

Using the standard normal probability table in Appendix A, Z can be used to calculate the probability that a project due date D can be met. The process used is similar to the one used for the previous example, with some additions:

1. Determine the activities that need to be accomplished to complete the project.

2. Determine the precedence relationships and estimated completion times for each activity. Create estimates for o, m, and p.
3. Construct a network diagram for the project.
4. Determine the critical path by identifying the path that takes the longest.
5. Determine the early start schedule and late start schedules by calculating ES, EF, LS, and LF for each activity, using T_e for the estimated times. Add this information to the network diagram, using the conventional notation.
6. Calculate the variances (σ^2) for the activity times.
7. Calculate the probability of completing by the desired due date D.

This process is demonstrated in Example 8.7.

Example 8.7 — Project Scheduling with Activity Time Uncertainty

In Example 8.6, activity time estimates were limited to one value, the most likely time estimate. The owners of the print shop were somewhat skeptical after seeing the results of the analysis, and they decided that it might be more realistic to admit that they were actually uncertain about their time estimates. With uncertainty in the time estimates, they wanted to know the probability of completing the project in 39 weeks, because that corresponded with the end of spring semester and would allow them more time to bring up the new operation.

Solution

The optimistic, most likely, and pessimistic activity times are presented in Exhibit 8.23 and are used to calculate T_e, the expected time. The activity variances are also calculated.

EXHIBIT 8.23 Expected Values and Variances of Time Estimates

Activity ID No.	Activity Description	Optimistic Estimate, o (weeks)	Most Likely Estimate, m (weeks)	Pessimistic Estimate, p (weeks)	Expected Time T_e (weeks)	Activity Variance Estimate, $\sigma_p^2 = [(p-o)/6]^2$
1	Needs analysis	3.00	4.00	5.00	4.00	0.11
2	Architect plans	8.00	10.00	12.00	10.00	0.44
3	Equipment selection	1.00	2.00	4.00	2.17	0.25
4	Building permits and zoning	3.00	4.00	6.00	4.17	0.25
5	Vendor ID and equipment order	2.00	3.00	4.00	3.00	0.11
6	Construction	13.00	16.00	20.00	16.17	1.36
7	Interior finish	3.00	4.00	6.00	4.17	0.25
8	Installation and setup	1.00	1.00	2.00	1.17	0.03

The values for T_e are used to calculate values for ES, EF, LS, and LF, just as was done in the previous example. These calculations are presented in Exhibit 8.24.

(continues)

Example 8.7 (continued)

EXHIBIT 8.24 Calculation of ES, EF, LS, LF, and Slack, Based on T_e

Activity	Activity Description	T_e	ES	EF	LS	LF	Slack
1	Needs analysis	4.00	0	4.00	0.00	4.00	0.00
2	Architect plans	10.00	4.00	14.00	4.00	14.00	0.00
3	Equipment selection	2.17	14.00	16.17	14.00	16.17	0.00
4	Building permits and zoning	4.17	14.00	18.17	15.00	19.17	1.00
5	Vendor ID and equipment order	3.00	16.17	19.17	16.17	19.17	0.00
6	Construction	16.17	19.17	35.34	19.17	35.34	0.00
7	Interior finish	4.17	35.34	39.51	35.34	39.51	0.00
8	Installation and setup	1.17	39.51	40.68	39.51	40.68	0.00

Early start and late start schedules are presented in Exhibit 8.24. Notice that the critical path does not change, even though some of the expected times are slightly different. The variance of the critical path consists of the sum of the variances along that path, activities 1, 2, 3, 5, 6, 7, 8, and is equal to 2.56 weeks. The standard deviation would be the square root of that variance, or 1.6.

The probability of completing the project in 39 weeks would be calculated using Equation 8.7, as follows:

$$Z = \frac{D - T_e}{\sigma_p}$$

$$= \frac{39 - 40.68}{1.6}$$

$$= \frac{-1.68}{1.6}$$

$$= -1.05$$

A look in Appendix B for a Z value of -1.05 shows that the probability of completing the project in 39 weeks is only about 14.6 percent.

Excel Tutor 8.7 demonstrates how Excel can be used to assist in this calculation.

www
OperationsNow
.com

Crashing Projects

Failure to complete a project on time almost always results in increased costs. The costs might take the form of a penalty imposed by the client expecting on-time completion, or they might be lost revenues. When it becomes clear to management that a project is on its way to missing a promised or needed completion date, some sort of intervention must be implemented to get the project back on track. A methodical approach to reducing project duration is a process called **crashing** the project.

Any attempt to reduce the project duration must focus on the time of activities on the critical path. The crashing process helps management decide which interventions will provide the greatest improvement for the least cost. Reducing the time required to complete an activity on the critical path is typically not without financial cost. Crash costs include anything that would be required to reduce the activity time. Such costs would cover additional labor or equipment, overtime costs, temporary employee costs, premiums paid for quicker response from outside contractors, and so on.

The crashing process determines how to reduce the project time by identifying the cheapest way to reduce the time of activities on the critical path. Reducing the time of an activity on the critical path can actually cause the critical path to change, however, because the time could become less than that of another path, which would make that other path critical. This complicates the crashing process somewhat. If more than one critical path exists, both must be reduced in order to reduce project duration. Example 8.8 provides an example of the crashing process.

Example 8.8

Crashing Projects

Exhibit 8.25 shows a network diagram of a project. To begin the crashing process, we must examine all of the activities on the critical path. We need to know the expected duration for each activity, the absolute minimum time in which each activity could be accomplished (called the **crash time**), and the additional cost per day of obtaining that crash time. This information is provided in Exhibit 8.26. The project duration is reduced one day at a time by selecting the activity on the critical path that requires the lowest additional cost.

EXHIBIT 8.25 Network to Crash

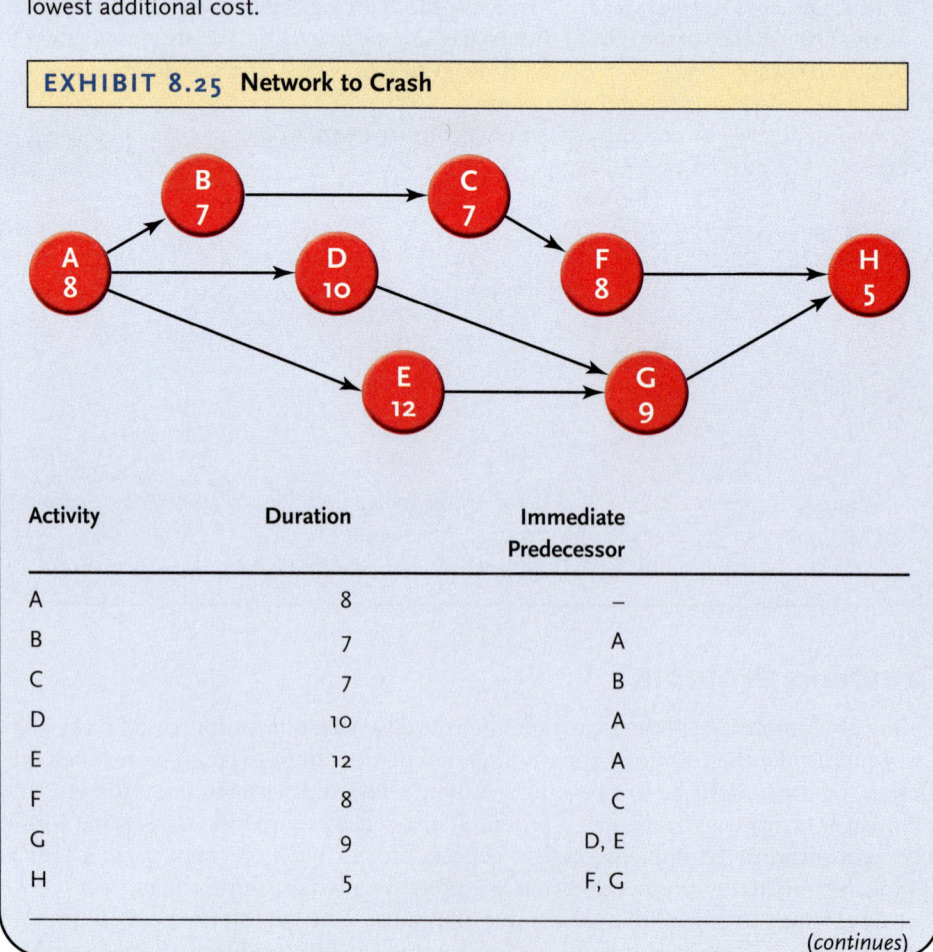

Activity	Duration	Immediate Predecessor
A	8	—
B	7	A
C	7	B
D	10	A
E	12	A
F	8	C
G	9	D, E
H	5	F, G

(continues)

Example 8.8 *(continued)*

EXHIBIT 8.26 Crash Time and Costs

Activity ID No.	Normal Time	Crash Time	Cost/Day ($)
A	8	7	400.00
B	7	5	300.00
C	7	6	250.00
D	10	6	350.00
E	12	10	500.00
F	8	7	350.00
G	9	8	400.00
H	5	3	450.00

The crashing process begins with a focus on the critical path. In this example, the critical path is ABCFH. Reduction in the times of any of those activities results in shorter project duration, so the focus is on the activities of ABCFH, identifying the activity with the lowest crash cost. As each reduction is made, we must examine the network for changes in the critical path or the existence of additional critical paths.

The lowest crash cost on the ABCFH path is activity C, which can be reduced from 7 days to 6, for $250. The duration of the ABCFH path is reduced from 35 days to 34, which ties it with the AEGH path. There are now two critical paths, both at 34 days. Reduction further will require a reduction in both critical paths. In the ABCFH path, the lowest crash cost is activity B, for $300. In the AEGH path, the lowest crash cost is a tie between A and G at $400. However, if we look at activities that are on both paths, such as A and H, reducing either reduces both critical paths. The crash cost of A is $400 and the crash cost of H is $450, so the lowest is A at $400. Activity A can be reduced from 8 to 7 days for $400. The critical path is still tied between ABCFH and AEGH, and it is now 33 days.

We are still left with activity H being in both paths, and it can be reduced to 4 days for $450. That reduces the critical path to 32 days, and it is still both ABCFH and AEGH. Activity H can be reduced again, from 4 days to 3 days, again affecting both paths at a cost of $450. The critical path is still ABCFH and AEGH and is 31 days. We are now in a situation where no remaining activities appear in both paths. Since the paths are both tied at 31 days, we must identify the low-cost activity in each one to reduce. In ABCFH the low-cost activity is reducing B from 7 to 6, for $300. In AEGH the low-cost activity is reducing G from 9 days to 8 for $450. ABCFH and AEGH are now tied for the critical path at 30 days. Reducing it further brings us back to B from 6 days to 5 for $300 and E from 12 days to 11 for $500. Again, we're still tied for the critical path, but at 29 days.

ABCFH and AEGH are still the two critical paths. In ABCFH our only choice is to reduce F from 8 days to 7 for $350. Our only remaining choice in AEGH is to reduce E again, from 11 to 10 days at a cost of $500. ABCFH and AEGH are now at 28 days, which is tied with the only other path ADGH. Since we cannot reduce ABCFH or AEGH any more, there is no point in reducing any other activity. The project duration cannot be reduced any further. The decisions made are summarized in Exhibit 8.27.

(continues)

Example 8.8 (continued)

EXHIBIT 8.27 Crashing Summary

Beginning critical path: ABCFH, 35 days

Step	Activity Crashed	Critical Path Before Activity Is Crashed	Critical Path After Activity Is Crashed	Project Duration After Activity Crashing (days)	Activity Crashing Cost ($)	Cumulative Project Crashing Cost ($)
1	C	AB**C**FH	ABCFH & AEGH	34	250	250
2	A	**A**BCFH & **A**EGH	ABCFH & AEGH	33	400	650
3	H	ABCF**H** & AEG**H**	ABCFH & AEGH	32	450	1,100
4	H	ABCF**H** & AEG**H**	ABCFH & AEGH	31	450	1,550
5	B G	A**B**CFH & AE**G**H	ABCFH & AEGH	30	300 450	1,850 2,300
6	B E	A**B**CFH & A**E**GH	ABCFH & AEGH	29	300 500	2,600 3,100
7	F E	ABC**F**H & A**E**GH	ABCFH & AEGH	28	350 500	3,450 3,950

Path	Project Duration									
ABCFH	35	34	33	32	31	30	30	29	29	28	28
AEGH	34	34	33	32	31	31	30	30	29	29	28
ADGH	28	28	28	28	28	28	28	28	28	28	28

Activity Crashed:		C	A	H	H	B	G	B	E	F	E
Crash Cost:		$250	$400	$450	$450	$300	$450	$300	$500	$350	$500
Cumulative Cost:		$250	$650	$1,100	$1,550	$1,850	$2,300	$2,600	$3,100	$3,450	$3,950

www.OperationsNow.com

The crashing process is demonstrated in a spreadsheet in Excel Tutor 8.8.

Project Management Caveats

Project management has become increasingly popular as businesses have become more focused on resource productivity, timeliness, and costs. Managers have recognized that by effectively managing projects, cash-to-cash cycles can be shortened and profitability can be increased. Several issues related to project management, however, should be of concern. Goldratt enumerates several issues that contribute to the ineffectiveness of project management efforts, even when network approaches like CPM are utilized.[3]

First, time estimates are just that, estimates. Estimates are frequently wrong. Time estimates are frequently very pessimistic and can be as much as double or triple the actual amount of time necessary to complete the activity. Activities made up of multiple tasks end up being padded much more than others. Second, early finishes tend not to be reported. Early finishes often get "absorbed" by resources, and even if a task is finished early, this will frequently not be reported to avoid starting the next task early. The effect is that projects aren't finished early. Third, any safety time, or "cushion," that is added to activities gets wasted. This is known as the "student syndrome." It is analogous to most professors' view of how students work on class projects—if a student asks for extra time on a project, it really doesn't do any good to give it to him because he will delay starting the project until the last possible moment anyway. The theory postulates that providing students with three weeks instead of three days to complete a project will not result in any more time being spent on the project. The similarity to project scheduling is that we typically try to protect project due dates by adding "cushions" to the activities, even though the cushion is often not needed and could have been reduced or eliminated with no negative impact on the project duration.

Another issue to recognize is that people on a particular project team are usually on other teams as well. Resources needed for a particular project are needed by other projects as well. A problem that crops up frequently when scheduling a project is the assumption that resources will be available when needed and as specified by the schedule. This is often not the case. If a resource is unavailable for an activity on the critical path, that activity must be delayed until the resource is available. If that activity is on the critical path, the project duration is extended. Project management software that can coordinate the demands of different projects on shared resources can aid in dealing with this problem.

CHAPTER SUMMARY

Clearly, timeliness is an important part of operations management. Promised due dates are met or missed because of the way resources are managed and decisions are made. Timeliness is an outcome of what management chooses to do. Effective or ineffective decision making will affect time-related measures. Quite often, time will be a factor in a decision because it is one side of a tradeoff. Do we want this now? Or that later? We can get it cheaper if we wait. Should we complete this order or that order? We only have time for one. Many decisions will pit time against money. Some decisions pit time against quality.

In this chapter, three groups of techniques were discussed. Dispatching or sequencing rules were introduced to demonstrate how jobs or orders in queue can be sequenced in different ways, depending on the performance measures that were most important. Techniques for managing queues of customers were introduced to provide a basis for improving that experience. Project management techniques were introduced to demonstrate how complex projects could be scheduled in ways that would help ensure timely completion.

Time is an integral component of value, it is important for competitive advantage, and it impacts financial and nonfinancial costs. Time is money, time is quality, and time has value. One of the difficulties in making tradeoffs is that the impact time has on value, competitiveness, or costs is often difficult to quantify. And, unfortunately for businesses that don't know any better, this can result in its importance going unrecognized.

270 UNIT TWO   Components of Value

KEY TERMS

- arrival process, 254
- backward scheduling, 245
- balking, 255
- calling population, 254
- cash-to-cash cycle, 237
- concurrent engineering, 242
- crashing, 265
- crash time, 266
- critical path, 259
- critical ratio (CR), 247
- earliest due date (EDD), 247
- early start schedule, 260
- first come, first served (FCFS), 246
- forward scheduling, 244
- Gantt chart, 245
- jockeying, 253
- late start schedule, 261
- network diagram, 258
- path, 259
- phase, 251
- project, 257
- project management, 257
- queue configuration, 251
- queue discipline, 253
- reneging, 255
- responsive, 232
- server, 251
- service process, 256
- shortest processing time (SPT), 247
- slack, 249
- slack per remaining operation, 249

REVIEW QUESTIONS

1. What is meant by "time is money" in the following scenarios:
    a. A business waiting for delivery of product components.
    b. A business waiting for the implementation of a new computer system.
    c. A new service design that can't be sold until the facility is remodeled.
    d. A consumer waiting for delivery of a mail-ordered product.
    e. A consumer waiting for a web page graphic to download.
2. How is flexibility related to timeliness?
3. Why is on-time delivery usually more important for business customers than for consumer customers?
4. What is the relationship between replenishment lead times and the amount of inventory a firm must carry? How is forecasting related to this relationship?
5. Waiting time for customers can impact a number of other business costs. What are they?
6. What is the impact of time on return on assets (ROA)?
7. What is the cash-to-cash cycle? Why is it important to profitability?
8. List some examples of business activities that add to the cash-to-cash cycle.
9. Provide an example of a negative cash-to-cash cycle.
10. What are the impacts of delayed quality feedback?
11. Why is the effective scheduling of resources critical to ROA?
12. Compare backward scheduling and forward scheduling.
13. What is a Gantt chart? How is it used?
14. Provide an example of a job sequencing rule based on due date.
15. Provide an example of a job sequencing rule based on estimated completion time.

16. Provide an example of a job sequencing rule based on both due date and estimated completion time.
17. What are jockeying, balking, and reneging as they apply to the behavior of customers in queue?
18. What can management do to make queues seem shorter to customers?
19. What is a project?
20. Why are network diagrams important in project management?
21. What is a path? What is slack? What is a critical path?
22. What is meant by crashing a project?

DISCUSSION QUESTIONS

1. Consider the products and services that you typically purchase. For which ones is timeliness a critical component of value? Why is it so important? Is it more important for services than products? Why?
2. What are some examples in your own life (athletics, work, artistic performance, schoolwork) when timely feedback is critical? What problems are created when the feedback is delayed?
3. Identify a process on your campus that you think takes too long. What are some possible changes to sequential activities to make them parallel? How much would the changes speed up the process?
4. As a student, what are your uses of backward and forward scheduling? How do you determine which to use?
5. How do the characteristics of the calling population, the arrival process, and the service process interact to determine the length and frequency of queues?
6. Identify examples of queues that do not incorporate methods that would make the customer's wait seem shorter. Propose changes to those queues to improve customer perceptions.

PROBLEMS

1. Big Screen Theater has set procedures for opening the movie house in preparation for customers. Management expects opening the theater to take no longer than 30 minutes for the two people involved (the assistant manager and the director of concessions). Activities required for opening are as follows:
   - The first activity for the assistant manager is to check for messages detailing any large groups that will be attending the theater. If there are messages, they must also be passed on to the director of concessions. Checking the messages takes the assistant manager about 5 minutes.
   - The assistant manager must then walk through the theater and verify that it is clean, an activity that takes approximately 10 minutes.
   - The assistant manager then prepares the movie projector, readying the first movie of the day, which takes the assistant manager up to the time when customers arrive.

- The theater operates using a computer system to print out tickets, and the first duty of the director of concessions is to start the computer system and properly input the correct data. Preparing the computer takes around 10 minutes.
- The director of concessions must then prepare the needed food, candy, and drinks for the incoming crowd, an activity that takes another 10 minutes. The director of concessions must also measure the food quantities to be consistent with the expected attendance, keeping in mind any messages passed on from the assistant manager.
- Finally, the director of concessions must prepare the cash register, an activity which will last until the first customer is seen.

Construct a Gantt chart that presents the needed activities in opening the theater.

2. Bob, Kelly, and Joe work for HC Consulting, which specializes in identifying problems with clients' customer service operations. Even though they work as a team, each performs a distinct function. Bob is always the first to interact with the clients, asking questions from appropriate employees. Kelly and Joe perform the next task, which is to observe the client company at work. While they observe the company, Bob examines the company's financial statements. Upon completion of these tasks, all three HC employees come together for a group discussion of the situation. When the problem is diagnosed, Kelly and Joe meet with the client company and present the findings, while Bob goes back to the office and completes documentation related to the job. Create a Gantt chart using this information.

3. Relo Inc. specializes in finding new office locations for its business clients. For each client, Relo must first understand the client's motivation for opening a new location. This is usually accomplished with a face-to-face interview. Relo must then familiarize itself with the client's industry by researching trends and competitive forces. Once Relo has an understanding of the client and its industry it can then look at specific geographic alternatives for the new facility. Relo narrows the field down to three locations, which are then investigated to determine costs for leasing or construction. When finished, Relo presents the findings to the client with hopes of retaining a consultancy role with the new facility development. Construct a Gantt chart for Relo's process.

4. The University Copy Shop prepares course packets for class. Determine the EDD sequence, as well as the average lateness and number of jobs late for the client orders.

Client	Order Arrival Sequence	Due Date	Estimated Completion Time (days)
MGT 235	1	10	3
MIS 365	2	5	3
FIN 112	3	2	2
ACC 205	4	8	4

5. Darcy is a freelance writer for several newspapers and magazines. Her schedule for next month, as well as the time she believes it will take to complete the assignments, follows.

Publication	Estimated Time Required (days)	Due Date
City Times	3	17
Nation-beat	6	8
Free News	4	15
The Shores	4	5
Monthly Press	2	23
The Star	5	19
Gossip	4	27

Determine the EDD sequence for the work she must complete. Calculate values for the average lateness and the number of jobs late.

6. Creative Colors is an interior design and decorating firm. Its next four projects are detailed below. Sequence the jobs using the SPT sequencing rule. What conclusions can you draw from the sequence?

Client	Order Arrival Sequence	Due Date	Estimated Completion Time (days)
Smith	1	6	4
Brown	2	4	2
Dewar	3	8	3
Walker	4	11	5

7. You have been hired by Advanced Technologies, a company that provides custom technology projects, and asked to explore the potential use of the SPT job-sequencing rule. The firm's next five jobs are detailed below. Explain whether the SPT rule is helpful in this scenario.

Client	Order Arrival	Due Date	Estimated Completion Time (days)
A&B Co.	1	14	2
Belco	2	8	6
Corr Int.	3	19	4
Dapp	4	24	10
Elly	5	10	7

8. Fancy Cakes bakes decorative cakes for parties and weddings. Jobs for the next two weeks are presented below. Arrange the jobs using the critical ratio rule. Compute the average lateness and the number of late jobs. What conclusions can be drawn from the results?

Client	Order Arrival Sequence	Due Date	Estimated Completion Time (days)
Aubin	1	5	4
Baldwin	2	8	4
Cross	3	9	3
Dampier	4	11	5
Ellman	5	14	2

9. Meta World Funds offers risk analysis and mutual funds to large institutional investors. The firm anticipates new projects and wants to schedule them efficiently. Below is a detailed table of their next five projects. Sequence the jobs using the critical ratio rule. Evaluate the performance of the rule.

Client	Order Arrival Sequence	Due Date	Estimated Completion Time (days)
Index	1	19	10
Technology	2	33	12
Global	3	26	8
Government	4	22	11
Energy	5	42	14

10. Read Only Co., a software development firm, constantly looks for the most accurate means to sequence their projects. From the table below use critical ratio, SPT, and EDD sequencing rules to sequence the orders. Provide your recommendation as to which rule is best by examining the total days late, number of jobs late, and average lateness to measure the rule's performance.

Client	Order Arrival Sequence	Due Date	Estimated Completion Time (days)
AIM	1	17	4
Beta	2	5	5
Coral	3	13	2
Draw-it	4	9	6
E-notes	5	15	3

11. As a new hire with College Book Binding, you have been asked to present a means to sequence pending jobs. The first order to come in is due on day 14 and will take 7 days to complete. The second job is due on day 29 and will take 5 days to complete. The third job is to be completed by day 7 and will take 2 days to finish. The fourth job is due on day 24 and will take 8 days to complete. The last job is to be finished by day 19 and will take 4 days to complete. Your challenge is to present an argument for using a sequencing rule. Choose the best rule as measured by the average lateness of jobs. Provide a rationale for the selected sequencing rule and explain why it is better than those rules not chosen.

12. Bass Clef Guitars makes custom guitars for its legendary clientele. Each guitar needs to complete four distinct operations, but completion time for each opera-

tion varies from one instrument to another. The table below provides information on the next five jobs. Calculate the slack and slack per remaining operation for each client's guitar.

Client	Order Arrival Sequence	Due Date	Estimated Completion Time (days)	Number of Remaining Operations
Timmy Hendricks	1	7	4	2
Don Mathews	2	11	6	4
Moses Moreno	3	21	8	4
Pat Dylan	4	16	2	4
Edy Van Whalen	5	17	5	4

13. As an expert on the subject of scheduling, you have been asked to explain when you would utilize slack per remaining operation. From the information below, sequence the jobs using slack per remaining operation and explain why it would be used.

Client	Order Arrival Sequence	Due Date	Estimated Completion Time (days)	Number of Remaining Operations
a	1	3	3	5
b	2	7	2	4
c	3	12	6	3
d	4	16	9	2
e	5	23	5	4

14. The Campus Post Office receives an average of 24 customers per hour. If the distribution follows the Poisson distribution, what is the probability that during any given hour it will receive 30 customers?

15. The Second State Bank gets an average of 41 customers per hour. The distribution follows the Poisson distribution. What is the probability that during any given hour, the bank will receive 50 customers?

16. The Roosevelt High School cheerleaders are having a car wash. If they get an average of 25 cars per hour, and the distribution follows the Poisson distribution, what is the probability that they will receive 40 cars in a given hour?

17. Tie has always dreamed of starting his own mortgage business. He has identified seven steps to complete before business can begin. Using the data below, construct a network diagram and determine the critical path.

Activity ID No.	Activity	Immediate Predecessors	Estimated Time (days)
1	Financing		5
2	Secure lenders	1	20
3	Lease space	1	10
4	Purchase supplies	3	1

5	Set up phones		4	4
6	Hire reps		2	20
7	Advertise		5,6	15

18. Innovative R&D markets new inventions. The following 10 activities are needed before an invention can be taken to market. Use the information to construct a network diagram, determine the early/late start/finish points, and find the critical path.

Activity ID No.	Activity Description	Immediate Predecessors	Estimated Time
1	Study feasibility		6
2	Gather information		4
3	Explore options		6
4	Define users	2	1
5	Narrow to one	3	1
6	Prototype	1, 4, 5	10
7	Internal test	6	5
8	External test	6	8
9	Measure performance	7, 8	5
10	Production	9	25

19. National Test Center is a leading research center for the study of communicable diseases. The research activities and their optimistic, most likely, and pessimistic times are given. Use the times to calculate the expected time and the variance.

Activity ID No.	Activity Description	Optimistic	Most Likely	Pessimistic
1	Take specimen	.5	1	3
2	Measure	1.5	2	4
3	Test	2.5	4	7
4	Analyze	3	5	7
5	Report	2	3	4

20. EZ Attorney provides its students with basic legal training so that they will be able to quickly negotiate settlements. The following chart provides EZ's estimation of the length of each activity (in hours) in the negotiation process. Use the information to calculate the ES, EF, LS, LF, and slack.

Activity ID No.	Activity Description	Optimistic	Most Likely	Pessimistic	T_e	Variance
1	Preparation	6.5	8.5	10.5	8.5	0.4444
2	Preliminary	3	5	7	5	0.4444
3	Common ground	2	5	8	5	1.0000
4	Issue at hand	8	10.5	13	10.5	0.6944
5	Agreement	2.5	4	7	4.25	0.5625

21. Bryan, the hockey player, is very interested in how long it takes to prepare for a game. The table below provides information on all of the activities leading up to the game. What is the probability that Bryan would be ready in 25 minutes?

Activity ID No.	Activity Description	Optimistic	Most Likely	Pessimistic	T_e	Variance
1	Dress	9	11	13	11	0.4444
2	Warmup	4	6	8	6	0.4444
3	Stretch	3	5	7	5	0.4444
4	Assignments	2	5	8	5	1.0000
5	Pregame	3	6	9	6	1.0000

22. Software Design assists companies with the implementation of new software products. Of course, time is of the essence and the company is on a very tight schedule. Use the following information to reduce the project duration as much as possible. What will it cost to reduce the project to that duration? The current critical path is 1, 2, 4, 5, 6.

Activity ID No.	Activity Description	Normal Time (days)	Crash Time (days)	Cost/Day ($)
1	ID needs	30	28	250
2	Research market	15	14	500
3	Narrow solutions	14	13	250
4	Feasibility	7	6	400
5	Prototype	60	59	800
6	Implementation	90	89	950

23. Sam is preparing to write a paper for class. Below is a table identifying the activities needed for his paper. Determine the project duration and the critical path. Given his work schedule, taking time off to write the paper will mean sacrificing income. Determine the lowest-cost approach for reducing the project by four days.

Activity ID No.	Activity Description	Predecessors	Normal Time (days)	Crash Time (days)	Cost/Day ($)
1	Choose topic		4	3	250
2	Outline	1	3	2	175
3	Research	1	7	5	300
4	Bibliography	2	2		
5	Write	3, 4	3	2	100

www.
OperationsNow
.com

INTERACTIVE ANALYSIS 8.1

THE SEQUENCING RULE INTERACTIVE MODEL

The Sequencing Rule Interactive Model, accessed through Chapter 8 of the *OperationsNow.com* website, provides a quick and easy way to compare the performance of several traditional sequencing rules. The techniques included for comparison are earliest due date (EDD), shortest processing time (SPT), critical ratio (CR), and first come, first served (FCFS). The user has the option of using the default data or entering new data for estimated completion time and due date. The user must also select the number of orders to be sequenced. By selecting the rule to be applied and clicking on the "schedule" button, the model resequences the orders and provides a color-coded Gantt chart of the resulting schedule. When orders are projected to be completed after their due date, a line showing the due date is also provided. Performance measures of total days late, number of orders late, and average lateness are provided.

Experiment 1: System Fundamentals

1. Use the default data for five orders to be sequenced, as shown below, and sequence the orders by earliest due date.

Order ID	Estimated Completion Time (days)	Due Date
A	5	9
B	3	6
C	11	17
D	4	11
E	7	29

   a. Record the performance measures and resequence by shortest processing time. How does the performance of the two rules compare on total days late, numbers of orders late, and average lateness?

   b. If your objective was to minimize lateness for the latest order, which rule would you select?

2. Again, use the default data for five orders to be sequenced, and sequence the orders by the critical ratio rule. Record the performance measures.

   a. Resequence the orders by first come, first served and compare the results.

   b. Rank the four rules for each performance measure. How does the performance of the four rules compare?

Experiment 2: Exploring Processing Time

1. Chapter 8 discusses three general approaches to order sequencing: focusing on processing time, focusing on due date, or combining the two. Using a rule that considers processing time makes sense, because the processing time dictates, to a great extent, whether the order will be completed on time. Using the default val-

ues for five orders, sequence the orders using the first come, first served rule and record the performance results. Resequence using the shortest processing time rule and record those results.

   a. Which rule performs best?

2. As new orders come in, they must be added into the sequence. Suppose that as order B was completed, a new order arrived. Delete the estimated completion time and due date for order B and replace them with an estimated processing time of 8 and a due date of 17. Resequence the orders, again using shortest processing time. What position does that order take in the sequence? What happens to the performance measures?

   a. Enter another order, in place of the current B order, that has a processing time that is longer than any of the current orders. What happens to it? What happens to the performance measures? What does this indicate for the shortest processing time rule? What is its flaw? How might you intervene to eliminate this problem?

Experiment 3: Exploring Due Date

1. A rule based on due date also makes sense, since the due date is one-half of the cause of an order being late. The most commonly used rule of this type is earliest due date (EDD). It basically gives priority to the order due the earliest. Set the model back to the default data for five orders.

   a. Earliest due date often provides the best results in terms of average lateness. Using the default values for five orders, record the performance measures for the EDD sequence and compare the results to those of the first come, first served sequence in Experiment 2. Increase the number of orders to six. Explain what happens in the sequence.

2. Compare the results of first come, first served, earliest due date, and shortest processing time for the default settings using four, five, and six orders. How do they compare?

Experiment 4: Exploring a Combination of Due Date and Processing Time

1. The critical ratio rule combines information from the due date and the processing time of each order to compute a ratio of the due date to the expected processing time. The resulting ratio provides a picture of the amount of extra time available to process the order. An order that is already late will have a critical ratio less than 1. The larger the ratio, the more extra time available. The orders are scheduled by the ratio, smallest is first. Sequence the default values for five orders using the critical ratio rules.

   a. Compare the results of the critical ratio rule to those of the EDD, SPT, and FCFS rules. How does it compare in this situation?

INTERACTIVE ANALYSIS 8.2

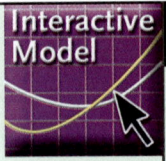
www.
OperationsNow
.com

THE WAITING LINE INTERACTIVE MODEL

The Waiting Line Interactive Model provides a rich environment for exploring service systems. The user can select between one- and two-phase systems. The simulator speed, which doesn't change the simulation outcome, allows the user to slow the system down to better observe interactions. The arrival rate is generated from a Poisson distribution. The arrival rate selection determines the parameter λ and is the number of arrivals per hour. The service rate is generated from a negative exponential distribution and is the number of customers served per hour. The service rate selection determines the parameter μ, which is the mean service rate. The service rate is generated from a negative exponential distribution and is the number of customers served per hour. The selection of NS1: or NS2: determines the number of servers for each phase of the system. Output measures are:

W_q = average time customers wait in line
W_s = average time customers spend in the system (waiting and being served)
L_q = average number of customers waiting in line for the service
L_s = average number of customers in the system (waiting and being served)

As the simulation runs, the number of customers in line is provided under each queue. The number of customers that have been through the system is presented under the last queue.

Experiment 1: System Fundamentals

1. Set the parameters equal to the values below:

   Number of phases: 1
   Speed: Slow
   Arrival rate: 8
   Service rate: 4
   NS1:   4

   Run the simulation, observing the system, until 100 customers have been served.

   a. Were all four servers ever busy at the same time? Did a waiting line ever form? How long did it get? What were the output measures for W_q, W_s, L_q, and L_s? Explain each.

2. Run the simulation with the same parameters except reduce the number of servers from 4 to 3. Did a waiting line ever form this time? How long did it get? What were the new output measures for W_q, W_s, L_q, and L_s? Explain the difference.

3. Run the simulation with the same parameters except reduce the number of servers from three to two. Did a waiting line form? How long did the line get? What were the new output measures for W_q, W_s, L_q, and L_s? Explain the change. What happened to the performance measures as each server was eliminated? Is this what you expected to happen?

4. Reset the parameters as follows:

   Number of phases: 2
   Speed: Slow
   Arrival rate: 4
   Service rate: 4
   NS1:   1
   NS2:   1

a. Carefully observe the simulation as it processes 100 customers. How long does the queue in front of the first server get? With arrival and service rates equal, why does a queue develop? Did you notice any instances of the second server being idle (yellow, rather than blue)? Why did this happen? After 100 customers, what were the output measures for W_q, W_s, L_q, and L_s?

b. Leave all parameters the same as in 4a, except reduce the service rate to 3 minutes. Again, observe the simulation as it processes 100 customers. How long does the queue in front of the first server get this time? Does a queue ever develop in front of the first server? Why did a queue develop? Did you notice any instances of either server being idle? Why did this happen? After 100 customers, what were the output measures W_q, W_s, L_q, and L_s? Compare them to the output measures for 4a. Explain how the differences relate to the change in service rate.

Experiment 2: The Serpentine Queue

Most fast-food restaurants, banks, and airline ticket counters have adopted a single-queue, multiple-server design that utilizes a long serpentine queue. The customer at the head of the line goes to the first open server. These systems are fair in that no one gains advantage by selecting the line with the fastest server. It also eliminates the problem of customers jumping from one line to another (jockeying).

1. Set the parameters as follows:

   Number of phases: 1
   Speed: Slow
   Arrival rate: 8
   Service rate: 2
   NS1:   4

   The casual observer would look at this configuration and conclude that everything should be fine. The system can serve eight customers per hour (four servers serving two each), and that is the arrival rate. Run the system until 100 customers have been served.

   a. What are the performance measures? Do you think they're acceptable?

   b. Reset the parameters as follows:

   Number of phases: 1
   Speed: Slow
   Arrival rate: 8
   Service rate: 3
   NS1:   4

   How would you judge the performance of this configuration from the standpoint of waiting time and line length, as well as resource utilization?

2. Set the parameters as follows:

   Number of phases: 2
   Speed: Slow
   Arrival rate: 8
   Service rate: 2
   NS1:   4
   NS2:   3

This system models what is essentially a two-phase system with a serpentine approach at each phase. Run the system, while observing what happens, until 100 customers have been served.

   a. Based on your observations while the system is running, how does the first queue compare to the second queue in terms of length? How would you explain this?

Experiment 3: Increasing the Number of Servers

1. Set the parameters equal to the values below:

Number of phases:	2
Speed:	Slow
Arrival rate:	4
Service rate:	4
NS1:	1
NS2:	1

   a. Run the simulation until 100 customers have been served. Record the output statistics. Reset the parameters as follows:

Number of phases:	2
Speed:	Slow
Arrival rate:	4
Service rate:	2
NS1:	2
NS2:	2

   Run the simulation until 100 customers have been served. Record the output statistics.

   b. Reset the parameters as follows:

Number of phases:	2
Speed:	Slow
Arrival rate:	6
Service rate:	2
NS1:	3
NS2:	3

   Run the simulation until 100 customers have been served. Record the output statistics.

   c. Reset the parameters as follows:

Number of phases:	2
Speed:	Slow
Arrival rate:	8
Service rate:	2
NS1:	4
NS2:	4

   Run the simulation until 100 customers have been served. Record the output statistics.

   How would you describe what happens when server rate is equal to arrival rate, but the number of servers required to meet that demand increases?

SELECTED REFERENCES

Fine, C. F. *ClockSpeed: Winning Industry Control in the Age of Temporary Advantage*. Reading, MA: Perseus Books, 1998.

Fitzsimmons, J. A., and Fitzsimmons, M. J. *Service Management: Operations, Strategy, and Information Technology*. New York: McGraw-Hill/Irwin, 2000.

Gido, J., and Clements, J. P. *Successful Project Management*. Cincinnati, OH: South-Western Publishing, 1999.

Gray, C. F., and Larson, E. W. *Project Management: The Managerial Process*. New York: McGraw-Hill/Irwin, 2000.

Katzenbach, J. R., and Smith, D. K. *The Wisdom of Teams*. New York: HarperCollins, 1999.

Meredith, J. R., and Mantel, S. J. *Project Management*. New York: John Wiley & Sons, 2000.

Olson, D. L. *Introduction to Information Systems Project Management*. New York: McGraw-Hill/Irwin, 2001.

Stalk, G., Jr., and Hout, T. M. *Competing Against Time*. New York: Free Press, 1990.

ENDNOTES

1. "Fix It and They Will Come," *The Wall Street Journal*, February 12, 2001, p. R4.
2. Adapted from D. H. Maister, "The Psychology of Waiting Lines," in J. A. Czepiel, M. R. Solomon, and C. F. Surprenant (eds.), *The Service Encounter* (Lexington, MA: Lexington Press, 1985), pp. 113–123.
3. E. M. Goldratt, *Critical Chain* (Great Barrington, MA: North River Press. 1997).

OperationsNow.com LEARNING ACTIVITIES

CHAPTER ENHANCEMENT RESOURCES
- Esources
- Reel Operations Video Clips
- Interactive Models
- Excel Tutors
- Supplementary Readings
- Links to Operations On Site Companies

OM EXPLORATION
- Check It Out
- OM in Action
- Online Business Tours
- Letters from the Top
- Putting It All Together: Virtual Case Studies
- Additional Reading

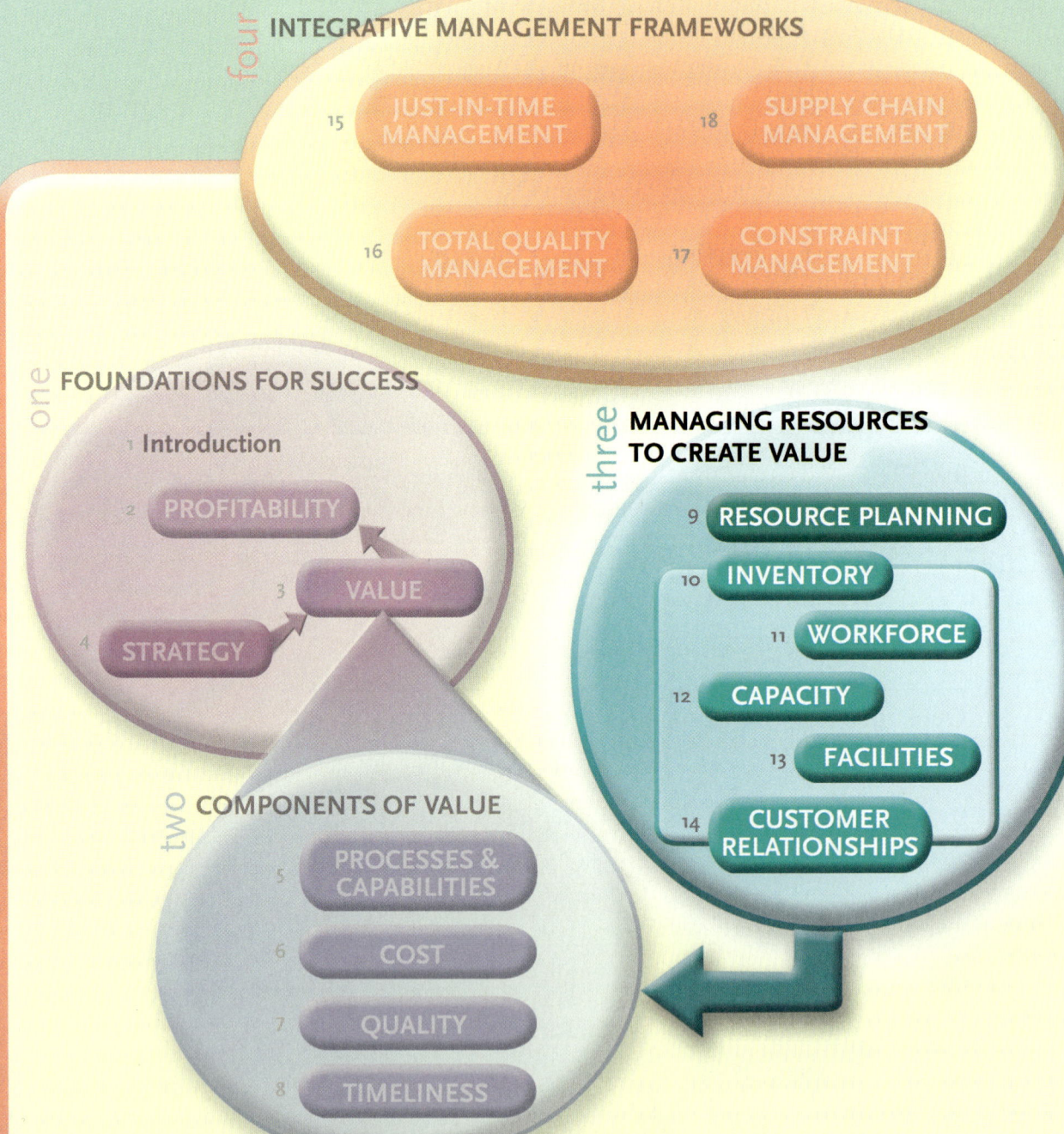

Managing Resources to Create Value

Chapter 9:
Resource Planning

Chapter 10:
Inventory

Chapter 11:
Workforce

Chapter 12:
Capacity

Chapter 13:
Facilities

Chapter 14:
Customer Relationships

INTRODUCTION

Unit 1 focused on foundations for the ultimate success of the firm. In a sense, these could be considered "prerequisites" that place Units 2, 3, and 4 into the appropriate context. Unit 2 focused on the components of value, from the perspective of the customer. These topics provided the basis for what customers value and are willing to pay for. In this unit, Unit 3, the focus shifts to the resources businesses use to create that value. First, we examine the concept of resource planning, with an emphasis on demand forecasting because it is that demand forecast that gives management a sense of how much of a particular resource will be needed. Next we examine five resources: inventory, workforce, capacity, facilities, and customer relationships, with the objective of making decisions that provide the best financial return on the investments in those resources. That financial return comes from the value created and the costs created. Creating the most value for the smallest investment, in other words making decisions so that these resources are productive, enhances business profitability.

The resource/profit model places resource planning at the head of Unit 3, which is devoted to the management of resources used in value creation. This chapter has important objectives as a prerequisite to examining each resource category. Without an understanding of the planning process and, most important, the role demand forecasting plays in that process, any resource plans would be unlikely to support the profitability, value, and strategy goals the business would have.

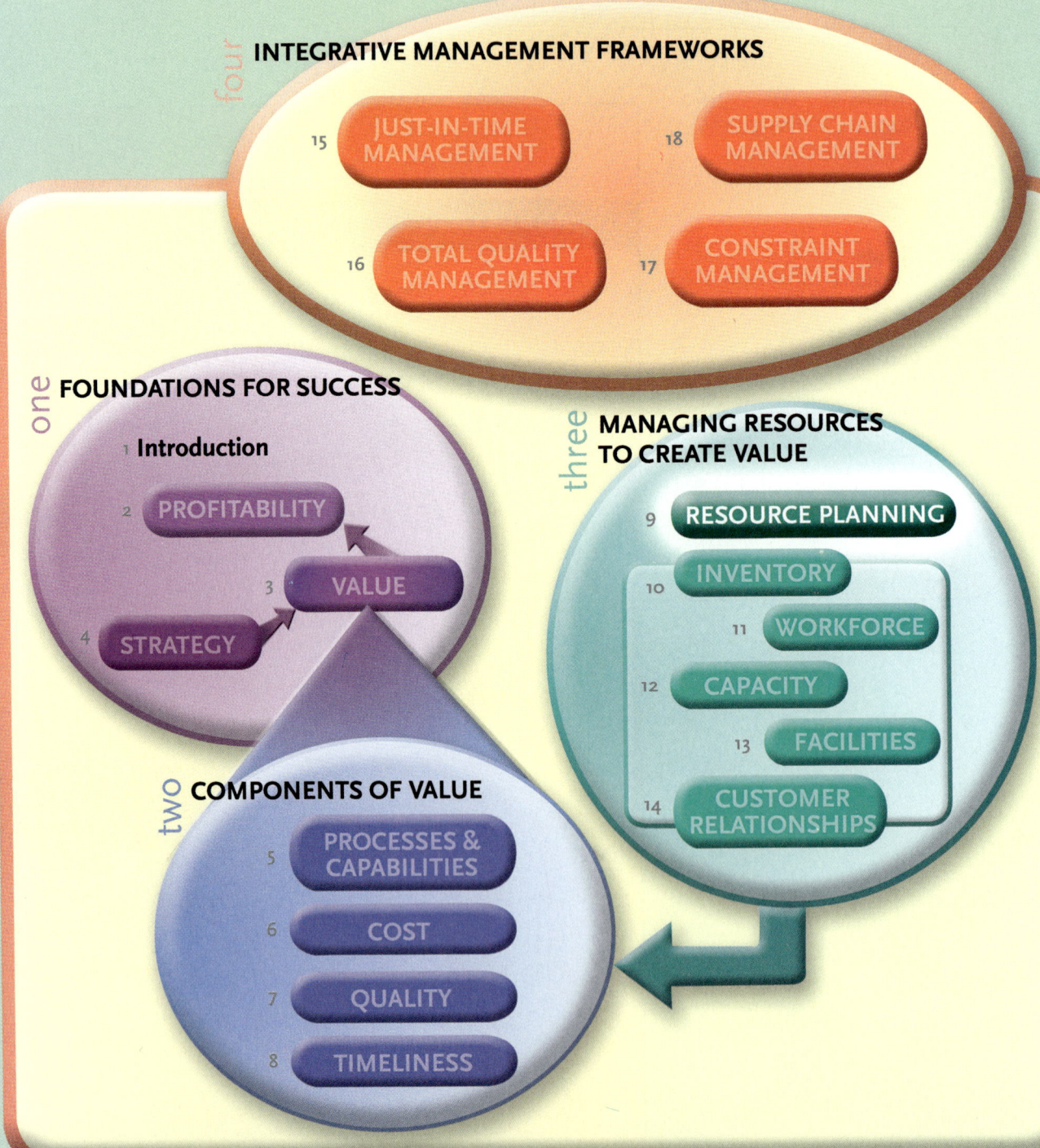

CHAPTER 9

Resource Planning

LEARNING OBJECTIVES

Upon completion of Chapter 9, you should be able to

- Describe the benefits of effective resource planning.
- Explain how the planning horizon affects planning tasks.
- Describe how lead times determine the planning horizon.
- Explain how product and service life cycles can aid in the planning process.
- Describe the different types of forecasting methods.
- Compute a causal forecast using simple linear regression.
- Recognize the components of a time series and appropriate forecasting techniques for each component.
- Compute forecasts using averages, exponential smoothing, seasonal indexes, and a multiplicative model.
- Compute measures of forecast accuracy.
- Describe how enterprise resource planning (ERP) systems benefit businesses.
- Explain the positive and negative aspects of implementing ERP systems.

Introduction: Why Do We Plan?
Planning Fundamentals
The Impact of Product and Service Life Cycles
A Strategy for More Successful Plans: Compressing Lead Times
Demand Forecasting
Causal Forecasting
Time Series Forecasting
Forecast Accuracy
Integrated Resource Planning Systems
Supply Chain Management
Chapter Summary

INTERNET RESOURCES

 Excel Tutors provide annotated spreadsheets for every solved problem that automatically load Excel.

 Esources provide an online version of the more traditional boxed insert.

 Reel Videos provide streaming video footage for company applications of chapter concepts.

 Interactive Models provide an experimental environment for quantitative concepts and simulations.

INTRODUCTION
Why Do We Plan?

This chapter lays the groundwork for the management of operations resources by accomplishing several objectives. First, it defines the task of resource planning, introducing the concept of planning horizon—how we know how far into the future plans must go. Second, the chapter identifies the critical links between effective resource planning and profitability measures. Third, the chapter examines demand forecasting concepts and techniques. These techniques are important because the demand forecast creates the foundation for many resource planning activities. Finally, this chapter introduces and develops a generic model for enterprise resource planning (ERP) systems, which are rapidly becoming a standard planning and management framework for businesses.

For our purposes, planning is the process of determining what is needed, and making arrangements to get it, in order to achieve objectives. Planning has become so ingrained in our lives that we do it without thinking. Human beings have progressed a long way from sitting in a cave thinking only about where their next meal will come from. With thousands of alternative ways to spend our time, some alternatives have naturally become more enjoyable than others. We have become sophisticated planners in our daily lives, without even realizing it. In business environments, the planning function can determine the success or failure of the firm. In a very general sense, a plan is an outline saying what we need to do in advance to enable us to accomplish something in the future. In Exhibit 9.1, the resource/profit model places resource planning prior to each of the operations resource categories because an understanding of resource planning is a prerequisite to making good resource decisions.

Plans can be quite general, or they can be very specific. They can be short term, dealing with tomorrow or next week, or they can address goals and objectives that extend years into the future.

An examination of planning processes, whether it's your plan for next Friday night or Bill Gates's plan for rolling out Windows 2010, will uncover some common characteristics. In both cases, some general goals are defined in terms of more specific objectives. Bill might be thinking, "2010 needs to be ready for roll out on time, with no bugs." You might be thinking, "I want to have a good time next Friday, because my Operations Management midterm, covering Chapters 1–9, will be over." In both of those situations, the goal must be broken down into more specific objectives in order to start the planning process. Let's leave Bill Gates out of this for now and concentrate on your needs. What must you do in order to enjoy Friday night? If you break that down, you might identify components that include places to go, friends to go with, money to spend, and transportation. Without any of these components of "going out and having a good time," the outcome could be disappointing. Each might require a different type of preparation in order to ensure that it can be done. Now is the time to decide where to go. Why? Because you might need advance tickets or a reservation.

This brings us to the sequence. Should you decide the places you wish to go first and then invite friends who'll like your idea? Or should you decide who's going and then decide where to go as a group? The answer is that it probably depends on what aspect of your Friday night is more important—the place or the people you're with. Should you decide where to go before knowing how much money you'll have? Or does the place you're going dictate how much money you'll need? As you can see, this becomes a complex process, and if it's this complex for your upcoming night out, think what poor Bill Gates must be going through. Complex as your planning process

EXHIBIT 9.1 Resource/Profit Model: Emphasis on Resource Planning

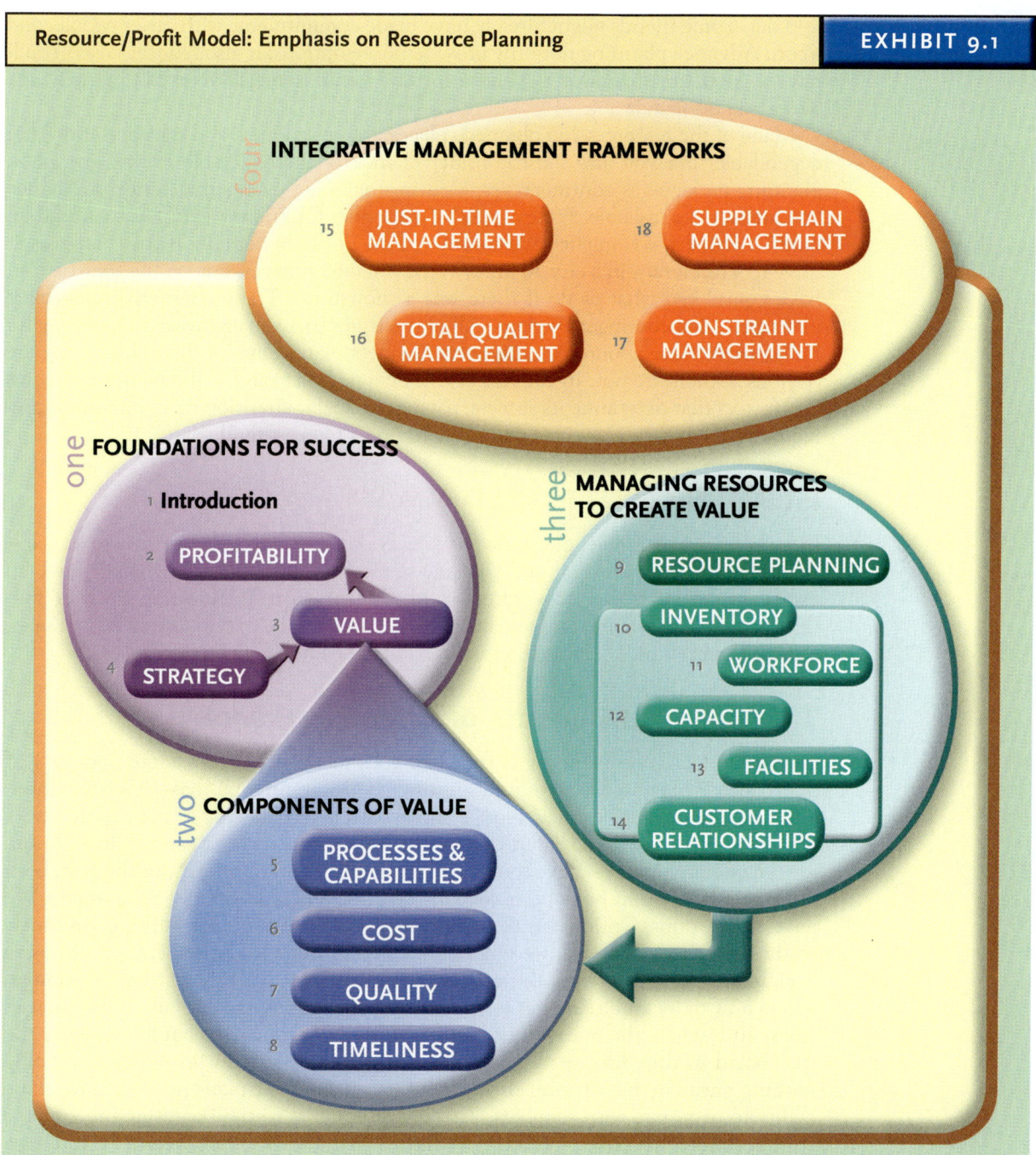

would appear if we attempted to model it in a flow diagram, you would nonetheless carry it out without even thinking about it.

You might spend a little effort planning for Friday night, but it's worth it because you want Friday night to be enjoyable. Some of your cohorts, however, won't spend a second thinking about Friday night until late Friday afternoon. Maybe they're really spontaneous or maybe they're not quite as sharp as you and maybe they just don't think ahead. In any case, their alternatives will be fewer than if they had started planning ahead of time. Some places to go might no longer be available because they're sold out. Some friends might already have made commitments with other people, and so on. Advance planning not only provides more options; it also reduces costs. You'll have a good time and won't spend a fortune, while some of your cohorts will stay home and do laundry.

Many of the resources you planned (places, friends, money, and transportation) are dependable, but you also must consider chance or unpredictable events known in planning parlance as contingencies. Contingencies are events that hinge on chance and are not controllable. For example, if your plan for Friday night was to attend an outdoor concert, you might have considered the possibility of rain. If your plan was to drive to a restaurant in a city 30 miles away, you might, depending on the time of year, have considered what to do if there was a snowstorm. These alternative or backup plans are called **contingency plans**. All of the issues that you addressed in planning for Friday night have counterparts in every business plan. Some of them, like costs, are obvious. Others are not. In the rest of this chapter, we examine the planning process and factors that determine its success, paying particular attention to an important prerequisite of business planning, that of obtaining a forecast for demand.

PLANNING FUNDAMENTALS

In our previous example, planning for your Friday night out, the worst-case scenario is that all of your plans fail and you stay home by yourself. You might not have an exciting time, but you'd recover from it. In a business setting, however, the total failure of a plan can be much more damaging. It could result in lost customers, lost sales, a missed opportunity, a lawsuit, or even a failed business.

The Financial Benefits of Effective Planning

One benefit of good planning is that like you, management has more options if it plans ahead. Suppose we were in a sporting goods retailing business. It's late winter, and we've noticed that a new type of snowboard is just starting to get popular. Several customers have asked about it in recent weeks, but we don't carry it. In addition, several of our employees have spoken of its popularity on the slopes. In the past, both pieces of information have been virtually certain indicators of upcoming trends. We have two options. Option 1 is to do nothing. If it turns out next fall that customers really want the snowboard, we will figure out then how to get some. Option 2 is to begin planning now to carry the snowboard next season. We'd need to make arrangements now to lock in a supplier for the snowboard so that in early fall we'd have it in stock. In essence, the question at hand is whether to devise a plan for stocking the snowboard in time for the next ski season. Making plans now, as opposed to doing nothing until fall, has several advantages. First, if we make plans now, we have some ability to negotiate with suppliers. This gives us access to the boards at a reasonable cost. Second, if we make plans now, we have a guaranteed supply. Third, we will have the boards early in the season when people are looking to upgrade their equipment, and we'll be one of the first stores with the board. Having that board gives us an opportunity to draw customers away from other shops because we'll have the board and they won't. Once the customers are in our store, they may purchase other accessories as well.

The preceding example exemplifies several aspects of the financial impact of planning. Once again, the most important financial measures for operations are profitability measures, and, once again, when we look at planning benefits from the standpoint of profitability, we see a direct impact on the same two profitability measures: profit margin and return on assets. Let's look at profit margin first. Remember, profit margin is equal to net income divided by sales. Net income is derived from net sales, minus the cost of goods sold and depreciation, minus interest paid, minus taxes. An advance plan to carry a new item like the snowboard has the potential to reduce costs *and* increase net sales, yielding a substantial boost to profit margin. Because of our plan, we get the boards at a lower cost, we get them early, and we can get the number we need. Net sales is increased, cost of goods sold is decreased.

This plan should also make a positive impact on return on assets. ROA is equal to net income divided by total assets. Net income rises as a result of this plan. Given that we're able to buy the boards at a reasonable cost, net income should rise substantially more than our total assets, even with a potential increase in inventory.

The primary positive impact of this plan is on net sales, but not all plans will have a direct impact on net income through net sales. For example, plans related to a new facility at a lower-cost location might affect only costs associated with that facility. Other plans might affect only machine capacity or labor. In general, plans related to resources that are used to create value provide a way to improve the reliability of obtaining those resources, a way to get those resources at lower cost, or opportunities to decide among an increased number of alternatives. More options mean more flexibility and more flexibility means an enhanced ability to respond to changes. The remaining chapters in this unit examine specific planning concepts and techniques related to the value-creating resources of inventory, workforce, capacity, facilities, and customer relationships. In each of these chapters, the specific impact that planning for that resource has on profitability is addressed.

Although it is true that the further ahead we can plan, the more options we have available, it is also true that the further ahead we plan, the less we know about future conditions. Think of your own planning activities. You can plan for this coming Friday night because you know something about it. It is difficult, if not impossible, for you to plan for a Friday night three months in the future because a lot can happen between now and then. You don't have enough knowledge about that night. In fact, you probably don't have any goals associated with that night to form the foundation for a plan. Exhibit 9.2 shows the relationships among planning horizon length, alternatives available, and certainty about outcomes. Options increase further in the future, but certainty decreases. This results in a tradeoff of sorts between increasing options and increasing uncertainty.

With that conflict in mind, planners have two means at their disposal for improving the outcome of a plan. First, they could try to improve the quality of knowledge far in the future, which would provide them greater certainty and allow them the luxury of considering more alternatives. The second approach would be to accept the fact that knowledge far in the future will always be suspect, and try to find ways of compressing the planning horizon so that planners can have more options without having to plan as far into the future. This means that options and alternatives must somehow be increased, even in the short term. These issues bring us to one of the more difficult questions that must be answered relative to planning: How far ahead must we plan? In other words, what is the best planning horizon?

Looking into the Future: The Planning Horizon

The distance into the future that we plan is known as the **planning horizon**. As a general rule of thumb, we should plan as far into the future as necessary to meet our objectives, but planning further ahead than necessary tends to result in plans that aren't very good or are irrelevant. How far is "necessary"? The minimum planning horizon, or the shortest distance into the future one can effectively plan, is determined by the lead time associated with obtaining resources necessary to meet your

| EXHIBIT 9.2 | **Relationships Among Planning Horizon, Alternatives, and Outcome Certainty** |

Planning Horizon

Short ———————————————————————————————— Long

Alternatives Available

Few ————————————————————————————————— Many

Certainty about Outcomes

High ————————————————————————————————— Low

objectives. The longer the lead time, the further out the minimum planning horizon. Let's look at an example.

Suppose we own a small brewery. One of our many objectives as a business is to ensure that we have sufficient capacity to meet demand. We do not want to forgo sales simply because we can't handle the demand. That would provide an excuse for our customers to try out our competitors. Capacity needs can be complex and vary widely in scope. One type of capacity need is the labor to run our equipment. Another capacity need is the capacity of our brewing and storage tanks. Another is the capacity of our bottling equipment. What would our planning horizon(s) look like?

Suppose we know that the lead time required to advertise job positions, interview, hire, and train new laborers is three weeks. For labor planning purposes, then, the minimum planning horizon for labor is three weeks. We must project our labor needs *at least* three weeks into the future, compare those needs to the labor we have available, and decide if we have enough. If we don't have enough, we must take action (advertise positions, interview, hire, and train). We could plan further than three weeks ahead, but our knowledge of labor needs further into the future is not as accurate. Moreover, we don't *need* to know further ahead—at least not from a labor planning perspective. What if we planned less than three weeks into the future, say, only one week? We might identify a labor shortage one week into the future, but since it would take three weeks to actually get the new labor up and running, we'd be short on labor for the two-week interim.

Now let's look at machine and storage capacity. The lead time for adding to machine or storage tank capacity is quite long. Our past experience has shown that from the time we identify a need for a large-scale piece of equipment to when it is installed, rigged, tested, calibrated, and brought into production is seven months. So, for the purposes of machine and storage tank capacity, our minimum planning horizon is seven months. What would happen if we planned only four months ahead? If we identified a shortage four months out, we'd react, but since it would take us seven months to get the equipment up and running, we'd miss three months of demand and incur all of the costs associated with losing those sales.

For machine capacity planning purposes, the minimum planning horizon will be seven months. We must project machinery and storage tank needs *at least* seven months into the future, compare those needs to the capacity we have available, and

CHAPTER 9 Resource Planning 293

> **Planning Is Complicated by Changes in Customer Behavior**
>
> Cost reduction efforts have always been a prime motivator of behavior, but the impact of recent reductions in business travel has surprised even experts. Increases in costs of air travel, combined with increases in available information via the Internet, have resulted in a reduction in business travel and a shift toward cheaper flights. Both shifts have made resource planning more difficult for airlines.
>
> Behavior changes among business travelers have been dramatic. For many, during the rapid expansion of the economy in the late 1990s price didn't matter. As the economy softened, however, many businesses cut travel and sought out bargains for necessary business trips. This has an especially significant impact on full-fare seats. Business travelers, who account for about 50 percent of all airline trips, create about 65 percent of the revenue. United Airlines calculated that about 9 percent of its passengers accounted for about 46 percent of its revenues.
>
> By mid-2001, the price of a business-fare ticket was nearly five times that of the lowest discount fare. This gap had doubled in only five years. Airline pricing strategists had mistakenly concluded that business travelers would travel no matter what. Despite those expectations, the percentage of passengers paying full-fare coach prices fell from 12 percent to 7 percent from 2000 to 2001. The percentage purchasing first-class tickets fell from 3 percent to 2 percent. The loss of high-priced seats has taken a toll on airline profits. Airlines monitor a measure known as the "domestic unit revenue," which measures the revenue generated per available seat mile. That measure dropped nearly 12 percent from 2000 to 2001. It dropped another 12 percent in June 2001 and another 12 percent in July.
>
> The ease of identifying lowest fares and purchasing tickets on the Internet makes this trend unlikely to reverse itself. Even when the economy improves, businesses that have found how easy it is to save money are not likely to go back to their old ways of traveling. For airlines, this drop in revenues, combined with increasing labor and fuel costs, will make profitability less likely and planning for the future more difficult.
>
> Source: "Fed Up with Airlines, Business Travelers Start to Fight Back," *The Wall Street Journal,* August 28, 2001, pp. A1, A4.

decide if we have enough. If we don't, we must begin the acquisition process. We could plan further than seven months out, but, again, our knowledge of needs further into the future is not as accurate. And, once again, we don't *need* to know further ahead, at least not from a machine and storage capacity planning perspective.

We probably hope to reach a point in our business where we have been so successful that we've added labor and machine and storage tank capacity to the point that we can't fit any more into our facility. Our capacity planning process now must include a new facility or an addition to the old one. Suddenly, we encounter a much longer planning horizon. Suppose we have the land and it makes sense to expand the existing facility. We do the research and find that the lead time for adding a new facility and bringing it into production would be 18 months. We must now plan with a minimum horizon of 18 months, and we must determine capacity needs 18 months into the future. This would be a critical stage for many businesses for several reasons. First, it's going to be a huge investment. Expanding when it is not needed could financially kill the business because of the added burden. Failing to expand when it is needed could also kill the business. What makes it worse is that 18 months out is a very long planning horizon. It is very difficult to determine accurate needs that far into the future. This is particularly true with products and services that have short life cycles. The impact that product and service life cycles have on planning is significant and is discussed in depth in the following section.

The example illustrates that there is no single planning horizon for a business. A business must be involved in planning for many different resources, potentially utilizing different planning horizons for each. Remember how important it is to reduce lead times? The increased accuracy associated with planning for the near future, when compared to the accuracy of planning for the distant future, results in better plan outcomes. This usually results in higher net sales and lower costs, all resulting in improved net income and ROA. In short, it means that what the firm wants to happen has a greater likelihood of actually happening. And, of course, profitability reflects that success.

THE IMPACT OF PRODUCT AND SERVICE LIFE CYCLES

When forming plans related to any product or service, one must consider how long the product or service will even exist. We're all familiar with products that become quickly obsolete. We've purchased them, only to wish that we'd waited. Electronics technologies (computers, video, music, TVs, cameras) change rapidly. Fashion-driven products may last only one season. Most products and services, even those that don't become obsolete quickly, go through what is commonly known as a product or service **life cycle**. Yes, services become obsolete also, sometimes because they are associated with products that become obsolete. For example, in the past, repair services worked on TVs, stereo systems, and the like. Today, as the cost for those items has come down, these repair-related services have disappeared.

As technology changes the way some services are delivered, we can expect to see some services disappear. How long will the need for travel agencies persist, as the percentage of airline tickets and hotel reservations made on the Internet increases? More changes in the service sector are sure to come as a result of service obsolescence.

Power plants require long production lead times, making it necessary to forecast power demand far into the future to maintain sufficient capacity, but also making it very likely that those demand forecasts will be inaccurate. Construction on this $5.5 billion nuclear power plant in Kungliao, Taiwan, was halted when it was one-third completed as politicians debated whether or not it was needed. Construction was restarted after a six-month hold.

Many B2B services that currently link customers to suppliers will disappear as technology enables direct linkages to be more efficient and cheaper.

Some services have disappeared because a product replaced them. Several years ago, flea treatment businesses were quite common, particularly in the southern United States. Anyone with a dog or a cat fought fleas. The most difficult challenge was to get rid of fleas in the environment where the animal lived, including the house, the carpet, and the yard. These businesses disappeared virtually overnight as veterinary pharmaceutical companies, like Ciba-Geigy Corporation, developed pills that pets could take once a month to kill fleas. Suppose, for another example, a synthetic oil good for 60,000 miles was developed. What would happen to the oil-change business? What would hap-

> **Are Second Phone Lines on the Declining Side of Their Life Cycle?**
>
> Product life cycles are often determinants of product demand. As the product goes through the natural progression of the cycle, demand can decline dramatically. The cycles are useful to aid in forecasting, but they can be interrupted by sudden technological changes. For example, businesses operated from homes were expected to create an increasing demand for additional phone lines for voice, fax, and computer connections. Many homes were increasing from one to two lines throughout the 1990s. By 1999, some 29 percent of households had second phone lines. However, two increasingly popular technologies, broadband Internet connections and cell phones, are turning that increase around.
>
> Some residential and in-home business customers are eliminating additional phone lines because they use cell phones exclusively and have no need for a traditional telephone. An added benefit is that the cell phone eliminates long-distance charges. For the first time in decades, the number of residential phone lines is actually decreasing, and it is decreasing at an accelerating rate.
>
> One might think that this wouldn't impact the providers much, since the same company often provides all of the services. Second phone lines, however, are extremely profitable. High-speed cable and broadband services have not yet been profitable. Unfortunately for the service providers, they are forced to cannibalize their own second-line customers to prevent competitors from doing the same thing.
>
> Source: "More Callers Cut Off Second Phone Lines for Cellphones, Cable Modems," *The Wall Street Journal*, November 15, 2001, p. B1.

pen to gas stations if fuel cell technology in automobiles became cost efficient? A diagram of a typical product or service life cycle is presented in Exhibit 9.3.

Exhibit 9.3 shows five stages in the life cycle. The **introduction stage** is defined by the product or service becoming known in the marketplace. Demand tends to be low in the introduction stage. It is followed by the **growth stage**, which covers that period of increased demand that occurs as consumers become aware of the product or service. With most products and services, there is a third stage, known as the **maturation stage**, which occurs when the market knows about the product or service and demand begins to level off. At this stage, demand has been satisfied. By this time, through product or service standardization, costs are reduced so that prices can be reduced. The fourth stage is the **saturation stage**. During this stage, demand begins to fall because the market has been saturated and alternatives have begun to appear and take away demand. The final stage, **decline**, occurs when the product or service is replaced by alternatives.

One might conclude that from a planning and profitability perspective, a business would be much better off if life cycles were long. If there were no competition or very little competition, that might be a correct conclusion. However, in markets where competitors are always giving chase, businesses actually try to speed up the cycle. For the business that can be first to market with a new product or service, a competitor is sure to follow. The leader gets the advantage during the introduction stage, and some of the growth stage, before competition begins to take away market share. From the leader's perspective, the best strategy is to introduce a replacement and repeat the process again. Short life cycles can create a successful "barrier of entry" to competitors trying to copy and take away market share. Exhibit 9.4 shows how life cycles can appear when a firm intentionally shortens them by introducing replacements.

EXHIBIT 9.3 Product Life Cycle

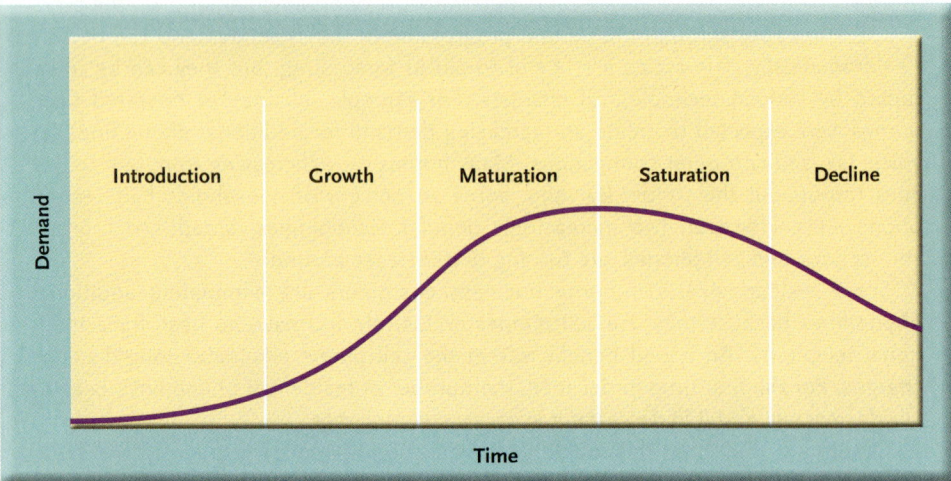

EXHIBIT 9.4 Product Life Cycles Interrupted by New-Product Introduction

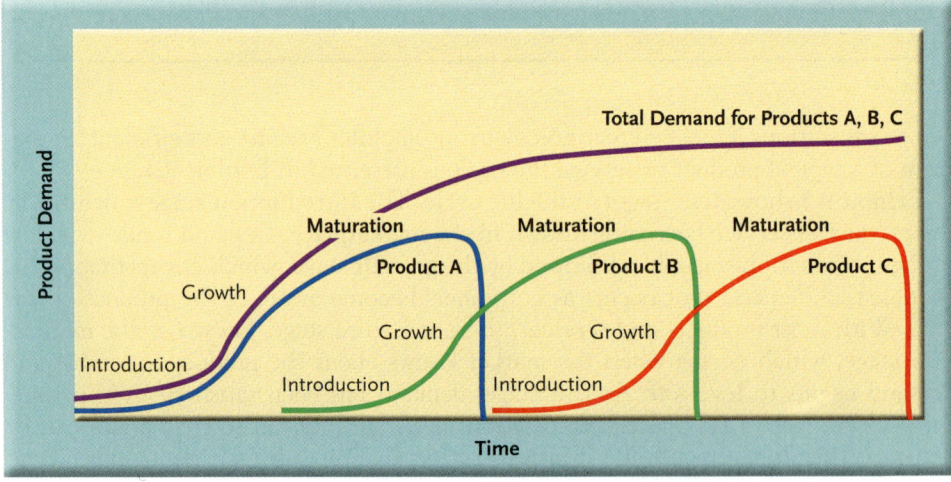

Obviously, from a consumer perspective, the services and products you are exposed to have very different life cycles. Most consumer services appear to have long life cycles, and most consumer products have very short ones. In general, both are becoming shorter. Services and products that are tightly linked to technology can be expected to have shorter and shorter life cycles. Some Internet-based services, for example, have already come and gone. Many disappeared because they never made a profit. From a life-cycle perspective, they never reached the growth stage. Some disappeared because others that were introduced hastened their decline stage.

The trend toward shorter product and service life cycles has had a substantial impact on the planning processes of businesses. Many businesses, particularly manufacturers, have found that they cannot maintain short product life cycles *and* sustain the resources required to produce them concurrently. The need to be flexible in environments of fast change is critical to the businesses' success. In addition, the high cost of production equipment requires substantial production volume to generate a sufficient financial return. Rather than investing in equipment that may be made obsolete by the short life cycle of products, many businesses outsource the production of those products. This strategy eliminates any conflict between paying for a piece of equipment and introducing a new product as a way to maintain market leadership.

A STRATEGY FOR MORE SUCCESSFUL PLANS: COMPRESSING LEAD TIMES

Certainly in an environment where the product life cycle may only be eight months long, a supplier that takes four months to bring a component into production cannot be tolerated. Likewise, no business can expect to be able to look 18 months into the future to predict demand so that a facility expansion can be started. Outsourcing plays an important role in making short-life-cycle environments tolerable, but effective planning is still necessary. For example, the minimum planning horizon for bringing a new product to market must include the lead time associated with getting a contract manufacturer with whom to outsource production. The shorter the lead time associated with making this arrangement, the quicker the product can be introduced to market. As a matter of fact, in virtually all business environments, whether the life cycle is short or long, compressing lead times leads to improved planning outcomes. Esource 9.1 provides an example of a business that profits from its ability to compress its customers' lead times.

www
OperationsNow
.com

Often lead times associated with acquiring resources are sufficiently long to require the business to forecast demand. When the response times promised to customers are shorter than the production lead time of the product or service, demand forecasts are also required. The accuracy of business plans will, in many ways, be dictated by the accuracy of forecasts. The following section provides an overview of forecast types, and presents several popular forecasting techniques.

DEMAND FORECASTING

Demand forecasting, like any type of forecasting, can be frustrating. Predicting the future is a stretch in any situation. Surprisingly, forecasting actually has its roots in heredity research done by Francis Galton in the late 1800s. Galton was a first cousin of Charles Darwin and for his entire 89 years (except for a brief period in the 1840s) he completely avoided traditional "work." He was the first to recognize the tendency of all systems to return to normalcy, now known as "regression to the mean," which later led to the concept of correlation. The concept of regression to the mean is critical to forecasting, because forecasts do exactly that: They examine what has happened, and from that, determine what is "normal." This seems logical, but three reasons make it difficult to determine this "return to normalcy." First, the return to normalcy can take place at an incredibly slow rate, making it difficult to know when, or if, it happens. Second, sometimes the return is so strong, it doesn't stop, but goes past "normal." And third, what is normal today may not be normal tomorrow.[1] The result is that even though systems seek out the normal state, it is difficult to know when it will happen, if it has ever happened, or if it will ever happen. We never really know if the demand we predicted was normal or not. This brings us to a universal truth about forecasting—forecasts are wrong. Despite the difficulty in forecasting demand, the demand for forecasting tools, in the form of computer software, is large. Esource 9.2 links to a provider of forecasting software that has been quite successful at meeting the needs of business planners.

www
OperationsNow
.com

Surveys are a very popular qualitative forecasting technique. Collecting opinions from customers in a shopping mall, for example, provides a focus on potential customers for a future store. Collecting data directly from shoppers, rather than using mail or phone surveys, yields data that truly represents opinions of future customers. The costs of gathering the data, however, are quite high when compared to other methods.

Planning for many resources, particularly those tied to capacity and inventory, depends heavily on demand forecasts. Increased emphasis on holding small supplies of inventory has increased the need for quick, frequent delivery of products. Maintaining minimum levels of raw materials and finished goods dictates that replenishment orders be placed promptly and accurately to provide an acceptable level of service. Such orders often depend on a demand forecast. Forecasting research, which has been a popular subject for academics for decades, makes it clear that different types of demand require different types of forecast. Some of the most common techniques are examined in this chapter. The importance of timely delivery and the desire to reduce inventory levels have motivated many businesses to reduce lead times, thereby reducing the planning horizon, which can enhance forecast accuracy more than increased sophistication of mathematical forecasting models.

Demand forecast methods can be categorized in two very general groups: qualitative and quantitative. **Qualitative forecasts**, such as expert opinion and customer surveys, are developed from nonquantitative information. Qualitative forecasts are used most often when no quantitative data exist. Such a situation might occur during the planning stages of a new product that has no usable history. **Quantitative forecasts** use mathematical models and are the most frequently used forecasts for demand forecasting. As a general rule, if quantitative data are available to use, a quantitative forecast will be the most accurate.

Quantitative forecasting techniques are generally divided into two groups, causal techniques and time series techniques. **Causal forecasting** techniques utilize extrinsic data as a predictor of demand. **Time series forecasting** techniques utilize only past demand data as a predictor of the future.

CAUSAL FORECASTING

Causal models that are used to forecast demand are generally based on regression analysis. The use of simple linear regression as a causal forecasting technique is best understood through the use of an example (see Example 9.1).

Causal forecasting methods provide an opportunity for managers to use external data for forecasting. This understanding of the relationship between demand and some form of external data creates a situation where management may be able to intervene and affect demand. Forecasters must be cautious, however, when developing causal forecasting models. The appearance of a relationship between demand and an external variable may be due to coincidence, rather than a true correlation.

TIME SERIES FORECASTING

A time series is simply a series of demand values from the past. Two years of weekly demands for a particular product would be a time series. Five days of hourly demand data for a bank's drive-up window would also be considered to be a time series. Use

Example 9.1

Causal Forecasting with Simple Linear Regression

A local distributor supplies beer for baseball games. Past experience has shown that beer sales are dependent on the number of attendees and on the weather. Since most games are sold out, the number of attendees doesn't help much in predicting sales. The hotter the day, though, the more beer sold. The sales data and a scatter diagram showing the relationship between beer sales and predicted daily high temperature are presented in Exhibit 9.5. Predicted daily high temperature is used rather than actual daily high temperature because *before the fact* the predicted high is the only temperature data available, and regression analysis can be used to describe the relationship between demand and the predicted, not the actual, high.

EXHIBIT 9.5 Data and Scatter Diagram Showing Relationship Between Beer Sales and High Temperature for Example 9.1

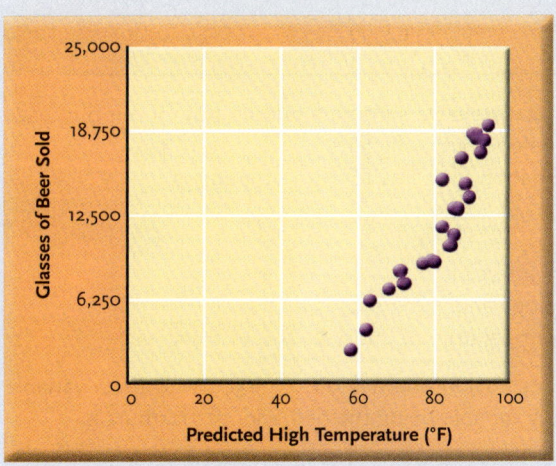

Predicted High Temperature	Beer Sales	Predicted High Temperature	Beer Sales
62	4,000	63	6,150
85	13,000	88	14,800
80	9,000	90	18,500
58	2,500	92	17,100
68	7,000	86	13,000
72	7,400	89	13,800
82	11,600	94	19,100
86	12,900	91	18,450
93	18,000	87	16,700
91	18,200	82	15,100
79	9,100	71	8,350
84	10,200	77	8,900
		85	11,000

(continues)

Example 9.1 (continued)

A model of the relationship between temperature and sales that will make it possible to predict the demand for beer, given a daily high temperature, is found by a regression analysis, which provides the formula for the line that best fits through the data points in Exhibit 9.5. The result of the regression analysis of the data from Exhibit 9.5 is provided in the partial Excel Regression Summary Output in Exhibit 9.6. Beer consumption for an 80-degree day is then computed.

EXHIBIT 9.6 Partial Excel Regression Analysis Output for Beer Sales for Example 9.1

Summary Output

	Coefficients
Y Intercept	−23,535
X Variable 1	438.4397

Excel provides an extensive summary output, but for our purposes, the Y intercept and X coefficient (slope) are sufficient.

The general equation for a line for this situation is

$$Y = a + bx \tag{9.1}$$

where
- a = Y intercept
- b = slope and
- x = temperature of interest

Using Excel's regression analysis on the data, with the x variable being the temperatures and the y variable being the demand, the formula is

$$Y = -23{,}535 + 438.4397x \tag{9.2}$$

For an 80-degree day, the demand forecast would be

$$Y = -23{,}535 + 438.4397(80) \tag{9.3}$$
$$= 11{,}540.2$$

Excel Tutor 9.1 shows how a spreadsheet can be used to aid in solving this problem.

www.OperationsNow.com

of any time series as the basis for demand forecasting requires an understanding of the components of the time series.

Components of a Time Series

There are four potential components of time series. One of the four, known as a **cycle**, is usually of marginal importance in demand forecasting. A cycle is a pattern of demand that repeats over a long period of time, such as a 20-year business cycle. These cyclical patterns clearly exist, but when forecasting demand for a product, a 20-year demand history is rarely available to work with, and if it were available, it would probably not be relevant. Given the reduction in product and service life cycles, in many cases even a one-year time series is hard to come by. Three remaining components of a time series are quite important, however, and consist of trend, seasonality, and random fluctuation.

A **trend** occurs when demand tends to be increasing or decreasing over time. During the growth stage of the life cycle, products and services have an upward trend. A downward trend would be indicative of the decline stage of the life cycle. Trends can also result from other factors independent of the product life cycle. Exhibit 9.7 is a graph of a time series with a trend.

Seasonality occurs when a pattern in the time series repeats itself at least once per year. When demand for a product is linked to holidays or seasons of the year, it is seasonality. Seasonality doesn't necessarily have to be based on an annual cycle, however. Banks often see increases for their services on Friday afternoons. Their demand pattern would repeat on a weekly cycle, but would also be considered to be seasonality. Exhibit 9.8 presents a time series with a seasonal pattern.

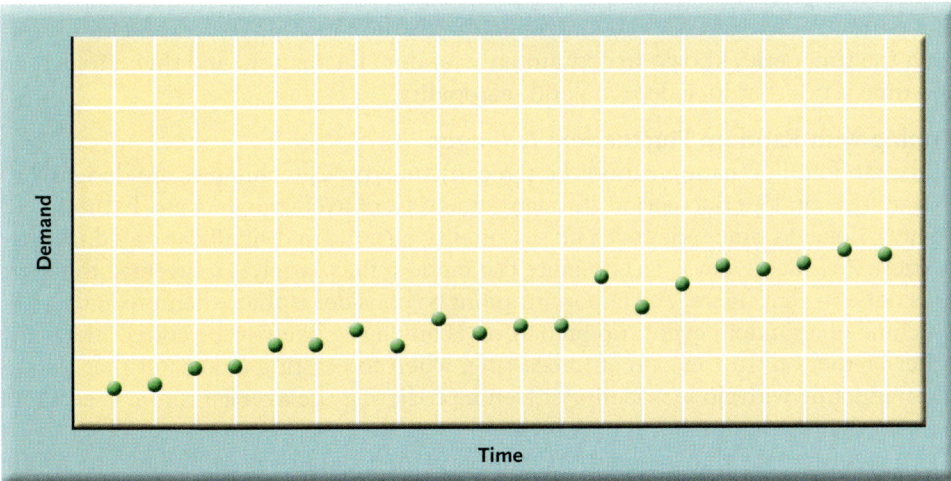

EXHIBIT 9.7 Example of a Time Series with Trend

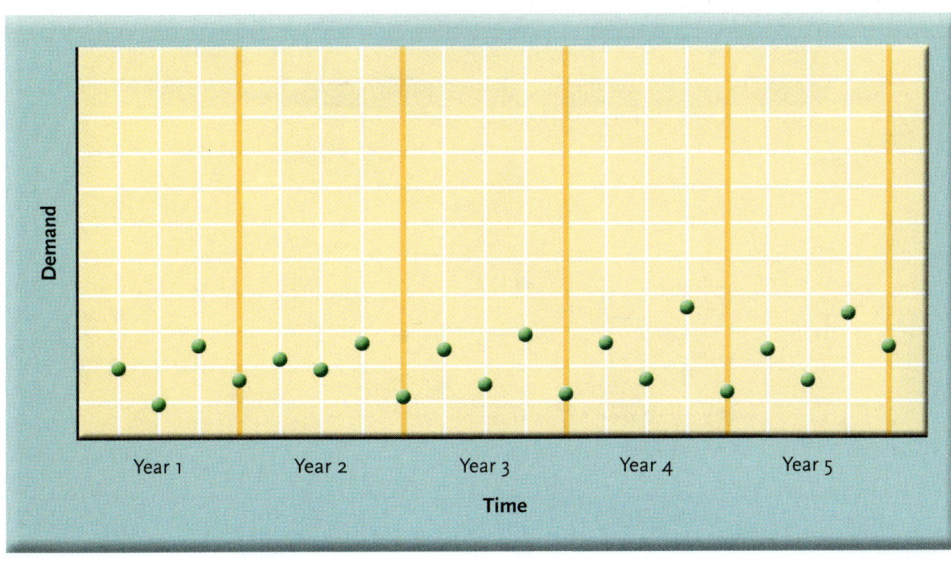

EXHIBIT 9.8 Example of a Time Series with Seasonality

Random fluctuation is the change in demand that does not result from cycle, trend, or seasonality. If the demand pattern does have an actual cause, we won't know it from looking at the data. Random fluctuation is present in virtually all time series, along with the other components. In some cases, random fluctuation can be significant enough to make it difficult to see trend or seasonality. Of the components of trend, seasonality, and random fluctuation, random fluctuation is the only one that cannot, by definition, be forecast. "Random" means that any outcome is equally likely. The outcome cannot be predicted. Exhibit 9.9 shows a time series that contains only random fluctuation. The more predominant the random fluctuation, and the less predominant trend and seasonality, the less useful the time series is for forecasting.

Interactive Model 9.1 provides an experimental environment for examining the impact of various amounts of seasonality, trend, and randomness in a time series.

Time Series Techniques

Time series forecasting techniques are designed to take advantage of the components of a particular demand. To present the most common techniques, it is useful to start with the time series known to contain only random fluctuation, and then progress to the time series that include trend and seasonality.

Coping with Random Fluctuation: Averages

Since random fluctuation cannot be forecast, time series techniques are designed to extract the random fluctuation through some type of averaging process. Exhibit 9.10 shows a demand time series with no seasonality or trend and significant random fluctuation. An effective way to eliminate the random fluctuation is to average the data, as is done in that figure. An important point to consider is that when predicting the outcome of a random event, no prediction is any more likely to be correct than any other prediction. In the case of forecasting, when forecasting a demand that fluctuates randomly with no seasonality or trend, predicting the average is just as accurate as any other prediction.

Despite the fact that random fluctuation cannot be predicted, the extent of the variability of that fluctuation, or the stability of the fluctuation, can be useful in making a prediction. When demand fluctuates randomly, it can fluctuate widely or nar-

EXHIBIT 9.9   **Example of a Time Series with Random Fluctuation**

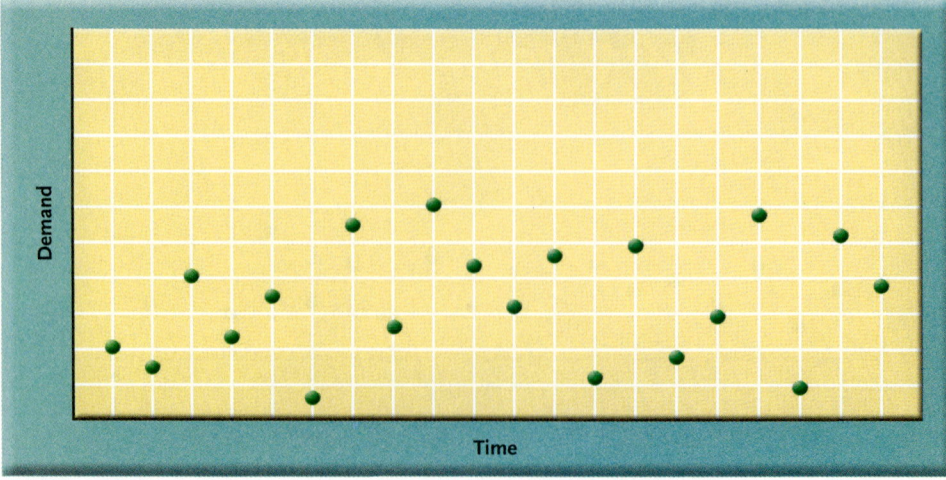

Demand with Random Fluctuation EXHIBIT 9.10

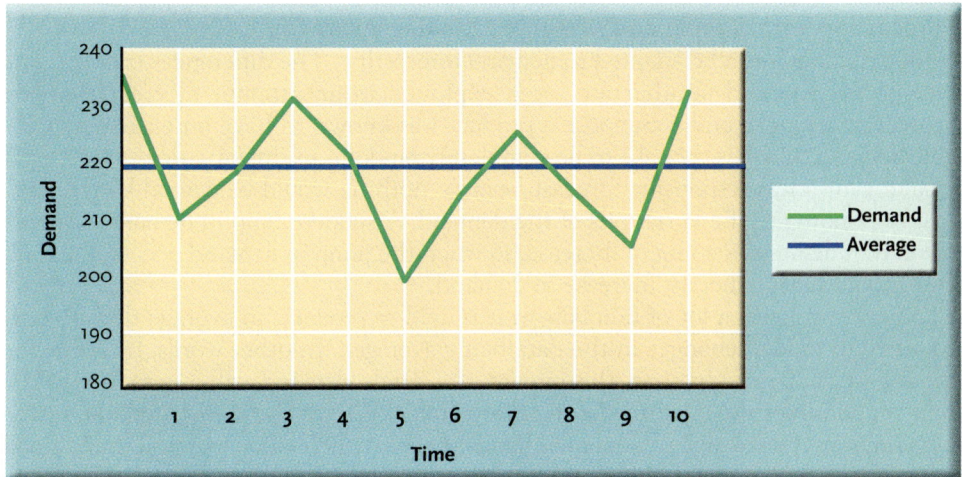

rowly. Exhibit 9.11 presents graphs of two different time series, both with the same average but with different amounts of variability. For forecasters of random demand, that variability is important. Even though randomness is present in demand, a substantial demand change might signify an actual demand shift, or it might just be random movement. When this occurs, the forecaster needs to know whether to utilize that information in forecasting or ignore it. The more variability and unpredictability in the demand, the less the forecaster is able to utilize changes in demand in forecasting the future.

Forecasts should be unresponsive to changes in demand when changes in demand are not indicative of anything in the future. If the changes do not provide valuable information, they should not affect forecasts. When demands are known to be relatively stable and a shift in demand is indicative of a true change, the forecaster wants

Variability of Time Series EXHIBIT 9.11

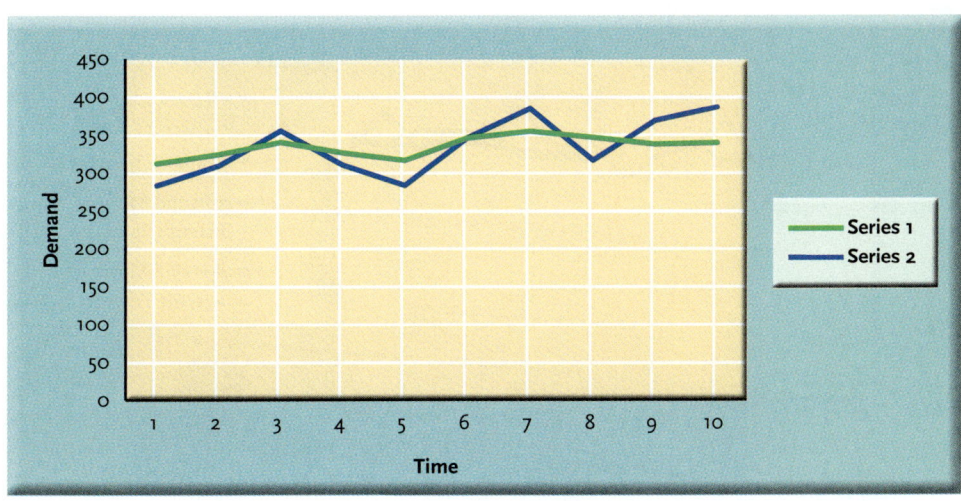

to be responsive to those changes. The degree to which a forecasting technique responds to demand changes is a factor in the design and selection of the forecasting approach.

Forecasting with Simple and Weighted Moving Averages

Various averages can be adapted to demand forecasting. The differences between one type of average and another are often exploited in an attempt to create varying degrees of responsiveness. Suppose a product was known to have an extremely variable demand that was thought to be completely random. In this situation, a forecaster would want a less responsive forecast because nothing would be gained by the forecast responding to the variations of the demand. A sudden jump in demand does not mean that demand is going to increase, so when the jump in demand occurs, the forecast should not predict an increase in demand.

An average with a lot of numbers in it is used to produce an average that is unresponsive to sudden changes in the data being averaged. In other words, by averaging more past demands together, the impact of a single demand value is reduced. The number of values included in the average is referred to as the n. An average with a larger n is less responsive to demand changes because each value averaged has a small impact on the average. On the other hand, when a small n is used, a change in one value can have a significant impact on the average. Let's look at an example. A possible technique when we do not want a responsive forecast might be an eight-period moving average. In that technique, the forecast for the upcoming period would be an average of the previous eight periods. If we wanted a responsive forecast, the forecaster would create a more responsive technique by averaging fewer periods to get the forecast. A three-period moving average might be used. That forecast would simply be the average of the previous three periods.

Exhibit 9.12 shows an eight-period moving average forecast and a three-period moving average forecast compared to the actual demand that followed each forecast. Notice how much more responsive to demand shifts the three-period moving average is. For example, following the high point in demand at period 11, the three-period average forecast responds by forecasting a demand for period 12 that is substantially higher than the forecast made for period 11. It has "responded" to the demand spike in period 11. The eight-period moving average forecast, however, does not respond as much to the

EXHIBIT 9.12   **Three-Period and Eight-Period Moving Average Forecasts**

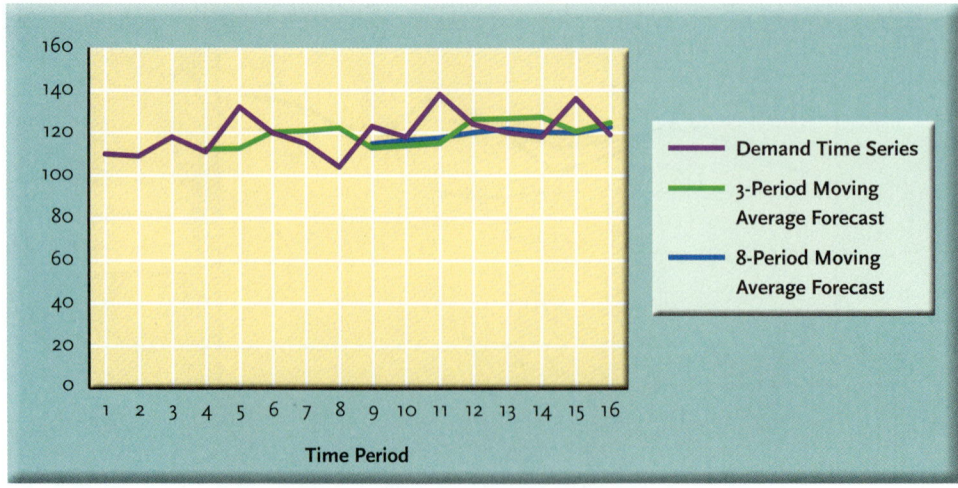

spike in period 11. Its forecast for period 12 is only slightly higher than the forecast for period 11. Also notice in Exhibit 9.12 that the line for the eight-period average is much smoother overall and fluctuates less than the three-period average.

Another approach to manipulating the responsiveness of an average is to use moving weighted averages. By assigning weights, whose sum must be 1.0, to be multiplied by the data points, the responsiveness can be manipulated, even though the same number of data points is used. Example 9.2 demonstrates this approach.

The forecast created in Example 9.2 gives much more weight to the recent demand of 146 and less to the smaller demands of the earlier periods. Weighted averages can be composed of any number of periods, and any weights, as long as the sum of the weights is equal to 1.

Simple Exponential Smoothing: A Sophisticated Weighted Moving Average

Exponential smoothing provides an alternative approach to moving weighted averages that is more easily adapted and requires storing only two data points. **Simple exponential smoothing** utilizes a constant called alpha (α) to provide the weights as designated by the user. The formula for simple exponential smoothing is

$$F_{t+1} = \alpha(A_t) + (1 - \alpha)F_t \tag{9.4}$$

Example 9.2

Calculating a Forecast with Moving Weighted Averages

Use a weighted average and the past four weeks' demand to predict the next week's demand. Demands for the past four weeks are:

Period	1	2	3	4
Demand	133	130	134	146

Solution

The forecast for period 5 could be computed using any of a number of different weighted averages. A simple average of the four demands would provide a forecast of 135.75. A weighted average, creating a more responsive forecast, might utilize weights of 0.5, 0.3, 0.1, and 0.1, as shown in Exhibit 9.13.

EXHIBIT 9.13 Solution to Example 9.2

Period	Demand	Weight	Forecast
1	133	0.1	13.3
2	130	0.1	13
3	134	0.3	40.2
4	146	0.5	73
5			139.5

The weighted average forecast of 139.5 for period 5 provides an example of how a more responsive forecast reacts to the demand increase in period 4. Excel Tutor 9.2 shows how moving weighted average forecasts can easily be completed in spreadsheets.

www
OperationsNow
.com

where F_{t+1} = forecast for the next time period
 α = smoothing constant, which must be greater than 0 and less than 1
 A_t = actual demand for the most recent period
 F_t = forecast for the most recent period

Some people find it easier to remember an equivalent formula:

$$F_{t+1} = F_t + \alpha(A_t - F_t) \qquad (9.5)$$

The logic is best understood by examining Equation 9.4. The smoothing constant, α, determines the relative weight assigned to the most recent demand. If $\alpha = 0.3$, for example, $1 - \alpha = 0.7$. A weighted average of the most recent demand and most recent forecast is created. Keep in mind that the most recent forecast, given the 0.7 weight, consists of the weighted average of the previous demand and previous forecast. In essence, this creates a weighted average giving the most recent demand a weight of 0.3 and spreading the remaining weight of 0.7 over all previous demands.

Examining the extremes offers further insight. If $\alpha = 1$, the forecast is equal to the most recent demand. This is also known as a naïve forecast. If $\alpha = 0$, the forecast is equal to the last period's forecast, giving no weight to the most recent demand. The value for α is typically between 0.1 and 0.5. The higher α makes the forecast more responsive to demand changes, just as a higher weight in the most recent period of a weighted average would make the forecast more responsive. The responsiveness with varying degrees of α is demonstrated in Exhibit 9.14, where forecasts with α values of 0.1 and 0.4 are shown against a shifting demand. The responsiveness of the higher α value is evident. Notice how the 0.4 alpha forecast immediately responds to the demand spikes at periods 13 and 20. Also note how the 0.4 alpha chases the rising demand at periods 23–25. Interactive Model 9.2 provides an opportunity to experiment with simple exponential smoothing as well as other forecasting techniques. Example 9.3 demonstrates the use of simple exponential smoothing.

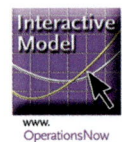

Adding Trend to the Exponential Smoothing Model

Although some time series have random fluctuation without any other evident time series components, many have random fluctuation as well as trend. An averaging

EXHIBIT 9.14 Comparison of 0.1 and 0.4 Alpha Values for Simple Exponential Smoothing

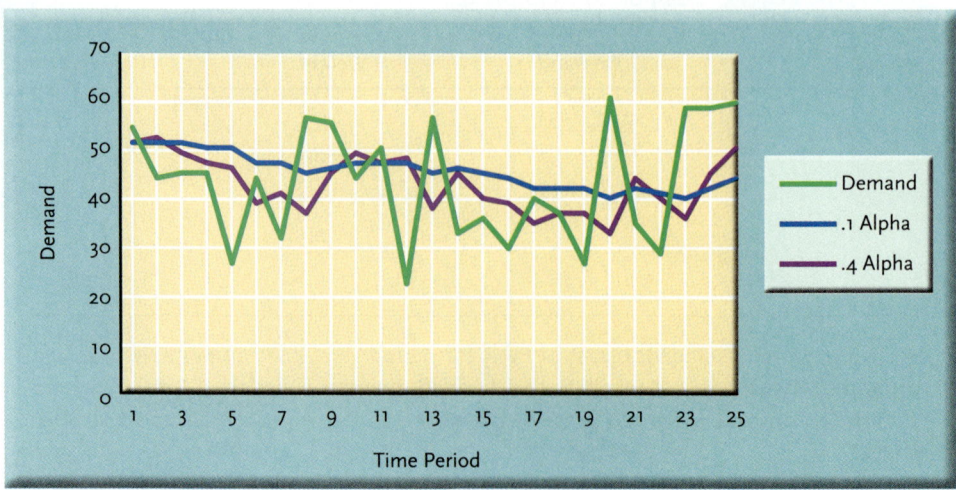

> **Example 9.3**
>
> ### Calculating a Forecast with Simple Exponential Smoothing
>
> A retailer recorded the following monthly demands for a particular CD player/changer.
>
> | Month | January | February | March | April | May | June |
> |--------|---------|----------|-------|-------|-----|------|
> | Demand | 100 | 110 | 115 | 104 | 112 | 117 |
>
> Forecast the demand for July using simple exponential smoothing with $\alpha = 0.3$ and an initial forecast of 90.
>
> **Solution**
>
> Using the equation for simple exponential smoothing,
>
> $$F_{t+1} = F_t + \alpha(A_t - F_t)$$
> $$F_2 = F_1 + \alpha(A_1 - F_1)$$
> $$= 90 + 0.3(100 - 90)$$
> $$= 93$$
>
> The process is continued in Exhibit 9.15, until the forecast for July (period 7) is determined.
>
> **EXHIBIT 9.15 Solution for Example 9.3**
>
> | Month | Period (t) | Demand (A_t) | Forecast (F_t) |
> |----------|------------|----------------|------------------|
> | January | 1 | 100 | 90.00 |
> | February | 2 | 110 | 93.00 |
> | March | 3 | 115 | 98.10 |
> | April | 4 | 104 | 103.17 |
> | May | 5 | 112 | 103.42 |
> | June | 6 | 117 | 105.99 |
> | July | | | 109.30 |
>
> Excel Tutor 9.3 demonstrates how to use spreadsheets to forecast with simple exponential smoothing.

www
OperationsNow
.com

technique, or simple exponential smoothing, should not be used for a time series containing a trend because each method ignores valuable information, resulting in a forecast that always lags behind. A modification to the exponential smoothing model, known as **trend-adjusted exponential smoothing** or **forecast including trend (FIT),** includes the trend in the forecast. In trend-adjusted exponential smoothing, a second constant, β, is used to include the trend component. The trend-adjusted exponential smoothing model separates the random fluctuation and trend components into two distinct parts. The formula for this model is

$$FIT_{t+1} = F_t + T_t \tag{9.6}$$

where F_t is the smoothed forecast, T_t is the trend estimate, and

$$F_t = FIT_{t+1} + \alpha(A_t - FIT_t) \tag{9.7}$$

$$T_t = T_{t-1} + \beta(\text{FIT}_t - \text{FIT}_{t-1} - T_{t-1}) \quad (9.8)$$

where α and β are smoothing constants. Notice that the trend component (T_t) of the trend-adjusted model is added to the smoothed forecast (F_t), and the smoothed forecast is calculated in the same way as in simple exponential smoothing. Example 9.4 demonstrates how this approach is used.

A time series with a trend component is also an appropriate application for use with a linear trend equation. By using the time period as the independent variable and demand as the dependent variable, the trend can quite easily be defined by the equation of the best-fitting line.

The linear trend equation is useful for predicting the impact the trend will have on demand—one application of simple linear regression.

Including Seasonality in the Demand Forecast

Seasonality is a common component in time series, and forecasters must address it as an element of information in predicting future demands. Seasonal indexes are used to

---

Example 9.4

Calculating a Forecast Using Trend-Adjusted Exponential Smoothing (FIT)

Suppose a 10-week time series for laptop demand at university bookstore was collected.

Week (t)	1	2	3	4	5	6	7	8	9	10
Demand (A)	25	29	30	34	39	38	41	42	46	48

Using $\alpha = 0.2$, $\beta = 0.9$, an initial trend (T_1) of 3, and an initial forecast (FIT_1) of 25, calculate the demand for period 11 using trend-adjusted exponential smoothing.

Solution

FIT_2 can be computed as follows:

$$\text{FIT}_2 = F_1 + T_1$$
$$= 25.00 + 3.00$$
$$= 28.00$$

FIT_3 is calculated as follows:

$$F_2 = \text{FIT}_2 + \alpha(A_2 - \text{FIT}_2)$$
$$= 28.00 + 0.2(29.00 - 28.00)$$
$$= 28.20$$

$$T_2 = T_1 + \beta(\text{FIT}_2 - \text{FIT}_1 - T_1)$$
$$= 3.00 + 0.9(28.00 - 25.00 - 3.00)$$
$$= 3.00$$

Therefore, to calculate FIT_3,

$$\text{FIT}_3 = F_2 + T_2$$
$$= 28.20 + 3.00$$
$$= 31.20$$

The process is continued for FIT_4 through FIT_{11} in Exhibit 9.16.

(continues)

Example 9.4 (continued)

EXHIBIT 9.16 Trend-Adjusted Forecast for Example 9.4

Week (t)	Demand (A_t)	F_t	T_t	FIT_t
1	25	25.00	3.00	25.00
2	29	28.20	3.00	28.00
3	30	30.96	3.18	31.20
4	34	34.11	2.96	34.14
5	39	37.46	2.94	37.08
6	38	39.92	3.29	40.40
7	41	42.76	2.85	43.20
8	42	44.89	3.46	45.62
9	46	47.08	1.81	47.35
10	48	48.71	1.56	48.89
11	?			50.27

A spreadsheet approach to using trend-adjusted exponential smoothing is provided in Excel Tutor 9.4.

model the seasonal pattern in a time series. If the time series consists of monthly data, each month will have a seasonal index. If the time series consists of hourly data, each hour will have a seasonal index. The seasonality is described by using the ratio of the actual demand for a period to the average demand across all periods for a given time horizon. Seasonal indexes are often calculated by averaging the ratios of demand for the specific time periods to the average demand to eliminate the possible impact of random fluctuations. This is another example of using averages as a way to eliminate random fluctuation. The resulting seasonal index provides a multiplicative relationship between actual demand for the period of interest and the average demand. Since random fluctuation has been eliminated through averaging, the variability remaining is assumed to be the result of the seasonal impact. A seasonal index of 1.8, for example, would mean that the demand for that period is, on the average, 1.8 times the average demand.

Seasonal indexes are used to generate a forecast for a particular period by multiplying the seasonal index by the average demand per period. The calculation of seasonal indexes and their use in forecasting are demonstrated in Example 9.5.

Dealing with Seasonality and Trend in a Time Series

There are many ways to forecast when seasonal and trend components are present in the time series. For example, we could combine the trend-adjusted exponential smoothing method with the seasonal indexes approach just used. Another common approach is to use a multiplicative model that combines the linear regression approach to forecasting trend with the seasonal indexes used to forecast seasonality. This approach utilizes the following steps:

1. Compute seasonal indexes for each period.
2. Remove the seasonal component from the time series (deseasonalize the data).

Example 9.5 — Calculating a Forecast Using Seasonal Indexes

The owner of a local tanning salon was interested in using seasonal indexes in forecasting daily walk-in demand to help plan for staffing needs for spring. The daily demand for the past four weeks is presented in Exhibit 9.17, as are the calculations for the seasonal indexes.

EXHIBIT 9.17 Calculation of Seasonal Indexes for Example 9.5

Day	Week 1 Walk-Ins	Week 2 Walk-Ins	Week 3 Walk-Ins	Week 4 Walk-Ins	Daily Average	Seasonal Index
Monday	5	7	3	4	4.75	0.34
Tuesday	6	9	6	7	7.00	0.51
Wednesday	12	10	9	13	11.00	0.80
Thursday	15	17	13	19	16.00	1.16
Friday	27	24	30	28	27.25	1.97
Saturday	15	20	16	17	17.00	1.23

Overall average demand: (332/24 = 13.83)

The salon owner has collected weekly demand data for several years and based on these data expects the daily average to go up to 20. The data show clear evidence of a seasonal pattern. Walk-in demand increases through each week, peaking on Fridays. What would the expected number of walk-ins be for each day?

Solution

The average daily demand is 13.83 walk-ins (332/24). The seasonal indexes for each day are created by computing an average demand for each day, and then dividing that average by the seasonal index. For Monday, for example, demands were 5, 7, 3, and 4 walk-ins, for an average of 4.75. Dividing 4.75 by the overall daily average of 13.83 provides a Monday seasonal index of .34. Thus, on the average, Monday walk-in demand was 0.32, or 32 percent of the average daily walk-in demand.

The remaining calculations are presented in Exhibit 9.18.

EXHIBIT 9.18 Calculation of Daily Walk-In Forecasts for Example 9.5

Day	Seasonal Index	Average Daily Demand	Daily Forecast
Monday	0.3434	20	6.87
Tuesday	0.5060	20	10.12
Wednesday	0.7952	20	15.91
Thursday	1.1566	20	23.14
Friday	1.9699	20	39.41
Saturday	1.2289	20	24.58

www.OperationsNow.com

Excel Tutor 9.5 shows how to use spreadsheets for determining seasonal indexes.

3. Model the trend component by using least squares regression on the deseasonalized data.
4. Determine the forecast by using the trend equation and seasonal indexes.

These steps are demonstrated in Example 9.6.

Example 9.6
Forecasting with a Multiplicative Model for Seasonality and Trend

Exhibit 9.19 provides four years of quarterly demand data for a large tax service. Using the multiplicative model for trend and seasonality, forecast the demand for period 17 (Q1 of the next year).

Solution

Included in Exhibit 9.19 are the calculations for seasonal indexes and the deseasonalized demand.

EXHIBIT 9.19 Combining Seasonality and Trend for Example 9.6

Season		Period (t)	Demand (A_t)	Demand/ Average Demand		Seasonal Index	Deseasonalized Demand
Yr1	Q1	1	482	1.61	Average	1.67	288.91
	Q2	2	213	0.71		0.77	278.13
	Q3	3	116	0.39		0.42	279.52
	Q4	4	335	1.12		1.15	291.09
Yr2	Q1	5	499	1.66		1.67	299.1
	Q2	6	225	0.75		0.77	293.8
	Q3	7	122	0.41		0.42	293.98
	Q4	8	344	1.15		1.15	298.91
Yr3	Q1	9	503	1.68		1.67	301.5
	Q2	10	237	0.79		0.77	309.47
	Q3	11	127	0.42		0.42	306.02
	Q4	12	349	1.16		1.15	303.26
Yr4	Q1	13	518	1.73		1.67	310.49
	Q2	14	244	0.81		0.77	318.61
	Q3	15	133	0.44		0.42	320.48
	Q4	16	353	1.18		1.15	306.73

Average Demand = 300

The regression analysis determines the best-fitting line through the deseasonalized demand. The general equation for that line is

$$Y = a + bt \tag{9.9}$$

where
Y = a point on the trend line
a = y intercept
b = slope
t = time period

(continues)

Example 9.6 (continued)

Using Excel's regression tool on the deseasonalized demand, with the time periods as the *x* variable, the *Y* intercept is calculated at 280.48 and the slope is 2.30. Given these factors, the equation for the line defining the trend of this demand data is

$$Y = a + bt$$
$$= 280.48 + 2.30t$$

The forecast is calculated by substituting the time period for *t* and multiplying the result by the appropriate seasonal index. If, for example, we needed a forecast for the first quarter of the next year (year 5), the following calculations would be made:

$$\text{Forecast} = [280.48 + 2.30(17)] \times 1.67$$
$$= 319.58 \times 1.67$$
$$= 533.70$$

The multiplicative model for forecasting with trend and seasonality is demonstrated in a spreadsheet environment in Excel Tutor 9.6.

www.OperationsNow.com

FORECAST ACCURACY

Virtually all forecasts will be wrong because all time series contain random fluctuation, and random fluctuation can't be forecast. However, the fact that plans are often based on forecasts motivates a business to forecast as accurately as possible. While one of the best ways to improve forecast accuracy is to reduce the time horizon, it is also important to match the technique being used to the characteristics of the particular time series used in the forecast. This is often accomplished by comparing the results of several forecasting approaches to see which one is most accurate.

Forecast accuracy can be measured in a number of ways, but the most frequently used approaches acknowledge that there are two separate types of forecast error. The first type of error, known as **absolute error**, is concerned with how far from the actual demand, on an absolute basis, the forecast tends to be. In other words, are we generally off by a few units or many units? The second type of error, known as **forecast bias**, is concerned with the general direction of error. Do we consistently forecast too high or too low? Or do we forecast high as often as low? Any examination of forecast accuracy will include a look at both types of error. The following discussion examines ways of measuring these two types of error.

Measuring Absolute Error

The measurement of the absolute error of a forecast can be obtained in several ways. The most popular measure of absolute error is the **mean absolute deviation (MAD)**, which is simply the average of the absolute values of the errors for each time period. The formula for computing the MAD is

$$\text{MAD} = \sum_{t=1}^{n} \frac{|A_t - F_t|}{n} \qquad (9.10)$$

In using Equation 9.10, the first step in computing the MAD is to calculate the error for past forecasts. Error is equal to the actual demand (A_t) minus the forecast demand (F_t). The second step is to take the absolute value of each error. Step three is to compute the mean of the absolute values. Example 9.7 demonstrates the MAD calculation.

Another commonly used measure of absolute forecast error is the *mean squared error* (MSE). Instead of computing the absolute value of the errors and averaging them, as in the MAD calculation, the errors are squared and then averaged:

$$\text{MSE} = \sum_{t=1}^{n} \frac{(A_t - F_t)^2}{n - 1} \qquad (9.11)$$

The calculation of the MSE is demonstrated in Example 9.8.

Example 9.7 Calculating Mean Absolute Deviation

A small retailer has kept weekly demand and forecast data for a particular set of skateboard wheels. Compute the MAD for the forecast.

Solution

Exhibit 9.20 lists the demand, forecast, and errors by subtracting the forecast from the demand. Absolute values of the errors are determined and then averaged. The resulting MAD is the average of the absolute values of the errors for the forecasting approach used.

EXHIBIT 9.20 MAD Calculation for Example 9.7

Period (t)	Demand (A_t)	Forecast (F_t)	Error ($A_t - F_t$)	Absolute Value of Error $\|A_t - F_t\|$
1	120	125	−5	5
2	134	131	3	3
3	138	133	5	5
4	125	134	−9	9
5	143	138	5	5
6	126	129	−3	3
7	136	132	4	4
8	140	132	5	8
				MAD = 5.25

A new forecast would be created for the next week. As soon as the actual demand occurs, error can be calculated. The absolute value of the new error term is then incorporated into a new MAD calculation for the week. The MAD is updated as each new forecast and demand occurs.

After eight periods, the MAD for the forecast is 5.25. This means that the average absolute error was 5.25. Given demands significantly above 100, this would be viewed as an accurate forecast.

Excel Tutor 9.7 shows how the MAD is calculated using a spreadsheet.

www
OperationsNow
.com

> **Example 9.8**
>
> **Calculating Mean Squared Error**
>
> Using the data from Example 9.7, calculate the MSE.
>
> **Solution**
>
> Exhibit 9.21 shows the calculation of the MSE for the data used in Example 9.6.
>
> **EXHIBIT 9.21** MSE Calculation for Example 9.8
>
> | Period | Demand | Forecast | Error | Error^2 |
> |--------|--------|----------|-------|-----------|
> | 1 | 120 | 125 | −5 | 25 |
> | 2 | 134 | 131 | 3 | 9 |
> | 3 | 138 | 133 | 5 | 25 |
> | 4 | 125 | 134 | −9 | 81 |
> | 5 | 143 | 138 | 5 | 25 |
> | 6 | 126 | 129 | −3 | 9 |
> | 7 | 136 | 132 | 4 | 16 |
> | 8 | 140 | 132 | 8 | 64 |
>
> MSE = 36.28571
>
>
> www.OperationsNow.com
>
> The MSE is calculated in a spreadsheet in Excel Tutor 9.8.

The objective for both MAD and MSE measures is a small number. The closer to zero, the better, but the size of the MAD or MSE is a function of the size of the demand. A MAD of 5, for example, if the demand is in the hundreds, is very good. However, a MAD of 5 would not be good if the demand is typically under 30.

Measuring Forecast Bias

Forecast bias is the tendency of a forecast to be too high or too low. A forecast should be unbiased. In other words, the forecast error should be neutral. It should forecast too high as often as it forecasts too low. Errors sum to zero in an unbiased forecast. Presence of bias in a forecast is an indication of a problem with the forecasting model being used or an indication that someone is intentionally trying to manipulate the forecast. There are several common approaches to measuring bias, with two techniques being most popular. The first approach is the **mean forecast error (MFE)**. The MFE is calculated by simply averaging the forecast errors, as demonstrated in Example 9.9.

The other common method for measuring forecast bias is the **running sum of forecast error (RSFE)**. The RSFE is a simple calculation that requires the errors to be summed periodically as each new forecast, actual demand, and error become available. Example 9.10 provides a demonstration of the RSFE calculation using the same data as above.

For the MFE and RSFE, the optimal measure is very close to zero. A positive number indicates that the forecast tends to be too low (actual demand minus the forecast is positive). A negative number (actual demand minus the forecast is negative) is an indication that the forecast is too high.

Example 9.9 Calculating Mean Forecast Error

Using the same data used in Example 9.7, calculate the MFE for the errors.

Solution

The errors sum to 8, and with an n of 8, the mean is 1. An MFE of 1 after eight demands and with demands of this size would be viewed as a good result. Exhibit 9.22 presents the results of this calculation.

EXHIBIT 9.22 MFE Calculation for Example 9.9

Period (t)	Demand (A_t)	Forecast (F_t)	Error ($A_t - F_t$)
1	120	125	−5
2	134	131	3
3	138	133	5
4	125	134	−9
5	143	138	5
6	126	129	−3
7	136	132	4
8	140	132	8 |//
			MFE = 1

Excel Tutor 9.9 demonstrates these calculations in a spreadsheet.

www.OperationsNow.com

INTEGRATED RESOURCE PLANNING SYSTEMS

Advances in computer technology and database management techniques have enabled software designers to integrate formerly separate planning and management systems into large systems known as enterprise systems (ESs) or enterprise resource planning (ERP) systems. With these systems, planning for all resources is accomplished from one common database. The impact on the way businesses function can be significant. Traditional resource management systems incorporated distinct systems to manage different resource groups. The problem with this approach is that different resources are not independent and decisions related to one need data related to another. The fact that the systems were separate often meant that the information was not the same either. One system would say one thing, and another system would say another. Updating a piece of information for a product—a labor standard, for example—meant updating that same piece of information in a variety of systems, inviting redundancy. It was virtually impossible to keep the same information on separate systems up-to-date and consistent. Decisions cannot be made in an integrative way when the systems do not talk to each other. ERP systems are designed to solve that problem. Esource 9.3 is one of the largest ERP system providers, offering business solutions to a variety of industries.

www.OperationsNow.com

Example 9.10 Calculating Running Sum of Forecast Error

Using the same data as in Example 9.7, calculate the RSFE for the errors.

Solution

As each period provides a new error value, it is added to the sum of the previous RSFE. Exhibit 9.23 presents the results for these data.

EXHIBIT 9.23 RSFE Calculation for Example 9.10

Period (t)	Demand (A_t)	Forecast (F_t)	Error ($A_t - F_t$)	RSFE
1	120	125	−5	−5
2	134	131	3	−2
3	138	133	5	3
4	125	134	−9	−6
5	143	138	5	−1
6	126	129	−3	−4
7	136	132	4	0
8	140	132	8	8

www
OperationsNow
.com

The most current RSFE, resulting from the error of period 8, would be 8. This value suggests that the forecast is somewhat biased and has a tendency to be a little too low. Excel Tutor 9.10 shows how to compute RSFE in a spreadsheet.

The unified database of an ERP system provides a common thread throughout the business and allows decisions to be made from an enterprise perspective. When the database is updated with new information, that information becomes the basis for all decisions. All decisions are made with current information. Everyone is working with the same numbers—the same set of facts. This is, without a doubt, a good thing because it gets all functions on the same page. There are always tradeoffs, however.

Despite the logic of such a system, ERP system implementation has not been entirely successful. ERP systems, for the most part, are not customized for a particular business. They are "off-the-shelf" systems. Some of the larger providers have created versions with aspects that are designed for particular industries, but they're not customized. The systems are too huge to customize to meet the needs of an individual company. Each firm must adjust its processes to meet the system's needs,[2] rather than the system being modified to meet the firm's needs. This has resulted in situations where the needs of the software drive business practices—the "tail wagging the dog" syndrome.

ERP systems were born in Europe, where businesses tend to be more tightly structured organizations than in the United States. This has led to problems in the United States, however. Modification of business practices to meet the system needs leads to one of two results. First, the new approach can be an improvement, as often happens. The techniques used to guide ERP system design are considered to be "best-practice" techniques. ERP system implementation, for some companies, has resulted in a reengineering of many of the business processes. There are some situations, however, particularly when businesses have developed a competitive niche and do something extremely well, when the practices mandated by the ERP software are not improvements and actually reduce the strategic advantages the firm has developed.[3] What makes things even worse is the fact that all of the major players in a particular industry may be using the same ERP system, which is mandating the same business processes. The concept of differentiating capabilities goes out the window if everyone does things exactly the same way and continues doing them because the ERP system says so.

The major providers of ERP systems in the large-business market include SAP, BAAN, PeopleSoft, Oracle, and J.D. Edwards. In addition to these ERP system providers, several companies focus on small and midsize businesses. There are also many companies in the business of producing add-on software to provide specific functions or to interact with preexisting (legacy) systems a company wishes to keep. Most of these companies provide alternatives for all major ERP systems. The large ERP systems function in a manner that is quite similar, so a close look at one of the leader's modules provides a good representative overview. Exhibit 9.24 lists and briefly summarizes SAP's R/3 (client–server version) system modules. Several modules are obviously closely related to operations decisions.

Exhibit 9.25 lists functions of Microsoft Great Plains software, a leading provider for small and midsize companies. The functions in this system are similar to those of SAP's R/3.

A tour of the functional modules of major providers of ERP systems leads to the conclusion that the different systems have basically the same objectives and, to a great extent, are similar. The modules and functions have slightly different names and might be organized in a slightly different manner, but they include the same set of business tasks and the same types of information.

EXHIBIT 9.24

SAP Modules

Asset Management: Captures information relating to depreciation, insurance, property values, etc.

Controlling: Includes cost center accounting, product cost controlling, and activity-based costing.

Financial Accounting: Includes general ledger, accounts receivable, accounts payable, and legal consolidations.

Human Resources: Includes personnel administration and planning and development.

Material Management: Includes inventory management, invoice management, invoice verification, and warehouse management.

Plant Maintenance: Includes equipment and technical objects, preventive maintenance, service management, and maintenance order management.

Production Planning: Includes sales and operations planning, material requirements planning, and capacity requirements planning.

Project System: Includes project tracking and budget management.

Quality Management: Includes quality certificates, inspection processing, planning tools, and quality notifications.

Sales and Distribution System: Includes sales management, logistics, transportation, and distribution requirements planning.

Source: D. E. O'Leary, *Enterprise Resource Planning Systems* (Cambridge, UK: Cambridge University Press, 2000), pp. 31–32.

EXHIBIT 9.25 — Microsoft Great Plains ERP Functions

Accounting and financial management	Multiple currencies
Advanced reporting and analysis	Payroll and/or ADP payroll integration
Budgeting	Paying bills and billing customers
Call center management	Project time and billing management
Selling online	Requisition, purchasing, and procurement
Employee self-service	Sales automation and customer relationship management
Customer service	Sales orders and fulfillment
Human resource management	Supply chain management
Inventory and stock levels	National accounts receivables
Manufacturing and resource management	

Source: Microsoft Great Plains Business Solutions, http://www.greatplains.com/solutions/, April 17, 2001.

Exhibit 9.26 provides a conceptual model of a generic ERP system, based on the advertised capabilities of several leading systems. Many of the functions of the ERP system seen in Exhibit 9.26 are closely related to operations decisions. ERP systems generate standard reports that are used for common decision-making processes. In fact, each module typically produces a standard set of reports. Many of these reports are utilized to make operations decisions, and many are based on data kept in the unified database, originating within operations. The availability of these reports depends on need and on cost issues.

The price of an ERP system often depends on the number of users that have access to it. Some companies convert ERP system reports to a format that they can put on their own Intranet to make the information available to others who do not have access to the ERP system. This is typically done for users who do not need access on a regular basis. Integration of the ERP system and a company Intranet is becoming more popular and more necessary. Depending on the ERP provider, other software may be able to access ERP reports to enable them to be read more easily and included in other types of reports.[4] Some reports, for example, are generated in Excel spreadsheet format. Others are generated in the format for particular groupware products for ease of integration into other reports.

The close links between operations and the ERP system, and the links between operations and other business functions *through* the ERP system, become more apparent to you as the management of resources is examined in more detail in this book. Exhibit 9.27 provides an ERP framework, with special focus on the five operations resources used to create value.

The use of ERP systems has gradually spread from manufacturing to the service sector and has become common even in the college and university setting. As a student, you may very likely interact with an ERP system. Systems created by PeopleSoft and Banner, for example, are designed specifically to provide a common database for room scheduling, student registration, advising, accounting, payroll, and even transcripts

Conceptual View of a Generic ERP System — **EXHIBIT 9.26**

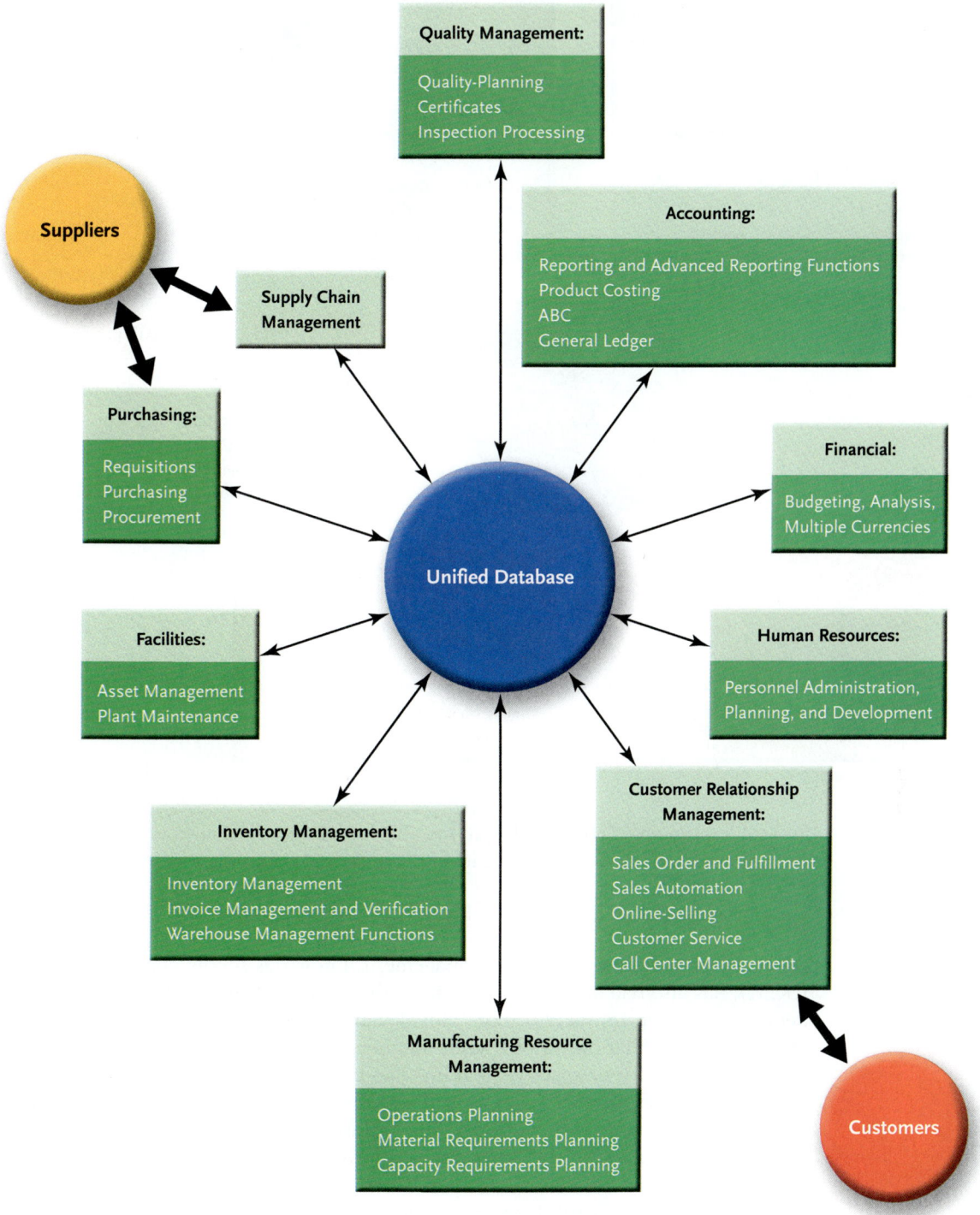

EXHIBIT 9.27 Operations Resources in an ERP System

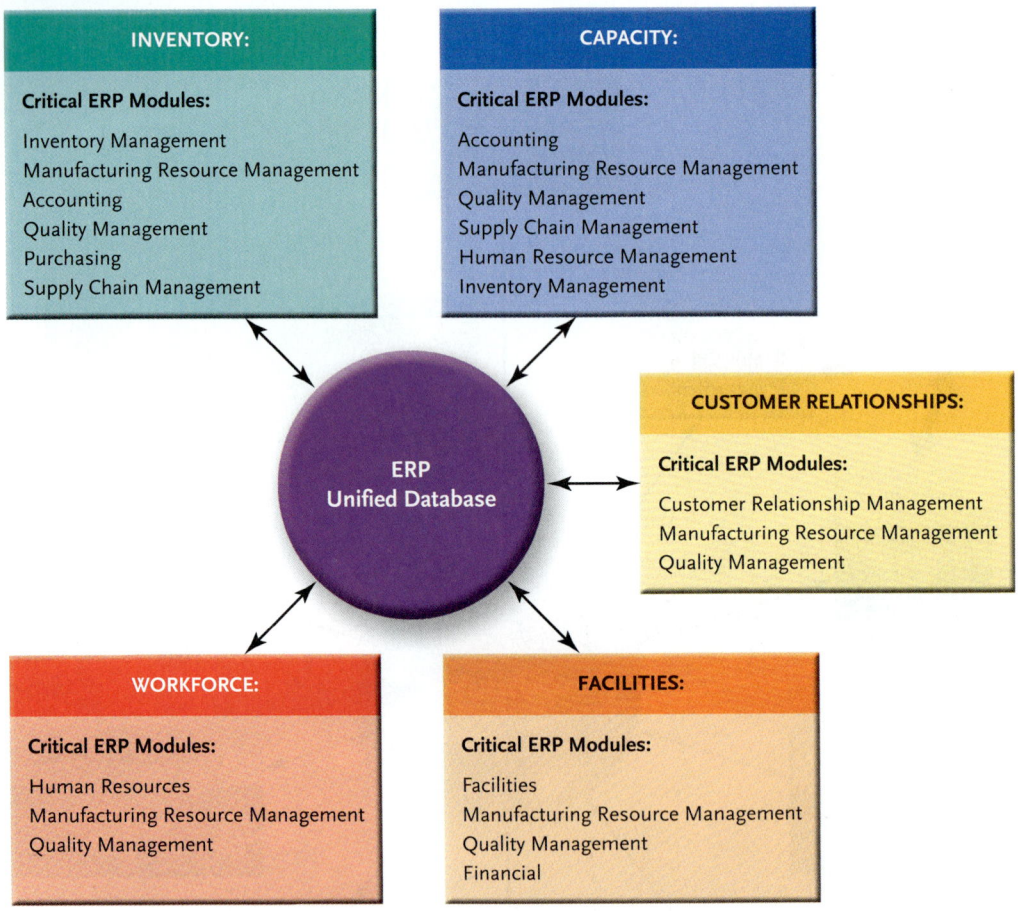

and student records. These ERP systems, just like those for businesses, are designed to integrate all aspects of the organization through one enterprisewide database.

SUPPLY CHAIN MANAGEMENT

A broad perspective on business management, known as supply chain management (SCM), has also had an integrative impact on business planning. SCM, discussed in detail in Chapter 18, takes a more global view of all decisions and pays particular attention to the relationships between suppliers and customers up and down the supply chain. With this perspective, and linkages between companies, planning within a company includes supplier issues as well as customer needs. Suppliers can have real-time access to customer schedules and can include customer needs when planning for resources. Customers, on the other hand, can have an accurate view of their suppliers' capabilities and know immediately if their suppliers can provide what they need. SCM has had a significant impact on resource planning because the resources of suppliers and customers can be integrated into the planning process. This is particularly important as suppliers and customers become more dependent on each other because of outsourcing and contractual agreements. The decision as to whether enough capacity exists to meet a customer's order, for example, cannot be resolved without understanding the implications an order will have for *supplier* capacity. Resource planning, under an SCM framework, expands considerably.

CHAPTER SUMMARY

Planning for operations resources is an important activity for any business. It can mean success or failure because it ultimately dictates how resources will be used and whether or not they will contribute to value creation. Successful plans—those that result in cost savings and an increase in alternatives—enhance profitability through increases in net sales and decreases in costs. They can enhance competitive opportunities by more closely matching resources to objectives. Plans that fail can result in money spent that can never be expected to provide a return, opportunities missed, and customers lost.

The primary input to most business plans is the forecast for demand, which often forms the basis for deciding how much of a particular resource will be needed. The accuracy of the forecast depends on several factors, but two important ones are the time horizon and the appropriateness of the model used. The accuracy of forecasts often determines the accuracy of plans, which dictate how well the availability of a resource matches customer needs. This match between resource availability and what customers want often controls such value attributes as processes and capabilities, costs, quality, and timeliness. The decisions that depend on accurate resource plans impact profitability measures. Having too few resources means that demand isn't met. Having too many resources means that resources are idle.

Planning for resources with a unified database, a framework known as enterprise resource planning (ERP), has the potential to improve the planning functions as well the business processes themselves. Despite costs and difficulties, ERP provides a way to integrate not only different business functions, but different businesses on different continents.

Successful planning alone does not ensure business success. Once plans are implemented, the actual results of the implementation must be compared to what was planned. If they are not what was planned, action must be taken to get plans and reality in sync. In the following chapters devoted to inventory, workforce, capacity, facilities, and customer relationships, planning techniques specifically designed for designated resources, along with other management decision-making techniques, are addressed.

KEY TERMS

absolute error, 312
causal forecast, 298
contingency plans, 290
cycle, 300
decline stage, 295
forecast bias, 312
forecast including trend (FIT), 307
growth stage, 295
introduction stage, 295
life cycle, 294
maturation stage, 295
mean absolute deviation (MAD), 312

mean forecast error (MFE), 314
planning horizon, 291
qualitative forecast, 298
quantitative forecast, 298
random fluctuation, 302
running sum of forecast error (RSFE), 314
saturation stage, 295
seasonality, 301
simple exponential smoothing, 305
times series forecasting, 298
trend, 301
trend-adjusted exponential smoothing, 307

REVIEW QUESTIONS

1. What are the financial benefits of good planning? How does good planning affect profitability measures?
2. What is meant by "planning horizon"? How is the minimum planning horizon determined?
3. Why are shorter planning horizons desirable from the standpoint of planning accuracy and success?
4. Describe the product life cycle. What are its stages?
5. How does the product life cycle affect planning?
6. As product life cycles have been compressed, how have planning processes been affected?
7. Why is lead time compression important?
8. Compare qualitative and quantitative forecasting approaches.
9. What is meant by "causal forecasting"?
10. What is a time series?
11. Describe the four components of a time series.
12. When a time series contains random fluctuation, but no other apparent time series components, what forecasting approach is most appropriate?
13. How should the alpha used in exponential smoothing be selected?
14. Describe how simple exponential smoothing is like a weighted moving average.
15. What are the two important aspects of forecast error? How are they measured?
16. What is an ERP system? Why is it useful?
17. What is meant by supply chain management?

DISCUSSION QUESTIONS

1. Describe a product life cycle you are familiar with. How long did the life cycle last? What was the reaction of the producer as the product progressed through its life cycle?
2. Identify current plans you have for semester break. What is the necessary timing of decisions that must be made relative to those plans? What are advantages and costs that could result from delaying those decisions?
3. How will you protect yourself from unexpected contingencies that could interfere with your semester break plans?
4. Describe the process you use to plan for financial needs associated with your education. How far ahead do you develop these plans? How do they influence your behavior?
5. How can one forecast be shown to be more accurate than another?
6. How do the components of a time series dictate the appropriate forecasting techniques to use?
7. What would you expect to result from using simple exponential smoothing to forecast a demand that has a trend?

PROBLEMS

1. Campus Bookstore tries to predict the number of books it should stock based on the number of classes requiring the book. A regression analysis provided the following equation for a particular book:

$$Y = 11.5441 + 19.6324X$$

Next semester, five classes will require the book as reading. What is the forecast for demand?

2. The City Foundation takes in donations from area businesses and distributes needed food and clothing to less fortunate people. Below is the data set, showing the amount donated with the size of the company. Using a spreadsheet, forecast the donations for a company with 50 employees.

Amount Donated ($)	Number of Employees
5,000.00	50
1,500.00	15
2,250.00	60
7,000.00	75
3,000.00	22
9,000.00	100
6,000.00	25
7,500.00	60
1,000.00	10
4,500.00	32

3. JT Outfitters sells jackets personalized with the customer's favorite college team. The company is determined to forecast its demand accurately. You have been asked to make a presentation on the use of simple linear regression as a causal forecasting technique. Use the following data in your presentation. Also, the company is considering lowering the current price of the jackets to $220. What will the demand be at that price?

Jackets Sold	Price ($)
450	$ 250.00
787	225.00
580	249.00
410	300.00
515	250.00
900	199.00
790	205.00

4. Grill King sells barbeque grills. Accurate demand forecasting is essential to the customer service level required by the company's customers. The company uses a four-week moving average technique. Use the information below to calculate the forecast for August.

Period	Demand	Weight
April	83	0.1
May	89	0.2
June	95	0.3
July	96	0.4

5. The Rid-em Race Car is a popular children's toy at Christmas time. The last six periods of demand are given below. Calculate the forecast for January using a three-week moving average and a six-week moving average. What conclusions can be drawn from comparing the results?

Period	Demand
July	275
August	290
September	280
October	299
November	350
December	550

6. The last six periods of demand for Tie's Tie Dyed are given below. Use the information to calculate three-week and six-week weighted moving averages. Explain the difference between the two measures.

Period	Demand	Three-Period Weight	Six-Period Weight
1	126		0.05
2	132		0.05
3	149		0.1
4	154	0.2	0.2
5	134	0.3	0.25
6	127	0.5	0.35

7. Dill Computers has seen the following pattern of demand for its computers. Provide three-period and six-period simple moving average forecasts for as many periods as possible. Graph the results. What conclusions can be drawn about the two different methods?

Period	Demand
1	149
2	153
3	147
4	148
5	154
6	187
7	164
8	152

Period	Demand
9	148
10	154
11	151
12	149

8. Books-N-Things sells schools supplies on campus. One of its biggest sellers is a blank computer disk. The demand for disks in the current period was 850, and the forecast was 782. Using simple exponential smoothing and a smoothing constant of 0.25, compute the next period's forecast.

9. E-Traders' World is an online investment service. The company anticipated demand for the current period to be 59 transactions. The demand was actually 49. Using simple exponential smoothing and an alpha of 0.4, forecast the next period's demand.

10. Mr. Pizza calculates demand for its pizzas in slices. Last month, Mr. Pizza sold 5,015 slices of its pizza. The company anticipates selling 5,125 slices for the current period. Use a simple exponential smoothing model with a smoothing constant of 0.1 to forecast demand. What is the result if you use a smoothing constant of 0.4?

11. The local health clinic experienced the five-week demand for its services presented in the table. Calculate the demand for period 6 using trend-adjusted exponential smoothing, using $\alpha = 0.2$, a $\beta = 0.6$, an initial trend of 1, and an initial forecast of 80.

Week	Demand (A)
1	80
2	82
3	84
4	81
5	79

12. A-Gear sells sweatshirts. The past eight weeks' demand is given below. You have been asked to develop a forecast using the exponential smoothing model with a trend adjustment. Develop the model using $\alpha = 0.1$ and $\beta = .9$. Use an initial trend value of 2 and an initial forecast of 144. Graph the actual demand with the forecast.

Week	Demand (A)
1	144
2	154
3	146
4	158
5	150
6	158
7	156
8	164

13. Ian's Eatery has the six-week demand history shown below. Using $\alpha = 0.1$, $\beta = 0.9$, an initial trend of 8, and an initial forecast of 900, forecast the demand for period 7 using trend-adjusted exponential smoothing.

Week	Demand (A)
1	799
2	852
3	878
4	912
5	942
6	994

14. Sno-Way is a snowplow service specializing in clearing residential driveways. Last year's monthly and quarterly demand is given below. Use the information to calculate the average quarterly sales and quarterly seasonal indexes. Explain what the seasonal indexes mean.

Quarter	Month 1	Month 2	Month 3
1	$12,451.00	$12,187.00	$8,754.00
2	3,420.00	452.00	–
3	–	–	324.00
4	987.00	6,450.00	10,651.00

15. The Daily News Corporation has recorded the following demand for its newspaper. Use the data provided to compute the seasonal index for each day of the week. The newspaper expects demand to go up to an average of 800 per day in week 5. Forecast the demand for each day of week 5.

Day	Week 1	Week 2	Week 3	Week 4
Sunday	945	968	924	957
Monday	675	642	634	661
Tuesday	624	687	698	614
Wednesday	648	683	619	664
Thursday	689	621	634	661
Friday	701	698	687	723
Saturday	754	731	768	722

16. 2-Wheelers rents bikes at a state park. Use the demand information given below to calculate the seasonal index for each month and forecast demand for the following year if average monthly demand is expected to increase to 20 rentals per month.

Month	Week 1	Week 2	Week 3	Week 4
Jan	0	0	0	0
Feb	0	0	0	4
March	8	12	12	14
April	14	16	16	20

Month	Week 1	Week 2	Week 3	Week 4
May	22	21	23	24
June	23	24	20	21
July	28	24	22	21
Aug	23	26	21	22
Sept	22	21	17	16
Oct	15	15	14	12
Nov	9	6	2	0
Dec	0	0	0	0

17. The Beach House sells products for pools and beach recreation. Sales of swimsuits for the last eight quarters are presented below. Use the data to compute seasonal indexes for each period. Forecast demand for the next quarter using the multiplicative model.

Quarter	Period	Demand
Q1	1	12
Q2	2	26
Q3	3	28
Q4	4	2
Q1	5	16
Q2	6	31
Q3	7	29
Q4	8	3
Average Demand	18.38	

18. The Springfield Homers, a professional football team, has been tracking sales of its merchandise for the past two years. The team identified trend and seasonality in the time series. Use the information below, along with the multiplicative model, to forecast sales for the upcoming year.

Season	Period	Demand ($)
Jan	1	64,976.00
Feb	2	26,567.00
March	3	16,314.00
April	4	9,007.00
May	5	14,599.00
June	6	11,092.00
July	7	18,377.00
Aug	8	32,789.00
Sept	9	75,312.00
Oct	10	68,980.00
Nov	11	72,134.00
Dec	12	81,613.00

Season	Period	Demand ($)
Jan	13	68,321.00
Feb	14	25,633.00
March	15	17,890.00
April	16	14,523.00
May	17	14,789.00
June	18	14,234.00
July	19	17,641.00
Aug	20	46,790.00
Sept	21	73,689.00
Oct	22	71,099.00
Nov	23	75,624.00
Dec	24	84,145.00

19. Rain-Stop Umbrellas has recorded sales data for the last two years. Graph the information and determine if there are both trend and seasonal components. Use the most appropriate method to forecast demand for the following year.

Season	Period	Demand
Spring	1	89
Summer	2	64
Fall	3	46
Winter	4	62
Spring	5	107
Summer	6	67
Fall	7	61
Winter	8	68

20. The forecasts and demands for the last six periods are given below for The Duckett Co. Calculate the error, the absolute error, and the MAD. Explain your results.

Period	Demand	Forecast
1	867	875
2	916	900
3	923	915
4	875	880
5	921	905
6	934	920

21. Hidden Beauty Nature Center has asked you to help forecast the number of visitors to the company's park. Using the information below, create a forecast for weeks 3 through 6 using a two-week moving average. Also forecast the demand for weeks 3 through 6 using simple exponential smoothing ($\alpha = 0.2$ and a forecast for week 2 of 175). Compute the MAD and mean forecast error for each method. Compare the accuracy of two forecasting methods.

Period	Demand
Week 1	189
Week 2	174
Week 3	186
Week 4	193
Week 5	191
Week 6	187

22. The information below is from the Aloe Corp. Calculate the error for the forecasts, the squared error, and the MSE.

Period	Demand	Forecast
1	62	65
2	67	65
3	64	67
4	71	67

23. The Music Man uses simple exponential smoothing to forecast the sale of CDs. The manager has proposed changing the α from 0.4 to 0.1. Using the information below, and a forecast in week 2 of 285, compare the two forecasting methods using the MAD and MFE.

Period	Demand
1	289
2	296
3	354
4	287
5	301
6	281
7	294
8	318

24. Super-Fresh, a local grocery store, forecasts its monthly electric bill. Using the information below, calculate a forecast for periods 3 through 12 using a two-month weighted average with the most recent month accounting for 70 percent of the importance of the forecast. Calculate the MAD and MFE for the forecasts. Comment on the results.

Period	Demand ($)
1	20,134.00
2	18,945.00
3	19,876.00
4	35,871.00
5	26,541.00
6	24,365.00

Period	Demand ($)
7	21,654.00
8	33,487.00
9	19,875.00
10	22,871.00
11	21,211.00
12	38,789.00

25. Citywide Bank tracks the number of customer transactions per day. Use the information below to calculate seasonal indexes for each day. Once completed, use the seasonal indexes to forecast the number of transactions the bank will have the following week in week 5.

Day	Week 1	Week 2	Week 3	Week 4
Monday	126	132	118	104
Tuesday	121	117	126	134
Wednesday	104	101	97	109
Thursday	109	87	111	104
Friday	187	189	198	183

At the end of week 5, actual demand was as follows: Monday, 143; Tuesday, 134; Wednesday, 124; Thursday, 101; Friday, 198. Calculate the MAD and MFE. Was the forecasting method biased?

26. The following table shows the forecasted number of students and the actual number of students enrolled in State University's MGT 100 course. Calculate the MAD and running sum of forecast error (RSFE). Explain the results.

Year	Actual	Expected
1985	67	65
1986	68	65
1987	71	65
1988	73	65
1989	63	65
1990	61	65
1991	62	65
1992	64	65
1993	68	65
1994	71	65

27. The city of Wasso has recorded the number of passengers using its public transportation system the past five days. Decide between two weighted average forecasting methods, one giving each of the last two periods equal weight, the other using a 70–30 split from the last two periods (70 percent for the most recent period). Calculate the MAD and RSFE. Which forecasting method is better? Explain your answer.

Day	Demand
1	387
2	364
3	399
4	412
5	393

28. The Blue-Notes are a small jazz band that have been playing together for a year. Last January, they believed that it would cost them $3,800 the first month to purchase the needed instruments and then $500 a month for lessons after that. It actually only cost them $3,456 the first month, but the monthly lesson costs varied greatly after that: $600, $700, $430, $530, $480, $94, $1,137, $415, $478, $784, and $723. Evaluate the accuracy of their initial cost predictions using the MAD and the RSFE. What do your answers say about the band's initial cost forecast?

29. Better-Built Construction Company forecasts the number of workers it believes it will need for each month. Last year's forecast and actual number of employees hired are given below. Use MSE and MFE to measure the forecast accuracy. What conclusions can be drawn from the measurements?

Month	Employees	Forecast
1	23	25
2	26	25
3	35	30
4	39	40
5	45	45
6	47	50
7	49	50
8	53	50
9	47	45
10	42	40
11	31	30
12	24	25

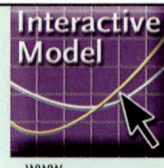
www.OperationsNow.com

INTERACTIVE ANALYSIS 9.1

THE TIME SERIES COMPONENTS INTERACTIVE MODEL

The Time Series Components Interactive Model is accessed through Chapter 9 of the *OperationsNow.com* website. It provides a conceptual view of the interaction among the three dominant components of a time series: random fluctuation, seasonality, and trend. The system inputs consist of a slider for each component, allowing the user to see how various combinations affect the appearance of the time series.

Experiment 1: System Fundamentals

1. Examine the graph of the time series with the sliders set to the default values.
    a. Center all three sliders. Describe the trend, seasonality, and random fluctuation present in the time series.
    b. Set the trend slider completely to the left and then move it completely to the right. What happens? Do random fluctuation and seasonality still exist?
2. Slide the trend slider all the way to the right. Center the seasonality slider.
    a. Slide the random fluctuation slider completely to the left, to eliminate random fluctuation from the time series. Describe what remains.
    b. Set the trend slider all the way to the right. Center the random fluctuation slider. This time, slide the seasonality completely to the left to eliminate it. Describe what remains.

Experiment 2: Component Interaction

1. Set the trend to its centered position. Slide the seasonality and random fluctuation sliders to the far left to eliminate them. You should be looking at a set of points in a straight line. Click on the right arrow on the trend slider so that the line is sloping upward, "one click" from being flat.
    a. Add random fluctuation one click at a time. How much random fluctuation does it take to totally hide the trend?
    b. Set the random fluctuation back to zero. Add seasonality one click at a time. Does the seasonality ever reach a point that effectively "hides" the trend? Why? What does this tell you about random fluctuation?
2. Set the trend back to its centered position. Set the seasonality slider completely to the left, then increase seasonality by one click. Set the random fluctuation slider completely to the left.
    a. Increase the random fluctuation one click at a time. Does it reach a point where seasonality disappears?
    b. Based on these experiments, which of the components of a time series can effectively hide the others?

INTERACTIVE ANALYSIS 9.2

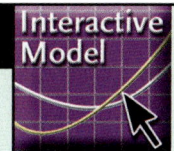
www.
OperationsNow
.com

THE FORECASTING TECHNIQUES INTERACTIVE MODEL

The Forecasting Techniques Interactive Model is accessed through Chapter 9 of the *OperationsNow.com* website. It provides an experimental environment for exploring four basic forecasting techniques. Exponential smoothing, trend-adjusted exponential smoothing, and linear trend equation techniques are provided for time series experimentation. Simple linear regression is provided for experimentation with a causal technique. Users of the Forecasting Techniques Interactive Model can input data by entering it directly into the data table or by dragging the blue dots representing demand on the graph. Depending on the situation, each method can be very useful. If the exponential smoothing or trend-adjusted exponential smoothing methods are chosen, the user selects the smoothing constant(s).

Outputs include the demand forecast data and graphical representation, as well as the mean forecast error (MFE) and the mean absolute deviation (MAD) as measures of forecast accuracy.

Experiment 1: System Fundamentals

1. Select exponential smoothing, leaving all data at the default starting values.
    a. The blue dots represent actual demand. The red dots represent the exponential smoothing forecast with $\alpha = 0.4$. The value of MAD is 4.52 and the MFE is 4.51. Drag the period 2 data point from 52 to 64. Slide it back and forth from 52 to 64 several times, observing what happens to the forecast. How is the forecast for period 3 affected? How does that compare to the forecast for periods 4 and 5? Observe what happens to the error for period 2 in the data table, and also what happens to the MAD and MFE as a result of this spike in demand. Explain what happens.
2. Reset the values to their defaults by clicking on the "reset" button. By dragging the demand data points, set the values for periods 3 through 9 to be 60. Explain what happens to the forecast and error measurements.
3. Set the values back to the default.
    a. Drag the period 1 demand data point up to 62. Explain what happens to the forecasts for periods 2 through 10.
    b. Drag the period 4 demand data point down to 42. Explain what happens to the forecasts for periods 5 through 10.

Experiment 2: Exploring Exponential Smoothing

Exponential smoothing is a popular forecasting technique, particularly when trying to smooth out the effects of random fluctuation. The degree to which randomness is smoothed dictates the responsiveness of the forecast and is controlled by the size of α. As was discussed in Chapter 9, a larger α (alpha) results in a greater weight being placed on the most recent demand and less on the previous forecasts.

1. Enter the following demand data into the table:

Period	1	2	3	4	5	6	7	8	9
Demand	56	52	58	63	55	55	60	56	62

Set the alpha to 0.2 and click on forecast.

a. Describe the impact the increasing demand at periods 3 and 4 has on periods 4 and 5. How does the forecast respond to the drop in demand that occurs in period 5?
b. Adjust the alpha from 0.2 to 0.6. Describe what happens to the forecasts.
2. Reset the demand values to their defaults by clicking on the "reset" button.
a. In period 2 the demand jumps from 44 to 52. For each value of alpha record the forecast for period 3. Describe what happens as the alpha changes and the responsiveness of the forecast increases.
b. Again, gradually change the alpha from 0.1 to 0.9, and observe what happens to the MFE. How does it change? Why is the forecast, no matter what alpha is used, biased?

Experiment 3: Exploring Trend-Adjusted Exponential Smoothing

Trend-adjusted exponential smoothing incorporates trend into the exponential smoothing forecast through the use of a second smoothing constant. The trend and random fluctuation components are treated quite separately in this model. The smoothed forecast is calculated exactly as in exponential smoothing, and then a trend component (T_t) is added. T_t is computed by adding to the previous trend component (T_{t-1}) a weighted difference between the previous two trend-adjusted forecasts and the previous trend. The weight used is beta (β).

1. Select trend-adjusted exponential smoothing and set the values to the defaults. Set the beta value to 0.1.
a. What does a beta of 0.1 mean? Adjust the alpha value from 0.1 up to 0.9, observing what happens to the forecast. How does it respond as alpha changes?
2. Set the alpha to 0.1. Adjust the beta value from 0.1 up to 0.9, observing what happens to the forecast. Describe what happens.

Experiment 4: Exploring the Linear Trend Equation

1. Set the values back to their default level. Select linear trend equation as the technique. The linear trend equation uses the timer period as the independent variable and computes the formula of the best-fitting line through the data. The model plots the line on the same graph as the demand data. Record the formula for the trend line.
a. Outliers can have a significant impact on the forecast when using a linear trend equation, depending on the location of the outlier. Drag the demand for period two from 52 to 62. What is the impact of that change on the trend formula? What is the impact on forecast accuracy?
b. Drag the demand for period 5 from 55 to 65. What is the impact of that change on the trend formula? What is the impact on forecast accuracy?
c. Drag the demand for period 9 from 62 to 72. Summarize the impact an outlier has on the formula for the trend and on the MFE and MAD. What clues would you look for in the MAD or MFE to possibly indicate the presence of an outlier in the data?
2. Whenever the linear trend equation is used, the number of periods to include in the analysis is critical. Trends change over time. Using too much data results in the forecast not responding to changes in trend. Using too little data runs the risk of the trend line changing as a result of random fluctuations.

a. Enter the following values as demand:

Period	1	2	3	4	5	6	7	8	9	10	11	12	13	14
Demand	44	52	50	54	55	55	60	56	64	69	67	71	72	71

Click on "forecast" and observe the graph. The trend equation is 44.44 + 2.07t. Record the MAD and MFE. Clearly this is an upward trend, rising just over two units per period. What is the demand forecast for period 20?

b. Suppose it was decided to use only the most recent nine periods to compute the linear trend equation. To do this, change periods 10 through 14 to "0" and enter the following demand data:

Period	1	2	3	4	5	6	7	8	9
Demand	55	60	56	64	69	67	71	72	71

Again, click on "forecast" and observe the results. What is the new equation? What are the new MAD and MFE? What is the forecast for period 20? Explain what happened.

Experiment 5: Exploring Simple Linear Regression

1. When using simple linear regression as a causal technique, one must be aware of all of the cautions that apply to the linear trend model. Outliers have the same impact. Using too many or too few data points in the analysis can have the same impact as well. Select simple linear regression.

    a. Drag demand points up and down on the graph. What changes are caused when points at either end of the data are moved? What is the impact of moving data points near the middle of the data?

    b. What happens to the MAD as points are dragged away from the line? What happens to the MFE? Why is it always 0? What would you conclude if you made the calculations for using this technique, used it to forecast demand, and very quickly discovered that your forecast was biased?

2. Set the values to the defaults by clicking on "reset." Outliers can be caused by aberrations in demand or by an input error. Key entry error is common and can have a huge impact on forecast accuracy. Record the regression equation and the MAD and MFE values for the default demand.

    a. Suppose the first data point, 46, had been mistakenly transposed. It should have been keyed in as 64. What impact would this have on the forecast?

    b. Explain the effects errors related to the Y intercept and errors related to the slope have on the MAD and MFE. Experiment with the model to reach your conclusions.

SELECTED REFERENCES

Bancroft, N. H., Seipt, H., and Sprengel, A. *Implementing SAP R/3.* Greenwich, CT: Manning Publications, 1998.

Bernstein, P. L. *Against the Gods: The Remarkable Story of Risk.* New York: John Wiley & Sons, 1998.

Hanke, J. E., and Reitsch, A. G. *Business Forecasting.* Upper Saddle River, NJ: Prentice Hall, 1998.

O'Leary, E. *Enterprise Resource Planning Systems.* Cambridge, UK: Cambridge University Press, 2000.

Turban, E., Lee, J., King, D., and Chung, H. M. *Electronic Commerce.* Upper Saddle River, NJ: Prentice Hall, 2000.

ENDNOTES

1. P. L. Bernstein, *Against the Gods: The Remarkable Story of Risk* (New York: John Wiley & Sons, 1998), pp. 152–172.
2. T. H. Davenport, "Putting the Enterprise into the Enterprise System," *Harvard Business Review*, July–August 1998, pp. 121–131.
3. Ibid.
4. D. E. O'Leary, *Enterprise Resource Planning Systems* (Cambridge, UK: Cambridge University Press, 2000), p. 63.

CHAPTER 9   **Resource Planning**   337

OperationsNow.com LEARNING ACTIVITIES

CHAPTER ENHANCEMENT RESOURCES
- Esources
- Reel Operations Video Clips
- Interactive Models
- Excel Tutors
- Supplementary Readings
- Links to Operations On Site Companies

OM EXPLORATION
- Check It Out
- OM in Action
- Online Business Tours
- Letters from the Top
- Putting It All Together: Virtual Case Studies
- Additional Readings

The resource/profit model presents inventory as the first of five resources used to create value. Inventory is an intriguing resource because it is an asset, but in many ways its role in the business is similar to that of a liability. Not enough inventory can be disastrous. Too much can be equally disastrous. Inventory serves many purposes, but its benefits come at great cost.

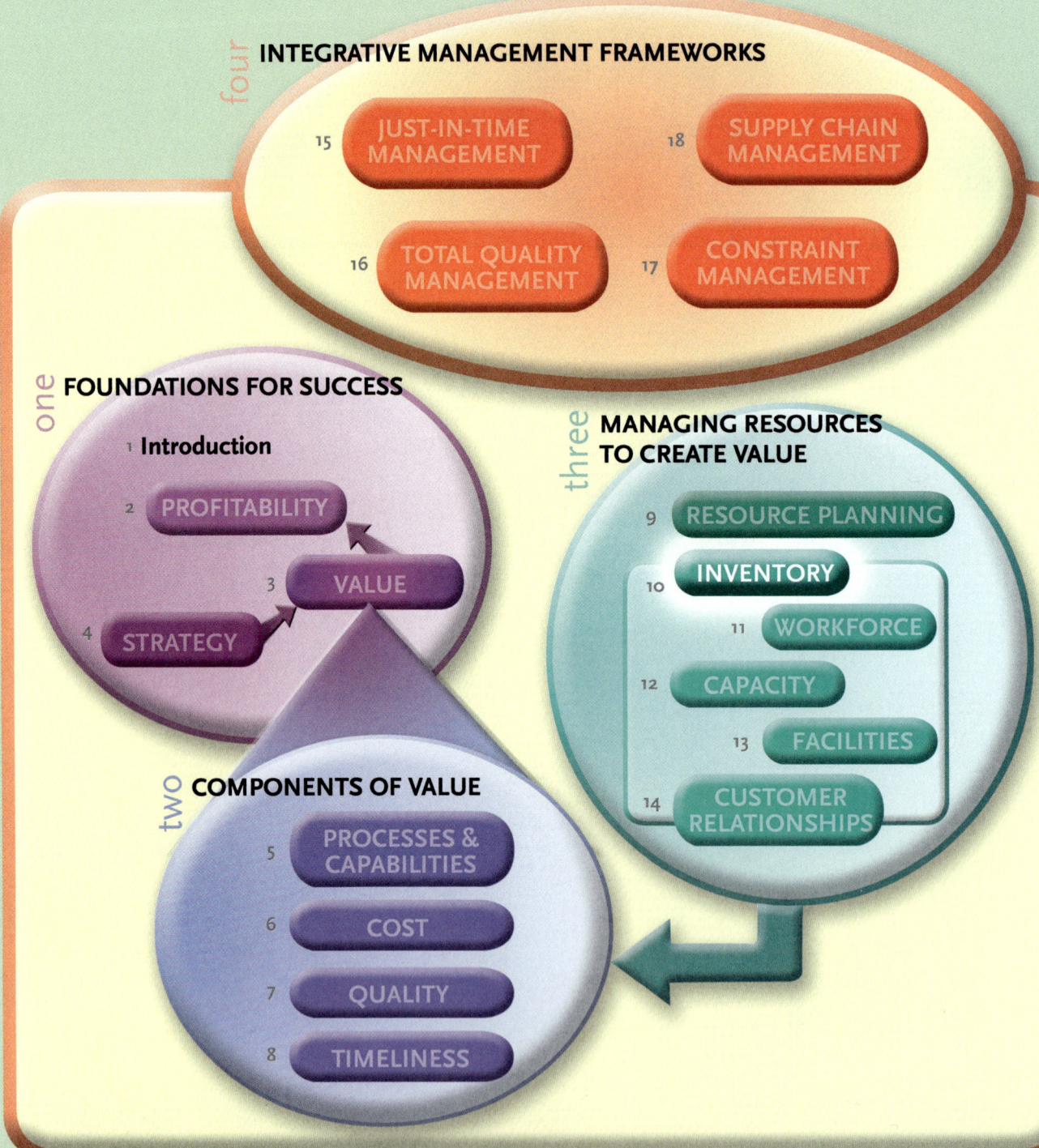

CHAPTER 10

Inventory

LEARNING OBJECTIVES

Upon completion of Chapter 10, you should be able to

_____ Explain why businesses carry inventory.

_____ Describe the costs associated with inventory.

_____ Compare independent and dependent demand inventory.

_____ Calculate days-of-supply.

_____ Explain how a reorder point system works.

_____ Describe the contribution made by a safety stock.

_____ Compute the reorder point for a desired service level.

_____ Make computations for the economic order quantity models.

_____ Describe weaknesses of the economic order quantity.

_____ Compute the appropriate order quantity for a fixed interval, variable quantity system.

_____ Describe the information inputs necessary to manage dependent demand inventory.

_____ Compute planned order releases using material requirements planning.

_____ Explain ABC analysis.

_____ Compute dollar days for a given inventory.

Introduction: A Balancing Act for Management
Why Should Businesses Carry Inventory?
Why Should Businesses Avoid Carrying Too Much Inventory?
Different Types of Inventory: Costs and Benefits
Retailing and Finished-Product Inventories
Component and Raw Materials Inventory
Inventory Decisions
Managing Independent Demand Inventory
Managing Dependent Demand Inventory
Prioritizing Inventory: ABC Analysis
Measuring Inventory Productivity
Chapter Summary

INTERNET RESOURCES

 Excel Tutors provide annotated spreadsheets for every solved problem that automatically load Excel.

 Esources provide an online version of the more traditional boxed insert.

 Reel Videos provide streaming video footage for company applications of chapter concepts.

 Interactive Models provide an experimental environment for quantitative concepts and simulations.

INTRODUCTION
A Balancing Act for Management

nventory, as shown in Exhibit 10.1, is the first of five resources traditionally controlled by operations. It is a critical resource in many ways. Its presence contributes to value because it reduces the wait time for a cus-

EXHIBIT 10.1 — The Role of Inventory in the Resource/Profit Model

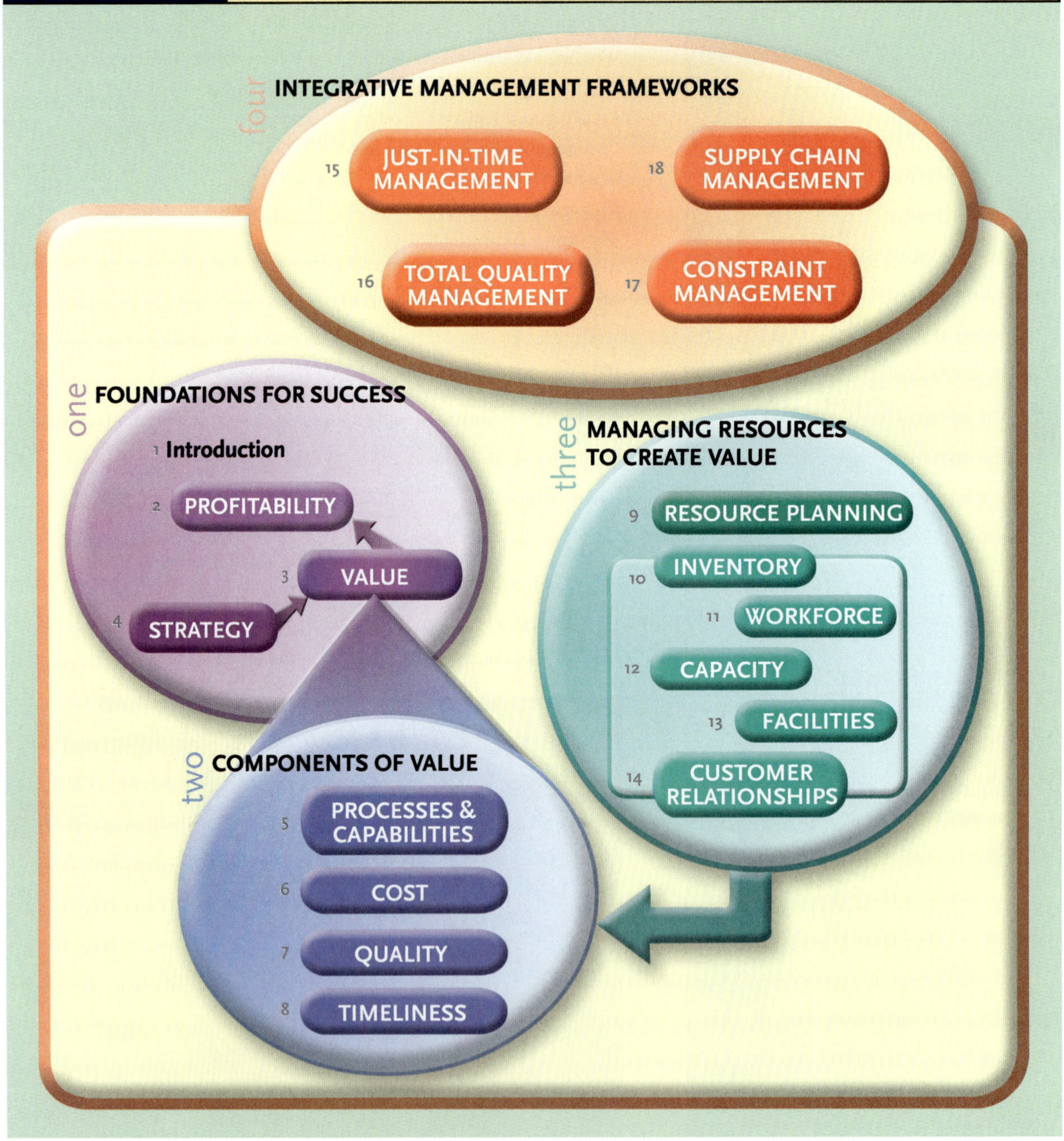

four — INTEGRATIVE MANAGEMENT FRAMEWORKS
- 15 JUST-IN-TIME MANAGEMENT
- 18 SUPPLY CHAIN MANAGEMENT
- 16 TOTAL QUALITY MANAGEMENT
- 17 CONSTRAINT MANAGEMENT

one — FOUNDATIONS FOR SUCCESS
- 1 Introduction
- 2 PROFITABILITY
- 3 VALUE
- 4 STRATEGY

three — MANAGING RESOURCES TO CREATE VALUE
- 9 RESOURCE PLANNING
- 10 INVENTORY
- 11 WORKFORCE
- 12 CAPACITY
- 13 FACILITIES
- 14 CUSTOMER RELATIONSHIPS

two — COMPONENTS OF VALUE
- 5 PROCESSES & CAPABILITIES
- 6 COST
- 7 QUALITY
- 8 TIMELINESS

tomer. It contributes to timeliness, response time, and other customer-service related factors as well. Surprisingly, its absence also contributes to value. The ability of a firm to react to market changes is enhanced if money has not been invested in inventory that could suddenly become obsolete. This is particularly true in markets with short product life cycles.

If the presence and absence of inventory both contribute to value, the amount of inventory held must be a difficult balancing act. Too little reduces the financial return received from the firm's other assets because sales are lost. Too much creates an investment in inventory that provides no financial return and may inhibit the firm's ability to respond to market changes. This chapter examines the different reasons companies hold inventory, the different types of inventory, costs and benefits associated with those inventory types, and techniques used to make critical inventory management decisions that enhance profitability.

WHY SHOULD BUSINESSES CARRY INVENTORY?

A general statement can be made that inventory of all types serves a function known as **decoupling**. Decoupling means that the inventory serves to break a direct dependency that one part of the supply chain may have on another. A direct dependency means that if one business entity supplies another with some input, and the supply stops for some reason, the other one will be immediately disrupted. This disruption potential is common within productive systems, companies, and supply chains. In today's manufacturing and service economies, low levels of inventory are desirable, and in most situations the low levels of inventory have a positive impact on the firm. Once in a while, however, something occurs to disrupt the continuous flow of goods necessary in a low-inventory environment. There's a strike, a natural disaster, a fire at a factory, or a recall of defective products that shifts a supplier's priorities. Inevitably, manufacturers and services that depend on suppliers of goods must find a balance between the benefits and risks associated with low levels of inventory.

The decoupling effect of inventory can enhance reliability and response time, leading to an increase in net sales. The increase in net sales can obviously result in enhanced net income and ROA. There is no free lunch, though.

WHY SHOULD BUSINESSES AVOID CARRYING TOO MUCH INVENTORY?

Just as there are general truths about the benefits of inventories, there are general truths about inventory costs. Inventory is an investment. In appropriate quantities, the investment can generate a substantial financial return. However, an investment in excess inventory is a very poor investment because the excess provides no financial return because its presence adds no value. In addition to the lack of a financial return, its associated costs can reduce net income. All inventory, for example, generates costs of storage and insurance. In most cases inventory drives several nonfinancial costs as well. It can reduce management's ability to make quick decisions, it can reduce flexibility, and it can reduce the firm's ability to adapt to changing market conditions. These costs vary with different types of inventory. The specific benefits and costs associated with inventory can be better understood if different types of inventory are examined in detail. The following discussion is devoted to specific types of inventory, their benefits, and their costs.

> ### Eliminating Inventory Through Mass Customization: Build-to-Order
>
> Excess inventory creates costs in virtually every product- and service-oriented industry. The more difficult it is to accurately forecast demand, the higher these costs are likely to be. Few industries battle this problem as much as the automobile industry, however. By eliminating the need to forecast and by building products to order, inventory can be reduced. Unfortunately, however, building products to order usually increases the time customers must wait for their products.
>
> A study by the business consulting firm McKinsey & Co. estimates that the costs associated with the discounts needed to sell excess stocks of finished cars might be as high as $80 billion per year. Nissan has calculated that switching its production completely over to build-to-order could save $3,600 per vehicle.
>
> Dell Computers offers customers products with options, but the options result from combining a few basic modules that are preassembled. The actual time to put together a Dell computer is about four minutes. Most of the customization comes in the form of software options. Cars, however, are much more complex than computers. Car customers come into a dealership with a much wider range of expectations in mind.
>
> In Germany, 60 percent of cars are built in response to a customer order. The proportion of built-to-order cars in Britain has increased from 10 percent to 32 percent in nine years. An analysis by the "DayCar" project, a research project examining auto leadtime reduction, has shown that of the 42 days it takes from order to delivery of a typical volume car, production takes only 2 days and delivery takes 5. The remaining days are consumed by paperwork, scheduling parts, and identifying time in the manufacturing process to actually accomplish the production. Renault currently offers customers the opportunity to alter their color choice and options on an ordered car as late as 14 days before production begins.
>
> While building to order may seem attractive, it can result in unsteady production. Inventory provides manufacturers with the ability to smooth production. Peaks and valleys in demand are smoothed by building inventory during slow periods that is sold off when demand is high. The inability to use this leveling approach would reduce the utilization on very expensive equipment. Utilization rates lower than 80 percent are typically considered to be unprofitable for auto makers.
>
> Auto makers really just need to get customers the exact car they want. They don't need to build it to customers' order. In most situations, a car matching their desires is probably sitting on a lot somewhere. The ability to locate it and deliver it quickly may provide a solution better than that of actually building it to their order.
>
> Source: "A Long March," *The Economist*, July 14, 2001, pp. 63–65.

DIFFERENT TYPES OF INVENTORY: COSTS AND BENEFITS

Different types of inventory serve different decoupling functions. Some inventories decouple a customer from a supplier. Other inventories decouple one machine from another. Still other inventories allow producers to delay costly commitment decisions or give management additional flexibility. All types of inventory have associated costs. Some costs are generic, occurring no matter what the inventory type. Others are specific to a certain inventory type.

Two costs associated with all types of inventory are order costs and carrying costs. **Order costs** are the administrative costs associated with ordering inventory: the costs of interacting with a supplier, writing up an order and invoice, and so on. Order costs are associated with the action of ordering and are independent of the size of the order. Order costs for a particular company go up if the company orders more frequently and go down if it orders less frequently. For manufacturers, cost analogous to the order costs is known as a **setup** or **changeover cost**. A changeover cost is the cost associated with preparing equipment to produce a quantity of a specific inventory item. No matter what that quantity or "batch" size, the cost of setting up the equipment will stay the same and will generally include labor, materials consumed in the changeover process, and lost production time on that piece of equipment.

Carrying costs are associated with the amount of inventory being held. They include insurance costs, storage costs, facility costs associated with the storage space used, and the opportunity cost of the dollars invested in inventory. Carrying costs are generally viewed as being a function of the average value of inventory. In fact, if it is assumed that the inventory level goes to zero prior to replenishment (this assumption is seldom true, but it's useful for this example), the average level of inventory is equal to one-half of the quantity ordered to replenish the inventory. This relationship is illustrated in Exhibit 10.2. As the average value of the inventory goes up, the carrying costs go up proportionately.

As you might have suspected, carrying costs and order costs are inversely related to each other. The larger the quantity ordered, the greater the average level of inventory, so the greater the carrying costs. However, as a larger quantity is ordered, orders occur less frequently, reducing the total order costs associated with the item.

A third cost associated with all inventories is the cost of not having it, which is called the **stockout cost**. Since demand is uncertain in many situations, there is always a chance of running out of inventory. Depending on the effects of a stockout, a variety of costs could be involved. In a B2C interaction, for example, the cost might be a lost sale or a dissatisfied customer. In a B2B relationship, a stockout might be expensive, resulting in a plant shutdown, employee layoff, and so on. Higher levels of inventory result in higher carrying costs but lower stockout costs.

A fourth cost that can be directly related to inventory level, the actual cost of purchasing the inventory item, is present only in certain situations. There are situations where quantity discounts make purchasing in large quantities attractive. Purchasing in large quantities when a quantity discount exists can lower the cost of the items but will increase the associated carrying costs. Again, one cost is traded for another.

Average Inventory as Q/2	EXHIBIT 10.2

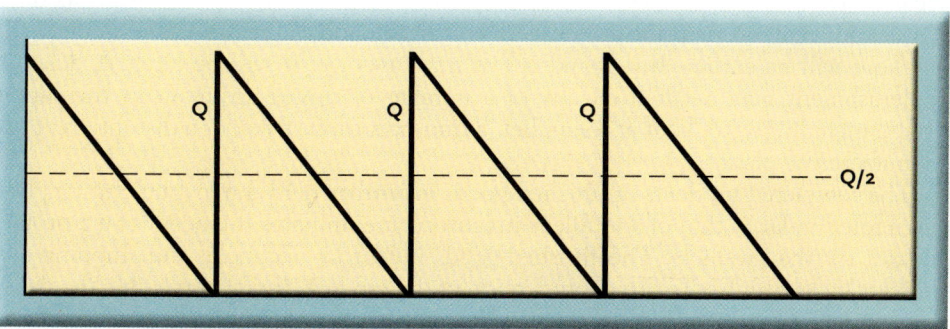

Costs associated with inventory are closely linked to time. This results in an ongoing goal for many businesses to reduce transportation time. For many logistics and shipping services, the ability to compress delivery times is an important competitive capability. Esource 10.1 provides an example of how one successful shipping service has succeeded in compressing its delivery times.

RETAILING AND FINISHED-PRODUCT INVENTORIES

Every day, most of us are exposed to a typical type of inventory—that held by a retailer. That inventory helps provide immediate gratification to the customer. Whereas a simple mail order business requires the customer to wait, when a company carries inventory the customer gets the product immediately. In addition to the enhanced response time for the customer, carrying inventory allows the customer to examine what will be purchased. The inventory held by the retailer decouples that retailer from its supplier, whether that supplier is a distribution center owned by the retail chain or a separate company. Stores that maintain only a very small amount of inventory depend more directly on the supplier because they need more frequent replenishments. A disruption in supply would have a much quicker impact on their ability to immediately respond to customer demands.

In some retail markets inventories are intentionally kept low, to conserve on storage space (reducing inventory-related costs) and to reduce the amount of money invested in inventory. In some situations, a practice known as **continuous replenishment** is used, whereby deliveries are made at extremely short intervals—daily, or even multiple times per day. Continuous replenishment in the retailing industry is similar to an approach known as just-in-time (JIT) delivery in manufacturing. It means that deliveries arrive frequently and in small quantities to enable a low average inventory level but still meet demand needs, as discussed in Chapter 2. The graph illustrating that effect is reproduced in Exhibit 10.3.

Inventory is often viewed and measured from a "time" perspective because it provides a supply or coverage for a given length of time. The rate of demand on that inventory, combined with the amount of inventory on hand, results in what is frequently called the "days-of-supply" or "weeks-of-supply" of inventory. When the amount of inventory on hand is viewed in this way, the issue of dependency on a supplier becomes crystal clear. Days-of-supply is simply the amount of inventory on hand divided by the average daily demand. Similarly, weeks-of-supply would be determined by dividing the inventory on hand quantity by the average weekly demand. The days-of-supply value tells, on average, how long it will be until inventory runs out. It also indicates the size of disruption that can be tolerated. Example 10.1 demonstrates the calculation of the days-of-supply.

Exhibit 10.4 is a diagram of a hardware retailer that has a six-day supply of floor cleaner. The manager knows that if the replenishment does not arrive within six days, a **stockout** may occur prior to the delivery. If demand is greater than average, the stockout will be earlier. If demand is less than average, it will be later. A delay in replenishment may result from any of a number of causes upstream in the supply chain, including a stockout at a supplier, a transportation strike, or a disruption at the manufacturing plant.

The completed-products or **finished-goods inventory** held at a manufacturing plant has a role similar to that of a retailer's inventory: it eliminates the need for a customer to wait for the products. The finished-goods inventory decouples the shipping and delivery systems from the actual production of the product. It makes possible the delivery of products even though production may be temporarily halted. It enables manu-

| Frequent Small Deliveries Versus Infrequent Large Deliveries | EXHIBIT 10.3 |

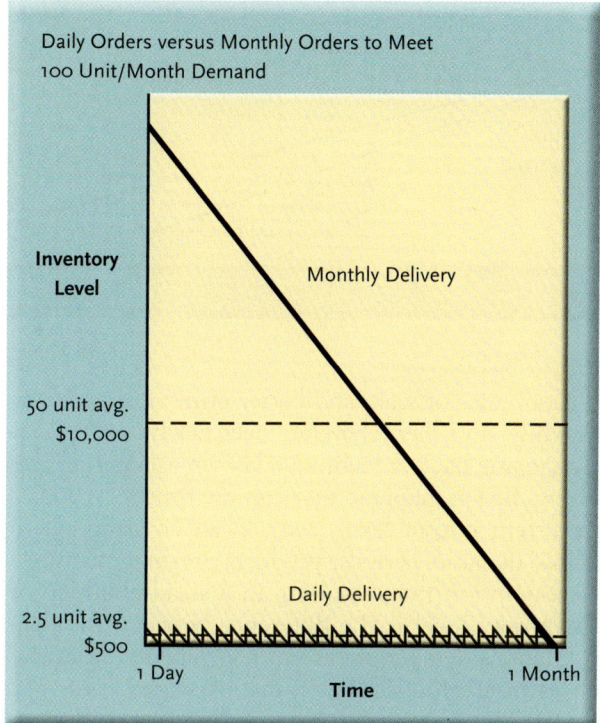

Example 10.1 Days-of-Supply Calculation

A convenience store sells, on average, 40 gallons of 2 percent milk per day. Some days demand is a few more, some days a few less. The store receives deliveries of milk every other day, equal to the amount sold the previous two days. On Tuesday evening, the store received a call from its supplier and was told that, due to problems at the plant, the delivery that should come on Wednesday would be delayed by one day. The store had 60 gallons of 2 percent on hand when the call came in. How long would that inventory be expected to last?

Solution

The days-of-supply calculation is

$$\frac{\text{On-Hand Inventory}}{\text{Average Daily Demand}} = \frac{60}{40}$$

$$= 1.5$$

Excel Tutor 10.1 shows how this calculation can be done in a spreadsheet.

| EXHIBIT 10.4 | Example of Days' Supply |

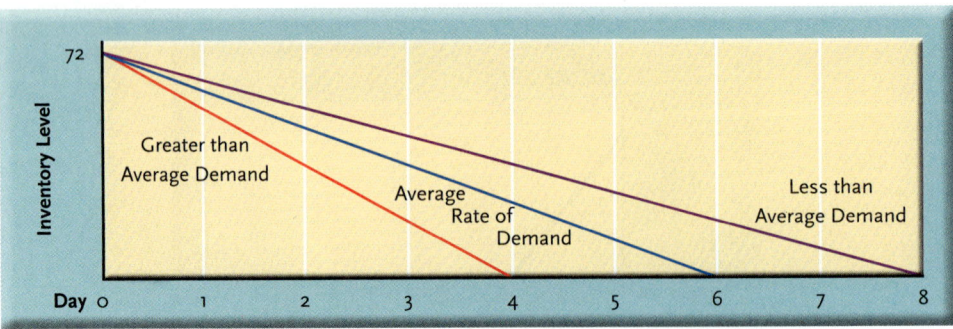

facturing to gain economies of scale and better utilize flexible equipment by making one product for a while, and then changing over machines to make another product for a while, then changing back, a technique known as **batch processing**.

Exhibit 10.5 shows how a manufacturer can use finished-goods inventory to operate at a more consistent output level, even in an environment of highly seasonal demand. During low demand periods, products are manufactured at a rate that is faster than the consumption rate, resulting in a steady buildup of finished-product inventory. The inventory level is the difference between the demand rate and the production rate. Then, as demand picks up, it is satisfied from the finished-product inventory as well as from products being manufactured. This approach, known as **level production**, results in a more stable workforce, as well as consistent capacity load on equipment.

Inventory held by a retailer or by a manufacturer as finished goods contributes to value in several ways. Obviously, the reduced response time that results from its presence increases perceived value for the customer. The added dependability is a benefit as well, particularly in a B2B transaction from a manufacturer. A promise of delivery for products already completed is much more certain to be met than one that requires production to take place before delivery. There are costs associated with these inventories as well, however, that must be weighed against the benefits.

The more inventory, the greater the days-of-supply, and the longer, on average, the inventory is held prior to being sold. Days-of-supply can be a positive when concern about reliability of supply exists, but it can be negative as well. Excess inventory

| EXHIBIT 10.5 | Inventory to Buffer Against Seasonal Demand |

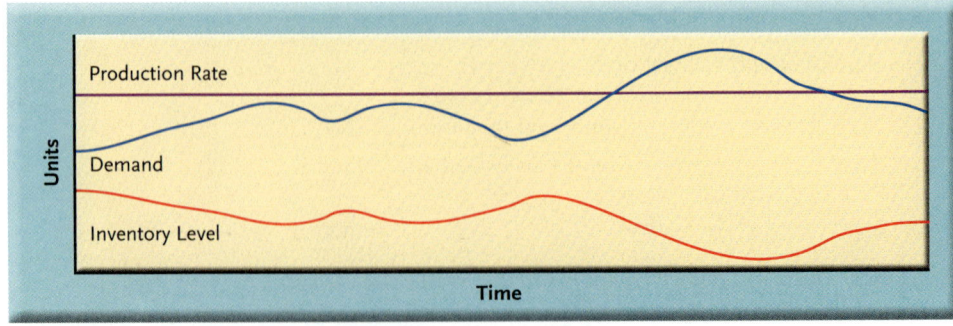

held for a long period of time has a greater chance of becoming obsolete and impossible to sell. The longer the days-of-supply, the more likely some of that inventory will be held too long. The more inventory held, the more room it takes to store it, resulting in a need for larger facilities. Storage-related costs go up. The productivity of the facilities used for inventory storage is zero, however, because no value is generated by square footage used to store excess inventory.

Excess retail inventory almost always results in price reductions to clear out old inventory. The Limited, like most clothing retailers, must present seasonal clothing far ahead of the start of the actual season. Invariably, clothing remains from the previous season. This excess inventory increases inventory levels, decreases inventory turns, and reduces the financial return from the inventory investment because the sales price on "out-of-season" clothing must be reduced.

Excess inventory can also increase the time to market for a new product by forcing a delay on its introduction. A new product introduced when a supply of its predecessor still exists makes the predecessor obsolete. If the business wishes to delay the new product's introduction to postpone the obsolescence of the existing product, valuable advantage gained by being first to market is lost. On the other hand, if the new product is introduced immediately, the inventory of the now-obsolete product becomes almost worthless. This phenomenon is equally destructive for manufacturers and services, particularly retailers of short-life-cycle products. No matter which choice management makes, to delay the new-product introduction or to introduce it despite the on-hand inventory of the old product, additional costs will be incurred directly as a result of that inventory.

Excess inventory also increases the cash-to-cash cycle. If a manufactured product is stored before being sold, the time it is stored adds to the length of the cycle. The days-of-supply of inventory can be a significant component of the cycle. One way to reduce the cash-to-cash cycle, particularly for make-to-stock manufacturers and for most retail inventories, is to reduce the days-of-supply of finished goods inventory.

Another often overlooked cost associated with inventory is the negative effect excess inventory has on product quality. This is a manifestation of the feedback delay concept introduced in Chapter 8. Large, infrequent deliveries of products are typically manufactured in a similar pattern. They are produced infrequently in large quantities. Likewise, if deliveries are made in frequent small quantities, manufacturers typically produce them in a similar pattern. Production in large quantities is dangerous from a quality perspective because if defects do exist, they are often not discovered until the entire quantity is produced and shipped. This results not only in greater waste and higher costs, but also in more difficulty in pinning down the actual cause of the defect, which makes it more difficult to prevent a recurrence.

Finished-product inventories of manufacturers and the stock inventories of retailers are similar in that their demands are both classified as **independent demand inventory**. In general, independent demand inventories are inventories whose demand comes directly from the market. It is not possible to know what the demand will be before the fact, and so it must be forecast. The techniques used to manage independent demand inventory, addressed later in this chapter, must include features to cope with the demand's probabilistic nature.

Another less obvious type of inventory, but also having independent demand, is the inventory of items consumed in the day-to-day activities that support a business. This inventory is known as **maintenance, repair, and operating (MRO) inventory**. For typical services, it would include paper, diskettes, forms for keeping records and receipts, cleaning supplies, and the plastic bags and boxes retailers put products in. For manufacturers, MRO inventories would include lubricants, tools, and repair parts. The demand for MRO inventories is very similar to the demand for the retailer's inventory and must be forecast in order to plan for those items.

Inventories like MRO and retail inventories are often consumed one unit at a time, making it difficult and time-consuming to pull inventory from warehouses. Automated order picking and sorting systems are often employed to meet high volumes of this type of demand. Transportation and shipping businesses, like UPS, and high-volume online retailers have a similar need for high-volume order filling or sorting capabilities. Esource 10.2 is a leading provider of systems and equipment for high-volume inventory and order sorting.

www.OperationsNow.com

COMPONENT AND RAW MATERIALS INVENTORY

Another distinct type of inventory is common in manufacturing and in many non-retailing services. These inventory items, known as component inventories and raw materials, also serve decoupling functions. Manufacturing inventories of purchased components and raw materials, for example, are held to decrease the direct dependence on the supplier of those goods. Similarly, a restaurant would maintain an inventory of raw food ingredients. For a hospital, a component inventory would consist of the disposable items and procedure kits, linens, pharmaceuticals, and the like. For an automobile producer, this inventory would consist of components purchased from other manufacturers, like tires, plastic parts, and brake systems.

Another type of inventory, known as **work-in-process inventory (WIP)**, is maintained to decouple manufacturing processing steps from each other and to account for products that are actually being processed at any given time. In many situations, both in services and manufacturing, items are processed in batches, rather than individually. For example, an insurance claims processing center might process claims through several stages. Rather than move each claim to the second step as soon as it completes the first, the claims processor might transfer claims in quantities of 20 from one stage to the next. These batches are known as **transfer batches**. Manufacturers often use transfer batches transferring materials from one work station to another. WIP inventory might also accumulate in front of manufacturing or service processes because of the inability of a particular processing step to keep up with demand. This occurs when the arrival rate at the process exceeds the processing rate. In some manufacturing processes, a brewery, for example, WIP inventory would include product that is actually in a process at any given time. WIP inventory can also exist as "pipeline" inventory. **Pipeline inventory** is inventory that is actually in pipelines (being transported

Work-in-process inventories, which consist of dependent demand items, provide manufacturers with the ability to "decouple" one work center from being directly dependent on another. Here, rear quarterpanels are being inspected prior to final assembly. The demand for rear quarterpanels is directly determined by the production schedule; however, there may also be some independent demand from body shops for replacement parts.

from one oil refinery to another, for example) or inventory being transported in trucks, trains, ships, or planes. For many businesses, particularly mail order retailers, Internet retailers, and B2B suppliers, much inventory can be in transit at any given time. Reducing the transit time reduces the level of inventory in the pipeline.

Inventoried items are given unique identifying numbers, known as part numbers or SKUs (stock-keeping units). SKUs enable the item to be identified and accounted for accurately. In some manufacturing situations, when an item is stored between processing steps, the SKU number actually changes after each processing step.

While the roles of raw materials, component, and WIP inventories differ from those of finished products, the costs and risks associated with carrying them are similar. Any inventoried item can become obsolete or, as a result of a short shelf life, spoil. If purchased in excess, the investment generates no financial return because it adds no value. WIP inventory, in particular, can be expensive because not only do the raw materials cost money, but the creation of the WIP inventory can use up operating capacity that may be in short supply. Scarce capacity used to create excess WIP inventory will not be available later to process inventory that is desperately needed.

Raw materials, component, and WIP inventories are known as **dependent demand inventory**. Dependent demand is not determined directly by the market, as is the case with independent demand, but rather by the demand for some other inventory item or by a production schedule intended to meet independent demand. Let's look at an example. The production of PCs requires a number of component items, including cases, hard drives, power supplies, motherboards, and sound cards. The demand for sound cards, for example, would be directly determined by the demand for completed computers. Suppose 439 PCs were needed to meet the forecasted demand for next week. Since one sound card is required for each PC, the demand for sound cards would be 439. The approaches used to manage dependent demand inventory do not need to cope with the uncertainty of a probabilistic demand. Demand for dependent demand is deterministic: We know *in advance* exactly what it will be.

Because dependent demand inventory is consumed in a deterministic environment, it is managed quite differently from independent demand inventory because it is consumed in a deterministic environment. Rather than being forecast in advance, it is simply calculated. Demand that can be calculated has no inherent error.

INVENTORY DECISIONS

Decisions that must be made to effectively manage inventory do not, on the surface, appear to be highly complex. In most cases only two questions need to be answered:

Pipeline inventories consist of goods that are in the process of "flowing" from one place to another. In this oil pipeline in Alaska, the length and size of the pipeline create a huge pipeline inventory. Pipeline inventories also include the inventory on trains, trucks, and ships when there is a constant amount in transit for consistent deliveries. In those cases, the existence of a pipeline inventory is not as obvious, but it is a significant amount of inventory nonetheless. In all reducing
tra
spe
inver
pipeli

> ### It's Not Just "When" and "How Many," but also "How" and "Where"
>
> The cost of transportation and related services amounts to 60 percent of the $1.1 trillion U.S. companies spend on logistics services. Internet technologies have enabled many companies to reduce these costs and have created opportunities that never existed before. The transport of inventories has always been an inefficient process. Moving goods from one city to another wastes resources because many trucks are traveling around empty. If one company needs to transport products from Boston to Milwaukee, for example, the truck eventually has to return to Boston. Unfortunately, the odds of identifying products that need to be shipped from Milwaukee to Boston are not always that great. In addition, the odds of the goods moving from Boston to Milwaukee exactly filling a truck are also pretty slim. Companies are rarely able to share the costs on transportation routes simply because companies with compatible needs can't identify each other. The Internet has drastically changed this scenario. Although the problem seems conceptually simple, matching of companies with complementary transportation needs (truck, rail, and ship) can be complex.
>
> Application server providers (ASPs) make extremely sophisticated software applications available to any company. Using this service, companies don't need to purchase the hardware and software. They are simply charged for their use. Logistics.com, a leading logistics ASP, is able to analyze the needs of many customers, utilizing the resources of many transportation companies (more than 60,000 trucks) to minimize costs.
>
> The ASP model has great potential for logistics and transportation management because the needs of many companies are very similar, even though the companies themselves may differ greatly. Businesses like Logistics.com provide a broad range of services for companies seeking to reduce logistics and transportation costs. Companies such as Wal-Mart Stores, Procter & Gamble, Compaq Computer Corporation, the Colgate-Palmolive Company, Kraft Foods, Quaker Oats Company, the Clorox Company, Georgia-Pacific Corporation, and The Limited utilize ASP services to help consolidate shipments, identify the lowest-cost carrier through online auctions, and optimize shipments using their applications.
>
> Source: "Shipment Fever," *CFO*, September 2001, pp. 29–30; http://www.logistics.com, September 19, 2001.

When should it be ordered? and *How many* should be ordered? In some cases, such as inventory placed in distribution centers, the question of *where* the inventory should be located must also be answered. The "when" and "how many" decisions for independent demand inventory are made in a different manner than decisions for dependent demand inventory. The following discussion provides a comprehensive overview of the techniques used for making these decisions.

MANAGING INDEPENDENT DEMAND INVENTORY

Many different approaches are used to determine when and how many to order for independent demand inventory. Two representative approaches will be examined for the purposes of an overview. Independent demand is, by definition, uncertain demand. No one knows in advance what the demand will be. Systems developed to manage inventory must include mechanisms that address demand uncertainty and also ensure that the inventory is available when needed. The percentage of demands that can be satisfied from on-hand inventory is known as the **service level**. When independent demand inventory is examined closely, you could conclude that it isn't actually the demand uncertainty that's the difficulty here. The fact that when you order you have to wait to get your order plays a role in the difficulty associated with managing that demand. In other words, there is a **replenishment lead time**. If we could get more inventory instantly, whenever we stocked out, stocking out wouldn't be a big deal. Or if demand were deterministic or known in advance for certain, it really would be no big deal to have to wait for the replenishment. In the real world, demand is uncertain *and* there is a replenishment lead time (which may also be uncertain), so we must develop mechanisms to deal with uncertainty.

A commonsense approach to avoiding a stockout when there is demand uncertainty and replenishment lead time hinges on several conclusions about determining when and how many units to order. First, we must recognize that "how many" we order can vary as a result of "how often" we order. If we order very frequently, for example, we can meet demand without ordering very much. If we order in small quantities, the "when" will most likely mean "soon."

Second, since we must wait a period of time for the order to arrive, we must order *before* we stockout. We must plan ahead. If we wait until we run out to order, we will be unable to satisfy demand during the replenishment lead time.

Third, the fact that there is variability of demand implies that order quantities or frequency must also vary to accommodate demand variability. For example, we can order in different size quantities each time we order, or we can order at different intervals, or we could do both. If demand is variable, however, and we want to order the same quantity every time we order, we *must* change the time interval between orders to react to demand changes. Likewise, if demand is variable and we want to order at fixed time intervals, we *must* be willing to change the order quantity to react to demand changes.

Two general approaches to making these decisions provide a nice overview of the many different systems used. They correspond to the issues just discussed and can be summed up as (1) fixed quantity, variable interval systems and (2) fixed interval, variable quantity systems.

Fixed Quantity, Variable Interval Systems

In a fixed quantity, variable interval system, the order quantity is the same each time an order is placed. However, to adapt to the varying rate of demand, the time interval between orders changes. A common implementation of this system is known as a **reorder point (ROP) model**. In a reorder point model, an order is placed whenever the level of inventory drops to a predetermined point. Whenever the inventory level reaches the reorder point, an order is placed. The rate of demand determines how long it takes for the inventory to drop to the level of the reorder point, hence the "variable interval." The rate of the demand after the order is placed determines whether a stockout will occur.

Determining when to reorder, in this case, means determining what the reorder point should be. A quick study of the purpose of the reorder point leads to a better understanding of how it should be determined. Recall from an earlier discussion that because there is a replenishment lead time (i.e., there is a time lapse between placing and receiving the order), the order must be placed prior to stocking out. The inventory must be sufficient to meet demand during that replenishment lead time. With this in mind, it should be clear that the order needs to be placed when there is still enough inventory on hand to meet the demand while we are waiting for the order to arrive. If the reorder point is calculated to be equal to the demand that would take place during the replenishment lead time, we'd have enough.

That logic is sound, and seems easy enough, but don't forget: We don't know for sure what the demand during lead time will be. It varies, but even though we don't know exactly what it is, we can still describe it and base our reorder point on what we know about it.

Just like any other demand, the demand during the replenishment lead time can be forecast. Depending on the situation, different types of forecasts could be used. The simplest case, and a common approach to solving this problem, is to use the average demand during the lead time. So if the average demand was 60 units per week, and the replenishment lead time was two weeks, the average demand during the lead time would be 120 units. If we set the reorder point to 120 units, we get an immediate lesson on the impact of variability. If the average demand during lead time was 120 units with *no* variability (in other words, it was always 120), a reorder point of 120 units would be fine. An order would be placed when the inventory dropped to 120, demand would consume the 120 units, and the new order would arrive just as that last unit was removed from inventory.

In the real world, if the average demand during lead time was 120, the demand during lead time would vary around the mean of 120. Sometimes it would be above 120 and sometimes it would be below 120. It would be normally distributed around 120 and its variability could be measured in the form of a standard deviation (σ). If 120 was used for the reorder point, it would be sufficient to satisfy the demand during lead time 50 percent of the time, since half of the demands would be above 120 and half would be below 120. Thus additional inventory must be added to increase the service level to above 50 percent (to meet demand in those 50 percent of the cases where demand exceeded 120). That additional inventory is known as a **safety stock.** Suppose, for the sake of an example, the average demand during lead time was 120 and had a standard deviation of 12. The distribution of this demand is shown in Exhibit 10.6.

Knowing the mean and standard deviation for demand that is normally distributed enables us to compute, quite easily, the probability that demand will be above a certain

EXHIBIT 10.6   Distribution of Demand During Lead Time

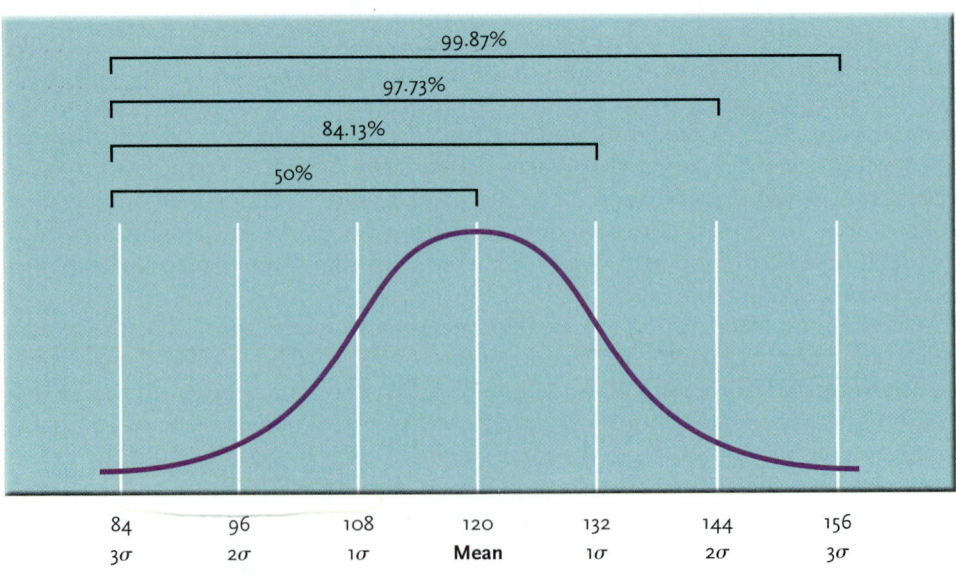

quantity. Using the normal probability table provided in Appendix A, we know that 84.13 percent of the demands during the replenishment lead time will be below the mean plus 1 standard deviation. In addition, we know that 97.73 percent of the demands will be below the mean plus 2 standard deviations. Thus 2 standard deviations would provide a service level of 97.73 percent. The formula for the reorder point is

$$\text{ROP} = \bar{d}_{LT} + \sigma_{LT} Z \tag{10.1}$$

where $\bar{d}_{LT}$ = average demand during the replenishment lead time
σ_{LT} = standard deviation of demand during the replenishment lead time
Z = number of standard deviations above the average demand during the replenishment lead time required for the desired service level

Exhibit 10.7 provides a diagram of how the basic reorder point system works. If we wanted a reorder point that would provide a 99 percent probability of exceeding the demand during the replenishment lead time (a 99 percent service level), it would need to be equal to the mean plus 2.33 standard deviations. In our example, that would be:

$$\begin{aligned}\text{ROP} &= \bar{d}_{LT} + \sigma_{LT} Z \\ &= 120 + 2.33(12) \\ &= 120 + 28 \\ &= 148\end{aligned}$$

An ROP of 148 would be sufficient to satisfy demand during the replenishment lead time with 99 percent confidence. This reorder point is shown, as it relates to the distribution of demand during lead time, in Exhibit 10.8.

One simplifying factor in the previous example is that the standard deviation of demand during the two-week lead time was provided. In most situations, the time units for the standard deviation would be the same as for the average. That is, both the average *and* standard deviation would be expressed as daily or weekly. If the average was on a daily basis, the standard deviation would also likely be on a daily basis. In the previous situation, if we had known only the weekly standard deviation of demand, we would need to convert it to the standard deviation for the two-week lead time. Unlike the mean, the standard deviation is not additive. So, if the weekly demand averaged 60 and had a standard deviation of 10, for example, the standard deviation over two weeks would *not* be 20. The variance (σ^2), however, is additive. So if the weekly standard deviation was 10, the variance would have been 100. The

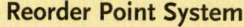

Reorder Point System

EXHIBIT 10.7

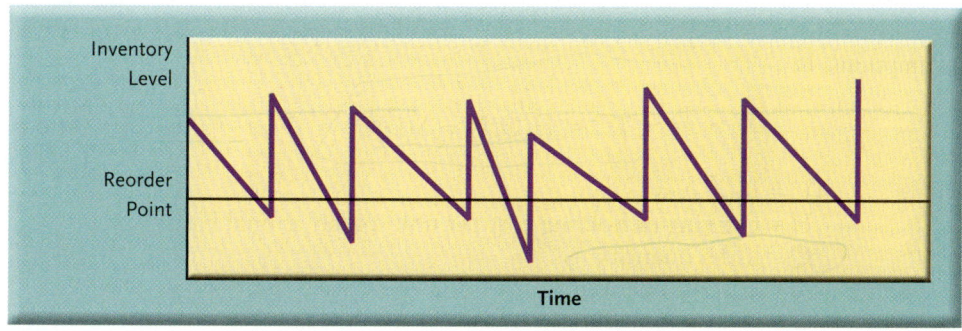

EXHIBIT 10.8 ROP at 2.33σ

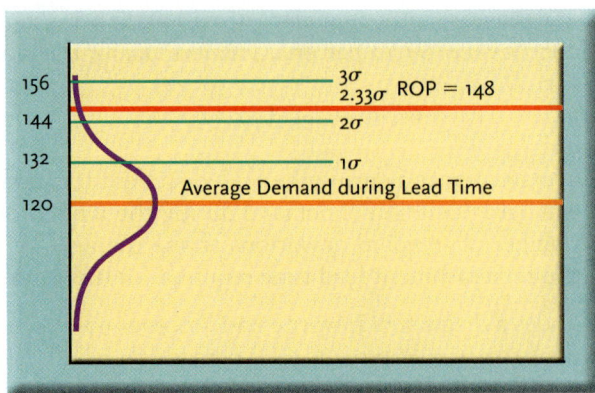

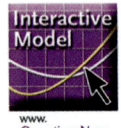

variance over the two-week lead time would be 200 and the standard deviation (σ) would then be 14.142 (the square root of 200).

Example 10.2 is another reorder point calculation to determine when to place an order.

Interactive Model 10.1 provides an opportunity to examine the impact service levels and replenishment lead times have on the reorder point.

The reorder point system tells us when an order should be released, but the order quantity still needs to be determined. A common approach to determining the quantity to order utilizes one of a set of techniques based on the **economic order quantity model**. Economic order quantity techniques identify the order quantity that will minimize the costs associated with the order size.

The simplest of the economic order quantity techniques is known as the basic economic order quantity. The basic economic order quantity (EOQ) makes the following assumptions in order to provide an optimal solution:

1. Annual demand is known.
2. Demand is even.
3. Lead time is constant.
4. There are no quantity discounts.
5. Only one product is involved.
6. Orders are received in single deliveries.

The assumptions confine the identified costs involved in the order quantity to only carrying costs and order costs. The formula for the total cost, given these assumptions, is:

$$TC = H(Q/2) + S(D/Q) \tag{10.2}$$

where TC = total cost
H = carrying or holding cost per unit, on an annual basis
Q = order quantity
S = cost of ordering
D = annual demand

> **Example 10.2**
>
> **Reorder Point Calculation**
>
> A local silk-screen operation wishes to utilize a reorder point system for managing the inventory of its most frequently used T-shirt. The replenishment lead time for this shirt is two weeks from the standard supplier. The average weekly demand is 62. The weekly standard deviation is 13. A 95 percent service level is desired. Complete the reorder point.
>
> **Solution**
>
> First the average and standard deviation for demand must be computed for the lead time. The weekly average demand is 62, so the average demand during the replenishment lead time is 124:
>
> $$\bar{d}_{LT} = 2(62)$$
> $$= 124$$
>
> Next, the standard deviation during the lead time must be calculated:
>
> $$\sigma_{LT} = \sqrt{\sigma^2 + \sigma^2}$$
> $$= \sqrt{(13^2 + 13^2)}$$
> $$= 18.38$$
>
> The value for Z, the number of standard deviations necessary for the desired service level, must be determined:
>
> $$Z_{.95} = 1.645 \quad \text{(from Appendix A)}$$
> $$\text{ROP} = \bar{d}_{LT} + \sigma_{LT}Z$$
> $$= 124 + 18.38478(1.645)$$
> $$= 154.243$$
>
> A noninteger solution should always be rounded up. Rounding down would provide slightly less than the desired service level. Thus
>
> $$\text{ROP} = 155 \text{ rounded up}$$
>
> Excel Tutor 10.2 solves this problem in a spreadsheet.

www
OperationsNow
.com

Typically, H is determined as a percentage of the value of the item. Exhibit 10.9 shows the relationships among the ordering cost, carrying costs, and total cost curve and it identifies the EOQ.

Carrying costs are typically 25–35 percent of the value of the item. In that scenario, the following formula might be used:

$$H = iP \qquad (10.3)$$

where
i = percentage used for determining carrying costs
P = purchase price of the item

By taking the first derivative with respect to Q of the total cost curve defined above to find the value of Q that minimizes cost, the formula for the EOQ is

$$\text{EOQ} = \sqrt{\frac{2DS}{H}} \qquad (10.4)$$

EXHIBIT 10.9 Carrying Costs, Ordering Cost, and Total Cost in EOQ

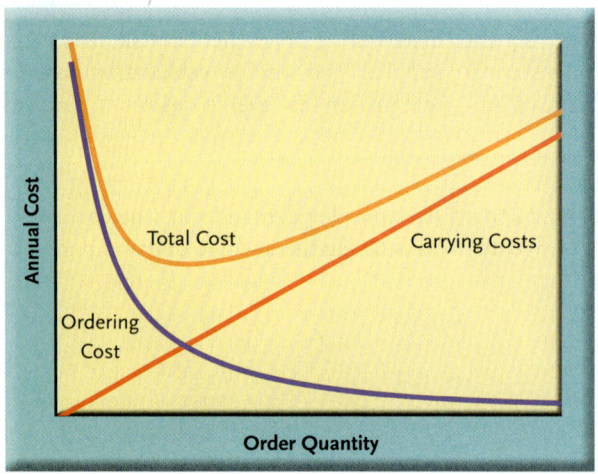

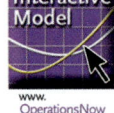

An economic order quantity problem is solved in Example 10.3.

Interactive Model 10.2 provides an experimental environment for manipulating EOQ input variables and immediately viewing the resulting impacts on the total cost curve.

The EOQ approach to determining order quantity has come under increasing scrutiny and has been criticized for inflating order quantities. The fact that it minimizes carrying costs and order costs, given that assumptions are met, cannot be denied, but many feel that it underestimates carrying costs by ignoring well-accepted nonfinancial costs of carrying inventory. Included among these costs not considered are costs of lost flexibility, increased quality feedback time, and increased lead times. As firms have become more familiar with continuous replenishment and JIT approaches, many have abandoned the logic of the EOQ formula in favor of ordering in very small quantities. Obviously, ordering in small quantities results in a high number of orders and higher order costs, but many firms have sought out ways to reduce order costs. However, the model does accurately portray the relationships among the costs it represents. The problem is that the model does not include all the relevant costs.

Various modifications of the basic EOQ model are used as the assumptions of the basic model are relaxed. One common variation is to incorporate a quantity discount model when quantity discounts affect the purchase price. The implication of this change is that in addition to the carrying and order costs being components of the total cost, the price is also affected. The following procedure is used to determine the low-cost order quantity when quantity discounts are available:

1. Compute the basic EOQ. It will fall within one of the price ranges specified by the supplier.
2. If the EOQ falls within the cheapest price range, the EOQ is the optimal order quantity.
3. If the EOQ does not fall within the cheapest price range, all price ranges having lower prices than the range the EOQ falls in must be evaluated.
4. The optimal quantity will be at the lowest allowable quantity of a price range. For each quantity, compute the total cost (carrying, order, and purchase price) for the quantity at each price break.

> **Example 10.3**
>
> **Economic Order Quantity Calculation**
>
> The University Bookstore wished to utilize the EOQ formula to determine the appropriate order quantity for its most popular backpack. Determine the EOQ given the following information:
>
> $$D = 600 \text{ per year}$$
> $$S = \$13 \text{ per order}$$
> $$H = \$3.25 \text{ per year}$$
>
> *(handwritten: $EOQ = \sqrt{\dfrac{2DS}{H}}$, $D = 1200$, $= 97.98$)*
>
> **Solution**
>
> $$EOQ = \sqrt{[2(600)(13)/(3.25)]}$$
> $$= \sqrt{4800}$$
> $$= 69.28203$$
>
> As is evident in Exhibit 10.9, the total cost curve is nearly flat at the bottom and rounding the EOQ off to an even quantity has little effect on the total cost associated with that quantity. In this case, the order quantity would be rounded up to 70.
>
> Excel Tutor 10.3 provides spreadsheet calculations for this problem.

www
OperationsNow
.com

The total cost equation for this model is

$$TC = D/Q(A) + Q/2(H) + DP \qquad (10.5)$$

where D = annual demand
Q = order quantity
A = cost per order
H = carrying cost
P = price per unit

The computation process for the quantity discount model is demonstrated in Example 10.4.

Fixed Interval, Variable Quantity Systems

An alternative to the fixed quantity, variable interval model, like the ROP approach, is the fixed interval, variable quantity system, sometimes referred to as a **periodic review system**. As mentioned earlier, if the order interval is fixed, the order quantity must vary to provide the system with the necessary adaptation to fluctuation demand. This means that the order quantity could potentially be different with each order. Such a system makes sense if the user needs to order at periodic intervals because of supplier shipment schedules or the need to combine orders for many different products into a single shipment.

There are several variations to the periodic review model, but we'll examine a fairly common one. In the periodic review model, just as in the ROP model, there is a need to satisfy demand during the replenishment lead time. We know that demand during the lead time is uncertain, so we will need to incorporate a safety stock, just as in the ROP system. Because demand varies from one order interval to another, the amount of inventory on hand when the order is placed will vary from one time to the

Example 10.4

Quantity Discount Model Calculation

A supplier of hard drives for a local computer supply store established the following price schedule:

1–20 units:	$229 each
21–60 units:	$210 each
61–120 units:	$199 each
120 units:	$175 each
Order cost:	$20 per order
Carrying cost:	$36 per unit per year
Annual demand:	476 units

What would the low-cost order quantity be?

Solution

1. Basic EOQ = $\sqrt{(2(20)(476))/36}$ = 22.997 (round to 23 units).

2. EOQ is in the range of the $210 price. All ranges having lower prices must be evaluated and compared.

   Total cost of ordering the EOQ is [$H(Q/2) + S(D/Q)$]

   $$TC = (476/23)20 + (23/2)36 + 476(210)$$
   $$= 413.91 + 414 + 99{,}960$$
   $$= \$100{,}787.91$$

   Total cost of ordering 61 units (the minimum allowable quantity for the next price range) is

   $$TC = (476/61)20 + (61/2)36 + 476(199)$$
   $$= 156.07 + 1{,}098 + 94{,}724$$
   $$= \$95{,}978.07$$

   Total cost of ordering 121 units (the minimum allowable quantity for the next price range) is

   $$TC = (476/121)20 + (121/2)36 + 476(175)$$
   $$= 78.68 + 2{,}178 + 83{,}300$$
   $$= 85{,}556.68$$

The low-cost order quantity is to order 121 units per order. At this quantity the cost savings from the quantity discount outweigh the increased carrying costs.

Excel Tutor 10.4 demonstrates how a spreadsheet can be used to determine the economic order quantity with quantity discounts.

www.OperationsNow.com

next. Recall in the ROP system that the order was placed when the inventory was at a specific point. It helps to examine this system conceptually first, and then through a mathematical formula.

The inventory ordered in this system must accomplish two things. First, it must satisfy demand during the order interval; second, it must satisfy demand during the replenishment lead time. Both demands are uncertain. An important point to recognize is that it may not be necessary to order the entire amount needed to satisfy the demand during the order interval and replenishment lead time because some inventory may already be on hand when the order is placed. Since that inventory can also be carried into the next interval to satisfy demand, it is subtracted from the order quantity. The formula is presented conceptually below, followed by its mathematical equivalent:

$$\text{Order Quantity} = \text{Expected Demand during Order Interval and Replenishment Lead Time} + \text{Safety Stock} - \text{Quantity on Hand}$$

$$Q = \bar{d}_{OI+LT} + \sigma_d Z \sqrt{(OI + LT)} - A \quad (10.6)$$

where $\bar{d}_{OI+LT}$ = average demand during the order interval and lead time
 σ_d = standard deviation of demand during the order interval and lead time
 Z = number of standard deviations required for the necessary service level (from Appendix A)
 OI = number of days in the order interval
 LT = replenishment lead time
 A = quantity of inventory on hand when the order is placed

Exhibit 10.10 provides a diagram of the periodic review model. The order quantity for a periodic review problem is computed in Example 10.5.

Example 10.5

Periodic Review Model Calculation

A local sporting goods store has located a supplier of athletic socks that can deliver every Friday, when it delivers other products to clothing stores in the area. The manager must place the order on Wednesday each week. The price charged for the socks is significantly cheaper than that charged by the current supplier, but the manager must convert to a periodic review system.

The store is open every day. Using the following information, calculate the new order quantity:

Average daily demand: 3.6 units

Lead time: 2 days

Standard deviation (over the order interval and lead time): 1.4

Inventory currently on hand: 5 units

Service level desired: 99%

Order interval: 7 days

Solution

$$Q = \bar{d}_{OI+LT} + \sigma_d Z \sqrt{(OI + LT)} - A$$
$$Q = 9(3.6) + 1.4(2.33)\sqrt{(9)} - 5$$
$$= 32.4 + 4.786 - 5$$
$$= 37.186$$
$$= 38 \quad \text{(rounded up)}$$

Excel Tutor 10.5 demonstrates how the order quantity for the periodic review model is calculated in a spreadsheet.

www
OperationsNow
.com

> **EXHIBIT 10.10** Periodic Review System

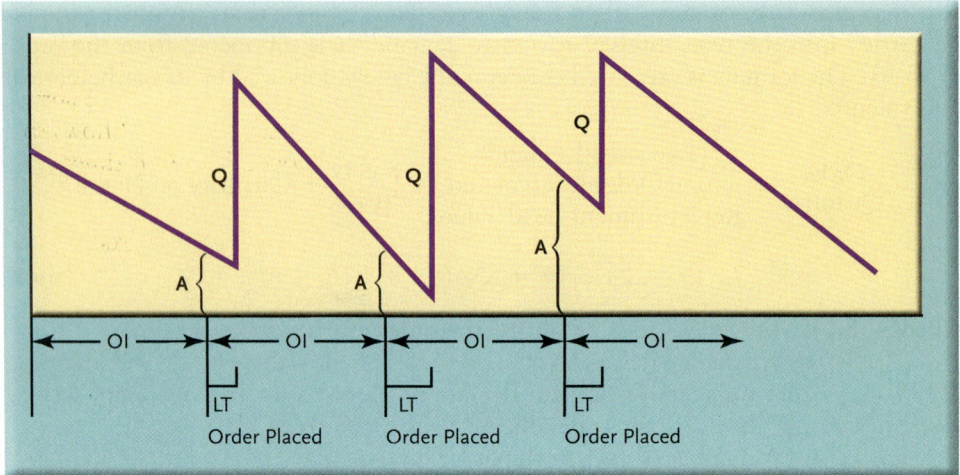

Note that the standard deviation may need to be converted from a daily or weekly standard amount to the standard deviation over the lead time and order interval. If that is necessary, the same technique used in the previous example would be employed.

MANAGING DEPENDENT DEMAND INVENTORY

As mentioned early in this chapter, dependent demand inventory is significantly different from independent demand. Because the demand for dependent demand inventory is derived from the production schedule of other items, it is deterministic. The approach used to determine the quantity and timing of orders is known as **material requirements planning (MRP)**. MRP logic is frequently used to determine orders for manufactured components as well as purchased components and raw materials.

As one might expect, MRP logic consists of two stages. First the quantity to order is determined, then the timing of the order is established. Once again, the questions that must be answered are How many? and When? The process used to determine the quantity is known as **netting**, or computing net requirements. Net requirements are computed by subtracting on-hand inventory from the total quantity needed. The timing of the order is computed with a process known as **backward scheduling**, which means that the replenishment lead time is subtracted from the due date to determine when the order must be released.

The netting and backward scheduling processes utilized in MRP logic require several pieces of information. First, the requirements for the end product must be known. This information typically comes from a production plan known as a **master production schedule (MPS)**, which is simply a statement of how many of each end item or product will be produced by the end of each time period. Second, the composition of the end product must be known so that the required components can be ordered. This information is obtained from a product structure file known as a **bill of material**. Third, the replenishment lead time and the current quantity on hand must be known. This information typically comes from a file that also contains information on the supplier, cost, and so on, known as an **inventory master file**. These inputs, shown in

Exhibit 10.11, are pulled together in MRP logic to provide the quantity and timing of orders that will ensure that components and raw materials arrive promptly and in the right quantities for the production of end products.

MRP logic typically starts with a master production schedule, similar to the one shown in Exhibit 10.12 for an inexpensive staple remover. The MPS shows the quantity of staple removers that are to be completed each week. The staple remover has four components: the outer jaw, the inner jaw, the connecting pin, and the spring. The product structure for the staple remover, presented in Exhibit 10.13, shows that it takes one of each component to produce the staple remover. The lead times associated with the components are:

Staple remover: 1 week
Outer jaw: 1 week
Inner jaw: 1 week
Connecting pin: 2 weeks
Spring: 2 weeks

Material Requirements Planning Inputs — EXHIBIT 10.11

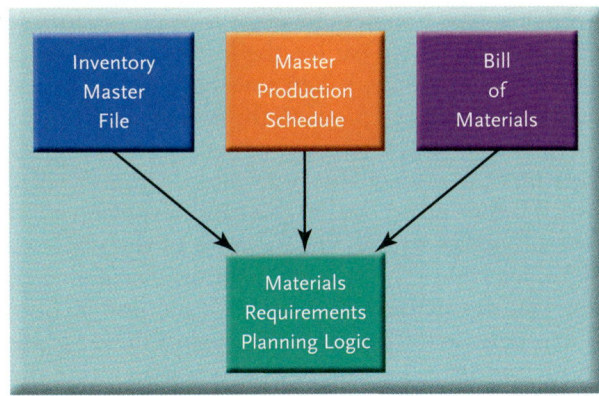

Master Production Schedule (MPS) for Staple Remover — EXHIBIT 10.12

Week	1	2	3	4	5	6	7	8
Quantity	0	45	62	35	64	52	67	62

Structure for Staple Remover — EXHIBIT 10.13

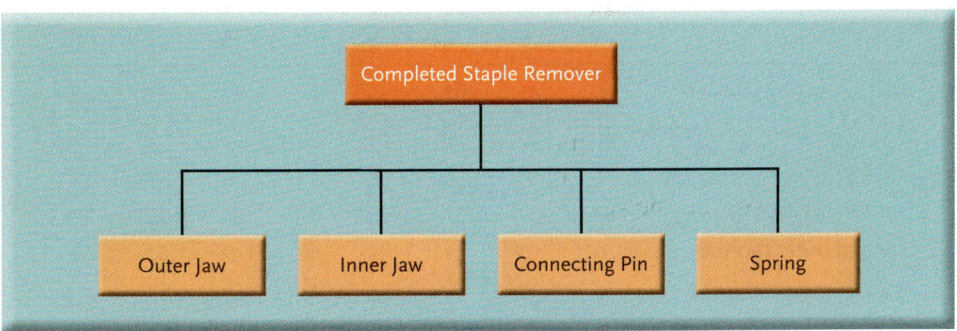

Also assume there are 75 units of the completed staple remover and 75 units of each component on hand currently.

The results of the logic used to compute the net requirements and establish the plan for when the orders will be released for just the staple remover are presented in Exhibit 10.14. The logic in this table is best described by looking at each row in the "MRP record." For the first row, **gross requirements** quantities for the completed staple remover come directly from the MPS for the staple remover. The gross requirements will be calculated differently for components of the staple remover. The **beginning on-hand inventory** is given as 75 units in period 1 for the completed staple remover. For the remaining periods, the weekly beginning on-hand inventory is equal to the **ending on-hand inventory** from the previous week. Ending on-hand inventory is equal to the beginning on-hand inventory plus planned order receipts minus gross requirements. The **net requirement** is equal to the gross requirement minus beginning on-hand inventory for that period. **Planned order receipt** is equal to the **planned order release** one lead time earlier. So, in this situation, the planned order receipt of 32 in week 3 is a result of the planned order release of 32 in week 2. The planned order release is equal to the net requirement for the lead time *later*. For example, the planned order release of 32 in week 2 is a result of the net requirement of 32 in week 3.

Exhibit 10.15 provides the complete logic for the end product and all three components. Notice that, as mentioned earlier, the lead time for the connecting pin and spring is two weeks, rather than one. When comparing the logic used for the components with the logic used in the end product, the primary difference is the calculation of the gross requirements.

Gross requirements for the components come directly from the planned order release of the "parent," which is the end product in this case. The planned order release for the staple remover is used because to start the assembly of the staple remover, all of the components must be available. The starting point for assembling the staple remover determines the due date for its components. The time line in Exhibit 10.16 aids in understanding the due dates associated with the staple remover product.

If the product structure were deeper, the gross requirements of the next lower level would be determined by their parents. If more than one unit of a particular component goes into its parent, then the gross requirement of that item is obtained from multiplying the planned order release of its parent by the quantity of units needed.

Notice that as soon as the initial starting inventory is consumed, ending and beginning on-hand inventory levels equal zero because the orders being placed are equal to the net requirement. Releasing an order exactly equal to the net requirement

EXHIBIT 10.14 **Quantity and Timing for Staple Remover Orders**

	Week 1	Week 2	Week 3	Week 4	Week 5	Week 6	Week 7	Week 8
Gross requirement	0	45	62	35	64	52	67	62
Beginning on-hand inventory	75	75	30	0	0	0	0	0
Ending on-hand inventory	75	30	0	0	0	0	0	0
Net requirements	0	0	32	35	64	52	67	62
Planned order receipts	0	0	32	35	64	52	67	62
Planned order releases	0	32	35	64	52	67	62	0

EXHIBIT 10.15 MRP Records for Staple Remover and Components

Staple Remover MRP Record	Week 1	Week 2	Week 3	Week 4	Week 5	Week 6	Week 7	Week 8
Gross requirement	0	45	62	35	64	52	67	62
Beginning on-hand inventory	75	75	30	0	0	0	0	0
Ending on-hand inventory	75	30	0	0	0	0	0	0
Net requirements	0	0	32	35	64	52	67	62
Planned order receipts	0	0	32	35	64	52	67	62
Planned order releases	0	32	35	64	52	67	62	0

Outer Jaw MRP Record	Week 1	Week 2	Week 3	Week 4	Week 5	Week 6	Week 7	Week 8
Gross requirement	0	32	35	64	52	67	62	0
Beginning on-hand inventory	75	75	43	8	0	0	0	0
Ending on-hand inventory	75	43	8	0	0	0	0	0
Net requirements	0	0	0	56	52	67	62	0
Planned order receipts	0	0	0	56	52	67	62	0
Planned order releases	0	0	56	52	67	62	0	0

Inner Jaw MRP Record	Week 1	Week 2	Week 3	Week 4	Week 5	Week 6	Week 7	Week 8
Gross requirement	0	32	35	64	52	67	62	0
Beginning on-hand inventory	75	75	43	8	0	0	0	0
Ending on-hand inventory	75	43	8	0	0	0	0	0
Net requirements	0	0	0	56	52	67	62	0
Planned order receipts	0	0	0	56	52	67	62	0
Planned order releases	0	0	56	52	67	62	0	0

Connecting Pin MRP Record	Week 1	Week 2	Week 3	Week 4	Week 5	Week 6	Week 7	Week 8
Gross requirement	0	32	35	64	52	67	62	0
Beginning on-hand inventory	75	75	43	8	0	0	0	0
Ending on-hand inventory	75	43	8	0	0	0	0	0
Net requirements	0	0	0	56	52	67	62	0
Planned order receipts	0	0	0	56	52	67	62	0
Planned order releases	0	56	52	67	62	0	0	0

(continues)

EXHIBIT 10.15	(Continued)							
Spring MRP Record	Week 1	Week 2	Week 3	Week 4	Week 5	Week 6	Week 7	Week 8
Gross requirement	0	32	35	64	52	67	62	0
Beginning on-hand inventory	75	75	43	8	0	0	0	0
Ending on-hand inventory	75	43	8	0	0	0	0	0
Net requirements	0	0	0	56	52	67	62	0
Planned order receipts	0	0	0	56	52	67	62	0
Planned order releases	0	56	52	67	62	0	0	0

EXHIBIT 10.16	Timeline for Staple Remover Component Orders

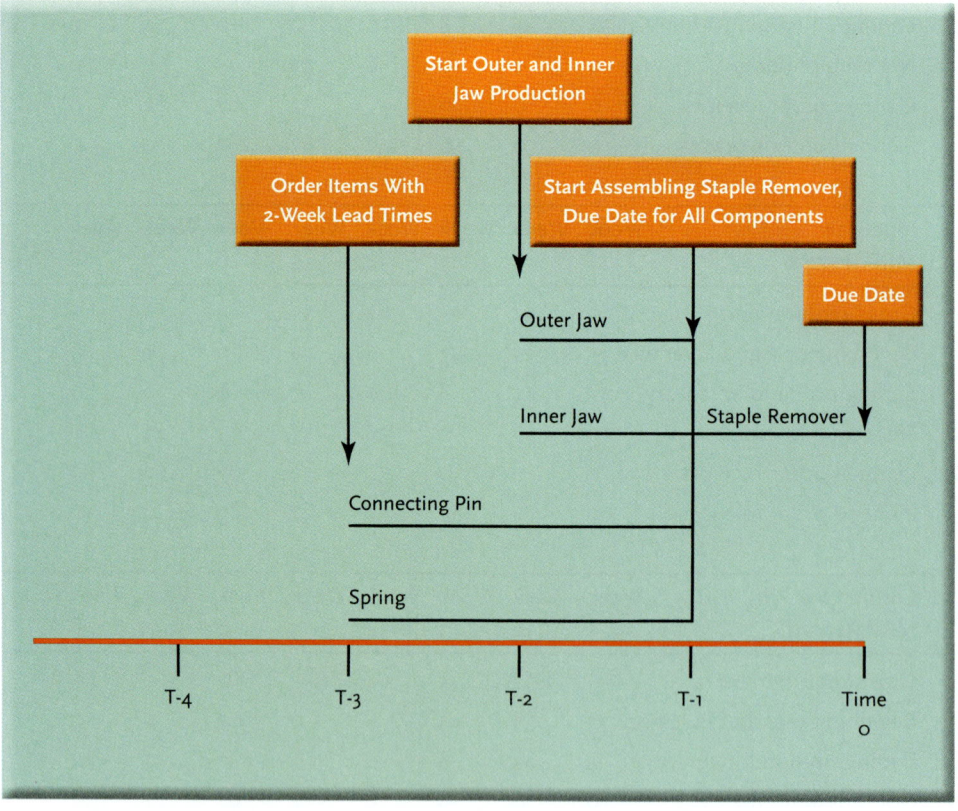

is known as **lot-for-lot ordering**. As an alternative to lot-for-lot ordering, various lot sizing methods could be used to manipulate order costs and holding costs, similar to managing independent demand.

In many situations, purchased components come in containers that hold a specified amount. Manufactured components are often produced in batches of a specified size.

Placing orders in multiples of fixed quantities is referred to as a **fixed-quantity order policy**. The use of such a policy will result in inventory being carried from period to period, resulting in higher inventory carrying costs than a lot-for-lot order policy. However, order costs and prices might be reduced by ordering in fixed quantities.

As products included in the MRP logic become more complex, the logic must accommodate various potential situations. One is that the same components might be used in different end products. To accurately account for this, MRP logic must proceed in a level-by-level rather than product-by-product fashion. In addition, since the gross requirements for a component may need to come from different parents, it must be built into the MRP logic as well.

Example 10.6 extends the previous demonstration of MRP logic. It includes the use of fixed-quantity order policies and also involves a situation where two end products share some components and where these components occur on different levels of the product.

In some situations, the demand for an inventory item can be both independent and dependent. Automobile components, for example, are needed for the production of finished automobiles but can have independent demand coming from dealer's service centers as well. Reel Operations Video 10.1 examines how Navistar manages dependent and independent demand inventories.

www.OperationsNow.com

The MRP software industry is a substantial one. Numerous companies market software and services associated with the management of dependent demand inventory. Esource 10.3 provides examples of two MRP software providers that describe the capabilities of their systems.

www.OperationsNow.com

Example 10.6 MRP Logic

Composite Specialties manufactures high-quality hockey sticks with graphite composite shafts and fiberglass-coated wooden blades. The #99 Senior Pro, modeled after the favorite stick of "The Great One" himself, is the top seller. Composite supplies the right- and left-handed versions of the #99 to ice arena pro shops and sporting goods stores. Exhibit 10.17 presents the master production schedule for both sticks.

EXHIBIT 10.17 MPS for #99R and #99L Hockey Sticks

	Week 1	Week 2	Week 3	Week 4	Week 5	Week 6	Week 7	Week 8
99R	460	525	540	560	610	550	580	670
99L	250	210	250	210	180	220	200	210

The #99 is a simple product, consisting of three major components at the final assembly stage: the composite shaft, the blade assembly, and a wooden extension plug that extends beyond the hollow handle shaft 4 inches so that players can adjust the length of the stick. The blade assembly consists of the wooden blade and lower shaft, which are assembled and then covered on each side with fiberglass. The blade itself is the only difference between the right- and left-hand versions. The product structures of both models are shown in Exhibit 10.18.

(continues)

Example 10.6 (continued)

EXHIBIT 10.18 Product Structures for #99R and #99L Hockey Sticks

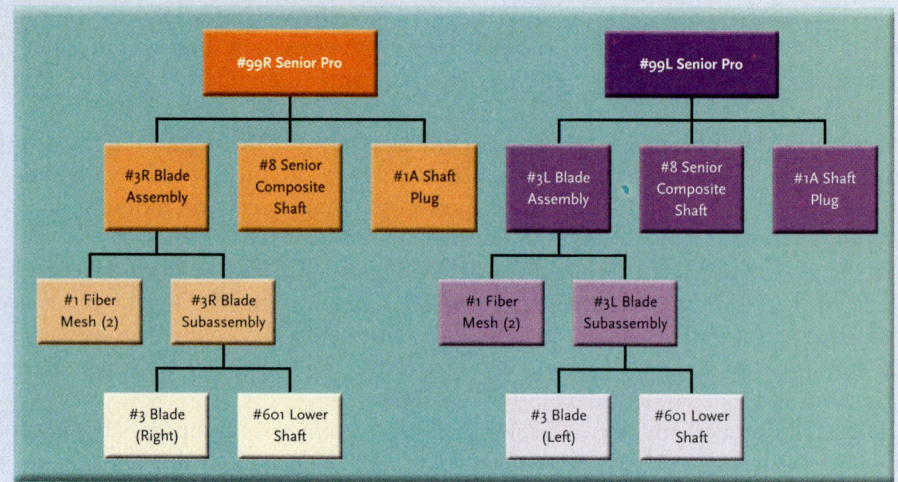

Most components are ordered lot-for-lot, but three are ordered with fixed-lot-size order policies.

Order policies and lead times are presented in Exhibit 10.19.

EXHIBIT 10.19 On-Hand Inventory, Lead Time, and Order Policy Information for #99R and #99L Hockey Sticks

SKU	On-Hand Inventory	Lead Time (weeks)	Order Policy
#99R Senior Pro Hockey Stick	500	1	Lot for lot
#99L Senior Pro Hockey Stick	500	1	Lot for lot
#3R Blade Assembly	600	1	Lot for lot
#3R Blade Assembly	500	1	Lot for lot
#8 Senior Composite Shaft	2,100	3	Lot for lot
#1A Shaft Plug	1,750	1	100
#1 Fiber Mesh	3,000	2	200
#3R Blade Subassembly	500	1	Lot for lot
#3L Blade Subassembly	500	1	Lot for lot
#3 Blade (Right)	1,100	2	Lot for lot
#3 Blade (Left)	900	2	Lot for lot
#601 Lower Shaft	500	1	Lot for lot

Using MRP logic, compute the planned order releases to meet the MPS for the #99R and #99L sticks.

(continues)

Example 10.6 (continued)

Solution

Exhibit 10.20 provides the MRP records for each SKU. Explanations of the logic follow the exhibit.

EXHIBIT 10.20 MRP Records For #99R and #99L Hockey Sticks and Components

#99R Senior Pro Hockey Stick MRP Record	LotSize = Lot for Lot			LeadTime = 1 week				
	Week 1	Week 2	Week 3	Week 4	Week 5	Week 6	Week 7	Week 8
Gross requirements	460	525	540	560	610	550	580	670
Beginning on-hand	500	40	0	0	0	0	0	0
Ending on-hand	40	0	0	0	0	0	0	0
Net requirements	0	485	540	560	610	550	580	670
Planned receipts	0	485	540	560	610	550	580	670
Planned releases	485	540	560	610	550	580	670	0

#99L Senior Pro Hockey Stick	LotSize = Lot for Lot			LeadTime = 1 week				
	Week 1	Week 2	Week 3	Week 4	Week 5	Week 6	Week 7	Week 8
Gross requirements	250	210	250	210	180	220	200	210
Beginning on-hand	500	250	40	0	0	0	0	0
Ending on-hand	250	40	0	0	0	0	0	0
Net requirements	0	0	210	210	180	220	200	210
Planned receipts	0	0	210	210	180	220	200	210
Planned releases	0	210	210	180	220	200	210	0

#3R Blade Assembly	LotSize = Lot for Lot			LeadTime = 1 week				
	Week 1	Week 2	Week 3	Week 4	Week 5	Week 6	Week 7	Week 8
Gross requirements	485	540	560	610	550	580	670	0
Beginning on-hand	600	115	0	0	0	0	0	0
Ending on-hand	115	0	0	0	0	0	0	0
Net requirements	0	425	560	610	550	580	670	0
Planned receipts	0	425	560	610	550	580	670	0
Planned releases	425	560	610	550	580	670	0	0

(continues)

Example 10.6 (continued)

#3L Blade Assembly

LotSize = Lot for Lot   LeadTime = 1 week

#3L Blade Assembly	Week 1	Week 2	Week 3	Week 4	Week 5	Week 6	Week 7	Week 8
Gross requirements	0	210	210	180	220	200	210	0
Beginning on-hand	500	500	290	80	0	0	0	0
Ending on-hand	500	290	80	0	0	0	0	0
Net requirements	0	0	0	100	220	200	210	0
Planned receipts	0	0	0	100	220	200	210	0
Planned releases	0	0	100	220	200	210	0	0

#8 Senior Composite Shaft

LotSize = Lot for Lot   LeadTime = 3 weeks

#8 Senior Composite Shaft	Week 1	Week 2	Week 3	Week 4	Week 5	Week 6	Week 7	Week 8
Gross requirements	485	750	770	790	770	780	880	0
Beginning on-hand	2100	1615	865	95	0	0	0	0
Ending on-hand	1615	865	95	0	0	0	0	0
Net requirements	0	0	0	695	770	780	880	0
Planned receipts	0	0	0	695	770	780	880	0
Planned releases	695	770	780	880	0	0	0	0

#1A Shaft Plug

LotSize = 100   LeadTime = 1 week

#1A Shaft Plug	Week 1	Week 2	Week 3	Week 4	Week 5	Week 6	Week 7	Week 8
Gross requirements	485	750	770	790	770	780	880	0
Beginning on-hand	1750	1265	515	45	55	85	5	25
Ending on-hand	1265	515	45	55	85	5	25	25
Net requirements	0	0	255	745	715	695	875	0
Planned receipts	0	0	300	800	800	700	900	0
Planned releases	0	300	800	800	700	900	0	0

#1 Fiber Mesh

LotSize = 200   LeadTime = 2 weeks

#1 Fiber Mesh	Week 1	Week 2	Week 3	Week 4	Week 5	Week 6	Week 7	Week 8
Gross requirements	850	1120	1420	1540	1560	1760	0	0
Beginning on-hand	3000	2150	1030	10	70	110	150	150
Ending on-hand	2150	1030	10	70	110	150	150	150
Net requirements	0	0	390	1530	1490	1650	0	0
Planned receipts	0	0	400	1600	1600	1800	0	0
Planned releases	400	1600	1600	1800	0	0	0	0

(continues)

Example 10.6

(continued)

#3R Blade Subassembly	LotSize = Lot for Lot			LeadTime = 1 week				
	Week 1	Week 2	Week 3	Week 4	Week 5	Week 6	Week 7	Week 8
Gross requirements	425	560	610	550	580	670	0	0
Beginning on-hand	500	75	0	0	0	0	0	0
Ending on-hand	75	0	0	0	0	0	0	0
Net requirements	0	485	610	550	580	670	0	0
Planned receipts	0	485	610	550	580	670	0	0
Planned releases	485	610	550	580	670	0	0	0

#3L Blade Subassembly	LotSize = Lot for Lot			LeadTime = 1 week				
	Week 1	Week 2	Week 3	Week 4	Week 5	Week 6	Week 7	Week 8
Gross requirements	0	0	100	220	200	210	0	0
Beginning on-hand	500	500	500	400	180	0	0	0
Ending on-hand	500	500	400	180	0	0	0	0
Net requirements	0	0	0	0	20	210	0	0
Planned receipts	0	0	0	0	20	210	0	0
Planned releases	0	0	0	20	210	0	0	0

#3 Blade (Right)	LotSize = Lot for Lot			LeadTime = 2 weeks				
	Week 1	Week 2	Week 3	Week 4	Week 5	Week 6	Week 7	Week 8
Gross requirements	485	610	500	580	670	0	0	0
Beginning on-hand	1100	615	5	0	0	0	0	0
Ending on-hand	615	5	0	0	0	0	0	0
Net requirements	0	0	545	580	670	0	0	0
Planned receipts	0	0	545	580	670	0	0	0
Planned releases	545	580	670	0	0	0	0	0

#3 Blade (Left)	LotSize = Lot for Lot			LeadTime = 2 weeks				
	Week 1	Week 2	Week 3	Week 4	Week 5	Week 6	Week 7	Week 8
Gross requirements	0	0	0	20	210	0	0	0
Beginning on-hand	900	900	900	900	880	670	670	670
Ending on-hand	900	900	900	880	670	670	670	670
Net requirements	0	0	0	20	210	0	0	0
Planned receipts	0	0	0	0	0	0	0	0
Planned releases	0	20	0	0	0	0	0	0

(continues)

Example 10.6 (continued)

#601 Lower Shaft	LotSize = Lot for Lot			LeadTime = 1 week				
	Week 1	Week 2	Week 3	Week 4	Week 5	Week 6	Week 7	Week 8
Gross requirements	485	610	550	600	880	0	0	0
Beginning on-hand	500	15	0	0	0	0	0	0
Ending on-hand	15	0	0	0	0	0	0	0
Net requirements	0	595	550	600	880	0	0	0
Planned receipts	0	595	550	600	880	0	0	0
Planned releases	595	550	600	880	0	0	0	0

EXCEL TUTOR
www.OperationsNow.com

Excel Tutor 10.6 demonstrates how MRP logic can be effectively created in an Excel spreadsheet.

PRIORITIZING INVENTORY: ABC ANALYSIS

The management of inventory can be expensive. The more sophisticated the system, the more expensive the management of the system. A reorder point system, for example, is a continuous-review system. Every time inventory is removed, a comparison is made between the actual level of inventory and the reorder point. A stockout can occur only during the replenishment lead time. A periodic review system, however, does not continuously monitor the inventory level. A stockout can potentially occur at any time. The differences in these systems result in cost differences. A simplistic approach might be to wait until a stockout occurs, and then reorder. A primitive form of a reorder point system is known as a **two-bin system**. When the first bin is emptied, a new order is placed. The second bin serves demand during the replenishment lead time.

A variety of inventory management systems are available and a company must decide which system to use. How does a company select the desired service level? One approach to making these decisions is a prioritization procedure known as ABC analysis (not to be confused with activity-based costing).

ABC analysis is based on the Pareto principle, which states that approximately 80 percent of the effects are the result of 20 percent of the causes. In an inventory situation, this translates into 80 percent of the dollar usage being associated with only 20 percent of the items. ABC analysis classifies inventory in order of importance. "A" items are the most important, "B" items are next, and "C" items are of relatively little importance. The relative importance of inventory items is generally linked to demand or dollar usage, but it could be linked to other critical issues, such as a particular customer, storage costs, or shelf life.

Generally, A items comprise about 10 percent or so of the inventory items. They are of extreme importance because they might account for as much as 50 percent of the cost. The B items are generally about 30–40 percent of the items, and C items are the remainder. Whether the items are A, B, or C will determine such issues as the type of inventory management system used, the service level used, and the number of suppliers or backup suppliers required.

MEASURING INVENTORY PRODUCTIVITY

Inventory productivity measures the amount of sales revenue generated from the inventory. Inventory productivity is generally measured in **inventory turns,** computed as sales divided by the average dollar level of inventory. The higher the inventory turns, the better. A higher number of turns simply means that the same amount of inventory, on average, is generating greater sales.

Since inventory is such a valuable asset, firms generally want to increase its productivity. Improving inventory turns is often mandated by top management. It results in reduced costs associated with inventory, increased profit margins, reduced assets and improved ROA. Increasing inventory turns almost always means reducing inventory. Rarely should it be interpreted as "increasing sales," although that would be even better. Unfortunately, all inventoried items don't contribute the same value to a business. Some are extremely important, while other items are just taking up space. Reducing the level of some inventory items will have no detrimental impact on sales, while reducing other items could actually result in reduced customer service caused by increasing stockouts. There are ways, however, to increase turnover in a manner that will not harm service quality or delivery reliability.

For manufacturers, inventory turnover is also related to lead time. If, for example, total manufacturing lead time was one week, the WIP inventory turns would be 52. Reducing lead time can result in a reduction of WIP inventory and improve the inventory productivity. Imagine the manufacturing facility as a large pipe. The pipe is always full, no matter how fast the contents flow. The faster the contents move, however, the greater the output, even though the volume inside the pipe is the same. Since the "output" is represented by sales (the numerator in the inventory turns equation), as output goes up, turns go up. One way manufacturers can reduce inventory is to reduce lead times by identifying non-value-adding steps in processes and implementing other time-saving practices, as discussed in Chapter 8. The inventory is in the system for a shorter time, resulting in a lower amount of inventory relative to sales. This same logic holds for the entire supply chain, from the basic manufacturers, who process raw materials, all the way through the assembler. Reduced time anywhere in the supply chain results in improved return on the inventory investment.

Another approach to improving the rate of flow of goods through a manufacturing operation or supply chain is to reduce the production and transfer batch sizes. Recall that the production batch size is the number of products produced before changing equipment over to produce something else. The transfer batch size is the number of products required before they will be transferred to the next processing step. As shown earlier, in Exhibit 10.3, more frequent delivery of smaller quantities anywhere in the supply chain improves the flow of goods. Rather than stopping and starting, goods begin to flow evenly. Using the pipe analogy again, we see that more can be moved through the pipe if its contents continue to flow evenly. Flow is a very apt term for the way materials move through manufacturing processes. Manufacturers seek to improve flow of materials. Some services actually view customers as "inventory" and seek to improve their flow as well.

The average level of finished goods and retailing inventories can obviously be reduced by carrying fewer of each item. The difficulty, however, is determining which items should receive the inventory reduction efforts. One approach is to focus strictly on the dollars. After all, the denominator of the inventory turns equation is the average value of inventory. By reducing the inventory level of high-dollar items, increasing inventory turnover is a quick result. However, the high-dollar items might also be the best sellers. Reduction in their quantity can have a negative impact on service level.

Another approach to the reduction of these types of inventory is to use a measure known as **dollar days**.[1] At the beginning of this chapter, inventory was described as an asset that sometimes behaved like a liability. The dollar-day method acknowledges this behavior and treats inventory like a loan. The total cost of a loan with a certain interest rate is determined by two factors: the size of the loan and its term. The total cost of inventory is determined in a similar way. It is dependent on the dollar value of inventory and how long the inventory is kept. Dollar days of inventory is computed by multiplying the dollar value of the inventory by the number of days until it will be sold. A firm wishing to increase inventory turns without detrimental effects on service level would seek to reduce dollar days. The dollar-day measure focuses equally on items with high dollar value *and* items that are slow movers. Items that are slow movers are those that do not contribute significantly to sales but have low turnover rates because they just sit in inventory. By using the dollar-day measure, it is possible for products with very different characteristics to be equally attractive for inventory reduction efforts. Example 10.7 demonstrates the computations necessary to determine the dollar days of inventory and also demonstrates how different products can create inventory costs in different ways.

Reducing inventory has a substantially different impact on the two items in the example because one is a fast mover and one is a slow mover. There is a six-day supply of the camcorder and a seven-week supply of the 35mm camera. Eliminating one unit of the 35mm camera reduces the dollar days by 10,500. Eliminating one unit of the camcorder reduces dollar days by 6,000 (12,000/2). The larger impact, however, will be in service quality, which will translate into net sales. Reducing the inventory of the camcorder will quickly reduce service level and net sales because of the short supply relative to the demand. Reducing inventory of the 35mm camera is of very little consequence because of its low demand. If the supply of the camcorder is reduced and net sales drop because of poor service, inventory turns could potentially be the same or even worse, because sales is in the numerator. Dollar days provides an excellent method of focusing on the right inventory for an inventory reduction effort. It acknowledges that there are two factors that account for inventory costs: the money invested in the inventory and the time it is invested.

Example 10.7 Dollar-Day Calculation

The value of a particular camcorder inventoried by an electronics shop is exactly $1,000, and annual demand is 730 units (an average of 2 units per day). Currently, there are 12 units in inventory. Another product, an autofocus 35mm camera, has a value of $214.29 and has an annual demand of 52 units (essentially one item every seven days) and 7 units on hand. What are the dollar days associated with each of these items?

Solution

For the camcorder, an average of 2 units are sold per day. So, 2 of the 12 units will be sold in one day, 2 more will be sold in two days, and so on. Exhibit 10.21 provides the completed dollar-day calculations. The 12 units of camcorder inventory create 42,000 dollar days.

(continues)

Example 10.7 (continued)

EXHIBIT 10.21 Dollar-Day Calculations for Camcorder

Number of Items	Days Until Sold	Dollar Days
2	1	2,000
2	2	4,000
2	3	6,000
2	4	8,000
2	5	10,000
2	6	12,000
Total dollar days		42,000

There are currently seven units of the 35mm camera on hand, selling one unit each day. Exhibit 10.22 shows that the dollar days created is 42,000.84 dollar days. The dollar days are virtually the same for the two items, but they are created by two very different product characteristics. The camcorder acquires dollar days from its high value. The 35mm camera gets its dollar days from the fact that demand is low, resulting in inventory that sits for a long time.

EXHIBIT 10.22 Dollar-Day Calculations for 35mm Camera

Number of Items	Days Until Sold	Dollar Days
1	7	1,500.03
1	14	3,000.06
1	21	4,500.09
1	28	6,000.12
1	35	7,500.15
1	42	9,000.18
1	49	10,500.21
Total dollar days		42,000.84

Excel Tutor 10.7 provides the Excel logic for the dollar-day calculation.

www
OperationsNow
.com

CHAPTER SUMMARY

This chapter examined inventory, the first of four critical resources used to create value. Two different types of inventory, dependent demand and independent demand, were recognized, and techniques used to manage them were examined. Since inventory is such an expensive asset and so costly to maintain, businesses strive to balance low inventory levels against appropriate levels of service. The financial impact of carrying too much inventory can be just as bad as the impact of losing sales from not carrying enough inventory.

Inventory is divided into two types: independent demand and dependent demand. Independent demand inventory is inventory whose demand is determined by the market. Dependent demand inventory is inventory whose demand is dictated by a production schedule for another item of inventory. The two types of inventory are managed differently because independent demand is uncertain, whereas dependent demand is deterministic. The systems used to manage these different types of inventory are described and demonstrated.

It is difficult to isolate the management of inventory from other productive resources because those other resources often consume and create inventory. It is also difficult to evaluate the productivity of resources and inventory because to be productive, many resources must create inventory. In any company, whether it be a manufacturer or a service, inventory is necessary: without it sales are lost and the business comes to a standstill. The resources that utilize inventory consist of the workforce, equipment capacity, and facilities—the other three categories that are examined in this unit. In the next chapter the workforce is examined as it adds value to business outputs.

KEY TERMS

- backward scheduling, 360
- batch processing, 345
- beginning on-hand inventory, 362
- bill of material, 360
- carrying cost, 343
- changeover cost, 343
- continuous replenishment, 344
- dependent demand inventory, 349
- decoupling, 341
- dollar days, 372
- economic order quantity model, 354
- ending on-hand inventory, 362
- finished-goods inventory, 344
- fixed-quantity order policy, 365
- gross requirements, 362
- independent demand inventory, 347
- inventory master file, 360
- inventory turns, 371
- level production, 346
- lot-for-lot ordering, 364
- maintenance, repair, and operating (MRO) inventory, 347
- master production schedule (MPS), 360
- material requirements planning (MRP), 360
- net requirements, 362
- netting, 360
- order cost, 343
- periodic review system, 357
- pipeline inventory, 348
- planned order receipt, 362
- planned order release, 362
- reorder point (ROP) model, 351
- replenishment lead time, 351
- safety stock, 352
- service level, 351
- stockout, 344
- stockout cost, 343
- transfer batch, 348
- two-bin system, 370
- work-in-process inventory (WIP), 348

REVIEW QUESTIONS

1. What is meant by decoupling? What is the role of inventory when decoupling is needed?
2. Describe the costs that comprise inventory order costs.
3. Describe the costs that contribute to inventory carrying costs.
4. What is a stockout cost?
5. What is continuous replenishment? In which business environment is it used?
6. What is meant by days-of-supply? How is it calculated?

7. What is batch production? Why do manufacturers use it?
8. How does excess inventory affect the cash-to-cash cycle?
9. What is the relationship between excess inventory and product quality?
10. What is independent demand inventory?
11. What is dependent demand inventory? How is it different from independent demand inventory?
12. What are pipeline inventories?
13. What is meant by the service level?
14. Describe the purpose of a safety stock. What impact does it have on inventory level?
15. What is the objective of the economic order quantity? What are its assumptions? What are its weaknesses?
16. Describe the informational inputs and logic of material requirements planning.
17. What resource decisions can be enhanced by using ABC analysis?

DISCUSSION QUESTIONS

1. Identify a product you keep on hand at home and do not want to be without. How many days-of-supply do you typically keep? What are the stockout costs? What are the costs of keeping too much?
2. How are the objectives of reorder point systems and MRP similar? How are they different? What characteristics of the demands of each determine the management methods used?
3. Discuss the linkage between forecast accuracy and inventory levels. What impact will an improvement in forecast accuracy have? What are some ways accuracy can be improved?
4. Why do some people argue that inventory should be treated as a liability instead of an asset? In what ways is the effect inventory has on a business similar to that of a debt?
5. Why does the dollar-day measure provide better direction for inventory reduction than the dollar value of the inventory item?

PROBLEMS

1. Mocha-Mocha is a local coffee shop. It sells an average of 239 cups of coffee per day. It receives a shipment of supply every two days. The store received a shipment this morning and currently has enough coffee on hand for 466 cups. If the demand is consistent with the average, will Mocha-Mocha be able to satisfy its customers until the next shipment?
2. Hathaway Services is not sure if it has the financial resources to stay in operation. It currently has $50,799 in liquid assets. The company has applied for a bank loan but does not yet know if it will receive any additional funding. If the company has an average expenditure of $12,095 per month, how long can it stay in operation without a loan?

3. Gas Guzzler is an independent gas station open seven days a week. The average weekly demand is 30,240 gallons. Every Monday a supply truck stops to fill the station's tanks. The station manager wants to begin each week with nine days' supply on hand. How many gallons should the station have on hand to start each week?

4. Ryan's Grill offers a regular special of 25-cent chicken wings. Average weekly demand for wings is 1,860, with a standard deviation of 11.4. Ryan's wing supplier requires orders to be placed one week before they are delivered. Calculate the reorder point if the restaurant would like to ensure a 99 percent service level.

5. Pads-N-Paper sells greeting cards for which it has an average weekly demand of 34 and a standard deviation of 9. The store would like to maintain at least a 97 percent service level. If the replenishment lead time on greeting cards is two weeks, what reorder point should be used?

6. The Stanfield Sluggers are a minor league pro baseball team. They currently use an average of 77 baseballs per week, with a standard deviation of 8.5. It takes a week's time to receive a shipment of new baseballs once ordered. What is the reorder point if the franchise would like a 90 percent service level?

7. Droid Robotics is a U.S. dealer in high-tech robotic components. Its parent company is located in Japan and supplies it with testing modules. Droid consumes an average of 125 testing modules per week, with a standard deviation of 5. It takes three weeks for an order of components to be shipped to Droid. Droid prides itself on delivering on time to its customers and must have no less than a 99.9 percent service level of testing modules. What should the reorder point be?

8. Dorm Accessories sells carpet for use in college dormitories. The average yearly demand for the carpet is 1,134. The cost per order is $30 and the inventory carrying cost is $7 per unit. Use the EOQ formula to calculate the appropriate order quantity.

9. Car USA would like to determine how many cars it should order at one time. The dealership sells an average of 10 cars per month. It costs the dealership $550 to place an order and $786 per year to carry a car in inventory. Compute the economic order quantity.

10. McMahon & Young is an area law firm. Its attorneys use 1,000 reams of paper a year. The cost of ordering from the local office supply company is $10 per order. It has calculated the annual carrying costs to be $1.25 per ream. What is the EOQ?

11. Fax & Phone sells telephone equipment and fax machines. It sells an average of five fax machines a month. Its supplier charges $49 per order but offers quantity discounts as follows:

    1–10 machines per order: $599 each

    10 + machines per order: $510 each

    The carrying costs for fax machines are $80 per unit. What is the EOQ?

12. Wiseman Bookstore has an annual demand of 250 for one of its selected hardback titles. The annual carrying cost of a single book is $4. The publishing company charges $5.50 per order. Calculate the EOQ if the publishing company charges $9.99 per book on orders of 1–20 and $9.29 per book on orders greater than 20.

13. Piper's Chips distributes snacks to grocery stores. The company uses a fixed-interval approach to replenishing inventory. You have been assigned to one of its clients. Use the following information to calculate the order quantity:

Average demand: 6 bags per day

Lead time: 2 days

Standard deviation of demand over the lead time: 2.4

Current inventory level: 24 bags

Service level: 95%

Order interval: 7 days

14. Harrington's Fine Jewelry orders most of its inventory from the same supplier. The supplier sends a representative to Harrington's every Monday to replenish stock. Given the following data, calculate the reorder quantity for the current order interval:

    Average demand: 3 pieces per day

    Lead time: 1 day

    Standard deviation: 1.89

    Current inventory level: 19

    Service level: 99%

    Order interval: 5 days

15. Sandlot Products produces toys for the beach. The Beach Combo 525 is a pail-and-shovel set perfect for a fun day in the sand. The combo is composed of three components: Pail 002, Handle 114, and Shovel 118. The Beach Combo requires one component for each finished product with the exception of the handle, of which there are two on the final product. Use the master production schedule below and MRP logic to compute the planned order releases for the components. There is a beginning inventory of 30 completed Beach Combos. Each of the components uses lot-for-lot ordering and has a one-week lead time.

Week	1	2	3	4	5	6	7	8
Demand	0	28	34	34	28	28	26	24

16. Safe Storage Inc. produces CD jewel cases. It is a simple product with only two components, a top and a bottom. The company operates on a lot-for-lot ordering system with a one-week lead time. There are currently 2,000 jewel cases on hand and ready for delivery. Use the following demand information and MRP logic to compute the planned order release schedule for the two components.

Week	1	2	3	4	5	6	7	8
Demand	0	1,450	800	1,050	875	1,200	950	850

17. Hanging Solutions manufactures products that help organize closets. Their best-known product is a wooden hanger. It is composed of a metal hook attached to a wooden support. The components are ordered lot-for-lot. The hooks are readily available with a one-week lead time but the supplier of the wooden supports can only offer a two-week lead time. The master production schedule is given below. Using MRP logic, calculate the planned order release schedule if there are 400 hangers currently in inventory.

Week	1	2	3	4	5	6	7	8
Demand	0	125	134	145	167	138	129	115

18. AM Tools produces two hammers, a regular and a deluxe. The regular hammer is composed of a wooden handle with a metal head. The deluxe consists of the same material but adds a rubber grip to the handle. The company uses lot-for-lot ordering

and can get the needed materials from its suppliers in one week. The production schedules for the two models of hammer are given below. If there are 50 regular hammers and 25 deluxe hammers currently on hand, what is the schedule of planned order releases?

Week	1	2	3	4	5	6	7	8
Hammer	0	45	51	53	48	62	49	52
Deluxe Hammer	0	21	26	27	22	24	27	31

19. Home Accents is a regional producer of doors for homes. The product structure is seen in Exhibit 10.23 and the master production schedule is given below. Using MRP logic, compute the planned order release schedule.

Week	1	2	3	4	5	6	7	8
Home Door	0	21	17	14	19	22	15	18

EXHIBIT 10.23

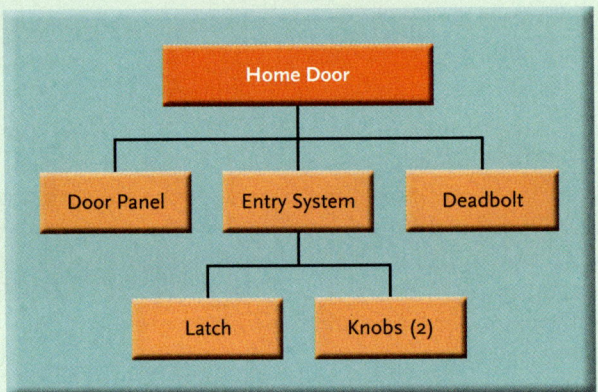

Component	Order Policy	On Hand
Home door	Lot-for-lot	25
Door panel	Lot-for-lot	0
Deadbolt	5	0
Entry system	Lot-for-lot	0
Latch	Lot-for-lot	30
Knobs	Lot-for-lot	15

20. Ray's Music currently has seven copies of pop singer Brianna Brinks's new CD. The CD has a value of $9.00 and the store expects to sell one copy every other day. Compute the dollar days of Brianna Brinks CDs.

21. The University Bookstore expects to sell six notebooks a day. The notebooks are valued at $2.50. The bookstore has 42 notebooks currently in stock. Calculate the dollar days associated with the notebooks.

22. Alberti Clothiers has seven shirts in inventory, valued at $22.00 each. The store expects to sell one shirt every eight days. Alberti also has 25 sweaters, valued at $48.00 each. Alberti anticipates selling five of these sweaters per day. Calculate the dollar days for each item. What is the reduction in dollar days if one unit of each item is eliminated from inventory?

INTERACTIVE ANALYSIS 10.1

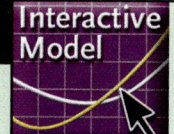
www.
OperationsNow
.com

THE REORDER POINT INTERACTIVE MODEL

The Reorder Point Interactive Model is accessed through Chapter 10 of the *OperationsNow.com* website. The Reorder Point Interactive Model provides an interactive environment in which to manipulate the various input parameters of the reorder point model and see the immediate results. The parameters of service level, standard deviation, and replenishment lead time can be adjusted to see the impact on the reorder point, the safety stock, and the average inventory level.

Experiment 1: System Fundamentals

1. Set the system parameters to these values:

Parameter	Value
Service level	99 percent
Standard deviation (weekly)	5
Replenishment lead time	1 week

   a. What is the reorder point with these parameters? Increase the lead time to two weeks. What happens to the reorder point?

   b. Increase the standard deviation from 5 to 8. What happens to the reorder point?

   c. Reduce the service level from 99 percent to 95 percent. What happens to the reorder point?

Experiment 2: The Impact of Service Level

1. The safety stock is a function of the variability of demand (σd_{LT}) and the service level desired. The safety stock affects the average level of inventory because the average level of inventory is equal to one-half the order quantity plus the safety stock. Set the parameters to these values:

Parameter	Value
Service level	85 percent
Standard deviation (weekly)	4
Replenishment lead time	2 weeks

   a. What is the reorder point and average level of inventory at these parameters? Increase the service level to 88 percent. What happens to the reorder point and average level of inventory?

   b. Increase the service level to 89 percent. What happens to the reorder point and average level of inventory? Increase the service level in 1 percent increments and graph the change in reorder point and average level of inventory. What is causing the change in the reorder point?

Experiment 3: The Impact of Demand Variability

The safety stock contributes to the reorder point and the average level of inventory. If no variability existed from period to period, there would be no uncertainty of demand and no need for a safety stock.

1. Set the parameters to these values:

Parameter	Value
Service level	95%
Standard deviation (weekly)	1
Replenishment lead time	3 weeks

    a. Record the values for the reorder point and average level of inventory. Incrementally change the standard deviation of demand by one-unit intervals, and record the corresponding changes to the reorder point and average level of demand. Describe the relationship between variability of demand, reorder point, and average level of inventory.

2. Set the parameters to these values:

Parameter	Value
Service level	95%
Standard deviation (weekly)	1
Replenishment lead time	1 week

    a. Record the values for the reorder point and average level of inventory. Repeat the process of incrementally changing the standard deviation of demand by one-unit intervals, and recording the corresponding changes to the reorder point and average level of demand. What impact does the replenishment lead time have on the relationship between variability of demand, reorder point, and average level of inventory?

Experiment 4: The Impact of Replenishment Lead Time

The reorder point is expected to satisfy demand during lead time. The longer that lead time, the greater the demand, and the higher the reorder point must be.

1. Set the parameters to these values:

Parameter	Value
Service level	95%
Standard deviation (weekly)	4
Replenishment lead time	1 week

    a. What happens to the reorder point when the replenishment lead time is increased to two weeks? three weeks? four weeks? Why is the standard deviation of demand during lead time changing?

    b. What happens to the average level of inventory as you move from one week, to two weeks, to three weeks, to four weeks?

INTERACTIVE ANALYSIS 10.2

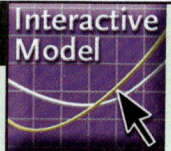

www.
OperationsNow
.com

THE ECONOMIC ORDER QUANTITY INTERACTIVE MODEL

The Economic Order Quantity Interactive Model is accessed through Chapter 10 of the *OperationsNow.com website*. The model provides an interactive environment to explore how the input parameters of carrying cost, demand, and order cost affect the economic order quantity. In the model, the user can change the values of the demand (D), the carrying cost (H), and the order cost (S) by manipulating slider buttons. The outcome is presented graphically, with the order quantity on the x axis and the total cost on the y axis.

Experiment 1: System Fundamentals

1. Set the default parameters to these values:

Parameter	Value
Carrying cost (H)	$9
Demand (D)	200
Order cost (S)	$20

   a. What is the economic order quantity at these parameter settings? What is the total carrying cost at this quantity? What is the order cost?

   b. From the shape of the total cost curve, do you think rounding the order quantity will have much of an impact on the total cost? Why or why not?

Experiment 2: The Impact of Carrying Cost

1. Set the parameters to these values:

Parameter	Value
Carrying cost (H)	$4
Demand (D)	200
Order cost (S)	$20

   a. What is the economic order point at these parameters?

   b. Incrementally increase the carrying cost, one dollar at a time, from $4 to $20. Graph your results. What is the relationship between carrying cost and the economic order quantity?

Experiment 3: The Impact of Order Cost

1. Set the parameters to these values:

Parameter	Value
Carrying cost (H)	$2
Demand (D)	200
Order cost (S)	$4

   a. What is the economic order quantity at these parameters? Increase the order cost to $5. What happens?

   b. Incrementally increase the order cost, one dollar at a time, to $20. Graph the economic order quantity for each corresponding order cost.

Experiment 4: The Impact of Demand

1. Set the parameters to these values:

Parameter	Value
Carrying cost (*H*)	$9
Demand (*D*)	200
Order cost (*S*)	$15

   a. Increase the demand to 220 units. What is the impact on the reorder point?

   b. Increase the demand, in increments of 20 units, from 220 to 400. Graph the results. What is the relationship between the economic order quantity and the demand?

SELECTED REFERENCES

Vollman, T., Berry, W. L., and Whybark, D. C. *Manufacturing Planning and Control Systems.* New York: McGraw-Hill, 1997.

Zipkin, P. H. *Foundations of Inventory Management.* New York: McGraw-Hill, 2000.

ENDNOTE

1. E. M. Goldratt and R. E. Fox, "The Fundamental Measurements," *The Theory of Constraints Journal*, August–September, 1988.

OperationsNow.com LEARNING ACTIVITIES

CHAPTER ENHANCEMENT RESOURCES
- Esources
- Reel Operations Video Clips
- Interactive Models
- Excel Tutors
- Supplementary Readings
- Links to Operations On Site Companies

OM EXPLORATION
- Check It Out
- OM in Action
- Online Business Tours
- Letters from the Top
- Putting It All Together: Virtual Case Studies
- Additional Readings

In the resource/profit model, workforce is represented as one of five resources necessary to create value. The workforce is, without question, as important as any other asset, and in many ways more important and more difficult to manage. After all, no other resources can get up and walk away from the business when dissatisfied. Managing a workforce is like no other challenge. It has the greatest potential, but it can also be the most difficult resource to utilize effectively.

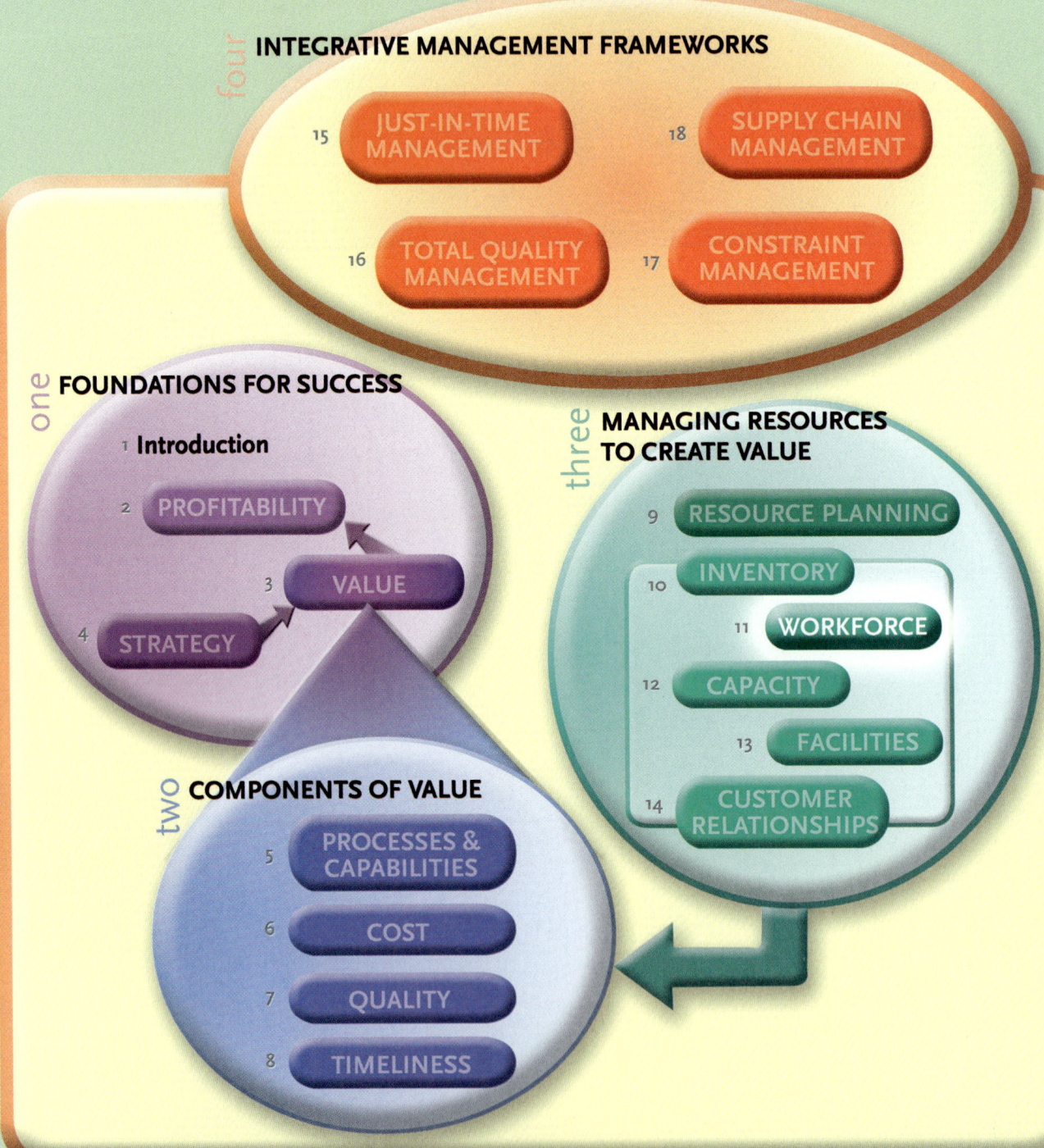

CHAPTER 1

Workforce

LEARNING OBJECTIVES

Upon completion of Chapter 11, you should be able to

_____ Describe how the workforce contributes to profitability.

_____ Explain how expectations for employees are increasing.

_____ Explain the impact the workforce has on value.

_____ Use the customer experience grid to describe the relationship between customers and employees.

_____ Describe why teams have become more important.

_____ Explain a structure for team processes.

_____ Describe the impacts of contingent workers.

_____ Describe why workforce productivity is important.

_____ Demonstrate how standard times are created.

_____ Make the necessary calculations to perform a work sampling study.

_____ Describe how learning rates can affect worker productivity.

_____ Calculate the amount of time a task will take, given a specified learning rate.

Introduction: Using the Workforce as a Key to Competitive Success
Employee/Customer Interaction, Value, and Profitability
The Employee Contribution to Value Attributes
Employee Interaction with Customers: A Prerequisite to Good Service
The Most Important Employee Contribution to Value: Sound Decisions
Increasing the Contribution of Employees Through Teams
Increased Need for Workforce Flexibility
Who's in Charge?
The New Working Environment
Workforce Productivity Improvement
Chapter Summary

INTERNET RESOURCES

 Excel Tutors provide annotated spreadsheets for every solved problem that automatically load Excel.

 Esources provide an online version of the more traditional boxed insert.

 Reel Videos provide streaming video footage for company applications of chapter concepts.

 Interactive Models provide an experimental environment for quantitative concepts and simulations.

INTRODUCTION

Using the Workforce as a Key to Competitive Success

Successful businesses recognize that their most valuable asset is their workforce. Clearly, the workforce is one of the most important resources for operations, as shown in Exhibit 11.1. The most successful CEOs have said this for decades, and some have actually meant it. The increasing importance of the workforce can be traced to several environmental pressures. First and foremost, as businesses become increasingly dependent on information and technology, related skills become more valuable, and competition for employees with those skills becomes fierce. We are in an information-based economy. Workers must have the skills to access and use the information and knowledge and must be able to keep up with the rapidly changing technologies utilized to manage it.

Second, as the business world becomes more networked, products become more like commodities, which makes differentiation on the basis of product quality or price more difficult. Market dominance shifts to the most innovative company. Innovation comes from ideas. Ideas come from people. Despite advances in recent years, we have yet to develop software that can come up with even the simplest idea.

Third, competition is, to a great extent, based on service-oriented value attributes. The market for high-quality employees is tight. Even for manufacturers, employees who can interact effectively with customers become key components of a successful strategy. Businesses seeking all ranges of workers, from minimum-wage workers to high-salaried specialists, struggle to fill positions with quality employees. To make matters worse, hiring someone is not the end of the process. Retaining a good employee becomes an ongoing challenge, because other businesses need good employees, too.

This chapter examines the workforce and its role in contributing to value and ultimately profitability. Included in that discussion are current issues that affect workforce management, such as the changing nature of the work environment, the increased use of teams, increasing needs for certain skills, job design characteristics, and workforce productivity improvement.

EMPLOYEE/CUSTOMER INTERACTION, VALUE, AND PROFITABILITY

As you certainly know by now, profitability depends on net income, which, in turn, depends on value, processes, and resources, as illustrated in Exhibit 11.1. No one can deny that employees are expensive, from a direct and indirect labor standpoint. The cost of direct labor varies tremendously, depending on the nature of the business, whether it's manufacturing- or service-oriented, and on other characteristics of the business. For example, in many manufacturing environments direct labor accounts for less than 10 percent of product costs. In other business environments, it can be the largest cost category. If the only value added by employees can be replaced by machines, however, it's no wonder some managers dream of the day when the factory doesn't even have lights in it. Given the desire most managers have to maximize utilization of resources, it's ironic that the full range of employee capability and talent is so often underutilized.

Without value, sales don't happen. As the business world becomes increasingly more connected through the Internet, anyone can buy anything from anyone else. Price differentials begin to disappear, because everyone is aware of the best prices. Product quality differentials disappear as well, because no one with inferior-quality products survives. Customers know what products and services are the best value,

CHAPTER 11   Workforce   387

The Role of Workforce in the Resource/Profit Model   EXHIBIT 11.1

four — INTEGRATIVE MANAGEMENT FRAMEWORKS
- 15 JUST-IN-TIME MANAGEMENT
- 18 SUPPLY CHAIN MANAGEMENT
- 16 TOTAL QUALITY MANAGEMENT
- 17 CONSTRAINT MANAGEMENT

one — FOUNDATIONS FOR SUCCESS
1. Introduction
2. PROFITABILITY
3. VALUE
4. STRATEGY

three — MANAGING RESOURCES TO CREATE VALUE
9. RESOURCE PLANNING
10. INVENTORY
11. WORKFORCE
12. CAPACITY
13. FACILITIES
14. CUSTOMER RELATIONSHIPS

two — COMPONENTS OF VALUE
5. PROCESSES & CAPABILITIES
6. COST
7. QUALITY
8. TIMELINESS

because they talk to each other via chat rooms, email, and bulletin boards. Location doesn't matter because a customer can click on anyone's website with equal ease. A business no longer competes only with those in its geographic region. The market consists of businesses with similar prices, quality, and products trying to differentiate themselves through whatever value attributes remain for differentiation. Exactly what does remain? For many businesses, the only thing left is service. Remember, in most businesses, value doesn't solely depend on outcomes. The processes a customer must go through to get the desired outcomes are equally important. How fast can I get it? How much do the people I talk to actually know about it? How pleasant is the interaction? Several studies have shown that service is an extremely important component of value in all types of B2B and B2C interactions, but even more so with Internet sales. Customer response, positive and negative, often results from service interactions with employees.

Employees make a tremendous difference in service encounters. In many cases, when the value added by customer–employee interactions is removed, there is no value differential left, and competitive advantage disappears. One way employees are wasted is in what management doesn't let them do. Despite the link between customers and value, in many companies, management does not want employees to interact with customers. Customers, however, are demanding these interactions. Employees want these interactions also, because talking to customers makes their job more interesting, and because they want to know the customers. People enjoy interacting with other people. It's fun. Unfortunately, managers often try to prevent these interactions because they sense a loss of control. They worry about what an employee might say. Sometimes they worry that an employee will tell the truth. But truth is what customers demand. Other customers will tell them the truth. They will find out the truth. It might as well come from the company and the workforce. Management's fear might be warranted if the employees do not have the skills or knowledge to effectively interact with customers. If that is the case, however, the business is probably doomed whether or not management succeeds at keeping employees away from customers. Employees need to be able to interact with customers.[1] Employees value companies that provide them with opportunities to expand their skills. Such companies are rewarded with high-quality employees.

Reduction of labor costs (direct and indirect) has always been a goal of businesses. Let's face it—reduction of all costs has been a goal of business, but labor gets the brunt of reductions because managers can always find an employee not working at 100 percent. The history of manufacturing technology leads one to believe that a primary goal has been to completely eliminate the need for direct labor. This has been accomplished by substituting capital investments, like automated machines, for people. This perspective almost seems reasonable in a product-oriented environment that has little need for interaction between customers and employees. And it definitely makes sense when the job is repetitive, boring, or dangerous. The elimination of labor in traditional manufacturing is not all that different from the trends in people-intensive business activities like marketing. Mass marketing strategies often eliminate the one-to-one interactions that characterized original "markets" where people assembled to discuss agricultural products they had to trade and sell. When the word "market" became a verb, the relationships among buyers and sellers changed drastically. Market shifted from being a place where people discussed and traded goods to something a company did to people. The Internet, however, is quickly reversing this trend. It is viewed as a "place" by many of its users. They "go" there. Where'd you get it? I got it on the Internet. An entity very dif-

Despite attempts to reduce customer interaction to improve efficiency, for many firms, customer interaction provides a way to differentiate from competitors. Small banks, like the one here, have been able to gain substantial market share in recent years by focusing on service activities that come only from the interactions between customers and highly skilled employees.

on site

Should Employees Talk to Customers?

The rapidly increasing ability of employees to talk directly to customers has created difficult issues for many businesses. Customers want the truth, and employees can often give it to them. Employees enjoy talking to customers. This is made faster and easier with Internet bulletin boards, listserves, and email. In May 2000, Jill Griffin, customer-service representative for American Airlines, registered with FlyerTalk, an online bulletin board for frequent fliers. She began to answer questions on her own time.

American Airlines officials were initially supportive, and Griffin had a loyal following on the site, but after a few months American became uneasy about her responding to questions and making statements without official authorization. In January 2001, she added a disclaimer to her responses, claiming that her responses weren't sanctioned by American or AMR, American's parent corporation. On March 29, 2001, she posted her last response, stating that her employer did not want her to post anymore.

An American Airlines spokesman expressed concern that she was passing on erroneous information and information that the company didn't want public. He expressed concern that if some of the information she passed on got into the hands of a competitor, American Airlines would be disadvantaged.

Other members of FlyerTalk, however, felt very differently. The publisher of *InsideFlyer* magazine, the host of the FlyerTalk forum, responded with "This is what customer service looks like in the 21st century." Other companies agree. Hilton Hotels has had a representative assigned to the FlyerTalk bulletin board since June 1999. Some companies assign someone to bulletin boards to "lurk" but not get actively involved. Delta, for example, monitors online discussions on several message boards but doesn't offer official responses. The gradual integration of this aspect of customer service into the mainstream of service and industrial markets is certain to cause problems. Although the businesses want to avoid "unofficial" information that could cause problems, customers don't believe "official" statements any more. They want the straight story from an individual, not a corporate entity. This is particularly true in an industry like air travel, where customers have more than enough reason to be skeptical.

While the question may be difficult for many companies, according to the authors of *The Cluetrain Manifesto,* it's a no-brainer. Companies must create the link so that customers can speak to individuals who have the answers to questions. The Internet has created an expectation that companies cannot ignore. To ignore it is to ignore their customers.

Source: "Should Workers Offer Unofficial Help Online?" *The Wall Street Journal,* April 17, 2001, pp. B1, B6; R. Levine, C. Locke, D. Searles, and D. Weinberger, *The Cluetrain Manifesto* (New York: Perseus Books, 2000).

---

ferent from other forms of media, like TV or radio, the Internet is much closer to being like the marketplace of old. Businesses have rapidly discovered that attempts to treat Internet marketing like TV advertising will fail. The Internet has brought employees and customers back in touch with each other for many businesses, when management allows it.

Do you remember the short-lived hyperbole of "push" technology? Probably not. It appeared in about 1998 as *the* way to use the Internet in marketing efforts. It's ancient history now. Users don't want it. Rather than a business disseminating one-way bullets of information to millions of potential customers, as is the case with TV advertising, customers expect two-way interaction on the Internet. They expect to talk to employees of the business. They expect to talk directly to people who know the answers to their questions, and, in most cases, those are the employees most familiar with the products and services—those who actually produce them. And, even though many businesses try to prevent it, employees can and want to talk directly to customers. That interaction has tremendous potential for product and service value and customer loyalty. Loyalty, after all, is often directed toward people, not legal entities like corporations. The interactions made possible by knowledgeable, committed employees may be one of the most important competitive advantages remaining.

THE EMPLOYEE CONTRIBUTION TO VALUE ATTRIBUTES

We know from Chapter 3 that customers value some product and service attributes more than others. What they value varies from customer to customer and also varies from business to business. The following list recaps the B2B and B2C value attributes presented in Chapter 3. Understanding the value added by the workforce requires understanding the link between those value attributes and the employees.

Cost	Style/fashion
Quality	Ethical issues
Response time	Technology
Dependability of delivery	Flexibility
Convenience	Personalization

Costs of products and service production are composed of materials, labor, and overhead expenses. Obviously the workforce, through its productivity, has an impact on labor and overhead costs. The greater the productivity, the lower the cost on a per-unit basis. Materials consumption and associated costs are often a function of the product and service design and the systems that process those materials. One of the most avoidable costs associated with material use is that associated with waste and poor quality. Ideas for preventing waste and improving quality are often best found at the lowest possible levels of the workforce. Major cost savings can be had by working smarter, not necessarily working harder. This is probably one of the most overlooked potentials of today's workforce. The workers on the frontlines have a wealth of knowledge. Unfortunately, many businesses get no financial return on that asset.

Quality, *response time*, and *dependability of delivery* often fall under the broader concept of product and service quality. Quality, in many ways, is not achieved by finishing a set of tasks that can easily be separated and assigned. It is a mentality that is instilled through a company culture. A culture is created from a common belief among employees. For many service encounters, the employee defines that interaction. Certainly product quality, response time, and delivery performance are dictated by various production and delivery systems, but without the emphasis on those attributes by employees, the firm will not excel. When disruptions and failures do take place, and a product or service quality level isn't up to expectations, or the delivery time is too long or late, the success of the recovery is entirely controlled by the intervening employees. The relationship established by the employees will determine the ultimate resolution.

Convenience, *style/fashion*, and *ethical issues* are value attributes that result more from strategic decisions and less from the day-to-day actions of employees. In the case of convenience, however, it is still up to the workforce to carry out the tasks necessary to provide it. When competing on the basis of style/fashion, a workforce that has the knowledge or interest about the product or service, especially from the perspective of being a user of the products, is of great help. When competing on ethical issues, it is important to have a workforce committed to the issues. Only a sympathetic workforce can effectively communicate the company's position. These workforce requirements may seem obvious, but they are not easily obtained. In a tight labor market, any additional qualifications that reduce the size of the pool of acceptable candidates make it more difficult and more costly to hire quality workers. For companies seeking to differentiate on the basis of these attributes, the characteristics of the workforce are extremely important.

Technology, *flexibility*, and *personalization* attributes are aspects of the product or service production system that require specific skills and capabilities on the part of employees. Employees who have direct impact on these value attributes will likely have job responsibilities that are specifically designed to enhance them. Technological skills are probably in the highest demand in today's workforce. Flexibility and personalization, in many cases, require technological capabilities as well because flexibility and personalization are often achieved through technological applications included in scheduling systems or customer relationship management (CRM) systems.

EMPLOYEE INTERACTION WITH CUSTOMERS: A PREREQUISITE TO GOOD SERVICE

The preceding discussion of the impact of employees on value attributes leads to the conclusion that trainable skills do not make the only difference between a value-adding employee and a non-value-adding employee. Knowledge is a requirement as well. Knowledge obtained on the job is often more important than the more formal knowledge a person brings to the company. Personality and attitude can also play a major role, particularly in customer contact situations. The combination of skills, knowledge, personality, and attitude, and their ultimate impact on the firm's ability to create the value attributes necessary to compete effectively, should make it obvious that an effective workforce truly is a firm's most valuable asset.

The link between the workforce and profitability can be made from the perspective of increasing value and decreasing costs, as has been done so far in this chapter, or from a broader and different perspective—that of customer loyalty. Much has been said about employee satisfaction and whether or not the satisfaction of employees ever has an impact on a firm's profitability. The **service–profit chain**[2] creates a sound logical link between employee satisfaction and profitability by demonstrating the link to customer loyalty that can be created by the workforce.

The service–profit chain, diagrammed in Exhibit 11.2, is not meant to be applicable only to services, excluding product-oriented companies, but is meant to address

EXHIBIT 11.2 Service–Profit Chain

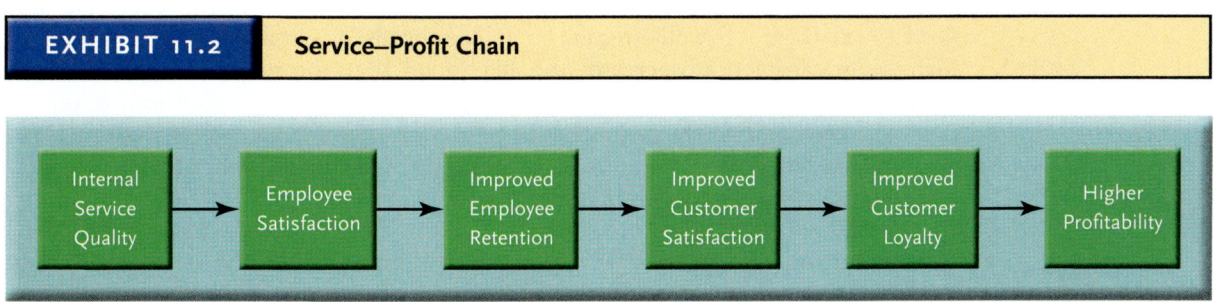

Source: Modified from G. W. Loveman, W. E. Sasser Jr., and L. A. Schlesinger, "Putting the Service–Profit Chain to Work," *Harvard Business Review*, March–April 1994, p. 166.

Cutting Employee Perks: With or Without Cutting Employee Morale

The concept of "internal quality" that maintains employee satisfaction and low employee turnover is often enhanced by a variety of employee perks. During the high point of the short-lived dot-com success era, perks included free lunches, coffee, massages, snacks, evening entertainment, and other benefits that seem unusual and extravagant in most situations. Some companies employed concierge services, costing as much as $100,000 per year, to assist employees with such tasks as vacation planning, buying tickets to entertainment events, and other personal activities that the employee would likely do at work. As companies began to experience financial difficulties, perks were the first things to go. In most cases, employees had little input in deciding which perks were withdrawn, and the changes had a negative impact on employee morale.

Reducing employee perks is a common means of cutting costs of items that do not have a significant return on investment. One Aetna Insurance office, for example, saves $400,000 per year by making employees buy their own coffee and tea. Excite@Home saves $165,000 per year by making employees pay 25 cents a can for soft drinks. In what would seem to be commonsense advice, experts recommend that when perks need to be cut, involving employees in the decision is important. Scaling back perks without totally eliminating them curbs negative reactions. Recommendations for cutting back on perks with a minimal impact on employee morale include the following:

- Scale back without entirely eliminating the perks.
- Ask employees which perks are the most important.
- Explain the cutbacks in the context of the business.
- Do not allow employees to learn about the cutbacks informally or through the grapevine.
- Do not make cuts that affect only lower-level employees.
- Do not assume that cuts will be a panacea for massive cost-cutting needs.
- Do not cut 401(k) matching funds, medical/dental care, day care, or flextime.

Source: M. Pole, "How to Cut Perks Without Killing Morale," *Fortune*, February 19, 2001, pp. 241–244.

---

the service-oriented activities of all companies. From Exhibit 11.2, the role of internal quality—in other words, treating employees well and getting them what they need to do their job well—results in higher levels of employee satisfaction. The increase in satisfaction decreases the likelihood that the employee will leave. A higher level of experience, resulting from improved employee retention, results in improved customer satisfaction, which comes from the increased value customers get from that interaction. That increase in satisfaction results in higher levels of loyalty and the higher level of profitability that accompanies it.

The role of internal quality and the concept of the internal customer is addressed in greater detail in Chapter 16, "Total Quality Management." The best companies to work for are always at an advantage because they get more job applicants, allowing them to be more selective. Esource 11.1 provides a reference to one of the more popular lists of the best companies to work for.

Customer loyalty is an often overlooked, but critically important result of operations. The feedback from customers frequently is something like "Your products are great, but I hate doing business with you." Customer loyalty doesn't result from evaluations like this. Companies focus on product-creation processes, but customer service processes get overlooked. The customer experience grid, adapted in Exhibit 11.3 to illustrate the impact of customer–employee interaction, provides an effective way to look at customer loyalty.[3] It demonstrates how the outcome and process combine to result in customer satisfaction of the overall experience. Each is only one component of the loyalty equation. The expectations also vary as customer interaction increases. In many cases, when the outcomes leave no opportunity for differentiation, processes become more important. Within the processes, the quantity and quality of employee interaction become an opportunity for differentiation. Invariably, the processes that make up the encounter depend on employees. The greater the interaction, the more critical the judgment and interaction skills of the employees, because expectations for customization increase as well.

One reaction of managers to this emphasis on customer loyalty might be that loyalty is too expensive to try to get. Businesses that try to develop loyalty have a completely different perspective. They view the customer relationship as a long-term asset with a lifetime value rather than a one-time source of revenue. Rather than sell one car to a customer, they want to transform that customer into a loyal customer and sell 10 or 12 cars over the next 25 years. What makes the customer loyalty goal even more

Customer Experience Grid with Customer Interaction Dimension — EXHIBIT 11.3

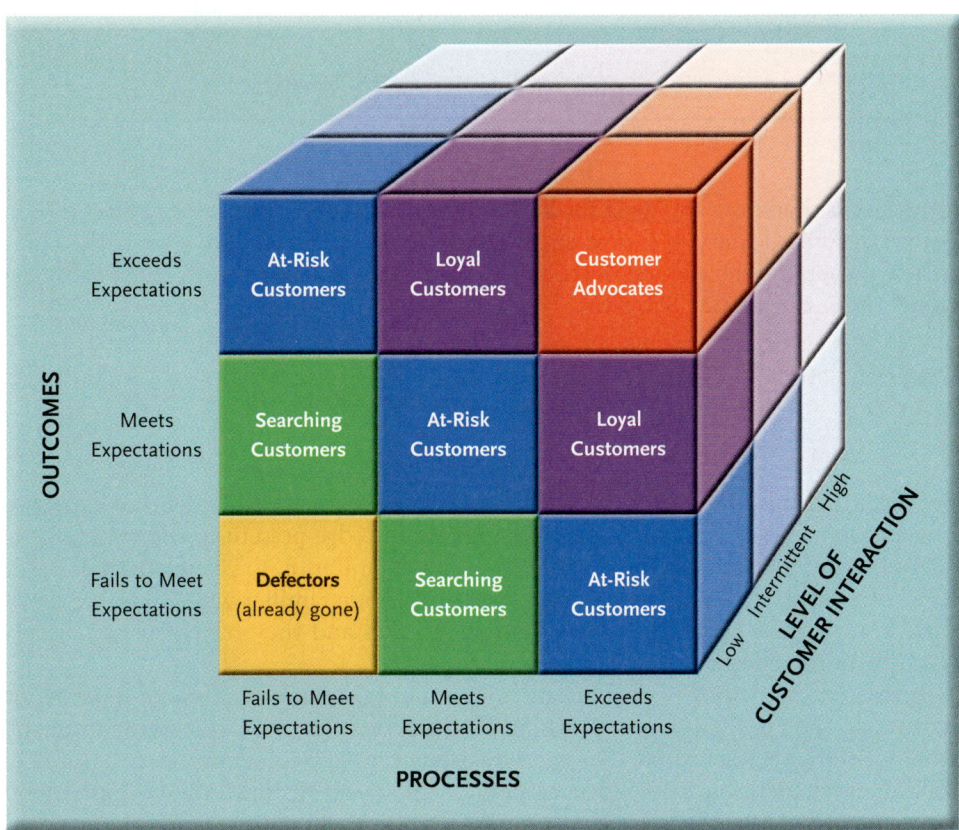

> ### Reducing Turnover in the Fast-Food Industry
>
> Employee work experience is important to good service and quality products. The service–profit chain provides an excellent framework for how this phenomenon eventually affects customer satisfaction. If you were to guess that one of the highest-turnover industries is fast food, you'd be right. Despite the fact that a high turnover rate is expected, it's still to management's benefit to reduce it. Several fast-food chains are trying to develop benefits packages that encourage employees to consider their jobs as a possible career. Burger King, for example, provides 401(k) retirement plans for workers in its 500 corporate restaurants and plans to launch a 401(k) plan for its 8,000 franchised restaurants. Tricon Global Restaurants, operator of Taco Bell, Pizza Hut, and KFC, offers some restaurant employees stock options and ties management bonuses to employee retention.
>
> In the mid-1990s, employee turnover rate for fast-food restaurants averaged over 200 percent (the average length of employment was about six months). Most restaurants have seen improvement in turnover rates, with some getting significantly below 200 percent. There are several benefits to these improvements. Average training costs per employee for Burger King, for example, are $400–800 per employee, so reduced turnover results in lower training costs. The average experience level of the employees goes up and so does quality. Profitability improves from the improved satisfaction of customers and from the reduction in labor costs.
>
> Increases in employee benefits have also resulted in an increase in the age of the employee. The average age of a Wendy's employee, for example, has crept up to between 27 and 28 years old. Restaurant management recognizes that it cannot provide quality levels that require a stable workforce from 16-year-olds. Attracting an older workforce requires more benefits and an opportunity for advancement.
>
> Source: "Fast Food Industry Pitches 'Burger Flipping' as a Career," *The Wall Street Journal,* May 29, 2001, pp. B1, B16.

attractive is that costs are lower for loyal customers. Unfortunately for managers who ignore customer loyalty, it is now easier than ever for a customer to try out the competition when the transaction outcome or process is unsatisfactory. In many cases the competition is just one click away.

THE MOST IMPORTANT EMPLOYEE CONTRIBUTION TO VALUE: SOUND DECISIONS

Successful organizations empower their workers to use their knowledge and expertise in decision making. The use of the talent and knowledge present in the workforce is enhanced by moving decisions downward in the organization to give workers at lower levels the authority to make decisions in areas they are familiar with. In many cases, their knowledge is specific to the situation at hand and they have a better understanding of the effects of the decision.

Increased interaction with customers is a natural outcome of moving decisions downward. The best answer to a customer's questions can often come only from the employee directly responsible for the production of that customer's product or service. Taking every question to a customer service employee frustrates the customer who waits endlessly as the customer service representative seeks out the employee who can best answer the question. This creates a delay that the customer shouldn't have. Putting the customer in direct contact with a knowledgeable and responsible employee familiar with the product or service provides a quick and accurate response.

Just as the employees who produce a product or service are often the most knowledgeable and most qualified to answer customers' questions, employees who work day-to-day with processes are often most qualified to help improve them. All aspects of business can be improved through significant contributions from employees on the front lines. For many firms, these improvement efforts have led to the use of project teams.

INCREASING THE CONTRIBUTION OF EMPLOYEES THROUGH TEAMS

In the late 1970s, Japanese auto manufacturers began increasing their market share in the United States by building cars that were well-designed, reliable, and of impeccable quality. Naturally, the U.S. auto manufacturers tried to figure out how they did it. One of the obvious differences was the way Japanese manufacturers used their employees. They had numerous small groups of employees working on product and process improvement projects. Suspecting that this was how the Japanese manufacturers created their quality culture, U.S. manufacturers and services embarked on a giant mission to implement employee work groups, called "quality circles," in all of their operations. Unfortunately for United States managers, quality circles were not the cause of the quality culture in Japan. Employees working in teams were, in fact, a result of that culture. In the United States, the quality circle fad gradually faded. We did come to realize, however, that using groups of employees to help improve quality levels and process productivity was a good idea. We just needed to figure out how to do it right. The result has been a steady increase in the use of project and improvement teams in U.S. businesses.

The use of teams has spread throughout the quality and process improvement efforts and has permeated new-product development, system implementation, and the management of virtually any small- or large-scale endeavor. Reengineering efforts, described in Chapter 5, are frequently accomplished by project teams. Total quality management (TQM) and just-in-time (JIT), two integrative management frameworks described in the final unit of this text, depend heavily on the expertise of well-trained worker teams. In many cases, the teams are intentionally composed of employees from different business functions to bring different perspectives, knowledge of different needs, and different areas of expertise to bear on the project. The desire to fully utilize employee knowledge and skills, combined with the increased recognition that many decisions have far-reaching impact across functional boundaries, has resulted in an increase in the use of cross-functional project teams.

Successful companies have learned that the development of a successful team requires much more than throwing workers together in a group and assigning them a task. Employees do not typically have the skills necessary to function well in that environment. A true team environment requires training and skill development to enable the employees to function effectively. The expertise needed does not end with knowledge about their particular business function. They need to know how to work in a team. They need to know how to make decisions in a team. The team skills are necessary for the team to fully utilize the talent and knowledge of its members. Without these skills, it is just a work group. Exhibit 11.4 presents a typical progression of the development of employee team capabilities.

Very little contribution is made by a team that hasn't been trained to effectively make decisions. In these situations virtually all of the work is done by the team leader.

EXHIBIT 11.4 Project Team Capabilities

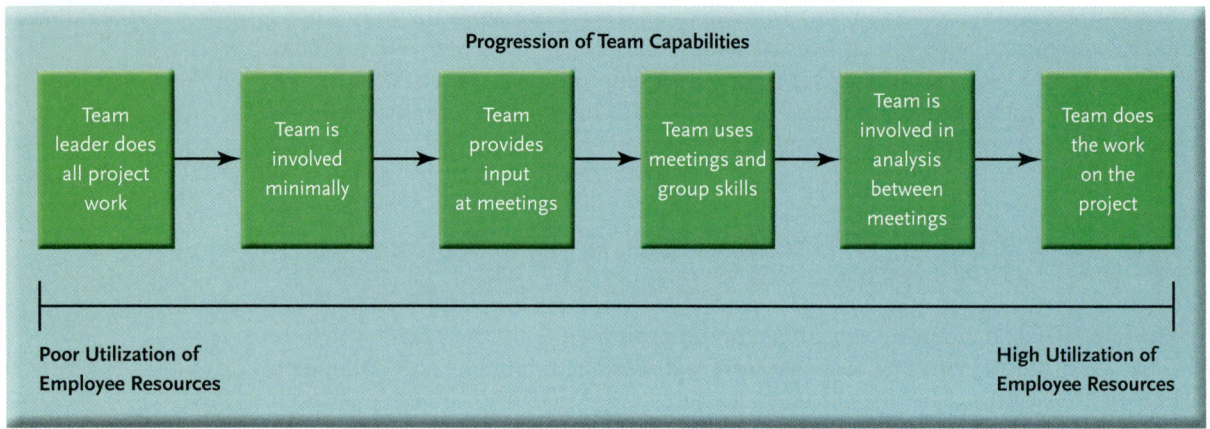

Source: Adapted from *Unleash the Power of Project Teams* (Cincinnati, OH: Association for Quality and Participation, 2000).

Team members, in addition to doing little work, are not contributing the most important thing they have to offer—their knowledge. Workers skilled in working in teams take on more responsibility until they reach a point where they can take on all team responsibilities. Failure to quickly move employees to make full contributions is no different from failure to use a piece of equipment to the fullest extent of its capabilities. An investment has been made in both cases and the owners of the firm have a right to expect that management will get the best return possible on that investment. Managers have been quick to realize that they do not always have the skills required to create effective teams in their organization. As a result, many outsource the training of employees so that they have the skills to effectively work in teams. Esource 11.2 provides an example of a company that specializes in training employees to work in teams.

Why Use Teams?

The advantages of using teams, rather than individuals, to accomplish business tasks must be understood in order to understand why businesses are so enthusiastic about their use. A primary advantage is that teams bring different perspectives along with different types of knowledge and expertise to the project. If a project has broad requirements, completion by an individual is unlikely to provide a result that meets all the requirements. In addition to the sum of the knowledge of a team, a team can be very creative in its actions. Members with different perspectives and different expertise can combine resources from different functional areas to contribute to a solution. This is not likely to happen with an individual.

A second advantage of using teams is that tasks can be assigned to the various members and the duration of the project can be reduced. In an effectively managed team, each member has responsibilities for "between-meeting" tasks. You've probably worked in student groups on projects when you've thought, "I could do this much quicker by myself," in which case you weren't working on a team, despite the fact that your professor may have called it that. That's the difference between a *group* of people working on a project and an effectively managed *team*. Teams actually get more done. Like any other resource, however, team management consists of a set of techniques that make effective team management possible and actually reduce the amount of management necessary. Attempting to utilize teams without the knowledge of these techniques will probably lead to a failed endeavor.

A third advantage of teams is known as "buy-in." You're probably familiar with the "not invented here" (NIH) syndrome. It's the phenomenon of trying to convince *someone else* that *your* idea is great. Had the other person thought of it, he'd think it was great, too. We all resist ideas or proposals from others, because we don't feel any ownership toward them. An important aspect of getting buy-in from others about a proposed change is to develop in them a sense of ownership. This can be accomplished only by involving them in deciding what the change should be. Granted, we can't involve everyone, but if we involve one person from a particular department, others in that department will have a greater sense of ownership than if they knew no one involved in the project. In summary, teams give us greater knowledge and a broader perspective, they give us greater capability, and they give us greater buy-in.

The use of teams has become so pervasive, it makes sense to categorize the use of teams into their various types and present some frameworks that will give a foundation of team processes. This discussion will not turn you into an expert on team functions, but it will give you a good introduction.

Appropriate Uses for Teams

When we look back at the advantages of using teams, it becomes clear that their advantages contribute most to implementing change. Most changes are intended to effect improvements. Change must occur for improvement to occur. It's that simple. Business improvements can be broken into two primary types.[4] The first type of improvement comes from **innovation**. Innovation is a dramatic change to something we do or something we produce. It is a new idea. Development and creation of innovation can be a project. The management of an innovation, making it come to fruition, is also a project. Innovations can come from individuals or teams, but those coming from teams have the added advantage of greater levels of creativity, broader perspective, and more knowledge behind them. The use of teams to create an innovation and infuse it into the business will enhance the results for the same reasons, but in this endeavor, buy-in is critical. The use of teams greatly improves that buy-in.

The second type of business improvement is known as **continuous improvement**. Continuous-improvement activities focus on existing processes and tasks, always seeking ways to improve them. In many cases, the improvement of business processes focuses on the elimination of non-value-adding (NVA) process steps. This focus speeds up the process and reduces costs. The result is enhanced value. Reel Operations Video 11.1 provides a real-world example of how Caterpillar has involved teams in its reengineering efforts.

For both types of improvement, the ability of a team to complete a project quickly is a function of how much time team members have to devote to it. If the only time team members have to work on a project is during weekly team meetings, because the rest of their job responsibilities keep them too busy or they're not allowed to work on it between meetings, not much can happen. If an individual is given the responsibility to complete the project, with no team involvement, and the individual is released from other responsibilities, the project could probably be completed faster. However, the result will suffer from the lack of knowledge, perspective, and buy-in, reducing the quality of the end result. Like anything else, you get what you pay for. The use of teams effectively requires a bigger resource investment than assigning a task to an individual, but the outcome is better.

Structure for Team Processes

In using teams to accomplish an improvement project, efforts must be organized so that resources are not wasted. Projects follow a life cycle, and that life cycle provides a structure for managing the project. Exhibit 11.5 is a diagram of a generic improvement project life cycle.[5]

Stage 1, the project identification stage, is initiated with the assignment of a project to a team, or a team selecting a project they wish to undertake. This stage also consists of the development of a mission or goals statement for the project, a description of the contribution that successful completion of the project will make to the organization, and the identification of all of the stakeholders. Stakeholders include anyone with a vested interest in the outcome.

Stage 2 consists of the analysis of the current situation. The specific activities depend on whether the project is of a problem-solving nature or is devoted to process improvement. A problem-solving project might be created in response to a variety of indicators or measures of performance. For example, a rash of customer complaints might trigger an effort to deal with a problem. A pattern of missed due date promises might result in a project team being formed to solve the problem. On the other hand, a process improvement focus might be an ongoing effort that isn't triggered by some event. For example, the specific steps differ slightly, depending on the focus. In a problem-solving project, for example, much of the effort will be spent on trying to determine the cause of the problem. For process improvement, however, that time would be spent identifying non-value-adding activities.

EXHIBIT 11.5   Project Life Cycle

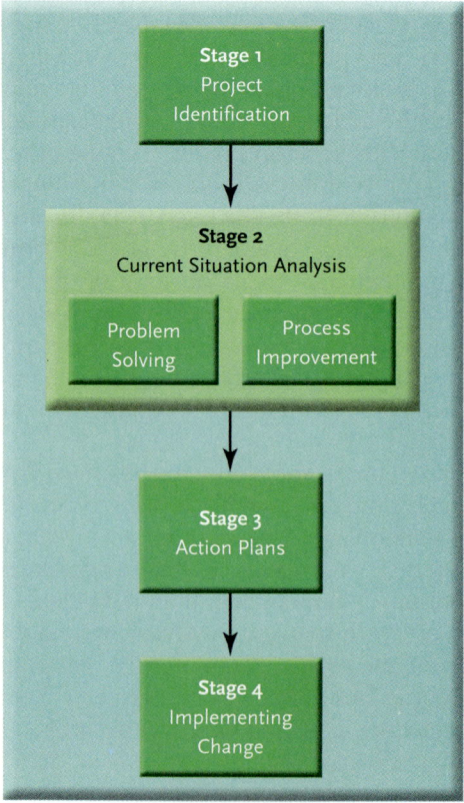

Stage 3 consists of creating the plan for taking action, whether the action is to solve a problem or provide improvement to a process. It proceeds from the identification of possible changes to make to the identification and selection of what changes will actually be implemented. Once selected, the change must be justified through the analysis of actual data.

Stage 4 is the implementation stage. It includes a plan for obtaining support and buy-in, a plan for implementing the changes, a plan for measuring and evaluating the results of the change recommended, and a plan for ensuring that the change is actually carried out. If it is a change in the way people do a particular task, for example, the plan should address what has to happen to make sure employees change their methods and ensure that the recommendations for change are actually carried out. Measures are then taken, and the results of the changes are analyzed. This creates information that can then be used to evaluate the effectiveness of the team. In other words, did the team's actions result in its goals being accomplished?

Team Decision-Making Tools

One outcome of the increase in the popularity of project teams has been the development of tools that can be used to aid in project team tasks. There are dozens, if not hundreds, of tools used by teams to aid in projects, but many have their roots in the traditional quality tools described in Chapter 7. Exhibit 11.6 provides a "refresher" of what those tools look like. An examination of the role the tools can play in a typical project provides a useful introduction to the use of team decision-making aids.

Each of the four stages of project life accomplishes distinct tasks. To accomplish these tasks, different tools are incorporated into the project activities. The first stage is to identify exactly what it is the team will do. A team whose objective is to focus on problems might use a Pareto chart to prioritize the results of customer complaints or performance measures to give them a sense of which item to address first. Similarly,

Traditional Quality Tools — EXHIBIT 11.6

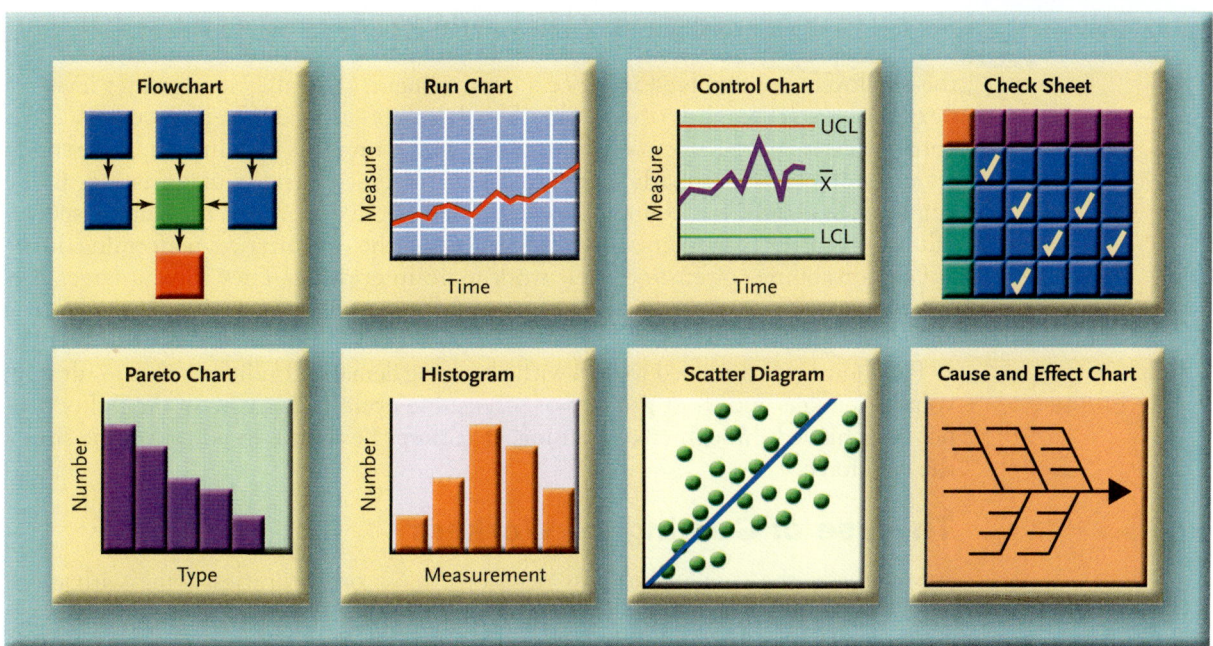

a control chart that indicates a process being out of control might form the basis for identifying and selecting a particular problem as an improvement-team focus. A check sheet might indicate too many instances of a particular undesirable event or condition. If the team has ongoing continuous-improvement responsibilities, a flowchart might initiate action to improve a process.

Stage 2 involves understanding the current situation, for problem solving and for process improvement efforts. For problem solving, analysis of run charts, Pareto charts, scatter diagrams, and histograms might lead to suggestions for possible causes. The cause and effect chart can aid in moving from possible causes to root causes. Once a root cause is suspected, run charts, Pareto charts, scatter diagrams, and histograms might again be used as validation tools. For process improvement, flowcharts and run charts will provide input into identifying non-value-adding activities.

Stage 3 requires the development of a solution to the problem or an elimination of the non-value-adding process steps. Selection of the appropriate changes to make might involve the use of several different tools, particularly the run chart, scatter diagram, or flowchart.

Stage 4 requires the development of buy-in among stakeholders and actions to ensure and evaluate results. Ensuring that the recommended changes actually take place might require that an ongoing use of control charts be implemented. To evaluate the impact of recommendations, the measures and tools used to identify the problem initially would be used again to provide a "before and after" view of the situation.

In addition to the traditional quality tools used to analyze data, other tools bring team members to convergence when making decisions. These consensus-building techniques strive to reduce the importance of opinion and move the team toward making objective decisions based on factual data. The training of teams is often outsourced to take advantage of the expertise offered by firms specializing in these skills.

INCREASED NEED FOR WORKFORCE FLEXIBILITY

The Use of Cross-Training

Flatter organization structures and increased involvement of employees in decision making requires employees to have skills in problem solving and data analysis. When the employees are involved in process improvement, they also need greater levels of flexibility to accomplish their jobs. Flexibility of individual employees is often enhanced through the use of **cross-training**, which involves training employees to do a variety of jobs. This greatly increases their contribution to the organization. If one employee is absent, for example, another employee can perform the same responsibilities. In addition, workers who move around in the organization performing different responsibilities often find their work more interesting. They have a larger perspective on what is done by the business and a larger sense of contribution to the company's goals.

Flexibility is also needed to deal with changing demand conditions that result from volatile markets and short product or service life cycles. This type of flexibility cannot be achieved through cross-training. It requires flexibility in adjusting the size of the workforce.

The Use of Contingent Workers

As is usually the case in business decisions, most opportunities come with costs. Tradeoffs abound in the area of workforce management. One of the more common and growing areas that offers great opportunities—but can also come at tremendous cost to product and service quality—is the use of temporary or **contingent workers**. Contingent workers are either temporary employees hired through a temporary agency or contractors who provide services so the company doesn't have to provide them for itself.

Formerly limited to hourly and low-skill positions, contingent workers now include employees of all abilities and salary levels, from filing clerks to engineers. The availability of a contingent workforce adds a tremendous amount of flexibility, enabling a firm to deal with seasonal demand fluctuations or implementation projects that are short-lived. It can also result in a myriad of problems deriving from a lack of training and preparation for the job. Abuses of temporary employees who receive a lower salary and fewer benefits than the people working right next to them can create a culture of resentful workers. Esource 11.3 provides an example of a service that offers temporary staffing to fill a variety of needs.

WHO'S IN CHARGE?

In many businesses, particularly those with high customer interaction, early process design decisions determine where the decision-making power lies. Exhibit 11.7 compares advantages and disadvantages that result from three alternative designs.

For businesses that require a great deal of customization, the customer will have great influence over the outcome and the interaction. In other businesses, the employee will be given the authority and responsibility to make decisions regarding the interaction and outcomes. In a third group of businesses, organizational rules and

EXHIBIT 11.7

Advantages and Disadvantages of Different Dominating Forces in Business Interactions

Impact	Interaction Dominating Force		
	Organization Rules and Policies	Contact Employee	Customer
Advantages	High efficiency Low cost of labor Low cost per unit of outcome High level of managerial control	Ability to customize More interaction Enhanced perceived value	Lower labor costs Enhanced sense of control for customer Enhanced perceived value
Disadvantages	Lack of flexibility No customization Low level of interaction Employees can't cope with unique situations Customers may be dissatisfied by lack of input	Less managerial control Higher labor cost High cost per unit of outcome	Low efficiency High costs per unit

Source: Adapted from J. A. Fitzsimmons, and M. J. Fitzsimmons, *Service Management: Operations, Strategy, and Information Technology* (New York: McGraw-Hill, 2001), pp. 204–206.

policies will restrict the employee and the customer from deviating from preestablished conventions. Although it isn't possible to select among these three alternatives for every business, choices made in the early stages of the service design process will set limits for how the customer, the contact employee, and the organization will dominate the interaction and outcomes.

The fact that the customer, employee, and organization can play different roles in the business encounter has implications for employee skills and characteristics. The employee capabilities needed for a business that allows the employee to set parameters and make decisions when working with a customer are very different from those needed if the employee and customer decisions are tightly bound by rules and policies.

THE NEW WORKING ENVIRONMENT

Businesses must respond to the specific needs of a customer, and this requires them to be more networked in order to provide the level of communication necessary. More information about what customers want and need is available. More information about what businesses offer is available also. In order to take competitive advantage of this information and use it to differentiate a business from competitors, employees must be prepared to use the information. They must be able to make decisions based on their own judgment of what the customer requires. They must not only be empowered to make the decision, but they must also be trained in how to make it. Despite the popularity of empowering employees, there is nothing worse than empowering an employee to make a decision and holding the employee accountable for the decision, but not providing the employee the training necessary to make the decision correctly. One of the most frustrating and threatening environments for employees is one where they do not feel comfortable about doing the job expected of them. It's unfair to the employee and it provides an unacceptable interaction for the customer. If employees are expected to do more, they must know more. In order to know more, they must be taught.

Increasing importance of customer–employee interactions, for competitive differentiation, means that employees must be capable of taking on these responsibilities. Employees must have judgment, they must be flexible, and they must be responsive to customer needs. As businesses expand globally, they must also move toward satisfying customers who have very different views of quality and very different wants and needs. The increasing diversity in the customer base is an important issue for brick and mortar firms as well as firms with strong Internet presence.

In addition to the increasing diversity among the customers, the workforce is also increasing in its diversity. Not only is the U.S. population becoming more diverse, but businesses are also locating in different cultures. Locating a business in a different country usually means hiring employees from that country. Managing a more diverse workforce requires an increased awareness of different cultures, different lifestyles, different languages, and different skills. The challenge for the firm is to take advantage of that diversity to add greater value, rather than letting the diversity of the workforce become a barrier.

WORKFORCE PRODUCTIVITY IMPROVEMENT

Like the productivity of any other asset, workforce productivity exists as a ratio of outputs to inputs. For many employees, productivity is measured as some form of "outcomes per hour" measure. For managers, productivity is often measured as the productivity of the assets that fall within their span of supervision. This includes productivity of employees, as well as equipment, facilities, and so on.

Employee productivity can be improved in a manner similar to that of any other asset—increase the numerator or decrease the denominator of the productivity ratio. Improving employee productivity generally means increasing the outputs, given the same amount of time. Surprisingly, this process usually does not require coercing the employee to work harder. Unlike jobs in the past, where the output was defined by the results of manual labor, many jobs today require interaction between a person and some form of equipment, which might be a computer, a telephone, or some other machine. The job might be to accomplish one set of tasks out of a much larger set that defines a completed product or service. In these situations, the output of an individual often hinges on the design of the system in which the person is placed. It results from the way one person fits into the system, the way that person's role is supported through appropriate work tools, and the way the systems in place provide an opportunity for that worker to be as productive as possible. In most cases, despite what managers may insist, lack of productivity for employees is the result of the systems in which they work, not their lack of ambition.

Productivity measures of individual resources are, by definition, local measures. Local measures often contradict each other and oppose the very goals sought by more global measures. Productivity measures frequently do this. Measuring the productivity of a call center employee, for example, might be accomplished by counting the number of calls per hour. Such a measurement would encourage the worker to try to shorten conversations with potential customers, thereby completing more calls per hour but also reducing the level of interaction customers expect. Both the performance measurement systems and reward–punishment systems are often critical in motivating employee behaviors. When not well designed, they can encourage the wrong behaviors.

Productivity Measurement and Improvement Tools

For some jobs, particularly those that are repetitive in nature, management and workers need a standard to provide a basis for training, evaluation, and comparison. The existence of a standard is important in jobs that produce high volumes because a slight improvement in productivity can result in significant output increases over time. Improvements in productivity can be obtained only if productivity is actually measured. In these situations, and in some nonrepetitive situations, a time standard is needed. A **time standard** defines the amount of time it should take to complete a task.

Time standards are frequently used in manufacturing environments where the job is repetitive, the materials are consistent, and the employee has little variability from one task to the next. The existence of the standard provides management with the ability to evaluate performance and also provides a critical piece of information to help in planning for the capacity necessary to meet demand. Efficiency, a commonly used measure, is the actual output divided by standard output. Measures that are based on a variance require determining the difference between actual output or actual cost and the standard output or standard cost. A standard is necessary to make any type of comparison. Standards can be created for employees in several ways. Two common approaches are stopwatch time studies and predetermined motion times.

Stopwatch Time Studies
Stopwatch time studies are based on actual observation of an employee for a long enough time to gather sufficient representative times for the task of interest. The period of time must include activities that are not completed with every repetition but are still parts of the job. Such activities include moving material, adjusting equipment or tools, and user maintenance tasks. The observations over that period of time are averaged to provide a measure known as **observed time**. To make the observed

time useful and representative of what would be expected of other workers, the observed time must be adjusted by incorporating a **performance rating**. The performance rating is based on how the observer perceives the employee being observed. If the observer feels that the employee being observed works at a pace faster than normal, the performance rating adjusts the observed time to be slower. If the observer feels that the employee is slower than a normal employee, the performance rating speeds up the observed time. The resultant time, after the performance rating has been applied to the observed time, is known as the **normal time**. It is simply the time that a typical worker would be expected to take to complete the task.

The **standard time** is computed by adjusting the normal time to incorporate **allowances**. Allowances are added as a percentage of the standard time to allow for personal time, restroom breaks, and rest periods. Example 11.1 demonstrates the calculation of a standard time utilizing stopwatch time study data.

Predetermined Motion Times

The second method of determining standards is to use **predetermined motion times**. Predetermined motion times avoid the negative aspects of stopwatch time studies. Employees generally do not like to be watched and timed. Accurate stopwatch time studies are also very difficult to implement and are prone to significant amounts of error. In addition, stopwatch time studies cannot be used to determine time standards for jobs that do not yet exist.

Predetermined motion times can be extracted from data gathered through years of observation. The predetermined motion times are created through detailed analysis of film footage of jobs. Jobs are broken into very small motions, which form the building blocks of virtually any job. The job of interest can be broken down into those motions, as can a new job that has never been performed, and the times for each motion can be determined. The time for the entire job is calculated by summing the times of all of its component motions. Predetermined motion times do not need to be

---

Example 11.1

Stopwatch Time Study Standard Time Calculation

In an effort to create a performance standard, the office manager for an insurance claims center performed a stopwatch time study for a claims reviewer position. The claims reviewer's essential responsibilities are to review each claim to ensure that all questions on the form are answered. The result of the stopwatch time study was that on average, each review took 34 seconds. The office manager judged the employee being observed to be 10 percent faster than the normal worker. Allowances for rest breaks, restroom breaks, and so on, are required to be 15 percent. Find the standard time for this job.

Solution

The *observed time* is equal to 34 seconds. To arrive at the *normal time*, the observed time must be adjusted by the performance rating. To adjust a normal time that is 10 percent fast to be equal to the time of a normal worker, an adjustment of 1.1 would be used:

$$34 \text{ seconds} \times 1.1 = 37.4 \text{ seconds}$$

The normal time is 37.4 seconds. Adding the 15 percent allowance, the *standard time* is

$$37.4 \text{ seconds} \times 1.15 = 43.01 \text{ seconds}$$

Excel Tutor 11.1 shows how this problem can be solved in a spreadsheet.

www.OperationsNow.com

adjusted using a performance rating because so many observations go into the creation of the times that they are considered representative of the normal worker.

In many nonrepetitive jobs, productivity is not a result of how fast employees work but is more related to how they spend their working time. Many white-collar workers and managers find that the parts of their job that are most important do not get the time required because other tasks get in the way. The first step toward increasing the productivity in these situations is to determine exactly how the employee is spending his/her time. **Work sampling** provides an effective way to accomplish that. If a sufficient quantity of random observations are made of a worker, and the observations are tallied, the resulting proportions of those categories are representative of the way that employee is utilized. It is important that the observations are truly random and an actual table of random numbers is used to generate the observation times. Failure to use real random observations will result in data not representative of what the employee actually does. Observing an employee "whenever you think about it" is not random. Example 11.2 demonstrates a work sampling implementation.

Example 11.2

Work Sampling

The divisional vice president for claims processing was concerned about how a particular claims office manager was spending his time. A random number table was used to create 200 random observation times over a four-week period. Categories for the activities were created based on the observations and observations were placed into the categories. Complete the work sampling study.

The resulting tallies follow:

Scheduling claims adjuster duties	21
Office personnel duties (payroll forms, employee evaluation, etc.)	14
Assisting with staff duties	36
Performing stopwatch time studies	44
One-on-one meetings with staff	10
Full staff meeting	8
Social chatting	13
On the phone	54

Solution

The observations are converted to the following percentages:

Scheduling claims adjuster duties	10.5%
Office personnel duties (payroll forms, employee evaluation, etc.)	7%
Assisting with staff duties	18%
Performing stopwatch time studies	22%
One-on-one meetings with staff	5%
Full staff meeting	4%
Social chatting	6.5%
On the phone	27%

Excel Tutor 11.2 shows how spreadsheets can aid in a work sampling study.

www
OperationsNow
.com

Managers are frequently surprised when they find out exactly how their employees are spending their time. Work sampling studies can provide an accurate view that can point to needed changes in the workplace. Here is a typical example of employees wasting time, while attempting to do their jobs. Excessive waiting for over-demanded office resources, like photocopiers, is a frequent discovery of work sampling studies.

The results of a work sampling study like the one in Example 11.2 can provide the impetus for the redesign of a job if it is clear that the employee being studied spends time that does not seem to match what that employee should be doing. For example, the employee studied spends a high proportion (27 percent) of the total time on the phone. If this takes time away from other activities deemed more important, ways to reduce phone time may need to be examined.

Learning Curves

An important aspect of worker productivity that often goes without notice is that over time, workers get better at what they do. You know from your own experiences that the first time you attempt something complicated, you need a long time to complete it. As you repeat the number of times you've done it, you get faster without it taking more effort. It actually gets easier. The phenomenon of the time required to complete a task getting shorter and shorter as the task is repeated is known as a **learning curve**. The **learning rate** determines the steepness of the learning curve and varies with different people and different types of tasks. Although learning curves are generally thought to apply to individuals, organizations also have learning curves, as do groups and teams.

As an example, if an individual's learning rate for a particular job was expected to be 90 percent, and it took 4 hours to complete the task the first time, it would take 3.6 hours the second time, 3.24 hours the fourth time, 2.916 hours the eighth time, and so on. The gain expressed by the learning rate is achieved every time the number of repetitions doubles, so a lower percentage means that learning is faster. Exhibit 11.8 provides the continuation of this pattern. Notice that absolute improvement gets smaller with each repetition because it takes more repetitions to double what has been done.

Exhibit 11.9 graphs the improvement with an 85 percent learning rate. As can be seen, an 85 percent learning rate is a "steep" learning curve. In other words, learning takes place very quickly. Exhibit 11.10 provides the same series, with a 97 percent learning curve. Notice the difference.

Learning Curve Pattern		EXHIBIT 11.8
Task Number	Time to Complete	
1	4.00	
2	3.40	
4	2.89	
8	2.46	
16	2.09	
32	1.77	
64	1.51	
128	1.28	
256	1.09	
516	0.93	
1,032	0.79	
2,064	0.67	

85 Percent Learning Curve — EXHIBIT 11.9

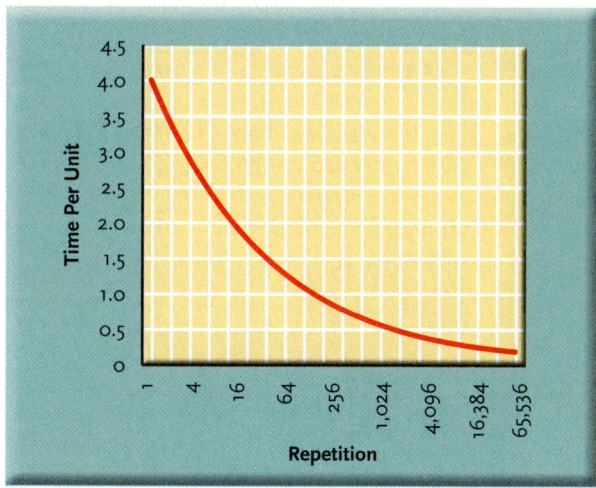

The equation for the learning curve is

$$T_n = T_1 n^r \quad (11.1)$$

where
- T_n = time in hours to produce the nth unit
- T_1 = time in hours to produce the first unit
- n = number of the unit of interest
- $r = \log l / \log 2$ where l is the expected learning rate

The use of the formula is demonstrated in Example 11.3.

The learning rate is almost always a prediction. No one ever really knows, in advance, how fast a person or group will learn. The fact that it is a prediction or forecast means

EXHIBIT 11.10 97 Percent Learning Curve

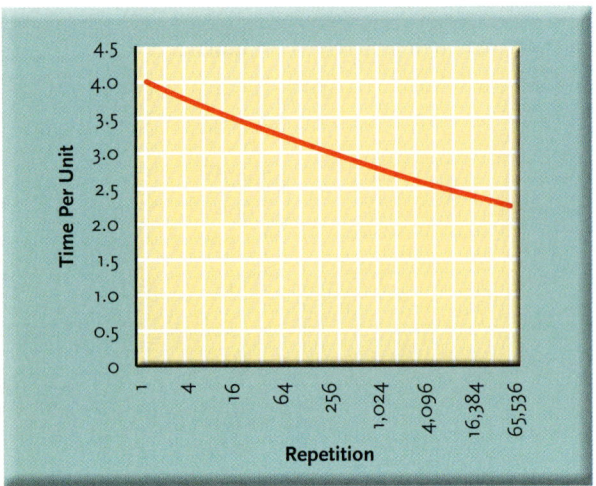

Example 11.3 Use of the Learning Curve Formula

A producer of machined components for missile trigger assemblies was considering the purchase of a new milling machine. New business had pushed capacity demands past what was available on existing equipment. A new relationship with a defense contractor, which appeared to be permanent, required the company to produce a component that needed more milling time than it had available. To assist in determining the capacity that would be needed on the milling machine, the owner decided to determine the time required per unit once the learning curve flattens out. Past experience gave the owner a high level of confidence in using a 96 percent learning rate. With the time for the first unit equal to 1.75 hours, what will be the time to produce the 300th unit?

Solution

$$T_n = T_1 n^r \qquad (11.1)$$

$$T_{300} = 1.75(300)^{\log 0.96/\log 2}$$

$$= 1.75(300)^{-0.0589}$$

$$= 1.75/300^{0.0589}$$

$$= 1.2506 \text{ hours}$$

www
OperationsNow
.com

Excel Tutor 11.3 provides an example of how learning curve calculations can be aided by using a spreadsheet.

that there will be error in estimating it. Error in estimating a learning rate can have a tremendous impact on the projected time it takes to do something many repetitions in the future. In the previous example, after 20 repetitions, the 97 percent learning rate resulted in the task taking 2.24 hours. Had the real learning rate been only 99 percent instead of 97 percent (an error of slightly over 2 percent), the actual time to complete the 20th unit would have been 3.30 instead of 2.24 hours (an increase of 47 percent). The total time to do all 20 repetitions would have actually been 72.84 hours instead of a projected 60.83 hours.

Learning curves are frequently used in bidding processes. A customer wants a bid on a customized or new product, and a learning curve is projected as a way to estimate total labor costs. In fact, bids submitted for government contracts are required to include learning effects. Obviously, as the previous example demonstrates, the error associated with the learning rate prediction can result in a huge error in projecting labor content and labor costs. It can also result in a drastic error in predicting the date of completion. The error can be the difference between profit and loss. It is common to project a learning rate range, rather than a point estimate, and project a range for the total amount of labor. Interactive Model 11.1 provides an interactive environment for experimenting with learning rates in a realistic bidding scenario.

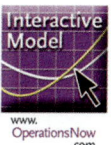

CHAPTER SUMMARY

This chapter considered the importance of the workforce as a resource used to create value. Through direct and indirect labor, as well as knowledge that can be applied to improvement, the workforce is generally thought of as a business's most valuable asset. It is the only asset that contributes directly to the value of the product or service and also contributes indirectly to the improvement of the use of other assets. The impact of the workforce is evident in each of the value attributes customers seek.

As businesses continue to utilize services to differentiate themselves from the competition, the importance of employee skills and ability to interact with customers increases. Employee interaction in service encounters plays a major role in building customer loyalty and improving profitability.

The environment in which workers must function is changing. Increased diversity among customers *and* employees adds to management's responsibilities and to the value-adding potential of the workforce. In addition to these changes, greater employee responsibility and the use of project teams increase the need for employee development and training. As the value of the employee asset increases, the need for productivity measurement and enhancement also increases. Various tools associated with productivity measurement and improvement were presented. Finally, a discussion of learning curves was presented, with tools that are required when utilizing learning curves to predict the time required to complete tasks.

In a labor market that is tight, the value of the workforce becomes even more important. But aren't all assets important? Inventory? Facilities? Capacity? Certainly, but the workforce is unique because it has free will and it can provide insight that improves the effectiveness of other resources.

KEY TERMS

allowance, 404
contingent workers, 401
continuous improvement, 397
cross-training, 400
innovation, 397
learning curve, 406
learning rate, 406
normal time, 404

observed time, 403
performance rating, 404
predetermined motion time, 404
service–profit chain, 391
standard time, 404
stopwatch time studies, 403
time standard, 403
work sampling, 405

REVIEW QUESTIONS

1. From a strategic perspective, why are employees critical in a service-based economy?
2. Why has customer service often become the most important competitive weapon?
3. How has the meaning of the term "market" changed? What type of "market" has the Internet created? What are customer expectations moving toward?
4. How does the service–profit chain relate to employee satisfaction?
5. Why are teams important for maximizing the contributions of the workforce?
6. Describe the steps of the improvement project life cycle.
7. What are the advantages and disadvantages of using contingent workers?
8. Describe the process of creating time standards from stopwatch time studies.
9. What is work sampling? Why is it important for managing worker productivity?
10. What is a learning curve? What are the dangers of depending on a learning curve for cost estimates?

DISCUSSION QUESTIONS

1. In jobs you have had, what have been the critical aspects of value added by the workers? Could they have been automated? What would have been lost if they had been automated?
2. If you imagine yourself in your first job after graduating, what value do you hope to offer the company? What value will you contribute to the products or services sold? Is that sufficient?
3. How can companies that are forced by demand fluctuations to use contingent workers avoid the problems that can accompany their use?

PROBLEMS

1. You have been asked by the manager of a bank to perform a stopwatch time study on its tellers. The average time for Carol was 1 minute, 37 seconds. She was judged to be the fastest teller, performing 20 percent faster than normal. Calculate the normal time for Carol and then compute a standard using a 12 percent allowance.
2. AAM Inc. performed a stopwatch time study on its production work stations and reported the results in the following table. Interpret the table and provide the standard time for each work station if a 10 percent allowance is required for rest breaks.

Work Station	Observed Time (seconds)	Performance Rating
1	89	10% faster
2	114	8% faster
3	140	6% slower
4	62	2% faster

3. You have been observing an employee, Kim, of the real estate agency of Walker & Smith. The employee is preparing a listing of houses that are for sale. It has taken Kim 15 minutes to complete the task and she is believed to be 30 percent faster than the typical employee. If an allowance of 5 percent is required, how long should it take the average employee to prepare a listing of houses for sale?

4. The sales manager for The Copy Co. used a random number table to find 250 observation times for one of his sales representatives. The results are given below. Complete the work sampling analysis by determining the proportion of time spent on each activity

Activity	Number of Observations
Cold calls	45
Calling on top customers	75
Demonstrating products	20
Phone canvassing	25
Follow-up calls	10
Driving	60
Social calls	15

5. You are the general manager for the Portsmouth Pilots, a minor league football team. You have been concerned with how your athletes spend their time at training camp and have asked an aide to conduct a work sampling study on two players, Jerry and Mike. The observations for the two players are presented below. Interpret the results.

	Number of Observations	
	Jerry	Mike
Practice	36	45
Lifting weights	19	30
Nutritionist	9	12
Sleep & recovery	14	18
Social	22	9
Films	28	21
Study playbook	22	15
Total	150	150

6. The Plant Manager at MRC Mfg. was given a proposal for a new machine. The new machine is advertised to be able to run 76 percent of the time, the rest being spent on changeover, loading, or emptying the machine. He was curious about the current equipment, so he made 200 random observations of its operation. The Plant Manager found the following results: loading machine, 15; emptying machine, 15; changeover, 8; break, 10; operating, 152. Should he expect the new machine to be better than the old machine?

7. An investment firm hired a new employee to put together an investment newsletter for its customers. The first time the employee put the newsletter together it took 2.3 hours. If the anticipated rate of learning is 92 percent, how long will it take the employee to put together the 50th newsletter?

8. College Painters is a student-run painting service that operates during the summer. Its first job took 11.4 hours to complete. The students will spend the entire summer painting houses in the same neighborhood, with similar houses, and expect to paint 50 of them before they go back to school. College Painters headquarters told them to anticipate a 98 percent learning curve. If that projection is accurate, how long will it take them to paint the last house in the neighborhood?

9. Ramsey is testing two video games for their degree of difficulty. The first game took him six hours to complete, and the manufacturer expects an 82 percent learning rate. The second game took only two hours to complete with an expected learning rate of 99 percent. Which game will take longer to play the 100th time it is played?

10. Carl has decided to read the top 75 mysteries of all time this summer. It took him 12 hours to read his first mystery. If the learning rate is 98 percent, how long will it take him to finish the last one? Assuming the 98 percent learning rate is correct, how many mysteries must Carl finish to cut two hours off his reading time?

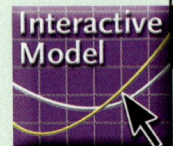
www.OperationsNow.com

INTERACTIVE ANALYSIS 11.1

THE LEARNING CURVE INTERACTIVE MODEL

The Learning Curve Interactive Model is accessed through Chapter 11 of the *OperationsNow.com* website. The model provides an interactive laboratory for exploring the effects learning rates have on a typical bidding scenario.

The model allows the user to specify the following parameters, provided here in their default settings:

Parameter	Value
Material cost per unit	$5,000
Labor hours per week	4,000
Hourly salary rate	$16
Weekly overhead	$45,000
Time for first unit	616.5
Bid price (1,000$)	$1,104.6
Number of units	125
Number of units	25

In addition, the user sets the learning rate using a slider button.

The system outputs include the learning rate selected, performance measures, project length, labor cost, overhead cost, materials cost, total cost, labor percentage, overhead percentage, materials percentage, and profit. The learning rate has a significant impact on the amount of labor required to complete the number of units specified in the order. The longer it takes to complete them, the higher the labor costs. That cost cuts into profit.

Experiment 1: System Fundamentals
1. Set the parameters at their default values and the learning rate at 90 percent.
   a. What is the project length at this learning rate?
   b. Improve the learning rate to 85 percent. What is the new project length?
2. Set the parameters at the default values and the learning rate at 90 percent.
   a. The current time for the first unit is 616.5 hours. Enter a starting time for the first unit as 500. What is the new project length? What is the average time per unit produced?
   b. Reset the parameters to their defaults, with the learning rate at 90 percent. Increase the time for the first unit to 660 hours. What is the new project length? What is the average time per unit produced?

Experiment 2: The Impact of Learning Rate on Financial Measures
1. Set the parameters to the default values. Set the learning rate to 90 percent.
   a. What is the project length? What is the labor cost per day? What is the total labor cost? What is the labor cost as a percentage of the total cost? What is the profit?
2. Improve the learning rate to 80 percent. What is the new project length? What is the new labor cost per day? What is the total labor cost? What is the labor cost as a percentage of the total cost? What is the new profit? What must the learning rate be in order to make a profit?
3. Keep the learning rate at 80 percent and all other parameters at their default values.
   a. If the company wishes to make a profit of $300,000, what must the bid price be? What would that mean for a per-unit cost to the customer?
   b. At the bidding price needed to make $300,000 in profit, and the corresponding cost per unit for the customer, what happens if the learning rate estimate was optimistic? Suppose it turned out that the learning rate was actually only 85 percent. What would happen to the profit?

Experiment 3: Economies of Scale
1. Set the parameters back to the default values. Set the learning rate at 90 percent.
   a. What is the cost per unit for the producer at the 90 percent learning rate? What is the project length?
   b. Increase the number of units in the order from 125 to 200. What is the new project length? What is the new cost per unit for the producer? Increase the number of units from 200 to 300 and then incrementally by 100 units up to 1,000 units. Compute the cost per unit at each quantity and graph the results. Describe the relationship between the number of units produced and cost per unit at a 90 percent learning rate.

c. Perform the same experiment as in 1b, using an 80 percent learning rate. How do the results compare?
2. Set the parameters back to the default values. Set the learning rate at 90 percent.
   a. What is the labor cost as a percentage of the total cost?
   b. Increase the number of units in the order from 125 to 200. What is the percentage of labor cost as a percentage of the total? Increase the number of units from 200 to 300 and then incrementally by 100 units up to 1,000 units. Record the labor cost as a percentage of the total cost at each quantity and graph the results. Describe the relationship between the labor cost percentage and the number of units produced produced at a 90 percent learning rate.
   c. Perform the same experiment as in 2b, using an 80 percent learning rate. How do the results compare?

SELECTED REFERENCES

Katzenbach, J. R., and Smith, D. K. *The Wisdom of Teams*. New York: HarperCollins, 1999.

Levine, R., Locke, C., Searles, D., and Weinberger, D. *The Cluetrain Manifesto*. New York: Perseus Books, 2000.

Zemke, R., and Connellan, T. *E-service*. New York: American Management Association, 2001.

ENDNOTES

1. For an interesting perspective on these interactions between customers and employees, see R. Levine, C. Locke, D. Searles, and D. Weinberger, *The Cluetrain Manifesto* (New York: Perseus Books, 2000).
2. G. W. Loveman, W. E. Sasser, Jr., and L. A. Schlesinger, "Putting the Service–Profit Chain to Work," *Harvard Business Review*, March–April 1994, p. 166.
3. R. Zemke and T. Connellan, *E-service* (New York: American Management Association, 2001), p. 28.
4. *Unleash the Power of Project Teams* (Cincinnati, OH: Association for Quality and Participation, 2000).
5. Ibid.

OperationsNow.com LEARNING ACTIVITIES

CHAPTER ENHANCEMENT RESOURCES
- Esources
- Reel Operations Video Clips
- Interactive Models
- Excel Tutors
- Supplementary Readings
- Links to Operations On Site Companies

OM EXPLORATION
- Check It Out
- OM in Action
- Online Business Tours
- Letters from the Top
- Putting It All Together: Virtual Case Studies
- Additional Readings

The resource/profit model places capacity as the third of five resources used to create value. Capacity, which results from the merging of resources, gives the business the ability to produce at a certain volume. Producing a product or service has no value unless it is produced in sufficient quantity within a certain time frame to meet the customers' needs. Capacity is not only important—it's also expensive. To ensure that capacity is generating the financial return necessary to justify its existence, it is always under close scrutiny.

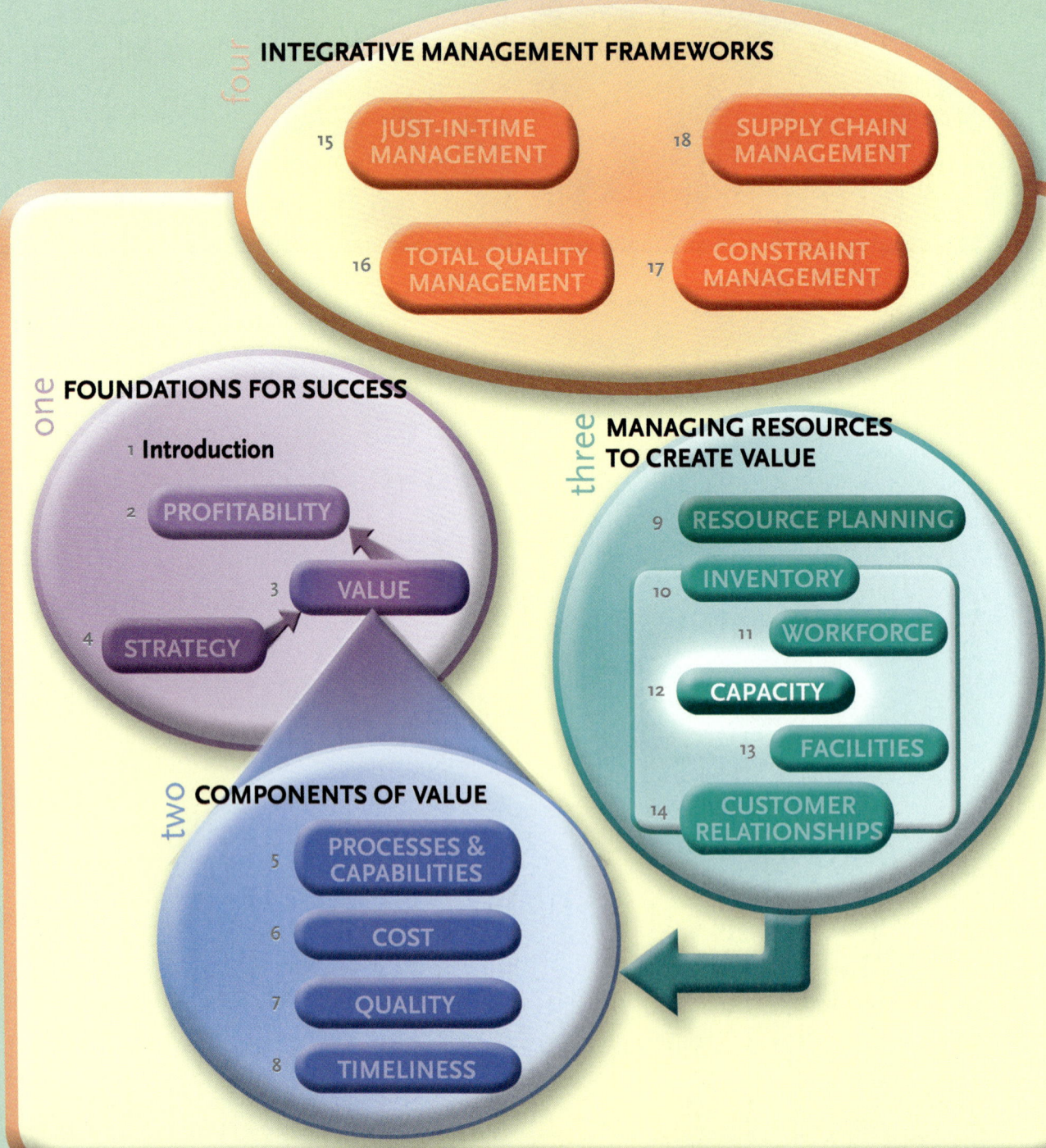

CHAPTER 12

Capacity

LEARNING OBJECTIVES

Upon completion of Chapter 12, you should be able to

- Define capacity and distinguish it from capability.
- Describe how capacity relates to value and profitability for B2C and B2B transactions.
- State how demand that varies from design capacity influences profitability.
- Describe the role individual resources and constraints play in determining system capacity.
- Make the calculations necessary to create demand chase and level production aggregate plans.
- Describe the information inputs and logic necessary for rough-cut capacity planning.
- Calculate required and available capacity for a rough-cut capacity plan.
- Describe the information inputs and logic necessary for capacity requirements planning.
- Calculate required and available capacity for a capacity requirements plan.
- Describe how yield management aids services in maximizing revenues.
- Perform the calculations to determine the number of customers to overbook.

Introduction: Matching Resource Availability to Market Demand
Capacity Defined
Capacity and Value
The Financial Impact of Capacity Decisions
Individual Resource Influence on System Capacity
A Broader View: Supply Chain Capacity
Managing the Demand–Capacity Match in Manufacturing
Managing the Demand–Capacity Match in Services
Current Trends in Capacity Management
Chapter Summary

INTERNET RESOURCES

 Excel Tutors provide annotated spreadsheets for every solved problem that automatically load Excel.

 Esources provide an online version of the more traditional boxed insert.

 Reel Videos provide streaming video footage for company applications of chapter concepts.

 Interactive Models provide an experimental environment for quantitative concepts and simulations.

INTRODUCTION
Matching Resource Availability to Market Demand

Capacity, shown in Exhibit 12.1 as the third of five resources used to create value, has different meanings in different contexts. It is sometimes viewed as being synonymous with capability, but there is a subtle difference. If a company determined that it couldn't produce a product, there might be several reasons. The company may have no experience with the product—a bicycle manufacturer producing computer hard drives, for example. Or the product might be a closer match to the company's abilities but still outside the company's scope of expertise. In such situations, capability implies "aptitude": Does the company have the knowledge and skills necessary to produce the product? Or the volume and timing may create problems, like when a hard drive manufacturer that is already overbooked with orders receives an order for more computer hard drives. Or a small manufacturer might receive a huge order: The order could probably be met eventually, but not in a reasonable amount of time. The ability to produce at a given volume in a specified amount of time is what we usually mean by "capacity."

Concerns about capacity are generally more specific than those about capability. Capacity concerns do not generally refer to issues like "Do we have the skills to do the job?" or "Do we have the technology to do the job?" because these questions have probably already been answered. The issue in question when dealing with capacity is usually "Do we have the skills, the technology, the equipment, or the space, *in sufficient volume*, to complete the job in the time allowed?" Or, for producers of more standardized products and services, "Can we meet the volume of demand, given the resources we have?" When the manager of a catering business asks her chef if the kitchen has the capacity to fulfill a large order of desserts, the issue isn't whether or not the chef has the capability to make the desired dessert; it's whether he has the capability to make *enough* desserts and make them in time to meet the customer order.

As has been discussed in previous chapters, capacity-related issues are the most significant difference between producing services and producing products. When producing products, capacity can be stored in the form of work-in-process and finished-goods inventory. For services, however, capacity usually can't be stored. It is available for the fleeting moment when it is created, and then it disappears. Planning for capacity, which is essentially planning for the necessary resources to meet expected demand, takes on a completely different level of difficulty for services. Services must match available capacity with demand and continue to do this as demand changes. If they miss either way, costs go up and profits disappear.

With all due respect to manufacturers, services really do have a more difficult task. It's not exactly easy for manufacturers either, though, because they must cope with changing demand, high costs associated with carrying inventory, and environments with high levels of customization that make it difficult to carry finished-product inventory.

In this chapter, several objectives are emphasized. First, capacity and its impact on value creation is addressed. Second, the impact of capacity decisions on financial performance are addressed. Third, the critical challenge of matching capacity and demand is analyzed and techniques to aid in that process are introduced for service and manufacturing environments. The chapter concludes with a discussion of capacity management and its role in enterprise resource planning (ERP) systems.

CAPACITY DEFINED

In most business settings, capacity is defined precisely in terms of a level of output per unit time. If this output level is sufficient to meet demand, we say that there is suffi-

EXHIBIT 12.1 The Role of Capacity in the Resource/Profit Model

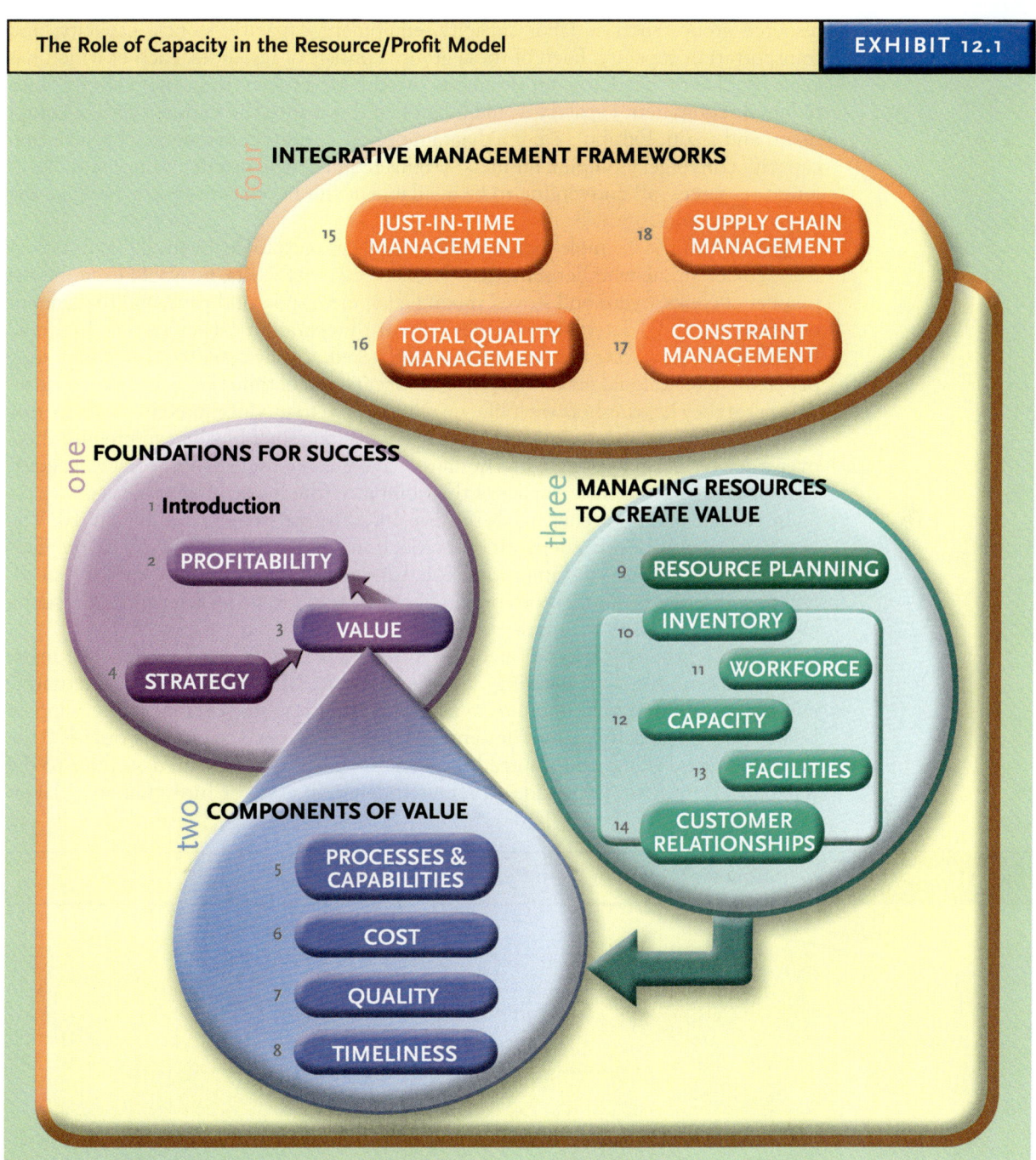

cient capacity. When viewing capacity this way, it must be recognized that many resources must converge to provide sufficient production capacity. Think of the resources that must come together to produce any product or service you purchase. Earlier in this text, in the discussion of processes and capabilities, the concept of pulling together resources from different parts of the business, to create capabilities, was discussed. Inclusion of capacity in the discussion means that each resource used to generate the capability must have the capacity to generate *enough* of the capability to meet demand. Capacity must be sufficient *in each resource* to meet demand. The capability to produce enough of a specific product might be the combined result of resource groups such as labor capacity, equipment capacity, storage capacity, and transportation capacity. Each of these groups consists of resources, each of which has capacity. Labor capacity, for example, would be broken into the various skills required. Equipment capacity would be broken down into the various types of equipment, and so on. Exhibit 12.2 is a diagram of how various components of production capacity converge. Complex business systems require the capacity of hundreds of different resources, all converging to be available at the necessary time, to produce the desired outcomes.

The chef in the example mentioned earlier clearly has to deal with different capacities. To determine whether sufficient "kitchen" capacity exists, he would examine the number of cooks, ovens and stoves, mixing equipment, pots and pans, and the amount of refrigeration. To determine whether sufficient preparation capacity exists, he would need to know how long the desserts could be stored. If they could be stored for a long period of time, he could make them over a longer period of time (low preparation capacity), but if they have a short shelf life, he must be able to produce more in a short period of time (high preparation capacity). If they have a long shelf life, he can produce them over a longer period of time, *but* he must have greater refrigerated storage capacity. Exhibit 12.3 illustrates the impact of this ability to store his finished products.

In Exhibit 12.3, our chef needs to have 1,000 desserts completed by day 10. The way he accomplishes this depends on production capacity and storage capacity. This example demonstrates the important role time plays in determining capacity needs and how interdependent various productive resources can be in determining capacity available and capacity required.

Obviously, the scenario pictured in Exhibit 12.3 provides two extremes of many possible alternatives to meeting the need for 1,000 desserts. Some alternative approaches could involve short-term access to other resources. For example, suppose he had storage capacity for 400 desserts. He would then need to produce only 600 the day they were due and could spread the remaining 400 over several days prior to the due date. He might also decide to rent refrigeration space or hire temporary labor.

EXHIBIT 12.2 Resources Merged to Form Production Capacity

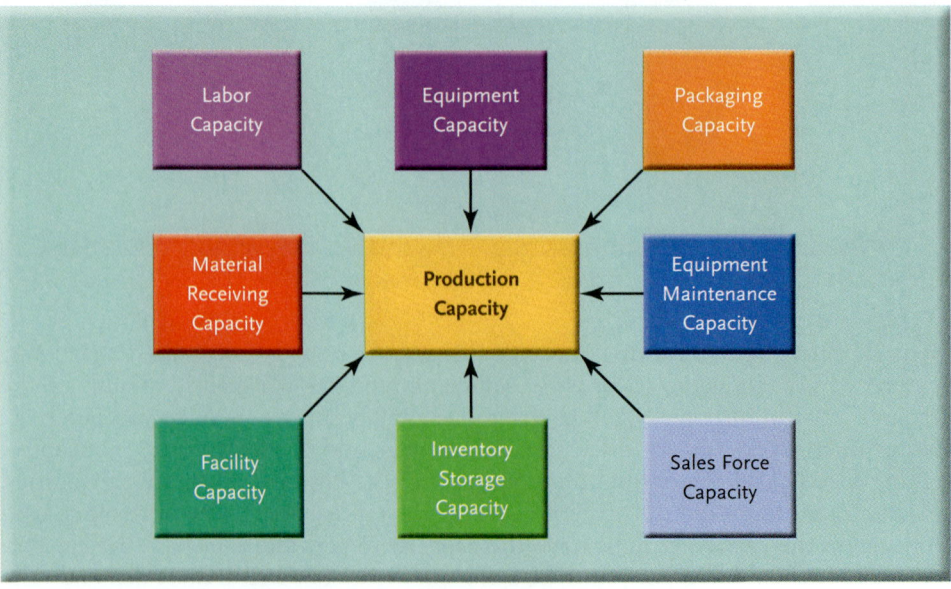

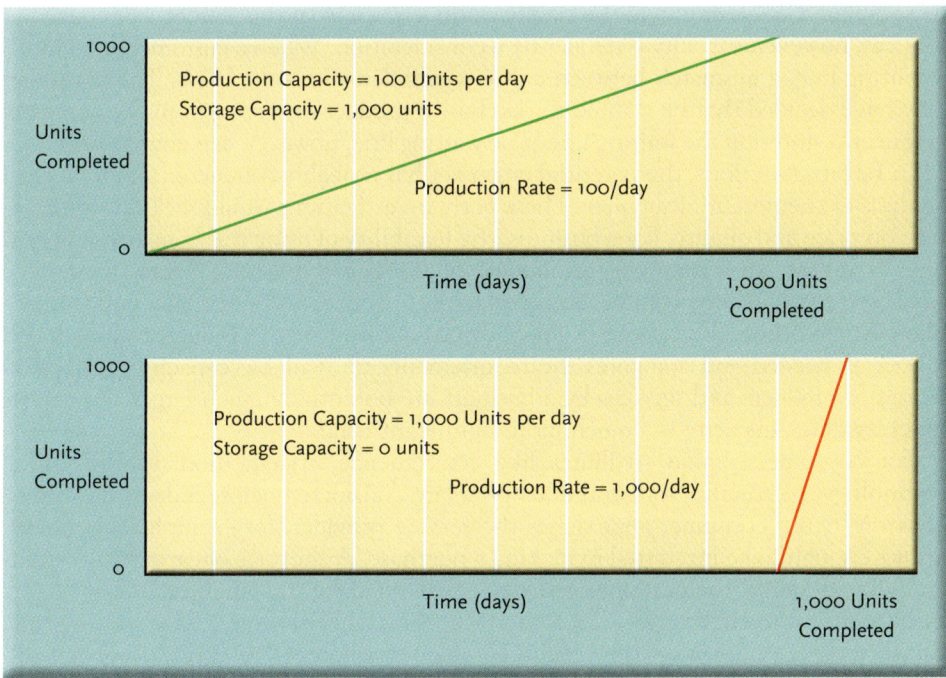

EXHIBIT 12.3 Production Rate Requirements Under Different Storage Capacities

The availability of either of these resources on a contingency basis would enhance his ability to cope with such a spike in demand.

CAPACITY AND VALUE

By the time a customer's request for products or services is viewed from a capacity perspective, questions regarding important value attributes should have already been answered. For example, a customer isn't likely to order computer hard drives from a bicycle manufacturer. If he does, he probably gets what he deserves. However, when a customer places an order for a particular product or service, even if that customer is a consumer like you or me, there is an implicit analysis of whether the company has the aptitude to produce the product or service desired.

We don't typically consider it in our decisions to purchase, but capacity issues greatly impact value attributes. This becomes evident when we examine the relationship between capacity and each value attribute. The following list provides the value attributes typically sought by consumers and business customers, as initially presented in Chapter 3:

Cost	Style/fashion
Quality	Ethical issues
Response time	Technology
Dependability of delivery	Flexibility
Convenience	Personalization

Capacity issues are addressed at different times during B2C and B2B purchases. As a result, capacity plays a different role in the ultimate decision to buy. For most consumer purchases, capacity issues are never addressed because the manufacturer's capacity is buffered by inventory in the supply chain, especially at the retailer. For consumer services, however, capacity is frequently a consideration. When a customer encounters a waiting line, a mismatch between capacity and demand is the cause. The consumer may have decided that he wanted to purchase a product or service from the company before encountering the waiting line. The waiting line, however, can change his mind.

In B2B transactions, the potential customer has probably conducted a more formal analysis of the potential supplier. These early investigations would seek out information on price and quality. For a business, the feasibility of using this company as a supplier is investigated from the standpoint of skills and needs. Capacity cannot be addressed until an actual conversation takes place between the customer and the supplier. At that time, the potential supplier finds out how many products or how much service is needed and compares the requirements to available capacity. Since purchases of products and services by a business are potentially much larger than those of a consumer, capacity is a much more significant issue.

For consumers, value attributes like convenience, style/fashion, ethical issues, technology, personalization, and even price are considered before a decision to purchase. When a consumer approaches the service provider, for example, she already knows enough to be interested in making a purchase. A shortage of capacity isn't generally known until the customer actually arrives to make the purchase.

In addition to the impact that a shortage of capacity can have on a waiting line, capacity has an impact on the remaining value attributes of response time, dependability of delivery, and flexibility. Notice that these are all time-related value attributes. Capacity often has less of an impact on *what* products or services can be produced than it has on *when* they can be produced. Since capacity is defined as output per unit time, a shortage of capacity generally means that production of the quantity desired is not feasible, given the amount of time available. With enough time, however, the quantity could probably be produced. The availability of capacity can provide flexibility that competitors lack. Esource 12.1 provides an example of a company that markets itself on flexibility that is directly related to available capacity.

www.
OperationsNow
.com

In the case of response time, the sooner an order can be started, the sooner it can be finished. An order can be started immediately only if the resources are immediately available. If they are not, meaning that they are already working on another order, the start will be delayed, delaying the finish. This is what causes a waiting line or queue. This is also known as a **backlog** in some industries.

Dependability of delivery is diminished when there is an increase in the variability of the response time. If the lead time to complete a promised service or order of products is very stable and dependable, it is unlikely that the response will take longer than expected. If it varies significantly, however, the prediction of how long it will take, which forms the basis for a delivery promise, has a higher probability of being wrong. What causes the variability in lead time? Usually variability results from disruptions that occur in the value chain. Delayed shipments of materials are one common cause; equipment breakdowns are another. In Chapter 10, the use of inventory buffers was described as a way to decouple process from these types of disruption. Buffers of excess capacity can also reduce the impact. If excess capacity exists, there will be some idle capacity. If there was a breakdown, the idle capacity could be pulled into use. The greater the capacity compared to demand, the greater the buffer and the greater the protection from the effects of the disruption.

In the case of flexibility, the immediate availability of resources is again important. A company can respond quickly to unusual demands only if it has available capacity.

If all capacity is being utilized, the company has no ability to respond. In each of the time-related value attributes, a company's ability to improve performance hinges on having available capacity. A buffer of available capacity offers strategic value to a company that competes on the basis of these quality attributes. Quick response, dependable response, and flexibility depend on a company's ability to respond on short notice. In some cases, buffers of inventory can enhance these capabilities. However, we've already discussed how finished-goods inventory actually reduces the firm's flexibility to respond to market changes with new-product introductions. A buffer of capacity does not have the same negative effect as a buffer of finished goods. Capacity kept in reserve to deal with disruptions and emergencies is known as **protective capacity**. Unfortunately, protective capacity tends to be in short supply because it is often viewed as an investment in resources that aren't providing a financial return. Protective capacity, because it isn't being used all the time, appears to create idle resources. This is, in fact, true. The resources are idle. However, without these idle resources, the firm cannot respond quickly to an unexpected demand on these resources. From a short-term perspective it appears that the idle resources should be eliminated, because high utilization of equipment results in quicker payback for the investment. Protective capacity provides a long-term financial return through its impact on various time-related value attributes, and protective capacity can increase value and increase market share. The ability to respond to a new customer who needs something immediately, or an old customer caught in a bind, can create a new level of customer loyalty.

THE FINANCIAL IMPACT OF CAPACITY DECISIONS

Reduced response time, improved dependability of delivery, and increased flexibility result in increased value. The increases in value result in enhanced market share, increases in net sales, and the resulting increases in net income and return on assets. In many cases, however, the impact of capacity can go beyond these service-oriented value attributes and influence cost and quality levels as well. In both cases, it is important to understand a specific type of capacity known as design capacity.

Design capacity is the rate of production the business was designed to accommodate on a long-term basis. For example, a manufacturing facility, by its size and the type and amount of production equipment it has, can produce products at a variety of output levels. But it was designed with a specific output level in mind. Producing at a rate less than the design capacity results in idle and unproductive resources. Because so many costs associated with production are fixed, the smaller volume of output results in higher costs per unit. Producing at a rate greater than the design capacity also results in problems. Equipment can incur excess wear and insufficient maintenance. Overtime may be required. Workers can be overwhelmed and facilities can get overcrowded. In cases of underproduction and overproduction, the resources are not used optimally, resulting in higher costs per unit than if the plant were operating at its design level. A match between the demand and the design capacity creates a situation known as the **best operating level**, the level at which costs per unit are at their lowest.

Matching demand to design capacity is even more critical for services. Overloading or underutilizing service resources can have similar impacts on costs. Resources that remain underutilized, including the workforce, do not generate the same financial return as when utilized fully. Resources overloaded have increased levels of wear and tear, and they don't get the maintenance needed to keep them in top running condition. A mismatch between demand and design capacity can be even more serious in the service sector because its effects go beyond simple cost issues.

The relationship between design capacity and demand is critical for many resources. Warehouses, for example, are not often thought of when considering capacity implications, but warehouses require a substantial facility investment. In situations like this one, when demand is far below capacity, storage costs per unit are extremely high because of the fixed costs that can't be spread out among large numbers of products stored.

Demand that is too low can result in inattentive employees and a business that doesn't deliver in a way that meets customer expectations. Restaurants, clubs, and entertainment-oriented businesses need customers to attract more customers. An empty restaurant, for example, warns potential customers that something is wrong with it. In experience-oriented businesses, customers expect interaction with others and, without that interaction, will not enjoy the experience as much. Overloading capacity in a service also has a negative impact. Queues form, increasing the wait time of customers. Interaction with the workforce drops to a lower level because the workforce is rushed. Less interaction means that customers will not be accommodated as well and are less likely to get the kind of treatment they are accustomed to. This is especially true with regular customers who have become used to being treated a certain way. This situation often results in moving employees from jobs that can be put off to jobs that can't wait. Workers from behind the scenes are moved to positions that require customer interaction. In many cases they don't have the same level of skills as the other employees, and customers end up getting lower levels of service. Exhibit 12.4 graphs various possible relationships between available capacity and demand.

To gain a more in-depth understanding of the importance design capacity plays, let's examine the profitability impact resulting from each zone presented in Exhibit 12.4. Zone A is a typical situation of demand being lower than design capacity. Besides the low net sales resulting from low demand, productive resources would be idle. The resulting impact is that the cost per unit associated with those resources would increase. Labor is underutilized, resulting in high labor costs per unit or a reduction in the labor force (a possible layoff). An important issue to consider is the duration of this condition. A short-term condition would not be serious, but if it continued, it would threaten broader profitability measures because costs, relative to sales, would be quite high.

Zone B is an almost perfect situation. One can't expect that demand would precisely equal design capacity over the long term, however. Manufacturers and services seek this relationship between demand and capacity.

Zone C is the opposite of Zone A. In Zone C demand is much higher than design capacity. For a manufacturer, equipment would be running faster and longer. Preventive maintenance tasks would be postponed, potentially resulting in long-term detrimental effects on the equipment. For labor to keep up, overtime would be needed. Overtime labor is paid at a higher rate than standard time labor, so labor costs per unit would increase. If this is a long-term situation, additional labor capacity would

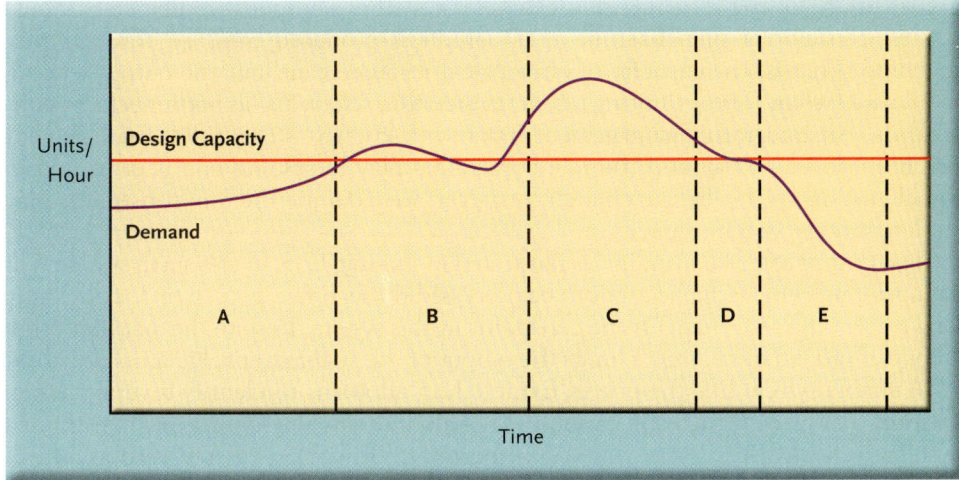

EXHIBIT 12.4 Demand and Design Capacity Relationships

be necessary, either through hiring permanent workers or through the use of a contingent workforce acquired through a temp agency. In either case, bringing on a significant number of untrained workers in a short period of time results in an underskilled workforce prone to problems. Included in those potential problems could be a decline in product and service quality, safety problems, and data recording mistakes. Anticipation of this condition would probably motivate a manufacturer to build up an inventory buffer to reduce the load on capacity.

At first glance Zone D seems to be a perfect situation, but the fact that it follows an overdemanded period means that it is really a recovery period. Tasks that would normally be done on an ongoing basis are delayed during high demand periods and a lull that follows offers an opportunity to catch up on those tasks. Even though demand isn't as high in Zone D, the load on the workforce could still be too high because they're trying to meet the demand and catch up on things that didn't get done during the preceding rush.

Zone E presents a serious drop in demand that could threaten the financial health of the business if prolonged. Demand that approaches only 50 percent of design capacity results in all of the cost increases discussed in Zone A but could also lead to quality problems that result from inattentive workers and associated morale problems. In addition, layoffs could result in the few remaining workers being given broader responsibilities, resulting in poor quality. If prolonged, the low demand would result in cash flow problems making it hard to cover the fixed costs associated with the design capacity.

Like many operations decisions, capacity planning involves tradeoff decisions. More capacity reduces response time and, in some ways, adds to a firm's flexibility. However, excess capacity increases costs, doesn't provide enough financial return, and can actually reduce flexibility if it is in the wrong form.

INDIVIDUAL RESOURCE INFLUENCE ON SYSTEM CAPACITY

In the previous discussions, the fact that service and manufacturing production capacity requires the convergence of numerous resources was mentioned. For many service- and manufacturing-oriented production systems, capacity results from the complex merger of resources. The overall capacity of the system is dependent on all of the individual resources used to create it. If one is missing, capacity is short. In many productive systems, the overall output of the system is constrained by the availability of one of the resources. For example, a factory's output could be constrained by the capacity of one machine if all products produced must go through that machine. That is, the capacity of one critical resource can limit the output level of the entire system. These limiting resources are often referred to as **bottlenecks** or **constraints**. An integrative management framework known as **constraint management** has been developed around the role constraints play in systems and is presented in detail in Chapter 17. In this chapter, however, we examine the role constraints play in determining system capacity.

The critical role of constraints is illustrated in Exhibit 12.5. In this small system that requires employment applications to be processed through five steps, step 3 is obviously slower than the rest. Step 3 is the constraint in this system. Despite the fact that other steps can process more, step 3 limits the output of the system to twelve units per hour.

A simple system like the one in Exhibit 12.5 allows us to identify several characteristics that result from a constraint. First of all, individual resources in a constrained system do not control their own utilization rates. Utilization is often used as a measure of capacity performance and is computed as the amount of time a resource is actually processing divided by the amount of time it could be processing. Step 4 has the potential to process one unit every four minutes—15 units per hour. The slower rate of step 3, however, can provide step 4 with only one unit every five minutes. Thus step 4 will process a unit in four minutes, then wait one minute for the next unit, then process it in four minutes, then wait, and so on. Step 4 will work four out of five minutes, for a utilization rate of 80 percent.

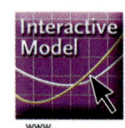

This phenomenon holds true for the processing steps that come before step 3 as well. Steps 1 and 2 are faster than step 3. If we feed applications into the system at the rate step 1 can process them, one every three minutes, the system can process them only as fast as step 3 (one unit every five minutes). The result of step 1 and step 2 processing applications faster than one every five minutes is simply a buildup of applications in front of step 3. This is shown in Exhibit 12.6. Notice also that the utilization of step 2 is limited by the capacity of step 1. Interactive Model 12.1 provides an opportunity to experiment with the impact a constraining work center can have in a productive system.

The second phenomenon created by the system constraint is that time lost by the constraint is lost for the entire system. Not only is the time lost, but it is lost forever. It can't be made up. This fact relates to the high level of utilization required of constraints. Since a constrained resource limits the system's output level, the constraint must be utilized 100 percent of the time to maximize the output of the system. If the constraint stops producing for any amount of time because of a breakdown or some

EXHIBIT 12.5   **Example of a Constrained System**

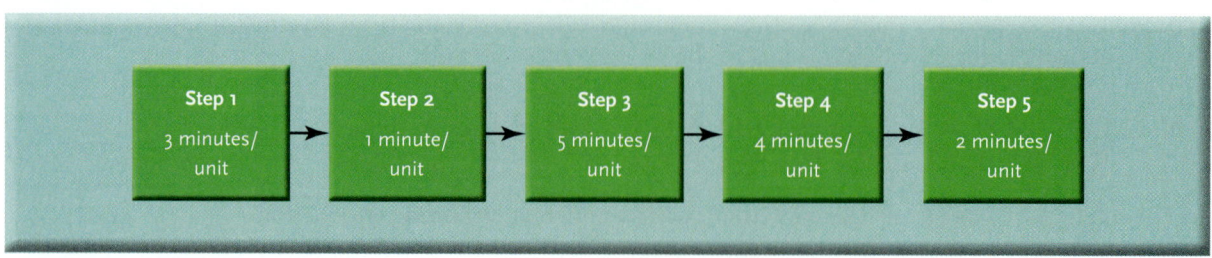

Example of a Constrained System with Excess Input	EXHIBIT 12.6

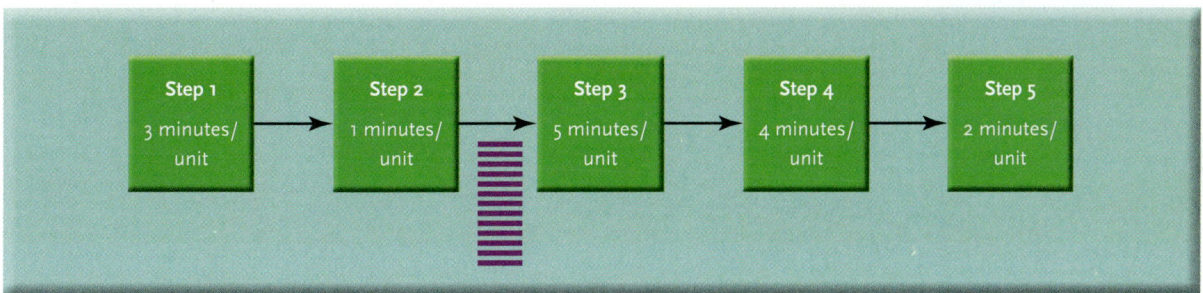

"Weakest Link" Analogy of Constrained System	EXHIBIT 12.7

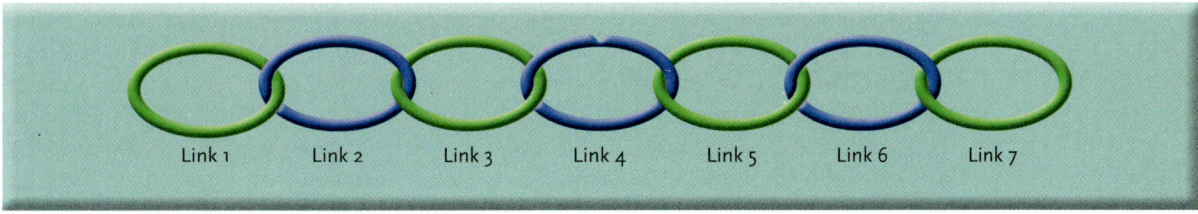

other reason, the result is the same as shutting down the entire system. For nonconstraints, a breakdown for a short amount of time is not serious because they are idle part of the time anyway. In fact, if a particular resource is a nonconstraint, it must be idle part of the time, since it can't produce faster than the constraint. Since the nonconstraints can work faster than the constraint, they can catch up again to make up for lost time if a disruption forces them to stop producing. The constraint, however, has no idle time available to get caught up.

One way to look at the capacity in a productive system is to use the analogy of a chain. The links of a chain can be of various strengths, but the strength of the chain is determined by the weakest link, as shown in Exhibit 12.7.

The chain analogy also illustrates a third phenomenon of constrained systems: Increasing the productivity or output of a nonconstraint does not help the system. Looking back at Exhibit 12.5, for example, what improvement would be gained by increasing the output of step 4 from 15 units per hour to 30 units per hour? Since step 4 receives units only every five minutes, an increase in capacity results in no improvement to the system, but just gives step 4 more time to be idle. More sophisticated approaches used to help manage constrained systems are discussed in detail in Chapter 17. If a system constraint is eliminated, a new one usually appears. Notice the weakest link (link 4) in Exhibit 12.7. If that link is strengthened (made faster), eventually another link replaces it as the "weakest" (slowest).

A BROADER VIEW: SUPPLY CHAIN CAPACITY

Just as one resource can constrain a productive system inside a business, one business can constrain an entire supply chain. The value added from various businesses in the

EXHIBIT 12.8 Weakest Link in a Supply Chain

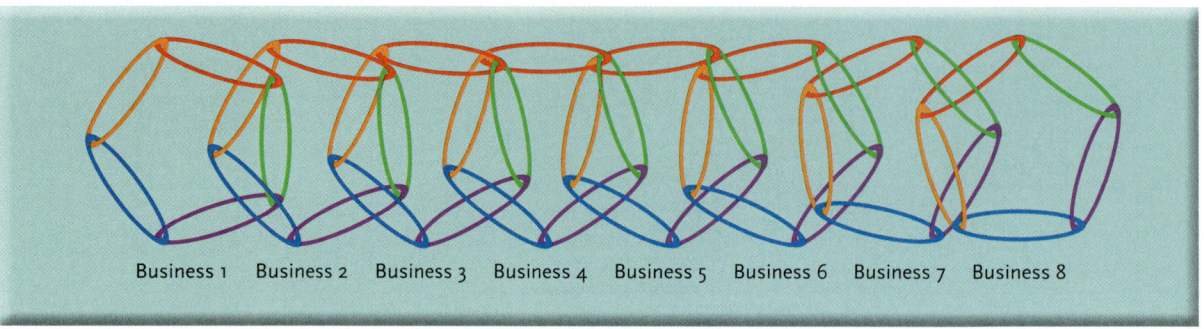

chain between raw materials and consumer products comes from a variety of resources in different companies. From basic manufacturer all the way to assembler and then to transportation services and to the ability of a retailer to stock its shelves, capacity defines the ability of the supply chain to accomplish its goal of adding value and getting it to the customer. Any link in the chain can be a constraint to what it can accomplish. Since any resource within a productive system can limit that system, the supply chain capacity can be limited by a specific resource within the chain. The supply chain, in effect, is a "chain of chains." The analogy presented in Exhibit 12.7 is extended to illustrate the complexities of supply chain capacity in Exhibit 12.8.

The difference in companies' abilities to utilize inventory as a means of leveling the effect of demand on capacity adds complexity to the supply chain capacity issue. The capacities required to complete all of the production functions within the supply chain are not just those required to produce products. Many are service-oriented capacities, such as transportation, distribution, and storage. Even though production capacity requirements can be leveled by utilizing finished-product inventories, demands on distribution systems cannot always be leveled in that way. Even though products can be produced ahead of time, they might not be amenable to shipping ahead of time. Within the supply chain, organizations utilize different strategies for minimizing costs associated with capacity and demand interactions. Naturally, these strategies differ between manufacturers and services. The following discussions examine common techniques for matching capacity and demand in these two environments.

MANAGING THE DEMAND–CAPACITY MATCH IN MANUFACTURING

The ability to buffer capacity from demand swings by utilizing inventory buildup creates an opportunity for manufacturers to examine their future capacity needs and create a plan for meeting them. This is typically done at an aggregate level, rather than at the individual product level, because forecasting into the future is much more accurate when done on an aggregate basis. **Aggregate demand** is the total demand, stated in some aggregate unit. An aggregate demand forecast is more accurate than forecasts of individual products because when forecasting at the aggregate level, the errors that would be associated with all of the individual product forecasts tend to cancel each other out. At the individual product level, some forecasts will be high and some low, but we won't know which until it's too late. At the aggregate level, we get the effect of averaging, and it reduces the random component.

Aggregate planning, as capacity planning at this level is known, uses inventory and variable labor level production to deal with demand fluctuations in an attempt to reduce costs. From Chapter 11, we know that carrying inventory can be beneficial, but it is also costly. Inventory can be used to eliminate the direct effects of demand fluctuation, but this method comes at a price. The more inventory we store, and the longer we store it, the greater the inventory carrying costs. But refusing to store inventory carries a price as well. Chasing demand by continuously adjusting capacity is not cost-free either. Hiring, training, and laying off workers are expensive activities. The more a company uses inventory to smooth production requirements, the less hiring and firing, but the higher the inventory carrying costs. Aggregate planning considers the interaction of these practices and attempts to reach low-cost solutions. Examination of the two extreme options provides insight into this technique.

Demand Chase Aggregate Planning

In the simplest approach, known as the **demand chase** approach to aggregate planning, production levels are changed to match changes in demand, so no inventory is needed to buffer against demand changes. Changes in production levels must be dealt with through hiring and laying off workers. Costs associated with this plan are the costs of hiring and laying off workers. Example 12.1 demonstrates this approach.

The demand chase strategy for aggregate planning is another one of those situations where all costs aren't quantifiable. The total costs for Example 12.1 are calculated to be $11,050. Common sense reveals other costs. In a tight labor market, what happens to workers who are laid off? They go to work somewhere else. Eventually, a business that experiences frequent layoff cycles will find that the only people willing to work there are those who are currently unable to get a job elsewhere. Most people

---

Example 12.1
Demand Chase Aggregate Plan

Quality Office Designs manufactures customized office fixtures. The company has created a "generic" configuration for aggregate planning purposes and has predicted the demand for next year, as presented in Exhibit 12.9. The labor required for each fixture is 1.2 hours. Assuming a 40-hour work week (160 hours per month) for employees, hiring costs of $475, and layoff costs of $400, management wishes to create a demand chase aggregate plan.

EXHIBIT 12.9 Quality Office Design Demand

Period	1	2	3	4	5	6	7	8	9	10	11	12
Demand forecast	1,400	1,300	1,600	1,280	2,000	2,400	2,550	1,990	1,750	1,600	1,600	1,850

Solution

The demand chase plan is constructed by first converting the units demanded each period into the required labor hours for that period. Once the required labor hours are determined, the number of workers needed is computed by dividing the labor hours required each month by 160. This result must be rounded up to a "whole" worker, since Quality can't hire partial employees. The results of these calculations are presented in Exhibit 12.10.

(continues)

Example 12.1 (continued)

EXHIBIT 12.10 Quality Office Design Labor Requirements

Period	1	2	3	4	5	6	7	8	9	10	11	12
Demand forecast	1,400	1,300	1,600	1,280	2,000	2,400	2,550	1,990	1,750	1,600	1,600	1,850
Labor hours required	1,680	1,560	1,920	1,536	2,400	2,880	3,060	2,388	2,100	1,920	1,920	2,220
Workers required	11	10	12	10	15	18	20	15	14	12	12	14

Costs are calculated by multiplying the number of hires each month by $475 and the number of layoffs by $400. Monthly costs are totaled. The results of the complete cost analysis are presented in Exhibit 12.11.

EXHIBIT 12.11 Cost Analysis of Demand Chase Aggregate Plan

Period	1	2	3	4	5	6	7	8	9	10	11	12
Demand forecast	1,400	1,300	1,600	1,280	2,000	2,400	2,550	1,990	1,750	1,600	1,600	1,850
Labor hours required	1,680	1,560	1,920	1,536	2,400	2,880	3,060	2,388	2,100	1,920	1,920	2,220
Workers required	11	10	12	10	15	18	20	15	14	12	12	14
Number of hires	0	0	2	0	5	3	2	0	0	0	0	2
Number of layoffs	0	1	0	2	0	0	0	5	1	2	0	0
Hiring cost		$0	$950	$0	$2,375	$1,425	$950	$0	$0	$0	$0	$950
Layoff cost		$400	$0	$800	$0	$0	$0	$2,000	$400	$800	$0	$0

Total hiring cost:	$6,650
Total layoff cost:	$4,400
Total plan cost:	$11,050

www.OperationsNow.com

Excel Tutor 12.1 demonstrates how a spreadsheet can aid in the development of a demand chase aggregate plan.

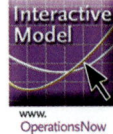
www.OperationsNow.com

will prefer a job that is more stable. The quality of the workforce is reduced by the cycle of layoffs and hirings. Training costs are included as a part of the hiring decision, but in virtually any job, experience translates into quality. Layoffs and rehires result in a lower overall experience level and the resulting lower quality level. The profit chain, described in Chapter 11, provides the logical links between employee experience, quality, customer loyalty, and profitability. For these reasons, a pure demand chase strategy is uncommon. Interactive Model 12.2 provides an experimen-

Level Production Aggregate Planning

The opposite extreme from the demand chase approach is to avoid hiring and firing and to deal with all of the demand fluctuations through a buffer of finished-product inventory. There are three potential kinds of cost associated with this approach. The first costs, once we determine the number of employees needed to produce the necessary units, are the hiring or firing costs associated with an initial labor adjustment. The second costs are those associated with carrying the inventory, including insurance, storage, and opportunity costs. They are typically calculated as a percentage of the average value of the inventory. The third cost associated with this plan is the cost of a stockout. Stockouts can occur with this plan, but they can be planned for. To plan months ahead to run out of something may seem foolish (and it would be), but keep in mind that this is a plan based on aggregate production to provide a close estimate of costs. It is ultimately based on a forecast of demand, and we know that forecasts are inaccurate. Stockouts do happen, and it makes sense to acknowledge that they can happen. Ultimately, at the execution stage several months in the future, effort would be taken to avoid the stockout.

The process required to create a **level production** aggregate plan takes advantage of our ability to store capacity from one period to the next in the form of inventory. To determine the number of units that need to be produced per period, we essentially determine the total number of units that need to be produced and divide that number by the number of time periods (days, weeks, or months). The number of units to be produced per period is translated into labor hours by multiplying the number of units by the time per unit. The total number of labor hours needed per period is translated into the number of workers needed by dividing the number of labor hours needed by the number of hours each employee works per period (8 hours per day, 40 hours per week, 160 hours per month, etc.). In Example 12.2, the scenario presented in the previous example forms the basis for a level production aggregate plan.

Example 12.2
Level Production Aggregate Plan

Quality Office Designs created a demand chase aggregate plan with total costs of $11,050. The company wants to create a level production plan for a comparison. The total number of units projected to be produced is 21,320. There is a total of 253 workdays in the year. Exhibit 12.12 reproduces the projected demand information from Example 12.1 and provides the total units to produce and the workdays per month.

EXHIBIT 12.12 Quality Office Design Demand

Period	1	2	3	4	5	6	7	8	9	10	11	12
Demand forecast	1,400	1,300	1,600	1,280	2,000	2,400	2,550	1,990	1,750	1,600	1,600	1,850

The labor required for each fixture is 1.2 hours. Hiring costs are $475, and layoff costs are $400. The initial staffing level is 11 employees. Inventory carrying costs associated with this plan have been determined to be $12 per unit per month.

(continues)

Example 12.2 (continued)

Solution

With 253 workdays available, and 21,320 units needed, 84.27 units (round up to 85) will need to be produced each day. Production of 85 units per day, at 1.2 hours per unit, requires 12.75 employees, rounded up to 13 workers. So an initial hiring of two workers will be required. The total number of units produced each month, based on the number of workdays each month and the daily production of 85 units, compared to the monthly demand, is presented in Exhibit 12.13. Included in Exhibit 12.13 are the resulting inventory levels and costs.

EXHIBIT 12.13 Results of Cost Analysis for Level Production Aggregate Plan

Period	1	2	3	4	5	6	7	8	9	10	11	12	Total
Demand forecast	1,400	1,300	1,600	1,280	2,000	2,400	2,550	1,990	1,750	1,600	1,600	1,850	21,320
Workdays	22	20	23	20	23	20	20	23	21	22	20	19	253
Monthly output	1,870	1,700	1,955	1,700	1,955	1,700	1,700	1,955	1,785	1,870	1,700	1,615	21,505
Beginning inventory	0	470	870	1,225	1,645	1,600	900	50	15	50	320	420	
Ending inventory	470	870	1,225	1,645	1,600	900	50	15	50	320	420	185	
Average inventory	235	670	1,047.5	1,435	1,622.5	1,250	475	32.5	32.5	185	370	302.5	
Carrying cost ($)	2,820	8,040	12,570	17,220	19,470	15,000	5,700	390	390	2,220	4,440	3,630	91,890

Average demand for each month is the beginning inventory plus the ending inventory, divided by 2. Notice that at the end of the year, more units have actually been produced than necessary. This results from the rounding up of the 12.75 workers to 13. The inventory carrying costs associated with this plan are substantial—$91,890. In addition, hiring the two new employees would cost $950, for a total cost of $92,840.

Excel Tutor 12.2 shows how the level production aggregate plan can be developed in a spreadsheet.

www.OperationsNow.com
EXCEL TUTOR

It is unlikely that either the demand chase or the level production aggregate plan will be totally acceptable. In most situations, the best solution turns out to be some hybrid of using inventory and adjusting the level of the workforce. For example, allowing one workforce adjustment in period 1 and another in period 6 and leveling the production for each six-month period presents a compromise. When the capability of using some overtime and some temporary workers is added, an infinite number of possible scenarios open up.

The financial impact of matching demand and capacity is illustrated quite well when the aggregate planning process is examined. The basic costs of production cannot be avoided. The inventory carrying costs are traded off against the costs associated with changing capacity in a quest for the "perfect match." We know, however, that the perfect match is not possible. The resulting capacity gives us a level of service that customers evaluate. Good service is viewed positively by customers, adds to their perception of value, and increases customer loyalty and the firm's market share. Stockouts, though sometimes unavoidable, reduce performance in the eyes of the customer and, given the importance of timeliness, are almost unacceptable. This is particularly true given the options for contingent capacity, discussed later in this chapter. Aggregate planning is very structured and explicitly addresses these costs. No matter what approach is used to match capacity and demand, however, the costs and financial impact are the same.

Detailed Capacity Planning in Manufacturing

While aggregate planning provides a mechanism for examining capacity and demand relationships in the long term, capacity–demand relationships must also be addressed on a detailed level in the short term. In many manufacturing environments, products are assembled from a combination of components, some that are purchased and others that are manufactured in-house. The purchased components do not directly affect capacity, but their availability or unavailability can affect the firm's ability to utilize capacity as scheduled. The most significant impact on manufacturing capacity comes from components and products that are manufactured in-house.

Detailed capacity planning processes are typically integrated with the detailed inventory calculations used to manage dependent demand inventory. Recall from Chapter 10 that dependent demand inventory (components and raw materials) is managed quite differently from independent demand inventory (end products and retail inventories). The logic used to determine when and how many to order for dependent demand inventory is known as material requirements planning (MRP). When the items are manufactured components for a product, the quantity and timing of the order have the direct result of creating a demand on capacity.

MRP creates an order to be released to manufacturing. This starts the actual manufacturing process. If the component must be ready by a certain date in order to assemble an end product, it must be produced beforehand. From MRP, the quantity needed and the timing are known. This information can be used to determine the required load on the resources used in the manufacturing processes. Once the capacity requirements are known, they can be compared to the capacity available, and a satisfactory match between capacity and demand can be developed.

Exhibit 12.14 illustrates the inputs of MRP. The primary outputs of the system presented in the exhibit are the quantities and timing of planned order releases for components and raw materials. The orders for components that are manufactured in-house create the demand that "loads up" manufacturing capacity. It should be no surprise, then, that the planned order releases that result from the MRP logic provide a primary input to detailed capacity planning for manufacturers. This approach is not the only approach to generating capacity requirements for manufacturers, however. The master production schedule can also be used to provide the product demand that can then be translated into capacity requirements. The mechanism used to translate the demand for products is a statement of the capacity required to produce a particular product or component. This can take several forms, but the most common is a **bill of capacity**. Recall from Chapter 10, in the discussion of MRP logic, that a primary input to that logic is the bill of material. The bill of material details the material components of any manufactured item. The bill of capacity is analogous to the bill of material in that it specifies the capacity components of the product.

There are two common approaches to capacity planning in manufacturing. The first, known as **rough-cut capacity planning**, utilizes the master production schedule

EXHIBIT 12.14 MRP Logic

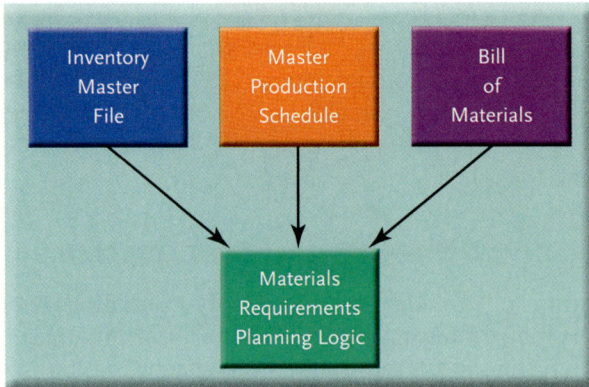

as the source of product demand information. In rough-cut capacity planning a capacity bill is created. This details all of the capacity required to manufacture the item specified in the master production schedule. For each resource utilized in the manufacture of the product, the total time required to produce all components and the finished product is calculated. These times are then multiplied by the quantity required in each time period to compute capacity needs for the period. These requirements are then compared to available capacity to identify potential problems.

Available capacity is generally calculated by converting the actual hours available on a particular work center into standard hours. Standard hours result from making two adjustments to the actual hours available. First, actual hours are adjusted to account for the historical utilization of the work center. An accurate view of the available capacity of a work center is desired. If a work center is typically utilized only 90 percent, because of maintenance, changeovers, and so on, then the available capacity should reflect that fact. Standard hours available should also recognize if a work center does not produce at 100 percent efficiency. Recall from Chapter 11 that efficiency is the actual output divided by the standard output. A work center that produces only 90 percent of the standard output will have an efficiency of 90 percent. In order for the capacity available to be an accurate reflection of reality, efficiency is also used as an adjustment to the actual hours. Example 12.3 provides a demonstration of the calculations used to compute required capacity for rough-cut capacity planning, as well as the available capacity.

Example 12.3 Rough-Cut Capacity Planning

Quality Pet Enclosures manufactures "crates" for dogs and cats. The crates come in various sizes and consist of heavy-gage galvanized wire formed into panels, which are then held together with snap clips. The crates are popular because they can be folded into a flat stack of panels within seconds. The firm has dedicated equipment for several of the more popular sizes, including the 24 × 40 crate (model 2440), which is the most popular. For the extremely large size (30 × 48) and some of the smaller sizes, one flexible manufacturing line is used. For the 2440 line, the utilization for all machines averages 93 percent. Efficiency is also consistent across all machines at 95 percent.

(continues)

Example 12.3 (continued)

The plant manager is considering the purchase of software that would enhance all capacity planning activities and wishes to create a prototype rough-cut capacity planning system as a test. Using the data provided below, determine the required and available capacity for the 2440 crate line.

Solution

The master production schedule is presented in Exhibit 12.15. The bill of capacity is presented in Exhibit 12.16. It is typically provided in hours required per unit of product.

EXHIBIT 12.15 Master Production Schedule for Model 2440

Week	1	2	3	4	5	6	7	8	9	10
2440 MPS	270	300	315	295	245	230	250	185	255	210

EXHIBIT 12.16 Bill of Capacity for Model 2440

Work Center	Time Required (hours)
Cutting	0.09
Forming	0.12
Grid assembly	0.15
Welding	0.13
Assembly	0.08

Capacity required, based on multiplying the quantity from the MPS times the processing time per unit from the bill of capacity, is presented in Exhibit 12.17.

EXHIBIT 12.17 Capacity Required for Model 2440 (in hours)

	Week									
Unit	1	2	3	4	5	6	7	8	9	10
Cutting	24.3	27	28.35	26.55	22.05	20.7	22.5	16.65	22.95	18.9
Forming	32.4	36	37.8	35.4	29.4	27.6	30	22.2	30.6	25.2
Grid assembly	40.5	45	47.25	44.25	36.75	34.5	37.5	27.75	38.25	31.5
Welding	35.1	39	40.95	38.35	31.85	29.9	32.5	24.05	33.15	27.3
Assembly	21.6	24	25.2	23.6	19.6	18.4	20	14.8	20.4	16.8

Capacity available is calculated by multiplying actual hours available by the historical utilization rate and by the historical efficiency. Calculations for capacity available are presented in Exhibit 12.18.

(continues)

Example 12.3 (continued)

EXHIBIT 12.18 Capacity Available on 2440 Line

Unit	Actual Hours Available	Historical Utilization	Historical Efficiency	Capacity (Standard Hours) Available
Cutting	40	0.93	0.95	35.34
Forming	40	0.93	0.95	35.34
Grid assembly	80	0.93	0.95	70.68
Welding	40	0.93	0.95	35.34
Assembly	40	0.93	0.95	35.34

Exhibit 12.19 provides the completed rough-cut capacity plan, which compares required capacity to available capacity for the 2440 line.

EXHIBIT 12.19 Rough-Cut Capacity Plan for 2440

	Week									
Unit	1	2	3	4	5	6	7	8	9	10
Cutting										
Required	24.3	27	28.35	26.55	22.05	20.7	22.5	16.65	22.95	18.9
Available	35.34	35.34	35.34	35.34	35.34	35.34	35.34	35.34	35.34	35.34
Forming										
Required	32.4	36	37.8	35.4	29.4	27.6	30	22.2	30.6	25.2
Available	35.34	35.34	35.34	35.34	35.34	35.34	35.34	35.34	35.34	35.34
Grid assembly										
Required	40.5	45	47.25	44.25	36.75	34.5	37.5	27.75	38.25	31.5
Available	70.68	70.68	70.68	70.68	70.68	70.68	70.68	70.68	70.68	70.68
Welding										
Required	35.1	39	40.95	38.35	31.85	29.9	32.5	24.05	33.15	27.3
Available	35.34	35.34	35.34	35.34	35.34	35.34	35.34	35.34	35.34	35.34
Assembly										
Required	21.6	24	25.2	23.6	19.6	18.4	20	14.8	20.4	16.8
Available	35.34	35.34	35.34	35.34	35.34	35.34	35.34	35.34	35.34	35.34

Excel Tutor 12.3 provides guidance for developing rough-cut capacity planning logic in a spreadsheet environment.

The rough-cut capacity plan for the entire plant would include the same logic and would cover all work centers in the plant. Work centers that are used in the production of several different products would incorporate the demand for those different products in the computation of the required capacity.

Rough-cut capacity planning is frequently used as a tool to ensure the master production schedule is feasible. Its analysis is quick but inaccurate. Several characteristics contribute to the inaccuracy of this approach. First, it ignores on-hand inventory, which would reduce the required capacity. Second, it ignores the possibility that actual production might not take place during the week the master production schedule shows the end product to be due.

A more detailed and accurate approach to capacity planning in a manufacturing environment is known as capacity requirements planning. **Capacity requirements planning (CRP)** is somewhat analogous to material requirements (MRP). It is completed at the component level rather than at the end-item level, using MRP planned order releases. CRP logic is similar to that of rough-cut capacity planning, but rather than using MPS demand data, it uses the planned order releases from MRP. Rather than bills of capacity, it uses the actual component routing data directly. Example 12.4 demonstrates CRP logic.

Example 12.4

Capacity Requirements Planning Calculations

A small fly rod manufacturer just implemented an MRP system to assist in managing its inventories. Its processes are quite simple, but it wishes to utilize the planned order releases from MRP to help plan for capacity. The processes are organized functionally and consist of three departments. The first department is handle assembly, where the rod blank is cemented into the handle and reel seat. The second department is the wrapping department, where guides are attached to the blank in a thread-wrapping process. The third is finishing, where an epoxy resin is used to coat the thread wraps and where decals are added. Exhibit 12.20 provides the product structure for the 9-foot 5-weight rod. The owner wishes to use the planned order releases from the new MRP system to compute capacity requirements for the three departments. In this experimental run, only one rod model is used for the sample calculations.

EXHIBIT 12.20 Product Structure for 9-foot 5-weight Fly Rod

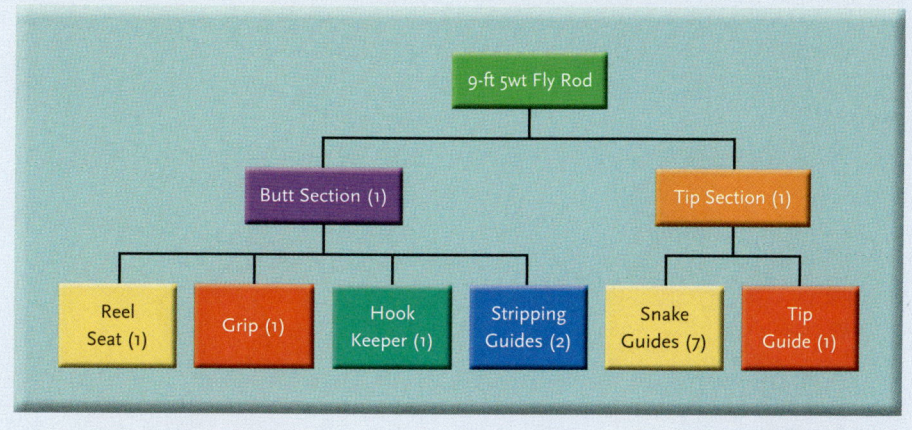

(continues)

Example 12.4 (continued)

Solution

The MRP logic generated the planned order releases seen in Exhibit 12.21.

EXHIBIT 12.21 Planned Order Releases for 9-foot 5-weight Fly Rod

	Week									
	1	2	3	4	5	6	7	8	9	10
Butt section	45	21	26	42	35	39	42	36	50	48
Tip section	45	21	26	42	35	39	42	36	50	48

Since all bottom-level components are purchased (guides, blanks, reel seats, and grips), only the assembly of the two sections requires capacity. The routings for the two sections are presented in Exhibit 12.22.

EXHIBIT 12.22 Routings for Fly Rod Components

	Handle Assembly	Wrapping (hours/unit)	Finishing (hours/unit)
Butt section	0.12	0.1	0.08
Tip section	0	0.25	0.12

By multiplying the quantity of each section from the MRP logic by the time per unit on each work center as given by the component routings, the requirements presented in Exhibit 12.23 were generated. Available capacity was calculated exactly as was done in Example 12.3, by multiplying actual hours by historical utilization and efficiencies.

Excel Tutor 12.4 demonstrates the capacity requirements planning method in Excel.

www.OperationsNow.com

EXHIBIT 12.23 Capacity Requirements Plan for Fly Rod Production

	Week									
	1	2	3	4	5	6	7	8	9	10
Handle Assembly										
Req'd for butt section	5.4	2.52	3.12	5.04	4.2	4.68	5.04	4.32	6	5.76
Req'd for tip section	0	0	0	0	0	0	0	0	0	0
Total required	5.4	2.52	3.12	5.04	4.2	4.68	5.04	4.32	6	5.76
Total available	36	36	36	36	36	36	36	36	36	36
Wrapping										
Req'd for butt section	4.5	2.1	2.6	4.2	3.5	3.9	4.2	3.6	5	4.8
Req'd for tip section	11.25	5.25	6.5	10.5	8.75	9.75	10.5	9	12.5	12
Total required	15.75	7.35	9.1	14.7	12.25	13.65	14.7	12.6	17.5	16.8
Total available	36	36	36	36	36	36	36	36	36	36
Finishing										
Req'd for butt section	3.6	1.68	2.08	3.36	2.8	3.12	3.36	2.88	4	3.84
Req'd for tip section	5.4	2.52	3.12	5.04	4.2	4.68	5.04	4.32	6	5.76
Total required	9	4.2	5.2	8.4	7	7.8	8.4	7.2	10	9.6
Total available	36	36	36	36	36	36	36	36	36	36

| Generic Manufacturing Planning and Control System | EXHIBIT 12.24 |

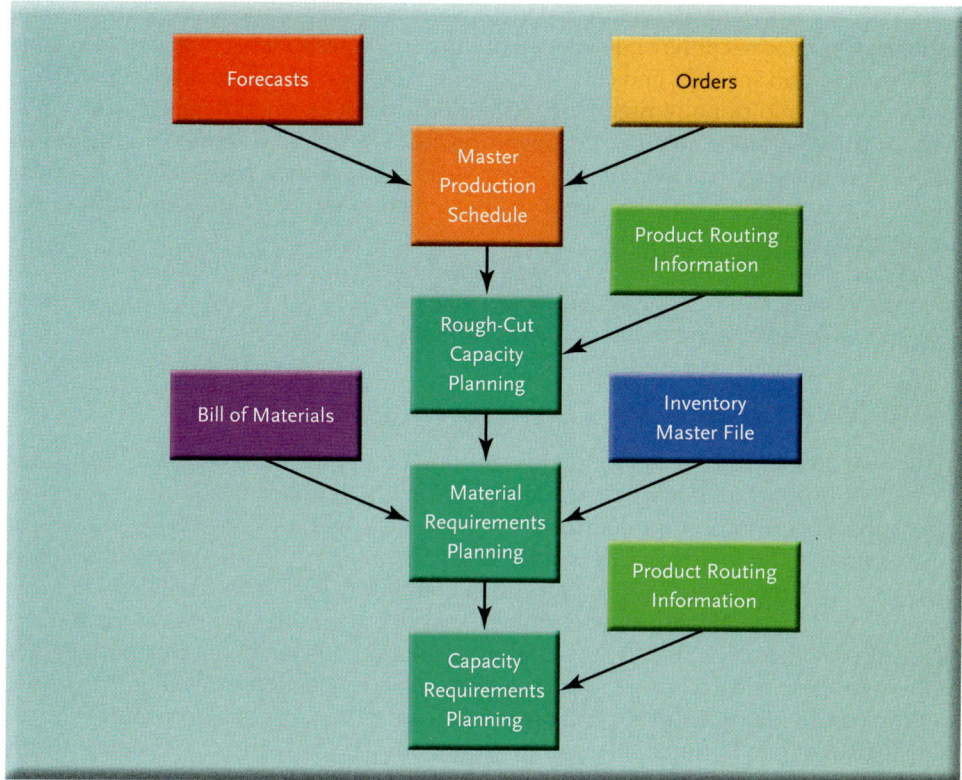

The capacity requirements planning method has two advantages over the rough-cut capacity planning method. Since the demand is derived from MRP planned order releases, inventory on hand is taken into account. In addition, timing more accurately reflects when the production will take place, because the lead times are taken into account in MRP logic.

Exhibit 12.24 shows the relationships between material and capacity planning functions within a generic production planning and control system.

Manufacturing production planning and control systems integrate materials planning and capacity planning. While the role of rough-cut capacity planning is used to validate the feasibility of the master production schedule, the role of CRP is to provide a more accurate comparison of available capacity and required capacity to help guide the actual execution of production orders.

During the execution of manufacturing orders, when the required work is being done, actual output levels are compared to plans and adjustments are made to ensure that output levels match the needs.

MANAGING THE DEMAND–CAPACITY MATCH IN SERVICES

Capacity management in services differs greatly from that in manufacturing, primarily because the load on capacity cannot be leveled by inventory buffering. The emphasis is on smoothing demand in an attempt to smooth its demand on capacity.

Many services adopt simple approaches to smoothing demand. These approaches include appointments or reservations. Appointments are generally required for professional services such as legal and medical services, where the professional's time is the capacity constraint. Reservations are typically required when space is the critical resource. Other services have developed pricing strategies to level demand. Weekday specials, weekend specials, and early-bird specials are used by different services to shift demand from traditionally high-demand periods to times when demand is low. For many of these services, much of the operating cost is fixed, so costs remain high even during low-demand times. Turning away customers during high-demand periods results in lost sales, so it makes sense to try to recoup some of that demand, even if the revenue generated is low.

Services that have high fixed costs and little marginal cost for additional customers have developed more sophisticated approaches to leveling demand. One of these approaches, known as yield management, is discussed in the following section.

Yield Management

In the year 2000, the 10 major U.S. airlines filled 72.8 percent of their seats.[1] This was the highest utilization in more than 50 years, but it is still indicative of a huge revenue-generating opportunity. One-fourth of their capacity was idle. Increasing the use of this resource would have resulted in a huge impact on profit because it would result in very little increase in cost. For services characterized by very high fixed costs but low variable costs for each additional customer served, a technique known as **yield management** provides an approach for matching demand to capacity. Hotels, airlines, car rental agencies, and resorts use yield management to maximize revenues. In those environments, any revenue lost from an empty seat, room, or car is lost forever. Even a small amount of additional sales adds to profitability because the cost associated with each individual customer is negligible. Yield management has also been considered as a means of leveling demand on health care facilities. Yield management utilizes different prices for different classes of fare, reservation systems, and overbooking to maximize revenues. Esource 12.2 provides a description of yield management as used by one airline.

www.OperationsNow.com

While the single empty seat on this flight might make it more pleasant for the passenger next to it, it also represents lost revenue. Since the additional passenger would add virtually no costs, any revenue gained through the sale of this seat would go directly to profitability. Yield management seeks to find that last passenger and fill this seat.

Yield management is a complex system that takes advantage of the characteristics of service markets to fill seats or rooms, recognizing that it is better to generate even a small amount of revenue from some capacity rather than let it go unused. When the customer base can be segmented into different classes, different prices can be identified for each class. A forecast of the demand at different prices is necessary to determine how many rooms or seats to sell at each price. Those who make reservations first receive the lowest prices. Prices can be adjusted during high-demand times to reduce demand or to shift demand to lower-demand times. Prices are also used to shift demand to different locations. Airlines, for example, take advantage of customers' willingness to drive to particular airports to get a lower airfare.

Overbooking

For services like airlines and hotels, reservations are used in an attempt to smooth demand on capacity. Despite reservations, a high no-show rate makes it necessary to overbook capacity. Overbooking means that the business takes more reservations than it has capacity for, with the assumption that some customers with reservations will not show up. In many situations, there is no cost to customers who fail to show. Many airline customers, for example, book seats on several flights because they don't know for sure which one they'll need. Then they either cancel at the last minute or just fail to show. In recent years, airlines have implemented a nonrefundable ticket policy for discount fares to discourage this behavior.

The empty seat or room created by the no-show results in a substantial opportunity loss if other customers are turned away. There are always tradeoffs, however. If seats are overbooked on a plane, and everyone shows up, someone is left off the plane.

Making Overbooking a Win–Win Situation

Overbooking, or, from the customer's perspective, "being bumped," is nowhere more abhorred than in the airline industry. Industry data kept by the U.S. Department of Transportation Air Travel Consumer Report shows that despite high levels of dissatisfaction, the frequency of "involuntary denied boardings" is increasing. The rate of bumps per 10,000 passengers was 0.88 in 1998 and in 1999, and it rose to 1.04 in 2000. Overbooking in the airline industry is a necessary evil. No-shows are common, despite the "no-refund" policies for discounted tickets. Full-fare tickets are still purchased by enough travelers to make no-shows (and the potential for turning down a passenger who could have filled that seat) a distinct possibility.

Bumps can be avoided if passengers volunteer to take a later flight. The trick is to offer incentives to encourage passengers to volunteer. Airlines are legally obligated only to find the passenger accommodation on the next available flight. If the flight is the last one for the day, they must provide overnight lodging and meals. They are under no obligation to provide other reimbursements.

In 1999, Delta Air Lines had the worst bump statistics in the industry with 15,607 involuntary denied boardings, 1.53 per 10,000 passengers. That was nearly double the industry average of 0.88. In 2000 the airline improved its performance to only 3,327 people, 0.33 per 10,000 passengers, and less than half of the industry average. How did it make such a dramatic turnaround? Delta adopted a flexible program called "Delta Dollars." The Delta Dollars program gives gate agents the authority and flexibility to offer from $250 to $1,000 as an incentive for volunteers to give up their seats. Rather than offer a fixed amount, as is done by some competitors, Delta can stage a sort of reverse auction, raising the incentive until someone takes advantage of it, eventually opening enough seats. The result is that each person relinquishing a seat can get up to $1,000 toward a future flight.

Despite Delta's progress on this aspect of quality service, it was ninth out of 11 major carriers in on-time arrivals (within 15 minutes of the scheduled time), with a 73.1 percent on-time rate. They had the most cancellations of the 11 major airlines, with 5.3 percent.

Source: "Not All Bumps Painful," *Cincinnati Enquirer*, May 20, 2001, pp. D1, D4; "Delta On-Time Record Still Poor," *Cincinnati Enquirer*, March 10, 2001, p. C1.

www.OperationsNow.com

"Bumping" or "walking" a customer happens whenever too many customers show up. The U.S. Department of Transportation provides specific regulations regarding the overbooking policies airlines use, as shown in Esource 12.3.

Overbooking is used to generate revenue from the empty rooms or seats created by the no-shows. It isn't as simple as just booking too many customers, however, because in addition to the costs associated with an empty room or seat, there are costs associated with turning customers away when more customers are overbooked than the space created by no-shows. The appropriate number to overbook is calculated by examining all possible outcomes related to different numbers of no-shows and selecting an overbooking strategy that minimizes the expected loss associated with no-shows. The number of overbookings that results in a "lowest expected loss" must be forecast. We know that forecasts tend to be wrong. Some forecasts are more wrong than others. In the overbooking problem, we examine past no-show records to identify the probabilities associated with different no-show rates. Since we know the costs associated with no-shows, and we know the costs associated with "bumping" customers when too many have been overbooked, we can compute the expected costs of different strategies. Example 12.5 demonstrates the process of determining the overbooking strategy with the lowest expected cost.

Overbooking is an automatic quality failure for any customer bumped. Any company overbooking must recognize this and have a recovery policy in place. In many cases, the bumped customer receives a benefit that results in enhanced value. For airline passengers, compensation in the form of a voucher is generally provided. In the hospitality and lodging industries, the accommodation that is provided is often better than the customer would have had if he had not been bumped.

Example 12.5 Overbooking

Rainbow Canyon Lodge management recognized that there was an increase in the number of no-shows during the past two years. They suspect that several hotels recently built in the area are causing this: When customers with reservations arrive at the canyon, some decide to stay at the newer hotels. Over the past year, no-shows averaged 1.56 per day. Actual no-show records are presented in Exhibit 12.25. Rainbow Canyon Lodge is in the heart of a major tourist area and has a very high occupancy rate. Management calculated the cost of a no-show to be $89. They made reciprocal arrangements with several hotels to take customers who are "bumped" from Rainbow Canyon Lodge. Management calculated the cost of lost goodwill plus the cost of the alternative lodging to be $110 per customer bumped.

EXHIBIT 12.25 No-Show History for Rainbow Canyon Lodge

Number of No-Shows	Frequency	Probability
0	152	0.42
1	88	0.24
2	55	0.15
3	39	0.11
4	26	0.07
5	5	0.01

(continues)

Example 12.5 (continued)

An average no-show rate of 1.56, with a cost per no-show of $89, results in an expected no-show loss of $138.84 per day, or $50,676.60 per year. Management wishes to develop a lowest expected loss overbooking strategy.

Solution

Exhibit 12.26 provides the expected opportunity costs associated with the probabilities of each no-show quantity if the reservations were overbooked by one. The expected opportunity cost for each number of no-shows is computed by multiplying the number of no-shows remaining after overbooking by one by the cost per no-show. The expected cost of bumping is computed by multiplying the number of customers bumped in each no-show scenario by the bumping cost. In Exhibit 12.26, the only scenario that can result in a customer being bumped is if there are zero no-shows. The total expected loss when overbooking by one would be $101.38 per night ($37,003.70 per year). This would present an expected annual savings of $13,672.90 over the current practice of not overbooking.

EXHIBIT 12.26 Expected Costs of Overbooking by One

Number of No-Shows	Probability	Number of Empty Rooms	Expected Opportunity Cost ($)	Expected Bumping Cost ($)
0	0.42	0	0.42(0) = 0	46.2
1	0.24	0	0.24(0) = 0	0
2	0.15	1	0.15(89) = 13.35	0
3	0.11	2	0.11(178) = 19.58	0
4	0.07	3	0.07(267) = 18.69	0
5	0.01	4	0.01(356) = 3.56	0
Sum			$55.18	$46.20
Total expected cost		$101.38		

Exhibit 12.27 provides the expected loss associated with a policy of overbooking by two each day. Expected losses per night are $143.72, substantially higher than overbooking by one. Overbooking by greater numbers would increase the expected loss. The best policy would be to overbook by one.

EXHIBIT 12.27 Expected Costs of Overbooking by Two

Number of No-Shows	Probability	Number of Empty Rooms	Expected Opportunity Cost ($)	Expected Bumping Cost ($)
0	0.42	0	0.42(0) = 0	92.4
1	0.24	0	0.24(0) = 0	26.4
2	0.15	1	1.15(0) = 0	0

(continues)

Example 12.5 (continued)

Number of No-Shows	Probability	Number of Empty Rooms	Expected Opportunity Cost ($)	Expected Bumping Cost ($)
3	0.11	2	2.11(89) = 9.79	0
4	0.07	3	3.07(178) = 12.46	0
5	0.01	4	4.01(267) = 2.67	0
Sum			$24.92	$118.80
Total expected cost		$143.72		

www.OperationsNow.com

Excel Tutor 12.5 shows the spreadsheet logic required to complete an over-booking problem.

CURRENT TRENDS IN CAPACITY MANAGEMENT

In today's quickly changing markets, firms need to be flexible enough to adapt to changes in customer needs, technologies, and competitors. For many manufacturers and services, this means that they cannot commit to permanent levels of resources. As a result, many resources are now available on a contingent basis. Employment agencies provide temporary workers to businesses that do not want to incur hiring and layoff costs that would be necessary given their demand fluctuations. Manufacturers often utilize contract manufacturers so they do not have to invest in production equipment that may soon be made obsolete by product advancements. They may even outsource basic components to eliminate the need to manufacture them themselves.

Contingent arrangements add to a firm's agility, but they can also have negative effects. Contingent workers can be the source of quality problems and dissatisfaction, particularly if they receive lower pay and benefits than their permanent cohorts. Contract manufacturing can be less reliable than in-house production and result in poor delivery performance and slower response. Transportation time can add significantly to the cash-to-cash cycle. For all capacity decisions, just like other operations decisions, tradeoffs must be made. Inherent in these tradeoffs are quantifiable *and* non-quantifiable costs.

CHAPTER SUMMARY

The matching of capacity and demand is one of the most difficult challenges facing business managers. Failure to have sufficient capacity can result in missed sales and dissatisfied customers. At best, customers come back later; at worst, they will try the competition and never return. The answer isn't necessarily to load up with more capacity to prevent this from happening because too much capacity brings its own problems. Idle capacity results in poor return on assets and higher costs that result in lower profitability. Any mismatch, in fact, can have devastating profitability implications. A key to managing capacity is to identify the amount of protective capacity needed and properly use the alternatives available for modifying either capacity or

om on site

What Should Happen to Employees When Demand Drops Suddenly?

As the technology markets turned down in late 2000, many technology-oriented companies found themselves with excess staff. Most were laid off. As the economy continued to slump, and then tried to cope with the aftermath of September 11, 2001, other segments of the U.S. economy took dramatic downturns. Travel-related industries, in particular, saw huge drops in demand. In the 30 days following September 11, companies announced the following anticipated layoffs:

Boeing	30,000
Cessna Aircraft	11,200
Raytheon	9,200
American Airlines	20,000
Bombardier Aerospace	4,100
United Airlines	20,000
Honeywell International	15,800
Continental Airlines	12,000
US Airways	11,000
Northwest Airlines	10,000
Advanced Micro Devices	2,300
Excite@Home	500

Many firms were accused of being unpatriotic by laying off workers, since layoffs would hurt an already-staggering economy. On the other hand, CEOs responded that carrying workers who weren't needed would do financial harm to the firm, reducing its value, which would have a worse impact on the economy. Although most companies lay off workers when they need to, some executives adopt a "no-layoff" policy.

Executives who refuse to lay off employees argue that this policy results in fierce loyalty, higher productivity from reduced turnover, higher levels of customer satisfaction, ability to recruit better employees, and greater innovation capability when the economy snaps back. The costs of layoffs can include severance and rehiring costs, lawsuits, loss of institutional memory, reduced trust in management, a lower-quality workforce when the economy recovers, and survivors who are risk-averse and paranoid.

The costs of layoffs and the benefits of avoiding them have begun to sink in. Many companies, even those that may ultimately lay off employees, have begun to cut costs elsewhere first, and make employee layoffs the last place to look for cost reduction.

Source: "Where Layoffs Are a Last Resort," *BusinessWeek*, October 8, 2001, p. 42; "Is It Unpatriotic to Lay Off Workers When the Nation Faces a Crisis?" *The Wall Street Journal*, October 2, 2001, pp. B1, B4; "Wichita: Not So Far from Ground Zero," *BusinessWeek*, October 8, 2001, p. 66.

---

demand to create a balance that provides sufficient financial return on resources *and* yields the flexibility, quick response, and good service so critical to customers.

This chapter explored several techniques to match capacity and demand. Traditional manufacturing-oriented approaches to capacity planning, known as rough-cut capacity planning and capacity requirements planning, form a critical part of material requirements planning systems. Services, in a difficult situation because services cannot be stored as inventory, utilize other techniques such as yield management and overbooking in an attempt to shift demand to meet available capacity. In all situations, the ability to meet the demand with the required quantity and in the required time frame characterizes the objectives of capacity management.

KEY TERMS

aggregate demand, 428
backlog, 422
best operating level, 423
bill of capacity, 433
bottleneck, 426
capacity requirements planning (CRP), 437
constraint, 426
constraint management, 426
demand chase, 429
design capacity, 423
level production, 431
protective capacity, 423
rough-cut capacity planning, 433
yield management, 440

REVIEW QUESTIONS

1. What is meant by the term "capacity"?
2. How does capacity differ from capability?
3. Why is the management of capacity more difficult for services than for manufacturing?
4. How does capacity affect value in B2B and B2C transactions?
5. What is the relationship between capacity and response time, dependability, and flexibility?
6. What is protective capacity?
7. How does design capacity relate to costs?
8. What are the possible consequences when demand rate varies from design capacity?
9. What role does a bottleneck or constraint play in determining system performance?
10. Describe how time lost on a constraint is lost by the entire system and is lost forever.
11. Describe how an analogy of a weakest link in a chain can be used to describe productivity improvement in a constrained system.
12. What is supply chain capacity?
13. What is aggregate planning?
14. Compare the level production and demand chase aggregate planning strategies.
15. What are the relevant costs in the aggregate planning process?
16. What are the informational inputs to the detailed capacity planning process used in manufacturing?
17. What are the differences between rough-cut capacity planning and capacity requirements planning?
18. What is yield management? What types of services use it?
19. What is the objective of overbooking? Describe the process of determining how many customers to overbook.

DISCUSSION QUESTIONS

1. How is capacity measured at your college or university?
2. Identify a business system you are familiar with. Does it ever suffer from too little capacity? What are the value implications when its demand is greater than its capacity?
3. In the system you identified for the previous question, what is its constraint? How could the capacity of the constraint be increased?
4. Students must manage their own capacity when demands on their time increase. What techniques do you use to match your personal capacity to the demands placed on it?

PROBLEMS

1. Time-Ticker Inc.'s workers handcraft watches for their customers. They use a demand chase aggregate planning approach, as shown below. The company's marketing department would like to run a promotion in month 3. The marketing department estimates that the promotion will generate an additional demand of 400 watches in that month. With a margin of $13, the promotion would generate a $5,200 increase in profit. Assuming 160 hours/worker/month, five labor hours per unit, and a current workforce of eight, will the promotion generate enough revenue to cover the hiring and firing costs associated with the increase in production?

	Month					
	1	2	3	4	5	6
Demand forecast	250	270	290	230	250	220
Labor hours required	1,250	1,350	1,450	1,150	1,250	1,100
Workers required	8	9	10	8	8	7
Number of hires	0	0	1	0	1	0
Number of layoffs	0	0	0	2	0	1
Hiring cost ($)	0	0	200	0	200	0
Layoff cost ($)	0	0	0	350	0	175
Total hiring cost	$400.00					
Total layoff cost	$525.00					
Total plan cost	$925.00					

2. Line Drive Co. makes baseball bats. Demand for the next six months is given in the table below. It takes 1.4 labor hours to complete a bat and Line Drive currently employs seven production workers, assuming 160 hours/worker/month. The hiring costs are $350, and the layoff costs are $275. Use the information given to create a demand chase aggregate plan. If Line Drive pays a $700 contract fee, an employment agency can lower the hiring costs to $290. Should Line Drive Co. use the employment agency?

Period	1	2	3	4	5	6
Demand forecast	800	1,050	1,400	1,800	760	590

3. Chase Services has the monthly demand given in the following table. Use that information to construct a level production aggregate plan. Each unit requires 3.6 hours of labor. Inventory carrying costs are $24 per unit per month, assuming 160 hours/worker/month. How many workers should Chase employ? What is the cost of this plan?

	Period											
	1	2	3	4	5	6	7	8	9	10	11	12
Demand	800	900	950	850	1,050	900	1,100	900	950	800	850	1,000
Work Days	20	20	22	21	22	21	20	22	21	20	21	21

4. Alco Industries uses a level production aggregate planning strategy. Alco's monthly demand information is given below. Each unit requires 6.5 hours of labor to complete. The inventory carrying costs are $45 per unit per month. Construct the aggregate plan. How many workers will the company employ? Assuming 160 hours/worker/month, how would your answer change if the company worked 21 days for the first six months and 20 days for the last six months?

	Period											
	1	2	3	4	5	6	7	8	9	10	11	12
Demand	2,200	2,100	2,200	2,200	2,100	1,800	2,200	2,300	2,200	1,900	2,200	2,200
Work Days	22	20	22	21	21	21	20	21	21	20	20	19

5. Buroni Construction would like to switch from a demand chase aggregate plan to a level production plan. The company believes that the money saved from eliminating the hiring and firing of workers will more than compensate for any inventory costs. Use the information given below to construct both models and decide which plan is more cost-effective. Assume in both cases that the needed number of workers for the first month are already employed.

	Period					
	1	2	3	4	5	6
Demand	800	900	1000	1050	890	875
Work days	23	24	23	24	22	23
Hiring cost	700					
Layoff cost	650					
Hours/unit	4					
Inventory carrying cost		$15/period				

6. Knightbridge Investments uses a hybrid aggregate planning strategy that consists of a level production plan, but adjusting the number of workers every 3 months. Use the information below to determine how many workers will be utilized during each of the three-month periods.

	Period					
	1	2	3	4	5	6
Demand	800	900	1,000	1,000	1,100	900
Work days	22	21	22	23	22	23
Hour/unit		7				
Inventory carrying cost		5				
Hiring cost		900				

7. Sta-Soft Inc. produces and sells hand-crafted pillows. Its product undergoes a three-step process. There is one work center for both cutting and stuffing, with two work centers for sewing. Each work center operates on a 40-hour workweek. Demand is given for the next six weeks, along with information on the needed processes. Assuming that the utilization is 94 percent and the efficiency is 96 percent for all processes, create a rough-cut capacity plan.

Week	1	2	3	4	5	6
Pillow	65	72	74	71	77	75

Work Center	Time Required (hours)
Cutting	0.25
Stuffing	0.45
Sewing	0.85

8. Three Pigs Co. manufactures decorative bricks for new homes. A supplier provides sheets of artificial brick material; Three Pigs must cut, bevel, and finish each brick. The company averages 96 percent utilization and 98 percent efficiency for the work centers. It has 40 hours of available capacity for the first two work centers and 80 hours for finishing. Using the following information, construct a rough-cut capacity plan. Do any of the work centers need additional capacity?

Week	1	2	3	4	5	6
Bricks	150	165	159	167	164	174

Work Center	Time Required (minutes)
Cutting	0.1
Beveling	0.14
Finishing	0.48

9. In-Focus caters to the weekend photographer, specializing in camera supplies and film development. As an added service the company allows customers to customize and personalize calendars. The calendars have become quite popular with a first period demand of 300, increasing by 10 percent for the next 5 periods (rounding up to the nearest whole number). The calendar production process requires scanning the needed photos, laying them out, and laminating the finished product. Using the following information, calculate a rough-cut capacity plan. Should the store add capacity to any of its work centers?

Work Center	Time Required (hours)	Actual Hours	Utilization	Efficiency
Scan	0.25	120	0.92	0.94
Layout	0.15	80	0.9	0.96
Laminate	0.35	160	0.87	0.82

10. Brite-Lights manufactures floor lamps. Each lamp consists of a base stand with two lamps at the top. Demand for the next six weeks for the floor lamps is 124, 126, 128, 132, 127, and 134. Planned order releases from Brite-Lights material requirements plan is below:

	Week					
	1	2	3	4	5	6
Base	124	126	128	132	127	134
Lamp	248	252	256	264	254	268

Use the planned order release data and the following routing and work center information to construct a capacity requirements plan.

Work Center	Painting	Assembly	Finishing
Base	0.07	0.15	0.05
Lamp	0.09	0.2	0.1

Work Center	Actual Hours Available	Utilization	Efficiency
Painting	40	0.96	0.96
Assembly	80	0.98	0.98
Finishing	40	0.97	0.95

11. Paddock Packaging assembles all of the packing boxes for Next-Day Deliveries. The standard packing box is made up of a top and a bottom portion. Each portion passes through three workstations: laying out the necessary materials, assembling the pieces, and checking the quality of the finished product. Historically there have been 39 hours available at each of the workstations. Use the planned order release data and the following routing to construct a capacity requirements plan.

	Week					
	1	2	3	4	5	6
Top	200	215	209	232	216	204
Bottom	200	215	209	232	216	204

	Layout	Assembly	Quality
Top (minutes)	0.04	0.05	0.02
Bottom (minutes)	0.06	0.08	0.02

12. Home-style Hotel has the following no-show records. The cost per no-show is $65 and the cost of bumping a customer is $80. Calculate the expected opportunity costs and the expected cost of bumping if the hotel implements a system of overbooking by one.

Number of No-Shows	Frequency	Probability
0	89	0.34
1	75	0.29
2	59	0.22
3	24	0.09
4	14	0.05
5	2	0.01

13. Yen's Chinese Restaurant noticed a number of no-shows during its busy dinner hours on Friday nights. The cost for each no-show is $54, and the cost of bumping a customer to a later time is projected to be $92. Use the following no-show history to devise an overbooking plan. The restaurant would like to overbook by only one or two dinners. Which is the lower-cost plan?

Number of No-Shows	Frequency
0	119
1	64
2	76
3	35
4	27
5	14

14. Fly-Hi Airlines has historically had a problem with no-shows on its flights. The airline's cost per no-show is $76, and the cost per passenger bumped is $102. Use the no-show records given in the first table below to construct the cost of a policy of overbooking by one.

Number	Frequency
0	75
1	145
2	62
3	25
4	16
5	2

The airline is considering changing its reservation policy and expects the no-shows to drop to the values shown below. What happens to the cost of the no-show plan? Should the airline still employ a policy of overbooking?

Number	Frequency
0	165
1	79
2	57
3	17
4	7
5	0

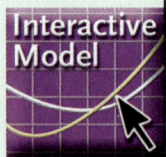

INTERACTIVE ANALYSIS 12.1

THE PRODUCTION LINE INTERACTIVE MODEL

The Constrained Production Line Interactive Model, found in Chapter 12 of the *OperationsNow.com* website, provides numerous opportunities to explore the subtleties of how constraints can appear in and affect productive systems. In the Constrained Production Line Interactive Model, the user has several alternatives for changing the nature of the system. The user can dictate the input rate for products entering the system as well as the processing time for each of the five work centers.

In addition, the user can dictate the variability of the input rate as well as the processing times. For example, if six minutes is selected for the processing time of a particular work center, with zero variability, every unit will be processed in six minutes. As variability for that work center is increased, from zero to slight, to moderate, and to extreme, the variability of the processing time increases around an average of six minutes per unit.

In addition to the input parameters of processing time and variability, the user has two controls of the simulation itself. The first is control of the speed of the clock running the simulation. Speeding up the clock simply means that the simulation clock runs faster. In addition, the pause button allows the user to temporarily stop the simulation and resume it again where it left off with the start button. The stop button stops the simulation and resets it to the starting condition.

Experiment 1: System Fundamentals

1. Set the input rate and processing time for all work centers at four minutes per unit with zero variability. Run the simulation for 100 simulator minutes.
   a. How many units were complete?
   b. Why weren't 25 units completed?
2. Set work center 3 to a six-minute processing time. Leave the variability at zero. Run the simulation for 100 simulator minutes.
   a. How many units were complete?
   b. What happens in front of work center 3?
   c. Repeat the 100-minute simulation with work center 3 processing at six minutes per unit, but reduce the input rate to one unit every six minutes. What happens?
3. Set the processing time of all work centers and the input rate to six minutes, with zero variability. Run the simulation for 100 simulator minutes.

a. How many units were complete?
   b. What determines the amount of units completed by the system in a set amount of time?

Experiment 2: Exploring the Impact of a System Constraint
1. Set the input rate and processing time for all work centers at four minutes per unit, with zero variability. Run the simulation for 100 simulator minutes.
   a. How many units were complete?
2. Reduce the processing time of any one of the five work centers to three minutes. Run the simulation for 100 simulator minutes.
   a. How many units were complete?
3. Reduce the processing time of an additional work center to three minutes. Run the simulation for 100 simulator minutes.
   a. How many units were complete?
   b. Why did a reduction in time not result in an improvement in system output?
   c. What does this tell you about investing in equipment to improve the speed of operations in service and manufacturing systems?

Experiment 3: Exploring Process Time Variability
1. Set all processing times and the input rate to the initial four-minute value with zero variability. Run the simulation for 100 simulator minutes.
   a. Examine the use of resources during this time. Does inventory build up anywhere?
   b. Are any of the work centers idle (white) during this time?
2. Leave the input rate and processing times at four minutes, but increase the variability of work center 3 to the extreme level. Run the simulation for 100 simulator minutes. Record the number of units produced.
   a. Observe the simulation runs. Does inventory build up anywhere? If so, where does it build up? Explain why this happens.
   b. After the initial startup phase, are any of the work centers ever idle? If so, which ones? Explain your observations.
   c. What implications does process time variability have for the productivity of resources?
3. Leave the input rate and processing times at four minutes, but increase the variability of all work centers and the input rate to the extreme level. Run the simulation five separate times for 100 simulator minutes each time. Record the results.
   a. How does this outcome differ from the previous simulation?
   b. Does inventory build up anywhere? If so, where does it build up? Explain why this happens.
   c. After the initial startup phase, are any of the work centers ever idle? If so, which ones? Explain the results.
   d. The average processing time for each work center is the same in the last two experiments. What is happening to make system output different? What implications does this have for the productivity of resources?

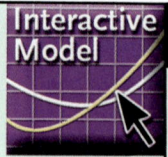
www.
OperationsNow
.com

INTERACTIVE ANALYSIS 12.2

THE AGGREGATE PLANNING INTERACTIVE MODEL

The Aggregate Planning Interactive Model is accessed through Chapter 12 of the *OperationsNow.com* website. The Aggregate Planning Interactive Model provides an environment that is simplified, but nevertheless offers the experimenter an almost infinite number of combinations of costs and resource availability for in-depth exploration of the different approaches to the problem of matching capacity to demand. The user can manipulate hiring cost, firing cost, inventory carrying costs per unit, available hours per day per worker, days per month, and hours per unit. In addition, the user can enter new demand data.

Experiment 1: Demand Chase Fundamentals

1. The demand chase strategy is at one extreme of the possible aggregate planning approaches. In this approach, employees are hired and fired as needed to meet the demand for each period. No inventory is carried from period to period.

    a. Given the starting values presented below, what is the total cost for the demand chase plan? Since no inventory is carried from period to period using the demand chase strategy, the costs incurred come from hiring and firing employees. Increase the hiring cost from $200 to $300. What happens to the cost of the demand chase plan?

Inventory carrying cost:	$8	Working hours/day/worker:	8
Hiring cost:	$200	Working days/month:	20
Firing cost:	$200	Hours/unit:	5

    b. Increase the firing cost from $200 to $300. What happens to the total cost of the plan?

2. The amount of hiring and firing that must take place from one period to the next is a function of the demand and three other parameters: hours/day/worker, days/month, and time/unit. An increase in the hours/day/worker or in the days/month would result in a reduction in the number of hires. Such a change would also likely result in overtime wages being paid. A decrease in the time/unit reduces the capacity needed, so fewer hires would be necessary. Set the starting parameters back to those used in 1, above.

    a. Increase the hours/day/worker from 8 to 9. What happens to the total cost of the plan?

    b. Set the starting parameters back again to those used in 1, above. Now increase the days/month to 21. What happens to the total cost of the plan?

    c. Set the starting parameters back again to those used in 1, above. Reduce the time per unit to 4. What happens to the total cost of the plan?

Experiment 2: Level Production Fundamentals

1. The level production plan is at the opposite end of the continuum of aggregate planning approaches. In this approach, expected demand for the entire year is divided by the number of periods to determine the output required per period to meet the annual demand by the end of the year. The number of workers needed is hired initially and then no other hires or fires occur for the year. Inventory is carried from low demand periods to high demand periods to meet the demand as

it fluctuates. In some periods inventory may actually go into the negative range, indicating unmet demand.

  a. Using the starting values presented below, what is the total cost for the level production plan? Why is it more expensive than the demand chase plan for the same parameters?

Inventory carrying cost:	$8	Working hours/day/worker:	8
Hiring cost:	$200	Working days/month:	20
Firing cost:	$200	Hours/unit:	5

  b. Which of the six parameters that can be changed in the model will have an impact on the cost of the level production plan?

2. If back orders were unacceptable, inventory would have to be produced prior to period 10.

  a. How many units are backordered during the year? How much inventory buildup would be necessary to prevent backorders?

  b. Building up inventory prior to the back orders would mean that we have ventured from a level production strategy. What would be some ways the inventory buildup could occur?

Experiment 3: Exploring Tradeoffs

1. The aggregate planning process is frequently a tradeoff between inventory carrying costs and personnel costs (hiring and firing, in this case). Set the parameters as follows:

Inventory carrying cost:	$6	Working hours/day/worker:	8
Hiring cost:	$250	Working days/month:	20
Firing cost:	$220	Hours/unit:	8

  a. What are the costs for the chase and level production plans with these input parameters?

  b. If inventory carrying costs are expected to rise, what must they rise to in order for the chase strategy to be the low-cost plan?

  c. If inventory carrying costs didn't increase, what would need to occur for the demand chase plan to be the low-cost strategy? What would the parameters be in order for that to occur?

2. One way to reduce the hiring and firing costs would be to increase the amount of work done by the employees. That could be done by increasing the hours per day or by increasing the days per month.

  a. What is the savings in hiring and firing (assuming no additional overtime cost) of adding two extra days per month?

  b. Reducing the processing time can have the same effect as increasing the amount of labor. Investing in automation may reduce the amount of time required for each unit, reducing labor costs overall, but also reducing the amount of hiring and firing. What would the savings in hiring and firing costs be if the processing time could be reduced from eight to seven hours? How many fewer people would be hired and fired during the year?

Experiment 4: Exploring a Level Demand

1. Set the input parameters as follows:

Inventory carrying cost:	$6	Working hours/day/worker:	8
Hiring cost:	$800	Working days/month:	20
Firing cost:	$400	Hours/unit:	10

a. Record the costs of the two plans.

b. Leave the input parameters the same, and enter the following demands for the 12 periods:

Period	Demand	Period	Demand
1	6,500	7	6,200
2	6,600	8	5,900
3	6,200	9	6,700
4	5,600	10	6,200
5	5,800	11	5,750
6	6,600	12	6,650

Click on the "solve" button. These demands sum to an annual demand of 74,700 units, identical to the previous demand. What are the costs for the two plans using this demand?

c. Why are both plans so much lower in cost than those related to previous demand? Why is the level production plan so low?

d. Leave all parameters the same and enter the following demands:

Period	Demand	Period	Demand
1	6,225	7	6,225
2	6,225	8	6,225
3	6,225	9	6,225
4	6,225	10	6,225
5	6,225	11	6,225
6	6,225	12	6,225

Click on the "solve button." Explain what has happened.

SELECTED REFERENCES

Shapiro, J. F. *Modeling the Supply Chain*. Pacific Grove, CA: Duxbury, 2001.

Sipper, D., and Bulfin, R. *Production: Planning, Control and Integration*. New York: McGraw-Hill, 1997.

ENDNOTE

1. "When Flying Too High with a Guy in the Sky Is the Thing to Do," *The Wall Street Journal*, February 14, 2001, p. A1.

CHAPTER 12   Capacity   457

OperationsNow.com LEARNING ACTIVITIES

CHAPTER ENHANCEMENT RESOURCES
- Esources
- Reel Operations Video Clips
- Interactive Models
- Excel Tutors
- Supplementary Readings
- Links to Operations On Site Companies

OM EXPLORATION
- Check It Out
- OM in Action
- Online Business Tours
- Letters from the Top
- Putting It All Together: Virtual Case Studies
- Additional Readings

The resource/profit model identifies facilities as the fourth of five critical resource categories that provide the necessary inputs to create value. Facility investments are among the most costly investments a business can make. Despite the implications facility decisions have on many of the value attributes customers seek, they are often taken for granted. The objectives of this chapter are to examine two critical decisions for facilities: the facility location and the facility layout. Both decisions are examined from the standpoint of financial impact and contribution to value. In addition, techniques used to assist in facility-related decisions are presented.

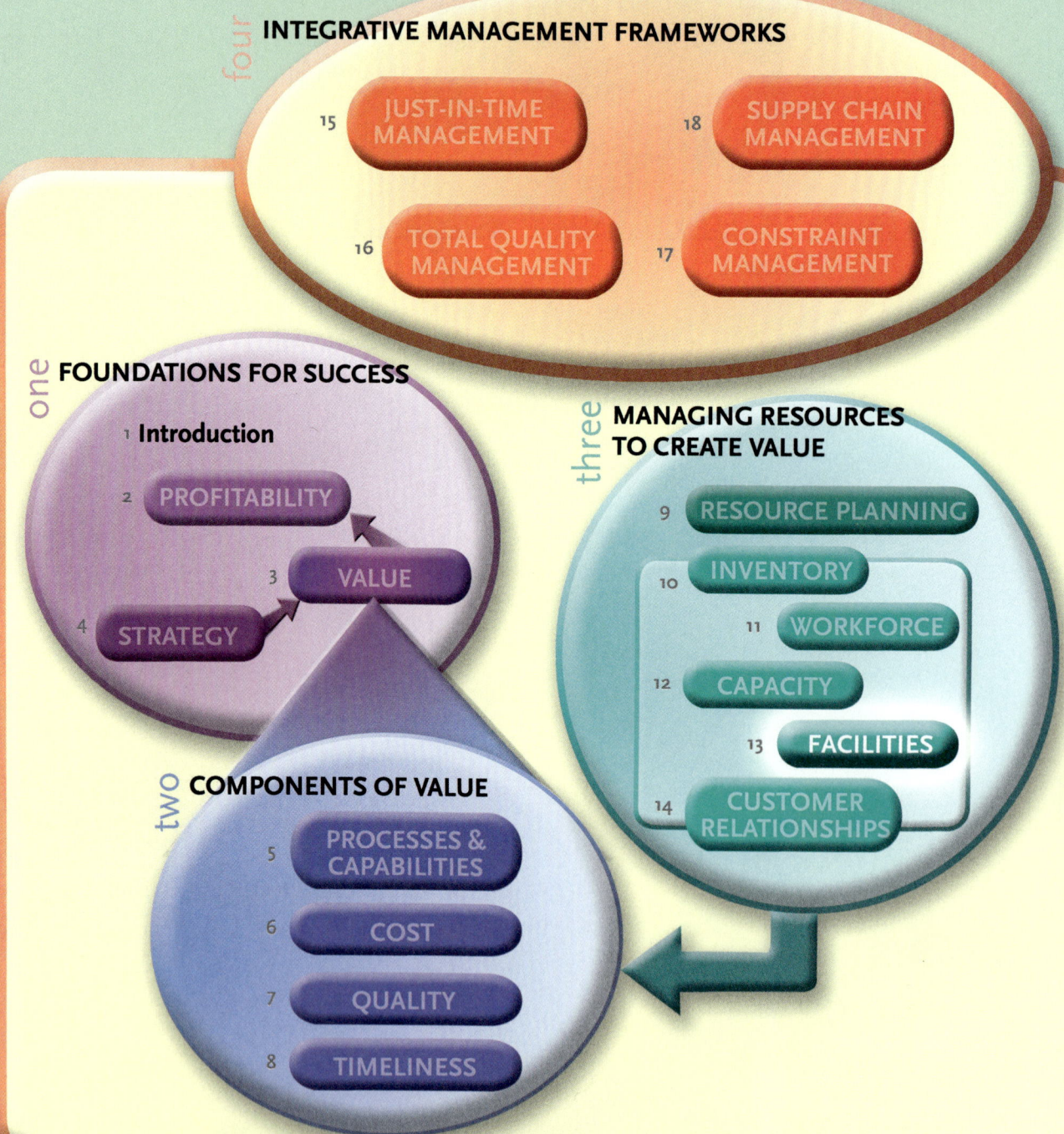

CHAPTER 13

Facilities

LEARNING OBJECTIVES

Upon completion of Chapter 13, you should be able to

____ Describe the impact facility decisions have on profitability and value.

____ Identify common decision criteria for business location decisions.

____ Explain why geographic information systems (GISs) benefit location decision making.

____ Use multifactor rating as a decision-making tool.

____ Perform the calculations necessary to use the center-of-gravity method.

____ Use decision tree analysis to aid in making a location decision.

____ Compute the breakeven point when comparing alternative locations.

____ Describe the strengths and weaknesses of process-oriented, product-oriented, and cellular layouts.

____ Utilize the cut-and-dry method and systematic layout planning for a process-oriented layout.

____ Determine the theoretical minimum number of work centers and balance a line in a product-oriented layout.

Introduction: Making Decisions for What May Be the Largest Investment
Strategic Importance of Facilities
Facility Location Decisions
Location Decision-Making Criteria
Location Decision-Making Techniques
Business Location Trends
Facility Layouts
Chapter Summary

INTERNET RESOURCES

 Excel Tutors provide annotated spreadsheets for every solved problem that automatically load Excel.

 Esources provide an online version of the more traditional boxed insert.

 Reel Videos provide streaming video footage for company applications of chapter concepts.

 Interactive Models provide an experimental environment for quantitative concepts and simulations.

INTRODUCTION

Making Decisions for What May Be the Largest Investment

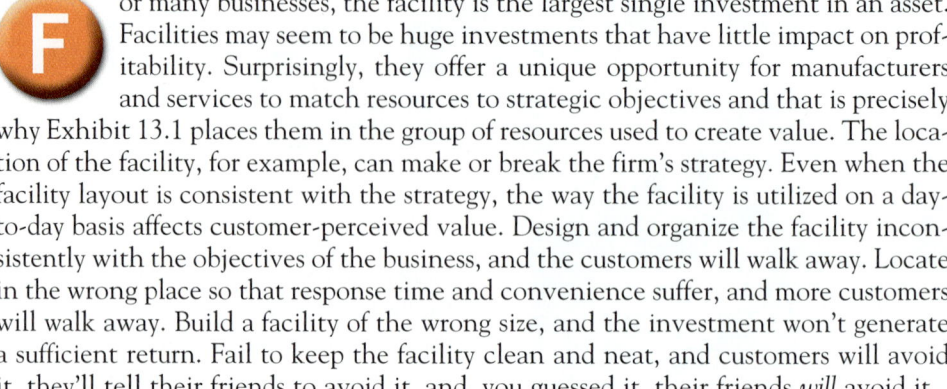

For many businesses, the facility is the largest single investment in an asset. Facilities may seem to be huge investments that have little impact on profitability. Surprisingly, they offer a unique opportunity for manufacturers and services to match resources to strategic objectives and that is precisely why Exhibit 13.1 places them in the group of resources used to create value. The location of the facility, for example, can make or break the firm's strategy. Even when the facility layout is consistent with the strategy, the way the facility is utilized on a day-to-day basis affects customer-perceived value. Design and organize the facility inconsistently with the objectives of the business, and the customers will walk away. Locate in the wrong place so that response time and convenience suffer, and more customers will walk away. Build a facility of the wrong size, and the investment won't generate a sufficient return. Fail to keep the facility clean and neat, and customers will avoid it, they'll tell their friends to avoid it, and, you guessed it, their friends *will* avoid it.

Facility-related decisions must be right the first time: Once they've been made, they are difficult and sometimes impossible to change. In many cases management must make the decisions before the business even exists, and they must make decisions that will remain valid years in the future.

STRATEGIC IMPORTANCE OF FACILITIES

Recall from Chapter 4 that a business strategy is essentially a plan to attract customers who have a certain set of value priorities. A cost leadership strategy, for example, seeks to attract customers who are very concerned with the cost of their purchases. This strategy will have an impact on a variety of long-term resource decisions. As discussed in Chapter 4, facility decisions were included as one of four structural decisions that had to be made when developing a strategy (along with capacity, process technology, and vertical integration/supplier relationships). The strategic importance of facility decisions becomes more clear as these decisions are linked to profitability. Not surprisingly, facility decisions dictate profitability through the impact they have on value and costs.

In Chapter 6, two key profitability measures were presented:

$$\text{Profit Margin} = \frac{\text{Net Income}}{\text{Sales}}$$

$$\text{Return on Assets} = \frac{\text{Net Income}}{\text{Total Assets}}$$

Both depend on net income:

$$\text{Net Income} = \text{Net Sales} - \text{Cost of Goods Sold} - \text{Depreciation} - \text{Interest Paid} - \text{Taxes}$$

As is the case with other operations resource decisions, facility decisions have two direct impacts on net income. Facilities contribute directly to the customer's perception of value through various value attributes. Customer-perceived value drives net

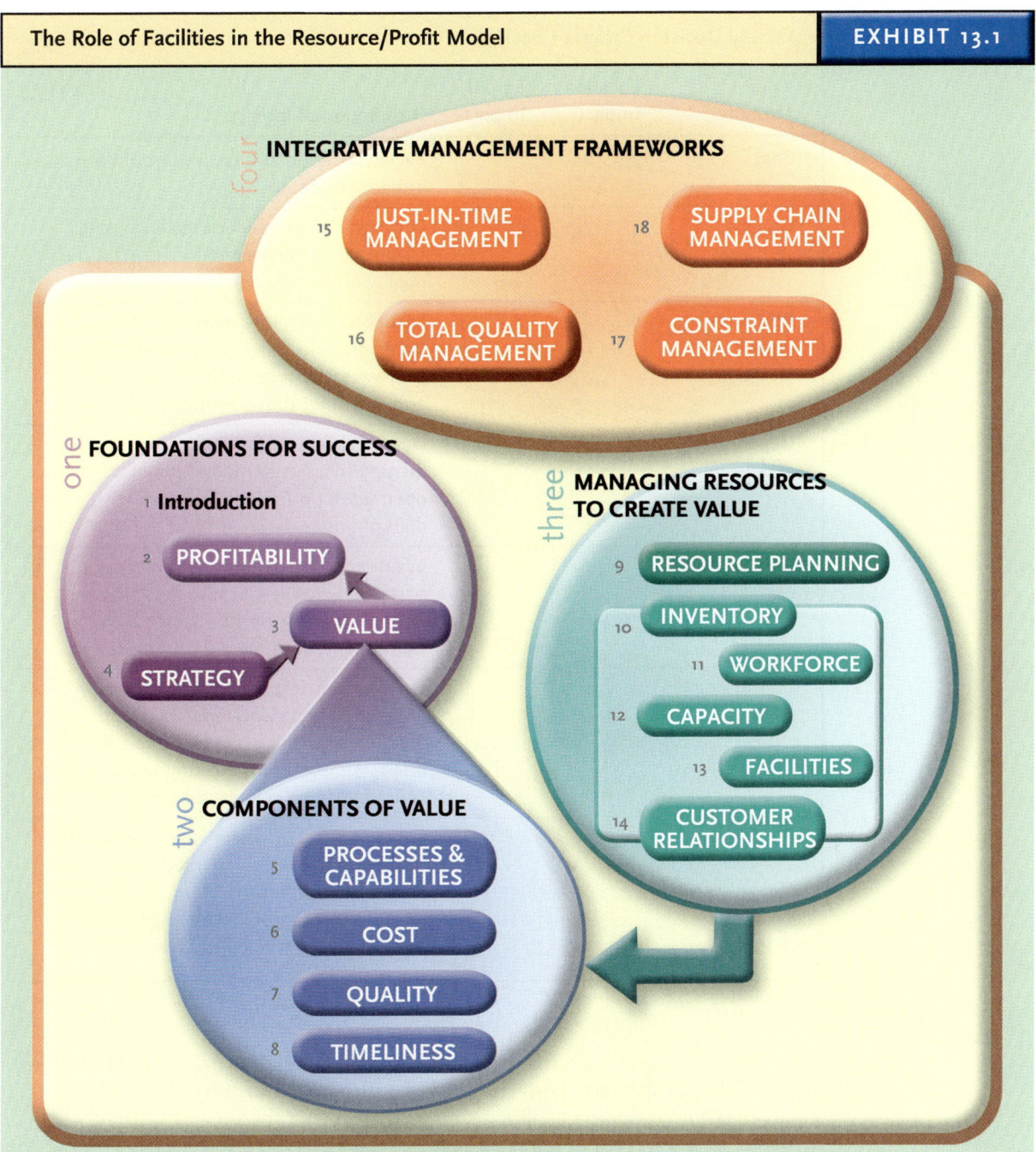

sales. Facilities also contribute directly to costs incurred by the business. They must be maintained. An increase in profitability improves the ratios between net income and sales and between net income and total assets. Profit margin and ROA are both affected by facility productivity through net income. Profit margin and ROA are also influenced by the facilities through their respective denominators, sales and total assets. Let's first examine the net income effect from facilities.

The primary impact any resource has on net income can be examined best from the standpoint of value added by that resource and costs linked to it. The B2C and

EXHIBIT 13.2	**Facility Decision Criteria Checklist**			
	Value Attribute	Location Impact	Layout Impact	Description of Impact
	Cost	✓	✓	Facility location and facility layout have an impact on costs.
	Quality	✓	✓	Location dictates service quality issues. Layout dictates flow and for services, the quality of the experience.
	Response time	✓	✓	Location determines distance and transportation times. Layout determines process effectiveness, as well as material and customer movement.
	Dependability of delivery	✓		Dependability is often a function of disruptions. Greater distances of transport open up opportunities for more disruptions.
	Convenience	✓		Location often dictates convenience, particularly for services, because the location translates into "nearness." Convenient often means close by.
	Ethical issues	✓		Location has implications for some ethical issues. Environmental impact is often a function of where a site is located. More often, the reason for locating in a foreign country may be perceived as exploitive.
	Flexibility	✓	✓	Some layouts, by design, are more flexible than others. Process-oriented layouts, in particular, are designed for flexibility. Some worker skills can be linked to geography and enhance a firm's flexibility.

B2B value attributes affected by facilities include price, quality, response time, dependability of delivery, convenience, ethical issues, and flexibility. Exhibit 13.2 summarizes corresponding facility decisions that impact these value attributes.

Value, we know, creates sales and market share. It is the driving force and is at the root of net income. Facilities are a key resource in the creation of that value but they do not exist independent of other resources that the facility houses. The influence of facilities on value extends to those resources and *through* those resources as well. Inventory, workforce, and capacity resources, for most businesses, are *inside* a facility. Location dictates where the inventory is kept and where the workforce and capacity are utilized. Facilities dictate where many services take place. Facility location, in fact, is important only if the location of other resources is important. If inventory needs to be placed west of Mitchell, South Dakota, on I90, that's where the facility needs to be located. For some businesses, location of workforce, inventory, and capacity isn't important, so the facility can be anywhere. This is particularly true for information-oriented services that do not depend on costly transportation of products or employees. In addition to the facility location, the way the facility allows other resources to be organized also contributes to their ability to create value. A close match between the facility and the goals of the business results in more productive resources, better processes, and better outcomes. These benefits translate directly into enhanced profitability.

Although we don't typically think about it this way, the location decision for the Olympic games can represent one of the largest-scale facility location decisions ever made. Facilities range from sports venues to housing, and include all of the issues a large business would consider, including transportation, access to support services, etc. Here, the Olympic Village is under construction in Athens, Greece, for the 2004 Summer Olympics. The sign reads "Olympic Village 2004."

The tradeoff to the values enhanced by facilities is the cost of facilities. For many businesses, facilities are one of the largest sources of costs. In addition to being a large up-front investment, they require ongoing maintenance. They consume power for light and heat, and they dictate many tax bills. The larger the facility, the greater these costs. The close link between facility size and facility-related costs results in a productivity measure of the ratio of output to square footage. Sales per square foot, for example, is equally relevant for a retail shop and a factory.

From a strategic perspective, the facility decisions are addressed by three broad decision categories—the location, the layout, and the design of the facility. A huge set of variables comes into play, however, making these seemingly simple decisions extremely complex. Unlike many other resource decisions, which can be made in a relatively objective manner, facility location decisions are more subjective and as disparate as tax rates at one extreme and the company president's favorite golf course at the other. Quite often, there is no single right answer. Location and layout are difficult to optimize because there is often no agreement on a single measure of performance. Facility design and layout decisions seek to create good solutions, but there is often no single optimal solution. The remainder of this chapter is devoted to facility location and facility design and layout decisions.

FACILITY LOCATION DECISIONS

The need for a facility location decision results from three possible scenarios, each resulting in different priorities for location. The three scenarios are a location for a new business, a location for a business that must relocate, and a location for a business expansion.

Locating a New Business

The new-business location is potentially the most challenging decision because there are more alternatives to consider and little information about future demand. Location decisions are often made as a progression of decisions, gradually narrowing down to a specific site. In many cases, an international location is possible, or even desirable, so the region of the world or specific country must be identified. From there, the target region within the country must be determined, followed by the state or location within the region, followed by the city, and, finally, within the city of choice, the site itself. For many companies, business inputs can drive the broad decisions concerning the country, region, or state.

For some businesses, characteristics of inputs and outputs can dictate location. A common input that can limit location choices is the raw material consumed by manufacturing processes, particularly when it is costly to transport. Some businesses create an output that cannot be transported economically. Manufacturers of very heavy, inexpensive items, like bricks and construction materials, must locate near their customers. This is true in the beverage industries as well, where each bottler supplies small geographic regions. Water is cheap but heavy and expensive to haul in bottles and cans. Other than water, the primary inputs are concentrated syrups, and transporting them over long distances is not as expensive as transporting the finished products. Some businesses, particularly services that require customer interaction, must locate near the customers because that is an expectation of the customer. A business dependent on tourism, for example, must locate where tourists will want to go.

Firms that depend on close B2B interactions must often locate near customers also. Rather than taking advantage of reduced transportation costs, however, this decision seeks to provide better service and more frequent deliveries of products. Proximity enhances such value attributes as response time, dependability of delivery, and flexibility. For manufacturers of easy-to-transport products, the location of the customer isn't an issue since their products can readily be shipped anywhere.

Some businesses must locate where they can hire employees with certain skills. High-technology businesses, for example, must locate where there are skilled workers. Craft-oriented furniture factories must locate where workers with these skills live. This is true for manufacturing firms as well as for services that require unusual or scarce talent. Businesses go where the talent is, resulting in geographic areas becoming centers for specific industries. The end result is that there is sufficient job potential to attract more people with talents that fit the needs of the businesses. There is also competition among the businesses for the best workers. In some cases, particularly for high-volume manufacturing of products that are relatively inexpensive to ship (clothing, for example), location is selected based on labor costs rather than labor talent.

Other businesses, particularly manufacturers that require heavy or difficult-to-transport raw materials, must locate near these raw materials to enable them to manage costs. Examples of these businesses include basic manufacturers like those that utilize minerals or agricultural products in their manufacturing processes. A similar situation results when a manufacturer must locate near a large water source so that water can be used for cooling purposes.

www
OperationsNow
.com

When services reduce the amount of required face-to-face interaction through expanded use of technology, their locations become less important. As the line of visibility moves toward the customer, the ever-increasing "behind the scenes" activities become a larger component of the business. Those activities do not need to consider proximity to the customer as part of the location decision. As a result, they can base the location decision on other factors. Esource 13.1 provides an example of how technology can eliminate facility location concerns.

In addition to the practical requirements driving location decisions, there are some that don't relate directly to a particular business yet often end up being the most important. At the top of these criteria are location characteristics that relate to quality of life. Climate, nearness to a large city, education systems, recreation, and so on, are all key considerations for these decisions.

In making a location decision for a new business, one difficulty is the need for predictions about its future. For example, from a capacity standpoint, it might be important to locate where expansion is possible, should expansion be needed in the future. Cost may be a more significant issue for a new business location simply because of the uncertainty about future cash flows. Availability of money may reduce the number of alternatives that can be considered.

Relocating an Existing Business

Business relocation decisions arise for several reasons. Sometimes management wants to relocate for financial reasons or because the availability of business inputs changes. In other situations, management may be forced to relocate because they've lost or can no longer afford the lease on a building.

In many ways, the relocation decision is similar to the decision for locating a new business; however, because the business is already up and running, more information is available. Many of the options considered initially will probably not be considered again. The business may need to be relocated in the same geographic area to avoid losing employees and customers. In most cases, demand patterns are known, as are customer characteristics and the rate of growth for capacity requirements. For some businesses, relocation would have no impact on these factors, but for others, particularly services that depend on foot or automobile traffic patterns, relocation can drastically affect demand. What was known to exist at the original location may have no relationship to what will happen at the new location.

For a business that needs to be near its customers, relocating may be problematic because there may be few choices. If building a new facility is not an option, the alternatives are limited to those facilities currently vacant. Even if constructing a new facility is feasible, placement of that facility is limited to property available, which may not be optimal.

Choosing a Location for Business Expansion

When the impetus behind a location decision is a need to expand, a choice must be made between expanding the current facility, building a new and bigger facility elsewhere, or becoming a multifacility business that will utilize the current facility as well as another one elsewhere. Expansion decisions are complex. Management must compare costs of expanding old facilities to costs of building new facilities and also consider the opportunities lost because of limitations of the old facility. For example, new technologies are typically more easily integrated into a new building. Given the chance to start from scratch, knowledge gained from experience often leads management to make significant changes in facility design. Many of the benefits of these opportunities are difficult to quantify.

The decision to become a multifacility business is particularly difficult because of the changes to management's job when a second facility is brought on line. Supervision and control issues change when management needs to be two places at once. The benefits, however, can include critical competitive advantages such as opening up new markets.

LOCATION DECISION-MAKING CRITERIA

Obviously, when beginning a location decision-making process, management has some idea of the scope of the alternatives to consider. Our coverage, however, starts with the broadest possible decision and progresses to the very small and narrow. One way to organize relocation decision-making factors is to examine a hierarchy of levels of decision alternatives that extends from international issues and possible countries, to regions within a country, to states, to city or community, and to the actual site. At each level, the criteria relevant to that level are considered. In the following discussion, we'll examine the criteria that traditionally have been the most important at each level, as well as a new technology that aids decision makers in merging these criteria.

om on site

New Markets Mean More Than Just Moving

Many factors enter into the decision to expand into other countries. Costs and political considerations are always important. Once a decision is made, however, how the firm does business must also be examined and adapted. Expanding Wal-Mart stores to Brazil, for example, is more than replicating a U.S.-style store. Each country has its own characteristics, and they will dictate what works and what doesn't.

Wal-Mart is the sixth-biggest mass merchandiser in Brazil, with $500 million sales in 2000. Since 1995 Wal-Mart opened 20 supercenters and Sam's Clubs in Brazil, and its plans include a new format called a Wal-Mart Todo Dia. *Todo dia* is Portuguese for "every day." These stores will be smaller and more warehouselike than a typical Wal-Mart supercenter, with concrete floors, no air-conditioning, and goods displayed in boxes. Todo Dias will sell goods at about 5 percent below the prices of competitors. The buildings can be built in less than three months. They will be attractive because the Brazilian income is low, customers cannot travel great distances to shop, and the stores will be neighborhood-focused.

Source: "Wal-Mart Gets Aggressive about Brazil," *The Wall Street Journal,* May 25, 2001, pp. A8, A12.

International Issues

Decisions that deal with locating in foreign countries can be broken down into two distinct situations: (1) a company wishes to do business in another country and must locate there in order to bring that to fruition, and (2) a company wishes to locate a facility in another country to gain some competitive advantage. Let's address the first scenario first.

Decisions to expand or relocate to a foreign country are becoming more common. As markets open up, opportunities open up as well. For some markets, businesses must have a physical presence in the country that houses the market. In these situations the decision is not about locating an operation in the country; it's about doing business in the country. If the decision is to do business there, then locating there is a foregone conclusion. The location decision then becomes one of *where* in that country.

The decision to do business in a foreign country, with a culture that could be drastically different from what a company is accustomed to, is a major one. It is a decision that has the potential to open up huge market opportunities but also has the potential to be a disaster. It is an expensive undertaking with high levels of uncertainty. Baazee.com provides a prime example of the differences between two cultures. Baazee.com is modeled after Ebay, the auction site, but is based in India. The auction market in India is drastically different from the U.S. market. In India, auctions are used almost exclusively for bankruptcy liquidations, so the concept of an online auction has a different meaning there than in the United States. In addition, very few Indian brands are well-known enough that people would buy them sight unseen. Baazee.com had to set up exchange centers in large cities so that transactions could be completed in person.[1]

The uncertainty doesn't stop with the market conditions. The workforce can also be significantly different from what management is used to. This includes skill and knowledge as well as cultural differences that affect business capabilities. The political and regulatory environment can also be drastically different from what management is accustomed to. Governments change. Monetary exchange rates change. Possibly the greatest contributor to risk is the fact that the state of the economy, the market, and the workforce may be changing in ways that take them all to a very different place in a short period of time. Despite all of the risks and uncertainty, businesses must recognize that they exist in a global economy. Competition is not limited to businesses in the United States. Market share does not mean *U.S. market share*. Location decisions related to expansion and growth must consider all location alternatives, not just those within U.S. boundaries.

A company may face an international location decision not to access the host country's markets, but to gain competitive advantage from something that country has to offer. Reasons for locating a facility in a foreign country tend to be dominated by cost issues such as tax advantages, lower labor costs, and lower materials costs. In addition to the expected cost reductions, a number of potential cost increases must be considered, including the skill and abilities of the labor force, political climate, quality of life for U.S. managers, tax climate, access to markets, site availability, access to process inputs, transportation costs, and transport time. Despite the popularity of moving operations overseas to gain labor cost reductions, there have also been moves back to the United States because the time required to ship completed products back to the United States was unacceptable. The increase in the cash-to-cash cycle can be substantial, reducing profitability.

Location decisions must consider global alternatives, but they can sometimes be motivated by unethical and exploitive goals. An example of such a decision is locating in a country that does not regulate pollution to cut costs associated with meeting the U.S. standards for clean air and water. Exploiting child labor to cut labor costs is another example. Customers are becoming increasingly aware of these situations and are beginning to reward ethical behavior by using the force of their own freedom of choice.

Domestic Location Decisions

Location decisions limited to the United States or North America have traditionally been based on criteria that relate to region, state, city or community, and to the actual site. Exhibit 13.3 (on page 469) summarizes the criteria traditionally considered in location decisions and the hierarchical level in which they are an issue. They are covered in greater detail in the following discussion.

For most manufacturing and service businesses, the capabilities, talent, and expertise of the workforce are a critical component of success. Locating where that resource is in short supply or nonexistent would be foolish. As jobs become more complex and more dependent on technological skills, the requirements of the labor force increase. This issue has to be a top priority for any location decision, and it is considered at the regional, state, and community level. It has become such a dominant criterion in business location decisions that many states are marketing the skills of their workforce as a way to attract new businesses. They know that the productivity of the workforce has a huge impact on the value created and on company profitability.

Labor costs are also a significant consideration, but because labor content varies from one business to the next, labor cost may or may not be a high priority. Labor costs vary from region to region, from state to state, and even from one city to the next. These differences can be substantial, particularly for labor-intensive producers of products or services. Labor organization (union versus nonunion) can also depend on location. Depending on the business, management may be particularly attracted to a workforce that has been willing to work with management on solving business problems.

Oops—Maybe That Move Was a Bad Idea

Much has been written about Xerox's fall from its May 1999 share price of $66 to its spring 2001 share price of around $7, which was only a few dollars above its share price 30 years earlier. The strategic snafus and leadership conflict that led to the firing of CEO G. Richard Thoman have been well-documented. It is enlightening, however, to look at some of the more concrete decisions that led up to Xerox's financial woes. One of the most interesting is the story of a location decision that went wrong.

Businesses often move operations to countries with low taxes. These moves have resulted in millions of dollars in tax savings for some companies. A look at a recent move by Xerox shows that there is always risk. Xerox initiated a plan to cut its worldwide tax rate to under 30 percent back in the late 1990s. By moving some operations to Ireland, it expected to increase net income by $800 million over five years. One of the biggest impacts was the creation of a call center in Dublin to serve all of Europe. Xerox also built a large manufacturing center to produce inkjet cartridges and other printer supplies. The move made Ireland the administrative parent of most of the European business.

The initiative backfired, however, as Xerox's weighted average of the worldwide tax rates rose from 31 percent in 1999 to 38 percent in 2000. The move to low-tax countries was dependent on an annual growth rate in pretax profit of 15 percent. The plan was to shift that growth in profit from high-tax countries (United States and Britain) to Ireland, which has tax rates of between 10 percent and 12.5 percent. Rather than grow at a 15 percent rate, however, Xerox had operating losses. Despite these losses, Xerox expected to return to profitability in the first half of 2001. The plan didn't work because a company with operating losses doesn't pay taxes, but records a tax benefit similar to an extraordinary gain. This is because the company can typically use the loss to recoup taxes paid in previous years or to reduce future taxes, but the losses can be used only to accrue tax benefits in the country where they were incurred. The company would like to record profits in low-tax countries, obviously, but it needs to record losses in high-tax countries so the losses can be used to reduce future or past taxes. If losses occur in a low-tax country, the tax benefit will also be low.

According to John Hodges, former deputy treasurer of Xerox's European operations, the plan was a big mistake. It was based on increasing revenues, and no one looked at what would happen if these revenues and profits didn't occur.

The lesson is simple. Clearly there are financial gains to be made by taking advantage of different tax regulations at different locations. This is true not only from one country to another, but even from state to state. However, just as there are advantages in moving, there can be equal or greater disadvantages. The advantages tend to get the most attention. When things are going well, reduced taxes may improve the situation. However, when things are going poorly, tax regulations can make things even worse. Basing a move decision on one criterion that provides an advantage only under certain circumstances is a recipe for disaster.

Source: "How a Xerox Plan to Reduce Taxes and Boost Profit Backfired," *The Wall Street Journal*, April 17, 2001, pp. C1, C15; "Less Red Ink for Xerox," *BusinessWeek.Com*, January 29, 2001; "Xerox: The Downfall," *BusinessWeek.Com*, March 5, 2001.

Location Decision Criteria Checklist					EXHIBIT 13.3
Criterion	**Region**	**State**	**City or Community**	**Site**	
Labor knowledge and talent	√	√	√		
Labor costs	√	√	√		
Other labor issues		√	√		
Business support services			√		
Quality-of-life issues	√	√	√		
Access to markets	√	√	√		
Access to transportation	√	√	√	√	
Education system		√	√		
Training infrastructure		√	√		
Regulatory climate	√	√	√		
Tax climate		√	√		
Utility availability			√	√	
Utility cost		√	√		
Incentives for new business		√	√		
Real estate costs		√	√		
Real estate availability		√	√		
Site-specific costs			√	√	

Increasingly, businesses outsource support services like payroll management, information technology, maintenance, and transportation services. The availability of these services can be a significant factor in the location decision. Absence of a particular service means that the business will have to do the function itself, increasing costs and diverting attention from core competencies.

When a business moves, at least some employees will move to the new location. Quality-of-life issues at the new location are usually considered in the relocation decision. What will it be like to live there? Are there leisure-time activities that are appealing and compatible with what the people like to do? Is the climate desirable? Is the community attractive? These criteria are difficult to quantify, but they can be among the most important.

For many businesses, particularly services that cannot "transport" what they produce, location near the market can be the factor that determines success or failure. Being half a block away from the flow of foot or automobile traffic can be the equivalent of being in Siberia. For such businesses, this is the only criterion that matters. Sometimes the city or community doesn't matter. The state doesn't matter. The region doesn't matter. The only issue is the site. If the site is a good one, any city in any state will be fine.

Access to transportation can also be important. Businesses whose employees must travel to customers and clients must have access to an airport. Businesses that ship products or receive inputs by truck must have close access to an interstate highway. Businesses that depend on rail deliveries must have rail access. Transportation, and access to various modes of transportation, often translates into reduced time in the cash-to-cash cycle. Speed it up to improve profitability. Cut it in half and the rate of financial return doubles.

Education plays a role in location decisions for two reasons. First, workers who will be transferred to a new location want assurance that the school system in place will provide a quality education for their children. Second, if the workforce needs special skills, the importance of vocational schools and universities is heightened.

From a cost standpoint, regulatory and tax climate can provide a dramatic boost or equally dramatic detriment to business success. Taxes are an issue of concern for virtually all businesses, and the tax regulations at the state and city level must be considered in location decisions. For some businesses, the regulatory environment can be important also.

For heavy consumers of electricity or natural gas, utility cost and availability can be a very important location criterion. Utility costs vary substantially from region to region, from state to state, and even from city to city. For manufacturers whose processes require substantial power use, these differences can have a significant impact on the bottom line.

www.OperationsNow.com

As states and communities have recognized the importance of economic growth and new businesses, many have elected to compete for them by offering various incentives that will be attractive to them. Included among incentives given by state and local governments are tax reductions and tax breaks, interest-free loans, facility or site upgrades, and education and training for potential employees. Although these incentives can turn into bidding wars between competing locations, they often provide enough financial benefit to be a significant factor in the decision-making process. Many states and regions actively market themselves to attract businesses. Esource 13.2 provides an example of how one state markets the talent and skills of its workforce in order to attract businesses.

As location issues get resolved, and a shortened list of potential alternatives at the regional, state, and city level becomes available, site considerations begin to dominate the decision-making process. The most dominant criteria at this point are the availability of a site and the cost of a site. Everything may look great for a given community, but if there is no land available, the other criteria don't matter. The same holds for high cost of land that is available. It can outweigh all other advantages of a particular city. In addition to the cost of the site itself, other site-specific costs may influence the final decision. For example, upgrading the site to meet the needs of a new facility may be too costly. Changing access to the site, including widening streets or adding stoplights, can increase site-related costs. A variety of costs can emerge at the last minute that are necessary to make a specific site compatible with what the business needs.

While the traditional cost-related criteria still drive many facility location decisions, other noncost criteria that are not as easy to quantify also play a role.[2] A rich and diverse local economy is important because many households are supported by two careers. Both partners must be able to find employment. Good schools are critical to attract an educated workforce. A quality education for their children is a top priority. Affordable housing is another critical criterion for business locations, since many employees might not be paid at high salary levels. The business must be able to attract employees at all levels. In many instances, the business needs to be able to attract workers from commuting distances. The site must be easy to commute to and mass transit is desirable. The ability to attract a diverse workforce means that the location must welcome ethnic, racial, and religious diversity. Businesses with specific talent requirements might need to locate near other employers in the same field to have access to pools of talent. For start-ups, nearness to venture capital firms can be important. For many businesses, easy access to north–south transportation routes is important because supply chains often cross the border into Mexico. Finally, many businesses look for cities that are regional centers of influence because they are more attractive for employees and are able to draw labor talent from the surrounding area.

Geographic Information Systems

A recent technological development has enhanced decision makers' ability to merge geographic information from a variety of sources. Geographic information systems (GISs) extract quantitative data from statistical databases for use in building sophisticated maps that present the information in a geographical context. Software can translate any database with population or geographic information to maps that assist in the identification of business locations. Data used include public information, such as U.S. census data, maps of streets, and other physical features, as well as private information, such as demographic information gathered through product sales. Merging the data sets aids in finding alternatives for business location decisions. Criteria are entered into a search query, and the result is a map that identifies all sites satisfying the criteria. Some systems also provide aerial photos of the sites.

In addition to business applications of this technology, many city and state governments have adapted this technology to make it easier for businesses to find sites. Cities make the service available online, so that businesses interested in locating there can identify potential sites. The complexities of location decisions, particularly when many variables are a concern, make traditional methods unusable. GIS technology can be customized to include virtually any statistics and convert them to a map format. Esource 13.3 provides online access to a GIS system specifically designed by a city to aid businesses in making location decisions.

www OperationsNow .com

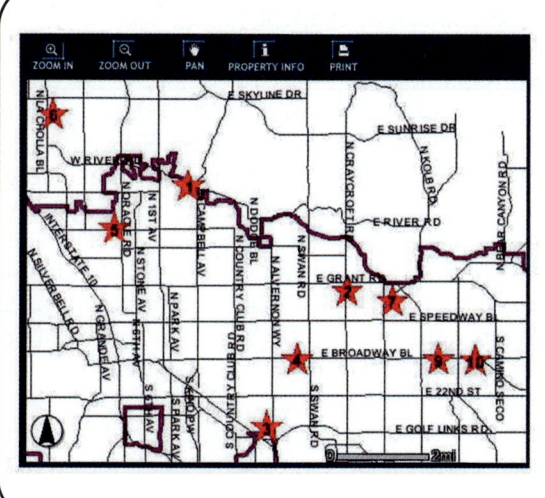

GISs have been adapted by many city governments to aid in their ability to attract business by making location-related information readily available. Here is a simple output from a city's GIS after a search for a 1500-square-foot office facility was initiated. Clicking on the address of each site provides an aerial photograph, ground photograph, and extensive facility details, such as actual size, year built, ceiling height, lease or sale price, and other amenities.

LOCATION DECISION-MAKING TECHNIQUES

The very nature of a location decision, whether it is for a new business, relocation, or expansion, is that the issues to be considered range from those that are easily quantified to those that are subjective and fuzzy. Transportation costs can be quantified. Quality of life can't. Site upgrade costs can be quantified. The quality of the school system can't. When it comes right down to it, the location of a business is where the owner or owners want it to be. The location might be consistent with the results of quantitative analysis, or it might be that the owner just likes the views better somewhere else despite the results of an extensive quantitative analysis of all criteria.

Many criteria in location decisions are compatible with quantitative analysis techniques, and several approaches are commonly used to help make the location decision more objective. For the most part, these approaches are general-purpose decision-making tools that fit very nicely into the location-decision scenario because they facilitate choosing from a list of alternatives. The tools that will be examined for location decisions are multifactor rating, the center-of-gravity method, decision trees, and breakeven analysis. Each of these techniques starts with a short list of alternatives and provides guidance in making the final cut.

Multifactor Rating

Location decisions are made after consideration of a broad range of information. No technique can provide a "best" solution, because there is no "best" solution. In many ways, location decisions can be evaluated only after the fact, because the suitability of the location depends on events that can only be predicted. Despite the fact that making the best decision may be impossible, making a good decision is obviously necessary. The variety of information to be considered makes it important to organize the information so the decision itself can be organized. The last thing any business wants is for an employee, four weeks after the move to the new facility, to point out a major shortcoming of the new facility: "The trucks that bring our products are too heavy for the street out front!" or "Did you know that they're going to reroute the highway so it won't be near our store any more?!" or "The dust from the manufacturing plant next door is ruining our paint finish!" No question, each of these would prompt the same response from management: "%#&*!! Why didn't we think of that earlier?!"

Multifactor rating provides a mechanism for considering a variety of factors with different levels of significance and incorporating them into a decision. It has many useful applications outside of location decisions, but for these types of decisions it is a good match. Multifactor rating starts with a list of issues or criteria (factors) to be considered in making the decision: condition of the building, cost of the building, nearness to transportation, and so on. This list should be extensive, made with the involvement of as many people as possible, and examined for completeness. The benefit of this process is not just that it provides guidance for the decision, but that it also forces decision makers to consider everything. Each factor is given an importance weighting between 0 and 1.0. The weights must sum to 1.0. A factor of little importance gets a low (closer to 0) weight; a factor of great importance gets a high (closer to 1.0) weight; factors of equal importance get equal weights.

Next, each of the alternative locations is given a score for each factor. For example, if a particular site has very good transportation access, that site might be given a score of 90 for transportation access. Another site, with not quite as good access, might be given a score of 85.

Next, the multifactor score for each location is computed by multiplying the importance weight for each factor by that factor's score and summing the results across all factors. The highest possible multifactor score for a particular location alternative would be 100. Example 13.1 demonstrates the use of this technique for a new business location decision.

Even though the multifactor rating technique appears objective because it provides quantitative results, it must be recognized as a subjective process. The weights

Example 13.1
Multifactor Rating for Tanning Salon Location

Tim Boyd, a local rental property owner, wants to open a small tanning salon. He's looking for a preexisting building that can be modified by constructing 12 tanning booths. He identified six criteria for decision making and gave them the importance weights shown in Exhibit 13.4.

EXHIBIT 13.4 Factors and Importance Weightings for Example 13.1

Factor	Important Weighting
Overall building condition	0.2
Ease of modification	0.2
Parking availability	0.2
Visibility/traffic	0.15
Electrical capacity	0.1
Cost	0.15

Tim identified four possible locations with buildings that are currently unoccupied. He scored each of the four alternatives on each factor. The scores are shown in Exhibit 13.5.

EXHIBIT 13.5 Factor Scores for Each Location for Example 13.1

	Scores			
Factor	Location 1	Location 2	Location 3	Location 4
Overall building condition	95	85	50	75
Ease of modification	80	90	75	85
Parking availability	60	70	90	95
Visibility/traffic	95	55	80	85
Electrical capacity	70	80	95	90
Cost	70	70	95	75

Solution:

The results of multiplying the factor scores for each location by the factor weights are presented in Exhibit 13.6. Location 4 turns out to be the highest scored location, with 84.

(continues)

Example 13.1 (continued)

EXHIBIT 13.6 Multifactor Scores for Each Location

Factor	Factor Weights	Scores			
		Location 1	Location 2	Location 3	Location 4
Overall building condition	0.2	95	85	50	75
Ease of modification	0.2	80	90	75	85
Parking availability	0.2	60	70	90	95
Visibility/traffic	0.15	95	55	80	85
Electrical capacity	0.1	70	80	95	90
Cost	0.15	70	70	95	75
Total score		78.75	75.75	78.75	84

www.OperationsNow.com

Excel Tutor 13.1 demonstrates the multifactor rating technique in Excel.

assigned and the scoring of each factor are subjective processes. Changing a weight or a score can result in a change in the solution. Nevertheless, the approach does increase the objectivity of the location decision, particularly if the establishment of the weights and scores involves several different individuals.

Center-of-Gravity Method

Nearness between suppliers and customers in B2B interactions improves supply chain efficiency and reduces the cash-to-cash cycle. Costs added anywhere in the supply chain are ultimately borne by the customer, and they diminish the perceived value of the product or service being purchased. One of the most relevant costs associated with customers and suppliers is the cost of transportation of goods. Transportation costs are typically a function of the weight of the product or item that is transported and the distance it must be transported. Sometimes, however, for lightweight but bulky products, volume is more important than weight.

Businesses that use centralized distribution centers (DCs) are particularly aware of these costs because they are continuously shipping from the DCs to stores. The placement of the DC is a critical piece of the cost picture for these firms. If the DC shipped exactly the same products and exactly the same quantities to each store, putting the DC in the exact center of the stores would make sense. However, this is typically not possible. Different stores sell different quantities and different mixes of products, so they require different shipments. The placement of the DC needs to consider different volume of goods shipped to different stores. For example, if one store needs a higher volumes of shipments than other stores, the DC should be closer to that store. An alternative perspective is placement of a store or factory considering shipments from suppliers that are already located. The issues are the same.

The center-of-gravity method identifies the best location for a single distribution center. In its simplest form, which is demonstrated in Example 13.2, it assumes inbound and outbound transportation costs are the same. The center of gravity, or "most central location," is found by calculating the X and Y coordinates for the distribution center to minimize transportation costs. The following formulas are used:

$$Cx = \frac{\sum d_{ix} V_i}{\sum V_i} \qquad (13.1)$$

$$Cy = \frac{\sum d_{iy} V_i}{\sum V_i} \qquad (13.2)$$

where
C_x = X coordinate of the center of gravity
C_y = Y coordinate of the center of gravity
d_{ix} = X coordinate of the ith location
d_{iy} = Y coordinate of the ith location
V_i = volume of goods moved to or from the ith location

A close look at these equations will show that this is essentially a weighted averaging technique for each coordinate, where the coordinate for each location is weighted by the number of trips. The products are summed, and the sum is divided by the total number of trips. Interactive Model 13.1 provides an interactive environment for experimenting with the center-of-gravity method.

Example 13.2

Center-of-Gravity Computation for Distribution Center Location

BrainFreez Beverages, a small regional bottler of high-energy drinks, is currently examining potential locations for a new facility. BrainFreez drinks are packaged in 12-ounce cans and 20-ounce bottles. BrainFreez can be purchased retail in 12-pack boxes of cans and 6-pack shrink-wrapped packages of 20-ounce bottles. BrainFreez has one supplier for each of the following inputs to its products: cardboard and paper goods, aluminum cans, plastic bottles and bottle tops, syrup concentrate. Using the following data, determine where BrainFreez should locate its new facility. Supplier locations are shown in Exhibit 13.7. Note that the locations are superimposed on a geographic grid. X and Y coordinates are listed in Exhibit 13.8. Truckloads per month of supplies coming from each supplier are presented in Exhibit 13.9.

EXHIBIT 13.7 Graphical Representation of Supplier Locations

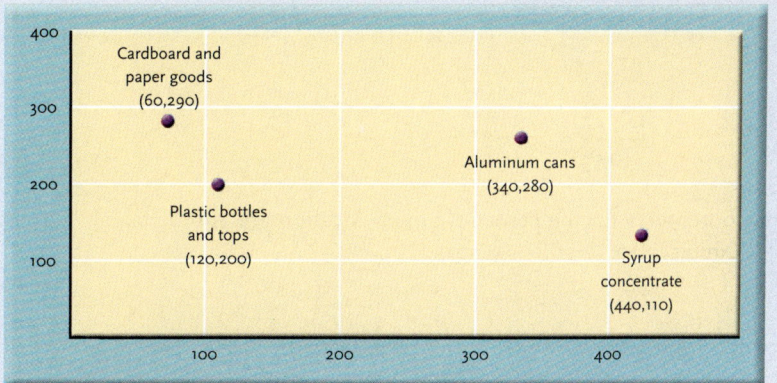

(continues)

Example 13.2 (continued)

EXHIBIT 13.8 X and Y Coordinates for Suppliers

Supplier	x	y
Cardboard and paper goods	60	290
Aluminum cans	340	280
Plastic bottles and tops	120	200
Syrup concentrate	440	110

EXHIBIT 13.9 Truckloads per Month

Supplier	Truckloads per month
Cardboard and paper goods	13
Aluminum cans	15
Plastic bottles and tops	19
Syrup concentrate	60

Solution

Using the data provided, for the first supplier, $d_{ix} = 60$, $d_{iy} = 290$, and $V_i = 13$. Using the remainder of the information provided, the coordinates for the center of gravity are calculated:

$$C_x = \frac{(60 \times 13) + (340 \times 15) + (120 \times 19) + (440 \times 60)}{13 + 15 + 19 + 60}$$

$$= \frac{34{,}560}{107} = 322.99$$

$$C_y = \frac{(290 \times 13) + (280 \times 15) + (200 \times 19) + (110 \times 60)}{13 + 15 + 19 + 60}$$

$$= \frac{14{,}977}{107} = 171.68$$

The coordinates for the center-of-gravity location are approximately (323, 172), as seen in Exhibit 13.10.

(continues)

Example 13.2 (continued)

EXHIBIT 13.10 Center-of-Gravity Location

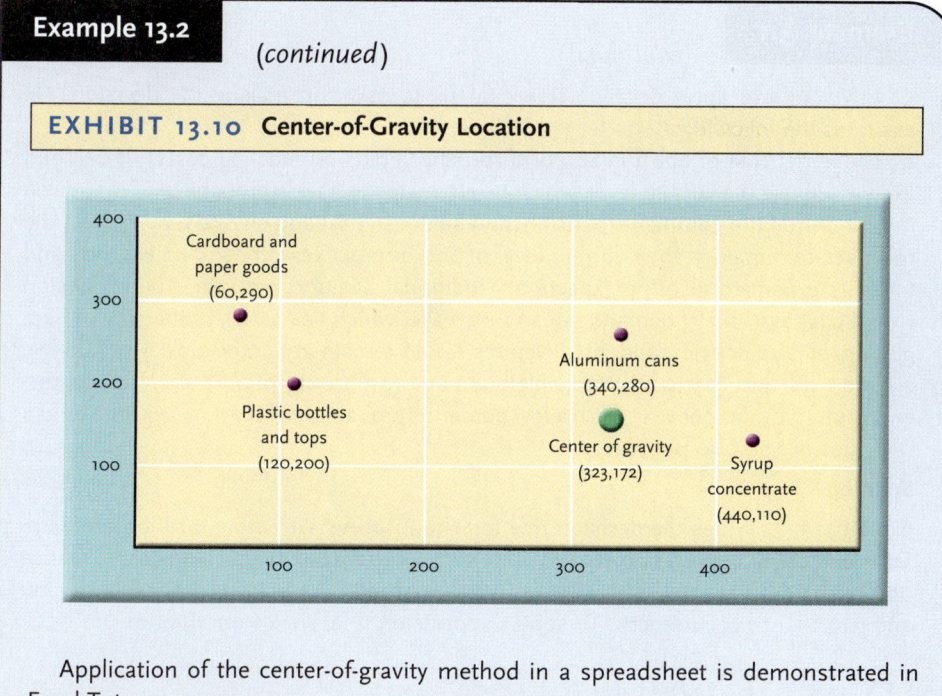

Application of the center-of-gravity method in a spreadsheet is demonstrated in Excel Tutor 13.2.

www.OperationsNow.com

Decision Tree Analysis

Decision tree analysis is a useful technique for organizing some location decisions by identifying expected revenues associated with each alternative. Decision trees are applicable to a wide variety of decisions where the outcomes of the choices are uncertain. Decision trees approach the calculation of expected revenues by multiplying the revenue expected for each alternative by the likelihood of its happening. This logic, combined with a "tree" structure for decision sequences and chance occurrences, forms the basis for decision tree analysis. Example 13.3 provides an example of decision tree analysis in a location decision.

Example 13.3 Decision Tree Analysis

The owner of The Gourmet Guy, a local gourmet food store, is confronted with a decision. The store opened nine years ago and has enjoyed steady growth. The store is adjacent to a large condominium complex that is expected to begin major expansion within the next year. Unfortunately, the expansion also means that Guy will lose his lease on the current facility and be forced to relocate. Guy identified two alternatives for relocation. Site 1 will cost $66,000 to purchase and an additional $14,000 to remodel with appropriate fixtures. It can handle the existing level of demand as is, but if demand were to increase, it would require an addition that would cost $55,000. Site 2 is large enough to handle any foreseeable demand increase. It can be purchased for $135,000, with no remodeling needed.

(continues)

Example 13.3 (continued)

Guy wants to apply decision tree analysis to assist in making the decision. He assumes the following:

1. The initial cost of Site 1 is $80,000 (purchase plus remodeling costs). If demand expands above the current level, which he estimates to have a probability of 0.75 given the condominium complex expansion, and he doesn't expand on Site 1, he expects the revenues to remain at their current level of $90,000 per year. If demand expands and Site 1 is expanded also, he expects an additional $65,000 per year. The expansion would cost $55,000. If demand doesn't increase, which has a 0.25 probability of happening, and he does expand, his revenues would remain at $90,000 per year.
2. Site 2 will cost $135,000. With a high demand (probability of 0.75) Guy expects revenues of $170,000 per year. With a low demand (probability of 0.25) he expects annual revenues of $80,000 per year.

Solution

Exhibit 13.11 provides the decision tree for The Gourmet Guy store location problem. Each branching point represents either a decision (represented by a box) or a chance occurrence (represented by a circle). In this example, there are two decision points and two chance occurrences. To solve the decision tree, work from right to left.

EXHIBIT 13.11 Decision Tree

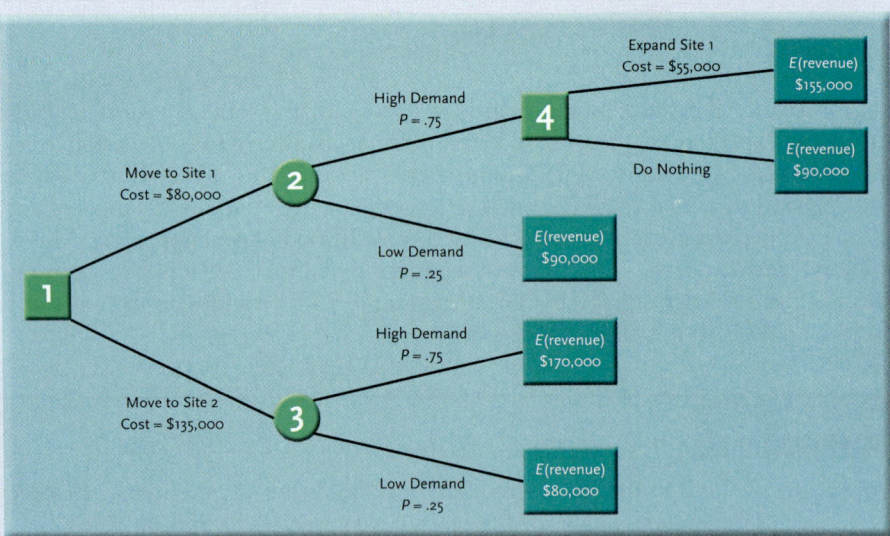

The first step is to determine the best decision at decision point 4, by determining the financial return for each of the two alternatives. The revenue generated by expanding Site 1 is

$$\$155,000 - \$55,000 = \$100,000$$

The revenue generated by doing nothing is $90,000. Since expansion has a higher expected value, it would be chosen and the do-nothing alternative would be pruned from the decision tree.

(continues)

Example 13.3 (continued)

The next step is to determine the expected values for moving to Site 1 and Site 2. The expected values of chance occurrences are determined by summing the products of the probabilities and the expected values branching from each decision point. The expected revenues of moving to Site 1 would be calculated as follows:

$$(0.75 \times \$100{,}000) + (0.25 \times \$90{,}000) = \$97{,}500$$

Subtracting the cost of Site 1:

$$\$97{,}500 - \$80{,}000 = \$17{,}500$$

To calculate the expected value of moving to Site 2, the same process is used:

$$(0.75 \times 170{,}000) + (0.25 \times \$80{,}000) = \$147{,}500$$

Subtracting the initial cost of Site 2 provides the expected value of moving to Site 2:

$$\$147{,}500 - \$135{,}000 = \$12{,}500$$

Moving to Site 1 has a higher expected value.

Excel Tutor 13.3 uses Excel to solve this problem.

www.OperationsNow.com

Breakeven Analysis

Breakeven analysis can be a useful tool for making location decisions. Back in Chapter 2, breakeven analysis was demonstrated in an example that compared three alternative suppliers of software. It can be used in a similar way when comparing location alternatives that have different fixed and variable costs. Different locations typically have different upfront costs associated with the purchase or upgrading of the facility and other capital items. They also have different variable costs. Materials, labor, and other resources may cost more at some locations than others. Example 13.4 demonstrates the use of breakeven analysis in a location problem.

Example 13.4 Location Breakeven Analysis

Ron Storch is a recent college graduate who worked for a landscaping company for the past four summers, earning money for school. He decided that a great way to gain managerial experience, and have fun, would be to run his own landscaping firm for a year or two before going back to school for an MBA. Through contacts and friends, he identified three alternative locations in three different states for starting his business. His previous employer helped him develop a plan and estimate material and labor costs for various jobs. With these data, he created a generic "job" that represents the typical new home landscaping job that will sustain his business. Ron also priced available equipment, labor rates, and material costs in each location. He developed the data presented in Exhibit 13.12 for use in his decision. His variable costs are based on labor rates, local landscaping materials costs, and 30 labor hours per job.

(continues)

Example 13.4 (continued)

EXHIBIT 13.12 Cost Data for Landscaping Location

Site No.	Fixed Costs($)	Labor Cost/Hour($)	Labor Cost/Job ($)	Materials Cost/Job ($)	Variable Cost/Job Total ($)
1	58,000	6.75	202.50	437.50	640.00
2	80,000	7.3	219.00	266.00	485.00
3	42,000	8.1	243.00	609.00	852.00

Solution

Exhibit 13.13 graphically illustrates his cost curves. Precise intersections for the cost curves are calculated below:

EXHIBIT 13.13 Cost Curves for Location Breakeven

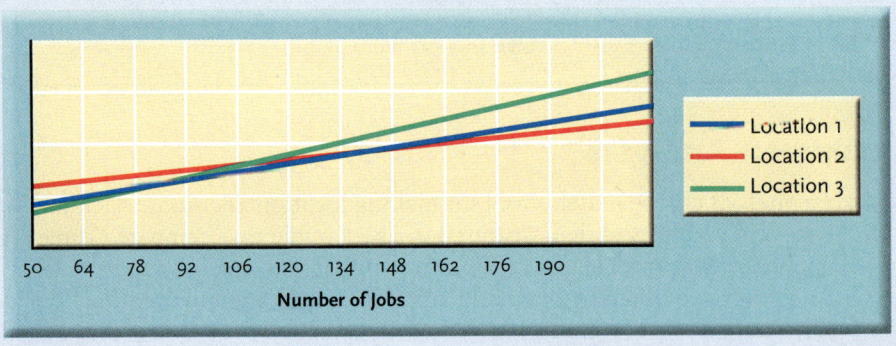

Site 1		Site 2
$58{,}000 + 640X$	$=$	$80{,}000 + 485X$
$640X$	$=$	$22{,}000 + 485X$
$155X$	$=$	$22{,}000$
X	$=$	141.9

Site 1		Site 3
$58{,}000 + 640X$	$=$	$42{,}000 + 852X$
$16{,}000 + 640X$	$=$	$852X$
$16{,}000$	$=$	$212X$
X	$=$	75.47

(continues)

> **Example 13.4** *(continued)*
>
> For an expected number of jobs fewer than 75, Site 3 is the low-cost site. From 75 jobs up to 142 jobs, Site 1 is the low-cost site. At volumes greater than 142 jobs, Site 2 is the best.
> This problem is solved in Excel in Excel Tutor 13.4.

www
OperationsNow
.com

BUSINESS LOCATION TRENDS

Increased use of the Internet in business has drastically changed the way businesses make location decisions. Although some businesses still utilize traditional criteria, many businesses are no longer bound by geographic limitations. Where they locate is still important, but the criteria can be weighted very differently. The types of workers that businesses need the most—those that help them create the most value—are engineers, investment analysts, technology workers, scientists, and other highly skilled, highly creative workers. These workers are particular about where they live simply because, well, they can be since their skills are in demand. Businesses that need them must locate where they live or where they'd like to live. Quality of life that would be attractive to these workers is now the most important criterion for the location of many businesses. In many cases these are smaller cities, like Seattle or Boston, but quite often they are the expensive suburbs of cities like Austin, Texas, or Raleigh, North Carolina. One characteristic that often sets these locations apart is that the communities are "wired." They've embraced the Internet and have an infrastructure in place. Taxes are low, crime is low, and the lifestyle is appealing to workers and management. These "edge cities" are really huge, well-planned, suburbs. Joel Kotkin, an expert on new-economy geography, refers to these cities as "nerdistans."[3] These communities are often close to major universities, which are sources of expertise as well as culture.

Even as the nerdistans are home to many businesses, small towns are gaining fast. Low taxes, low costs, low crime, and simple lifestyles have made cities in the West and Midwest more attractive. Nevada, Montana, Colorado, and the Dakotas have a higher concentration of high-tech workers than Massachusetts.[4] The cities of choice are quite diverse, but in most cases they are far from the urban environments that once attracted businesses. Fort Collins, Colorado, is a classic example of the new type of city that is attracting business. It offers good schools, a clean environment, outdoor recreation, and a quality of life that is desirable.[5]

Attractive locations may not remain attractive forever. Popularity itself can change an area to such a great extent that it destroys its attractiveness. Silicon Valley is a great example. Its popularity among the newly rich raised property values and property taxes to the extent that teachers and government workers could no longer afford to live there. Businesses began to shy away from locating there because the typical worker would have to commute 40 miles from the nearest affordable place to live. As technology continues to change the geography by making it easier to telecommute and cheaper to transport goods, and as communication problems between disjointed departments and businesses are eliminated, priorities for location decisions will continue to shift.

FACILITY LAYOUTS

The location of a facility dictates part of its contribution to value, but as we discussed in Chapter 5, distinctive capabilities are created by the general layout of the facility

www.OperationsNow.com

and whether it should be process-oriented, product-oriented, or cellular. Processes, which dictate value, must exist within the limits set by the general layout choice. Layout decisions at the time of the facility design, as well as during improvement efforts, can increase the productivity of many different resources. Reel Operations Video 13.1 investigates the benefits of facility layout decisions made by Bernard, a manufacturer of water cooling equipment.

Even after the general decision is made, more decisions remain. Precisely how the general layout will incorporate equipment and specific functions must be decided. The work environment is also important. For some resources, location of the resource can dictate productivity measures. For example, work centers that are far apart may result in unnecessary transporting of materials between them. For human resource productivity, the decisions made during the layout process can have other effects. Lighting, noise, ventilation, and other aesthetic factors can influence employee perceptions of their environment. Many of these factors have a direct impact on productivity.

Frequently these specific layout decisions become part of the work of employee teams devoted to process improvement. In some cases, the vendors that supply manufacturing equipment become involved in these decisions. In the following sections, the strengths and weaknesses of each kind of general layout will be reviewed, as well as decisions regarding those layouts and the techniques used to make those decisions.

Office Layouts Change to Reduce Noise Levels

In the 1980s and 1990s the trend toward open offices reached its peak as many office cubicles were constructed of short, movable architectural walls.

The result was a feeling of openness that was intended to promote an atmosphere that would encourage cooperation and teamwork. Recently, however, many employees and managers have begun to retreat from this layout because of noise. In a study conducted by the American Society of Interior Designers, 70 percent of respondents indicated that lower noise levels would increase their productivity, but 81 percent of the business executives were unaware that a noise problem existed.

Employee productivity is reduced by other employees talking, phone calls are interrupted by noise, and, in general, employees desire more "acoustical privacy." Employees complain more about noise than lighting, air conditioning, and lack of space. Offices are staffed at high densities to reduce costs. Employees in open cubicles sometimes use speaker phones and typically speak louder when using them. In addition, telephones, fax machines, beepers, file drawers, keyboards, printers, and many other objects also contribute to the level of noise in office settings.

In response to concern about office noise levels, low architectural walls are being replaced by walls that extend all the way to the ceiling, and managers are separating groups of employees who have similar noise-level needs. Small soundproof conference rooms are also being constructed. Herman Miller, an office furniture manufacturer, noted that sales of short cubicle panels have been declining since 1996, while sales of taller panels have been on the increase.

In addition to structural changes, many companies are masking noise by installing "white-noise" machines. Dynasound, a producer of noise-masking systems, has had a sixfold increase in sales since 1994.

Source: "Shut Up So We Can Do Our Jobs!" *The Wall Street Journal*, August 29, 2001, pp. B1, B8; "ASID Sound Solutions," http://www.dynasound.com/SoundSolutions.pdf.

Process-Oriented Layouts

A process-oriented layout is characterized by functional departments. It enables the firm to adapt the sequence of operations to meet particular needs of customers who desire a customized product or service. Exhibit 13.14 presents a typical process-oriented layout.

The functional nature of the layout makes it possible for a customer or product to be routed through departments in any sequence necessary to fulfill the processing requirements. For example, an order could enter the printing business illustrated in Exhibit 13.15 at the design department, and then go to printing, then binding, and finally packaging and shipping. On the other hand, an order for a standard product that doesn't get bound might start at paper storage, go directly to printing, and then move to packaging and shipping. The layout offers great flexibility.

After the general decision to adopt a process-oriented layout has been made, decisions remain for making that layout the best it can be. The strength of the process-oriented layout is its ability to utilize the functional departments in any sequence desired. This strength can result in a tremendous amount of material movement or, in the case of a service, customer movement from one department to another that could be some distance away. The arrangement of departments within the process-oriented layout will dictate the costs associated with transporting customers and products through the system. These costs can be substantial and a well-designed layout can have a dramatic impact on them.

The primary objective in determining the relative locations of departments in a process-oriented layout is to locate close together those departments that interact the most and to locate at a distance those that don't interact or that need to be separate from each other. This logic applies to both manufacturing and service layouts, including the layout of professional offices. Consulting firms, architectural firms, legal firms,

EXHIBIT 13.14 Process-Oriented Layout from Chapter 5

and so on, have various experts that are pulled together to work on projects. It makes sense to locate those that most frequently interact closer to each other.

The frequency of the interaction or transportation, combined with the distance between the locations, establishes the transportation or movement costs associated with their relative positions in the layout. Not surprisingly, layout decisions attempt to minimize these costs. This process is generally a "cut-and-try" approach to obtaining a good layout, but it cannot guarantee the best layout as an outcome. In an operation with only six departments, there would be 6! (720) possible positions for the six departments.

In the cut-and-try approach, two matrices are initially constructed. One provides the frequency of the interaction between each pair of departments. The other provides the distances between all potential locations or rooms in the facility. This approach utilizes several modifications of the layout to improve it. A third matrix, called a total-distance matrix, contains the products of the frequency of interaction and the distance for each pair of potential locations. These distances are summed to provide a total distance of travel for each proposed layout. The total distance associated with alternative layouts can be compared and the best one selected. Example 13.5 demonstrates this process.

Example 13.5 — Cut-and-Try Layout Process

Exhibit 13.15 is a diagram of a proposed layout for a printing business. The operation has six departments. Print jobs are moved, usually by forklift truck, from one department to the next one in their routing.

EXHIBIT 13.15 Proposed Layout for a Printing Business

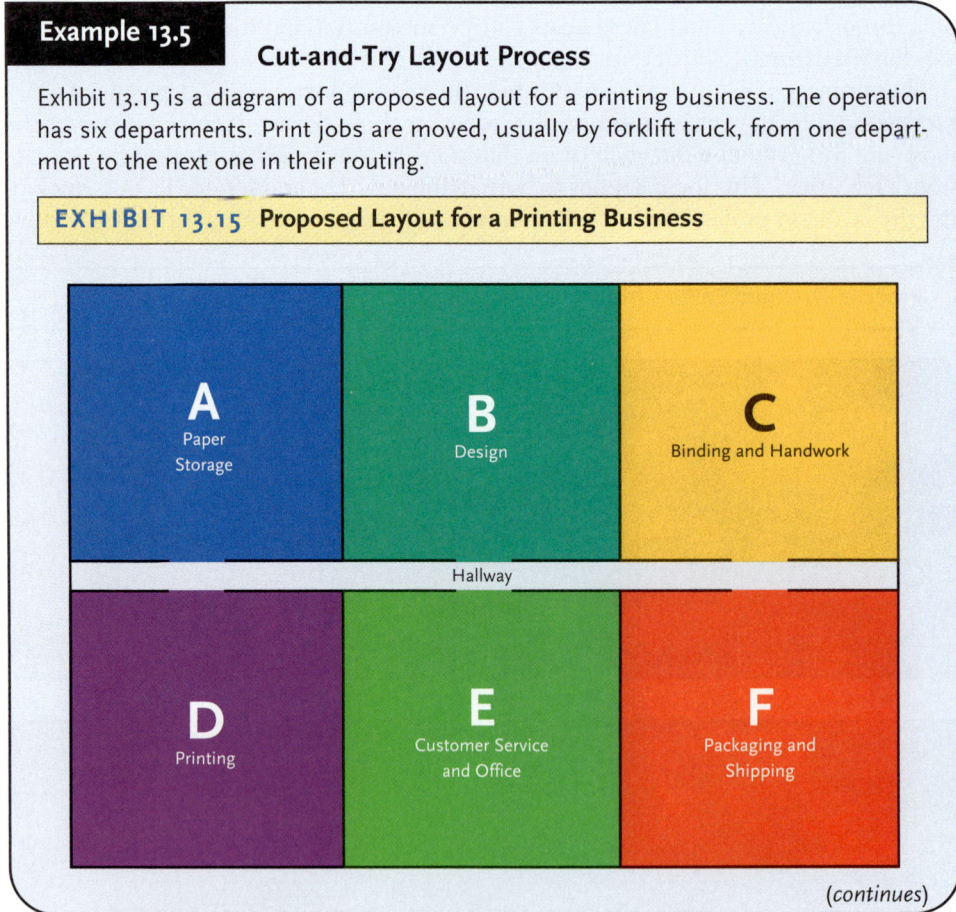

(continues)

Example 13.5 (continued)

Use the trips matrix presented in Exhibit 13.16, and the distance matrix for the proposed layout in Exhibit 13.17 to compute the total distance associated with this layout. How can the layout be improved?

EXHIBIT 13.16 Trips Matrix for Printing Business

	Trips per Month					
	Paper Storage	Design	Binding and Handwork	Printing	Customer Service	Packaging and Shipping
Paper Storage	0	0	60	260	20	50
Design		0	12	10	15	10
Binding and Handwork			0	310	8	440
Printing				0	6	560
Customer Service					0	5
Packaging and Shipping						0

EXHIBIT 13.17 Distance Matrix for Proposed Layout

	Distances (feet)					
	A	B	C	D	E	F
A	0	30	60	15	40	70
B	30	0	30	40	15	40
C	60	30	0	70	40	15
D	15	40	70	0	30	60
E	40	15	40	30	0	30
F	70	40	15	60	30	0

Solution

The total distance matrix is obtained by multiplying the number of trips by the distance, as seen in Exhibit 13.18.

(continues)

Example 13.5 (continued)

EXHIBIT 13.18 Total Distance Matrix for Proposed Layout

	Paper Storage	Design	Binding and Handwork	Printing	Customer Service	Packaging and Shipping
Paper Storage	0	0	3,600	3,900	800	3,500
Design			0	360	400	225	400
Binding and Handwork			0	21,700	320	6,600
Printing				0	180	33,600
Customer Service					0	150
Packaging and Shipping						0

Total distance = 75,735

An examination of the interactions would probably lead to a change in the layout to move several departments closer together. For example, the high level of interaction between printing and binding/handwork, paper storage and printing, binding/handwork and packaging/shipping, and printing and packaging/shipping makes those pairs of departments very attractive to have in close proximity. An improvement can be made by making the changes shown in Exhibit 13.19.

EXHIBIT 13.19 Improved Layout

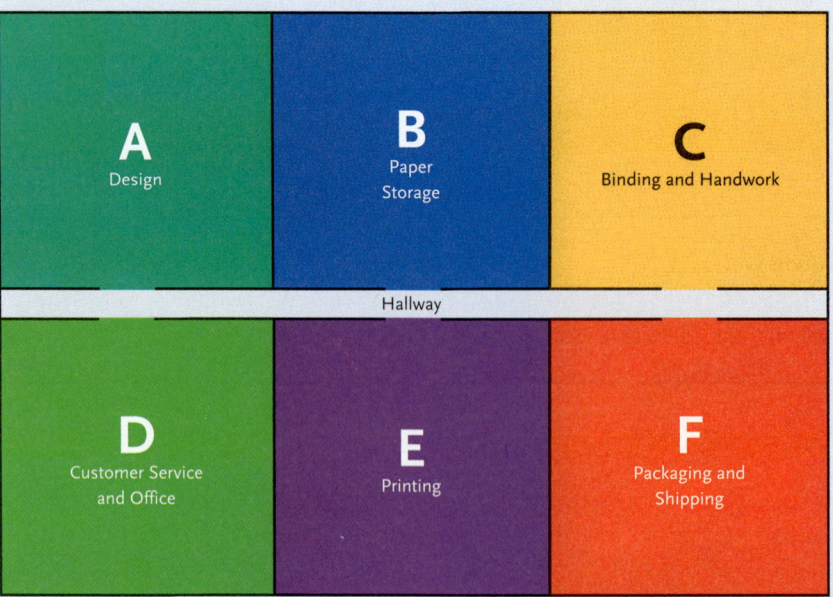

(continues)

Example 13.5 (continued)

Exhibit 13.20 provides the updated total distance matrix, reflecting the changes made in Exhibit 13.9, showing a total monthly distance reduction from 75,735 feet to 47,935 feet. This is a reduction of almost 37 percent and would contribute a proportional reduction in costs linked to that material movement.

EXHIBIT 13.20 Total Distance Matrix for Improved Layout

	Distance (feet)					
	Design	Paper Storage	Binding and Handwork	Customer Service	Printing	Packaging and Shipping
Design	0	0	720	225	400	700
Paper Storage		0	1,800	800	3,900	2,000
Binding and Handwork			0	1,050	12,400	6,600
Customer Service				0	240	300
Printing					0	16,800
Packaging and Shipping						0

Total distance = 47,935

This process of trial-and-error improvement would continue until it appeared that a good solution was generated. Another improvement would be to move printing and packaging/shipping so that they are immediately across from each other rather than next to each other, trading places between with the binding/handwork department and the printing department. Since there are more trips between printing and packaging/shipping than there are between binding/handwork and packaging/shipping, this would reduce the total distance as well. This cut-and-try improvement process would be continued until a satisfactory layout was obtained.

Excel Tutor 13.5 demonstrates how this problem can be solved in a spreadsheet.

www.OperationsNow.com

Other approaches are also used to develop process-oriented layouts. Some identify relationships between pairs of departments by rating the importance of the pairs being next to each other and then use a cut-and-try approach to moving them around to generate good alternative layouts. One popular approach that utilizes this technique is systematic layout planning (SLP).[6] SLP starts with a relationships matrix with each pair of departments and assigns a "closeness desirability" rating of A, E, I, O, U, or X, where A is absolutely necessary, E is especially important, I is important, O is OK, U is unimportant, and X means that they should not be close to each other. The ratings are illustrated in a diagram through the use of lines connecting each department. The printing business layout is examined using this technique in Example 13.6.

In addition to the manual approaches to layout planning, computer packages are available to aid in the layout process. A very popular one, Computerized Relative Allocation of Facilities Technique (CRAFT)[7] starts with the equivalent of a total distance or total cost matrix and makes swaps between pairs of departments. It continues to make swaps until no improvement is gained. It is basically a computerized approach to the cut-and-try method. Each of the approaches provides a structure and

Example 13.6 SLP Technique for Process-Oriented Layout

Using SLP, determine an improved layout for the printing business.

Solution

Exhibit 13.21 shows the closeness desirability matrix that has been developed from the trips matrix provided for the previous example in Exhibit 13.16. The more trips per month, the stronger the closeness desirability rating.

EXHIBIT 13.21 Closeness Desirability Matrix

	Closeness Desirability Ratings					
	Paper Storage	Design	Binding and Handwork	Printing	Customer Service	Packaging and Shipping
Paper Storage		U	I	E	O	I
Design			O	O	O	O
Binding and Handwork				E	U	A
Printing					U	A
Customer Service						U
Packaging and Shipping						

The initial layout proposal is presented in Exhibit 13.22, with the appropriate connectors.

EXHIBIT 13.22 Initial Layout Proposal with SLP Convention Connecting Lines

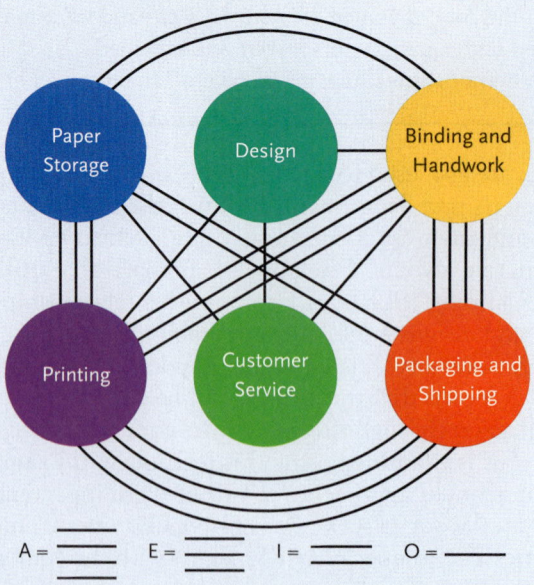

(continues)

Example 13.6   (continued)

The next iteration on this layout would strive to reduce the distance between departments with high closeness desirability ratings (connected by four lines or three lines). The first move can be to move printing to the right side of the layout. Exhibit 13.23 shows this step as an improvement.

EXHIBIT 13.23 First Iteration Improvement Using SLP

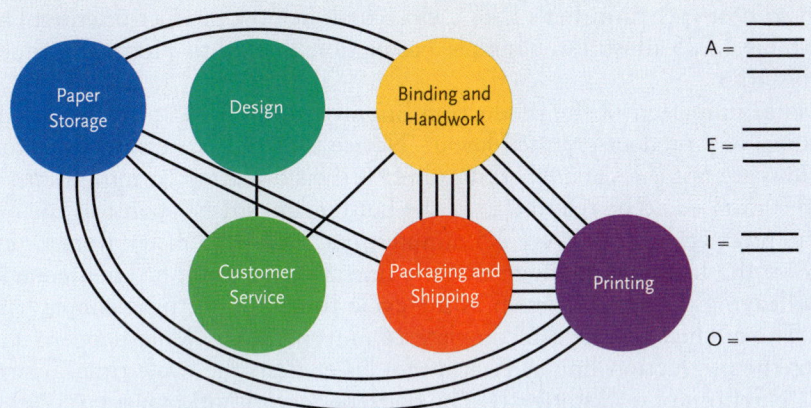

The process would continue in a trial-and-error fashion until the layout was believed to be satisfactory. The next improvement would be to move paper storage to the right side, to reduce the length of its connection to printing. The only connection lengthened by this move would be the single line connection to customer service, which is less important than the other relationships paper storage has. This change is shown in Exhibit 13.24.

EXHIBIT 13.24 Second Iteration Improvement Using SLP

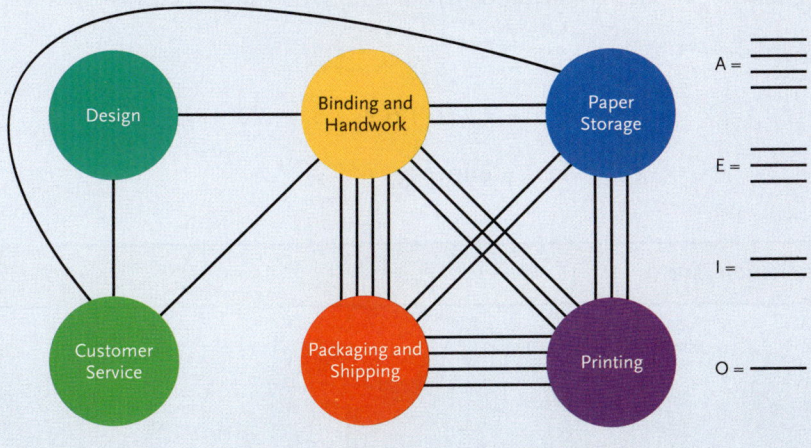

This process would continue if another obvious beneficial move was noticed.

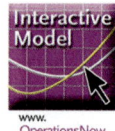

some objectivity to the process, but none guarantees optimal results. Interactive Model 13.2 provides an experimental environment for examining the process-oriented layout problem.

Product-Oriented Layouts

Product-oriented layouts take the form of assembly or production lines in many manufacturing operations. Products flow through a large number of workstations, each adding components and labor to what will eventually be a finished product. These layouts have little flexibility, but when designed correctly they can provide high volumes at low costs per unit. Let's take a close look at how product-oriented layouts work. Exhibit 13.25 illustrates a simple production line, with processing times for each workstation.

A close examination of the production line in Exhibit 13.25 provides insight to the workings of a product-oriented layout. Notice that the processing times for the workstations are not the same. Workstation D is the slowest, at 2.5 minutes per unit. This workstation could be referred to as the **bottleneck**, since it controls the output rate of the production line. Every 2.5 minutes, one unit will emerge from D and be passed down the line, eventually to exit the line at workstation F. The frequency of a product leaving the line is known as the **cycle time**, and in this example it is 2.5 minutes. The production line can complete 24 units per hour. What happens if products enter the production line at A at a rate faster than the cycle time? They will accumulate in front of workstation D. The bottleneck workstation plays a critical role by determining the utilization possible on the other workstations. Since it makes no sense to accumulate products in front of workstation D, the input rate into the line needs to be one unit every 2.5 minutes. Workstation A will actually only work 1.8 minutes out of every 2.5 minutes, for a utilization rate of 72 percent. Workstation B works 2.2 out of 2.5 minutes for a utilization rate of 88 percent. Workstation C has a utilization rate of 64 percent (the lowest of the workstations). Workstation D will work 100 percent of the time. E will have a utilization rate of 88 percent, and workstation F will be utilized 76 percent of the time. The low utilization that results from the differences in processing times is known as **balance delay**. The overall utilization of the entire line (U) can be computed by dividing the total amount of time actually spent performing tasks by the total time in the system. The amount of actual processing for the product is calculated by summing the times (t) for each task:

$$T = \Sigma t \tag{13.3}$$

$$= 1.8 + 2.2 + 1.6 + 2.5 + 2.2 + 1.9$$

$$= 12.2 \text{ minutes}$$

EXHIBIT 13.25 Production Line

A	B	C	D	E	F
1.8 minutes	2.2 minutes	1.6 minutes	2.5 minutes	2.2 minutes	1.9 minutes

Each product is in the system for 15 minutes (2.5 minutes each for six workstations). This is also often referred to as the **production lead time**. The production lead time can be calculated by multiplying the cycle time by the number of work centers:

$$\text{Production Lead Time} = C \times N \tag{13.4}$$

$$= 6 \times 2.5$$

$$= 15 \text{ minutes}$$

Where C = cycle time
N = number of workstations in the production line

Thus

$$U = \frac{T}{C \times N} \tag{13.5}$$

$$= \frac{12.2}{15.0}$$

$$= 81.3\%$$

The overall utilization of 81.3 percent is not acceptable for a layout whose strength is low cost per unit. High-cost equipment required for this type of layout needs a higher utilization rate to generate the financial return needed to provide a payback on the capital investment.

Suppose some of the work done at workstation D could be done at workstation C. What would be the impact of moving 0.3 minute of work from D to C? Let's find out. Exhibit 13.26 illustrates this change. Since the bottleneck (BDE) is now 7.2 minutes, this subtle change reduces the cycle time from 2.5 to 2.2 minutes. Output per hour increases from 24 to 27 units per hour and production lead time drops from 15 minutes to 13.2 minutes. The overall utilization improves to 92.4 percent (12.2/13.2 minutes). The small modification that caused all of these improvements simply resulted from a better-balanced line. The key to high levels of productivity in product-oriented layout is to balance the times required of each workstation in a process known as **line balancing**.

You were probably already thinking that in the real world no one could just "move" work from one workstation to another. You're right. Line balancing must be considered at the design stage in order to assign work as equally as possible. The first step in line balancing is to define the work necessary to complete the product in terms of very small tasks known as **work elements**. The work elements are defined precisely,

Production Line Improved (in minutes) EXHIBIT 13.26

A	B	C	D	E	F
1.8 minutes	2.2 minutes	1.9 minutes	2.2 minutes	2.2 minutes	1.9 minutes

and precedence relationships are established in much the same way as was done when creating project network diagrams. Elemental times are identified for each work element. To determine how the elements will be grouped into workstations, the minimum number of workstations must be determined. This is based on the cycle time needed to meet output requirements. The greater the output rate, the shorter the cycle time must be. The shorter the cycle time, the greater the number of workstations necessary to complete all of the processing that needs to be done. Balancing a preexisting line or new production line requires the following steps:

1. Identify the tasks, work elements, and precedence relationships by using a precedence chart.
2. Determine the cycle time (C) necessary to satisfy output requirements. This is accomplished using the following equation:

$$C = \frac{\text{Production Time Available per Day}}{\text{Units of Output Required per Day}} \quad (13.6)$$

3. Determine the theoretical minimum number of workstations (N_{min}) by using the equation

$$N_{min} = \frac{T}{C} \quad (13.7)$$

4. Assign the tasks to workstations.
5. Evaluate the utilization of the line.

Example 13.7 demonstrates the line balancing process.

Line balancing appears to be very precise on paper; in reality, however, it isn't quite that precise. Several complicating factors interfere. First of all, even though a workstation is defined as taking 3.95 minutes, that is an average. Since people, not robots, are performing the tasks, there will be variability at all workstations. This will increase balance delay. Second, different materials and slightly different levels of equipment performance can contribute to balance delay. In some cases, a line will be used for more than one product. One will be run for a while, and then the equipment

Example 13.7 Line Balancing

Hollow Logs is a manufacturer of cedar deck furniture owned by Julie Olsen. The company has been operating for six years. Initially, the business was laid out in a typical process-oriented fashion, to allow for flexibility. Over time, Julie came to realize that almost 90 percent of the volume came from a single model of chair and a single model of table. Several months ago she subcontracted out the sawing and milling of all cedar components for these two products. Her production process now consists of the assembly and finish only. She decided to downsize the functional departments used to make other models and to convert the chair and table assembly and finish to a production line approach.

Her first task is to develop a balanced line for the table. An examination of past demand and current orders on hand led Julie to believe that she needs to be able to complete 120 units per day on a standard eight-hour day, five-day week schedule. Her shop foreman and lead production operator developed a precise description of the work elements required for the table assembly. These data are presented in Exhibit 13.27. Using these data complete the line balancing process.

(continues)

Example 13.7 (continued)

EXHIBIT 13.27 Assembly Work Elements for Deck Table

Step	Description	Time, t (minutes)
1	Inspect top board kit	0.5
2	Sequence top boards in jig	0.6
3	Insert top braces in jig	0.3
4	Screw braces to top boards (16 screws)	3.6
5	Remove top assembly	0.2
6	Inspect bottom sawbuck stand boards	0.5
7	Insert left end X boards into jig	0.4
8	Drill, insert, and tighten center bolt	1.25
9	Remove left end assembly from jig	0.4
10	Insert right end X boards into jig	0.5
11	Drill, insert, and tighten center bolt	1.25
12	Remove right end assembly from jig	0.4
13	Attach center brace connecting left and right X boards	2.3
14	Attach hinges to top using placement jig	3.6
15	Attach base assembly to hinges	1.3
16	Inspect	0.7
17	Package	1.8

Solution

Precedence relationships are presented in Exhibit 13.28, and the production process is diagramed in Exhibit 13.29.

EXHIBIT 13.28 Deck Table Assembly Precedence Relationships

Step	Required Predecessors
1	0
2	1
3	2
4	3
5	4
6	0
7	6
8	7
9	8
10	6

(continues)

Example 13.7 (continued)

Step	Required Predecessors
11	10
12	11
13	12
14	5
15	14
16	15
17	16

EXHIBIT 13.29 Diagram of Deck Table Assembly Process

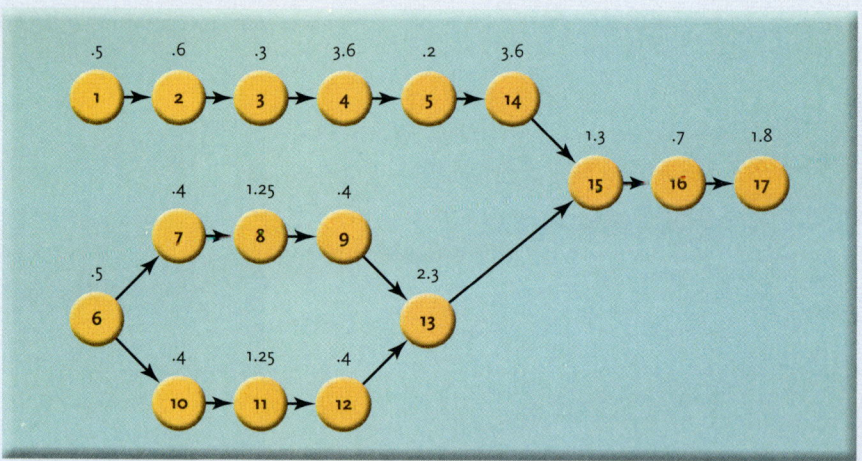

After the precedence relationships are determined and charted, the cycle time (C) needed to meet output requirements is determined:

$$C = \frac{480 \text{ minutes per day}}{120 \text{ units required per day}}$$

$$= 4 \text{ minutes}$$

The next step is to determine the theoretical minimum number of workstations:

$$N_{min} = \frac{T}{C}$$

$$= \frac{19.6}{4}$$

$$= 4.90$$

(continues)

Example 13.7 (continued)

The theoretical minimum number of workstations is the number required to get the total amount of work done (*T*) and meet the output rate (*C*) required. Any fractional number of workstations must be rounded up. In this case, the theoretical minimum number of workstations would be rounded up to five. There is no guarantee that the work could actually be done in only five workstations. Precedence relationships may prevent that. However, with more than five workstations, there will be significantly more idle time on workstations, reducing overall utilization.

The next step is to assign work elements to workstations. The first attempt will be to group the work elements, striving for groups that sum to the cycle time of four minutes. This will be done as they are assigned to the minimum number of workstations, five. Precedence relationships must be kept in mind when making these assignments. Exhibit 13.30 shows a first attempt. The resulting production line, with workstation times, is presented in Exhibit 13.31. This line will have a cycle time of 4.0 minutes, that of the slowest workstation (2).

EXHIBIT 13.30 First Iteration at Grouping Work Elements at Workstations

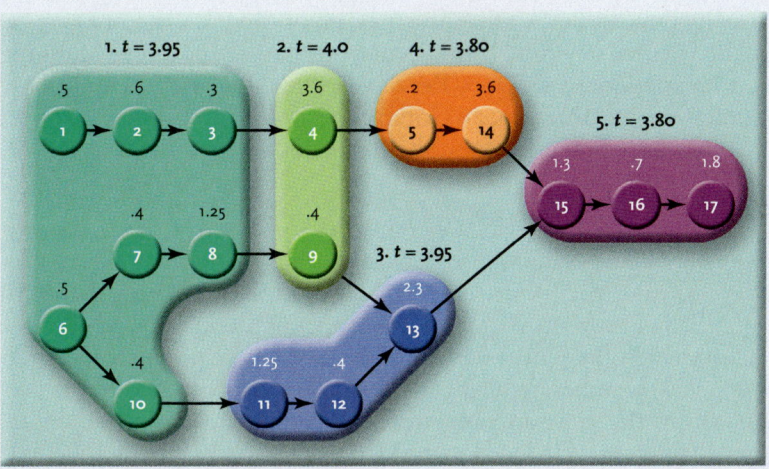

EXHIBIT 13.31 New Production Line for Hollow Logs Table Assembly (in minutes)

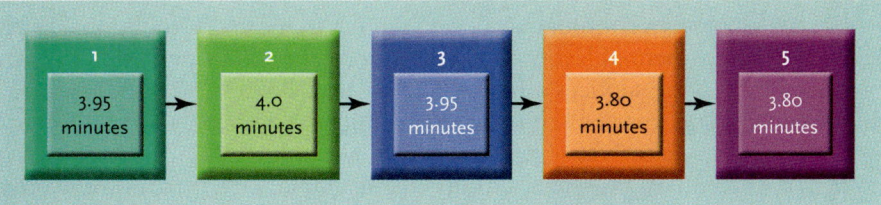

(continues)

Example 13.7

(continued)

This arrangement appears to be good. The resulting production line meets the output requirements of 120 units per day. Overall utilization is 92.5 percent (18.5/20). There is little room for improvement. For example, bringing work elements 4 and 5 together leaves work element 9 to be recombined. The only place for 9 would be combining it with 14. The result is no improvement because we still end up with a cycle time of 4.0 minutes. In addition, precedence relationships become a problem. There is no solution that can eliminate the 4.0-minute maximum in a workstation.

This is an excellent example of how small work element times make it possible to come up with a better balance. The perfectly balanced line, in this situation, would have a cycle time of 3.7 minutes, which might be more feasible if work element times were smaller. The negative aspect of small work element times is that tasks that logically fit together might be split up.

Excel Tutor 13.7 demonstrates how the line balancing problem can be aided by a spreadsheet.

www.OperationsNow.com

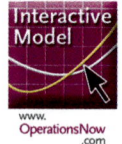
www.OperationsNow.com

will be changed over for another product. Obtaining a perfect balance in this situation is virtually impossible. Worker absenteeism or the presence of a new worker can also upset the balance of a line. Workers may need to be moved to fine-tune a line to account for inexperienced workers. Because of these real-world conditions, line balancing is often an ongoing process. Interactive Model 13.3 provides an interactive environment for experimenting with the line balancing problem.

Cellular Layouts

Cellular layouts offer a compromise between product-oriented and process-oriented layouts. Beyond that, they offer some capabilities that are better than either of the alternatives. Cellular layouts require that a family of products be produced in a "cell" that has all of the resources necessary to produce all of the products in the family. The resources are close together, reducing material transport costs, but the sequence of the movement within the cell can vary, creating an opportunity for flexibility. In addition to the advantages of reduced material transport and increased flexibility, workers can be expected to operate more than one type of resource. In contrast to the workstations in a production line, the work centers in a cell are less dependent on each other, reducing the potential impact of one disruption on other machines. In a low-inventory "lean" environment, a breakdown on one machine can quickly result in the rest running out of material.

Service Layouts

The objectives of a service layout may be very similar to those of a traditional product-oriented or process-oriented layout in manufacturing. Product-oriented layouts strive for a flow, and in some services a flow is also desired. Process-oriented layouts offer greater flexibility and in some services that flexibility is desired as well. In other services, however, the objectives of the layout may not be to enhance the efficiency of customer movement. Retail store layouts, for example, strive to move customers through the store to expose them to more products and increase the likelihood of a purchase. Certain high-frequency products (milk and bread, for example) are placed to lure the customer to the back of the store. The customer is forced to pass other merchandise along the way.

Different types of retail stores use different strategies for moving customers. Much of this customer movement is controlled by the layout of the aisles and traffic patterns. It may seem trivial, but remember, productivity of the facility for most retailers is measured in sales per square foot. Increased sales translate directly into an increase in the ROA.

"Flow" Drives Layout for Kohl's

Facility layout discussions often focus on manufacturing and the cost savings that result from more efficient transportation of inventory. Facility layouts can also enhance productivity in the service sector. Kohl's Corporation, a discount department store chain, is currently gaining ground to shift from a Midwest to a national entity. It, along with Target, is expected to continue its growth pattern as sales shift from high-end stores as consumers pay close attention to prices. Success for Kohl's, such as the same-store sales gain of nearly 15 percent in December 2000, is primarily a result of facility layout decisions. The aisle design is modeled after a figure 8 racetrack, to provide a route that takes shoppers through all departments, keeps them on one floor, and allows them quick access in and out of the store. The layout, illustrated in Exhibit 13.32, consists of a route that is about a quarter-mile long. Wide aisles leave plenty of room for carts. The middle aisles divide the track and provide a shortcut for shoppers who don't want to finish the entire route.

EXHIBIT 13.32 Kohl's Quarter-Mile Track

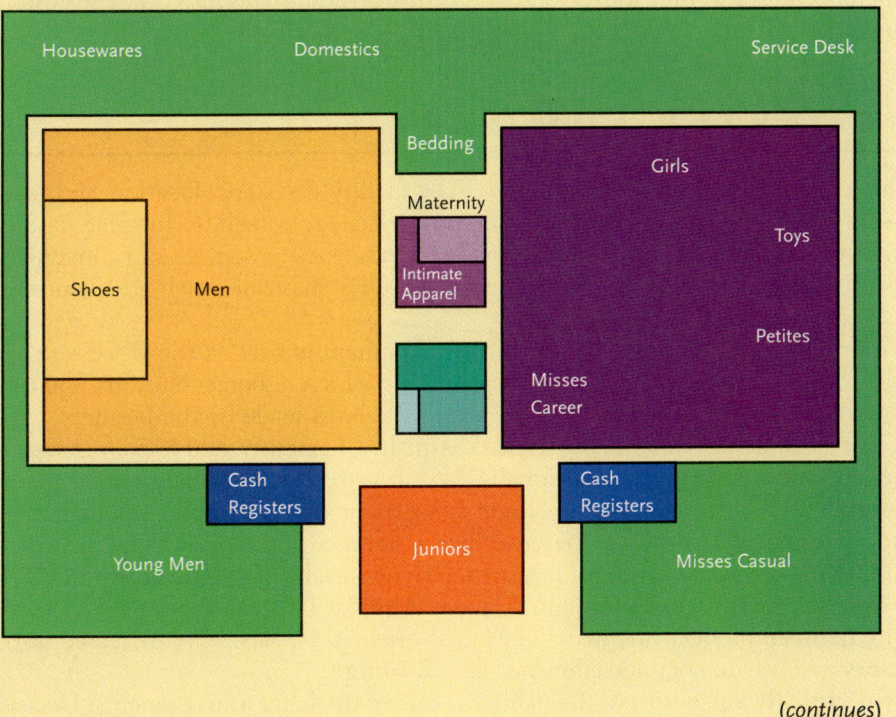

(continues)

> **(Continued)**
>
> The quarter-mile track in Kohl's compares to routes that are double in competing stores. In the Kohl's layout, each department is restricted to five or fewer display racks around the track. The result is a smaller, simpler layout and a more productive facility. Sales per square foot, a standard retail facility performance measure, reached $279 for Kohl's, compared to $220 for Target Corporation's Marshall Fields, $147 for Dillard's Inc., and $192 for May Department Stores Co. Kohl's pays particular attention to keeping aisles wide and racks far apart, avoiding the crowded appearance of many of its competitors. The use of tiered racks creates an amphitheater look that allows customers to see more merchandise. Colored clothing is always displayed in the same sequence: from light to dark. Unlike many stores, Kohl's does not allow employees to straighten up displays throughout the day—that is reserved for night crews. Daytime employees are expected to concentrate on customer service. A 2-P.M. recovery effort, which involves everyone, is the only time displays are straightened during the day.
>
> Source: "Retail," *BusinessWeek.com*, January 8, 2001; "Kohl's Retail Racetrack," *The Wall Street Journal*, March 1, 2000, pp. B1, B6.

Layouts like those used in retailing are not different from those used in the warehousing environment. When employees must "pick" orders to be shipped from hundreds or thousands of products, the layout of the warehouse can make a tremendous difference in travel time for the order picker, which translates into time the customer must wait.

CHAPTER SUMMARY

This chapter has been devoted to two key facility decisions: location and layout. Facility location dictates many of the costs related to a facility. In some cases the impact is on other value attributes as well, including response time and convenience. Location decisions must consider a variety of issues, many of which are quantifiable, but many are purely subjective.

Facility layout, on the other hand, has a dominant impact on the processes within the facility. Layouts provide the structure within which resources must fit. The layout is often a result of strategic decisions that have been made by the business. Layout decisions influence such value attributes as quality, flexibility, and response time. The product-oriented layout is traditionally used to gain efficiencies and reduce per-unit costs. Line balancing is an important component of the product layout decision. Process-oriented layouts, on the other hand, are used to enhance flexibility. Determining where departments are located relative to each other is an important aspect of determining the process-oriented layout. Cellular layouts, which offer a compromise between product-oriented and process-oriented layouts, have increased in popularity as a way to combine efficiency and flexibility.

In virtually any business, the facility is one of the biggest investments. Decisions related to its location and layout affect the financial performance of the firm because of the size of the investment and the impact the decisions have on customer-perceived value.

KEY TERMS

balance delay, 490
bottleneck, 490
cycle time, 490
line balancing, 491
production lead time, 491
work elements, 491

REVIEW QUESTIONS

1. Why are facility decisions important to the financial success of a business?
2. What impact do facility decisions have on value attributes?
3. Why is it usually impossible to identify an objective "optimal" facility location decision?
4. What are the situations that can require location decisions for new facilities?
5. How do process inputs and outputs affect facility location decisions? Describe examples for each.
6. Describe the hierarchy of business location decisions that is often addressed during a facility location decision process.
7. What are the issues that relate to each level of the location decision hierarchy?
8. What is meant by a "multifactor rating" approach to making location decisions? What are the weaknesses of the technique?
9. What types of location decision can be aided by the center-of-gravity technique? How does the center-of-gravity technique work?
10. How can location decisions be aided by decision tree analysis?
11. Give an example of how breakeven analysis might be used to aid in a facility location decision.
12. How can geographic information systems help in the location decision process?
13. What is meant by a process-oriented layout?
14. How does the cut-and-try method of determining the process-oriented layout work?
15. Describe how the systematic layout planning (SLP) approach to layout planning works.
16. What is a product-oriented layout?
17. What is cycle time? How is it determined?
18. What is the objective of line balancing?
19. Why do cellular layouts provide an attractive compromise between product-oriented and process-oriented layouts?

DISCUSSION QUESTIONS

1. Identify a business you are familiar with that has an excellent facility. What parts of the facility contribute to the business's success?
2. Identify a business that has made poor facility decisions. How does the facility affect the success of that business?
3. Select pairs of competing businesses in your community. How does location affect the competitive relationship of these businesses?
4. What are the comparative strengths and weaknesses of process-oriented and product-oriented layouts? Identify an example of each. Are these strengths and weaknesses supported by these examples?
5. Suppose you are on a site selection committee for C.J. Pennyman, a designer retailer. The committee has had difficulty agreeing on a recommendation for a new store. Explain the logic and benefits of multifactor rating and describe how it could be used to help them solve their problem.
6. A colleague at Fotor's Financial Products has criticized a manufacturing client for using line balancing because line balancing is not a precise process. Do you agree or disagree? Explain.
7. Compare and contrast the cut-and-try layout approach and SLP.
8. You have been hired as a consultant by Tasty Ice-Cream, to aid in the search for a new location. An employee of Tasty argues that decision trees should not be used in this case, because Tasty is a risk-averse organization. That is, Tasty does not want to suffer any losses in revenue. The employee also stated that decision trees do not account for potential losses in revenue and therefore should not be used in the decision. Do you agree or disagree? Explain your answer.
9. A consultant to your company stated that a breakeven analysis is the most accurate technique to choosing new site locations and has no flaws associated with it. Do you agree? Explain your answer.
10. For the following businesses, identify the optimal location in your community and provide a justification for your decision.
    a. Bookstore
    b. Drive-through fast-food restaurant
    c. Convenience store
    d. Grocery store
    e. Electronics and computer repair shop
    f. Prison
    g. Auto repair shop
    h. Soft drink bottler
    i. Conversion van factory

PROBLEMS

1. Dan, a recent college graduate, is starting his own computer repair business and wishes to purchase office space for his new company. Use the following table and the multifactor rating method to determine the best location.

Factor	Weight	Site 1	Site 2	Site 3
Cost	0.4	9	8	6
Traffic	0.2	5	6	9
Scalability	0.2	6	8	9
Access to customers	0.2	8	5	9

2. Bryant Bookstore plans to implement an ecommerce website to serve its customers. Bryant wants to use a multifactor rating system to determine the best web-hosting choice and identified five criteria weighted as follows: storage space, 0.1; cost, 0.15; reliability, 0.3; support, 0.2; and speed of site, 0.25. Four web-hosting services are being evaluated. Use the ratings to determine the best choice for Bryant Bookstore.

Criteria	Site 1	Site 2	Site 3	Site 4
Storage	95	90	80	90
Cost	90	85	85	95
Reliability	75	85	95	90
Support	85	90	85	85
Speed	75	90	90	90

3. ShopMor Superstores is planning on building a new warehouse. It currently has four regional distribution centers, with locations and anticipated deliveries as given in the table below. Calculate the center of gravity to determine where the new warehouse should be located. Plot the four distribution centers and the new warehouse.

Regional Centers	X	Y	Deliveries
North	100	200	12
South	120	40	24
East	20	80	18
West	180	140	9

4. Samson Industries would like to locate a new facility close to its suppliers. Data on location and deliveries are presented below. Use the data to calculate the center of gravity. Explain how the new location can help lower transportation costs.

Suppliers	X	Y	Deliveries
Adco	280	200	30
Driam	160	40	20
Moritt	50	80	20
Flamdin	120	160	15

5. Kesey Products asked you to assist in selecting a new location using the center-of-gravity method. The company's largest question centers around the different transportation costs it incurs when delivering products to its customers. Explain how transportation costs could be considered using the center-of-gravity method.

6. Tri-State Bank would like to install a new ATM machine. There are two possible locations for the machine. Location 1 will cost $15,000. There are three possible revenue outcomes: a 45 percent probability of $45,000, a 35 percent probability of $85,000, and a 20 percent probability of $160,000. Location 2 will cost $20,000 with a 30 percent probability of $80,000 in revenue and a 70 percent probability of revenues of $110,000. Use a decision tree to decide which location the bank should use for its ATM.

7. University Pharmacy would like your assistance in solving the decision tree below. Which is the best alternative?

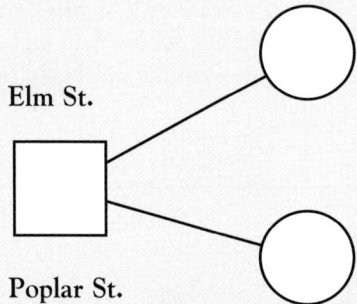

Elm St.
- 20% probability of $60,000 revenue
- 25% probability of $130,000 revenue
- 25% probability of $125,000 revenue
- 30% probability of $90,000 revenue

Poplar St.
- 30% probability of $30,000 revenue
- 45% probability of $110,000 revenue
- 25% probability of $170,000 revenue

8. Snuggle Sweaters is planning on starting a new line of sweaters in a new facility. The company identified three possible location sites, with the respective information for each site given below. Labor and material costs are provided per sweater. Use the information and breakeven analysis to decide which facility should be opened if the company forecasts 7,900 sweaters being sold.

Site	Fixed Costs ($)	Labor Cost ($/hour)	Labor Cost per Sweater ($)	Materials Cost per Sweater ($)	Total Variable Cost per Sweater ($)
1	525,000	6.75	11.00	24.00	35.00
2	540,000	7.3	11.00	22.00	33.00
3	560,000	8.1	9.00	21.00	30.00

9. Doran Design is a successful engineering firm that would like to expand to new markets. It plans on opening a new location at one of three possible sites. Doran anticipates that the new facility will complete 600 jobs per year. Use a breakeven analysis to calculate which location should be chosen.

Site	Fixed Costs/ Year ($)	Labor Costs ($/hour)	Labor Cost/ Job ($)	Materials Cost/ Job ($)	Total Variable Cost/ Job ($)
1	90,000	6.75	84.00	235.00	319.00
2	78,000	7.3	96.00	247.00	343.00
3	70,000	8.1	102.00	242.00	344.00

10. Jacque's Gear, a hockey skate shop, wants to open a new store at one of three possible locations. Use breakeven analysis to find the range of sales volume necessary to minimize costs at each location.

Site	Fixed Costs ($)	Labor Costs ($/hr)	Labor Costs ($)	Materials Costs ($)	Variable Costs ($)
1	105,000	12	700.00	1,100.00	1,800.00
2	130,000	11	600.00	900.00	1,500.00
3	145,000	12	700.00	800.00	1,500.00

11. Morris Machining's plant diagram is below. A distance of 20 feet separates departments that are next to each other. Departments across the center hall from each other are separated by 10 feet, and those that are diagonal from each other are separated by 30 feet. Use the trips matrix and the cut-and-try layout method to create a diagram that would reduce the total distance.

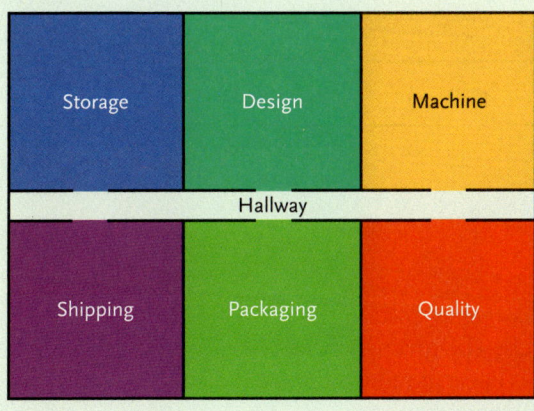

	Storage	Design	Machine	Shipping	Packaging	Quality
Storage	0	45	30	5	15	50
Design		0	60	0	0	10
Machine			0	20	15	50
Shipping				0	65	30
Packaging					0	60
Quality						0

12. Café Dijon has the following layout, trips matrix, and total distance matrix for its restaurant. Use this information to develop a layout that will reduce the total distance.

Trips Matrix

	Delivery	Dining	Restroom	Kitchen
Delivery	0	10	4	20
Dining		0	15	30
Restroom			0	5
Kitchen				0

Distance Matrix

	Delivery	Dining	Restroom	Kitchen
Delivery	0	10	10	20
Dining		0	20	10
Restroom			0	10
Kitchen				0

13. Paisley Products makes custom-designed ties. The company's current layout is shown below. Use the given information and the cut-and-try layout method to design a facility that will reduce the total distance.

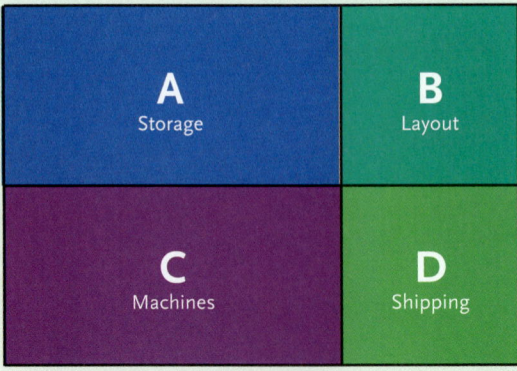

Trips Matrix

	Storage	Layout	Machines	Shipping
Storage	0	50	5	0
Layout		0	25	10
Machines			0	25
Shipping				0

Distance Matrix

	A	B	C	D
A	0	10	5	15
B		0	15	5
C			0	10
D				0

14. Nordic Products would like help in organizing a production layout. The company gave its departments the following closeness desirability ratings. Use this information and the SLP process to identify a good layout.

	Warehouse	Engineering	Production	Shipping
Warehouse		A	I	I
Engineering			E	U
Production				O
Shipping				

15. Use the following closeness desirability ratings and SLP to help Canine Collars Co. determine a layout for a production facility.

	Receiving	Staging	Production	Quality	Shipping
Receiving		A	O	U	A
Staging			A	U	U
Production				I	O
Quality					E
Shipping					

16. Best-Books Bookstore offers customers a large selection of books, their favorite coffees, and a lounge area where they can drink and read. Use SLP to lay out the store according to the given desirability ratings.

	Receiving	Shelves	Food and Drink	Lounge
Receiving		A	O	O
Shelves			E	E
Food & Drink				A
Lounge				

17. Starling Tennis Co. makes tennis rackets. The Baseline is its most popular model. The company anticipates that it needs to produce 80 rackets in an eight-hour day to meet demand. The total amount of work needed per racket is 30 minutes. What is the theoretical minimum number of workstations required to get the total amount of work done?

18. Spirit Recordings makes and sells CDs of colleges' fight songs. Use the information below to group elemental tasks into work centers to form the most balanced line possible. What is the cycle time of the line?

Step	Description	Predecessors	Time (minutes)
1	Set up equipment	0	5
2	Acoustic check	1	15
3	Record	0	20
4	Playback	3	30
5	Package	2, 4	5

19. Saf-Home manufactures door handles. It anticipates a need for 68 handles per day to satisfy demand. The following nine processes are involved in the manufacturing process. Use the information and the line balancing technique to create a diagram of the work centers needed and steps included in each work center to meet demand.

Step	Description	Predecessors	Time (minutes)
1	Mold	0	1
2	Shave	1	0.5
3	Drill	1, 2	1
4	Size	0	2
5	Grind	4	4
6	Paint	1, 2, 3	3.5
7	Lubricate	4, 5	1
8	Inspect Fit	1, 2, 3, 4, 5, 6, 7	4
9	Package	1, 2, 3, 4, 5, 6, 7, 8	3

20. Frame-N-Sav makes picture frames for the posters and prints that the store sells. The store needs to make 10 frames a day in its eight hours of available time to satisfy its customers. Each frame takes two hours to make. What is the theoretical minimum number of workstations required to get the total amount of work done?

INTERACTIVE ANALYSIS 13.1

THE CENTER-OF-GRAVITY INTERACTIVE MODEL

www.
OperationsNow
.com

The Center-of-Gravity Interactive Model is accessed through Chapter 13 of the OperationsNow.com website. It is based on a location decision involving a central distribution center (shown in red) that must provide shipments to four retail destinations (shown in blue). It provides a visual example of the center-of-gravity model. The user of this model has very simple inputs.

As system inputs, the location of any of the shipping destinations can be changed by entering coordinates into the table or by simply dragging the destination on the map. In addition, the quantity of deliveries per week can also be changed. The default values are:

Destination	X Coordinate	Y Coordinate	Weekly Quantity
D1	20	20	800
D2	30	50	900
D3	50	40	200
D4	77	39	100

Experiment 1: System Fundamentals
1. Set the parameters to their default values.
   a. The distribution center is currently located close to destinations D1 and D2, and a significant distance from D4. Explain why this occurs.
   b. Move D4 30 miles to the south, from (80, 50) to (80, 20). How much does the distribution center move?
2. Set the parameters back to their defaults.
   a. Record the location of the distribution center. Move D2 40 miles north, from (30, 50) to (30, 90). What happens to the distribution center?
   b. Set the parameters back to their defaults. Change the quantity of D2 from 900 to 200. Again, move D2 40 miles north, from (30, 50) to (30, 90). What happens to the distribution center? Explain why the result is different from that in 2a above.

Experiment 2: Exploring the Impact of Shipment Quantity
1. Set the parameters back to their default values.
   a. Currently, destination D1 requires four times as many shipments as D3. Move D1 40 miles to the east, from (20, 20) to (60, 20). What is the impact on the location of the distribution center? What are its new coordinates? How far did it move?
   b. Set the parameters back to their defaults. Move destination D3 40 miles to the east, from (50, 40) to (90, 40). What is the impact on the location of the distribution center? What are its new coordinates? How far did it move?
2. Set the parameters back to their default values.
   a. Move D4 40 miles to the south, from (80, 50) to (80, 10). What is the impact on the distribution center location?
   b. Move D2 40 miles to the south, from (30, 50) to (30,10). What is the impact on the distribution center location?

c. Based on the two previous experiments, what is the relationship between quantity of shipments and the effect of the destination location on the distribution center location?

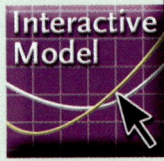

INTERACTIVE ANALYSIS 13.2

THE PROCESS-ORIENTED LAYOUT INTERACTIVE MODEL

The Process-Oriented Layout Interactive Model is accessed through Chapter 13 of the OperationsNow.com website. It offers an interactive approach to the analysis of transportation requirements for a simple six-department facility layout scenario in a print shop environment. User input parameters in this model are restricted to the demand for each of three products and the locations of each of six departments. The default values for demand are 100 units/month for product X, product Y, and product Z. The routings for each of the three products are provided. The number of trips required between departments is a function of the monthly demand for a product and the product's routing. So, if a particular product routing specifies transporting the order from paper storage to printing, and there was a demand of 200 orders per month, there would be 200 trips from paper to printing per month resulting from that product. The other products may add more, depending on their routings.

Total distances are computed as the number of trips between two departments per month multiplied by the distance between the two departments, as determined by a particular layout alternative. Departments can be moved from one location "room" to another by simply dragging the department to another location. When a department is dragged to another room, the department already there moves to the room just vacated. By swapping departments in this manner, any layout desired can be created. The distance and cost matrices update automatically with each move. In addition, the cells in the total distance matrix light up to show any distances changed by a move. If new demands are entered, the "update" function recalculates the distance and cost outcomes.

Experiment 1: System Fundamentals

1. the default settings are demand X = 100, demand Y = 100, demand Z = 100. The default layout is

Location	Department
A	Paper storage
B	Design
C	Packaging
D	Printing
E	Service
F	Binding

a. Given the routings presented, identify a department that you think should be as close as possible to the paper storage department. Does "as close as possible" mean adjacent to each other or across the hall from each other? Why do you think the two departments should be as close as possible to each other? Make a change to the layout so that they are actually as close together as they can be. What happens to the total distance for the layout when this move is made?

b. Identify another department that should be close to paper storage. Why do you think it should be close to printing? Move it as close as possible, while maintaining the relationship between paper and the department you identified for 1a. Is the total distance improved again? If so, by how much?

c. What happens if the two departments you identified to be close to printing swap places? Is the total distance improved? Explain why it is more important for one than the other to be closest to paper.

2. Start with the layout as it was at the end of Experiment 1 above.
   a. Record the layout. What is the total monthly distance for it?
   b. Examine the routings. Can you identify any other changes that might improve it? Try them. What is the best layout you can come up with? What is the total distance? Explain, in terms of the demand and the routings, why your changes resulted in an improvement.

3. Set the layout back to the default setting.
   a. What is the total distance for product X? Identify the layout that minimizes the total distance for X. What is it?
   b. Identify the layout that minimizes the total distance for Y. What is it?
   c. Identify the layout that minimizes the total distance for Z. What is it?

Experiment 2: The Impact of Routing on the Need for Departments to Be Close

1. Set the demand to the defaults of X = 100, Y = 100, and Z = 100. The routings for the three products are

   X: Design → Paper Storage → Binding → Printing → Packaging
   Y: Design → Paper Storage → Printing → Service → Binding → Packaging
   Z: Paper Storage → Binding → Service → Packaging

   a. Examine the three routings closely. From the routings, create a matrix similar to the following, and rate the importance of departments being close to each other. Use the SLP notation from this chapter.

	Paper Storage	Design	Binding	Printing	Service	Packaging
Paper storage	———					
Design	———	———				
Binding	———	———	———			
Printing	———	———	———	———		
Service	———	———	———	———	———	
Packaging	———	———	———	———	———	———

Explain why you came up with the ratings you have.

b. Create guidelines for arranging the layout by matching each SLP rating with one of the following potential department relationships:
- Immediately across from each other
- Immediately next to each other
- Diagonal across and one over from each other
- Opposite ends of the same side
- Diagonal opposite ends of the hall

2. Make the layout to meet your guidelines.
   a. Can more than one layout be created to meet your guidelines? What are the other layouts that satisfy your guidelines? When you actually arrange them, do they all have the same total distance?

Experiment 3: The Effects of Product Mix

1. The composition of demand and the proportions of the various products can have a significant impact on transportation of goods from one department or work center to another. This results from the various routings needed to produce those products. Obviously, in a dynamic environment with frequent changes in the product mix, the layout cannot be changing all of the time to keep up. However, when identifying the best layout, it is important to consider the layout that will best meet the most likely mix of products.

Arrange the layout as below:

Location	Department
A	Design
B	Binding
C	Service
D	Paper storage
E	Printing
F	Packaging

   a. This layout is very good for the product mix of X = 100, Y = 100, Z = 100. Change the product demands to X = 100, Y = 250, Z = 100. What is the total distance for this product mix with this layout?
   b. How can the layout be improved? Identify the best layout for this product mix. What is the total distance for the best layout? Explain why the improvements worked.
   c. Identify the worst possible layout for this product mix. What is the total distance? How does it compare to the best layout for this product mix?

INTERACTIVE ANALYSIS 13.3

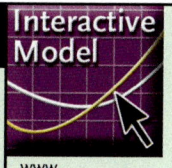

www.
OperationsNow
.com

THE LINE BALANCING INTERACTIVE MODEL

The Line Balancing Interactive Model is accessed through Chapter 13 of the OperationsNow.com website. It provides a useful laboratory for experimenting with a simple, five-work-center production line. It is made even simpler by the lack of variability in work center processing times. This simplicity enables the observer to see precisely how balance among work center processing times can affect resources in a product-oriented layout.

The Line Balancing Interactive Model offers the user only one parameter to change: the processing times for the work centers. The input rate is controlled by the slowest work center. The output rate is also dictated by the slowest work center through its determination of the cycle time. Each work center's processing time can be set at any time, from one to eight minutes per unit. The key output measures include the utilization for each work center, the system utilization, and the output of the system.

In addition to the input parameter of processing time, the user has two controls of the simulation itself. The first is control of the speed of the clock running the simulation. Speeding up the clock simply means that the simulation clock runs faster. In addition, the pause button allows the user to temporarily stop the simulation and resume it again where it left off with the start button. The stop button stops the simulation and resets it to the starting condition.

Experiment 1: System Fundamentals

1. Set the processing times for all work centers at two minutes. Start the simulation and run it for 100 simulator minutes.
   a. How many units were completed? Why did the system not complete a quantity equal to 100 divided by the processing time?
2. Reset the processing times to four minutes at all work centers. Start the simulation and run it for 100 simulator minutes.
   a. How many units were completed? Develop a formula for predicting the units that will be produced for any processing time, when all work centers process at the same rate. Include the effect of the system filling up with material.
3. Change the processing time of each work center to another setting. Use your formula to predict your results. Run the simulator using those settings.
   a. Is your formula correct?

Experiment 2: Balance Delay

1. Balance delay, as described in Chapter 13, is caused by an imbalance in the processing times of the work centers. It results in less-than-optimal use of resources. Work centers are idle as a result, and flow of inventory can become intermittent. Set all of the work center processing times at two minutes, with the exception of work center 4, which should be set at three minutes. Run the simulation for 100 simulator minutes at the normal speed.
   a. What is the cycle time? What is the output after 100 simulator minutes? Explain why system utilization is now at 73.3 percent.
   b. Change the processing time for work center 4 to four minutes. What is the utilization for the entire system? Explain the result.

2. Set the processing times at two minutes for work centers 1, 3, and 5 and four minutes for work centers 2 and 4.
   a. What is the utilization for each work center? What is the system utilization? Explain the result.
   b. What is the relationship between the utilization of the fastest work centers and the utilization of the system?

SELECTED REFERENCES

Bowersox, D. J., Closs, D. J, and Cooper, M. B. *Supply Chain Logistics Management.* New York: McGraw-Hill/Irwin, 2002.

Francis, R. L., and White, J. A. *Facility Layout and Location: An Analytical Approach.* Englewood Cliffs, NJ: Prentice Hall, 1992.

Kotkin, J. *The New Geography.* New York: Random House, 2000.

Schmenner, R. W. *Making Business Location Decisions.* Englewood Cliffs, NJ: Prentice Hall, 1982.

Shapiro, Jeremy F. *Modeling the Supply Chain.* Pacific Grove, CA: Duxbury Press, 2001.

ENDNOTES

1. "Lost in the Translation," *The Wall Street Journal,* February 12, 2001, p. R12.
2. "When Deciding Where to Put a Business, Companies Better Not Ignore the Obvious: Where Would Employees Like to Live?" *The Wall Street Journal,* October 15, 2001, p. R14.
3. J. Kotkin, *The New Geography* (New York: Random House, 2000).
4. Ibid.
5. "The Rockies Emerge as Pocket of Prosperity in a Slowing Economy," *The Wall Street Journal,* June 6, 2001, pp. A1, A8.
6. R. Muther, *Systematic Layout Planning* (Boston: Industrial Education Institute, 1961).
7. R. L. Francis and J. A. White, *Facility Layout and Location: An Analytical Approach* (Englewood Cliffs, NJ: Prentice Hall, 1992).

CHAPTER 13 Facilities 513

OperationsNow.com LEARNING ACTIVITIES

CHAPTER ENHANCEMENT RESOURCES
- Esources
- Reel Operations Video Clips
- Interactive Models
- Excel Tutors
- Supplementary Readings
- Links to Operations On Site Companies

OM EXPLORATION
- Check It Out
- OM in Action
- Online Business Tours
- Letters from the Top
- Putting It All Together: Virtual Case Studies
- Additional Readings

The resource/profit model places customer relationships as the fifth of five resources that are used to create value. Customer relationships are included as an operations resource for two primary reasons. First, businesses invest heavily in developing customer relationships because of the financial return associated with customer loyalty and, as with any other investment, business owners expect financial return. Second, the relationships a business has with its customers are dominated by experiences customers have, and those experiences have their roots in processes.

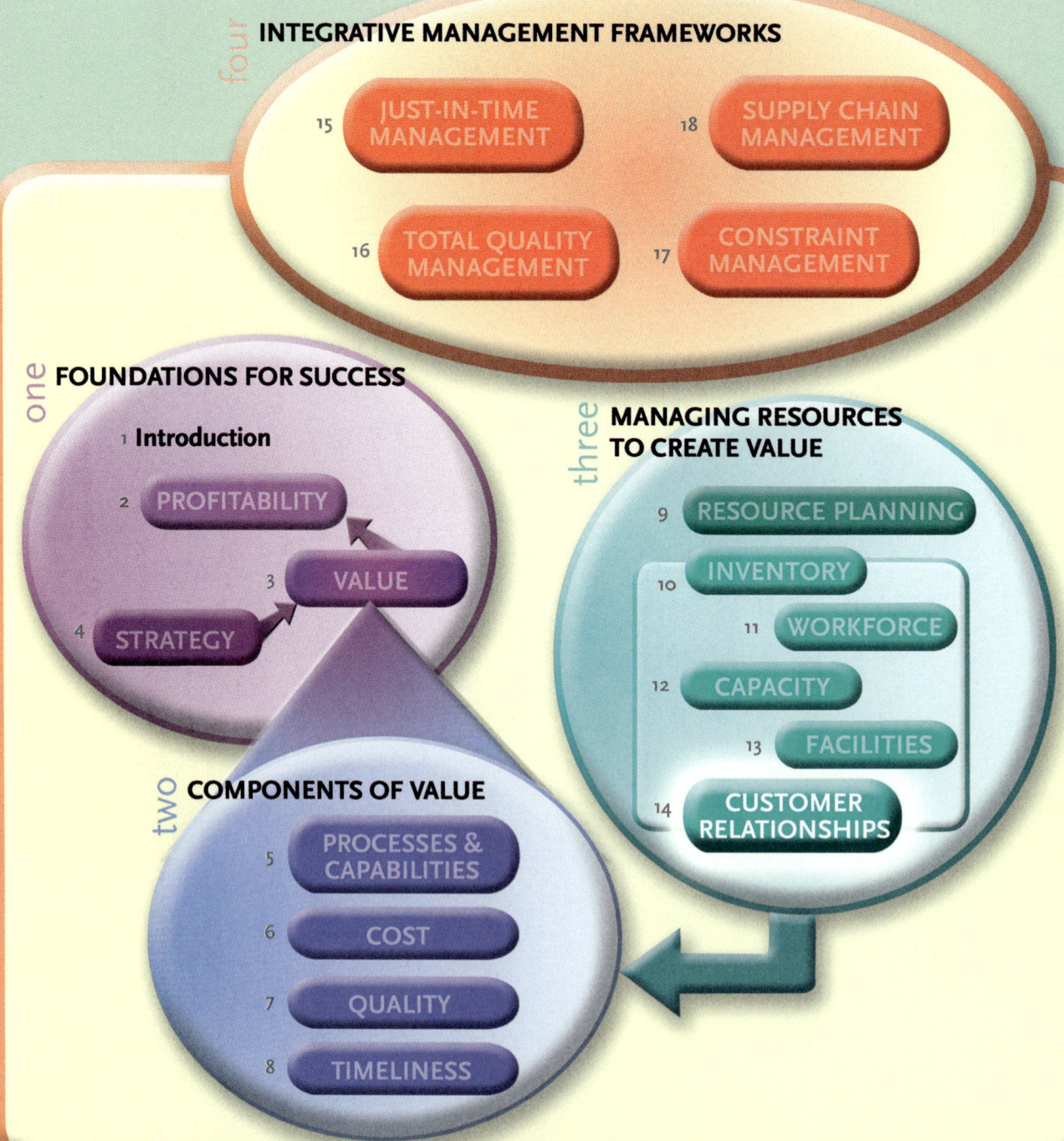

CHAPTER 14

Customer Relationships

LEARNING OBJECTIVES

Upon completion of Chapter 14, you should be able to

- Describe the importance of both sides of the customer relationship.
- Explain the four approaches to extending customer relationships.
- Describe the four phases of customer loyalty and the vulnerabilities of each.
- Describe how profitability is enhanced by customer loyalty.
- Explain how customer relationship management enhances the value of customer relationships and increases profitability.
- Describe how customer relationship management enhances the productivity of all other operations resources.
- Describe how customer relationship management enhances other interactions between the customer and the business.

Introduction: The Value of Strong Customer Relationships
Perceived Value: A Prerequisite to a Relationship
Extending Customer Relationships
Customer Loyalty and Profitability
Customer Loyalty: A Cycle of Value Enhancement
Customer Relationship Management: Investing in the Valuable Customers
Chapter Summary

INTERNET RESOURCES

 Excel Tutors provide annotated spreadsheets for every solved problem that automatically load Excel.

 Esources provide an online version of the more traditional boxed insert.

 Reel Videos provide streaming video footage for company applications of chapter concepts.

 Interactive Models provide an experimental environment for quantitative concepts and simulations.

INTRODUCTION

The Value of Strong Customer Relationships

All business resources should be utilized with the creation of value in mind. Customer perceptions of the value created can be measured by the strength of the relationship between the company and the customer. The customer relationship that develops, partly as a result of that value, requires a substantial investment to maintain. Its presence, however, increases the customer's perception of value, and for this reason it is presented in Exhibit 14.1 as the fifth of five resources managed to create value.

The relationship a firm has with its customers goes beyond merely providing them with value. A relationship is two-sided, and the relationship between a customer and a business must include value the business offers the customer and value the customer offers the business. Just as companies tailor the level of value offered to customers to strengthen their relationship, customers also offer different levels of value. The interaction between the value offered by a customer and the value offered by the business creates the basis for profitability.

A business cannot have a relationship with a group of customers, however. Its relationships are with individuals. Customer relationship management must go beyond strategic objectives that identify a target group of customers with a particular prioritization of value attributes. The relationship must be with a person, not with a group of people who share a common characteristic. This chapter examines how the business interacts with the individual customer, develops that relationship, and then uses that relationship to leverage greater profitability through operations.

The importance of customer relationships increases as competition for customers increases. Many businesses envision each customer as a potential long-term source of income, rather than as a one-time purchaser. One of the early champions of this concept was Carl Sewell.[1] In his story of how he became the largest Cadillac dealer in the United States, he stressed the development of ongoing, long-term relationships with his customers.

It may surprise you, but long-term customer relationships result from processes and experiences, not from what company spokespersons say. Talk doesn't do it. Satisfaction with the processes and experiences surrounding a purchased product is necessary for a long-term relationship, but it isn't sufficient. Also insufficient are the processes and experiences surrounding a purchased service. Experiences must surpass merely meeting customer expectations: They must delight the customer to cement a long-term relationship.

For a car dealership, a long-term relationship might result in the purchase of 15 automobiles over a 30-year period and a stream of cash that could approach half a million dollars. From a profitability standpoint, it is easy to think, "That gives us 15 times as much as we would have gotten from only one sale." But from a profitability standpoint, it gives us more than that. One person who buys 15 automobiles over a 30-year period is far more profitable than 15 automobiles bought by 15 different people over the same 30 years.

If the customer who returns consistently is very profitable, there must also be customers who are far less profitable. There must also be some who aren't profitable at all. This brings us to two objectives of customer relationship management. The first is determining what the individual customer values. The second is determining the value of the individual customer. If either is missing, there is no relationship. In the long run, both must exist for the business to survive.

EXHIBIT 14.1 The Role of Customer Relationships in the Resource/Profit Model

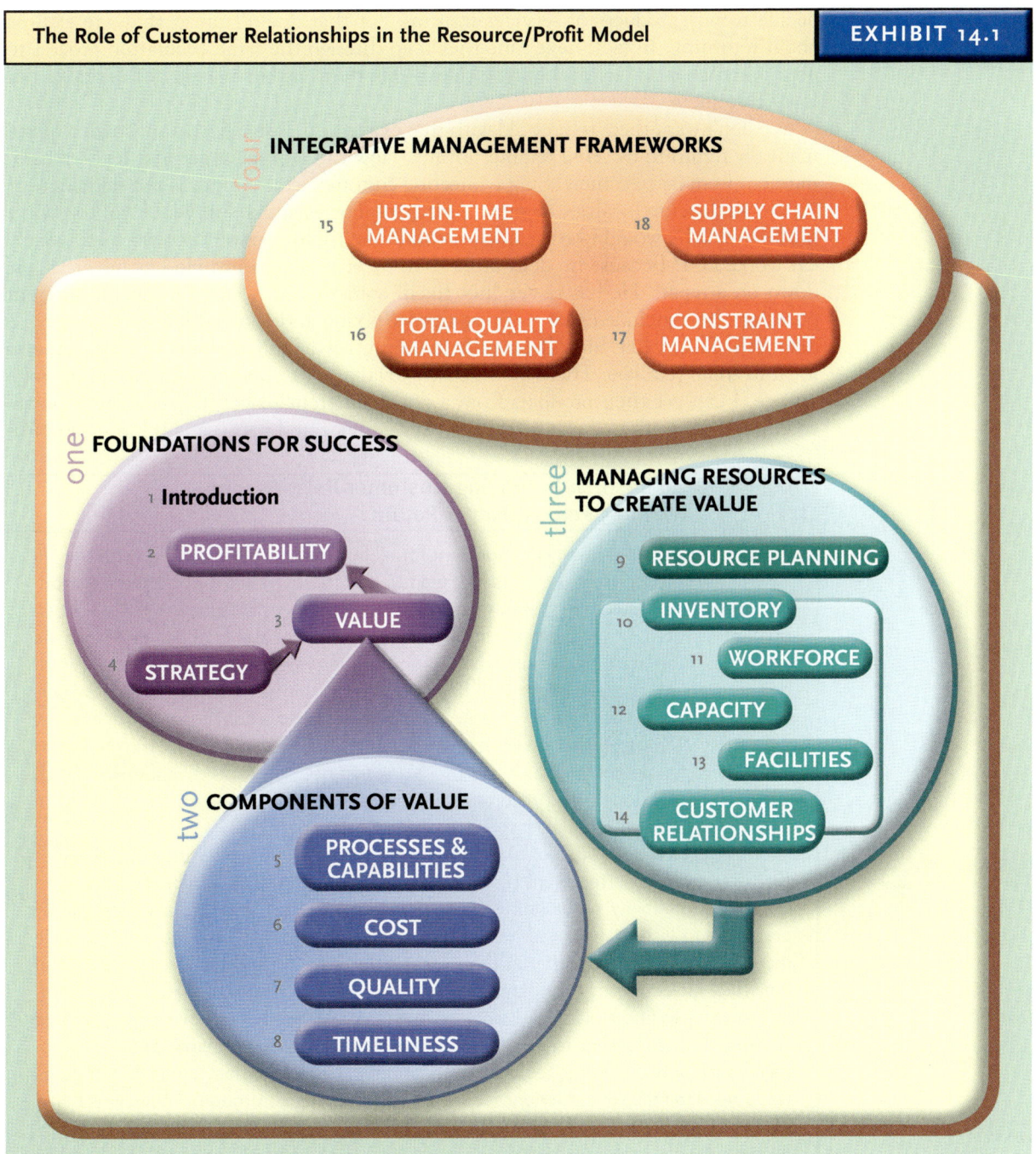

PERCEIVED VALUE: A PREREQUISITE TO A RELATIONSHIP

We speak of value often: how value attributes are defined by the customer, how customers define it differently, and how they define it in terms of product and service characteristics that are most important to them. The product and service characteristics originate with inventory, workforce, capacity, and facilities. Customers may decide to buy products or services from us, but that doesn't mean they are excited about returning. In fact, next time they'll go through the same evaluation process to determine what to buy and maybe they'll buy from us, but maybe not. They're not loyal customers.

We don't want them to proceed with that evaluation. Instead, we want them to automatically return to us. That requires loyalty. How can a business get that level of commitment from its customers? Simply meeting customer expectations is not sufficient.

We all develop loyalties to some businesses. For example, I'm very loyal to my car mechanic. Why would I be loyal when sometimes I have to wait two weeks to get my car worked on? Because he does more than meet expectations. He has never let me down on a repair. He has never "not fixed" something. In fact, on several different occasions he concluded that nothing needed fixing and charged me nothing for the diagnosis. Plus, I like him. If I didn't like him, I wouldn't be loyal to him. I'm also loyal to some retailers. Those that get my loyalty have gone beyond providing good service. I can get their products from a dozen different places, maybe even at lower cost. I'm loyal to them because they give me advice and because it is fun to do busi-

Ski Resorts: Improving Customer Relationships When 85 Percent Never Return

Customer loyalty is important for all businesses, but particularly for the ski resort industry, which is engaged in a battle to improve customer relationships. The industry has been plagued with a lack of growth since 1978—about 50 million visitors per year, despite improved skis that are easier to control and the growth in snowboarding, which accounts for about 25 percent of those visits. (Without snowboarding there might well have been a substantial decline.) In fact, 85 percent of first-time skiers never return. No other business would tolerate such a low return rate. Some experts believe that the amount of planning, packing, traveling, and lifting of heavy ski gear makes a trip to a ski resort not only expensive, but too much work. The operations of ski resorts require vacationers to get up early and stand in lines for equipment rentals, lessons, lift tickets, lifts, and meals.

Intrawest Corp., owner of ski resorts at Stratton Mountain (Vermont), Whistler (British Columbia), Tremblant (Quebec), and Copper Mountain (Colorado), hopes to improve profitability by boosting resort attendance. After studying a typical family preparing to visit an Intrawest resort, and following them with a video camera while there, the company learned that their vacation was hectic and hard work. Results of the study include recommendations to provide pet-sitting services based on the family's inability to find a place for its dog to stay. In addition, the firm plans to offer large seasonal storage lockers, to eliminate much of the packing and transportation of equipment, and more child-oriented accommodations. One of the most significant findings was a need to make the experience more social, including communal dining, which had existed at many ski resorts, and a "village-centered" model. The village-centered business model has proven to be successful for Intrawest. After its adoption, reservations grew at a 76 percent rate during the year from March 31, 2000, to March 31, 2001. Sales of property at resort sites grew as well. In the 90 days preceding July 1, 2001, Intrawest sold $233 million in property. Some 70 percent of the units offered for sale were sold. Prices per square foot were up 11 percent over the previous year.

Source: "In Pursuit of Hassle-Free Slopes," *The Wall Street Journal*, March 16, 2001, pp. B1, B4; "Intrawest Reports an 18% Increase in Nine-Month Income from Continuing Operations," http://biz.yahoo.com/prnews/010710/va293.html, May 14, 2001; "Intrawest Sells Record US$233 Million in Real Estate in Past 90 Days" http://biz.yahoo.com/prnews/010710/va293.html, July 10, 2001.

ness with them. They make money from me and I enjoy doing business with them, so it is a good relationship. We both benefit from the relationship, and that's what makes it successful. If I don't enjoy doing business with them, it's not a good relationship for me. If they don't profit from me, it's not a good relationship for them. Should I try to negotiate prices that eliminate their profit? No, because they need to profit to stay in business.

EXTENDING CUSTOMER RELATIONSHIPS

Brown describes four different approaches to extending the customer relationship. Exhibit 14.2 briefly describes each.[2]

Marriott has been a leader in the use of customer relationship management as a means of increasing the value provided to customers by anticipating their needs and satisfying them.

Win Back or Save

The win-back or save situation creates an interesting dilemma for management. In this situation, a customer has defected or is about to defect. Recovery policies and actions play a role in the win-back or save effort. A recovery provides the basis for a save. A win-back effort is much more difficult and much more costly than the recovery, however. The win-back is necessary when the recovery or save doesn't work or is never attempted. Studies indicate that win-backs are more successful if contact is made within the first week after the defection. Some customers are very susceptible to win-back efforts, whereas others, known as "churners," switch frequently no matter what efforts are expended to retain them.

Information available on customers helps identify those whose usage rate is dropping as potential targets for saving before they actually defect and a win-back is needed. If a change in a customer's usage is detected, an intervention to save that customer might be worthwhile. The change in usage must be detectable, however, and

EXHIBIT 14.2

Extending Relationships	
Win Back or Save:	A customer is on the verge of defecting, or has already defected to a competitor. This is an effort to win the customer back or keep him or her from leaving.
Prospecting:	A customer currently patronizes a competitor or patronizes no one. This is an effort to get a new customer.
Loyalty Building:	A current customer is deemed to be a valuable customer. This is a customized "loyalty" program created for this customer.
Cross-Sell/Upsell:	A current customer is deemed amenable to further purchases. This is an effort to sell the person more.

this requires accurate usage data. This type of action is frequently taken by credit card companies when they suspect a customer is about to defect. Usage data may indicate that a customer paid off a large amount of balance, which may indicate that the customer is about to close the account. A large payment often triggers an offer of reduced interest rates to save the customer.

Prospecting

Prospecting is an attempt to win new customers. Segmentation and selectivity are important components of any prospecting effort. **Segmentation** is the identification of different types of potential customers and is necessary to provide focus for the effort. Without it, the effort won't succeed at an acceptable rate, or too much money will be spent trying to attract customers who aren't good targets. Selectivity involves identifying what the customer wants and determining how valuable the customer is. Selectivity, for example, can reduce the impact of payment defaults or bad credit. The goal is to target customers to increase the likelihood that new customer acquisition efforts bear fruit. We should not target customers whom we might regret having, for example, customers with bad credit.

Loyalty Building

Loyalty building is initiated with value-based segmentation. In other words, we determine which customers are the most valuable, and then decide what can be spent to build their loyalty.

If customer loyalty were easy to achieve, everybody would have it. Loyalty is more than a customer just patronizing a particular business. Loyalty withstands the efforts of competitors to get the customer to switch. Oliver provides an excellent definition that fits B2C as well as B2B relationships:

> *Customer loyalty is a deeply held commitment to rebuy or repatronize a preferred product or service consistently in the future, despite situational influences and marketing efforts having the potential to cause switching behavior.*[3]

Oliver describes four phases of customer loyalty.[4] Phase one is **cognitive loyalty**. Cognitive loyalty is not very strong because it is based on information rather than experiences. Since it is based on information (information about price is an example), more attractive information about a competitor can cause the customer to switch. A better sales pitch promoting lower costs or better quality may be sufficient to overcome cognitive loyalty.

Phase two is **affective loyalty**. Affective loyalty is ingrained in the customer's mind as affect and not just based on cognition. Affect is anchored. In their minds customers have linked the business to positive outcomes they've experienced. When they think of the business, they don't recall things that have been said to them, as in the cognitive phase; they recall actual outcomes they've experienced. Affective loyalty is more difficult for competitors to change, but intermittent periods of dissatisfaction from poor outcomes may be sufficient to result in switching.

Oliver describes phase three loyalty as **conative loyalty**. Conative loyalty occurs when a customer has a deep behavioral commitment to buy from a particular business. Experiences have created an automatic association with the product or service. At this stage, the behavior has become habitual.

The fourth and final phase of customer loyalty is **action loyalty**. In this phase, loyalty is sustained by commitment and by the force of inertia. The customer has psy-

> **A Case Study in Losing Customer Loyalty**
>
> Most retailers have gone through periods of declining sales. Virtually all retailers must cope with defectors. The Gap's combination of style, quality, and price made it the most successful apparel retailer for years. Few businesses, however, have gone from being so popular to losing so many customers as The Gap in 2000 and 2001. Net income for the first nine months of 2001 dropped 96 percent compared with the previous year.
>
> Anecdotal evidence seems clear. Apparel shoppers—not noted for loyalty—had a very simple reason to defect. The Gap no longer carried the clothing that had attracted them in the first place. Most customers have the same complaint: The Gap has moved to styles and colors that are for adolescents, not for the 20- to 30-year-olds who had been the store's mainstay. Glitter jeans and "avant-garde" looks are not what 20-somethings can wear to work. So, for many customers, The Gap no longer offered the styles they wanted.
>
> Quality also became suspect. Customers complain about a reduced level of quality. This was instigated somewhat by The Gap's introduction of the bargain alternative, Old Navy. As customers realized that the company has lower-quality clothing made for the Old Navy chain, they began to suspect that the quality had been downgraded at The Gap as well. Gap officials deny that they reduced quality.
>
> Old Navy's cost leader strategy created huge sales at first, but very quickly competitors matched and even beat their prices. A February 2000 study showed that featured products at Target were 27 percent below Old Navy's prices.
>
> The lesson is a strong one. Many customers are loyal, but they are creatures of habit (the conative stage). For them, dissatisfaction will mean defection. For a retailer with a good reputation, delivering the goods is necessary to maintain the reputation it desires.
>
> Source: "Gap's Image Is Wearing Out," *The Wall Street Journal*, December 6, 2001, pp. B1, B4.

chological "ownership" in the business, and even periods of dissatisfaction are not likely to result in switching.

One of the worst mistakes a business can make is to force a customer to try out the competition. An examination of the phases of loyalty provides the reason why it is so dangerous. At any of the four loyalty phases, if we *force* the customer to try out the competition, we've interrupted the loyalty development process. Stage one is based on information. Forcing the customer to go to a competitor gives the customer new information. At stage two, periods of satisfaction may disrupt the loyalty-building process. If customers are denied what they seek, they will undoubtedly be dissatisfied. Even at phases three and four, when the customer is committed to buying from the company, if the company doesn't have what they seek, or is too busy to provide it, customers may have no choice but to go elsewhere. If the new experience is good, a customer's loyalty may change.

Exhibit 14.3 provides a model of the four phases of loyalty, the actions that serve to maintain customers, and the threats or "vulnerabilities" that can result in switching. Notice that for the second, third, and fourth phases, a "trial" use of a competitor is a vulnerability. If a business forces its customers to seek out a trial use of the competition, the business itself is to blame for the lost customer.

In services with employee–customer interaction **interpersonal loyalty** can come into play. In this environment, loyalty can be a much stronger force because a relationship

EXHIBIT 14.3 Phases of Loyalty, Sustainers, and Vulnerabilities

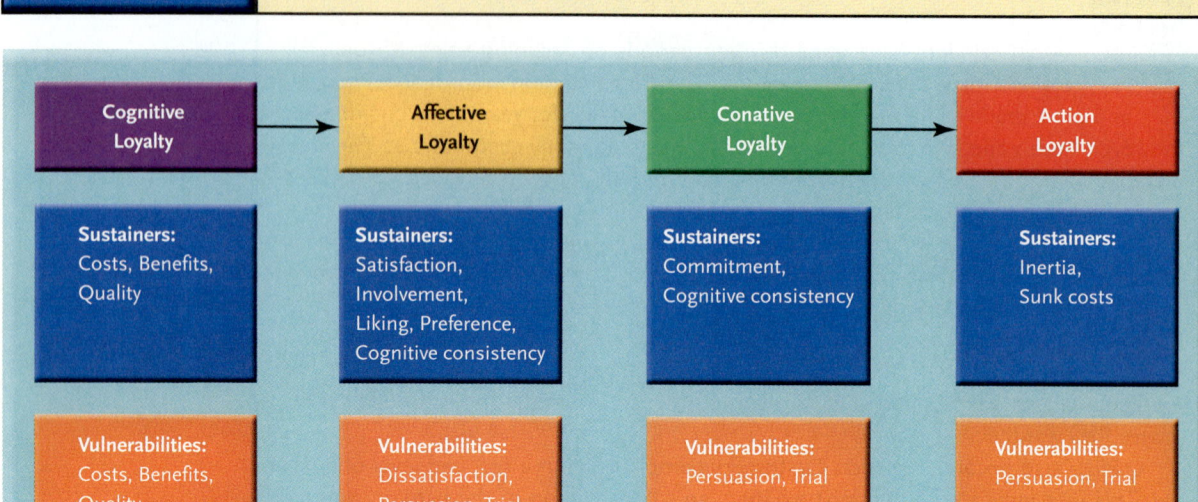

Source: Adapted from R. L. Oliver, *Satisfaction: A Behavioral Perspective on the Consumer* (New York: McGraw-Hill/Irwin, 1997), p. 394.

with an individual can be much stronger than a relationship with a business. Customers have additional expectations for this type of relationship, and when these expectations are met, the loyalty is enhanced.

Despite the importance of loyalty and recognition of how it develops, research has not shown that some customers are more likely to be loyal than others. Loyalty appears to result from prices, quality, services, and experience, not from customer characteristics. Loyalty must be earned with each customer.

Even very loyal customers will defect if they have no choice. Forcing a customer to try out the competition is the first step toward losing that customer. Once experience is gained elsewhere, new loyalty can begin to develop.

> **Increased Loyalty through Increased Convenience**
>
> Small changes in customer processes can change a strategy into one that prioritizes speed and convenience. Mobil Oil, now a part of ExxonMobil, began an effort to do just that in 1996 when it began to develop the Speedpass wireless transaction system. Mobil Speedpass is a small tag that attaches to a keychain. Users of the Speedpass follow these simple directions:
>
> 1. Wave the Key Tag at the Speedpass pump panel marked "Place Speedpass Here."
> 2. The pump recognizes you electronically and instantly activates.
> 3. Choose your grade of gas and start pumping.
> 4. You'll be billed automatically to the credit card of your choice.
>
> By 2001, Mobil Speedpass had 5 million users. The key advantage is a reduction of the time required to purchase gas. This is achieved by eliminating the need for the customer to get a credit card from a wallet or purse and eliminating the credit card approval time. Speedpass holders average one visit per month more than nonusers. Increased revenues have justified the $15,000 investment in the technology required of each station.
>
> Unfortunately, the technology is easy to copy. Other companies sell the technology, and Shell is testing it at several stations. Mobil has been down this road before. It invested heavily in "pay-at-the-pump" technology in the early 1990s and others simply copied it. It is now leveraging the customer relationships achieved through the use of the technology, rather than the technology itself. It considers its key assets the customer database and the brand. Speedpass was accepted at 400 Chicago-area McDonald's restaurants in the fall of 2001. ExxonMobil is depending on the network effect. The more users, the more valuable Speedpass becomes. As the number of users increases, other businesses become more interested. As more businesses use Speedpass, more customers will be interested. Unlike many programs designed to increase customer loyalty, Speedpass offers no financial incentive, just convenience. The goal is simply to make everything happen faster.
>
> Source: "Pay as You Go," *Fast Company*, November 2001 (online edition), http://www.wallisco.com/speedpass/.

Cross-Sell/Upsell

Cross-sell/upsell efforts strive to identify complementary or enhanced products or services that would interest a customer. The objective is to determine increased levels of value that the customer would move up to. The efforts are critical because the customers already have a relationship with the firm. The cost of the sale is much less than selling the same product or service through prospecting because less effort needs to be spent. Customers who accept cross-sell or upsell increase their profitability to the business.

While the objective of all four approaches is to extend the length of the relationship, the cost per success is different for each approach. The results of PricewaterhouseCoopers research summarized in Exhibit 14.4 show clearly why the duration of the relationship is so important.

Profitability is enhanced with improved customer retention. Profitability is a function of inputs and outputs, both of which are affected by customer loyalty. A simple example provides clear picture of the benefits. Suppose a particular service costs $200 per year. Using the profitability enhancement figures from Exhibit 14.4, and focusing on a customer group of 10 people, we see that customers who do not stay for a full year incur a financial loss. When they are retained for an entire year, their profitability becomes positive, but on a cumulative basis, they are still not "in the black." As they stay on each additional year, however, their profitability increases on a percentage basis *and* their cumulative profitability grows dramatically. This is illustrated numerically in Exhibit 14.5 and graphically in Exhibit 14.6

EXHIBIT 14.4 Profitability and Customer Retention

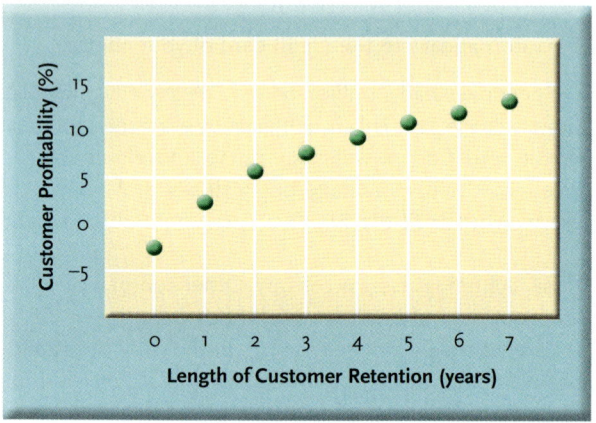

Source: Adapted from Brown, S. A., *Customer Relationship Management*, Toronto: John Wiley & Sons, 2000.

EXHIBIT 14.5 Effect of Customer Retention on Profitability

Customer Retention Level	Service Cost ($)	Profitability (%)	Yearly Profit ($)	Cumulative Profit ($)
Year 0 profit for 10 customers who stay 0 years	$200	−0.03	−600	−600
Year 1 profit for 10 customers who stay 1 year	200	0.015	300	−300
Year 2 profit for 10 customers who stay 2 years	200	0.06	1,200	900
Year 3 profit for 10 customers who stay 3 years	200	0.07	1,400	2,300
Year 4 profit for 10 customers who stay 4 years	200	0.09	1,800	4,100
Year 5 profit for 10 customers who stay 5 years	200	0.108	2,160	6,260
Year 6 profit for 10 customers who stay 6 years	200	0.115	2,300	8,560
Year 7 profit for 10 customers who stay 7 years	200	0.135	2,700	11,260

Graphical Representation of Cumulative Profit — EXHIBIT 14.6

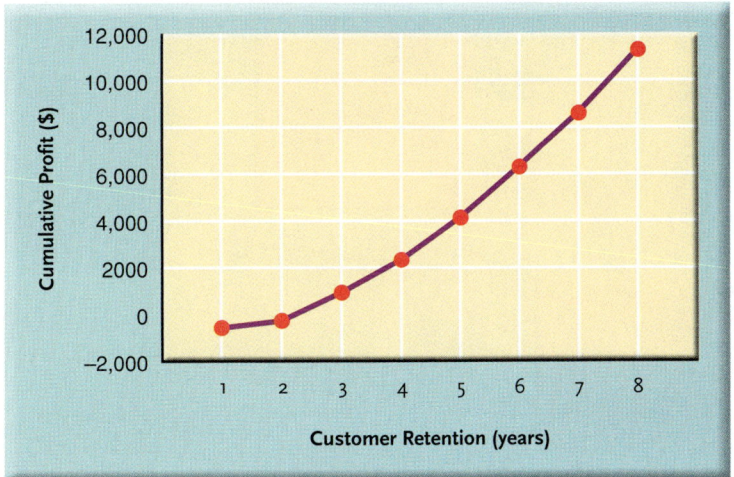

CUSTOMER LOYALTY AND PROFITABILITY

New-customer acquisition, which is the first phase of obtaining customers, is usually assigned to marketing. This is an expensive way to gain customers because targeting can never be completely accurate. Businesses always invest in potential customers that never materialize. The value attributes used to persuade customers are limited and price is often the most important. For services, the customer cannot be certain about any other value attributes before the service occurs. The customer must base the purchase decision on price along with a prediction, resting on other information, of what the experience will be. That information typically comes from a company spokesperson. Depending on the industry, costs of acquiring a new customer can range from twice to 10 times as expensive as the cost of retaining a current one.[5]

Customer retention efforts involve more people and more business functions than customer acquisition, and they create more opportunities to convince the customer to stay. Customer experience is the basis for retention efforts. The returning customer knows what the value attributes are if the company has delivered them in the past. As the customer becomes more loyal, retention costs decline.

The impact of customer retention on costs and revenues associated with that particular customer are obvious, but the cost of new-customer acquisition is reduced as well. Why? Because loyal customers become advocates and take on the role of company spokespersons. Exhibit 14.7 illustrates this process.

As the process repeats, new-customer acquisitions increase, but the cost of each new customer is reduced because of the effect of customer advocates. The advocate serves as an information source for new customers (recall that they are at the first phase of customer loyalty, which is based on information). As information sources, customer advocates more reliably predict what the experience will be than would information obtained from a traditional company spokesman. The advocate actually is a company spokesman, but a more credible one, because of his or her perceived objectivity. The voice of company advocates is sometimes referred to as "buzz". Companies love to generate buzz because it's believed to be more effective than advertisement and it costs

EXHIBIT 14.7 Loyalty/Growth Cycle

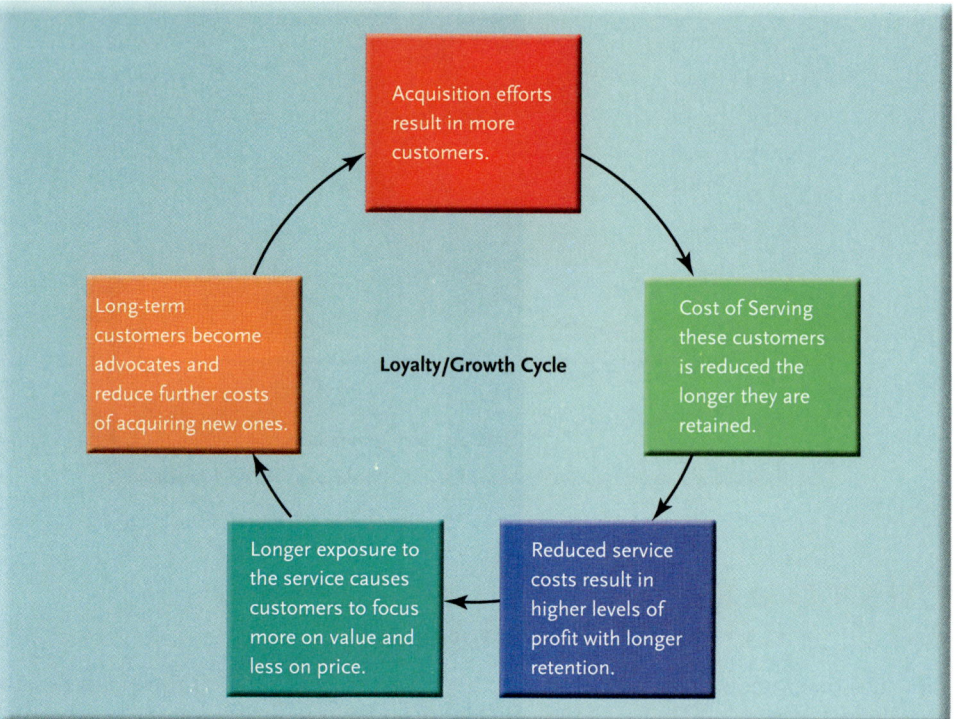

much less. Several online services have evolved to take advantage of customers' willingness to post positive and negative feedback on the Internet. Esource 14.1 provides an example of a widely used product and service feedback site.

The value of customer loyalty is quite convincing when industry-specific data are examined. In a study commissioned for *Fortune* magazine, research showed that a 5 percent increase in loyalty in certain industries resulted in an average gain in lifetime profits per customer of 73 percent. The specific profit increases are presented in Exhibit 14.8.

If the retained customer has the potential to add profitability to the firm, certainly the lost customer can do the opposite. Another study showed that 5 percent swings in customer retention rates resulted in earnings swings of 25 percent to 100 percent.[6] In both directions! The lost customer creates a need to acquire another. The very disgruntled defector can create as much negative word of mouth as the advocate can create buzz. It used to be a common rule of thumb that dissatisfied customers told 10 others. Today, through email, bulletin boards, and websites, negative word of mouth can reach thousands.

CUSTOMER LOYALTY: A CYCLE OF VALUE ENHANCEMENT

In addition to the increased revenues and reduced costs associated with loyal customers, customer loyalty also enhances the ability of other resources to create value. Let's first examine this phenomenon for all operations management resource groups.

EXHIBIT 14.8 Lifetime Profit per Customer Improvement from 5 Percent Increase in Loyalty

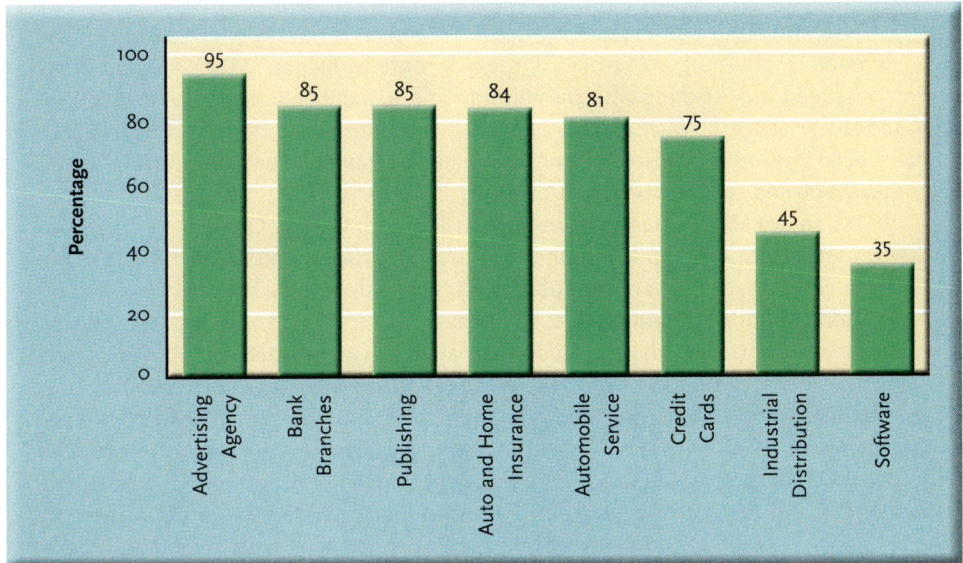

Customer loyalty improves inventory productivity because businesses with loyal customers see those customers again and again. This gives them better knowledge about how customers utilize their products and services, allowing more accurate forecasts of what the customers' current and future needs are. Improved forecast accuracy reduces inventory requirements to cope with uncertainty. It also means more accurate production planning, which translates into better due-date performance and fewer inventory shortages. The accurate forecast of customer needs improves quality, which translates into a lower defect rate and lower inventory levels.

Workforce productivity is also enhanced by the development of customer loyalty. Loyal customers communicate more, giving the workforce more information, enabling employees to add more value to the experiences of all customers. In addition, customer loyalty and employee loyalty feed on each other. Employees get positive feedback from customers, resulting in better performance and a higher level of job satisfaction. Higher levels of satisfaction result in less employee attrition, a workforce with more experience, and, again, more value for the customer. Another advantage of customer loyalty to the employee is that when businesses make the commitment to build loyal customers, they are also making a commitment to building loyalty among employees.

Customer loyalty enhances capacity productivity in two ways. First, demand forecast accuracy results in more accurate capacity planning and a closer match between capacity and demand. This is particularly beneficial in services, where mismatches between capacity and demand cannot be buffered by finished-goods inventory. The improved match between capacity and demand results in improved machine utilizations for manufacturers and enhanced financial return on machine investments. Second, uncertainty about what customers want can result in capacity being wasted on things that aren't really important. Enhanced knowledge about customers helps the business accurately prioritize what gets done, reducing wasted capacity.

Knowledge obtained from loyal customers makes it possible to more accurately link facility layout decisions to customer desires. This not only affects facility productivity,

om on site

97X—A Broadcasting Phenomenon

Customer loyalty means different things to different businesses. Some talk about it but don't really go after it. To others, it's a way of life. For the niche company, churning customers is a quick route to failure. WOXY-FM radio has demonstrated how sticking with the mission and patiently building a loyal customer base lead to success. With an overwhelming commitment to its customers, WOXY has defied the odds stacked against a small, independent broadcaster in today's corporate-owned broadcasting environment.

WOXY (97.7 FM) broadcasts from the small town of Oxford, Ohio, and reaches the Dayton and Cincinnati markets. Since 1983, owners Doug and Linda Balogh maintained a course set to attract serious alternative music lovers. They have been committed to being original and unique. No sleaze, no shock, no hype, and, most of all, no corporate-controlled playlists. Just alternative music selected for play by people who love alternative music. They've created what has become one of the last truly independent, truly alternative radio stations. Despite an industry that has seen the largest owner of radio stations go from owning 39 stations to owning more than 1,200, WOXY has remained fiercely independent. It doesn't succumb to the corporate model of sacrificing art to produce more money in a hurry. As Doug puts it, selling only vanilla, chocolate, and strawberry may be an efficient revenue model, but it creates a wonderful opportunity for those who have a distinctly unusual flavor.

Doug and Linda's business reflects their own ethics and values. Their continuous belief that they have a responsibility to meet listener needs has been rewarded with overwhelming accolades and customer loyalty. And their belief created a successful model for generating revenue. Program manager Keri Valmassei describes their sound as "the widest variety of quality alternative music possible, without regard to label, gender, nationality, etc. If it's good, we're playing it, period."

By the mid-1990s, *USA Today, Rolling Stone, SPIN Magazine,* and the *New York Times* continued to rank WOXY as one of the best and one of the only truly independent and alternative radio stations on the planet. Despite the critical acclaim, however, the WOXY signal could reach only so far. Lovers of alternative music loved the station, word of mouth and positive press spread the word, but signal range was limited. And then came the Internet.

WOXY launched its website in 1996. It started streaming audio over the Internet in 1998. For WOXY (www.woxy.com) the potential to broadcast over the Internet meant two things: broadcasts were no longer limited geographically, and the great customer support and loyalty that had been generated by word of mouth could now expand exponentially. The power of customer advocates could reach critical mass. Instead of one person telling a friend, one person could tell hundreds or thousands. And no matter where they lived, they could tune in and listen. And that is precisely what has happened.

While Doug and Linda had been patiently waiting for that critical mass, their efforts were not going unnoticed. Alternative music lovers all over the United States and the world were tuning in online and emailing their feelings. From Virginia:

> The music you guys play is so routinely solid that I can happily just sit back and listen . . . And I'm working like heck to spread the word.

From California:

> I had given up on radio over 3 years ago . . . nothing more than corporate entities trying to push bad music down our throats . . . A friend let me know about you yesterday and I have not stopped listening yet.

(continues)

(Continued)

From Texas:

I am spreading the gospel re: 97X . . . I tell all my friends about 97X on the web.

WOXY was beyond being just noticed. In October 2001, AOL 7.0 was launched and it included RADIO@AOL. In addition to AOL-owned content, eight radio stations were also included. WOXY radio was one of the content partners. Despite thousands of corporate-owned stations, the original content of a small-town station had grown a brand name so distinctive that it was an obvious choice. As Doug Balogh describes the story, the most important message is a very short one: "It was no accident." WOXY success didn't just happen. The owners recognized a set of potential customers whose needs weren't being met. They went after those customers and got their loyalty and trust. Customer loyalty was the key. They became advocates. They spread the word, and that can only happen when the customer is delighted with the product.

Source: http://www.woxy.com, "WOXY Cincinnati: The Spirit of Independence Lives On," *Virtually Alternative*, and Author Interviews with Doug Balogh.

---

but enhances the effectiveness of processes as well. Facility location decisions can also be enhanced by customer loyalty. The location decision itself can be enhanced because knowledge obtained from loyal customers can be used in making the decision. The success of the location decision can also be affected because loyal customers are more likely to seek out a new or relocated facility. Word of mouth then elevates the chances for success for the new facility.

CUSTOMER RELATIONSHIP MANAGEMENT: INVESTING IN THE VALUABLE CUSTOMERS

The customer most valuable to a business is the loyal customer; thus there are benefits to recognizing the value of loyal customers. Like any investor, businesses must understand what the financial return on a customer is and what they can afford to spend for that return. They can typically afford to spend more for a potentially loyal customer than they can for one who is likely to switch any day.

Businesses create budgets detailing how much they can afford to spend on marketing, advertising, promotions, warranty repair, and other incentives designed to attract and retain customers. The difference between those approaches and customer relationship management (CRM) is that CRM aims at the individual rather than the market at large or some demographic group. Software firms providing CRM solutions abound. Esource 14.2 provides an example of one of the many businesses offering CRM software systems.

www
OperationsNow
.com

Data gathered during the actual transaction with customers can be valuable, and the fact is, the more loyal the customer, the more data can be obtained. Data gathered can be analyzed and provide information to help identify the most valuable customers. This data analysis is frequently referred to as **data mining**, a critical task for operations because the information is gained during interactions with the customer. It isn't gathered later with a phone call or collected in customer surveys or based on what customers say they like. It's based on what they have done. For the product-oriented company, the data collection process is integrated into the services associated with the product purchase. For the high-customer-contact service, it is part of the entire service encounter.

Investors recognize that there are times when an investment in the entire market, as in an index fund, makes sense. Diversification reduces risk. There are times, however, when an investor wants to invest only in certain sectors or only in certain companies because good information indicates that a better financial return is possible there. This logic holds for investments in customers as well. Diet Coke provides a good example. Research by the Coca-Cola Company showed that 33 percent of its Diet Coke drinkers consumed 84 percent of the total amount of Diet Coke consumed.[7] Studies of credit card profits have shown similar results. It's the Pareto principle: A small percentage of the customers are responsible for a large percentage of the profits. This small group of customers deserves special attention and is worth the cost of that attention.

You may have noticed that in certain situations, some people get better service than others. Frequent-fliers wait in shorter ticket lines and have access to comfortable lounges. You might not be aware of this, but loyal retail customers wait in shorter phone queues when they need customer service and often get better treatment when they need special services. The catalogs loyal customers receive are different from those of nonloyal customers. Loyal customers get more frequent contact, more personal contact, and they often receive a quicker response when they have a problem.

Many customers do not view different treatment positively. They do not appreciate it when someone else receives better service, and they think they are entitled to it as well. Equity sensitivity can be so important that in some cases, it has resulted in different pricing methods. Several automobile companies, for example, have switched to absolute pricing and eliminated the haggling that is typical in the industry. Customers become dissatisfied when they discover that someone else got a better deal than they did. Customer dissatisfaction from perceived inequity is particularly strong when it comes to receiving perks that have obvious value. For the business trying to develop loyalty in customers, knowing that perceived inequity can result in dissatisfaction is very important. Dissatisfaction, after all, is the worst enemy of loyalty in its early phases of development.

Because newly acquired customers are at the first phase of loyalty (cognitive, based on information rather than experience), they're still sensitive to price. In return for less contact with employees, and less attention, they should receive lower prices. This is often perceived as more equitable by equity-sensitive customers, and many will view this as value enhancement. It may actually increase their loyalty to the point where experience, rather than price, is most important.

We have a paradox. If we treat customers who have demonstrated loyalty better, they stay with us. It makes sense to invest more in these customers because the return is greater. However, if our actions result in other "less-loyal" customers becoming dissatisfied, they will probably not move beyond phase one of customer loyalty. The result is that we're not developing new loyal customers, we're merely retaining those that are already loyal. Businesses will always have defectors. A certain percentage of customers come and go. Models to predict this churning phenomenon form the basis for much of our marketing effort. After all, the churning (away from competitors) provides us with an opportunity for new-customer acquisition. To build loyalty, we must recognize that different customers have different needs. They have a different set of values. New customers are more tuned in to price. Loyal customers are more inclined to look at total value. Providing different levels of service to each doesn't have to mean "more" for one and "less" for the other. It can be geared to meet their needs.

The successful business needs to attract new customers, convert new customers to loyal customers, and then retain them. But paying attention solely to loyal customers and ignoring the rest isn't going to be effective in the long run. Learning more about loyal customers should not have negative impacts on the satisfaction level of new acquisitions. The opposite result should. As more information is learned about what customers need, it should be transferred down to the entire organization. This cycle of increasing knowledge about customers leads to increased loyalty and higher profitability. A focus on building loyalty rather than on customers known to be "transient" adds to perceived value and profitability.

Information Technology: The Enabling Force Behind CRM

Knowing and responding to customer needs at the individual level requires making information available to everyone who might need it. For this to happen, the information must be collected, analyzed, and made immediately available for anyone who might need it. *Anyone* is key, since customer information is critical to a variety of business processes. This can happen only when a centralized customer database is in place. The data must be accessible by various functions in order to tell them what customers want *and* gather more information. For many businesses, the customer data becomes a significant part of the unified ERP database. Exhibit 14.9 shows how the customer database interacts with various business functions.

Business process improvement efforts must be customer-focused, and customer information made available by CRM can contribute to the success of those improvement efforts. Many aspects of customer satisfaction go beyond the quality of the product or service being purchased to encompass the ease of doing business. How easy it is to purchase a product or service can be as important as the product or service itself. This is particularly true in B2B relationships, where processes like invoicing, shipping, scheduling, and component design are very important. The development of new and improved business processes and their standardization across the business can be

Customer Database and Associated Functions EXHIBIT 14.9

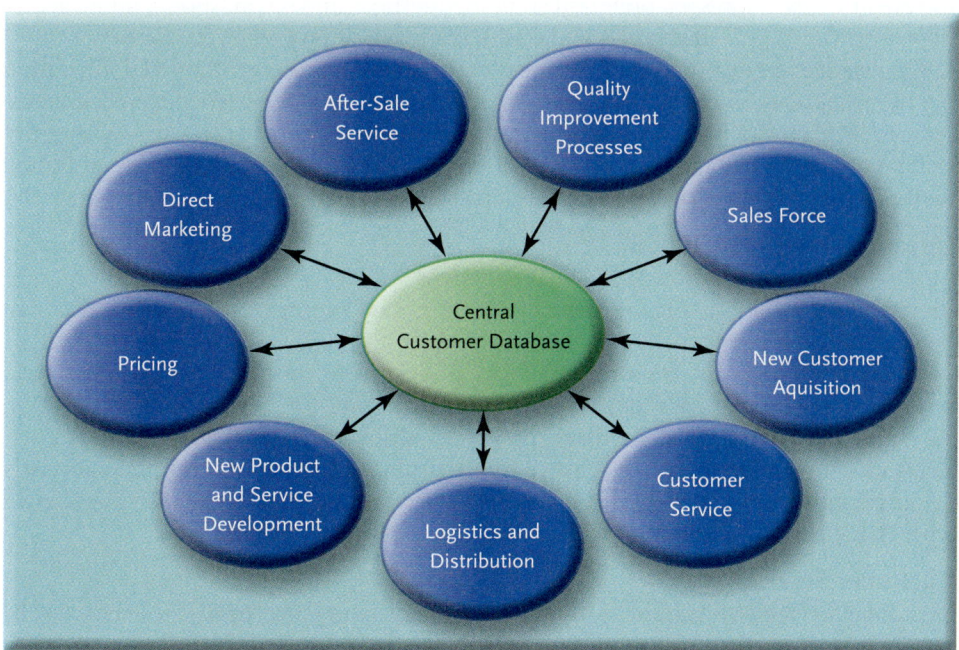

www.OperationsNow.com

enhanced through CRM data. We've all encountered companies that are easy to do business with, as well as some that are difficult to do business with. Esource 14.3 provides an example of why one business with an excellent reputation is so easy to do business with.

Each business process can enhance or detract from perceived value. Those processes that require customer contact provide information that directly contributes to the CRM database. In the following sections the CRM impact on each interaction presented in Exhibit 14.9 is explained.

Product and Service Quality Improvement

An understanding of the link between specific customers and quality expectations provides appropriate focus for quality improvement efforts. Different customers have different quality specifications, particularly for products. In many cases, quality levels must be set to meet the specifications of the most demanding customers. The result is that less demanding customers get higher quality than they need and, as a result, must pay for something they don't value. When identifying the quality problem to improve, for example, priorities for improvement projects should take into account the customers that would be concerned about a particular problem. Specific problems a particular customer has had with a process can be examined and contribute toward the improvement.

Sales Force

Sales-related decisions can benefit substantially from information gleaned from customer purchasing history. The sales function for B2C and B2B transactions can be enhanced by knowledge of previous purchases and interactions by other members of the sales force. Field sales often take place in the customer's business setting. Immediate access to the sales history can eliminate delays that would result from having to get the information and then return. In addition, new purchases often depend on old purchases. Model numbers and specific descriptions of previous purchases should be available to the sales force. In many B2C businesses, these functions are handled by a call center, so immediate access to customer data by call center staff can increase the opportunities for sales and speed up the purchasing process. Information regarding credit cards, addresses, preferred shipping method, and so on, should all be accessible. For web-based sales it can make an already quick process even quicker.

Knowledge about purchasing patterns can also contribute to improved allocation of sales resources. Sales staff with particular attributes can be assigned to specific customers. The method of purchasing (on-site versus telephone orders versus Internet orders) often dictates demand on sales functions. Knowledge of changing purchasing methods can help in assigning sales resources most effectively.

New-Customer Acquisition

New-customer acquisition frequently involves targeting groups of potential customers. Data from existing customers provide a good source of information that can be used to identify potential new customers. Like the resources needed in any other costly business process, resources devoted to new-customer acquisition must yield results. Many companies require a specific success rate for new-product acquisition programs in order to sustain those programs. Knowledge from existing customers helps identify target groups and, since information also exists on customers recently acquired, the acquisition methods that have proven most effective can be aligned with the appropriate target groups.

Customer Service

Customer service efforts benefit from access to customer data because the data can be analyzed to determine the services that provide the most benefit and that are most important to the more profitable customers. Since customers then move toward higher levels of loyalty and advocacy, receiving expected product or service attributes will give them satisfaction, but will not necessarily "delight" them. Being delighted often comes from how well they are treated before, during, and after the sale. Customer services that go above and beyond expectations provide that opportunity.

Logistics and Distribution

In many instances logistics and distribution decisions include determining which channels (mail, Internet, UPS, magazine, newspaper, web, face-to-face, etc.) to use to deliver products, services, and information. Knowledge of individual preferences is useful in planning for future needs and for determining appropriate channels for new-customer acquisitions. Moving customers to more expensive channels or lower-cost channels requires customer-specific information about other choices they've made or other characteristics related to their likelihood of switching to a competitor.

New-Product and New-Service Development

Enhanced knowledge of customers reduces risks associated with new-product and service development by increasing the likelihood that the results will be compatible with customers' requirements. Access to customer data provides development teams with data on wants, needs, likes, and dislikes of current products. Past enhancements and customization provide direction for new products and services. Quite often, information about specific customers can enable new-product and service development to better anticipate future needs of those customers. The result is not only that the new product or service is more likely to be perceived as valuable, but it can also be launched to the market earlier. The resulting early entrance to the market enhances the product's competitive advantage.

Product and Service Pricing

Companies that develop customer loyalty and access customer information sell products and services of higher value and typically have lower costs. This gives them the option to sell at a lower price, which they need not exercise. The ability to readily access customer information allows them to make an educated decision about whether to offer a lower price to a particular customer. With the information available, the decision can be based on previous transactions, customer history, and customer value.

Direct Marketing

Direct marketing efforts are aided by access to customer data as well. Companies with a loyal customer base and well-developed customer data are able to use that information for product and service development. Those companies have a broader selection of products and services and more opportunities to cross-sell and upsell. Access to the information gives the sales force better technological skills, more information about customer needs and expectations, and an improved ability to anticipate. All told, the sales force knows the customer better, provides customers with more relevant information about products and services, and has a greater likelihood of landing a sale.

After-Sale Service

After-sale service is enhanced by access to customer information because that information contains a history of the customers' relationships with the firm, including what they purchased, when they purchased, and any previous after-sale service interactions. Even if the contact person is different each time a customer accesses after-sale service, that person can see what occurred before. This eliminates redundant activities and speeds up processing and results. All lead to increased value for the customer and profitability for the business.

Outsourcing CRM

Customer relationship management is frequently outsourced to companies specializing in software with extensive CRM, call center, and data warehousing capabilities. The advantage to outsourcing these services is similar to the advantages cited by companies that outsource manufacturing functions. Just as a short product life-cycle can make a manufacturing machine obsolete, rapid changes related to CRM technologies can also make them obsolete. Staff training, facilities, equipment, and software needs change as the capabilities of this technology advance. Avoiding the investment by outsourcing the service eliminates that uncertainty. It also provides an opportunity for the company to maintain its CRM efforts at the cutting edge by utilizing a company that has that expertise as its core competency.

CRM in an Enterprise Resource Planning Environment

Customer relationship management is a significant component in an enterprise resource planning system. The unified database for all business activities is a natural environment for storing and accessing customer information. The integration of CRM into the ERP environment is important to enhance two aspects of CRM. On the one hand, it improves the value customers require by accessing other information stored in ERP's unified database. Cost data and transportation data, for example, are used to make decisions that enhance value for the customer. On the other hand, determining a customer's worth to the company is enhanced by accessing other ERP data. Credit history, for example, can be a significant influence on customer value.

CHAPTER SUMMARY

Value creation is at the heart of profitability for any business, and the ability to create more value for less money has a significant and immediate impact on profitability. Loyal customers contribute to profitability in two ways. First, as they move through four phases of loyalty, their priorities shift from information they receive about the company to their own experiences with the company. As loyalty grows, they become easier to satisfy, less concerned about price, and less likely to defect. Loyal customers also enhance a business's ability to attract new customers because loyal customers become customer advocates. They provide the information new customers seek and, because they are viewed as being more objective than company representatives, the information is more effective. Customer loyalty also affects management's ability to make decisions regarding other resources because the processes that use those resources can be improved.

Advances in technology have resulted in a structured approach to managing customer interactions known as customer relationship management. CRM allows the business to collect information about customer interactions and target its capabilities at customers who value those capabilities most. CRM also enables businesses to identify the most valuable customers and invest in developing their loyalty. Some customers have great potential for loyalty and profitability. Others have little potential, and investment in building that loyalty will not likely yield a positive financial return. The difficulty in managing this process is that the business must recognize that satisfaction is a prerequisite to loyalty. If, through treatment that varies from customer to customer, a customer becomes dissatisfied, that customer will never be loyal. Care must be taken to identify new customers with potential to become loyal and nurture those customers, while at the same time providing enhanced value to those who are already loyal.

KEY TERMS

action loyalty, 520
affective loyalty, 520
cognitive loyalty, 520
conative loyalty, 520

data mining, 529
interpersonal loyalty, 521
segmentation, 520

REVIEW QUESTIONS

1. What is customer loyalty?
2. Describe ways businesses extend customer relationships.
3. Describe the four phases of customer loyalty and their characteristics.
4. Describe how customer loyalty improves profitability.
5. Why does customer loyalty reduce the cost of new-customer acquisition?
6. What is "buzz"? Why is it more effective than advertising?
7. What impact has the Internet had on buzz?
8. How does interpersonal loyalty affect customer loyalty?
9. How can customer loyalty enhance the productivity of other operations resources?
10. What are the two objectives of customer relationship management?
11. Why might customer relationship management efforts inhibit new-customer acquisition? How can that be avoided?
12. How does information technology support customer loyalty development?

DISCUSSION QUESTIONS

1. Identify the business you are most loyal to. Why are you loyal to the business? What does it do that has contributed to your loyalty? Is it because of the product or service the business offers? Or is it something else?
2. Try to dissect your loyalty to that business. Is your loyalty to people? Or is it to the business itself? If certain people left the business, would your loyalty disappear?
3. What would the business have to do to lose your loyalty? Has it ever done that? What is your reaction when it doesn't meet your expectations?
4. Identify a business that you have just recently begun to interact with. Do you think you will become a loyal customer? Why or why not?
5. What expectations do you have that a business should know about if it wants to make you a loyal customer? Do you think those expectations are common among other customers as well?

SELECTED REFERENCES

Barrenechea, M. J. *E-business or Out of Business*. New York: McGraw-Hill, 2001.

Brown, S. A. *Customer Relationship Management*. Toronto: John Wiley & Sons, 2000.

Oliver, R. L. *Satisfaction: A Behavioral Perspective on the Consumer*. New York: McGraw-Hill/Irwin, 1997.

Sewell, C., and Brown, P. B. *Customers for Life*. New York: Simon & Schuster, 1990.

Zemke, R., and Connellan, T. *E-service*. New York: Amacom, 2001.

ENDNOTES

1. C. Sewell and P. B. Brown, *Customers for Life* (New York: Simon & Schuster, 1990).
2. S. A. Brown, *Customer Relationship Management* (Toronto: John Wiley & Sons, 2000).
3. R. L. Oliver, *Satisfaction: A Behavioral Perspective on the Consumer* (New York: McGraw-Hill/Irwin, 1997), p. 392.
4. Ibid., pp. 392–397.
5. Deloitte Research, *Making Customer Loyalty Real* (New York: Deloitte & Touche, 1999).
6. "When Loyalty Erodes, So Do Profits," *BusinessWeek*, August 13, 2001, p. 8.
7. Brown, *Customer Relationship Management*, pp. 20–21.

CHAPTER 14 Customer Relationships

OperationsNow.com LEARNING ACTIVITIES

CHAPTER ENHANCEMENT RESOURCES
- Esources
- Reel Operations Video Clips
- Interactive Models
- Excel Tutors
- Supplementary Readings
- Links to Operations On Site Companies

OM EXPLORATION
- Check It Out
- OM in Action
- Online Business Tours
- Letters from the Top
- Putting It All Together: Virtual Case Studies
- Additional Readings

UNIT 4

four — INTEGRATIVE MANAGEMENT FRAMEWORKS

- 15 JUST-IN-TIME MANAGEMENT
- 18 SUPPLY CHAIN MANAGEMENT
- 16 TOTAL QUALITY MANAGEMENT
- 17 CONSTRAINT MANAGEMENT

one — FOUNDATIONS FOR SUCCESS

- 1 Introduction
- 2 PROFITABILITY
- 3 VALUE
- 4 STRATEGY

three — MANAGING RESOURCES TO CREATE VALUE

- 9 RESOURCE PLANNING
- 10 INVENTORY
- 11 WORKFORCE
- 12 CAPACITY
- 13 FACILITIES
- 14 CUSTOMER RELATIONSHIPS

two — COMPONENTS OF VALUE

- 5 PROCESSES & CAPABILITIES
- 6 COST
- 7 QUALITY
- 8 TIMELINESS

Integrative Management Frameworks

Chapter 15:
Just-in-Time Management

Chapter 16:
Total Quality Management

Chapter 17:
Constraint Management

Chapter 18:
Supply Chain Management

INTRODUCTION

The link between day-to-day decisions and global performance measures like profit margin and return on assets is direct in the sense that day-to-day decisions clearly affect global performance measures. However, for the decision maker, it is very difficult to evaluate decision alternatives on the basis of the impacts on global performance measures. The cause–effect relationship between specific resource decisions and profitability is difficult to establish because of the complexities of the business environment. The four integrative management frameworks discussed in Unit 4 provide decision-making guidance that helps to align specific resource decisions with profitability goals. Each offers guidelines that are easy to interpret for day-to-day decision making and, if followed, are consistent with profitability goals, providing the necessary link between decision making and global business performance measures.

Units 1, 2, and 3 stress the need to utilize resources to obtain an acceptable financial return. In this chapter, just-in-time management is examined as the first of four integrative frameworks in the resource/profit model. Many of what are currently considered to be lean management practices have evolved from the JIT philosophy, which was imported from Japan in the 1980s. JIT is an important concept in operations management because it provides a framework for efficient, waste-free management of processes and applies to manufacturing and services as well.

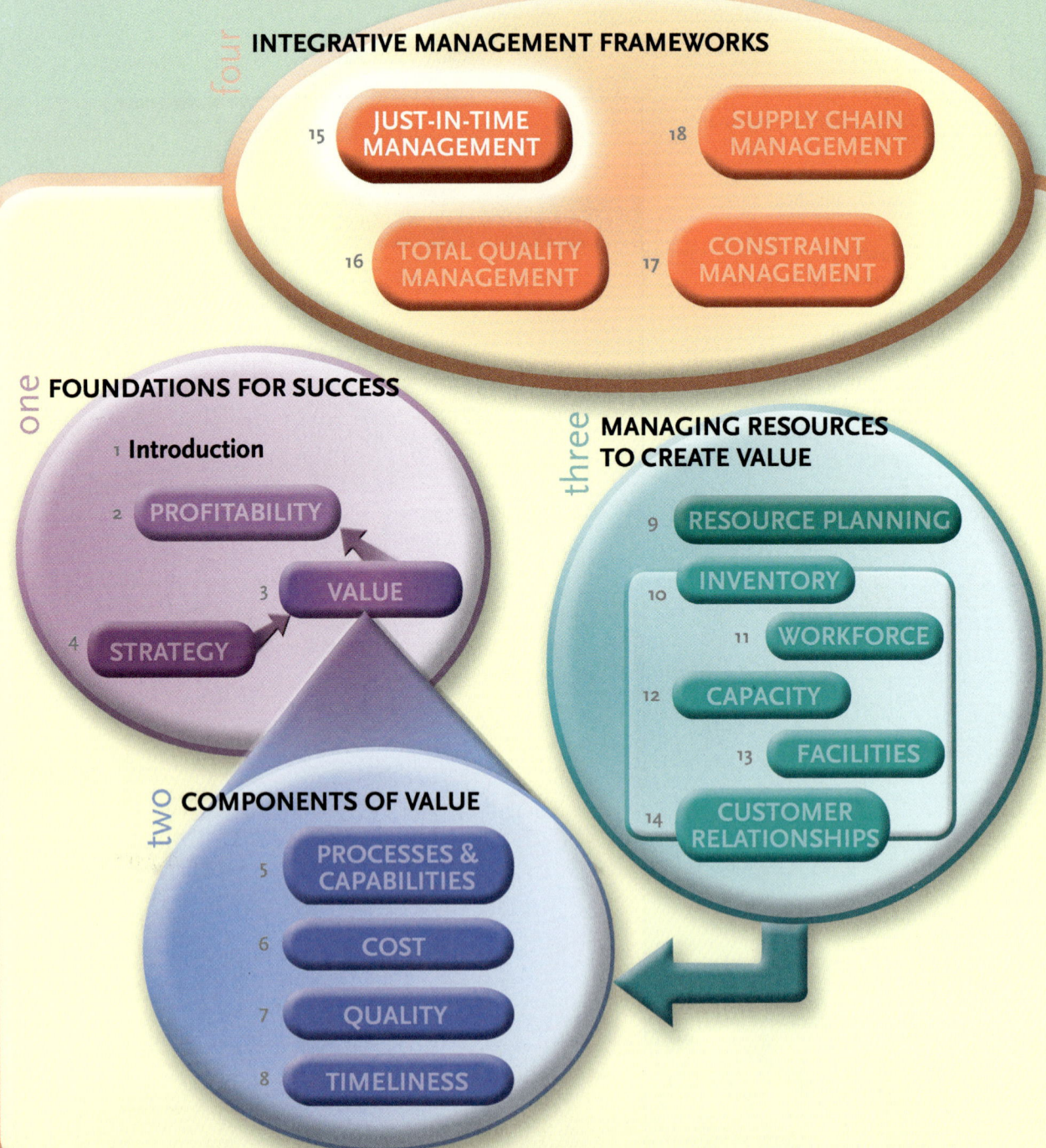

CHAPTER 15

Just-in-Time Management

LEARNING OBJECTIVES

Upon completion of Chapter 15, you should be able to

_____ Describe the overriding objective of just-in-time management (JIT).

_____ State the wastes that were the focus of Toyota's original version of JIT.

_____ Describe the enterprisewide JIT techniques and explain how each affects wastes in the business.

_____ Describe the inventory-focused JIT techniques and explain how each reduces inventory waste.

_____ Describe the workforce-focused JIT techniques and explain how each reduces workforce waste.

_____ Describe the capacity-focused JIT techniques and explain how each reduces capacity waste.

_____ Describe the facility-focused JIT techniques and explain how each reduces facility waste.

Introduction: A Management Framework for Waste Elimination
Eliminate Waste: The Focus of the JIT System
JIT Waste Reduction Techniques
Enterprisewide JIT Techniques
Inventory-Focused Techniques
Workforce-Focused Techniques
Capacity-Focused Techniques
Facility-Focused Techniques
Chapter Summary

INTERNET RESOURCES

 Excel Tutors provide annotated spreadsheets for every solved problem that automatically load Excel.

 Esources provide an online version of the more traditional boxed insert.

 Reel Videos provide streaming video footage for company applications of chapter concepts.

 Interactive Models provide an experimental environment for quantitative concepts and simulations.

INTRODUCTION

A Management Framework for Waste Elimination

Just-in-time (JIT) practices were initially imported from Japan in the early 1980s as an attempt to copy the successful Japanese approach to automobile production. Early attempts to copy the Japanese approach were seldom effective because U.S. manufacturers didn't recognize the sophistication of the system. Instead, they viewed it as a few specific techniques that could easily be copied. As time went on, U.S. manufacturers began to comprehend the magnitude of JIT and implement it as an integrated way of thinking rather than a "quick fix," and they began to benefit from its effects. A prerequisite to understanding JIT is recognizing its overriding objective of eliminating waste. This contrasts to the common perception that JIT's focus is limited to inventory reduction. JIT is predominantly a manufacturing management framework, but many aspects of it have become popular in the service sector. For that reason, it is presented as the first integrative management framework in Exhibit 15.1.

JIT accomplishes waste reduction by improving process productivity, reducing inventory, improving quality, and increasing worker involvement. In this chapter, the JIT system is dissected, the various wastes that it strives to eliminate are discussed, and the techniques used are examined.

ELIMINATE WASTE: THE FOCUS OF THE JIT SYSTEM

The roots of JIT can be traced to the production system developed by Toyota and modified over the years by many companies. Despite the modifications, a look at the focus of the initial Toyota system provides an excellent overview of the types of waste JIT seeks to eradicate. Exhibit 15.2 lists the types of waste Toyota's original vision of JIT focused on reducing.[1] Each waste reduction focus is described in turn.

Overproduction waste is caused by producing in excess of demand or by producing items before they are needed. The waste of producing too much is obvious. It creates excess inventory and wastes capacity on products that have no demand. Producing too early creates similar wastes. Early production adds to the inventory levels and adds time to the cash-to-cash cycle. If the orders produced early cannot be shipped, they must sit around taking up valuable space, reducing the financial return on the facility investment. There is also a risk of damage that will detract from the quality of the products. If products are shipped early, they inflate the inventories of the customer by getting there early and sitting in storage. This action anywhere in the supply chain will have a negative impact. It's not unusual for U.S. manufacturers to produce and ship early. Sometimes this behavior is motivated by the need to meet monthly or quarterly shipping goals. Management pulls orders from next month ahead, which increases the shipments for the current month. Obviously, this creates fewer shipments for the next month, resulting in a need to do it again.

Waiting time waste results from customer orders, inventory, or completed products waiting in queue for a process to begin. While a product or order is waiting, no value is being added, but financial costs are mounting and the wait time for the customer is increasing. The added wait time results in a reduction in value for the customer, as well as an increase in the delay to obtain the financial return associated with the products. In most environments, but particularly those that incorporate process-oriented layouts, wait time can be many times greater than the actual processing time. This results not only in long lead times, but in completion times that

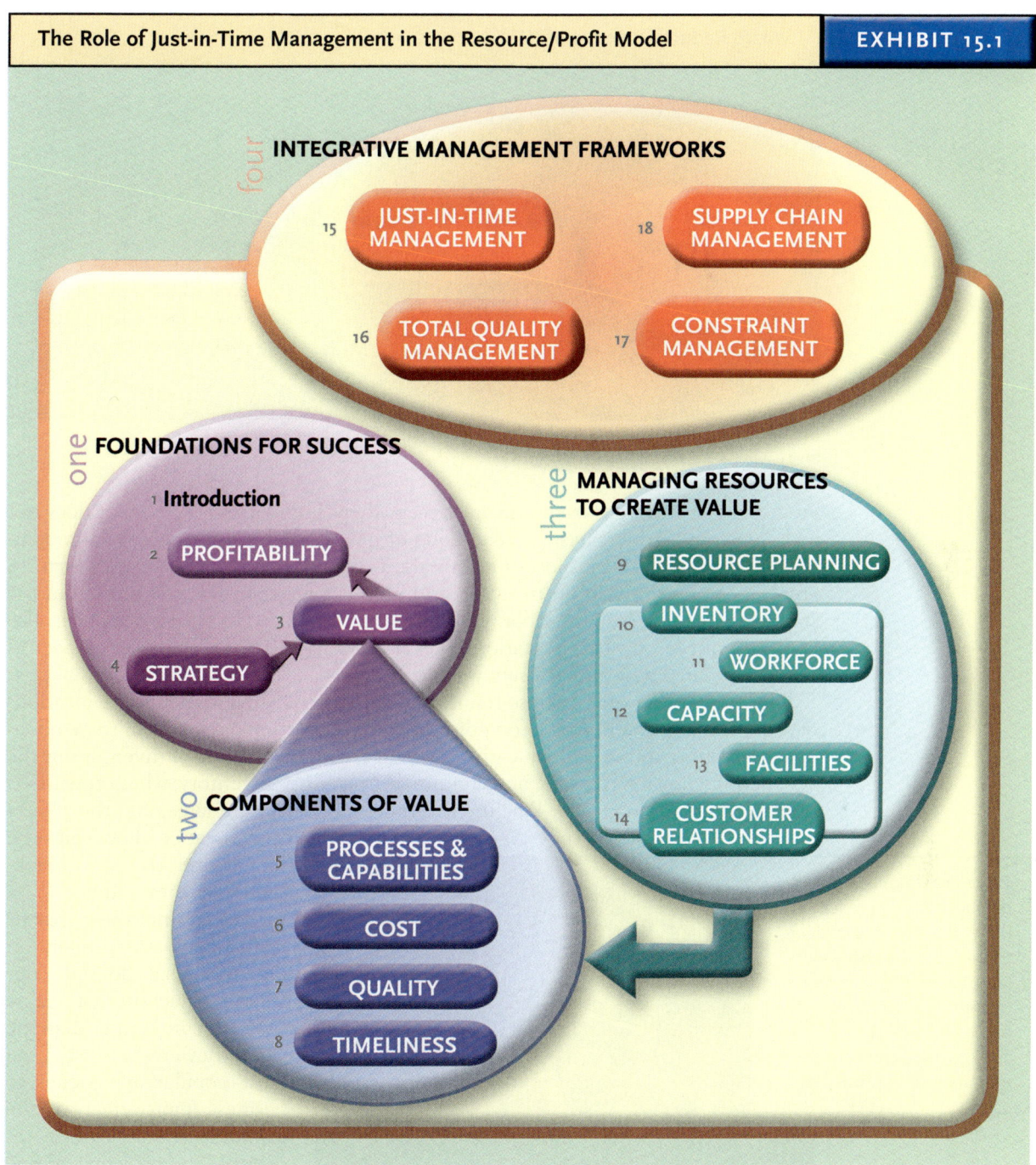

are variable and difficult to predict. This inaccuracy contributes to the need to hold more inventory, which increases costs even more. In addition, delivery reliability, response time, and other service-related value attributes suffer. Inventory that is waiting has a significant impact on costs. In the automobile industry, the time vehicles wait before being shipped to dealerships is known as "dwell time". The cost associated with dwell time has been estimated to be as high as $10 per vehicle per day.[2]

Transportation waste results from excessive material handling and material movement. This may be caused by ineffective facility layouts, requiring extensive

EXHIBIT 15.2 Waste Reduction Focus of JIT

movement of materials from one area to another. This increases costs but does not add value, and it increases the likelihood of quality problems stemming from damage. Excess material transportation can also be the result of poor process design. In any case, transportation of inventory and products is expensive, not only from the standpoint of the cost for labor, equipment, and fuel to do the moving, but also because unnecessary transportation takes a lot of time. It has the same impact as waste associated with unnecessary waiting time.

Transportation waste can also result from decisions leading to ineffective locations of suppliers or warehouses. Long-distance transportation can add a tremendous amount of time to the cash-to-cash cycle and create high levels of inventory in the system by adding a substantial and continuous "pipeline" inventory, which consists of products that are in transit. Pipeline inventories can be quite large, and the greater the distance between the source and the destination, the larger they will be.

Toyota has pioneered JIT management approaches to the extent that it is evident throughout the company. Minimal inventory, a clean, waste-free environment, and processes free of non-value-adding steps characterize the manufacturing processes.

Processing waste results from steps in production processes that do not contribute value or that create costs that are greater than the value they create. One of the most popular approaches to business improvement is the examination of processes in search of non-value-adding steps. These steps are important to identify and eliminate because they consume labor and processing time, have potential to create quality problems, consume time on expensive resources while providing no financial benefit, and tie up equipment capacity that could be used to add value to other products. This aspect of JIT has taken on a life of its own in a variety of ways. Few businesses have succeeded without concentrated efforts to eliminate non-value-adding steps in processes. This initiative has its roots in JIT.

Inventory waste consists of excess inventory, over and above that which is necessary. It wreaks havoc with costs, lead times, quality, and flexibility. Inventory used to buffer against uncertainties can hide the very problems that create those uncertainties. Better system reliability results in less need for the inventory and improves business performance at all levels. Improved system reliability also results in processes being more predictable, which improves levels of profitability. The creation of the excess inventory, by definition, requires the use of capacity and labor. Those resources end up being wasted as well, because the excess inventory they create doesn't get sold. Wasted resources increase costs, bringing down profit margin and ROA.

Possibly the biggest benefits of reducing inventory come from not having inventory to cover up problems. Over the years, in most businesses, lack of reliability of suppliers, of individual work centers, of quality, and other problems have been dealt with by adding inventory. Inventory has often served as a "coping mechanism". As long as that inventory remains, it's difficult to identify those problems. When inventory is reduced, however, problems surface immediately. They become obvious, and they can then be solved.

Unnecessary motion waste deals with human resources and how workers perform job tasks. When jobs require repetitive activities, ineffective job design can result in substantial wastes of labor resources over time. The resulting ineffective use of labor increases the product or order costs, decreasing the value to the customer or decreasing the company's profitability. Eliminating unnecessary labor results in an increase in available capacity and a reduction in the demand for capacity.

Product defect waste results from products that do not meet customer specifications for quality. Defective products create costs by wasting inventory, labor, and capacity on products that can't be sold. In addition, they create more demand on the labor and capacity that must be used to repair them. Rework of defective parts increases the processing time associated with their production, lengthening lead time, and increasing the level of inventory in the system, all contributing to higher costs and lower profitability.

Operations Resources and Waste

It should be no surprise that the seven categories of waste just described have substantial impact on inventory, workforce, capacity, and facilities. In addition to the direct impact on these resources, customer relationships may be the most severely affected because waste reduces value. Reel Operations Video 15.1 provides a cross section of the types of waste eliminated by JIT in an implementation at Allied Signal.

In addition to the elimination of waste, JIT also attempts to increase the involvement of employees in the decision-making process by recognizing the value of "local" knowledge. Local knowledge is knowledge possessed by employees who work with certain processes every day. They understand the quirks and idiosyncrasies others not working in the process would never be aware of. Waste elimination typically results from the knowledge and expertise of workers with local knowledge. Workers in the trenches are often the most familiar with those resources and can contribute substantially to their improvement. Employee involvement is frequently implemented through process improvement teams. In fact, one of the first JIT techniques adopted by U.S. manufacturers was employee improvement teams known at that time as "quality circles." The phenomenal growth of employee teams in the United States can trace its roots back to the introduction of JIT.

JIT WASTE REDUCTION TECHNIQUES

Associated with the import of JIT to U.S. businesses were a number of techniques. Many of these techniques have not remained exclusive to JIT. They have become so popular that they are often used independently of JIT, particularly in the service sector. Some of the more widely accepted techniques, such as the focus on eliminating non-value-adding steps in processes and some of the tools associated with quality improvement, have been described in other chapters in this text. In most cases, U.S. businesses have found that for a given situation, some JIT techniques are more appropriate than others. They are not all independent, however. Many JIT tools are related to others. Some are prerequisites to others, in fact. JIT is often viewed as a toolbox with an assortment of techniques that can be applied in many different situations. All of the tools are good, but each has a specific use. Each technique is geared toward waste reduction within a particular resource group, but as we know, a technique can't impact one resource without having an impact on the others. The toolbox analogy can be extended. An individual tool can solve a specific problem, but knowledge about all of the tools is far more valuable than knowledge of just one. Wrenches, for example, are great for tightening bolts but don't work well for driving nails. On the other hand, if two boards are to be attached with screws, a saw is used first to cut the boards to length. A drill is used next to drill holes for the screw. A screwdriver is used last to turn the screw. All of the tools have a task, but they depend on each other. A narrowly trained "screwdriver operator" wouldn't be able to accomplish much. All of the techniques generally associated with JIT are shown in the model in Exhibit 15.3, grouped by resource focus.

An explanation of the model presented in Exhibit 15.3 provides a perspective on JIT as an integrated system, rather than just a toolbox. The JIT techniques range from very narrowly focused to strategic and broad-based. Exhibit 15.3 shows how two of the broader techniques have an impact on virtually all of the resources by their effects on the values of the business. Each of the remaining techniques can be thought of as serving specific waste-reduction purposes for inventory, workforce, capacity, or facilities. They all have a cumulative impact on profitability because the waste elimination reduces costs and increases value.

The implementation of any complex system, JIT included, is a challenging task. Success depends on a variety of factors. The significance of the change to a JIT environment is well documented in Reel Operations Video 15.2, which chronicles a JIT implementation at Tri-State Manufacturing.

The remainder of this chapter is devoted to the detailed examination of each technique and its impact on the targeted resource.

ENTERPRISEWIDE JIT TECHNIQUES
Quality Management

Describing effective quality management as a component of JIT is a bit like saying Texas is a state in the southwestern United States. The Southwest probably couldn't exist without Texas, but if you ask some people from Texas they'd probably be quite confident that they could get along by themselves. Quality is more of a prerequisite to JIT than a part of it. JIT can't exist without effective quality management, but quality management functions are emphasized in many businesses not incorporating JIT techniques.

As a prerequisite to JIT, a commitment to quality is necessary in all aspects of the business. Poor quality anywhere, even within transactions inside the business, may eventually find its way to the customer. High levels of quality reduce the amount of inventory needed, and service quality results in on-time delivery of inventory. Quality extends to record keeping and inventory accuracy as well. The list goes on. Quality

EXHIBIT 15.3 JIT Techniques and Their Impact on Operations Resources

JIT Techniques

Total Quality Management / Kaizen →
- Matching Production to Demand
- Kanban
- Component Standardization
- Small-Batch Production
- Reduced Changeover Times
- Frequent Deliveries
- Paperless Transactions
- Improved Supplier Relationships
→ Inventory

- Employee Involvement
- Employee Cross-Training
- Improvement Teams
→ Workforce

- Process Focus
- Eliminate Nonvalue-adding steps
- Automation
- Small-Scale Equipment
- Protective Capacity
- Level Loading of Capacity
- Increased Preventative Maintenance
→ Capacity

- Cellular Layouts
- U-Shaped Production Lines
→ Facilities

Inventory, Workforce, Capacity, Facilities → Customer Relationships

---

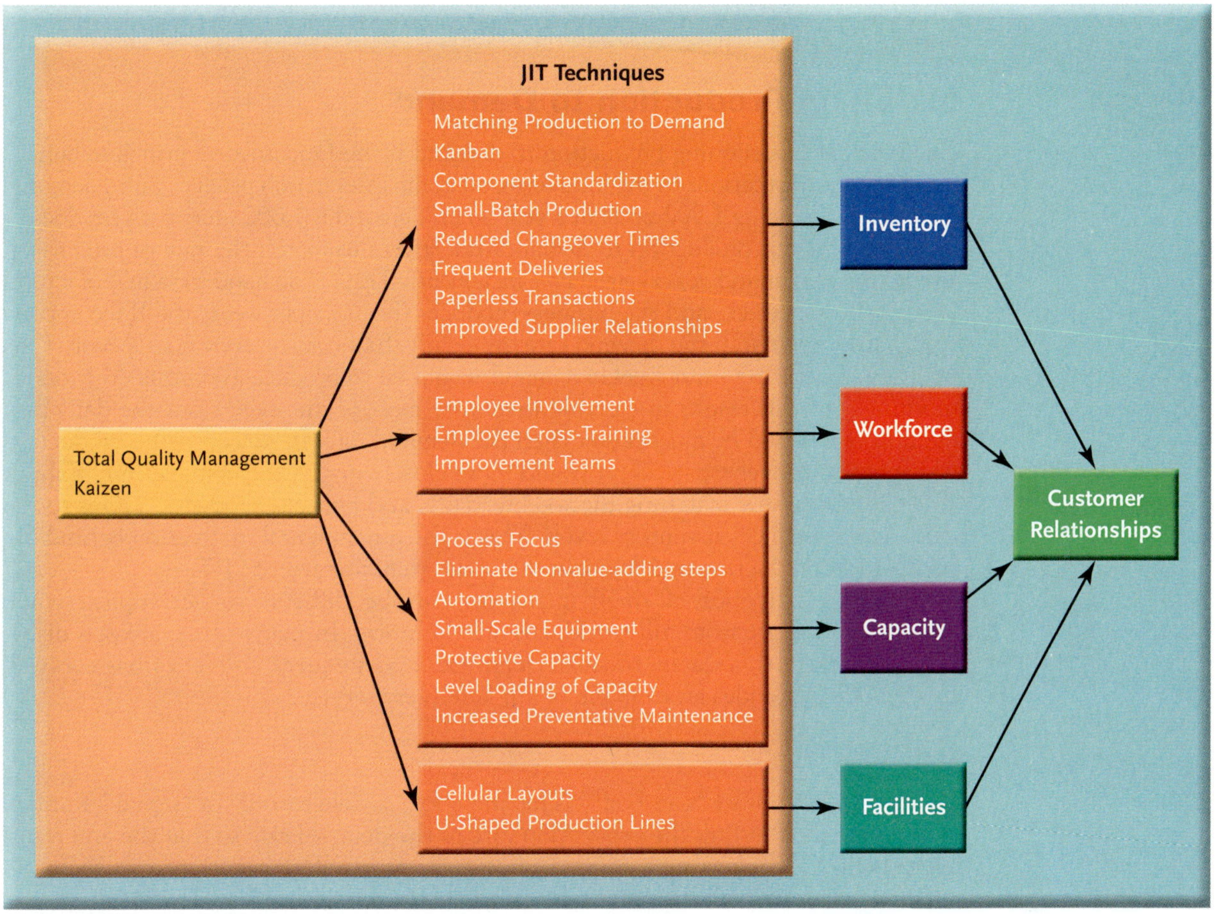

management influences the workforce because it changes the way workers do their jobs. It gives them responsibility for ensuring quality and empowers them to make improvements that eliminate waste. It provides them with tools that help improve quality. Quality management affects capacity because it reduces the amount of capacity wasted on defective products. Quality management has an impact on facilities because quality extends to housekeeping and facility maintenance. The facility, like any other resource, must be maintained with utmost care, or that lack of care will eventually affect quality and reach the customer. Reel Operations Video 15.3 provides an insider's view of how one approach to managing quality, known as total quality management (TQM), and JIT interact at Bernard Welding and Equipment Company.

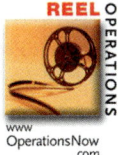
www.OperationsNow.com

Kaizen

Kaizen (pronounced ki-zen) is a Japanese philosophy that translates into "continuous improvement." Continuous improvement implies that a business should always strive to make everything better, and this mentality extends through all resources. The business should continuously strive to reduce inventory, the workforce should constantly strive for improvement, capacity should seek higher levels of productivity, and facilities should be made more productive. Nothing should be considered "good enough" because there is always room for improvement. In addition to the kaizen "attitude," some businesses utilize kaizen workshops or the "kaizen blitz" approach to completely overhaul processes. A kaizen blitz is a two- or three-day marathon of tearing down an entire department and completely redesigning its processes.

INVENTORY-FOCUSED TECHNIQUES
Matching Production to Demand

The concept of matching production to demand is the fundamental principle behind inventory minimization. In the long term, all companies match production to demand. However, producing 1,000 units in a year when demand is 1,000 units per year doesn't necessarily match production to demand. JIT strives to match the rate of production to the rate of demand *at very small time increments*. Thus, if demand for a manufacturer is 100 units per week, and the business produces five days per week, the JIT company would strive to match the demand rate on a daily, half-day, or even hourly basis. One way to meet the 100-unit weekly demand would be to produce 100 units on Monday morning. But this results in carrying inventory most of the week since the daily production rate would be much faster than the demand rate. If, however, the production was spread out over the week, it would more closely match the demand rate. Exhibit 15.4 illustrates how matching the weekly, daily, and half-day production rates to the demand rate reduces inventory levels. This is the fundamental motivation behind the small-batch production and frequent deliveries that characterize JIT.

Frequent deliveries of small quantities can be difficult to accomplish when economies of scale from full truckloads are the norm. In many urban areas, a distribution industry that caters to small quantities and frequent deliveries has evolved. Esource 15.1 provides an example of a JIT delivery service.

Kanban

Kanban (pronounced "kon-bon") is Japanese for "visible record" or "signal." Kanban systems are used to link the production rate to the demand rate so that the end result is production of only what is needed when it is needed. This contrasts with the more

JIT has spawned an entire industry of transportation specialists. Con-way Southern Express (CSE) provides next- and second-day deliveries of small, less-than-truckload quantities. Here, Rubbermaid takes advantage of CSE capabilities to make small frequent deliveries possible.

EXHIBIT 15.4 Comparison of Delivery Schedules

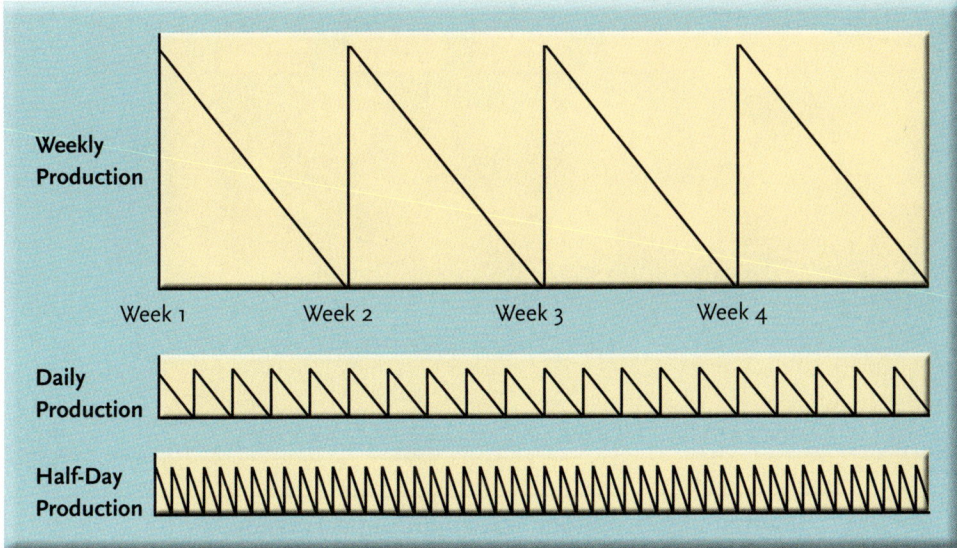

traditional U.S. approach which forecasts demand and then produces in a batch to meet the forecast. In that situation, products are "pushed" through the system and then sold. In a kanban system, the demand "pulls" products through the system. Many variations of the basic kanban system exist, but all are based on similar logic.

Kanban systems utilize small buffers of inventory between work centers, departments, and manufacturing plants. The unique characteristic about each inventory buffer is that it has a maximum size determined by management. When the maximum size of a particular inventory buffer is reached, no more inventory can be added. So, if a particular work center produces parts that go into a buffer between it and the next work center, when the buffer is full, it must stop producing. The signal to produce to replenish the buffer is created when the buffer drops below full. This signal is incorporated in the system through a very simple, visible means of detecting when the buffer is full or not. The signal that it is less than full authorizes the feeding work center to begin to produce. Let's look at an example. Exhibit 15.5 shows a simple production line with seven work centers (WCs). At the end of the line is a container that holds six finished products. Between each pair of work centers there is also a container that holds six parts. Each part must be processed through all seven work centers and is then shipped to a neighboring factory for assembly into an automobile.

As one item of finished product is removed from the buffer following WC7, the empty space in the buffer authorizes WC7 to replenish it. WC7 requires a unit from the buffer between WC7 and WC6. As soon as the worker removes that unit, the buffer following WC6 is less than full, which is the authorization to produce. Production at WC6 will require a unit from the preceding buffer (the one between WC5 and WC6). This authorizes WC5 to produce. This "pulling" action, triggered by the demand for the finished product, proceeds all the way back through the line. The kanban in this case is the open space in the buffer container and is the authorization to produce.

Interactive Model 15.1 provides an interactive environment for experimenting with a kanban system.

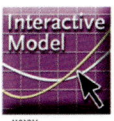

EXHIBIT 15.5   Kanban System

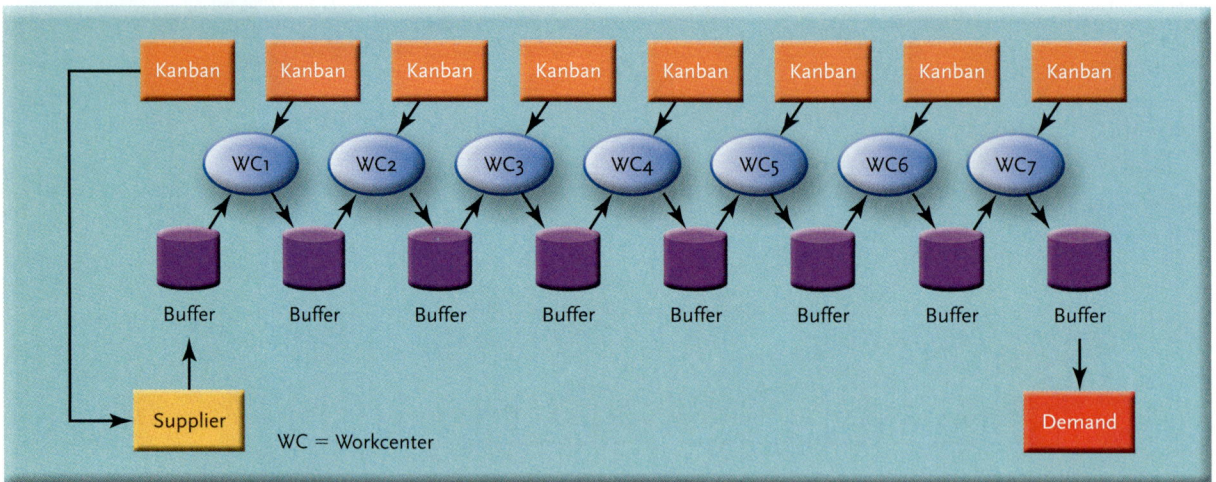

WC = Workcenter

> ### Maintaining Inventory Access during a Tragedy
>
> The events of Tuesday, September 11, 2001, changed many aspects of life in the United States. For some businesses disruptions in transportation, particularly during the first week following the tragedy, tested their philosophy of low levels of inventory. At 2:00 p.m., the day of the attack, Chrysler announced that it was closing all its U.S. plants for the day.
>
> At DaimlerChrysler's plants, inventories of raw materials and parts are kept at very low levels, to reduce costs and improve quality levels. Flow of inventory into the plants, necessary to keep lines running and workers employed, depends on frequent deliveries. Parts that come from Canadian suppliers must cross the border. Increased security resulted in border waiting lines up to 18 hours at Ambassador Bridge. One particular part, a steering gear needed for the Ram pickup, was already in a tenuous situation. TRW, the supplier, was having difficulties with one of its suppliers, which flew the part to the TRW plant in Virginia. Chrysler had been contracting to fly the parts from Virginia to its plant in Saltillo, Mexico. But U.S. airspace was closed on Tuesday afternoon.
>
> To keep the parts flowing, Chrysler utilized an expedited trucking service which employed two drivers per truck, each legally allowed to drive 10 hours straight per 24-hour period. It also told 150 of its largest suppliers to send extra parts to Chrysler plants to increase the size of the inventory buffer.
>
> By the morning of September 12, all three U.S. auto makers, through their lobbyists, had begun pleading with U.S. officials to increase the efficiency of the customs checks at the Canadian border. The response was immediate. Canadian Pacific Railway offered to set up an emergency shuttle through the Windsor–Detroit tunnel, bypassing the Ambassador Bridge bottleneck. Over a four-day period, 110 trailers were moved through the tunnel between the United States and Canada.
>
> The events of September 11 forced many businesses to change their short-term and long-term business practices. For many, particularly those depending on a far-reaching network of suppliers, the practice of reducing inventory to minimum levels had to be reconsidered. After all, inventory serves to buffer against uncertainties, so if uncertainties and the potential for disruptions increase, buffers must be expanded.
>
> Source: "Chrysler Averts a Parts Crisis," *The Wall Street Journal,* September 24, 2001, pp. B1, B4.

The number of items allowed in each buffer determines the total amount of work-in-process inventory in the system, as shown in Exhibit 15.6. In the example, maximum buffer size of six parts in each of the buffers limits the amount of work-in-process inventory to 42 units. Management can increase that amount by changing the maximum buffer size (a larger container or an additional container). Note that all buffers do not need to be the same size. There may be a legitimate reason why one buffer would be a different size than another.

Kanban systems can also link together work centers that are not physically adjacent to each other. There are many scenarios where work centers or suppliers provide parts but are a long distance away. The distance need not diminish the applicability of kanban as a means of authorizing deliveries of component parts and raw materials. The system tightly links all inventory production and delivery, as illustrated in Exhibit 15.7.

When work centers are not located next to each other, the signal to produce can take the form of a card or electronic message which is posted when a buffer is not at its maximum level. The fundamental principle is that only the demand for the item authorizes its production. Kanban systems are well-suited for repetitive manufacturing environments but not for manufacturing environments where there is a great deal of customization and variability from one product to another.

Component Standardization

Even in high-volume, mass production situations, customers are offered choices of different product models. Automotive manufacturers, for example, offer several different models to choose from. Even though the models are different, many of the components serve the same function. For example, the steering wheel on a Honda Accord and on a Honda Odyssey can be identical. Many small parts, including fasteners, interior trim components, knobs and buttons, light fixtures, and even frame and exterior trim components, can be the same if the vehicles are designed with that in mind. Parts standardization provides a number of benefits for a manufacturer. First, it reduces the number of different items that must be inventoried. This reduces the amount of record keeping necessary, the number of orders and deliveries, and the number of suppliers. The result is lower costs. In addition, particularly in industries like the auto industry,

Inventory Levels in Kanban System EXHIBIT 15.6

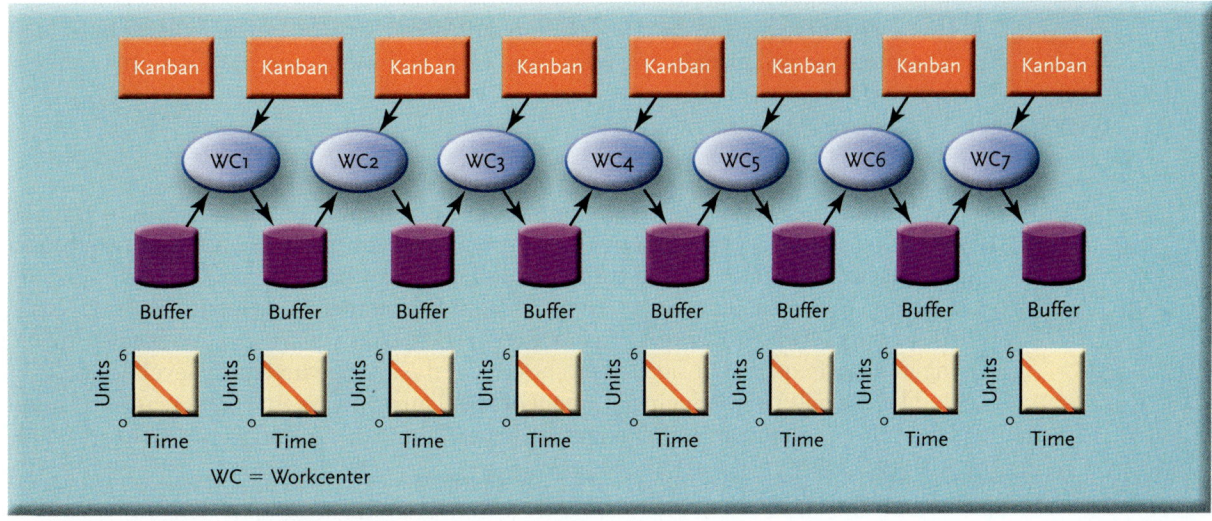

EXHIBIT 15.7 Kanban System Extending to Suppliers

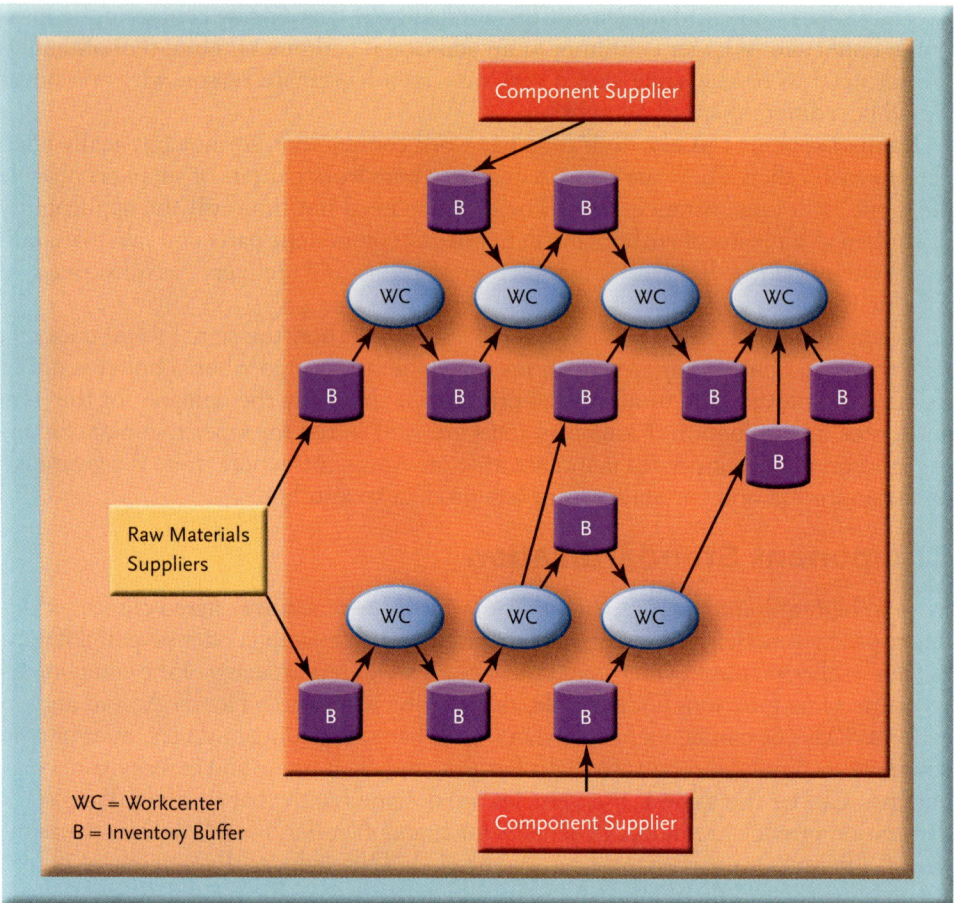

inventories of repair and replacement parts must be maintained for years after the car has been produced. Service centers must have access to original equipment replacement parts to provide expected levels of after-sale service to customers. An increase in parts standardization for any industry that produces a variety of products will benefit inventory reduction efforts. Total inventory investment can be reduced by at least 50 percent as well as reducing associated costs and increasing productivity of inventory resources.

Small-Batch Production

Small-batch production is the primary means of matching production rate to demand rate. The ability to produce a small quantity of parts or products and then switch over equipment to produce a small batch of another part or product enables a manufacturer to match the demand rate in relatively small time increments. As mentioned previously, the average level of inventory is a function of the quantity produced in a batch. Producing in more frequent but smaller batches drives the average inventory level down.

The difficulty in producing in frequent small quantities is that it increases the number of times equipment must be changed over. This can cut into the capacity available for actual production and reduce the financial return on the equipment, since equipment costs are spread over the number of units produced. Reducing the number of units per batch increases the per-unit costs for that batch. Small-batch production becomes economical only when changeover times can be reduced sufficiently.

Reduced Changeover Times

U.S. manufacturers who adopted JIT and small-batch production quickly discovered that virtually all of their capacity could be devoted to changeovers (with little left for actual production) unless they made dramatic reductions in changeover times. For most U.S. manufacturers, changeover processes had received very little previous attention and there was plenty of room for improvement. Manufacturers often found that with a modest amount of effort, changeovers that formerly took several hours could be accomplished in just a few minutes. This had an immediate effect of shortening production runs, smoothing out the flow of materials through the plant, and reducing inventory levels.

The process of changing equipment from producing one product to producing another is similar to any process in that it can be analyzed and improved. Early JIT manufacturers found many ways to speed up changeover processes, ranging from special "setup teams" that would practice to gain expertise, to developing fixtures that eliminate painstaking adjustments that are part of the changeover process. Changeover time reduction has become an integral aspect of JIT and in some industries has even led to the adoption of a setup improvement process known as single-minute exchange of dies (SMED).

Frequent Deliveries

Frequent deliveries from suppliers create the same effect on inventories of raw materials and purchased component parts as does small-batch production on inventories of work-in-process finished goods. Frequent replenishment of small quantities results in a smoother flow of materials through the system and a rate of production that more closely matches the rate of demand. Deliveries of raw materials and component parts are pulled into the system just like work-in-process inventory is pulled through it. The smooth flow of small quantities of inventory that provide benefits to a manufacturing plant can provide the same benefits to the entire supply chain if extended. In fact, if JIT methods are restricted solely to the internal aspects of a manufacturing plant, with no impact on supplier deliveries, the impact is to merely move excess inventory from one place to another, and the benefits to the customer don't materialize because costs are not reduced in the supply chain.

Paperless Transactions

In order to produce in small batches, changeover times must be reduced, because each production batch has associated costs. More batches, even though smaller, will result in escalating changeover costs unless the cost of each changeover is reduced substantially. Similarly, each delivery from suppliers has fixed costs that result from the activities related to the transaction. One way to reduce these costs is to eliminate the "paper processing" that traditionally accompanies them. By switching from paper invoices to an electronic process known as **electronic data interchange (EDI)**, much of the administrative cost associated with these orders can be eliminated. EDI is not actually an original component of the JIT toolkit, but many manufacturers have identified it as a beneficial application for JIT environments.

A Precious Metal Disaster

Stockpiling inventory is associated with many risks. The inventory can become obsolete because of new technologies, changes in the marketplace, or new regulations. On the other hand, unreliable suppliers can make stockpiling attractive. Stockpiling inventory can also appear attractive when prices for the items appear to be increasing. All of these issues played a role for the Ford Motor Company, leading up to its 2002 announcement of a $1 billion writeoff for a stockpile of palladium.

Palladium is a precious metal that is used in catalytic converters that clean car emissions. Prices for palladium, much of which comes from arctic Russia, have been notoriously volatile. In response to supply uncertainties, Ford's purchasing staff built up stockpiles of inventory. Meanwhile, engineers worked to develop methods to reduce the need for palladium. The engineers succeeded, and by late 2001 Ford had developed technologies that reduced its dependency on palladium. That's the good news. The bad news is that prices for palladium dropped drastically in 2001 and 2002, meaning that all of the palladium Ford bought was now worth much less than it had paid for it.

In the 1980s catalytic converters used platinum instead of palladium. Palladium is similar to platinum but cheaper. Its price stayed around $100 an ounce until the late 1980s. As more cars depended on palladium for clean emissions (about one ounce per car was needed), demand for palladium climbed. From 1992 to 1996, demand increased by a factor of 5, to 2.4 million ounces. Prices rose, but because Russia had stockpiles, no one worried about shortages. In 1997, however, the Russian government held up shipments. Prices surged to $350 per ounce. By 1999 prices reached $700 per ounce and in January 2001 prices topped $1,000 per ounce. By this time, Ford was stockpiling. Meanwhile, Ford engineers were making progress. Palladium requirements were cut in half because of better chemistry.

After their January 2001 peak, palladium prices began to fall and reached $350 by summer. Ford was overstocked with palladium that had little value.

Sources: "Beyond Explorer Woes, Ford Misses Key Turns in Buyers, Technology," *The Wall Street Journal*, January 14, 2002, pp. A1, A8. "How Ford's Big Batch of Rare Metal Led to a $1 Billion Write-Off," *The Wall Street Journal*, January 14, 2002, pp. A1, A8.

Improved Supplier Relationships

Suppliers to JIT manufacturers have expectations for profit margin, return on assets, and return on equity, so to meet the frequent delivery needs of a JIT customer requires a significant change in the way they do business. Delivering raw materials and purchased components frequently, often several times per day, requires good communication between the supplier and customer. Beyond that, because of the investment in the change, the supplier needs a commitment from the customer that the relationship will not disappear at the end of the year. Supplier relationships in a JIT environment have several characteristics that improve the situation for both parties involved.

One characteristic that sums up the relationship between suppliers and customers in a JIT environment is that they behave more like business partners. They collaborate by providing each other with production schedules, helping each other in new product design projects, and providing expertise for each other when dealing with product quality. It is not unusual to find the supplier's employees in the customer's plant and the customer's employees in the supplier's plant. Reel Operations Video 15.4

provides an example of the close interaction between customer and supplier in a JIT environment. In this video, Toyota and Flex-n-Gates team up to improve processes.

In addition to the dramatic increase in communication, the relationship is longer lasting and more exclusive. Long-term supplier relationships require directed efforts to make the relationship last. Many businesses provide descriptions of the type of relationships they seek with suppliers. Esource 15.2 provides an example of how one company describes the importance of its supplier relationships.

www.OperationsNow.com

For a supplier to make the changes necessary to meet the needs of a JIT manufacturer, it must also become a JIT manufacturer. After all, it wouldn't make sense for the supplier to produce in large, infrequent batches and then deliver them in small quantities several times a day. The inventory has to be somewhere, and it would simply be in the finished-goods warehouse of the supplier, even though it would be delivered JIT. From a supply chain cost perspective, that would be no better than delivering it all at once to the customer's warehouse. JIT practices must be incorporated upstream in the supply chain in order to provide true benefits.

WORKFORCE-FOCUSED TECHNIQUES
Employee Involvement

The concept of waste elimination, the focal point of JIT, is applied to all resources. Human resources can be wasted as much as any other, and knowledge and talent are

om on site — Supplier Relationships: Key to Successful Inventory Reduction

Well-developed supplier relationships are a prerequisite to a firm's ability to reduce on-hand inventories and depend on the frequent, low-quantity deliveries of suppliers. If a disruption occurs or a supplier is not dependable, the result can be catastrophic. Supplier relationships often go beyond a long-term contract and must include access to information that formerly was restricted. Autoliv, a North American unit of a Swedish producer of auto safety equipment, used to struggle with high levels of inventory and constant shortages of materials that came from 125 suppliers. High-priced "rush" shipments were commonplace ways of dealing with parts shortages.

Beginning in 2000, Autoliv management made their inventories visible to their vendors through a secure Internet access. Every hour, Autoliv uploads its inventory data to SupplySolutions, Inc., a software and service provider. SupplySolutions transforms the data into information usable by Autoliv suppliers. Vendors are now able to get immediate information about Autoliv's inventory levels. Information includes minimum and maximum inventory information for every item, so vendors can anticipate needed shipments. Vendors have permission to ship at any time the system indicates that inventory is needed. In fact, it is the vendor's responsibility to ship. By October, downtime from shortages was reduced and rush shipments of inventory had declined by 95 percent.

Some suppliers have balked at the new requirements. Access to SupplySolutions data is not free; it costs suppliers about $200 per month. In addition, some do not think they should have the responsibility to control their customer's inventory. They maintain that that is the customer's responsibility. Autoliv's response is that it may seek out other suppliers to replace those intransigent suppliers.

Source: "Bumpy Ride," *The Wall Street Journal*, May 21, 2001, p. R21; http://www.autolive.com.

just as likely or more likely to be wasted than labor. JIT uses employee involvement in all aspects of the business to ensure that nothing is overlooked and the implications of decisions are understood at all levels. Although the broad enterprise view possessed by upper-level employees is critical for good decision making, the detailed impact of decisions on customer interactions and specific processes must also be considered, and this perspective can be obtained only from the employees who take part in those interactions and work in those processes.

Employee Cross-Training

We've discussed the importance of a pull system in reducing inventory waste. One critical aspect of inventory management is to not produce products or components unless they are needed. This is a worthy objective, but it is difficult for management to idle workers who are being paid $18 an hour to produce. Businesses don't want excess inventory, but they also don't want to pay workers for doing nothing. Cross-training, which teaches employees to do several different jobs, offers an alternative to having idle employees. If a particular work center has no demand, the operator can go elsewhere in the manufacturing facility, to operate a work center that has demand. The more jobs an employee can do, the more valuable that employee.

Labor contracts can present barriers to cross-training because they may establish strict work rules that specifically outline the jobs that employees are allowed to do. As the need for cross-training has increased, many contracts have relaxed the strict nature of work rules to allow more flexibility and a better utilization of the workforce.

Improvement Teams

Employee improvement teams utilize employee knowledge and talent to achieve the continuous improvement or kaizen attitude that forms a foundation for JIT. Implicit in the utilization of employee improvement teams is a commitment to train employees in improvement processes and problem-solving techniques. The problem-solving techniques taught to employees, the respect given to them by management, and the authority delegated ensure that processes and quality are maintained and improved to provide a valuable resource to the company.

CAPACITY-FOCUSED TECHNIQUES
Process Focus

JIT focuses on process expertise, rather than expertise in producing a particular product. A process focus means that the firm builds process expertise and organizes its business and manufacturing plants around that focus. The concept of focused factories means that the factories are divided into small subfactories, each of which concentrates on the processing methods that it does well. Focused factories do not try to do all types of processing, as is often the case in traditional U.S. manufacturing plants, although they may manufacture a wide variety of products if those products have similar processing requirements. This emphasis on process excellence gives the JIT firm an advantage in capabilities and value creation. Focused factories become experts at certain processes and gain a reputation for that capability. This focus creates lean, productive, low-cost processes that can create differentiating capabilities.

Eliminate Non-Value-Adding Steps

The elimination of non-value-adding process steps is at the root of every productivity improvement effort. Managers who have improved productivity can thank JIT for this commonsense approach to business process improvement. Processing steps that do not add value exemplify one of the most common forms of waste in business. The waste present in many businesses is caused by an assumption that whatever has been done historically must be the correct way to do it. JIT companies recognize that this isn't necessarily the case. Elimination of the non-value-adding steps opens up capacity, reduces costs, and increases ROA.

Automation

Although not a tactic that is exclusive to JIT firms, many have utilized automated processes for repetitive or dangerous jobs. Casual observers may claim that this shows a disrespect for employees, because it replaces them with machines, but the opposite is a better description of what's going on. Japanese manufacturers believed that employees should be used for their knowledge and talent, and that making people perform jobs that could be accomplished by machine actually showed disrespect. Since some aspects of JIT fit repetitive manufacturing environments better than those that require flexibility, automated equipment is better suited. JIT manufacturers face difficult decisions when automating processes, however. Automated equipment is expensive and usually relatively inflexible. As processing needs change, most automated equipment is too inflexible to adapt. In some cases, automated equipment has been "traded in" for employees who can better adapt to different needs.

Small-Scale Equipment

Much of JIT is devoted to producing at exactly the rate of demand. That desire drives many business decisions. In many manufacturing processes a machine can be run at only one speed—fast. It is either running at that output rate, or it is turned off. If the rate of demand slows, the machine output must be slowed or inventory will accumulate. Reducing the machine's output rate can be accomplished only by turning the machine off.

Let's look at a straightforward example. Suppose a machine has a capacity of 2,000 units per week but the demand is only 1,000 units per week. The only option is to run the machine 50 percent of the time. This could be done by scheduling the machine 2-1/2 days on and 2-1/2 days off, or some other equivalent combination. No matter what the approach, while the machine is running, it is producing at twice the rate of demand. This creates a buildup of inventory that is ultimately consumed by demand, but inventory builds up nonetheless. Contrast this situation with one in which management buys two machines, each with a capacity of 1,000 units per week. They now have the flexibility to produce at 2,000 units per week or at 1,000 units per week, matching demand and not building up inventory. If management had purchased 10 machines, each with a capacity of 200 units per week, they would have even more flexibility to adapt to changing demand rates without producing at rates faster than the consumption rate.

Protective Capacity

For U.S. manufacturers that have converted from traditional manufacturing to JIT, one of the most difficult changes has been to eliminate excess inventory by increasing capacity a small amount. In Japan, where JIT got its start in the 1950s, there is simply no room for excess inventory. In order to respond quickly to customer needs, some excess capacity was needed. For U.S. manufacturers, who traditionally rely on machine utilization as a performance measure because of the link to cost per unit, this has been difficult to accept. The greater the utilization, the more units to absorb the costs and the lower the apparent cost per unit. Utilization, however, has encouraged production in excess of demand, which results in inventory. Rather than carry excess inventory, JIT manufacturers carry protective capacity. From the standpoint of meeting unexpected demand, capacity and inventory are equally effective. Protective capacity, however, doesn't have the negative impact on flexibility and quality that results from inventory.

Level Loading of Capacity

Whenever a manufacturer limits the amount of finished-goods inventory, adjusting to varying demand levels becomes difficult. Manufacturers that do not carry finished goods are almost in the same situation as services when it comes to coping with demand variability. Recall the two aggregate planning strategies discussed in Chapter 12, the demand chase and the level production strategy. The level production strategy required the manufacturer to build up inventory during low-demand periods for use to help meet demand during peak periods. This option is obviously not an alternative for JIT firms, because of the large amount of inventory required.

The alternative is the demand chase strategy. Traditionally, Japanese firms guaranteed lifetime employment, which made it impossible to lay off workers in slow periods and hire them back in fast periods. Although lifetime employment is no longer guaranteed in Japanese firms (and never was in U.S. firms), we know how detrimental that hire–fire pattern of employee treatment can be on workforce quality. (Before long, the only available job candidates are those who can't get permanent employment anywhere else.) The alternative is to somehow create a level demand for production. There are several approaches to doing this, keeping in mind that the load doesn't have to be perfectly level. Many JIT manufacturers level the load for a time period and then adjust it to another level for a period of time. Overtime hours and contingent workers can absorb some fluctuation in the production output. Another approach is to manufacture complementary products that provide seasonal cycles that are out of phase with each other. Manufacture motorcycles for the summer and snowmobiles for the winter, for example.

Increased Preventive Maintenance

The reduction of inventory, particular work-in-process inventory, eliminates any decoupling that may have been accomplished by the inventory between work centers. Without decoupling, downstream work centers are directly dependent on upstream work centers, so any machine breakdown can quickly bring an entire production process to a halt. One approach to reducing the potential for a production line stoppage when there is little inventory is to reduce machine breakdowns by increasing the amount of preventive maintenance. This is a good example of one method to reduce disruptions when inventory cannot be used as a means to mitigate the effects of a disruption. In some cases, particularly when equipment must be utilized at a high level, preventive maintenance activities are scheduled into the machine's activities just as if it were a customer order, or it is scheduled during second or third shifts when the plant is not producing or is producing at a reduced capacity.

Preventive maintenance typically requires that equipment be shut down, resulting in an impact on capacity. That capacity is not productive when it is being maintained, so it is important to schedule preventive maintenance carefully. The complexities of integrating preventive maintenance schedules with production schedules has resulted in the creation of a software industry that specializes in scheduling preventive maintenance. Esource 15.3 provides an example of how a preventive maintenance software vendor describes the software's function.

FACILITY-FOCUSED TECHNIQUES

Cellular Layouts

JIT implementation has an impact on just about every aspect of a business. Changing the facility is one way for a business to adapt to the needs of JIT. In Chapter 5, cellular layouts were introduced as a compromise between product- and process-oriented layouts. Cellular layouts utilize work cells, which contain small groups of machines that provide all the capability necessary to produce a family of products. Cellular layouts are particularly attractive in JIT environments for several reasons. They virtually eliminate the material movement that is often a waste of transportation. Cells utilize small-scale equipment, which increases the firm's ability to adjust to demand changes if necessary. In cellular manufacturing it is common to make workers responsible for tasks that are broad, rather than the very narrow tasks common in product-oriented assembly lines. The closeness of the machines also makes it easy to teach all cell members to run all pieces of equipment. This cross-training of employees improves the reliability of the cells, allowing them to continue if a worker is absent. In the event of a downturn in demand, the number of workers in the cell can be reduced to slow down the cell's output.

U-Shaped Production Lines

JIT manufacturers often design their work cells and their product-oriented process in U-shaped layouts. Exhibit 15.8 compares the traditional U.S. layout to a JIT layout.

Unlike traditional U.S. manufacturing plants that utilize "straight lines" of equipment, with raw materials incoming at one end and packaging and shipping at the

Comparison of U-shaped and Traditional Production Lines — EXHIBIT 15.8

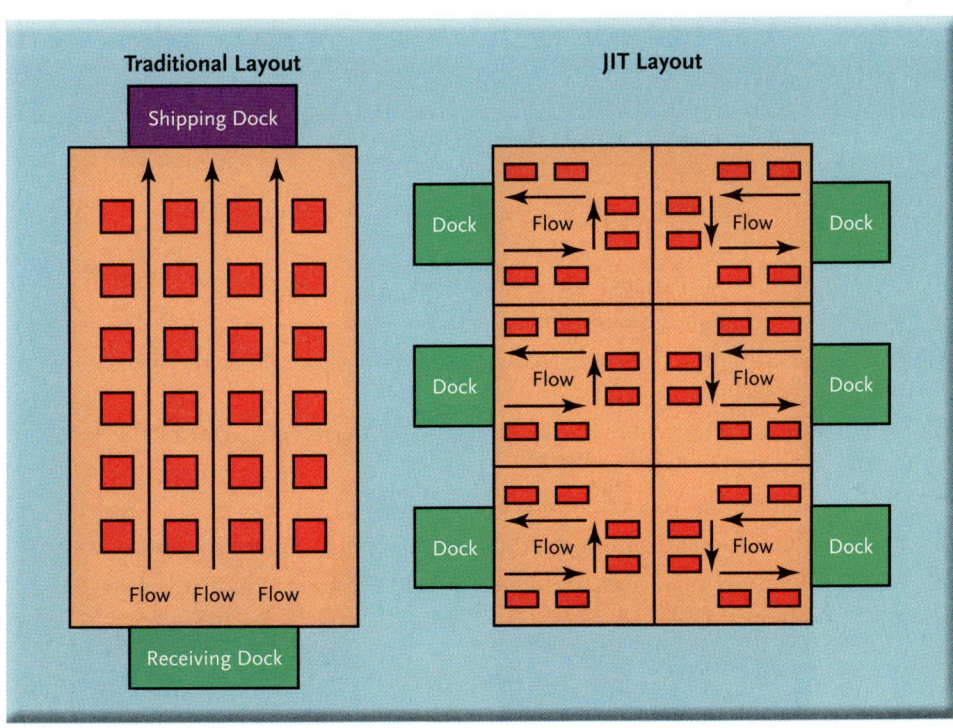

other, U-shape lines allow incoming materials and shipping to be located near each other. In addition, if the lines and facility are configured correctly, shipping and receiving can be done right at the production line, which eliminates transporting inventory and finished products to the shipping dock area. The advantages of the U-shaped lines go beyond the elimination of transportation waste. Elimination of unnecessary steps in material processing and movement reduces the potential for damage.

CHAPTER SUMMARY

JIT accomplishes its goal of waste reduction by applying a number of techniques that focus on inventory, workforce, capacity, and facilities. Many of the techniques have received broad acceptance outside the JIT environment. Other techniques, however, are known only to committed JIT users. Do not conclude, however, that just because JIT is a philosophy and a broad-based system, its techniques cannot be used unless the entire system is adopted. That is certainly not the case. A tremendous amount of benefit can be obtained from selective adoption of JIT techniques. As mentioned earlier, JIT is a toolbox and its contents should be used whenever there is a close match between the JIT tool and the problem to be fixed.

KEY TERMS

electronic data interchange (EDI), 553
inventory waste, 545
kanban, 548
overproduction waste, 542
processing waste, 544

product defect waste, 545
transportation waste, 543
unnecessary motion waste, 545
waiting time waste, 542

REVIEW QUESTIONS

1. What is the overall objective of JIT?
2. What are the different types of waste JIT strives to eliminate? Give examples of each.
3. Describe the JIT techniques that have broad implications for waste elimination.
4. Which JIT techniques focus on inventory reduction?
5. Why is matching the demand rate and the production rate at the root of inventory reduction?
6. How does a kanban system work? How does management control the levels of inventory in that system?
7. How does inventory reduction improve quality?
8. How does the standardization of product components reduce inventory waste?
9. What is meant by small-batch production? How does it reduce inventory?
10. Why are reduced changeover times important to maintain small-batch production?

11. How do frequent deliveries of inventory support the goal of matching the production rate to the rate of demand?
12. How does the electronic transfer of information support inventory reduction efforts?
13. What are the characteristics of supplier relationships in a JIT environment?
14. Describe the elements of JIT that support employee involvement. Why is employee involvement important to JIT?
15. Identify the JIT techniques that assist in eliminating the waste of capacity.
16. How does JIT improve the productivity of facilities? What specific facility layout approaches aid in this effort?

DISCUSSION QUESTIONS

1. Identify ways JIT has been implemented in the service sector. How has this affected you as a customer?
2. JIT's reduction of inventory has been criticized for resulting in plant shutdowns during crisis situations. Should JIT be eliminated? If not, how should it be modified?
3. What would be the results of the inventory waste elimination efforts of a JIT effort if quality levels weren't high?
4. How does JIT enhance product value for customers?
5. How can services benefit from the waste reduction of JIT?
6. Why is it important for all businesses in a supply chain to implement JIT? What happens if they don't?
7. Explain how JIT's inventory reduction techniques affect raw materials, work-in-process, and finished-goods inventories.
8. What is the logic behind a "pull" system? How could it be used in a make-to-stock system?
9. Identify the JIT techniques that would be appropriate and those that would not be appropriate for implementation in services.

INTERACTIVE ANALYSIS 15.1

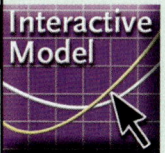

THE KANBAN SYSTEM INTERACTIVE MODEL

The Kanban System Interactive Model, found in Chapter 15 of the *Operations-Now.com* website, provides extensive simulation capabilities to experiment with the basic functions of a typical kanban system. As discussed in Chapter 15, a kanban system is a "pull" system. Its pulling function is the result of the authorization to produce only if the buffer immediately after a work center is less than full. As demand removes a unit of product from the finished-products inventory buffer, it creates an authorization for work center 5 to replenish it. Work center 5 removes a unit from the inventory buffer that feeds it, authorizing work center 4 to replenish it. This creates a chain reaction that goes all the way back to work center 1.

The key interacting variables in the system are process variability and the maximum number of units in each buffer (known as the kanban size). If there is no process variability, the kanban size can be small, even as low as one unit. As variability increases, a work center can run out of work to do if the buffer before it runs out of inventory.

In addition to the input parameters of processing time and variability, and maximum buffer size, the user has two controls of the simulation itself. The first is control of the speed of the clock running the simulation. Speeding up the clock simply means that the simulation clock runs faster. In addition, the pause button allows the user to temporarily stop the simulation and resume it again where it left off with the start button. The stop button stops the simulation and resets it to the starting condition.

Experiment 1: System Fundamentals

1. Set the parameters for processing time, variability, and maximum buffer size to their default levels of four minutes for each work center and the output rate, zero variability, and three units in each buffer, as shown below. Set the simulation rate on "slow."

Parameter	Setting
Buffer size	3
Work center 1 processing time	4
Work center 2 processing time	4
Work center 3 processing time	4
Work center 4 processing time	4
Work center 5 processing time	4
Demand Rate	4
Work center 1 process variability	zero
Work center 2 process variability	zero
Work center 3 process variability	zero
Work center 4 process variability	zero
Work center 5 process variability	zero
Work center 1 breakdown severity	zero
Work center 2 breakdown severity	zero
Work center 3 breakdown severity	zero
Work center 4 breakdown severity	zero
Work center 5 breakdown severity	zero
Simulation rate	Slow

   a. Start the simulation. In your own words, describe what is happening. Stop the simulation.

2. Stop the simulation and set the demand rate to one unit every six minutes. Leave the processing times at four minutes for all work centers. Leave the process time variability and breakdown severity at zero. Start the simulation. Whenever a work center box is gray, it means that it is idle.

   a. Are work centers ever idle? Why?

b. Using the pause button, pause the simulation while work centers are idle. Given the way a kanban system is supposed to work, why are the work centers idle? Stop the simulation.
3. Reset all settings back to the default values of a four-minute demand rate, zero processing time variability, and four-minute processing times on all work centers except work center 3. Set the processing time on work center 3 to one minute. Start the simulation.
   a. How does the system function differently than in 1b?
   b. What is happening at work center 3 and at the inventory buffer immediately after work center 3? Explain.

Experiment 2: Unbalanced Conditions in Kanban Systems

1. It should be no surprise that in a kanban system slower work centers and faster work centers have an impact on other work centers. Adding inconsistency in processing times provides interesting outcomes that aid in understanding the subtleties of this system. Set the parameters as shown below:

Parameter	Setting
Buffer size	3
Work center 1 processing time	4
Work center 2 processing time	8
Work center 3 processing time	4
Work center 4 processing time	8
Work center 5 processing time	4
Demand rate	4
Work center 1 process variability	zero
Work center 2 process variability	zero
Work center 3 process variability	zero
Work center 4 process variability	zero
Work center 5 process variability	zero
Work center 1 breakdown severity	zero
Work center 2 breakdown severity	zero
Work center 3 breakdown severity	zero
Work center 4 breakdown severity	zero
Work center 5 breakdown severity	zero
Simulation rate	Normal

   a. Start the simulation and let it run for 100 simulator minutes. Observe what happens to the use of the work centers and the inventory buffers as it runs. What is the output after 100 minutes? Stop the simulation.
   b. Leave the parameters as they are in 1a, with the exception of the maximum buffer size. Change it to 2 units. Run the simulation for 100 simulator minutes. Does the system appear to behave any differently? What is the output? Why is it different?

c. Again, leave the parameters the same except for the maximum buffer size. Reduce it to 1 unit. Run the simulation again for 100 simulator minutes. Observe what happens. What is the output in that length of time? Explain what happens.

d. Based on the previous three simulation runs, what does the buffer do to aid in the utilization of work centers? Is it needed?

Experiment 3: Process Variability in Kanban Systems

1. Inventory buffers provide a decoupling function that is extremely beneficial when there is uncertainty in the system. In most production systems, variability of processing times and other disruptions add sufficient uncertainty to make inventory buffers beneficial. Set the parameters as shown below:

Parameter	Setting
Buffer size	1
Work center 1 processing time	4
Work center 2 processing time	4
Work center 3 processing time	4
Work center 4 processing time	4
Work center 5 processing time	4
Demand rate	4
Work center 1 process variability	zero
Work center 2 process variability	zero
Work center 3 process variability	Extreme
Work center 4 process variability	zero
Work center 5 process variability	zero
Work center 1 breakdown severity	zero
Work center 2 breakdown severity	zero
Work center 3 breakdown severity	Severe
Work center 4 breakdown severity	zero
Work center 5 breakdown severity	zero
Simulation rate	Normal

a. Run the simulation for 100 simulator minutes. What is the output? What do you observe to be the effect of the variability at work center 3?

b. Leave the parameters as is, with the exception of work center 5. Increase its variability to extreme and downtime to severe. You now should have the maximum variability and downtime severity for work centers 3 and 5. Run the simulation for 100 simulator minutes. What is the output? What was the impact of having high variability on two work centers?

c. Now add an extreme level of variability and downtime severity to all five work centers. Run the simulation for 100 simulator minutes. What is the new level of output? What happens to output as extreme levels of process variability and breakdowns are added to the system?

d. Leave the variability and downtime settings at their maximum level. Increase the buffer maximum size from 1 to 2, and run the simulation for 100 simulator minutes. What is the output?
2. Increase the buffer maximum to 5 units and run the simulation for another 100 simulator minutes. What happens? Explain the relationship between variability and disruptions, inventory buffer size, and system productivity.

SELECTED REFERENCES

Finch, B. J., and Luebbe, R. L. *Operations Management: Competing in a Changing Environment*. Orlando, FL: Dryden Press, 1995.

Hall, R. *Zero Inventories*. Homewood, IL: Dow Jones-Irwin, 1983.

Monden, Y. *The Toyota Production System*. Atlanta, GA: Industrial Engineering and Management Press, 1983.

Ohno, T., and Mito, S. *Just-in-Time for Today and Tomorrow*. Cambridge, MA: Productivity Press, 1988.

Suzaki, K. *The New Manufacturing Challenge*. New York: Free Press, 1987.

Womack, J. P., Jones, D. T., and Ross, D. *The Machine That Changed the World*. New York: HarperCollins Publishers, 1990.

ENDNOTES

1. K. Suzaki, *The New Manufacturing Challenge* (New York: Free Press, 1987), p. 8.
2. A. K. Reese, "Needle in a Supply Chain Haystack," *Isource* (http://www.isourceonline.com/magazine/), January 2002.

OperationsNow.com LEARNING ACTIVITIES

CHAPTER ENHANCEMENT RESOURCES
- Esources
- Reel Operations Video Clips
- Interactive Models
- Excel Tutors
- Supplementary Readings
- Links to Operations On Site Companies

OM EXPLORATION
- Check It Out
- OM in Action
- Online Business Tours
- Letters from the Top
- Putting It All Together: Virtual Case Studies
- Additional Readings

The resource/profit model identifies total quality management (TQM) as the second integrative management framework. The commitment of the Japanese to quality, and their expertise with the tools needed to make quality happen, took U.S. manufacturers by surprise in the early 1980s. They attempted a quick fix, but U.S. manufacturers soon found instead that high quality levels required a dramatic change in company culture. They learned that the role of TQM is to develop high levels of quality by turning the traditional culture into one that stresses quality in every task.

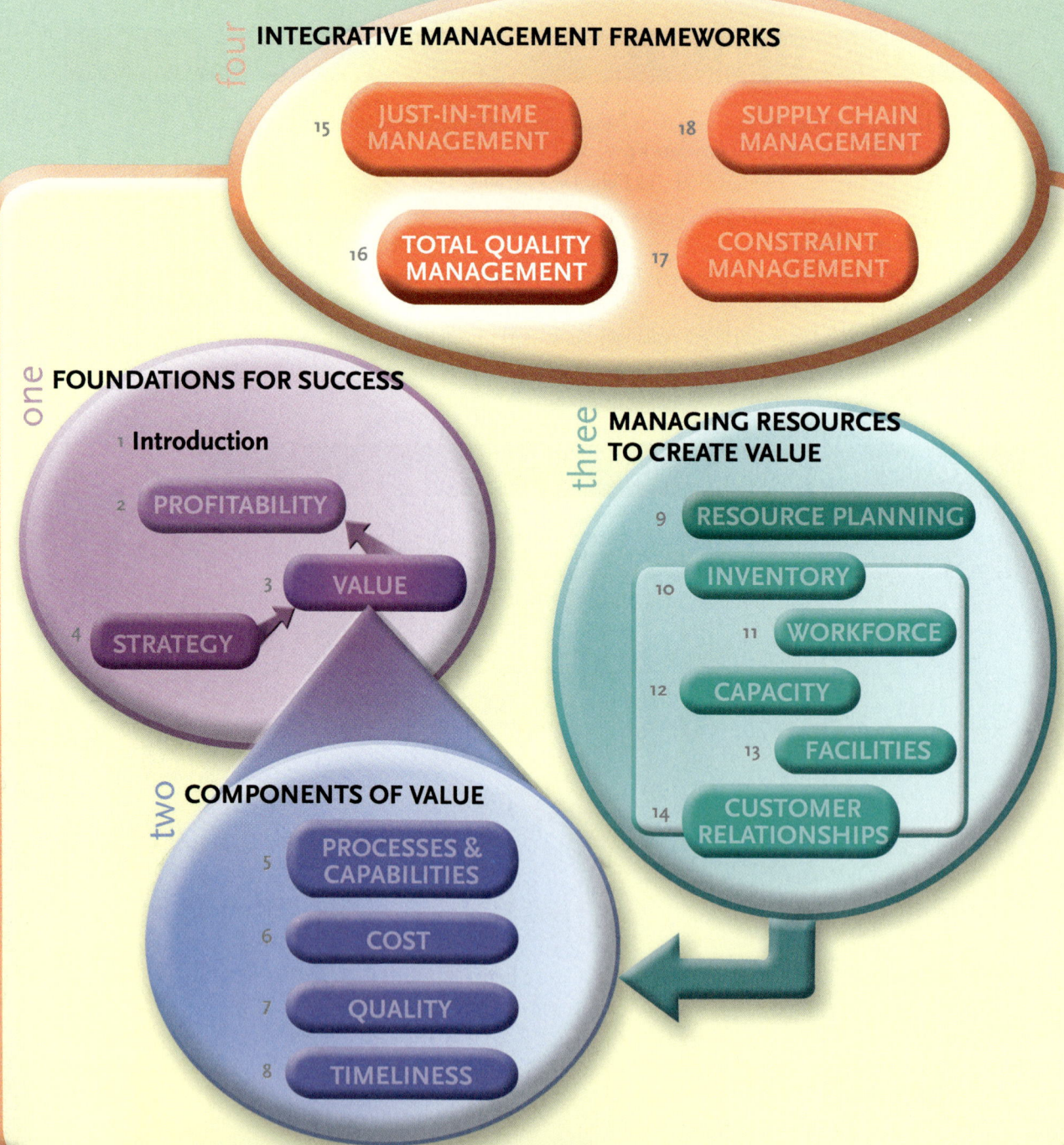

CHAPTER 16

Total Quality Management

LEARNING OBJECTIVES

Upon completion of Chapter 16, you should be able to

- State the contributions Shewhart, Deming, Juran, and Crosby made to total quality management (TQM).
- Explain the importance of internal and external customers and the role each plays in TQM.
- Describe the three principles of TQM.
- Explain how the supportive approaches support TQM's principles.
- Explain how the PDCA cycle is used to obtain continuous improvement.
- Describe the seven steps of the quality improvement story.
- List examples of the quality tools used at each quality improvement story step.
- Describe industry-focused and process-focused benchmarking.
- Explain how certification programs can provide structure for quality improvement.
- State the criteria used for the Malcolm Baldrige National Quality Award.

Introduction: Building a Culture of Continuous Improvement
A Brief History of TQM
Components of TQM
An Enterprise View of Quality
The TQM Process
Obtaining Continuous Improvement
Benchmarking
Quality Certification Programs
Quality Awards
Chapter Summary

INTERNET RESOURCES

 Excel Tutors provide annotated spreadsheets for every solved problem that automatically load Excel.

 Esources provide an online version of the more traditional boxed insert.

 Reel Videos provide streaming video footage for company applications of chapter concepts.

 Interactive Models provide an experimental environment for quantitative concepts and simulations.

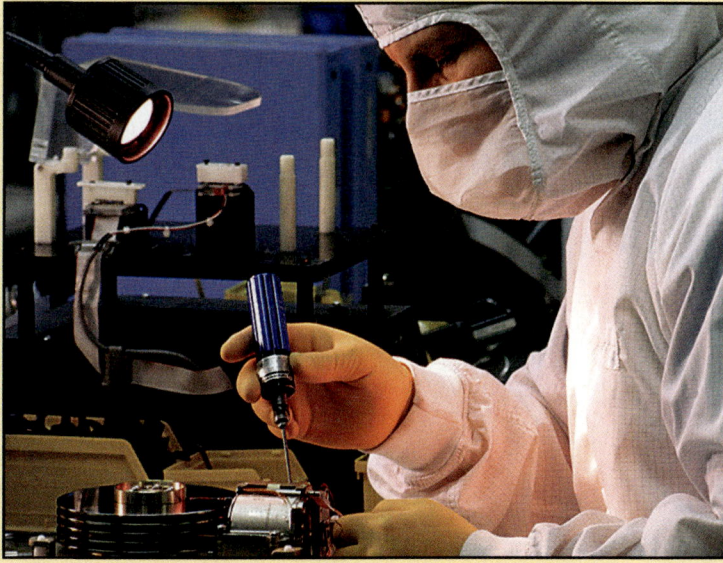

INTRODUCTION
Building a Culture of Continuous Improvement

Chapter 7 examined quality as one of the four components of value. Conformance to customer specifications and expectations was identified as a way of defining quality that is useful to business. That quality definition allows us to measure it, control it, manage it, specify it to suppliers, *and* ask customers to evaluate it. If we don't know precisely what quality is, efforts to improve it will bear no worthwhile fruit. Conformance to customer specifications and expectations—that's what quality is. Now, what's total quality management? Total quality management (TQM) goes beyond meeting customer expectations to provide an integrative management framework, as shown in Exhibit 16.1, that facilitates that end result. The framework provided by TQM provides goods and services that satisfy customers by meeting their expectations, so it provides a mechanism for achieving quality. However, the TQM framework also has an impact on the other components of value: processes and capabilities, costs, and timeliness. How does that happen?

Product or service quality is an end to be measured and achieved, but TQM is a process. Some consider it to be a management philosophy; others consider it to be a business culture. Either way, TQM helps managers create a setting that embraces customer expectations as the most important consideration. In this chapter, we examine how TQM works by looking at the principles of its founders, the approaches used to implement it, and some of the techniques that comprise it.

A BRIEF HISTORY OF TQM

Total quality management can be traced back to the post–World War II reconstruction of Japan. Japan's economy was completely devastated by the war, and Japanese leaders recognized the necessity to produce exports in order to survive. Business leaders from the United States, including some quality experts, were invited to Japan by government leaders to teach quality practices. Japanese manufacturers embraced these quality practices to the extent that Japanese goods, previously known for their poor quality, became accepted among the best in the world. Despite the fact that the experts who taught the Japanese manufacturers how to produce quality products were from the United States, most manufacturers in the United States did not embrace quality concepts until they began to lose market share to Japanese products in the late 1970s and early 1980s. In some cases, entire industries were lost to Japanese competitors because U.S. products were of such inferior quality. As markets began to disappear, U.S. manufacturers began to pay attention to their own experts. Reel Operations Video 16.1 examines Honda's approach to creating an environment of continuous improvement.

The development of TQM in the United States can best be examined by looking at these experts and their philosophies. Although many people have contributed to TQM's development, its proliferation can be traced to four individuals: Walter A. Shewhart, W. Edwards Deming, Joseph M. Juran, and Philip B. Crosby.

Walter A. Shewhart

Walter Shewhart was a Bell Labs statistician during the 1920s and 1930s. His primary contribution to product and service quality was the recognition that variability existed in all manufacturing processes and that statistical tools could help explain that variability. Shewhart developed the use of statistical process control charts, which provide an opportunity to control the variability of processes. Despite the fact that Shewhart developed much of the foundation for quality control, his impact is

CHAPTER 16 Total Quality Management

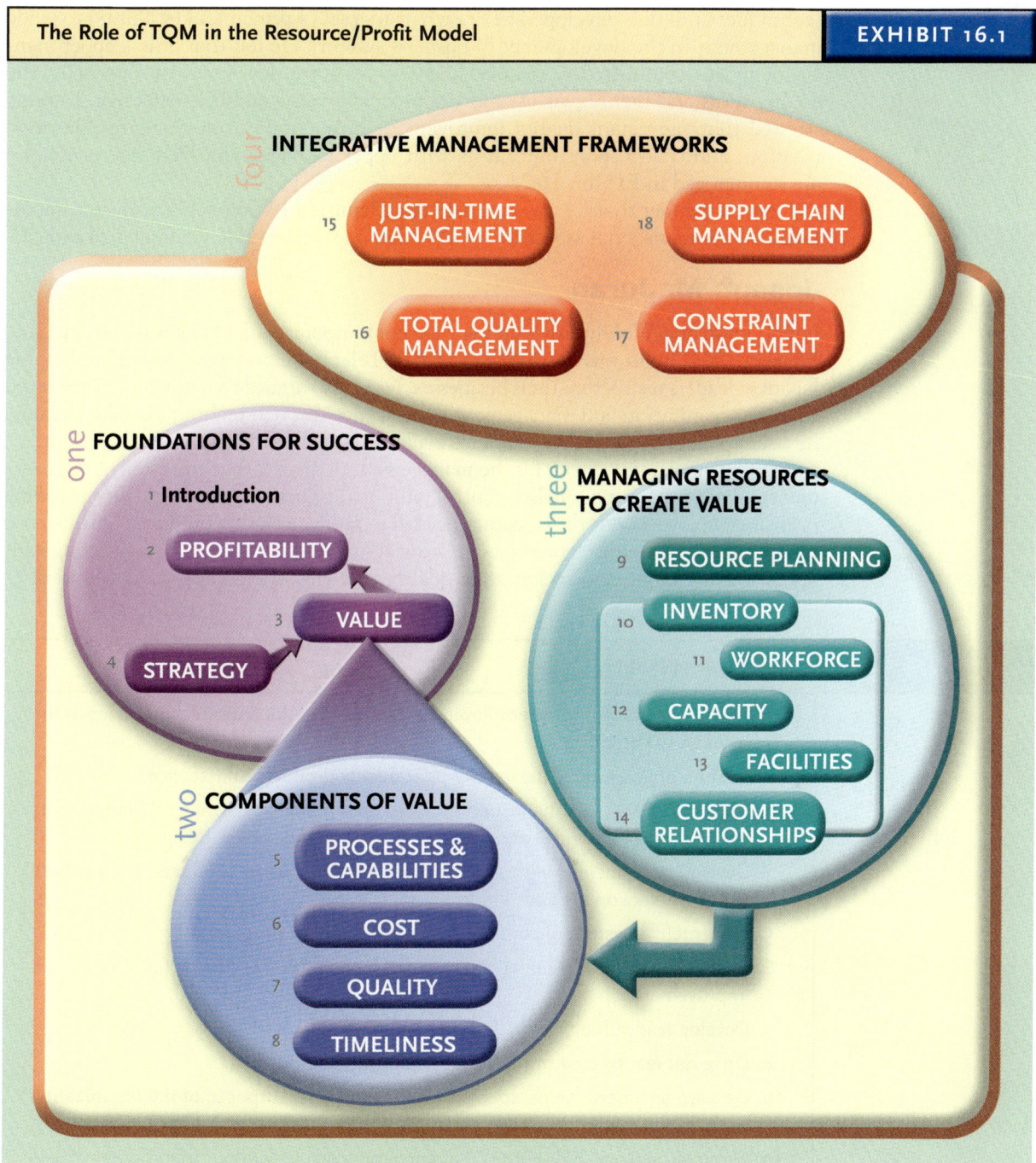

EXHIBIT 16.1 The Role of TQM in the Resource/Profit Model

often viewed as less than that of the other people involved in TQM. This is primarily because he was not a "crusader" for quality like the others, and because he died in 1967, before the concept of TQM had become popular in the United States.

W. Edwards Deming

W. Edwards Deming, a statistician who had studied the work of Shewhart, was one of the principal trainers of Japanese manufacturers in the 1950s. Deming extended the techniques and tools developed by Shewhart to a set of principles (14 points) to guide management in the development of business systems. He felt that unless upper management was committed to quality, and systems were developed to support it, the quality tools and techniques used at the process level would be ineffective. Deming stressed that significant quality improvement only comes from changing the organization, and that responsibility rests with upper management. Deming's principles are summarized in Exhibit 16.2.

Despite the fact that he was a statistician, Deming's 14 points place greater importance on the managerial aspects of quality than on statistics. Dr. Deming died in 1993.

Joseph M. Juran

Joseph Juran and W. Edwards Deming were contemporaries. Deming was born in 1900, Juran in 1904. Juran was an employee of Bell Telephone and was involved in helping Japanese leaders restructure their businesses. Juran also argued that quality was achieved through organization and management systems, not through techniques. Like Deming, he believed that most quality problems could be traced to ineffective management.

Juran created a framework for the management of quality that consisted of three elements: quality planning, quality control, and quality improvement. Quality planning provides employees with the direction needed to produce quality products. Quality control evaluates the performance by comparing actual results to goals and correcting variances. Quality improvement identifies quality problems, their causes, and solutions.

EXHIBIT 16.2

Deming's 14 Points

1. Create and publish to all employees a statement of the aims and purposes of the company or organization.
2. Adopt a philosophy of preventing poor quality products and service.
3. Understand the role inspection plays in quality management and eliminate its need by utilizing control and improving product and service design.
4. Develop relationships with suppliers that provide quality products. Do not base supplier selection on price alone.
5. Implement a system of continuous improvement of processes.
6. Provide employee training that teaches the skills required for continuous improvement.
7. Develop leadership.
8. Drive out fear by creating a culture of innovation and trust.
9. Develop an enterprise perspective on the aims and purposes of the organization by utilizing the efforts of teams that break down departmental barriers.
10. Eliminate slogans and themes that encourage results without training employees correctly.
11. Eliminate numerical quotas.
12. Improve employee pride by eliminating barriers to good workmanship.
13. Encourage education and improvement for everyone.
14. Take action at the top level of management to accomplish the transformation.

Source: W. E. Deming, *Out of the Crisis* (Cambridge, MA: MIT Press, 1986).

Crosby's Absolutes   EXHIBIT 16.3

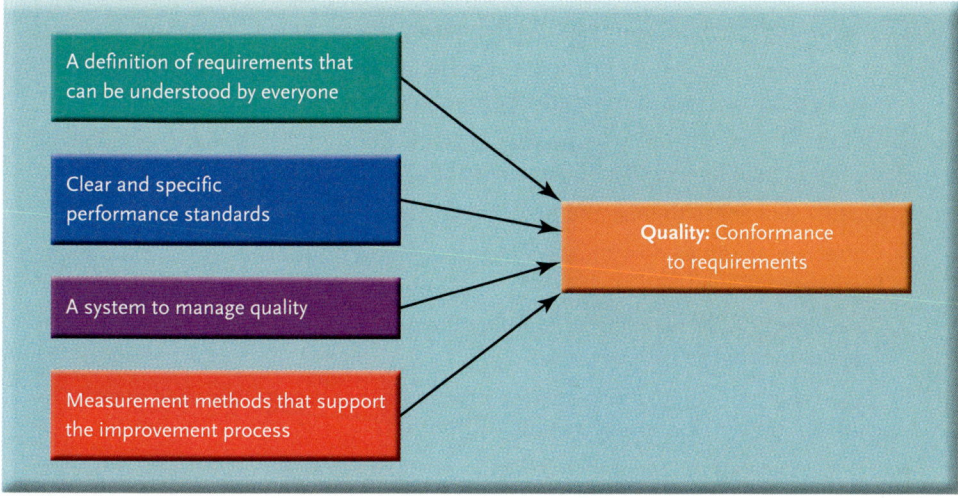

Source: J. MacDonald and J. Piggott, *Global Quality: The New Management Culture* (San Diego: Pfeiffer, 1993), p. 99.

Philip B. Crosby

The contributions of Philip Crosby are dominated by his influence on the education and attitudes of top management, not the development of techniques, as was the case with the previous three quality "gurus." Crosby's career started in 1952. He worked for various manufacturing firms, culminating at ITT as corporate vice president of quality. In 1979 he started his new firm, Philip Crosby Associates, following the wide acclaim of his book *Quality Is Free*. Crosby's quality philosophy is built around four "absolutes," briefly presented in Exhibit 16.3.

Crosby's approach is also summarized in a set of 14 points, presented in Exhibit 16.4. It emphasizes a "zero-defect" program that is initiated with a celebration and emphasizes motivation, education, and recognition.

COMPONENTS OF TQM

The TQM framework is based on three principles.[1] The first is **customer focus**, which means precisely what it says. The customer determines what quality is. The customer focus principle goes beyond our traditional view of the customer, however, by distinguishing between internal and external customers.

Every action in a business has a customer. A memo is generated for someone and that person is an **internal customer**. Raw material inventory retrieved from a warehouse is retrieved for someone, and that person is an internal customer. Sick leave records are kept accurately for someone to access and use, and that person is an internal customer. If the quality needs of internal customers are not met, the firm cannot expect to meet the needs of external customers either. **External customers** are the consumers the business typically thinks of as "customers"—those who buy products and services. The external customer is the ultimate recipient of quality. Poor internal quality eventually makes its way to external customers.

Like other capabilities that add value, capabilities that contribute to internal and external value are often outsourced to provide the best possible outcomes. Esource16.1

www.OperationsNow.com

> **EXHIBIT 16.4**   **Crosby's 14 Points**
>
> 1. Management commitment to make it clear where management stands on quality.
> 2. Quality improvement teams to run the quality improvement programs.
> 3. Quality measurement to provide a display of current and potential nonconformance problems in a manner that permits objective evaluation and action.
> 4. Utilize the Cost of Quality framework to define the ingredients of the cost of quality and explain its use as a management tool.
> 5. Quality awareness to raise the personal concern felt by all employees.
> 6. Corrective action to provide a systematic method of resolving forever the problems that are identified.
> 7. Zero-defects (ZD) planning to examine the activities that must be conducted in preparation for the zero-defects program.
> 8. Supervisor training to define the type of training that supervisors need in order to carry out their part of the program.
> 9. ZD day to create an event that will let all employees realize that there has been a change.
> 10. Goal setting to turn pledges and commitments into action.
> 11. Error-cause removal to give the individual employee a method of communicating to management the situations that make it difficult to improve.
> 12. Recognition to appreciate those who participate.
> 13. Quality councils to bring together the professional-quality people for communication on a regular basis.
> 14. Do it over again to emphasize that the quality improvement program never ends.
>
> Source: Adapted from P. B. Crosby, *Quality Is Free* (New York: McGraw-Hill, 1979).

provides an example of a company that focuses on fulfilling some of the less obvious aspects of internal and external value.

The second principle is **continuous process improvement**. Improvement of service- and product-oriented production processes focuses on the elimination of variability. Variability is enemy number one of quality. If there is one overriding principle of obtaining outcomes that meet customer expectations, the elimination of variability would be it. TQM extends that objective even further, however, to make it never-ending. Reduction of variability is always desirable. If reduction is achieved, more reduction would be even better. Meeting customer expectations requires that the outcomes of processes be the same every time. Outcomes must also be predictable. To be predictable they must be consistent, but a variable process is unpredictable. To eliminate variability, a variety of techniques are used to bring processes and work methods under control.

The third principle is **total involvement**, which is a culture that embraces the customer's view of quality in all aspects of the business. This requires a commitment at all levels of the firm, from the very top to the very bottom. All employees must have the knowledge, capabilities, and authority to improve processes. This extends upstream in the supply chain to include suppliers and contractors as well. The "local knowledge" that exists among employees provides an excellent resource when tapped. The resultant improvements extend to all corners of the business.

As shown in Exhibit 16.5, in a TQM environment the business utilizes resources (inventory, workforce, capacity, facilities, and customer relationships) with the customer's needs as the top priority. The resources are managed within a priority of doing things right the first time.

AN ENTERPRISE VIEW OF QUALITY

Total quality management (TQM) is an enterprise view of quality that radiates from the top down; it doesn't just reside within the functional units. The complexities of quality management are demonstrated by the many different types of quality. Dimensions of quality for services and products were discussed in Chapter 7 and are presented in Exhibit 16.6.

Resource Contributions to TQM — EXHIBIT 16.5

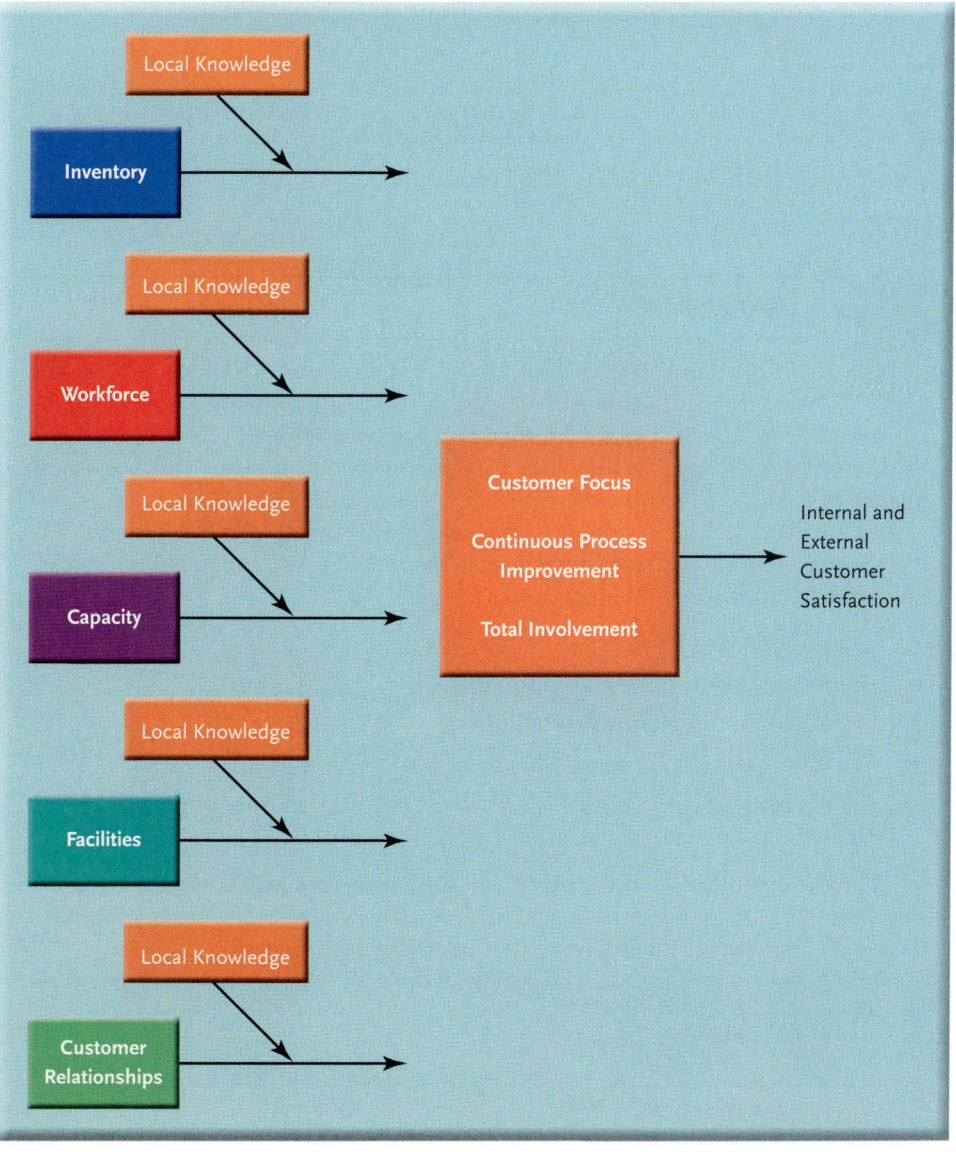

EXHIBIT 16.6 **Dimensions of Quality for Products and Services**

Source: Adapted from D. A. Garvin, "What Does Product Quality Really Mean?" *Sloan Management Review* 26 (Fall 1984), pp. 29–30, P. E. Pisek, "Defining Quality at the Marketing Development Interface," *Quality Progress* 20 (June 1987), pp. 28–36, and J. A. Fitzsimmons and M. J. Fitzsimmons, *Service Management* (New York: McGraw-Hill, 2001), p. 45.

TQM Results

Nelson Nameplates is a Los Angeles manufacturer of a variety of products, including nameplates and membrane switches that are used on electronic controls. Nelson was started in 1946 and has gone through a history of market and technology changes. It began its TQM effort in 1990 in response to management's desire to take a more proactive stance toward quality.

Traditionally, Nelson employees were reluctant to point out quality problems. Involvement with Philip Crosby Associates II, Inc., has resulted in numerous improvements in performance, including:

- Tripled revenue in 10 years.
- Fourfold drop in employee turnover.
- Threefold reduction in product returns.
- Improved quality at suppliers through Nelson's involvement.
- Achieved literacy in English for 100 employees (out of 300) who hadn't been English-literate through education.

A major component of Nelson's improvement process is the "error-cause removal" (ECR), in which employees identify causes of quality problems. More than 500 ECRs have been identified; more than 400 have been resolved.

During the 10-year effort, cost of quality dropped from 30 percent to 18 percent of sales.

Source: http://www.nelsonusa.com/about/index.htm, February 6, 2002; http://www.philipcrosby.com/main.htm, February 6, 2002.

Quality dimensions specific to products include performance, features, durability, and serviceability. The **performance** dimension of quality results from specific characteristics and capabilities of the product or service. Performance for a product may include the actual functions the product is able to perform. Performance for a service refers to the ability to respond accurately to customer needs. **Features** are additional capabilities that can be added to a product or service. Additional capabilities that go beyond the basic functional level, or additional services that add to the basic service, are considered features. The **durability** dimension describes how long a product will last under different conditions. **Serviceability** is a measure of effort required to repair a product.

Service-specific quality dimensions include assurance and empathy. **Assurance** relates to the level of trust and confidence generated by employees that customers interact with. **Empathy** is the approachability and sensitivity employees demonstrate.

Quality dimensions that are shared between product and services include reliability, responsiveness, reputation, tangibles, and aesthetics. The **reliability** dimension addresses the consistency of the performance. **Responsiveness** addresses the company's ability to respond promptly. **Reputation** summarizes the business's performance history. **Tangibles** are the physical facilities, equipment, and written material the customer comes in contact with. The **aesthetic** dimension covers aspects like the look, sound, or smell of a product, or the way it feels. Aesthetics go beyond the functional characteristics of a product and include subjective, ancillary characteristics.

For the customer, the dimensions just described combine to form an overall impression that results in satisfaction or dissatisfaction. Each is important to varying degrees, depending on the nature of the product or service. For the business lacking a unifying structure, however, they may be viewed independently by different functions, but the customer doesn't view them independently. The dimensions of quality combine to provide an overall level of satisfaction with quality, which contributes to the overall perception of value. We know, however, that quality is not the only component of value. Since the customer doesn't view the quality dimensions independently, decisions that dictate them can't be made independently either. They are related and intertwined, despite the fact that each may be more closely linked to one particular business function than others. Ultimately, the customer makes a decision based on the *total* perceived value of the interaction.

Without TQM and without recognition of the internal customer, the desire to provide the best product or service quality to the external customer may fall short and lead to a less than optimal situation. Each business function can have a different perspective of what quality means. For example, marketing may place a very high priority on product and service features and options. Engineering may place a higher priority on conformance to specifications. Shipping may place the highest priority on meeting the promised delivery date. Each may be willing to sacrifice another criterion to improve its favorite. Their concept of the internal customer steps in. The recognition that tasks and processes serve other aspects of the business, and are of critical importance, provides a unifying framework that improves the total value package, including the processes and capabilities, costs, timeliness, and ultimately customer relationships. The internal customer perspective results in improvements in all business processes, even those that do not directly serve the customer. As shown in Exhibit 16.7, these process improvements reduce costs. These improvements would not take place without the recognition of the importance of the internal customer.

As one of four components of value, the impact of quality on profitability is simple—as quality is enhanced, value is enhanced, increasing net sales. The impact of TQM is greater, however, because of the inclusion of internal customers. The recognition of internal customers implicit in TQM creates a closer relationship between quality and the

> **EXHIBIT 16.7** The Impact of Internal and External Customer Focus on Profitability

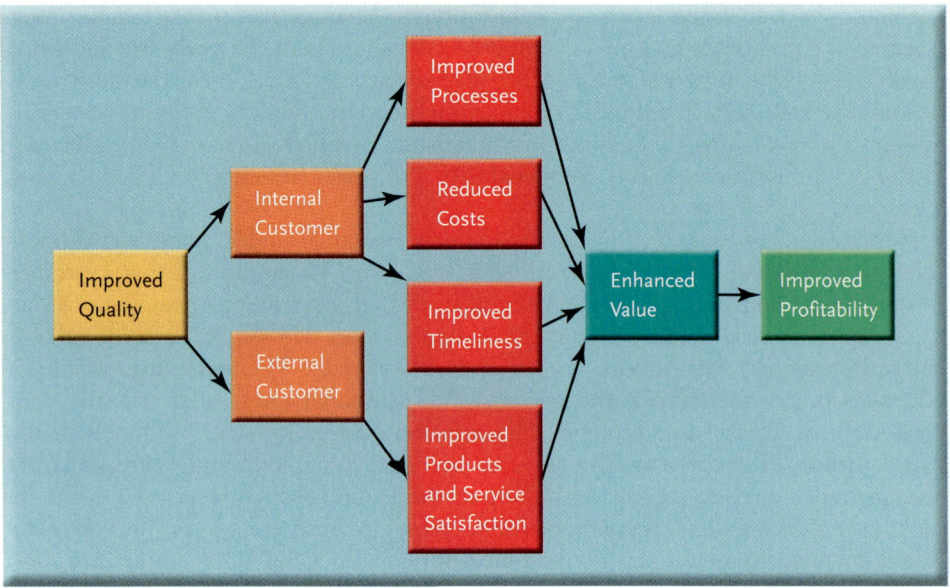

other components of value: processes and capabilities, cost, and timeliness, as described above. TQM enhances all four value components. The result is a greater impact on value than could be had by merely improving quality for the external customer.

THE TQM PROCESS

This ongoing process of TQM requires more than the principles of customer focus, process improvement, and total involvement. A number of supportive approaches are used to adhere to these principles, including top management commitment, employee involvement, employee training and development, reward and recognition, measurement, and a framework for using the quality tools presented in Chapter 7. Exhibit 16.8 shows how the three principles of TQM are supported by these approaches.

Top management commitment has often been cited as a missing component in failed TQM implementations. Without top management commitment, other priorities take precedence over the principles of TQM. The TQM effort dies very quickly as employees notice that management doesn't give it top priority. It doesn't take long for employees to abandon the principles when it is obvious to them that top management doesn't follow them. Employee involvement, in a manner similar to that employed by JIT, improves processes that impact internal and external customers. Local knowledge is valuable in improving these processes. Process and quality improvement teams are universal in TQM environments. To support employee involvement, training and development are crucial. The processes and analyses to solve quality problems are not simplistic. Most employees need training and practice in using these techniques. The expectation that employees are involved in the TQM process must be included in the company's reward and recognition systems. Management will get the behavior it rewards. If TQM is to become the culture, it must become part of the cultural norm. This will take place only if it is a part of the reward structure.

The continuous improvement effort driven by TQM is not a haphazard "let's change things and see what happens" type of environment. Improvement can come

Supportive Approaches to Three Principles of Quality — EXHIBIT 16.8

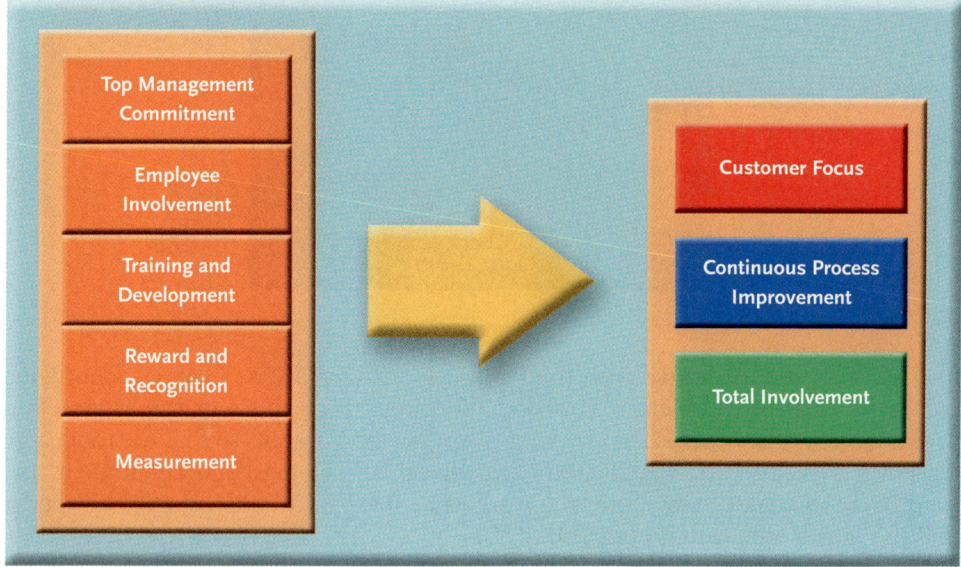

only from the recognition of problems, and problems can be recognized and verified only from objective data. Obtaining the data requires a well-developed measurement system. Accurate measurement is a prerequisite to making decisions related to improvement. Without accurate measurement, problems can't be identified and solutions can't be generated and tested to see if they actually worked.

Not surprisingly, instituting a cycle of continuous improvement of processes and a continuous effort to find and eliminate problems affecting internal and external customers is not easy. It requires an organizing structure such as those examined in the following section.

OBTAINING CONTINUOUS IMPROVEMENT

The Plan, Do, Check, Act Cycle

The most frequently used framework for guiding improvement is Shewhart's Plan, Do, Check, Act (PDCA) cycle, presented in Exhibit 16.9. The PDCA cycle creates a structure for the continuous improvement process that reinforces the use of data in making decisions.

The first stage of the PDCA cycle, Plan, is probably the most difficult. Three important tasks are completed in the Plan stage. The first task is problem identification and validation. This is potentially the most important of all improvement tasks because if it is not done correctly, there will be no improvement *and* a tremendous amount of time will have been wasted. Problem identification should be an obvious first step, but it must include validation. Problem validation means confirmation that the problem is a concern and does, in fact, exist.

The second task within the Plan stage is to gain a thorough understanding of the current situation. An understanding of the problem, how it impacts other aspects of the business, and how it is impacted by other aspects of the business establishes direction for the improvement process.

| EXHIBIT 16.9 | Shewhart's PDCA Cycle |

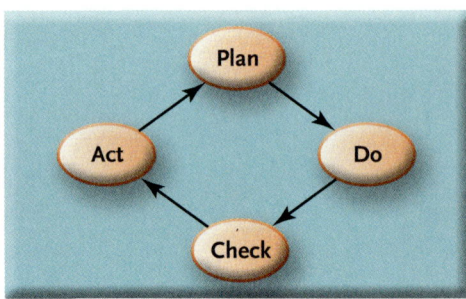

The third task associated with the Plan stage is the analysis of causes. Identifying root causes for any problem is always challenging. Since apparent causes are often symptoms of deeper causes, the challenge is to "peel the onion," so that the root cause is what is ultimately attacked. Figuring out what the problem is, understanding it, and identifying the cause summarizes the work to be done in the Plan stage. No wonder it is the most difficult to accomplish.

The Do stage is pretty straightforward when compared to its predecessor. The Do stage requires that the corrective action or proposed solution to the problem be implemented. That's it. If it's a process improvement, the change is made. If it's the elimination of the cause of some other problem, the action is taken to eliminate the cause.

The Check stage is also straightforward. After the Do stage is complete and a change has been made, the role of the Check stage is to see if that change has had the desired result. Did the change actually improve the process? Did it eliminate the cause of the problem? Is the problem gone? Like the problem identification and validation task, checking the results requires data and measurements.

The Act stage is where the improvement becomes enterprisewide. If the Check stage verified that the change had the desired impact, the first step in the Act stage is to standardize the change throughout the business. Thus, if a process change resulted in an improvement, that change should become part of the standard operating procedures for similar processes throughout the organization. If the action eliminated a problem, that action should become a standard operating procedure everywhere else as well. The second step in the Act stage is to bring the effort to its conclusion and then go back to the Plan stage to identify a new focus. Depending on the organization, concluding the cycle may require that a report be created or a presentation to management be made.

The Quality Improvement Story

Defining the PDCA cycle in terms of the seven steps just described has created an improvement process that is virtually universal with TQM-oriented firms. The seven steps have become known as the Quality Improvement (QI) story.[2] Exhibit 16.10 shows the QI story as it relates to the PDCA cycle.

The popularity of the QI story, particularly with employee quality and productivity improvement teams, has established it as the standard process used throughout many TQM environments. Employees, however, must be able to accomplish its seven steps in order for it to be effective. The eight quality tools presented in Chapter 7 provide the means for accomplishing its objectives. The eight tools are presented in Exhibit 16.11 as a quick review. For in-depth coverage, refer back to Chapter 7.

PDCA Cycle and QI Story

EXHIBIT 16.10

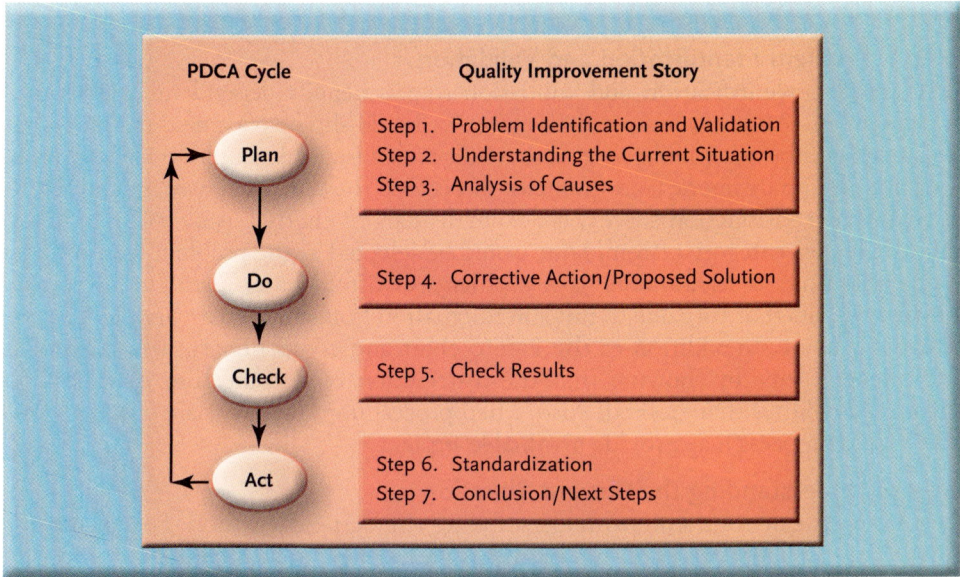

Quality Tool Overview

EXHIBIT 16.11

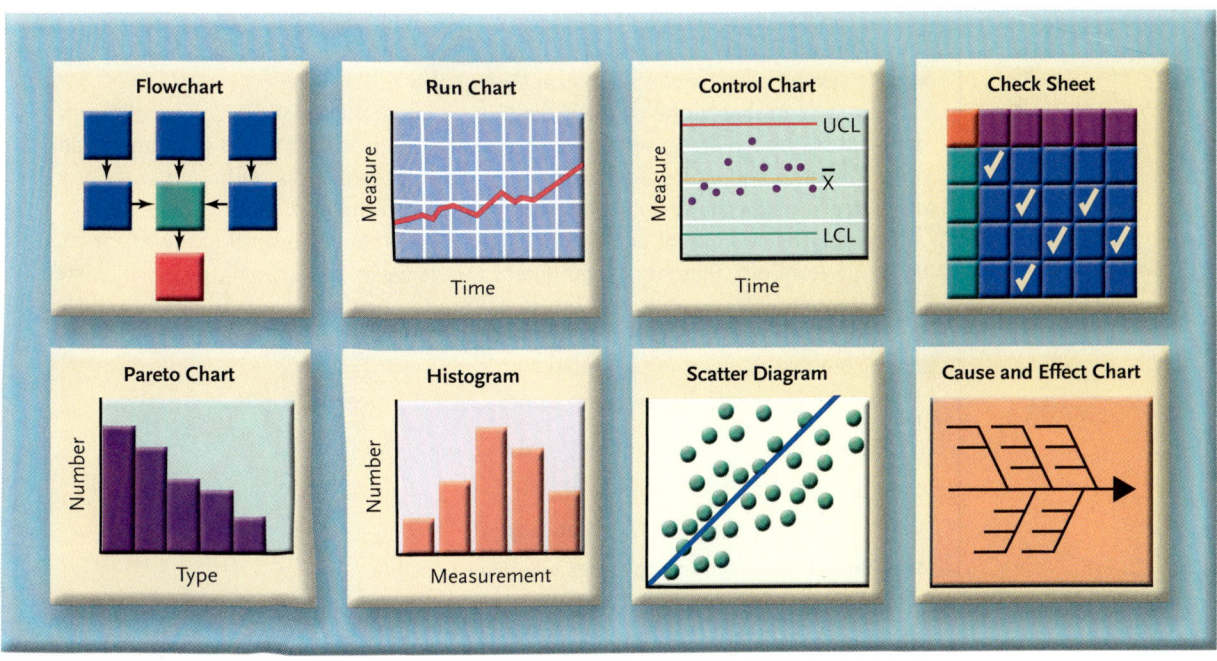

The quality tools are useful in completing the QI story. Some can be used in all seven of the steps in the QI story, whereas others are specific in their contribution to the improvement process. In the following discussion, the tools used in each step are described.

Step 1. Problem Identification and Validation

The problem identification and validation step is heavily dependent on data and measurement. After all, if a problem exists, it should show up as measurements that are outside of the acceptable range. Pareto charts are frequently used to identify problems for an improvement team to focus on because they prioritize issues. The results of a customer satisfaction survey, for example, can be charted using a Pareto chart, and the largest category of complaint would be selected as the problem to eliminate. Variability that is nonrandom is a problem. Control charts distinguish between process outputs that vary due to random fluctuation from those that vary due to some assignable cause. In addition to the Pareto chart and control chart, histograms also indicate problems by showing that the distribution of one measure is wider (has greater variability) than desired. Also, when process improvements are sought, a flow chart of the process may provide a valuable input.

Step 2. Understanding the Current Situation

Several tools can contribute to understanding the current situation. For example, a flow chart can almost certainly aid in understanding a problem situation or process to

---

Standardizing Election Processes

The TQM focus on systems, standards, and elimination of variability provides interesting insights on the 2000 U.S. presidential election, which resulted in chaos from misinterpreted ballots, miscounted ballots, malfunctioning machines, and resulting uncertainty. Who better to examine what went wrong than the American Society for Quality (ASQ)? An examination of the areas for improvement reveals several obvious conditions causing quality problems.

First, and probably one of the most important characteristics, is the lack of standardized systems. For example, there are between 4,000 and 5,000 separate jurisdictions, with some jurisdictions having more than 100 precincts. Although strict procedures are in place, they vary from one jurisdiction to the next.

Second, the equipment and technology used in about one-third of the precincts is up to 40 years old. Punchcard equipment that is worn, in ill repair, and inconsistent in function provides opportunity for variability and poor quality. In addition to the lack of standardized processes and old equipment, standards and procedures related to ballot counting vary among precincts.

ASQ recommends five steps for improving the process:

1. Define what constitutes quality in the voting process.
2. Seek relevant and reliable data.
3. Examine all processes systematically.
4. Standardize election processes wherever possible.
5. Develop the will to improve continuously and to apply needed resources to the task.

Source: American Society for Quality, "Election Reform," http://www.asq.org/news/election/fix.html, March 7, 2002. Used by permission.

be improved. A run chart can aid in understanding how measures vary over time, which can be quite useful for later steps in the QI story process. Histograms can also aid in this step because they provide a different view of the data. Quantitative data are often difficult to understand until they are converted to a graphical representation. Under certain situations, Pareto charts and scatter diagrams might also be useful.

Step 3. Analysis of Causes
The analysis of causes is challenging because it requires that the data gathered be used to determine exactly what is causing the problem. Two of the seven tools are particularly useful here. The first is the scatter diagram, which is used to identify relationships between two variables. It serves as a good screening device because if something is suspected as the cause of something else, the two must be correlated. Causality cannot exist without a relationship. The fact that two variables are correlated, however, doesn't necessarily mean that one causes the other.

Also, the cause and effect diagram provides an organized procedure for identifying potential causes and eventually getting to the root cause. Because of the popular use of employee teams in the continuous improvement process, the cause-and-effect diagram often provides a brainstorming tool for cause identification.

Step 4. Corrective Action/Proposed Solution
The corrective action/proposed solution step is taken when the data analysis is completed. The most useful tool for this step is a flowchart if the process is being changed, for example.

Step 5. Check Results
This step can potentially utilize any of the tools. In order to conclude that the action had the desirable results, data must be collected for validation measures taken after the change and compared to measures taken before the change to see if the problem was eliminated or the process improved. This step could require the use of flowcharts, run charts, Pareto charts, histograms, or control charts. All would be used to complete "before-and-after" comparisons for evaluation.

Step 6. Standardization
If step 5 showed that the changes were successful, standardization would take place. Depending on the changes, implementation might require slight modification to meet the needs of different contexts. In that case, it might be necessary to repeat some of the work done in step 4. If implementation were a duplication of the initial changes, no further data analysis would be needed.

Step 7. Conclusion/Next Steps
Depending on the requirements placed on the employees, the report or presentation would include all of the tools used in the process. Creating an improvement summary based on these seven steps gives the process its name and results in a story of quality improvement. Identification of the next improvement would require going back to step 1 and following the process again. Exhibit 16.12 summarizes the link between the seven quality tools and the steps in the QI story.

BENCHMARKING

Improvement efforts are often better received and more successful if there is a goal or objective to strive for. This is true for quality improvement efforts as well as business process improvements that would benefit only internal customers. One way to identify goals is to identify "best practices" through a process known as **benchmarking**. Two different types of benchmark are commonly used. The first type, **industry-focused**

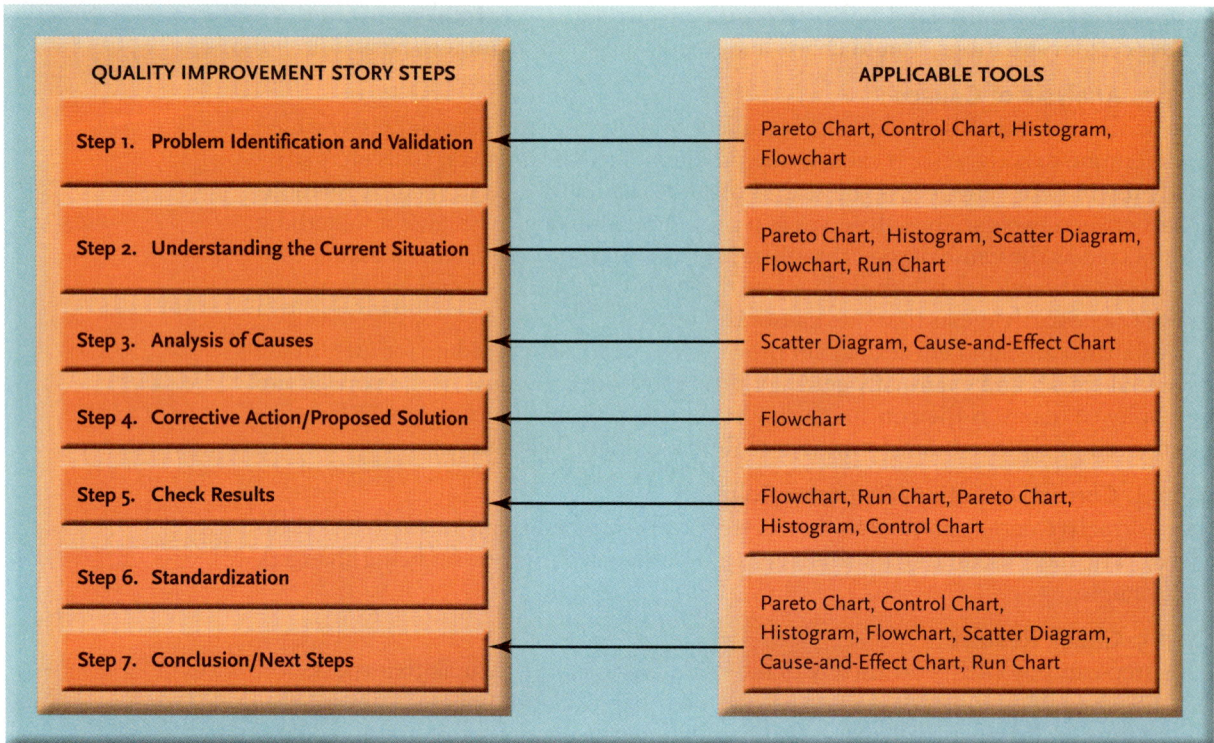

EXHIBIT 16.12 QI Story and Applicable Tools

www.OperationsNow.com

benchmarking, seeks to identify the best practices among competitors. One of the more difficult aspects of benchmarking is identifying processes to benchmark. Numerous benchmarking services have evolved to aid companies seeking benchmarking information. Esource 16.2 provides an example of an Internet service for companies seeking to benchmark their business processes.

The house of quality, introduced in Chapter 5 as a part of the quality function deployment process and reproduced from Chapter 7 in Exhibit 16.13, is used to link product and service design to customer needs and requires industry-focused benchmarks in two places. Near the bottom of the house is a space for "Competitive Evaluations." This requires that target relationships for measures be compared to those of the competition. On the right side is the "Competitive Evaluation of WHAT/HOW Relationships." Both of these competitive evaluations rely on best-practice data about competitors obtained through benchmarking.

The Internet has made it much easier to identify benchmarks through a variety of industry-focused organizations. As an example, Exhibit 16.14 lists industry-focused benchmarking organizations cited at one of many benchmarking websites.

The second type of benchmarking, known as **process-focused benchmarking,** is used when a business wants to identify a best practice for a process that is not industry-specific. Many business processes are generic. For example, the way phone centers are managed for mail order retailers is similar no matter what the product. The operation of warehouses is similar from one industry to the next. Process-focused benchmarking provides a way for companies to identify best practices that are world class, even if no competitor has a good system in place. It is usually easier to get access to benchmarking

| House of Quality | EXHIBIT 16.13 |

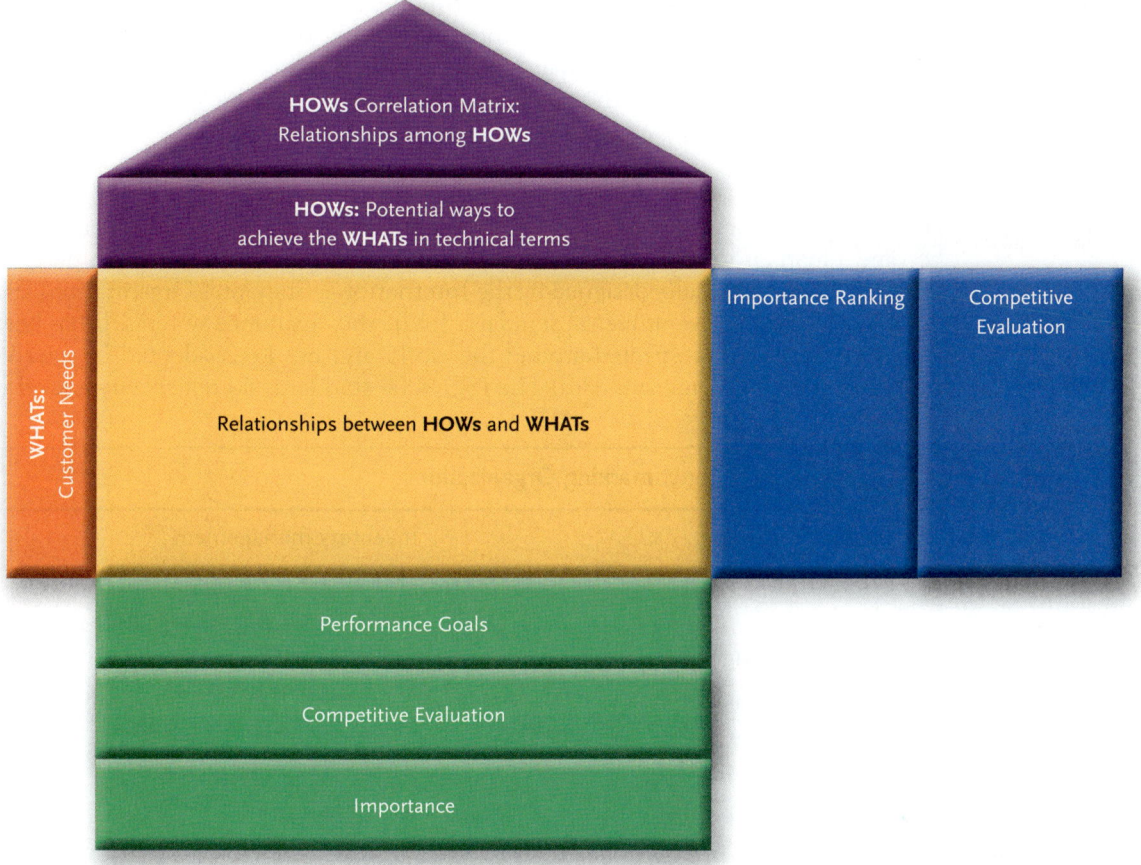

| Industry-Focused Benchmarking Organizations | EXHIBIT 16.14 |

Airlines	Financial services	Oil and gas
Airports	Government	Petrochemical
Aerospace	Health care	Pharmaceutical
Automotive	Higher education	Retail
Banking	Hospitality	Retention
Broadcasting	Insurance	Software
Cable and satellite television	Internet	Sport
	ISP	Telecommunications
Computer hardware manufacturing	Magazine	Transportation
	Manufacturing	Water utility
Defense	Natural gas	Wireless
Electric utility	Newspapers	Yellow pages
Energy	Not-for-profit	

Source: The Benchmarking Network, "The Benchmarking Resource Guide," http://www.well.com/user/benchmar/, May 21, 2001.

partners for process-focused benchmarking because there is no competitive advantage to be lost by sharing that information. Many of the processes closely related to operations management are selected for process-focused benchmarking because of their impact on quality. Many organizations offering members access to best practices for specific business processes have been formed. Exhibit 16.15 lists operations-related processes that are now such popular benchmarking targets that they have organizations devoted specifically to them.

QUALITY CERTIFICATION PROGRAMS

For many companies, particularly those that interact globally, quality certification has become a mandatory way of doing business. The most popular certification program is ISO 9000. As originally designed by the International Standards Organization, ISO 9000 was a series of five universal standards for quality assurance systems. It has been widely accepted and respected around the world and has been adopted by over 90 countries as the national standard. The ISO 9000 standards do not specify a level of

EXHIBIT 16.15 Process-focused Benchmarking Organizations

Agile manufacturing	Inventory management
B2B	Lean manufacturing
B2C	Procurement and supply chain management
Call center management	
Customer satisfaction	Process management
Customer service	Product development
Distribution and logistics	Relationship management
Facilities and real estate	Six sigma
Global operations	

Source: The Benchmarking Network, "The Benchmarking Resource Guide," http://www.well.com/user/benchmar/, May 21, 2001.

ISO certification has become a hallmark in many industries. Although it doesn't guarantee product quality for automotive parts suppliers, it provides proof that quality systems are in place. Here, DaimlerChrysler advertises its ISO certification.

product or service quality. Instead, they specify a set of quality assurance systems that must be in place. By requiring quality systems, they ensure that the certified company has the infrastructure, knowledge, and capability to produce quality products and services. The standards are identical for all companies, no matter what size or industry. The standards have been popular because customers can be confident that their suppliers have quality assurance systems in place. When the company gets certified, new markets open up. For U.S. companies doing business internationally, ISO 9000 certification is virtually required. Esource 16.3 provides an example of a company that obtained ISO certification to broaden its ability to market its products to quality-oriented customers.

The ISO 9000 standards are developed and monitored by the International Standards Organization. The National Institute for Standards and Technology is the U.S. representative on that organization. The U.S. version of the ISO 9000 standards was developed by the American National Standards Institute (ANSI). The original five components of the ISO 9000 series of standards are presented in Exhibit 16.16.

The ISO 9000 standards received a major overhaul in 2000, resulting in the discontinuation of ISO 9002 and ISO 9003. In addition, ISO 9001 was replaced with one standard: ISO 9000 2000. The very complex 20-section set of requirements was reorganized into a more logical five sections. The original ISO 9000 standards had been criticized because they did not mandate continuous improvement or any level of actual product or service quality. Both criticisms were valid. The new ISO 9000 2000 standards are much more customer-oriented and address customer satisfaction in greater detail. In addition, the new standards mandate communication with customers and measurement of customer satisfaction. The ISO 9000 2000 standard also emphasizes continuous improvement. While the old standards implicitly expected organizations to make improvements, the new standard makes that requirement explicit. The standard now requires evaluation of the effectiveness of the quality management system and systematic improvement of that system. New requirements and modifications to old ones have definitely changed the tone of the standards. Terminology was changed as well, to make the standards more understandable. Exhibit 16.17 summarizes the requirements that were modified or changed. The nature of these changes shows the new emphases of the standards.

EXHIBIT 16.16

Original ISO 9000 Standards

ISO 9000: Quality management and quality assurance standards.
- Part 1: Guidelines for selection and use.
- Part 2: Generic guidelines for the application of ISO 9000, ISO 9002, and ISO 9003.
- Part 3: Guidelines for the application of ISO 9001 to the development, supply, and maintenance of software.
- Part 4: Guide to dependability program management.

ISO 9001: Quality system-model for quality assurance in design, development, production, installation, and servicing.

ISO 9002: Quality system-model for quality assurance in production, installation, and servicing.

ISO 9003: Quality system-model for quality assurance in final inspection and test.

ISO 9004: Development of quality management systems.

EXHIBIT 16.17	**Summary of Changed and Modified Criteria in ISO 9000 2000**
	Communicate with customers
	Evaluate the effectiveness of quality management system
	Evaluate the effectiveness of training
	Evaluate the suitability of quality management system
	Identify customer requirements
	Identify quality management system improvements
	Improve quality management system
	Meet customer requirements
	Meet regulatory requirements
	Meet statutory requirements
	Monitor and measure customer satisfaction
	Monitor and measure processes
	Provide quality infrastructure
	Provide a quality work environment
	Support internal communication

Just as the ISO 9000 series requires quality management systems, its counterpart ISO 14000 requires environmental management systems. The requirements of ISO 14000 guide organizations in formulating policies that take into account environmental impact legislation. Just as ISO 9000 doesn't specify quality performance criteria, ISO 14000 doesn't specify environmental performance. It applies to the environmental aspects that business can control.

QUALITY AWARDS

Many businesses accept the challenge of winning a quality award as motivation to instill quality into the organization's culture. There are many quality awards, ranging from state and local awards to national and international. The most prestigious quality award in the United States is the Malcolm Baldrige National Quality Award.

The Malcolm Baldrige National Quality Award

The Malcolm Baldrige National Quality Improvement Act was signed into law in 1987. Its award, managed by the U.S. Department of Commerce, is intended to increase the awareness of quality as an important component of competitiveness, to share information about successes, and to promote understanding of the requirements for quality. It accomplishes these objectives by publicizing and increasing public awareness of successes achieved by the winners of the award. No more than two awards can be given annually in each of five categories. The categories originally were manufacturing companies and their subsidiaries, service companies and their subsidiaries, and small businesses. In 1998 categories for educational and health care organizations were added.

The Baldrige program and award framework comprise an excellent structure for developing a quality-driven organization. This has become a popular means of improving quality, even for organizations not intending to apply for the award. The Baldrige award embraces the following values:[3]

- Visionary leadership
- Customer-driven excellence
- Organizational and personal learning
- Valuing employees and partners
- Agility
- Focus on the future
- Managing for innovation
- Management by fact
- Focus on results and value creation
- Systems perspective
- Public responsibility and citizenship

The Malcolm Baldrige National Quality Award is presented annually. Clarke American Checks, a manufacturing firm, receives the award in the presence of Commerce Secretary Don Evans and President Bush.

These values are translated into seven categories of award criteria:

- Leadership
- Strategic planning
- Customer and market focus
- Information and analysis
- Human resource focus
- Process management
- Business results

The model used to illustrate how these categories fit together is presented in Exhibit 16.18.

Exhibit 16.19 provides an overview of the way the award criteria are scored. Each item is scored based on points for the approach and deployment of the item and points for the actual results. The maximum total score is 1,000.

Each year the winners are announced with much publicity and fanfare. Exhibit 16.20 lists recent award winners. The performance of Baldrige winners provides evidence of the impact a quality emphasis can have on profitability. The National Institute of Standards and Technology (NIST) maintains a "Baldrige Index" to monitor the financial performance of Baldrige Award winners and compare their performance to the Standard & Poor's 500. The Baldrige Index is a fictitious stock fund made up of publicly traded U.S. companies that have received the Malcolm Baldrige National Quality Award between 1990 and 1999. In the latest study, NIST invested a hypothetical $1,000 in each of the whole-company winners (ADAC Laboratories, Eastman Chemical Company, Federal Express Corp., and Solectron Corp.). Another hypothetical $1,000 was invested in the S&P 500. The investments were tracked from the first business day of the month following the announcement of award recipients through December 1, 2000. Adjustments were made for stock splits. The Baldrige Index outperformed the S&P 500 by a ratio of 4.4 to 1. In another study comparing the performance of the whole-company winners and the 18 subsidiary company winners to the S&P 500, the Baldrige companies outperformed the S&P by a ratio of 4.2 to 1.

The Baldrige Award does not have a lock on the impact of quality on financial performance. A recent study of 600 publicly traded firms that have won quality awards,

EXHIBIT 16.18 — Malcom Baldrige National Quality Award

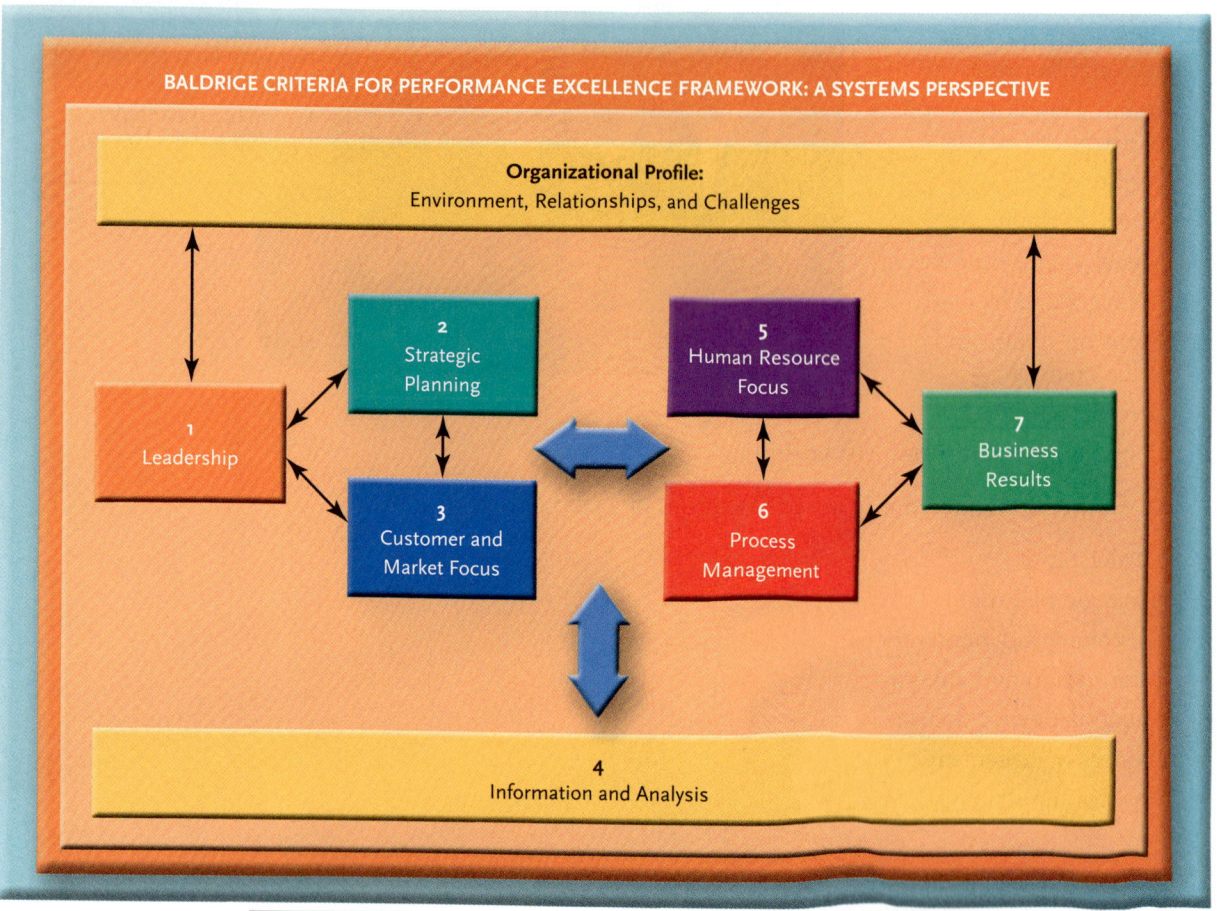

Source: Baldrige National Quality Program Criteria for Performance Excellence, 2001, p. 5, http://www.quality.nist.gov/PDF_files/2002_Business_Criteria.pdf.

including the Baldrige, showed that award recipients experienced a 44 percent higher stock price return, 48 percent higher growth in operating income, and 37 percent higher growth in sales than a control group of firms similar in size and operating in the same industries.[4]

The Quality Cup

In addition to the Baldrige National Quality Award, most states have implemented quality award programs that encourage businesses to seek quality reputations. There are also numerous industry-specific quality awards. One prestigious award, the Quality Cup, is a national award that focuses on the accomplishments of teams. The Quality Cup is awarded to up to three teams per year in each of the following categories:

- Education
- Government
- Health care
- Manufacturing industry

EXHIBIT 16.19 Baldrige Award Criteria and Scoring Summary

Criterion	Total Points	Item	Item Point Value
Leadership	120	Organizational leadership	80
		Public responsibility and citizenship	40
Strategic planning	85	Strategy development	40
		Strategy deployment	45
Customer and market focus	85	Customer and market knowledge	40
		Customer relationships and satisfaction	45
Information and analysis	90	Measurement and analysis of organizational performance	50
		Information management	40
Human resource focus	73	Work systems	23
		Employee education, training, and development	25
		Employee well-being and satisfaction	25
Process management	85	Product and service processes	45
		Business processes	25
		Support processes	15
Business results	450	Customer-focused results	125
		Financial and market results	125
		Human resource results	80
		Organizational effectiveness results	120

- Service industry
- Small businesses (fewer than 500 employees)

CHAPTER SUMMARY

The quality of products and services has come to dominate the competitive efforts of businesses. This chapter has provided an overview of TQM, a management framework employed to create a culture committed to quality in all aspects of the business. TQM is achieved in different ways, including certification programs and award programs. TQM's focus on continuous improvement and its reliance on quality tools and performance measurement create a culture of quality-mindedness. The TQM culture, when permeated throughout the business, creates a focus on internal *and* external quality. That focus provides benefits beyond those obtained from simply producing high-quality outputs. It creates enhancements to processes and capabilities, costs, and timeliness as well. As we know, process quality improvement, when combined with

EXHIBIT 16.20 — Baldrige Award Winners

Year	Manufacturing	Service	Small Business
1995	Armstrong World Industries, Inc., Building Products Operation Corning Incorporated, Telecommunications Products Division		
1996	ADAC Laboratories	Dana Commercial Credit Corporation	Custom Research Inc. Trident Precision Manufacturing, Inc.
1997	3M Dental Products Division Solectron Corporation	Merrill Lynch Credit Corporation Xerox Business Services	
1998	Boeing Airlift and Tanker Programs Solar Turbines Incorporated		Texas Nameplate Company, Inc.
1999	STMicroelectronics, Inc.—Region Americas	BI The Ritz-Carlton Hotel Company, L.L.C.	Sunny Fresh Foods
2000	Dana Corporation—Spicer Driveshaft Division KARLEE Company, Inc.	Operations Management International, Inc.	Los Alamos National Bank

product and service quality, enhances the entire value package. This increase in value translates into improved levels of profitability and overall improvements in financial measures for the business.

KEY TERMS

aesthetics, 575
assurance, 575
benchmarking, 581
continuous process improvement, 572
customer focus, 571
durability, 575
empathy, 575
features, 575
external customer, 571
industry-focused benchmarking, 581

internal customer, 571
performance, 575
process-focused benchmarking, 582
reliability, 575
reputation, 575
responsiveness, 575
serviceability, 575
tangibles, 575
total involvement, 572

REVIEW QUESTIONS

1. Describe the impact of the four major contributors to TQM.
2. Why is the recognition of the internal customer critical to TQM?
3. Explain the importance of eliminating variability in a TQM environment.
4. What role does total involvement play in creating a culture supportive of TQM?
5. Describe the following dimensions of quality:
   a. Performance
   b. Reliability
   c. Serviceability
   d. Response
   e. Features
   f. Durability
   g. Aesthetics
   h. Reputation
6. How does TQM enhance the value components of processes and capabilities, cost, and timeliness?
7. Describe the PDCA cycle. How does it relate to the Quality Improvement story?
8. What are the two different types of benchmarking? How are they used?
9. What role have quality certification programs had in improving quality?
10. What is ISO 9000? Why would a company be interested in getting ISO 9000–certified?
11. Describe the criteria of the Baldrige Award.

DISCUSSION QUESTIONS

1. From your work experiences, identify instances where you or your colleagues ignored an internal customer and it resulted in poor quality for the external customer.
2. Why is a step-by-step process like the QI story important in accomplishing objectives?
3. Why do award programs like the Malcolm Baldrige Quality Award get criticized?
4. Why must TQM be a commitment that crosses departmental boundaries?
5. Can company culture alone, with no knowledge of statistical techniques, succeed in improving product and service quality?

SELECTED REFERENCES

Aguayo, R., *Dr. Deming: The American Who Taught the Japanese About Quality*. New York: Simon & Schuster, 1991.

Crosby, P. *Quality Is Free*. New York: McGraw-Hill, 1979.

Juran, J. M. *Juran on Planning for Quality*. New York: Free Press, 1988.

Tenner, A. R., and DeToro, I. J. *Total Quality Management*. Reading, MA: Addison-Wesley, 1992.

ENDNOTES

1. Adapted from A. R. Tenner and I. J. De Toro, *Total Quality Management* (Reading, MA: Addison-Wesley, 1992).
2. GOAL/QPC, *Total Quality Control in Japan*, Research Report No. 89-10-10 (Metheun, MA: Author, 1989).
3. Business Criteria for Performance Excellence, http://www.quality.nist.gov/Criteria.htm, March 20, 2002.
4. Eighth NIST Stock Investment Study, http://www.quality.nist.gov/Stock_Studies.htm, March 20, 2002.

CHAPTER 16 Total Quality Management

OperationsNow.com LEARNING ACTIVITIES

CHAPTER ENHANCEMENT RESOURCES
- Esources
- Reel Operations Video Clips
- Interactive Models
- Excel Tutors
- Supplementary Readings
- Links to Operations On Site Companies

OM EXPLORATION
- Check It Out
- OM in Action
- Online Business Tours
- Letters from the Top
- Putting It All Together: Virtual Case Studies
- Additional Readings

The resource/profit model identifies constraint management as the third of four integrative management frameworks. Constraint management is often viewed as a focusing framework, but the nature of its focus has such broad implications that its influence spans functional boundaries. Objectives of constraint management are more directly linked to profitability than the other integrative frameworks. Despite a controversial history, constraint management has had a broad impact on resource decision making.

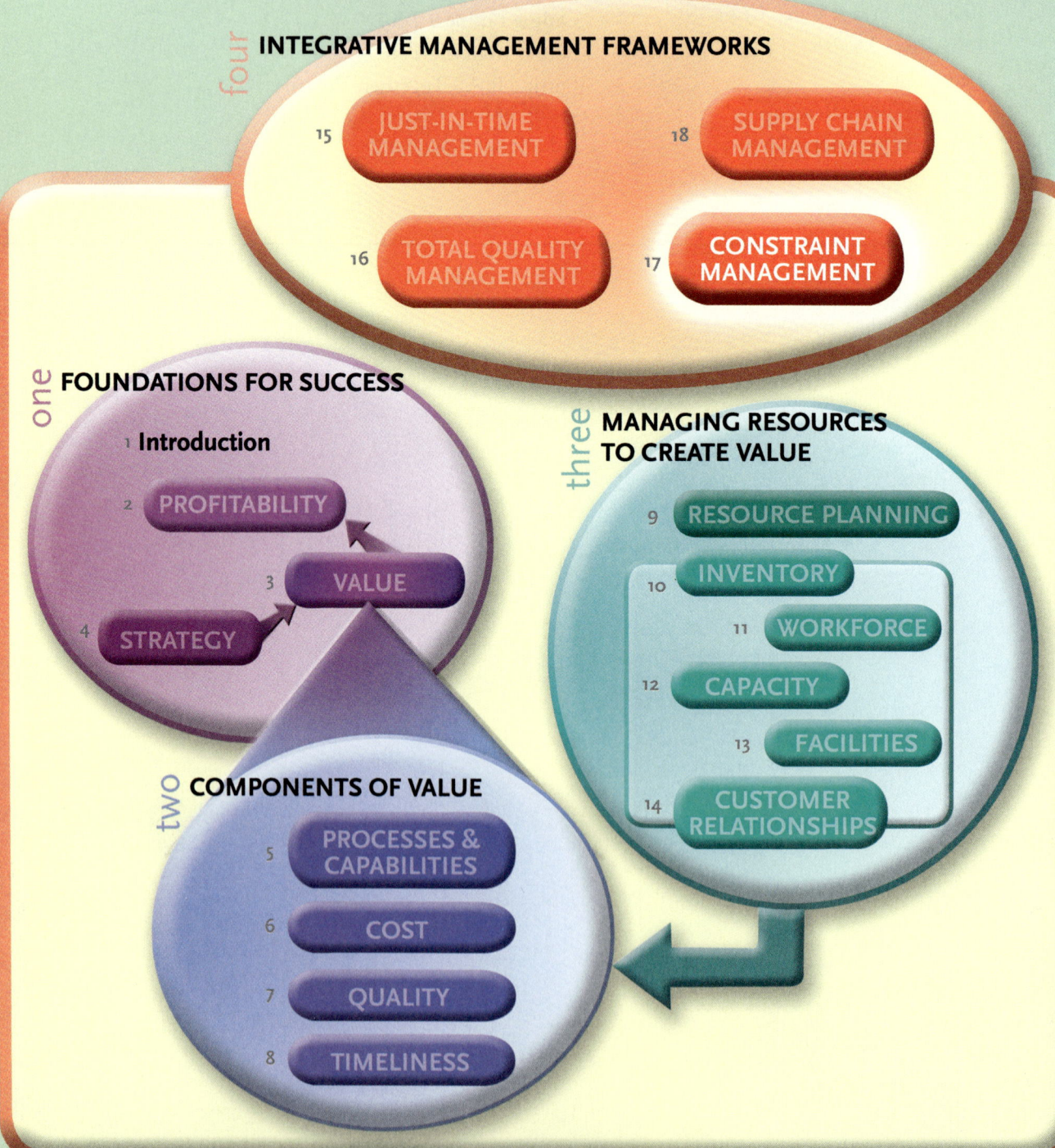

CHAPTER 17

Constraint Management

LEARNING OBJECTIVES

Upon completion of Chapter 17, you should be able to

_____ Define a constraint.

_____ Compare utilization and activation from a constraint management perspective.

_____ Describe the global measures of throughput, inventory, and operating expense, and compare them to traditional global measures.

_____ Explain the five-step focusing process of constraint management.

_____ Explain how systems can be protected from disruptions by using time buffers.

_____ Describe how time buffers function and how they affect the exploitation of a constraint.

_____ Explain what is meant by a constraint buffer, a shipping buffer, and an assembly buffer.

_____ Differentiate between a production batch and a transfer batch.

_____ Compute the appropriate product mix for a constrained production system.

_____ Compare the kanban system used in JIT to the buffering system used in constraint management.

Introduction: Maximizing System Output
Defining a Constraint
Global Performance Measures
The Constraint Management Focusing Process
The Role of Disruptions in Productive Systems
Protecting the System from Disruptions
Buffering to Protect Constraints
Constraint Management and Batch Sizes
The Role of the Constraint: A Product Mix Example
JIT and Constraint Management
Chapter Summary

INTERNET RESOURCES

 Excel Tutors provide annotated spreadsheets for every solved problem that automatically load Excel.

 Esources provide an online version of the more traditional boxed insert.

 Reel Videos provide streaming video footage for company applications of chapter concepts.

 Interactive Models provide an experimental environment for quantitative concepts and simulations.

INTRODUCTION

Maximizing System Output

Unlike TQM and JIT, which were developed by the contributions of many different people, the development of constraint management (CM) can be credited to one individual, Eliahu Goldratt. Goldratt, an Israeli physicist, is the author of the 1984 book *The Goal*.[1] A combination of a business novel and a love story, *The Goal* became extremely popular. It tells the story of a manufacturing plant manager trying to save an unprofitable plant from being closed down—an interesting tale about the importance of constraints in a business. Unlike most business paperbacks that claim a very brief period of fame, *The Goal* is still very popular. Despite its age, *The Goal* is still a frequent listing on *BusinessWeek*'s bestseller list.

Following the publication of *The Goal*, constraint management, or the theory of constraints, as it is also known, began to get increasing attention from managers. As a part of that increasing attention, numerous extensions and techniques were developed to help effectively manage constraints until a concise framework for managing resources evolved. The existence of this framework led to the inclusion of constraint management as the third integrative management framework in Exhibit 17.1. The evolution of constraint management led to the proliferation of consulting firms specializing in helping businesses manage their constraints. Esource 17.1 provides an example of such a consulting firm and describes its consulting focus.

www.OperationsNow.com

DEFINING A CONSTRAINT

A **constraint** is defined succinctly as anything that inhibits a system's progress toward its goals. Obviously, before a system's constraint can be identified, the system's goals must be understood. Placing the constraint in the context of system goals broadens the applicability of constraint management to include systems whose goals go beyond "profit" or "making money," as is the case for many business systems. Education and other not-for-profit systems are feasible applications for constraint management.

Defined as anything that inhibits a system's progress toward its goals, the role a constraint plays in any system becomes very important. The system's output, as measured by its goals, is limited by the constraint(s) of that system. A system's constraint can actually take many forms. It could be a resource, a policy, an input to the system, or some external force. For example, if one goal of your university is to graduate accounting majors, a lack of faculty or a lack of classroom space could be a constraint. A lack of applicants to enter the accounting program could be a constraint as well, but it might be a symptom of a policy constraint—not providing enough financial aid to students. Or it might be due to the fact that accounting firms are not currently recruiting or hiring students from your university, so students do not want to major in accounting.

Constraint management is a framework for managing the constraints of a system in a way that maximizes the system's accomplishment of its goals. The fact that it manages the most important part of the system, the part that determines its output, means that constraint management is actually a way of focusing on the most critical aspects of the system.

The role a constraint plays in a simple productive system is easily portrayed in an example. Exhibit 17.2 diagrams a simple production system. Suppose that we could sell every unit we produce in this system. Given a goal of producing as many units as possible, the system portrayed in Exhibit 17.2 is constrained by work center 3, which

EXHIBIT 17.1 The Role of Constraint Management in the Resource/Profit Model

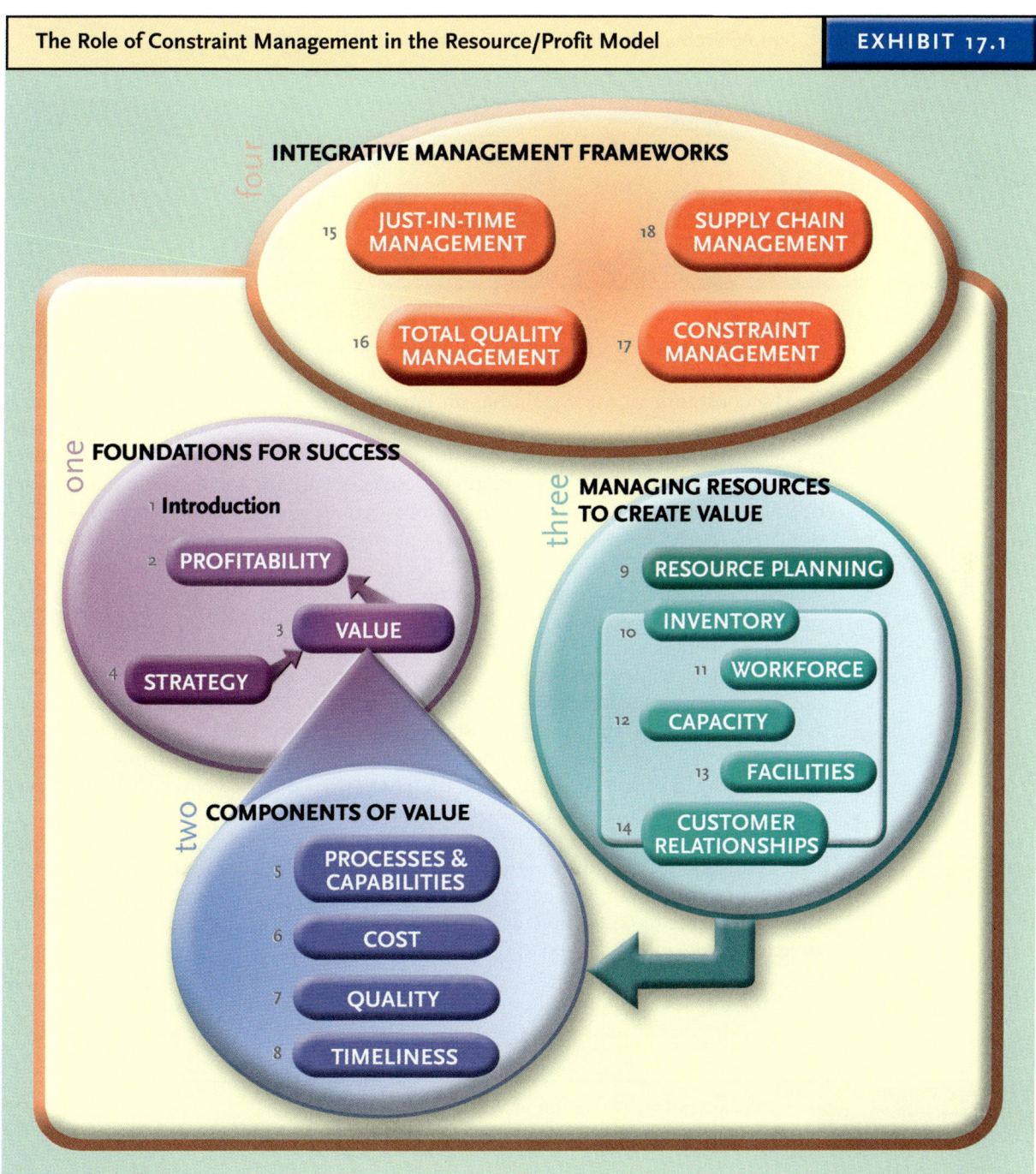

takes nine minutes per unit. The result is that a unit exits the system every nine minutes, despite shorter processing times by other work centers. The role of work center 3 goes beyond restricting the rate of output of the system. Work center 1, for example, could process a unit every six minutes, but close examination shows that it would not make sense for it to do that. Material would exit work center 1 at a rate of one unit per six minutes but would not be able to exit the system at that rate. A queue of inventory would build up in front of work centers 2 and 3, and it would grow indefinitely as long as the input rate exceeded the output rate. The logical approach would

EXHIBIT 17.2 — Simple Productive System with Constraint (minutes per unit)

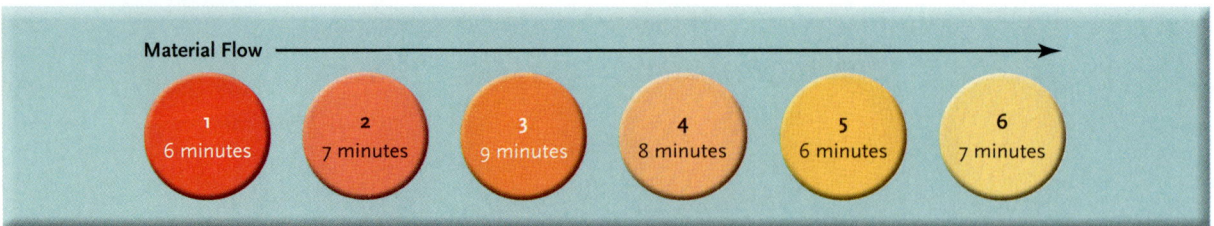

be to allow work center 1 to process one unit only every nine minutes, since any more than that would not increase the system's output.

The constraint in the system has an impact on many performance measures. For example, it is commonplace to incorporate "utilization" as a measure of equipment productivity. We already know that utilizing work center 1 at a 100 percent level (processing one unit every six minutes) doesn't provide any more system output than utilizing it at a 66 percent level (producing one unit every nine minutes). This phenomenon is so important in the constraint management framework that two concepts, utilization and activation, have been redefined to help understand it. In a constraint management context, **utilization** means that the operation of a resource contributes to the goals of the system. **Activation** of a resource means that the resource is being used but does not contribute to the system's goals. In this situation, work center 1 could be activated at 100 percent but it could be utilized only to a level of 66 percent. The utilization level of work center 2 is also determined by work center 3. It will be constrained to processing a unit every nine minutes, the same as work center 1. It will process each unit in seven minutes, and then wait two minutes before receiving the next unit. Its utilization, therefore, will be 78 percent. Exhibit 17.3 provides utilization data for each work center.

The effect that a constraint has on work center performance is important. It is an excellent example of how an attempt to optimize a local performance measure, like work center utilization, can actually harm a more global performance measure. Imagine the increase in costs (inventory carrying costs, quality costs, facility costs) if the inventory were allowed to build up because input rate exceeded output rate. Imagine also the impact on timeliness as queues were allowed to grow longer and longer. The resulting impact on profitability (from net sales as well as costs) would be devastating, despite the fact that the utilizations on work centers 1 and 2 were high. This is

EXHIBIT 17.3 — Constraint's Determination of Work Center Utilization

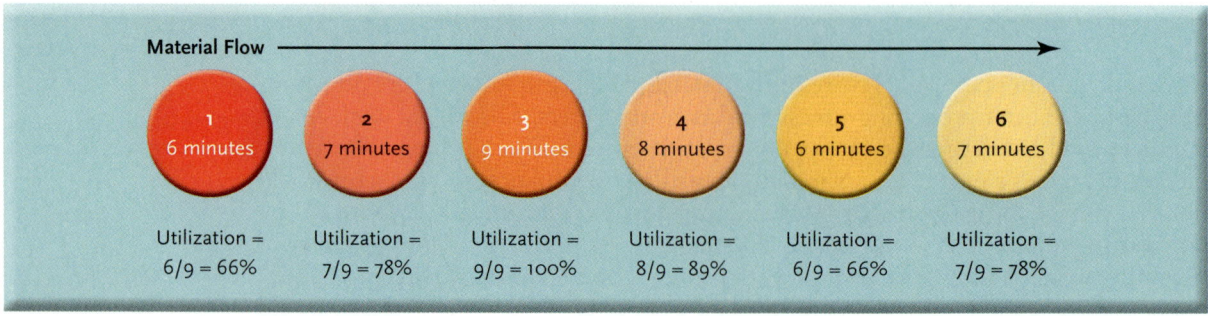

This refinery in Malaysia utilizes a proprietary delayed coking technology to maximize production of diesel fuel, which is in high demand in the region. That technology increases the capacity of the entire refinery system. The refinery is a joint venture of Conoco, Petronas (the Malaysian national oil company), and Statoil (the Norwegian national oil company).

such an important concept in constraint management that a new set of global performance measures was developed for it.

The impact of the constraint on other resources is made even more clear when an effort is made to improve the system's performance. Suppose we decided to improve work center 3 to speed up its processing time. Reducing it from nine minutes to eight minutes improves the output of the system. However, any further reduction in the processing time of work center 3 would not improve system performance. Why? Because a system constraint acts like the weakest link in a chain. Efforts to improve a link will increase the strength of the chain only as long as it is the weakest link. As soon as it is strengthened to the point that it is no longer the weakest, further improvement to that link does no good. The "new" weakest link must be identified. When improvements are being considered for a constraint, the same logic holds. Improving a constraint will increase the output of a system, but only as long as it is still the constraint. Eventually, increasing the capability of the constraint will cause the constraint to move somewhere else. Improve work center 3, and the new constraint becomes work center 4.

Increasing the output of a nonconstraint is a frequent result of capital investment decisions that seek to automate processes. Money is invested to reduce labor costs, but the only way to maintain run time is to activate the resource beyond the level it can be utilized. The result is no return on the improvement investment because the system output hasn't been changed. The investment may actually have a negative impact because pressure to utilize the resource may result in the production of excess inventory.

GLOBAL PERFORMANCE MEASURES

Constraint management decisions depend on three global performance measures: throughput, inventory, and operating expense. In a constraint management context, **throughput (T)** is defined as the rate at which the system generates money through sales. With this in mind, production over and above that which could be consumed by demand is not considered throughput because it can't be sold. **Inventory (I)** is defined as money invested in things the system intends to sell. **Operating expense**

(OE) is defined as money the system spends in turning inventory into throughput. These definitions differ from the traditional nomenclature. For example, throughput traditionally means the rate at which products are produced, regardless of whether or not they are sold. The constraint management definition forces management to consider the production rate and the rate at which they can be sold. The constraint management definition for inventory includes money invested in equipment and facilities, because they may ultimately be sold as well. Traditional inventory definitions do not include facilities and equipment. The definitions have been changed to include a more direct means of measuring global performance and eliminate behaviors and "games" that are commonly used to improve performance of narrow and short-term measures, although they are known to be detrimental to long-term success. Despite the differences, the constraint management global measures can be equated to more traditional measures. These relationships are presented in Exhibit 17.4.

A widely held myth in business is that if all of the local measures are optimized, the result will be the optimization of global measures. We know from previous discussions that this is not true. The constraint management focus on global measures provides a more consistent link between day-to-day decisions and the broad performance of the firm. Constraint management eliminates the emphasis on local performance measures that aren't consistent with enterprise goals.

www.OperationsNow.com

The constraint management perspective has modified the definitions of a variety of terms to better meet its needs. As a result, numerous glossaries of constraint management terms have been developed. Esource 17.2 provides such a glossary.

THE CONSTRAINT MANAGEMENT FOCUSING PROCESS

The constraint management framework includes a system improvement process that focuses on the constraint. The five-step process is

Step 1: Identify the constraint.

Step 2: Exploit the constraint.

Step 3: Elevate the constraint.

Step 4: Subordinate all other decisions to step 2 and step 3.

Step 5: If, in steps 2 through 4, the constraint is eliminated, go back to step 1.

EXHIBIT 17.4 Constraint Management Global Measures and Traditional Measures

Traditional Measure	Constraint Management Measure
Net Profit	Throughput − Operating Expense
Return on Investment	$\dfrac{\text{Throughput} - \text{Operating Expense}}{\text{Inventory}}$
Inventory Turns	$\dfrac{\text{Throughput}}{\text{Inventory}}$
Productivity	$\dfrac{\text{Throughput}}{\text{Operating Expense}}$

Step 1. Identification

The identification of the constraint is a critical step in the focusing process. Constraints are often obvious, like those that result from the shortage of a resource. In more complex environments, however, an analysis may be needed to identify the constraint. The analysis compares the demand for a resource with the available capacity. Any resource that does not have sufficient capacity to meet demand would be considered a constraint. In manufacturing, constraints often have queues of inventory in front of them. A similar situation can be found in many services. Nonresource constraints, however, can be more difficult to identify. Identification of a policy as a constraint, for example, might require an approach similar to TQM to identify the root cause of a problem. There can be more than one constraint in a system.

Step 2. Exploitation

The exploitation of a constraint means that it should be used to its fullest extent. That includes trying to prevent it from ever being idle, since shutting down a work center that is a constraint would have the same impact as shutting down the entire system. Every effort should be made to ensure that the constraint never runs out of materials to process. Every effort should be made to ensure that capacity of the constraint isn't wasted on products that already have quality problems.

The exploitation of a policy constraint is a different process. A policy, for example, can't be used more effectively. The exploitation of a policy constraint requires that the policy must be eliminated or modified so that it no longer poses a constraint.

Step 3. Elevation

The exploitation of a constraint often creates enough additional capacity to eliminate it as a constraint. There are times, however, when exploitation isn't enough. Elevation means actually increasing the capacity of the constrained resource. Maybe that involves buying additional capacity. If cash is the constraint, it might be necessary to take out a loan. If supply of materials is a constraint, a new supplier may be needed, even if the materials cost more from that supplier. In any case, elevation requires a financial investment to increase the availability of the constraint above what could be gained by mere exploitation. Investment in additional capacity for a constrained resource can have a big return because of its direct impact on increasing the system's throughput. Other work centers that have been idle because of the role the constraint plays in the system may now be utilized more, simply because of this one investment.

Step 4. Subordination

Exploiting and/or elevating a constraint increases throughput. Maintaining the increased level of constrained resource output, however, may require an adjustment in the way other resources are used. It may require the establishment of new policies and procedures. The subordination step is designed to give such a high priority to exploitation and subordination that any decision made should be examined to see if it would have a negative impact on those efforts. Those decisions should always be subordinated to the exploitation of the constraint.

Step 5. Repeat

From the "weakest link" analogy, we know that if we keep strengthening a link, eventually it won't be the weakest one. Management of the system through the five-step focusing process must recognize that the same phenomenon can occur here. Prior to

Constraint Management at Amazon.com

The concept of matching all production rates to the rate of the constraint is critical in a large or complex system that has, at its core, one critical resource. This is the case at Amazon.com's warehouses. At the center of the order picking, sorting, and packaging process is a Crisplant sorting machine that reads product barcodes, routes them to one of 2,100 chutes for orders, and signals operators when an order is ready to be packaged. Crisplant sorting machines are used in airport luggage sorting, post offices, and in manufacturing and warehouse environments for sorting inventory. The Crisplant machine at Amazon.com is the warehouse constraint. If flow rates of products into the machine exceed the machine's capacity, a backup occurs. If flow rates are too slow, the machine's capacity isn't fully utilized and system output suffers.

A critical by-product of effective sorting is errors. In 2000, some 10 percent of the orders contained errors that resulted in workers searching for missing items and restocking wrong ones. New software has reduced errors to less than 5 percent.

The Crisplant machine works with batches of from 500 to 2,000 orders. Employees feed items onto conveyors and the Crisplant machine scans the items' barcodes and directs each item to an appropriate chute. When an order in a chute is complete, workers must remove the items and package them. If workers remove packages too slowly, the chute is not available for a new order. Every function of the warehouse seeks to avoid delays that would reduce efficiency of the Crisplant machine. The flow in and out of the machine is so critical that a new job—flowmeister—was created, to maintain a cadence or rhythm. The flowmeister ensures that the workers removing completed orders keep up with the rate items are coming into the machine.

The focus on flow resulted in the warehouse being able to package 200,000 items on peak days in December 2001. That was a 30 percent increase over the previous year with one-third fewer workers.

Source: "Amazon Ships to Sorting Machine Beat," *New York Times on the Web,* January 21, 2002; www.crisplant.com, January 20, 2002.

Mother Nature is the source of many disruptions that can affect business systems and supply chains. Tropical storm Allison provided many such disruptions for Houston, Texas, in the summer of 2001. B2B suppliers were unable to make deliveries and manufacturers with low levels of inventory were forced to stop production.

making any further adjustment to improve the output of the constrained resource, we need to make sure that resource still is the constraint. When exploitation or elevation causes another resource to become the constraint, the process must focus on the new constrained resource.

THE ROLE OF DISRUPTIONS IN PRODUCTIVE SYSTEMS

In any system that utilizes resources, disruptions can wreak havoc. Machines can break down, deliveries can be late, quality problems can arise, and workers can be absent. This has traditionally been referred to as "Murphy," from Murphy's law. Murphy's law states that if something can go wrong, it will. Disruptions exist in many forms, but they have the same impact on the system—they create delays, which ultimately add to the amount of time needed to complete a task. Obviously, the elimination of these types of disruption is a concern for managers. Finding the causes of these disruptions is a major thrust of both the TQM and the JIT frameworks.

There is another type of disruption, however, that is addressed by constraint management in a manner that is different from that of other management frameworks. Random fluctuation is present in many aspects of business processes, including the amount of time needed to complete the process. Random fluctuation can create disruptions. Within a series of processing steps random fluctuation cannot be completely eliminated, so the system must be able to cope with it. If we look back at the simple system presented earlier in Exhibits 17.2 and 17.3, the constrained resource is a consistent problem that we understand quite well. The system looks predictable, but if we add variability into the picture, the system becomes more complex. Exhibit 17.5 shows variability in that system.

Imagine the following scenario. On average, work center 1 completes a unit in six minutes and work center 2 completes a unit in seven minutes. There will be instances for each when units are completed in less time than the average and in more time than the average. The statistical fluctuation that takes place at each work center (with the exception of work station 4) has an impact on each of the other work centers as well. Suppose, for example, that work center 1 completes a unit in 6 minutes,

Simple System with Processing Variability — EXHIBIT 17.5

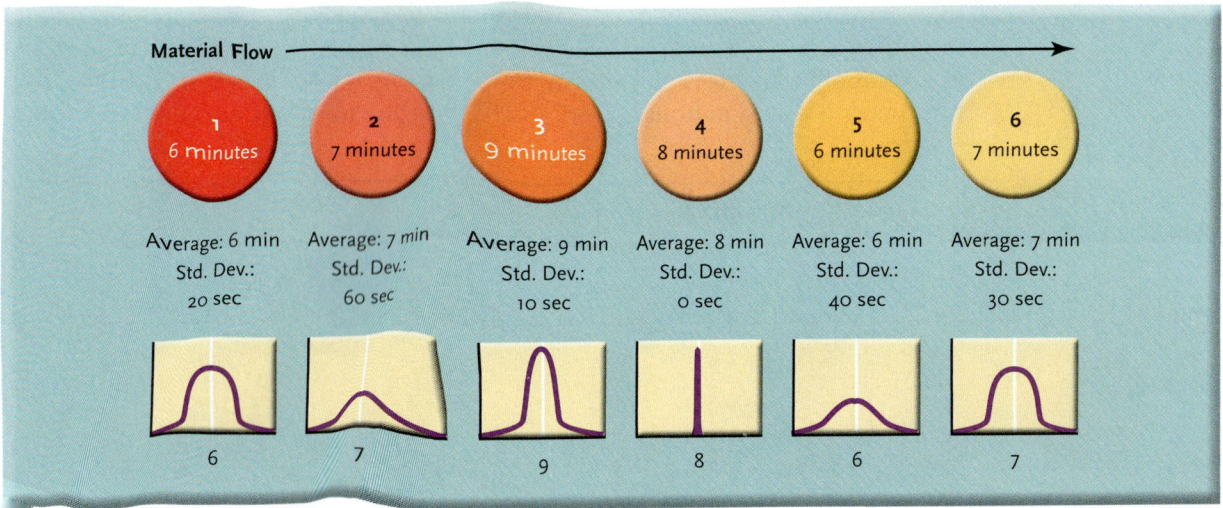

20 seconds, which is within the expected variation. The completion time will delay by 20 seconds when work center 2 can start work on that unit. Sometimes a work center will take longer to process a unit, and sometimes it will take less time than average. The impact of the statistical fluctuations tends to increase as we move toward work center 6. It accumulates. This phenomenon is recognized as the impact of **statistical fluctuation among dependent events** in constraint management. Its effect can be substantial because the disruptions it causes can be substantial.

PROTECTING THE SYSTEM FROM DISRUPTIONS

All disruptions, including those from unexpected events and the accumulation of statistical fluctuation, have an impact on the system. Nonconstraints, because they have excess capacity, can experience a level of disruption without reducing system output. For example, work center 5 has idle time that can be used to catch up if it is forced to periodically shut down because of a lack of material or a breakdown. A constrained resource, however, has no idle time. Work center 3 is utilized 100 percent of the time and has no idle time to enable it to catch up from downtime due to lack of material or other reasons. Thus the constraint must be protected from these disruptions. The approach constraint management uses to protect constrained resources from disruptions is to **decouple**, or "disconnect," them from the rest of the system with inventory.

BUFFERING TO PROTECT CONSTRAINTS

Disruptions to systems can generally be measured by their duration. An hour's disruption results in delays of an hour. Any scheme to protect a constraint must recognize that the amount of protection must also be measured by time. We could protect a constraint from a 1-hour disruption or a 20-hour disruption or an *x*-hour disruption if we deemed the duration appropriate. That protection comes from a buffer of inventory known as a **time buffer**. A time buffer decouples, for a specified amount of time, the constrained resource from being directly dependent on the work centers that supply it. The role of the buffer can be best understand by going back to the system examined in Exhibit 17.5.

Work center 3 is clearly the constraint of that system. It can be idled by a disruption occurring at either work center 1 or work center 2. A disruption of either would shut off the supply of materials to work center 3 and idle it. Because it should be working 100 percent of the time to meet demand, it has no way to catch up the time it lost as a result of being idle. Lost time on the constraint is lost forever. In Exhibit 17.6 a time buffer is placed in front of work center 3 to provide protection from this threat.

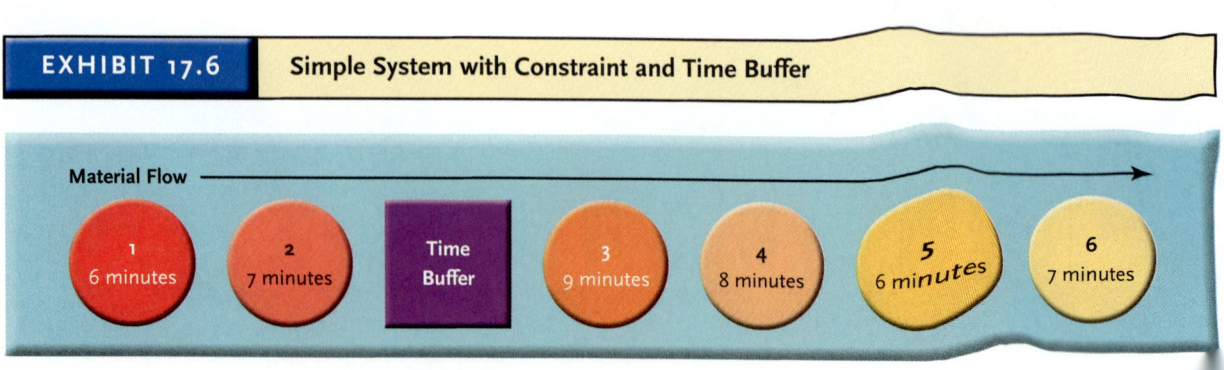

EXHIBIT 17.6 | **Simple System with Constraint and Time Buffer**

The time buffer performs an important and interesting task. The first, and maybe most critical, decision regarding the time buffer should be to determine its potential size. How much protection is needed? That question can be answered only when the potential time of the disruptions is known. For example, if there is a possibility that work center 1 could break down and be down for eight hours, it would create an eight-hour disruption that could idle work center 3. The only way to prevent such a disruption to work center 3 would be to keep a buffer of work in front of work center 3 that would keep it busy working for eight hours. In our situation, given that it takes work center 3 nine minutes per unit, work center 3 could process 53.3 units (let's round up to 54) in an eight-hour period. Thus to protect the constraint from an eight-hour disruption, we'd keep an eight-hour time buffer (that would be equal to 54 units of inventory) in front of it. Since work centers 1 and 2 can process units faster than work center 3, they could build up that amount of inventory by processing faster than work center 3, then back off to produce at the rate of one unit every nine minutes. Inventory would then flow into and out of the buffer at the same rate of one unit every nine minutes, as shown in Exhibit 17.7.

If a disruption caused by a breakdown at work center 1 or 2, or a disruption in raw material supply, stopped the inflow, the constrained resource (work center 3) would be able to continue unaffected for up to eight hours. During the time of disruption, the buffer would be gradually reduced by the production rate of work center 3. When the disruption ended, the production rate for work centers 1 and 2 would be stepped up to replenish the buffer back to its eight-hour level.

In an environment that must fulfill orders by a certain due date, however, it becomes more difficult. Suppose our system was identical to that of the previous example, except that we produce to fill specific orders. Orders vary in size, but suppose we have an order for 27 units due 14 days from now. The role of the time buffer continues to be to protect the constraint from disruptions of the same time, but it also protects our due date from those disruptions. Suppose each work center produces 54 units per day in our system. That's a nine-minute cycle time for the system during an eight-hour workday. With no time buffer in place, the order would move through each work center in four hours. If the order were due on day 14, we would start it on day 11 because it would take three days to get through the six work centers.

With an eight-hour time buffer in place, time has been added to the order's processing time. Since there are already eight hours of inventory in front of work center 3 when our order finishes work center 2, it must wait in that queue for eight hours. Work center 3 processes a unit every nine minutes, and our order comes out of work center 2, one unit every nine minutes. With an eight-hour time buffer in place, we need to start our order on day 10 because it will now take four days to get through the system. If a disruption of less than eight hours takes place, it will not result in our

| Inventory Flow In and Out of a Time Buffer | EXHIBIT 17.7 |

Material Flow →

1 — 6 minutes → 2 — 7 minutes → (1 unit every 9 minutes) → 8-hour Time Buffer 54 units → (1 unit every 9 minutes) → 3 — 9 minutes → 4 — 8 minutes → 5 — 6 minutes → 6 — 7 minutes

order being late. The effect of the buffer, in this case, is to trigger us to start the order one day earlier, giving us eight hours of slack in our schedule. A disruption at work center 1 or 2 will mean our order will not arrive at work center 3 when planned; however, the plan specified for the order to arrive there (and be placed in an eight-hour queue) eight hours before it was actually needed. Exhibit 17.8 shows the times that would be associated with our order.

As long as the order enters the time buffer prior to day 12, it can be completed on time because it can be started at work center 3 as soon as it enters the queue in front of it. The effect of the time buffer is that we release the order into the system one day early. That extra day of slack allows it to tolerate disruptions in work center 1 or 2, as long as they are less than eight hours (a day) in duration. Since other orders are entering the time buffer from other work centers, our order being late would not necessarily idle work center 3. In constraint management parlance, this particular type of time buffer is known as a **constraint buffer**.

The constraint is protected from up to a one-day disruption at work center 1 or 2. The due date is also protected from up to a one-day disruption at work center 1 or 2. If disruptions could be greater, the time buffer should be greater.

The sizing of time buffers is an iterative process. If random checks on the one-day time buffer in the example showed that it was always full (always had eight hours of work in it), that would mean that it was too big. If there had been a disruption, the buffer would slowly have been drained by the constraint, and it would have less than eight hours' content. If it always contained eight hours of inventory, that would indicate that there are never disruptions, meaning that the buffer isn't needed or that its size could be reduced. The goal is to have a buffer that, on average, is roughly two-thirds full. A buffer that averages about two-thirds full indicates that its size is sufficient to cover a serious disruption but not so large that most of it is never used.

The order due on day 14 would be late if there were disruptions after the constrained resource at work center 3, 4, 5, or 6. The order could be protected from these disruptions by using another time buffer immediately after the final processing step but immediately before shipping. This buffer is known as a **shipping buffer**. Suppose we determined that one day of protection was needed for potential disruptions at these work centers. Exhibit 17.9 shows the shipping buffer added to the system.

Notice that adding an eight-hour shipping buffer results in adding an additional day to the lead time when the order must be released into the system. With this change, the due date would be protected from disruptions anywhere in the system. The shipping buffer offers protection from disruptions that could come from work

EXHIBIT 17.8   Order Processing in System with Time Buffer

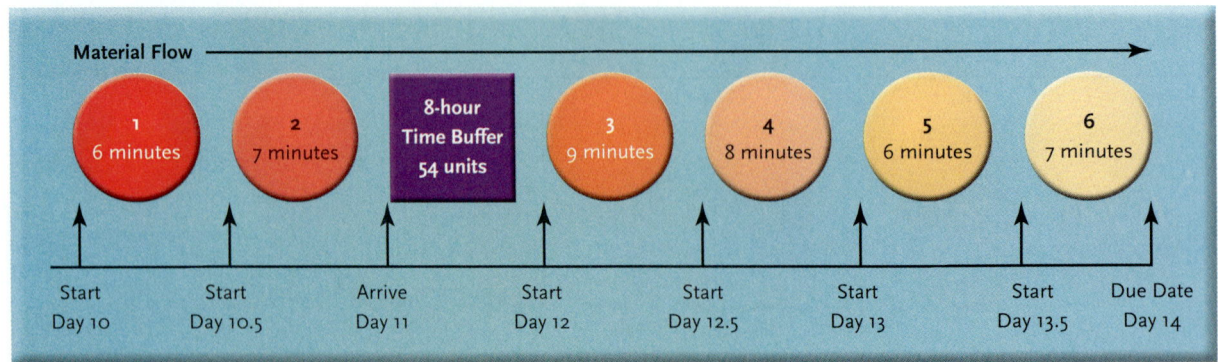

				EXHIBIT 17.9
System with Shipping Buffer Added				

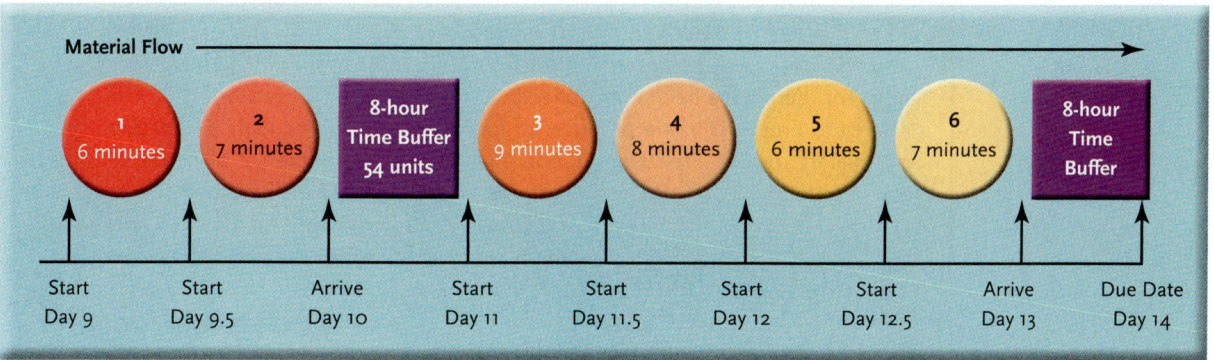

center 3, 4, 5, or 6. The constraint buffer protects from disruptions at work center 1 or 2 and protects the constraint from being idle as well. In fact, if a disruption at work center 1 or 2 lasted longer than one day, the shipping buffer would provide an additional day of protection. Interactive Model 17.1 provides an environment for experimenting with buffers in constrained systems.

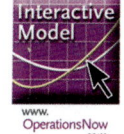

When parts go through constrained resources, it is a good practice to move them through the remaining work centers as quickly as possible. This is generally not difficult, because remaining work centers are not constrained, so there should be no waiting lines. Assembly points, however, can sometimes cause delays. When a component that has been processed by a constrained resource reaches an assembly point, it is possible that the component it is to be assembled with is not yet there. To prevent this type of delay from happening, some constraint management systems include a buffer of components that did not go through constrained resources in front of assembly points. This helps to ensure that components that have been through constrained resources are not delayed. This buffer is known as an **assembly buffer**. Buffers can also serve as a tool for identifying potentially late orders that need to be expedited. An order that is late in arriving to a buffer is a signal that disruptions have occurred. Identifying orders that should be in buffers, but aren't, helps identify potentially late orders.

CONSTRAINT MANAGEMENT AND BATCH SIZES

The advantages of small-batch production and small batches for delivery were addressed in the previous chapter, but recognition of the role played by constraints in productive systems makes a second look worthwhile. Constraint management recognizes that there are, in fact, two distinctly different types of inventory batches and two distinctly different types of decisions to make. The number of units produced before changing equipment over to produce something else is known as a **production batch**. The number of units transferred at a time to another step in the production process is a **transfer batch**.

We know that the larger the production batch, the less frequently a piece of equipment must undergo a setup or changeover. This reduces the time the equipment must be stopped during these changeovers, increasing its utilization. For a constraint, increasing the production batch size increases its utilization, and this is a form of

> ### A Constraint Management Case
>
> Constraint management has attracted numerous advocates because of its almost immediate impact on resource productivity and profitability. It has been criticized, however, for providing short-term solutions to business problems. Yet there have been many anecdotal cases and "success stories."
>
> Oregon Freeze Dry is a producer of food products (particularly backpacking foods and military meals). Freeze-dried food goes through a simple set of processes. Fresh food is processed (wet processing) and is then "flash frozen" and then subjected to a vacuum chamber, which removes moisture. The process removes moisture and oxygen, reducing causes of spoilage. In addition, 90 percent of the weight is removed, making it easier and cheaper to transport. At Oregon Freeze Dry, food products move from a wet processing area to freezing and then to drying. The drying process varies from 8 to as many as 50 hours, resulting in variable product flows and a large amount of work-in-process inventory. Freezing, in effect, became a queue for the drying process. Quality problems were frequent because of the reliance on temporary workers. Work-in-process inventories were also high. In response to the problems, management implemented constraint management to help manage the processes and control inventory.
>
> Although the dryers were identified as the constrained resource, the freezers and dryers were treated as one. The dryers were scheduled, and the freezer schedule (the step immediately prior to drying) was scheduled to meet the dryer schedule. Buffers were maintained at the freezers to protect the constraint from being idle. Material was released into the wet processing step only at the rate the dryer could process it. This reduced inventory accumulating in front of the drying process (at the freezer) and also stabilized product flows. Stability of product flows made it easier to schedule capacity and labor. The link between the input rate and the rate of processing at the constraint is often maintained using a system known as "drum-buffer-rope" (DBR). DBR ensures that the flow of materials into the system does not exceed the constraint's capabilities. At Oregon Freeze Dry, the links required were enhanced through the use of the enterprise resource planning (ERP) system. ERP's centralized database and continuous updating created very rapid feedback and real-time access to production information.
>
> Source: Michael Umble and Elisabeth Umble, "Integrating Enterprise Resources Planning and Theory of Constraints: A Case Study," *Production and Inventory Management Journal*, Second Quarter, 2001, pp. 43–48; http://www.ofd.com/gci/index.html, March 12, 2002.

exploitation. For other resources, however, since they are nonconstraints and have idle time at their disposal, smaller production batch sizes are more desirable. They result in lower levels of inventory, improved quality, and so on. The best scenario is that all of the nonconstraint idle time be used for changeovers. In that way, the smallest possible production batch sizes are used, minimizing inventory levels, but not allowing changeovers to cut into time needed for actual production.

Transfer batches should always be as small as possible. Reducing the size of the transfer batch creates a more even flow of materials through the system and also reduces the likelihood that work centers would have to sit idle waiting for materials to be delivered while large transfer batches accumulate. When transfer batches are large, the movement from one resource to the next becomes infrequent, which in some cases can result in a nonconstraint being turned into a constraint because all of its idle time is consumed waiting for work to arrive. In effect, it gets "starved" while waiting for a delivery. In time, when the delivery arrives, the time left to process it may be insufficient.

THE ROLE OF THE CONSTRAINT: A PRODUCT MIX EXAMPLE

In Goldratt's first book, *The Goal*,[2] a problem was introduced to demonstrate the impact of constraints on traditional thinking. The problem has become a virtual classic and its solution frequently surprises even the most experienced managers. This problem is presented in Example 17.1.

Example 17.1

Product Mix Problem

Exhibit 17.10 provides a model of a simple manufacturing system that produces two products, P and Q. Product P sells for $90 per unit and Q sells for $100 per unit. There is a weekly demand for 100 Ps and 50 Qs.

EXHIBIT 17.10 Production System for Example 17.1

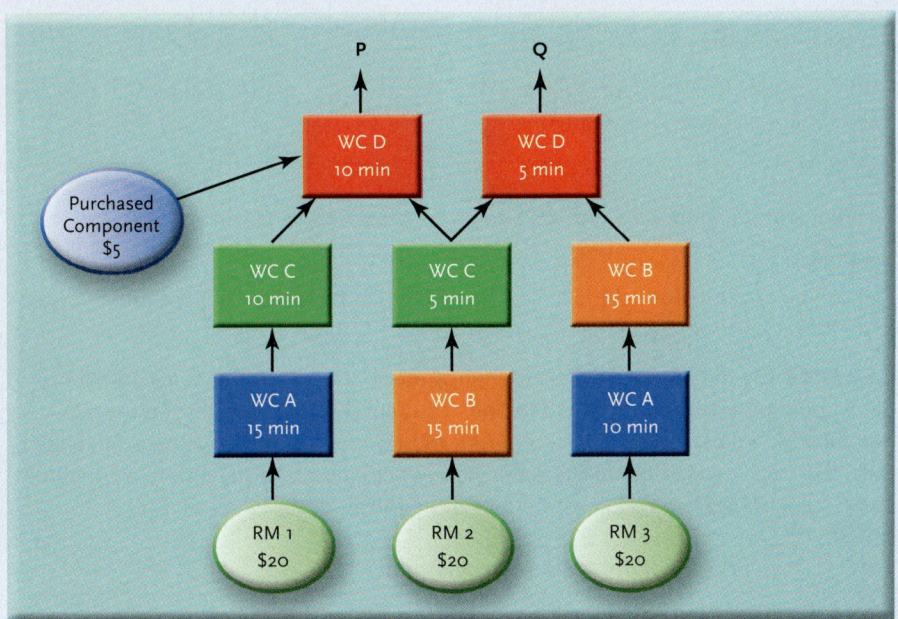

Manufacturing P requires two raw materials (raw material 1 and 2), each costing $20. In addition, P uses a purchased component that costs $5 per unit. Manufacturing Q also requires two raw materials (raw material 2 and 3). Raw material 2 is used in P and Q. Raw material 3 also costs $20.

Four work centers, A, B, C, and D, are used to manufacture the products. Each has 2,400 minutes (40 hours) available each week. Each work center (WC) has two tasks to perform, with no changeover required when switching between tasks. For example, WCA is used in a 15-minute process on raw material 1 to produce a P and WC A is also used in a 10-minute process on raw material 3 to produce a Q. Producing P requires that raw material 1 be processed first at WC A, then at WC C. Raw material 2 is processed first at WC B and then at WC C. The two are then assembled, along with the $5 purchased component, at WC D. They are then complete and can be sold. To manufacture a Q, raw material 2 is processed first at WC B, then at WC C. Raw material 3

(continues)

Example 17.1 (continued)

is processed first at WC A, then at WC B. The two are assembled at WC D and then sold. Operating expense for the week, including everything except materials costs, is $6,000. These values are summarized in Exhibit 17.11.

EXHIBIT 17.11 Production System Data

	P	Q
Market demand	100	50
Selling price	$90	$100
Raw materials costs		
RM 1	$20	
RM 2	$20	$20
RM 3		$20
Purchased component	$5	

Time available on each work center: 2,400 minutes

Operating expense per week: $6,000

What combination of Ps and Qs should be produced to maximize profit?

Solution

The solution to the product mix problem is obtained by completing the first two steps of the five-step focusing process outlined earlier.

Step 1. Identify the constraint. The identification of the constraint is accomplished in this situation by computing the demand requirements on each resource (work centers, raw materials, and purchased parts) and comparing them to the availability of each. Any resource unable to meet the weekly demand is, by definition, a constraint. The results of these calculations are presented in Exhibit 17.12.

EXHIBIT 17.12 Identification of Constraint

Product Demand	Required Time on WC A	Required Time on WC B	Required Time on WC C	Required Time on WC D	Required RM 1	Required RM 2	Required RM 3	Required Purchase Components
100 P	1,500	1,500	1,500	1,000	100	100	0	100
50 Q	500	1,500	250	250	0	50	50	0
Total required	2,000	3,000	1,750	1,250	100	150	50	100
Available	2,400	2,400	2,400	2,400	Unlimited	Unlimited	Unlimited	Unlimited
Problem?	OK	Problem	OK	OK	OK	OK	OK	OK

(continues)

Example 17.1 (continued)

In this example situation, since there are no limitations on the availability of raw materials and purchased parts, a constraint can only be one of the work centers. With only 2,400 minutes available on each work center, WC B is the constraint because it requires 3,000 minutes to meet demand and only 2,400 minutes are available.

Step 2. Exploit the constraint. Exploitation means getting the most out of the constraint in terms of the system's goals. The goal of this system is to maximize profit. So the constraint should be utilized in the way that yields the most profit. Constraint management utilizes a technique known as obtaining the best return per unit of the constraint. In this situation, the "return" sought is a financial one. The "units" of the constraint are minutes of use. A calculation of the dollar return per minute of time on the constraint is made for products P and Q to determine which one best exploits work center B. This calculation is presented in Exhibit 17.13. To make the calculation, the contribution margin (selling price minus materials cost) is computed for each end product and divided by the number of minutes work center B is used to produce it. The result shows that product P yields $3 per minute on the constraint and product Q yields $2 per minute.

EXHIBIT 17.13 Calculation of Dollar Return per Constraint Minute

	P	Q
Contribution margin	$90−$45=$45	$100−$60=$40
Minutes on B	15	30
Return per constraint minute	$45/15 = $3 per minute	$60/30 = $2 per minute

Since B is the constraint, we must use all 2,400 minutes, no matter what product mix is used. The difference in return per minute means that we can spend 1,500 minutes at WC B making P for $3 per minute, and the remaining 900 minutes making Q for $2 per minute, or the reverse—spend 1,500 minutes at WC B making Q for $2 per minute and then the remaining 900 minutes making P for $3 per minute. Obviously, the most profitable choice is the first. If we select P as the most profitable way to utilize the constraint, 1,500 minutes will be used to meet its demand. That leaves 900 minutes to be used producing product Q. At 30 minutes on WC B for each Q, a total of 30 units of Q can be produced in that amount of time. The product mix that maximizes profit is 100 Ps and 30 Qs. Exhibit 17.14 provides the calculations for profit.

(continues)

> **Example 17.1** *(continued)*
>
> **EXHIBIT 17.14 Profit Calculations for Example 17.1**
>
> | | |
> |---|---|
> | 100 P: | 100 × $45 = $4,500 |
> | 30 Q: | 30 × $60 = $1,800 |
> | Total | $6,300 |
> | Minus operating expenses | −$6,000 |
> | Profit | $300 |
>
> Excel Tutor 17.1 demonstrates how Excel can be used to aid in solving the product mix problem.

The results of Example 17.1 provide insight into the importance of constraints. A comparison of this solution to a solution using more traditional measures is useful. The contribution margins of P and Q are $45 and $60, respectively. The solution we obtained results in a weekly profit of $300, as shown in Exhibit 17.14. A solution based on contribution margin would have led us to produce as many Qs as possible. The profit using that solution is actually a loss of $300. Clearly, in this situation, focusing on the contribution margin to obtain the most profitable product would have provided the wrong solution. Similarly, a sales commission system can also encourage the wrong behavior. A commission system based on selling price or contribution margin would encourage sales reps to sell Q instead of P, which would be exactly the wrong thing to do.

JIT AND CONSTRAINT MANAGEMENT

The JIT and constraint management frameworks do not conflict and, despite differences of areas of focus, overlap somewhat. The buffering process used by constraint management is similar to the kanban system used in JIT systems in that each controls inventory and dictates that production be equal to that required by the rate of demand. Kanban provides small buffers between each work center, while constraint management provides buffers only at critical points as protection from disruptions. JIT systems typically have excess capacity (no constraints) and provide a larger buffer at the finished-goods point. This is similar to a shipping buffer used in constraint management. In a constraint management system, if all internal constraints were eliminated, there would be no constraint buffer, only a shipping buffer. In a kanban environment, if there were a constraint, the natural reaction of management would probably be to increase the maximum size of the buffer in front of the constrained resource to counteract problems caused by a small buffer. That change would begin to resemble the constraint management approach. The key difference between the two approaches is that they represent different perspectives: JIT focuses on the elimination of waste as its top priority, whereas constraint management focuses on maximizing throughput through the management of system constraints.

CHAPTER SUMMARY

Constraint management, a framework that focuses on maximizing system output by managing the system constraints, was examined and explained in this chapter. Like TQM, which emphasizes quality, and JIT, which emphasizes waste elimination, co straint management provides a useful perspective that makes managers aware of constraints, their impact, and how they can be managed to enhance the productivity of the system as a whole.

The five focusing steps of constraint management can be applied to effectively improve system performance by focusing on the system constraint. The use of inventory or time buffers protects the constrained resource from upstream disruptions that could force it to be idle.

The second step of the five-step focusing process, exploitation, can have particularly broad implications for management decisions, including capital budgeting, product mix decisions, and resource scheduling. A close examination of constraint management and use of the five focusing steps as a way to enhance systemwide productivity often contradicts more traditional measures used to make decisions. The role of a constraint in a system, for example, can cause traditional measures such as contribution margin to lead to an incorrect result. The financial return per unit of the constrained resource provides a means of exploiting a constraint in terms of profit goals.

KEY TERMS

activation, 598
assembly buffer, 607
constraint, 596
constraint buffer, 605
constraint management, 596
decouple, 604
inventory, 599
operating expense, 599
production patch, 607
shipping buffer, 606
statistical fluctuation among dependent events, 603
throughput, 599
time buffer, 604
transfer patch, 607
utilization, 598

REVIEW QUESTIONS

1. What is a "constraint"?
2. Describe the weakest link analogy as it applies to constraint management.
3. What is meant by "utilization" and "activation"?
4. Define "throughput," "inventory," and "operating expenses" from a constraint management perspective.
5. Describe the five steps of the constraint management focusing process and the meaning of each.
6. What is the relationship between statistical fluctuations and dependent events?
7. What is a time buffer?
8. How can time buffers help exploit a constraint?
9. Define "constraint buffer," "shipping buffer," and "assembly buffer."
10. What is meant by "transfer batch" and "production batch"? What role does a constrained resource play in determining the sizes of these different batches?
11. How does constraint management compare to JIT?

DISCUSSION QUESTIONS

1. Identify a constraint in a process you interact with (for example, food service, lines at the recreation center, your favorite fast-food restaurant). How would you exploit the constraint to improve system productivity?
2. Identify systems that you interact with that must cope with disruptions. How could buffers be used to lessen that impact?
3. In the product mix problem demonstrated in Example 17.1, describe why traditional financial measures would lead to the wrong answer.

PROBLEMS

1. Dee-Lish Apple Orchard offers a three-step process to sell its apples as illustrated below. The first workstation is the picker, which collects the apples from the trees. The second step is a quality station, which inspects the apples for flaws. The last step is to package the apples for market. What is the maximum amount of apples that this system can ready for market in an hour?

2. Dr. Wahle sets up patient appointments every 15 minutes. The patient must go through the following steps: sign in, see the doctor, and pay for the visit. If the first patient arrives at 10:00, when will the fourth patient be able to leave? What is the constraint in the system? If the first patient arrives at 10:00, how many patients will be waiting in the waiting room at noon?

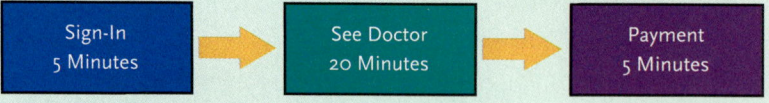

3. The Taco Hut has a Monday night special of 25-cent tacos. The steps for making tacos are outlined below, beginning with adding ground beef to the shell, topping with lettuce, cheese, and tomatoes, and then packaging. Which of the workstations will be utilized 100 percent? What will be the utilization of the others if input rate is restricted to the rate of the constrained resource?

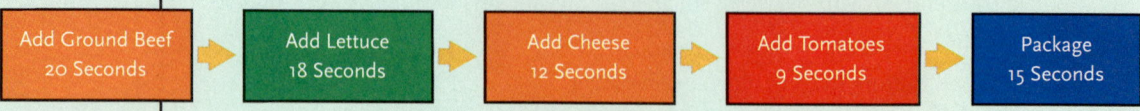

4. Paper-Giant makes paper notebooks for students. Notebook production is a three-step process. First, 500 sheets of paper must be counted and aligned, a process that takes 55 seconds. Holes must then be punched in the paper, which takes 35 seconds. Finally, the wire binding must be attached to the paper, taking 120 seconds. Calculate the utilization for each of the workstations. What is the constraint in the system? What is the utilization rate for each work center if it must maximize throughput?

5. Active Inc. manufactures two products, a wiffle bat and ball. To make a wiffle ball, processes at two workstations must be completed: 5 minutes of molding and 5 minutes of cutting. The wiffle bat requires 10 minutes of molding and 5 minutes of coloring. The company needs to produce 190 bats and 125 wiffle balls per week to meet demand. There are 2,400 minutes available at each work center each week. Find the constraint. If an engineering change can decrease the molding time on the bat by 1 minute by increasing the coloring time from 5 to 10 minutes, should Active undertake the change?

6. Woodrow Woodworking produces countertops and the backsplashes that accompany them. The company can produce up to 130 backsplashes and 150 counters per week to meet demand. A backsplash requires 8 minutes on the cutter and 7 minutes of finishing. Countertops require 9 minutes of cutting, 5 minutes on the glue press, and 12 minutes of finishing. A backsplash costs $25 to manufacture and sells for $40. A counter sells for $70 and costs $35. Determine the constraint and the best product mix. What is the profit for the best product mix?

7. Tuff-T's makes two styles of customized T-shirts. The 001 is a plain white shirt selling for $14 and costing $4. Material for the shirt must first be cut, which takes 18 minutes, and then the shirt can be sewn, a process that takes 24 minutes. The 004 is a tie-dyed shirt with a customized logo selling for $24 and costing $6. The shirt must go through the same process as the 001, but cutting takes an additional minute, and sewing an additional two. The colored shirt must also be dyed, which takes 35 minutes, and the logo must be made and ironed on, taking another 12 minutes. Overall, there is a demand for 70 style 001's and 50 style 004's per week. Find the constraint and determine the product mix that maximizes profit.

INTERACTIVE ANALYSIS 17.1

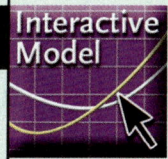

THE CONSTRAINT MANAGEMENT INTERACTIVE MODEL

The Constraint Management Interactive Model is accessed through Chapter 17 of the OperationsNow.com website. It provides an interactive environment for experimenting with various combinations of constraint buffers that can aid in the exploitation of system constraints.

In the Constraint Management Buffer Interactive Model, the user has several opportunities to control the model's behavior. The input rate and processing times at each of the five work centers can be varied from one to eight minutes per unit. The variability of each can be controlled as well, and has options of zero, slight, moderate, and extreme. In addition to the variability, breakdowns can be zero, small, moderate, or severe. Increasing breakdown severity increases the frequency and duration of breakdowns. The user also has the ability to create buffers in front of any work center by establishing the beginning level of inventory. The buffer size can range from zero to five units. Time buffers can be created by combining the number of units with the time per unit at that work center. For example, a buffer of four units in front of a work center that was set at 5 minutes per unit would provide a 20-minute time buffer. When the system is stopped, the quantity of products produced by the system and the utilization for each work center are provided. The user also has the option to dictate the simulator clock speed and can pause the simulation.

Experiment 1: System Fundamentals

1. Set the parameters to the default values, as shown below.

	Initial Inventory	Processing Time	Variability	Breakdown Severity
Input	0	4	zero	
WC 1	0	4	zero	zero
WC 2	0	4	zero	zero
WC 3	0	4	zero	zero
WC 4	0	4	zero	zero
WC 5	0	4	zero	zero

   a. Run the simulation for 100 simulator minutes. How many products are completed?

   b. Increase the processing time for WC 3 from four to five minutes. What happens to the number of products finished? What happens to the level of inventory in the system? What happens to the utilization of each work center?

   c. Change the input rate to one unit every 5 minutes (leaving WC 3 at five minutes also). What happens now? What does that indicate about the role of the constraint and the system input rate? How do utilization rates change for each work center?

2. Set the parameters back to the default values, as shown below.

	Initial Inventory	Processing Time	Variability	Breakdown Severity
Input	0	4	zero	
WC 1	0	4	zero	zero
WC 2	0	4	zero	zero
WC 3	0	4	zero	zero
WC 4	0	4	zero	zero
WC 5	0	4	zero	zero

   a. Increase the processing time variability for WC 3 to the extreme level. Run the simulation for 100 simulator minutes. What is the finished-product output? How does this compare to the results from 1a? What happens to inventory in the system? How does process time variability affect inventory levels at the various work centers? How are work center utilizations affected?

   b. Increase the variability of WC 3 even more by changing the breakdown severity to severe. Run the simulation for 100 simulator minutes. What is the new finished-product output? How does this compare to the results from 2a? What happens to inventory in the system? How are the work centers affected by increased variability? How are work center utilizations affected by this change?

Experiment 2: Using Inventory Buffers to Isolate Constraints from Disruptions

1. Set the parameters to the values shown below.

	Initial Inventory	Processing Time	Variability	Breakdown Severity
Input	0	6	zero	
WC 1	0	4	zero	zero
WC 2	0	4	zero	zero
WC 3	0	6	zero	zero
WC 4	0	4	zero	zero
WC 5	0	4	zero	zero

   a. Run the simulation for 100 simulator minutes. How many products are finished?

2. Set the parameters to the values shown below.

	Initial Inventory	Processing Time	Variability	Breakdown Severity
Input	0	6	zero	
WC 1	0	4	Extreme	Severe
WC 2	0	4	Extreme	Severe
WC 3	0	6	zero	zero
WC 4	0	4	zero	zero
WC 5	0	4	zero	zero

   a. Run the simulation for 100 simulator minutes. How many products are finished? What happens to WC 3 as a result of the increased variability and disruptions present in the work centers that precede it? Do you notice idle time on WC 3? What is the utilization of WC 3?

3. Set the parameters to the values shown below.

	Initial Inventory	Processing Time	Variability	Breakdown Severity
Input	3	6	zero	
WC 1	3	4	Extreme	Severe
WC 2	3	4	Extreme	Severe
WC 3	3	6	zero	zero
WC 4	3	4	zero	zero
WC 5	3	4	zero	zero

   Start with 5 units of inventory in front of WC 3.

   a. Run the simulation for 100 simulator minutes. How many products are finished? Do you notice as much idle time on WC 3? What is the new utilization of WC 3?

4. Reset the parameters as shown below.

	Initial Inventory	Processing Time	Variability	Breakdown Severity
Input	0	6	zero	
WC 1	0	4	Extreme	Severe
WC 2	0	4	Extreme	Severe
WC 3	2	6	zero	zero
WC 4	0	4	zero	zero
WC 5	0	4	zero	zero

Start with 2 units of inventory in front of WC 3.

   a. Run the simulation for 100 simulator minutes and observe what happens. How many products are finished? Does a buffer of two units prior to WC 3 effectively decouple it from disruptions? Do you any notice idle time on WC 3? What is the utilization of WC 3?

5. Reset the parameters as shown below.

	Initial Inventory	Processing Time	Variability	Breakdown Severity
Input	0	6	zero	
WC 1	0	4	Extreme	Severe
WC 2	0	4	Extreme	Severe
WC 3	4	6	zero	zero
WC 4	0	4	zero	zero
WC 5	0	4	zero	zero

Start with 4 units of inventory in front of WC 3.

   a. Run the simulation for 100 simulator minutes. How many products are finished?
   b. Does a buffer of 4 units prior to WC 3 effectively isolate it from disruptions? Do you notice idle time on WC 3? What is the new utilization of WC 3?

Experiment 3: The Cumulative Effect of Disruptions

1. Begin with the parameters set to the values shown below.

	Initial Inventory	Processing Time	Variability	Breakdown Severity
Input	0	4	Extreme	
WC 1	0	4	Extreme	Severe
WC 2	0	6	zero	zero
WC 3	0	4	zero	zero
WC 4	0	4	zero	zero
WC 5	0	4	zero	zero

Start with no inventory in buffers.
   a. Run the simulation for 100 simulator minutes. How many products were complete?
   b. How does that compare to the same configuration with zero variability and zero breakdowns for all work centers? Would you conclude that the difference is due to processing variability and disruptions?
2. Begin with the parameters set to the values shown below.

	Initial Inventory	Processing Time	Variability	Breakdown Severity
Input	0	4	Extreme	Severe
WC 1	0	4	Extreme	Severe
WC 2	0	4	Extreme	Severe
WC 3	0	6	zero	zero
WC 4	0	4	zero	zero
WC 5	0	4	zero	zero

   a. As you can see, the constraint has been moved. Perform the same experiment as in 1a. What happens?
3. Set the parameters to the values shown below.

	Initial Inventory	Processing Time	Variability	Breakdown Severity
Input	0	4	Extreme	Severe
WC 1	0	4	Extreme	Severe
WC 2	0	4	Extreme	Severe
WC 3	0	4	Extreme	Severe
WC 4	0	6	zero	zero
WC 5	0	4	zero	zero

   a. Run the simulation for 100 simulator minutes. What happens?
   b. Is the effect of these changes caused by increased variability? Or by moving the constraint? How could you find out for sure? Perform the necessary experiments to confirm your hypothesis.

SELECTED REFERENCES

Goldratt, E. M. *Critical Chain.* Croton-on-Hudson, N.Y.: North River Press, 1997.

Goldratt, E. M. *The Goal,* 2nd Rev. Ed. Croton-on-Hudson, N.Y.: North River Press, 1992.

Goldratt, E. M. *Theory of Constraints.* Croton-on-Hudson, N.Y.: North River Press, 1990.

Umble, M. M., and Srikanth, M. L. *Synchronous Manufacturing.* Cincinnati, OH: South-Western Publishing, 1990.

ENDNOTES

1. E. M. Goldratt, *The Goal,* 2nd rev. ed. (Croton-on-Hudson, N.Y.: North River Press, 1992).
2. Ibid.

CHAPTER 17 **Constraint Management** 621

OperationsNow.com LEARNING ACTIVITIES

CHAPTER ENHANCEMENT RESOURCES
- Esources
- Reel Operations Video Clips
- Interactive Models
- Excel Tutors
- Supplementary Readings
- Links to Operations On Site Companies

OM EXPLORATION
- Check It Out
- OM in Action
- Online Business Tours
- Letters from the Top
- Putting It All Together: Virtual Case Studies
- Additional Reading

Supply chain management (SCM) is identified by the resource/profit model as the fourth and final integrative management framework. Like its predecessors, JIT, TQM, and constraint management, SCM provides managers with yet another perspective from which they can judge actions and predict outcomes. SCM recognizes that the impact of decisions does not stop at the wall of the factory but extends beyond, and that waste and non-value-adding activities cannot be hidden or excluded from the ultimate goal of the value chain.

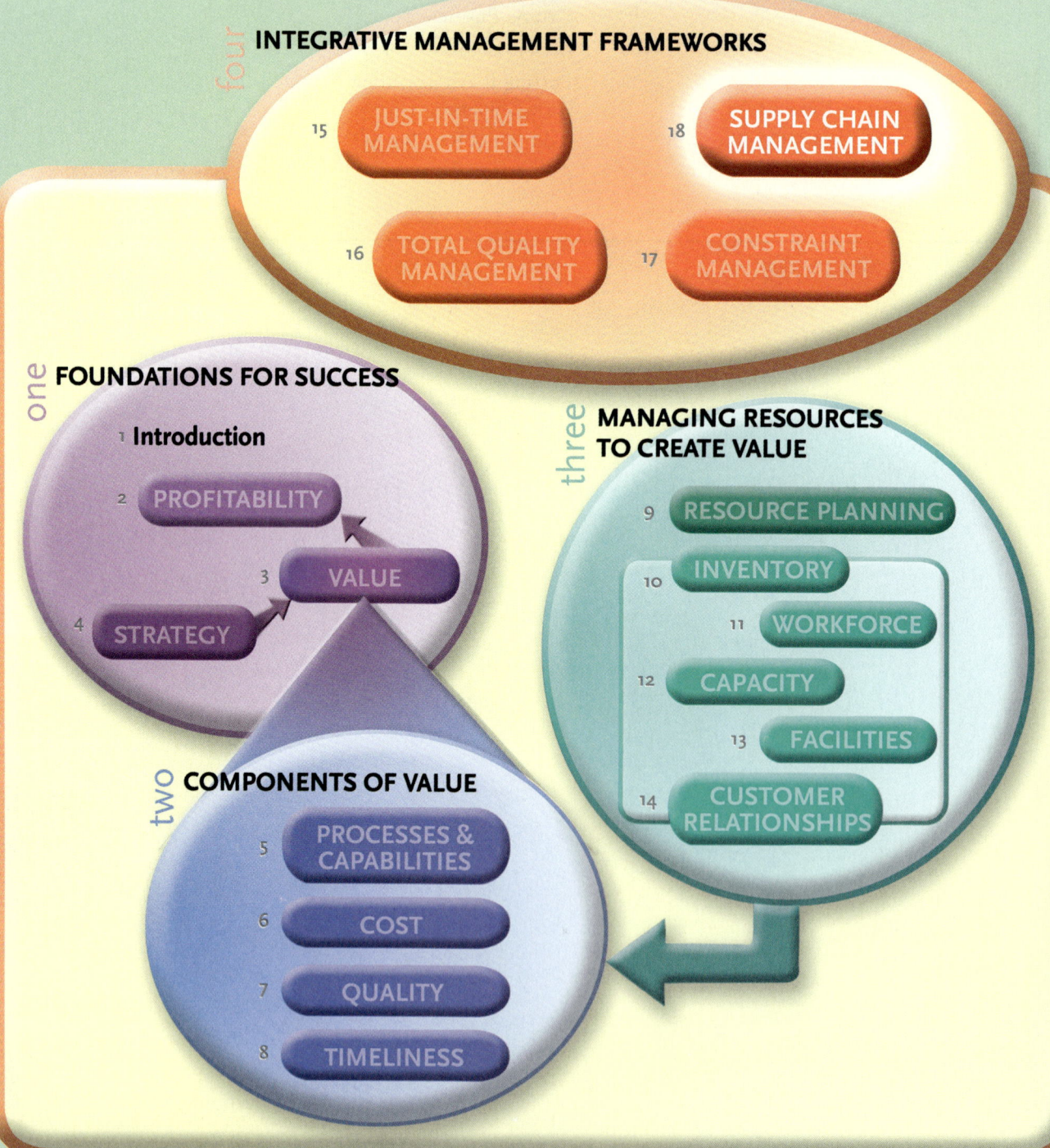

CHAPTER 18

Supply Chain Management

LEARNING OBJECTIVES

Upon completion of Chapter 18, you should be able to

- Explain the motivating forces behind the adoption of supply chain management (SCM).
- List examples of how customer actions affect suppliers and how supplier actions affect customers.
- Explain the seven critical decision areas of SCM.
- Describe an example of a supply chain and identify points of interaction between buyers and suppliers.
- Explain the bullwhip effect and its possible causes.
- Describe risk pooling and the implications it has for distribution networks.

Introduction: A Systemwide Perspective
Supply Chain Management: The Motivating Forces
Supply Chain Management Components
Supply Chain Management: A Typical Example
Extending the Supply Chain Globally
A Closer Look at the Bullwhip Effect
A Closer Look at Risk Pooling
Chapter Summary

INTERNET RESOURCES

 Excel Tutors provide annotated spreadsheets for every solved problem that automatically load Excel.

 Esources provide an online version of the more traditional boxed insert.

 Reel Videos provide streaming video footage for company applications of chapter concepts.

 Interactive Models provide an experimental environment for quantitative concepts and simulations.

INTRODUCTION

A Systemwide Perspective

As information technologies have made it possible for customers and suppliers in B2B relationships to communicate quickly and effectively, the advantages and benefits gained from doing so have become not only apparent, but expected. Goods and services travel between manufacturers, warehouses, distributors, wholesalers, and retailers. That has been obvious as long as they've existed. Businesses have long known who their suppliers were and who their customers were. What hasn't been as obvious, however, is the impact that decisions thought to be internal had on others. Supply chain management evolved into the fourth integrative management framework depicted in Exhibit 18.1 as managers began to recognize the interactions present in supply chains. The ability to tightly link buyers and sellers together through ongoing communication has enabled businesses to consider the effect decisions made within each business had on the other businesses.

The supply chain, as defined in Chapter 3,

> encompasses all activities associated with the flow and transformation of goods from the raw material stage (extraction), through to the end user, as well as the associated information flows. Material and information flow both up and down the supply chain.[1]

The generic supply chain initially presented in Chapter 3 is reproduced in Exhibit 18.2. Each arrow signifies the potential flow of materials from suppliers to customers. A flow of information, however, travels in the opposite direction of each arrow. Effective supply chain management depends as much on this flow of information as it does on the flow of materials. Even though only some activities in the chain add value, all add costs. The objective of supply chain management is to optimize performance of the chain to add as much value as possible for the least cost possible. This can occur only if the perspective used in decision making is broadened to include the entire chain. This systemwide perspective is critical because many pressures and conflicts encourage managers to place decisions internal to their own businesses at a priority above that of the supply chain. Gains from these decisions are short term, however. A long-term perspective recognizes that if a decision improves performance for an individual business while increasing overall costs for the supply chain, the result will be increased costs for the customer and harm done throughout the chain. The only way decisions can be made with this supply chain perspective instead of just a company or plant perspective is if the appropriate information is available.

Supply chain management is not an easy framework to successfully implement. From the perspective of productivity, however, it has become recognized as very important. An examination of why supply chain management is needed provides an excellent introduction to what supply chain management can do.

SUPPLY CHAIN MANAGEMENT: THE MOTIVATING FORCES

Change is brought about by many factors. External forces often force managers to adopt new ways of acting and thinking. Sudden recognition of the "better way" can sometimes be enough to change behavior. The ability to do something that was previously impossible can also be enough of a catalyst to change the way things are done.

EXHIBIT 18.1 The Role of Supply Chain Management in the Resource/Profit Model

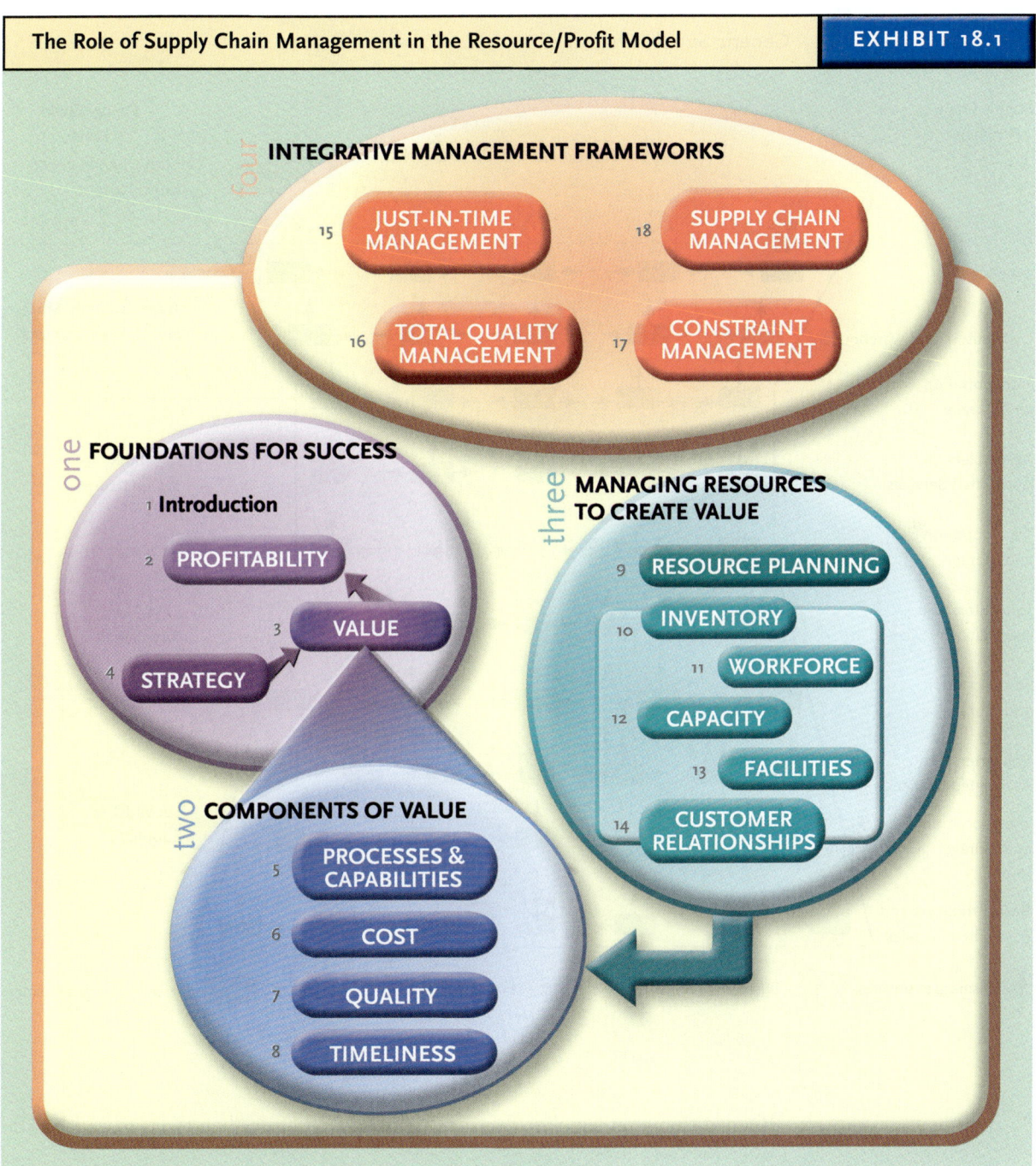

Supply chain management is a dramatic change in behavior from more traditional management approaches and has been motivated by a variety of conditions, fitting all of these descriptions. The most important reasons for the adoption of supply chain management can be summarized as follows:

1. Increased competition to meet customer expectations for value.
2. Recognition that customer decisions and actions often dictate costs and limitations for suppliers.

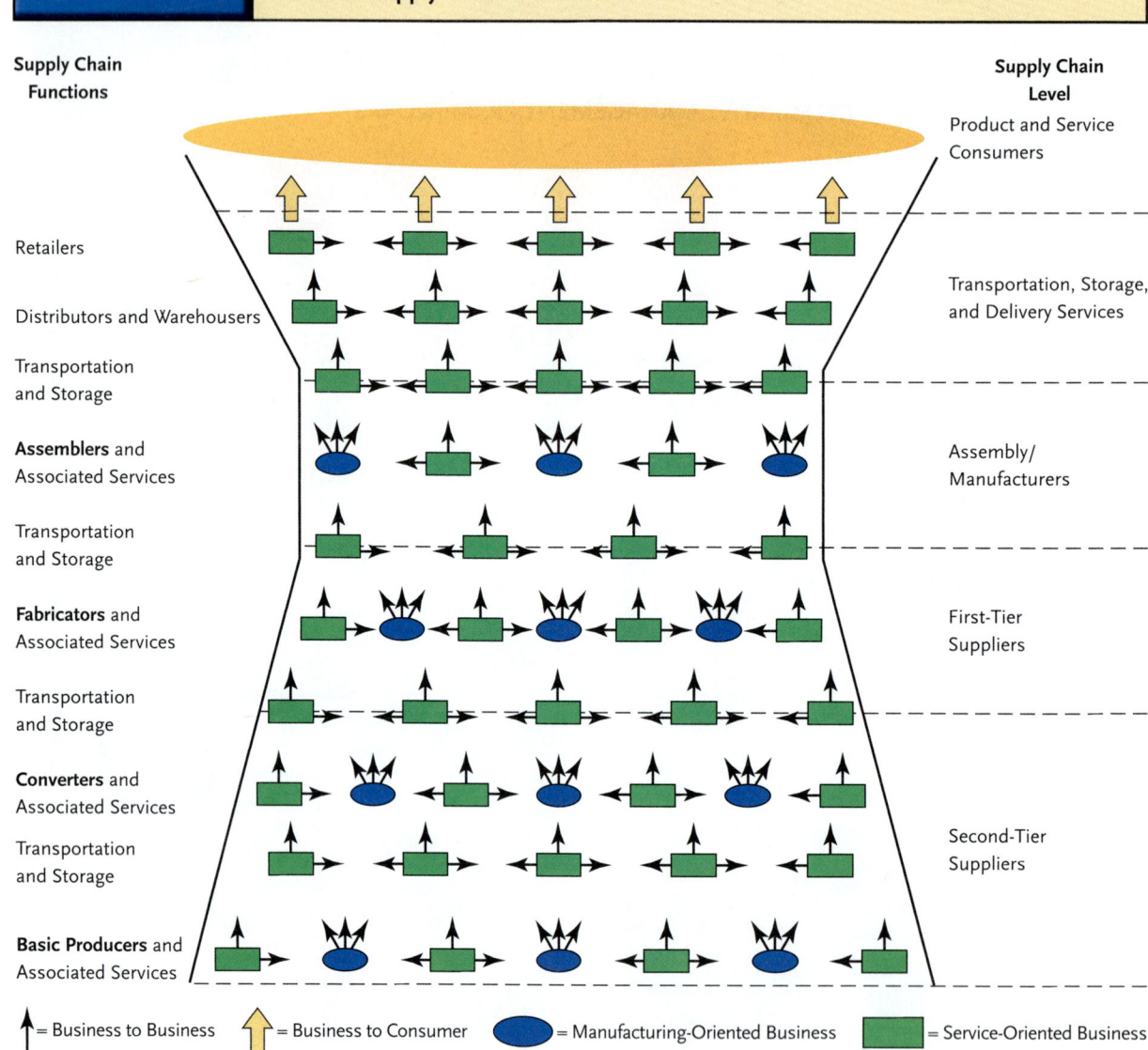

EXHIBIT 18.2 — Generic Supply Chain

3. Recognition that supplier decisions and actions often dictate costs and limitations for customers.
4. Increased potential for timely communication and feedback brought about by technological advances.

A brief discussion of each is presented in turn.

Increased Competition

As domestic markets turned into global markets, businesses initially saw potential for a tremendous opportunity to reach more people with their products and services. Very quickly, however, they realized that along with more potential customers came more competitors. Most did not view intensified competition as an opportunity, but it really was. Customers who are exposed to better products and services elevate their expectations. Businesses that want to continue to compete must improve the value of their products. That comes through enhanced processes and capabilities, lower costs for customers, better quality, and greater timeliness. One company stretches a bit, customers like it, and the competitors must respond. Customer expectations follow the components of value: processes and capabilities, price, quality, and timeliness. If anyone improves on any of them, expectations rise. As each is enhanced in the competitive process, competitors must catch up. This came at a time when businesses, wisely, were focusing more on core competencies in hopes of doing better at what they already did well. Outsourcing was increasing. The paradox is that as value needed to increase, the businesses were passing off much of the value-adding processes to others. Clearly, closer relationships were necessary to make this work.

Businesses sought greater and greater levels of productivity, in order to provide increasing levels of value. This was not limited to B2C companies but included B2B companies as well. Suppliers were pushed and pushed to do better, do it quicker, and do it for less. For many companies, familiarity and experiences with just-in-time (JIT) techniques had led to closer relationships with suppliers. Clearly, the productivity and time requirements being passed down from customers were placing demands on what the suppliers were doing and could do. Productivity was being lost. Costs were added. The decisions and expectations of customers sometimes prevent suppliers from doing things that could actually add value. Suppliers, eager to please, often incurred unnecessary costs trying to meet the needs of their customers. In many cases, their actions weren't really necessary and didn't add value to the product.

What can be viewed as insensitivity among trading partners to each other's needs went in both directions. Not only did suppliers often have to jump through unnecessary hoops for customers, but customers also incurred costs because of supplier decisions and actions. The simplest and most direct costs for customers were related to the delivery patterns of the supplier. Infrequent large quantities versus frequent small quantities, for example, had a tremendous impact on inventory levels for the customer. Decisions made independently clearly provided suboptimal conditions for all parties involved in the supply chain.

On the surface, it appears that supply chain management efforts have been motivated most directly by two of the value attributes: cost and timeliness. Lowering the price to the consumer often requires cost reduction. This creates a need to eliminate non-value-adding steps throughout the production network. Increasing pressures to reduce inventories require quicker and more reliable deliveries from suppliers. No doubt, these are important pressures that have contributed to the need for supply chain management, but they're not the only reasons.

It doesn't take long for a savvy manager to realize that the actions of someone else in the supply chain result in cost increases within that manager's firm. So the manager initiates a conversation. Maybe it's with a supplier who gets orders for products in a format that's incompatible with his computer system. Or maybe if the orders arrived an hour earlier, the shipment could go out today rather than tomorrow. Or maybe a customer could save many hours of labor if the delivery was packaged in a different sequence. In many cases things are done a certain way because that's the way they've always been done. Or maybe the demands placed on the supplier by the customer cause excess work and increase costs. When a supplier or a customer asks about making a change, the response often is "Oh, I didn't know that caused a problem for you. Sure, we can change the way we do that. No big deal." That's the very beginning of supply chain management—suppliers and customers talking. Esource 18.1 provides an example of a supplier of a broad range of manufactures that excels at communication and partnership.

Reduction of costs throughout the supply chain requires a reduction in inventory to minimize those costs as well. Reducing production costs has often made outsourcing more attractive because of differences in labor costs and other production costs. Outsourcing also enables a firm to focus on its core competencies by handing off other work to those who are better at it. Outsourcing, however, can be detrimental when it comes to inventory costs and to the timeliness component of value. Outsourcing reduces reliability and adds transportation time. Inventory protects from those uncertainties. Transportation, however, takes time. Time means delays. Timeliness is even more critical when outsourcing production to the labor force in foreign countries. In some situations, the need for timeliness may require management to forgo opportunities for cheaper labor elsewhere simply because of the transportation time.

The emphasis on cost and timeliness enhancement in the supply chain does not mean that the value components of processes, capabilities, and quality are ignored. That is not the case at all. Much of the effort that goes into an effective supply chain management program is spent working with suppliers to improve all four components of value. In fact, supply chain management is composed of a variety of actions that enhance all aspects of value. In addition to the profitability potential gained from increased product value, cost reductions also contribute to enhanced profitability.

It is very common for U.S. businesses to spend 20 to 30 percent of their revenues on the acquisition of goods from outside suppliers. For manufacturers, 60 percent is typical.[2] A small cost savings in purchases can have a dramatic impact on the bottom line. Consider the following example presented in Exhibit 18.3. This company has sales revenue of $12,520,000 and total purchases of $7,200,000. Total salary and wages are $2,400,000, and financial and other costs are $960,000. Profit before taxes was also $960,000. A 6 percent savings in the cost of supplies, which goes directly to profit, provides a 45 percent increase in before-tax profits. These direct reductions in costs that can stem from better relationships with suppliers are not the only cost savings. Indirect cost savings appear in various areas of the business, including reduced material consumption, reduced labor, and reduced overhead costs that can result from better delivery service, shorter response times, lower inventories, and improved utilization of equipment.[3] Supply chain management has increased in attractiveness as businesses recognize the bottom-line impact. It can have a significant effect on profitability, particularly as companies have squeezed out costs in most other areas. Amazon.com provides an excellent example. Amazon's first profits ever, in the fourth quarter of 2001, are credited largely to supply chain management efforts.

These simplistic and direct impacts on costs are very enticing to managers. However, supply chain management goes even further to enhance value. Exactly how value and profitability are enhanced depends on the specific situation, but an examination of the components of supply chain management provides insight into how it improves value for the customer.

The Impact of Customers on Suppliers

Suppliers began to realize that demands placed on them by their customers actually inhibited their ability to be good suppliers. Lack of communication and an adversarial relationship created an "us-against-them" attitude. In addition to problems that seemed to have obvious causes, another one was recognized. It seemed that even though demand at the consumer end of the supply chain was relatively stable, the variability of demand upstream got increasingly greater. This phenomenon, known as the **bullwhip effect**, can detract from the productivity of the entire supply chain and results from several different customer behaviors. The bullwhip effect is examined in detail later in this chapter.

EXHIBIT 18.3 Supply Savings Example

Sales revenue	$12,520,000
Total purchases	$7,200,000
Total salaries and wages	$2,400,000
Financial and other costs	$960,000
Profit before taxes	$960,000
6% savings in supply costs	$432,000
Impact on profit	45% increase

Breakdown of Total Revenue of $12,520,000

- Total Purchases: $7,200,000
- Total Salaries and Wages: $3,400,000
- Financial and Other Costs: $960,000
- Profit Before Taxes: $960,000

om on site — SCM and Profit for Amazon

The likelihood of finally documenting a profit seemed low for Amazon in 2001, despite CEO Jeff Bezos's claim that it would happen. Analysts expected no profit until at least 2003. Then, in the fourth quarter of 2001, the profit was undeniable—even though Amazon offered a 20 percent discount on books costing $20 or more during the fourth quarter.

One of the biggest improvements for Amazon, in the area of operations, was the culmination of efforts to improve logistics and supply chain management. Prior to 2001, some 12 percent of Amazon's inventory ended up going to the wrong place. This added costs and delayed deliveries. Inventory management improvements reduced this to 4 percent in 2001 even as sales increased. Between November 9 and December 21, 2001, shoppers purchased 37.9 million items. As a result, the cost of fulfilling orders dropped by 15 percent ($22 million) from 2000 to 2001.

Amazon also streamlined its processes for sorting orders. By reducing the time to get all of the components of an order into the system, the number of orders Amazon is able to ship increased. In 2001 Amazon was able to ship 35 percent more items with the same number of workers, driving up labor productivity. Even with these improvements, however, experts estimate that the Amazon distribution system is still operating at less than 40 percent of its capacity.

Source: www.amazon.com; "How Amazon Cleared the Profitability Hurdle," *BusinessWeek*, Online edition, February 4, 2002; "How Hard Should Amazon Swing," *BusinessWeek*, Online edition, January 14, 2002.

The Impact of Suppliers on Customers

Just as the ordering actions of upstream supply chain entities can have a huge impact on the lives of their suppliers, the responses of suppliers can create sweet dreams or nightmares for their customers. Many possible events can have a negative impact on downstream customers. Most have an immediate impact that is obvious. A missed delivery due date, defective products, or raw material shortages can result in missed shipments or delays and can create a dissatisfied consumer. Unreliability within the chain typically results in the customer increasing inventory to reduce the direct dependencies that can contribute to the problems. Inventory will always be important in supply chains, but part of effective supply chain management is determining how to get the greatest benefit from the least cost. This involves decisions about inventory placement in the system—geographical placement at each storage level, as well as which levels in the network to use for storage. Correct placement can improve performance within the chain, reduce costs, and reduce the impact of disruptions.

The most feared of all supplier responses to product demand occurs when the supplier cannot respond. These instances are rare, but they can happen. Every year, natural disasters idle manufacturing plants. Those plants supply others. Whether the disaster is a fire, a flood, a tornado, or an earthquake, entire supply chains can be brought to a halt. This is particularly true when a supply chain depends on a sole supplier for a critical part, as is often the case in JIT environments. In these instances, good relationships with suppliers can prevent a business disaster.

Technological Advances

As managers became aware of the need for integration of decision making, and some were actually attempting it, the quick rise of the Internet provided a means of having immediate access to information that was previously out of reach or too late in arriving to do any good. The Internet made it possible for a supplier to look at the same information that the customer looked at. Rather than forecast demands based on previous orders from a customer, a supplier could actually view the production schedule and eliminate forecasting altogether. And the supplier's supplier could do the same thing. The combination of a need *and* the capability to satisfy it resulted in a surge in the popularity of supply chain management.

SUPPLY CHAIN MANAGEMENT COMPONENTS

Supply chain management can be broken down into the following eight critical decision-making areas:

- Distribution network configuration
- Inventory management
- Distribution strategy
- Strategic partnering
- Cooperative product design
- Information management
- Policy, procedure, and product standardization
- Electronic commerce[4]

Combined, they provide a powerful force that increases product value and enhances profitability throughout the supply chain. The following sections provide a brief overview of each component.

> **Communication Enhances Supply Chain Connections**
>
> Internet-based communication has had a profound impact on the connectivity of businesses desiring supply relationships. It has enabled companies to maintain real-time communication of schedules and demand, it has reduced non-value-adding activities, and it has reduced the time required for transactions. Examples of increased efficiency abound.
>
> Engineers working for IBM suppliers who had examined blueprints of components at IBM facilities before submitting bids for the work now receive blueprints on line. They communicate online with IBM engineers and are encouraged to suggest improvements that can reduce costs for IBM. If changes are accepted, they are immediately made available to other bidders.
>
> The enhanced ability of companies to communicate directly to each other, and buy and sell what each needs, would have never happened without the Internet companies designed to pull them together. CheMatch.com is an excellent example. CheMatch is an exchange and information resource for buying and selling bulk commodity chemicals, polymers, and fuel products. It acts as a miniature stock exchange—an independent neutral third party providing access to commodity chemicals, polymers, and fuel products traded on its exchange.
>
> The trading of products for B2B transactions has become commonplace, but other types of trading exist as well. Yet2.com has created the first global marketplace for the exchange of intellectual assets. Designed to save companies the cost of R&D that has already been performed by someone else, Yet2.com lists, licenses, and sells rights to use inventions by companies who invest millions in R&D but often find that their inventions don't generate revenues because no one knows about them.
>
> Source: "E-purchasing Saves Businesses Billions," *USA Today*, February 7, 2000, pp. 1A, 2A; http://chematch.com/home.jhtml, September 20, 2001; http://www.yet2.com/PSUser/y2_aboutus.htm?page=com, September 20, 2001.

Distribution Network Configuration

A traditional narrow view of the management or product supply concerned itself with getting the product out of the factory door on time. Obviously, a supply chain management strategy extends far beyond that view. It is concerned with everything that happens to that product, from raw material to consumer, within manufacturing plants and warehouses and between those manufacturing plants and warehouses. The fact is that many of the costs incurred and much of the time consumed takes place between those facilities. Products and their components travel great distances. One of the most important tasks for supply chain management is to determine what those distances will be and how that travel will take place so that value can be maximized and costs can be minimized. This requires that a distribution network be designed for the present *and* future needs of the supply chain.

The distribution network includes warehouses, production facilities, retailers, and the inventory that flows between them. Configuring the network requires decisions related to the location of the warehouse and production facilities, where production should take place, where and in what quantities inventories should be kept, and the means by which it is transported from one place to another. What makes these decisions more complex, however, is that the configuration must meet current needs and future needs. This requires the use of forecasting to predict the impact that future demand will have on the network requirements.

UNIT FOUR Integrative Management Frameworks

Inventory Management

As was investigated in detail in Chapter 10, inventory management can be accomplished by determining when to order and how many to order. Inventory management in the supply chain differs only in the information inputs used to help make those two decisions at all levels of the supply chain. For example, for a warehouse, how many units should be ordered? When should they be ordered? What are the risks associated with the order? What safety stocks should be held and why? Should safety stocks be equal for all products warehoused? When choices exist, where should inventory be held? Which warehouse? Or should it be held in the manufacturer's finished-goods warehouse, in a distribution center, or somewhere between? Or should the retailer hold it? These are just a few of the many questions that must be answered relative to inventory management in the broad supply chain management environment.

Distribution Strategy

Distribution strategies address the approach used to distribute products to other places. For example, retailer-owned warehouses might take shipments from suppliers and hold them until ordered by the retail stores. This strategy is known as **warehousing**. On the other hand, retailers might take shipments directly from manufacturers' suppliers, in a strategy known as **direct shipment**. A third alternative, made popular by Wal-Mart, is called **cross-docking**. A cross-docking strategy ships continuously from suppliers to warehouses, where the products are redirected and delivered to the retailers in continuous shipments.[5] These three approaches are illustrated in Exhibit 18.4.

The most sophisticated of the three strategies is cross-docking. It requires excellent communication links between suppliers and retailers. It depends on a very reliable transportation system to ensure continuous delivery of goods. Demand forecasts are critical,

EXHIBIT 18.4 Distribution Strategies

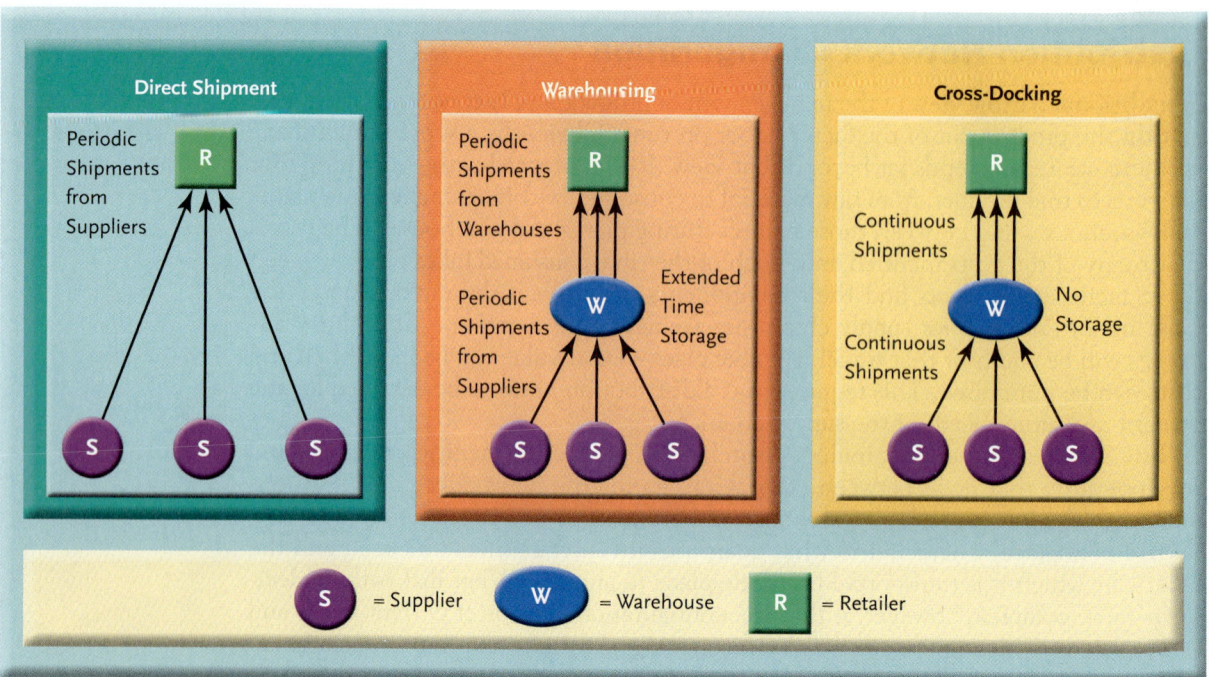

and in many instances they are based on direct data from point-of-sale (POS) systems at the retailer. Cross-docking strategies are most suitable for large distribution systems with many retailers and large volumes of goods. Small distribution systems would be required to deliver in less than full truckloads, making transportation costs prohibitive.

Distribution system decisions affect pipeline inventory levels as well as customer service in a classic tradeoff. This Pepsi distribution center in Boston, MA, illustrates how flows of products can be affected by the capacity of individual components of the supply chain. Notice the side-access trailers that allow easy loading and unloading of a variety of products.

The distribution strategy selected has implications for a variety of resources. The strengths of a warehousing strategy are risk pooling and reducing inbound transportation costs. **Risk pooling**, in short, is based on the fact that if inventory is held in one warehouse to service a large number of retailers, lower levels of inventory can be held than if the inventory was held at each retailer. This is caused by the fact that with a large number of retailers, demands that are higher than expected are canceled out by those that are lower than expected. The more retailers the warehouse serves, the greater the benefit from risk pooling. Overall, the inventory in the warehouse is sufficient to meet all of the demands. Inbound transportation costs are reduced because all shipments are coming from the same place.

A direct shipment strategy eliminates all warehousing costs, but the penalty is that inventory service levels at each store require high levels of safety stock. Overall, much more inventory is required to obtain an acceptable service level. In addition, economies of scale are difficult to gain for shipments because they can be coming from many different places. In a cross-docking strategy, no advantage is gained from risk pooling, but that weakness is often offset by the very frequent shipments and more accurate forecasts. Risk pooling is examined in more detail in a later section of this chapter.

Strategic Partnering

Developing "partners" rather than just hiring suppliers is at the heart of supply chain management. Relationships create an opportunity for communication. Communication enhances productivity improvement and cooperation. As mutual dependence develops, the supplier depends on the customer and the customer depends on the supplier. When it progresses past a simple financial relationship to include each helping the other being better at what they do, it becomes even stronger. These benefits are obvious to enlightened managers, but even a simplistic examination of the costs associated with switching to a new supplier provides support for maintaining long relationships. Several of these costs are listed in Exhibit 18.5.[6]

The costs associated with changing suppliers clearly are varied. Many are direct and immediate, others indirect and long term. Some may never even be recognized; nevertheless, they are significant.

Building a network of reliable suppliers and building solid relationships with them forms a foundation for supply chain management. For many supply chains, the size of the business and its influence is the greatest at the customer end. Automotive supply chains, for example, are dominated by the automobile assemblers: Ford, Daimler-Chrysler, General Motors, Toyota, Honda, Nissan. This continues to be true even

EXHIBIT 18.5	Costs of Switching Suppliers
Equipment expense for the new supplier	Updating engineering drawings
Equipment installation and transfer	Training supplier employees
Inventory buildup at customer to cover transition to new supplier	Developing new supply chain linkage (communication, data, etc.)
Quality validation/certification of new supplier	Costs of transition (time, contracts, travel, negotiations)
Process engineering expenses for new supplier	Costs of dissolution with old supplier
Product redesign	

Source: Laseter, T. M., *Balanced Sourcing*. (San Francisco: Jossey-Bass, 1998), p. 4.

www.OperationsNow.com

though there are thousands of suppliers. A similar phenomenon exists in electronics industries. Supply chains ruled by Motorola or Dell or Hewlett Packard consist of hundreds of suppliers. Historically, in those types of supply chains, the rule was for suppliers to do what they were told. Their customers' approach was very authoritarian and was dominated by the desire for low prices. The suppliers had to adapt their production to what the customer demanded. Today, even the most powerful customers have recognized that in B2B interactions, it pays to have a broader perspective on decision making. Supply chain management requires that relationships with suppliers be based on sharing similar goals, mutual dependence, and knowledge of the suppliers' competency. Esource 18.2 provides an example of how businesses develop specific guidelines for their suppliers.

Businesses take different approaches to supplier development, depending on their priorities. Laseter provides a matrix of approaches used to develop purchasing relationships.[7] It recognizes a frequent conflict between their commitment to the price of the supplies and their commitment to a cooperative relationship. This supplier relationship matrix, presented in Exhibit 18.6, points out how only a balance between commitment to low prices and commitment to the relationship can be effective. Too much importance for either risks the other. For the customer who pays no attention to the relationship and cares only about price, improvement can't happen and product value suffers as a result. The supplier feels resentful and abused. Ultimately, the supplier looks for another customer. For the customer who cares nothing about price and only about the relationship, there is no incentive for the supplier to provide a good price because the customer doesn't seem to care. The supplier makes out like a bandit, but the customer suffers from high material costs. Again, the consumer doesn't get good value, but this time it's because of product cost issues.

Certification programs are a common approach to developing balanced supplier relationships. There are numerous certification programs in existence. Chrysler's SCORE (Supplier Cost Reduction) is a famous example. In the SCORE program suppliers are encouraged to submit cost saving ideas worth 5 percent of their annual sales to Chrysler. Chrysler gets 50 percent of the savings. The supplier gets the other 50 percent.

Many customers utilize their expertise in supplier development efforts as another way to build balanced relationships. The customer frequently has more resources at hand to help suppliers deal with problems, quality improvement, employee training,

Supplier Relationship Matrix

EXHIBIT 18.6

	Commitment to Competitive Pricing	
Commitment to a Cooperative Relationship	**Low**	**High**
High	**Trust-Based Partnerships** • Supplier dominated • Unclear rationale for improvement • Assumes congruence of supplier goals • Supplier may capture all of the value creation	**Balanced Sourcing** • Uses supplier capabilities completely • Drives improvement at customer and supplier • Requires high capability customer
Low	**Unleveraged Purchasing** • Unmotivated, unstructured • Traditional "clerical" mentality of purchasing • "Price taker" • Leaves lots of money on the table	**Darwinian Rivalry** • Adversarial • Customer dominated • Requires purchasing clout • Eliminates lethargy, but may cause resentment • Does not result in improvement

and so on. In all cases, supplier development and certification programs result in improved productivity and quality, which flow downstream with the products, helping everyone in the chain.

Cooperative Product Design

Product design, in order to provide an end result of products that meet the customers' needs and are capable of being produced efficiently and effectively, often involves the concurrent engineering of products and processes. Quality function deployment (QFD) links product and process design to customer requirements. For many manufacturers, particularly those who depend on outsourcing to increase the value of their products, the component designs are as critical as those of the finished products. The design of components, for example, can dictate the requirements for assembly equipment. When more than one supplier of a particular component exists, the components must be designed so that they can be produced by all suppliers. Increasingly, new-product design efforts require the involvement of suppliers. This is not just to ensure that the components are manufacturable. In many cases, the suppliers can provide insight that will improve the products, reduce costs, and, most important, reduce time. These interactions and supplier investments of time can be expected only when the supplier and customer have a mutually beneficial relationship.

Information Management

Much of the motivation behind supply chain management is linked to the availability of technology that can collect, store, and communicate data that can enhance product value. There are really three decisions:

1. What data should be collected? In other words, what data can aid in increasing value through enhanced processes and capabilities, reduced costs, improved quality, or enhanced timeliness?
2. How should the data be stored? Current trends favor enterprise resource planning (ERP) systems as a means of maintaining a centralized database that all users can access. Supply-related data are critical to a variety of decision areas, so utilizing the ERP environment makes a lot of sense.
3. With whom is data shared? This question addresses issues related to data access. Clearly, suppliers can benefit from access to demand data of their customers. They can benefit from production schedule access and inventory levels as well.

On a more technical note, once these decisions have been made, how the data are accessed by outside entities must be addressed. The Internet provides many alternatives for sharing and accessing such data, but each alternative raises security issues. Communication issues must be dealt with in both directions. It isn't enough for suppliers to have information about customers. Customers also need information about suppliers. Inventory levels and capacity of suppliers, for example, are critical pieces of information if customers are going to be able to respond to the requests of *their* customers.

In many cases, numerical data are useless without the proper analysis. The development of decision support technologies, including statistical analysis tools, optimization tools, and simulation capabilities, can be useful in turning raw data into information that can add value to products and increase the value that can be shared with the entire supply chain.

Policy, Procedure, and Product Standardization

Long-term interaction between suppliers and customers, particularly in B2B situations where customers are fed components to assemble, creates situations that can point out conflicts and incompatibilities between business processes and priorities. Businesses design their processes with the best of intentions, but not all businesses arrive at the same processes to accomplish similar goals. The development of relationships between suppliers and customers allows them to learn about each other's business processes and adapt theirs to be compatible. An ongoing relationship with a customer or a supplier requires that each be easy to do business with. If either is difficult, the relationship will not be productive. Supplier relationships can benefit from best-practice benchmarks which result in enhanced productivity for both parties and easy "handshaking" between partners' communication systems through commonality of systems. ERP systems frequently provide a means of accomplishing this. Suppliers utilize the same system as their customers. This creates advantages of data sharing and enhances business process compatibility, but, as mentioned earlier in this book, it can restrict firms' flexibility to improve business processes.

Standardization of processes makes for higher levels of productivity; but standardization of products and parts can contribute to productivity as well. In many industries, a major portion of inventory is made up of very small, inexpensive components that are used throughout the product line. Fasteners (nuts, bolts, clips), for example, are used in huge quantities in the auto industry. Standardization of these components has long been a major goal of manufacturing firms. Standardization across the entire supply chain can have a significant impact on inventory levels and associated costs.

Electronic Commerce

Many of the benefits of supply chain management are tied to time reductions. Electronic commerce can contribute significantly to those improvements. Electronic funds transfers speed up the cash-to-cash cycle and, when combined with electronic order processing, make continuous replenishment systems much more economical. Small, frequent orders reduce inventory levels, but the administrative costs of processing them can be large. Eliminating the "paper pushing" that traditionally documents interactions between suppliers and customers reduces costs and speeds up the process. Dedicated B2B sites on the Internet make it possible for customers to identify potential suppliers and customers. Suppliers auction off goods in traditional online auctions. Customers find low-cost suppliers through reverse auctions. Esource 18.3 provides an example of each auction type.

www.OperationsNow.com

SUPPLY CHAIN MANAGEMENT: A TYPICAL EXAMPLE

A better perspective on what the components of supply chain management mean for a business and its suppliers can be gained by being specific. The generic supply chain from Exhibit 18.2 is an excellent starting point for examining the extent of the supply chain management impact.

Pacers, a popular brand of athletic shoes, are sold primarily through national chains of athletic shoe stores. The shoe production facilities are somewhat vertically integrated, performing fabrication and assembly operations in one plant. Pacers purchases components (leather, fabric, composite material for soles, foam, laces, and so forth) in bulk from a number of different suppliers. Pacers then does all cutting, coating, and coloring. It also sews (assembles) all products. Exhibit 18.7 is the generic supply chain modified to represent Pacers's supply chain.

A review of various decisions and their impacts shows how a supply chain management perspective can enhance value and reduce costs for a company like Pacers. Many decisions can take place at the downstream or consumer end of the chain. For example, suppose a large retail chain, one of Pacers's largest customers, decides to have a promotion four months in the future. That decision will have numerous implications for Pacers and its suppliers. First, Pacers must revise demand forecasts to include the increase in sales that will result from that promotion. The impact of promotions is particularly hard to forecast, so the best approach will be to examine past promotions held by this customer. They will also expect a "postpromotion lag" in demand coming from customers who bought products early in response to the promotion. Knowing the dates of the promotion is not specific enough information for Pacers, however.

Pacers needs to know when the retailer will need the inventory in its stores. Knowing when the inventory will need to be in stores, Pacers can determine when it will need to be completed. Pacers also needs to know *which* of its distribution centers to ship to. This will have an impact on when the inventory must be shipped from the Pacers facility because the retailer's warehouses could be scattered throughout the United States. Once Pacers knows where to ship to, it can decide where in the manufacturing system the inventory should be produced. When this is known, it can examine the capacity at that facility and determine when it is feasible to produce the order. Capacity limitations in the optimal facility may preclude Pacers from producing

EXHIBIT 18.7　Pacers's Supply Chain

Supply Chain Functions

- Retailers
- Distributors and Warehousers
- Transportation and Storage
- **Assemblers** and Associated Services
- Transportation and Storage
- **Fabricators** and Associated Services
- Transportation and Storage
- **Converters** and Associated Services
- Transportation and Storage
- **Basic Producers** and Associated Services

Supply Chain Level

- Product and Service Consumers
- Transportation, Storage, and Delivery Services
- Striders Assembly and Fabrications Operations
- First-Tier Suppliers
- Second-Tier Suppliers

↑ = Business to Business　⇧ = Business to Consumer　● = Manufacturing-Oriented Business　▮ = Service-Oriented Business

there, however. It may be forced to produce at another facility that has available capacity. If Pacers's production facilities typically produce in small batches and maintain a smooth pattern of production, this large promotion may disrupt the pattern. The sooner Pacers can begin to integrate it into production runs, the less of an impact it will have on the other orders that must be fulfilled. However, the further ahead Pacers produces it, the higher the inventory level in the supply chain, because someone must store it until it is sold. The results of these decisions, to a great extent, will be dictated by the *distribution network configuration, inventory management,* and *the distribution strategy.*

By moving upstream in the supply chain (away from the consumer) and toward the suppliers, it is apparent that the impact of this promotion could extend beyond Pacers's warehousing and manufacturing facilities. Raw material transportation and storage capacity, as well as the capacity of suppliers, will also be affected by this promotion. Its impact will spread like ripples on a pond. Transportation and storage capacity between suppliers and facilities must be able to absorb the increased flow of product. Depending on where the company plans to manufacture the product, specific supply transportation channels and warehousing locations may be affected. Some transportation channels may not have the capacity to absorb the impact, resulting in using a combination of different channels or providers. Manufacturing schedules for Pacers's suppliers most certainly will need to adjust to the additional demands placed on them by this promotion. They will need to determine when and where their production will occur. Production patterns in their facilities (large batch versus small batch), raw material delivery patterns from their suppliers, and even the availability of raw materials can be affected. Their suppliers, in turn, may have to adjust to supply them with what they need. At any point, if there is a situation that prevents a particular entity in the supply chain from doing what needs to be done, the order is at risk of being late. These issues are part of the *strategic partnering* Pacers has developed and its *information management* processes. The ease of working with those suppliers and the efficiency of these interactions will be dictated by the *policy, procedure,* and *product standardization* decisions made in past interactions. Suppliers may utilize electronic commerce capabilities in locating and purchasing their raw materials.

Finally, depending on the nature of the promotion, it is possible that Pacers may actually be required to design a product exclusive to the promotion. In that case, working with its suppliers through *cooperative product design* will ensure that the product meets customer requirements and can be produced effectively.

Since we know that Pacers is a major player in the athletic shoe industry, it should be no surprise that a promotion by one store chain is one of many promotions that it must deal with annually. This is a way of life for Pacers. A promotion at a major customer may cause a blip in demand, but many customers have promotions and the demand for each fluctuates somewhat, so the total centralized demand for Pacers's products should be relatively stable. This is the effect of risk pooling. Maintaining a stable load on production capacity is one of the most important things Pacers can do to maintain high levels of productivity.

While customer decisions affect upstream supplier productivity in the supply chain, supplier decisions and actions can affect downstream productivity. Suppose that the day before Pacers was informed of this promotion, its primary supplier of leather informed Pacers of a shortage of shipments from South America. Earthquakes, tornadoes, fires, floods, government regulations, and simple management error at suppliers can have major impacts on customers. But something as simple as a supplier changing its supplier can also have a significant impact. In a network as complex as a supply chain can be, the seemingly unimportant decisions can cause major problems.

EXTENDING THE SUPPLY CHAIN GLOBALLY

Inclusion of foreign suppliers in the supply chain can have substantial benefits as well as risks. A global supply chain is mandatory as a business extends its markets to foreign countries. The impact of a global extension of the supply chain depends on how it is extended. Is the customer end of the supply chain extended? Or is the supplier end extended?

Extending the customer base into foreign countries has the potential to increase the size of markets, but it is rarely accomplished just by shipping products over and selling them. Many businesses have found that different cultures prefer different types of services and products. Values differ. Wal-Mart, for example has struggled with its expansions into South America, particularly Brazil and Argentina.[8] One of the causes of its problems is that it has had a difficult time reaching volumes sufficient to allow it to keep costs down. Stocking a wide variety of products is difficult because of a distribution system not configured as well as it is in the U.S. operation. In South America, most Wal-Mart shipments come directly from the manufacturer, rather than through a cross-docking system used in the United States. Some stores in South America receive 300 deliveries per day, compared to 7 at U.S. stores. Other problems exemplify typical "glitches" businesses often encounter but don't anticipate when extending their customer base internationally. Many businesses find that the distribution network configuration is forced to be different than they're used to and that transferring the distribution strategy they have in the U.S. is impossible. The end result in many instances is difficulty getting timely deliveries. To make matters worse, the technology infrastructure may inhibit the business from utilizing the information and communication capabilities its distribution and inventory management systems depend on.

Extending the supplier end of the supply chain brings its own set of issues. Technology and communication systems can certainly have an effect here as well. Complicating things further is a diffuse distribution network, adding the impact of greater transportation times. One of the biggest hurdles, however, is the development of the close relationships that can only come from strategic partnering efforts. Cooperative product design, made even more critical if the business is also extending its markets internationally, is complicated by distance and by culture differences. Policy, procedure, and product standardization can be a terrific hurdle that is difficult enough when dealing with domestic suppliers, but becomes even more problematic when dealing with businesses that have operated in a completely different culture.

Despite the difficulties in extending the supply chain management paradigm internationally, effective business management in a global setting needs the very benefits supply chain management can offer. Government and regulatory shifts toward free trade have made these extensions more common and more desirable. The U.S. economy has become a subset of the global economy. Businesses cannot afford to not take advantage of the customers and suppliers. If they avoid them, their competitors won't.

For businesses in the United States, expanding the supplier base to foreign countries can be a more difficult decision. Foreign suppliers can add value and reduce costs in a number of ways. Labor costs might be lower, for example. Some products are available in certain geographic regions and a local supplier is the only way a business can obtain them. The benefits can be too attractive to pass up, but do not come free.

A CLOSER LOOK AT THE BULLWHIP EFFECT

At each level of a supply chain, the variability of the purchases a company makes is often greater then the variability of the demand that consumes its products. When this is true for each company in the supply chain, the bullwhip effect results, and demand increases in variability at each level, as illustrated in Exhibit 18.8.

The causes of the bullwhip effect have been a source of interest to researchers, because eliminating the causes would eliminate the effect. Lee and colleagues propose four likely causes:[9]

- Demand forecast updating
- Order batching
- Price fluctuation
- Rationing and shortage gaming

Reduced Time Can Mean Reduced Opportunity for Disruptions in Tightly Linked Supply Chains

Disruptions in supply have always been on the radar screen of low-inventory businesses. In fact, the need to minimize these disruptions and create a stable supply source has been a motivating force behind supply chain management efforts. Reducing the time required for a delivery reduces the potential for disruption. Despite the need for time reductions in getting products to market, many companies use contract manufacturers to minimize investment in equipment that may quickly become obsolete as products go through accelerated life cycles. The result is a serious dilemma.

On one hand, manufacturers of products need to subcontract some manufacturing tasks in order to focus on processes they do best and avoid equipment investments that may not provide financial return. Outsourcing manufacturing increases lead times, however, because of the transportation time that is injected into the supply chain. To make things worse, many of the contract manufacturers used are located in China or other Asian countries. Delivery from Asia to the United States is two weeks by ship. Air freight is prohibitively expensive.

The need to speed up deliveries has resulted in the cheap labor costs associated with Asia no longer being sufficient to attract manufacturers. Many have chosen to identify closer suppliers. For an increasing number, that has led to contract manufacturers in Guadalajara, Mexico. Unlike border towns, whose workforce is typically unstable, Guadalajara has a stable workforce supported by seven universities and dozens of technical schools.

The link between time and potential disruptions has become even more critical as terrorism has become a possible cause of supply disruption. Many companies were affected by the September 11, 2001, terrorist attacks. Auto manufacturers, food producers, and others faced delays on deliveries coming from Canada. Just-in-time environments were hit even worse because their inventories were lower and could not absorb disruptions for as long. As the potential for disruptions and the uncertainty associated with them increases, the need for effective supply chain management increases as well.

Inventory buffers will need to be increased, but the focus should be on the most critical parts and those that would be affected most, like those coming from single international sources. Manufacturers must pay closer attention to where their incoming parts are coming from. Since one of the biggest disruptions has been delays at international borders, manufacturers may need to investigate domestic or regional suppliers as a primary or secondary source. Transportation strategies may need to be broadened. If regulations associated with shipping cargo on passenger flights change, shipping on cargo flights may be necessary. Enhanced knowledge of security and customs operations along international borders can also aid in minimizing disruptions. Increased levels of communication with suppliers can add to the information that has previously been limited to forecasts. Enhanced relationships provide a basis for better communication and quicker reaction to any type of disruption.

Source: "When Just-in-Time becomes Just-in-Case," *The Wall Street Journal*, October 22, 2001, p. A18; "How a Need for Speed Turned Guadalajara into a High-Tech Hub," *The Wall Street Journal*, March 2, 2002, pp. A1, A8.

| EXHIBIT 18.8 | **Bullwhip Effect** |

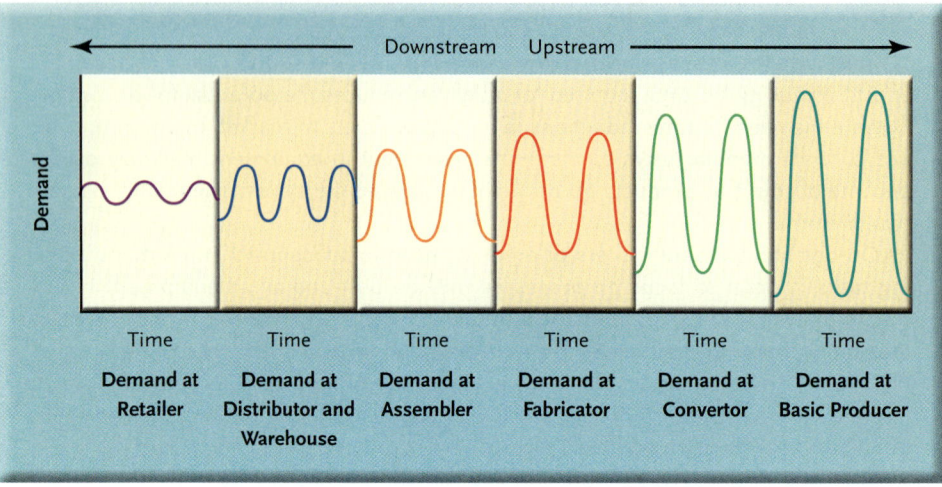

The impact of forecast updating is direct. Forecasts, which provide input to the businesses' production scheduling, inventory management, and capacity planning efforts, is typically based on previous demand, determined by previous customer orders. As orders for products are increased, demand forecasts are adjusted and orders for suppliers are adjusted as well. In addition to meeting the demand, however, orders from the suppliers must also fill increasing safety stocks. This is made even worse by long replenishment lead times. The longer the lead times, the more uncertain the demand and the greater the safety stocks. At each level of the supply chain, this phenomenon increases the bullwhip effect.

As customer needs deplete the inventory, inventory goes out at a relatively smooth rate. The orders to replenish that inventory, however, do not go out as frequently. Inventory is ordered in batches. Batch ordering occurs because of high transaction costs on orders and the need for full truckloads when orders are delivered. Order batching also occurs as a result of the time periods utilized in performance measuring systems. Salespersons may submit orders periodically, but they will always submit them at the end of the time period used in measuring their performance. The result of all batch ordering is that the orders are released in a very "lumpy" fashion, reflected in a lumpy demand on the supplier who must fulfill those orders. That supplier, in return, allows demand to accumulate prior to releasing orders, and the effect is magnified.

Businesses often buy before they need to because suppliers offer pricing advantages. Suppliers offer promotions or special prices. In addition to purchasing ahead of time, discount prices can also encourage customers to buy more than is needed. In both cases, purchases exceed demand. In both cases, the act triggers a bigger effect as it moves through the supply chain.

In many industries, customers live in fear of supply shortages. They know that if a supply shortage does occur for a critical component, the suppliers will ration the part and they won't get as many as they need. In response, they order ahead and in larger quantities than they need in anticipation of the shortage. Then, if the shortage doesn't happen, they cancel and reduce orders. The result is that the demand on the supplier fluctuates significantly—and much more than the actual demand on the customer's products.

It is important to restate that value added anywhere in the supply chain is critical to the value received by the customer. Similarly, costs added anywhere trickle down to costs borne by the customer. No matter what the cause of the bullwhip effect present in a particular supply chain, the negative impact on value that results from the bullwhip effect can be huge and can rear its ugly head in many unsuspected ways. The implications of the bullwhip effect can be best understood by examining its impact on each of the four components of value: process and capabilities, costs, quality, and timeliness.

The impact demand fluctuation has on processes and capabilities can be direct and can have significant implications for the competitive success of the firm. First, all businesses seek a level load on their capacity that matches their design capacity. Demands that go up and down make it extremely difficult or impossible to maintain this level load. This is particularly true if the variability is coming from batch ordering triggered by periodic customer orders. Most customers will be on similar cycles, compounding the problem. Effort spent on constantly fluctuating output to meet spiking demand patterns takes attention away from other needs, such as process improvement and productivity enhancement. The business is placed in a feast-or-famine mode, neither of which is good for productivity.

Orders that are placed early or that are larger than demand would dictate result in a loss of flexibility. Studies show that in some industries, months of demand can be met by inventory held within the supply chain. Thus if a product innovation occurred, it would be months before it could get to market. In this situation the development of unique capabilities that could be very competitive in the marketplace is nullified by the presence of the excess inventory. No matter how creative the product designers, no matter how innovative their product improvement, it can't get to market soon enough.

We know that a mismatch between demand and design capacity results in an increased cost per unit, whether the demand is lower than design capacity or higher than design capacity. This occurs for many reasons, including the need for overtime, temporary help, and increased load on machines. Demand that is too low results in a potential cash shortage, increases costs of short-term debt, and reduces the financial return on investments in equipment. Inventory carrying costs increased by batch purchasing, purchasing ahead to take advantage of price differentials, and higher safety stocks not only increase inventory carrying costs for the business making the purchase, but also add to the total amount of inventory in the supply chain. As we know, costs added anywhere find their way to the customer.

Large amounts of fluctuation in the demand of upstream businesses may make the load on production so uneven that the firm is required to lay off employees during low demand periods. This can diminish the quality of the workforce as good employees are lost to businesses that can offer better job security. Businesses that are constantly gearing up or gearing down in response to demand shifts are not very responsive because they can be caught going the wrong direction. They try to predict what's going to happen to demand next, and they invariably make a mistake. They are put in a reactive position that does not give them the flexibility to respond quickly to real customer needs.

The impact of the bullwhip effect has other ramifications for timeliness. One of the most important is its impact on the cash-to-cash cycle. The bullwhip effect invariably results in increased levels of inventory throughout the supply chain. Increased demand fluctuation, whatever the cause, elicits a response that includes adjusting demand forecasts upward and increasing safety stock to prevent stockouts. The cash-to-cash cycle, which dictates the financial return rate on all investments, including inventory, depends on a high inventory turnover rate. The bullwhip effect

POS data collection provides immediate retail demand information for manufacturers, reducing the bullwhip effect. Levi Strauss utilizes POS data collection and its own software to link retail sales directly to manufacturing. The result has reduced inventory levels and increased sales.

has an even worse effect on inventory than high inventory levels in one business because it creates a situation where all upstream businesses in the supply chain have increasing amounts of excess inventory. Days-of-supply expands as a cushion to protect the business from the high level of demand fluctuation. The result is a long cash-to-cash cycle, diminishing financial returns, and a decrease in the agility necessary to respond to market dynamics.

A key to eliminating the bullwhip effect and a key to any supply chain management effort is an increase in information supplied by businesses to their suppliers. Rather than suppliers creating demand forecasts from order histories, they should have access to their customers' actual orders. This can happen in several ways: by making those orders available for access by suppliers electronically, for example, or by allowing suppliers direct access to POS (point-of-sale) data collected continuously at the cash registers of retail stores. Suppliers can then immediately produce and ship based on actual customer demand data, rather than use forecasts created from a history of batched orders.

Closer relationships with suppliers can result in elimination of price discounts, thereby eliminating the motivation to order ahead or order in larger-than-necessary quantities. The result is beneficial for both companies involved. Inventory is reduced for the customer, who can now better link purchases to needs, and demand on production capacity is smoother for the supplier.

Traditional inventory reduction approaches, including reducing the transaction costs associated with orders, can lessen the need to order in large batches. In addition, identifying economical avenues for shipping smaller quantities can help, as can eliminating the penalties associated with shipping less than full truckloads. Very frequent deliveries of small quantities, known as continuous replenishment, are one approach used to smooth out demands on suppliers. This is common when a cross-docking distribution strategy is employed. Suppliers have access to actual sales data from customers and replenish on a daily or more frequent basis.

A CLOSER LOOK AT RISK POOLING

As mentioned earlier, the uncertainty associated with customer demand must be accommodated through inventory safety stocks, wherever that inventory happens to be. If, for example, each retailer maintained inventory that was replenished through direct shipments, the safety stock at each retailer must cope with demand variability. If all of the retailers were supplied from a central warehouse, safety stocks could be less because the *aggregated* variability would be less. High demand at one place would cancel out low demand at another place.

The benefits of risk pooling consist of the costs saved by the reduced levels of inventory and the higher service level. Let's look at a simple example. Pacers has two warehouses in the northeastern United States to serve retailers there. The company is considering a merger of the two. To determine if such a merger makes sense, Pacers would need to determine the impact such a merger would have on inventory costs. As we know, safety stocks are required in inventory management systems to deal with variability.

For each product warehoused by Pacers, inventory is held at each warehouse. Recall from Chapter 10 that in a reorder point system, on average, the safety stock is not used, so the average amount of inventory is increased by the amount of the safety stock. Suppose for a particular product the safety stock was 200 units at one warehouse and 120 units at another. The variability of demand results in inventory carrying costs on 320 units. Combining the warehouses results in less variability of demand at the centralized warehouse because all demand now comes to one place, and there is a greater likelihood that high and low demands will cancel each other out. The result is that the same service level can be had by carrying less than 320 units. The risk pooling phenomenon can be explored in Interactive Model 18.1.

Ultimately, whether the decision to centralize makes financial sense depends on the savings across all product lines compared to the costs associated with facility modifications and changes in transportation costs.

CHAPTER SUMMARY

Because of increasing global competition, supply chain management has expanded to become a framework to allow businesses to go beyond decisions that offer short-term value enhancement to providing long-term enhancement to the entire supply chain. Just as businesses have gone through the realization that what is best for one function may not be the best for the business, they have come to realize that what is best for one business may not be the best for the supply chain. And ultimately, since the customer receives the value added by the entire chain, that's what matters most.

This chapter provided an overview of supply chain management as a perspective that guides decision making by broadening the scope of decision impact. Like TQM, JIT, and constraint management, it provides a framework for managers to judge their actions, leading to improved value for the customer and improved profitability for themselves.

KEY TERMS

bullwhip effect, 628
cross-docking, 632
direct shipment, 632
risk pooling, 633
warehousing, 632

REVIEW QUESTIONS

1. What pressures have resulted in supply chain management being adopted by an increasing number of companies?
2. Why does supply chain management provide a competitive advantage to firms using it?
3. Provide examples of how the actions of customers impact suppliers.
4. Provide examples of how the actions of suppliers impact customers.
5. Describe the decision-making components of supply chain management.
6. What are the three alternative distribution strategies? Describe how each one works.
7. What is meant by risk pooling? How does distribution strategy affect risk pooling?
8. What is strategic partnering? Why is it important to supply chain management?
9. What are some of the common challenges that accompany a global extension of the supply chain?
10. What is the bullwhip effect? What are some of its causes?

DISCUSSION QUESTIONS

1. Identify a common consumer item you recently purchased. Trace the product back through its supply chain. Try to identify all of the cost-adding and value-adding steps along its route through the network of product and service suppliers.
2. Identify a business that chose to vertically integrate rather than outsource for its supplies. What are the advantages and disadvantages of vertical integration? What would be the advantages and disadvantages for it if it chose to outsource?
3. Identify the external suppliers for your university. What relationships does your university have with these businesses? Is it a strategic partner with any businesses? How can you tell?

INTERACTIVE ANALYSIS 18.1

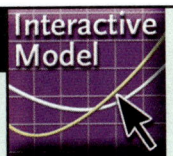
www.
OperationsNow
.com

THE RISK POOLING INTERACTIVE MODEL

The Risk Pooling Interactive Model is accessed through Chapter 18 of the *Operations-Now.com* website. It provides a simple demonstration of the impact of risk pooling on the systemwide inventory of two products when alternatives for inventory location are available. The users of the Risk Pooling Interactive Model are provided with several input parameters. First, the desired service level can be selected using a slider button. The selection between retailer, regional distribution centers (DCs), and the centralized distribution center can also be made using the drop-down box. The weekly demand and the standard deviation for each of the two products is entered via the table.

The scenario provides three options for storing inventory in a small distribution network. The first option is to keep all inventory at the four retailers. Each retailer has a reorder point system with safety stocks dictated by the service level selected. The second alternative is to store inventory at the two regional distribution centers. Each serves two of the retailers. The regional distribution centers also manage the inventory with a reorder point system with safety stocks dictated by the service level selected. The third alternative is to keep all inventory at the centralized distribution center. It is also managed using a reorder point system.

Experiment 1: System Fundamentals

1. Set the service level to 85 percent. Leave product demand and standard deviation values at the default levels.
   a. Compare the system inventory level for the three alternatives of retailer, regional distribution center, and centralized distribution center. How do they compare?
2. Increase the service level to 90 percent and perform the same comparison. Leave product demand and standard deviation values at the default levels.
   a. Compare the system inventory level for the three alternatives of retailer, regional distribution center, and centralized distribution center. How do they compare?
3. Increase the service level to 95 percent and perform the same comparison. Leave product demand and standard deviation values at the default levels.
   a. What impact does the increase in service level have on the difference in inventory levels for the three alternatives?

Experiment 2: The Impact of Demand Variability on Risk Pooling

1. Set the service level to 85 percent. Leave product demand at the default values. Double each standard deviation.
   a. What is the level of system inventory for each alternative inventory location? How has it changed as a result of the variability being increased?
2. Change the service level to 90 percent and then 95 percent, monitoring the changes in inventory level for each location alternative.
   a. What are the relationships among nearness of inventory to the customer, demand variability, and service level?

SELECTED REFERENCES

Handfield, R. B., and Nichols, E. L. *Introduction to Supply Chain Management.* Upper Saddle River, NJ: Prentice Hall, 1999.

Laseter, T. M. *Balanced Sourcing.* San Francisco: Jossey-Bass, 1998.

Leenders, M. R., and Blenkhorn, D. L. *Reverse Marketing.* New York: Free Press, 1988.

Simchi-Levi, D., Kaminsky, P., and Simchi-Levi, E. *Designing and Managing the Supply Chain.* New York: McGraw-Hill, 2000.

ENDNOTES

1. R. B. Handfield and E. L. Nichols, *Introduction to Supply Chain Management* (Upper Saddle River, NJ: Prentice Hall, 1999), p. 2.
2. M. R. Leenders and D. L. Blenkhorn, *Reverse Marketing* (New York: Free Press, 1988), p. 8.
3. Ibid, p. 11.
4. Adapted from D. Simchi-Levi, P. Kaminksy, and E. Simchi-Levi, *Designing and Managing the Supply Chain* (New York: McGraw-Hill, 2000), pp. 8–10.
5. Ibid, pp. 112–115.
6. Ibid, p. 4.
7. Laseter, T. M., *Balanced Sourcing* (San Francisco: Jossey-Bass Publishers, 1998), p. 4.
8. "Wal-Mart Gets Aggressive about Brazil," *The Wall Street Journal,* May 25, 2001, pp. A8, A12; also described in Simchi-Levi, Kaminsky, and Simchi-Levi, *Designing and Managing the Supply Chain.*
9. H. L. Lee, V. Padmanabhan, and S. Whang, "The Bullwhip Effect in Supply Chains," *Sloan Management Review,* Spring 1997.

APPENDIX A

Areas of the Standard Normal Distribution

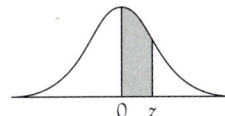

An entry in the table is the proportion under the entire curve that is between $z = 0$ and a positive value of z. Areas for negative values of z are obtained by symmetry.

z	.00	.01	.02	.03	.04	.05	.06	.07	.08	.09
0.0	.0000	.0040	.0080	.0120	.0160	.0199	.0239	.0279	.0319	.0359
0.1	.0398	.0438	.0478	.0517	.0557	.0596	.0636	.0675	.0714	.0753
0.2	.0793	.0832	.0871	.0910	.0948	.0987	.1026	.1064	.1103	.1141
0.3	.1179	.1217	.1255	.1293	.1331	.1386	.1406	.1443	.1480	.1517
0.4	.1554	.1591	.1628	.1664	.1700	.1738	.1772	.1808	.1844	.1879
0.5	.1915	.1950	.1985	.2019	.2054	.2088	.2123	.2157	.2190	.2224
0.6	.2257	.2291	.2324	.2357	.2389	.2422	.2454	.2486	.2517	.2549
0.7	.2580	.2611	.2642	.2673	.2703	.2734	.2764	.2794	.2823	.2852
0.8	.2881	.2910	.2939	.2967	.2995	.3023	.3051	.3078	.3106	.3133
0.9	.3159	.3186	.3212	.3238	.3264	.3289	.3315	.3340	.3365	.3389
1.0	.3413	.3438	.3461	.3485	.3508	.3531	.3554	.3577	.3599	.3621
1.1	.3643	.3665	.3686	.3708	.3729	.3749	.3770	.3790	.3810	.3830
1.2	.3849	.3869	.3888	.3907	.3925	.3944	.3962	.3980	.3997	.4015
1.3	.4032	.4049	.4066	.4082	.4099	.4115	.4131	.4147	.4162	.4177
1.4	.4192	.4207	.4222	.4236	.4251	.4265	.4279	.4292	.4306	.4319
1.5	.4332	.4345	.4357	.4370	.4382	.4394	.4406	.4418	.4429	.4441
1.6	.4452	.4463	.4474	.4484	.4495	.4505	.4515	.4525	.4535	.4545
1.7	.4454	.4564	.4573	.4582	.4591	.4599	.4608	.4616	.4625	.4633
1.8	.4641	.4649	.4656	.4664	.4671	.4678	.4686	.4693	.4699	.4706
1.9	.4713	.4719	.4726	.4732	.4738	.4744	.4750	.4756	.4761	.4767
2.0	.4772	.4778	.4783	.4788	.4793	.4798	.4803	.4808	.4812	.4817
2.1	.4821	.4826	.4830	.4834	.4838	.4842	.4846	.4850	.4854	.4857
2.2	.4861	.4864	.4868	.4871	.4875	.4878	.4881	.4884	.4887	.4890
2.3	.4893	.4896	.4898	.4901	.4904	.4906	.4909	.4911	.4913	.4916
2.4	.4918	.4920	.4922	.4925	.4927	.4929	.4931	.4932	.4934	.4936
2.5	.4938	.4940	.4941	.4943	.4945	.4946	.4948	.4949	.4951	.4952
2.6	.4953	.4955	.4956	.4957	.4959	.4960	.4961	.4962	.4963	.4964
2.7	.4965	.4966	.4967	.4968	.4969	.4970	.4971	.4972	.4973	.4974
2.8	.4974	.4975	.4976	.4977	.4977	.4978	.4979	.4979	.4980	.4981
2.9	.4981	.4982	.4982	.4983	.4984	.4984	.4985	.4985	.4986	.4986
3.0	.4987	.4987	.4987	.4988	.4988	.4989	.4989	.4989	.4990	.4990

APPENDIX B

Areas of the Cumulative Standard Normal Distribution

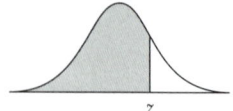

An entry in the table is the proportion under the curve cumulated from the negative tail.

z	G(z)	z	G(z)	z	G(z)
−4.00	0.00003	−2.50	0.00621	−1.00	0.15866
−3.95	0.00004	−2.45	0.00714	−0.95	0.17106
−3.90	0.00005	−2.40	0.00820	−0.90	0.18406
−3.85	0.00006	−2.35	0.00939	−0.85	0.19766
−3.80	0.00007	−2.30	0.01072	−0.80	0.21186
−3.75	0.00009	−2.25	0.01222	−0.75	0.22663
−3.70	0.00011	−2.20	0.01390	−0.70	0.24196
−3.65	0.00013	−2.15	0.01578	−0.65	0.25785
−3.60	0.00016	−2.10	0.01786	−0.60	0.27425
−3.55	0.00019	−2.05	0.02018	−0.55	0.29116
−3.50	0.00023	−2.00	0.02275	−0.50	0.30854
−3.45	0.00028	−1.95	0.02559	−0.45	0.32636
−3.40	0.00034	−1.90	0.02872	−0.40	0.34458
−3.35	0.00040	−1.85	0.03216	−0.35	0.36317
−3.30	0.00048	−1.80	0.03593	−0.30	0.38209
−3.25	0.00058	−1.75	0.04006	−0.25	0.40129
−3.20	0.00069	−1.70	0.04457	−0.20	0.42074
−3.15	0.00082	−1.65	0.04947	−0.15	0.44038
−3.10	0.00097	−1.60	0.05480	−0.10	0.46017
−3.05	0.00114	−1.55	0.06057	−0.05	0.48006
−3.00	0.00135	−1.50	0.06681	0.00	0.50000
−2.95	0.00159	−1.45	0.07353	0.05	0.51994
−2.90	0.00187	−1.40	0.08076	0.10	0.53983
−2.85	0.00219	−1.35	0.08851	0.15	0.55962
−2.80	0.00256	−1.30	0.09680	0.20	0.57926
−2.75	0.00298	−1.25	0.10565	0.25	0.59871
−2.70	0.00347	−1.20	0.11507	0.30	0.61791
−2.65	0.00402	−1.15	0.12507	0.35	0.63683
−2.60	0.00466	−1.10	0.13567	0.40	0.65542
−2.55	0.00539	−1.05	0.14686	0.45	0.67364

z	G(z)	z	G(z)	z	G(z)
0.50	0.69146	1.70	0.95543	2.90	0.99813
0.55	0.70884	1.75	0.95994	2.95	0.99841
0.60	0.72575	1.80	0.96407	3.00	0.99865
0.65	0.74215	1.85	0.96784	3.05	0.99886
0.70	0.75804	1.90	0.97128	3.10	0.99903
0.75	0.77337	1.95	0.97441	3.15	0.99918
0.80	0.78814	2.00	0.97725	3.20	0.99931
0.85	0.80234	2.05	0.97982	3.25	0.99942
0.90	0.81594	2.10	0.98214	3.30	0.99952
0.95	0.82894	2.15	0.98422	3.35	0.99960
1.00	0.84134	2.20	0.98610	3.40	0.99966
1.05	0.85314	2.25	0.98778	3.45	0.99972
1.10	0.86433	2.30	0.98928	3.50	0.99977
1.15	0.87493	2.35	0.99061	3.55	0.99981
1.20	0.88493	2.40	0.99180	3.60	0.99984
1.25	0.89435	2.45	0.99286	3.65	0.99987
1.30	0.90320	2.50	0.99379	3.70	0.99989
1.35	0.91149	2.55	0.99461	3.75	0.99991
1.40	0.91924	2.60	0.99534	3.80	0.99993
1.45	0.92647	2.65	0.99598	3.85	0.99994
1.50	0.93319	2.70	0.99653	3.90	0.99995
1.55	0.93943	2.75	0.99702	3.95	0.99996
1.60	0.94520	2.80	0.99744	4.00	0.99997
1.65	0.95053	2.85	0.99781		

GLOSSARY

absolute error   The absolute value of the forecast error.

acceptable quality level (AQL)   In acceptance sampling, it identifies the quality level required in order for lots to be considered to be good. See *acceptance sampling*.

acceptance sampling   Extracting a sample group from a large quantity of products or components of interest. Also known as a "lot," and, based on the quality level of the sample group, the entire lot is either good or bad.

action loyalty   The fourth phase of customer loyalty sustained by commitment and inertia.

activation   Running a machine or resource when it doesn't contribute to throughput.

activity drivers   Used to measure the demands that cost objects place on activities and to assign the cost of associated activities to cost objects. See *cost object*.

actual costs   Past payments for currently owned resources.

aesthetics   A dimension of quality that includes looks, sound, and smells.

affective loyalty   The second phase of customer loyalty when loyalty is anchored in experiences.

aggregate demand   The total demand for all products or services.

aggregate planning   A capacity planning tool that uses inventory and variable labor to deal with demand fluctuations.

allowance   When constructing a time standard using a stopwatch time study or predetermined motion times, the addition of time to the standard for personal, restroom, and other time.

appraisal costs   Costs associated with product inspection, testing, and auditing of quality-related systems.

AQL   See *acceptable quality level*.

arrival process   The pattern in which or frequency with which customers arrive at the queue.

assembler   The final step of the four stages of product value creation, which puts together the outputs of fabricators.

assemble-to-order   Producing major components of a product prior to receiving an order and assembling the product to meet a specific order.

assembly buffer   A time buffer placed immediately prior to an assembly for nonconstrained components.

assembly line   A narrowly defined manufacturing assembly process made up of equipment with little flexibility in a product-oriented layout.

assurance   A dimension of quality that relates to the level of trust or confidence generated by employees.

backlog   A queue of orders waiting to be processed.

backward scheduling   When a completion date or due date is known and that date must determine a start date.

balance delay   In a product-oriented layout, this is the lost resource utilization resulting from differences in processing time at each work center. See *line balancing*.

balking   When a customer views a queue and does not enter it because it is too long.

basic producer   A manufacturer that extracts raw materials from natural resources.

batch processing   A system in which a group of identical products or customers is processed through one step in the process and then the entire group moves to the next step.

beginning on-hand inventory   The quantity of inventory on hand at the beginning of a time period.

benchmarking   Identification of best practices of other companies.

best operating level   The level of demand or "load" on a system that results in the lowest cost per unit produced or processed.

bill of capacity   A statement of the time required on each resource needed to produce a product.

bill of material   In material requirements planning, this is a computer file containing information about the materials required to produce a product or component.

bottleneck   A constraint in a production system.

BPA   See *business process analysis*.

breakeven analysis   An analytical process that compares the fixed and variable costs of alternatives in order to identify the best alternative for a given volume of output.

bullwhip effect   The increasing variability of demand as one moves upstream in a supply chain.

business process analysis (BPA)   A productivity improvement approach that focuses on large processes and the transitions between different departments.

business strategy   Defines the range of activities for a business, setting priorities so that it accomplishes the overall corporate strategy.

calling population   The population of arriving customers or orders.

capabilities   The abilities a business has that result from its processes. Capabilities create value.

capability chain   The capabilities added by all members of a supply chain.

capability index   A measure of process capability.

capacity   The level of productive output of an organization in a specified period of time.

capacity requirements planning   A detailed capacity planning approach in manufacturing that uses the planned order

GLOSSARY

releases from MRP to provide the quantity of units that must be produced.

carrying cost   Costs associated with carrying inventory.

cash-to-cash cycle   The amount of time between the cash outlay required for purchasing direct materials or inventory consumed during the production of the product or service and the actual receipt of the payment when the product or service is sold.

causal forecast   A forecast that uses extrinsic data as a predictor of demand.

cause and effect diagram   A tool used to aid in the identification of root causes or quality problems.

cellular layout   A layout in which products whose processes require similar resources are grouped into product families. Each cell contains all the resources necessary to produce products in that family.

changeover cost   The cost of changing equipment from producing one product or service to another.

changeover time   The time required to change equipment from producing one product or service to another.

check sheet   A quality analysis tool used to tally occurrences of interest.

cognitive loyalty   The first phase of customer loyalty based on information customers receive.

competitive priorities   Key value attributes that are highly influenced by operations management: cost, quality, dependability of delivery, flexibility, and response time.

conative loyalty   The third stage of customer loyalty when action results from habit and behavioral commitment

concurrent engineering   Performing product and service development engineering functions in tandem to reduce time and improve communication.

constraint   Anything that inhibits a system's progress toward its goals.

constraint buffer   A time buffer placed immediately prior to a constraint.

constraint management   A framework for managing the constraints of a system in a way that maximizes the system's accomplishment of its goals.

consumer's risk   In acceptance sampling, the probability of accepting a bad lot, designated as β.

contingency plans   Alternative or back-up plans to be used if an unexpected event makes the normal plans infeasible.

contingent workers   Temporary workers employed by an agency and contracted to work for another firm.

continuous improvement   A process of always seeking ways to improve existing processes and tasks.

continuous process improvement   Ongoing improvement efforts for service-oriented and product-oriented production processes that focus on the elimination of variability.

continuous processing   In a continuous processing environment, this is any equipment or workstation that is dedicated to one product or service, yielding high levels of efficiency.

continuous replenishment   The delivery of inventory, frequently in small quantities.

control chart   A specific type of run chart used to plot measurements or test outcomes against time and distinguish between variability caused by random fluctuation and variability that has an assignable cause. See *run chart*.

control limits   In a process control chart, these are typically three standard deviations above and below the process mean.

converter   The second stage of product value creation, which refines natural resource inputs.

core competencies   Those things a firm does very well and that distinguish it from competitors.

corporate strategy   In the broadest strategy, it defines the businesses that a corporation will engage in and how resources will be expended.

cost   The expenses associated with ownership.

cost leader strategy   A strategy that seeks to price goods and services lower than competitors.

cost object   An item for which costs are measured and assigned.

cost of quality   All of the costs associated with maintaining the quality of goods and services.

cost per unit   Total cost for producing the units of interest divided by the number of units produced.

cost traceability   The ease with which costs can be assigned to cost objects.

CR   See *critical ratio*.

crash time   The absolute minimum time in which each activity could be accomplished.

crashing   A methodical approach to reducing a project's duration.

critical path   The path that takes the longest.

critical ratio (CR)   A sequencing rule that prioritizes by the ratio of the time remaining to the time needed to complete the job. The smallest ratio goes first.

CRM   See *customer relationships management*.

cross training   Training employees to do a variety of jobs.

cross-docking   Continuous shipment from suppliers to warehouses, where goods are redirected and delivered to retailers in continuous shipments.

customer focus   The first principle of total quality management, which dictates that the customer determines what quality is.

customer relationships   The relationships a business develops with its customers, often measured by the degree of customer loyalty.

customer relationships management (CRM)   Systems designed to improve relationships with customers and improve the business's ability to identify valuable customers. They include call center management software, sales tracking, and customer service.

cycle   A component of a time series that is a pattern that repeats over a long period of time.

cycle time   The frequency of products emerging completed from a product-oriented layout.

data mining   Analysis of data generated by customer interaction.

decline   The final stage of a product or service life cycle as demand disappears.

decouple   To reduce the direct dependency of a process step on its predecessor.

demand chase   An aggregate planning approach that uses hiring and firing of employees to increase and decrease output to match fluctuating demand.

dependability of delivery   The ability of the firm to deliver products and services to the customer when promised.

dependent demand inventory   Inventory whose demand is determined by the production schedule for finished products. Dependent demand items usually are components and raw materials.

design capacity   The capacity a facility is designed to accommodate on an ongoing basis.

design for manufacturability (DFM)   The practice of designing products with the capabilities of manufacturing processes in mind.

DFM   See *design for manufacturability*.

differentiating capabilities   Capabilities possessed by a firm that distinguish it from its competitors.

differentiating strategy   A strategy that seeks to create products and services that are different from those of competitors.

direct labor   Labor that can be traced directly to the good or service being produced.

direct materials   Materials that can be traced directly to the good or service being produced.

direct shipment   Shipping directly from manufacturer suppliers to retailers.

dollar days   The dollar value of an item in inventory multiplied by the number of days until it will be sold.

durability   How long a product will last.

earliest due date (EDD)   A sequencing rule that prioritizes customers or jobs by the due date, earliest first.

early start schedule   In project management calculations, this is the completion of the early start and early finish times. Also known as the forward pass.

economic order quantity model   An approach used to determine an order quantity that minimizes the sum of ordering and carrying costs.

economic value added (EVA)   A productivity measure that indicates whether or not a business is creating wealth from its capital. It is equal to the after-tax operating profit minus the annual cost of capital.

EDD   See *earliest due date*.

EDI   See *electronic data interchange*.

efficiency   The ratio of actual output to standard output.

electronic data interchange (EDI)   Electronic exchange of information between customers and suppliers instead of paper transactions.

empathy   A dimension of quality that results from the approachability and sensitivity of employees.

ending on hand inventory   The quantity of inventory on hand at the end of a time period.

EVA   See *economic value added*.

expected costs   Forecasted payments for future resources.

experience detractors   In moment-of-truth analysis, when an experience viewed by the customer is viewed as a detractor or as something that signifies a reduction in the quality of service.

experience enhancers   In moment-of-truth analysis, these are experiences that make the customer feel good about the interaction and make the interaction better.

external customer   Consumers and businesses that buy products and services.

external failure costs   Costs incurred when a customer is exposed to poor quality.

fabricator   The third stage of product value creation which takes inputs from converters and transforms them into components used by assemblers.

facilities   The buildings and structures that house various aspects of a business.

FCFS   See *first come, first served*.

feature   A dimension of quality that consists of additional capabilities of products or services that can be added.

finished good inventory   Inventory consisting of products that have completed all stages of production.

first come, first served (FCFS)   A sequencing rule that prioritizes by when a person or job arrived in the queue.

FIT   See *forecast including trend*.

fixed costs   Costs that are not affected by volume.

fixed quantity order policy   In material requirements planning, rather than ordering the quantity of the net requirements, orders are placed in increments of a fixed quantity.

flow chart   A diagram of the steps in a process.

focus strategy   A strategy that targets a small segment of the market with products or services.

forecast bias   The tendency of a forecast to be too high or too low.

GLOSSARY

forecast including trend (FIT)   Trend-adjusted exponential smoothing.

forward scheduling   A technique used when a start date is known, and a completion date needs to be determined.

functional layout   A process-oriented layout.

functional strategy   A strategy that establishes the link between functional decision making and business strategy.

Gantt chart   A horizontal bar graph with time on the x-axis and the different resources on the y axis. It displays the amount of time required on each resource and when that time is required.

gross requirements   In material requirements planning, the total quantity needed to meet demand.

growth stage   The second stage of a product or service life cycle, where demand begins to increase.

histogram   A bar graph that plots a measurement on the y axis and the frequency of the occurrence of the measurement on the x axis.

independent demand inventory   Inventory whose demand is dictated by the marketplace.

industry-focused benchmarking   The identification of the best practices among competitors.

innovation   A dramatic change from a new idea.

integrative management framework   A management approach or "philosophy" that guides day-to-day decisions in a way that is consistent with a firm's profitability goals. Examples include just-in-time, total quality management, constraint management, and supply chain management.

internal customer   An entity of a business that receives an output of some other part of the same business.

interpersonal loyalty   Loyalty to an individual that a customer has dealt with, rather than to the business.

introduction stage   The first stage of a product or service life cycle.

inventory (constraint management definition)   Money invested in things the system intends to sell.

inventory (traditional definition)   Materials used in the production of products and services. Examples include raw materials inventory, work-in-process inventory, and finished goods inventory.

inventory master file   In material requirements planning, this is a computer file containing information about an inventory item such as the quantity on hand, the cost, and so on.

inventory turns   A measure of inventory productivity computed by dividing sales by the average value of inventory.

inventory waste   Waste that consists of excess inventory over and above that which is necessary.

job shop   A manufacturer, typically a process-oriented layout, that is able to produce custom tools and equipment for others because of its flexibility.

jockeying   When customers switch lines hoping to move faster.

kanban   A system used to link production rate to demand.

Kano model   A business model that proposes that there are actually three important levels of quality characteristics for customers: must-be, one-dimensional, and delighters.

keiretsu   The close-knit networks of suppliers of Japanese manufacturers.

late start schedule   In project management computations, this is the computing of the late start and late finish values. Also known as the backward pass.

lean production   Producing at minimum cost.

learning curve   A curve that shows the reduction in the time it takes to complete a task as the number of times it has been completed increases.

learning rate   The amount of improvement obtained as a task is repeated.

level production   An aggregate planning approach that uses inventory stored from period to period to reduce the need to change the output rate as demand changes.

life cycle   A pattern of demand growth and decline that occurs from the introduction of a product to its obsolescence.

line balancing   A process used to balance the times among work centers in a product-oriented layout to reduce balance delay. See *balance delay*.

line of visibility   The separation between service activities that take place in the "back room" and those that are exposed to the customer.

lot-for-lot ordering   In material requirements planning, ordering exactly the amount of the net requirements.

lot tolerance percent defective (LTPD)   In acceptance sampling, the level of quality in the lot that would be unacceptable to the customer. See *acceptance sampling*.

LTPD   See *lot tolerance percent defective*.

machine utilization   A productivity measure for machines that is equal to actual running time divided by time available.

MAD   See *mean absolute deviation*.

maintenance, repair, and operating inventory (MRO)   Inventory that consists of items consumed in the day-to-day activities of a business.

make-to-order   Producing a product when an order is received.

make-to-stock   Producing a product before an order is received and storing the product.

maquiladoras   Foreign-owned (typically U.S.-owned) manufacturing plants in Mexico.

master production schedule (MPS)   A schedule of end products that must be completed in a specific time period.

material requirements planning (MPR)   An inventory management approach used to manage dependent demand inventory that plans order releases for the future based on production schedules.

maturation stage   The third stage of a product or service life cycle when demand begins to level off.

mean absolute deviation (MAD)   A measure of the absolute forecast error that is the mean of the absolute values of the forecast errors.

mean forecast error (MFE)   A measure of forecast bias that is the mean of the forecast errors.

MFE   See *mean forecast error.*

moment-of-truth analysis   The identification of the critical instances when a customer judges service quality and determines the experience enhancers, standard expectations, and experience detractors.

MPS   See *master production schedule.*

MRO   See *maintenance, repair, and operating inventory.*

MRP   See *material requirements planning.*

multi-factor rating   A decision-making technique used for considering a variety of factors by assigning each factor a level of importance.

net present value (NPV)   The difference between the market value of a product or service and the cost of creating it.

net requirements   In material requirements planning, gross requirements minus beginning on-hand inventory.

netting   The process of computing net requirements.

network diagram   A diagram similar to a flow chart that illustrates the steps in a project.

nonproduction costs   The costs of selling and administration.

normal time   In a time study, this is the observed time after adjustment by the performance rating.

NPV   See *net present value.*

observed time   When performing a time study, this is the average of the times of observations.

operating characteristics curve   Used in the development of acceptance sampling plans, this is a graph that demonstrates how well the plan discriminates between good and bad quality by showing the probability of accepting a lot of LTPD quality (a bad lot) and the probability of rejecting a lot of AQL quality (a good lot).

operating expenses   In constraint management, this is the money the system spends turning inventory into throughput.

order cost   The fixed cost associated with ordering inventory.

order loser   Product or service characteristics or attributes that repel particular customers.

order qualifier   Product or service characteristics that are necessary, but not sufficient to result in winning the order.

order winner   A product or service characteristic that is most important to a particular customer and results in the customer ordering.

out-of-pocket costs   Cash payments made for resources.

overhead   All nondirect costs that exist after direct labor and direct materials have been identified.

overproduction waste   The waste caused by producing in excess of demand.

Pareto analysis   A process used to separate the relatively few important problems from the many unimportant ones.

Pareto chart   A bar graph used to categorize data and help establish priorities.

path   A sequence of activities that begins at the start of the project and goes to its end.

performance   A dimension of quality that results from specific characteristics and capabilities of the product or service.

performance rating   When performing time studies, this is an adjustment made to take into account whether the observed worker was faster or slower than normal.

period costs   Costs of resources used in nonproduction elements of a business.

periodic review system   An independent demand management system that orders inventory on fixed time intervals.

phase   A distinct step in a process that requires a separate queue.

pipeline inventory   Inventory in transit.

planned order receipt   In material requirements planning, this is the planned receipt of material that results from a planned order release.

planned order release   In material requirements planning, this is the order planned to be released to satisfy a future net requirement.

planning horizon   The distance into the future one plans.

poka-yoke   A device that makes it impossible or nearly impossible to do something incorrectly.

predetermined motion time   The time required to complete small aspects of tasks collected from a large number of observations and stored in a database so that future time standards can be created without needing a stopwatch time study.

prevention costs   Costs associated with efforts to prevent errors or defects from happening.

process capability   The ability of a process to consistently meet customer expectations, demonstrated by the control limits being within the customer specifications.

processes   Organized tasks accomplished by grouping resources together.

processing waste   The waste that results from steps in production processes that do not contribute value or that create costs that are greater than the value they create.

process-oriented layout A layout that is organized by the function of each resource, allowing steps to be done in any sequence.

producer's risk In acceptance sampling, this is the probability of rejecting a good lot, indicated by α.

product costs Costs of resources used to make products.

product defect waste The waste of capacity, inventory, and labor resulting from products that do not meet customer specifications.

production batch The quantity produced at a workcenter before changing over to produce something else.

production costs Costs associated with the actual production of goods or services.

production lead time The amount of time a product spends in a productive system in order to be completed.

productivity A measure of how well inputs are used by a business, typically the ratio of an output to the input of interest.

product-oriented layout A layout that provides the necessary resources in a fixed sequence that matches the sequence of the steps required to produce the product or service.

profit margin Profit generated per dollar of sales.

profitability A measure of the productivity of money invested in a business, typically a ratio of net income to some input such as net sales or total assets.

project A set of activities aimed at meeting a goal, with a defined beginning and end.

project management A variety of techniques that recognize the dependencies present among the project activities and manage those activities in order to complete the project on time.

protective capacity A layer of capacity above that which is absolutely required to meet known demand, providing the firm with the ability to handle occasional problems and enabling them to handle special requests.

QFD See *quality function deployment*.

qualitative forecast A forecast based on qualitative information.

quality Meeting customer expectations.

quality function deployment (QFD) A widely used approach that translates customer needs into product and service designs that guide the corresponding process requirements.

quantitative forecast A forecast based on quantitative data.

queue configuration The physical design of the lines and servers in a queuing system.

queue discipline The rules that management enforces to determine the next customer served in a queue.

random fluctuation Unpredictable variation in demand this is not due to trend, seasonality, or cycle.

recovery The way a business deals with an external failure when trying to satisfy the customer despite the failure.

recovery plan Policies for how employees are to deal with quality failures so that customers will return.

reengineering Starting from a clean slate to improve a process.

reliability A dimension of quality resulting from a company's consistency of performance.

reneging When a customer joins the queue, but then leaves it because the wait was too long.

reorder point model An independent demand inventory management system that reorders when inventory drops to a specific level.

repetitive processing Processing on a continuous basis.

replenishment lead time The time required to receive inventory that has been ordered.

reputation A dimension of quality resulting from a company's performance history.

resource driver A tool used to measure demands placed on resources by activities and to assign the costs of those resources to activities.

response time The time required to complete a customer's request.

responsive The ability to respond quickly to change, to customer needs, and to internal and external forces.

responsiveness A dimension of quality resulting from the company's ability to respond quickly.

return on assets (ROA) Profit per dollar of assets.

return on equity (ROE) Profit per dollar of equity.

risk pooling Inventory held in one warehouse to service a large number of retailers requires less inventory than if held at the individual retailers.

ROA See *return on assets*.

ROE See *return on equity*.

rough-cut capacity planning A detailed capacity planning approach used in manufacturing that uses the master production schedule to provide the quantity of units that must be produced.

RSFE See *running sum of forecast error*.

run chart A plot of a variable of interest on the y axis and time on the x axis.

running sum of forecast error (RSFE) A measure of forecast bias that is the sum of forecast error, and is updated as each new error is calculated.

safety stock Additional inventory used to help meet demand uncertainty.

saturation The fourth stage of a product or service life cycle when demand shifts to the beginning of its decline.

scatter diagram A chart that seeks to identify relationships between variables by plotting one variable on the *x* axis and another on the *y* axis.

seasonality A pattern in a times series that repeats itself at least once a year.

segmentation Identification of different groups of customers based on their characteristics.

server A resource that is able to complete the process or service that customers or jobs wait in queue for.

service blueprint A type of flow diagram used for services that identifies decision points, failure points, and the line of visibility.

service encounter The interaction and the processes in which the customer is involved.

service level The percent of orders satisfied from existing inventory.

service process The capacity of the server(s), the distribution of service times, and other behaviors of the server that affect the number of customers the server can handle.

service–profit chain A framework used to link employee satisfaction to profitability.

serviceability A dimension of quality that consists of the amount of effort required to repair a product.

setup time The time required to change equipment from producing one product or service to another.

shipping buffer A time buffer immediately prior to shipping.

shortest processing time A sequencing rule that gives highest priority to the job with the shortest expected processing time.

simple exponential smoothing A sophisticated type of moving average that uses a smoothing constant to weight the previous demand and establish the responsiveness of the forecast.

six sigma quality An approach used to improve quality by reducing the likelihood of a defect occurring as a result of random fluctuation. In six sigma quality, six standard deviations above and below the mean are required to be within the customer's specifications.

slack Time until due minus the expected processing time. As a sequencing rule, the highest priority is given to the job with the least amount of slack.

slack per remaining operation Slack divided by the number of operations remaining until the job or order is completed.

specifications Precisely written expectations for a product or service used as the standard for quality evaluation.

standard A measure that should be achieved.

standard expectation In moment-of-truth analysis, these are experiences that are expected and taken for granted by customers.

standard time The result of a stopwatch time study after an adjustment by the performance rating and after allowances have been made.

statistical fluctuation among dependent events Disruptions caused by accumulating variability among processing times of processes that depend on each other.

statistical process control A preventive approach to managing quality by monitoring processes in a way that identifies potential problems before defects are even created.

stockout An instance when demand cannot be satisfied by existing inventory.

stockout cost The cost associated with not having inventory when a customer demands it.

stopwatch time study The process of developing a time standard by actually observing and timing workers.

strategy The means by which a company positions itself for future profitability.

substitute quality characteristics In quality function deployment, these are terms used to translate the customer needs into a description of the product or service that is in technical language.

supply chain The path of value creation, from basic producer through consumer, including all transportation and logistics services that connect them.

testing A specific type of inspection used when a visual inspection cannot reveal whether products meet specifications.

throughput In constraint management, dollars generated by sales.

time buffer A buffer of inventory that will keep a resource busy for a specified amount of time.

time standard The expected time for a worker to complete a task.

timeliness The speed at which a business completes tasks and the degree to which it completes tasks on schedule and as promised.

times series forecasting Using past demand to forecast the future.

total costs The costs of all resources obtained in a particular period.

total involvement A commitment at all levels of the firm, from the very top to the very bottom.

transfer batch The quantity produced at a workcenter before transferring the products to the next step in the process.

transportation waste The waste that results from excessive materials handling and movement.

trend A component of a time series that causes demand to increase or decrease.

trend adjusted exponential smoothing An exponential smoothing technique that includes a smoothing constant for trend.

two-bin system A primitive reorder point inventory system in which two containers of inventory are kept. An order for more is placed when one container becomes empty. See *reorder point model*.

unnecessary motion waste The waste of human resources caused by unnecessary labor due to ineffective job design.

utilization (constraint management definition) The time a resource is used and contributing to throughput divided by the time the resource was available.

utilization (traditional definition) The time a resource is used divided by the time the resource was available.

value The amount a customer is willing to pay for a product or service, sometimes thought of as benefits divided by cost.

variable costs Costs that increase or decrease as units produced increase or decrease.

variance The difference between desired cost or consumption rate and the actual cost or consumption rate.

variance analysis A process used to compare actual consumption of inventory and capacity to ideal consumption levels.

waiting time waste The waste that results from customer orders, inventory, or completed products waiting in queue for a process to begin.

warehousing Holding inventory received from suppliers in warehouses until it is needed by retailers.

work elements Small tasks that make up process steps.

work sampling A process of recording what a worker is doing to determine how employee time is spent.

workforce The employees required to produce a product or service.

work-in-process inventory Inventory that has begun processing, but has not yet completed it.

yield management An approach used in capital-intensive services that attempts to obtain maximum revenues through differential pricing, reservation systems, and overbooking.

NAME INDEX

The letter *n* following a page number indicates reference to a note.

A

Aguayo, R., 592
Aquilano, N. J., 124n

B

Balogh, Doug, 528, 529
Balogh, Linda, 528
Bancroft, N. H., 336
Bank, D., 94
Barrenechea, M. J., 536
Bergeron, B. P., 228
Bernstein, P. L., 336
Berry, L. L., 229
Berry, W. L., 382
Bezos, Jeff, 629
Blenkhorn, D. L., 648
Bowersox, D. J., 512
Brocka, B., 210n, 228
Brocka, M. S., 210n, 228
Brown, P. B., 536
Brown, S. A., 519, 524n, 536
Bulfin, R., 456
Bulkeley, W. M., 94
Bush, George W., 587

C

Carlzon, Jan, 217, 228, 229
Chase, R. B., 124n
Chew, W. B., 70
Chung, H. M., 336
Clark, K. B., 106n
Clements, J. P., 283
Closs, D. J., 512
Cohen, L., 153n, 157, 228, 229
Connellan, T., 229, 414, 536
Cooper, M. B., 512
Crosby, Philip B., 571, 572, 592
Czepiel, J. A., 283

D

Davenport, T. H., 336
Deming, W. Edwards, 569–570
DeToro, I. J., 592

E

Evans, Don, 587

F

Finch, B. J., 565
Fine, Charles H., 154, 157, 283
Fitzsimmons, J. A., 94, 127, 186n, 187n, 283, 574n
Fitzsimmons, M. J., 94, 127, 186n, 187n, 283, 574n
Fox, R. E., 382
Francis, R. L., 512
Friedland, J., 95

G

Galton, Francis, 297
Garvin, D. A., 184, 186n, 187n, 229, 574n
Gates, Bill, 288
Gido, J., 283
Goldratt, Eliahu, 268, 283, 382, 596, 609, 620
Gray, C. F., 283
Griffin, Jill, 289

H

Hagerty, J. R., 94
Hall, R., 565
Handfield, R. B., 94, 648
Hanke, J. E., 336
Hansen, D. R., 70, 180
Hayes, R. H., 106n, 123n, 143n
Heskett, J. L., 87, 95, 127
Hill, Terry, 101, 127, 157
Hodges, John, 468
Hout, T. M., 283

J

Jones, D. T., 565
Jones, T. O., 95, 127
Jordan, B. D., 70, 180
Juran, J. M., 228, 570, 592

K

Kaminsky, P., 648
Kano, Noriaki, 212
Kaplan, R. S., 70
Katzenbach, J. R., 283, 414
King, D., 336
Kotkin, J., 512

L

Larson, E. W., 283
Laseter, T. M., 634n, 648
Lee, H. L., 640, 648
Lee, J., 336
Leenders, M. R., 648

Levine, R., 389n, 414
Levinson, Kathy, 84
Locke, C., 389n, 414
Loveman, G. W., 95, 127, 391n, 414
Luebbe, R. L., 565

M

MacDonald, J., 571n
McWilliams, G., 95
Mantel, S. J., 283
Meredith, J. R., 283
Mito, S., 565
Monden, Y., 565
Mowen, Maryanne M., 70, 180
Muther, R., 512

N

Nardelli, Bob, 82
Nichols, E. L., 94, 648
Norton, D. P., 70

O

Ohno, T., 565
O'Leary, D. E., 317n, 336
Oliver, R. L., 520, 522n, 536
Olson, D. L., 283

P

Padmanabhan, V., 648
Parasuraman, V., 229
Piggott, J., 571n
Pisek, P. E., 184, 186n, 187n, 574n
Pole, M., 392
Porter, Michael, 101, 127

Q

Quick, R., 94

R

Reese, A. K., 565
Reitsch, A. G., 336
Ross, D., 565
Ross, S. A., 70, 180

S

Sasser, W. E., Jr., 95, 127, 391n, 414
Schaaf, D., 229

Schlesinger, L. A., 95, 127, 391n, 414
Schmenner, R. W., 512
Searles, D., 389n, 414
Seipt, H., 336
Sewell, Carl, 516, 536
Shapiro, J. F., 456, 512
Shewhart, Walter A., 568–569, 577–578
Shostack, G. L., 157
Simchi-Levi, D., 648
Simchi-Levi, E., 648
Sipper, D., 456
Smith, D. K., 283, 414
Solomon, M. R., 283
Sprengel, A., 336
Srikanth, M. L., 620
Stalk, G., Jr., 283
Stone, G. P., 80, 94
Surprenant, C. F., 283
Suzaki, K., 565

T

Tenner, A. R., 592
Thoman, G. Richard, 468
Turban, E., 336

U

Umble, Elizabeth, 608n
Umble, Michael M., 608n, 620

V

Valmassei, Keri, 528
Vollman, T., 382

W

Weinberger, D., 389n, 414
Westerfield, R. W., 70, 180
Whang, S., 648
Wheelwright, S. C., 106n, 123n, 127, 143n
White, J. A., 512
Whybark, D. C., 382
Womack, J. P., 565

Z

Zeithaml, V. A., 229
Zemke, R., 229, 414, 536
Zipkin, P. H., 382

SUBJECT INDEX

The letter *n* following a page number indicates reference to a note.

A

ABC analysis of inventory, 370–371
Abercrombie & Fitch, 85
Absolute error, 312
  measuring, 312–314
ABTCO, 104
Acceptable quality level (AQL), 211
Acceptance sampling, 210, 211
Action loyalty, 520–521
Activation, 598
Activities, 165–166
Activity drivers, 168, 169
Activity-based costing (ABC), 168
Actual costs, 163
ADAC Laboratories, 587
Adobe Systems, 55
Aesthetics, 575
Affective loyalty, 520
Aggregate demand, 428–429
Aggregate planning:
  demand chase, 429–431
  International Model, 454–456
  level production, 431–433
Airline industry, 244, 441
Allied Signal, 545
Allowances, 404
Amazon.com, 29, 132, 135, 602, 629
American Forest and Paper Association, 84
American Journal of Sociology, 94
American National Standards Institute (ANSI), 585
American Society for Quality (ASQ), 580
American Society for Quality Control (ASQC), 24
APICS-The Performance Advantage, 215n
Application server providers (ASPs), 350
Appraisal costs, 191–192, 193
Archer Daniels Midland (ADM), 86, 95
Arrival process, 254–255
  probability for, 255
Assemblers, 74
Assemble-to-order, 143
Assembly buffer, 607
Assembly lines, 142
Assurance, 575
Autoliv, 555
Automation, 557
Automobile industry, 188–189, 342, 395, 516
Average costs, 163–164

B

Backlog, 422
Backward scheduling, 245, 360
Balance delay, 490
Balanced scorecard (BSC), 59, 174
  benefits of, 175
Baldridge Award, 586–590
Baldridge Index, 587
Balking, 255
Bankruptcy, 36–37

Barnes & Noble, 135
Basic producers, 74
Batch processing, 346
Batch production, 142
  constraint management and, 607–608
  small-, 552–553
Beginning on-hand inventory, 362
Benchmarking, 581–584
  industry-focused, 581–582, 583
  process-focused, 582, 584
Benefits, 13
Bernard Welding and Equipment Company, 547
Best operating level, 423–424
Bill of capacity, 433
Bill of material, 360
Borders, 15
Bottlenecks, 426, 490
Breakeven analysis, 56–59
  for facilities location, 479–480
  Interactive Model, 68–70
Broadcasting industry, 528–529
Buffers, 604–607
  assembly, 607
  constraint, 606
  Constraint Management Interactive Model and, 615–619
  inventory flow and, 605
  order processing in system with, 606
  shipping, 606–607
  simple system with, 604
  time, 604–607
Builder's Square, 81
Build-to-order; *see* Customization
Bullwhip effect, 628, 640–644
Burger King, 394
Business method patents, 135
Business outputs, 24–28
  customers and, 28, 29
  products, 25
  services, 25–28
Business process analysis (BPA), 151
Business strategy, 99–100, 101–102
Business travel, 293
Business Week, 32, 33, 135n, 445n, 468n, 498n, 536, 629
Business-to-business (B2B) transactions, 28
  outsourcing and, 77
  value and; *see* Customer determination of value, business value attributes
Business-to-consumer (B2C) transactions, 28

C

Calling population, 254
Canadian Pacific Railway, 550
Capabilities, 14
  as component of value, 14–16, 91
  differentiating, 15
  processes versus, 132–134; *see also* Processes
Capability chain, 154–155

Capability index, 202–205
  calculation, 203, 205
  formula for, 203
Capacity, 19, 417–457
  Aggregate Planning Interactive Model, 454–456
  backlog and, 422
  best operating level and, 423–424
  competitive priorities and, 109–110
  constraints and, 426–427
  current trends in management of, 444
  defined, 418–421
  demand-capacity match:
    in manufacturing; *see* Demand-capacity match in manufacturing
    in services; *see* Demand-capacity match in services
  design, 109, 423–425
  financial impact of decisions, 423–425
  individual resource influence on, 425–427
  introduction, 418
  just-in-time management and; *see* Just-in-time management, capacity-focused techniques
  matching resource availability to market demand, 418
  Production Line Interactive Model, 452–453
  production rate requirements and, 421
  profitability from, 50–52
  protective, 110, 423
  resource/profit model and, 419
  resources merged to form production, 420
  supply chain, 427–428
  value and, 421–423
Capacity requirements planning (CRP), 437
  calculations for, 437–438
Carrying costs, 343
Cash-to-cash cycle, 89, 237–238
Category killer retailers, 81
Caterpillar, 170, 397
Causal forecasting, 298
  with simple linear regression, 299–300
Cause and effect diagrams, 195
  example of, 196
Cellular layout, 140, 496
  conceptual view of, 141
  JIT management and, 559
Center-of-gravity method for location decisions, 474–477
  computation of, 475–477
  Interactive Model, 507–508
Changeover costs, 343
Changeover time, 142
  reduced, 553
Check sheets, 198–199
CheMatch, 631
Chrysler, 85, 550, 584, 634
Cincinnati Enquirer, 441n
Cisco Systems, 89
Clothing industry, 103, 521
Coca-Cola, 530

663

Cognitive loyalty, 520
Coldwater Creek, 103
Competitive priorities, 108
Completed-products inventory, 344–348
Component inventory, 348–349
Component standardization, 551–552
Computerized numerically controlled (CNC) machines, 139
Conative loyalty, 520
Concurrent engineering, 152
    timeliness and, 242–243
    traditional development compared to, 153
Conoco, 599
Constraint buffer, 606
Constraint management, 22, 426, 595–621
    activation and, 598
    at Amazon.com, 602
    batch sizes and, 607–608
    buffers and; see Buffers
    case study of, 608
    defined, 596–599
    disruptions and, 603–604
        Mother Nature and, 602
        protecting the system from, 604
    focusing process, 600–603
    global performance measures, 599–600
    Interactive Model, 615–619
    introduction, 596
    JIT and, 612
    maximizing system output, 596
    product mix example of, 609–612
    resource/profit model and, 597
    simple productive system, 596–599
        with constraints, 598, 604
        with processing variability, 603
        with time buffer, 604
    utilization and, 598
Constraints, 426–427
    defined, 596–599
    examples of, 426, 427
    Production Line Interactive Model, 452–453
    "weakest link" analogy, 427
Consumer Reports, 188
Consumer's risk, 211
Contingency plans, 290
Contingent workers, 400–401
Continuous improvement, 397
Continuous process improvement, 572; see also Total quality management (TQM)
Continuous processing, 142
Continuous replenishment, 45, 344
    graph of, 345
Control charts, 199–210
Control limits, 201–202
Convenience as a value attribute, 81, 83
Converters, 74
Con-way Southern Express (CSE), 548
Cooperative product design, 635
Core competencies, 114

Corporate strategy, 99, 100
Cost, 16, 158–180; see also specific costs
    average, 163–164
    capacity and, 109–110
    defined, 162
    facilities and, 111
    fixed, 56
    human resources and, 116
    introduction, 160–161
    new product or service development and, 119
    nonfinancial, 173–174
    operations; see Operations cost
    paying for value, 160–161
    per unit, 173
    perceived value and, 161–164
        "costs," 162, 163–164
        profitability and, 162–163
    performance/reward system and, 120
    price and, 81, 163, 164
    process technology and, 112
    product, 169–170
    production planning/inventory control and, 118
    productivity improvement and reduction of, 170–173
    quality and, 117
    resource/profit model and, 160
    supply chain management and, 627–628
    tradeoffs, 173
    types of, 163
    as value attribute, 16–17, 92
        for businesses, 86–87
        for consumers, 81
    value chain and, 164–166
    variable, 56
    variance analysis and, 171–173, 178–180
    vertical integration/supplier relationships and, 114
Cost leader strategy, 101
Cost object, 166
    resource costs and, 169
Cost of capital, weighted average, 43–44
Cost of quality (COQ), 190–193
    appraisal costs, 191–192
    external failure costs, 190
    internal failure costs, 191
    prevention costs, 192–193
    relationship of categories of, 193
Cost per unit, 173
Cost traceability, 167–168
Crash time, 266
Crashing projects, 265–268
Critical path, 259–262
Critical path method (CPM), 258
    calculations for, 260–262
Critical ratio (CR), 247
    job sequencing using, 249
Crosby, Philip B., 571
    "absolutes" of, 571
    14 points of, 572
Cross-docking, 632–633

Cross-functional teams, 28–29
Cross-sell/upsell, 519, 523–525
Cross-training, 400
Customer determination of value, 74, 78–95
    business output/customer matrix, 78
    business value attributes, 85–90
        cost, 86–87
        defined, 86
        dependability of delivery, 88
        flexibility, 89
        list of, 86
        primary and secondary, 90, 102
        quality, 87
        response time, 88–89
    consumer value attributes, 80–85
        convenience, 81, 83
        cost, 81
        ethical issues, 83–84
        list of, 80, 161
        personalization, 83
        primary and secondary, 90, 102
        quality, 81
        response time, 83
        style and fashion, 84–85
        technology, 85
    strategy and; see Strategy
    value creation and, 90–92
    value transfer model, 91
Customer focus, 571–572; see also Total quality management (TQM)
Customer loyalty, 391–394
    action, 520–521
    affective, 520
    building, 519, 520–523
    cognitive, 520
    conative, 520
    as a cycle of value enhancements, 526–529
    increased convenience and, 523
    interpersonal, 521–522
    losing, 521
    loyalty/growth cycle, 525, 526
    profitability and, 525–526, 527
    sustainers, vulnerabilities and, 521, 522
Customer relationship management (CRM), 529–534
    breakeven analysis and, 57–58
    data mining and, 529–530
    enabling force behind; see Information technology
    enterprise resource planning and, 534
    outsourcing, 534
    quality and, 218–219
Customer relationships, 20, 515–537
    with employees, 386–395
    extending, 519–526
        cross-sell/upsell, 519, 523–525
        loyalty building, 519, 520–523
        prospecting, 519, 520
        win back or save, 519–520
    introduction, 516
    loyalty; see Customer loyalty

SUBJECT INDEX

management of; *see* Customer relationship management (CRM)
perceived value and, 517–519
profitability from, 53, 523–525
resource/profit model and, 517
value of strong, 516
Customer service, 5–6; *see also* Service encounters
Customers, 28
business output and, 29
external, 571–572
internal, 571–572
suppliers and, 628, 630
Customization:
eliminating inventory through, 342
layout alternatives and, 138–150
Cut-and-try layout, 484–487
Cycle, 300
Cycle time, 490

D

DaimlerChrysler, 85, 550, 584, 634
Data mining, 529–530
Days-of-supply, 344
calculation of, 345
example of, 346
Decision tree analysis, 477–479
Decline stage of life cycle, 295, 296
Decoupling, 341, 342, 604
Defective products, 187, 189, 545
Dell Computer, 26, 342
Delta Air Lines, 441
Demand chase, 429–431
Demand collection system, 12
Demand forecasting, 297–298
Demand linkages, 142–143
Demand-capacity match in manufacturing, 428–439
aggregate demand and, 428
aggregate planning and; *see* Aggregate planning
bill of capacity, 433
capacity requirements planning and, 437–439
detailed capacity planning, 433–439
generic planning and control system, 439
material requirements planning and, 433, 434
rough-cut capacity planning and, 433–437
Demand-capacity match in services, 439–44
overbooking, 441–444
yield management, 440–441
Demand-production match, 548
Deming, W. Edwards, 569–570
14 points of, 570
Dependability of delivery:
capacity and, 110
facilities and, 112
process technology and, 112–113
production planning/inventory control and, 118

quality and, 117–118
as a value attribute, 88
vertical integration/supplier relationship and, 115
Dependent demand inventory, 349
backward scheduling and, 360
bill of material and, 360
inventory master file and, 360
master production schedule and, 360
material requirements planning and, 360–370
netting and, 360
Design capacity, 109, 423–425
Designing for manufacturability (DFM), 145–146
Detroit Diesel, 187
Differentiation strategy, 101, 135–137
Direct labor, 169
Direct materials, 169
Direct shipment, 632
Direct-to-customer model, 5
Disk drives, 40
Disney World, 42
Disruptions, 603–604
supply chain management and, 641
Distribution centers (DCs), 474–475
location of, 474–477
Distribution network configuration, 631
Distribution strategy, 632–633
Dollar days, 372
calculation of, 372–373
Domino's Pizza, 137
"dot.coms," 7–8
Durability, 575

E

Earliest due date (EDD), 247
Early start schedule, 260–262
Earnings per share (EPS), 41
Eastern Chemical Company, 587
Ebay, 7, 12
Economic order quantity (EOQ) model, 354–357
calculation, 357
Interactive, 381–382
Economic value added (EVA), 43–44
equation for, 43
Economist, The, 342n
Efficiency, 50–52
calculation of, 52
equation for, 51
Electronic commerce, 637
Electronic data interchange (EDI), 553
Empathy, 575
Employees; *see* Workforce
Ending on-hand inventory, 362
Enterprise resource planning (ERP) systems, 315–320
conceptual view of, 319
customer relationship management and, 534
at Microsoft, 318

operations resources in, 320
at SAP, 317
supply chain management and, 636
Environmental forces, 22–24
changing, 104–105
globalization, 22–23
Internal, 23
natural environment, 23–24
regional pressures, 24
Error-cause removal (ECR), 574
Ethics as a value attribute, 83–84
E-Trade, 84
Expected costs, 163
Experience detractors, 218
Experience enhancers, 218
External customers, 571–572
profitability and, 576
External failure costs, 190, 193
ExxonMobil, 523

F

Fabricators, 74
Facilities, 19–20, 459–513
competitive priorities and, 111–112
decision making, 460
criteria checklist, 462
introduction, 460
just-in-time management of, 559–560
layouts for; *see* Layout alternatives
location of, 463–481
breakeven analysis for, 479–481
business expansion, 465
center-of-gravity method for, 474–477, 507–508
criteria checklist, 469
decision tree analysis for, 477–479
domestic issues, 467, 469–471
geographic information systems, 471
international issues, 466–467, 468
multifactor rating method for, 472–474
new businesses, 463–464
relocating an existing business, 465
trends in, 481
profitability from, 52–53
resource/profit model and, 461
strategic importance of, 460–463
value attributes and, 460–463
Fashion industry, 240
Fast Company, 7n, 523
Fast-food industry, 394
Features, 575
Federal Express Corp., 587
Federal Signal, 25
Feedback delay, 239–240
Finished-goods inventory, 344–348
First Chicago Bank, 125
First come, first served (FCFS), 246
queue discipline and, 253–254
Fixed costs, 56
Fixed-quantity order policy, 365

Flexibility:
    capacity and, 110
    facilities and, 112
    human resources and, 116–117
    layout alternatives and, 138–150
    new product or service development and, 119–120
    organization system and, 121
    process technology and, 113
    production planning/inventory control and, 118–119
    quality and, 118
    timeliness and, 232
    as a value attribute, 89
    vertical integration/supplier relationships and, 115
Flex-n-Gates, 555
Flextronics International Ltd., 89
Flowcharts, 193
    example of, 194
Focus strategy, 101, 103
Ford, 5, 554
Forecast bias, 312
    measuring, 314–316
Forecast including trend (FIT), 307–312
Forecasting, 38, 89, 297–315
    accuracy of, 312–315
        absolute error, 312–314
        forecast bias, 312, 314–316
    causal, 298
        with simple linear regression, 299–300
    demand, 297–298
    Interactive Model, 333–335
    qualitative, 298
    quantitative, 298
    time series and; *see* Time series forecasting
Forest Stewardship Council, 84
Fortune, 136n, 392n
Forward scheduling, 244–245
Frequent deliveries, 553
Functional layout, 138–140
Functional strategy, 100, 102–105

G

Gantt chart, 245, 258
Gap, The, 521
General Electric (GE), 100, 215
General Motors, 5
Gentex, 188
Geographic information systems (GISs), 471
Globalization:
    as environmental force, 22–23
    supply chain management and, 639–640
Goal, The (Goldratt), 596, 609, 620
Goals, 98
Green labeling, 83–84
Gross requirements, 362
Growth stage of life cycle, 295, 296

H

Harry Potter phenomenon, 79
Harvard Business Review, 70, 95, 127, 157, 336, 391n, 414
Heijunka, 188
Hennes & Mauritz (H&M), 240
Hewlett-Packard, 89
Histograms, 198
    example of, 199
Home Depot, 82, 84
Honda, 200, 213, 551
House of quality, 146–150
    benchmarking and, 582, 583
Huffman Corporation, 234
Human resources; *see* Workforce

I

IBM, 631
Independent demand inventory, 347
    economic order quantity model, 354–357
    fixed interval, variable quantity systems, 357–360
    fixed quantity, variable interval systems, 351–357
    managing, 350–360
    periodic review system, 357–360
    reorder point model, 351, 353
    replenishment lead time and, 351–353
    service level and, 351
Industry-focused benchmarking, 581–582
    house of quality and, 583
    organizations, 583
Information management, 636
Information technology, 531–533
    after-sale service, 533
    customer database and, 531
    customer service, 532–533
    direct marketing, 533
    logistics and distribution, 533
    new-customer acquisition, 532
    new-product and new-service development, 533
    product and service pricing, 533
    product and service quality improvement, 532
    sales force, 532
Infrastructural strategic decisions, 105–108; *see also* Strategy, competitive priorities and
    list of, 106
Innovation, 397
Institute for Highway Safety, 192
Integrative management frameworks, 20–22, 539; *see also* Constraint management; Just-in-time (JIT) management; Supply chains; Total quality management (TQM)
Intermediaries, 86
Internal customers, 571–572
    profitability and, 576

Internal failure costs, 191, 193
Internal Revenue Service (IRS), 167
International Standards Organization (ISO 9000), 584–586
    changed and modified, 586
    original, 585
Internet, 5, 8, 386–387
    broadcasting in, 528–529
    cost and, 163, 164
    employee-customer interaction and, 386–390
    as environmental force, 23
    quality and, 190, 218
    service and, 387–388
    timeliness and, 232, 251
    value and, 77, 83, 85, 86
Interpersonal loyalty, 521–522
Intrawest Corp., 518
Introduction stage of life cycle, 295, 296
Inventory, 18, 339–383, 599–600
    ABC analysis, 370–371
    as balancing act for management, 340–341
    beginning on-hand, 362
    competitive priorities and, 118–119
    component, 348–349
    costs and benefits of, 342–344
    customization and, 341
    decisions, 349–350
    decoupling and, 341, 342
    dependent demand; *see* Dependent demand inventory
    dollar days, 372–373
    ending on-hand, 362
    finished-goods, 344–348
    as global performance measure, 599–600
    independent demand; *see* Independent demand inventory
    introduction, 340–341
    just-in-time; *see* Just-in-time (JIT) management, inventory-focused techniques
    maintenance, repair, and operating, 347–348
    measuring productivity of, 371–373
    pipeline, 348–349
    prioritizing, 370–371
    profitability from, 45–47
    quality, productivity, and reduction of, 188–189
    raw materials, 348–349
    reasons for carrying/not carrying, 341
    resource/profit model and, 340
    retailing, 344–348
    safety stock, 54, 352
    scheduling and, 250–251
    service level of, 54
    stockout, 54, 344
    stockpiling, 554
    supply chain management and, 632
    transportation of, 350
    turnover, 47

SUBJECT INDEX

two-bin system, 370
work-in-process, 348, 349
Inventory master file, 360
Inventory turns, 371
Inventory waste, 545
Isource, 565

J

J. D. Power and Associates, 188
Job sequencing, 246–250
    critical ratio, 247, 249
    earliest due date, 247
    first come, first served, 246
    Interactive Model, 278–279
    process-oriented layout for, 246
    shortest processing time, 247, 248
    slack per remaining operation, 249–250
Job shop, 142
Jockeying, 253
Johnson & Johnson, 89
Journal of Marketing, 229
Juran, Joseph M., 570
Just For Feet, 81
Just-in-time (JIT) management, 21–22, 344, 541–565
    capacity-focused techniques, 556–558
        automation, 557
        eliminating non-value-adding steps, 556–557
        increased preventive maintenance, 558
        level loading of capacity, 558
        process focus, 556
        protective capacity, 557–558
        small-scale equipment, 557
    constraint management and, 612
    enterprisewide techniques:
        kaizen, 547–548
        quality management, 546–547
    facility-focused techniques, 559–560
        cellular layouts, 559
        U-shaped production lines, 559–560
    introduction, 542
    inventory-focused techniques, 45, 548–555
        component standardization, 551–552
        frequent deliveries, 553
        improved supplier relationships, 554–555
        kanban, 548–552, 561–565
        matching production to demand, 548, 549
        paperless transactions, 553
        reduced changeover times, 553
        small-batch production, 552–553
        during a tragedy, 550
    operative resources and, 545, 547
    resource/profit model and, 543
    waste reduction and; *see* Waste reduction
    workforce-focused techniques, 555–556
        employee cross-training, 556
        employee involvement, 555–556
        improvement teams, 556

K

Kaizen, 547–548
Kanban, 548–552
    extending to suppliers, 552
    Interactive Model, 561–565
    inventory levels in, 551
Kano model, 212–213
Keiretsu, 6
Kohl's, 497–498
Krispy Kreme, 85

L

Lands' End, 144
Late start schedule, 261–262
Law of unintended consequences, 108
Layout alternatives, 137–140, 481–498
    cellular, 140, 141, 496, 559
    noise levels and, 482
    process oriented; *see* Process-oriented layout
    product oriented; *see* Product-oriented layout
    service, 496–498
    U-shaped production lines, 559–560
Lead time, 297
    distribution of demand during, 352
    production, 491
    replenishment, 351–353
Lean manufacturing, 188
Lean production, 170
Learning curves, 406–409
    85 percent, 407
    equation for, 407
    Interactive Model, 412–414
    97 percent, 408
    patterns, 407
    use of formula, 408
Learning rate, 406
Level production, 346, 431–433
Levi Strauss, 644
Life cycle of products and services, 294–297
    improvement project, 398–399
    new product introduction and, 296
    stages in, 295
    team processes and, 398–399
Limited, Inc., The, 85
Line balancing, 491–496
    Interactive Model, 511–512
Line of visibility, 111
Local knowledge, 545
Lot tolerance percent defective (LTPD), 211
Lot-for-lot ordering, 364
Loyalty; *see* Customer loyalty

M

McDonald's, 137, 152, 153
Machine utilization, 50
    calculation of, 51
    equation for, 50

McKinsey & Co., 342
Maintenance, repair, and operating (MRO) inventory, 347–348
Make/market or order/deliver loop, 238
Make-to-order (MTO), 142, 143
Make-to-stock (MTS), 142–143
Making Customer Loyalty Real, 32
Malcolm Baldrige National Quality Award, 586–590
    award criteria and scoring, 589
    values of, 587, 588
    winners of, 590
Manufacturers, 5, 6, 24, 25
    strategic tradeoffs for, 122–124
Maquiladoras, 28, 89
Marriott, 519
Master production schedule (MPS), 360
    example of, 361
Material requirements planning (MRP), 360–370
    capacity and, 433, 434
Maturation stage of life cycle, 295, 296
Mean absolute deviation (MAD), 312–314
    calculating, 313
Mean forecast error (MFE), 314
    calculating, 315
Mean squared error (MSE), 313
    calculating, 314
Microsoft, 318
Middlemen, 86
Midrange Enterprise, 215n
Mobil Oil, 523
Moment-of-truth analysis, 217–218
Motorola, 215
Multifactor rating for location decision, 472–474
Murphy's law, 603

N

National Institute of Standards and Technology (NIST), 585, 587
Natural environment, 23–24
Nelson Nameplates, 574
Net income, 9, 161
    cost and profitability, 162–163
    equation for, 41
Net present value (NPV), 11–12, 36
Net requirement, 362
Netting, 360
Network diagram, 258
    example of, 259
New product or service development:
    competitive priorities and, 119–120
    design for, 145–146
    requirements for, 144–145
New York Times, The, 95, 104, 206n
97X, 528–529
Nissan, 342
Nucor Steel, 52
Nonproduction costs, 169
Normal time, 404

O

Oba, Hajime, 188
Objectives, strategic, 134
Observed time, 403–404
Old Navy, 521
Olympic games, 463
Operating characteristics (OC) curve, 211
    example of, 212
Operating decisions; *see* Strategy
Operating expense (OE), 599–600
Operating resources, profitability from, 44–53
Operations cost, 166–170
    activity drivers and, 168, 169
    assigning, 166–167
    component of product cost, 169–170
    cost object and, 166, 169
    direct, 167–168
    indirect, 168–169
    resource drivers and, 167–168, 169
Operations management, 1–33
    business outputs, 24–28
    as critical to a career in business, 4–8
    cross-functional teams, 28–29
    customers, 28
    integrative management frameworks; *see* Integrative management frameworks
    interaction among processes, 28–30
    introduction, 4–8
    new business environment and, 8–9
    resource/profit model; *see* Resource/profit model
Operations strategy, 102–105
    list of, 106
OperationsNow.com, 4–8
Order costs, 343
Order losers, 101
Order qualifiers, 101, 135–137
Order winners, 101, 135–137
Order-taking process, 240–243
    concurrent engineering and, 242–243
    illustrated, 241
    with parallel processing, 240, 242
    with reduced time on tasks, 240, 241
Oregon Freeze Dry, 608
Organization system, competitive priorities and, 121–122
Out-of-pocket costs, 163
Outsourcing, 6, 27–28, 87
    competitive priorities and, 113–115
    customer relationship management, 534
    supply chains and, 77, 628, 629
Overbooking, 441–444
    example of, 442–444
    as a win-win situation, 441
Overhead, 169–170
Overproduction waste, 542

P

Pacers, 637–639, 645
Pacific Lumber Company, 84
Palladium, 554
Paperless transactions, 553
Pareto analysis, 196
    example of, 197–198
Pareto charts, 195–196
    example of, 196, 198
Part deployment, 147–148
Patents, 135
Path, 259
PayPal, 7
Pepsi, 633
Performance, 575
Performance measures, global, 599–600
Performance rating, 404
Performance/reward system, competitive priorities and, 120–121
Period costs, 163
Periodic review system, 357–360
    calculation, 359
    diagram of, 360
Personalization as a value attribute, 83
Petronas, 599
Phase, 251
Pipeline inventory, 348–349
Plan, Do, Check, Act (PDCA) cycle, 577–578
    Quality Improvement and, 579
Planned order receipt, 362
Planned order release, 362
Planning horizon, 291–294
Poka-yoke, 152–154
Predetermined motion times, 404–406
Prevention costs, 192–193
Preventive maintenance, 558
Price, 13
    cost and, 81, 163, 164
PricewaterhouseCoopers, 523
Process capability, 202
Process control charts, 199–210
    example of, 202
    Interactive Model, 228
Process planning, 148–149
Processes, 11–12, 131–155
    capabilities versus, 132–134
        strategic objectives versus, 134
    capability chains and, 154–155
    competitive priorities and, 112–113
    as component of value, 14–16, 91
    general layout decisions, 137–150
        demand linkages and, 142–143
        mixing product and process, 140
        new-process requirements, 144–145
        process oriented, 137, 138–140
        product, service, and process design, 145–146
        product oriented, 137–138
        quality function deployment; *see* Quality function deployment (QFD)
        service process considerations, 143–144
        volume requirements and, 140–142
    improvement tools, 150–154
        business process analysis, 151
        concurrent engineering, 152
        poka-yoke, 152–154
        reengineering, 151–152
    improving, 13
    interaction among, 28–30
    introduction, 132
    JIT focus on, 556
    order qualifiers and order winners, 135–137
    profit margin and, 42
    resource/profit model and, 130
    service blueprinting and, 154, 155
    technology and, 112–113
Process-focused benchmarking, 582, 584
    organizations, 584
Processing waste, 544–545
Process-oriented layout, 137, 138–140, 483–490
    conceptual view of, 139
    cut-and-try approach, 484–487
    illustrated, 246, 483
    Interactive Model, 508–510
    job sequencing and; *see* Job sequencing
    mixing product-oriented and, 140
    systematic layout planning approach, 487–489
Producer's risk, 211
Product costs, 163
    components of, 169–170
Product defect waste, 545
Product planning, 146–147
Production and Inventory Management Journal, 608n
Production batch, 607–608
Production costs, 169
Production lead time, 491
Production lines, 490
    improved, 491
    U-shaped, 559–560
Production planning:
    competitive priorities and, 118–119
    demand and, 548
    quality function deployment, 150
Productivity, 41
    improvement in, 54–56
        cost reduction in, 170–173
        workforce; *see* Workforce, productivity improvement
    local versus global, 53–54
    measures of, 48–52
    quality, inventory reduction and, 188–189
Product-oriented layout, 137–138, 490–496
    balance delay and, 490
    bottlenecks and, 490
    conceptual view of, 138
    cycle time and, 490
    illustrated, 490, 491
    line balancing and, 491–496
    mixing process-oriented and, 140

production lead time and, 491
work elements and, 491–492
Product/process matrix, 123–124, 142, 143
Products, 25
    development of new, 119–120
    information technology and, 532–533
    in-house production of, 79–80
    life cycle of, 294–297
    quality of, 184
        defective, 187, 189
        dimensions of, 186, 187, 574, 575
    services compared to, 27
Profit, 7–8
    profitability and, 9, 40–41
Profit margin, 41–42
    equation for, 41
    time and, 232–237
Profitability, 9, 35–71, 40–41
    adaptation and, 40
    breakeven analysis and, 56–59
    cost and, 162–163
    customer relationships and, 53, 523–525
    improvement in, 54–56
    internal and external customers and, 576
    introduction, 36–40
    loyalty and, 525–526, 527
    measures of, 40–44
        balanced scorecard, 59
        economic value added, 43–44
        local versus global, 53–54
        profit margin; see Profit margin
        return on assets; see Return on assets
        return on equity, 43
    from operating resources, 44–53
        capacity, 50–52
        customer relationships, 53
        facilities, 52–53
        inventory, 45–47
        workforce, 47–50
    productivity and, 41
    quality and, 186–189
    realistic cost/benefit decision, 39
    resource/profit model and, 9–11
    time and, 232–238
    timeliness and, 232–238
    value and investment results, 36–40
Program evaluation and review technique (PERT), 258
Project management, 257–269
    caveats, 268–269
    crashing projects, 265–268
    developing the network, 258–263
    key objectives of, 257–258
    scheduling, 258
        sequence for, 262
        with uncertain time estimates, 263–265
Projects, 141, 257
Prospecting, 519, 520
Protective capacity, 110, 423

Q

Qualitative forecasts, 298
Quality, 17, 182–229
    acceptable quality level, 211
    acceptance sampling, 210, 211
    awards for, 586–590
    capacity and, 110
    as component of value, 17, 92, 184–186
        for businesses, 87
        for consumers, 81
    consumer's risk, 11
    cost of; see Cost of quality (COQ)
    customer relationship management, 218–219
    facilities and, 111
    general purpose analysis tools, 193
        cause and effect diagram, 195, 196
        check sheets, 198–199
        control charts, 199–200
        flowcharts, 193, 194
        histograms, 198, 199
        Pareto analysis, 196, 197–198
        Pareto charts, 195–196
        run charts, 194–195
        scatter diagrams, 199
    human resources and, 116
    introduction, 184
    Kano model and, 212–213
    lot tolerance percent defective, 211
    new product or service development and, 119
    operating characteristics curve, 211, 212
    performance/reward system and, 120–121
    proaction versus reaction in management, 189–190
    process technology and, 112
    producer's risk, 211
    product, 184
        defective, 187, 189
        dimensions of, 186, 187
    production planning/inventory control and, 118
    productivity, inventory reduction, 188–189
    profitability and, 186–189
    recovery and, 190, 219–220
    resource/profit model and, 185
    service, 184
        defective, 189
        dimensions of, 186, 187
    service-oriented improvement in, 216–218
        moment-of-truth analysis and, 217–218
        service blueprinting and, 216–217
    six sigma, 212, 213–216
    statistical process control, 200–210, 228
    strategic decisions, 117–118
    substitute quality characteristics, 147
    total quality; see Total quality management (TQM)
    total quality management, 220
    vertical integration/supplier relationships and, 114–115
Quality certification programs, 584–586
Quality circles, 395
Quality Cup, 588–589
Quality function deployment (QFD), 146–150, 192
    conceptual model of, 145
    part deployment, 147–148
    process planning, 148–149
    product planning, 146–147
    production planning, 150
Quality Improvement (QI) story, 578
    PDCA cycle and, 579
    steps in, 580–582
    tool overview, 579, 582
Quality management, 546–547
    total, 22, 220, 395, 547
Quality Progress, 229, 574n
Quantitative forecasts, 298
    causal, 298
        with simple linear regression, 299–300
    time series; see Time series forecasting
Quantity discount model, 356–357
    calculation, 358
Queue configuration, 251–253
Queue discipline, 253–254
Queues:
    at airports, 244
    arrival process, 254–255
    balking, 255
    calling population, 254
    Interactive Model, 255, 280–282
    jockeying in, 253
    managing, 251–256
    multiple-phase system, 251–253
    multiple-server system, 251, 252
    physical features of, 251–256
    psychological features of, 256–257
    reneging, 255
    service process, 255–256

R

Random fluctuations, 302
    coping with, 302–304
    as disruption, 603
    example of, 302
Raw materials, 348–349
R-chart, 204–210
    construction of, 208–210
Recovery, 190, 219–220
Recovery plan, 219–220
Reengineering, 45, 151–152
    project teams, 155
Regional pressures, 24
Regression to the mean, 297
Reliability, 575
Renault, 342
Reneging, 255

SUBJECT INDEX

Reorder point (ROP) model, 351
    calculation, 353, 355
    Interactive, 379–380
Repetitive processing, 142
Replenishment lead time, 351–353
Reputation, 575
Resource drivers, 167–168, 169
Resource management, 17–20; see also Capacity; Customer relationships; Facilities; Inventory; Resource planning; Workforce
Resource planning, 287–337
    changes in customer behavior and, 293
    contingency plans, 290
    enterprise resource planning systems, 315–320
    financial benefits of, 290–291
    forecasting; see Forecasting
    fundamentals of, 290–294
    integrated systems, 315–320
    introduction, 288–290
    lead time and, 297
    planning horizon and, 291–294
    product and service life cycles and, 294–297
    resource/profit model and, 298
    supply chain management, 320–321
Resource scheduling, 250–251
Resource/profit model, 9–24; see also specific aspects of the model
    components of value, 14–17
    environmental forces, 22–24
    foundations for success, 9–13
    illustrated, 10
    integrative management frameworks, 20–22
    managing resources to create value, 17–20
    in review, 24
Response time; see also Timeliness
    capacity and, 110
    facilities and, 112
    new product or service development and, 120
    organization system and, 122
    process technology and, 113
    production planning/inventory control and, 119
    quality and, 118
    as a value attribute:
        for businesses, 88–89
        for consumers, 83
    vertical integration/supplier relationships and, 115
Responsiveness, 232, 575
Retail inventory, 344–348
Return on assets (ROA), 42–43
    equation for, 41
    increasing, 55
    time and, 237
Return on equity (ROE), 43
    equation for, 41

Return to normalcy, 297
Risk, 38–39
Risk pooling, 633, 645
    Interactive Model, 647
Rough-cut capacity planning, 433–437
Run charts, 194–195
    example of, 195
Running sum of forecast error (RSFE), 314
    calculating, 316

S

Safety stock, 54, 352
Sales price, 163
Sampling, acceptance, 210, 211
SAP, 317
Saturation stage of life cycle, 295, 296
Scatter diagrams, 199
    example of, 200
Scheduling, 243–245
    backward, 245
    forward, 244–245
    project, 258
    resource, 250–251
Seasonal products, 236
Seasonality, 301
    calculating, 310
    inventory and, 346
    multiplicative model and, 311–312
    weighted moving average forecasting and, 308–312
Second phone lines, 295
Segmentation, 520
September 11, 104, 445, 550, 641
Server, 251
Service blueprinting, 154, 193, 216–217
    example of, 155, 217
Service encounters, 216–218
    employee-customer interaction, 386–395
    moment-of-truth analysis and, 217–218
    service blueprinting and, 216–217
Service layouts, 496–498
Service level, 54, 351
Service Performance Improvement (SPI), 82
Service process, 255–256
Service system design matrix, 124–125
Serviceability, 575
Service-profit chain, 87
    workforce and, 391–392
Services, 5, 6, 24, 25–28
    development of new, 119–120
    information technology and, 532–533
    life cycle of, 294–297
    products and, 27
    quality and, 184
        defective, 189
        dimensions of, 186, 187, 574, 575
    strategic tradeoffs for, 124–125
Setup costs, 343
Setup time, 142
Shewhart, Walter A., 568–569
    Plan, Do, Check, Act cycle, 577–578
Shipping buffer, 606–607

Shortest processing time (SPT), 247
    job sequencing using, 248
Simple exponential smoothing, 305–306
    adding seasonality to, 308–312
    adding trend to, 306–312
    calculation of, 307
Six sigma (6σ) quality, 212, 213–216
    meaning of, 215
Ski resorts, 518
Slack, 249
Slack per remaining operation, 249–250
    job sequencing using, 250
Sloan Management Review, 229, 574n
Small-batch production, 552–553
Small-scale equipment, 557
Solectron Corp., 587
Sony, 89
Specifications, 87
Speed, 6
Speedpass, 523
Sports Authority, 81
Standard expectation, 218
Standard time, 404
Standardization, 551–552
    in elections, 580
    supply chain management and, 636–637
Standards, 170–171
Starbucks, 77
Statistical fluctuation among dependent events, 604
Statistical process control (SPC), 200–210
Statoil, 599
Steel Dynamics, 135
Steel industry, 136
Stockout, 54, 344
Stockout cost, 343
Stockpiling inventory, 554
Stopwatch time studies, 403–404
    calculation of, 404
Strategic partnering, 633–635
Strategy, 97–125
    business, 99–100, 101–102
    competitive priorities and, 105–122
        capacity, 109–110
        complexity of relationships among, 122
        facility, 111–112
        human resources, 115–117
        new product or service development, 119–120
        organization system, 121–122
        performance/reward system, 120–121
        process technology, 112–113
        production planning/inventory control, 118–119
        quality, 117–118
        supplier relationships, 113–115
        vertical integration, 113–115
    corporate, 99, 100
    cost leader, 101
    differentiation, 101
    focus, 101, 103

SUBJECT INDEX

functional, 100, 102–105
goals and, 98
hierarchy of, 99–105
introduction, 98
operations, 102–105
   list of, 106
as plan for creating value, 98
resource/profit model and, 13, 99
strategic tradeoffs:
   for manufacturers, 122–124
   for processes; *see* Processes, general layout decisions
   for services, 124–125
Structural strategic decisions, 105–108; *see also* Strategy, competitive priorities and
   list of, 106
Style and fashion as value attributes, 84–85
Substitute quality characteristics, 147
Supplier relationship matrix, 634, 635
Suppliers, 77
   customers and, 628, 630
   relationship with, 113–115
      improved, 554–555
   strategic partnering with, 633–635
Supply chains, 74–78
   capacity of, 427–428
   components of, 74
   comprehensive definition of, 75
   defined, 624
   generic model of, 76, 626
   management of; *see* Supply-chain management
   outsourcing and, 77
Supply-chain management, 22, 320–321, 623–649
   bullwhip effect, 628, 640–644
   communication and, 631
   components of, 630–637
      cooperative product design, 635
      distribution network configuration, 631
      distribution strategy, 632–633
      electronic commerce, 637
      information management, 636
      inventory management, 632
      policy, procedure, and product standardization, 636–637
      strategic partnering, 633–635
   disruptions and, 641
   example of, 637–639
   generic supply chain, 76, 626
   global extension of, 639–640
   introduction, 624
   motivating forces, 624–630
      impact of customers on supplies, 628
      impact of suppliers on customers, 630
      increased competition, 626–628
      technological advances, 630
   resource/profit model and, 625
   risk pooling and, 633, 645
      Interactive Model, 647
   systemwide perspective, 624

SupplySolutions, Inc., 555
Systematic layout planning (SLP), 487–489

T

Tangibles, 575
Tasks, 15
Taxes, facilities location and, 468
Teams, 395–400
   advantages of, 396–397
   appropriate uses for, 397
   buy-in, 397
   continuous improvement and, 397
   decision-making tools, 399–400
   innovation and, 397
   project, 395–396
   structure for processes, 398–399
Technology:
   information; *see* Information technology
   supply chain management and, 630
   as a value attribute, 85
Test Track, 257
Testing, 191–192
Theory of constraints; *see* Constraint management
3Com, 89
Throughput (T), 599–600
Time buffer, 604–607
Time series forecasting, 298–312
   averages, 302–312
      seasonality, 308–312
      simple and weighted moving, 304–306
      simple exponential smoothing, 305–307
      trends, 306–309
   components of, 300–302, 332
   random fluctuations and, 302–304
   seasonality and, 301
   techniques, 302–312
   trends and, 301
Time standard, 403
Timeliness, 17, 231–283
   better tools enhance, 234
   as a component of value, 17, 92
      for businesses, 88–89
      for consumers, 83
   feedback delay, 239–240
   flexibility and, 232
   Gantt chart and, 245
   introduction, 232
   job sequencing and; *see* Job sequencing
   money and, 232
   order-taking; *see* Order-taking process
   profitability and, 232–238
      cash-to-cash cycle, 237–238
      profit margin, 232–237
      return on assets, 237
   project management; *see* Project management
   resource/profit model and, 233
   responsiveness and, 232

scheduling and, 243–245
   backward, 245
   forward, 244–245
   resource, 250–251
supply chain management and, 627–628
time reduction strategies, 240–243
"Time-to-market," 88–89, 240
Todo Dias, 466
Total costs, 163
   cost per unit versus, 173
Total involvement, 572; *see also* Total quality management (TQM)
Total quality management (TQM), 22, 220, 395, 547, 567–593
   benchmarking, 581–584
   brief history of, 568–572
      Crosby, 571, 572
      Deming, 569–570
      Juran, 570
      Shewhart, 568–569
   components of, 571–573
   culture of continuous improvement, 568
   dimensions of quality for products and services, 574, 575
   enterprise view of, 573–576
   introduction, 568
   obtaining continuous improvement, 577–578
   Plan, Do, Check, Act cycle, 577–578, 579
   positive results from, 574
   process of, 576–577
   quality awards, 586–590
      Malcolm Baldrige National Quality Award, 586–590
      Quality Cup, 588–589
   quality certification programs, 584–586
   Quality Improvement; *see* Quality Improvement (QI) story
   resource contributions to, 573
   resource/profit model and, 569
Toyota, 5, 188–189
   JIT system at, 542, 544, 555
Toys "R" Us, 81
Transfer batches, 348, 607–608
Transportation costs, 350
Transportation waste, 543–544
Trek, 74
Trend, 301
   multiplicative model and, 311–312
   weighted moving average forecasting and, 306–312
Trend-adjusted exponential smoothing, 307–311
Tricon Global Restaurants, 394
Tri-State Manufacturing, 145, 546
Two-bin system, 370

U

UAL (United Airlines), 167, 245, 293
Uncertainty, 38–39
United Airlines, 167, 245, 293

United Parcel Service (UPS), 5–6
Unnecessary motion waste, 545
USA Today, 631
Utilization, 50
  calculation of, 51
  constraint management and, 598
  equation for, 50

V

Value, 73–95
  components of, 14–17
    capabilities, 14–16, 91
    cost, 16–17, 92
    processes of, 14–16, 91
    quality, 17, 92, 184–186
    timeliness, 17, 92
  customer determination of; *see* Customer determination of value
  facilities, 19–20, 460–463
  introduction, 74
  managing resources to create, 17–20, 132
    capacity, 19, 421–423
    customer relationships, 20
    inventory, 18
    resource planning, 20
    workforce, 19, 390–391
  paying for, 160–161
  perceived, 517–519
    cost and, 161–164
  plan for creating; *see* Strategy
  resource/profit model and, 11–13, 75
  supply chains and, 74–78
Value chain, 164–166
  illustrated, 165
Value transfer model, 91
Variability, 572
Variable costs, 56
Variance, 170
Variance analysis, 171–173
  example of, 172
  illustrated, 171
  Interactive Model of, 178–180
Vertical integration, 6
  competitive priorities and, 113–115
"Voice of the customer" (VOC), 146–147

W

Waiting lines; *see also* Queues
  at airports, 244
  Interactive Model, 280–282

Waiting time, 236
Waiting time waste, 542–543
Wall Street Journal, The, 7n, 32, 33, 40n, 55n, 70, 82n, 94, 95, 127, 135n, 164n, 167n, 234n, 240n, 244n, 293n, 295n, 389n, 394n, 445n, 456, 466n, 468n, 482n, 498n, 512, 518n, 521n, 550n, 554n, 555n, 641n
Wal-Mart, 81, 466, 639–640
Warehousing, 632
Washburn Guitar, 139
Waste:
  inventory, 545
  operations resources and, 545
  overproduction, 542
  processing, 544–545
  product defect, 545
  transportation, 543–544
  unnecessary motion, 545
  waiting time, 542–543
Waste reduction, 542–565
  as the focus of JIT system, 542–545
  JIT techniques for; *see* Just-in-time (JIT) management
  management framework for, 542
Weakest link:
  constrained system, 427
  supply chain, 428
Web's Best, 32
Weighted moving average forecasting, 304–312
  simple exponential smoothing and, 305–312
  three- and eight-period, 304–305
Wendy's, 394
Wilson tennis balls, 206
Win back or save, 519–520
Work elements, 491–492
Work sampling, 405–406
Workforce, 19, 385–415
  competitive priorities and, 115–117
  competitive success and, 386
  contingent workers and, 400–401
  cross-training, 400
  customer experience grid and, 393
  customer loyalty and, 391–394
  decision-making power and, 401–402
  drop in demand and, 445

employee-customer interaction, 386–395
  as a prerequisite to good service, 391–394
  sound decisions and, 394–395
flexibility and, 400–401
introduction, 386
just-in-time management and, 555–556
  employee cross-training, 556
  employee involvement, 555–556
  improvement teams, 556
new working environment, 402
perks, 392
productivity improvement, 402–409
  allowance, 404
  learning curves; *see* Learning curves
  normal time, 404
  observed time, 403–404
  performance rating, 404
  predetermined motion times, 404–406
  standard time, 404
  stopwatch time studies, 403–404
  time standards, 403
  work sampling, 405–406
profitability from, 47–50, 386–390
reducing turnover, 394
resource/profit model and, 387
satisfaction of, 391–392
service-profit chain, 391–392
teams and; *see* Teams
value attributes and, 390–391
Work-in-process (WIP) inventory, 348, 349
World Wide Web, 7

X

X-bar chart, 201–209
  construction of, 208–209
  example of, 202
Xerox, 468

Y

Yield management, 440–441

Z

Zara, 240

TEXT AND WEBSITE LINKAGES

 **Esources**  **Reel Operations**  **Excel Tutors** 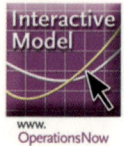 **Interactive Models**

The following icons placed in the text indicate a resource related to the topic at hand that is explored on the website.

Federal Signal: A Manufacturing Operations Tour

First Chicago: A Blend of Service and Manufacturing Operations

Nucor Steel: Technology Advancements Improve Productivity and Profitability of Resources

Trek Uses Numerous Approaches to Match Value Produced to Customers' Value Needs

ABTCO's Strategy is Overhauled by New Owners Working to Save It

Manufacturing Strategies Depend on Matching Resources with Volume, Flexibility, and Product Variety Needs

First Chicago National Bank Utilizes All Aspects of the Service System Design Matrix

McDonalds Completes Kitchen Makeover to Meet Changing Customer Expectations

Process-Oriented Manufacturing at Washburn Guitars

TriState Turns Effective Process Design into High Quality Products

McDonald's: Re-engineering the Process to Meet Customer Needs

Lean Production Provides a Structured Cost Reduction Methodology

Detroit Diesel: Designing and Producing Quality

Honda: Proactive Quality Management to Reduce Failure Costs

Statistical Process Control Extends to Monitoring Even Door Closing Speed at Honda

United Airlines: Scheduling Complex Resources in a Service

Complex Projects Almost Always Bring Surprises: The Alton Bridge Project

Management of Manufacturing and Service Parts Inventory

Caterpillar: Team-based Reengineering for Process Improvement

Genesis Systems: Cellular Layouts Improve Productivity and Capacity

Bernard: Production Process and Inventory Storage Layout Improvement

Federal Signal: JIT to Reduce Inventory and Eliminate Waste

Tristate Implements JIT to Reduce Inventory Levels and Transportation

Bernard Welding Equipment Company Combines JIT and TQM in a Successful Change of Culture

Honda: Structured Process for Continuous Improvement

Flex-n-gate Gets Assistance from Toyota in Implementing JIT

Technology Assists APL in Transporting High Volumes of Goods Containers

---

Breakeven Analysis Interactive Model
Variance Analysis Interactive Model
The X-bar and R Chart Interactive Model
Sequencing Rules Interactive Model
Waiting Line Interactive Model
Time Series Components Interactive Model
Forecasting Techniques Interactive Model
The Reorder Point Interactive Model
Economic Order Quantity Interactive Model

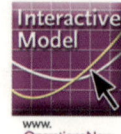

Learning Curve Interactive Model
Production Line Interactive Model
Aggregate Planning Interactive Model
Center of Gravity Interactive Model
Process-Oriented Layout Interactive Model
Line Balancing Interactive Model
Kanban System Interactive Model
Constraint Management Interactive Model
Risk Pooling Interactive Model